THE OXFORD ENCYCLOPEDIA OF ISLAM AND POLITICS

THE OXFORD ENCYCLOPEDIA OF ISLAM AND POLITICS

Emad El-Din Shahin

EDITOR IN CHIEF

Volume 2

Laskar Jihad–Zaytūnah

OXFORD

UNIVERSITY PRESS

OXFORD
UNIVERSITY PRESS

Oxford University Press is a department of the University of Oxford.
It furthers the University's objective of excellence in research,
scholarship, and education by publishing worldwide.

Oxford New York
Auckland Cape Town Dar es Salaam Hong Kong Karachi
Kuala Lumpur Madrid Melbourne Mexico City Nairobi
New Delhi Shanghai Taipei Toronto

With offices in
Argentina Austria Brazil Chile Czech Republic France Greece
Guatemala Hungary Italy Japan Poland Portugal Singapore
South Korea Switzerland Thailand Turkey Ukraine Vietnam

Oxford is a registered trademark of Oxford University Press in the UK and certain other countries.

Published by Oxford University Press, Inc.
198 Madison Avenue, New York, NY 10016
www.oup.com

Library of Congress Cataloging-in-Publication Data
The Oxford encyclopedia of Islam and politics / Emad El-Din Shahin, editor in Chief.
volumes cm
Includes bibliographical references and index.
To be complete in 2 volumes—ECIP data.
ISBN 978-0-19-973935-6 (set : alk. paper)—ISBN 978-0-19-999805-0 (v.1 : alk. paper)—
ISBN 978-0-19-999806-7 (v.2 : alk. paper)
1. Islam and politics—Encyclopedias. I. Shahin, Emad Eldin, 1957-
BP173.7.O94 2013
297.2'72—dc23 2013016398

Printed in the United States of America
on acid-free paper

Common Abbreviations Used in This Work

AD	*anno Domini,* in the year of the Lord
AH	*Anno Hijra,* in the year of migration from Meccato to Medina
b.	born
BCE	before the common era (= BC)
c.	*circa,* about, approximately
CE	common era (= AD)
cf.	*confer,* compare
d.	died
diss.	dissertation
ed.	editor (pl., eds), edition
f.	and following (pl., ff.)
fl.	*floruit,* flourished
l.	line (pl., ll.)
n.	Note
n.d.	no date
no.	Number
n.p.	no place
n.s.	new series
p.	page (pl., pp.)
pt.	Part
rev.	Revised
ser.	Series
supp.	Supplement
vol.	volume (pl., vols.)

The Oxford Encyclopedia of Islam and Politics

L

LASKAR JIHAD. Laskar Jihad (Holy Warriors) was founded in Indonesia in 2000 as the paramilitary wing of the Forum Komunikasi Ahlus Sunnah Wal-Jamaah (FKAWJ, Sunni Communication Forum). The FKAWJ was established on 14 February 1999 in Solo (in Java) in response to the crises that befell Muslims in Ambon, Poso, and Maluku and inability of the government to deal with the conflict. Although there was a long history of Christian-Muslim antipathy in eastern Indonesia, this conflict was set off when a mob of Christians attacked Muslims who were praying in a mosque on the eve of ʿĪd al-Fiṭr. The ensuing violence between Christians and Muslims claimed thousands of lives, displaced large numbers of villagers, forced conversions, particularly among Christians, and resulted in burned houses, banks, schools, cars, markets, and sacred places.

Jaʿfar Umar Thalib, the founder of both FKAWJ and Laskar Jihad, reflected the narrow, more puritanical and less pluralistic interpretation of the Salafīs. He was educated at a Salafī/Wahhābī-oriented institution in Jakarta and continued his studies at the Maududi Institute in Lahore, Pakistan, where his exposure to Salafī thought continued. In 1987–1989, he joined the Afghan war against the Soviet Union as an expression of Muslim solidarity. Thalib met *mujāhidīn* from all over the world, including Osama Bin Laden. His organization was not associated with Bin Laden or al-Qaʿida, however, because Thalib was drawn to the Salafī-oriented Jamāʿat al-Daʿwah ilā al-Qurʾān wa-Ahl al-Ḥadīth faction of the *mujāhidīn*. From Afghanistan he returned to Indonesia and headed the al-Irsyad *pesantren* (Islamic boarding school) in Salatiga, Java. Not satisfied with his new appointment, he traveled to Saudi Arabia and Yemen to consolidate his ties with Salafī-oriented scholars in the Middle East. He returned to Indonesia and established a *pesantren* in Yogyakarta. By this time, his Salafī and Wahhābī thoughts had crystallized and were shaping his views on Islam and its relationship with the state.

As Laskar Jihad was grounded in the tradition of Ahlus Sunnah Wal-Jamaah, it gained support in many parts of Indonesia. It is difficult to judge the number of its members, but it appears to have had three to seven thousand at its height, although it claimed up to twenty thousand. Membership in Laskar Jihad started with regular Salafī-oriented religious meetings in various cities in Indonesia, and the FKAWJ trained the religious cadres in *tawḥīd* (the unity of God) at several *pesantren* affiliated with Thalib. While the members of Laskar Jihad were being recruited and receiving paramilitary training in Bogor and Yogyakarta, Laskar Jihad officials sought permission from the government to engage in a physical and revolutionary *jihād* in Ambon, Central Sulawesi, and Maluku. Though the FKAWJ actively sought the state's intervention in the Maluku and Ambon crises, the Indonesian governments led by Bacharuddin Jusuf Habibie (May 1998–October 1999) and Abdurrahman Wahid (October 1999–July 2011) failed to resolve the problem; elements of the Indonesian military provided some arms and training. Salafī-Wahhābī scholars in Saudi Arabia and Yemen issued seven *fatwas* (religious opinions) that rendered *jihād* in Maluku an obligation for individual Muslims (*farḍ ʿayn*) because the government failed to resolve the conflict.

While Laskar Jihad was established to aid Muslims in the conflict areas, its general purpose was to embody the virtues of *ahl al-sunnah wa-al-jamāʿah* (those who follow the *sunnah* of the Prophet and his community) in all aspects of life in order to bring Muslims back to pristine Islam based on the Qurʾān and the *sunnah*. "*Sunnah*" here refers not only to the tradition as exemplified by the Prophet Muḥammad but also to *al-salaf al-ṣāliḥ* (virtuous early Muslim scholars). In the organization's view, improvement of the individual would eventually prepare the Muslim community for the implementation of Islam at all levels. This Salafī ideology is widely shared by more militant Islamic organizations, including Darul Islam, Front Pembela Islam (Islamic Defense Front, formed in 1998), and Majelis Mujahidin Indonesia (Mujāhidīn Council of Indonesia, formed in 2002). While these organizations have called for the establishment of an Islamic state, Laskar Jihad continued to profess loyalty to the Indonesian government, though it did call for the application of Sharīʿah throughout the Republic of Indonesia. It is within this context of defending the integrity of the nation that Laskar Jihad sent its cadres to Maluku and Papua, although there were numerous reports charging its members with anti-Christian activities in Poso, Maluku, and Ambon.

On 5 October 2002, Laskar Jihad was disbanded, although there have been different explanations for its end, including divisions among *ʿulamāʾ* who previously supported it, Thalib's own view that it had strayed from Salafī principles, the view that it had accomplished its mission, and government pressure.

[*See also* Indonesia; *and* Salafī Movements.]

BIBLIOGRAPHY

Abuza, Zachary. *Militant Islam in Southeast Asia: Crucible of Terror*. Boulder, Colo.: Lynne Rienner, 2003.

Hasan, Noorhaidi. *Laskar Jihad: Islam, Militancy, and the Quest for Identity in Post-New Order Indonesia*. Ithaca, N.Y.: Southeast Asia Program, Cornell University, 2006.

Jamhari, and Jajang Jahroni. *Gerakan Salafi Radikal di Indonesia*. Jakarta: RajaGrafindo Persada, 2004.

Mulyadi, Sukidi. "Violence under the Banner of Religion: The Case of Laskar Jihad and Laskar Kristus." *Studia Islamika* 10, no. 2 (2003): 75–110.

ETIN ANWAR
Updated by FRED R. VON DER MEHDEN

LEBANON. Lebanon recognizes eighteen separate sects or confessional groups within its political system. In addition to fourteen Christian denominations, which account for approximately 35 percent of the country's population, there are Sunnīs, Shīʿī, Druze, ʿAlawīs, and Ismāʿīlīs.

An individual's political identity in contemporary Lebanon is defined largely in sectarian terms. The 1989 Taif Accord, which set the framework for ending the 1975–1990 civil war, preserved the distribution of political offices among confessional groups. Thus the presidency remained the sole domain of the Maronite Christians, the office of prime minister continued to be filled by a Sunnī Muslim, and the speaker of the parliament was to be Shīʿī Muslim. The relative power of these offices changed somewhat, but the underlying principle of confessional distribution of political office and privilege was maintained. Religion thus continues to be a primary factor in defining Lebanese politics and society.

Sunnī Muslims. Although Sunnīs represent only about one-quarter of the Lebanese population, until the 1980s they were the dominant Muslim sect. Concentrated for the most part in the coastal cities—Tripoli, Sidon, and especially Beirut—they were favored during four hundred years of Ottoman rule, and their leaders were senior partners in the founding of the modern republic. The unwritten National Pact (al-Mīthāq al-Waṭanī) of 1943, which defined the terms of confessional power sharing in the independent state, was an agreement between the ranking Sunnī, Riyāḍ al-Ṣulḥ, and his Maronite counterpart, Bechara al-Khoury. Al-Ṣulḥ and al-Khoury became Lebanon's first prime minister and president, respectively.

In 1920, France, holding a League of Nations mandate over Lebanon, created Greater Lebanon (Le Grand Liban) in order to establish a viable state under Maronite domination. The Sunnīs (joined by some Shīʿīs) mounted resistance to the decision, preferring to be part of a greater Syria. As a result, the 1943 independence of Lebanon entailed a compromise between the Sunnīs' preference for an Arab identity for the independent state and the Maronites' preference for sustaining links with the West and France in particular.

Early Sunnī prominence was reflected not only in the allocation of the position of prime minister but also in religious leadership. Reflecting its Ottoman heritage, the *muftī* of the republic is a state employee, and the office is filled by a senior Sunnī cleric, usually one trained at al-Azhar. The Lebanese Sunnīs generally follow the Shāfiʿī school of Islamic law (*madhhab*), although some Sunnīs in the north follow the Mālikī school.

During the civil war, only a few Sunnī *ʿulamāʾ* (religious scholars) were engaged in organizing paramilitary forces. In Tripoli, Shaykh Saʿīd Shaʿbān (d. 1998) founded the Islamic Unity Movement (Ḥarakāt al-Tawḥīd al-Islāmīyah). Shaʿbān, who was known for his militant views, maintained especially close ties with the Islamic Republic of Iran, and among the Sunnī *ʿulamāʾ*, he was one of Iran's closest allies in Lebanon. He was succeeded upon his death by his son Bilāl. The Assembly of Muslim Clergymen (Tajammuʿ al-ʿUlamāʾ al-Muslimīn) led by Shaykh Māhir Ḥammūd, a Sunnī, and Shaykh Zuhayr Kanj, a Shīʿī, is committed to Muslim unity and argues that Sunnī-Shīʿī differences are merely juridical. Also noteworthy is the older Islamic Group (al-Jamāʿah al-Islāmīyah) that grew out of the Muslim Brotherhood (Ikhwān al-Muslimīn). The Brotherhood, dominated by laypeople, has enjoyed a notable following among Lebanon's Sunnīs but has generally maintained a low public profile. It was led by the scholar Fatḥī Yakan, a former member of parliament, until his death in 2009.

Shīʿī Muslims. The Shīʿī lived for centuries on the periphery of Lebanon. Until the twentieth century, they were concentrated in the south and in the Bekáa Valley, where most of them lived in poverty. In the south, the heartland of Shiism in Lebanon, the Shīʿī comprised a large peasantry engaged in agricultural labor and subsistence farming in the hills and valleys of Jabal ʿĀmil (a region around the city of al-Nabaṭīyah). The region is an important historic center for Shīʿī scholarship.

According to the census of 1932, the last official census conducted in Lebanon, the Shīʿī were the third-largest confessional group in Lebanon and so were allocated the position of speaker of the national assembly or parliament in the National Pact. Despite their numbers, the Shīʿī were subordinate to the Sunnīs, who enjoyed generally higher social and economic status. Today the Shīʿī population is roughly equal in size to the Sunnī population, and both hold an equal number of seats in the parliament. The growth of this population has continued, post-Taif, to challenge the historic demographic logic of a political system with a Maronite president and Sunnī prime minister.

In 1967 the Lebanese parliament voted to create the Supreme Shīʿī Council (al-Majlis al-Shīʿī al-Aʿlā). The council began activity in 1969 under the leadership of Mūsā al-Ṣadr. Its founding signaled new autonomy for the Shīʿī community in Lebanon, which would no longer be overseen by the Islamic Council and the *muftī* of the republic. In 1974 al-Ṣadr created the Movement of the Deprived (Ḥarakat al-Maḥrūmīn), a dynamic force in Lebanese politics and the forerunner of Amal, the populist Shīʿī movement. Two political parties nominally represent the Shīʿī community in Lebanon: Amal and Ḥizbullāh. Ḥizbullāh, the more influential of the two, receives support from Iran and is presided over by its secretary-general Ḥasan Naṣrallāh.

Druze. The Druze faith, an early offshoot of Ismāʿīlī Shiism, had its origins in Fāṭimid Egypt. The largest single concentration of Druze is in Lebanon, where they comprise about 5 percent of the population. The highest legal authority among the Druze is the Mashyākhat al-ʿAql. In the 1950s and 1960s, two men shared this position, one representing the Jumblattīs and the other the Yazbakīs, two of the most prominent Druze families in Lebanon. The *shaykh al-ʿaql* heads a High Council that brings together distinguished men of religion with secular notables. The High Council is the counterpart to the Sunnī Islamic Council and the Shīʿī Supreme Council, and like those institutions it supervises the dispensation of justice and charity, oversees religious trusts, and administers confessional schools. The council draws a salary from the Beirut government.

The Mashyākhat al-ʿAql plays an important role in linking the Druze community to the state, but the moral consensus of the Druze is sustained by the *ajāwīd*, the religious specialists, who number about one for every hundred people. Each Druze village maintains a *majlis* that meets weekly, on Thursday evenings. The *majlis* combines elements of a prayer meeting and a town meeting and is the forum where local issues are discussed. Major issues that confront the Druze as a whole are dealt with at a *khalwah*, a meeting of *ajāwīd*. The Druze distinguish between *shaykh*s of religion (*shuyūkh al-dīn*) and *shaykh*s of the highway (*shuyūkh al-ṭarīq*), the latter wielding coercive power; when the community is at risk, the *shaykh*s of religion predominate. Thus Druze *ajāwīd* have not played a significant role in organizing political or paramilitary organizations.

ʿAlawīs. Historically the ruling minority in Syria, the ʿAlawīs were numerically insignificant in Lebanon into the early 1980s, when they numbered about twenty thousand. However, with the growing influence of Syria in Lebanon, particularly after the Gulf War of 1990–1991, the ʿAlawīs rose in importance and in number. Today, as many as one hundred thousand live mostly in northern Lebanon. In the 1992 parliamentary elections, the ʿAlawī community was allocated two seats out of 128, marking the first time they enjoyed formal political representation in Lebanon.

Twenty-First Century Developments. Various factors have exacerbated sectarian animosities in Lebanon. The rise of Ḥizbullāh—notorious for terrorist acts like the kidnapping of innocent foreigners in the 1980s, yet a participant in Lebanese political life and the leader of the resistance struggle that finally prompted a unilateral Israeli withdrawal from its occupation zone in southern Lebanon in 2000—is one. Equally important, regional developments—including the persistence of the Arab-Israeli conflict, the Anglo-American invasion of Iraq, and the Syrian civil war—have heightened tensions in Lebanon.

Anti-Syrian, prodemocracy demonstrations beginning in February 2005, following the assassination of the former prime minister Rafīq al-Ḥarīrī, prompted the withdrawal of Syrian military and intelligence forces from the country in compliance with United Nations Security Council Resolution 1559 (September 2004). However, this movement, referred to as both the Independence Intifada and the Cedar Revolution, resulted in few truly diplomatic reforms and instead solidified a new political fault line between the pro-Western 14 March Coalition and the pro-Syrian 8 March Coalition. The system of confessionalism, or consociational democracy, in 2013 (whereby power is distributed evenly between Muslim and Christian communities and then subdivided among sects) remains as entrenched as ever.

The parliamentary elections of 2005 granted the 14 March Coalition led by Saʿd Ḥarīrī, son of the late prime minister, 72 out of 128 seats in the parliament. The rival pro-Syrian bloc, led by the Shīʿī parties Amal and Ḥizbullāh, along with the Free Patriotic Movement of General Michel Aoun, supported by Christian voters, won the other fifty-six seats and received the majority of the popular vote.

The new government, however, fell in late 2006, with the resignation of 8 March ministers from the cabinet and the start of an eighteen-month Ḥizbullāh-led sit-in protest in the downtown area of the capital. This political deadlock was followed by a series of violent conflicts in May 2008, with Ḥizbullāh and allied parties occupying large parts of Beirut. Shaykh Ḥammād bin Khalīfah Āl Thānī, the emir of Qatar, brokered an end to this crisis on 21 May 2008, in what became known as the Doha Agreement. All Lebanese factions agreed on a national-unity government with Fouad Siniora as prime minister and Michel Sleiman as president.

With 55 percent voter turnout in the next elections in 2009, the 14 March Coalition won seventy-one seats. Despite this electoral victory, Saʿd Ḥarīrī and his allies could neither avoid nor sideline Ḥizbullāh. Indeed, in November, after more than four months of negotiations, an agreement was reached whereby 14 March received fifteen ministerial posts, the Ḥizbullāh-led 8 March opposition ten posts, and President Sleiman was requested to nominate five "neutral" politicians to bring the total cabinet to thirty persons. Immediately after the new government formed, Druze leader Walīd Jumblatt, with his bloc of ten parliamentary seats, left the 14 March Coalition, resulting in a parliamentary configuration in which neither 14 March nor 8 March held a majority of seats.

Popular protests in neighboring Syria on 15 March 2011, calling for the ouster of President Bashar al-Assad, led to swift and violent reprisals from the Syrian government. The escalation through 2011 of a wave of protests into a full-scale civil war in Syria exacerbated tensions between competing Lebanese political interests. Pro-Syrian and anti-Syrian movements formed along confessional lines and some Lebanese parties played a more direct role in the conflict: arming combatants, or in some instances, sending fighters, to bolster the ranks of regime forces, the oppositionist Free Syrian Army, or one of a number of radical Islamist groups, such as Jabhat al-Nusra. Ḥizbullāh, in particular, played a key role in securing a victory for the regime in the pivotal battle of Al-Qusayr in June 2013. The crisis in Syria had a significant impact on the Lebanese scene, with occasional violence between 2011–2013 in mixed areas of the country, such as in the adjacent and predominately Sunnī Bab al-Tibbaneh and predominately ʿAlawī Jabal Muḥsin neighborhoods in Tripoli. Lebanon, like Syria's other neighbors, also hosted hundreds of thousands of Syrian refugees.

Lebanon's diverse confessional makeup has made the country particularly susceptible to outside intervention. With a colonial history of the French supporting the Maronite Christians and the British supporting the Druze, outside parties play a strong interventionist role. The United States and other Western powers have supported the predominately Sunnī and Christian 14 March movement while Iran and Syria support Ḥizbullāh for religious and ideological reasons and also as a proxy in the regional contestation with Israel. As such, the future of Lebanon and relations between confessional groups will no doubt depend as much on regional developments as on internal politicking.

[*See also* Amal; Druze; Faḍlallāh, Muḥammad Ḥusayn; Ḥizbullāh; *and* Ṣadr, Mūsā al-.]

BIBLIOGRAPHY

Deeb, Lara. *An Enchanted Modern: Gender and Public Piety in Shiʿi Lebanon*. Princeton, N.J.: Princeton University Press, 2006.

Haddad, Simon. "The Political Consequences of Electoral Laws in Fragmented Societies: Lebanon's 2009 Elections." *Journal of Social Political, and Economic Studies* 35, no. 1 (Spring 2010): 45–78.

Hanf, Theodor. *Coexistence in Wartime Lebanon: Decline of a State and Rise of a Nation*. Translated by John Richardson. London: Centre for Lebanese Studies, 1993.

Khalaf, Samir. *Civil and Uncivil Violence in Lebanon: A History of the Internationalization of Communal Conflict*. New York: Columbia University Press, 2002.

Makarem, Sami Nasib. *The Druze Faith*. Delmar, N.Y.: Caravan, 1974.

Norton, Augustus Richard. *Hezbollah: A Short History*. Princeton, N.J.: Princeton University Press, 2007.

Picard, Elizabeth. *Lebanon, a Shattered Country: Myths and Realities of the Wars in Lebanon*. Translated by Franklin Philip. Rev. ed. New York: Holmes & Meier, 2002.

Rougier, Bernard. *Everyday Jihad: The Rise of Militant Islam among Palestinians in Lebanon*. Translated by Pascale Ghazaleh. Cambridge, Mass.: Harvard University Press, 2007.

Traboulsi, Fawwaz. *A History of Modern Lebanon*. London: Pluto, 2007.

Zayn, Muḥammad Ḥusayn. *Al-Shīʿah fī al-tārīkh*. Beirut: Dār al-Āthār, 1979.

Zisser, Eyal. *Lebanon: The Challenge of Independence*. London: I. B. Tauris, 2000.

AUGUSTUS RICHARD NORTON
Updated by TAYLOR LONG
and AHMAD MOUSSALLI

LIBRARIES. *See* Education, Muslim.

LIBYA. Islam in nineteenth-century Libya—known at the time as the regions of Cyrenaica, Tripolitania, and Fazzān—was marked by Sunnī orthodoxy in its urban areas (primarily Tripoli, Benghazi, and the mercantile centers of Sabhā and Murzuq in Fazzān) and various heterodox and more populist interpretations in the rural hinterlands and among the nomadic tribes of the desert areas. The latter reinterpreted and adapted the austerity of Sunnī Islam to the Islamic practices of the regions' tribal communities. Small pockets of Ibāḍī Muslims dotted the Tripolitanian landscape.

The second Ottoman occupation, of 1835, meant primarily to forestall European colonial designs after the French invasion of neighboring Algeria in 1830, resulted in the first manifestations of both anti-Ottomanism and anti-Western sentiments expressed in overtly Islamic terms. This identification of a popular expression of Islam with political opposition became a defining characteristic of politics in Libya—a characteristic that marked not only the anticolonialist struggle and the Sanūsī monarchy after independence, but played a significant role in Muʿammar al-Qadhdhāfī's Jamāhīrīyah as well.

The Sanūsīyah. Sayyid Muḥammad ibn ʿAlī al-Sanūsī, an Algerian religious scholar who had traveled to Mecca, founded the Sanūsī order in 1842 in part to defend Islam against foreign encroachments and simultaneously to revitalize and purify the religion. Isolated Cyrenaica—outside European influence and only nominally under Ottoman suzerainty—provided the ideal locale for a religious movement that relied in part on the doctrine of *hijrah* ("withdrawal," in emulation of the Prophet Muḥammad's flight from Mecca to Medina) to settle among the tribes of the territory's hinterlands.

For almost nine decades the Sanūsī order was a powerful Islamic revivalist movement that combined both economic and religious elements as it spread across Cyrenaica, Fazzān, and parts of rural Tripolitania. Its economic importance, pointed out by Emrys Peters, resulted from the order's manipulation of tribal power over the trading routes that ran from the Sahara via Cyrenaica to the Libyan coast. Peters delineated a system of alliance patterns among local tribal leaders and *shaykhs* that allowed the order to dominate both local and long-distance trade. The order's religious relevance to the local tribes was expressed through its incorporation of the use of *shurafāʾ* (descendants from the Prophet Muḥammad who acquire thereby some of his qualities) and of *mrabtin* (local pious individuals endowed with saintly qualities).

By the end of the nineteenth century the Sanūsī order, centered first in Jaghbūb and then in the even more isolated desert oasis of al-Kufrah, in 1895 became the dominant religious and political power in Cyrenaica. As part of its mission it imposed a previously unknown degree of Sunnī orthodoxy among its rural adherents and paved the way for the further spread of Sunnī practice into Wadai and Tibesti, areas now part of modern Chad. The declining Ottoman Empire unofficially agreed to what Evans-Pritchard described as a "Turco-Sanusi condominium." With its property officially recognized by the Ottomans as *waqf* (religious endowment), the order came to symbolize orthodox Islam wherever its *zawāyā* (lodges) were found.

By the early part of the twentieth century only some of the *ʿulamāʾ* in the regions' urban centers could challenge the hegemony the Sanūsī had established. Not surprisingly the Sanūsī order led the local resistance, particularly in Cyrenaica, to the Italian invasion after the Ottoman Empire abandoned its efforts to do so in 1912. Although the Sanūsī leadership eventually fled to Egypt, it left behind a number of individual *shaykhs*—such as ʿUmar al-Mukhtār—who continued the struggle against the fascists until 1931.

Due in part to the Sanūsī alliance with the British in World War II, and because of the Great Powers' determination that Libya should not fall once more under Italian control, the Kingdom of Libya was proclaimed in 1951, with King Muḥammad Idrīs al-Sanūsī, the grandson of the order's founder, as its head. More concerned with scholarly pursuits, matters of religious importance—such as the creation of an Islamic university in al-Bayḍāʾ—and personal piety, Idrīs proved unable to effectively face the demands of a younger generation imbued with a growing sense of nationalism and an oil economy that grew at a phenomenal pace after the first marketing of oil in 1961. On the eve of the Qadhdhāfī coup in 1969 the monarchy had become a political anachronism and, significantly, the confluence of religion and the growing political opposition to the West remained an important feature of the military regime that succeeded it.

Qadhdhāfī's Revolution and Islam. Indeed, Qadhdhāfī's "revolution" was originally considered one of the earliest examples of the political renewal of Islam since the North African countries obtained their independence in the 1950s and 1960s. The Libyan leader was not trained in Islamic jurisprudence and had only a cursory knowledge of Islamic theology. His knowledge and interpretations of Islam reflected, primarily, the recent history of his country and of the Sanūsī kingdom.

The earliest pronouncements of the regime included a number of nationalist as well as Islamic references and the substantive measures initially taken by the regime—among them the revival of Qur'ānic criminal penalties and the banning of alcohol and nightclubs—indicated an open admittance of Islam as a guiding force in the country's political life. Although Islam would clearly be part of the revolution's ideology, it was mentioned only briefly in Article 2 of the constitutional proclamation issued by the revolutionary government on 11 December 1969, and then simply as "the religion of the state." Despite the fact that Qadhdhāfī himself on numerous occasions referred to the importance of Islam to his revolution, the unveiling of his political program during the Libyan Intellectual Seminar in May 1970 made only perfunctory references to Islam—except in the context of Qur'ānic education, which the government initially left untouched.

Both events hinted at the fact that the reformism of Qadhdhāfī and his revolutionary officers (if they were to be considered Islamic reformers), consisted of a highly idiosyncratic, politicized interpretation of Islam. Islam in Libya since 1969 can thus be characterized as both a conscious choice to promote political mobilization and as the embodiment of moral commitments by the revolution's leadership. The regime firmly believed that its search for legitimacy could only be achieved within Libya's highly conservative society if it could demonstrate its adherence to Islamic principles.

Simultaneously, however, this search for legitimacy also entailed the evisceration of all potential competitors by reducing regional and tribal power and identification—in particular the rural religious elites formerly affiliated with the Sanūsī lodges and the orthodox *'ulamā'* in the country's urban centers. The imposition of a new bureaucratic structure after 1970 was meant in part to secure the first objective. The latter, although already foreshadowed by expressions of distrust made by the regime vis-à-vis the *'ulamā'* during the 1970 Libyan Intellectual Seminar, took until early 1975 when they were removed from committees set up to reform the country's legal system. By that time Qadhdhāfī had already taken a number of measures that put his experiments at odds with Sunnī Islamic practices elsewhere.

Part of Qadhdhāfī's initiatives involved a series of legal reforms that dated back to a decree issued shortly after the 1969 revolution that called for the implementation of Sharī'ah law; this was extended by the Islamization of Libyan law in October 1971. The new regulations, derived from Mālikī legal practice, called for the maintenance of existing laws if they agreed with Sharī'ah principles and for the use of customary law (*'urf*) when applicable. In essence the regime devised a two-track approach by arguing that matters of religious doctrine were inviolable but that "secular" issues could be subjected to *ijtihād*, or innovative reasoning. Similarly, Qadhdhāfī was less willing to accept *ḥadīth*, *sunnah*, *ijmā'*, and *qiyās* and pronounced them unnecessary accretions to Islam. In particular he argued that only part of the *sunnah* could be considered a constitutive part of Sharī'ah, arguing that *ijtihād* was an acceptable means of broadening its scope in the modern world. In a celebrated discussion with the country's *'ulamā'* at the Mulay Muḥammad Mosque in Tripoli in July 1978 Qadhdhāfī reiterated most of these points.

Islam, Qadhdhāfī argued, should not simply reassert traditional values but should become a progressive force. As such the Libyan leader clearly saw the revival of Sharīʿah law as a means for both ideological renewal and greater political legitimacy. And it was this populist reinterpretation of Islamic law, devoid of specialized jurists, that assumed increasing importance throughout the 1970s and 1980s and that made every individual—in line with the regime's populist aspirations—a potential *mujtahid*, an individual capable of interpreting and innovating Islamic doctrine and law. These legal reforms in effect afforded the Libyan regime the opportunity to carefully control independent religious organizations. By taking control of *waqf* property through special legislation in 1972 and 1973 the regime further reduced the already diminished impact of the urban *ʿulamāʾ*. The *ʿulamāʾ*, now bereft of the financial basis of the religious establishment, for all practical purposes became state employees in Libya and lost whatever cultural, financial, and political autonomy they had once possessed. The Libyan state assumed the role of patron of the religious establishment, heavily subsidizing religious life and religious observance after 1970—including pilgrims performing the *ḥajj* and the construction of a significant number of new mosques.

As Qadhdhāfī started to conceptualize ideas that eventually resulted in the Third Universal Theory and the Green Books—political action based on Islam that would replace both capitalism and communism—his statements on Islam and political action based on Islam grew bolder. At the April 1973 Zuwārah speech, which ushered in his cultural revolution, Qadhdhāfī revealed the principles on which the country's political system would be based: Arab unity, direct popular democracy, and Islamic socialism. According to the Libyan leader the new theory would solve once and for all the contradiction inherent in a secular concept of the state caught between *dīn* (religion) and *dawlah* (state): Islam would serve as the source of inspiration for political renewal and innovation, and as a means of legitimizing the regime's political institutions. Qadhdhāfī's vision of egalitarian individualism—visible in the country's political institutions that were run directly by the people represented in People's Congresses and in Islam through the application of individual *ijtihād*—was repeated in the Green Book, which was implicitly based on Islamic doctrine.

The creation of the Jamāhīrīyah in 1977 was the culmination of this egalitarian process and augured in a new stage of Qadhdhāfī's interpretation of Islam. The economic aspects of his Green Book, which included the abolition of private property, were seen by the *ʿulamāʾ* as contradictory to Islam, and they objected to Qadhdhāfī's determination to use the Green Book's principles as an alternative to the traditional teachings of Sharīʿah law. In response Qadhdhāfī increased his own interpretations of Islam and declared in 1977, for example, that the Libyan calendar would start with the death of the Prophet Muḥammad in 632 rather than the customary date of the *hijrah* in 622. He finally mounted an all-out offensive against the power of the *ʿulamāʾ*. In early 1978 he argued that, because the Qurʾān was written in Arabic, there was no need for expert interpretation. The Qurʾān was declared the sole source of Sharīʿah law; the *sunnah*, as well as *qiyās*, *ijmāʿ*, and *ḥadīth* were rejected as errors. The mosques were put under popular control; the status of women in divorce cases was declared equal to that of men; and the *ḥajj* to Mecca was no longer considered a pillar of Islam.

As on all other occasions Qadhdhāfī's "innovations" served political as well as religious purposes: they afforded the regime greater legitimacy for whatever actions it took in secular matters and simultaneously freed it from the constraints of Islamic doctrine and tradition, which

Qadhdhāfī argued were outdated and open to individual interpretation. Although the reaction of the *ʿulamāʾ* within Libya remained necessarily muted, Qadhdhāfī's actions in time would be labeled by the country's underground Islamist movements as *bidaʿ*—heretical innovations. By the mid-1980s followers of these movements, including among others, the Ḥizb al-Taḥrīr al-Islāmī and the local version of the al-Ikhwān al-Muslimūn, were increasingly targeted and on several occasions publicly executed by the regime.

Throughout the 1990s the Qadhdhāfī regime faced opposition from a number of different groups, including Islamist fundamentalist movements consisting largely of Libyans who had fought against the Soviets in Afghanistan. In response it steered a middle course between hardline religious opponents and the general population, which was generally opposed to militant Islam. As it refuted militant Islamist authority through an anti-Islamist campaign, the regime in 1994 extended the application of Islamic law and granted new powers to religious leaders, including the right to issue religious decrees. In 1997 it passed a series of measures that authorized collective punishment for anyone harboring Islamists. By the end of the decade most of the Islamist opposition to the regime had been eliminated. As the country sought rapprochement with the West after 2003, the focus and relevance of whatever Islamist opposition to the Qadhdhāfī regime still existed was gradually lost, and by 2010 the regime felt sufficiently confident to release over two hundred imprisoned Islamists. The 17 February Revolution, which developed in 2011 and led eventually to the overthrow of the Qadhdhāfī regime, was largely nonideological in origin and direction with very little public support for the development of an Islamist alternative.

Assessment. Islam in Libya in the nineteenth and twentieth centuries shows the lingering impact of the country's historical legacy. During the colonial period in particular, the two competing religious establishments—the Sanūsī-allied *shaykhs* and the urban-based, orthodox *ʿulamāʾ*—cooperated with the British and the Italians respectively, and as a result undermined confidence among young Libyans who grew up during the Arab nationalist period that they could serve as trustworthy political interlocutors.

Qadhdhāfī's pronouncements on Islam after 1969 referred to this earlier historical period. In particular the pro-Western attitude and weak nationalist credentials of the Sanūsī monarchy indelibly marked the Libyan leader as he grew up in the country's hinterland, and resulted in his suspicion of any type of organized religious groups in the country, and eventually led to their evisceration in the mid-1990s. It also resulted in Qadhdhāfī's strong conviction, maintained throughout his tenure in office, that religious affairs were clearly both within the purview of the government and subject to personal interpretation.

Soon after the 1969 coup, Qadhdhāfī adopted a highly activist political stance in which he proclaimed himself a mediator between different interpretations of Islamic precepts. His insistence on the right of personal interpretation—that fused both his political and religious aspirations—necessitated a number of doctrinal interpretations that pitted him both against his country's *ʿulamāʾ* and much of the orthodox Sunnī religious establishment throughout the Arab world. It resulted in a political process in which the Libyan leader simply imposed his own views on Libyan religious leaders and the country's population alike. The Islamic precepts that Qadhdhāfī had originally advocated as valuable in themselves assumed an evocative symbolism in Libya, and anchored within the teachings of the Third Universal Theory, became a political instrument of the regime.

Despite this Islam in Libya today is not undergoing a religious revival by radical means. Qadhdhāfī sought simply to extend a long tradition of government that is based on and legitimated by religious precepts. If his attitude toward Islam was considered radical, it was primarily because his overall political, secular ambitions also were viewed as radical. As the latter lost their urgency and coherence in the late 1990s when Libya's confrontation with the West subsided, the former were viewed, increasingly, as an idiosyncratic, popular reinterpretation of Islam that was steeped in the egalitarian tradition Qadhdhāfī had grown up in.

In the post-Qadhdhāfī era, Libya can be expected to continue its tradition of governance grounded in and legitimized by religious precepts. The Draft Constitutional Charter for the Transitional Stage, unveiled in August 2011, guides the interim national government until a permanent charter is approved. A promising document in its commitment to popular sovereignty, civil liberties, and human rights, the draft charter calls for an independent, democratic state with Islam as the state religion and Sharīʿah as the principal source of legislation. In a homogenous Islamic society like Libya, which is conservative in outlook and deeply religious in nature, core elements of the draft charter will almost certainly be found in the permanent constitution.

BIBLIOGRAPHY

Ayoub, Mahmoud M. *Islam and the Third Universal Theory: The Religious Thought of Muʿammar al-Qadhdhafi*. London: KPI Limited, 1987.

Brahimi, Alia. "Islam in Libya." In *Islamist Radicalisation in North Africa: Politics and Process*, edited by George Joffé, pp. 9–27. London and New York: Routledge, 2012.

Evans-Pritchard, E. E. *The Sanusi of Cyrenaica*. Oxford: Clarendon Press, 1949.

Mason, John P. *Island of the Blest: Islam in a Libyan Oasis Community*. Athens: Ohio University: Center for International Studies, 1977.

Mayer, Ann Elizabeth. *Islamic Law in Libya: Analyses of Selected Laws Enacted since the 1969 Revolution*. London: School of Oriental and African Studies, 1977.

Pargeter, Alison. "Qadhafi and Political Islam in Libya." In *Libya since 1969: Qadhafi's Revolution Revisited*, edited by Dirk Vandewalle, pp. 83–104. New York: Palgrave Macmillan, 2008.

Peters, Emrys L. *The Bedouin of Cyrenaica: Studies in Personal and Corporate Power*. Edited by Jack Goody and Emanuel Marx. Cambridge, U.K., and New York: Cambridge University Press, 1990.

Qadhdhāfī, Muʿammar al-. *The Green Book* (*Kitāb al-akhdar*). Tripoli: World Center for Studies and Research of the Green Book, 1980.

St. John, Ronald Bruce. *Libya: Continuity and Change*. London and New York: Routledge, 2011.

St. John, Ronald Bruce. *Libya: From Colony to Revolution*. Rev. ed. Oxford: Oneworld, 2012.

Vandewalle, Dirk. *A History of Modern Libya*. Cambridge, U.K., and New York: Cambridge University Press, 2006.

Vikør, Knut S. *Sufi and Scholar on the Desert Edge: Muhammad b. ʿAlī al-Sanūsī and His Brotherhood*. Evanston, Ill.: Northwestern University Press, 1995.

DIRK VANDEWALLE
Updated by RONALD BRUCE ST JOHN

LOOSEN AND BIND, THOSE WHO. *See* Ahl al-Ḥall wa-al-ʿAqd.

LOYA JIRGA. *Loya jirga* is a Pushto term used in Afghanistan meaning "great council" and refers to an assembly of notable figures from throughout the country. The mythology of the *loya jirga* dates back several centuries, but in its modern guise it has served largely to legitimate a preexisting elite consensus. Such assemblies met in 1921 to ratify a treaty with the United Kingdom and in 1941 to ratify the expulsion of Axis nationals. A 1964 *loya jirga* endorsed a new constitution. During and after the Soviet-Afghan war of the 1980s, the idea of a *loya jirga* as a source of legitimacy was undermined from several directions.

In Kabul the communist regime used the term to describe a number of patently unrepresentative gatherings that predictably endorsed the regime's policies, something which tainted the concept in many Afghans' eyes. When meeting in 1989 in Rawalpindi, Pakistan, in response to the Soviet withdrawal from Afghanistan, Sunnī resistance parties from Afghanistan preferred to use the word *shūrā* to describe their gathering, with some hinting that a *loya jirga* was an instrument of Pushtun domination. The term almost disappeared in the immediate post-communist period because the Taliban showed no interest at all in consulting with others.

The displacement of the Taliban regime in November 2001 created the need for a pathway to new political arrangements, and the starting point was a conference of non-Taliban Afghan political actors, meeting under UN auspices, that was held in Bonn in late November and early December of that year. The agreement they finalized sought to use the perceived traditional legitimacy of the *loya jirga* in two distinct ways. First it provided for the holding of an "Emergency Loya Jirga" to lift the status of what in Bonn was labeled an "Interim Administration" to that of a "Transitional Administration." Second it provided for a "Constitutional Loya Jirga" to endorse a new constitution for the country. Each of these was held in due course, but neither quite matched the ideal of a *loya jirga* that had been in circulation, largely because behind-the-scenes actors—armed militia leaders and US officials in particular—played a large role in shaping the outcomes. Each gathering was notable for the presence of articulate women delegates. Their other notable feature was the use of indirect "election" procedures to choose delegates, but this meant that disappointment at manipulation by the powerful was all the more acute.

The 2004 Constitution moved to formalize the institution of *loya jirga*; Article 110 describes the *loya jirga* as the highest manifestation of the will of the people of Afghanistan and provides that it should be composed of members of the National Assembly and chairpersons of provincial and district councils. Its responsibilities under Article 111 are to amend the constitution, impeach the president, and take decisions on "the independence, national sovereignty, territorial integrity and supreme interests of the country." Much speculation has circulated about how these powers might be used, but with many critics of President Hamid Karzai holding seats in the National Assembly, he showed little interest in activating this kind of *loya jirga*. However he did not abandon the idea altogether. In June 2010 he convoked a "Peace Jirga" that authorized the establishment of a "High Peace Council," and more controversially, in November 2011, he brought together a group of supporters he called a *loya jirga*—quite distinct in composition from the *loya jirga* envisaged by the 2004 Constitution—to pronounce on the idea of a strategic partnership with the United States. This was little more than a piece of theater.

In twenty-first-century Afghanistan, the capacity of a *loya jirga* to generate widespread support for a government or its policies—in other words, to create political legitimacy—is far from clear. Such hopes are premised on a number of assumptions: that Afghanistan is a tribal society with Pushtuns dominant; that Pushtun leadership patterns remain stable; that the *loya jirga* is a traditional Pushtun institution of real salience; and that tradition remains an effective device for generating legitimacy. All these assumptions can be challenged. First claims that Afghanistan is a tribal society are easily overstated. While some ethnic groups such as Pushtuns have tribal structures within them, others do not. Furthermore while Pushtuns are almost certainly the largest ethnic group in the country, they do not comprise an absolute majority of the population. Second traditional Pushtun tribal leadership structures have been seriously disrupted in recent decades by armed attack, by forced migration, and by the rise of challengers such as the Taliban, or armed strongmen with links to wider political movements or the global economy. Third the history of the *loya jirga* suggests that it is to some degree at least an invented tradition for an imagined community, which may blunt its legitimating potential. Finally in a globalizing world in which young Afghans are increasingly exposed to influences that no earlier generation had encountered, the relevance of tradition is increasingly questionable.

BIBLIOGRAPHY

Buchholz, Benjamin. "Thoughts on Afghanistan's *Loya Jirga*: A Myth?" *Asien* 104 (July 2007): 23–33.

Hanifi, M. Jamil. "Colonial Production of Hegemony through the 'Loya Jerga' in Afghanistan." *Iranian Studies* 37, no. 2 (2004): 295–322.

Noelle-Karimi, Christine. "The Loya Jirga: An Effective Political Tool? A Historical Overview." In *Afghanistan: A Country Without a State?*, edited by Christine Noelle-Karimi, Conrad Schetter, and Reinhard Schlangenweit, pp. 37–52. Frankfurt, Germany: IKO (Verlag für Interkulturelle Kommunikation), 2002.

Reshtia, Sayed Qassem. "La Lôye Jerga: Ses Origines et son Rôle Historique dans l'Evolution de la Société Afghane." *Central Asian Survey* 7, nos. 2–3 (1988): 5–19.

WILLIAM MALEY

M

MADRASA. *See* Education, Muslim.

MAHDĪ. *See* Religious Beliefs.

MAHDĪ, AL-ṢĀDIQ AL-. (1936–) is a Sudanese Islamic thinker and contemporary political leader. As a great-grandson of the Sudanese Mahdī Muḥammad Aḥmad ibn ʿAbd Allāh (d. 1885), al-Ṣādiq was born into a leading Islamic family and trained for his leadership role from birth. He received a broad traditional Muslim education and later a modern one at Victoria College in Alexandria. He then studied at the University of Khartoum and graduated from St. Johns College, Oxford, where he studied philosophy, politics, and economics. Al-Ṣādiq rose to prominence in 1961 following the death of his father, Imam al-Ṣiddīq al-Mahdī. The *shūrā* council of the Anṣār (a Sudanese Islamic movement, originally the followers of Muḥammad Aḥmad, the Mahdī) decided that he was too young to become their imam and appointed his uncle al-Hādī instead. With the leadership divided and al-Ṣādiq heading the Ummah Party, a split within the Ummah and the Anṣār became unavoidable. It paved the way for a long-term pact between al-Ṣādiq and Ḥasan al-Turābī, the leader of Sudan's Muslim Brothers. This was probably one of the factors that led al-Ṣādiq, a presumed liberal, to announce his intention, on becoming prime minister in 1966, to promulgate an Islamic constitution and found an Islamic state. Al-Ṣādiq and his followers were defeated in the 1968 elections and had to seek reconciliation with his conservative uncle. This seems to have turned him into a conservative, and the Ummah-Anṣār coalition was as autocratic in the 1980s as it had been under previous imams. As prime minister after the 1986 elections, al-Ṣādiq was in full control of both the Anṣār and the Ummah. His failure to lead on the most crucial issues, the Islamic nature of the state and its interethnic and interreligious relations, probably caused his downfall in June 1989.

Al-Ṣādiq was the most prominent leader to oppose the so-called *Sharīʿah* laws implemented by President Jaʿfar Nimeiri in September 1983. He denounced them as un-Islamic because *Sharīʿah* could be implemented only in a just society in which Muslims were not forced to steal in order to survive. He failed to abolish these laws, however, while he was prime minister in 1986–1989 because of his ambivalence and inability to introduce alternative ones first. He assumed that he would lose popular support if he submitted to southern and secularist demands for unconditional abrogation. He tried to run again for office, this time for the presidency in 2010, but to no avail. He is still very much engaged in the politics of Sudan and often tries to impose himself on the political landscape by offering solutions to the Darfur crisis. Yet because of the weakness of his position vis-à-vis the other more powerful elements in the country, he remains but a marginalized intellectual whose tenure in politics has merely subordinated idealism for real-politik.

Al-Ṣādiq has expressed his views on the Islamic state in many of his writings, and in these his ideology is far more liberal and progressive than his political career would suggest. He ruled that modern formulation of *Sharī'ah* should be entrusted to universities, with lay scholarly supervision; otherwise *Sharī'ah* will wither away, and Muslim leaders will have abdicated their trust. Islamic states may be traditional, modernizing, or revolutionary, as long as they abide by the general constitutional principles of Islam and as long as their legal systems are based on a traditional or modern formulation of *Sharī'ah*. Following a detailed elaboration of al-Ṣādiq's views on human rights "one may suggest that al-Ṣādiq seems to be of the opinion that the Ḥudūd (legal punishments for serious crimes) may—even should—be frozen."

In the sphere of economics two principles should be applied. First wealth is collectively owned by humanity, and while individual ownership is legitimate, society has to provide for the poor. Second it is mandatory to implement special injunctions, such as *zakāt* (alms-giving), inheritance laws, and the prohibition of usury. Hence there is no contradiction in an economic system that is both Islamic and modern. Islamic international relations, according to al-Ṣādiq, are to be based on peaceful coexistence; war is justified to deter aggression and is not permitted as a way of enforcing Islam. Even pagans are not to be converted by force. In Islamic international relations there are four basic principles: human brotherhood, the supremacy of justice, the irreversibility of contracts, and reciprocity. Finally al-Ṣādiq regards *taqlīd*, the uncritical adoption of a tradition or a legal decision, as a great curse. He claims that when non-Muslim opinion refers to Islamic fundamentalism, it is *taqlīd* they have in mind and that it should therefore be abolished.

[*See also* Sudan; *and* Turābī, Ḥasan al-.]

BIBLIOGRAPHY

Works by al-Ṣādiq al-Mahdī

"Islam—Society and Change." In *Voices of Resurgent Islam*, edited by John L. Esposito, pp. 230–240. New York and Oxford: Oxford University Press, 1983.

Yas'alūnaka 'an al-Mahdīyah. Beirut: Dār, al-Qaḍāyā, 1975.

Secondary Works

Esposito, John L., and John O. Voll. *Islam and Democracy*. New York: Oxford University Press, 1996.

Esposito, John L., and John O. Voll. *Makers of Contemporary Islam*. New York: Oxford University Press, 2001.

Ibrahim, Hassan Ahmed. "An Overview of al-Sadiq al-Mahdi's Islamic Discourse." In *The Blackwell Companion to Contemporary Islamic Thought*, edited by Ibrahim M. Abu Rabi', pp. 161–174. Malden, Mass., and Oxford: Blackwell, 2006.

Johnson, Douglas H. *The Root Causes of Sudan's Civil Wars*. Bloomington: Indiana University Press, 2003.

Lesch, Ann Mosely. *The Sudan: Contested National Identities*. Bloomington: Indiana University Press, 1998.

Warburg, Gabriel R. *Islam, Sectarianism, and Politics in Sudan since the Mahdiyya*. London: Hurst, 2003.

Gabriel R. Warburg
Updated by Khaled M. G. Keshk

MAHATHIR BIN MOHAMED. Mahathir bin Mohamed (1925–) was born 20 December

1925 in Alor Setar, Kedah, Malaysia. As the prime minister of Malaysia from 1981 to 2003, he is credited with engineering Malaysia's rapid modernization symbolized, among others things, by a multimedia super corridor, Kuala Lumpur International Airport and its adjacent Sepang International Race Circuit, and the Petronas Twin Towers, which was, until 2003, the tallest building in the world. He embraced an export-oriented market strategy that propelled Malaysia into the world's top twenty trading nations and enhanced the living standards of its citizens.

The son of a schoolmaster, Mahathir attended a Malay school in Sebrang, Perak, before enrolling in Sultan Abdul Hamid College, Alor Setar, Kedah. In 1947 Mahathir entered the King Edward VII College of Medicine in Singapore, where he met Siti Hasmah Mohd Ali, whom he married in 1956. After graduation in 1953 Mahthir entered government medical service, which he left in 1957 and established the Maha Clinic, which earned him popularity. He was first elected to parliament in 1964 and reelected in 1974, and he held several ministerial posts in the 1970s. He was elected president of the United Malays National Organisation (UMNO) in 1981 and, on 16 July 1981, became the fourth prime minister of Malaysia. Unlike his predecessors who were members of the royal families, Mahthir was a commoner, a "rebel and troublemaker" with a modest social background. He led the ruling coalition, Barisan Nasional (BN), to win all the consecutive elections with a two-thirds majority of seats in the parliament.

Mahathir did face several threats to his rule but overcame these challenges. The most serious challenge to Mahathir's rule was mounted by Anwar Ibrahim, the deputy prime minister. The split was preceded by the 1997–1998 financial crisis. Anwar was supportive of open markets and international investment while Mahathir preferred a home-grown solution. A bitter struggle ensued, with Anwar Ibrahim launching a reform movement (*reformasi*). Mahathir sacked Anwar from the post of deputy prime minister, expelled him from UMNO, and finally had him arrested.

Mahathir's long tenure as the prime minister gave Malaysia the political stability needed for economic growth. He welcomed foreign investment, reformed the tax structure, reduced trade tariffs, and privatized numerous state-owned enterprises. The New Economic Policy, which had encouraged Malay economic success, was replaced in 1991 by the New Development Policy, which emphasized general economic growth and the elimination of poverty. Under Mahathir's leadership Malaysia prospered economically with a growing manufacturing sector and its own national car, the Proton. He unveiled Vision 2020 in 1991, a blueprint for Malaysia to achieve the status of a developed nation by the year 2020.

Mahathir urged Malaysians to strive for a balance between spirituality and material well-being. He launched a policy of Islamization, in 1982, with the aim of inculcating Islamic values and enhancing the integrity of the management in government. He also embarked upon the Clean, Efficient, and Trustworthy campaign to improve the quality of work. He emphasized the need for the Muslims and Malays to acquire knowledge. He asked Muslims to absorb the scientific knowledge of the West and the values of orderliness, discipline, and firm social organization in order to regain the lost glory of Islamic civilization.

Mahathir as prime minister, was outspoken and blunt. He was active in international affairs, especially in the Association of Southeast Asian Nations (ASEAN) and the Asia-Pacific Economic Cooperation (APEC) forum. He spoke in favor of nonalignment and the economic development of the less developed. He criticized the West for trying to impose liberal democracy and neoliberal economics on developing nations. He was critical of the West for its double standards in the

Middle East, for the excesses of globalization, and for hypocrisy over human-rights practices.

Mahathir is also a prolific writer. He wrote articles for the *Straits Times* and *Sunday Times* in Singapore and also contributed monthly articles to the *Mainichi Daily News* of Japan, compiled in his *Reflections on Asia* (2001), explaining how Malaysia went against the economic orthodoxy and challenged the theology of the free market. Altogether he has authored seventeen books.

Bibliography

Work by Mohamed Mahathir

Mahathir bin Mohamed. A *Doctor in the House: The Memoirs of Tun Dr. Mahathir Mohamad*. Selangor, Malaysia: MPH Group, 2011.

Secondary Works

Khoo, Boo Tek. *Paradoxes of Mahathirism: An Intellectual Biography of Mahathir Mohamad*. Kuala Lumpur: Oxford University Press, 2003.

Wain, Barry. *Malaysian Maverick: Mahathir Mohamad in Turbulent Times*. Basingstoke, U.K., and New York: Palgrave Macmillan, 2009.

Welsh, Bridget, ed. *Reflections: The Mahathir Years*. Washington, D.C.: South East Asia Studies Program, Johns Hopkins University, 2004.

Yu, Eugene. *Mahathir Mohamad: An Illustrated Biography*. Selangor, Malaysia: MPH Publishing, 2008.

Abdul Rashid Moten

Majlis. In the pre-Islamic and early Islamic periods the Arabic term *majlis* ("place of seating; session") was used for the assembly of the tribal chief or notables, later that of the ruler who held court, either in an entertaining sense, with scholars holding learned debates and poets declaiming their poems, or in a governing sense, to receive petitioners who required a public audience with the sovereign. By the fifteenth century at least, *majlis* was used in premodern states for a governing body. The encyclopedist Aḥmad al-Qalqashandī (d. 1418) includes in his fourteen-volume work *Ṣubḥ al-aʿshā* a description of the powers enjoyed by the Sublime Council (*al-majlis al-ʿāla*) of the Mamlūk vice-sultan Kitbughā al-Manṣūrī, to wit, "to promulgate government orders concerning such matters as legal affairs, governance, tax collection, public safety and innovations" (Tsugitaka 1997, p. 108). From this usage *majlis* came to refer to a constituent assembly or elected parliament, in which sense it is first found in the promulgation in 1866 of an "Assembly of Delegates" (*majlis shūrā al-nuwwāb*) by Khedive Ismāʿīl Pasha of Egypt, whose seventy-five members were elected for three-year terms.

This Egyptian body was followed by the first Ottoman parliament, convened in 1877, which according to the constitution of 1876 was intended to have two chambers: an elected chamber of delegates and an appointed chamber of notables. In practice the elected chamber's role in governing was limited by ministerial powers and the sultan's veto. The parliament was dissolved by sultanic decree one year later, in 1878; when the sultan himself was removed from power in 1908, the parliament was reconvened and it functioned until 1920, at which time the Ottoman Empire was breaking up and it was replaced by Turkey's Grand National Assembly, a unicameral legislative body known simply as the Meclis.

With the collapse of the Ottoman Empire many of its constituent lands were colonized and parliaments were inaugurated under the watchful eyes of the alien powers. Many were elected bodies—of men by men since few women across the region enjoyed suffrage—and had legislative powers, and despite upheavals in the political realm of most Muslim lands have remained standing, even if largely as a facade, as in Syria after the military coups of 1949 and in Iraq after 1979 where under Saddam Hussein only Baʿath party members, or those who swore allegiance to the Baʿath party, were allowed to run for election to the National Assembly (*al-majlis al-waṭanī*). In the monarchies of the Gulf states, Kuwait and Bahrain being exceptions, the *majlis* has only an advisory role and is generally composed, sometimes partially, of appointees. Oman's Majlis al-Shūrā is an elected body that until 2011 had only advisory powers, while Qatar's establishment of a parliament, which was granted by the first constitution of 2003, has been continually postponed, with elections promised in 2007 and now in 2013.

In Iran the parliament is also called Majles, its full name being Majles-e Shorā-ye Eslāmī. It was founded in 1906 as a bicameral institution and was continued as a unicameral parliament in the Islamic Republic, which overthrew the prerevolutionary regime of the Shah in 1979. Unlike many of its counterparts, the Majles of revolutionary Iran has never been dissolved and has consistently held elections every four years since the first Majles convened in 1980. Although the parliamentary elections are generally considered free, both the candidates who stand for election and all laws that are proposed or passed by Parliament are vetted, and can be struck down, by the Guardian Council.

In Ismāʿīlī usage *majlis* has a particular connotation, not shared by the other sectarian branches of Islam; it refers to a "formal session of religious instruction, the place of it, and also to the lecture or sermon read in it" (Madelung, 1986, p. 1033). An early treatise by Muḥammad ibn ʿAbd al-Karīm al-Shahrastānī (d. 1153) entitled *Majlis-i maktūb*, which was discovered in 1964, is an example of such a sermon, in this case delivered to a Twelver Shīʿī audience circa 1145. The *majlis* was institutionalized by the Fāṭimids, whose chief propagandist of the religion (*dāʿī al-duʿāt*) would prepare and deliver a sermon twice weekly, at which time payment of a tax called *najwā* was collected.

[*See also* Constitutions and Constitutionalism; Elections; Governance; Representation; *and* Women in Politics.]

BIBLIOGRAPHY

Baktiari, Bahman. *Parliamentary Politics in Revolutionary Iran: The Institutionalization of Factional Politics*. Gainesville: University Press of Florida, 1996.

Karpat, Kemal H. "The Ottoman Parliament of 1877." In his *Studies on Ottoman Social and Political History: Selected Articles and Essays*, pp. 75–89. Leiden, Netherlands: E. J. Brill, 2002.

Lazarus-Yafeh, Hava, et al., eds. *The Majlis: Interreligious Encounters in Medieval Islam*. Wiesbaden: Harrassowitz, 1999.

Madelung, Wilferd. "Madjlis." *Encyclopaedia of Islam*. 2d ed. Vol. 5, pp. 1031–1082. Leiden, Netherlands: E. J. Brill, 1986.

Shahrastānī, Muḥammad ibn ʿAbd al-Karīm. *Majlis: Discours sur l'ordre et la création*. Translated by Diane Steigerwald. Sainte-Foy, Que.: Presses de Université de Laval, 1998.

Tsugitaka, Sato. *State and Rural Society in Medieval Islam: Sultans, Muqtaʿs, and Fallahun*. Leiden, Netherlands, and New York: E. J. Brill, 1997.

Peri Bearman

Majlisī, Muḥammad Bāqir al-.

(c. 1627–1699), influential Shīʿī theologian of the late Ṣafavid period (1501–1722) and one of the most important *ḥadīth* scholars of Imāmī "Twelver" Shiism.

Muḥammad Bāqir al-Majlisī, also referred to as Allamah Majlisī and Majlisī the Second, was born in Isfahan to a clerical family from Lebanon. His father, Muḥammad Taqī al-Majlisī (c. 1594–1659) known as Majlisī the First, was the Friday prayer leader in Isfahan, with leanings toward the Akhbārīyah school of Shīʿī theology, and allegedly Ṣūfī inclinations, as well. Muḥammad studied the Qurʾān and jurisprudence with his father, receiving licenses to refer to and report *ḥadīth* from notable contemporaries including Mullā Muḥsin Fayḍ al-Kāshānī (d. 1680), Sayyid Mīrzā Jazā'irī (c. 1640–1701), Shaykh Ḥurr-i Āmulī (c. 1624–1693), and Muḥammad Ṭāhir Qummī (d. 1686), all of whom were prominent Akhbārī traditionalist *ḥadīth* scholars, appointed to the position of *shaykh al-Islām* in their respective cities.

Muḥammad Bāqir al-Majlisī was a prolific writer in both Persian and Arabic. He is widely recognized for compiling one of the most comprehensive collections of Shīʿī *ḥadīth*, a massive 110-volume encyclopedia called the *Bihār al-anwār* (The Sea of Lights), which included all the recorded traditions of the imams that Majlisī could find (regardless of the strength of their respective chains of transmission).

According to the Akhbārīyah school, the role of clerics was essentially apolitical, but al-Majlisī wielded considerable political power. He was appointed *shaykh al-Islām* of Isfahan by both Shah Sultan Ḥusayn and Shah Sulaymān. Despite his father's alleged connections to Sufism, Muḥammad Bāqir al-Majlisī was a vociferous opponent of Sufism and Sunnism, becoming one of the most influential proponents of Shiism as a national identity. He promoted rituals and customs unique to Imāmī Shiism as it exists today, including visitation/pilgrimage to the tombs of Shīʿī saints, and popular mourning sermons commemorating the tragedies at the Battle of Karbala.

Al-Majlisī promoted an essentially Akhbārīyah legalist theology, creating normative pressures on those who were not Shīʿī and those who disputed his interpretation of Shiism. In al-Majlisī's perspective the Prophet and his successors were infallible beings, and the accounts of their sayings and doings (*aḥādīth*) were the chief sources of appropriate jurisprudence. Human beings are innately irrational and corrupt and unable to determine what is permissible without guidance; therefore the role of *ijtihād* (reason in Shīʿī jurisprudence) was designated only to the elite jurists whose position became divinely ordained, implicit representatives of the Prophet's missing successor, the Twelfth Imam.

Thus, disputing al-Majlisī's theology was tantamount to disputing the infallible. Al-Majlisī's oppression of Sufism and philosophy, as well as his promotion of new Shīʿī rituals, helped replace the popularity of gnostic mysticism/Sufism with institutionalized legalism in dominant Shīʿī discourse. Al-Majlisī's influence on Shīʿī theology, the weight of *ḥadīth* for determining law, and the elevated role of the jurist greatly influenced Iranian religious culture. Al-Majlisi remains a controversial figure for advocates and critics of Iranian clerical hierocracy and authority in Shīʿī discourse, all of whom look to al-Majlisī's precedence.

BIBLIOGRAPHY

Works of Muḥammad Bāqir al-Majlisī

Biḥār al-anwār al-jāmiʿah li-durar akhbār al-aʾimmah al-aṭhār. Beirut: Dār al-Taʿārif li-al-Maṭbūʿāt, 2001.

Essence of Life: A Translation of Ain al-hayat. Qom, Iran: Ansariyan Publications, 2005.

Hayat al-Qulub: Stories of the Prophets, Characteristics and Circumstances of the Prophets and Their Successors. Qom, Iran: Ansariyan Publications, 2003.

Secondary Works

Brown, Jonathan A.C., *Hadith: Muhammad's Legacy in the Medieval and Modern World*. Oxford: Oneworld Publications, 2009, pp. 132–133.

Karanjia, Ramiyar P. "Majlesi, Moḥammad-Bāqer." In Encyclopædia Iranica, online edition, 2011. http://www.iranicaonline.org/articles/majlesi-mohammad-baqer.

AARON ALBERT HALEY

MAJLIS ULAM INDONESIA. The Indonesian Council of Ulama (*Majelis ʿUlamaʾ*

Indonesia or MUI) was formed in 1975 during the military-dominated New Order. Authorities saw it as a means of transmitting government policies to the Islamic community and controlling dissident Islamic elements. The regime did not want the MUI to attach itself to any political party. During the New Order era, the MUI was closely identified with the Ministry of Religion and from its outset the Council has received the majority of its funding from the state. With the return to democracy after 1998 the MUI has been more independent, but has expanded its authority over Islamic matters. Indonesia's present president, Susilo Bambang Yudhoyono, has sought the advice of the MUI and stated that the organization is central in matters regarding the Islamic faith.

The MUI is administered by a board of directors and an advisory group that contains representatives from almost all the major Islamic organizations, including the Muhammadiyah and Nahdatul Ulama as well as more militant groups such as the Islamic Defenders Front and the Majelis Mujahidin Indonesia. It excludes Islamic groups that the MUI considers "deviant," such as the Aḥmadīyah. There are approximately 150 branches with independent authority.

The MUI also has a series of boards and institutes that provide additional authority and state funding. The most prominent of these is the National Syariah Board and the Institute to Study Food, Medicine and Cosmetics. The MUI is also involved in administering the *ḥajj*.

The Council is well known for its *fatāwā*, which originate among the small Fatwa Commission of the MUI at the annual conference (the national conference held every five years), or by individual members. The annual and national conferences reflect more discussion and tend to have greater weight, although no *fatāwā* are legally binding unless backed by state action.

MUI *fatāwā* tend to reflect a conservative interpretation of Islam and an agenda that seeks to foster a less pluralistic religious environment. It has been most vigorous in attacking what it sees as heretical interpretations of Islam such as the Aḥmadīyah and Shiism. Support for the MUI's campaign against heresy has come from high government leaders including the president and attorney general. It's most well-known effort to define Islam has been its long-term campaign to ban the Aḥmadīyah from practicing in Indonesia. This effort can be observed in MUI *fatāwā* of 1980 and 2002, in numerous statements by the organization's leaders, and tacit support of violent actions against the Aḥmadīyah. It has actively pressured the government to pass legislation to reinforce this position. There have been no such efforts to ban other religions, although Muslims have been discouraged from participating in some aspects of interfaith interaction as illustrated by the Jakarta branch invoking a 1981 *fatwa* banning Muslims from attending Christmas celebrations or giving Christians greetings. It does not seek to suppress Christianity, Buddhism, or Hinduism but is wary of possible efforts to convert Muslims. At the local level there have been isolated threats against Christian churches. However, the MUI rejects terrorism and considers suicide bombing as *ḥarām* (forbidden).

Also well publicized has been the MUI 2005 *fatwa* criticizing pluralism, liberalism, and secularism. These concepts are seen as encouraging a secular environment, leading believers to seek answers outside of Islam and allowing religious freedom to all sects including those adhering to heretical interpretations of Islam. The MUI's conservative social agenda has included opposition to homosexuality, pornography, and the use of alcohol, immodest clothing, and nightclubs during Ramadan. Prominent members have supported female circumcision. At the international level it has defended Islamic causes and defended Islam against perceived attacks, leading to the condemnation of American actions in the Middle East post-9/11.

The MUI has not been without detractors. There have been complaints about too many *fatāwā*, an issue that the organization sought to redress. Often individual MUI members have issued what many would consider trivial statements, such as declaring speed bumps *ḥarām*. At times the organization is erroneously linked to *fatāwā* by other bodies. More liberal Muslims, such as the Liberal Islam Network, have criticized the organization's stand on pluralism, liberalism, and liberal democracy. The MUI has also been confronted by those who believe that it concentrates too much on *ḥalāl* (permissible) and *ḥarām* and insufficiently on broader social issues such as poverty and corruption.

BIBLIOGRAPHY

Gillespie, Piers. "Current Issues in Indonesian Islam: Analysing the 2005 Council of Indonesian Ulama Fatwa No. 7 Opposing Pluralism, Liberalism and Secularism." *Journal of Islamic Studies* 18, no. 2 (2007): 202–240.

Hooker, M. B. *Indonesian Islam: Social Change through Contemporary Fatawa*. Honolulu: University of Hawaii Press, 2003.

Lindsey, Tim. "Monopolising Islam: The Indonesian Ulama Council and State Regulation of the 'Islamic' Economy." *Bulletin of Indonesian Economic Studies* 48, no. 2 (2012): 253–274.

Means, Gordon P. *Political Islam in Southeast Asia*. Boulder, Colo.: Lynne Rienner. 2009.

Fred R. von der Mehden

MALAYSIA. The Malay Peninsula before the imposition of British rule in the late nineteenth century comprised traditional Malay states under the control of hereditary Malay sultans. In these states Islam, which had spread to this part of the world during the twelfth to fourteenth centuries, was already strongly established at all levels of society. Aspects of Islamic law were observed to varying degrees, although elements of pre-Islamic culture still existed among the people. Among the sacred powers of the Malay rulers was responsibility for the defense and good governance of Islam as the state religion.

The role of the religious scholar was essentially that of faithfully preserving, transmitting, translating, and commenting on the classical from Mecca that he learned, mastered, and largely memorized. The intellectual tradition and paradigm of religious *taqlīd* (faithful preservation and imitation of traditional opinions regarded as authoritative and orthodox) was nurtured in the Malay kingdoms.

Arabic Texts. The inclination toward *taṣawwūf* (Islamic mysticism, Ṣūfism) and the popularity of Ṣūfī *ṭarīqahs* (brotherhoods) among the Malays was fostered by Ṣūfī-oriented Muslim preachers and scholars and reflected in the preeminent position of the twelfth-century scholar al-Ghazālī's thought in the Malay-Indonesian archipelago. Because of the unifying thrust of al-Ghazālī's intellectual contributions, many great figures of Islamic learning in the Malay states from the seventeenth century through the nineteenth pursued a tradition of Islamic learning in which *fiqh* (jurisprudence), *taṣawwūf*, and *kalām* (theology) were integrated.

What formal education existed for the Malay community during the early part of the nineteenth century was purely Islamic religious, centered on the reading and memorization of the Qurʾān and the learning of basic religious rituals such as prayer, fasting, *zakāt*, and the *ḥajj*. The mosque was the only site of such education until the emergence of the *pondok* (private residential religious seminary) in the late nineteenth century and the *madrasah* (school, pl. *madāris*) in the beginning of the twentieth century.

British Colonial Period. The Muslim states of the Malay Peninsula outside the three Straits Settlements—the island of Penang (acquired in 1786), the island of Singapore (1819), and Melaka (Malacca, 1824)—remained free from British interference until the latter part of the nineteenth century. The Pangkor Agreement of 1874 signaled the imposition of British rule on the Malay states of the peninsula. It provided for the appointment of a British resident to the Malay state; it was incumbent upon the Malay ruler (sultan) to ask his advice and act upon it in all matters "other than those touching Malay Religion and Custom." This led to the creation of a new religio-legal bureaucracy subservient to the royal palace and subordinate to the traditional Malay elites close to the palace. This bureaucratization of Islam served to strengthen the control of the Malay sultan and the secular traditional elite over the religious life of the people.

Perceiving British rule as essentially one of infidel dominance supported by Christian evangelism, the Malay religious leaders and scholars generally adopted a hostile attitude toward Western culture. Consequently they mobilized their resources to strengthen and defend the Islamic identity of the masses by building their own *pondoks* and *madāris* with independent curricula and financial resources. Except in areas where the spirit of *jihād* against British colonialism or Siamese expansionism in the north was generated by a few prominent religious scholars around the turn of the century, an attitude of resignation and submission to British rule prevailed among both the Malay rulers and the masses.

Khan Trust for Culture. The beginning of the twentieth century witnessed the emergence of an Islamic reform (*iṣlāḥ*) movement that began to criticize the socioeconomic backwardness and religious conservatism of traditional Malay society of the time. This new socioreligious activism began when several religious scholars studying in the Middle East came under the powerful influence of the revivalist and reformist ideas of Jamāl al-Dīn al-Afghānī and Muḥammad ʿAbduh at the close of the nineteenth century; others were earlier exposed to the puritanical teachings of the Wahhābī movement. From their base in Singapore and later in Penang, the reformers pioneered the establishment of modern *madāris* whose curriculum differed radically from the *pondok* system, with the introduction of several modern subjects and a new method of learning and teaching religion. This modernization of religious education and the spread of reformist writings and thought through the new media of magazines and newspapers had far-reaching social and political consequences.

The religious bureaucracy and the traditional *ʿulamāʾ* (scholars) were accustomed to some religious practices regarded by the reformists as *bidʿah* (unlawful innovation), and they tolerated some degree of accommodation with local traditions that were perceived by the reformists as *khurāfāt* (superstitions and accretions). They opposed the views and activities of the reformists, popularly called Kaum muda (the Young Group). The call for greater exercise of independent religious reasoning (*ijtihād*) with direct reference to the Qurʾān and the *sunnah* and less reliance on a single *madhhab* (legal school) was strongly resisted by the traditionalists, who came to be known as Kaum Tua (the Old Group). In their efforts to rouse the Malay community from its intellectual slumber and socioeconomic inferiority to the immigrant non-Muslim communities in the urban centers, the reformists also came to criticize and challenge the political order of the British colonialists. Seriously inhibited by British colonial policy coupled with opposition from both the traditionalists and Malay secular elites, Islamic reformism in British Malaya was unable to become an effective social force.

The Japanese interregnum during World War II, though traumatic, did not seriously alter the position of Islam among the Malays. The Islamic reformist spirit and Pan-Islamic advocacy were suppressed while Malay nationalist sentiments gathered momentum. Postwar Malay nationalism of a conservative orientation saw the foundation of the United Malay Nationalist Organization (UMNO) in 1946. The British formed the Federation of Malaya in 1948 after its Malayan Union proposal was rejected by the Malays. They arrested both the radical Malay nationalist leaders and the proponents of an Islamic political party, Hizbul Muslimin, which was banned a few months after its formation in 1948. The Pan-Malayan Islamic Party (Partai Islam se Malaysia, better known as PAS) originally developed from the defection of the *ʿulamāʾ* faction in UMNO in 1951 and became a registered political party in 1955. Its emergence marked another turning point in the development of Islamic thought in the Malay states.

Independence. The British granted independence to the Federation of Malaya in 1957, with Singapore becoming a separate colony, and thus began the era of parliamentary democracy and constitutional monarchy. In 1963 Malaysia came into being, with the inclusion of Singapore (until mid-1965) and the two Bornean states of Sabah and Sarawak.

The total population of Malaysia, according to 2011 estimates, was 29.27 million compared to 18.38 million in 1991. Malaysia is multiethnic and multireligious and is characterized by an almost complete identification of religion with ethnicity. The Muslim portion, comprising mainly ethnic Malays, was 61.3 percent in 2010, Buddhists, mainly ethnic Chinese, 19.8 percent, and ethnic Indians Hindus 6.3 percent. The Christians (9.2 percent) come mainly from the indigenous Kadazans of Sabah and the Ibans of Sarawak, although, like Islam, Christianity has followers among all of the country's ethnic groups except the Malays.

Although the position of Islam as the official religion of post-independence Malaysia—with the Malay rulers of each state serving as the guardians of Islamic religion and Malay custom—was guaranteed in the constitution, only some aspects of the life of the Muslim community and the nation were influenced by Islamic values and norms. The government under the leadership of Tunku Abdul Rahman with the support of the British was committed to a secular vision of the new nation and vigorously opposed the Islamic political struggle and ideals. As such, it came under strong attack from the PAS and other Islamically oriented Malay organizations. PAS became part of the coalition government of the National Front in 1973. The government under the second prime minister of Malaysia, Tun Abdul Razak, established the Islamic Centre, which formed an important part of the Islamic Religious Affairs section of the prime minister's department. Tun Abdul Razak's government gave increased attention to the educational, social, and economic development of the Malay Muslims, in part to accommodate the demands coming from PAS within the government and from the *daʿwah* (Islamic proselytization) movement outside it. After leaving the coalition in 1977, rivalry between PAS and UMNO became a major factor in framing government Islamic policies.

Daʿwah. The assertive and generally antiestablishment *daʿwah* movement emerged in the 1970s through the activities of youth organizations in secular educational institutions, including the National Association of Malaysian Muslim Students (PKPIM), the Islamic Representative Council (IRC), and the Malaysian Muslim Youth Movement (ABIM), established in 1971. ABIM became the dominant student *dakwah* organization under the leadership of Anwar Ibrahim, who underscored a more flexible and pluralist approach than many of its more conservative membership. It represented a new phase in Islamic thought and action, but its vision of Islam as a complete and holistic way of life was in fact a continuation and elaboration of earlier reformist and revivalist movements in the Middle East and Pakistan. Complementing the Islamic political movement in the country, the youth-led *daʿwah* organizations pressed for the greater application of Islamic laws and values in national life and articulated the holistic Islamic perspective of social, economic, and spiritual development. While the scope of Islamic religiosity was widened to embrace all aspects of life, the intensity of religious life was simultaneously emphasized by *daʿwah* proponents. Thus the form and content of Islamic life were noticeably affected. The government under Tun Hussein Onn at first viewed the new phenomenon negatively, and was extremely wary of the political effect of assertive, Malay-dominated *daʿwah* on the multiracial nation and its own political strength. One of the central government's responses was to initiate its own *daʿwah*-oriented institutions and activities under the aegis of the Islamic Centre and in cooperation with government-linked Muslim missionary organizations. The Ministry of Education was also progressively improving the teaching of Islam in the schools; it established the Faculty of Islamic Studies in the National University of Malaysia in 1970, opening up new opportunities for Islamically committed graduates to work in the civil service.

The resurgence of the holistic Islamic consciousness, spearheaded by the *daʿwah* movement was reinforced in the 1970s by the Afghan War, increased funding of religious activity from the Middle East and the 1979 victory of the Islamic Revolution in Iran. There was demand for the establishment of more Islamic institutions in the country and the government under Tun Hussein Onn made some concessions.

The Mahathir Administration. After a decade of Islamic resurgence, affecting both religion and politics in the Malay community, Mohamed Mahathir was deeply aware of its long-term implications for UMNO and its legitimacy in the view of the Malays, whose Islamic consciousness was clearly on the rise. PAS continued to insist on the full implementation of the Sharīʿah and the establishment of an Islamic state in Malaysia. When PAS asserted that UMNO was a secular party without Islamic credentials, Mahathir took steps to nurture the Islamic identity of his own party.

He brought into UMNO Anwar Ibrahim, the charismatic leader of ABIM and an articulate spokesman of nonpartisan *daʿwah* in the 1970s. His wooing of Anwar and ABIM was a strategy calculated to strengthen the Islamic credentials of his government and to "out-Islam" PAS in its Islamic challenge. With the help of Anwar, Mahathir largely succeeded in both. The creation of the Islamic Bank and the establishment of the International Islamic University in 1983, followed by that of the International Institute of Islamic Thought and Civilization in 1987, were the immediate results of Anwar's direct involvement in Mahathir's administration.

The creation of these institutions was in line with the Mahathir administration's new program known as the "Islamization Policy." In the domain of law, he declared that "Islamic laws are for Muslims and meant for their personal laws, but laws of the nation, although not Islamically-based can be used as long as they do not come into conflict with Islamic principles." In line with his Islamization policy and with this stand on Islamic law, Mahathir established the Sharīʿah and Civil Technical Committee with the objectives of upgrading the status of Shariʿah courts and ensuring all laws of the country would be in conformity with Islam. In a controversial statement, criticized by both PAS and non-Muslim groups, he declared that Malaysia was already an Islamic state.

Most important to Mahathir, however, was Malaysia's economic development, which is the legacy of his rule that is best remembered and most widely acknowledged. His political aim was "to make Islam in Malaysia synonymous with economic progress and modernization." Under his twenty-two-year rule Malaysia witnessed the most significant Islamic and economic transformations in its history. Malaysia in 2010 was the sixteenth-largest trading nation in the world. With economic progress and independence, Malaysia under Mahathir was free to pursue an independent foreign policy that was openly critical of Western powers. From its architectural feat of building the tallest twin towers in the world to its political feat of championing global Muslim interests in international forums, Mahathir's Malaysia had succeeded in attracting attention from the worldwide Muslim *ummah*.

In 1998, however, Mahathir faced the biggest crisis of his political career following a political feud he had with Anwar, his heir apparent. Mahathir fired Anwar from both the government and the UMNO and Anwar was convicted of corruption and sodomy, although many viewed the charges as politically motivated. He had served six years of his fifteen-year sentence when he was released on 2 September 2004, upon his acquittal of the sodomy charge by the federal court.

Into the Twenty-first Century. Mahathir resigned voluntarily as prime minister on 1 October 2003, having been Malaysia's longest-serving prime minister. He was succeeded by Abdullah Badawi, whose advocation of Islam Hadhari (civilizational Islam) was presented as a new approach to the development and governance of Islam, emphasizing "civilizational" development of Islam instead. Islam Hadhari's ten principles stress healthy spiritual development, good governance, mastery of knowledge, economic development, better quality of life, protection of the rights of minority groups and women, cultural and moral integrity, environmental protection, and strong national defense. Unlike the reception of Mahathir's Islamization policy, Islam Hadhari has generated more controversy in the Muslim community than among the non-Muslims. Critics have termed it a new sect and an unacceptable interpretation of Islam and said that the call for a moderate was a redundancy because Islam is inherently moderate.

When Badawi's successor Najib Abdul Razak came into office in 2009, he stated that he would continue Islam Hadhari. He has presented Malaysia as a model of moderate, modern Islam. Although he has stated that Islam guides Malaysia's policies, he has advocated a more inclusive nation under the banner of "1Malaysia."

Malaysia's biggest challenge in the new century is to maintain interethnic and interreligious peace in the light of new religious, political, social, and economic developments.

[*See also* Daʿwah; Partai Islam se Malaysia; *and* United Malays National Organization.]

BIBLIOGRAPHY

Abdullah Ahmad Badawi. *Islam Hadhari: A Model Approach for Development and Progress*. Singapore: MPH Group Publishing, 2006.

Al-Attas, Syed Muhammad Naguib. *Preliminary Statement of a General Theory of the Islamization of the Malay-Indonesian Archipelago*. Kuala Lumpur: Dewan Bahasa dan Pustaka, 1969.

Bakar, Osman. "Islam and Political Legitimacy in Malaysia." In *Islam and Political Legitimacy*, edited by Shahram Akbarzadeh and Abdullah Saeed, pp. 127–146. London and New York: Routledge Curzon, 2003.

Liow, Joseph Chinyong. *Piety and Politics: Islamism in Contemporary Malaysia*. Oxford and New York: Oxford University Press, 2009.

Mauzy, D. K., and R. S. Milne. "The Mahathir Administration in Malaysia: Discipline Through Islam." *Pacific Affairs* 56, no. 4 (Winter 1983–1984): 617–648.

Muhammad Kamal Hassan. *Moral and Ethical Issues in Human Resource Development.* Kuala Lumpur: Institut Kajian Dasar Malaysia, 1993.

Muhammad Kamal Hassan. "The Response of Muslim Youth Organizations to Political Change: HMI in Indonesia and ABIM in Malaysia." In *Islam and the Political Economy of Meaning: Comparative Studies of Muslim Discourse,* edited by William R. Roff, pp. 180–196. London: Croom Helm, 1987.

Riddell, Peter G. *Islam and the Malay-Indonesian World: Transmission and Responses.* London: Hurst, 2001.

Roff, William R. *The Origins of Malay Nationalism.* 2d ed. Kuala Lumpur and Oxford: Oxford University Press, 1994.

M. Kamal Hassan
and Osman Bakar
Updated by Fred R. von der Mehden

Malcolm X. (1925–1965), born Malcolm Little, also known as El-Hajj Malik El-Shabazz, was an African American Muslim leader, civil and human rights advocate, Pan-Africanist, and Pan-Islamist. The life of America's most conspicuous Muslim in the 1960s was shaped by resentment of white (European American) racism and a determination to improve the lives of African Americans. Malcolm was born in Omaha, Nebraska, to uneducated, poor, Christian, "black nationalist" (Garveyite) parents whose unfortunate destinies affected him throughout his life. He believed that whites had murdered his father and unjustly placed his mother in an insane asylum and himself and his siblings in different foster homes. At the age of fifteen, when Malcolm finished the eighth grade, he knew that he was disinclined toward formal education and established religion. He chose a life of vice and crime.

It was Malcolm's imprisonment for larceny (1946–1952) that marked the beginning of his intellectual and social transformation. Prison was the "academy" where he read Western and Eastern philosophy and literature, as well as works on Christianity, genetics, and American slavery, and where he improved his oral skills. The scope of his readings may have exceeded that of the average American undergraduate. His informal studies introduced him to Islamic precepts and Muslim heroic history.

Encouraged by his siblings and an inmate, Malcolm converted in 1948 to the doctrines of the Honorable Elijah Muhammad (d. 1975), leader of the Nation of Islam, and by the time he was paroled, he had dropped the name "Little," which he considered his "slave name," and adopted the surname "X," representing his lost tribal name.

Malcolm was attracted by Muhammad's principal claims that God is a black man (often called Master W. F. Muhammad) who will liberate African Americans and destroy Satan—their white oppressors—and that Elijah Muhammad was his messenger. Malcolm was equally fascinated by Muhammad's verbal boldness and his sanction of retaliatory, not aggressive, violence. Malcolm's social experiences, intellectual accomplishments, and dedication to his leader qualified him for an ascendant position in the Nation.

Muhammad's appointment of Malcolm X to the leadership of Temple Number Seven (in mid-1954) in the Harlem district of New York City was crucial to his and the Nation's fame. As third world and American political activism expanded in the late 1950s and early 1960s, Malcolm became increasingly brazen in his denunciation of racism and publicly supportive of African American, African, and Muslim liberation movements. Some of his speeches tested his leader's protective policies of political inaction and avoidance of unnecessary contact with Sunnī Muslims. Nonetheless Muhammad recognized the benefits of giving him a margin of freedom, provided Malcolm's loyalty was evident.

From 1959 onward, however, Malcolm allowed his eagerness for modification of Muhammad's policies and his own popularity to make his loyalty questionable. His short visits to Saudi Arabia and African countries as Muhammad's emissary, and the national broadcast of "The Hate That Hate Produced" (1959), his most effective television interview, strengthened his political attractiveness. Malcolm was disappointed that Elijah Muhammad's 1959 visit to Muslim countries, and his performance of the Lesser Pilgrimage (*'umrah*), did not result in significant political changes in the Nation.

Under the watchful eyes of envious Nation officials, Malcolm gradually modified his administration of Muhammad's Mosque Number Seven. Although he continued to respond sharply to Sunnī Muslim condemnation of the Nation's theology, he instituted regular Arabic instruction and maintained close contact with Muslim diplomats. Furthermore Malcolm deemphasized the Nation's doctrine of "the satanic nature of whites" and instructed his assistant ministers in African and Asian cultures and current affairs. These modifications were indicative of the less restrained, sociopolitical activist role he wished to play.

In November 1963 Malcolm provided his detractors in the Nation, along with Elijah Muhammad, with an excuse to rid themselves of what they perceived as a threat to their power. Contrary to his leader's directive not to comment on the murder of President John F. Kennedy, Malcolm compared it to "chickens coming home to roost." Although he claimed that his remark was inadvertent, it reflected his impatience with Muhammad's political restrictions. Yet he was neither organizationally nor financially prepared for his suspension that December. His withdrawal from the Nation in March 1964 represented his determination to be an effective political activist and his realization that he was not indispensable to Muhammad's movement. His vindictive exposure of Muhammad's immorality, about which he had heard in the 1950s, did not much augment his meager following or his prestige.

Malcolm's public confrontation with Muhammad was not essentially doctrinal. Months after his withdrawal from the Nation, he continually acknowledged Muhammad as his spiritual leader, and he asserted that their differences were primarily political and moral.

After separating from the Nation, Malcolm's most urgent concerns were his Islamic credibility, funds, and his racist image. He probably thought his conversion to Sunnī Islam and his pilgrimage (*ḥajj*) in 1964 would help to resolve these problems and reconcile him with Muslims internationally. Now known as El-Hajj Malik El-Shabazz, his acts of piety, his celebrated letter from Mecca, and his meetings with Muslim heads of state and Islamic officials apparently were not given much laudatory coverage in the Arabic press. Malcolm knew that Muslim dignitaries wished him well and recognized the Islamic legitimacy of his sociopolitical concerns, but their belated and parsimonious response to his need for material and moral support negatively affected the growth of his short-lived Muslim Mosque, Inc., and Organization of Afro-American Unity (founded in March and June 1964, respectively, now apparently defunct).

Immigrant Muslims, whom Malcolm had charged two years earlier with deliberate disinclination toward proselytizing among African Americans, were unconvinced of his Islamic sincerity. Most American Sunnī Muslims were similarly unresponsive. Despite their admiration of his advocacy of civil and human rights, which the Organization of African Unity resolved to support in the United Nations, Malcolm's recent past and his conversion attracted few of them to the Muslim Mosque, Inc.

It is debatable whether Malik completely abandoned the notion of an organic relationship between European and American whites and Satan. Malcolm had seen phenotypically white Muslims—and African Americans—and accepted them as brothers long before his travels abroad. Minimally his post-pilgrimage statements indicate his increased preparedness not to offend potential supporters.

The influence of Malcolm X's persona, rather than that of El-Hajj Malik El-Shabazz, is most observable among non-Muslims and Muslims alike. Under pressure from mainly non-Muslim African Americans, New York City preserved and dedicated a portion of the Audubon Ballroom, where assassins' bullets cut short Malcolm's last speech. His birthday and his assassination on 21 February 1965 by members of the Nation of Islam with the apparent complicity of American authorities are widely remembered. He was given a Muslim burial by an obscure African American Sunnī organization. The Sunnī Muslim community was conspicuously underrepresented at his funeral, which was held in a church. He is immortalized by reprints of his best-selling *Autobiography*, his speeches, and biographies; streets, schools, and other buildings, including the former Mosque Number Seven, bear his name. Muslims reproach non-Muslims for their projection of El-Hajj Malik El-Shabazz as an ethnocentric revolutionary whose primary concern was civil and human rights, not Islamic proselytization (*daʿwah*).

Spike Lee's internationally acclaimed film *Malcolm X* (1992) generated the most varied discussion of Malcolm since his death. Many immigrant and American Muslims, notably Imam Warith Deen Mohammed (d. 2008), have confirmed Malcolm's Islamic genuineness. Minister Louis Farrakhan (b. 1933) continues to speak ill of Malcolm's attitude toward Elijah Muhammad's immorality; he cautions that Lee's film may cause further division in the present Nation of Islam, which he leads. Both Imam Mohammed and Minister Farrakhan claim to continue Malcolm's social and political work. Although both "Malcolm X" and "El-Hajj Malik El-Shabazz" are considered martyrs, the life of the latter was too brief, and thus his legacy too meager, to compete with "Malcolm" for an exalted place in the collective Muslim memory.

[*See also* Nation of Islam.]

Bibliography

Works of Malcolm X

The Autobiography of Malcolm X. With the assistance of Alex Haley. New York: Grove Press, 1965. Written by Alex Haley based on a series of interviews with Malcolm X shortly before his death.

Malcolm X Speaks. Edited by George Breitman. New York: Grove Press, 1965. Useful collection of his post-Nation religious and political thought.

*The End of White World Supremacy: Four Spee*ches. Edited with an introduction by Benjamin Karim. New York: Arcade Publishing, 1971. Rare representation of his doctrinal and social thought before his conversion to Sunnī Islam.

February, 1965, the Final Speeches. New York: Pathfinder Press, 1992. The latest and most useful compilation of Malcolm's last presentations abroad.

Secondary Works

Carson, Clayborne. *Malcolm X: The FBI File*. Edited by David Gallen. New York: Carroll & Graf, 1991.

Clarke, John Henrik, ed. *Malcolm X: The Man and His Times*. Trenton, N.J.: Africa World Press, 1990. The best collection to date of essays by individuals associated with Malcolm in the United States and abroad, including his widow.

Cone, James H. *Martin & Malcolm & America: A Dream or a Nightmare?* Maryknoll, N.Y.: Orbis Books, 1991. Outstanding analysis by a renowned African American exponent of Christian liberation theology.

Evanzz, Karl. *The Judas Factor: The Plot to Kill Malcolm X*. New York: Thunder's Mouth, 1992 Goldman, Peter. *The Death and Life of Malcolm X*. New York: Harper, 1973.

Jaaber, Hjeshaam. *The Final Chapter: I Buried Malcolm (Haj Malik El-Shabazz)*. Jersey City, N.J.: New Ming Productions, 1993.

Karim, Benjamin, Peter Skutches, and David Gallen. *Remembering Malcolm*. New York: Carroll & Graf, 1992.

Kly, Y. N., ed. *The Black Book: The True Political Philosophy of Malcolm X (El Hajj Malik El Shabazz).* Atlanta: Clarity Press, 1986. A Muslim's interpretation of Malcolm's religiosocial and political doctrines.

Lomax, Louis E. *To Kill a Black Man.* Los Angeles: Holloway House, 1968. The earliest and fullest comparative analysis of the thoughts of Malcolm X and Martin Luther King by a close associate of both men.

Lomax, Louis E. *When the Word is Given: A Report on Elijah Muhammad, Malcolm X, and the Black Muslim World.* New York: New American Library, 1963.

Muḥammad, Akbar. In *The Islamic Impact*, edited by Yvonne Y. Haddad, Bryon Haines, and Ellison Findly. Syracuse, N.Y.: Syracuse University Press, 1984.Perry, Bruce. *Malcolm: The Life of a Man Who Changed Black America.* Barrytown, N.Y.: Station Hill Press, 1991.

Terrill, Robert. *Malcolm X: Inventing Radical Judgment.* East Lansing: Michigan State University Press, 2004.

Tyner, James A. *The Geography of Malcolm X: Black Radicalism and the Remaking of American Space.* New York: Routledge, 2006.

AKBAR MUHAMMAD

MALIK. *See* Schools of Jurisprudence, *subentry* Sunni Schools of Jurisprudence.

MAMLŪK STATE. A regime controlled by slave soldiers (sing. *mamlūk*, pl. *mamālīk*, "one owned") governed Egypt, Syria, southeastern Asia Minor, and western Arabia (the Hejaz) from 1250 to 1517. Founded by officers (*amīrs*) of the Ayyūbid sultan Ṣalāḥ al-Din al-Ayyūbī (d. 1193), the Mamlūk State was born under the shadow of usurpation. Fearing their displacement by Ṣalāḥ's heir Tūrān-Shāh, these officers, who had attained high rank in their former master's Baḥrīya regiment, assassinated the legitimate claimant and designated one of their own as sultan. The first two sultans, Aybak and Quṭuz, were preoccupied with quelling internal rebellion by their own subordinates and external rivalry by surviving Ayyūbid princes in Syria. Quṭuz's lieutenant Baybars won renown following his victory over invading Mongols at ʿAyn Jālūt (Spring of Goliath) in Palestine, but soon thereafter he murdered his sovereign and began to formalize his administration.

Sultan Baybars (r. 1260–1277) spent much of his reign battling the Crusader states in Syria-Palestine and securing his eastern frontiers against invasions from Il-Khanid Iran. Yet he did not neglect the infrastructure of his regime. The Nile Valley's agrarian resources were inventoried, and the Ayyūbid system of land allotments to militarists (*iqṭāʿ*) was restructured. In consequence of Baybars's policies and those of his major successors, Qalāwūn (r. 1279–1290) and al-Nāṣir Muḥammad (r. 1310–1341), a state far more centralized than its Ayyūbid predecessor was created in the central Arab lands. Moreover, Baybars offered haven in Cairo to an uncle of the last ʿAbbāsid caliph in Baghdad (dispatched by the Mongols in 1258), and so the orthodox caliphate was revived in Egypt—but under the Mamlūk sultan's strict control. The caliph now functioned solely as the sultan's legitimator, thereby mitigating the seizure that had sullied the origins of his office.

Until the mid-fifteenth century the Mamlūk State flourished as the undisputed military power of the central Muslim world. Although the regime recruited its ruling oligarchy from men who were imported as slaves, and therefore never surmounted the sedition and intrigue that had given it birth, the Mamlūk sultanate stabilized the political order in this turbulent zone for 267 years. Until around 1340, when the Black Death decimated the populace of both Egypt and Syria, the regime enjoyed an era of prosperity. Agrarian productivity was high, and the trade linking South Asia with the Mediterranean poured copious revenues into the government's coffers. The

Mamlūk autocrat was acknowledged as the paramount monarch of Sunnī Islam because of his dominion over all three holy cities (Mecca, Medina, and Jerusalem). No foreign competitor in Europe or Southwest Asia posed any tangible threat to Mamlūk suzerainty until the final decade of the fifteenth century, when the international balance of power altered radically. Because Mamlūk factional quarreling was confined largely to the military elite, the mass of the population and its productive sectors remained unscathed until insurmountable fiscal crises compelled the regime to adopt predatory measures to stave off bankruptcy. Cairo, Damascus, and Aleppo flourished as brilliant centers of culture, while the literary arts experienced a "silver age" of refinement. The Mamlūk elite invested heavily in charitable endowments (*awqāf*) that supported a sophisticated religio-academic class in these urban centers. Cairo in particular cast a cosmopolitan lure across the Islamic world, attracting scholars to its schools from afar.

The sultanate's economy never recovered fully from the famines and plagues of the later fourteenth century. Whether the regime could have devised long-term strategies rather than short-term expedients to surmount these disasters—had its elite been less preoccupied with disputes among cadres—remains a debated issue. Certainly the emergence of the formidable Ottoman military threat in Asia Minor, plus the growing maritime menace from Europe, transcended the Mamlūks' powers of deterrence. Thus, after more than one hundred years of stop-gap efforts to recover its former glory, the Mamlūk sultanate was defeated in 1516 at Marj Dābiq in Syria by the Ottoman monarch Selim I. Cairo fell to Selim the following year. Today historians castigate the Mamlūk State for its acceleration of economic decline in the central Arab lands. Yet this regime indelibly shaped the bureaucracy and administrative profile of Egypt into modern times. The sultanate imparted a legacy of security to these regions that later governments have sought with less success to emulate.

[*See also* Egypt; *and* Ottoman Empire.]

BIBLIOGRAPHY

Ayalon, David. *Studies on the Mamlūks of Egypt (1250–1517)*. London: Variorum Reprints, 1977. Collected articles by the leading authority on the Mamlūk institution.

Irwin, Robert. *The Middle East in the Middle Ages: The Early Mamluk Sultanate, 1250–1382*. London: Croom Helm, 1986. Political survey of the Baḥrī Mamlūk era.

Lapidus, Ira M. *Muslim Cities in the Later Middle Ages*. Cambridge, Mass.: Harvard University Press, 1967. Insightful description of urban society under Mamlūk rule, with an extensive bibliography.

Petry, Carl F. *The Civilian Elite of Cairo in the Later Middle Ages*. Princeton, N.J.: Princeton University Press, 1981. Quantitative analysis of the scholastic elite (*ʿulamāʾ*) during the Mamlūk period.

Petry, Carl F. *Protectors or Praetorians?: The Last Mamlūk sultans and Egypt's Waning as a Great Power*. Albany: State University of New York Press, 1994.

Wasserstein, David J., and Ami Ayalon, eds. *Mamluks and Ottomans: Studies in Honour of Michael Winter*. London: Routledge, 2006.

CARL F. PETRY
Revised by KHALED M. G. KESHK

MAQĀṢID AL-SHARĪʿAH. *See* Sharīʿah.

MARTYRDOM. Like Judaism and Christianity, Islam accords a special status to those who sacrifice their lives in the service of their religion. Early sources (Qurʾān and *ḥadīth* [traditions]) and the auxiliary sources (*sīrah* [biography of Muḥammad], *maghāzī* [accounts of military campaigns], *ʿilm al-rijāl* [biographies of narrators], and *tafsīr* [exegesis]) all underline the value of life and the ultimate price paid to sacrifice it.

The meaning of *shahīd* (martyr), which appears no less than fifty-six times in singular, plural, and adverbial forms in the Qurʾān, is "eyewitness" or "witness" in a legal sense. Apart from the direct reference to the plural *shuhadāʾ*, however, the Qurʾānic valorization of *ṣabr* (endurance in times of difficulty) and the related theme of the suffering of all the prophets at the hands of persecutors supports reverence of martyrdom, long suffering, self-sacrifice, and patience.

Mahmoud Ayoub (1978) has pointed out that, even in the earliest portion of the Qurʾān, there is a divine confirmation of the ideal of martyrdom (Q 85:3–8). The most important verse dealing with martyrdom is one in which the word *shuhadāʾ* (witnesses) is interpreted by many exegetes to mean "martyrs." Qurʾān 4:69 says "Whosoever obeys God, and the Messenger—they are with those whom God has blessed. Prophets, just men, martyrs [*shuhadāʾ*], the righteous; good companions they!" (A. J. Arberry's translation). Arberry (d. 1969), faithful to the exegetical tradition, unhesitatingly uses "martyrs" to translate *shuhadāʾ*, whereas other translators, such as Yusuf ʿAlī (d. 1953), more cautiously use the English word "witnesses" instead.

The doctrine of the Hereafter (*al-ākhirah*) caused Muḥammad much trouble with his early audiences, who stubbornly refused to accept the idea of life beyond the grave. Islam thus deemed "vainglory" the pre-Islamic Arab literary and cultural motif of *fakhr* (honor or pride in prowess on the field of tribal warfare) and replaced it with a glorification of the pious dedication to the struggle for the promotion of the Word of God. In the *ḥadīth* collection of the ninth-century Persian compiler Muslim ibn al-Ḥajjāj, the author quotes the prophet Muḥammad: "Whosoever partakes of the battle from desire of glory or in order to show his courage, is no martyr; a martyr is only he who fights in order that Allāh's Word may be prevalent" (Wensinck, 1941, p. 95) that, according to al-Ḥajjāj, expressely clarified the prophet's understanding. The change in ethos indicated between the period of Jāhilīyah and the Islamic era is analogous to the change Christianity wrought in the pagan world.

Thus martyrdom in Islam is intimately connected with the rewards of Paradise. This is clear in the *ḥadīth* literature, which served as a basis for the final elaboration of the doctrine of martyrdom by the *fuqahāʾ* (legal scholars) of Islam. Indeed the *ḥadīth* literature is vastly more supportive of and unambiguous about martyrdom than is the Qurʾān. There are countless explicit statements attributed to the Prophet that make it clear those who die for Islam enjoy a special rank.

As a result Muslims esteem martyrdom and associate it with eternal rewards. Islamic respect for martyrdom can be ritualistic or devotional, as in the case of the *taʿzīyah* (consolation) commemorations in Shiism, or historical, as in the manner in which all Muslims idealize the formative struggle of the early band of Muslims under the leadership of Muḥammad. It can also be existential: that is, Muslims may seek to become martyrs, to better earn spiritual solace. The ideal of martyrdom can be read into the very name of the religion: *Islām* means submission to the will of God. And the primary—not to say archetypal—act of submission is, according to the Islamic tradition, Abraham's willingness to sacrifice his son, and, presumably, his son's willingness to comply, thereby rendering that son (unidentified in the Qurʾān) a martyr or, more accurately, one who was willing to become a martyr.

There have been times in the Islamic community when the ideal of martyrdom was "socialized." Within the larger Sunnī tradition, the personal ethos and ideal of martyrdom became quiescent as a religious motif. Even though Sunnī theologians recognized the power of the idea and even perpetuated the veneration of the early martyrs of Islam—such as Ḥamza ibn ʿAbd al-Muṭṭallib, the original *sayyid al-shuhadā*ʾ (Prince of Martyrs, a title now most familiarly attached to the hero par excellence of the Shīʿī, Ḥusayn ibn ʿAlī)—and the veneration of the sacrifices made by the early community as acts of martyrdom, they nonetheless rigorously opposed the cultivation of a contemporary cult of martyrdom in their respective societies by emphasizing the illegality of suicide and equating the seeking of a martyr's death with it. This was, no doubt, at least partly in response to the activities of rebellious groups such as the Khawārij (Khārijīs) who were disruptive to the greater unity of Muslims, the *ahl al-sunnat wa-al-jamāʿat* (the people of the [Prophet Muḥammad's] tradition and the greater Muslim community—what may be called "catholic Islam"). The same theologians elevated the accomplishment of moral and ethical challenges as equal or even preferable to death: fasting, regularity in prayer, reading the Qurʾān, filial devotion, and rectitude in the collection of taxes. The rank of martyr could thus be sought in the normal acts of worship: the ritual perfection and purity of motive with which these were performed then determined how close a believer might come to being granted the prize of martyrdom.

In addition, books of *ḥadīth* list categories of believers whose deaths occur in such a violent or painful way that they are counted as martyrs. According to Wensinck, such a death can be of five, seven, or eight types. The most explicit list is from the *Muwaṭṭa*ʾ of Mālik ibn Anas (d. 795): The martyrs are seven, apart from death in Allāh's way. He that dies as a victim of an epidemic is a martyr; he that dies by being drowned is a martyr; he that dies from pleurisy is a martyr; he that dies from diarrhea is a martyr; he that dies by fire is a martyr; he that dies by being struck by a wall falling into ruins is a martyr; the woman who dies in childbed is a martyr.

It is indicative of this transition that none of the "Rightly Guided" Caliphs, the first four caliphs of Sunnī tradition, is typically given the rank or title of martyr. This is interesting because Abū Bakr, the first caliph, is the only one of the four not to have been killed in an open act of violence, which gives credence to later interpretations of the phenomenon by scholars. In keeping with Islam's communal ethos, martyrdom is treated by the *fuqahā*ʾ as not necessarily or most importantly a means for achieving individual salvation or felicity in the next world. Rather it has the pragmatic value of ensuring the continued existence of the group through communal defense.

Shīʿī Islam, however, is often identified by the way in which the ideal of martyrdom has been kept a vital element of belief. The potency of the ideal here can be seen by referring to the only Islamic movement of the modern period to have acquired a universally recognized distinct or non-Islamic identity—the Bahāʾī faith. In this religion, which began in a Shīʿī milieu, the ideal of martyrdom is retained as an important element of contemporary religious belief. Shiism, especially since the establishment of the Ṣafavid dynasty at the beginning of the sixteenth century, elaborated the motif of cultivated martyrdom as a religious and cultural ideal to an unprecedented degree. The Twelver Shīʿī list of martyrs begins with Abel (Qābīl) and continues through history to include the prophet Muḥammad and eleven of the twelve imams, the exception being the still-expected Twelfth Imam. Within Shiism the visiting of the graves of the martyrs—preeminently but not exclusively the imams—has special religious significance, as do weeping for them (or even pretending to weep) and suffering distresses similar to those of Ḥusayn and his companions, such as thirst. Indeed, according to some contemporary Shīʿī authorities, the true meaning of the mystical term *fanā'* (annihilation, selflessness) is none other than the sacrifice of the physical life in the path of Islam (as related in a speech by Ayatollah Sayyid Maḥmud Ṭāleqāni [d. 1979]).

The theme of martyrdom is important in Sufism. The Islamic world is adorned with thousands of shrines (sg., *mashhad*) to pious Muslims who have been regarded as martyrs, though not all places known as *mashhad* claim to hold the remains of a bona fide martyr. (In Turkish, for example, *meshed* is a word for "cemetery" in general.) These tombs are the objects of special veneration and pilgrimage, the practice of which is traced to the Prophet himself, who is said to have visited the graves of the martyrs of the Battle of Uḥud interred in al-Baqīʿ cemetery in Mecca to pay special homage to them. In Sufism, however, martyrdom acquires many of the same features associated with the type of the martyr-hero exemplified by Jesus in the Gospel accounts of the Passion, the most important example here being that of al-Ḥusayn ibn Manṣūr al-Ḥallāj—whose act of martyrdom is frequently conflated with that of Ḥusayn ibn ʿAlī—who was crucified in Baghdad in the early tenth century and has been "kept alive" as an ideal of piety and spiritual valor not only in the Ṣūfī tradition but in aspects of wider Islamic culture as well. But there have been many others, including his son Manṣūr ibn Manṣūr al-Ḥallāj, Suhrawardī "al-Maqtūl" of Aleppo (d. 1191), ʿAyn al-Quẓātok Hamadānī, ʿImād al-Dīn Nesîmî in Turkey, ʿAbd al-Ḥaqq Ibn Sabʿīn in Spain, and Sarmad in Mughal India, to name a few of the most famous. Even at the time of Ḥallāj's crucifixion, visitation to the tombs of martyrs was such a firmly established practice that Ḥallāj's remains were cremated and the ashes scattered on the Euphrates so that no tomb to him could be erected that might become the object of a cult. The recent study of the fourteenth-century Indian Ṣūfī martyr Masʿūd Beg shows the literary process involved in the acknowledgment of a saint as also a martyr.

Martyrdom Today. Islam is based on bearing witness to the truth of God's most recent revelation through his final prophet Muḥammad. Insofar as the most dramatic—and according to some the most meaningful—form of bearing witness has to do so with one's *nafs* (self, soul, life), then Islam is also based on martyrdom. But, as we have seen, the act of bearing witness is accomplished in Islam in a number of ways, ranging from the uttering of the words *lā ilāha illā Allāh wa-Muḥammad rasūl Allāh* (there is no god but God, and Muḥammad is the messenger of God) to the ultimate act of witnessing, the sacrificing of one's own life for the establishment or defense of Islamic ideals. Between these two possibilities are a number of other acts and gestures that have been recognized by *fuqahā'* as constituting *shahādah* under the Islamic holy law, Sharīʿah. These other acts include dying during pilgrimage, dying from various particularly virulent and painful diseases, for women dying during childbirth, and so forth.

Today Islam is distinguished among the world religions by the intensity with which martyrdom, in the sense of relinquishing one's life for faith, is consciously kept alive and cultivated. The motif within Sunnī Islam has been seen to reside—obviously quite erroneously, especially in light of recent history—chiefly in the veneration of the struggles of the early Islamic community with the Meccan Arabs and their *jāhilī* culture. With the severe dislocations experienced by a large part of the Muslim world since the eighteenth century, a new era of the understanding of martyrdom has arrived. In some ways the importance of the theme in the contemporary world transcends the divisions of Sunnī, Shīʿī, and Ṣūfī.

Martyrdom was a prominent theme in the recent Iran-Iraq War (1980–1988); both sides relied heavily on the ideal to motivate military troops. Since 1994 the theme has achieved even more prominence with the rise of terrorist groups describing themselves as Islamic. The most prominent and dramatic example has been the destruction of the World Trade Center in New York City on 11 September 2001. While the prize of martyrdom continues to inspire those involved in the Palestinian opposition to Israel and the American-led wars in Iraq and Afghanistan, and in light of contemporary challenges that mistakenly associated suicide operations against "unbelievers" with martyrdom, leading theologians in the more conservative schools of thought revised their interpretations to revert back to the essential view that moral and ethical accomplishments were preferable to death. Saudi clergymen such as ʿAbd al-ʿAzīz ibn Bāz, Muḥammad bin Ṣāliḥ al-ʿUthaymīn, and Ṣāliḥ bin Fawzān al-Fawzān, all members of the kingdom's Council of Senior Scholars and the Permanent Committee of Scholars, prohibited suicide bombings as a legitimate form of "*jihād*," insisting that committing such acts were fighting for the sake of Satan. Martyrdom operations were frowned upon elsewhere throughout the Muslim world, although more extremist practitioners continued to stand by the practice.

In general, while martyrdom does not figure prominently in the Qurʾān, tradition holds that one who has died in the service of Islam is distinguished from other Muslims in the life after death in several ways:

1. A martyr is spared the postmortem interrogation by the angels Munkar and Nakīr;
2. A martyr bypasses purgatory (*barzakh*) and, on death, proceeds directly to the highest station in Paradise, nearest the divine throne;
3. This station is called in a *ḥadīth* "the most beautiful abode" and the *dār al-shuhadāʾ* (abode of martyrs);
4. Martyrs' wounds will glow red and smell of musk on the Day of Judgment;
5. Of all the inhabitants of Paradise, only the martyrs wish for, and are theoretically allowed, to return to earth in order to suffer martyrdom (again);
6. Through meritorious acts, a martyr is rendered free of sin and therefore does not require the Prophet's intercession (*shafāʿah*);
7. Some traditions even portray notable martyrs as intercessors for others;
8. Because of their purity, martyrs are buried in the clothes in which they died and are not washed before burial;
9. According to al-Ghazālī, a martyr enjoys the third highest position in the afterlife, just below the prophets and the *ʿulamāʾ* (religious scholars); according to an earlier authority (Abū Ṭālib al-Makkī, d. 996), the martyrs rank second as intercessors after the prophets.

Such traditions appear to gain popularity during times of extreme sociopolitical turmoil, although contemporary interpretations increasingly tolerated the practice to its nonviolent features.

[*See also* Jihād.]

BIBLIOGRAPHY

Aghaie, Kamran Scot. *The Martyrs of Karbala: Shīʿī Symbols and Rituals in Modern Iran*. Seattle: University of Washington Press, 2004.

Aghaie, Kamran Scot, ed. *The Women of Karbala: Ritual Performance and Symbolic Discourses in Modern Shīʿī Islam*. Austin: University of Texas Press, 2005.

Allen, Lori. "There Are Many Reasons Why: Suicide Bombers and Martyrs in Palestine." *Middle East Report* 223 (2002): 34–37.

Arnold, Thomas W. "Saints and Martyrs (Muhammadan in India)." In *Encyclopaedia of Religion and Ethics*, edited by James Hastings, vol. 11, pp. 68–73. Edinburgh: T. and T. Clark, 1911/1958.

Ayoub, Mahmoud M. "Martyrdom in Christianity and Islam." In *Religious Resurgence: Contemporary Cases in Islam, Christianity, and Judaism*, edited by Richard Antoun and Mary Elaine Hegland, pp. 67–77. Syracuse, N.Y.: Syracuse University Press, 1987.

Ayoub, Mahmoud M. *Redemptive Suffering in Islām: A Study of the Devotional Aspects of ʿĀshūrāʾ in Twelver Shīʿism*. The Hague: Mouton, 1978.

Bethel, Fereshteh Taheri. "A Psychological Theory of Martyrdom." *World Order* 20, no. 3–4 (Spring–Summer 1986): 5–25.

Björkman, W. "Shāhid." In *Shorter Encyclopaedia of Islam*, edited by H. A. R. Gibb and J. H. Kramers, pp. 517–518. Leiden, Netherlands: E. J. Brill, 1953.

Chelkowski, Peter, ed. *Taʿziyeh: Ritual and Drama in Iran*. New York: New York University Press, 1979.

Cook, David. *Martyrdom in Islam*. Cambridge, U.K., and New York: Cambridge University Press, 2007.

Dorraj, Manochehr. "Symbolic and Utilitarian Political Value of a Tradition: Martyrdom in the Iranian Political Culture." *The Review of Politics* 59, no. 3 (1997): 489–521.

Ernst, Carl W. "From Hagiography to Martyrology: Conflicting Testimonies to a Sufi Martyr of the Delhi Sultanate." *History of Religions* 24 (1985): 308–327.

Firestone, Reuven. "Merit, Mimesis, and Martyrdom: Aspects of Shiʿite Meta-Historical Exegesis on Abraham's Sacrifice in Light of Jewish, Christian, and Sunni Muslim Tradition." *Journal of the American Academy of Religion* 66, no. 1 (1998): 93–116.

Klausner, Samuel Z. "Martyrdom." In *The Encyclopedia of Religion*, edited by Mircea Eliade, vol. 9, pp. 230–238. New York: Macmillan, 1987.

Lane Fox, Robin. *Pagans and Christians*. New York: Knopf, 1987.

Massignon, Louis. *The Passion of al-Ḥallāj: Mystic and Martyr of Islam*. Translated by Herbert Mason. 4 vols. Princeton, N.J.: Princeton University Press, 1982.

Nabīl Zarandī, Muḥammad. *The Dawn-Breakers: Nabīl's Narrative of the Early Days of the Baháʼí Faith*. Translated and edited by Shoghi Effendi. New York: Baháʼí Publications Committee, 1953.

Pannewick, Friederike, ed. *Martyrdom in Literature: Visions of Death and Meaningful Suffering in Europe and the Middle East from Antiquity to Modernity*. Wiesbaden, Germany: Reichert Verlag, 2004.

Patton, Walter M. "Saints and Martyrs (Muhammadan)." In *Encyclopaedia of Religion and Ethics*, edited by James Hastings, vol. 11, pp. 63–68. Edinburgh: T. and T. Clark, 1911/1958.

Sachedina, Abdulaziz Abdulhussein. *Islamic Messianism: The Idea of the Madhī in Twelver Shiʿism*. Albany: State University of New York Press, 1981.

Shuhadāʾ thawrat 1919 [Martyrs of the 1919 Insurrection]. Cairo: al-Hayʾah al-Miṣrīyah al-ʿĀmmah lil-Kitāb, 1984.

Ṭāleqāni, Maḥmūd, Murtadā Muṭahharī, and ʿAlī Sharīʿatī. *Jihād and Shahādat: Struggle and Martyrdom in Islam*. Edited by Mehdi Abedi and Gary Legenhausen. Houston: Institute for Research and Islamic Studies, 1986.

Wensinck, A. J. "The Oriental Doctrine of the Martyrs." In his *Semietische Studien uit de Nalatenschap*, pp. 91–113. Leiden, Netherlands: A. W. Sijthoff, 1941.

B. TODD LAWSON
Updated by JOSEPH A. KÉCHICHIAN

MASJID JĀMIʿ. Although it is not necessary to convene in a public sanctuary for the five daily prayers (*ṣalāt*), which can be performed anywhere, individually or communally, the mosque (*masjid*, lit. "place of prostration") has become the primary building of worship for Muslims. The mosque functions both as place of worship and as meeting-place for the community, for social, educational, and political purposes; for the early Muslim community, it replaced the agora of ancient cities. From early times, the ruler's oath of allegiance (*bayʿa*) took place in the mosque, as did the weekly Friday sermon (*khuṭba*) in which the ruler's name was confirmed. From the mosque, governors and caliphs addressed Muslims on matters of political importance; in the mosque, business was concluded, legal scholars held their study-circles, and banquets were given. In contemporary times, the mosque still has the additional functions of a haven for the disadvantaged, a center for religious education of young and old, and a community center.

From the beginning, politics and religion were inseparable, combined as they were in one person, the Prophet Muḥammad. The mosque, therefore, has always been a place of both realms, such that in early times it was frequently built next to the governor's palace and paid for by the ruler's funds, and the caliph or his delegate, the governor, would ascend the pulpit (*minbar*) to deliver the Friday sermon or to make official announcements. The public nature of the Friday midday prayer, and the address made during the sitting, were instituted by Muḥammad in Medina, building upon the custom of Friday being the market-day, when large numbers of the faithful were gathered in one place (Goitein 1968).

The Friday prayer (*ṣalāt al-jumʿa*), which is mandatory for every adult male Muslim (Shiite Islam makes an exception if no Imam is present), came to be conducted in a large, congregational mosque, known as the *masjid jāmiʿ* (< Ar. *jamaʿa* "to assemble"), or Friday mosque. In the early Islamic period, only one Friday mosque in a community was permitted, since the address to the congregation was to be conducted by the ruler of that community. With the growth of the Muslim population, however, this became increasingly untenable. The tenth-century geographer al-Muqaddasī (1994, p. 182) remarked on the numbers of people preparing for Friday prayer in al-Fusṭāṭ:

> I once heard it said that there pray in front of the imam on Friday close to ten thousand people. I did not believe it until I went out with the foremost of those bustling to the Sūq al-Ṭayr (Bird Market), and saw for myself that the matter was just about as has been stated. And being late, one day, I was strenuously repairing to the Friday prayers, and I found the lines of people in the markets extending to more than a thousand cubits [approx. one-fourth of a mile] from the mosque.

The jurists debated the permissibility of allowing more than one Friday mosque in large towns or even in villages, and until the nineteenth century the admissibility of several Friday mosques in one city was contested (Johansen 1999, p. 99). With the advent of more Friday mosques, the caliph and governor delegated their role to the prayer leader (*imām*) and sermonizer (*khaṭīb*).

The Friday mosque is built on a grand scale to accommodate the large numbers of believers and was in historical times the tallest and most visible building in town. Traditionally, and especially in Iran, the Friday mosque is part of the bustling bazaar complex. Due to its size and grandeur, until the tenth century CE the caliph himself had to agree to the erection of a Friday mosque (Hillenbrand 1994, p. 44), and because of its importance in the Muslim community, Christian conquerors would typically convert the Friday mosque into a cathedral.

Because the congregation was gathered together during the Friday prayer service, the sermon was often used historically to mobilize the masses in one way or another, whether to emphasize issues of morality or to provoke and appeal to political action. For this reason, throughout history the government has attempted to control the Friday sermon. Exemplary of this today is the clerical structure in Iran, instituted by Ayatollah Khomeini in 1979 and reporting to the Supreme Leader, which appoints the Friday prayer leaders and supervises the Friday prayers, in order to ensure that all Friday sermons are in line with the government's view. In Sunni countries, such as Egypt, Saudi Arabia, and Jordan, the Ministry of Religious Affairs has the same role.

[*See also* Khuṭbah; *and* Religious Beliefs.]

BIBLIOGRAPHY

Encyclopaedia of Islam, 2d ed. "Masdjid." Leiden: Brill, 1960–2004. Volume 6, 644–707.

Goitein, S. D. *Studies in Islamic History and Institutions*. Leiden: E. J. Brill, 1968. Chapter five, "The Origin and Nature of the Muslim Friday Worship."

Hillenbrand, Robert. *Islamic Architecture: Form, Function, and Meaning*. New York: Columbia University Press, 1994.

Johansen, Baber. *Contingency in a Sacred Law: Legal and Ethical Norms in the Muslim* Fiqh. Leiden: Brill, 1999. Chapter one, "The City and Its Norms."

al-Muqaddasī, *The Best Divisions for Knowledge of the Regions (Aḥsan al-Taqāsīm fī Maʿrifat al-Aqālīm)*. Tr. Basil Anthony Collins. Reading, U.K.: Garnet, 1994.

Ram, Haggay. *Myth and Mobilization in Revolutionary Iran: The Use of the Friday Congregational Sermon*. Washington, D.C.: American University Press, 1994.

PERI BEARMAN

MAṢLAḤAH. *See* Sharīʿah.

MASYUMI PARTY. The Masyumi (Partai Majelis Syuro Muslimin Indonesia, or Council of Indonesian Muslim Associations) was founded on 7 November 1945. It was initially an umbrella organization that included disparate Islamic groups including the traditional Nahdlatul Ulama (Awakening of Ulama or NU) and the modernist Muhammadiyah. During the first years of the republic, it had the largest number of delegates to the national legislature. The Masyumi promoted an Islamic state and the obligation to uphold the Sharīʿah. However, there were differences between the traditional and modernist elements of the organization and the Nahdlatul Ulama left to form its own party in 1952.

The smaller Masyumi came to manifest several characteristics. It s members articulated a more modernist approach to Islam in Indonesia. It supported an Islamic state and the obligation to uphold the Sharīʿah, differing in its principles from more secular organizations in the republic. However, it generally presented a tolerant interpretation of Islam and a willingness to cooperate with other non-Islamic elements. Although it included a conservative constituency from the indigenous business community and large local landowners, the Masyumi leadership tended to foster a form of Islamic socialism. The majority of them expressed support for a mixed economy with protection of both workers and small businesses, but suspicion of foreign capital. A minority was more focused upon Islamic education and more purely religious programs. Ethnically, the Masyumi found its base outside Java, by far the most populous island in the archipelago, and its leaders sought to limit the influence of the Javanese who dominated at the executive level of the republic. Finally, it remained a strong supporter of democratic ideals throughout its existence and confronted those in power who sought to limit democracy.

During the early 1950s there were a series of unstable government coalitions and the Masyumi displayed its willingness to work with non Islamic partners. It participated in five of the six ruling party coalitions and held a succession of cabinet posts, including three prime ministerships, and included such notables as Mohammad Natsir and Mohammad Hatta, who later became vice president. These Masyumi-led governments were in power prior to national elections that were first held in 1955. The results of that vote displayed both the general fragmentation of the electorate and the divisions within the Islamic community. Four parties received approximately 75 percent of the votes, although a total of 28 parties were represented in the new parliament. Masyumi and Nahdlatul Ulama split the great majority of the Islamic vote with the former receiving 20.9 percent and the latter 18.4 percent of the electorate. This gave the Masyumi 57 seats in a legislature totaling 257. The other two major parties were the Partai Nasional Indonesia (PNI or National Party of Indonesia) with 22.2 percent and the Partai Kommunis Indonesia (PKI or Communist Party of Indonesia) with 16.4 percent.

The unstable political pattern that followed the elections led to stalemate and open rebellion against the government, particularly on Sumatra and Sulawesi. Sections of the Masyumi along with major elements in its leadership participated in these antigovernment actions, which were quickly defeated by national military forces. Meeting rejection of his policies and seeking to reinforce his power, in 1958 then-President Sukarno inaugurated a nondemocratic system called Guided Democracy. Parliament was eliminated and most democratic rights were curtailed as Sukarno rejected pluralist democracy. The 1945 constitution, with its strong presidential powers, was restored by decree. The Masyumi was in the forefront of those opposing the president's new structure and because of that and its participation in earlier rebellions the party was banned in 1960. Key members of the party's leadership were arrested and not released until after the military supplanted Sukarno in 1967–1968. At that time there were efforts to reestablish the party, but the new military-dominated government (the New Order) refused to restore it. Elements of the Masyumi did, however, participate in the Muslim Party of Indonesia (PMI or Partai Muslimin Indonesia-Parmusi), which was active during the New Order, although they were not allowed to attain leadership roles.

BIBLIOGRAPHY

Feith, Herbert. *The Decline of Constitutional Democracy in Indonesia*. Ithaca, N.Y.: Cornell University Press, 1962.

Kahin, George McTurnan. *Nationalism and Revolution in Indonesia*. Ithaca, N.Y.: Cornell University Press, 1952.

Lev, Daniel. *The Transition to Guided Democracy: Indonesian Politics, 1957–1959*. Ithaca, N.Y.: Cornell University Press, 1966.

FRED R. VON DER MEHDEN

MĀWARDĪ, ABŪ AL-ḤASAN AL-. Al-Māwardī (974–1058) was an eminent Shāfiʿite Sunnī jurist, chief judge of Baghdad under the Būyids, caliphal envoy and adviser, and author of notable contributions in jurisprudence, theology (*kalām*), politics, exegesis, and literature. He was born and partly educated in Basra and died in Baghdad. He served as a judge in a few towns before assuming the chief judgeship in Baghdad. In 1038 he was awarded the sobriquet (*laqab*) of *aqḍā ʾl-quḍāt* ("supreme judge" or "the best of judges"), even as some doubted the legality of this title. Ironically, he is much admired for his courageous *fatwa* against the Būyid Jalāl al-Dawlah's demand from al-Qāʾim to be granted the title *shāhanshāh* (*mālik al-mulk*, the king of kings) on the grounds that it befits only God. Al-Māwardī was on several occasions chosen by the caliph al-Qādir (r. 991–1031) and the caliph al-Qāʾim (r. 1031–1074) to perform diplomatic missions to the Būyids and, once, to the Seljuks.

Intellectually, he was a thinker of some originality who knew politics both in theory and practice, read widely not only in Islamic but also Greek and Persian ethical and political traditions and tried to synthesize them, not always successfully, in his unusually numerous treatises on politics and ethics. Al-Māwardī's independence is evidenced by his pro-Muʿtazilite opinions on the issue of the objectivity and rationality of ethical knowledge in contrast with the Ashʿarite doctrine of ethical subjectivism and a soft spot for the free-will doctrine (in his orthodox critics' view, he inclined toward Qadarism and Muʿtazilism). Yet he sided with the Ashʿarites on, among other issues, the createdness of the Qurʾān. While later Shāfiʿite biographers defended his Ashʿarism, in his works he never refers to himself as an Ashʿarite but frequently as a Shāfiʿite. Some have suggested that his doctrine on the relationship between reason and revelation was much closer to Ḥanafite Māturīdism in charting a middle course between Muʿtazilism and Ashʿarism. Al-Māwardī seems to have disliked the traditionalist (anti-*kalām*) branch of Sunnism championed by the Ḥanbalites, and his authoritative work on the caliphate, *al-Aḥkām al-sulṭānīyah* (henceforth, *Aḥkām*), stands out for completely ignoring the Ḥanbalite opinion while including the Mālikite and Ḥanafite opinions along with his own Shāfiʿite school. Al-Māwardī's *Aḥkām* has received much attention, but close readings of al-Māwardī's entire oeuvre have been rare in modern scholarship. Owing particularly to his notorious concession to legitimize a usurper in *Aḥkām*, modern commentators see him as attempting to legitimize the status quo and legalize the illegal. While his *Aḥkām* reflects the formal Sunnī approach to the caliphate, the statecraft literature written by al-Māwardī draws on a wide array of Islamic and extra-Islamic sources in a framework that looks more like that of the state-centered secretaries like Ibn al-Muqaffaʿ (d. 756) or Qudāma ibn Jaʿfar (d. 948) than his own in *Aḥkām*. This framework is essentially indebted to the familiar Near Eastern, in particular Persian, model of kingship, and while it does frequently draw on Islamic scriptural sources, it treats it as one mine among many of political wisdom. His thought in these writings is by no means "secular" and deems religion and state twins and mutually necessary, but one cannot fail to notice the sharp disjunction in style, authorities, and concerns between the Greco-Persian heritage in his statecraft literature and the Arab-Islamic heritage in his legal and theological writings. In *Aḥkām*, al-Māwardī prohibits calling the caliph "God's caliph," in accordance with the Sunnī doctrine, and insists that it be "the caliph of God's messenger." In his treatise on statecraft, *Tashīl*, however, he presents a different model of political authority, quoting the Persian emperor Ardshīr ibn Bābak's pledge of allegiance with his governors that "religion and kingship are twins" and asserting that "the king is God's caliph in his lands."

Riḍwān al-Sayyid establishes the following chronology of al-Māwardī's social and political writings (al-Māwardī, 1990, p. 82):

1014–1029: Juristic writings, such as *al-Ḥāwī* (a detailed treatment of the Shāfiʿite school) and *al-Iqnāʿ* (written at the request of the caliph al-Qādir as a compendium of the Shāfiʿite school).

1030s: This was a prolific period that resulted in a few works on ethics and politics. *Adab al-dunyā wa-l-dīn* (The Ethics of Worldly and Religious Life), a work on ethics, with important discussion on the nature of intellect and the formation of human community; *Naṣīḥat al-mulūk* (Counsel for Princes), whose attribution to al-Māwardī is disputed; and his final advice work, *Tashīl*.

1040s: In this period he produced two mature advice works, *Qawānīn al-wizāra* (Rules of the Vizierate), addressed to viziers, and then *Tashīl al-naẓar wa-taʿjīl al-ẓafar*, addressed to kings. The latter was probably written for the Būyid prince Jalāl al-Dawlah (415–435) who was on good terms with al-Māwardī.

1050s: *al-Aḥkām al-sulṭānīyah* (Ordinances of Government), a compilation of Sunnī theological and legal discourses pertaining to government.

In his *Qawānīn al-wizāra*, al-Māwardī addresses the office of vizierate that had existed since the ʿAbbāsids. He distinguishes the vizierate of execution (*tanfīdh*), which is of a limited transfer of authority for the purpose of execution of specific functions, and the vizierate of delegation (*tafwīḍ*), which is the delegation of all the authority related to a certain function or region by the sovereign to the vizier. In *Aḥkām* he writes that the vizier of execution may be a non-Muslim but the vizier of delegation cannot. The second section deals with protection—of the king from friends and enemies, of the vizier himself from his peers, and of the subjects from fear and disorder. The third section treats the vizier's attributes; the fourth, caution; the fifth and sixth, appointment and dismissal, respectively; the seventh, the vizierate of execution; and the eighth, claims on the vizier. Al-Māwardī exhorts the vizier to piety, truthfulness, justice, and concern for the afterlife.

Tashīl resembles the *Qawānīn* but is addressed to a ruler rather than to a vizier. It consists of two parts, on the ethical qualities (*akhlāq*) that the ruler should cultivate, and the governance he should pursue. The first part is not simply influenced by the widespread infiltration of Hellenistic and Greek influence among the intellectuals of the age but is based directly on Aristotelian views taken from the ninth-century translations of Aristotle's masterpiece *Nicomachean Ethics* and some of Galen's writings. He further draws on Plato's theory that reduces ethics to four essential traits: *tamyīz* (prudence), *najdah* (helping others), *ʿiffah* (chastity), and *ʿadl* (justice). These are the sources and categories on which most Muslim writers of the age on ethics drew, placing all ethics in the context of Aristotle's golden mean (*wasaṭiyyah*), for which they found ample references in scriptural materials.

In his works on ethics and politics al-Māwardī's reflections on social, economic, and anthropological foundations of political society are marked by significant originality, although his originality tends to be synthetic rather than radical in nature. Articulating a widespread view among authors schooled in the sciences of ethics and practical philosophy, al-Māwardī presents rulership in the context of the differences among people and their resultant needs for cooperation. He discusses virtues, including the motivation for acquiring them; the beginning of virtues, he writes, is reason, and the result of them, justice. The principles of sovereignty rest on two matters: governance, which consists of cultivation of the lands, protection of the subjects, management of the army, and assessing wealth; and its foundation, which consists of religion, power, and wealth. Al-Māwardī's authorities and examples in all of this literature comprise Qurʾānic verses and *ḥadīth*, the *ʿAhd Ardashīr* and other Iranian materials, the sayings of caliphs and secretaries, Plato and Aristotle, and unnamed Indian kings and philosophers.

Al-Māwardī's influential *al-Aḥkām al-sulṭānīyah* has long been considered by subsequent scholars an authoritative—and for some, *the* authoritative—expression of the classical Sunnī theory of caliphate. Before al-Māwardī, the issue of imamate had been discussed in works on *kalām*. His treatise, however, is not a theological treatise but a new legal genre altogether, in which issues previously discussed in theology (nature, election, and the role of the caliph/imam) were united with those in jurisprudence for the first time. After al-Māwardī, there began to appear, inconsistently, brief chapters on imamate in standard juristic manuals, at least among the Shāfiʿites and the Ḥanbalites—due perhaps to the concentration of these schools in Baghdad, where the caliphal drama mostly took place.

The Sunnī caliphate discourse had been created almost exclusively by Ashʿarite theologians, who happened to be Shāfiʿite and Mālikite in jurisprudence, as Sunnī theological polemics against the Muʿtazilah, the Shīʿī and the Khārijites. By al-Māwardī's time the general parameters of the discourse had been settled in the writings of al-Bāqillānī and al-Baghdādī. Al-Māwardī's primary intention was the defense of the existing Sunnī caliphal institution against the possibility of irrelevance or extinction. He sought to project an aura of general agreement among the Sunnīs and moved the debate from the realm of theology to the realm of practice and jurisprudence. To that end he made a few subtle but significant innovations in his approach to the standard issues. These were:

1. One key contention of the Ashʿarite theologians had been that the imamate is an obligation by revelation not reason.

Al-Māwardī's view, as noted above, was closer to that of the Muʿtazilah and that is why, contrary to common perception, al-Māwardī states both opinions without committing to any, thus avoiding provocation.

2. Like the majority of Sunnī theologians, he rejected the possibility of the coexistence of more than one imam and affirmed the usual list of requirements for the imam of Qurayshite descent, capability of *ijtihād*, probity, and competence in leadership in war and peace.
3. In an innovation that changed the very nature of the institution of the caliphate, al-Māwardī famously accepted the imamate of someone overpowered and confined (*ḥajr*) by another who is not openly rebellious and disobedient. This was an unveiled concession to the Būyid control of Baghdad but also a veiled warning to the Būyids, and possibly the Seljuks, to watch their limits.
4. An equally important innovation that gives a sense of al-Māwardī's overall direction is in the case of the agency that appointed the next imam. On this question there were two central questions: the identity and qualifications of those who elected the caliph (*ahl al-ikhtiyār* or *ahl al-ḥall wa-l-ʿaqd*, lit. "those who untie and tie") and whether the caliph could be appointed through testamentary designation by the reigning caliph (*naṣṣ*).

The proper way to appoint the next caliph had, in Sunniī doctrine, been election by some number of electors followed by the oath of allegiance (*bayʿah*) by all Muslims. Al-Māwardī rejects that the "appointment of a caliph requires the contract *(bayaʾa)* of the majority of untiers and tiers from every city, so that the agreement on the caliph may be general and submission to him imamate by consensus" (*Aḥkām*, 33-4); since the involvement of the entire Muslim community was not needed in the case of the appointment of Abū Bakr, it could not be a requirement. Al-Māwardī was the first not only to claim a consensus on the issue but also to consider designation a method of appointment independent of confirmation by the electors.

In all the above departures from earlier Sunnī opinions, al-Māwardī seems to be insulating systematically the imamate from the will of the community or the whims of the caliph-makers—namely, the sultans. Three aspects of al-Māwardī's caliphate theory stand out as distinct from what his predecessors and contemporaries wrote on the subject: (1) he moves discourse of the caliphate from theology to jurisprudence; (2) he sanctifies and ritualizes the imamate by allowing the separation of caliphal authority from effective power to govern; and (3) the community completely disappears from his theory. Al-Māwardī's interest is to wed theory to reality and sustain the caliphate as much as possible and so he makes the formal aspect of the appointment an easy to carry out ritual. That his political program looks odd and unrealistic is not because it is divorced from practice, but precisely because he was trying to wed theory to practice without challenging either too much.

Bibliography

Works of Abū al-Ḥasan al-Māwardī

Tashīl al-naẓar wa-taʿjīl al-ẓafar fī akhlāq al-malik wa-siyāsat al-mulk. Edited by Riḍwān al-Sayyid. Beirut: Dār al-ʿUlūm al-ʿArabīyah, 1987.

al-Aḥkām al-sulṭānīyah. Edited by Khālid ʿAbd al-ʿAlmī. Beirut: Dār al-Kitāb al-ʿArabī, 1990.

Secondary Works

Anjum, Ovamir. *Politics, Law and Reason in Islamic Thought: The Taymiyyan Moment*. Cambridge, U.K., and New York: Cambridge University Press, 2012.

Brockelmann, C. "al-Māwardī, Abū 'l-Ḥasan ʿAlī b. Muḥammad b. Ḥabīb." In *Encyclopaedia of Islam*. Vol. 6, p. 869. Leiden: E. J. Brill, 1986.

Crone, Patricia. *God's Rule: Government and Islam*. New York: Columbia University Press, 2004.

Dumayjī, ʿAbd Allah b. ʿUmar b. Sulaymān al-. *al-Imāmah al-ʿuẓmā ʿinda ahl al-sunnah wa-l-jamāʿah*. Riyadh: Dār Ṭība, 1987.

Gibb, H. A. R. *Studies on the Civilization of Islam*. Edited by Stanford J. Shaw and William R. Polk. Boston: Beacon Press, 1962.

Hallaq, Wael B. "Caliphs, Jurists and the Saljuqs in the Political Thought of Juwayni." *The Muslim World* 74, no. 1 (1984): 26–41.

Hurvitz, Nimrod. *Competing Texts: The Relationship between al-Māwardī's and Abū Yaʿlā's al-Aḥkām al-Sulṭāniyya*. Cambridge, Mass.: Harvard Law School, Islamic Studies Program, 2007.

Lambton, Ann K. S. *State and Government in Medieval Islam: An Introduction to the Study of Islamic Political Theory: The Jurists*. Oxford and New York: Oxford University Press, 1981.

Marlow, Louise. "Advice and Advice Literature." In *Encyclopaedia of Islam Three*, edited by Grudrun Krämer et al. Leiden: Brill, 2012. http://referenceworks.brillonline.com/entries/encyclopaedia-of-islam-3/advice-and-advice-literature-COM-206.

Mikhail, Hanna, *Politics and Revelation: Māwardī and After*. Edinburgh: Edinburgh University Press, 1995.

Sayyid, Riḍwān al-. "Introduction." In al-Māwardī, *Tasʿhil al-naẓar*. Beirut: Dār al-ʿUlūm al-ʿArabīyah, 1987.

OVAMIR ANJUM

MAWDŪDĪ, SAYYID ABŪ AL-AʿLĀ.

Sayyid Abū al-Aʿlā Mawdūdī (1903–1979) (also rendered from Urdu as Abuʿl-Aʿla Maudūdī), Islamic ideologue and politician, was an influential and prolific contemporary Muslim thinker. His interpretations contributed greatly to Islamic revivalist thought and influenced Muslim thinkers and activists from Morocco to Indonesia. His impact is evident in the exegesis of Sayyid Quṭb of Egypt, as well as in the ideas and actions of Algerian, Iranian, Malaysian, and Sudanese revivalist activists. Mawdūdī's sway left an impact in South Asia where his ideas took shape. Jamāʿat-i Islāmī (the Islamic Party), the organization that embodied his ideology for five decades, played a significant role in the history and politics of Pakistan, India, Bangladesh, Sri Lanka, and the South Asian communities of the Persian Gulf states, Great Britain, and North America.

Early Life. Mawdūdī was born in Aurangabad, Deccan (now Maharashtra), on 25 September 1903, into a notable family of Delhi that traced their lineage to the great Chishtī Ṣūfī saints who played a prominent role in the conversion of many Indians to Islam. The Mawdūdīs were close to the Mughal court, especially during the reign of the last ruler of that dynasty, Bahādur Shāh Ẓafar. The family, which had suffered greatly during the 1858 British attacks, continued to identify with the glories of Muslim history in India and was not reconciled to British rule over the domain of the Mughals. Mawdūdī's mother was also from a notable family of Delhi that settled in the Deccan and served generations of *niẓāms* (hereditary rulers of Hyderabad). The Indo-Islamic cultural roots of the family, its identification with the glorious heritage of Muslim rule over India, its aristocratic pretensions, and its disdain for British rule shaped Mawdūdī's worldview.

Mawdūdī's father, Sayyid Aḥmad Ḥasan, was among the first to attend the Muslim Anglo-Oriental College at Aligarh and to embark on Sayyid Aḥmad Khān's experiment in Islamic modernism. His stint at Aligarh, however, did not last long, because he left the school to earn a law degree in Allahabad. After completing his studies, Aḥmad Ḥasan delved into Sufism and for a time abandoned his career to devote himself to worship at the shrine of Niẓāmuddīn Auliyāʾ in Delhi. Aḥmad Ḥasan's puritanical streak and love of Sufism created a powerful religious and ascetic environment in which his children were nurtured. Aḥmad Ḥasan, moreover, took great pains to rear his children in the Muslim *sharīf* (notable) culture and to provide them a classical education, intentionally excluding English from their curriculum. They were introduced to Arabic, Urdu, and religious texts. Mawdūdī's mastery of Arabic was such that, at the age of fourteen, he translated the Egyptian thinker Qāsim Amīn's work *Al-marʾah al-jadīdah* (The New Woman) into Urdu.

At the age of eleven the young Mawdūdī enrolled at the Madrasah-i Fauqaniyah in Aurangabad, where he was introduced to modern education. He was compelled to abandon formal learning at the age of sixteen because of his father's death, but he remained acutely interested in writing and politics. His interests were then secular and focused solely on the issue of nationalism. In 1918 and 1919 he praised Hindu Congress leaders, notably Gandhi and Madan Muhan Malaviya, and joined his brother Abulkhair in Bijnor to begin a career in journalism. Soon after that the brothers moved to Delhi in 1918, where Mawdūdī was exposed to a variety of intellectual currents in the Muslim community, and he became acquainted with modernist writings as well as with the activities of the independence movement. In 1919 he moved to Jabalpur to work for the pro-Congress weekly *Taj*. There he became fully active in the Khilāfat movement as he mobilized Muslims to support the Congress Party. His passionate articles eventually led to the closure of the weekly.

Mawdūdī then returned to Delhi, where he befriended important Khilāfat activists such as Muḥammad ʿAlī, with whom Mawdūdī cooperated briefly. He continued to show interest in the independence movement, albeit increasingly from a Muslim standpoint. For example, he briefly joined the Tahrik-i Hijrat protest movement, which encouraged Muslims to emigrate from British India (*dār al-ḥarb*, abode of war) to Muslim-ruled (*dār al-Islām*, abode of Islam) Afghanistan. In 1921 Mawdūdī met senior leaders of the Jamʿīyatul ʿUlamāʾ-i Hind, *mawlānās* Muftī Kifāyatullāh and Aḥmad Saʿīd. The eminent *ʿulamāʾ* recognized Mawdūdī's talents and invited him to edit the Jamʿīyat's official newspaper, *Muslim*, and later its successor *al-Jamīʿyat*. Mawdūdī remained in the service of the Jamʿīyat until 1924, as he developed a more acute awareness of Muslim political consciousness. Gradually he became more actively involved in the affairs of his faith, writing on the plight of Muslims in India, the predicament of Turks in the face of European imperialism, and the wonder of Muslim rule in India. His tone was communalist and political, not revivalist as his later writings illustrated.

These years were also a period of learning and intellectual growth for Mawdūdī. He learned English and delved into Western works, while his association with the Jamʿīyat also encouraged him to acquire a formal religious education. Toward that end he commenced the *dars-i niẓāmī* (syllabus of education of the *ʿulamāʾ* in India), first with the renowned ʿAbdussalām Niyāzī, and later at Delhi's Fatihpuri Madrasah. In 1926 he received his certificate in religious training (*ijāzah*), thus becoming a Deobandī *ʿalim*. Interestingly Mawdūdī never acknowledged his status as one of the *ʿulamāʾ*, and his education in the Deobandī tradition did not come to light until after his death.

Communalism. The collapse of the Khilāfat movement in 1924 was a turning point in Mawdūdī's life. He lost faith in nationalism, which he believed had led Turks and Egyptians to undermine Muslim unity, and came to suspect the Congress Party of manipulating nationalist sentiments to serve exclusive Hindu interests. His views thus became openly communalist, revealing opprobrium for the movement and its allies. At this time he found himself at odds with the Jamʿīyat and decided to part ways with his Deobandī mentors who, importantly, supported the Congress Party to end British rule in India.

No less opposed to British colonial control, Mawdūdī advocated an Islamic anti-imperialist platform that asserted opposition to colonialism while safeguarding Muslim interests. The communalist rhetoric soon imbued Mawdūdī with a sense of mission, permitting him to express views discretely. When in 1925 a young Muslim activist assassinated the Hindu revivalist leader Swami Shradhanand, because the latter advocated to reconvert low-caste converts to Islam back to Hinduism, the assassination and its widespread criticism of Islam as a religion of violence by the Indian press, mobilized him. Angered by this response and summoned to action by Muḥammad ʿAlī's sermon at Delhi's Jamiʿ Mosque encouraging Muslims to defend their faith, Mawdūdī took it upon himself to clarify to critics Islam's position on the use of violence. The result was his famous treatise on war and peace, violence, and *jihād* in Islam, *al-Jihād fī al-Islām* (Jihād in Islam). The treatise remains one of the most articulate expositions of this theme by a revivalist thinker; it received accolades from the Muslim community and confirmed Mawdūdī's place among the Muslim literati.

Mawdūdī became convinced that his vocation lay in leading his community to political and religious salvation. The direction which this endeavor was to take was not, however, entirely clear. In 1928 he completed a number of translation projects, historical accounts of Hyderabad, and religious texts at the behest of the *nizām*'s government. His most important contribution was a seminal introduction to Islam, *Risālah-yi dīnīyāt* (translated as *Towards Understanding Islam*). It was in Hyderabad that he first grew a beard, adopted Indo-Muslim attire, and underwent a conversion experience that was religious in content though motivated by his understanding of political imperatives. The political situation in the city, the last remnant of Muslim rule in India, was precarious at the time as the majority Hindu population asserted itself, while the power of the *nizām* was on the wane. Mawdūdī was not unaffected by what he witnessed in his birthplace and became convinced that the decline of Muslim power stemmed from the corruption introduced into Islam, along with centuries of dross that obscured the faith's true teachings. Conversely the salvation of Muslim culture lay in the restitution of Islamic institutions and practices, once the culture was cleansed of unsavory influences that sapped its power. He therefore encouraged the *nizām*'s government to reform Hyderabad's Islamic institutions and to promote the true teachings of the faith. Witnessing inaction disheartened Mawdūdī, which led him to lose trust in existing Muslim political structures, as he looked instead for an alternative.

Mawdūdī's revivalist position was radical communalism. It asserted Muslim rights, proposed a program for promoting and safeguarding them, and demanded the severance of all cultural, social, and political ties with Hindus in the interest of purifying Islam. He went so far as to advocate a separate cultural homeland for Indian Muslims.

Darul-Islam and Jamāʿat-i Islāmī. In 1932 Mawdūdī purchased the journal *Tarjumān al-Qurʾān* (Interpreter of the Qurʾān) that became a forum for his views. Still the rapid changes that characterized the passing of the Raj convinced Mawdūdī that the pen alone was unlikely to affect the course of events. He thus became interested in an organization that articulated his ideas. In 1938 he agreed to head Darul-Islam, a religious education project conceived by Muhammad Iqbal at Pathankot, a hamlet in Punjab. At Darul-Islam Mawdūdī devised a model Islamic community, which he hoped would spearhead the reform of the faith in India. Meanwhile he remained intensely interested in politics, became embroiled in the struggle between the Pakistan Movement and Muslims of the

Congress Party, always maintaining his independence of thought from both positions. He first lambasted Muslim supporters of the Congress, many of whom were his mentors in the Jamʿīyatul ʿUlamāʾ-i Hind, for betraying the Muslim cause. Later he turned his attention to the Muslim League, which he chastised for its secularist communalism. As a result of Mawdūdī's activism the project acquired an increasingly political tone, leading him to leave Pathankot for more direct political activity in Lahore. There he taught at the Islāmīyah College and joined in debates over the future of the Muslim community. In August 1941 Mawdūdī, with a number of young *ʿulamāʾ* and Muslim literati, formed the Jamāʿat-i Islāmī (Islamic Party) in Pathankot.

After Partition. When India was partitioned Mawdūdī divided the Jamāʿat into independent Indian and Pakistani units. He moved to Lahore and replaced the communalist agenda with a campaign to establish an Islamic state. During Pakistan's early years Mawdūdī did much to mobilize public opinion for the cause of Islam, pushing the *ʿulamāʾ* to demand an Islamic constitution. He was soon identified as an enemy of the state, accused of opposing Pakistan, and of being a subversive tool of India. Between 1948 and 1950 he was imprisoned for refusing to lend religious legitimacy to the government's military campaign in Kashmir, and imprisoned once again in 1954, this time tried and sentenced to death for his role in instigating the 1953–1954 disturbances against the Aḥmadīyah in Punjab. His sentence was later commuted and he was released from prison in 1955, although he was incarcerated in both 1964 and 1967 for challenging the regime of Ayub Khan.

In 1969 Mawdūdī instructed the Jamāʿat to launch a national anti-left campaign to forestall the Awami League's effort to gain independence for East Pakistan and to keep the Pakistan Peoples' Party out of power. The Jamāʿat failed on both counts: it lost the 1970 elections and was overshadowed by the left. Taking stock of the defeat, and after serving thirty years at the helm of the Jamāʿat, Mawdūdī stepped down as the president (*amīr*) of the party. Although he continued to exercise much power in the Jamāʿat, his remaining years were dedicated to writing, and he died in Buffalo, New York, on 22 September 1979. His funeral later that month in Pakistan drew a crowd of more than 1 million as he was buried in his house in the Ichhrah neighborhood of Lahore.

Throughout his years of political activity Mawdūdī produced many articles, pamphlets, and books. His compositions not only made him the foremost revivalist thinker of his time but further confirmed his place as an important force in traditional religious scholarship. His Qurʾānic translation and commentary, *Tafhīm al-Qurʾān* (translated as *Understanding the Qurʾān*), begun in 1942 and completed in 1972, remains one of the most widely read Qurʾānic commentaries in Urdu today.

Assessment. In his numerous works Mawdūdī elaborated his views on religion, society, economy, and politics, which constituted an interpretive reading of Islam that sought to mobilize faith for the purpose of political action. His ideological perspective, one of the most prolific and systematic articulations of the revivalist position, left its marks on revivalism across the Muslim world. Indeed the contours of Islam's discourses with socialism and capitalism were first defined by him, as was much of the terminology associated with Islamic revivalism, including "Islamic revolution," "Islamic state," and "Islamic ideology."

Mawdūdī's reading of Islam began with a radical exegesis. His vision was chiliastic (millenarian) and dialectic, in that it saw the battle between Islam and un-Islam (*kufr*)—both the West and the Hindu culture of India—as the central force in the historical progression of Muslim societies. This struggle, argued Mawdūdī, would culminate in an Islamic state, which would in turn initiate broad reforms in society, thereby establishing a utopian Islamic order. With this agenda Mawdūdī rationalized Islam into a stringent belief system, predicated upon absolute obedience to the will of God, and amounting to a command structure that aimed to transform society and politics. By reinterpreting such key concepts as divinity (*ilāh*), god/lord (*rabb*), worship (*ʿibādah*), and religion (*dīn*), he recast the meaning of the faith so that social action became the logical end of religious piety. Religion itself became the vehicle of social action. Despite the radicalism of his vision and his polemic on Islamic revolution, Mawdūdī's approach to politics throughout his career remained irenic. He continued to believe that social change would not result from mobilizing the masses to topple the existing order, but from taking political power and effecting broad reforms from the top down. In Mawdūdī's conception Islamic revolution was to unfold within the existing state structures rather than after their destruction. He disparaged the use of violence in promoting the cause of Islam and defined the ideal Islamic state as a "theodemocracy" or a "democratic caliphate." Moreover he believed that education rather than revolutionary action was the keystone to Islamic activism. In this regard Mawdūdī's position, as manifested in Jamāʿat's politics, stood in contrast to Ayatollah Ruhollah Khomeini's example; it provided Islamic revivalism with an alternate paradigm for social action that prevailed among revivalists.

[*See also* Jamāʿat-i Islāmī; Jamʿīyatul ʿUlamāʾ-i Hind; Khilāfat Movement; *and* Pakistan.]

BIBLIOGRAPHY

Works of Abū al-Aʿla Mawdūdī

Musalmān aur maujūdah siyāsī kashmakash [Muslims and the Current Political Struggle]. 3 vols. Lahore: Risālah Tarjumānulqurʾan, 1938–1940.

Towards Understanding Islam. Edited and translated by Khurshid Ahmad. Lahore: Islamic Publications, 1960 (English translation of *Risālah-yi dīnīyāt*).

A Short History of the Revivalist Movement in Islam. Translated by al-Ashʿari. Lahore: Islamic Publications, 1963 (English translation of *Tajdīd va iḥyāʿ-i dīn*).

The Moral Foundations of the Islamic Movement. Lahore: Islamic Publications, 1976 (English translation of *Taḥrīk-i Islāmī kī akhlāqī bunyāden*).

Towards Understanding the Qurʾān: English Version of Tafhīm al-Qurʾān. Translated and edited by Zafar Ishaq Ansari. Leicester, U.K.: Islamic Foundation, 1988.

Secondary Works

Abūlāfāq. *Sayyid Abūl aʿlā Maudūdī: Savāniḥ, afkār, taḥrīk* [Sayyid Abū al-Aʿlā Mawdūdī: Biography, Thought, Movement]. Lahore: Islamic Publications, 1971.

Adams, Charles J. "The Ideology of Mawlana Mawdūdī." In *South Asian Politics and Religion*, edited by Donald Eugene Smith, pp. 371–397. Princeton, N.J.: Princeton University Press, 1966.

Adams, Charles J. "Mawdūdī and the Islamic State." In *Voices of Resurgent Islam*, edited by John L. Esposito, pp. 99–133. New York: Oxford University Press, 1983.

Ahmad, Aziz. "Mawdudi and Orthodox Fundamentalism of Pakistan." *Middle East Journal* 21, no. 3 (Summer 1967): 369–380.

"ʿAllāma Mawdūdī and Contemporary Pakistan." Special issue of *The Muslim World* 93, nos. 3–4 (July 2003): 351–561.

Gilani, Sayyid Asad. *Maududi: Thought and Movement*. Translated by Hasan Muizuddin Qazil. Lahore: Farooq Hasan Gilani, 1978.

Hasan, Masudul. *Sayyid Abul Aʿala Maududi and His Thought*. 2 vols. Lahore: Islamic Publications, 1984.

Jackson, Roy. *Mawlana Mawdudi and Political Islam: Authority and the Islamic State*. London and New York: Routledge, 2011.

Nasr, Seyyed Vali Reza. *Mawdudi and the Making of Islamic Revivalism*. New York: Oxford University Press, 1996.

SEYYED VALI REZA NASR
Revised by JOSEPH A. KÉCHICHIAN

Ministry of Islamic Affairs. Because the Prophet united all earthly authority in his persona and only delegated to one of his followers when he deemed it necessary, serious dilemmas were created at his death, including on how best to administer the religious realm. Abū Bakr, who succeeded Muḥammad as imam of the Muslim community introduced the first institutions, though it was Muʿawiyah who combined the Bedouin custom of proclamation by the heads of families with the Byzantine tradition to elect successors through heredity. The caliphate thus emerged, even if its powers were not clearly defined, which, in turn, required imagination to run the community.

Umayyad and ʿAbbāsid rulers organized the state and its various institutions to uphold the public good (*maṣlaḥah*), which necessitated that they become sovereigns, thereby gaining unlimited powers. Caliphs assigned the leadership of the Friday prayer and the *khuṭbah* to an imam, Qurʾānic justice to a *qāḍī*, the gathering of taxes to a *ʿamil*, the command of the army and the administration in general to an *amīr*. A ruler was assisted by a *wazīr* (vizier or counselor) who under the ʿAbbāsids received no special delegation of power, but who was assigned additional responsibilities as the empire expanded. It was under the Mamlūks and the Ottomans that viziers became powerful ministers.

Gradually *wazīrs* engaged in organizing their affairs to best serve nascent departments that filled various courts. Duties expanded to secure revenues that satisfied masters anxious to invest in public works such as roads, bridges, canals, irrigation schemes, and monuments to posterity. While local associations saw to the construction and repair of mosques and monuments that were necessary to the ordered life of the community, the hope for rewards in the next world, which was acknowledged in Islam, prompted many to donate portions of possessions theoretically acquired by legal means to benefit the less fortunate. New mosques, aqueducts, and reservoirs were built for the benefit of pilgrims near roads going to the holy cities. Bridges, rest houses, *madāris*, monasteries for Ṣūfīs, and hospitals were all likewise developed. It was to ensure the continued existence of these facilities that means of endowments (*awqāf*) were also created

The current ministry of *awqaf* affairs developed with the introduction of the modern nation-state after the collapse of the Ottoman Empire, as each independent country added a special department to look after endowments. In Jordan, for example, *awqāf* affairs were formerly organized under the Ottoman Empire through the administration of the 19 Jumada II, 1280 Hijri Law, which remained in force until 1946 when the Kingdom of Jordan passed its own Islamic Awqaf Law. According to this Hashemite edict, *awqāf* affairs and financial matters related to them fell under independent regulations, whose funds would not be mixed with other public resources. Presumably the purpose was to safeguard and protect *awqāf* holdings from loss, enabling the nascent ministry to fulfill its mission while seeing to its total autonomy.

Among the many objectives of ministries of Islamic affairs none were as important as the maintenance, development, preservation, and management of mosques and *awqāf* funds. Other key functions included the development of mosques to deliver the message of Islamic education; the ability to strengthen morals through the teachings of Islam and guidance of the faith; the desire to nurture and solidify Islamic mannerisms in the private as well as public lives of all Muslims; the support of public Islamic functions and the scriptures that called for the establishment of religious institutes and schools to teach scriptures; and the aspiration to spread Islamic culture and preserve Islamic heritage to reveal the role of Islam in the elevation of mankind and bring Muslims closer to their faith.

Toward the end of the twentieth century the ministry of Islamic affairs blended in with the ministry of justice in several countries, although most Muslim countries preferred to separate the two. In Saudi Arabia, for example, the ministry of justice administered Sharīʿah law and the provision of legal services although in most Muslim countries, such administration was usually undertaken by Islamic affairs offices. Because Saudi Arabia hosted the holy cities of Mecca and Medina, the ministry's full name in the kingdom was the Ministry of Pilgrimage (*Ḥajj*) and Endowments (*Awqāf*), whereas in most Muslim countries, and to avoid schisms as well as emphasize tolerance and forgiveness, the more common nomenclature of *wazarat al-shuʾun al-islamīyah* (Islamic affairs) was formally updated to *shuʾun dīnīyah* (religious affairs).

For many Muslim countries, the ministry of Islamic affairs was responsible for the organization of the annual pilgrimage to Mecca although, for Riyadh, the burden was somewhat different: to be accountable for the provision of facilities for the visit of all Muslim pilgrims to the holy cities. For most ministries, however, the chief mission was to assume responsibility for building and maintaining mosques throughout their respective countries, as well as the administration of land held by religious trust, which was often significant.

BIBLIOGRAPHY

Dūrī, ʿAbd al-ʿAzīz al-. *Early Islamic Institutions: Administration and Taxation from the Caliphate to the Umayyads and Abbasids*. Translated by Razia Ali. London: I. B. Tauris, 2011.

Gaudefroy-Demombynes, Maurice. *Muslim Institutions*. 6 vols., vol. 3: *Law and Institutions*. London: Routledge, 2007.

JOSEPH A. KÉCHICHIAN

MINORITIES IN MUSLIM STATES.

Generally speaking, the term "minority" refers to a group of people within a community or country differing from the main population in religion, language, ethnicity, political persuasion, etc. The modern usage of "minority" emerged in a European context in the mid-nineteenth century and expresses the notion of a vulnerable and marginalized specific group within a society. According to a United Nations definition offered in 1977, a minority is: "A group numerically inferior to the rest of the population of a State, in a non-dominant position, whose members—being nationals of the State—possess ethnic, religious or linguistic characteristics differing from those of the rest of the population and show, if only implicitly, a sense of solidarity, directed towards preserving their culture, traditions, religion or language" ("Minority Rights: International Standards and Guidance for Implementation," UN Human Rights Commission, Office of the High Commissioner New York and Geneva, 2010, p. 2).

In premodern Islamic states the concept of a minority was mainly traced back to the religious minorities and the condition of non-Muslims. In general terms modern Muslim states approved newly founded civil societies instead of religious society in which the Muslims and people of different faiths enjoyed equal rights as equal citizens.

Notwithstanding in Muslim societies the minority issue continues to be sensitive, raising considerable controversy due to a widespread attitude to refuse to recognize non-religious concepts in this respect. Scholarship in the field of the religious minorities in Islam has tended to treat the issue as linked to traditional views, regarding it as unchanged over time, up to the present. Curiously there is a convergence of views between two apparently conflicting factions in this regard: On the one hand there are the Islamist political movements, such as al-Jihād in

Egypt, and Muslim scholars, who are hostile toward non-Muslims and advocate the reimposition of the *dhimmah* regulations; and on the other are some Western scholars and ideologues who are critical toward Islam, which is regarded by them as a monolith. Both of them advocate the traditional practice of the *dhimmah* agreement as applied unchangingly over all the times and places of the Islamic era.

Indeed the status and treatment of minorities is something different with respect to their status under Islamic law (*fiqh*). Islamic juristic discourses on political issues are a natural product of the historical processes of the Islamic political and legal experience. Traditional views, classical Islamic thinking, and regional practice are often confused: It is the historical conditions that tend to produce religious tolerance or intolerance, not only the theological dimension. Indeed the study of the minorities in the Islamic world has up until now suffered from either an exclusively theoretical legalistic approach based upon the classical insights in the *fiqh*, both in terms of academic dissertations and Western and Islamic public opinion debates. As a part of anti-Islamic discourses Western European media seem to show a particular interest in the treatment of religious minorities in Muslim states, within the frame of a human rights debate, which perpetuates a stereotyped and ahistorical view of Muslim world as unrelated to history.

Prevailing classic Islamic thought of pluralism is inclusive, and recognizes religious minorities which enjoy Qurʾānic protection with a secondary status. Islam has traditionally been tolerant of religious differences within the Islamic community (*ummah*) and to a certain extent even encouraged them (for purposes that were fiscal, conviction, and so on). But, as in premodern states, the minority groups are still classified exclusively by religious affiliation within the dichotomy Muslim/non-Muslim.

The status of non-Muslims in Muslim societies, territorially defined as "Abode of Islam" (*dār al-islām*), has varied greatly over time and space. Legal theory has never been uniform throughout the Muslim world and has often been far removed from practice. The population of the first Islamic empires (Umayyad, ʿAbbāsid, and so on) was heterogeneous in religion, language, and social structure. As the faith of the Muslim sovereigns and of the ruling elite, Islam was the dominant religion, but the non-Muslim minorities retained an important place within the political structure of the state. There was also a substantial population of non-Christian roots, such as the Druze, the Hindus, or the several Jewish sects. Linguistic groups were as varied and overlapping as the religious communities. Moreover, Islam has a Sunnī majority (85 percent) and a Shīʿī minority (15 percent). But, as a legal and political discipline of minority, these kinds of differences were hardly taken into account. In other words there does not seem to be any rule about homogeneity according to the origin or activity of the inhabitants, except in those cases where a district was inhabited by a community of a distinct religious or ethnic minority. Therefore during Islamic history special rights are granted only to non-Muslims.

Islamic Theory and Practice. Muslim people emerged as a minority, persecuted and forced to flee from Mecca to Medina because of their new religion. Following the death of the Prophet Muḥammad in 632, Islam emerged over the decades after a period of gestation. Islamic society took shape through a process of dialogue with the other religious traditions. New territories were annexed to the growing Islamic state and the Muslims living within its borders were a minority. It took them several centuries to become the majority: It was in the three centuries that followed the ʿAbbāsid revolution (750) that non-Muslims were reduced to minority status in most areas of the Near and Middle East.

The basis of the classical juridical treatment of non-Muslims in Islam depends on Islamic sources, like the Qurʾān and the Prophetic tradition (Sunnah), but also on secondary sources. According to the rules of *fiqh* the world is divided into two main territorial entities, the dār-al islām ("Abode of Islam"), and the dār-al ḥarb ("Abode of War").

The inhabitants of the dār-al islām were divided into three main categories: Muslims, having access to state positions; non-Muslim subjects living under Islamic jurisdiction, who were granted a legal protection (the *dhimmah*); and foreigners living temporarily in Islamic territory (*mustamin*). Although they belonged normally to enemy territory, they were granted a safe-conduct protecting their property and lives, together with the practice of their religion, respecting the Qurʾānic principle "No compulsion in religion" (sūrah 2:256).

The "people of the book" were required to pay two tributes: a land tax (kharāj) and a poll tax (jizyah). The various schools of law varied considerably as to the definition of the legal rights and obligations of the protected people (dhimmīs). On the basis of the Qurʾānic injunctions Muslim scholars advocate that the religious persecution of a confessional minority is a justification for war.

Early Modern Islamic Attitudes Toward Minorities: The Ottomans as a Case Study. The policies of the Muslim states of the past toward their non-Muslim subjects were based on the precedent of the early Islamic states, but with certain innovations in this respect. The Islamic empires of the early modern age, like the Ottoman, the Ṣafavid, and the Moghul, were a mosaic of ethnic and religious groups governed by a Muslim elite, dominating the army and the administration, heterogeneous conglomerates of lands and peoples. They administered large non-Muslim populations which, in many areas, outnumbered Muslims.

Non-Muslim residents were tolerated as long as they lacked public visibility. In different times many Christians and Jews reached positions of power, but non-Muslims, as groups, did not enjoy full equality. This paradigm of hierarchical structure was challenged in the mid-nineteenth century, when there was a process of legal codification (tanzimat) toward formal individual equality before the civil law. The three leading non-Muslim monotheistic religious communities—the Jewish, the Greek Orthodox, and the Armenian—were established as recognized dhimmī (in Ottoman Turkish, zimmi) communities, known as millets (from the Qurʾānic term millah, meaning in Ottoman Turkish "nation") and led by their proper religious dignitary. Within each millet communities were responsible for educational and fiscal issues, as well internal personal legal matters (marriage, divorce, inheritance, etc.). Recent scholarship on the Ottoman Empire has debated the origins of the institution of the millet. New historical evidence suggests that the institution of millet, as a centralized institution, first appeared only in the seventeenth century and became prevalent only in the nineteenth century.

As the Turkish scholar Selim Deringil has pointed out, in the end of their history the Ottomans adopted the archimperialist mind-set of their European enemies, conceiving its periphery as a colonial setting. The peoples of distant peripheries, such as the nomadic Turkmen tribes of eastern regions and the Bedouins of Arab provinces, were construed as uncivilized and savage and in need of a civilizing mission. It was a new type of rule about homogeneity according to the origin of the inhabitants, considered an ethnic minority even in an Islamic context.

Dhimmitude. Recent political Islamophobia, under the impact of political Islam linked to the ideas of war on terror and the security state, which especially emerged after 11 September 2001, revamped the Islamophobic Orientalist approach of Western scholars of the nineteenth century. Despite Europe's growing Muslim minority population—as a faith group it is a minority in democratic secular states, with protected rights, including the right to practice their religion—there is a widespread attitude to demonize them as the unassimilable and disloyal inner enemy.

In 1982 the Maronite Lebanese president Bachir Gemayel (Bashīr al-Jimayal) had coined the Islamophobic neologism "dhimmitude." The term was later introduced into pseudo-academic and polemist discourse by the Egyptian writer Bat Yeʾor, who devoted several of her writings to the topic of persecution and ill treatment of minorities in all the Islamic world at all times. Her clear message is that Islam is not a tolerant religion, fostering aggressive actions toward those populations who do not embrace Islam. She based her works upon a documentation of Islamic sources and various dhimmi communities from all areas of Muslim rule, but she also ignored all those sources supporting the opposite view. In other words sources like those proposed by the Egyptian writer can be used to prove exactly the contrary of what Bat Yeʾor has tried to demonstrate. Even leading contemporary scholars of the history of the Jewish communities of medieval Islam, such as Mark R. Cohen and Abraham Udovitch, have criticized the term "dhimmitude" as misleading and Islamophobic.

The minority issue in Muslim countries raises serious questions in the West resulting in much negative press for Islam as a religion. The constitutions of many Muslim countries are thought to contradict the Universal Declaration on Human Rights and to ignore civil rights standards. At the other end of the spectrum, there are Muslim intellectuals seeking ways to legitimize full legal and political equality of Muslims and non-Muslims in Islamic terms. They clearly look at the public good (maṣlaḥah) and claim the need for a radical ijtihād (individual effort into legal issues) that takes into account the intentions of the norms of the past, rather than the technical details of fiqh and the letter of the law. Their primary concern is to avoid the public disorder (fitnah).

The Minority Issue in Modern Muslim States. The balance of power between different Islamist trends, as well as the degree to which regimes are under pressure from Islamist groups, have a major part to play in determining the status of non-Muslims in the modern Islamic world, where very few Muslim countries claim to have an Islamic constitution.

For instance in modern Egypt al-Azhar Islamic University contributed to the Islamic debate, highlighting the concept of citizenship in the Islamic discourse. Prominent Sunnī religious reformists, such as Muḥammad ʿAbduh (1849–1905) and one of his disciples, Maḥmūd Shaltūt (1893–1963), focused on the traditional status of the protected (dhimmī) community associating it with the concept of citizenship. The term muwāṭin, in its literal sense, has been often used as meaning a non-Muslims sharing the same waṭan (homeland) as Muslims, but not as citizens sharing the same legal and political status. In 1985 the renowned Egyptian political analyst Fahmī Huwaydī tried to find the causes and solutions to tension between Muslims and non-Muslims in Islamic countries by putting on the same level the concepts of dhimmī and muwāṭin. More recently the Grand Mufti of Egypt, ʿAlī Jumʿa (Gomaa), has said that what he calls the "paradigm of al-Azhar" is a traditionally inclusive approach that accommodates and contrasts drastically Islamism as a polarizing and exclusivist force.

Another example is Pakistan, which is a country created for Muslims out of the subcontinent of India and is constitutionally declared an Islamic state. Despite recent legislative attempts to Islamize society, the country remains essentially secular in character. There the minority issue is a question of Islamist rhetoric to obtain the support of the masses, as is evident by the fact that the Ministry of Minorities is usually headed by a minister who is either Christian or Hindu.

The Republic of Turkey's unique history as a secular democracy with a Sunnī majority creates interesting institutional patterns with regard to its policies on religious minorities, both non-Sunnī and non-Muslim. According to the 1923 Treaty of Lausanne, the Republic of Turkey does not grant the minority legal status to Muslim minorities, both ethnic and linguistic, such as the Kurds or the Alevis, which constitute the largest of minorities.

Today one-third of Muslims live as minorities in the non-Muslim world. In nations where Muslims are in a minority, such as southern Thailand or the Philippines, many young Muslim women have adopted Islamic dress to indicate their resistance to the prevailing national political culture.

There is a convergence of opinion within the Muslim-Christian encounter debate to consider modern confessionalism, by its nature, as undermining national unity and obstructing democratic development. The prevailing opinion in the dialogue circles is that the citizens of a united nation, no matter which confession they are part of, must join in dialogue to solve their common problems.

BIBLIOGRAPHY

General Works

Fattal, Antoine. *Le statut légal des non-musulmans en pays d'Islam*. Recherches publiées sous la direction de l'Institut de Lettres Orientales de Beyrouth. Beirut: Imprimerie Catholique, 1958. Contains an extensive bibliography of legal and historical literature.

Huwaydī, Fahmī. *Muwāṭinūn lā dhimmiyyūn*. Cairo: Dār al-Shurūq, 2005.

Khadduri, Majid. *War and Peace in the Law of Islam*. Baltimore: Johns Hopkins University Press, 1955.

Komeili, Mahadi. *Rights of Minorities in Islam*. Repr. New Delhi: Kanishka, 2009.

The Ottoman Period

Ayed, Saleh bin Hussain, al-. *The Rights of Non-Muslims in the Islamic World*. Translated by Alexandra Alosh. Riyadh: Dar Eshbelia, 2002.

Deringil, Selim. "'They Live in a State of Nomadism and Savagery': The Late Ottoman Empire and the Post-colonial Debate." *Comparative Studies in Society and History* 45 (2003): 311–342.

Single Case Studies in the Modern Islamic World

Aragon, Lorraine V. *Fields of the Lord: Animism, Christian Minorities and State Development in Indonesia*. Honolulu: University of Hawaii Press, 2000.

Gabriel, Theodore P. C. *Christian Citizens in an Islamic State: The Pakistan Experience*. Aldershot, U.K., and Burlington, Vt.: Ashgate, 2007.

Hassan, Farooq. "Islam: A Religion of Tolerance or Terrorism (an Analytical and Critical Study)." *Interdisciplinary Journal of Contemporary Research in Business* 3, no. 10 (February 2012). http://journal-archieves15.webs.com/822-830.pdf.

Shatzmiller, Maya. *Nationalism and Minority Identities in Islamic Societies*. Studies in Nationalism and Ethnic Conflict. Montreal: McGill-Queen's University Press, 2005.

Tanthowi, Pramono U. *Muslims and Tolerance: Non-Muslim Minorities under Shariah in Indonesia*. Islam in Southeast Asia: Views from Within. Chiang Mai, Thailand: Silkworm Books, 2008.

On the Polemist Debate on Dhimmitude and the Clash of Civilizations

Cohen, Mark R. "Modern Myths of Muslim Anti-Semitism." In *Muslim Attitudes to Jews and Israel: The Ambivalences of Rejection, Antagonism, Tolerance and Cooperation*, edited by Moshe Ma'oz. Brighton, U.K.: Sussex Academic Press, 2010.

Fekete, Liz. *A Suitable Enemy: Racism, Migration and Islamophobia in Europe*. London and New York: Pluto Press, 2009.

Kaya, Ayhan. *Islam, Migration and Integration: The Age of Securitization*. Migration, Minorities and Citizenship. Houndmills, U.K.: Palgrave Macmillan, 2009.

NICOLA MELIS

Minority Fiqh. The jurisprudence of Muslim minorities (Ar. *fiqh al-aqallīyyāt*) is a contemporary Muslim legal discourse that responds through the interpretive method called *ijtihād* to the challenge of private and public issues facing Muslims living in the West. It is generally held that the concept of *fiqh al-aqalliyyāt* was first used in 1994 by Ṭāhā Jābir al-ʿAlwānī (b. 1935), an Iraqi Sunni jurist resident in the United States, to provide legitimacy for the participation of Muslims in American elections. Within the literature of *fiqh al-aqalliyyāt*, it is possible to distinguish between legal theory and legal practice. As theory, *fiqh al-aqalliyyāt* takes the form of a formulation of its sources, methodology, and application. As legal practice, it is a corpus of legal opinions, *fatwas*, on specific issues. The key element in both is the attempt to reconcile rules of Islamic law, regarded as general and universal by jurists who advocate *fiqh al-aqalliyyāt*, with the political and social conditions of Muslims in the West. For these jurists, *fiqh al-aqalliyyāt* is a particular jurisprudence (*fiqh*) tailored to particular individuals and groups, and its *fatwas* are meant to be specific to these individuals and groups. For this reason, *fiqh al-aqalliyyāt* is not perceived as a competitor to traditional Muslim jurisprudence. Rather, it uses the same sources as its traditional counterpart, only its focus is on principles and cases that provide flexible answers to problems faced by Muslims in a minority context.

With regard to its sources, *fiqh al-aqalliyyāt* has recourse to the primary sources of Sunni law, namely, the Qurʾān, sunna, consensus (*ijmāʿ*), and analogy (*qiyās*), and to secondary sources such as public interest (*maṣlaḥa*), juristic preference (*istiḥsān*), custom (*ʿurf*), the opinion of a Companion of the Prophet, etc. However, *fiqh al-aqalliyyāt* is highly selective in its employment of Islamic legal sources. One can look at *fiqh al-aqalliyyāt* from a closed-source perspective and from an open-source perspective. In the first case, it seems to draw on a set of traditional sources and principles used in Islamic law to formulate rules for exceptional juridical cases, especially in mandatory situations or in the absence of revealed text. In this respect, it is to be compared to *fiqh al-ḍarūra* (the jurisprudence of necessary cases) since it deals with one of the exceptional cases (*ḥālāt istithnāʾiyya*), viz. that of Muslims not living in Muslim lands. In this sense, necessity is the closed dimension of *fiqh al-aqalliyyāt* —it upholds traditional legal theory and practice, is reactive, and remains within the bounds of the legal principle of averting hardship (*mashaqqa*).

Maṣlaḥa, or public interest, in particular, is a central issue and approach in *fiqh al-aqalliyyāt*. Theoreticians of *fiqh al-aqalliyyāt* have argued that it allows a pragmatic and adaptive attitude toward the norms and institutions of Western societies. They often reiterate the idea that when interests change, legal opinions should also change, according to time, place, and circumstances. As a result, public interest opens legal theory and practice to interaction with the context, seeking simplicity and proactiveness.

Although the supporters of *fiqh al-aqalliyyāt* emphasize the role of the individual in legal awareness and application, it is mostly a collective jurisprudence. Cases of pronouncements of individual jurists are rare. The major role is played by two organs: the ECFR (European Council for Fatwa and Research) in Western Europe and the AMJA (Assembly of Muslim Jurists in America) in North America. This collective character of *fiqh al-aqallīyyāt* signals a deliberative approach that negotiates three conditions: the legacy of traditional *fiqh*, the social condition of Muslim minorities in the West, and the legal obligations of these Muslims toward the laws of Western societies.

Founders. Credit should be given to al-ʿAlwānī for laying the foundations of *fiqh al-aqalliyyāt*. In 1999 he published an article entitled "Madkhal ilā fiqh al-*aqalliyyāt*: Naẓarāt taʾsīsiyya" (An Introduction to the *Fiqh* of Minorities: Foundational Insights), which presented the first results of his reflections on this new subsection of *fiqh*. A year later he published a booklet *Fī fiqh al-aqalliyyāt al-muslima* (translated into English as "Towards a *Fiqh* for Minorities: Some Basic Reflections," 2003), in which he argues for the necessity of *ijtihād* for Muslims living in the West. He is mainly concerned with the kind of constructive relations Muslims residing in the West should establish with non-Muslims. It should be noted that al-ʿAlwānī is above all a specialist in *uṣūl al-fiqh*, legal theory, and therefore his interest in the theoretical aspects of *fiqh al-aqalliyyāt* is obvious. His intellectual project is to construct a new *ijtihād* relying on a Qurʾānic methodology that interacts with social and natural sciences. For him, the purpose of *fiqh al-aqalliyyāt* is to develop a set of methodologies that make Islamic law and ethics flexible enough to be applied in the Western context.

The Egyptian jurist and preacher Yūsuf al-Qaraḍāwī (b. 1926), author of one of the major foundational texts, *Fī fiqh al-aqalliyyāt al-muslima: ḥayāt al-muslimīn wasaṭ al-mujtamaʿāt al-ukhrā* (On the *Fiqh* of Muslim Minorities: The Life of Muslims among Other Societies, 2001), is more focused on legal practice. In al-Qaraḍāwī's legal understanding, *fiqh al-aqalliyyāt* is part of the scholarship on *taysīr al-fiqh li-l-muslim al-muʿāṣir* (facilitating *fiqh* for contemporary Muslims). He shares with al-ʿAlwānī the idea of the centrality of *ijtihād* to shed a new light on modern political and social issues. Nevertheless, in developing his "modern *fiqh*" al-Qaraḍāwī draws more on his legal experience as a mufti. Al-Qaraḍāwī's formula is to combine traditional *fiqh* with an emphasis on public interest and moderation. Often he is led to accept concessions for modernists on a number of issues, such as those of women and the state. Additionally, al-Qaraḍāwī conceives his *fiqh al-aqalliyyāt* as complementary to his book *al-Aqalliyyāt al-dīniyya wa-l-ḥall al-islāmī* (Religious Minorities and the Islamic Solution, 3d ed., 1998), which discusses the Islamic answer to the question of non-Muslims living in Muslim societies. Above all, in respect to his interest in Western Europe, al-Qaraḍāwī seems to be motivated by a concern about the religiosity of Muslims, and especially about their secularization.

Other recent contributions to the discourse mostly treat the same issues discussed by al-ʿAlwānī and al-Qaraḍāwī. Close to the latter stands the Mauritanian jurist ʿAbd Allāh b. al-Shaykh al-Maḥfūẓ Ibn Bayya (b. 1935), who published *Ṣināʿat al-fatwā wa-fiqh al-aqalliyyāt* (The *Fatwa* Industry and the Jurisprudence of Minorities) in 2007. Others, mostly from Lebanon, Egypt, Tunisia, and Morocco (e.g., Khālid ʿAbd al-Qādir, Ṣalāḥ al-Dīn ʿAbd al-Ḥalīm, ʿAbd al-ʿāṭī Ashraf, ʿAbd al-Majīd al-Najjār, and Ismāʿīl al-Ḥasanī), generally stick to the line of reasoning elaborated by the founders. Thus most of the *fiqh al-aqalliyyāt* literature in Arabic lacks direct contact with Muslim minorities in the West. Markedly, these authors try to replace the necessary social component in *fiqh al-aqalliyyāt* with a philological corpus of terms and sources. Their methodology seems to be a set of concepts and ready-to-wear processes that they apply to any sort of *fiqh*. Accordingly, the deliberative link that is based on an embodiment of *fiqh* in everyday life is completely absent; the *fiqh* and the society to which it applies belong to two different realms.

The Jurisprudence of Muslim Minorities in Application. In a decision (5/12) issued in 2004, the ECFR affirmed the special importance of *fiqh al- aqalliyyāt*, since it leads to recognition of the Muslim presence in non-Muslim countries and to the application of Islamic legal provisions in that reality. The ECFR also affirmed the authority of al-ʿAlwānī, al-Qaraḍāwī, and Ibn Bayya. The council agreed that the concept of *fiqh al-aqalliyyāt* is valid insofar as it concerns itself with legal issues related to Muslims who live outside Muslim countries. Generally speaking, the ECFR employs two methods to formulate a decision in cases involving Muslim minorities in the West. Either its jurists issue a legal opinion, *iftā*ʾ, in answer to a question posed by an individual or a group of people (*mustaftī*) through such communication media as mail, email, and the telephone; or it deliberates in lengthy collective discussions of more controversial questions. In all its decisions, the ECFR looks to provide Muslims in the West with a way to take part in Western culture without assimilation, and thus, as part of a strategy of public relations, it follows a conciliatory line with regard to Western societies. As is true for deliberative bodies of *fiqh* in the Muslim world that rely on collective *ijtihād*, legal diversity characterizes the ECFR's deliberations. A result is eclecticism, typical of juristic councils whose members come from different legal backgrounds. Many of the prominent scholars of the ECFR were neither born nor raised in Europe, and most actually live in Muslim countries. Thus the ECFR reflects a variation on modern Islamic jurisprudence, seen within the project of *fiqh* renewal.

With time, more European Muslim jurists will emerge. However, in the absence of a solid training in Islamic law in Europe, the ECFR is obliged to recruit authorities from the Arab world. For the moment, the structure and function of the ECFR seem to be under the sway of non-European jurists. In the French headscarf controversy of 2004, the ECFR did not go beyond a traditional *fiqhī* attitude. It condemned the French decision to ban visible religious signs and advised Muslims living in France to stand up for their legitimate rights, to express their opposition, through peaceful and legal means, to what it deemed an unjust law. In other matters, however, the ECFR did cross the red line, as in its *fatwa* permitting a conventional mortgage in circumstances of necessity (*ḍarūra*), which bypassed the prohibition of *ribā*, usury, in Islamic law.

The Boundaries of *Fiqh al-Aqalliyyāt*. Traditional *fiqh* has limited recourse to custom, which is restricted to cases where scriptural rules are missing. However, when scriptural rules are based on custom, it is permitted to change the legal provisions as the custom changes. Al-Qaraḍāwī's *fatwa* allowing a Muslim woman living in the West to remain married to a non-Muslim (which is strictly forbidden in the Qurʾān) particularly disturbed conservative Muslims, who contest the legitimacy of *fiqh al-aqalliyyāt* and criticize its pragmatic reasoning. They argue that Western reality should not be the source of Islamic legislation, only its subject matter, which is covered by traditional *fiqh* in the same way other areas are. The pragmatism of al-Qaraḍāwī's reliance in the above-mentioned *fatwa* on weighing differing interests, and finding the stronger interest in Islam's maintaining social ties in the West between Muslims and non-Muslims, is rejected by the conservatives. Of course, conservatives assail the idea of integration into Western societies to begin with, and, accordingly, any principle that enables Muslims, under Islamic terms, to interact with these societies.

Inasmuch as it is a legal discourse for a specific community (Arabic-speaking Muslims), *fiqh al-aqalliyyāt* does not fully grasp the complex Muslim reality of western European societies. It also does not follow the evolution of religiosity among young Muslims living in the West. Rather, the legal process adopted by *fiqh al-aqalliyyāt* focuses on preserving Muslim identity, the call to Islam, relations with non-Muslims, and providing Muslims with legal knowledge. As such, it is a preaching *fiqh*, *fiqh daʿwa* so to speak. In many respects, *fiqh al-aqalliyyāt* appears to be a pretext to establish ways of communication between Muslims over daily matters and to prevent an overwhelming secularization of Muslims in the

West. Many European Muslim voices are critical of the involvement of Islamic institutions, such as al-Azhar and Muslim *fiqh* councils, in *fatwa* committees and in the making of *fiqh al-aqalliyyāt*. Nevertheless, pluralism and deliberation, which characterize the sessions of the ECFR and the AMJA, could, if open to young European Muslims, play a significant role in the life of Muslims living in the West. Furthermore, any development of *fiqh al-aqalliyyāt* should consider the secular public space in the West and should find a way to work in accordance with it.

[*See also Fiqh.*]

BIBLIOGRAPHY

Albrecht, Sarah. *Islamisches Minderheitenrecht: Yūsuf al-Qaraḍāwīs Konzept des fiqh al-aqallīyāt*. Würzburg: Ergon Verlag, 2010.

al-ʿAlwānī, Ṭāhā Jābir. *Fī fiqh al-aqalliyyāt al-muslima*. Cairo: Dār Nahḍat Miṣr, 2000.

Bruinessen, Martin van, and Stefano Allievi, eds. *Producing Islamic Knowledge: Transmission and Dissemination in Western Europe*. Abingdon, Oxon: Routledge, 2011.

Caeiro, Alexandre. "The Power of European *Fatwās*: The Minority *Fiqh* Project and the Making of an Islamic Counterpublic." *International Journal of Middle Eastern Studies* 42 (2010): 435–449.

Gräf, Bettina, and Jakob Skovgaard-Petersen, eds. *Global Mufti: The Phenomenon of Yūsuf al-Qaraḍāwī*. New York: Columbia University Press, 2009.

Ibn Bayya, ʿAbd Allāh ibn al-Shaykh al-Maḥfūẓ. *Ṣināʿat al-fatwā wa-fiqh al-aqalliyyāt*. Jiddah: Dār al-Minhāj, 2007.

March, Andrew F. "Sources of Moral Obligation to non-Muslims in the 'Jurisprudence of Muslim Minorities' (*Fiqh al-aqallīyyāt*) Discourse." *Islamic Law and Society* 16 (2009): 34–94.

Masud, Muhammad Khalid. "Islamic Law and Muslim Minorities." *ISIM Newsletter* 11.2 (2002): 17.

al-Qaraḍāwī, Yūsuf. *Fi fiqh al-aqallīyyāt al-muslima: ḥayat al-muslimīn wasaṭ al-mujtmaʿāt al-ukhrā*. Cairo: Dār al-Shurūq, 2001.

ECFR [http://www.e-cfr.org].

Abdessamad Belhaj

Mirrors for Princes. The practice of providing political know-how to those in authority may be traced to ancient times. Among the first to do this are the Chinese Confucian writers of the classical age who sought to gain high office ostensibly to reform government institutions. Mencius, the philosopher who defended ideas first put forward by Confucius, visited rulers to dispense advice on good governance. Even more significant were the writers of the Legalist school of Chinese thought, such as Lord Shang and Han Fei, who held high office only to suffer tragic deaths. Another classic of the advisory genre from ancient China is *The Art of War* by Sun Tzu, who aimed "to reach invincibility, victory without battle, and unassailable strength through understanding of the physics, politics, and psychology of conflict" (1988, p. vii). Not surprisingly, the Chinese classic retained its fame as a sourcebook of guidance in military strategy, politics, and even business, almost rivaling Niccolò Machiavelli's celebrated magnum opus *The Prince*, perhaps the best known *Fürstenspiegel*, or "mirror for princes," a genre of political literature in which the writer offers advice to the prince to enable the latter to sustain his leadership role, govern more effectively, and secure his realm. Remarkably, and under the guise of offering practical advice, many of these authors made significant contributions to the field of political philosophy and the art of governance.

Advice to Rulers. Providing advice to rulers became a universal phenomenon that developed across the centuries throughout the world. Among the ancient Egyptians, Babylonians, Chinese, Indians, and Persians, the focal power of the ruler was beyond question. In Greek political philosophy, Plato pioneered consideration of the ruler's central role in governing the city-state. To Plato, the philosopher-king was the ideal type of ruler, combining theoretical wisdom with practical political experience, a partial embodiment of which was Alexander the Great, pupil of Aristotle, who had in turn been a student of Plato. Plato's concept of the philosopher-king had a formative impact on both Islamic and Western political thought. In the Muslim context, Abū Naṣr al-Fārābī synthesized the Platonic and Islamic notions of the ideal ruler as one who is prophet/lawgiver/imam, all combined. This formulation reappeared in different forms in the writings of Ibn Sīnā, Ibn Bājjah, and Ibn Rushd.

The rise and progressive expansion of Arab power in the decades after the death of the Prophet Muḥammad confronted successive Muslim caliphs and sultans with complex problems of governance and administration over an immense realm of countries and peoples, stretching from Spain to Central Asia. In the context of the multifaceted challenges of rulership and the struggles for power among ruling factions, both official and unofficial advisors emerged in key roles within and on the periphery of the ruling elite. Although some of these advisors were lay functionaries, others belonged to the clerical class (ʿulamāʾ), who dispensed advice on governance according to Islamic law—a practice that harked back to the beginnings of the Caliphate. Among these luminaries, a dozen left behind a rich literature that represents much of the collective political thought and experience of Muslim thinkers and practitioners of the art and science of governance during the centuries of Islam's ascendance.

The fundamental question that confronted rulers was the role of political leadership in the historical process and the extent to which governors went to change history. In fact, most were preoccupied with their intrinsic abilities to shape their respective political process. Although the Platonic notion of the ideal ruler found a practical reaffirmation in Plutarch, whose measure of great men included heroism in war, grace, dignity, and generosity, it was not until the fourteenth and fifteenth centuries that the leadership theme reemerged forcefully in Western political discourse, particularly in the writings of Niccolò Machiavelli and, later, Thomas Hobbes, who shared a belief in the practical necessity of effective rulership to establish a stable and secure political order. In the aftermath of the French Revolution and the ensuing Napoleonic wars, a renewed focus on heroic leadership was propounded by Georg Friedrich Hegel and Thomas Carlyle, who saw the march of history as being determined by "great men." These notions inspired Western leaders to seek added powers and, in an ironic twist, to solicit ideological justifications from learned men.

To be sure, theorists persuasively argued that leaders were a necessary and permanent feature in all societies, even if it should be noted that there could not be "a leadership for all seasons." As Charles de Montesquieu and Max Weber postulated, leadership was a dynamic function that varied in nature, scope, and importance, depending on the developmental phase of a given society. Consequently, a leader's power and locus of action was determined by his personal attributes and the conditions prevailing in his political environment. Clearly, times of crisis and turmoil required a much greater leadership role than periods of stability and normalcy. Indeed, as Weber theorized, conditions of social crisis provided an opportunity for the rise of charismatic leaders with a message of salvation to establish a new political order.

Muslim "Mirrors for Princes" (*Adab*). One of the earliest Muslim contributors to the genre of "mirrors for princes" literature was ʿAbd Allāh Ibn al-Muqaffaʿ (720–757), a Persian convert to Islam. This brilliant secretary to the uncle of Caliph al-Manṣūr was a pioneering figure who propelled the emergence of classical Arabic literature through his translations from Persian, such as the Indo-Persian epic *Kalīlah wa Dimnah*, as well as his authorship of several *Fürstenspiegels* on the art of government. Of special significance were Ibn al-Muqaffa'’s *al-Adab al-Kabīr* (Great literature), *al-Adab al-Saghīr* (Lesser literature), and *Risālah fī al-Sahābah* (Epistles of the companions), which are replete with political advice to the caliph and his courtiers, and which were derived from *khudaynāmah* chronicles of Persian kings and his own experience and involvement in the affairs of state that caused his early demise at the hands of his enemies. Yet Ibn al-Muqaffa'’s writings established a powerful precedent to be followed by subsequent authors of tomes to advise rulers, including al-Jāḥiẓ, Ibn Qutaybah, Tayfur, Ibn Abī al-Rabī', Ibn 'Abd Rabbih, al-Māwardī, Kai Ka'us, Niẓām al-Mulk, al-Ghazālī, al-Ṭurṭūshī, Ibn Ẓafar, Ibn Jamā'ah, Ibn al-Tiqtaqāh, and al-Dawānī, among others. The most significant precedent Ibn al-Muqaffa' set for this long list of distinguished Muslim writers was to transform the absolutist model of Persian kingship into a more humanistic practice of rulership constrained by Islamic faith with its laws, obligations, and equality of all believers before God.

A most worthy successor to Ibn al-Muqaffa' was Abū 'Uthmān 'Amr al-Jāḥiẓ (776–868), a famous and prolific writer of *adab* literature, Mu'tazilī theology and political discourse. Born and educated in Basra in an obscure family of mawālī from the Banū Kinānah and probably of Abyssinian origin, al-Jāḥiẓ owed his sobriquet to a malformation of the eyes (the renowned Mu'tazili theologian suffered from hemiplegia, a total paralysis of the arm, leg, and trunk on the left side of his body, which explained his facial deformation). Despite his handicap, however, he demonstrated "an invincible desire for learning and a remarkably inquisitive mind [that] urged him towards a life of independence and, much to his family's despair, idleness." According to a leading historian, al-Jāḥiẓ's "precocious intelligence won him admittance to Mu'tazilī circles and bourgeois salons," where he helped "define thorny 'problems confronting the Muslim conscience at that time' ranging from how best to harmonize faith and reason, the delicate question of the Caliphate and the even more difficult and defining issue of various 'conflicts between Islamic sects and the claims of the non-Arabs' " (Pellat, 1965, p. 385). In time, al-Jāḥiẓ won recognition for his voluminous writings, which provided comprehensive advice to the caliphs al-Ma'mūn and al-Mutawakkil on how to govern, the qualities of the ideal Muslim ruler, the behavior of courtiers, the practices of effective governance as expressed in his *Kitab al-Taj* (Book of the crown), and other contributions. Though his physical appearance may have affected his career in the 'Abbāsid court, al-Jāḥiẓ's role as an éminence grise accorded him regular access to members of the ruling elite. Al-Jāḥiẓ thus came to occupy a key place in Muslim political thought as his ability to manipulate rhetoric and humor, his gift of providing useful advice without offending, and his capacity to overcome natural handicaps were instrumental in making his talents useful to the 'Abbāsid cause.

After al-Jāḥiẓ, the most notable exponent of *adab* writing was Abu Muhammad 'Abd Allāh Ibn Qutaybah al-Daynuri (828–889). Born in Kufa, Iraq, this Ḥanbalī theologian of Iranian descent and leading *qāḍī* was instrumental in Caliph al-Mutawakkil's campaign to replace Mu'tazilī ideology with Sunnī traditionalism. Despite his espousal of orthodoxy, as an official ideologue of the new order, Ibn Qutaybah was an eclectic intellectual who also wrote on secular subjects. He studied philology and was the first representative of the eclectic school of Baghdad philologists that succeeded the Kufa and Basra schools of rationalist thinking (*ahl al-ra'y*), while jurisprudence (*fiqh*) was under development. Although engaged in theological polemic, Ibn Qutaybah's chief works were directed to the training of an ideal clerk who would loyally serve his ruler. Four of his studies that may be said to form a series were geared towards that objective: (1) the *Adab al-Kātib* (Training of the clerk) provided detailed instruction on writing and was a useful compendium of Arabic style; (2) the *Kitāb al-Maʿārif* (Book of knowledge) described how an advisor ought to gather knowledge to better serve his leader; (3) the *Kitāb al-Shiʿr wal-Shuʿarāʾ* (Book of poetry and poets) highlighted the critical importance of poetry as a form of communication; and (4) the most important study of the set, the *ʿUyūn al-Akhbār* (Sources of information), dealt in ten chapters with lordship, war, nobility, character, science and eloquence, asceticism, friendship, requests, food, and women. This was a heavily illustrated volume with examples from history, poetry, and both Arabic and Persian proverbs. Ibn Qutaybah was greatly influenced by Ibn al-Muqaffaʿ and al-Jāḥiẓ and the Indo-Iranian antecedents, although his Arabic prose was superior for its simplicity, facility, and modernity.

A contemporary of Ibn Qutaybah, Aḥmad Abū Ṭāḥir Tayfur (819–893) was a historian and *littérateur* of Baghdad whose career brought him into contact with high officials. Of particular relevance was a letter Tayfur wrote to his son, who was a provincial governor during the caliphate of al-Maʾmūn, which offered detailed advice about the ruler's duties and the maxims of good governance.

Another jurist of this period was Shihāb al-Dīn Aḥmad Ibn Abī al-Rabīʿ (d. 894). An advisor to the Caliph ʿAbbās VIII al-Muʿtaṣim, the son of Hārūn al-Rashīd, Ibn Abī al-Rabīʿ authored the *Sulūk al-Mālik fī Tadbīr al-Mamālik* (A king's behavior to govern kingdoms). Ibn Abī al-Rabīʿ relied on Greek philosophy, which asserted that man possessed civic attributes, but placed his discourse within an Islamic context. Man, posited Ibn Abī al-Rabīʿ, was capable, but more so when he relied on God. Likewise, he asserted that rulers were capable of governing, but did so more effectively and justly when they applied God's laws.

Among the few Andalusian writers of works on princely conduct was Abu ʿUmar Aḥmad Ibn ʿAbu Rabbi (860–940) of Córdoba, Spain, who followed the *adab* tradition of al-Jāḥiẓ and Ibn Qutaybah. He lived during the apogee of Arab rule on the Iberian Peninsula under the Marwānid dynasty. For three decades, Ibn ʿAbu Rabbi was an official panegyrist of Marwānid rulers and served as laureate of Caliph ʿAbd al-Raḥmān III (912–961). His *al-ʿIqd al-Farīd* (The unique necklace) remained an encyclopedic compilation of knowledge that included chapters on government, good conduct, war, and rulership.

Few Muslim thinkers left as large an impact on contemporary Muslim societies as Abū al-Ḥasan al-Māwardī (974–1058), a Shāfiʿī jurisprudent (*faqīh*) from Basra, Iraq. This eminent *qāḍī* of great learning and author of seminal books on Islamic law and government discussed various principles of political science, with special references to the duties of caliphs, their chief ministers, and other viziers. His *Al-Aḥkām al-Sulṭāniyah* (Princely rules), followed by the *Qawānīn al-Wizārah wa-Siyāsat al-Mulk* (Ministerial laws and the politics of authority), paved the way for future studies. Perhaps unparalleled, al-Māwardī's *Nasīhat al-Mulūk* (The advice of kings) was a key volume for every aspiring Muslim official. Importantly, this corpus highlighted the dynamic relationships between various social groups and government representatives, as well as the myriad measures required in different situations to strengthen the ruler's power to ensure victory. Al-Māwardī's proficiency in jurisprudence, ethics, political science, and literature proved useful in securing respectable posts throughout his long life. As a trusted advisor in the ʿAbbāsid court in Baghdad and in most of his writings, al-Māwardī sought to strengthen Sunnism and the power of the caliphs against the sultans and provincial governors. He was entrusted with critical diplomatic missions by the caliphs al-Qādir (991–1031) and al-Qā'im (1031–1074) to negotiate with emerging rivals such as the Shīʿah Būyid rulers of Iraq. A man of upright reputation and modesty, al-Māwardī effectively assumed the combined functions of political theorist, jurist, diplomat, and court counselor. Considered the author of the "doctrine of necessity" in Muslim political theory, ostensibly because he believed that unlimited powers delegated to regional governors tended to create chaos, al-Māwardī supported a strong caliphate. Yet he also favored clear principles for the election of a caliph, though he identified key qualities for "voters," including the necessity of a certain degree of intellect and the demonstration of sound character.

Despite al-Māwardī's best efforts, the ʿAbbāsid Caliphate declined in the eleventh century, and lost power to rising Seljuk sultans. The period of Seljuk ascendance produced two major advisory tomes by non-Arab writers—the *Qabusnamah* of ʿUnsur al-Maʿali Kai Ka'us (b. 1020) and the *Siyasatnamah* of Abu ʿAli al-Hasan al-Tusi Niẓām al-Mulk (1018–1092). Kai Ka'us was the penultimate governor of the Ziyarid dynasty that ruled the southern littoral of the Caspian Sea under the Seljuks. Written in the Persian *andarz* style (giving counsel to rulers), the *Qabusnamah* was intended to provide practical guidance to his son and successor, Gilan Shah. The book's introduction and forty-four chapters covered a wide range of topics, including kingship, leadership in battle, and administration. Since its appearance in 1083, the *Qabusnamah* has stood as a work readily accessible on account of its direct style, numerous aphorisms, and historical anecdotes, and remained popular particularly in Persia and the Ottoman Empire.

An equally renowned "mirror" was the *Siyasatnamah* or *Siyar al-Muluk* (The history of kings), written by Abu ʿAli al-Hasan al-Tusi Niẓām al-Mulk, the famous minister of the Seljuk sultans Alp Arslan and Malik Shah. After Alp Arslan was assassinated in 1072, the ruthless Niẓām al-Mulk dominated Malik Shah and, in effect, became the actual ruler of the Seljuk Empire. Written in 1091–1092, just prior to Niẓām al-Mulk's own assassination, the *Siyasatnamah* detailed in fifty chapters advice to the sultan and the shortcomings and failures of Seljuk rule, which he vainly sought to correct. The addition of eleven chapters a year after the *Siyasatnamah* was first published in 1092 highlighted Niẓām al-Mulk's sense of failure in providing a sound system of governance, as dangers threatened the empire, especially from the Ismāʿīlīs who rose against Seljuk rule. Still, Niẓām al-Mulk, like Cardinal Richelieu in France several centuries later, was a patron of the arts, generously supporting poets and writers. Remarkably, he also founded several colleges whose ethos and teachings were based on the Ashʿarī *kalām* (dialectical theology) and the Shāfiʿī school of law, to which he adhered. These *Madrasahs*, including the famous al-Niẓāmīyah of Baghdad, contributed greatly to the Sunnī revival in the central and eastern lands of Islam.

One of the foremost theologians of Islam, Abū Ḥāmid al-Ghazālī (1058–1111) hovered, perhaps, over his many peers as a distinguished reformer of the faith. In 1091, al-Ghazālī was sent by Niẓām al-Mulk to teach at the al-Niẓāmīyah *Madrasah*in Baghdad. Although popular within both religious and political circles, al-Ghazālī sought to distance himself from the vicissitudes of government affairs. He left teaching after experiencing an intense spiritual struggle and took up the mystical life of the Ṣūfī for twelve years. Al-Ghazālī returned to teaching and produced several major studies, including his most important work, *Iḥyā' ʿUlūm al-Dīn* (The revival of the religious sciences). A semiautobiographical work, *al-Munqidh min al-Ḍalāl* (Deliverance from error) was also composed, although his *Nasīhat al-Mulūk* (Advice to kings) set standards for kingly behavior and provided guidance on dealing with ministers and subjects. Despite his high stature, al-Ghazālī remained uninvolved in government work and political affairs because of his true calling as a religious reformer, mystic, and thinker who successfully reconciled Sufism with Islamic orthodoxy.

An equally influential philosopher was Abu Bakr Muḥammad al-Ṭurṭūshī (1059–1126) who was born in Spain but who settled in Alexandria, Egypt, where he educated many disciples including such famous figures as Ibn al-ʿArabī and Ibn Tūmart (d. 1130), the future Mahdi of the Muwaḥḥidūn movement in North Africa. Al-Ṭurṭūshī wrote *Sirāj al-Mulūk* (Lamp for rulers), a large compilation (sixty-four chapters) of moral maxims, anecdotes, and advice on rulership dedicated to his patron, the counselor al-Maʾmūn ibn al-Baṭāʾiḥī. The encyclopedic dimensions of Ṭurṭūshī's book provided considerable material for Muslim political thinkers of subsequent generations. Though Ibn Khaldūn criticized al-Ṭurṭūshī in the *Muqaddimah*, allegedly for being a compiler without originality, he himself benefited from the wealth of historical information and political insights contained in the *Sirāj al-Mulū*.

Ironically, one of the more erudite Muslim philosophers, Ibn Ẓafar al-Ṣiqillī who was born in Sicily in 1104, was "rediscovered" by Gaetano Mosca, the influential Italian political scientist who developed the theory of elitismand the doctrine of the political class in the late nineteenth century, as he drew parallels between Ibn Ẓafar's *Sulwān al-Muṭāʿ fī ʿUdwān al-Atbāʿ* (Consolation for the ruler during the hostility of subjects) and Machiavelli's *The Prince*. Mosca, who founded the modern field of elite studies, was instrumental in building upon the intellectual legacy of his great Italian predecessor from Florence. Yet, as a Sicilian, Mosca also became keenly interested in exploring the contributions of mediaeval Arab thinkers to the field of political science. In reading the *Sulwān*, Mosca discovered "a Machiavellism more refined than that of the Florentine Secretary" (Mosca, 1936, pp. 26–27) a powerful endorsement Ibn Ẓafar's work after the passage of eight centuries. Ṣiqillī was, like the Florentine, an unlucky man, as those in power seldom appreciated his wisdom and loyalty. According to ʿImād al-Dīn al-Iṣfahānī, who knew Ibn Ẓafar personally, the Sicilian was "a mighty genius," and Ibn Khallikan, the great chronicler, praised him as "an accomplished scholar." In the *Sulwān*, the ruler facing opposition is advised to (1) trust in God (*tawfid*) and advance resolutely if the cause is just or abandon it if it is unjust; (2) adopt fortitude (*taʾassi*) and face crises until they are over; (3) rely on patience (*sabr*); (4) practice contentment (*rida*); and (5) practice self-denial (*zuhd*) to give up the vanity of earthly benefits.

Ibn Ẓafar al-Ṣiqillī was al-Ṭurṭūshī's immediate chronological successor and, as such, provided the intellectual link between the long line of *Fürstenspiegel* authors going back to Ibn al-Muqaffaʿ and subsequent writers of the "mirror" or related genres such as Ibn Jamāʿah, Ibn al-Tiqtaqāh, Ibn Taymīyah, and al-Dawānī.

A direct intellectual descendant of al-Māwardī and al-Ghazālī, Badr al-Dīn Ibn Jamāʿah was a Shāfiʿī jurist, theologian, and teacher, whose book on constitutional law, *Taḥrīr al-Aḥkām fī Tadbīr Ahl al-Islām* (The formulation of orders to guide Muslims), outlined the ruler's obligations towards his subjects as well as his need to seek advice from the "ulamāʾ in legal matters. Although a conservative theologian, Ibn Jamāʿah was also a pragmatist, offering rulers worldly counsel in the genre of the "mirror for princes."

Born of noble lineage, Ṣāfī al-Dīn Muḥammad ibn ʿAlī ibn Ṭabāṭabah, known as Ibn al-Tiqtaqāh, was the Shīʿah representative (*naqīb*) of al-Ḥillah in Iraq. During his visit to Mosul, he wrote *Al-Fakhrī* (On the systems of government and muslim dynasties), for Fakhr al-Dīn ʿIsa ibn Ibrahim, the ruler of the city. It included a *Fürstenspiegel* and a history of caliphs and *wazīrs*, with detailed biographies. Despite his Shīʿah allegiances, Ibn al-Tiqtaqāh provided realistic assessments of the factors responsible for the successes or failures of rulers in Islamic history. In order to ensure the ruler's success, Ibn al-Tiqtaqāh listed ten qualities based not only on moral standards but also on mastery of the art of rulership. Ibn al-Tiqtaqāh was concerned with practical politics needed to sustain the ruler and his state, and had considerable influence on the work of Ibn Khaldūn.

Like several of his predecessors, Taqī al-Dīn Aḥmad ibn Taymīyah, the preeminent but highly controversial Ḥanbalī theologian and jurisconsult, played a significant role in influencing successive rulers and affairs of state in both Syria and Egypt and, more recently, within Islamist circles. Although Ibn Taymīyah did not write strictly in the "mirror" genre, his voluminous publications, religious edicts (*fatwas*), and personal involvement in political affairs, doctrinal polemics, and military campaigns made him a controversial figure who faced frequent persecution and imprisonment. As an activist advocate of Ḥanbalī puritanism, Ibn Taymīyah emphasized that rulers should always be guided by Islam's teachings, which would require them to seek advice from the ʿulamāʾ as the guardians of the faith. Ibn Taymīyah's doctrinal and political legacies left a formative impact on Islamic political thought and society, particularly in the development of contemporary revivalist ideologies and movements, which is why it was important to dwell on his many contributions.

Finally, a less known Muslim philosopher, Muḥammad ibn Asʿad Jalāl al-Dīn al-Dawānī (1427–1503), the *qāḍī* of Fars, is worthy of attention, too. Dawānī's *Akhlaq-i Jalili* (Practical philosophy), which was a popular version of Naṣīr al-Dīn al-Ṭūsī's *Akhlaq-i Nasiri*, was composed for Uzun Ḥasan, the Aq Qoyunlu ruler. To al-Dawānī, a righteous ruler was necessary to maintain "the equipoise of the world," as he courageously argued that, in addition to righteousness, the ruler—clearly, Uzun Ḥasan—ought to learn certain practical rules of governance to enjoy his power under God's Sharīʿah. Moreover, he argued that a ruler needed supreme law as well as monetary power to govern effectively; he must also have and display unique qualities, including those that would allow him to lead "men to perfection." Importantly, al-Dawānī did not simply identify force as a tool for rulership but, like Ibn Ẓafar, defined good government as one that was based on God's justice. He boldly called on the just ruler to become "the shadow of God upon earth, His representative (*khalīfat Allāh*), and the deputy (*nāʾib*) of the Prophet Muḥammad." Al-Dawānī's work remained valuable since he summarized much of the literary heritage of Islam, including political philosophy, law, and practical wisdom on rulership. As such, his work represented the culmination of intellectual currents until the fourteenth century, when Muslim power passed on to the Ottoman Turks and Persian shahs.

BIBLIOGRAPHY

Al-Bassam, Sulayman. *Kalila wa Dimna, or The Mirror for Princes*. London: Oberon, 2008.

Donohue, John J., and John L. Esposito, eds. *Islam in Transition: Muslim Perspectives*. New York: Oxford University Press, 1982.

Gabrielli, F. "Ibn al-Muqaffaʿ." In *The Encyclopaedia of Islam*, edited by H. A. R. Gibb, pp. 883–885. Rev. ed. Vol. 3. Leiden, Netherlands: E. J. Brill, 1965.

Al-Ghazālī, Abū Ḥāmid. *Deliverance from Error: Five Key Texts Including His Spiritual Autobiography*, al-Munqidh min al-Dalal. Translated by R. J. McCarthy. Louisville, Ky.: Fons Vitae, 2004.

Al-Ghazālī, Abū Ḥāmid. *Ghazālī's Book of Counsel for Kings*. Translated by F. R. C. Bagley. London: Oxford University Press, 1964.

Griffel, Frank. *Al-Ghazālī's Philosophical Theology*. New York: Oxford University Press, 2009.

'Adil Fathi Thabit 'Abdal-Hafiz. *Shar'iyyat al-Sulta fil-Islam* [Legitimation of authority in Islam]. Alexandria, Egypt: Dar a Jami'at al-Jadida lil-Nashr, 1996.

Hourani, Albert. *Arabic Thought in the Liberal Age, 1798–1939*. New York: Cambridge University Press, 1983.

Ibn al-Tiqtaqah, Muhammad ibn 'Ali. *Al Fakhri: On the Systems of Government and the Moslem Dynasties*. Translated by C. E. J. Whitting. London: Luzac, 1947.

Ibn Khaldûn. *The Muqaddimah: An Introduction to History*. Translated by Franz Rosenthal. Abridged and edited by N. J. Dawood. Princeton, N.J.: Princeton University Press, 1967.

Ibn Qutaybah, Abu Muhammad 'Abdallah. *Ibn Kutaiba's Adab-al-Kâtib* [Training of the clerk]. Edited by Max Grünert. Leiden, Netherlands: E. J. Brill, 1900.

Kéchichian, Joseph, and R. Hrair Dekmejian. *The Just Prince: A Manual of Leadership, Including an Authoritative English Translation of the Sulwān al-Muta' fi 'Udwan al-Atba' (Consolation for the Ruler During the Hostility of Subjects) by Muhammad Ibn Zafar al-Siqilli*. London: Saqi, 2003.

Keshk, Muhammad Jalal. *Al-Sa'udiyyun wal-hal al-Islami*. Washington, D.C.: n.p. 1982.

Lecomte, G. "Ibn Kutayba." In *The Encyclopaedia of Islam*, edited by H. A. R. Gibb, pp. 844–847. Rev. ed. Vol. 3. Leiden, Netherlands: E. J. Brill, 1965.

Machiavelli, Niccolò. *The Prince*. Translated by George Bull. London: Penguin, 1999.

al-Māwardi. *The Ordinances of Government*. Translated by Wafaa H. Wahba. Reading, U.K.: Garnet, 2000.

Mosca, G. *Histoire des Doctrines Politiques*, Paris: Payot, 1936, pp. 26–27. [my translation of: "…et l'autre d'une machiavelisme plus raffinée que celui du secrétaire florentin"]

al-Munajjid, Salah al-Din, ed. *Shaykh al-Islam Ibn Taymiyyah: Siratuhuh wa Akhbaruhuh 'inda al-Mu'arrikhin*. Beirut: Dar al-Kitab al-'Arabi, 1976.

Pellat, Ch. "Al-Djahiz." In *The Encyclopaedia of Islam*, edited by H. A. R. Gibb, p. 385. Rev. ed. Vol. 2. Leiden, Netherlands: E. J. Brill, 1965.

Rosenthal, Erwin I. J. *Political Thought in Medieval Islam: An Introductory Outline*. Westport, Conn.: Greenwood, 1985.

Sun Tzu. *The Art of War*. Translated by Thomas Cleary. Boston: Shambhala, 1988.

Joseph A. Kéchichian

Modernity. Islamic modernists advocate flexible, continuous reinterpretation of Islam so that Muslims may develop institutions of education, law, and politics suitable to modern conditions. Modernizing tendencies appeared in the last decades of the nineteenth century in response to westernizing regimes and European rule. Elite Muslim culture was evolving into separate westernized and traditional spheres that modernists sought to unify. To validate their reexamination of Islam's sources among traditionalists, Muslim modernists declared that modernism constituted a return to true Islam as originally preached and practiced, a claim put forth by many reform movements throughout Islamic history. Modernism's distinction among such movements lies in the philosophical and political liberalism displayed by its expositors, in contrast to the tendency in late twentieth-century Islamist discourse to regard liberalism as alien to Islam. To win the support of Muslims attracted to Western culture, modernists argued that the recovery of true Islam would generate the requisite dynamism needed to restore Muslim societies to an honored place in the world. Modernism, then, begins with the assumption widely held by nineteenth- and twentieth-century Muslims that the Muslim world had become backward in relation to the West and that in order to restore equilibrium between the two societies, it was necessary to adapt the practices, institutions, and artifacts associated with European power to an Islamic milieu.

Nineteenth-century Beginnings. Such adaptation began in Egypt and the Ottoman Empire during the first half of the nineteenth century. In the 1860s some Muslims objected to the inclusion of manners and customs in the inventory of items borrowed from Europe. Such Muslims anticipated that indiscriminate imitation of Europe would lead to Western culture supplanting Muslim culture and to the erasure of Islam. These Muslims argued for a more judicious selection of features to be adopted, for distinguishing between the kernel of modern practices and the husk of Western culture. They held that the scientific and technological underpinnings of European power were reducible to categories of knowledge and practice that Muslims could learn without damaging Islam's integrity. Moreover these modernists asserted that modern European science had developed on the basis of classical Islamic learning transmitted to Europe through Muslim Spain. Therefore, were Muslims to learn modern sciences, they would reclaim their own heritage.

This reference to Islam's Golden Age of learning is related to another element in modernist thought, namely the revival of Islam's rationalist philosophical tradition, which distinguished between knowledge attained from revelation and knowledge acquired through the exercise of reason. Since Islamic beliefs and practices derived from revelation, they could not clash with any conclusions acquired through rational thought. One strain within modernism even asserted that revealed knowledge is essentially rational, that is, it could be attained by the exercise of reason.

Modernists authenticated their ideas with yet another appeal to Islamic history by claiming to return to Islam's original principles. In this respect they were putting their own stamp on the eighteenth-century tendency to emphasize strict adherence to beliefs and practices as defined by scripture: the Qurʾān and the *sunnah*. Early modern scripturalist movements included the Wahhābīs in Arabia, Shāh Walī Allāh's circle in India, and reformist Ṣūfī orders throughout the Muslim world. In modernist hands the scriptural orientation legitimized criticism of current beliefs and practices as deviations from the pristine Islam of *al-salaf al-ṣāliḥ* (the pious ancestors).

Early Proponents in Government. The earliest formulations of Islamic modernism issued from Egypt and the Ottoman Empire, the first Muslim lands to initiate reforms of bureaucratic and military institutions along European lines. In the 1860s Rifāʿah Rāfiʿ al-Ṭahṭāwī (1801–1873), a leading Egyptian education official, restated classical Islamic philosophy's view on the complementary relationship between reason and revelation, thereby giving Islamic sanction to the study of European sciences, the striving for technological progress, and the rationalization of government institutions for the sake of advancing society. Al-Ṭahṭāwī also wrote that Muslims who studied modern science and technology would be retrieving knowledge Arabs had imparted to Europe centuries earlier. With respect to Islamic law, he urged religious scholars to exercise *ijtihād* (independent reasoning) in order to adapt religious law to changing conditions. Furthermore al-Ṭahṭāwī called for educational reform, in particular the provision of primary education for all boys and girls. He argued that educating girls would benefit society, because educated women would be more suitable wives and better mothers, and they would contribute to economic production.

In North Africa Khayr al-Dīn al-Tūnisī's (1810–1889) position as a high minister in the reforming autonomous regime of Tunisia during the 1870s was comparable to al-Ṭahṭāwī's in Egypt. In 1875 Khayr al-Dīn established Sadiki College, one of the first schools to combine Islamic and modern scientific topics. Its graduates provided the core of Tunisia's small modernist movement for the next few decades. In addition Khayr al-Dīn introduced liberal political thought to modernism by claiming that parliamentary government and a free press accorded with Islam.

While Khayr al-Dīn and al-Ṭahṭāwī advanced modernist ideas as high officials in modernizing states, the modernist movement known as the Young Ottomans in Istanbul represented lower-level bureaucrats. The Ottoman movement to rationalize bureaucratic and military institutions, known as the Tanzimat (1839–1876), was dominated by a handful of high-ranking officials. The Young Ottomans agreed with the Tanzimat programs designed to rationalize administration in order to enable the Ottoman Empire to fend off European encroachments, but they objected to high officials' adoption of Western manners. In the late 1860s the Young Ottomans called for a liberal political regime similar to European constitutional monarchies that limited sovereigns' powers with elected parliaments. Given their opposition to wholesale adoption of European ways, the Young Ottomans justified the introduction of liberal political principles by claiming that they were part of Islam. Thus their leading writer, Mehmet Namık Kemal (1840–1888), interpreted the Islamic concepts of *shūrā* (consultation) and *bayʿah* (oath of allegiance) to mean an elected parliament and popular sovereignty.

Modernist Intellectuals. Modernist ideas were taken up by men outside official circles in the Ottoman Empire's Arab provinces toward the end of the nineteenth century. In Damascus, Beirut, and Baghdad a handful of progressive religious scholars (Jamāl al-Dīn al-Qāsimī [1866–1914], Ṭāhir al-Jazāʾirī [1852–1920], ʿAbd al-Qādir al-Maghribī [1867–1956], and Maḥmūd Shukrī al-Ālūsī [1857–1924]) called for educational and legal reform, upheld the compatibility of Islam and reason, and favored a liberal political system in terms similar to those laid out by the Young Ottomans. The major impetus for modernism in these circles was alarm at the marginalization of religious scholars in the new Ottoman order. Their aim was to demonstrate the relevance of their expertise in Islamic law to a modernizing Ottoman state.

Jamāl al-Dīn al-Afghānī (1838–1897) brought to modernism a new sense of activism and political resistance to European domination. Born in Iran, he did not belong to any Muslim state's reformist bureaucracy or to a local corps of religious scholars; rather, he restlessly roamed from India to Istanbul spreading his call for an activist ethos and a positive attitude to modern science. Like al-Ṭahṭāwī, al-Afghānī drew on classical Islamic philosophy and promoted its revival to open Muslims' minds to the necessity of acquiring modern knowledge. His chief contribution to modernism was to imbue it with an anti-imperialist strain, because he lived during an era when European armies were conquering Muslim lands from Tunisia to central Asia. To combat European aggression Muslims had to shake off fatalistic attitudes and embrace an activist ethos, individually and collectively. This voluntaristic spirit became characteristic of modernism in the assertion that Muslims must take responsibility for their own welfare rather than passively accept foreign domination as a fate decreed by God. Al-Afghānī succeeded in spreading his views and reputation through political journalism and teaching, but he failed in his bids to gain influence over Muslim rulers. Without an organized base or institutional backing, his conspiratorial approach to political agitation proved fruitless.

Egypt. Islamic modernism underwent its richest development in a Middle Eastern context at the hands of al-Afghānī's Egyptian disciple Muḥammad ʿAbduh (1849–1905). His formulations of modernist thought in the fields of law, education, and theology provided the intellectual bases for modernist trends throughout the Muslim world. ʿAbduh believed that European wealth and power stemmed from achievements in education and science. Consequently Muslims could overcome European domination only by promoting a positive attitude to modern learning and its application in society. A few years after Great Britain occupied Egypt in 1882, his gradualist approach gained the support of British authorities, who secured his appointment to official positions to promote educational and legal reform. Serving on an administrative supervisory committee of al-Azhar (the Arab world's most prestigious center of Islamic learning), ʿAbduh attempted to bring together customary religious education and modern learning, but his opponents thwarted him. His theological writings asserted the harmony of reason and Islam, demonstrating that all rational knowledge, including modern science, accords with Islam. To substantiate this view ʿAbduh's Qurʾānic exegesis claimed that the Qurʾān anticipated modern scientific knowledge: for instance the prohibition of alcohol accords with modern medicine's conclusions about alcohol's damaging effects on health. As for such classic Islamic theological issues as the nature of God and His attributes, ʿAbduh discouraged speculation, because their subject lay beyond the limits of rational comprehension. In the legal sphere, where ʿAbduh served as chief jurisprudent (*muftī*) of Egypt, he flexibly interpreted Islamic law to show that Muslims could adapt to modern circumstances and still remain true to their faith.

ʿAbduh's thought contained a tension between scrupulous adherence to the authority of religion and a willingness to accommodate to the demands of modernity. The generation of Muslims in Egypt influenced by ʿAbduh tended to emphasize one or another of these elements. Muḥammad Rashīd Riḍā (1865–1935), who came to Egypt from Syria in 1897 to join ʿAbduh's reformist circle, developed the religious element in his influential journal, *al-Manār*. In the first three decades of the twentieth century, Egypt's political and cultural elites leaned toward secularism, as they sought to separate religion from politics. Rashīd Riḍā reacted by reinforcing scriptural authority, thereby safeguarding the integrity of Islam. He particularly sought to demonstrate the suitability of Islamic law to modern government, and he stressed the reform of religious practices and beliefs. Most of ʿAbduh's disciples (lawyers, teachers, and government officials), however, traveled down the path to secularism, bending their interpretation of Islam to demonstrate its compatibility with modern life. It seems as though this split stemmed from opposing sources of authority: Islamic scripture and the exigencies of modern life. A second source for this split lay in modernists' call for a return to the way of the first generation of Muslims, the *salaf*. Modernists validated their views by calling for a return to Islam's scriptural sources, the Qurʾān and the *sunnah*. For Rashīd Riḍā this meant close study of those sources to define a core of concepts that would safeguard Islam's integrity. This method, however, gave secularists license to interpret the sources to suit their liberal temperament. Hence in 1925 ʿAlī ʿAbd al-Rāziq (1888–1966) cited scripture to justify Turkey's abolition of the caliphate and the separation of religion and politics. Islamic scripture contains enough general statements and ambiguities to allow for both secular and religious interpretations.

India. As in the Middle East Muslims in India confronted European domination, which became virtually complete when Great Britain abolished the Mughal dynasty following the 1857 Revolt. A second impetus to modernism in India lay in missionaries' criticisms of Islam, which led to a tradition of public debates between missionaries and Muslim scholars. Indian modernism emerged in full bloom in the works of Sayyid Aḥmad Khān (1817–1898), who aimed to convince the British to overcome their distrust of Muslims in the wake of the 1857 Revolt and to persuade Muslims to open their minds to Western ideas. Aḥmad Khān argued that Islam's teachings concerning God, the Prophet, and the Qur'ān are compatible with modern science, which involves discovery of "the work of God" in natural laws. Since God is the author of both natural laws and the Qur'ān, the two exist in harmony. In general Aḥmad Khān would bend the meaning of scripture to suit the conclusions of reason to a greater extent than 'Abduh, who often declared that only God knows the truth when reason and revelation appear to conflict.

Aḥmad Khān's major achievement was the establishment in 1875 of the Muhammadan Anglo-Oriental College at Aligarh, which was intended to train Muslims for government service, thereby restoring them to the roles they filled in Mughal times as administrators and officials. Because Aḥmad Khān's religious ideas were so controversial, however, the task of teaching Islamic subjects was entrusted to more orthodox scholars, and the desired blend of modern learning with a modernist religious orientation did not emerge. Other Aligarh modernists introduced 'Abduh's and Rashīd Riḍā's writings to the curriculum, worked for the flexible interpretation of Islamic law, and advocated improvements in women's status in matters of education, veiling, seclusion, and marriage.

In the first half of the twentieth century Indian modernists had to face the question of how to sustain the Muslim community under a non-Muslim regime, be it the existing British one or an envisioned Hindu-majority state. One group, led by Muhammad Iqbal (1875–1938), argued that Indian Muslims comprise a distinct nation and must live in a Muslim state. Followers of this view struggled for the creation of Pakistan as a separate Muslim polity. The other group, whose spokesman was Abū al-Kalām Āzād (1888–1958), held that Muslims should join with Hindus to combat British rule and struggle for a unified, composite nation. Although this fundamental issue divided them, both groups interpreted the juridical concept of *ijmā'* (consensus) to indicate that whether Muslims formed a separate state or lived in a Hindu majority state, they should live under a democracy.

Indonesia. Indonesia, at the eastern end of the Muslim world, gradually came under Dutch rule during the nineteenth century. Once again European domination and missionary activities stimulated rethinking among Muslims, and a modernist movement emerged. In addition more regular steamship service to the Middle East increased the flow of Indonesian Muslims traveling for pilgrimage and study. On their return many Indonesians brought with them the new reformist teachings circulating in Cairo and Mecca. Indonesia's most important modernist movement, the Muhammadiyah, was founded in 1912 in Jogjakarta by Hadji Ahmad Dahlan (1868–1923), who had resided in Egypt during the 1890s and met Muḥammad 'Abduh. He resembled 'Abduh and Aḥmad Khān in avoiding involvement in nationalist politics in order to avoid suppression by colonial authorities. The Muhammadiyah established a network of modernist schools to combine instruction in religion and modern sciences. To demonstrate support for improving women's status, it set up schools for girls. The Muhammadiyah also advocated legal reform through a return to the Qur'ān and the *sunnah* and the exercise of *ijtihād*. Because Indonesian Islam confronted local animist and Hindu traditions that survived among nominal Muslims, the Muhammadiyah tended over time to focus more on purifying religious practices and beliefs than on spreading modernist interpretations.

Conflicts with Other Ideologies. Around the turn of the twentieth century modernists in Egypt, India, and Indonesia accommodated themselves to European rule because of their conviction that it was futile to seek independence until Muslims had thoroughly assimilated true Islam. Nationalists in each land would accuse the modernists of compromising with European powers and thereby prolonging foreign rule. This criticism cost the modernists dearly in the contest to influence popular opinion. In the first half of the twentieth century nationalist forces grew stronger and eclipsed modernist influence. In large measure modernism's limitations stemmed from its character as an elitist intellectual response to Western power, whereas nationalists used symbols and rhetoric designed to appeal to a broader spectrum of society.

In the 1920s Islamic modernism began to split into three distinct movements. One of them, secularism, aimed to push Islam out of the public sphere and to limit expressions of private spiritual devotion. The most famous secularist leader, Mustafa Kemal Atatürk of Turkey, banned headscarves, Ṣūfī orders, and other Islamic practices in the 1920s, while bringing the religious establishment under stricter control of the state than it had been under Ottoman rulers. A second movement, Islamic liberalism, sought to reconcile Islamic faith and modern liberal norms such as democracy and human rights. Among the most famous early exponents of this position was ʿAlī ʿAbd al-Rāziq, a scholar at al-Azhar in Eygpt, who argued in the 1920s that Islamic sources left methods of governance for humans to devise. A third movement, Islamic revivalism, adopted modern ideals such as human equality, republicanism, and socioeconomic development—as well as modern methods of administration and communication—in an attempt to reconstruct the honor and glory they saw in the early Islamic period. Among the most famous revivalist leaders of the twentieth century were Ḥasan al-Bannā of Egypt and Sayyid Abū al-ʿAlā Mawdūdī of India (and later Pakistan), who founded the first large-scale Islamist organizations in the late 1920s and early 1930s, respectively.

Current State of Modernism. Today Islamic modernism remains splintered into these mutually hostile movements. At the same time its offshoots have grown to dominate the political and social lives of most Islamic societies. By the end of the twentieth century relatively few Muslims adhered to the traditional positions that modernists had campaigned against a century earlier, such as monarchism, suspicion of mass education, loyalty to jurisprudential precedent, and disregard for Western technology. But as modernist principles carried the day, modernism itself came to be derided as overly Western-oriented and insufficiently authentic, even by some Muslim intellectuals who themselves espouse Western-derived global norms such as democracy and human rights. In the late nineteenth and early twentieth centuries Islamic modernists argued that aspects of Islam, if properly understood, were consistent with European models. In the late twentieth and early twenty-first centuries, by contrast, the inheritors of modernism argued that aspects of global norms, if properly understood, are consistent with Islamic models.

[*See also* ʿAbd al-Rāziq, ʿAlī; ʿAbduh, Muḥammad; Afghānī, Jamāl al-Dīn al-; Aḥmad Khān, Sayyid; Atatürk, Mustafa Kemal; Āzād Abū al-Kalām; Bannā, Ḥasan al-; Egypt; India; Indonesia; Iqbal, Muhammad; Muhammadiyah; Nationalism; Ottoman Empire; Rashīd Riḍā, Muḥammad; Sufism; Tanzimat; Turkey; *and* Wahhābīyah.]

BIBLIOGRAPHY

Commins, David Dean. *Islamic Reform: Politics and Social Change in Late Ottoman Syria*. New York: Oxford University Press, 1990.

Khalid, Adeeb. *The Politics of Muslim Cultural Reform: Jadidism in Central Asia*. Berkeley: University of California Press, 1998.

Kurzman, Charles, ed. *Liberal Islam: A Source Book*. New York: Oxford University Press, 1998.

Kurzman, Charles, ed. *Modernist Islam, 1840–1940: A Sourcebook*. New York: Oxford University Press, 2002.

Moaddel, Mansoor. *Islamic Modernism, Nationalism, and Fundamentalism: Episode and Discourse*. Chicago: University of Chicago Press, 2005.
Weismann, Itzchak. *Taste of Modernity: Sufism, Salafiyya, & Arabism in Late Ottoman Damascus*. Boston: Brill, 2000.

DAVID COMMINS
Updated by CHARLES KURZMAN

MONARCHY. Monarchy, in the sense of hereditary rule by one man, was almost universally accepted as the natural form of government throughout the premodern Islamic world. As in Judaism and Christianity, ultimate sovereignty (*mulk*) belonged to God alone (e.g., Q 3:26, 3:189, 5:17–18; cf., e.g., Ps. 47:9, 103:19, Rev. 19:16). However, again as in many other premodern (and some modern) polities, God's authority was delegated to a representative on earth, whose relationship with the divine elevated him above others. The Qur'ān's "Obey God, and obey the Messenger, and those charged with authority [*ūlā al-amr*] among you" (Q 4:59) was often adduced in support of obedience to the ruler, as was the (non-canonical) *ḥadīth* beginning "Government [or the Sultan] is God's shadow on earth" (*al-sulṭān ẓill Allāh fī al-arḍ*). In modern times over forty countries, including ten with majority Muslim populations, are governed by some form of monarchy.

Formative Period (c. 600–c. 900). After the death of Muḥammad (d. 632) authority was vested in a series of rulers from the Prophet's tribe of Quraysh. By the 660s the caliphs were formally styled "God's Servant" (*ʿabd Allāh*) and "Commander of the Faithful" (*amīr al-muʾminīn*). "God's Deputy," or "caliph" (*khalīfat Allāh*), is first securely attested on rare coins from the 690s but tends to occur mainly in court poetry and chancery prose. Following the ʿAbbāsid Revolution (750), an alternative rendering, *khalīfat rasūl Allāh* (Successor to God's Prophet), gained a normative status among religious scholars. The caliph could also be styled *imām* (leader) and his office *al-imāmat al-kubrāʾ* (the greater imamate), to distinguish it from ordinary prayer leadership.

Although the title "king" (*malik*) often occurs with a positive sense in panegyric from the Umayyad period (661–750) and frequently in the ʿAbbāsid period (750–1258), the caliphs eschewed it as a formal title. This appears to reflect a view that kingship (*mulk*) was something properly belonging to God and that "king" was not an appropriate title for someone ruling on God's behalf; monarchs perceived to be worldly and illegitimate, including non-Muslim rulers, were often referred to as kings in contrast to legitimate caliphs or imams.

Despite this distinction, in practice the caliphs perpetuated the characteristics of pre-Islamic kingship. Pre-Islamic kings had made similar claims to represent God on earth and, in the case of the Roman emperor, also to be God's servant (Gk., *doulos*). As in Roman and Iranian monarchy inheritance was a necessary qualification for the caliphate. Open, in classical Sunnī thought, to any member of Quraysh (the kin group of God's Prophet), the caliphate was in fact further restricted to specific Qurashī dynasties. They ruled as monarchical figureheads, elevated by the symbolic trappings of universal kingship, particularly in forms deriving from the Sassanian tradition. In their panegyrics the ancient Near Eastern trope of the king as the sacred source of justice, fertility, and prosperity are recurrent themes, as are images of the monarch as the center of the universe and the guide to salvation.

The Classical Period (c. 900–c. 1250). As regional potentates became independent during the ninth and tenth centuries, new forms of monarchy developed, often legitimated by diplomatic relations with the ʿAbbāsids. In the mid-ninth century, the ʿAbbāsid caliphs had imitated Sassanian precedent by bestowing crowns on senior military commanders and on regional rulers, such as the Armenian kings. In the tenth century, both the Sāmānids (c. 875–1005) and the Būyids (932–1062) revived the Iranian title *shāhanshāh* or *malik al-mulūk* (King of Kings), as well as *malik* in various other composite forms, such as *al-malik al-mu'ayyad min al-samā'* (The King Protected by Heaven). Later eastern successor states, including the Ghaznavids (977–1186), the Khwārazm shāhs (1017–1231), and the Seljuks (1040–1194), continued to use the title *malik* and its composites; it also spread west, being adopted by the Shīʿī Fāṭimid caliphs (909–1171) in the late eleventh century. At the same time, *sulṭān* (government, power) had evolved into a formal title, adopted by the Seljuks who had supplanted the Būyids in dominating ʿAbbāsid Iraq. Increasingly elaborate chains of royal and noble epithets are a feature of the period, lamented by some contemporaries.

These developments, as well as the presence of rival caliphates, prompted Sunnī political treatises, such as those by al-Bāqillānī (d. 1013) and al-Māwardī (d. 1058), which acknowledged the legitimacy of the caliphs' delegation of military power and addressed the problem of multiple claimants to the caliphate. The same period also produced Hilāl al-Muḥassin Ṣābi''s (d. 1056) *Rusūm dār al-khilāfah* (trans. *The Rules and Regulations of the ʿAbbasid Court*, 1977), which discussed court protocol, including ceremonials for encounters between the ʿAbbāsid caliph and military commanders. In the wake of the Seljuk conquest al-Ghazālī (d. 1111) composed a political theory that prioritized the preservation of Muslim religious and social life, and was resigned to accepting arbitrary military rule: the caliph was appointed by a sultan who ruled through brute "power" (*shawka*); in turn the sultan was legitimated by his acknowledging the caliph's authority in the Friday prayer and on the coinage.

Middle and Early Modern Period (c. 1250–c. 1800). When the Mongols extinguished the Iraqi ʿAbbāsid caliphate in 1258, the ʿAbbāsid line became of only local significance: the Mamlūks (1260–1517) claimed that the ʿAbbāsids delegated authority to them in Egypt, as did some other North African rulers. However, in the western Islamic lands, dynasties such as the Mu'minid leaders of the Almohads (1130–1269) had already adopted the titles *khalīfah* (in the sense of successor to their founder, rather than the Prophet) and *amīr al-mu'minīn*; both titles remained in use in North and West Africa thereafter. In the central and eastern Islamic lands Turkic and Mongol universal monarchic traditions were fused with Perso-Islamic political culture. By the mid-sixteenth century three major dynastic empires all articulated their authority in terms of universal monarchy, which combined narrowly "Islamic" elements with the monarchic traditions of the regions they ruled: the Ottoman sultans (c. 1280–1924) in Anatolia and the Mediterranean, and the Ṣafavid (1501–1722) and Mughal (1526–1858) shahs in Iran and India, respectively. The Ottomans formally claimed the Sunnī caliphate (after the 1540s), breaking with the classical tradition that the caliph should be from the Quraysh. Panegyric poetry, advice literature, *shāhnāmahs* (books of kings), and other related genres were produced at all these royal courts, and established classical texts, such as the *Naṣīhat al-mulūk* and the *Kitāb al-tāj*, circulated widely.

Modern Period (after 1800). Both European expansion and social and economic change challenged traditional Islamic monarchies: the British deposed the Mughal emperor in 1858; in the Ottoman Empire and in Qājār Iran (1796–1925), various reforms were attempted, including the formulation of constitutions (in 1876 and 1906, respectively). Following defeat in World War I a military coup ended the Ottoman sultanate (1922) and the caliphate (1924), replacing them with a secular republic. Across the former Ottoman territories, new monarchies were installed with the support of European powers, notably the kingdom of Saudi Arabia (1932). Beyond the former Ottoman territories, older monarchies include the kingdom of Morocco and the sultanate of Oman; the former, ruled by a dynasty that has held power since 1666, became a constitutional monarchy in 1962; the Āl Bū Saʿīd have held power in Oman since the mid-eighteenth century. In Iran a form of constitutional monarchy persisted under the Pahlavi shahs (1925–1979) until the revolution that installed the Islamic Republic. In Southeast Asia, Brunei and Malaysia are majority-Muslim monarchies.

BIBLIOGRAPHY

Ayalon, Ami. "Malik in Modern Middle Eastern Titulature." *Die Welt des Islams* n.s. 23–24 (1984): 306–319.

Al-Azmeh, Aziz. *Muslim Kingship: Power and the Sacred in Muslim, Christian and Pagan Polities.* London and New York: I. B. Tauris, 1997.

Bāshā, Ḥasan. *al-Alqāb al-Islāmīyah fī al-taʾrīkh wa-al-wathāʾiq wa-al-āthār.* Cairo: Dār al-Nahḍah al-ʿArabīyah, 1978.

Bosworth, Clifford E. *The New Islamic Dynasties: A Chronological and Genealogical Manual.* Edinburgh: Edinburgh University Press, 1996.

Broadbridge, Anne F. *Kingship and Ideology in the Islamic and Mongol Worlds.* Cambridge, U.K., and New York: Cambridge University Press, 2008.

Crone, Patricia. *Medieval Islamic Political Thought.* New ed. Edinburgh: Edinburgh University Press, 2005.

Marlow, Louise. "Advice and Advice Literature." In *Encyclopaedia of Islam THREE*, edited by Kate Fleet et al. Leiden, Netherlands: Brill, 2012.http://referenceworks.brillonline.com/entries/encyclopaedia-of-islam-3/advice-and-advice-literature-COM_0026.

Marsham, Andrew. *Rituals of Islamic Monarchy: Accession and Succession in the First Muslim Empire.* Edinburgh: Edinburgh University Press, 2009.

Newman, Andrew J. *Safavid Iran: Rebirth of a Persian Empire.* London and New York: I. B. Tauris, 2009.

Andrew Marsham

Montazeri, Hossein ʿAlī. (1922–2009), a prominent Shīʿī Muslim cleric who played a pivotal role in the Iranian Revolution of 1979 and in the establishment of the Islamic Republic of Iran. In 1982 he was declared by the Assembly of Experts as the intended successor to Ayatollah Ruhollah Khomeini (1902–1989) in the office of supreme leader of the country, but he was forced to resign this position in 1989. By the time of his death in December 2009, however, Montazeri had emerged as a major dissident cleric who advocated for the rights of religious minorities and women and publicly challenged the legitimacy of the Islamic Republic as a true Islamic state.

Montazeri was born into a peasant family in Najafābād, central Iran, in 1922. He began his theological studies at the seminary school of Isfahan in 1937 and in 1944 moved to Qom, the principal center of Shīʿī learning in Iran, where he completed his training in jurisprudence under the supervision of Khomeini. In the early 1950s, as the move to nationalize the Iranian oil industry gained strength, Montazeri became increasingly active in the political arena, following his mentor, Khomeini. In response to the shah's White Revolution of 1963, sociopolitical reforms that included attempts to westernize Iranian society, Montazeri's political activism, and opposition to the Pahlavi monarchy intensified. When Khomeini was arrested and exiled in 1964, Montazeri, along with other midranking and younger clerics, continued to criticize the regime. He was imprisoned in 1975 but released during the 1979 revolution.

After the overthrow of the shah, Montazeri played a leading role in drafting the new constitution, which gave substantial authority to the Shīʿī *ʿulamāʾ* (religious scholars). Montazeri was a staunch advocate of Khomeini's doctrine of *wilāyat al-faqīh*, which makes a senior Shīʿī cleric the head of state. Montazeri served for seven years as Khomeini's intended successor. However, in March 1989 Montazeri resigned from his post after being pressured by Khomeini to do so. The reasons for Montazeri's ouster included his outspoken support for his son-in-law, Mehdi Hashemi, who had exposed the role of the chairman of the Iranian parliament, ʿAlī Akbar Hāshimī Rafsanjānī, in the Iran-Contra affair. Also Montazeri's candid criticisms of the state's domestic and foreign policy, especially the execution of political dissidents, contributed to his fall.

After Khomeini's death in 1989 Montazeri largely kept a low profile but returned to full public view in 1994 when he issued a letter to Ayatollah ʿAlī Khameneʾi (1939–), Khomeini's successor. In it he questioned Khameneʾi's authority and argued that because Islam enjoins the separation of powers, power in the Iranian government should be distributed among the various branches of government. The election of the reformist president Muḥammad Khatami (1943–) in 1997 brought new opportunities for Montazeri to advance his political agenda. In response the regime placed him under house arrest, a sentence that lasted until 2003. During his imprisonment Montazeri continued to support the reformist movement while criticizing the government for its domestic and foreign policies.

Between 2003 and 2009, Montazeri's political activism largely involved the writing of numerous works on Islam and politics, some of which were posted on his personal website. In one of his important works, *Risālah-ʾi huqūq* (Treatise on Law), he argued for the compatibility of human rights and Islamic law, claiming that Islam not only recognizes human rights in principle, but also advances the rights of women, the elderly, children, and even animals. Following the government crackdown on the pro-democracy protests after the disputed 2009 presidential elections, Montazeri famously declared the Islamic Republic to be neither Islamic nor a republic. Montazeri died on 19 December 2009. Thousands of mourners attended his funeral at Qom two days later, many chanting antigovernment slogans and calling for the downfall of dictatorship.

BIBLIOGRAPHY

Work of Hossein ʿAlī Montazeri

Secondary Works

Abdo, Geneive. "Re-Thinking the Islamic Republic: A 'Conversation' with Ayatollah Hussain ʿAlī Montazeri." *Middle East Journal* 55, no. 1 (2001): 1–27.

Akhavi, Shahrough. "The Thought and Role of Ayatollah Hossein ʿAlī Montazeri in the Politics of Post-1979 Iran." *Iranian Studies* 41, no. 5 (2008): 645–666.

Davari, Mahmood T. *The Political Thought of Ayatullah Murtaza Mutahhari: An Iranian Theoretician of the Islamic State*. London and New York: Routledge, 2005.

Gheissari, Ali, and Vali Nasr. *Democracy in Iran: History and the Quest for Liberty*. Oxford and New York: Oxford University Press, 2006.

Risālah-ʾi huqūq. Tehran: Saraie, 2004.

BABAK RAHIMI

MOROCCO. The population of Morocco, about 32.3 million in 2012, is more than 99 percent Sunnī Muslim. There is a tiny Jewish minority but no indigenous Christian minority. Moreover, there are no significant religious differences between the Berbers, found primarily in the mountains, and the Arabic-speaking population. Islamic fundamentalist movements have challenged the monarchy since the 1970s, movements whose strength as well as diversity and influence on Moroccan society became more visible in the 1990s, when King Ḥasan II (d. 1999) initiated a process of liberalization of the political system.

One very influential model of the history of Islam in Morocco was that of Ernest Gellner (d. 1995), who viewed Moroccan Islam as having oscillated throughout history between the puritanical, scripturalist religion of the literate urban bourgeoisie and the ritualistic, anthropolatrous religion of the illiterate rural tribes. According to Gellner, orthodoxy revolved around Holy Scripture and thus entailed literacy. It was strictly monotheistic and egalitarian (among believers), and it emphasized moderation and sobriety and abstention from ritual excesses. In this form of Islam, there were no intermediaries between the believer and God. In contrast, the more anthropolatrous popular Islam stressed hierarchy and mediation between the believer and God. The mediators were Ṣūfī *shaykhs*, saints, and *shurafāʾ* (*sharīfs*). This form of Islam was characterized by ritual indulgence, in contrast to the puritanism of urban orthodoxy.

In Gellner's model, Moroccan tribes nestled in mountains as well as deserts periodically revolted against the reigning dynasty in the name of the puritanical Islam normally associated with urbanized masses. This was possible because the ideals of urban orthodoxy were always present among rural tribes even though they were subordinate to the norms of popular belief. Once successful, the puritanical revivalist movements would eventually revert to the anthropolatrous popular religion, once more vulnerable to puritanical revolt. Gellner viewed this "pendulum swing" as having been unhinged by "modernity." The modern state monopolized violence, whereas precolonial authority did not; consequently, the authority of the tribes diminished, as did that of the saints who formerly mediated their conflicts.

Puritanical reformist movements, as Gellner pointed out, periodically emerged to advocate a return to the pristine Islam of the Qurʾān and sunnah—Ibn Yāsīn's Almoravids and Ibn Tūmart's Almohads are the most obvious examples. At the same time, Gellner overlooked the fact that no such movements managed to seize and retain control of the Moroccan state since the Almohads did in the middle of the twelfth century.

More important, Gellner attempted to impose on the whole of Moroccan history the relationship between popular and orthodox Islam that he observed in the 1950s and 1960s. On the basis of his fieldwork among the High Atlas Berbers, he saw Sufism as a distinctive component of popular religion; in fact, as shown by Vincent Cornell (1998), it had pervaded both popular and orthodox Islam from at least the fifteenth century through the early decades of the twentieth. Most of the *ʿulamāʾ* whom Gellner viewed as embodying orthodoxy were themselves Ṣūfī mystics. Some *ʿulamāʾ* periodically criticized certain ritual manifestations of Sufism, notably the cult of saints and the practices linked to intercession. The Ṣūfīs persecuted by *ʿulamāʾ* were typically renowned *ʿulamāʾ* themselves, often from the same urban elite as their persecutors. In Morocco, the contrast between high and low culture cannot be superimposed on the contrast between Ṣūfīs and Salafī. This becomes obvious when one examines the principal attempts at Islamic reform from the late eighteenth through the early twentieth century.

Forerunners of Twentieth-century Reformism. Islamic reformism in Morocco began as early as the revivalism of the Almoravids in the eleventh century and the Almohads in the twelfth; however, modern reformism is usually thought to begin with Sultan Sīdī Muḥammad ibn ʿAbd Allāh (r. 1757–1790), who insisted on the strict application of Islamic law and the elimination of heretical innovations. Sīdī Muḥammad also condemned charlatans who used Sufism to exploit the masses and "extremist Ṣūfīs" who did not conform to Islamic law. At the same time, he was himself a member of the relatively orthodox Nāṣirīyah Ṣūfī order and regularly visited the tombs of saints.

Sīdī Muḥammad's son Mawlāy Sulaymān (r. 1792–1822) was also a reformer, who condemned heretical innovations (*bidʿah*) and stressed the need to conform to the Qurʾān and sunnah. He also criticized the popular Ṣūfī orders and banned their festivals in honor of saints on the grounds that rhythmic dancing and the mixing of men and women at such gatherings were contrary to the Qurʾān and sunnah.

Mawlāy Sulaymān did not ban the visitation of saints; however, he specified rules governing such practices. Although he condemned many aspects of popular Sufism, he also belonged to the Nāṣirīyah, with his reformist being approach considerably less radical than that of the Wahhābīs or of Morocco's twentieth-century Salafīs. Nevertheless, even his relatively moderate demands for a return to the Islam of the Prophet disturbed many Moroccan *ʿulamāʾ*.

Salafī Reformism. The Salafīyah reformist movement spread to Morocco in the late nineteenth and early twentieth century. Its most important feature was the critique of the cult of saints, seeking to rationalize the interpretation of Islam through a return to the sources and their explanation without mediation. This trend insisted on *ḥadīth*, rather than *fiqh*, which was seen as a rigid set of rules with no connection to the revealed sources or to the reality of Moroccan society. For members of the early trend, adherence to nationalism was not systematic, but Salafī reformism became intertwined with nationalism in the 1930s. Salafī *ʿulamāʾ* such as Abū Shuʿayb al-Dukkālī (d. 1937) disapproved of non-Muslim control the Islamic world, and their country in particular, but they did little to stop the European onslaught that befell North Africa.

In contrast, Ṣūfī *shaykh*s, such as Sīdī Muḥammad ibn ʿAbd al-Kabīr al-Kattānī (d. 1909) and Aḥmad al-Hībah (d. 1919), died leading resistance to colonial rule. The conventional generalization that Ṣūfī *shaykh*s collaborated with the French and the Spanish against the Salafī nationalists reflects the situation in the 1940s, but not that of the early decades of anticolonial resistance. Importantly, the convergence of Sufism and resistance against foreign occupiers is illustrated by the case of Sīdī Muḥammad ibn Jaʿfar al-Kattānī, best known for two books, *Salwat al-anfās* (Solace of the Souls), published in 1899, and *Naṣīḥat ahl al-Islām* (Frank Counsel to the People of Islam), first published in 1908. The first work celebrates the saints, Ṣūfīs, *shurafāʾ*, and *ʿulamāʾ* buried in Fez; the second calls for a return to the pristine Islam of the Prophet.

The Salafī movement eventually merged with Moroccan nationalism, as embodied by the Istiqlāl Party and its most famous leader, Muḥammad ʿAllāl al-Fāsī. Once Morocco regained its independence in 1956, King Muḥammad V (d. 1961) and his successor, Ḥasan II (d. 1999), curbed the influence of this party, but it has remained a political force, winning 60 out of 395 seats in the 2011 parliamentary elections. At the same time, the monarchy has distanced itself from Salafī discourse and practice in the wake of the 16 May 2003 Casablanca bombings, isolating the movement and closing down its separate groups.

Fundamentalist Movements. In 1969, ʿAbd al-Karīm Mutiʿ founded the Shabībah Islāmīyah (Islamic Youth), an extremist religious movement that eventually became a legal opposition party, calling for Islamic virtues in politics and public affairs. Shabībah was influenced ideologically by the writings of the Egyptian Sayyid Quṭb, and it became influential among Moroccan students. The assassination of trade unionist ʿUmar ibn Jallūn in 1975 allegedly by some of its members led to the exile of Mutīʿ and to the disbanding of the movement.

Over the next few years, former members of the Shabībah worked to form a legal political party. As part of a wider process of political liberalization in the mid-1990s, the monarchy finally authorized the formation of their party, which in

1998 took the name Party of Justice and Development (PJD). Since then, the PJD has participated in legislative and municipal elections, consistently increasing its parliamentary representation from nine seats in 1997 to 107 in 2011. The PJD's ideology is similar to that of the Egyptian Muslim Brotherhood. Accepting the legitimacy of the monarchy, the PJD works within the legal framework and under the authority of the commander of the faithful to promote democratic, social, and economic reform.

Unlike the Party of Justice and Development, the al-ʿAdl wa-al-Iḥsān (Justice and Benevolence, or Justice and Charity) movement has never formalized its political role in Morocco. ʿAbd al-Salām Yāsīn (b. 1928) had in 1965 what he called a "spiritual crisis." After reading a wide range of mystical texts, Yāsīn joined the Ṣūfī Būshīshīyah brotherhood, becoming a follower of Shaykh al-Ḥājj al-ʿAbbās. Yāsīn left the order in 1971 to begin an activist career of his own.

In 1974, Yāsīn wrote a *risālah* (epistle or letter) to King Ḥasan II entitled *Al-Islām, aw, al-ūfān: Risālah maftūḥah ilā malik al-maghrib* (Islam, or The Deluge: An Open Epistle to the King of Morocco). Its basic message was simple and familiar. Yāsīn argued that the Muslims' problems were the result of their having deviated from Islam. If they returned to the laws of God and stopped imitating the West, the oppression of the poor by the rich would vanish, as would the domination of Morocco by the West, the state of terror in which Moroccans lived, and the squatter settlements ringing Morocco's cities. In short, everything that was bad would be good.

Yāsīn spent three and a half years (1974–1977) in an insane asylum because of his epistle. Once released, he resumed his campaign for a strictly Islamic polity in Morocco, but he no longer criticized the king directly. In 1979 he began publishing an Islamic review titled *Al-Jamāḥah* (The Group), but it was banned in 1983. The government also prohibited Yāsīn from preaching in mosques. In December 1983, he began publishing another newspaper titled *Al-Ṣubḥ* (The Dawn), but it, too, was soon banned. Sentenced to two years in prison, he was released in January 1986.

In 2000, Muḥammad VI, who acceded to the throne in July 1999, freed Yāsīn, who had been under house arrest. Before his release, Yāsīn posted a memorandum on his website in which he offered criticism of Ḥasan II's rule and offered advice to Muḥammad VI. Compared to his 1974 epistle, this letter was much shorter, less rhetorical, and devoid of religious content. The integration of the PJD into the electoral arena has tended to isolate the Justice and Benevolence movement; at the same time, both movements have continued to pursue political objectives aimed at reforming Morocco's socioeconomic and political system.

In recent years, political reforms have tended to favor perpetuating political authoritarianism at the expense of broader political inclusion in Morocco, enabling the monarchy to maintain its position as the arbiter of political life. The monarchy continues to enjoy broad social and religious esteem, while varied religious traditions complicate the development of a mass Islamic discourse. Islamic movements are divided between those willing to participate in the political system and those who remain dissident. The May 2003 Casablanca attacks also revealed the existence of local Islamist elements, enjoying transnational inspiration if not transnational ties, with a more radical agenda. The divisions in Islamic ranks have enabled the monarchy to contain organized political Islam; however, the institutional reforms instituted by the monarchy have also enabled Islamists to demonstrate impressive powers of electoral mobilization. In the process, the role of the commander of the faithful has been undermined with religious authorities—*ʿulamāʾ* and Islamists—carrying on discussions on the definition and implementation of Islam in public life. Early in the twentieth century, the sultan was venerated for his *barakah* (blessing; spiritual power), and although this is in part still true today, the king of Morocco is respected now more as the guarantor of the unity of the nation.

[*See also* Islam and Politics in the Middle East and North Africa; *and* Yāsīn, ʿAbd al-Salām.]

BIBLIOGRAPHY

Cornell, Vincent J. *Realm of the Saint: Power and Authority in Moroccan Sufism*. Austin: University of Texas Press, 1998.

El Mansour, Mohamed. *Morocco in the Reign of Mawley Sulayman*. Wisbech, U.K.: Middle East & North African Studies Press, 1990.

Gellner, Ernest. *Saints of the Atlas*. Chicago: University of Chicago Press, 1969.

Laroui, Abdallah. *Les origines sociales et culturelles du nationalisme marocain, 1830–1912*. Paris: Maspero, 1977.

Linn, Rachel. "Morocco's Radicalised Political Movements." In *Islamist Radicalisation in North Africa: Politics and Process*, edited by George Joffé, pp. 138–159. London: Routledge, 2012.

Munson, Henry, Jr. *Religion and Power in Morocco*. New Haven, Conn.: Yale University Press, 1993.

Tozy, Mohamed. *Monarchie et Islam politique au Maroc*. Paris: Presses de la Fondation Nationale des Sciences Politiques, 1999.

Wegner, Eva. *Islamist Opposition in Authoritarian Regimes: The Party of Justice and Development in Morocco*. Syracuse, N.Y.: Syracuse University Press, 2011.

Zeghal, Malika. *Islamism in Morocco: Religion, Authoritarianism, and Electoral Politics*. Translated by George Holoch. Princeton, N.J.: Markus Wiener, 2008.

Henry Munson Jr.
and Malika Zeghal
Revised by Ronald Bruce St John

Moro Islamic Liberation Front.

The Moro Islamic Liberation Front (MILF) is considered the largest Muslim movement in the Philippines, with an estimated membership ranging from fifteen to forty thousand drawn largely from among the Maguindanao and Maranao tribes from Mindanao. Its governing body is the Central Committee headed by Chairman al-Haj Murad Ebrahim, who was elected after the death of the founding chair, Hashim Salamat, in 2003.

The MILF started in 1977 as a result of a power struggle within the Moro National Liberation Front (MNLF) between its chairman, Nur Misuari, and vice-chairman, Hashim Salamat. A major issue in the dispute was the ideological orientation of the MNLF, which has been described as secular with Marxist-Maoist leanings, although it was identified as a Muslim movement. Salamat and several followers broke off from the MNLF and established the New MNLF. In 1984, they renamed the organization the Moro Islamic Liberation Front. The word "Moro," a derogatory term used by Spanish colonizers, has been appropriated by southern Philippine Muslims to refer to their political, cultural, and religious identity and aspirations. The Islamic orientation of the MILF can be traced to the background of its founder, Salamat, who was educated in the Philippines and at al-Azhar University in Egypt, where he received both bachelor's and master's degrees in Islamic philosophy in the 1960s. As a student in Egypt, he was influenced by the writings of Ḥasan al-Bannā and Sayyid Quṭb of Egypt's Muslim Brotherhood, and Abū al-Aʿlā Mawdūdī, founder of the Jamāʿat-i Islāmī, South Asia's leading Islamist organization. He returned to the Philippines and eventually became one of the organizers of the MNLF.

In 1984, the MILF declared that it was engaged in a *jihād* and that their objective was to establish an Islamic state in the Bangsamoro (Moro nation) homeland where the Sharīʿah would be implemented. In pursuance of this goal, the MILF established several camps in Mindanao with an administrative setup including a justice system, schools, farms, and mosques. These camps, which were viewed as building blocks of an Islamic society, also serve as training grounds for its Bangsamoro Islamic Armed Forces (BIAF), whose commander in chief is the chairman of the MILF Central Committee.

The MILF protested the 1996 Final Peace Agreement between the Philippine government and the MNLF. The latter accepted autonomy, but the MILF persisted with its demand for a separate Islamic state and became the major player in the continuing conflict in the south. The Philippine government then felt compelled to negotiate a separate peace agreement with the MILF.

In 2000, during the term of President Joseph Estrada, the military overran MILF's major base, Camp Abu Bakr, and several other training camps. The attack was a major setback for the MILF, but it did not eliminate the movement; rather, it contributed to its rise to prominence after disappointed MNLF members and other sympathizers opted to support the movement. In 2001, President Gloria Macapagal Arroyo resumed peace negotiations with the MILF, with more Muslim participation and the involvement of Malaysia and Libya and later the United States and Japan. The negotiations were marred by ceasefire violations and bombings, for which the government blamed the MILF, as well as disagreements that resulted in suspension of talks several times. In 2008, the Philippine government and the MILF were about to sign a Memorandum of Agreement on the Ancestral Domain of the 2001 Tripoli Agreement, but the Supreme Court issued a restraining order preventing the government from concluding the agreement and ruled the draft agreement unconstitutional. The agreement involved more autonomy than the previous government-MNLF accord and introduced the notion of a "substate," with the Bangsamoro Juridical Entity (BJE) as the authority over Moro ancestral domains. The Philippine government withdrew its support for the agreement and dismantled the negotiating panel while requiring that the MILF disarm before the talks could continue. The MILF response was renewed fighting, resulting in the death and displacement of people in the affected areas in Mindanao.

Another point of contention in MILF-government relations is the reported linkages between the MILF and international extremists such as the Jemaah Islamiyah (JI). Before his death, Salamat issued a statement rejecting terrorism, which the current chair, al-Haj Murad Ebrahim has reiterated.

In August 2011, President Simeon Benigno Aquino met with MILF leaders in Tokyo. Since then, representatives of the MILF and the Philippine government have been meeting in Kuala Lumpur, with security, rehabilitation of areas affected by the conflict, and ancestral lands as major items for discussion. Another major subject is the creation of a political entity that would replace the Autonomous Region in Muslim Mindanao (ARMM). The ARMM was created during the term of President Corazón Aquino as part of the Final Peace Agreement of 1996. However, the ongoing activities of breakaway factions of the MILF like the Bangsamoro Islamic Freedom Fighters (BIFF) led by Ameril Umbra Kato, who left the MILF after it opted for an autonomous region instead of the previous demand for a separate Islamic state, plus various issues such as wealth sharing between the Philippine government and the envisioned political entity, continue to threaten the peace process.

[*See also* Philippines.]

Bibliography

Abinales, Patricio N. *Orthodoxy and History in the Muslim-Mindanao Narrative.* Quezon City, Philippines: Ateneo de Manila University Press, 2010.

Gaerlan, Kristina, and Mara Stankovitch, eds. *Rebels, Warlords, and Ulama: A Reader on Muslim Separatism and the War in Southern Philippines*. Quezon City, Philippines: Institute for Popular Democracy, 2000.

Institute for Autonomy and Governance. "Understanding the MOA-AD." Special issue, *Autonomy and Peace Review* 44, no. 3 (July-September 2008).

Mastura, Michael O. *Bangsamoro Quest: The Birth of the Moro Islamic Liberation Front*. Penang: Research and Education for Peace, Universiti Sains Malaysia, 2012.

McKenna, Thomas. *Muslims Rulers and Rebels: Everyday Politics and Armed Separatism in the Southern Philippines*. Berkeley: University of California Press, 1998.

Santos, Soliman M., Jr. *The Moro Islamic Challenge: Constitutional Rethinking for the Mindanao Peace Process*. Quezon City: University of the Philippines, 2001.

Vivienne SM. Angeles

Moro National Liberation Front.

The beginnings of the Moro National Liberation Front (MNLF) can be traced to 1969, when a group of ninety young, progressive Muslims went to Sabah, part of the Sultanate of Sulu, located on the northern portion of the island of Borneo (and often considered one of the thirteen member states of Malaysia), for military training. Nur Misuari, a former student activist and instructor at the University of the Philippines, emerged as chairman of the group, which included the chief minister of Sabah, Tun Mustapha, and Libya's president, Muʿammar al-Qadhdhāfī, among its early supporters.

The MNLF aimed to preserve Moro interests and cultural identity in a country that witnessed religious and political animosity between the Christian majority and its Muslim minority. For some observers, the MNLF was also a response to the acceleration of national integration and development programs during the 1950s and 1960s, which resulted in an influx of Christian settlers into predominantly Moro areas in Mindanao, Sulu, and Palawan. The Moros were suspicious of the government's motives behind integration and feared the destruction of their Muslim community (*ummah*). Consequently, the movement protested continuing government marginalization and neglect of Muslim areas, which perpetuated problems like economic underdevelopment and low literacy rates.

In 1974, the Central Committee of the MNLF issued a manifesto declaring the establishment of an independent Bangsa Moro Republik (an Islamic state, which would make implementing Sharīʿah its main goal). With support from several member countries of the Organization of the Islamic Conference (OIC) although the OIC itself never called for any type of war, the MNLF was able to engage in a full-scale war from 1973 to 1976, which forced the Philippine government to sign the Tripoli Agreement conceding full autonomy to Moroland.

The Philippine government, however, failed to abide by the Tripoli Agreement; the ceasefire collapsed, and fighting resumed in late 1977. In the same year, Misuari's leadership was challenged and other factions—the Moro Islamic Liberation Front (MILF) and the MNLF-Reformist Group (MNLF-RG)—emerged. In the early 1990s, leading members of the MNLF split to form the core of the Abu Sayyaf Group (ASG).

Under President Corazón Aquino, the Philippine government was mandated by the 1987 constitution to grant limited autonomy to Muslims in the south. This resulted in Republic Act 6734, providing for the autonomous region in Muslim Mindanao. The act required a plebiscite, and only four provinces voted to be included in the autonomous region. Still, the MNLF dissociated itself from the institution of the autonomy provisions, and called on the different Moro factions to unite in a renewed armed struggle for an independent Moro state.

In 1996, under President Fidel Ramos, the Philippine government and the MNLF signed a peace agreement and Misuari was elected governor of the Autonomous Region of Muslim Mindanao (ARMM). By November 2001, after what proved to be a period of neglect, Misuari accused President Gloria Arroyo of reneging on the peace agreement and launched a new rebellion in the south. He was later arrested in Malaysia and deported to the Philippines, where he was jailed on charges of rebellion. A council of fifteen MNLF Central Committee members wrested the chairmanship from Misuari a few weeks later and installed Farouk Hussein as Chairman. The council recognized Misuari again in 2006 then ousted him once more in 2008 when it chose Muslimin Sema as its leader. Misuari was released from prison and placed under house arrest in 2008. In 2009, he was acquitted of the rebellion charges but continues to be recognized by the mass base of the MNLF and the OIC as head of the movement.

The MNLF-led movement must be credited with some success in terms of the recognition achieved for Philippine Muslims locally and internationally. These include the official recognition of Islam as part of Philippine heritage and Moro culture, the establishment of *Sharīʿah* courts, and the granting of limited autonomy. Filipino Muslims have also received educational and economic assistance from Muslim countries, and the MNLF itself has been given observer status in the OIC. Factionalism in the movement continues, however, due to different responses to the government, varying positions on the negotiations with the Moro Islamic Liberation Front, reactions to Abu Sayyaf activities, and the perceived failure of the government to implement the terms of the 1996 Final Peace Agreement. In addition to the group that recognizes Misuari as chairman, there are also the MNLF-Sema faction (also known as EC15) and the MNLF-Islamic Command Council, among others.

[*See also* Philippines.]

BIBLIOGRAPHY

Abinales, Patricio N. *Orthodoxy and History in the Muslim-Mindanao Narrative.* Quezon City, Philippines: Ateneo de Manila University Press, 2010.

Angeles, Vivienne SM. "The State, the Moro National Liberation Front, and Islamic Resurgence in the Philippines." In *Religious Fundamentalism in Developing Countries*, edited by Santosh C. Saha and Thomas K. Carr, pp. 185–200. Westport, Conn.: Greenwood, 2001.

Che Man, W. K. *Muslim Separatism: The Moros of Southern Philippines and the Malays of Southern Thailand.* Singapore: Oxford University Press, 1990.

Gaerlan, Kristina, and Mara Stankovitch, eds. *Rebels, Warlords, and Ulama: A Reader on Muslim Separatism and the War in Southern Philippines.* Quezon City, Philippines: Institute for Popular Democracy, 2000.

Gomez, Hilario M., Jr. *The Moro Rebellion and the Search for Peace: A Study on Christian-Muslim Relations in the Philippines.* Zamboanga City, Philippines: Silsilah, 2000.

Tuazon, Bobby M. ed. *The Moro Reader: History and the Contemporary Struggles of the Bangsamoro People.* Quezon City: CenPeg Books, 2008.

W. K. CHE MAN
Updated by VIVIENNE SM. ANGELES

MOSSADEGH, MOHAMMAD. Mohammad Mossadegh Mirzā Hidāyat Allāh Khān (1882–1967) is viewed by most Iranians and Arabs as a hero and a nationalist who attempted to free Iran from the influences of foreign powers. He is remembered for his opposition to the practices and policies of the Anglo-Iranian Oil Company (AIOC). He came from a prominent family with close ties to the royal family of the Qājār dynasty (1785–1925). In 1892, Nāṣir al-Dīn Shāh (1831–1896), in recognition for his late father's service to the crown, bestowed upon Mossadegh the title of "Moṣṣadegh al-Salṭāneh." He received his doctorate of law from the University of Neuchâtel in Switzerland, and he taught at the University of Tehran at the start of World War I, before his storied political career.

Mossadegh was first elected to represent Isfahan in the newly inaugurated Majlis (Parliament) of Iran in 1907. He was chosen to serve as deputy leader of the Jamʿīyat-i Insāniyat (Humanitarian Society). His vehement opposition to the Anglo-Persian Treaty of 1919 endeared him to the masses. Also due to this political stand, he gained public trust and was endorsed by the people of Shīrāz to become the governor of Fārs Province. He was later appointed finance minister in the government of Aḥmad Qavan (Qavām al-Salṭāneh) in 1921, and then foreign minister in the government of Moshīr-al-Dawlah in June 1923.

In 1925, he opposed the efforts of Reza Shah Pahlavi (d. 1944) to introduce legislation to dissolve the Qājār dynasty and appoint himself as shah/king of the Imperial State of Persia. Mossadegh argued that this act ran counter to the 1906 Iranian constitution.

In 1944, during the reign of the second and last shah of the Pahlavi dynasty, Muhammad Reza Shah (d. 1980), Mossadegh was once again elected to parliament. He led the Jebhe Melli (National Front of Iran), an organization he had formed with nineteen other nationalists. Jebhe Melli aimed to establish democracy and end foreign influence in Iranian politics.

Throughout his political career, Mossadegh opposed the British oil company's domination of Iran's resources and strived for the nationalization of his country's oil. His persistence in challenging the Anglo-Iranian Oil Company was inspired by the fact that most of Iran's oil reserves in the Persian Gulf area had been developed by the AIOC for export to Britain and that Iran was getting little from the AIOC for its oil. The AIOC refused to offer a 50-50 profit-sharing deal with Iran as Aramco had done with Saudi Arabia. Adding to anger over Iran's defeat and occupation by the Allied powers, these factors solidified the issue of nationalization as the most important in postwar Iran.

On 28 April 1951, the Majlis appointed Mossadegh prime minister. The rising popularity of Mossadegh worried the shah. In order to avoid hostilities and rivalry over political power, the shah appointed Mossadegh to the premiership. Mossadegh's new administration introduced a range of social reforms, such as unemployment compensation, the requirement of factory owners to pay benefits to sick and injured workers, and abolition of forced labor.

Mossadegh's government refused to allow the British any role in the Iranian oil industry, which escalated the confrontation between Iran and Britain. The British noticed Mossadegh's popular support had and feared his success, since his reform plan and oil nationalization were in opposition to British interests. Britain's attempts to oust Mossadegh failed until they sought America's help.

A period of turmoil began in Iran, and tension began to escalate within the Majlis when, on 16 July 1952, during the royal endorsement of his new cabinet, Mossadegh insisted on the constitutional prerogative of the prime minister to name a minister of war and chief of staff, something the shah had done hitherto. The shah refused, and Mossadegh announced his resignation, appealing directly to the public for support, pronouncing that in the present situation, the struggle started by the Iranian people could not be brought to a victorious conclusion.

Aḥmad Qavam was appointed Iran's new prime minister. Many national movements and Islamist, communist (Tudeh Party), and nationalist groups mobilized themselves and called for mass demonstrations throughout the country in favor of Mossadegh, which lasted for five days. Many were killed or suffered serious injuries. As a result the shah dismissed Aḥmad Qavam and reappointed Mossadegh, granting him the full control of the military he had previously demanded.

Mossadegh implemented a reform policy and oil nationalization, declaring the British an enemy and severing all diplomatic relations with them. In March 1953, the CIA's Near East and Africa division chief, Kermit Roosevelt Jr., arrived in Tehran to direct a plot, known as "Operation Ajax," aimed at convincing Iran's monarch to issue a decree to dismiss Mossadegh from office. In August 1953, the shah formally dismissed the prime minister, Mossadegh, in a written decree, an act explicitly permitted under the constitution. He signed two decrees, one dismissing Mossadegh and the other nominating the CIA's choice, General Fazlollāh Zahedi, as prime minister.

Mossadegh was tried and convicted of treason by the shah's military court. On 21 December 1953, he was sentenced to death, but his sentence was later commuted to three years' solitary confinement in a military prison. Subsequently, he was kept under house arrest at his Aḥmadābād residence, where he died on 5 March 1967.

BIBLIOGRAPHY

Diba, Farhad. *Mohammad Mossadegh: A Political Biography.* London: Croom Helm, 1986.

Elm, Mostafa. *Oil, Power, and Principle: Iran's Oil Nationalization and Its Aftermath.* Syracuse, N.Y.: Syracuse University Press, 1992.

Gasiorowski, Mark J., and Malcolm Byrne. *Mohammad Mosaddeq and the 1953 Coup in Iran.* Syracuse, N.Y.: Syracuse University Press, 2004.

Katouzian, Homa. *Musaddiq and the Struggle for Power in Iran.* London: I. B. Tauris, 1990.

Saikal, Amin. *The Rise and Fall of the Shah: Iran from Autocracy to Religious Rule.* Rev. ed. Princeton, N.J.: Princeton University Press, 2009.

Zabih, Sepehr. *The Mossadegh Era: Roots of the Iranian Revolution.* Chicago: Lake View, 1982.

Labeeb Ahmed Bsoul

Movement for National Reform.

The Movement for National Reform (MNR; Ḥarakat al-Iṣlāḥ al-Waṭanī) is a moderate Islamist political party in Algeria that was founded by Shaykh Abdallah Djaballah in 1999. Djaballah, a moderate Islamist who was born in 1956, in Skikdah, Algeria, started his activism on Algerian campuses in the 1970s, to study "Islamic sciences." The origins of the MNR go back to al-Nahḍah Association for Cultural and Social Reform, which Djaballah established in 1988.

In 1989, he founded his own party—the Islamic Renaissance Movement (Ḥarakat al-Nahḍah al-Islāmīyah). With al-Nahḍah, Djaballah won thirty-four seats during the 1997 legislative elections, making it the fourth largest power in parliament. In 1999 a major split took place between the party leadership over the issue of the presidential elections. Djaballah, in opposition to some party leaders, refused to support Abdelaziz Bouteflika and he broke away from al-Nahḍah.

It was at this point that he created the MNR. Just before founding the MNR, Djaballah ran for president (1999) as an independent candidate, although he withdrew at the last moment to join all opposition figures refusing to participate in what they determined was a rigged electoral process. In the 2002 legislative elections, the MNR became the third most powerful political force and leader of all Islamist parties, with forty-three seats in parliament, although the party was swept under, five years later, following Djaballah's dismissal, as he insisted on maintaining an independent position from the government. In fact, in 2007, the MNR won three out of 389 seats, allegedly punished by constituents for cooperating with the government. Djaballah, who finished third in the 2004 presidential elections with 5 percent of the votes, formed another opposition group, al-Iṣlāḥ, in 2007, which became the Front of Justice and Development in 2011.

In 2011, the MNR adopted a pro-government stance, thus losing credibility as an opposition party. Still, MNR cadres engaged in *mushārakah* (partnership) with the state, a notion that was interpreted as a practical step by those who wished to work within the law and as a conciliatory one by those who opposed the government. The party's challenge in the post-Djaballah era, under Ahmad Abdesalam and Muhammad Boulahia, was to restore the MNR as a credible opposition party that could win a few dozen seats in the parliamentary elections.

Bibliography

Boubekeur, Amel. "Political Islam in Algeria." Working Document 268. Brussels, Belgium: Center for European Policy Studies, May 2007.

Ḥarakat al-Iṣlāḥ al-Waṭanī. *Al-Barnāmaj al-siyāsī* (Political program). Algiers: MNR, 2004.

Joseph A. Kéchichian

Movement for the Society of Peace. The Movement for the Society of Peace (MSP, also formerly known as Hamas) is an Islamist movement and a political party in Algeria. Although the MSP was founded in 1997, its predecessor organization was founded in 1990, by Mahmoud Nahnah. Then known as the Ḥarakāt li-Mujtamaʿ Islāmī, or the Movement for an Islamic Society, Hamas was ably led by Mahfoud Nahnah, who remained leader of both movements until his death in 2003. Nahnah's political orientation could be described as that of a moderate Islamist, given his and the organization's commitment in the social domain to the dissemination and encouragement of Islamic values, as well as its practice in the political domain of participating in electoral processes and partnering with secular parties in coalition governments. As the leader of the movement and the party, Nahnah embraced moderation and rejected violence in his Islamist approach to politics, which would contrast with other Islamist movements in Algeria, including the Front Islamique du Salut (FIS), the Groupe Islamiste Armée (GIA), the Groupe Salafiste pour la Prédication et le Combat (GSPC), and al-Qaʿida in the Islamic Maghreb (AQIM), all of which at various times chose to challenge the Algerian regime by force of arms. Aboujerra Soltani became the leader of the MSP after Nahnah's death.

The MSP has chosen a path of critique and compromise rather than open confrontation with the Algerian government. Nahnah's orientation toward compromise became established in 1988 when he rejected an invitation by Ali Belhadj, a leader within the more contentious FIS, to join that party. With the founding of Hamas in 1990 and then the MSP in 1997, Nahnah and members of these two parties encouraged reform within the Algerian regime, with MSP activities focusing on a dual social and political orientation. In social affairs, the MSP emphasizes educational and charitable work, while in the political domain it functions as a policy-oriented group eager to introduce reforms from within.

In Algeria, the MSP has sought to embody a moderate expression of Islamism, while advocating economic and political reforms that it believes will lead to the amelioration of the social and economic conditions of Algeria's working classes. By contrast, rival organizations chose a more confrontational or violent orientation, including al-Qiyām (founded by Hashemi Tidjani) and al-Qiyām's successors, the FIS, the Armed Islamic Movement (MIA), the GIA, the GSPC, and AQIM.

Rather than resorting to armed force, the MSP has chosen to participate in parliamentary politics. When parliamentary elections were restored by the Algerian regime in 1997, the MSP and another moderate Islamist party called the Ḥarakāt al-Nahḍah (Ennahda) ran for office in those elections. These two parties were then criticized by other Islamist parties who thought that it was improper for them to contest elections within a regime that was not fully committed to democratic processes. In that 1997 election, the MSP won sixty-nine seats in parliament, while al-Nahḍah secured thirty-four seats. With their success at the polls, the MSP decided to join in the formation of a coalition government with two secular parties, the Front Nationale de Liberation (FLN) and the Rassamblement Nationale pour la Démocratie (RND). After the May 2002 parliamentary elections, the MSP's vote tally declined, as it only won thirty-eight seats. During the same 1997 elections, al-Nahḍah fell short, with only one seat. The 1997 elections also saw the rise of a new Islamist party called Iṣlāḥ (led by Adballah Djaballah), which won forty-three seats. In the election that was held in May 2012, the MSP abandoned its coalition partners, creating instead a new "Green Alliance" with three other Islamist parties: al-Nahḍah, al-Iṣlāḥ, and the Front for Justice and Development. Results proved devastating. With low voter turnout and under the specter of allegations of electoral fraud, the Green Alliance of the Islamist parties barely managed to elect fifty-nine parliamentarians, while the ruling FLN party emerged the winner with 220 seats.

In the 2012 parliamentary elections in Algeria the MSP's vote tally declined significantly. This result can be attributed to a variety of factors: low voter turnout, disillusion with the MSP's capability to ameliorate economic conditions, general fatigue and malaise among Algerian voters, and possible vote manipulation on behalf of the Algerian government.

BIBLIOGRAPHY

Boubekeur, Amel. *Political Islam in Algeria*. Centre for European Policy Studies, CEPS Working Document no. 268. Brussels: Centre for European Policy Studies, 2007. http://www.ceps.eu/book/political-islam-algeria.

Hamladji, Noura. *Co-optation, Repression, and Authoritarian Regime's Survival: The Case of the Islamist MSP-Hamas in Algeria*. European University Institute Working Paper SPS no. 2002/7. San Domenico, Italy: European University Institute, 2002. http://cadmus.eui.eu/bitstream/handle/1814/327/sps20027.pdf?sequence=1.

Layachi, Azzedine. "Political Liberalisation and the Islamist Movement in Algeria." *Journal of North African Studies* 9, no. 2 (2004): 46–67.

Tayekh, Ray. "Islamism in Algeria: A Struggle between Hope and Agony." *Middle East Policy* 10, no. 2 (June 2003): 62–75.

Ricardo Laremont

Mu'amalat. *See* Sharīʿah.

Mudaraba. *See* Islamic Finance.

Mughal Empire. The Mughals ruled from 1526 to 1858; they brought Timurid and Mongol (Mughal) traditions of power and governance from Iran and Central Asia into India. By the mid-seventeenth century they ruled between 100 and 150 million people. In terms of population and resources, this empire outstripped the contemporary Islamic empires of the Ottomans and the Ṣafavids and was matched only by that of Ming China. At its height, Mughal authority embraced most of the subcontinent. The reasons for imperial success were a successful revenue system and an effective partnership between the emperors and the nobility, a portion of whom were Hindu.

Origin and Development. The empire was founded by Timurid prince Ẓahīruddīn Muḥammad Bābur (1483–1530), who descended, on his father's side, from Timur through Abū Saʿīd of Herāt; his grandfather on his mother's side was Yūnus Khān of Tashkent, great khan of the Mongols and thirteenth in line of succession from Chinggis Khan. After failing for more than two decades to reconquer his family patrimony in Transoxiana, in 1519 Bābur turned to India, where there was substantial Rajput opposition to the Lōdī Afghan rulers. After several probing raids, Bābur conquered northern India in two great battles, Panipat against the Afghans in 1526, and Khānu'ā against the Rajputs in 1527. Bābur's son Humāyūn (1508–1556) failed to consolidate the Mughal position against the Afghans in the face of competition from his brother princes and was driven out of northern India in 1540. In 1555, after exile in Sind and at the Ṣafavid court in Iran, followed by the establishment of a political base in Kabul, he invaded India, defeated the Afghans, and reestablished the dynasty. In 1556 Humāyūn's son Akbar (1542–1605) began a long reign, during which he expanded Mughal territories from Afghanistan's Helmand River in the west to Bengal's Brahmaputra River in the east, and from the Deccan's Godavari River in the south to the Himalayan Mountains in the north; he also developed a sophisticated system of taxation and governance that supported the empire for over one hundred years.

Akbar's son Jahāngīr (1569–1627) brought no significant expansion of Mughal territory, emphasizing instead consolidation. In 1628, after a bloody succession struggle, Shāh Jahān (1529–1666) succeeded his father. A successful general, he was conspicuously proud of ruling most of India, of commanding overwhelming military power, and possessing great wealth. His reign saw some expansion of Mughal authority to the north, east, and south, but a notable failure to extend it toward the family in Transoxiana, to the northwest. Internally, he developed a more distinctively Islamic political culture and sought to express the grandeur of his empire both at court and through architecture. Shāh Jahān's third son, Awrangzīb (1618–1707), won a particularly bitter succession struggle, which was prompted not by the death of his father but by an illness that set off a succession rivalry between his four sons. In his reign of forty-nine years Awrangzīb extended Mughal territories to the far south, expanding them by one quarter, or 220,000 square miles, and in consequence shifted the empire's center of gravity southward. He continued his father's development of an Islamic political culture and presided over a society that grew steadily wealthier but more frequently revolted against its rulers.

After Awrangzīb died, there were four succession struggles in the years 1707–1720. Local revolts increased. Mughal viceroys in Hyderabad, Bengal, and Awadh declared independence. Over the subsequent century the Mughal emperors became puppets of competing local forces—Marāthās, Rajputs, Rohilla Afghans, and the rulers of Awadh. Eventually, in 1803, the British defeated the Marāthās under the walls of Shahjahanabad Delhi. The Mughals were confined to the city until 1858 after the Mutiny uprising overthrew the British. Through the long period of decline, although powerless, they remained a source of authority.

Imperial Legacy. Scholars do not agree over why the Mughal empire imploded between 1707 and 1720. What is clear, however, is that a complex series of interrelated events was involved, in which the following played a part: revolts of regional groups—Sikhs, Jāts, Rajputs, Marāthās; four debilitating wars of succession at the center; a breakdown of imperial administration in the localities; increasing difficulty in collecting revenue; a growing dearth of treasure at the center; and the emperor's growing inability to fund *jāgīrs* for his *manṣabdārs* and to pay the salaries of his troops. All this took place in a society that was richer and increasingly able to equip itself to resist central power. Thus, in a short space of time, the center found itself no longer able to impose its will upon the empire.

The Mughal Empire left a legacy to India of the idea of political power embracing the whole Subcontinent and, particularly in the reign of Akbar, of one that equally embraced all its people. The empire, along with the Delhi Sultanate, as Richard Eaton has demonstrated, created the framework within which over one-third of the subcontinent's populatio became Muslim, at the same time becoming one-third of the Muslim population of the world.

The British took over and adapted many Mughal governing practices, among them the *durbar*. Consciousness of the Mughal imperial legacy contributed to the development of Britain's imperial monarchy. During the Mughal period, India stopped being merely a receiver of Islamic influences from outside and came, as the ideas of Aḥmad Sirhindī were conveyed by Mawlānā Khālid Baghdādī to the Caucasus and Anatolia and those of eighteenth-century Indian developments in *maʿqūlāt* (Islamic rational scholarship) sciences were transported to Cairo and Damascus, India came to be a transmitter to the Islamic world as well. This role has continued to the present day.

[*See also* Sirhindī, Aḥmad.]

BIBLIOGRAPHY

Alam, Muzaffar. *The Languages of Political Islam: India, 1200–1800*. Chicago: University of Chicago Press, 2004

Alam, Muzaffar, and Sanjay Subrahmanyam, eds. *The Mughal State, 1526–1750*. New Delhi: Oxford University Press, 1998.

Alam, Muzaffar, and Sanjay Subrahmanyam. *Writing the Mughal World: Studies on Culture and Politics*. New York: Columbia University Press, 2011.

Balabanlilar, Lisa. *Imperial Identity in the Mughal Empire: Memory and Dynastic Politics in Early Modern South and Central Asia*. London: I. B. Tauris, 2012.

Dale, Stephen F. *The Garden of the Eight Paradises: Bābur and the Culture of Empire in Central Asia, Afghanistan, and India, 1483–1530*. Leiden: E. J. Brill, 2004.

Gommans, Jos. *Mughal Warfare: Indian Frontiers and Highroads to Empire, 1500–1700*. London: Routledge, 2002.

Koch, Ebba. *The Complete Taj Mahal and the Riverfront Gardens of Agra*. London: Thames & Hudson, 2006.

Lal, Ruby. *Domesticity and Power in the Early Mughal World*. Cambridge, U.K.: Cambridge University Press, 2005.

Robinson, Francis. *The Mughal Emperors and the Islamic Dynasties of India, Iran, and Central Asia, 1206–1925*. London: Thames & Hudson, 2007.

Robinson, Francis. *The ʿUlama of Farangi Mahall and Islamic Culture in South Asia*. London: Hurst, 2001.

Stronge, Susan. *Painting for the Mughal Emperor: The Art of the Book, 1560–1660*. London: V&A, 2002.

FRANCIS ROBINSON

MUḤAMMAD. Abū Qāsim Muḥammad ibn ʿAbd Allāh was born in the year 570 CE in the town of Mecca in Arabia, which was at the time a cosmopolitan center of commercial and religious activity. In the year 610, he announced that he had been visited by an angel of revelation (Gabriel). In 613 he began to preach his message among members of his tribe. In 622, having been rejected by the majority of his people, he left Mecca in dire circumstances on the invitation of rival clans in Medina, who offered him refuge, accepted his call to prophethood, and supported his subsequent conflict with the Meccans. Eight years later, in the year 630, Muḥammad returned triumphantly to Mecca to establish the religion of Abraham of the one true God. In 632, Muḥammad died with nearly the entire Arabian Peninsula under his sway.

By the year 711, Muḥammad's followers were leading conquests through Persia, Central Asia, and into India on the east, as well as through North Africa and into Spain on the west. The spectacular pace of Arab conquests after Muḥammad's death and subsequent Arabization of learning and culture in the broad expanse of North Africa, Middle East, and Central Asia has been the subject of much speculation. Secular historians identify several causes for the rapid conquests, typically a combination of the fervent nature of the Arab mission and the exhausted nature of both the Byzantine and Persian Empires, which had been embroiled in fierce competition for influence at the time. For believers, the conquests are evidence of the truth of Muḥammad's message—a conviction that hinges hopes for the success of future Muslim expansion on true belief and righteous conduct.

Life before Prophethood. Traditional biographical sources contain little information about Muḥammad's childhood. It is reported that his father died before he was born and he lost his mother at the age of six. Raised first by his grandfather ʿAbd al-Muṭṭalib and then by his uncle Abū Ṭālib, the leaders of the Hāshimī clan of the Quraysh tribe, Muḥammad grew up in a relatively influential family. Nonetheless, as an orphan he remained vulnerable, a condition that may have helped shape his concern for the less fortunate, which was to become a central feature of his prophetic call. In his youth, Muḥammad came to be known as "the trustworthy" (*al-Amīn*) on account of his forthrightness and honesty. As a young man, he joined hands in a pact (*ḥilf al-fuḍūl*) with other members of his tribe in defense of foreigners who were being exploited and had no legal recourse in the prevailing social order of Mecca. It is reported that later in his career, Muḥammad reaffirmed his commitment to the pact, which became a significant precedent for Muslims to enter into pacts with non-Muslims for the purpose of upholding virtue and justice.

Call to Prophethood. At the age of forty, in the year 610 CE, Muḥammad confided to his family that he had received revelations from God. His wife Khadījah, close friend Abū Bakr, and cousin ʿAlī were among the first to accept his claim without reservation. For the first three years of prophethood (*nubūwah*), Muḥammad preached to a small group of family and friends before announcing his role as God's messenger (*rasūl*) to the rest of his tribe. This sequence of closed preaching to trusted confidants followed by open call (*daʿwah*) is seen as an initial phase that is necessary for spiritual development (*tazkīyah*and *tarbīyah*), a program that has been incorporated into the methodology of some Islamic movements today.

Muḥammad's call was rejected by the majority of influential individuals of Mecca, among them ʿAmr b. Hishām (remembered as Abū Jahl, "the father of ignorance"), an influential member of the Makhzūm clan, and his uncle ʿAbd al-ʿUzzā (referred to as Abū Lahab, "the father of flame"). As Muḥammad's mission picked up steam, opposition also increased. Two of Muḥammad's daughters, who were married to two of Abū Lahab's sons, were humiliatingly divorced on account of his prophetic activity. In the face of mounting ridicule and insult, Muḥammad is reported to have preached tolerance and even kindness, a spirit that is embodied in the Qurʾān (41:34).

As opposition turned to outright persecution, the weaker contingent among Muḥammad's followers migrated to Abyssinia to seek protection under the authority of a just Christian kingdom. Asylum was duly granted to these early emigrants, serving as an example for the permissibility of Muslims seeking refuge among non-Muslims when necessary. Even Muḥammad continued to live under the protection of his uncle Abū Ṭālib, a non-Muslim who never embraced the prophetic call. For this, the entire Hāshimī clan, along with the rest of the followers of Muḥammad, were eventually boycotted. Muḥammad continued to preach patience in the face of adversity, but also sought help from outside Mecca in the neighboring township of Ṭāʾif, which was rebuffed violently by its inhabitants. In the same year, 620 CE, about a decade after his call to prophethood, Muḥammad lost his wife and comforter, Khadījah, as well as his uncle and protector, Abū Ṭālib. Remembered as "the year of sorrow" (*ʿām al-ḥuzn*), this year marks the climax of God's process of testing the prophet and the community of believers in Mecca. Islamist activists—patterning the trajectory of their struggle on the life of the Prophet—anticipate similar trials in their faith-based efforts to transform the world. It is this period in Mecca that also serves as a model for advocates of nonviolence as a means of social and political change in Islam. In particular, Muḥammad's response to the angel who offered to crush Ṭāʾif after its people had violently rejected him has been noted as mirroring the response of Jesus when he was on the cross.

Muḥammad's central religious teachings in this period were the belief in one God (*tawḥīd*), the institution of prophethood (*risālah*), and the life hereafter (*ākhirah*). Muḥammad's teachings had strong social, political, and economic implications. He taught that women and men were both equally God's creation and accountable before God as individuals (33:35); that people must give charity and shun usury (2:261–281); the less fortunate are to be cared for (107); people should not deal in fraud (83:1–3), hoard wealth (104), or renege on their debts and promises (2:177, 23:8); and that God and God's messengers were to be obeyed (64:12 and passim), even though worldly leaders commonly remain heedless because of their love for wealth and power (7:60–127 and passim).

Emigration (*Hijrah*) and the Formation of a Community (*Ummah*). The emigration from Mecca to Medina, or the *hijrah*, is a landmark event in the life of Muḥammad. It serves as a key shift in context that both Muslim and non-Muslim scholars draw on to provide a framework for his life and message. The second caliph, ʿUmar ibn al-Khaṭṭāb (r. 634–644), selected the *hijrah* as the starting point for the Muslim calendar, indicating that it is this event that resulted in the formation of the Muslims as a distinct "community" or "nation" (*ummah*), an event that is echoed in revelations of the Qurʾān dated to roughly this period (2:143, 22:78). William Montgomery Watt has contrasted Muḥammad's life in Mecca, "Muḥammad as Prophet" (610–622), with what was to follow, "Muḥammad as Statesman" (622–632), in Medina.

The *hijrah* was instigated by two rival tribes (Aws and Khazraj), who extended an invitation to Muḥammad to move to Medina to arbitrate disputes. In exchange, the tribes were invited to accept Muḥammad as God's messenger, believe in his revelations, and support his cause. Among the residents of Medina were also Jewish tribes, with whom Muḥammad felt a natural affinity because of their common ancestor Abraham, as well as their common belief in One God and shared sacred history. After arriving in Medina, Muḥammad made two critical, one might say revolutionary, political moves. First, he joined each of the Meccan emigrants (pl. *muhājirūn*) in a relationship of brotherhood to a Medinan "Helper" (pl., Anṣār). In this way, a new "super-tribe" *ummah* was born that had its moorings in faith rather than blood relations. Second, he drafted a "constitution" (*mīthāq*) that included the Jewish tribes, affirmed his role as the final arbiter of disputes, bound them all together as one community (*ummah*) for the defense of Medina, but nonetheless gave each tribe relative autonomy to manage its own affairs.

At the same time, Muḥammad began to marry again, a process that had already begun after the death of Khadījah, with whom he had remained monogamous during their twenty-six year marriage. Muḥammad is reported to have married up to about a dozen women before the end of his life, including the young ʿĀʾishah, who was a tender six years old at the time of the marriage and nine (according to most sources) when the marriage was consummated. Muḥammad's marriages have been the subject of many polemics against Islam. They have, however, been explained in political terms, both in Muslim apologetics and by sympathetic Western scholars. His marriage to ʿĀʾishah was not atypical for its time but was of foundational significance for the Islamic tradition, because she lived a long life after Muḥammad's death and transmitted intimate details about his life that would have otherwise been lost. Politically, she was the daughter of his best friend and companion, Abū Bakr, who eventually became the first caliph after Muḥammad's death. Other marriages, such as the one to the daughter of Abū Sufyān, Muḥammad's chief rival in Mecca, served as a means for reconciliation among enemies.

Battles and Raids. The Meccans were merchants, and their trade routes to the north ran past Medina. One of Muḥammad's moves early on in Medina was to organize raids (*ghazw*) against his own tribe and its allies. It was unprecedented for a tribe to be raided by one of its own, and equally rare for the tribe of Quraysh to be raided at all, because they were custodians of gods at the Kaʿbah (a shrine built by Abraham) and hosts of the annual pilgrimage and trade in Mecca. Although the significance of the raids has been debated, with some designating them as mere Arab "sport," other analysts of Muḥammad's political strategy view them as part of a larger mission to liberate Mecca for the believers in order to establish the religion of the one true God. Muḥammad did not personally participate in all of the raids, and on one such occasion, at Nakhlah, his followers engaged in a skirmish, in spite of Muḥammad's instruction to merely scout, which resulted in the shedding of Meccan blood at the hands of Muslims in one of the four "Sacred Months." Although Muḥammad is said to have been aggrieved by the incident, the Qurʾān legitimized the action by stating that "oppression is worse than slaughter" (2:191). The Qurʾān further empowered Muḥammad and the believers to engage in armed conflict because "they had been wronged" (3:195, 22:39).

The botched raid at Nakhlah strengthened the hand of the "hawks" in Mecca to attack Muḥammad at his new base in Medina. The ensuing Battle of Badr, in which the two armies clashed head-on for the first time, resulted in the decapitation of the Meccan leadership and an overwhelming victory for Muḥammad. Muḥammad is reported to have defeated the Meccan army with a force that was vastly outnumbered. News of the success spread throughout the land. The Battle of Badr, which took place in the holy month ofRamaḍān, is remembered as "the distinguishing day" (*yawm al-furqān*). Badr also highlights a few qualities of Muḥammad as a political and military leader. He was a risk taker, willing to enter into an all-or-nothing military encounter out of conviction and deep faith in God. He led by persuasion, not by coercion, and adjusted his strategy on the battlefield based on advice from foot-soldiers to gain tactical advantage. He also initiated a propaganda campaign in a nearby village to compel the opposing force to engage him in battle or suffer moral defeat, thereby reducing their options while enhancing his own.

The prisoners of war that Muḥammad's army captured were ransomed or released after they performed service for the Muslims, which reportedly included the option of providing instruction on how to read or write to the illiterate. The battle may have been won, but the war was still on. The efforts of Muḥammad developed into the doctrine of *jihād fī sabīl Allāh*, or an all-out "struggle in the path of God," which involves every action of the believer to submit to the will of God, be it spiritual or military. Together with the Qurʾān and founding of a new *ummah*, the doctrine of *jihād* has been a cornerstone of Muḥammad's legacy. The following year, the Meccans returned to avenge their humiliation and fallen leaders at Badr in the Battle of Uḥud. Once again, Muḥammad took the counsel of his followers but, against his better judgment, left the city to engage the enemy out in the open. A contingent of hypocrites abandoned Muḥammad at the eleventh hour, but the believers nonetheless managed to place themselves in a tactically superior position on the field and gain the upper hand. However, after an initial period of success, dissention among the ranks of Muḥammad's army led to a reversal of fortunes. Muḥammad suffered personal injury that resulted in the momentary loss of consciousness. He retreated and managed to save himself and his army from annihilation.

Two years later, in the fifth year after the *hijrah*, the Meccans returned with an enormous force, together with their allies from Arabia, to finish the job. On the advice of a Persian companion, Salmān al-Farisī, Muḥammad chose to defend the city by building a trench around its most vulnerable points and relying on Jewish allies for defense from the rear. The strategy succeeded but involved deception on the part of Muḥammad to sow dissent among the ranks of the enemy. This behavior has been considered by Muslims as exceptional and specific to times of conflict and imminent danger. An example of this exceptionalism is when Muḥammad is reported to have given a special sword to one of his followers to create havoc among his enemy. The warrior, Abū Dujānah of the Khazraj, "strutted up and down between the ranks," indicating his intent to inflict great slaughter, to which Muḥammad replied: "That is a gait which God detesteth, save at a time and place as this" (Lings, 2006, p. 184).

After each of the three major battles mentioned above, Muḥammad took action against the three major Jewish tribes, one by one, for undermining his position in Medina or for all-out treason. He expelled two of them from the city, but executed the entire population of adult males of the third (Banū Qurayẓah), taking their women, children, and possessions as spoils of war for the community of believers. Muslim tradition maintains that the actions were retaliatory, in accordance with accepted norms of the time, and consistent with Jewish laws for treason, instead of universal examples of ad hoc savagery. Some scholars have seen in these episodes more sinister traits. They argue that Muḥammad desired to eliminate the Jewish tribes because they did not accept him as God's messenger and undermined his legitimacy as a messenger of God in Medina. However, such negative interpretations of Muḥammad's character and motives are extraneous to the traditional sources, which have embedded within their narratives specific acts of betrayal that prompted each incident. These episodes were not taken as precedents for carte-blanche aggression against Jews in the Sharīʿah, but they are periodically accentuated by fringe elements to invoke hatred in times of religious tension and conflict.

Truce (*Ṣulḥ*) and Conquest (*Fatḥ*). In year six of the *hijrah*, Muḥammad led a large number of his followers (said to be approximately 1,400) in a peaceful pilgrimage to Mecca after having a religious vision or dream (*ru'yah*). This was not the first time that Muḥammad had based a major act on a dream, a pattern that Muslim religious and political leaders were to follow throughout Islamic history. Muḥammad and his companions went, inspired, unarmed into the bosom of the enemy. The venture could have ended in disaster, but it turned out to be a brilliant strategic move. Viewed theologically, Muḥammad entrusted himself into the care of God and merely followed instructions given to him in a dream. Viewed from the lens of secular history, Muḥammad gambled that the slaughter of unarmed pilgrims would simply not take place because it would result in an unacceptable loss of prestige for the tribe of Quraysh. As custodians of the Kaʿbah and of the pilgrimage, the Quraysh were obligated to serve as hosts to any party seeking to visit the holy shrine without hostile intentions. Representatives of the Quraysh met Muḥammad outside Mecca in a settlement known as the Ḥudaybīyah. The two parties entered into a ten-year truce whose terms appeared to be heavily in favor of the Meccans. In spite of the reluctance of his companions, albeit with the wholehearted support of one of his wives, Umm Salamah (of the Makhzūm clan, whose leader, Abū Jahl, had been slain at Badr), Muḥammad ratified the treaty. For one, the Meccans were forced to recognize him as an equal to be negotiated with. Further, the truce allowed Muḥammad to stabilize his place in Medina, forge new alliances, and neutralize threats that had developed on other fronts.

In this manner, within a period of two years after the truce of Ḥudabīyah and in the eighth year after the *hijrah*, Muḥammad was able to return to Mecca victorious. The last two years of his life involved "mopping-up" operations in strongholds of the peninsula, such as Ṭāʾif, and in reconciling various constituencies to his leadership, such as the Christians of Najrān. Before his death, Muḥammad had commissioned an army to march northward toward Syria. The army departed, but only after his death, a symbol of his mission to the rest of humanity, which was to be carried on by those who came after him. In one *ḥadīth*, Muḥammad is reported to have said: "I am the messenger of God to the Arabs specifically, and to the rest of humanity generally." This report, and others like it, have served the missionary ambitions of Muslims to take God's message to the entire world.

The Qurʾān calls the Muḥammad "an excellent example" for the believers (33:21). Devout Muslims seek to follow his way, or *sunnah*, in all aspects of their lives: appearance and dress, manners and behavior, ritual and worship, leadership and politics. Muḥammad's legacy encompasses these various dimensions, and has been appropriated in diverse ways to suit individual persuasions and historical contexts. In the modern world, Muḥammad serves as a model for both individual virtue and social reform. Advocates of Islamic revolution tend to pattern their movements in stages to mirror Muḥammad's life narrative. Others see the paradigm of socialism in his life of symbolic poverty, or conversely, identify the roots of democracy in Muḥammad's practice of consultation (*shūrā*) with his companions. For the Shīʿah, Muḥammad's role as a religious and political leader rightfully belongs to his descendants, unlike Sunnīs, who see authority as vested in the body of Muslims (particularly the scholars or *ʿulamāʾ*) collectively. For Sunnī traditionalists, Muḥammad is a "universal model" to be emulated in all aspects of life, mediated by an unbroken chain of interpretation through history that maintained a balance of power with political authority whose objective was to safeguard the Sharīʿah. Muslim tradition as a whole, considers Muḥammad's forgiving nature as paramount. He is reported to have said, "If you have mercy on those on earth, the One who is in heaven will have mercy on you." The Qurʾān calls Muḥammad "a mercy to the worlds" (Q. 21:107), and it is primarily through this lens that Muslims of all persuasions remain anchored to the one they call their beloved, and the beloved of God (*ḥabīb Allāh*).

BIBLIOGRAPHY

Afzaal, Ahmed. "The Origin of Islam as a Social Movement." *Islamic Studies* 42 (2003): 203–243.

Armstrong, Karen. *Muhammad: A Prophet for Our Time*. New York: HarperCollins, 2006.

Brown, Jonathan A. C. *Hadith: Muhammad's Legacy in the Medieval and Modern World*. Oxford: Oneworld, 2009.

Donner, Fred M. *Muhammad and the Believers: At the Origins of Islam*. Cambridge, Mass.: Belknap Press of Harvard University Press, 2010.

Khalidi, Tarif. *Images of Muhammad: Narratives of the Prophet in Islam across the Centuries*. New York: Doubleday, 2009.

Ibn Hishām, ʿAbd al-Malik. *The Life of Muhammad: A Translation of Iṣḥāq's Sīrat rasūl Allāh*. Translated and edited by Alfred Guillaume. Karachi: Oxford University Press, 1967.

Lings, Martin. *Muhammad: His Life Based on the Earliest Sources*. Rev. ed. Rochester, Vt.: Inner Traditions, 2006.

Mazrui, Al-Amin Ali. *The Content of Character: Ethical Sayings of the Prophet Muhammad*. Translated by Hamza Yusuf. San Francisco: Sandala, 2005.

Motzki, Harald, ed. *The Biography of Muḥammad: The Issue of the Sources*. Leiden, Netherlands: Brill, 2000.

Powers, David S. *Muḥammad Is Not the Father of Any of Your Men: The Making of the Last Prophet*. Philadelphia: University of Pennsylvania Press, 2009.

Safi, Omid. *Memories of Muhammad: Why the Prophet Matters*. New York: HarperCollins, 2009.

MAHAN MIRZA

MUHAMMADIYAH. Muhammadiyah is one of the largest and oldest Muslim organizations in Indonesia. It was founded in Yogyakarta in 1912 by Ahmad Dahlan (1869–1923), a religious teacher (*kiyayi*) who was concerned for religious reform. In 1920 it began to expand beyond Yogyakarta to the whole of Java and in 1925 beyond Java. By 1925 it had twenty-nine branches with four thousand members. By the early twenty-first century it had some 30 million members. It is highly organized, with a Central Board of Leadership chosen by a triennial (earlier annual) national congress and comparable structures at provincial, district, and branch levels. It has councils for the major activities, such as *dakwah* (propagation of Islam), education, and the like, and also separate organizations for women, youth, and so on.

It was formed during what is often called the "national awakening" (c. 1900–1930), when many political and social groups were formed to deal with the situation under modern colonial rule. The first was Budi Utomo (1908), a Javanist cultural and educational group of which Dahlan was a member. Others, with which Muhammadiyah interacted, included the politically activist Sarekat Islam (1911), Persatuan Islam (1923), similar to the Muhammadiyah but stricter, the Communist Party (1920), which Muhammadiyah strongly opposed, Sukarno's Indonesian Nationalist Party (1927), and Nahdlatul Ulama (1926). This last is a traditionalist group founded in conscious reaction to the modernist groups such as Muhammadiyah and has been its main competitor over the years. It has some 40 million members or more in the early twenty-first century.

As a modernist reform movement Muhammadiyah accepts the Qurʾān and the *sunnah* as the only unquestioned religious authorities and rejects as *bidʿah* (innovation) many popular customs, including various forms of magic and charms, certain rituals for the dead, and the ubiquitous *slametan* (ceremonial meals). It also disapproves of the Ṣūfī *tarekats* (orders). It calls for *ijtihād* (interpretive effort) based directly on the Qurʾān and *sunnah*, not necessarily following the interpretations of the four traditional *madhhab*s (schools of Islamic law). It has a council, Majlis Tarjih, to give *fatwas* (juristic opinions) on this basis. It gladly accepts and uses modern scientific ideas and methods. In these things it reflects the ideas of Muḥammad ʿAbduh and other Middle Eastern reformers, who influenced the early leaders of the movement, but these ideas are worked out in response to the Indonesian context. Christian missionaries, whose activities increased in the early twentieth century, have been seen as a major challenge but have also provided models for many activities.

From the beginning, Muhammadiyah has, as an organization, avoided direct political involvement and has focused on educational, social, and *dakwah* activities, although at times it has had some identification with political parties. It has developed a system of modern-style schools (in contrast to the traditional *pesantrens*) from kindergarten to university level, teaching mainly secular subjects along with religion. It formed a scout movement, Hizbul Wathan, in 1918 and a women's group called Aisyiyah between 1918 and 1922. A social service department was set up in 1918 and established its first orphanage in 1922 and first clinic in 1926. Since then, in addition to orphanages and clinics the Muhammadiyah has come to run hospitals, health centers, family planning agencies, and other services. Since the Muhammadiyah was nonpolitical, it was viewed relatively favorably by the Dutch colonial authorities and received some financial aid from them, for which more political groups criticized it.

Up until the early 1930s there was considerable conflict among the various religious organizations, but after that cooperation increased, partly because of greater pressure from the colonial government. In 1937 several groups, including Muhammadiyah, formed the MIAI (Supreme Council of Muslims of Indonesia).

The Japanese, during their occupation of Indonesia from 1942 to 1945, sought Muslim support in ways that strengthened the Muslims politically. They forced the various Islamic organizations, including Muhammadiyah, to come together into a single organization, Masyumi (Supreme Indonesian Council of Islam).

In the ensuing war for independence (1945–1949), secular and Islamic groups struggled together, though Muhammadiyah and other existing groups did not participate as organizations. After independence there developed a three-cornered contest between Islamic parties calling for an Islamic state, Sukarno's Nationalist Party based on Pancasila, and the Communist Party. Muhammadiyah maintained its connection with Masyumi, now a political party, but Nahdlatul Ulama withdrew in 1952. In the national election in 1955 the Islamic parties gained 42.5 percent of the vote, less than they had expected. In 1957 Sukarno introduced his "guided democracy," and in 1960 Masyumi was forced to disband, while Muhammadiyah narrowly escaped this fate. The struggle culminated in the brutal events of 1965–1966 when many Communist followers were slaughtered, often by Muslim youth groups. Muhammadiyah declared the struggle a *jihād* but did not justify the excesses.

Under Suharto's New Order, Muhammadiyah returned to its clearly apolitical stance, expanding its membership and activities. As of 1984 it claimed to have some twelve thousand schools at all levels and over eight hundred other institutions. It is said to have displayed relatively little creative religious or ideological thinking during this time, however. When Suharto in 1985 compelled all religious organizations to accept Pancasila as their sole basis, Muhammadiyah acquiesced with considerable reluctance, in contrast to Nahdlatul Ulama's more ready acceptance.

After the fall of the New Order, in which Muhammadiyah's leader played a prominent role, the organization once again associated itself with a political party, as did Nahdlatul Ulama. Neither party calls for an Islamic state, however, though some others do. In 1999 the Muslim parties together got 38 percent of the vote, with Muhammadiyah's National Mandate Party (PAN) getting 7.4 percent. In the 2004 and 2009 elections it received 6.4 percent and 6.0 percent, respectively.

Muhammadiyah and Nahdlatul Ulama constitute "the stable centre of Indonesia's Muslim community" (van Bruinessen, 2003), and their supporters tend to be active also in secular civic activities, though there is also a revived neo-Salafī trend in Muhammadiyah. Many feel that Muhammadiyah is still less dynamic and innovative than in its early years and that it faces the challenge of rediscovering or reformulating its identity and role.

BIBLIOGRAPHY

Nakamura, Mitsuo. *The Crescent Arises over the Banyan Tree: A Study of the Muhammadiyah Movement in a Central Javanese Town*. Yogyakarta, Indonesia: Gadjah Mada University Press, 1983. Anthropological study of Muhammadiyah in a particular town, stressing the degree to which the organization fits into its Javanese environment. Perceptive and informative.

Noer, Deliar. *The Modernist Muslim Movement in Indonesia, 1900–1942*. Singapore: Oxford University Press, 1973. Detailed account of several movements and organizations, including Muhammadiyah.

Peacock, James L. *Purifying the Faith: The Muhammadijah Movement in Indonesia*. Menlo Park, Calif.: Benjamin/Cummings, 1978.

van Bruinessen, Martin. "Post-Suharto Muslim Engagements with Civil Society and Democratisation." Paper presented at the Third International Conference and Workshop "Indonesia in Transition," organized by the KNAW and Labsosio, Universitas Indonesia, August 24–28, 2003. Universitas Indonesia, Depok. http://www.hum.uu.nl/medewerkers/m.vanbruinessen/publications/Post_Suharto_Islam_and_civil_society.htm. Study covering several groups including Muhammadiyah.

WILLIAM E. SHEPARD

MUHTASIB.

See Ḥisbah.

MUJĀHIDĪN-I KHALQ.

The origins of the Sāzmān-i Mujāhidīn-i Khalq Īrān (MEK), currently led by Maryam and Masʿūd Rajavī from its political headquarters in Paris, can be traced back to the 1950s. The overthrow of the democratically elected government of Mohammad Mosaddegh in August 1953 by a U.S. and British-led military coup, followed by the repressive policies of the Shah Muhammad Reza Pahlavi's regime against the nonviolent opposition, prompted some members of the religious group within the Liberation Movement of Iran (LMI) to reconsider their strategies in the struggle against Pahlavi rule. Motivated by the success of revolutionaries in Cuba and the rise of armed guerilla organizations in Latin America and Asia, younger LMI activists, all university students, believed that guerilla warfare was the only effective strategy of resistance against a regime with a large-scale bureaucracy and a powerful army and police force.

Searching for a new strategy this generation of Muslim activists formed an underground reading group that, alongside the Qurʾān, studied the works of leftist revolutionaries across the globe. Its purpose was to formulate a new ideology as well as establish leadership that could launch a revolution to pave the path for the creation of a classless society that eliminated human exploitation. After six years of *kār-e feshōrdeh-e īdeʾūlūzhīk* (intense ideological activity) efforts, the members of the reading group led by Mohammad Hanifnejad announced the formation of the MEK in September 1965. They identified their ideology as *Eslām-e rāstīn-e enqelābī* (the true revolutionary Islam).

This form of "true revolutionary Islam," which borrowed generously from Marxism, was perceived as the only ideology capable of liberating the Iranian people from domestic reactionary forces and foreign imperialism as well as establishing a *jāmāʿah-e bītabaq-e tūhīdī* (a classless society based on monotheistic order). Integrating Marxist teachings into their interpretations of the Qurʾān, the Mujāhidīn defined the history of societies as one of conflict between exploiters and the exploited. Marxist guerrilla fighters in Latin America and Vietnam were seen as allies in the struggle for the creation of a classless society, while Muslim rulers like Muhammad Reza Pahlavi and later

Ruhollah Khomeini were foes. Their heavy reliance on Marxism lent them the title of Islamic Marxists from both regimes.

Mainly through university networks, the founders of the organization, who predominantly originated from the traditional and religious middle and lower middle classes, recruited new members and set up covert cells in Tehran, the political heart of the country. These resistance cells received ideological and political education in addition to basic military training from those members who had served their obligatory service in the army. More advanced training in guerrilla warfare followed when several members of the organization joined the Palestinian Liberation Organization in Lebanon and the Palestinian Occupied Territories. To their misfortune and surprise all three founders and nearly half of the original 150 members were arrested when the shah's secret police infiltrated the organization in 1971, before any military operations were carried out. Of the seventy members who were arrested and tried, several were sentenced to death and executed in Tehran soon thereafter.

Afterward a number of surviving members denounced Islam and declared Marxism the sole ideology of the organization. This ideological schism and competition for organizational resources turned into a violent clash and resulted in the death of two Mujāhidīn activists. Eventually the Marxist members founded a new organization and split off from the Muslim faction, although the remaining Muslim members were able to launch several attacks against foreign and domestic targets in the 1970s. More importantly they were able to recruit new members and play a crucial role in the final days of the revolutionary struggle on the streets of Tehran in February 1979.

The large expansion of the MEK's social base and networks across the country occurred during the relatively open political atmosphere of post-revolutionary Iran, from February 1979 to June 1981. During this period the MEK established offices in nearly every province throughout Iran and formed the largest opposition to the newly established Islamic Republic (IR) through coalitions with liberal and secular individuals and groups. Their most prominent ally was the incumbent president of the IR, Abol-Hasan Bani Sadr. While prior to the 1979 revolution the number of fulltime affiliates of the MEK barely reached several hundred, full-time activists were estimated to have reached tens of thousands during the 1980s. It was then that the MEK turned to what it called imposed armed struggle, after the IR rulers resorted to repressive policies. As a result of violent clashes, mass arrests, and the executions of thousands of MEK affiliates and other leftist organizations, many activists went into hiding or left their country. Among these individuals was the leader of the MEK, Masʿūd Rajavī, who fled to Paris. While in exile the group's leadership founded the National Council of Resistance of Iran in the summer of 1981, and the National Liberation Army (NLA) in Iraq in 1987, with the aim of violently overthrowing the Islamic state and forming a Democratic Islamic Republic. From its main base in Iraq the NLA launched several large scale military operations against Iranian targets along the Iran-Iraq border. However the MEK's military opportunities from its main Iraqi base known as Camp Ashraf withered when Iran accepted UN Resolution 598 and agreed to a ceasefire with Iraq in June 1988. According to a recent estimate (RAND, 2009) the MEK deployed nearly ten thousand members and supporters, both at Camp Ashraf as well as in exile communities in the West. Since the late 1980s dozens of defectors along with several Iran observers blamed the organization for human rights violations and cult-like behavior. The MEK vehemently denounced these accusations as propaganda stemming from the Islamic regime.

Since the end of the Iran-Iraq War in 1988 the activities of the Mujāhidīn-i Khalq have been limited to mostly diplomatic actions in the West. Occasionally some members of the group have been arrested in Iran and several have been executed since the early 1990s for their alleged involvement in the organization, such as distribution of fliers and financial support. The group has strong support in the European Parliament and US Congress, which both played key roles in removing the MEK from the list of Foreign Terrorist Organizations both in the European Union and, most recently, in the US. Although it is still the largest well-organized group in exile among the opposition to the Islamic Republic, the organization has not been able to launch noteworthy activities in the country due to the strict measures of the regime.

[*See also* Iranian Revolution of 1979.]

BIBLIOGRAPHY

Abrahamian, Ervand. *The Iranian Mojahedin*. New Haven, Conn.: Yale University Press, 1989.

Banisadr, Masoud. *Masoud: Memoirs of an Iranian Rebel*. London: Saqi Books, 2004.

Goulka, Jeremiah, et al. *The Mujahedin-e Khalq in Iraq: A Policy Conundrum*. Santa Monica, Calif.: RAND National Defense Research Institute, 2009. http://www.rand.org/content/dam/rand/pubs/monographs/2009/RAND_MG871.pdf.

Mujāhidīn-i Khalq. *Bonyangozaran* [The Founders]. Mojahedin-e Khalq Online Library. http://mojahedin.org/pages/library.aspx.

Nejathosseini, Mohsen. *Bar Faraz-e Khalij-e Fars* [Above the Persian Gulf]. Tehran: Nai Publishers, 2000.

HAMID REZAI

MUJAHIDUN. *See* Jihād.

MUKHTĀR, ʿUMAR AL-.

ʿUmar al-Mukhtār ibn ʿUmar al-Minifī (c. 1858–1931), a Libyan resistance leader, grew up in a religious family connected to the Sanūsīyah Ṣūfī order in Cyrenaica (eastern Libya). He came from the ʿĀʾilat Farḥāt branch of the Minifīyah, an independent client tribe. ʿUmar studied at the lodge of Zanzūr, moving on to the Sanūsī capital and university of Jaghbūb in 1887, then moving with the leadership to Kufra, in the Libyan desert, in 1895.

Two years later he was appointed *shaykh* of the al-Qaṣūr lodge in western Cyrenaica, in the territory of the unruly ʿAbīd tribe. ʿUmar succeeded in solidifying the authority of the order in the region. His success noted, he was again called south in 1899, when the order was expanding into Borku (northern Chad). He was appointed *shaykh* of the ʿAyn Qalakkah lodge. Here he had his first military experiences fighting the French forces. In 1903 he moved back to al-Qaṣūr as *shaykh* of the lodge.

When the Italians invaded Libya in 1911, ʿUmar led the ʿAbīd in the ensuing *jihād*, By the time World War I ended in a truce in 1917, ʿUmar had gained great influence with Muḥammad Idrīs, the new leader of the Sanūsīyah. In 1923 the Italians reopened hostilities. Idrīs went into exile in Egypt and appointed ʿUmar one of the leaders for the campaign in Cyrenaica. Already more than sixty years old, as *nāʾib al-ʿāmm* (general representative) he became a charismatic figure who inspired the tribes to join and maintain the struggle.

ʿUmar, known as Assad al-Sahara (The Lion of the Desert), displayed considerable tactical skill and was able to lead the mostly tribal units in a campaign that for more than six years confounded the Italians in spite of their great numerical and material superiority. Eventually his guerilla forces started to be worn down as food became scarce and vital ammunitions ran out, and in 1929, after a series of defeats, ʿUmar asked for truce negotiations. They led nowhere, and after three months he resumed fighting. But

Italian superiority was now evident, in particular after they began rounding up the Bedouin population in concentration camps in 1930 and cut off supply lines by closing the Egyptian border with barbed wire. ʿUmar's fighters became hunted groups, and on 11 September 1931 ʿUmar himself was captured in a chance encounter. He was brought to Benghazi, submitted to a mock trial, and hanged publicly on 16 September, at Solush. After his death the resistance crumbled within three months, and ʿUmar became a martyr of the Cyrenaican rebellion.

What made ʿUmar al-Mukhtār such a charismatic leader was a combination of religious authority and personal skill. Although the forces he led were largely tribal, he himself came from a relatively minor, client tribe. His first military power was based on the ʿAbīd tribe, among whom he was the leader of the Sanūsī Ṣūfī lodge. ʿUmar did not venture outside Libya to defy order, but simply defended his land. While he did not articulate novel ideas, he was a devoted practitioner of freedom, and his basic understanding of authority compelled him to fight and die for his nation.

[*See also* Libya; *and* Sanūsīyah.]

BIBLIOGRAPHY

Ahmida, Ali Abdullatif. *The Making of Modern Libya: State Formation, Colonization, and Resistance, 1830–1932*. 2d ed. Albany: State University of New York Press, 2009.

Del Boca, Angelo. *Gli Italiani in Libia*. 2 vols. Rome: Laterza Figli, 1986–1988. Thorough study of the period from an Italian point of view.

Evans-Pritchard, E. E. *The Sanusi of Cyrenaica*. Oxford: Clarendon Press, 1949. Still the major study of the period in English.

Lion of the Desert. 25th Anniversary Edition DVD. Directed by Moustapha Akkad. 1981; Burbank, Calif.: Starz/Anchor Bay, 2005. This historically accurate movie stars Anthony Quinn, Oliver Reed, and Irene Papas.

Santarelli, Enzo, et al. *Omar al-Mukhtar: The Italian Reconquest of Libya*. London: Darf, 1986. Concentrates on the last years of the war, using Italian sources in a critical perspective.

Vandewalle, Dirk. *A History of Modern Libya*. Cambridge, U.K., and New York: Cambridge University Press, 2006.

KNUT S. VIKØR
Updated by JOSEPH A. KÉCHICHIAN

MULLAH OMAR. (b. c. 1959) is the spiritual and political leader of the Sunnī fundamentalist Taliban movement of Afghanistan. Omar was Afghanistan's de facto head of state from 1996 to 2001. He is an ethnic Pashtun belonging to the Hotak subtribe of the Ghilzai branch of the Pashtun tribal confederation. He is thought to have been born to a landless peasant family in the village of Nodeh (some reports suggest that his birthplace was Singesar, also near Kandahār) in Kandahār province. Mullah Omar has been wanted by U.S. authorities for harboring Osama Bin Laden and his al-Qaʿida organization, which are believed to be responsible for the 11 September 2001 terrorist attacks on New York and Washington. Omar is reported to be hiding in the mountainous Pakistan-Afghanistan border regions.

Mullah Omar remains an enigmatic personality. Despite his role as one of the founders of the Taliban, little is publicly known about him. There are few photographs of Mullah Omar, as the Taliban's strict interpretation of Sunnī Islam discourages making images of human beings. During his tenure as *amīr* (leader) of Afghanistan, Mullah Omar seldom left Kandahār and almost never met with non-Muslims.

Omar started his career as an Islamic militant by becoming a local subcommander with the Younis Khalis faction of the Ḥizb-i Islāmī party of the anti-Soviet Mujāhidīn in the 1980s.The Ḥizb-i Islāmī was the recipient of a large amount of U.S.,

Saudi, and Pakistani financial and military assistance during the war against the Soviet-sponsored regime in Kabul. After the withdrawal of Soviet troops from Afghanistan in 1989, Omar continued to fight against the Soviet-backed Najibullah regime between 1989 and 1992. He was wounded in action four times and lost an eye in the anti-Soviet struggle. After he was disabled, Omar is believed to have studied and taught in a Deobandī *madrasah* (Islamic seminary) in the Pakistani border city of Quetta in the early 1990s.

The Soviet withdrawal from Afghanistan and the subsequent collapse of the Najibullah regime in 1992 eroded any semblance of central authority in the country as various *mujāhidīn* factions vied for power. The anarchical situation in Afghanistan facilitated Mullah Omar's rise to prominence with the emergence of the ethnically Pashtun-dominated Taliban between 1993 and 1994. The Taliban's recruits came from the Wahhābī-influenced Deobandī Qur'ānic schools in Afghanistan and Pakistan and from the Afghan refugee camps in Pakistan. Mullah Omar claimed to have formed the Taliban in order to rid Afghanistan of the rampant corruption and anarchy that had emerged as a result of the internecine civil war among rival Islamist factions. According to the Taliban's version of its origins, Muhammad Omar, then a village *mullah* in Kandahār, responded to pleas for assistance in freeing two girls kidnapped and assaulted by a local militia commander. Omar gathered a group of religious students, or *ṭālibs*, of the local *madrasah* and organized an attack on the commander that resulted in the girls' freedom and the subsequent execution of the commander. Mullah Omar is perceived to be genuinely firm in his constrained vision of "orthodox" Sunnī Islam influenced by the Wahhābī school. Omar's Pakistani and Afghan sympathizers have created a legend of the *mullah*'s charisma, piety, and dedication to Islam.

At the regional level, Pakistan backed Mullah Omar and the Taliban movement (known in Pashto as Da Afghanistano da Talibano Islami Tehrik) in the 1990s as the Pakistani military elite saw Mullah Omar as a loyal client who would aid its geostrategic objective in post-Soviet Afghanistan. Moreover, Mullah Omar's strict Deobandī interpretation of Sunnī Islam was also supported by Pakistan's close Arab allies Saudi Arabia and the United Arab Emirates. These countries felt some ideological affinity with his interpretation of Islam, and strategically they regarded the Taliban as a counter to their regional rival, Shīʿī Iran.

Relying on Pakistani military assistance in the areas of weapons supply, tactical direction, and training, the Taliban under the leadership of Mullah Omar were able to occupy large parts of Afghanistan in the mid-1990s. In April 1996, supporters of Mullah Omar bestowed on him the title Amīr al-Muʾminīn (commander of the faithful) after he took a cloak alleged to be that of the Prophet Muḥammad from a chest in a shrine in Kandahār and wore it. An Afghan legend held that whoever could retrieve the cloak from the chest would be the great leader of the Muslims. Mullah Omar renamed Afghanistan the Islamic Emirate of Afghanistan in October 1997. However, he continued to reside in Kandahār and did not move to Kabul, which has been the capital of Afghanistan for over 150 years. Under Mullah Omar's rule, lawlessness and crime diminished in the parts of Afghanistan administered by the Taliban, but fighting and the suffering of civilians from the destruction of war continued.

Osama Bin Laden and his terrorist al-Qaʿida network were able to expand without hindrance under the safe sanctuary extended by Mullah Omar in the period between 1996 and 2001. Mullah Omar's association with Bin Laden went back to their time as resistance fighters against the Soviet occupation of Afghanistan between 1979 and 1989. After the 11 September 2001, attacks, Washington gave Mullah Omar an ultimatum to hand over Bin Laden or to face a U.S. military assault. Mullah Omar rejected Washington's ultimatum while his erstwhile Pakistani allies abandoned him and allied themselves with the United States. In October 2001 Operation Enduring Freedom removed Mullah Omar's Taliban regime from power. Omar declared that he and his Taliban forces would fight to the death rather than submit to U.S. demands to turn over Osama Bin Laden.

Mullah Omar went into hiding after the toppling of the Taliban regime. He escaped from an oncoming battalion of U.S. Marines by riding off on a motorbike, even though he reportedly has only one functioning leg. The United States government has offered a reward of up to $10 million for information leading to his capture.

The Taliban faction associated with Mullah Omar continued to operate against the U.S. and NATO coalition forces based in Afghanistan after the toppling of Mullah Omar's regime in late 2001. Some captured Taliban claimed in January 2007 that the Directorate for Inter-Services Intelligence (ISI) of the Pakistani military was still protecting Mullah Omar. This corroborates a similar allegation made by the president of Afghanistan, Hamid Karzai, in 2006, although the government of Pakistan vehemently denied it.

Mullah Omar has proclaimed a *jihād* against the U.S. and NATO "occupying forces" and the U.S.-installed Afghan regime of President Karzai. He continues to have the allegiance of prominent pro-Taliban military commanders in the region, including his former enemy Gulbuddin Hekmatyar. Numerous statements reportedly from Omar have been released. In June 2006 a statement regarding the death of Abū Muṣʿab al-Zarqāwī in Iraq hailed al-Zarqāwī as a martyr and claimed that the resistance movements in Afghanistan and Iraq "will not be weakened." In August 2007, Omar reportedly issued a statement through an intermediary on the eighty-eighth anniversary of Afghanistan's independence from Britain encouraging resistance against the "foreign colonial occupation" of Afghanistan.

There were unsubstantiated claims in 2010 that Mullah Omar was based somewhere in Pakistan. Some reports have again suggested that the ISI is backing Mullah Omar and the Taliban's Supreme Council, known as the Quetta Shura (allegedly based in the Pakistani city of Quetta), as well as the Taliban-linked Haqqani group in the North Waziristan Agency of Pakistan's Federally Administered Tribal Areas. The Pakistani government, however, again categorically denied these reports. Nonetheless, Pakistan's alleged covert support for Mullah Omar and other Sunnī Pashtun anticoalition groups in Afghanistan could be intended to help Pakistan retain its influence in Afghanistan in the wake of the U.S. government's decision to scale down its military operations in that country beginning in 2014.

In January 2010, media reports suggested that Mullah Omar was now willing to back talks with the United States in order to end the almost decade-long conflict between the Taliban and the U.S.-led NATO forces. However, these reports were denied by the Taliban.

Despite the Obama administration's 2010–2011 military surge in Afghanistan and the U.S. military's increased collaboration with its NATO allies in stabilizing the situation in that strife-torn country, Mullah Omar has eluded all U.S. attempts to apprehend him.

In a message marking the end of Ramaḍān, the Islamic month of fasting, in September 2010, Omar urged Afghans who fought against the Soviet occupation in the 1980s, many of whom were now allied with the U.S.-backed government of President Hamid Karzai, to join the Taliban's campaign against the U.S./NATO forces. Nevertheless, leaving aside Mullah Omar's increasingly contradictory declared positions, there were high-level negotiations between the Karzai regime and all major factions of the Taliban in 2010 in an attempt to end the Afghan conflict. According to various reports, even Mullah Omar's faction of the Taliban has also been involved in a new U.S.-led negotiations process initiated in 2011. These talks with the Taliban are aimed at stabilizing Afghanistan in the wake of the drawdown of NATO's military forces in that country beginning in 2014.

[*See also* Afghanistan; Ḥizb-i Islāmī Afghānistān; *and* Taliban.]

BIBLIOGRAPHY

Coll, Steve. *Ghost Wars: The Secret History of the CIA, Afghanistan, and Bin Laden, from the Soviet Invasion to September 10, 2001*. New York: Penguin, 2004. One of the best-documented studies of U.S. policy toward Afghanistan, based partly on official declassified sources and interviews that are not found in other publications.

Giustozzi, Antonio, ed. *Decoding the New Taliban: Insights from the Afghan Field*. London: Hurst, 2009. An informative work on the evolution of the neo-Taliban in Afghanistan.

Goodson, Larry P. *Afghanistan's Endless War: State Failure, Regional Politics, and the Rise of the Taliban*. Rev. ed. Seattle: University of Washington Press, 2001. A balanced account role of the Taliban in the Afghan conflict in the 1990s.

Griffin, Michael. *Reaping the Whirlwind: Afghanistan, Al Qaʿida and the Holy War*. Rev. ed. London: Pluto, 2003. A general study of post-Soviet Afghan politics and foreign intervention in Afghan affairs.

Hussain, Rizwan. *Pakistan and the Emergence of Islamic Militancy in Afghanistan*. Aldershot, U.K.: Ashgate, 2005. A detailed analysis of Pakistani policy toward Afghanistan from 1947 to 2001.

Rashid, Ahmed. *Taliban: Islam, Oil and the New Great Game in Central Asia*. London: I. B. Taurus, 2000. A well-researched journalistic account of the rise of the Taliban in the 1990s.

Waldman, Matt. *The Sun in the Sky: The Relationship between Pakistan's ISI and Afghan Insurgents*. Crisis States Discussion Paper 18. London: Crisis States Research Centre, June 2010. Includes a brief analysis of the alleged links of Mullah Omar's faction of the Taliban with the Pakistani military establishment.

Walsh, Declan. "Afghan Taliban Leader Ready to End al-Qaida Ties, Says Former Trainer." *Guardian*, 29 January 2010.

Zaeef, Abdul Salam. *My Life with the Taliban*. Edited by Alex Strick van Linschoten and Felix Kuehn. New York: Columbia University Press, 2010. This is an autobiography of a senior member of the Taliban that provides insight into the workings of Afghanistan's Taliban regime (1996–2001) under the leadership of Mullah Muhammad Omar.

RIZWAN HUSSAIN

MURABAHA. *See* Islamic Finance.

MURJIʾITES. The Murjiʾites are the followers of a Muslim sect that probably emerged in the second half of the eighth century CE, including some early prominent scholars reported to have subscribed to Murjiʾī views; for example, Abū Ḥanīfah al-Nuʿmān (d. 767), the eponymous founder of what is today the largest Sunnī legal school, the Ḥanafī. What may be the earliest Murjiʾī treatise was attributed to al-Ḥasan ibn Muḥammad ibn al-Ḥanafīyah (d. c. 719), a grandson of ʿAlī ibn Abī Ṭālib, the Prophet Muḥammad's cousin and son-in-law and the first imam in Shīʿī Islam. Medieval Muslim sources distinguish among various Murjiʾī subsects, each having its own religious and political idiosyncrasies. It is generally believed that the name of the sect was derived from the verb *arjaʾa* (defer or postpone). Based on Qurʾān 106:9 ("And there are others who await Allāh's decree, whether he will punish them, or forgive them"), the Murjiʾites, a name given to them by their detractors, are said to have deferred the status of grave sinners to the Day of Judgment, when God, knowing people's intentions and the circumstances of their acts, will pass judgment on them. Additionally, a basic doctrinal principle of the Murjiʾites was their view on the relationship between faith and acts. Whereas some Muslim sects held that one's acts both influenced and were indicative of one's faith, the Murjiʾites held that there was no necessary correlation between faith and acts, such that all Muslims—as long as they identify themselves as such—should be treated as believers regardless of how they actually behave. Moreover, some early scholars reportedly affiliated with Murjiʾism held predestinarian views, maintaining that people do not have full freedom to choose their acts.

The doctrines of the Muji'ites were most likely a reaction to the civil wars that plagued the first Islamic century. Some Muslim sects passed judgment on who was right and wrong in those wars. The Murjiʾites, however, abstained from condemning or siding with any particular side, preferring to regard all as believers and defer the judgment on their schisms to God. According to epistles attributed to some early scholars believed to have followed Murjiʾī views, reports about these schisms were not sufficient to constitute conclusive evidence for or against the parties involved. This lack of certitude meant that Muslims should abstain from either passing judgment on or fighting with one side against another. Furthermore, their belief in the distinction between faith and acts meant that they considered all Muslims to be believers regardless of their acts, which acts usually follow from a certain interpretation of religious texts.

Murjiʾī views thus had clear political implications. To abstain from judging people's faith on the basis of their acts meant that members of Muslim communities who failed to observe the instructions of Islam should not be harassed by other members of the community or by the rulers. Furthermore, regardless of their behavior, Muslim rulers must be treated as true believers and obeyed accordingly, a thesis that predestination, which reduces the liability of human beings for their actions, furthers even more. On the basis of these beliefs, the Murjiʾites have generally been regarded as quietists, a view that is contradicted by reports about their participation in some revolts in the late Umayyad period in the first half of the eighth century. Be this as it may, we do know that their quietism did not necessarily lead them to support Muslim rulers against their opponents. Additionally, while suspension of judgment on Muslims was not satisfying for parties involved in civil wars, it meant that the Murjiʾites were in a better position to avoid the extremism of other sects, which more often than not led to political divisions and civil strife. Remarkably, Sunnī Muslims like to present themselves as moderates among extremist sects. In fact, the Sunnī reading of the early schisms is partly based on the Murjiʾī approach towards the same subject.

Debates over the nature and requirement of faiths are at the heart of modern encounters between Islamist groups, particularly violent ones, and Muslim regimes. Violent Islamist groups generally justify using violence against Muslim rulers (and at times Muslim citizens) on account of their acts that, in their understanding, contradict the teachings of Islam, such as adopting non-Islamic legal codes or collaborating with non-Muslim foreign powers. Official Sunnī religious scholars usually condemn these views, relying for the logic of their condemnations on Murjiʾī views. Religious freedom and tolerance are central issues in the religious discourse of these scholars, and they generally require that all citizens, Muslim citizens in this case, be treated as true believers as long as they profess Islam and regardless of the compatibility of their views and acts with the teachings of Islam. Therefore, in the legal systems of most Muslim countries today, the mere profession of faith suffices to avert a legal charge of blasphemy, a view that Muslim "modernists" uphold wholeheartedly. This discourse demonstrates the striking doctrinal and political similarities between Sunnism and Murji'ism. However, it ignores medieval Sunnī presentations of the Murji'ites as a deviant sect whose extremist views equate pious and impious believers. However, facing the repugnant reality that some early scholars whom they held in high esteem may have had Murji'ī inclinations, medieval Sunnī scholars distinguished between "orthodox" and "unorthodox" Murji'ites. Unlike the latter, the former did not judge faith on the basis of actions, but agreed that actions can in principle affect faith, a view that some Sunnī scholars also maintained.

BIBLIOGRAPHY

Agha, Saleh Said. "A Viewpoint of the Murji'a in the Umayyad Period: Evolution through Application." *Journal of Islamic Studies* 8, no. 1 (1998): 1–42.

Ash'arī, Abū al-Ḥasan al-. *Maqālāt al-islamīyīn*. Beirut: al-Maktabah al-'Aṣrīyah, 1990. See esp. pp. 213–234.

Cook, Michael. "Activism and Quietism in Islam: The Case of the Early Murji'a." In *Islam and Power*, edited by Alexander S. Cudsi and Ali E. Hillal Dessouki, pp. 15–23. London: Croom Helm, 1981.

Cook, Michael. *Early Muslim Dogma: A Source-Critical Study*. Cambridge, U.K.: Cambridge University Press, 1981.

van Ess, Joseph. "Das *Kitāb al-irǧā'* des Ḥasan b. Muḥammad b. al-Hanafiyya." *Arabica* 21 (1974); 48–51.

Watt, W. Montgomery. *The Formative Period of Islamic Thought*. Edinburgh: Edinburgh University Press, 1973.

AMR OSMAN

MUSHARAKA. *See* Islamic Finance.

MUSLIM BROTHERHOOD. Founded in Ismailia, Egypt, in 1928 by Ḥasan al-Bannā (1906–1949), the Society of the Muslim Brothers (Jamā'at al-Ikhwān al-Muslimūn) is the most prominent Islamic activist organization within the broader field of religious social movements in Egypt, with branch organizations throughout the Arab world. The movement was initially proclaimed as a religious and philanthropic organization that aimed to instill Egyptian society with Islamic values through popular preaching and charitable institutions. Its emergence, however, was part of a widespread reaction to alarming developments that swept through the Muslim world. European domination of the Middle East and the division of Arab territories following World War I, along with the fall of the Islamic caliphate, gave rise to the need for societal efforts to resist growing Western influence on Muslim societies.

As a teacher and gifted orator, al-Bannā was able to attract to his movement members of the local intelligentsia, as well as some artisans and workers. The Ikhwān expressed interest in public affairs and developed a distinctive conception of the comprehensiveness of Islam that contrasted with that of both the established clergy and the conventional philanthropic charities. Al-Bannā called for an activist Islam that impacted all levels of society. He considered the Islamic state a significant component of the desired order, but Ikhwān leaders did not consider the assumption of political power an imminent possibility. The tasks of moral reform (*iṣlāḥ al-nufūs*) and of agreeing on an Islamic methodology (*minhāj islāmī*) must have seemed more appropriate for that early stage in the group's evolution. It was at this time that al-Bannā raised official ire by emphasizing the need to "guide" the state.

The Ikhwān did not identify itself as a political party, although it frequently acted like one. Its activities acquired a distinct political character in the late 1930s, with the publication of the weekly *al-Nadhīr* (The Warner), which occasionally threatened to "fight any politician or organization that did not work for the support of Islam and the restoration of its glory." Its support for absolute obedience (*al-ṭāʿah*) to the leader and its tight organizational pattern—which linked the highest level of the Guidance Council to the most basic level of the *usrah* ("family," or cell)—were likened to those of fascist organizations.

Just before World War II, the Ikhwān boasted more than three hundred branches, although it had been careful not to antagonize the government. Its leaders avoided confrontation with the British, while building up their own organizational and paramilitary capacity, especially the "Secret Apparatus." In the 1940s, the Ikhwān became the most popular and respected nationalist force opposing British imperialism and military occupation, as well as Zionism in Palestine. Its standing grew as both the Wafd and the palace, closely associated with the British, were largely discredited as nationalist forces. By 1947, the Ikhwān's official membership rolls reached seventy-five thousand, and with the formation of roaming scouts (*jawwālah*), their presence became felt in the streets. The organization built its own companies, factories, schools, and health facilities, and rose within the ranks of various institutions, including trade unions and the armed forces, to such a degree that by the end of the 1940s, it was considered by many to be "a state within a state." Parallel to these efforts, it escalated militant attacks on colonial interests in Egypt. Cairo responded by dissolving the Brotherhood, as the confrontation between the two reached a peak late in 1948, after the assassination of Prime Minister Maḥmūd Fahmī al-Nuqrashī. Al-Bannā was in turn gunned down in February 1949, probably at the hands of government agents. Importantly, Ikhwān membership had reached almost a half million active associates (*ʿuḍw ʿāmil*) that year, with another half million sympathizers throughout Egypt.

Leadership. Egyptian leaders and intellectuals of the Ikhwān were among the most influential twentieth-century political figures. After his assassination on 12 February 1949, al-Bannā was succeeded as general guide (*al-murshid al-ʿāmm*) by Ḥasan al-Huḍaybī (d. 1973), a respected judge elected as a consensus figure to bridge the growing divisions within the Muslim Brotherhood. His son, Maʾmūn al-Huḍaybī, became the official spokesperson of the Ikhwān and was a future general guide as well. The elder Huḍaybī was succeeded by a charismatic attorney and movement elder, ʿUmar al-Tilimsānī (d. 1986), who successfully shepherded the organization through the transformative period of the 1970s. Mustafa Mashhur, also a member of the organization's formative generation played a pivotal role throughout the 1980s, under the leadership of Ḥāmid Abū al-Naṣr (d. 1996), before assuming the position of general guide until his death in 2002. Muḥammad Mahdī ʿĀkif, an Ikhwān member elected to the Egyptian parliament in 1987, became secretary-general of the organization in 1996. Like many leaders of the Muslim Brotherhood, he spent several years in prison but was released in 1999, eventually assuming the top post in 2002. In 2010, ʿĀkif became the first general guide to step down from the position, all previous holders having died while in office. He was succeeded by Muḥammad Badīʿ, a longstanding Muslim Brotherhood activist and member of the Guidance Bureau who became the eighth general guide. While none of the Muslim Brotherhood's leaders have departed too dramatically from Bannā's original message and example of leadership, the more recent general guides, beginning with Muṣṭafā Mashhūr, who assumed the post in 1986, the organization began to put more emphasis on internal consolidation of power and the solidification of its structural hierarchy at the expense of outreach and engagement of the broader society. This is explained in part by the fact that these recent leaders emerged out of the organization's Secret Apparatus, whose activities had historically been outside of the purview of even Bannā himself.

Sayyid Quṭb (d. 1966), a rising Ikhwān intellectual during the 1950s, joined the Ikhwān after al-Bannā's assassination in 1949 and became its chief spokesman after its second dissolution in 1954. On orders from President Gamal Abdel Nasser, who loathed his ideas and feared his growing influence, Quṭb was executed in 1966.

Political Participation. After Sadat succeeded Nasser in 1970, he released the Ikhwān leadership from prison and sought the group's support, primarily to buttress his antileftist initiatives. The first wave of leaders was released in 1971, including al-Tilimsānī, who had been tortured in Nasser's prisons. Nevertheless, Sadat maintained the Ikhwān's "illegal" status as a political party, even refusing to convert it into a *jamʿīyah* (private voluntary organization) registered with the Ministry of Social Affairs. The popular assembly was tolerated as long as nooses were maintained around its leaders' necks. By 1979, amid increasing criticism of his peace initiative with Israel, Sadat offered to recognize the Ikhwān officially, as well as to appoint al-Tilimsānī to the Shūrā Council (the upper chamber of parliament). As with most presidential offers, a condition was attached, namely that the Brotherhood moderate its criticism of Sadat's policies; al-Tilimsānī rejected the overture. An acceptance would have placed the Ikhwān under direct government control and given the Ministry of Social Affairs power to dissolve any organization at will, confiscate its properties, and change its board of directors, and al-Tilimsānī would have been beholden to the president rather than to the group's constituency or the public at large.

Al-Tilimsānī and top Ikhwān leaders were subjected to Sadat's fury in September 1981, when approximately 1,500 Egyptian intellectuals, journalists, and activists of all political stripes were arrested, allegedly for crimes against the state. Senior officials were quickly released after Sadat's assassination on October 6, after it was established that the Ikhwān was not implicated in that attack. In fact, by 1981, the Brotherhood established itself as a nonviolent opposition movement, as al-Tilimsānī moved the organization into the mainstream of political and social life. Under his leadership, the Muslim Brotherhood accepted political pluralism and parliamentary democracy. Because it was still banned, the Ikhwān formed an opposition alliance with the Wafd Party in order to compete in the 1984 parliamentary elections. Interestingly, the alliance gained sixty-five seats (out of 450), seven of which were earmarked for Muslim Brotherhood members. This victory transformed the alliance into a respectable opposition to the National Democratic Party (NDP) and President Hosni Mubarak.

The coalition collapsed by 1987, and the Muslim Brotherhood formed the Islamic Alliance with the Socialist Labor Party and the Liberal Party, in order to organize new plebiscites. The Brotherhood enjoyed a dominant position in this alliance, which emboldened it to present and defend a ten-point platform to implement Sharīʿah. *Al-islām huwa al-ḥall* (Islam is the solution) was the only campaign slogan for the alliance. The brothers reached out to the Coptic Christian community at this time as they refined their political agenda. The second of the ten points called for "full equal rights and obligations between Muslims and their Coptic brothers," and the only Copt at the top of any party list elected in 1987 was on the Islamic Alliance list. Although the Ikhwān joined other opposition parties in boycotting the 1990 elections, they returned to the democratic process in the mid-1990s, underscoring the necessity for political moderation.

Despite frequent police harassment and arrests, Ikhwān candidates left their mark on the Egyptian parliament. In 2005, they participated in pro-democracy demonstrations with the Kifāyah (Enough) movement, which was first established in 2004 at the grassroots level. The movement objected to the NDP decision to appoint Gamal Mubarak, the president's son, as its secretary-general in preparation for an eventual succession to the country's highest post. Such courageous opposition to the NDP was made possible by the results of the 2005 parliamentary elections, when Brotherhood candidates won eighty-eight seats, or 20 percent of the total, to form the largest opposition bloc. What was even more remarkable was that this gain was made despite clear violations of process, including the physical prevention of citizens from casting their ballots and the arrests of thousands.

In 2011, as millions of Egyptians took to the streets to seek the overthrow of the Mubarak regime, the Muslim Brotherhood's leadership wavered before committing to the popular nonviolent protest movement, emboldened in part by its youth contingent. Following eighteen momentous days of protests, which featured several violent confrontations with state security forces, Mubarak resigned from his three-decade rule, handing over power to the Supreme Council of the Armed Forces (SCAF), which appointed a caretaker government pending free and democratic elections.

Almost immediately, the Muslim Brotherhood announced the formation of its official political wing, the Freedom and Justice Party (FJP), and declared its intentions to compete in parliamentary elections (it later reversed course on its original decision not to field a presidential candidate) and help shape the future of a democratic Egypt. During the early phase of a postauthoritarian system in Egypt, the Muslim Brotherhood emerged as by far the most organized and widely supported political faction in the country, garnering nearly half of the seats in parliament, more than twice the nearest competitor. A longstanding Muslim Brotherhood figure, Saʿad al-Katatny, became the Speaker of Parliament in late 2011. As the country faced mounting economic, social, and political problems, the FJP was poised to play a crucial role in determining the future course of the country. Following the dissolution of the parliament by the Supreme Constitutional Court and the subsequent election of Mohamed Morsi as Egypt's first president in the post-Mubarak era, the Muslim Brotherhood mobilized its members and supporters in solidarity with Morsi, especially in the face of rising opposition from liberal forces.

Regional Impact. Soon after its founding, the Muslim Brotherhood movement spread into the countries adjoining Egypt, and it remains the main Pan-Arab Islamic movement. Its charter stipulates that it is a "universal Islamic assembly" (*hay'ah islāmīyah jamʿīyah*) rather than an Egyptian or even an Arab organization. It actively established branches from the mid-1930s onward, following visits by its leaders to Syria, Lebanon, Palestine, Jordan, Iraq, Yemen, and elsewhere, and set up special tents in Mecca during the pilgrimage seasons in the 1940s and 1950s to greet, entertain, and enlist pilgrim delegates from all over the Muslim world. Arab students, attracted to the movement while studying in Egypt, carried their ideas back to their countries. The Pan-Arab activities of the Ikhwān were stepped up during the Palestine War of 1948, to which it contributed volunteers. From then on, the Ikhwān did its best to support affiliated movements in other Arab countries when they were persecuted, an activity that was soon caught up in inter-Arab politics. The movement also had appeal in North Africa, especially in Morocco—where it had close relations with the Istiqlāl Party—and was not unknown in Tunisia, Algeria, and parts of the Horn of Africa. Sympathetic groups, with similar orientations, flourished in India, Malaysia, Indonesia, the Philippines, and of course Pakistan, where the Jamāʿat-i Islāmī shares the Ikhwān ideology. More recently, the Ikhwān has made inroads in Europe and the Americas. The following sections will provide brief studies of three cases of the Muslim Brotherhood's expansion into other Arab countries: Syria, Jordan, and Sudan.

Syria. From its beginnings, the Muslim Brotherhood in Syria has acted as an opposition movement but has never held any official position of power. The Brotherhood traces its origins to the late 1930s, when the Syrian people were struggling for independence from French rule. To address the severe problems facing Syria's urban, predominantly Sunnī populace, there arose a variety of social and political associations. Some of these were benevolent societies (*jamīʿyāt*), headed by religious scholars with formal training in Islamic law. On the eve of Syria's independence, one of these, the Dār al-Arqām, moved to Damascus, where it merged with other Islamist associations and, at a 1944 conference, renamed itself the Muslim Brotherhood (Ikhwān al-Muslimūn). Syrian students who studied in Cairo became familiar with the ideas of Ḥasan al-Bannā. One such student was Muṣṭafā al-Sibāʿī, who became the Syrian Brotherhood's first general supervisor (*al-murāqib al-ʿamm*).

The earliest objectives of the Muslim Brotherhood in Syria were to nurture Islamic morals and ethics, to reform the state bureaucracy by applying laws and regulations fairly, and to bring about national independence. Such ideas were disseminated through neighborhood schools and periodicals associated with the Brotherhood. The Arab military defeat in Palestine in 1948 enabled the Brotherhood to expand its following in Syrian cities and towns, especially in Damascus, where during the 1950s its representatives consistently won a fifth of the parliamentary seats allotted to the capital and its environs. Throughout this period, the Muslim Brotherhood competed with communists, Baʿthists, Nasserists, and other forces disenchanted with the veteran nationalists who had governed Syria since independence in 1946.

The Baʿth Party's seizure of power in 1963 focused the Muslim Brotherhood's attention squarely on the more radical economic and social policies introduced by this avowedly secular political movement, as well as on the party's insertion of large numbers of provincial cadres into the central administration. In the aftermath of Syria's defeat in the Arab-Israeli War of 1967 and the rise of a more pragmatic wing of the Baʿth Party led by Hafez al-Assad, the Muslim Brotherhood soon expressed its misgivings with the new regime. An explicitly secular constitution promulgated in 1973 provoked widespread popular protest. During the mid-1970s, the Brotherhood's northern militants escalated the level of violence directed against the regime. This phase in the Muslim Brotherhood's struggle against the Baʿthist order is closely identified with the leadership of ʿAdnān Saʿd al-Dīn, a teacher and writer from Hama, who had become general supervisor in a disputed election in 1971. In the face of escalating violence, the government decreed in July 1980 that anyone found to be connected to the Muslim Brotherhood would be sentenced to death. The regime then cracked down on the Brotherhood, using its formidable armed forces and security services. Six years of terror and counterterror culminated in a confrontation between the Muslim Brotherhood and the Assad regime in the socially conservative Sunnī stronghold of Hama. In February 1982, militants affiliated with the Brotherhood proclaimed an armed uprising and seized control of large parts of the city. It took elite military and security forces two weeks to crush the rebellion, killing between five and twenty thousand civilians and razing the central business district and historic grand mosque. The showdown dealt a devastating blow to the Brotherhood, and put the regime's adversaries on notice that the authorities would tolerate no overt challenge to Baʿth Party rule.

By the early 1990s, contacts between the Brotherhood and the authorities became more frequent, and in December 1995 the general supervisor, Shaykh ʿAbd al-Fattaḥ Abū Ghudah, returned to Damascus from Saudi Arabia, pledging not to engage in overtly political activity. Activists in London then elected ʿAlī Ṣadr al-Dīn al-Bayanūnī to the post of general supervisor. As the decade ended, leading figures of the Brotherhood expressed increasingly moderate sentiments. Following the election of Bashar al-Assad to the presidency in July 2000, the general supervisor told reporters that the Muslim Brotherhood did not even have to be permitted to operate legally inside Syria; it would be enough to come up with some kind of "formula" that would allow the organization to "express its views" concerning public issues.

In May 2001, the Muslim Brotherhood published a Covenant of National Honor, which called for the creation in Syria of a "modern state" (*dawlah ḥadīthīyah*), in which "free and honest ballot boxes are the basis for the rotation of power between all the sons of the homeland." The document made no mention of the concept of *shūrā*, nor of the implementation of Islamic law (Sharīʿah). An April 2005 statement once again demanded "free and fair elections" and the termination of the draconian state of emergency that had been imposed in 1963. The general supervisor announced in January 2006 that the Brotherhood had decided to join forces with Syria's exiled former vice president, ʿAbd al-Ḥalīm Khaddām, in a campaign to replace the Baʿthist regime with a democratic system. In taking this step, the Brotherhood allied themselves with the liberal activists who had issued the Damascus Declaration in October 2005.

Ultimately, the Muslim Brotherhood's ability to effect meaningful political change in Syria will depend on how deftly the regime led by President Bashar al-Assad wields the carrot and the stick. In the post–Cold War era, the Syrian government no longer enjoys the largesse and protection of the Soviet Union. United States pressure on Syria to negotiate a less than favorable settlement with Israel, particularly in the aftermath of the second Palestinian uprising of 2000 and the February 2005 assassination of former Lebanese prime minister Rafīq Ḥarīrī, seems unlikely to loosen the Baʿth Party's grip on power. The launch of popular protests in March 2011 and the ensuing violent crackdown by the Assad regime has placed the Muslim Brotherhood at the forefront of a new opposition force, led by the political leadership in exile by the Syrian National Council. This makeshift organization has gained considerable international support in the form of economic aid and political pressure on the Assad regime to enact genuine democratic reforms or face the prospects of a prolonged civil conflict and possible international intervention. With the rise in violent confrontations between the regime and anti-Assad rebels, the Muslim Brotherhood provided logistical and military support to the opposition forces with the aim of turning the tide within the war and ensuring Assad's defeat.

Jordan. An enduring feature of Jordanian political life for more than sixty years, the Muslim Brotherhood in Jordan was created as part of an effort by Ḥasan al-Bannā to form additional bases of support for his movement. In the early 1940s, members of the Egyptian Muslim Brotherhood were sent to both Palestine and Jordan to establish new branches. In 1946, the first Jordanian branch was founded in the town of Salt; further centers were then established in Amman, Irbid, and Kayak. The leadership of the Muslim Brotherhood was indigenous, and the first head of the organization was a prominent cleric, Ḥājj ʿAbd al-Laṭīf al-Qurah (d. 1953). Ḥājj al-Qurah led an eight-member *majlis* (ruling council), which directed the new movement.

King Abdullah (r. 1946–1951) extended tacit approval to the organization but warned that it would be rescinded if the activities of the Muslim Brotherhood strayed from the spiritual to the political. At this point the Muslim Brotherhood was essentially a religious organization with a reformist educational agenda. Following the death of Ḥājj al-Qurah in 1953, a new leader, ʿAbd al-Raḥmān al-Khalīfah, an attorney, was appointed. His appointment signaled the transfer of leadership into the hands of educated professionals, a trend that has continued into the twenty-first century. Increasingly close relations between the Muslim Brotherhood and the monarchy were the most striking feature under the leadership of al-Khalīfah. In official recognition of the Muslim Brotherhood's support against leftist movements, King Hussein exempted the organization from the banning of political parties in 1957. The Brotherhood was exempted because it was officially registered as a charity, although in practice its activities were indistinguishable from those of a political party.

Following the 1967 Arab-Israeli War and Israel's occupation of the West Bank of the Jordan River and Gaza Strip territories, the Palestine Liberation Organization (PLO) established strongholds among the refugee community in Jordan, and the relationship between the Muslim Brotherhood and the monarchy was strengthened. During times of crisis, such as Black September in 1970, when the Jordanian army fought Palestinian guerrillas, the king counted on the Muslim Brotherhood as a staunch ally. The group's leaders lent legitimacy to the Jordanian monarchy by recognizing its authority to quash dissenting forces and backing its political and economic policies.

After a shaky decade of recrimination of the regime by the Muslim Brotherhood and repression by the monarchy utilizing Jordan's intelligence services, relations between the two improved by the end of the 1980s. Following a severe economic crisis, the king's decision to hold the first elections in over twenty-two years gave the Muslim Brotherhood an opportunity to participate in electoral politics. The Muslim Brotherhood won twenty-two out of eighty seats in parliament.

By the spring of 1990 the parliament had taken on a life of its own as deputies, led by the Islamic bloc, investigated allegations of government corruption and denial of civil liberties.

The summer 1990 Iraqi invasion of Kuwait presented the organization with a difficult political dilemma centering on conflicting pressures from local constituents and financial backers in the conservative Gulf regimes. Inasmuch as the Muslim Brotherhood initially condemned Saddam Hussein's invasion of Kuwait, many were bewildered when it reversed course, staging mass protests and demonstrations condemning the stationing of American forces in Saudi Arabia and calling upon the king to support Iraq in the face of an impending foreign invasion. The king, in recognition of the groundswell of public opinion, supported Iraq and also gave the Muslim Brotherhood five cabinet appointments including the ministers of education, religious affairs, health, social development, and justice.

The Brotherhood's period of influence was short-lived, however, lasting six months. Having survived the Gulf War crisis, the king reconsolidated his position at the expense of the Islamists. In June 1991, he dismissed the cabinet and asked the foreign minister, Tahir al-Masri, a Palestinian who supported peace with Israel, to form a new government. Predictably, the Brotherhood refused to join a government that would negotiate with Israel. Another important step taken by the king was the approval of a National Charter. The charter legalized political parties but prohibited those with connections, financial or otherwise, outside Jordan. These limitations were aimed directly at the Muslim Brotherhood, which in December 1992 formed a separate political party, the Islamic Action Front (IAF), under the leadership of Ishaq Farhan, that further confirmed its commitment to the parliamentary system. The IAF, as distinct from the Muslim Brotherhood, conformed to the requirements of the National Charter. The party's goals, unsurprisingly, were identical to those of the Brotherhood, and the party's founders, mostly professionals or civil servants, were mostly Brotherhood members and a few independent Islamists.

The IAF and most other opposition parties that opposed the monarchy's revisions to the electoral law boycotted the 1997 elections in protest. Parliamentary politics in Jordan have remained dominated under the rule of King Abdullah II by conservative East Bank Hashemite loyalists. The election law has not been relaxed to allow for greater representation of ideological candidates, though the IAF returned to full electoral participation in 2003. In that election, the party secured seventeen seats in the expanded parliament, including one for the only woman candidate in the IAF. Realizing they could make little impact in parliament, the Muslim Brotherhood focused on a strategy of building its strength in the professional infrastructure of educational, service, and sociocultural institutions. Toward that end, it took over the leadership of almost every professional association in Jordan and reached out to a wide and diverse public, ranging from the educated middle classes to the poorest Palestinian refugees.

The election of a Ḥamās majority to the Palestinian parliament in January 2006 seemed to embolden the IAF. Ḥamās and the Jordanian Brotherhood have maintained close ties, and the IAF has deplored King Abdullah II's boycott of Ḥamās. Statements issued by the IAF, now under the leadership of Hamzeh Mansour, praising the election of Ḥamās and promising to challenge the Jordanian electoral law, reflect a new boldness in the organization's rhetoric and a more direct challenge to monarchical rule than ever before, calling for the establishment of a new regime that would bring a referendum to the Jordanian people seeking to overturn the 1994 Israel-Jordan peace treaty. Largely in response to internal pressures as well as developments around the region, the king proposed wide-ranging constitutional reforms that would limit the monarchy's power and establish greater representation of the people within the parliamentary system. Critics within Jordan have viewed these reforms as largely cosmetic, however, failing to address the root of the problems within the Jordanian political system.

Sudan. It was in the 1940s that Sudanese students studying in Cairo started their own branch of the Muslim Brothers. Jamāl al-Dīn al-Sanhūrī and al-Ṣādiq ʿAbd Allāh ʿAbd al-Mājid were among its earliest propagators, and in 1946 they were sent by the Egyptian movement to recruit members in Sudan. Early adherents came primarily from the rural areas of northern Sudan and were deeply committed to Ṣūfī Islam and opposed to communism. The Sudanese Muslim Brothers were officially founded at the ʿĪd Conference on 21 August 1954, two years after the Free Officers Revolution in Egypt. Al-Rāshid al-Ṭāhir, one of the Brothers' most prominent student leaders, later became the movement's general supervisor.

After the 1958 military takeover, led by General Ibrāhīm ʿAbbūd, the army's chief of staff, the Muslim Brothers were allowed at first to continue their activities, as a religious movement, while all political parties were banned. However, on 9 November 1959, al-Ṭāhir plotted to overthrow the regime with an illegal cell within the army, composed of Muslim Brothers, Communists, and others. The plotters were arrested, and the Muslim Brothers lost their cadres in the army as well as their freedom to act.

The next important stage in their history started in 1964 when Ḥasan al-Turābī and several leading Brothers returned from their studies abroad. Al-Turābī, who had joined the Brothers while an undergraduate at Khartoum University College in 1954, had completed his postgraduate studies in Europe and returned to Sudan with a Ph.D. in constitutional law and an appointment in the School of Law at Khartoum University. There he emerged as the most effective spokesman of the Brothers at the university and started to promote peaceful settlement in the south. Most of the mass demonstrations of students and sympathizers in October 1964, which ultimately led to the civilian revolution and the downfall of General ʿAbbūd, were led by the Muslim Brothers from the university.

They founded the Islamic Charter Front (ICF) in October 1964, with al-Turābī as secretary-general. In the years 1965–1968 the ICF cooperated with al-Ṣādiq al-Mahdī's wing of the Ummah Party in its anticommunist drive and in promoting an Islamic constitution. Following the May 1969 military coup, led by Colonel Jaʿfar Nimeiri and his communist allies, some of the Brotherhood's leaders, including al-Turābī, were at first arrested. Al-Turābī concentrated his efforts on restructuring the Brothers in such a manner that the old guard lost whatever influence it still had while his followers, who had joined in the 1960s, were moved to top positions. Al-Turābī and those Brothers who remained in Sudan were thus well prepared for Nimeiri's move toward an "Islamic path" in the mid-1970s. Lack of democracy did not trouble al-Turābī and his colleagues since they realized that they could not rely on the traditionalist parties, the Ummah and the DUP, in their fight for an Islamic state.

The Sudanese Brothers founded the National Islamic Front (NIF) following the failure of the anti-Nimeiri coup led by the Anṣār in July 1976. The appointment of Rāshid al-Ṭāḥir, the one-time leader of the Muslim Brothers, as deputy president and prime minister in that year was also an indication of change. Al-Ṭāḥir, though no longer a member, was generally thought of as such by the population. Once national reconciliation became official policy in July 1977, the Brothers were well prepared and grasped whatever positions the government offered. Ḥasan al-Turābī himself was appointed attorney general in 1979, while many of his colleagues accepted positions in the judiciary, in the educational and financial systems, and in the Sudan Socialist Union (SSU). In the 1986 elections, the NIF came in a close third, after the Ummah and the DUP.

The Islamist Revolution in Sudan was not a popular uprising as in Iran but a military coup, brought about by al-Turābī and his supporters in the NIF with the military might of a group of army officers and men led by ʿUmar Ḥasan al-Bashīr. Al-Turābī, along with the leaders of other political parties, was imprisoned but received special favors and continued to help his colleagues in the government to conduct the affairs of state. Al-Bashīr's move against the Sudanese Bar Association, undertaken with al-Turābī's full consent, was to emasculate it and appoint instead fellow Islamists, headed by Jalāl ʿAlī Luṭfī. Under Luṭfī the Special Courts Act was inaugurated, and seventy-five new assistant magistrates with sweeping powers were appointed to supervise the new courts and to impose on Sudan an Islamist judicial system embracing all civil and criminal courts. In November 1989, while still in his cell at Kober Prison, al-Turābī played an influential role in the creation of the International Organization for Muslim Women, thereby enforcing his views on women's equality in Islam.

Al-Turābī organized and headed the Popular Arab and Islamic Congress (PAIC) in 1991, which he declared would coordinate all anti-imperialist movements in the Muslim world and guide them toward Islamic revolution. The first congress was convened in Khartoum, which had the only international airport through which all citizens of Arab states were free to enter without visas. After the first Gulf War, Sudan became a center for extremist antiestablishment Muslim leaders who viewed the Arab League and Saudi Arabia, which had cooperated with the West during that war, as having betrayed the Arab-Islamic cause.

In 2000 Ḥasan al-Turābī was imprisoned once again, and the al-Turābī era seemed to have come to an end. As he reemerged as a figure of opposition to the increasingly isolated al-Bashīr regime, al-Turābī was regularly imprisoned or placed under house arrest for fear that his supporters could rally behind him and destabilize the government. This was the case in 2004, during the Sudanese civil war and more recently in 2011, during the height of the Arab uprisings across the Middle East and North Africa, which al-Bashīr feared could spread to Sudan under al-Turābī's charismatic leadership.

BIBLIOGRAPHY

Abd-Allah, Umar F. *The Islamic Struggle in Syria.* Berkeley, Calif.: Mizan, 1983.

Awadi, Hesham al-. *In Pursuit of Legitimacy: The Muslim Brothers and Mubarak, 1982–2000.* London: I. B. Tauris, 2004.

Baker, Raymond William. *Islam without Fear: Egypt and the New Islamists.* Cambridge, Mass.: Harvard University Press, 2003.

Bayat, Asef. *Making Islam Democratic: Social Movements and the Post-Islamist Turn.* Stanford, Calif.: Stanford University Press, 2007.

Boulby, Marion. *The Muslim Brotherhood and the Kings of Jordan, 1945–1993.* Atlanta, Ga.: Scholars Press, 1999.

Brynjar, Lia. *The Society of the Muslim Brothers in Egypt: The Rise of an Islamist Mass Movement, 1928–1942.* Reading, U.K.: Ithaca, 1998.

Burr, J. Millard, and Robert O. Collins. *Revolutionary Sudan: Hasan al-Turabi and the Islamist State, 1989–2000.* Leiden, Netherlands: E. J. Brill, 2003.

Calvert, John. *Sayyid Qutb and the Origins of Radical Islamism.* New York: Columbia University Press, 2010.

Clark, Janine A. *Islam, Charity, and Activism: Middle-class Networks and Social Welfare in Egypt, Jordan, and Yemen.* Bloomington: Indiana University Press, 2004.

Commins, David Dean. *Islamic Reform: Politics and Social Change in Late Ottoman Syria.* New York: Oxford University Press, 1990.

Eickelman, Dale F., and James P. Piscatori. *Muslim Politics.* Princeton, N.J.: Princeton University Press, 1996.

Esposito, John L. *Islam and Politics.* 4th ed. Syracuse, N.Y.: Syracuse University Press, 1998.

Gerges, Fawaz A. *Journey of the Jihadist: Inside Muslim Militancy.* Orlando Fla.: Harcourt Trade, 2006.

Ikhwanweb. http://www.ikhwanweb.com/. The English website of the Ikhwān.

Kepel, Gilles. *Muslim Extremism in Egypt: The Prophet and Pharaoh.* Translated by Jon Rothschild. Rev. ed. Berkeley: University of California Press, 2003.

Layish, Aharon, and Gabriel R. Warburg. *The Reinstatement of Islamic Law in Sudan Under Numayrī: An Evaluation of a Legal Experiment in the Light of Its Historical Context, Methodology, and Repercussions.* Leiden, Netherlands: E. J. Brill, 2002.

Pargeter, Alison. *The Muslim Brotherhood: The Burden of Tradition.* London: Saqi, 2010.

Schwedler, Jillian. *Faith in Moderation: Islamist Parties in Jordan and Yemen.* Cambridge, U.K.: Cambridge University Press, 2006.

Teitelbaum, Joshua. "The Muslim Brotherhood and the 'Struggle for Syria,' 1947–1958: Between Accommodation and Ideology." *Middle Eastern Studies* 40 (May 2004): 134–158.

Turabi, Hassan al-. "The Islamic State." In *Voices of Resurgent Islam,* edited by John L. Esposito, pp. 241–251. New York: Oxford University Press, 1983.

Vidino, Lorenzo. "The Muslim Brotherhood's Conquest of Europe." *Middle East Quarterly* 12, no. 1 (Winter 2005), pp. 25–34. http://www.meforum.org/article/687.

Warburg, Gabriel. *Islam, Sectarianism, and Politics in Sudan since the Mahdiyya.* London: Hurst, 2003.

Wickham, Carrie Rosefsky. *Mobilizing Islam: Religion, Activism, and Political Change in Egypt.* New York: Columbia University Press, 2002.

Wiktorowicz, Quintan, ed. *Islamic Activism: A Social Movement Theory Approach.* Bloomington: Indiana University Press, 2004.

Wiktorowicz, Quintan. *The Management of Islamic Activism: Salafis, the Muslim Brotherhood, and State Power in Jordan*. Albany: State University of New York Press, 2001.

Wolf, Susanne. "The Muslim Brotherhood in the Sudan." Master's thesis, University of Hamburg, 1990.

Zisser, Eyal. "Syria, the Ba'th Regime, and the Islamic Movement: Stepping on a New Path?" *Muslim World* 95 (January 2005): 43–65.

Zollner, Barbara H. E. *The Muslim Brotherhood: Hasan al-Hudaybi and Ideology*. New York: Routledge, 2009.

Abdullah A. Al-Arian

Muslim-Christian Relations. Intentional, structured encounters between Muslims and Christians are generally termed "Muslim-Christian dialogue." Interfaith dialogue is a conversation in which two or more parties seek to express their views accurately and to listen respectfully to their counterparts. Since the second half of the twentieth century, organized dialogue meetings have proliferated at the local, regional, and international levels, although these meetings have varied significantly in their organization, focus, and venue, as well as in the composition of participants.

Several motives have propelled the contemporary dialogue movement. These include the desires to foster understanding, to stimulate communication, to correct stereotypes, to work on specific problems of mutual concern, to explore similarities and differences, and to facilitate means of witness and cooperation. The pragmatic need for better understanding and cooperation among adherents to the world's two largest communities of faith—Christianity and Islam—is particularly acute. Together Christians and Muslims comprise almost half the world's population, so the way in which they relate is bound to have profound consequences for both communities and for the world.

The dynamics of interfaith encounters between Muslims and Hindus, Muslims and Jews, and Muslims and Christians differ. Their historic relationships as well as their major theological, social, and political concerns vary markedly. Contemporary initiatives in Muslim-Christian dialogue can be understood best in the larger context that can be established by a brief overview of dominant themes in Muslim-Christian encounters.

Historical Background. Muslim-Christian dialogue dates back to the rise of Islam in the seventh century. Rooted as both traditions are in the monotheism of the patriarch Abraham, Muslims and Christians share a common heritage. The history of Muslim-Christian interaction includes periods of great tension, hostility, and open war as well as times of uneasy toleration, peaceful coexistence, and cooperation.

Islamic self-understanding incorporates an awareness of and direct link with the biblical tradition. Muḥammad, his companions, and subsequent generations of Muslims have been guided by the Qurʾān, which they have understood as a continuation and completion of God's revelations to humankind. The Qurʾān speaks of many prophets (*anbiyāʾ*, sg. *nabī*) and messengers (*rusul*, sg. *rasūl*) who functioned as agents of God's revelation. Particular emphasis is laid on the revelations through Moses (the Torah) and Jesus (the Gospel) and their respective communities of faith, or "People of the Book" (*ahl al-kitāb*).

The Qurʾān includes positive affirmations for the People of the Book, including the promise that Jews and Christians who have faith, trust in God and the Last Day, and do what is righteous, "shall have their reward" (2:62 and 5:69). The different religious communities are explained as a part of God's plan; if God had so willed, the Qurʾān asserts, humankind would be one community. Diversity among the communities provides a test for people of faith: "Compete with one another in good works. To God you shall all return and He will tell you (the truth) about that which you have been disputing" (5:48).

The Qur'ān states that "there shall be no compulsion in religious matters" (2:256). Peaceful coexistence is affirmed (106:1–6). At the same time, the People of the Book are urged to "come to a common word" on the understanding of the unity of God (*tawḥīd*) and proper worship (e.g., 3:64, 4:171, 5:82, and 29:46). Christians, in particular, are chided for having distorted the revelation of God. Traditional Christian doctrines of the divinity of Jesus and the Trinity are depicted as compromising the unity and transcendence of God (e.g., 5:72–75, 5:117, and 112:3). There are also verses urging Muslims to fight, under certain circumstances, those who have been given a book but "practice not the religion of truth" (9:29).

While the Qur'ān provides a framework for Muslims' understanding of Christians and Christianity, particular political, economic, and social considerations have shaped the encounter in each setting. Circumstances and relationships between Muslims and Christians in Egypt, for example, cannot be equated casually with those in Lebanon over the same centuries. Relationships in Egypt, a religious and intellectual center of the Islamic world, were subject to distinctive dynamics not found elsewhere. Cairo, known as the "city of a thousand minarets," is home to al-Azhar, the mosque and university that have been a bastion of Sunnī orthodoxy through much of Islamic history. Still, the Coptic Orthodox Christians in Egypt comprise the largest Christian community in the Arabic-speaking world, representing 9 percent of the total population of 82 million in 2011. As members of an Oriental Orthodox church, the Copts have been completely independent of both the Roman Catholic and the Eastern (Greek, Russian, and Serbian) Orthodox churches since the middle of the fifth century. By contrast, the mountains of Lebanon provided safe haven for a wide range of religious groups—including numerous Catholic, Orthodox, and Protestant Christian communities after the nineteenth century, various Sunnī and Shīʿī Muslims, and the Druze—for more than a thousand years. As minority communities threatened by Christian crusaders or Muslim conquerors or more recent colonial powers, inhabitants of Lebanon have coexisted, cooperated, and clashed in many ways. An examination of Muslim-Christian relations in Spain or the former Yugoslavia or contemporary Indonesia, the world's largest Muslim country, further illustrates the need for careful, contextual analysis.

Historically, Christians living under Islamic rule were usually treated as "protected peoples" (*dhimmī*); the practical implications of *dhimmī* status fluctuated from time to time and from place to place. Even in the best of circumstances, however, it was difficult for Christians and Muslims to engage one another as equals in dialogue.

With few exceptions, Islamic literature that is focused on Christianity has been polemical. The writings of the celebrated fourteenth-century Muslim scholar Ibn Taymīyah (d. 1328 CE) illustrate the point. In his book *al-Jawāb al-ṣaḥīḥ li-man baddala dīn al-masīḥ* (The Correct Answer to Those Who Changed the Religion of Christ), Ibn Taymīyah catalogs the major Islamic theological and philosophical criticisms of Christianity: altering the divine revelation, propagating errant doctrine, and making grievous mistakes in religious practices.

On the Christian side, the advent of Islam in the seventh century presented major challenges, which altered the religious balance of power in several regions of the world. In the short space of a century, Islam transformed the character and culture of many lands from northern India to Spain, disrupted the unity of the Mediterranean world, and displaced the axis of Christendom to the north. Furthermore, Islam challenged

Christian assumptions, since Muslims were successful in both their military and political expansions, but also because their religion presented a puzzling and threatening new intellectual position.

Mutually negative depictions notwithstanding, there were a few more positive voices among medieval Christians. Saint Francis of Assisi (d. 1226), who visited the sultan of Egypt in the midst of the Crusades, instructed his brothers to live among Muslims in peace, avoiding quarrels and disputes. Deep animosity toward Islam was pervasive, however. Martin Luther (d. 1546) wrote several treatises attacking Islam, the Qurʾān, and Muḥammad, motivated in part by the threat of Ottoman Turks advancing on Europe. Luther held the long-standing view that Islam as a post-Christian religion was false by definition.

Nineteenth and Twentieth Centuries. Several developments in the nineteenth and twentieth centuries set the stage for contemporary Muslim-Christian dialogue. First, constantly improving transportation and communication facilitated international commerce and unprecedented levels of migration. Second, scholars gathered a wealth of information on diverse religious practices and belief systems. Although Western studies of Islam were often far from objective, significant changes have occurred. With more accurate information in hand, many non-Muslim scholars concluded that Muḥammad was sincere and devout, challenging the prevailing Western view that he was a shrewd and sinister charlatan. Similarly, the scope and reliability of information on Christianity has broadened the horizons of many Muslim scholars during the past century.

A third major factor contributing to the new context arose from the modern missionary movement among Western Christians. The experience of personal contact with Muslims led many missionaries to reassess their presuppositions. Participants in the three twentieth-century world missionary conferences (Edinburgh in 1910, Jerusalem in 1928, and Tambaram, India, in 1938) wrestled with questions of witness and service in the midst of religious diversity. These conferences stimulated debate and paved the way for ecumenical efforts at interfaith understanding under the auspices of the World Council of Churches (WCC), founded in 1948.

Organized Dialogue Movement. The dialogue movement began during the 1950s when the WCC and the Vatican organized a number of meetings between Christian leaders and representatives of other religious traditions. These initial efforts resulted in the formation of new institutions. In 1964, Pope Paul VI established a Secretariat for Non-Christian Religions to study religious traditions, provide resources, and promote interreligious dialogue through education and by facilitating local efforts by Catholics. Several major documents adopted at Vatican II (1962–1965) focused on interfaith relations. On 25 October 1974, the late King Fayṣal ibn ʿAbd al-ʿAzīz Āl Saʿūd's foremost religious advisors initiated contacts with Catholic officials, when Shaykh Muḥammad Āl Harakan (who became minister of justice), Shaykh Rashīd bin Khunayn (an undersecretary in the same ministry), Shaykh Muḥammad bin Jubayr (the late head of the Majlis al-Shūrā), and Shaykh ʿAbd Āl Musnad (who eventually chaired the Religious Studies Department at Imam Muḥammad University and later became a member of the Higher Council of ʿUlamāʾ), visited Pope Paul VI. At the time, the four Saudi religious scholars participated in the Catholic Church's dialogue between Christians and Muslims, part of a carefully laid out discourse between the two communities. In June 1973, King Fayṣal visited Rome, where the Islamic Cultural Center received approval for construction. The dialogue continued when on 24 April 1974, Fayṣal received, in Riyadh, Cardinal Pignedoli, the president of the Vatican Office of Non-Christian Affairs, who conveyed "the regards of His Holiness, moved by a profound belief in the unification of Islamic and Christian worlds in the worship of a single God, to His Majesty King Faisal as supreme head of the Islamic World." The most visible Christian leader during the last quarter of the twentieth century, Pope John Paul II, was a strong advocate for the new approach to interfaith relations. During his papacy (1978–2005), John Paul II traveled to 117 countries, including several Muslim countries. Remarkably, John Paul II was the first pope to visit a mosque, in Damascus in 2001, illustrating his strong desire for dialogue. Indeed, the spirit of his approach to Islam was evident in a 1985 speech delivered to over eighty thousand Muslims at a soccer stadium in Casablanca, when he declared:

> We believe in the same God, the one God, the Living God who created the world.... In a world which desires unity and peace, but experiences a thousand tensions and conflicts, should not believers come together? Dialogue between Christians and Muslims is today more urgent than ever. It flows from fidelity to God. Too often in the past, we have opposed each other in polemics and wars. I believe that today God invites us to change old practices. We must respect each other and we must stimulate each other in good works on the path to righteousness. (Pope John Paul II, Casablanca, Morocco, 19 August 1985)

In 1989, John Paul II reorganized the Secretariat for Non-Christian Religions and renamed it the Pontifical Council for Interreligious Dialogue.

Modes of Dialogue. While the nature of the encounter differs from place to place and over time, most organized efforts adhere to a particular type of dialogue. As the interfaith dialogue movement emerged, organizers and participants developed several distinctive yet interrelated modes.

"Parliamentary dialogue" is carried on by the large assemblies convened for interfaith discussion. The earliest example was the 1893 World's Parliament of Religions in Chicago. Such gatherings became more frequent in the late twentieth and early twenty-first centuries under the auspices of multifaith organizations such as the World Conference on Religion and Peace and the World Congress of Faiths.

"Institutional dialogue" is the organized effort to initiate and facilitate various kinds of dialogue meetings. In addition to its immediate focus, this approach also seeks to establish and nurture communication between institutional representatives of religious organizations.

"Theological dialogue" includes structured meetings in which theological and philosophical issues are the primary focus. Muslims and Christians, for example, may concentrate on understandings of God, Jesus, revelation, human responsibility in society, and so forth.

"Dialogue in community" and "the dialogue of life" are inclusive categories concentrating on practical issues of common concern—for example, the proper relationship between religion and the state, the rights of religious minorities, issues arising from interreligious marriage, appropriate approaches to mission and witness, and religious values and public education.

"Spiritual dialogue" is concerned with developing, nourishing, and deepening spiritual life through interfaith encounters.

Obstacles. The organized dialogue movement represents a new chapter in the long history between Muslims and Christians. Intentional efforts to understand and cooperate are hopeful signs, particularly for religious communities with a history of mutual antipathy.

Many Muslims are wary of the entire enterprise because of the long history of enmity and the more recent experiences of colonialism. Contemporary political machinations involving the

United States or other major Western powers also create problems for many would-be Muslim participants. Still other Muslims suspect that dialogue is a new guise for Christian missionary activity.

Although the primary impetus for organized dialogue originated largely with Christians and church-related bodies, many conceptual and theological obstacles remain. Some Christians argue that dialogue weakens or undermines Christian mission and witness. For many, the perception of Islam as inherently threatening is deeply ingrained; they are unwilling or unable to move beyond stereotypes or to distinguish between sympathetic and hostile counterparts in the other community.

The horrific attacks of 11 September 2001 on the World Trade Center in New York and the Pentagon in Arlington, Virginia, marked a major turning point in Muslim-Christian relations. In the United States, thousands of churches formed study programs on Islam; many initiated dialogue programs and constructive projects (e.g., churches, mosques, and synagogues together building houses for low-income neighbors).

At the same time, the voices of some highly audible Christian and Muslim leaders became more polemical. Those overtly rejecting the other religion as "false," "demonic," or "evil" found followings in their respective communities. Still, dramatic efforts were made when the custodian of the Two Holy Mosques, ʿAbd Allāh ibn ʿAbd al-ʿAzīz met Pope Benedict XVI at the Vatican on 6 November 2007, as an immense taboo was eradicated between Islam and Catholicism. Beyond its historic dimension, it was fair to ask whether the two men were harbingers of coexistence or whether the meeting was an example of an impossible dialogue. Like Fayṣal before him, ʿAbd Allāh believed in acculturating the kingdom's Muslim scholars with other civilizations, to foster genuine harmony among them. Yet ʿAbd Allāh's task was more urgent, after the erudite and scholarly Pope Benedict XVI broadcast controversial views about non-Catholic beliefs. In fact, the pontiff's exceptionally controversial September 2006 speech at Regensburg University in his native Germany, in which he quoted Emperor Manuel II Paleologos (r. 1391–1425) of the Byzantine Empire to offer judgments on the Prophet, complicated and delayed whatever progress was made in the past. The crusader ruler, who may have held some relevance in the fourteenth century, could not be perceived as a paragon of moral authority in the twenty-first. Of course, the pope repeatedly stressed that the Byzantine emperor's words were not his own, and expressed regret for any offences his utterances caused throughout the Muslim World, even if the Saudi went out of his way to build bridges.

In June 2008, the Saudi ruler invited several Muslim scholars, led by Grand Mufti ʿAbd al-ʿAzīz Āl al-Shaykh, to endorse a call for opening a dialogue with people of other faiths at the start of a historic three-day summit at al-Safah Palace, a step that was followed by a conference in Madrid, cosponsored with the Spanish government, to enlarge his outreach initiatives to defuse interfaith tensions, improve Islam's tarnished political image in the aftermath of 9/11, and restore respect for religious values. Critically, the Saudi announced that the three-day meeting would include Muslim, Christian, and Jewish clerics, as well as representatives of Eastern religions.

Today, Muslim-Christian dialogue represents a new and major effort to understand and cooperate with others in increasingly interdependent and religiously diverse countries. The newness of dialogue and the absence of conceptual clarity have required experimentation. Questions about planning, organization, representation, and topics of discussion need thoughtful consideration and careful collaboration. Through trial and error, advocates of interfaith dialogue in Asia, Africa, Europe, and North

America continue to refine the process. Many local, regional, and international dialogue groups have developed guidelines to address common concerns and avoid pitfalls to further enhance harmony among the world's leading faiths.

BIBLIOGRAPHY

Cragg, Kenneth. *The Call of the Minaret*. 2d ed. Maryknoll, N.Y.: Orbis, 1985. First published 1956. Groundbreaking book challenging Christians to take Islam seriously and on its own terms.

Donner, Fred M. *Muhammad and the Believers: At the Origins of Islam*. Cambridge, Mass.: Belknap Press of Harvard University Press, 2010.

Haddad, Yvonne Yazbeck, and Wadi Zaidan Haddad, eds. *Christian-Muslim Encounters*. Gainesville: University Press of Florida, 1995. An invaluable collection of twenty-eight articles exploring scriptural, theological, historical, and contemporary dimensions of Christian-Muslim relations.

Ibn Taymīyah, Aḥmad. *A Muslim Theologian's Response to Christianity: Ibn Taymiyya's* al-Jawab Al-Sahih. Edited and translated by Thomas F. Michel. Delmar, N.Y.: Caravan, 1984.

Islam and Christian-Muslim Relations. Birmingham, U.K, 1990–. Quarterly journal covering a wide range of historical and contemporary aspects of Christian-Muslim issues.

Islamochristiana. Rome, 1975–. Scholarly annual journal produced by the Pontifico Istituto di Studi Arabi e d'Islamistica. Articles, notices, and reviews are in English, French, and Arabic.

Jukko, Risto. *Trinity in Unity in Christian-Muslim Relations: The Work of the Pontifical Council for Interreligious Dialogue*. Leiden, Netherlands: Brill, 2007.

Mohammed, Ovey N. *Muslim-Christian Relations: Past, Present, Future*. Maryknoll, N.Y.: Orbis, 1999.

The Muslim World. Hartford, Conn., 1911–. Indispensable quarterly journal devoted to the study of Islam and Christian-Muslim relations past and present.

Sherwin, Byron L, and Harold Kasimow, eds. *John Paul II and Interreligious Dialogue*. Maryknoll, N.Y.: Orbis, 1999.

Volf, Miroslav, Ghazi bin Muhammad, and Melissa Yarrington. *A Common Word: Muslims and Christians on Loving God and Neighbor*. Grand Rapids, Mich.: Wm. B. Eerdmans, 2009.

Watt, William Montgomery. *Muslim-Christian Encounters: Perceptions and Misperceptions*. London: Routledge, 1991. Reflections by a prominent Christian scholar of Islam.

CHARLES A. KIMBALL
Updated by JOSEPH A. KÉCHICHIAN

MUSLIM-JEWISH RELATIONS. The Israeli-Palestinian conflict colors the current state of Muslim-Jewish relations, shading certain parts of an intertwined history and highlighting instances of strife, as well as of reconciliation. This coloration can be perceived in multiple images of Muslim-Jewish relations. A recurrent image is one of animosity in which present conflict appears an inevitable result of religious foundations.

The expression of animosity can take the form of statements such as "The Jews deny Muslim authenticity by refusing to read Deuteronomy 18 as foretelling the arrival of Muḥammad," or "The Jews follow a corrupted Torah that demands conquest," or "Muslims have battled Jews since the time of the Prophet Muḥammad," or "The Qurʾān encourages the hatred of Jews." Such arguments and others more virulent appear in religious booklets that circulate widely and often initiate first contact between pious Jews and Muslims. Among the less pious and more affluent, a parallel impulse assumes a completely different cast. Here Biblical and Qurʾānic parallels attest to a shared spiritual life, the culture of Andalusia represents a golden age, and the memories of Jews from Muslim lands offer paradigms for future interactions. These arguments, at times, speak polemically to religious nationalisms and, at other times, present an alternate reality based on the interpretation of religious texts. Both species of argument, however diametrical, address the Israeli-Arab conflict, whether they name it or not.

How then to speak of Muslim-Jewish relations? Gil Anidjar has suggested that it may well be impossible since Christian thought has determined the social positions of Judaism and Islam. Must Muslim-Jewish relations then be conceived in postcolonial or, more magnanimously, trilateral terms? Many scholars of early Islam stress the religious lexicon shared by Christians, Jews, and Muslims in the Arabian Peninsula. With a common repertoire of stories, each group sought self-definition by varying the themes of a collective narrative. This helps to explain why a set of identical religious ancestors does not breed harmony, but it fails to explain the impact of the shared story. The notion of the three as "Abrahamic religions" distills a complex legacy by identifying a common founding ancestor. What, in fact, does Abraham bequeath his variegated religious descendants? More psychologically inclined scholars have spoken to the dysfunction inherent in a founding family in which two wives and their sons compete for the preference of Abraham and God alike. Exile and willingness to be sacrificed characterize this coveted preference.

An account of the many parallels between Islam and Judaism has not yet been provided. To date, comparisons have been more localized and focused on philology, legal tenets, or philosophy. A good part of the shared tradition results from a founding tribal social structure that memorializes battles and recounts family dramas. Thus the experiences of ancestors/prophets like Abraham, Isaac, Jacob, Joseph, and Moses were recognizable to early Muslims and Jews and were reflected in social norms. The centrality of the tribal history ensures vivid alliances even in nontribal social settings. Sustained practices resulted in similar scripture, and the laws contained in scripture governed most aspects of life. Practice and tradition then go a long way toward accounting for textual parallels in Jewish and Muslim sacred books. Of course, authority also plays a large role in Islam and Judaism. Legal and narrative opinions alike require a lineage of respected sages to support them. Both Judaism and Islam preserve revelation in a book, which means that authorized exegesis is a path to God.

Revelation in Islam and Judaism follows a similar path: God speaks to a prophet on a mountain who in turn produces a scriptural record to guide adherents. Moses's halting speech and Muḥammad's illiteracy prove that the prophet is a medium and that a human being, no matter how exalted, cannot be a manifestation of God. The Qurʾān and the Torah differ more in genre than in content. In the Qurʾān, revelation unfolds in a highly structured poetic form dense with meaning. Although widely characterized as the world's first prose narrative, the Torah also contains legal compendia, poetry, and proverb. Even parallel stories like that of Joseph have a different effect on readers due to the variant genres of poetry and prose.

Judaism and Islam revere a transcendent God through a strict monotheism. With mandated daily prayers, sacred seasons, and family law, both religions command significant identitarian aspects. Local culture and religion exert mutual influence at the same time that a global religious community arises from a relatively closed canon of sacred writings. Where Islam seeks to expand the community—the *ummah*—Judaism limits proselytizing by maintaining that Jews share an ethnic and a genetic background. In both cases, the modern merger of religion and nationalism has enabled religious law to function as state law and transformed the perception and experience of religion as a result. It is increasingly difficult to think of contemporary Islam outside the frameworks of Saudi Wahhābīyah, Iranian Shīʿī, or the Egyptian Muslim Brotherhood, etc. Similarly, Zionism in general and religious Zionism more particularly impact Jewish experience and perception.

The entanglement of Judaism and Islam with politics manifests itself nowhere more strongly than in Jerusalem, the only remaining Middle Eastern city where significant numbers of Muslims and Jews meet. Such meetings are rarely of a harmonious nature. While the tensions of Jerusalem arise from political dispute, divergent religious narratives underlie or at least lend pathos to the political. The Temple Mount/ Ḥaram al-Sharīf represents for Jews the site where the Temple once stood and marks for Muslims the Night Journey of the Prophet Muḥammad from Mecca to Jerusalem and his subsequent ascent to heaven. The sacred mount is one and the same, yet serves as a site where the divergence of Judaism and Islam becomes most apparent. The excavation of tunnels that once facilitated the passage of priests from one end of the Temple to the other and the restrictions on who can enter the Dome of the Rock and al-Aqṣā, the two mosques on the mount, seem to one group as essential preservation and to the other as a violation of religious autonomy.

Note how Islam and Judaism alike support tradition through the stability of scripture and the centrality of textual study. The Torah, the Qurʾān, and their supporting exegetical literatures are complex works with multiple simultaneous positions. The preservation of tradition also entails fluctuation. This means that there is no set or predetermined trajectory that Muslim-Jewish relations must follow. Such relationships can be revived, maintained, or transformed all within the framework of tradition.

BIBLIOGRAPHY

Adang, Camilla. "The Proofs of Prophethood." In *Muslim Writers on Judaism and the Hebrew Bible: From Ibn Rabban to Ibn Hazm*, pp. 139–191. Leiden, Netherlands: E. J. Brill, 1996.

Anidjar, Gil. *The Jew, the Arab: A History of the Enemy*. Stanford, Calif.: Stanford University Press, 2003.

Bakhos, Carol. *Ishmael on the Border: Rabbinic Portrayals of the First Arab*. Albany: State University of New York Press, 2006.

Cole, Peter, trans. and ed. *The Dream of the Poem: Hebrew Poetry from Muslim and Christian Spain, 950–1492*. Princeton, N.J.: Princeton University Press, 2007.

Firestone, Reuven. "Comparative Studies in Bible and Qur'an: A Fresh Look at Genesis 22 in Light of Sura 37." In *Judaism and Islam: Boundaries, Communication, and Interaction; Essays in Honor of William M. Brinner*, edited by Benjamin H. Hary, John L. Hayes, and Fred Astren, pp. 169–184. Leiden, Netherlands: Brill, 2000.

Khan, Irfan Ahmad. "The Qur'anic View of Moses as a Messenger." In *Jewish-Muslim Encounters: History, Philosophy, and Culture*, edited by Charles Selengut, pp. 35–50. St. Paul, Minn.: Paragon House, 2001.

Menocal, María Rosa. *The Ornament of the World: How Muslims, Jews, and Christians Created a Culture of Tolerance in Medieval Spain*. Boston: Little, Brown, 2002.

Mir, Mustansir. "Kabbalah and Sufism: A Comparative Look at Jewish and Islamic Mysticism." In *Jewish-Muslim Encounters: History, Philosophy and Culture*, edited by Charles Selengut, pp. 165–179. St. Paul, Minn.: Paragon House, 2001.

Rahman, Fazlur. *Major Themes of the Qurʾān*. Minneapolis: Bibliotheca Islamica, 1980.

Stillman, Norman A., comp. *The Jews of Arab Lands: A History and Source Book*. Philadelphia: Jewish Publication Society of America, 1979.

Wasserstrom, Steven M. *Between Muslim and Jew: The Problem of Symbiosis under Early Islam*. Princeton, N.J.: Princeton University Press, 1995.

Wheeler, Brannon M. *Moses in the Quran and Islamic Exegesis*. London: RoutledgeCurzon, 2002.

Rachel Havrelock

Muslim League. *See* India; Pakistan.

Muslim Political History. What follows is a history of Muslim regimes, political ideas, and institutions from the beginning of Islam until the nineteenth century. Islam was born as a message that called its followers to unite, preach, mobilize, and worship under the leadership of its prophet, Muḥammad, at first in persecution as a minority and then as a struggling community of believers in Medina. This struggle has been enshrined as symbolic and normative in the religious and cultural memory of Muslims, reported and commented upon in the two religious sources of Islam, the Qur'ān and the Prophet's model (*sunnah*), and reflected in the structure of Islamic law. Thus Islam was born as a political and politically triumphant message. The birth of the first Muslim government is dated to the crucial moment of the flight (*hijra*) of the persecuted Meccan Muslim community to Medina, then called Yathrib, in the year 622. Instrumental in inviting him was the influential portion of the two Arab tribes of the town that had embraced Islam prior to the Prophet's arrival, but he was acceptable even to the nonbelievers of the city as an arbiter and peacemaker between two the long-warring tribes. Muḥammad began his fledgling political leadership by forging a political alliance out of the disparate tribes of Medina, including the two pagan and three Jewish tribes, as well as various allies in the suburbs, thus creating a document that has been called by some the first written constitution in history (for questions surrounding the authenticity of this document, see al-ʿUmarī, 1991, vol. 2, p.102). The Pact of Medina is a document of notable political genius, allowing the Prophet to establish his authority with a light hand. It declared the followers of Islam to be a community above tribal and clan affiliations, but acknowledged the existing organization of other tribes, called on all signatories to unite in defending Medina against invaders, recognized the existing tribal norms relating to mutual transgressions, accorded each tribe the right to manage its own affairs and conflicts, and declared the Prophet to be the arbiter in case of disputes between tribes. In the various ensuing disputes within Medina and against the Meccans, the Prophet led the Muslim community through diplomacy and military action to victory which, once Mecca fell to the Muslims in the eighth year of Hijra, expanded, after a couple of fateful battles, to the rest of Arabia.

Within the Muslim community the Prophet wielded complete authority, including spheres we may recognize as "religious" as well as "political," whereas his authority over the other tribes was, by virtue of the fact that they did not believe in his message, political, negotiated, and fluid. Within his community his authority was based on his prophetic calling and repeatedly asserted in the Qur'ān, "Obey God and obey the Messenger" (3:32), "Those who swear allegiance to you [Muḥammad], covenant with God" (48:10), "Whoever obeys the Messenger, obeys God" (4:80), and so on.

By 632, when the Prophet passed away, the Muslim community had established its authority over much of the Arabian Peninsula, and the Qur'ān was seen as having laid out the foundations of a religion (beliefs and rituals), a political entity, as well as a legal system. The Qur'ān addresses not just ritual and belief, which are its primary concerns, but emphatically pronounces on all aspects of life ranging from political, economic, and social to spiritual and intellectual. It establishes political practices such as *shūrā*, or consultation (3:159; 42:38), calls the believers to obey their political authorities within limits (4:59; 4:83), and calls on them to maintain unity and mutual bonds of fraternity, and assigns to them collectively a mission of "commanding right and forbidding wrong" assigned to the believing community (*ummah*) as a whole (3:110). The economic commandments include the prohibition of usury or interest (2:278–279), the establishment of private property and punishment for theft (5:38), the practice of a mandatory alms tax (*zakāt*), established "So that the wealth may not accumulate to the wealthy amongst you" (59:7). In the social realm it establishes an extended family structure and regulates marriage, divorce, inheritance, and family relations generally and in great detail. It is, furthermore, a self-reflective document that declares itself to be divine, infallible, deliberately composed, universal, and absolutely essential for any claim of relationship to God, whose laws must be embraced in totality and without arbitrarily rejecting any of its parts, thus making it problematic for any political aspirant to claim authority, political or religious, except on its terms. Furthermore the Qur'ān's egalitarian teachings and its direct availability to ordinary believers without an authorized priesthood to interpret it made it difficult for political authorities to claim religious monopoly.

The Caliphate. After the demise of the Prophet Muḥammad (632), his Companions differed on his succession, a dispute that became, in hindsight, a point of sectarian division. Due to the paucity of the sources and the sectarian nature of historiography, it is difficult to get a conclusive picture of these developments. On the whole the Prophet's successors (*khulafā'*, sing. *khalīfah* or *khilāfah*; henceforth caliph/s) followed his policies loyally without claiming his full religious authority but serving, nonetheless, as political as well as limited religious authorities. The first four caliphs, known as the Rightly Guided Caliphs (*rāshidūn*) by the Sunnīs, are: Abū Bakr (r. 632–634); 'Umar ibn al-Khaṭṭāb (r. 634–644); 'Uthmān ibn 'Affān (r. 644–656); and 'Alī ibn Abī Ṭālib (r. 656–661).

The Qur'ān and most likely the Prophet himself having been silent on the subject, it was the conduct and decisions of Abū Bakr that helped define the role of the Prophet's successor to a large degree. The first defining moment was Abū Bakr's purported deployment of the Qur'ānic verse in the wake of the Prophet's demise which reminded believers that the mission of Islam was not to be over with the life of the Prophet (3:144). Abū Bakr's decisiveness against the so-called apostate tribes settled another fundamental question for centuries to come, if not forever. The question ultimately was whether allegiance to the Medinan state, the expression of the political unity of the community (*ummah*), was part and parcel of being Muslim; Abū Bakr's answer was a decisive yes—although the implications of this affirmation remained ambiguous. A third intervention by the first caliph, equally significant but less appreciated, was his explication of the role of the caliph in his inauguration speech: "I have been given charge over you while I am not the best of you. If I do well, support me, and if I err, straighten me... obey me so long as I obey Allāh and His Messenger—but if I disobey Allāh and His Messenger, you have no obligation to obey me" (al-Tabarī, 1993, p. 11).

This statement of Abū Bakr responded to a central question about the nature of the office of Prophet's successor, namely whether or not that office carried with it any inherently divine authority that gave an infallible character to its occupier. What's more, the guardian of the community, in this view, had a custodian: the *ummah* itself. This view of political authority, found in the Qur'ān and the early practice and continuous with Arab nomadic egalitarianism, can be called the community-centered view. It contrasts with the alternative, ruler-centered, perspective that prevailed in the Near East generally at the time and came to gradually dominate the Umayyad and 'Abbāsid perceptions. These two views corresponded with the two sources of hierarchy that inevitably developed, one based on seniority or precedence (*sābiqa*) and excellence (*faḍīla*) in Islam, and the other based on political power, which was to soon fall into the hands of those excelling in political acumen and tribal power play rather than piety. The two different logics of power set in motion by the meteoric rise of

Islamic rule grew into rebellion. Some disaffected contingents from Egypt accused the third caliph, ʿUthmān, of nepotism. One version of this history, necessarily based on extrapolation from scanty sources, holds that ʿUthmān's policies came to rely, in the face of an expanding and diverse empire, on the strong tribal loyalty of his fatefully powerful Umayyad clan, thus excluding the pious in favor of the loyal. The fourth caliph, ʿAlī, inherited a turbulent office and was unable, due possibly to his idealism, or naïveté, to rein in the conflicts arising from the murder of the third caliph. ʿUthmān had come from the Umayyad clan of the Quraysh, which had been since before Islam the more powerful rival to the Prophet's clan, the Hāshimīs, and due to this rivalry its powerful members had opposed Islam until the final conquest of Mecca. Muʿāwiya ibn Abī Sufyān (d. 680), ʿUthmān's cousin who was then the governor of Syria, demanded that ʿAlī execute or hand over ʿUthmān's assassins, but ʿAlī found himself in a position abandoned by many of the senior Companions and surrounded by the rebels who had an active role in his very election. The military conflict between ʿAlī and Muʿāwiya, in particular the Battle of Ṣiffīn, was to become the single most fateful and divisive event in Islamic history, wreaking havoc on the unity and psyche of the Muslim community that never could fully recover from what came to be known as the First Fitnah of Islam (656–661), which had begun with ʿUthmān's assassination and did not cease until ʿAlī's assassination and the transfer of power to Muʿāwiya. Muʿāwiya is a highly contested figure, villainized by the pro-ʿAlid party that came to call itself *shīʿat ʿAlī* (Alī's partisans) or simply Shīʿa, but has been evaluated with ambivalence by the Sunnīs (for a historiographically more nuanced view of Muʿāwiya, see Keshk).

The Umayyads (661–750). Whatever the actual events, many have looked back to conclude that ʿAlī's piety, idealism, and otherworldliness were overcome by the political shrewdness of his rivals, while he needed to wrestle with the contingencies of governing and keeping together a rapidly expanding Islamic empire. Muʿāwiya's political skill reined in the centrifugal forces that might have ended the unity of the nascent Muslim state and Islam's political project altogether but it did so at the cost of some of the ideals of Islam. His reign nonetheless provided the peace and stability that ʿAlī had been unable to secure, which is probably what silenced his many critics among the senior Companions. Muʿāwiya's appointment of his son Yazīd as his designated successor (*walī al-ʿahd*) without the proper consultation (*shūrā*) that had been expected both in Islamic and Arab tribal tradition was a fateful act that set Islamic history on a dynastic path. From a different perspective it was perhaps inevitable that Islam's egalitarian political ideal, ensconced in the piety of its first rulers rather than in robust institutions, would give way to the political norms of the time in a diverse, expanding, and conflict-ridden empire. The tragic killing by an army of Yazīd's of ʿAlī's son and the Prophet's grandson, al-Ḥasan (d. 680), who had set out along with his family in order to lead a rebellion brewing in Kufa against Yazīd, later served to give this conflict theological significance. The psychological ramifications of the slaughter of the Prophet's grandson by an army of the Prophet's successor, whatever the political context, have since been tremendous and potent.

Three types of political norms seem to underlie the extremely contentious history of the period: those associated with the Umayyads or those generally concerned with the unity, peace, and defense of the caliphate sided with the Umayyads; those associated with the ʿAlīds moved further toward political idealism and theological radicalism; while a third political rationale underlay the concerns of those who belonged to neither type of elite and, resenting the elitism and partisanship of both sides, yearned for the equality and consultation (*shūrā*) of the Arab tradition endorsed by the Qurʾān, the Prophet, and the early caliphs.

The egalitarian impulse in its most radical form was expressed in the Khārijīs, a group of Arab tribes that had seceded from ʿAlī's army under the premise that he should not have accepted human arbitration (*taḥkīm*) with Muʿāwiya's army, for he had been in the right by God's book and, since "Judgment (*ḥukm*) belongs to none but God" (6:57; 12:40; 12:67), no human arbitration could be justified. The Khārijīs increasingly leaned toward greater hostility and fanaticism, excommunicating sinners and deeming the majority of Muslims who disagreed with them legitimate targets of bloodshed, threatened and were fought by all subsequent caliphs, including ʿAlī and Muʿāwiya. The Khārijīs' grievances can be attributed to two factors: the tribal dynamics and the monopolization of wealth and power by the Qurashī elite, and the Khārijīs' own fanatic proclivities and rigid interpretation of the Qurʾān; the two factors, doubtless, fed each other. Notwithstanding their egalitarianism, violent behavior and fanaticism were perhaps more than any other factors responsible for dampening the Muslim majority's enthusiasm for such causes. The demand for *shūrā* had not been the sole monopoly of the Khārijīs, and it seems to have been the rallying cry for most of the more than a dozen major rebellions during the ninety years of Umayyad rule. The nearly successful revolt of ʿAbd Allāh ibn al-Zubayr (d. 692) and the temporary establishment of his caliphate had begun in the name of general *shūrā*, as had other major revolts like that of ʿAbd al-Raḥmān ibn al-Ashʿath (d. 704). The Qādarī rebels, like the Jabrī, had called for general *shūrā* along with Umayyad injustice as their grievances. Khārijī fanaticism, along with the failure of most of the revolts, however, made *shūrā* a threat to unity and stability, and an unpopular option in itself. The rulers rejected *shūrā* except as an internal family consultation, whereas the Shīʿīs, not as serious a threat at first as the Khārijīs, rejected it even more forcefully than the Umayyads in favor of the guidance of an imam whose piety could be guaranteed, or, as the doctrine developed during the eighth century, who was infallible due to his descent from the Prophet. The Marwānids, a clan of the Umayyads, came to power after the almost-successful revolt of Ibn al-Zubayr, and, facing a tremendous deficit of legitimacy, drew on the claims of their office as caliphs by claiming to be God's appointed deputies and on renewed *jihād* at the frontiers.

The most extraordinary Umayyad in Muslim tradition is ʿUmar ibn ʿAbd al-ʿAzīz or ʿUmar II (d. 719), who stands out for having righted all that had gone wrong in Umayyad practice since the *rāshidūn* caliphs, thus earning him the honorary title of Fifth Rightly Guided Caliph; he became the yardsticks against which all the vices of the Umayyads could be measured. There is little reason to doubt the general outline of the account of ʿUmar II's life and reforms, which, even if exaggerated, depicts how the eighth-century *ʿulamāʾ*, when these accounts were reduced to writing, saw their political predicament. Among his most remarkable acts, according to some accounts, after being bequeathed the caliphate, was to give it up, as the ideal Muslim caliph should, and leave the matter to the *shūrā* of the Muslims.

The ʿAbbāsids (ruled 749–945; reigned 749–1258, and in Cairo 1261–1517). The ʿAbbāsids inherited in the eighth century the Umayyad problems and eagerly adopted and developed the emerging Umayyad solutions but increasingly employed the Persian-Sassanid political heritage and wisdom, which included a highly stratified social ideal, a professional army (composed, in this case, of imported Turkish slaves), religion as an arm of government, and a divinized emperor. One new and major challenge for the ʿAbbāsids was that posed by the increasingly consolidated group of the Sunnī *ʿulamāʾ*, more cautiously referred to, at this early stage, as the "proto-Sunnīs." The proto-Sunnīs began to claim authority as the chief guardians of the tradition, the *sunnah*, but were labeled by their contemporary detractors, the rationalist theologians, as the *nābiṭa* (a general term for an emergent, threatening populist current) or the *ṭughām* (rabble). They were a result of the consolidation of different moderate ideological tendencies that consolidated against the radical alternatives that had, in making sense of the First Fitnah, rejected one or more groups of Companions, such as the Khārijīs (who denounced Qurashī leadership generally and were fought by both ʿAlī and the Umayyads) and the proto-Shīʿī (who denounced the Umayyads and all the Companions of the Prophet except those who supported ʿAlī). The new grouping was diverse in its attitude toward the First Fitnah and was, at its core, the tradition-centered group (*ahl al-ḥadīth*) that most admired the Companions who had remained neutral in the ʿAlī-Muʿāwiya conflict, and gradually incorporated those who were moderately pro-ʿAlid as well as those that had been pro-Umayyad. The confrontation between the ʿAbbāsid caliph al-Maʾmūn (d. 833) and the proto-Sunnīs, led by a particularly unassuming and ascetic *ḥadīth* scholar from Baghdad, Aḥmad ibn Ḥanbal, was precipitated by the ambitious caliph's desire to claim the religious authority that the Shīʿī had granted their religious imams, but rarely had any Sunnī caliph ever wielded or claimed it. Al-Maʾmūn, a brilliant and ambitious rationalist theologian and scientist, desperate for legitimacy, inspired by the absolutist ideals from his Persian upbringing, and threatened by the growing religious and moral authority of the traditionalists, chose the issue of the "createdness of the Qurʾān" (*khalq al-Qurʾān*) as the most likely to demonstrate and put an end to their simple-minded faith that amounted, in his view, to polytheism (*shirk*). Aḥmad's heroic persistence, ever since the stuff of legend, had exactly the opposite effect, and the Sunnī *ʿulamāʾ* were never again challenged for authority by a caliph in this way. With the rise of the military patronage states created by invading horse warriors in the next century, the nature and legitimacy of rule so changed that such a challenge was no longer possible or necessary.

During the ninth century, the ʿAbbāsid caliphate fragmented. Based, even at its height, on delicate alliances, the cracks were progressively aggravated by a number of factors, including the agricultural decline in the Iraqi hinterland, the perpetual problem of dynastic succession that invited fraternal warfare and palace intrigues, fiscal mismanagement by bureaucratic families, and the economic burden of maintaining professional armies comprised of unruly Turkish slaves. In the event the fragmentation manifested itself as provincial governors sought independence, followed by the rise of various kingdoms (Būyids, Fāṭimids, Ḥamdānids) during the tenth century, that were established by military adventurers who expressed their opposition in theological terms as Shīʿī—thus marking the tenth century as the Shīʿī century. There soon followed a series of Central Asian nomadic invasions.

The process of provincial independence is instructive in shedding light on the nature of ʿAbbāsid rule. Al-Maʾmūn's Khorāsānian governor Ṭāhir, who had been a key ally in his rebellion against his brother al-Amīn, claimed de facto independence (by omitting al-Maʾmūn's name from the Friday sermon) but was allowed to pass the governorship to his son, thus establishing his claim to a dynasty that lasted for half a century and, due to the inability of its last dynastic representative, was handed to the Sāmānids, who had originated as a local landowning power in Balkh, in northern Afghanistan. The caliphs depended on these Iranian dynasties in Khorāsān to keep in check the Shīʿī *duʿāt* from the Caspian region (Gīlān), in the north, and the Khārijī-leaning raiders, Ṣaffarids, from Sīstān,in the south. The Ṣaffarid ʿAmr ibn Layth succeeded in taking Nishapur from the Ṭāhirids in 873, and the caliph in Baghdad was compelled to accept him as his governor in Sīstān, Khorāsān, and Fārs. The ambitious Ṣaffarid coveted Transoxiana but was defeated by the Sāmānids and lost its territories, except the original base in Sīstān, where the Ṣaffarids lasted for six more centuries. A similar dynamic ensued in the southwest in Egypt, where the governor Aḥmad ibn Ṭūlūn established his dynasty right over governorship which lasted for less than half a century. The rising Shīʿī threat proved decisive in both wings, leading to the rule of the Būyids in the east and the center and Fāṭimids in the west in North Africa and Egypt, putting an end to ʿAbbāsid power, although not their reign, in the tenth century that has therefore been called the Shīʿī century. It was during this period in Baghdad, at the end of the High ʿAbbāsid caliphate and the Būyid period and in the face of the rising Shīʿī theological and political threat, that the caliphate theories were articulated by Sunnī theologians.

The Sultanistic, or Military Patronage, Period (Tenth–Fifteenth Centuries). The Būyids, mercenaries of Persian stock and Twelver Shīʿī background, took over the east and Baghdad itself but left the Sunnī caliph in place, rather than inviting a Shīʿī imam who would have used the Shīʿī creed and lorded it over them. The Ghaznavid dynasty was created in Afghanistan on the eastern border of Sāmānid dynasty by rebellious Turkish slave commanders of the Sāmānids. Under Maḥmūd's (d. 998) consummate military leadership, the Ghaznavids reached their height, annexing Khwārizm in the north and Ray and Hamadān from the Būyids in the west, thus creating the largest kingdom in the region, whose administrative apparatus was based on Persian

Major Dynasties in Muslim History

Independent Dynasties during the High ʿAbbāssid Caliphate (Eighth–Tenth Centuries)

***To the west*:** Spanish Umayyads (756–1031); Idrīsids (Morocco, 789–926); Ṭūlūnids (Egypt, under ʿAbbāsid tutelage, 868–905)

***To the east*:** Ṭāhirids (Khorāsān, under ʿAbbāsid tutelage, 821–73); Sāmānids (Khorāsān and Transoxania, under ʿAbbāsid tutelage, 819–1005); Ṣaffārids (Sīstān, 867–c. 1495)

***Anti-ʿAbbāsid Shīʿī dynasties (the Shīʿī century)*:** Fāṭimids (Egypt, Syria, and North Africa, 909–1171); Ḥamdānids (Upper Syria and parts of Iraq, 905–1004); Būyids (Persia and Iraq, 932–1062); Rassids or Zaydīs of Yemen (9th–20th centuries)

Sultanic Period Dynasties (Tenth–Thirteenth Centuries)

***To the east*:** Ghaznavids (Khorāsān, Afghanistan, northern India, 977–1186); Ghūrīds (Khorāsān, Afghanistan, northern India, c. 1000–1215); the Delhi Sultans (northern India, 1206–1555)

***To the west*:** Almoravids or al-Murābiṭūn (North Africa and Spain, 1056–1147); Almohads or al-Muwaḥḥidūn (North Africa and Spain, 1130–1269); Marinids (Morocco, 1196–1549); Ḥafṣids (Tunisia and Algeria, 1228–1574)

***Sunni Military Patronage dynasties in the center*:** Seljuks (Iraq and Persia, 1038–1194); Ayyūbids (Egypt, Syria, Diyarbakir, 1169–1250 in Egypt and Syria, lasting elsewhere until the 13th–15th centuries)

Post-Mongol Dynasties (Thirteenth–Fifteenth Centuries)

Mamlūks (Egypt and Syria, 1250–1517); Mongol Il-Khanid (Persia, 1256–1353); Mongol Golden Horde (southern Russia, western China, 1226–1502); Tīmūrids (Persia and Tranoxania, 1370–1506); Aq Qoyunlu (Diyarbakir, eastern Anatolia, Azerbaijan, 1378–1508)

Early Modern Period ("Gunpowder") Empires (Fifteenth–Nineteenth Centuries)

Safavids (Persia, 1501–1732); Qājārs (Persia, 1779–1924); Mughals (India, 1526–1857); Ottomans (1300s–1924)

Source: Bosworth, 1980.

administrative heritage, thus distancing the Ghaznavids from their pagan Turkish steppe background. Maḥmūd's son, however, lost Khorāsān and Khwārizm to another wave of nomadic Turkish invasions from the north, and the Seljuks, and the Ghaznavids thereafter turned their attention eastward to northern India.

Next came the Seljuks, the nomad tribes from the Central Asian steppe that had been previously kept in check by Tranoxanian governor dynasties such as the Sāmānids. The Seljuks had entered Ghaznavid service in 1030s, but in keeping with their nomadic ways proceeded to plunder Khorāsān. The large Ghaznavid army being no match for the Seljuks' agility, they eventually occupied the cities and defeated the Ghaznavids and then the Būyids, entering Baghdad in 1058. These uncouth barbarian saviors were received by the ʿAbbāsid caliph with some gratitude and much trepidation. Given that the Seljuk arrival in the Muslim world inaugurated a new era, this apprehension was warranted. The Seljuks entered the lands of Islam not as slaves imported by the ʿAbbāsids, as had been the case so far, but as intact Turkish tribal groups that had already converted to Sunnī Islam and who could therefore, given the situation in Baghdad, claim the ideological role of the saviors of the Sunnī caliphate and of Sunnī Islam against the Shīʿī and against the Byzantine threat. By defeating the Būyids and warding off the much more ominous Fāṭimid threat from Egypt and, ultimately, the historic victory against Byzantium at Manzikert in 1071 (which had been likely motivated by geopolitical rather than religious reasons), the Seljuks could now lay claim to a kind of pragmatic legitimacy as defenders of Islam. The Seljuks gave final form to the characteristic institutions and patterns of governance of the Middle East, in particular under the able Persian vizier Niẓām al-Mulk, by inserting themselves as legitimate sultans through shrewd religious politics, supporting and balancing legal and theological schools through the crucial instruments of endowing *madrasahs* for the teaching of Sunnī jurisprudence and auxiliary sciences and thus patronize the *ʿulamāʾ* and *khānqāh* to support the Ṣūfīs, thus effecting what has come to be known as the "Sunnī Revival." (For a critique of this intentionalist view, see Chamberlain, 2005.)

Political models and thought. During this era the central lands of Islam suffered from two major invasions by nomad warriors, the Crusades, and the destruction of the whole region by the Mongols. In fact, the social, cultural, and political institutions that emerged during this period spread to the rest of the Muslim world, putting an end to the diversity of the immediate post-ʿAbbāsid period and characterizing Islamic societies until the modern period. The statecraft of the period was the consequence of an uncomfortable mix of various sociopolitical cultures: 1) The Persian-Sassanid model, reflected in the great Persian epic of kings, the *Shāhnāmah* by Firdawsī, to the Turkish Ghaznavid Sultan Maḥmūd in the early eleventh century, and the mirrors-for-princes genre, such as *Siyasat-namah*, written by the influential Persian vizier of the Seljuks, Niẓām al-Mulk (d. 1092). This model had been based on the ideal of an absolutist monarch, stratified society, and religion as the imperial ideology; 2) The Central Asian nomadic tribal, or Turkmen, model, which was the ethnicity that provided rulers and their armies to much of the Islamic world for more than a millennium (tenth–nineteenth centuries). Unlike its more egalitarian Arab counterpart, Turkmen tribal organization had been hierarchical and hence more compatible with Persian statecraft. The ruler in this model reigned as the senior member of the dynastic clan whereas other male members of the family shared political power as governors of regions. Succession was not by generally accepted rule as seniority or primogeniture but by acclamation by leaders of the polity of the most astute, decisive, and militarily effective member of the household; the potential successors often battled to prove their right, a literal survival of the fittest to rule. The Arab tribal model of the Umayyads and in most cases the ʿAbbāsids, in contrast, had generally led to consultative succession, and even the reigning caliphs felt bound by the testamentary designations of their predecessors; and 3) In the political practice of this period the substantive political teachings of Islam, either as ensconced in the scriptural texts or the practice of the *rāshidūn*, or as redacted and theorized in the Sunnī caliphate discourse, played only a minor role. This arrangement in which the political power rested with the military elite and religious authority with the *ʿulamā*ʾ has been claimed by some scholars as "secularization" and others in the similar vein as a "medieval Islamic constitution" of sorts. But this is an unpersuasive reading of a complex situation. It is impossible to deny the complete infusion of the political ideas and practices of the period with religious ideas in general and Islam in particular, ranging from the caliphate politics of the sultans, the caliph's formal (but merely ceremonial) bestowal of the patent of investiture to the sultans, the essential grounding of the legitimacy of the sultan's power as the defender of Islam, and the actual substance of the laws governing the social and economic fabric of the Islamic world, all derived from the Sharīʿah or was justified in its terms.

The absence of a direct role of Islamic political imperatives in medieval statecraft can be understood as a function of how theory, practice, and interests came to be aligned. To be sure the invading "barbarian" sultans could not claim the formal legitimacy required by the caliphate discourse, which required a Qurashī lineage for the Sunnīs among other things. Nor would the ambitious sultans have been willing to submit unilaterally to the substantive requirements of the laws of Islam as elaborated by the social elite, the *ʿulamā*ʾ, of the conquered cities. The Shīʿī Būyids' preference for a Sunnī caliph under house arrest over a Shīʿī imam neatly demonstrates the obvious primacy of politics over ideology for the rulers of the period, if not for others. But the *ʿulamā*ʾ, for their part, did not, on the whole, wish to extend their political theory to include the sultans as legitimate rulers either (exceptions being al-Juwaynī, Ibn Taymīyah, and Ṭarṭūshī). Driven partly by a mix of theoretical conservatism, mistrust of commonsense reason, fear of challenges to their authority, internal divisions, and, most of all, the fear of the manipulation of Islamic doctrine by reasons of power, the *ʿulamā*ʾ mainstream did not for the whole of the medieval era adopt an alternative to the caliphate theory, opting rather to accord a certain functional (or substantive) legitimacy to the rulers in return for the latter's defense of the laws and lands of Islam.

The Post-Mongol World (Thirteenth–Fifteenth Centuries). The late medieval era or post-Mongol period is largely continuous with the early medieval period in its institutions and ideas. An important institutional development was the rise of military slaves as rulers in the Syro-Egyptian world.

Mamlūks. The Mamlūk sultanate had its origins in the bodyguard (*ḥalqa*) of Ṣalāḥ al-Dīn al-Ayyūbī (1240–1249), Ṣalaḥ al-Dīn's son. The Mamlūks superseded the Ayyūbids in Egypt and Syria under the constraint of two military crises: the crusade of Saint Louis (1249–1250) and the Mongol invasion of Syria (1259–1260). They led an expeditionary force into Palestine, and defeated the Mongols at ʿAyn Jālūt in 1260. Ẓāhir Baybars was the effective founder of the Mamlūk sultanate. In his comparatively long reign (1260–1277), a high degree of internal stability, contrasting with the political vicissitudes of the previous decade, allowed the establishment of the characteristic political structure and institutions of the regime. The central and essential institution of Mamlūk society under both the sultanate and the Ottomans was the military household. This consisted of *mamlūks* obtained, trained, and emancipated by a master (*ustādh*), to whom they remained attached by loyalty and more formally by legal clientage (*walāʾ*). The second bond of loyalty created by the Mamlūk household was the comradeship (*khushdāshiyya*) existing among the *mamlūks* as brothers-in-arms. The principal households were those of the sultans (the Royal Mamlūks), designated from the *laqab* of the founding master, for example, the Ṣāliḥīyah of al-Malik al-Ṣāliḥ Ayyūb, and the Ẓāhirīyah of al-Malik al-Ẓāhir Baybars. Since the *mamlūks* were immigrants, recruited principally from a single ethnic group (originally the Qipchaq Turks, subsequently the Circassians), they formed, in effect, an alien tribe. The factional struggles among the different households, which form a recurrent feature of Mamlūk history, bear some analogy to clan warfare. The *mamlūks* depended upon their master for patronage and advancement, while the master depended upon his *mamlūks* for the maintenance of his own power and security.

During Baybar's rule the Mamlūk sultanate was threatened by the Mongol Il-Khans in the east and by the remains of the Frankish states on the Syro-Palestinian coast. Of the two, the Mongols were by far the greater danger. Two of Baybars's internal aims were to legitimize his rule and to establish a dynasty. He failed in the latter but succeeded in the former by installing an ʿAbbāsid prince as caliph in Cairo, and receiving from him a formal delegation of plenary powers as the universal sultan of Islam (June 1261). The princes were recognized willy-nilly as caliphs in Egypt and Syria until (and even beyond) the Ottoman conquest. By his transistion of the caliphate to Cairo, Baybars placed the supreme legitimating authority in Sunnī Islam under the control of the sultan. Thereafter the caliph played an essential, if formal, part in the accession observances of the Mamlūk sultans.

In terms of ruling institutions the Mamlūk institution was the logical peak of the system of a military household constituted by military slaves that had been in place since ʿAbbāsid times. Only now the principle of dynastic succession was curbed in favor of a *mamlūk* commander acclaimed as sultan (i.e., a member of a powerful synthetic family made up of master and slaves rather than the actual biological family of the sultan succeeded). The rationale for such system was that unlike members of established households in the society, the military slaves, kept apart from the society, had but one loyalty, to the master. The rule of "slaves on horses" has been seen as symptom of a tragic failure of political institutions and hence thought in the Islamic world.

In contrast to the loose Ayyūbid family confederacy of autonomous principalities, the provinces of the Mamlūk sultanate were under close central control, being administered by governors of *mamlūk* origin serving as the sultan's delegates (sing. *nāʾib al-salṭana*). When the danger from the Frankish states and the Mongols came to an end, and the sultans became sedentary in Cairo, their governmental functions became more important than leadership in war. The inveterate rivalry and violence of the Mamlūk households characterized this period, getting worse during transitional periods. The distinctive characteristic of the administrative system was the overriding control exercised by the sultan through Mamlūk *amīrs*. Even the sons of Mamlūks (*awlād al-nās*) corrupted for the purpose of warfare by society and civilization, were excluded from power struggles. The military households, including that of the sultan, were maintained by assignments of landed revenue (sing. *iqṭāʿ*). It was the Royal Mamlūks who were promoted to emirates and appointed to the top offices at court and in the provinces. Although their tenure of office was individually precarious, and their assignments were never in this period hereditary or life tenures, these magnates were always potential opponents of the sultan. Repeated attempts to establish a species of contractual relationship by obtaining an accession compact at the installation of a sultan were never effective in practice; hence many reigns ended in factional revolt, and the deposition (or even murder) of the ruler. The growing economic weakness of the fifteenth century has been ascribed to political factors, the factional conflicts of the magnates, resulting in enfeebled administration, and hence in the decay of agriculture. Its causes may alternatively be attributed to the heavy mortality occasioned by successive epidemics of plague.

In 1517 the Ottoman Sultan Selim I defeated the Mamlūks, turning Egypt and Syria into Ottoman provinces. The Ottoman conquest, however, was not followed by the extirpation of the *mamlūk*s, and the recruitment and the formation of *mamlūk* military households continued and provided part of the armed forces of Egypt. The heads of the Mamlūk establishment, nominally twenty-four in number, bore the Ottoman designation of *sanjak beg*; the *beylik* emerged as a factor of great political importance in the middle decades of the seventeenth century (a period of Ottoman weakness), and the old pattern of Mamlūk factionalism reappeared, along with the inveterate hostilities between the leading households. Their ascendancy in Egypt ultimately ended with their massacre by Muḥammad ʿAlī Pasha in 1812.

Gunpowder Empires (Fifteenth–Eighteenth Centuries). The post-Mongol Muslim world, divided as it came to be by the Mongol onslaught between Persianate east and Arabic west, was transformed in the early modern period by the rise of three great empires: the Mughals in South Asia, the Ṣafavids in Persia, and the Ottomans in the west. The three empires shared basic features such as Turkic dynastic origins, Persianate political culture, and the central place of Islam in terms of social organization and legal culture.

Osman Bey (d. 1324), a minor chieftain on the Byzantine border in Anatolia, and Safī al-Dīn (d. 1336), a Sunnī-Shāfiʿī Ṣūfī master in Ardabil (in northwestern Iran), the eponymous founders of the Ottoman and Ṣafavid dynasties, respectively, arose about the same time and drew on a similar social reservoir, the Oghuz (*ghuzz* in Arabic) Turks, who had started moving to the eastern Caspian region in the tenth century and whose more successful cousins had established the Seljuk Empire, and who had been settling in Anatolia since the Seljuk Alp Arslan's defeat of the Byzantines in 1071. The Ottoman *ghuzza* arose, exploiting their geopolitical advantage through constant warfare for two centuries against non-Muslim neighbors to the west and other Turkmens in Anatolia, whereas the Ṣafavid religious order consolidated its power by taking over its ally, the Aq Qoyunlu dynasty, and effecting what has been called the greatest religious revolution since the rise of Islam itself. The religious warfare (*ghazw*) was a minor justification for the Ottoman expansion, whereas religious conversion to Twelver Shiism of their subjects throughout Iran was the very basis of Ṣafavid legitimacy and rule. This drastic and almost unheard of forced mass conversion in Islamic history provided two durable advantages to the Ṣafavids: it transcended the deep cleavage in society between the settled Persian and nomadic Turkmen populations, and it provided a rationale for subverting the Sunnī Islam of the townsmen whose loyalties might have otherwise sided with the Sunnī Ottoman rivals. Of the three empires only the Ṣafavids ruled over an entirely Muslim population and on the basis of a primarily religious ideology; the Ottomans had non-Muslim Europeans as half their subjects, whereas the Mughals ruled over a large non-Muslim majority.

The clash between Ottoman military organization and Ṣafavī religious fervor provided the main backdrop to west Asian history from the fifteenth to the eighteenth centuries.

The Ottomans stand out in institutional development, creativity, and emphasis. Rising from the rough frontier rather than the more sophisticated Persianized centers of culture, the Ottoman court was Turkish; the scribes maintained Persian traditions in bureaucracy and literature, but Turkish was important, for the first time, not only in these domains but also among Turkish *ʿulamāʾ*, where it was never replaced fully by Arabic. Like all Turco-Persian systems the Ottoman Empire was stratified: the ruling elite, the secretarial class, and the subjects. The ruling elite drew from the Ottoman house exclusively, hence other ethnic Turks, unlike all other Perso-Turkish states, were not free to rise up the ladder as military or ruling elites but were limited to pursuing the *madrasah* education and secretarial path as scribes or the *ʿulamāʾ*; the military-administrative elite was now comprised by a new "Roman" race, Turkish-speaking and Muslim, but with non-Muslim, non-Turkish origins, for Turks were now Muslim and a majority. Neither Muslims nor protected minorities (*dhimmī*s) could be traditionally enslaved, which meant that the Ottomans not only procured military slaves from outside their borders through traditional methods, such as the taking of prisoners of war and purchase, but also invented a new mechanism, *devşirme* (lit. gathering), of taking young men from rural Christian areas, not always by force, and drafting them into the sultan's household exclusively. These slaves later came to occupy the top posts in provincial and central governments and constituted their own households, with wives of similar backgrounds, thus resulting into a new race of European, Christian-born workers who were "Ottoman" in every other respect.

Between 1590 and 1639 the Ottomans and the Ṣafavids engaged in hostilities that did not change their boundaries so much as bring them closer in their modes of seeking legitimacy; the Ṣafavids learned from Ottoman organization and recruited Georgian slave-soldiers, whereas the Ottomans, so far content with their "Roman" identity, turned to honing their religious-ideological basis. Muḥammad al-Fātiḥ (Mehmed II Fatih), having conquered Constantinople in 1453—a conquest that had been prophesied in Prophetic traditions since early times—already granted a religiously comfortable foundation, and the taking from the Mamlūks of the traditional Islamic lands, Egypt, Syria, and the Hjiaz in 1517, helped in the mid-sixteenth century upgrade the claim of the Ottoman sultan to being the "chief of the believers" and the supreme caliph of all Muslims. The great Sultan Süleyman, titled Kanuni (the Lawgiver), wished to ensure that his sultanic *qānūn* was in accordance with the Islamic Sharīʿah. The "classic" Ottoman model of taxation had been generally along egalitarian agrarian lines, collecting taxes in monetary form in proportion to one's landholdings (the ratio of the tax rates of poor, middle-class, and well-off being 1:2:4), but the large amount of cash required to pay the colossal sultanic military household, in addition to the costs of inconclusive wars against the Hapsburgs in the west and Ṣafavids in the east, led the Ottomans around 1600 to return to a more familiar model of large land grants in return for military service.

The place of the *ʿulamāʾ* in the Muslim empires is a crucial variable in explaining later developments; the religious foundation of the Ṣafavid Empire, which the Qājār kings could not claim, leaving the Shīʿī *ʿulamāʾ* of the region with far greater social and economic authority and independence vis-à-vis the kings, whereas the Sunnī *ʿulamāʾ* of the Ottoman Empire had been incorporated into the state structure as functionaries.

They administered both God's Sharīʿah and the sultan's *qānūn* and were rotated from one place to another and thus barred from establishing independent power bases; those, like the Arab *ʿulamāʾ*, who preferred to stay in their local posts, were excluded from high offices. When the eighteenth-century Damascene *ʿulamāʾ* petitioned to be considered for higher offices at the center of power, the sultan replied that they were welcome to such consideration provided they learned Turkish and joined the provincial rotation.

Early reformism. The rise of large empires and the conversion of more peoples to Islam, doubling the size of the Islamic world since its early expansion in the eighth century, was accompanied by a tolerant and syncretic mood, evident in the Mughal Emperor Akbar's toying with the idea of creating a new religion by harmonizing Islam and Hinduism. For these and other reasons the mood had turned against religious syncretism by the seventeenth century. Another major social transformation had been introduced by the new empires. In the military patronage state era of the previous six centuries, Islamic societies had been largely self-governed, and the authority of military rulers, despite their ruthlessness and segregation from their subjects, was local, limited, and negotiated; the sultans often needed the real socioreligious leaders of society, the *ʿulamāʾ*, as much as the latter needed the former for upholding Islamic law, defense, and internal order. The Ottoman Empire co-opted the *ʿulamāʾ* into the imperial bureaucracy, rendering the remaining independent or locally oriented *ʿulamāʾ* ineffective. Previously an ʿIzz al-Dīn ibn ʿAbd al-Salām (d. 1262) or an Ibn Taymīyah (d. 1328) could threaten and fruitfully challenge the sultan; such moralizing challenges by individuals now seemed unimaginable.

A few important reformist movements, therefore, emerged that were to have a lasting impact until today. Aḥmad Sirhindī (d. 1624) of India rose against Akbar's syncretism and campaigned, through Ṣūfī and scholarly networking and preaching, to establish Sufism strictly on the basis of the *sunnah* of the Prophet. By the eighteenth century the long-standing dialogue between the mystic and syncretic tradition of Ibn al-ʿArabī bordering on pantheism and the *sunnah*-based Sufism of the kind endorsed by Sirhindī gained new momentum and was often resolved in the favor of the latter, prompting a consequent rise in the attention given to *ḥadīth* studies. The revivalist *ḥadīth* scholarship at the religious centers of Islam, in Mecca and Medina, reinvigorated by scholarly networks from India to Morocco and by a pro-*ḥadīth* in Sufism, fed a number of reformist movements across the Muslim world, such as those of Muḥammad ibn ʿAbd al-Wahhāb (d. 1792) in Arabia, Usuman Dan Fodio (d. 1817) in West Africa, Muḥammad ibn ʿAlī al-Sanūsī (d. 1859) in North Africa, and the Farāʾiẓī movement in East Bengal by Ḥājjī Shariatullah (d. 1840), among others. Most of these movements were anti-imperialist and internal to the Islamic world, with no direct reference to the European threat in their agendas. Of these the movement of Ibn ʿAbd al-Wahhāb captured the center and attained notable political success after its alliance with the family of Muḥammad ibn Saʿūd rising even after its first suppression by Muḥammad ʿAlī's Egyptian army in 1818. The modern-day Saudi kingdom established in 1932 is based on the resurrection of the same alliance under the leadership of ʿAbd al-ʿAzīz ibn Saʿūd. No other early modern reformist movement resulted in a similar, direct political presence on the modern scene, but many contributed to reformist and revivalist trends during the twentieth century that continue to shape and indeed dominate Muslim religious thought.

State-centered reformism. Assuming that the source of European power was its modern armies, Muslim rulers like the Ottoman Sultan Maḥmud II

(1808–1839) and his vassal in Egypt, Muḥammad (Mehmet) ʿAlī (1805–1849), tried to emulate the West by creating military training schools staffed by Europeans. Delegations were sent to Europe to study languages, sciences, and politics. Translation bureaus and printing presses were established to make technical information more accessible. Thus military modernization was followed by attempts to modernize administration, law, education, and economy. These reforms were imposed top-down by a small ruling elite but rejected for myriad reasons by the more conservative sectors of the government, military, and society and, in particular, the *ʿulamāʾ*. This led to a more thorough and ruthless modernization attempt by Maḥmud's son, Abdülmecid, known as Tanzimat (reorganizations). Islamic institutions were not so much supplanted as made irrelevant by the establishment of state-sponsored, modern, European-inspired counterparts: new secular schools to train military personnel and members of the nascent bureaucracy, land reforms, new legal codes and courts to regulate civil, commercial, and penal affairs ushered in dramatic changes. The creation of a westernized elite backfired on the sultan and led to the demand and then promulgation of the First Ottoman Constitution in 1876. Sultan Abdülhamid II (1876–1909) soon abolished the constitution and turned against the reforms, accentuating the Islamic aspect of this multiple-personality empire, while implementing some reforms such as the spread of public education.

The Ottomans' light-handed, pluralistic imperialism, so familiar to the Near East for centuries, was designed for and provided overall stability and peace, but proved no match for the nation-state, the ultimate war machine created by the combination of technology and capitalism and the training fields of European religious warfare. The Ottoman elite on the whole at first resisted, then compromised as little as they felt necessary, and ultimately conceded that survival lay in submission to the European model, abolishing in 1924 even the symbol of the caliphate and extirpating Islam as much as possible from society. The top-down reform attempts followed a similar but less dramatic trajectory elsewhere in the Muslim world: Turkey's Mustafa Kemal Atatürk inspired the Pahlavis of Iran (1925–1979), but the stronger and economically independent *ʿulamāʾ* class was able to lead, or co-opt, a popular revolution against "westoxification" of the shahs, leading to the Islamic Revolution of 1979—remarkable for being the only religious revolution of modern times.

[*See also* Imamate, Theories of the; *and* Sovereignty.]

BIBLIOGRAPHY

Anjum, Ovamir. *Politics, Law and Community in Islamic Thought: The Taymiyyan Moment.* Cambridge, U.K., and New York: Cambridge University Press, 2012.

Bosworth, C. E. *Islamic Dynasties: A Chronological and Genealogical Handbook.* Rev. ed. Edinburgh: Edinburgh University Press, 1980.

Chamberlain, Michael M. *Knowledge and Social Practice in Medieval Damascus, 1190–1350.* Cambridge, U.K., and New York: Cambridge University Press, 1994.

Chamberlain, Michael M. "Military Patronage States and the Political Economy of the Frontier, 1000–1250." In *A Companion to the History of the Middle East,* edited by Youssef Choueiri. Malden, Mass., and Oxford: Blackwell Publishing, 2005.

Cooperson, Michael. *Al-Maʾmun.* Oxford: Oneworld, 2005.

Crone, Patricia. *God's Rule: Government and Islam: Six Centuries of Medieval Islamic Political Thought.* New York: Columbia University Press, 2004.

Crone, Patricia. *Slaves on Horses: The Evolution of the Islamic Polity.* Cambridge, U.K., and New York: Cambridge University Press, 1980.

Crone, Patricia, and Martin Hinds. *God's Caliph: Religious Authority in the First Centuries of Islam.* Cambridge, U.K., and New York: Cambridge University Press, 1986.

Donner, Fred McGraw. *The Early Islamic Conquests*. Princeton, N.J.: Princeton University Press, 1981.

Donohue, John J. *The Buwayhid Dynasty in Iraq 334 H./945 to 403 H./1012: Shaping Institutions for the Future*. Islamic History and Civilization, vol. 44. Leiden: Brill, 2003.

Esposito, John L. *Islam and Politics*. 4th ed. Syracuse, N.Y.: Syracuse University Press,1998.

Gibb, H. A. R. *Studies on the Civilization of Islam*. Edited by Stanford J. Shaw and William R. Polk. Boston: Beacon Press, 1962.

Ḥakam, ʿAbd Allāh ibn ʿAbd al-. *Sīrat ʿUmar ibn ʿAbd al-ʿAzīz*. Edited by Aḥmad ʿUbayd. Beirut: ʿĀlam al-Kutub, 1984.

Heck, Paul L. *The Construction of Knowledge in Islamic Civilization: Qudāma b. Jaʿfar and his Kitāb al-Kharāj wa-ṣināʿat al-kitāba*. Leiden: Brill, 2002.

Hillenbrand, Carol. "Islamic Orthodoxy or Realpolitik? Al-Ghazālī's Views on Government." *IRAN* 26 (1988): 81–94.

Hodgson, Marshall G. S. *The Venture of Islam: Conscience and History in a World Civilization*. 3 vols. Chicago: University of Chicago Press, 1974.

Holt, P. M. " Mamlūks." In *Encyclopaedia of Islam*. 2d ed. Brill Online, 2012.

Humphreys, R. Stephen. *From Saladin to the Mongols: The Ayyubids of Damascus, 1193–1260*. Albany: State University of New York Press, 1977.

Kennedy, Hugh. *The Prophet and the Age of the Caliphates: The Islamic Near East from the Sixth to the Eleventh Century*. 2d ed. Harlow, U.K., and New York: Longman/Pearson, 2004.

Keshk, Khaled. *The Historians' Muʿāwiya: The Depiction of Muʿāwiya in the Early Islamic Sources*. Saarbrücken, Germany: VDM, Verlag Dr. Müller, 2008.

Kunt, Metin. "Ottomans and Safavids: States, Statecraft, and Societies." In *A Companion to the History of the Middle East*, edited by Youssef Choueiri, pp. 192–206. Malden, Mass., and Oxford: Blackwell Publishing, 2005.

Lambton, Ann K. S. *State and Government in Medieval Islam: An Introduction to the Study of Islamic Political Theory: The Jurists*. Oxford and New York: Oxford University Press, 1981.

Lapidus, Ira M. "The Separation of State and Religion in the Development of Early Islamic Society." *International Journal of Middle East Studies* 6, no. 4 (1975): 363–385.

Lewis, Bernard. *The Political Language of Islam*. Chicago: University of Chicago Press, 1988.

Madelung, Wilferd. *The Succession to Muhammad: A Study of the Early Caliphate*. Cambridge, U.K., and New York: Cambridge University Press, 1997.

Makdisi, George. "The Sunni Revival." In *Islamic Civilization, 950–1150*, edited by D. S. Richards, 155–168. Oxford: Cassirer, 1973.

Murad, H. Q. "Ethico-Religious Ideas of ʿUmar II." Ph.D. diss., McGill University, 1981.

Nagal, Tilman. *Studien zum Minderheitenprobleme im Islam*. Vol. 2: *Rechtleitung und Kalifat*. Bonn: Orientalischen Seminar der Universität Bonn, 1975.

Sayyid, Riḍwān al-. *Al-Jamāʿa wa-al-mujtamaʿ wa-al-dawla*. Dār al-Kitāb al-ʿArabī, 1997.

Tabarī. *The History of al-Tabarī = Taʾrīkh al-rusul waʾl mulūk*. 40 vols., vol. 10, translated by F. Donner. Albany: State University Press of New York, 1993.

ʿUmarī, Akram Ḍiyāʾ al-. *Madīnan Society at the Time of the Prophet*. Translated by Hudā Khattāb. 2 vols. Herndon, Va.: International Institution of Islamic Thought, 1991.

Zaman, Muhammad Qasim. *Religion and Politics under the Early ʿAbbāsids: The Emergence of the Proto-Sunnī Elite*. New York: Brill, 1997.

Ovamir Anjum

Muslim Political Thought. The history of Muslim political thought spans more than fourteen centuries and has evolved in response to diverse theoretical and practical stimuli. Despite the many changes in the conception of political authority and organization, Muslim political thought maintains a remarkable affinity to the early prophetic ethos and remains concerned with reconciling the transcendental values of the Islamic revelation with the political demands of an evolving social structure and culture.

Muslim political thought has always been subject to outside influences and ready to embrace ideas from outside its political and cultural experience. This embrace, however, always involved unwavering adherence to ethical traditions that were grounded in the religious parameters of Islam. Therefore, political debate has always been concerned with subordinating political authority to a transcendental law rooted in an overarching conception of *Sharīʿah* (Islamic law) and a free expression of religiosity.

The outstanding feature of Muslim political thought has been the relentless efforts to subjugate political action to moral evaluation and demands. This feature of Muslim thinking was not lost on the most profound philosopher of history, G. W. F. Hegel. Hegel characterized Islamic interest in reconciling the secular and the moral as the "Mohammedan principle" and the "enlightenment of the Oriental World" and thought that Islamic historical precedent influenced the later efforts by the Enlightenment philosophers to do the same:

> We must therefore regard [the reconciliation of the secular and spiritual] as commencing rather in the enormous contrast between the spiritual, religious principle, and the barbarian Real World. For Spirit as the consciousness of an inner World is, at the commencement, itself still in an abstract form. All that is *secular* is consequently given over to rudeness and capricious violence. The *Mohammedan* principle—the enlightenment of the Oriental World—is the first to contravene this barbarism and caprice. We find it developing itself later and more rapidly than Christianity; for the latter needed eight centuries to grow up into a political form. (Hegel, 2007, p. 109)

The following entry is intended to provide not a complete catalogue of the prevailing political ideas throughout the long history of Muslim political thought but a glimpse into the overall progress of Islamic political thinking and the prevailing ideas that shaped political thinking among Muslims.

Greek Influence and the Search for the Ideal State. Early political writings by Muslim philosophers and scholars emerged in the context of intellectual exchange with Greek philosophy. The extensive translation of Greek work under the caliph al-Maʾmūn exposed Muslims to Greek political philosophy. This exposure stimulated political thinking in the quest of finding an ideal political arrangement. Al-Fārābī's political writings provide an important insight into the Greek influence on early Muslim political philosophy.

Abū Naṣr al-Fārābī (c. 870–950) was a leading Muslim philosopher who devoted his most important philosophical work to political issues. His *al-Madīnah al-fāḍilah* remains one of most fascinating political writings of all times. His impact on later Muslim philosophers was so great that he was often referred to as the "Second Teacher," the first being Aristotle. Al-Fārābī's philosophical writings represent a creative synthesis of the philosophy of Plato and Aristotle, but he "broke completely with Greek metaphysics in favor of philosophical approach rooted in methodology." *Al-Madīnah al-fāḍilah*, Al-Fārābī's major work, was undoubtedly inspired by Plato's *Republic*. The similarity between the two works was, however, more in form than in substance. Like Plato, al-Fārābī employs in his work the notion of the "ideal state" and insists that such a state must be governed by a ruler that combines the mental power of a philosopher with the political strength of a king. Al-Fārābī, nonetheless, replaces the philosopher-king of Plato with the prophet-imam, a person who combines the moral insights of a prophet with the leadership capacity of an imam. Al-Fārābī argues that the ideal state resembles the city-state of Medina as it was ruled by Prophet Muḥammad.

Al-Fārābī describes in Platonic terms the qualities necessary for the ruler: he should possess innate virtues to rule with justice and fairness; he should be a good orator and should perfect himself until his soul unites with the active intellect; he should have both a strong physique and an astute mind; and he should love learning and truth and be above materialism. Reviewing the various qualities enumerated by al-Fārābī, it is evident that the ideal ruler he describes is analogous to Plato's philosopher-king.

Following in the footsteps of Plato, al-Fārābī distinguishes between perfect and corrupt states. He identifies three perfect states and qualifies them, in accordance with their size, into: *ʿuzmā* (the greatest), *wustā* (the medium), and *sughrā* (the smallest). These states are then contrasted with four different types of corrupt city: the ignorant city (*al-madīnah al-jāhilīyah*), the dissolute city (*al-madīnah al-fāsiqah*), the hypocritical city (*al-madīnah al-mubaddalah*), and the straying city (*al-madīnah al-ḍāllah*). These correspond closely to Plato's fourfold division of the world into imperfect cities in the *Republic*, namely, timarchy, oligarchy, democracy, and monarchy.

Al-Fārābī relates the quality of life of the city to the moral disposition of its inhabitants. The souls of the inhabitants of corrupt cities are lacking in moral commitment, and are hence subject to internal conflict and torment, which are manifested in the constant divisions and turmoil that distinguish these cities. Similarly, al-Fārābī identifies happiness (*saʿādah*) as the overarching value for measuring the quality of life in the various city types. He further entertains the possibility of moving from a virtuous community, through a virtuous city, and ultimately to a virtuous world. The virtuous city (*al-madīnah al-fāḍilah*) is distinguished from the others in that its inhabitants cooperate to achieve happiness. The virtuous world (*al-maʿmūrah al-fāḍilah*) is achieved when all cities collaborate to achieve happiness.

Richard Walzer explores the themes of happiness in the writing of both Plato and al-Fārābī and finds an important difference in their approaches. He argues that Plato limited the experience of supreme happiness to philosophers who were able to achieve proper understanding of the world. Al-Fārābī, similarly, taught that supreme happiness was the lot of the ideal ruler whose intellect is united with the Active Intellect. Walzer, however, insists that al-Fārābī "does not confine his interest to the felicity of the first ruler: he is equally concerned with the felicity of all the five classes which make up the perfect state" (introduction to al-Fārābī, 1985, pp. 409–410).

Political Legitimacy and the Foundation of Political Authority. The influence of Greek political ideas on Muslim political philosophy was confined to a small circle of intellectual elites within Muslim society and was seen as irrelevant to the immediate concerns of a growing empire plagued by a fierce struggle among the various clans of the Quraysh tribe. The immediate concern for most Muslim scholars was the issue of political legitimacy, as various political groups vied for political control of the state.

Early writings on the question of political legitimacy reflected the ongoing struggle between the Shīʿī and Sunnī sects of Islam. Early Shīʿī scholars insisted that the question of political legitimacy was essentially a religious question to be decided by consulting Islamic traditions. They employed a number of traditions that confined political leadership to the house of the Prophet. The struggle between al-Ḥusayn, the grandson of the prophet, and Yazīd ibn Muʿāwiyah, the founder of the Umayyad dynasty, was taken as a reference point. Shīʿī scholars insisted that the Prophet designated ʿAlī as his successor and that his descendants through al-Ḥusayn were the legitimate claimants to the *imāmah* (the highest political leadership). Sunnī scholars insisted, however, that political legitimacy of the leader (imam) is grounded in people's consent and that the leader is determined through the process of selection (*ikhtiyār*) and declaration of allegiance (*bayʿah*). The debate between the Shīʿī and Sunnī branches of Islam has been highly fraught, and each side sought to vindicate its approach by citing scriptures and by referencing historical evidence and rational arguments. Much of the Sunnī political literature that has reached us was apparently compiled as a reaction to Shīʿī claims.

Many of the Shīʿī claims of hereditary religious leadership were grounded in a metaphoric reading of the Islamic sources or on the basis of statements by the Prophet that designated his cousin ʿAlī as the designated successor to the prophet. Sunnī scholars rejected any religious or scriptural foundation for political legitimacy, and invoked procedural conditions and personal criteria for the selection of political leaders.

The conventional Sunnī attitude toward the Shīʿī claim of *imāmah* can be found in the refutation of Abū Bakr al-Bāqillānī in his book *al-Tamhīd fī al-radd ʿalā al-mulḥidah al-muʿaṭṭilah wa-al-rāfiḍah wa-al-khawārij wa-al-muʿtazilah*, which would become the standard treatise on political legitimacy. Al-Bāqillānī's refutation depends mainly on demonstrating the speculative nature and contradictions of the sources adopted by the Shīʿī scholars. He insists that if the Prophet had designated ʿAlī, his command would have been obligatory for all Muslims, and he would have proclaimed it publically in front of a large number of his companions instead of secretly informing one two people, as the Shīʿī scholars insist. Had he declared his successor, al-Bāqillānī asserted, the knowledge would have been spread and became known to every companion, in the same manner that *ṣalāḥ* (prayer), *zakāh* (alms), fasting, and other religious obligations are known. The act of designating a successor would have become known to the entire Muslim community in the same fashion as the appointing of important judges, army commanders, and governors by the Prophet.

Al-Bāqillānī's arguments led the way for the majority of Muslim scholars within the Sunnī tradition to treat political authority as temporal, lacking any religious significance or consequence. While the majority of Muslim writers would avoid referring to political authority in Islamic history as secular, they would readily describe it as "civil" (*madanīyah*).

ʿAbd al-Maʿālī al-Juwaynī, in his book *Ghiyāth al-umam fī al-tiyāth al-ẓulam*, makes a similar argument to refute the claims of designation. He contends that such a claim can be sustained on the basis of any of three types of evidence: irrevocable text of the Qurʾān, preponderance of prophetic statement (*ḥadīth mutawātir*), or established consensus among companions. Because none of the above is available, the claims of designation are unfounded.

The Shīʿī theory of *imāmah* posits a divinely ordained and guided political authority that resembles theocracy. The imam in the Shīʿī tradition is an infallible human being with direct access to divine guidance similar to that claimed by the Prophet. Indeed, Shīʿī scholars initially argued that the need for continuous divine guidance necessitated the presence of the guided imam. This argument, based on the principle of divine favor, insists that the Muslim community is in constant need of a "referential authority" that can clarify the divine will on new issues it confronts. Because human beings are fallible, it is necessary, the argument goes, for an imam to be appointed by God as an expression of his favor to his servants. The presence of an imam in every age to guide and direct the believers is inevitable. Al-Kulaynī quotes Imām al-Ṣādiq as saying, "The earth cannot be without an imam so that if the believers misinterpreted the divine command he would correct them and if they neglect a duty he would guide them." Similarly, al-Kulaynī attributes to al-Ṣādiq the statement "Should the imam be taken away for a moment it would have set the earth in turmoil."

The disappearance of the imam prevented the creation of a theocratic authority and turned Shiism for many centuries toward political quietism, until Khomeini succeeded in reengaging

Shiism with politics in the middle of the twentieth century through the theory of the "*wilāyat al-faqīh*" (guardianship of the jurist). The theory of *wilāyat al-faqīh*, which Khomeini articulated in his book *al-Ḥukūmah al-islāmīyah*, attaches political legitimacy to the election by the community of the political leadership represented by Muslim jurists (*faqīhs*). Though the theory insists on that the *wilāyat al-faqīh* is decided partially by the election of the *ummah* and partially by appointment by God, who determines the necessary qualities of the *faqīh*, the election of the *faqīh*, from a procedural perspective, is not different from that of *ahl al-ḥall wa-al-ʿaqd* (the notables) in the classical theory.

Classical Theory of Government. The classical political theory is that which the jurists of the Sunnī majority developed under the title of the rules of *imāmah*, or sultanic rules. This theory was jointly developed by several Islamic jurists led by Abū Bakr al-Bāqillānī, Abū Yaʿlā al-Farrāʾ, ʿAbd al-Maʿālī Juwaynī, and others. But the most definitive formulation of this theory is found in *Kitāb al-aḥkām al-sulṭānīyah wa-al-wilāyāt al-dīnīyah* by Abū al-Ḥasan al-Māwardī (972–1058). The classical theory of *imāmah* is based on the following five principles.

First, the election of the imam is a collective duty assigned to the *ummah* (community). According to Islamic law, the *ummah* is responsible for the establishment of the *imāmah*. However, the duty of the *ummah* in this respect is a collective one. If some people perform this duty, it is no longer a duty for the rest of the community. The *imāmah* is the succession to the prophethood for protecting religion and managing earthly affairs. The contract of the *imāmah* for the one who would fulfill it from among the *ummah* is necessary by consensus, though the mute are excluded. Al-Māwardī adds that "if it is established that the *imāmah* is a duty, then it is a collective duty like *jihād* and acquisition of knowledge. If it is performed by the qualified persons the duty will be discharged collectively."

Second, the task of electing the imam is restricted to two groups: electors, or the *ahl al-ḥall wa-al-ʿaqd* (the elite of the community) and *ahl al-imāmah* (community leaders). Al-Māwardī says, "If it is discharged by someone qualified for the same, the duty will be discharged collectively. If it is not discharged by any, there remain two groups of people, namely *ahl-ikhtiyar* [the people of selection] who have to elect an imam for the *ummah*, and *ahl-al-imamah*, one of whom has to stand for the *imāmah*. The people other than these two groups are not to be blamed or charged if the imāmahis delayed."

Third, *ahl al-ikhtiyār* are appointed according to three conditions: "extensive probity of their character; knowledge of the requirements of the position; and... wisdom which enables them to elect the most capable person for the post."

Fourth, *ahl al-imāmah* are designated on the basis of seven conditions.

> One, the propensity to knowledge that enables him to do make *ijtihād* for new developments and situations; healthy senses including that of ears, eyes and tongue so that he can do whatever he realizes by them; freedom of organs and limbs from defects, affecting his ability to act; fifth, wisdom to rule the subjects and manage the interests; sixth, bravery and courage to protect the Sharīʿah and fight with the enemies; [and] seventh, lineage, that is he should be a Quarayshī [member of the tribe of Quraysh], because of the text and*ijmāʿ*.

Fifth, the selection of the imam can be lawful in one of two ways, either *mubāyaʿah* (pledge of allegiance) of *ahl al-ḥall wa-al-ʿaqd* for the one whom they elect for *imāmah* or nomination by the former imam of the latter.

The Popular Foundation of Political Authority. In the history of Islamic thought, the question of the popular basis of political authority and the procedural requirements of legitimacy was hotly debated three centuries after the demise of Rashīdī rule. Perhaps the first serious political study in the history of political thought in Islam are the opinions put down by Abū Bakr al-Bāqillānī in his book *al-Tamhīd* under the heading *imāmah*. In this book, written in the eleventh century, we come across the fundamentals of the classical theory that reach its advanced stage in Māwardī's *al-Aḥkām al-sulṭānīyah*. The classical theory deals with the questions relating to those responsible for electing the caliph (*khalīfah*) under the heading *ahl al-ʿaqd wa-al-ḥall* (people who tie and loosen) or *ahl al-ikhtiyār* (people of selection). For them three qualifications, as discussed above, are stipulated, namely, the requirements for sound opinion and wisdom, the competence to manage the public interests, and popular support. Classical theory was ambiguous as to how popular support to be decided. It is often equivocal regarding the method of selecting the group assigned the task of electing the imam. Al-Māwardī does not tell us, for instance, whether the distinction is a defined and regulated process or a spontaneous one. If it is spontaneous, then *ahl al-ikhtiyār* may constitute the majority of population, particularly if the decision regarding the fulfillment of the three aforementioned requirements is left to the personal judgment of the individuals concerned. On the other hand, if the distinction of *ahl al-ikhtiyār* is a regulated process, then it will be necessary for the *ummah* as a whole to participate in the process of electing *ahl al-ikhtiyār*. Thus participation in the election process becomes an individual duty.

Second, the distinction made by al-Māwardī between *ahl al-ikhtiyār* and *ahl al-imāmah* is problematic in that the characteristics of *ahl al-ikhtiyār* also include characteristics of *ahl al-imāmah*. Therefore, the membership of *ahl al-imāmah* cannot be fully separated from the membership of *ahl al-ikhtiyār*, because the member of the *imāmah* group will have the right to participate in the deliberation of the *ikhtiyār* group. Accordingly, the separation of *ahl al-imāmah* from *ahl al-ikhtiyār* is an arbitrary and haphazard distinction.

The differentiation between the Muslim community into *ahl al-imāmah* and *ahl al-ikhtiyār* espoused by al-Māwardī is untenable, as it reveals a disconnect between the general theory of government among premodern Muslim scholars and actual political processes and practices. The theory hence serves to disguise the political reality of Muslim society and gives legitimacy to the rampant usurpation of political authority. It also provides a confused conceptualization of the political structure of the Muslim society. It effect, the theory reduced the political representation in the selection process to a single person empowered to choose the head of state on his own. The artificial reduction of the category of *ahl al-ḥall wa-al-ʿaqd* to a single individual was effectively an abdication of the principle of majority. It justified this reduction by insisting that any attempt to locate a defensible number between the entire community and one person is futile. This assumption would later be considered invalid, as is examined below.

Despite the fact that al-Juwaynī succeeded in finding a defensible middle between "all" and "one," the classical theory did not take this solution into consideration. Rather, it overlooked it and stuck to the theorization of al Bāqillānī. Abū al-Maʿālī al-Juwaynī was successful in solving the problem that confronted his teacher Abū Bakr al-Bāqillānī through induction of the power variable in the quantitative equation of *ahl al-ḥall wa-al-ʿaqd*.

Al-Juwaynī's analysis of political power reflects a profound understanding of the sources of the stability and instability of the state. He links the number required to select the imam to social force and interprets the quantitative determination of the *shūrā* council as the power to implement the decision and affirm the authority in the face of the opposition of rivals and the rise of the rebels. Accordingly, al-Juwaynī argues that the necessary number must be determined in such a way that the council members can muster effective support by the different forces and various population groups. Defining the number of *ahl al-ikhtiyār* as a few individuals, or dozens or hundreds of persons, without considering their popular base and the political forces these people represent, is an error arising from a disastrous ignorance of the structure of reality and patterns of political mobilization in society.

This thorough analysis of the determinants of the number of persons required for participation in election is repeated in the writings of Abū Ḥāmid al-Ghazālī, who contends that the number of selectors is simply decided by the majority. So the required number is that number which is necessary and sufficient to represent the public. Al-Ghazālī says:

> What we prefer is that one person pledging the *bay'ah* to the imam can be sufficient if that one person has a following large enough to overcome opposition, and if the support is such that if he turns to a direction, all the public would turn to the same direction with him. Nobody goes against him except those who do not care for his opposition. Therefore, if one person who is followed and obeyed as described above, pledges the *bay'ah*, it will be sufficient because his agreement entails the agreement of the public. If this purpose cannot be realized but by two or three persons, their agreement will be necessary. The target is not the dignitaries and important personalities of the people but acquisition of strength of the imam by the followers and supporters. This is achieved by exercising influence and inducing obedience. We maintain that when 'Umar pledged allegiance to Abū Bakr, the *imāmah* was not confirmed merely due to his *bay'ah* but rather due to the fact that hands came in succession to the *bay'ah* because of his initiative. Had the persons other than 'Umar not pledged, and all the people remained opposed or divided equally, the *imāmah* would not have been concluded. The reasons being that the prerequisite of the agreement is the existence of power and might, and inclination of the hearts to obedience and correspondence of manifest to the hidden on the *bay'ah*. The objective for which we require the imam is to bring together all the different opinions amidst of fusion of likes and dislikes. All these depend on the might and power and the power is achieved only through agreement of the majority of noteworthy persons of all the ages.

The solution to the size of the popular basis of political authority lies in the notion of the "*shūrā* council," which has gained wide support among Muslim intellectuals in modern times. This notion not only helps solve the problem of number but also helps in determining the identity of the *shūrā* members and the task assigned to them. The membership of the *shūrā* council cannot be determined on the basis of purely theoretical qualifications such as moral character, knowledge, and wisdom, as was perceived by many of the early political jurists, but rather must be made on the basis of understanding the relationship between the political forces of the *ummah*, which constitute the source from which the authority of the *shūrā* members is derived, and the *shūrā* council entrusted with political decision making. In this sense the evolving political understanding of the relationship of the general public and the political authority that represents them no longer embraces the theoretical requirements stipulated by the classical theory. Rather, it depends on the political positions of political leaders and their ability to effectively respond to the political demands of the public and the social groups they represent, as well as on the extent of public support and cooperation they enjoy.

To look at membership in vital political institutions, such as the *shūrā* council and executive power, in the framework of purely theoretical qualifications ignores the fact that the ability of the participants in these institutions to translate their decisions into actions depends on the political support the enjoy. The act of resolving problems and settling disputes cannot be confined to those who possess judgment but depends mainly on the ability of those who hold political office to translate their decisions into concrete actions. Possession of opinion and knowledge qualifies individuals to be a counsel whose opinion is sought because of his or her expertise but does not automatically endow them with political authority, which can only be obtained by passion of political power and political clout.

It should be evident that the equation of the *ahl al-shūrā* with the jurists as mentioned in the writings of classical and modern scholars has arisen from confusing the function of juristic knowledge with that of the political representation or *shūrā*. The function of juristic authority posited by classical political theory is therefore confined to deducing general precepts and rulings from authoritative texts, whereas the function of the political *shūrā* is connected with the ability to respond to the aspirations and concerns of the people, determining the priorities of political action, evaluating the balance of power and to mobilize energies and unite the ranks. A scholar can perform the function of the *shūrā* provided that he possesses the qualities of leadership and aptitudes and could win the support and cooperation of the political forces at play on the ground.

By the same token, the members of *shūrā* must have the minimum degree or standard of knowledge in order to carry out their duties and function in a proper fashion. This, however, does not make any difference to the fundamental fact that we endeavor to elaborate—that the qualification necessary for performing the juristic role and the qualification required for performing the *shūrā* function do not necessarily correspond to each other. Ibn Khaldūn recognized the vast difference between the academic authority of jurists and scholars and the political authority of *ahl al-ḥall wa-al-ʿaqd* and explained this difference precisely and thoroughly. Ibn Khaldūn says that *ḥall* and *ʿaqd* (the power to tie and loosen, or decision-making power) is indeed for those who are capable of acting upon it and translating it into political actions. The person who does not have power can neither resolve problems nor settle disputes. Only Sharīʿah rulings and decrees can be sought from him. He goes on to say:

> Some may think that the reality is otherwise and that the exclusion of the jurists and scholars by kings from the *shūrā* (political counsel) is not desirable. The prophet has already said: the scholars are inheritors of the prophets. This must be known that the case is not as is thought to be. The rule of the king and sultan is carried on according to the requirement of the nature and temperament of the population and society, otherwise it will be away from the politics. The civic nature of these people's role does not require anything of that kind, because the Shura, and *ahl al-ḥall wa-al-ʿaqd* are only for the one who possesses group solidarity on the strength of which he can manage affairs, resolve disputes, act or leave. As for one who does not enjoy group solidarity nor possesses group protection, and is dependent on others, what does he have to do with the *shūrā* and what does his inclusion in the *shūrā* means, except the consultation with him in the Sharīʿah rulings which is found in *istiftāʾ*. As for his consultation in political matters he is far away from it due to absence of group feeling.

Ibn Khaldūn and the Sociology of the State. Ibn Khaldūn's efforts to identify the patterns of historical change and social collaboration moved the study of society and the state beyond relying on textual evidence and analysis and laid the foundation for social analysis. He calls the new approach to understanding social and historical development that he introduced the "science of social building" (*ʿilm al-ʿumrān*). The new science consisted in observations he recorded in his *Muqaddimah* in the form of general rules he derived from observing historical communities. These observations gave rise to a new conception of political organization, or the state, that markedly departed from the normative conception elaborated by early Muslim historical and scholars.

Ibn Khaldūn explains the basis of political power by introducing the concept of "group solidarity" (*ʿaṣabīyah*). He locates political power in group dynamics, namely, the willingness of the members of the group to render full support for maintaining the well-being of the entire group. Any group in which members identify their well-being and survival with that of their group enjoys a higher level of social solidarity and is in a better position to overcome other groups under the right historical conditions. Ibn Khaldūn believes that groups that are physically challenged, such as the Arab tribes who live in the desert and rely on the strength of the member of their tribes for defense and sustenance. He anchors group solidarity in both human nature and group dynamics, and notes the differences in the mechanisms of self-defense between the city and the desert.

Living under difficult conditions that require every tribe member to assume responsibility for the collective security of the tribe toughens people as they develop the mental ability required to live with constant risk. This, combined with the uncertain food supply and the need to endure occasional shortages of provisions, raises the level of endurance among Arab tribesmen, giving them an advantage in any power confrontation with people who grow up in protected cities. For this reason, Ibn Khaldūn concluded, powerful states and dynasties were historically established by strong tribes. The demise of the state is, therefore, connected with the decline of mental toughness, along with tribal ties, with the development of the state and the successions of new generations of statesmen who were born under conditions of safety and plenty. The founders of the established state lose control over their political power in the course of the struggle with new claimants to power who come from strong tribes that are still living facing adverse conditions away from the comforts of protected and prosperous cities.

Ibn Khaldūn does not dismiss religion from his historical analysis but sees it as a source of moral certitude and strength. Religion is an element of political power insofar as it provides an additional moral grounding to the groups (or dynasties) that seek political dominance, and as overarching moral principles that bring people of different tribal and ethnic solidarities into a similar normative order. The social foundation of power, he insisted, is always central, even with prophetic missions. He therefore concluded that religious movements that are incognizant of the social foundation of political power are incapable of founding states by the sheer charisma of their leaders.

Ibn Khaldūn was among a handful of Muslim historians who employed empirical analysis in developing political ideas and theories around the fifteenth century. Several centuries would pass before Muslim scholars employed his methodology. His thinking would eventually reach Muslim scholars through the writings of modern Western thinkers who were the first to develop the empirical analysis of society and the state into a more advanced form of political reasoning.

Modern Islamic Thought and Political Reform. The watershed between classical and modern Islamic political thought can be found in the writings of Jamāl al-Dīn al-Afghānī and Muḥammad ʿAbduh. Al-Afghānī (1838–1897) studied Islamic sciences in various parts of Afghanistan, Persia, and Iraq. When he was eighteen years of age, he went to India, where he was exposed to European sciences. Al-Afghānī led an active life, traveling throughout the Muslim world and Europe, propagating his reformist ideas and searching for fertile soil in which his ideas could flourish. He arrived in Cairo in March of 1871, where he stayed until his expulsion by Khedive Tawfīq in September 1879, because of his political activism. Despite the relatively short period of time al-Afghānī spent in Egypt, he made a lasting impact there, for his ideas were embraced and nurtured by Egypt's leading figures, the most prominent of whom was Muḥammad ʿAbduh.

Al-Afghānī, along with his eminent disciple ʿAbduh, endeavored to combat fatalism, which plagued the bulk of Muslim societies by the turn of the nineteenth century. It was widely accepted then that Muslim decadence was natural, as it reflected an advanced stage in the continuous moral decline since the time of the Prophet. It was also believed that this trend was inevitable and beyond human control. Al-Afghānī rejected this interpretation of history, advocated by traditionalists, insisting that Muslim decadence had been precipitated by moral and intellectual decline, and that the superiority of the West and its triumph over the Muslims was a temporary stage in the continual struggle between the East and the West. He attributed Western military superiority to its scientific advancement, arguing that the French and English had been able to conquer Muslim lands not by virtue of being French or English, but because of their superior and more advanced scientific capabilities. Furthermore, al-Afghānī saw a positive aspect of the rivalry between the East and the West, contending that the Western invasion of Muslim lands had a stimulating effect on Muslims and would eventually awaken them from the state of slumber that had dominated their lives for centuries.

Al-Afghānī recognized, however, that scientific development could not be achieved merely by training Muslims to use Western technology. Technology and scientific innovations are mere artifacts, reflecting the ethos of a people and their philosophical outlook. What was needed for the Muslims to progress was a new spirit and direction:

> If a community did not have a philosophy, and all the individuals of that community were learned in the sciences with particular subjects, those sciences could not last in that community for a century.... The Ottoman government and the Khedivate of Egypt have been opening schools for the teaching of the new sciences of a period of sixty years, and they are yet to receive any benefit from those sciences.

Al-Afghānī ascribed the Muslim failure to catch up with the West in science and technology to their deficient outlook and faulty perspective, arguing that Islam had created in the early Muslims the desire to acquire knowledge. Thus, they quickly assumed a leading role in scientific research, first by appropriating the sciences of the Greeks, Persians, and Indians, and later by taking these sciences to new frontiers. He accused contemporary Muslim scholars (*ʿulamāʾ*) of wasting time and energy on trivial matters, instead of addressing the important questions and issues confronting the Muslim community (*ummah*). He therefore called the *ʿulamāʾ* to probe for the causes of Muslim decline, instead of occupying their minds with minutiae and subtleties. Rather than providing strong leadership for the community, he proclaimed, the *ʿulamāʾ* have deprived the *ummah* of technology, allowing the West thereby to surpass the Muslims in military capacity. "Ignorance has no alternative," he wrote, "but to prostrate itself humbly before science and to acknowledge its submission."

The government al-Afghānī advocated was based on, and defined by, Islamic law. Under such government, the ruler was obliged to consult the *ummah* and to work toward promoting the common good. The ruler's principal task was to safeguard the Islamic law:

> The ruler of the Muslims will be their religious, holy, and divine law that makes no distinction among people. This will also be the summary of the ideas of the nation. A Muslim ruler has no other privilege than that of being the most ardent of all in safeguarding the sacred law and defending it.

Afghani's concerns with political reform were primarily concerning educational reform as a prerequisite for any sociopolitical change. Ironically, however, most of those inspired by him were interested in political reform, and had thus paid little, if any, attention to reforming the ideas and practices underlying Muslim backwardness. Perhaps the only exception was Muḥammad ʿAbduh, who devoted the later years of his life to reforming religious ideas and practices, emphasizing education as the principal approach to social change.

ʿAbduh, the most influential Egyptian scholar in the nineteenth and early twentieth centuries, joined his teacher in his attack on traditionalist *ʿulamāʾ* who depicted "European" sciences as perverted and admonished Muslims to refrain from learning them. "The truth is where there is proof," ʿAbduh proclaimed, "and those who forbid science and knowledge to protect religion are really the enemies of religion." ʿAbduh agreed with al-Afghānī that the decline of the Muslim community stemmed from its deficient educational system, which discouraged rational reasoning and suppressed intellectual curiosity. He emphasized that such an educational system was incompatible with Islamic teachings, which honor reason to the extent of giving it the authority to judge the validity and truth of religious claims.

But if the *ʿulamāʾ* were partly responsible for the decline of the *ummah*, the rulers also shared in this responsibility, for they had placed their self-interests before those of the *ummah*, and hence allowed the division of the Muslim world into small entities. It is incumbent upon Muslims by their faith, he asserted, to come together under one banner and join forces to meet the challenge of imperialism. Al-Afghānī contended that the division of the Muslim world into small units defies the teachings of Islam, and thus should not be condoned by Muslims.

> Actually, the schisms and divisions, which have occurred in Muslim states, originate only from the failure of rulers who deviate from the solid principles on which the Islamic faith is built and stray from the path followed by their early ancestors.

The division of the Muslim world into small states, he maintained, was artificial, induced by the struggle for power among various rulers. As such, this division did not reflect the real sentiments of the Muslim masses, who had been, on the contrary, united from the very beginning only by the bonds of Islam, disregarding any other type of bonds such as race or ethnicity.

Al-Afghānī's main goal throughout his life was the unification of the Muslim peoples under one Islamic government. Establishing a unified Islamic state, he thought, could be the first step toward reforming the decadent condition of the Muslims. He believed that such a state could revitalize the Muslim *ummah* and mobilize the masses to meet the European challenge. To achieve this goal, al-Afghānī tried first to persuade the rulers of India, Persia, and Egypt, as well as Sultan Abdülhamid, the head of the Ottoman state (with whom he had a close personal relationship) to Islamize the practices and policies of their governments. He soon realized that Muslim rulers were neither receptive to his ideas nor interested in Islamic reform. Gradually, he began to address his reformist ideas to Muslim intellectuals in particular, and the public in general. In 1879, he established the first Egyptian political party, al-Ḥizb al-Waṭanī al-Ḥurr (the National Liberal Party).

Evidently, al-Afghānī's political activities provoked the wrath of Tawfīq, the khedive of Egypt, who expelled al-Afghānī from Egypt in the same year. After leaving the country that had provided him with his most receptive audience, al-Afghānī spent two years in India before moving to Paris, where he was joined by Muḥammad ʿAbduh; together they established an Arabic newspaper called *al-ʿUrwah al-Wuthqā* (The Indissoluble Bond). The newspaper was distributed throughout the Muslim world, especially in Egypt and India. Al-ʿUrwah was also the name of a clandestine organization headed by al-Afghānī himself. This organization helped in financing and distributing the newspaper, and was dedicated to two objectives: the struggle against imperialism and the unification of the Muslim community. The newspaper was forced to stop publishing after eighteen issues when the British authorities in Egypt and India enacted severe measures to prevent its distribution. The possession of one issue of the newspaper, for instance, was punishable in India by a fine of £100 and two years' imprisonment.

The Rise of Radical Muslim Political Thought. Postcolonial rule in many Muslim countries witnessed increased hostility between secular, Westernizing forces and Islamically oriented social forces. This conflict led to the banning and persecution of Islamic groups, most notably the Muslim Brotherhood. It was against the background of the violent model of secularization that the current Islamic model of development emerged and matured. The model of change, which continues to be dominant within the rank of Islamists, is epitomized in the writings of Sayyid Quṭb. Quṭb organizes his system of ideas around three key concepts: "*jāhilī* society," "Islamic society," and "the Islamic vanguard."

Quṭb contends that all societies could be subsumed under one of two, mutually exclusive, societies: Islamic and *jāhilī*. Quṭb developed the concept of *jāhilīyah* or *jāhilī* society, to analyze modern society and expose its shortcomings and deficiencies. The term *jāhilīyah* was first introduced in the Qurʾān in reference to the faithlessness of pre-Islamic Arab society and its ignorance of divine guidance. Sayyid Quṭb, however, adapted the term and redefined it. According to Quṭb, a *jāhilī* society is one that has been established on rules, principles, and customs that have been founded by man without regard to, or in ignorance of, divine guidance. In such a society, Quṭb argues, man's unrestrained greed and self-aggrandizement become the overwhelming forces that dominate the social, economic, and political relationships among its members, leading to injustice and exploitation of some persons, classes, races, or nations by others.

> [*Jāhilīyah*'s] roots are in human desires, which do not let people come out of their ignorance and self-importance, or in the interests of some persons or some classes or some nations or some races, whose interest prevails over the demand of justice, truth and goodness.

Islamic society, on the other hand, is based on harmony between God and man, the unity of religious and sociopolitical principles, and man's duty to his fellow man and to God. Quṭb defines Islamic society as one in which Islamic law (Sharīʿah) rules, and where Qurʾānic and prophetic injunctions are observed and practiced.

> [The] Muslim community does not denote a land which is the abode of Islam, nor is it a people whose forefathers lived under the Islamic system at some earlier time. It is the name of a group of people whose manners, ideas and concepts, rules and regulations,

values and criteria, are all derived from an Islamic source.

But how does this process of the resurrection of Islamic society begin? How can Islam replace *jāhilīyah*? Quṭb's answer was that bringing an Islamic society to life requires the emergence of an Islamic vanguard.

The transformation of the *jāhilī* society into an Islamic one is not a natural process that takes place apart from human efforts, Quṭb stresses. Nor is it a supernatural process carried out directly by divine power in isolation of human agency. Rather, changing the prevailing conditions from *jāhilī* to Islamic is a long and tedious process that requires the struggle of the Muslim masses. The struggle to establish an Islamic society, Quṭb contends, should be initiated and led by a vanguard. The vanguard must confront the *jāhilī* society on two levels: theoretically, by refuting the ideas and arguments of the *jāhilīyah* and exposing its corruption, and practically, through a well-organized movement, equipped with all the strength it can acquire, to combat a powerful *jāhilīyah*.

When *jāhilīyah* takes the form not of a theory but of an active movement in this fashion, then any attempt to abolish this *jāhilīyah* and to bring people back to God that presents Islam merely as a theory will be undesirable, and indeed useless. *Jāhilīyah* controls the practical world, and for its support there is a living and active organization. In this situation, mere theoretical efforts to fight it cannot even be equal, much less superior, to it.

What is troubling about Quṭb's model is that it reduces the problems facing Muslim society to a simplistic struggle between good and evil, faith and infidelity, or morality and immorality. No more do these problems appear as cultural and civilizational problems, resulting from a drastic decline in the intellectual, industrial, and organizational capacities of the Muslim people, alongside the moral decline in Muslim character. With Quṭb, the problems of the Muslim society became exclusively moral problems, and could be solved simply when a significant number of people declare their commitment to the "Islamic worldview."

Quṭb went on to redefine the terms "development" and "underdevelopment," and to introduce new criteria for advancement and progress. A developed society, Quṭb insisted, is not a society that is on the cutting edge of material production, but one that displays moral superiority. A society that is high in science and technology but low in morality is backward, while a society that is high in morality but low in science and material production is advanced. By defining the question of development this way, Quṭb was able to take away the guilt associated with underdevelopment and provide a quick fix to a seemingly complex and intricate situation. The feeling of relief and self-confidence came, however, at the cost of sacrificing clarity and sound judgment. As a result, many Islamist groups began to see their role in terms of converting the *jāhilī* society to Islam, and engaging in a fierce and frequently bloody struggle with political authorities. Advancement and progress are no longer to be accomplished by emphasizing science, industry, innovation, education, and social reform, but through revolution.

While the currently dominant Islamic model draws its conception of reform from the Qur'ānic framework of historical change, the model is completely impervious to the interconnectedness of the moral sphere and other spheres of collective life. Thus the dominant Islamic model articulated by Quṭb separates moral development from material advancement, while portraying social change in terms of growth in the number of individuals who renounce their allegiance to *jāhilī* society and declare their commitment to Islam.

The simplistic nature of the model stems from the fact that it neglects to gauge the impact of social structure on the process of institutionalization of moral principles. The advocates of the model failed to take note of the structural differences between the society that witnessed the early institutionalization of the Islamic ideals and the one in force today. As a result of this ahistorical approach to understanding social change, the dominant model almost completely ignores the need to identify the patterns of historical change, so as to develop a model that allows organizational and technological development along with moral.

Founding Democratic Tradition within Islamic Normative Framework. There are increasingly dominant views among mainstream Muslim scholars and intellectuals that strongly emphasize the importance of laying a pluralist and democratic foundation for modern Muslim society and the need to ground this foundation in and Islamic worldview and ethics. Leading Muslim intellectuals and scholars insist, to the total bewilderment to their modernist counterparts, that Islam is not only compatible with a scientific, pluralist, and democratic society, but that its reform is a prerequisite for such a society.

The views of contemporary Muslim intellectuals and scholars continue to mature in the direction of recognizing human dignity and reciprocity in society. Fahmī Huwaydī, a leading journalist in the Arab World and a respected Muslim reformist, addressed the question of equality between Muslims and non-Muslims in his book *Muwaṭinūn lā dhimmīyūn* (Citizens, not *Dhimmīs*). Huwaydī rejects the *dhimmī* classification of non-Muslims as a historically relevant concept and demonstrates, by referring to Islamic sources, that non-Muslims in a Muslim political order enjoy full citizenship rights on par with Muslims. The views advanced by Huwaydī are supported by the views of Rāshid al-Ghannūshī, the founder and leader of the main Islamic opposition in Tunisia, who stresses that non-Muslims enjoy equal citizenship with the Muslim majority. Al-Ghannūshī also advocates the right of women to participate on equal footing with men in public life. "There is nothing in Islam," he writes, "that justifies the exclusion of half of the Muslim society from participating and acting in the public sphere. In fact, to do this is to do injustice to Islam and its community in the first place, and to women [secondarily]." Similar arguments for gender equality can be seen in the writings of leading Shīʿī jurists, including Murtażā Muṭahharī, Muḥammad Khatami, and Muḥammad Mahdī Shams al-Dīn.

The effort to ground in Islamic tradition a liberal outlook toward political rights is not limited to scholars in Arab society, where Sunnī Islam prevails, but can also be found in Iran, where Shiism dominates. Take for instance the views advanced by Mahmoud Soroush in debating a Persian modernist, Hamid Paydar, on the question of compatibility of Islam and democracy. Paydar, who advances a purely Western secular view of the role of religion in society, contends that the fact that religion considers itself "the cradle of the truth" and subsumes opposing beliefs under the categories of "apostasy, idolatry, and delusion" makes it incompatible with democratic government. Soroush responds by rejecting the dichotomy between democracy and religion as false, since it is possible for someone to "consider an idea absolutely false while judging its bearer blameless, respectable, and even commendable."

The question for Soroush and many Muslim intellectuals is not whether Islam is compatible with democracy, but whether values and beliefs that advance intolerance and promote the imposition of faith by the state are Islamic. Any call to impose faith on people is an instance of manifest error, because faith and imposition stand in complete contradiction to one another. Faith is a matter of the heart, and no one should be forced to confess a particular faith, let alone be penalized or chastised for not doing so, because using force in this case lead to negating the very state one intends to achieve. Liberty is indeed a precondition for faith and must therefore be a religious duty to obtain and defend. Without liberty faith will be reduce to external mimicry and spiritless and artificial religiosity. Similarly, without freedom religious law loses its authenticity and social dynamics stagnate. This is because religious law is fundamentally a matter of internal commitment and personal volition. Freedom is also a precondition for religious law, because religious understanding of both faith and law are not decided in any centralized and closed system, but through and open and free debate among the advocates of various interpretations and commitments.

Bibliography

Afghānī, Jamāl al-Dīn al-. "Lecture on Teaching and Learning." In *An Islamic Response to Imperialism: Political and Religious Writings of Sayyid Jamāl ad-Dīn "al-Afghānī,"* edited by Nikki R. Keddie, pp. 101–108. Berkeley: University of California Press, 1968.

Black, Antony. *The History of Islamic Political Thought: From the Prophet to the Present*. 2d ed. Edinburgh: Edinburgh University Press, 2011.

Donohue, John J., and John L. Esposito. *Islam in Transition: Muslim Perspectives*. 2d ed. New York: Oxford University Press, 2007.

Esposito, John L. *Islam and Politics: Contemporary Issues in the Middle East*. 4th ed. Syracuse, N.Y.: Syracuse University Press, 1998.

Euben, Roxanne L., and Muhammad Qasim Zaman, eds. *Princeton Readings in Islamist Thought: Texts and Contexts from al-Banna to Bin Laden*. Princeton, N.J.: Princeton University Press, 2009.

Fārābī, al-. *Al-Farabi on the Perfect State: Abū Naṣr al-Fārābī's Mabādi' ārā' ahl al-madīna al-fāḍila*. Translated by Richard Walzer. Oxford: Clarendon, 1985.

Hegel, Georg. *The Philosophy of History*. Translated by J. Sibree. New York: Cosmo Classics, 2007.

Ibn Taymīyah, Aḥmad. *The Political Shariyah on Reforming the Ruler and the Ruled*. Translated by Umar Farrukh. Beirut: Dār al-Fiqh, 2005.

Māwardī, al-. *The Ordinances of Government*. Translated by Wafaa H. Wahba. Reading, U.K.: Garnet, 2000.

Safi, Louay M. *Tensions and Transitions in the Muslim World*. Dallas, Tex.: University Press of America, 2003.

Watt, W. Montgomery. *Islamic Political Thought*. Edinburgh: Edinburgh University Press, 1998.

Zaman, Muhammad Qasim. *Modern Islamic Thought in a Radical Age: Religious Authority and Internal Criticism*. Cambridge, U.K.: Cambridge University Press, 2012.

Louay M. Safi

Muslim Students Association of North America.

As immigration from Muslim countries to the United States increased after World War II, Muslim students began to organize themselves on American campuses. In 1963, the Muslim Students Association of the United States and Canada (today: MSA National) was founded at the University of Illinois at Urbana-Champaign as an initiative to provide a platform for these campus-based organizations scattered all over North America. Although few Muslim students from less than twenty local Muslim students' association (MSA) organizations were present at the inaugural meeting, MSA National grew rapidly. MSAs all over North America started to affiliate under the umbrella of MSA National, those affiliations being fostered at annual conventions. After immigration laws were relaxed in 1965, immigration from various Muslim countries increased. Hence, in the 1970s, MSA National was no longer just a Muslim students' organization but an organization with a large share of Muslim professionals. Accordingly, MSA National was involved in the formation of organizations for Muslim professionals, such as the Islamic Medical Association, the Association of Muslim Social Scientists, and the Association of Muslim Scientists and Engineers, as well as the North American Islamic Trust. Gradually, the organization found itself unable to respond to the different needs emerging from its diverse membership base. Consequentially, the Islamic Society of North America was founded in 1982 at the nineteenth annual MSA National convention to cater to the needs of the nonstudents, in order for MSA National to return to concentrating on its original clientele.

MSA National is a nonprofit organization, overseen by an executive committee consisting of a board of directors as well as zonal representatives. In 2012 there were around two hundred MSA chapters in the United States and Canada affiliated with MSA National. MSA National organizes regional, zonal, and continental conferences bringing Muslim students together and addressing their needs. MSA National assists Muslim students by building their local MSA chapters. Affiliated chapters are self-organized, MSA National playing the role of a mentor and leadership builder. Affiliated chapters benefit from privileges in MSA National elections.

Aside from the regular conferences, MSA National has more recently focused on social media to connect and build a community of Muslim students in North America.

MSA National's main purpose is to increase the Muslim-friendliness of university campuses. Main focal points are the recognition of Islamic holidays, the establishment of prayer rooms, and the accessibility to *ḥalāl* food. The organization provides guidelines for reaching those goals for the benefit of the local MSA-affiliated chapters.

Additionally, MSA National pursues several national projects in the field of community building and awareness raising. More recently, MSA National has also begun to focus increasingly on issues such as interfaith relations (together with Interfaith Youth Core) and environmentalism, as well as civic engagement and political activism. Those issues provide potential platforms for future alliances with Muslim as well as non-Muslim partners.

BIBLIOGRAPHY

Ba-Yunus, Ilyas, and Kassim Kone. *Muslims in the United States*. Westport, Conn.: Greenwood, 2006.

Muslim Students Association of the United States and Canada [http://msanational.org/] (accessed June 2012).

SABINA VON FISCHER

MUSLIM WORLD LEAGUE. *See* Congresses.

MUṬAHHARĪ, MURTAẒĀ. Ayatollah Murtaẓā Muṭahharī (1920–1979) was born in Fariman, a village in the province of Khorāsān, Iran. He studied in Mashhad and at the Hawẓah-i ʿIlmīyah Seminary in Qom before taking up a teaching position at Tehran University. He was also a professor of philosophy at Tehran State Faculty of Theology. A disciple and colleague of Ayatollah Ruhollah Khomeini (1902–1989), Muṭahharī served time in prison for participating in the anti-Shah uprisings of 1964 and 1975.

Muṭahharī was a cofounder of the famous lecture hall, the Ḥusaynīyah-i Irshād, and a founding member of the Combatant Clergy Association, a revolutionary group of clerics who strove to create a theocratic government based on Khomeini's concept of Islamic governance—*vilāyat-i faqīh* (rule of the jurist). As an early supporter, Muṭahharī chaired the Revolutionary Council, serving as Khomeini's representative until Muṭahharī's assassination in 1979.

Muṭahharī was a gifted speaker and a prolific writer throughout his life, engaging in a wide range of topics, including ontology, epistemology, and philosophy as well as Qur'ānic exegesis, politics, economics, social issues, women's rights, and sexual ethics. He saw Islam as a complete, all-encompassing way of life, and believed that only elite jurists were qualified to lead an Islamic government.

While the Iranian Revolution was fomented by a diverse group of ideologues, Muṭahharī was an articulate writer and thinker, representing the populist clerics who came to dominate Iran's sociopolitical scene in the aftermath of the revolution. His works are still cited as representative of the Islamic Republic's core ideology.

Muṭahharī's unique appeal came from his thoughtful rhetoric. He was well educated and familiar with Western philosophies and political theory, of which he was critical. While his positions were rigid and typical of hardline clerics, he supported his arguments for orthodoxy rationally and persuasively, instead of confining his arguments to Islamic doctrine and polemics. On the topic of women's rights, for example, Muṭahharī emphasized natural gender inequality, and defended orthodox practices and traditions (compulsory veiling, inheritance, polygamy, and unilateral rights of divorce) not only by citing the Qur'ān but discussing generalized physical, emotional, and psychological traits and differences that appealed to traditional family values and patriarchal sensibilities. He defended compulsory veiling, describing it as a benefit to society, and women in general, by eliminating sexual tension, curbing the temptations of illicit sex, and avoiding related social ills and their consequences. Muṭahharī defined women's rights as those that were associated with home life and the family. He denounced Western sexual ethics as permissive, materialistic, and exploitative; a commoditization of the female body at the expense of family virtues.

Muṭahharī's arguments regarding natural inequality applied to his views of society and economics as well. He believed that economic inequality was a natural social condition, and that human beings were each endowed with their own gifts and potential. He took no issue with the state collecting legitimate taxes, supporting the rule of law, or administering public property and natural resources with respect to private ownership. Moreover, he favored limited interference in the market economy, though not to the disadvantage of the state. Muṭahharī's position on private property set him apart from most other popular Iranian revolutionary groups at the time, which were concerned with social justice, and more influenced by Marxist ideology. The popular revolutionary current favored nationalization of property to varying degrees. Leading groups, including Maoists and the Tudeh (Iranian), secular liberals as well as religious groups like the Mujāhidīn (the future Mujāhidīn-i Khalq), and even eminent clerics like Muḥammad Bāqir al-Ṣadr of Iraq, Maḥmud Ṭāleqāni, and another famous revolutionary ideologue, ʿAlī Sharīʿatī (1933–1977) all concluded that ownership and inequality were the chief sources of social ills that befell the Islamic Republic.

Muṭahharī saw Marxism and Western ideologies such as liberalism and nationalism as dangerous and incompatible with a truly Islamic government. He was suspicious of the various Islamic-leftist groups and particularly leery of ʿAlī Sharīʿatī, a popular lay preacher famous for his sermons at the Ḥusaynīyah-i Irshād. Sharīʿatī was highly critical of the clerical establishment, and incorporated Marxist concepts of class disparity and historical determinism into a revolutionary ideal of "Red" Shiism.

Shortly after the revolution triumphed, most militant groups were marginalized by Khomeini or consumed by violent power struggles. On 1 May 1979 Murtaẓā Muṭahharī was shot by a member of a group called the Furqān. The anniversary of his death was proclaimed National Teacher's Day in his honor.

BIBLIOGRAPHY

Dabashi, Hamid. *Shiʿism: A Religion of Protest*. Cambridge, Mass.: Belknap Press of Harvard University Press, 2010.

Davari, Mahmood T. *The Political Thought of Ayatullah Murtaẓā Mutahhari: An Iranian Theoretician of the Islamic State*. London: Routledge, 2005.

Mirsepassi, Ali. *Intellectual Discourse and the Politics of Modernization: Negotiating Modernity in Iran*. Cambridge, U.K.: Cambridge University Press, 2000.

Muṭahharī, Murtaẓā. *Understanding Islamic Sciences: Philosophy, Theology, Mysticism, Morality, Jurisprudence*. London: Saqi, 2002.

AARON ALBERT HALEY

MUʿTAZILAH. The Muʿtazilah were a major theological school of Islam that was renowned for its development of dialectical theology (*ʿilm al-kalām*) that sought to explain revelation through the use of human reason (*ʿaql*). It emerged from obscure beginnings in the middle of eighth century and lasted as an independent school into the twelfth century. The origin of the term Muʿtazilah—meaning those who set themselves apart or those who stand aside—remains as little known as that of the school itself. One account relates how Wāṣil b. ʿAṭā' (d. 748–749), or his student ʿAmr b. ʿUbayd (d. 761), set himself apart (*iʿtazala*) from the study circle of al-Ḥasan al-Baṣrī (d. 728) in disagreement about the status of the grave sinner. Despite its unfounded historicity, this story was widely circulated, by both the Muʿtazilah and others, in explanation of their origins and name. As a whole, the Muʿtazilah were distinguished by an abstract scholasticism that rarely engaged real-world concerns and practical details.

Theological Principles. In the first part of the ninth century Abū al-Hudhayl al-ʿAllāf (d. 840, 842, 847, or 849/850), the first systematizer of Muʿtazilī thought, identified five principles that were shared by the Muʿtazilah, marking them as a self-consciously separate group. These principles, subsequently ascribed to earlier Muʿtazilī figures, include the following:

(1) The first principle proclaims divine oneness (*tawḥīd*). On the one hand, it consists of interpreting the many attributes of God in the Qurʾān as existing only metaphorically (*majāz*), lest multiple entities are affirmed in God. These attributes, therefore, have no existence outside of oneness, such that God hears, sees, and knows through His essence and not through them. On the other hand this principle implies God's transcendence (*tanzīh*) so that verses describing God in human terms or as having a body, such as His "having a hand" ("God's hand is above theirs," 10:48) or "sitting on the throne" ("the Merciful sat on the throne," 5:20) also have to be understood metaphorically. The double implications of this principle brought against the Muʿtazilah the accusation of divesting God of His nature (*taʿṭīl*).

One of the more historically controversial consequences of this principle was the doctrine that the Qurʾān was the "created speech of God" and not part of His essence, since speech as they saw it was one of God's attributes of action. Proclaiming that God's speech is eternal would entail its coeternity with Him, and that, they argued, would be nothing less than proclaiming a duality in God. In political terms, this controversy played out in the *miḥnah* (833–849) instituted by the ʿAbbāsid caliph al-Maʾmūn (r. 812–833), who (under the influence of the Muʿtazilah) unsuccessfully attempted to diminish the sway of the *ḥadīth* folk (*ahl al-ḥadīth*) in Baghdad by enforcing acceptance of this principle. The episode spoke to both the elite and abstract nature of Muʿtazilī doctrines as well as their willingness to forcibly impose their ideas on the general population. This tendency is discussed in greater depth below.

(2) The second principle, divine justice (*ʿadl*), imposes on God the moral imperative of doing what is already known by reason to be just and good. It also pronounces man to be the creator of his actions, namely, having free will, for God would not be just had He created man's evil deeds and then held him responsible for them. On the basis of this principle, critics accused the Muʿtazilah of denying divine will.

(3) The third principle, the punishment and threat (*waʿd wa al-waʿīd*), implies that God punishes whoever transgresses His command in line with His promise in the Qurʾān. According to the opponents of the Muʿtazilah, this principle set limitations on God's absolute will (including His mercy) and undermined the Prophet or the Imams (for the Imāmī/Twelver Shīʿah) ability to intercede on behalf of believers.

(4) The fourth principle, the "intermediate position" (*manzilah bayn al-manzilatayn*), categorizes the grave sinner as neither a believer nor an unbeliever but a *fāsiq* (mortal sinner). The Muʿtazilah did not ostracize the *fāsiq* from the Muslim community in legal matters—for example, the funeral prayer is said for him—but they deemed him condemned to eternal damnation in hell.

(5) The fifth principle necessitates the responsibility of intervening in the affairs of the community, namely, enjoining good and forbidding wrong. It is noteworthy that this principle was adopted with various degrees of intensity by other Muslim groups. This principle had broad political ramifications that were best exemplified in the Zaydī Shīʿah imamates of Yemen and the Caspian.

This schemata of five principles is somewhat misleading. In actuality, the first and second principles are the foundational bedrock of Muʿtazilism. Belief in the absolute unity of God underlies the Muʿtazilī conception of God as well as their exegesis of the Qurʾān and so extends far beyond a simple affirmation of monotheism. The Muʿtazilī insistence on a God that is just in a manner that humans can rationally understand and adheres to a system of morality that aligns with human reasoning leads directly to the third and fifth principles outlined above. Moreover, the combination of these three principles (i.e., the second, third, and fifth) produced the Muʿtazilī belief that the community had an obligation to overthrow an unjust imām even by use of force. The fourth principle is best characterized as a historical remnant of the earliest formulations of Muʿtazilism.

Heterogeneity and Periodization. Despite the principles described above, the Muʿtazilah were far from a homogeneous or unified school of thought. Experimentation and heterogeneity marked their middle period in particular, which extended from the beginning of the ninth century up until the end of the *miḥnah*. For example, Ibrāhīm b. Sayyār al-Naẓẓām (d. between 835 and 845) opposed the atomist world view of Muʿtazilah. In his description of human action, Dirār b. ʿAmr (d. 749) resisted the Muʿtazilah doctrine of free will and prefigured the "acquisition" doctrine (*kasb*) of Abū al-Ḥasan al-Ashʿarī (d. 936). The third phase in the development of the Muʿtazilah, usually described as the "classical" or "scholastic" period, is marked by efforts to build a coherent system of thought around the competing efforts of two schools: the Basran school, with Abū ʿAlī al-Jubbāʾī (d. 915–916) and his son Abū Hāshim (d. 933), and the Baghdadi school with Abū al-Qāsim al-Kaʿbī al-Balkhī (d. 931). As discussed below, it was the doctrines of the Basrans as formulated by Abū Hāshim that thrived and prevailed within Shīʿī theology.

The classical or scholastic period of the Muʿtazilah came to an end with the Seljuk dynasty (eleventh–twelfth centuries), but the movement remained vibrant throughout the Muslim world, particularly in Iran. It was only with the Mongol invasions of the thirteenth century the Muʿtazilah disappeared as a distinctive and independent school of thought.

The Muʿtazilah, the Shīʿah, and Political Activism. Muʿtazilism remained influential among the Shīʿah, and it is here (especially with the Zaydīs) that the political potential of the movement was most fully actualized. Muʿtazilī influence was sometimes projected back to the eighth century, with claims that Zayd b. ʿAlī (d. 740) studied with Wāṣil b. ʿAṭāʾ, but it likely first emerged in the ninth century. Recent scholarship has disputed the Muʿtazilism of Qāsim b. Ibrāhīm al-Rassī (d. 960), leaving al-Hādī ilaʾl-Ḥaqq (d. 911)—the founder of the first Zaydī state in Yemen—as the first Zaydī *imām* unambiguously associated with Muʿtazilī ideas. Echoes of Muʿtazilī theology are also found among the Caspian Zaydīs by (at the very latest) al-Muʾayyad Aḥmad b. al-Ḥusayn (d. 1020). While accepting the broader theological tenets of Muʿtazilism outlined above, the Zaydīs placed a particular emphasis on the principles of divine justice and enjoining good/forbidding wrong, which justified (and even necessitated) the overthrow of an unjust ruler via armed insurrection under the leadership of a qualified candidate for the imamate. Rhetoric highlighting free will, the desire to establish justice, and the duty to enjoin good/forbid wrong became staples of the oaths of allegiance administered by most Zaydī *imāms*. Whereas Zaydism incorporated Muʿtazilī theological beliefs almost in their entirety, it also anchored those principles in the reality of political rule. Thus in the Caspian regions and Yemen, Muʿtazilī ideals were often muted or altered to account for the complexities of actual governance. At times, Muʿtazilism served to legitimize violent suppression of dissenting voices (e.g., the thirteenth-century persecution of the Muṭarrifī Zaydīs by the Zaydī imām Manṣūr ʿAbd Allāh b. Ḥamza—d. 1217) in the name of forbidding wrong and enjoining good. Contemporary Zaydī scholars continue to define their school primarily in terms of Muʿtazilī theological principles.

The Imāmī/Twelver Shīʿah adopted a less politicized understanding of Muʿtazilism beginning in the late tenth century with al-Shaykh al-Mufīd (d. 1022) and (especially) al-Sharīf al-Murtaḍā (d. 1045). The Twelvers/Imāmīs accepted many of the theological principles detailed above, particularly the Muʿtazilī conception of divine justice, but they dissented on issues such as the nature of legitimate political authority (the imamate) and continued to affirm the intercession of the *imāms* on behalf of their followers. They also advocated political quietism in the absence of the *imām*. In this regard, it may be argued that the Imāmī/Twelvers are strongly influenced by Muʿtazilī thought, while the Zaydīs are in many ways their closest modern descendants.

Modern Developments. In the nineteenth century, Sunnī Islamic reformists such as Muḥammad ʿAbduh (d. 1905) adopted the "rationalism" of Muʿtazilī doctrines in order to ground their reform agenda in Islamic history (see his *Risālat al-tawḥīd*). These Sunnī neo-Muʿtazilī thinkers utilized the Muʿtazilah (in a selective manner) to justify a reformed orthodoxy among Sunnī Muslims. With respect to the Shīʿah, Muʿtazilism retains its influence in Zaydism, although the previous centuries have witnessed a "Sunnification" movement that has attempted to mute its political activism. Since the mid-twentieth century, Imāmī/Twelver Shiism has experienced a politicization in which the activist interpretation of divine justice is increasingly invoked despite the continued absence of the Twelfth Imam.

BIBLIOGRAPHY

Cook, Michael. *Commanding Right and Forbidding Wrong in Islamic Thought*. Cambridge, U.K.: Cambridge University Press, 2000. The chapters on the

Mu'tazilah and the Zaydīs are particularly useful for understanding the abstract scholasticism of the former and its actualization by the latter.

Ess, Josef van. "Mu'tazilites." In *Encyclopedia of Religion*, edited by Mircea Eliade, vol. 10, 220–229. New York: Macmillan, 1987. This article expounds the doctrines of the Mu'tazilah and outlines their history with great clarity and detail.

Ess, Josef van. *Theologie und Gesellschaft im 2. und 3. Jahrhundert Hidschra: Eine Geschichte des religiösen Denkens im frühen Islam*. 6 vols. Berlin: Walter de Gruyter, 1991–1997. The most comprehensive intellectual and social history of the Mu'tazilah up to the middle of the ninth century. The fourth volume includes an exhaustive survey of secondary literature and primary sources on the Mu'tazilah, as well as a thematic discussion of their doctrines.

Frank, Richard MacDonough. *Beings and Their Attributes: The Teaching of the Basrian School of the Mu'tazila in the Classical Period*. Albany: State University of New York Press, 1978. This work sheds light on the innovative teachings of Abū Hāshim al-Jubbā'ī on the divine attributes, specifically his doctrine of the states (*aḥwāl*), through a close examination of the original Arabic.

Gimaret, Daniel. "Mu'tazila." In *Encyclopaedia of Islam*, edited by H. A. R. Gibb, vol. 7., pp. 783–793. 2d ed. Leiden, Netherlands: E. J. Brill, 1993. This study remains relevant with a good bibliography of primary texts.

Madelung, Wilferd. *Der Imam al-Qāsim ibn Ibrāhīm und die Glaubenslehre der Zaiditen*. Berlin: Walter de Gruyter, 1965. This is the definitive work on the relationship between the Zaydī Shī'ah and the Mu'tazilah.

Madelung, Wilferd. *Religious Schools and Sects in Medieval Islam*. London: Variorum, 1985. A number of articles in this collection of previously published studies are still seminal for an understanding of Mu'tazilism, particularly in the Iranian context.

Martin, Richard C., and Mark R. Woodward. *Defenders of Reason in Islam: Mu'tazilism from Medieval School to Modern Symbol*. Oxford: Oneworld, 1997. This work includes a full translation of 'Abd al-Jabbār's summary of his *Uṣūl al-khamsah* (The Five Principles), a brief history of the Mu'tazilah, and a discussion of a neo-Mu'tazilah text.

McDermott, Martin J. *The Theology of al-Shaikh al-Mufīd (d. 413/1022)*. Beirut: Dar el-Machreq, 1978. McDermott provides the most comprehensive exposition of the Twelver Shī'ī views of al-Shaykh al-Mufīd, who adopted much of Baghdadi Mu'tazilism, and compares Baghdadi Mu'tazilah doctrines to those of the Basrans.

Peters, J. R. T. M. *God's Created Speech: A Study in the Speculative Theology of the Mu'tazilî Qâdî l-gudât Abûl-Hasan 'Abd al-Jabbâr bn Ahmad al-Hamadânî*. Leiden, Netherlands: Brill, 1976. This monograph is primarily an exposition of the Basran Mu'tazilah 'Abd al-Jabbār's (d. 1025) doctrine on the createdness of the Qur'ān as presented in volume 7 of his major work *al-Mughnī fī abwāb al-tawḥīd wa al-'adl*. It also includes a fairly accessible exposition for the nonspecialist of Basran Mu'tazilī theology as represented by 'Abd al-Jabbār, with a particular focus on epistemology, ontology, and theodicy.

RACHA EL OMARI
and NAJAM HAIDER

MUTTAHIDA MAJLIS-I AMAL. National and provincial elections were held throughout Pakistan in October 2002. An Islamist political coalition, the Muttahida Majlis-i Amal (MMA; United Action Council), was voted into office in the provincial election in the Northwest Frontier Province (NWFP; now Khyber Pakhtunkhwa), shared power in a coalition government in the province of Baluchistan, and came to head the opposition in the National Assembly. Of the 124 members of the NWFP Provincial Assembly, seventy were from the MMA and fifty-four from the opposition. In Baluchistan, the MMA joined a coalition government, as it did not win that provincial election outright.

This unprecedented outcome was the first time in Pakistan's fifty-five-year history that an Islamist political party had won a significant election. To some, the MMA's victory was perceived as a boon by those who admonished the government of Pakistan's continuing support of the U.S. military invasion of Afghanistan, whereas others regarded it as a reaction to the growing "Punjabification" of political power relations in Pakhtun areas of the country. Another key factor contributing to the MMA's electoral success was that key members of the MMA's constituent parties for the first time came together and formed an electoral alliance and did not run against each other, which in the past resulted in dividing the "Islamist" vote.

In 1993, Qāzī Ḥusain Aḥmad of the Jamā'at-i Islāmī formed the Islamic Front to focus on social development concerns in Pakhtun areas. Seven years later, Mawlānā Samīul Ḥaq created the Pakistan-Afghanistan Defense Council, which brought together the Islamic Front and other constituent groups in response to the West's criticism, in particular, of the Taliban government in Afghanistan and of Osama Bin Laden. Following the U.S. invasion of Afghanistan in October 2001, the coalition became the MMA, consisting of six Islamist parties: Jamā'at-i Islāmī, Jam'īyatul 'Ulamā'-i Islām (Faẕlur Raḥmān group), Jam'īyatul 'Ulamā'-i Islām (Samīul Ḥaq group), Jam'īyatul-'Ulamā'-i Pākistān, Markazī Jam'īyat Ahl-i Ḥadīth, and Tehrik Nifaz Fiqah Jaferiya (a Shī'ah party).

The constituent political parties campaigned "to implement an Islamic system and to protect Islamic values," prioritizing promoting the Islamization process, greater provincial autonomy, various social issues (e.g., lower unemployment and inflation rates), as well arranging for "healthy entertainment and mental, psychological, and moral mentoring of the youth," and to end "unwanted restrictions on independent journalism and freedom of speech, and that journalism be made according to religious and national values" (MMA, 2002, "Constitution of MMA"). Its campaign promises laid the foundation for two of the most important pieces of legislation that it would introduce, the provincial Sharī'ah Law and the Hisba Bill.

Six months after taking office, the MMA government passed its Sharī'ah Law, a framework to reform education and encourage greater personal piety, transform the economy into one based on Islam, and "put an end to corruption, embezzlement and malpractices of the provincial government." In addition, the provincial government would enact "necessary legislation... to wipe out vulgarity and lawlessness" (MMA, 2003, "Draft Report on Islamization").

The Hisba Act was developed to ensure implementation of both the Sharī'ah Law and various other plans to promote Islamization. It proposed to create a new ombudsman's office to "advocate virtue (*amr bi-al-ma'rūf*)" and ensure that "social evils, injustices, and the misuse of powers could be checked properly" (MMA, 2003, "Draft Report on Islamization"). Pakistan's federal Council on Islamic Ideology issued a judgment on the Hisba Bill in September 2004, deeming it "unconstitutionally vague." It was concerned with the possibility of the Hisba Force opening the door to havoc (*mufasid*), creating a dangerous state of indeterminacy with the result that "in the course of making laws, at any time, any government, whatsoever, can use these laws to obtain its political objectives in an unfair manner" (Council of Islamic Ideology, 2004). Its greatest concern was with the arbitrariness that could result from both the Hisba Act and the Hisba Force and the inclusion of moral and ethical issues about which there is no consensus or agreement, as the Hisba Bill "has not defined what good and evil are," and it cannot do this on an ad hoc basis, as "arbitrariness would bring disgrace to the institution" (Council of Islamic Ideology, 2004).

In mid-November 2003, one of the MMA's constituent members, the Shī'ah group Tehrik Nifaz Fiqah Jaferiya, was banned in Pakistan as a terrorist organization. The Jam'īyatul-'Ulamā'-i Pākistān was weakened by the death of its leader, Aḥmad Nurānī, the following month. The Jam'īyatul 'Ulamā'-i Islām—Samīul Ḥaq periodically disassociated itself from the coalition while it still held office. Importantly, the MMA government opened a political space within which extremist Islamist groups, such as Maulana Fazlullah's Tehrik-e-Taliban Pakistan faction in Swat, were allowed to operate freely.

The MMA fared poorly in the 2007 elections and has effectively disintegrated, but its constituent groups keep stating they will contest elections together in the future.

BIBLIOGRAPHY

Council of Islamic Ideology, Government of Pakistan. "Judgement on Proposed Hasba Act." September 2004. In Urdu, translated by Juan Cole.

Muttahida Majlis-i Amal. "Constitution of MMA." 2002. In Urdu, translated by Anita Weiss.

Muttahida Majlis-i Amal. "Draft Report on Islamization in NWFP." 2003. In Urdu, translated by Ayesha Attique.

ANITA WEISS

N

NABHĀNĪ, TAQĪ AL-DĪN AL-. Muḥammad Taqī al-Dīn bin Ibrahīm al-Nabhānī (1905–1977), was born in Ijzim, a village near Haifa, and died 20 December 1977 in Beirut. He was the founder of the Islamic Liberation Party (Ḥizb al-Taḥrīr al-Islāmī), a small but durable political movement that embodied the conjuncture of Islamist activism and Palestinian yearning for a homeland and reversing the outcome of the 1948 war.

After a religious education, he served as a judge in the *sharīʿah* court of Haifa during the British Mandate. During the early 1940s he went to Egypt, where he studied at al-Azhar University and joined the Muslim Brotherhood. He returned to Haifa and became a leading figure in the local branch of the Muslim Brothers until the partition of Palestine in 1948. At some time during the chaotic year of partition he moved first to Nablus and then to Jerusalem, where he taught religion at the Ibrahimiya School. In 1950 he composed his first work, *Inqādh filasṭīn* (Saving Palestine). He left the Muslim Brotherhood shortly thereafter and founded the Islamic Liberation Party in Jerusalem with other dissident Muslim Brothers in 1952 for the dual purposes of establishing an Islamic state and liberating Palestine. From its initial base in the Jordanian-ruled West Bank, the party spread to Lebanon, Syria, Iraq, Egypt, Tunisia, and Turkey. This geographical expansion correlated to a broadening of the party's focus from a primary concern with Palestine to the project of setting up an Islamic state that would restore Islamic order throughout the Muslim world.

Even though the party never attained legal status in Jordan, it remained active until the 1967 war. During that time it strove to spread Nabhānī's ideas by running clandestine study groups and distributing leaflets. The party also ran candidates as independents in elections for the Chamber of Deputies in 1954 and 1956; in both elections, the party won a single seat. In November 1953, official pressure induced al-Nabhānī to leave the country for Syria, where he stayed until 1959, when he moved to Lebanon to organize the party there. He was never allowed back into Jordan, but his party continued to spread his teachings. Although the party spread widely, it never won the large following it sought and expected, even during a period when other Islamist groups enjoyed growing influence. Nonetheless, the party did produce an elaborate and detailed program for instituting and managing an Islamic state.

His teachings contain several broad themes. One theme is to persuade Muslims, whose minds have been colonized and Westernized, that Islam is preferable to capitalism or socialism as the basis for a modern political, economic, and social order. A second theme is to analyze Muslim history with a view to identifying the causes of contemporary political weakness. A third theme concerns the measures Muslims should take to restore Islam through an Islamic state. British plots in particular and Western imperialist conspiracies in general, according to al-Nabhānī, pervaded the Muslim world and ultimately explain its main lines of political development. The idea that Britain and Europe viewed a strong caliphate as a danger to their designs on the Muslim world frequently appears in al-Nabhānī's later works. Another recurring theme is al-Nabhānī's belief that nationalism was introduced to the Muslim world in order to divide Muslims and leave them vulnerable to European conquest. He believed that the liberation of Palestine can be achieved only after reversing the effects of nationalism through a political transformation of the Arab states. Such a transformation of Arab politics depends on a corresponding revolution in Muslim society. He attributes Arab malaise to confusion in the realm of ideas. Thus, it will be sincere and able thinkers who begin the process of social reform and bring it to schools, factories, farms, and homes. The starting point for this social movement is an inspired individual who serves as leader of a vanguard that then influences the rest of society. As the influence of the vanguard grows, it will turn into an organized political party that takes over Arab countries and unites them.

The most salient proposition that has come to define al-Nabhānī's party is the call to reestablish a unified Islamic caliphate. Unlike the Muslim Brotherhood of the Arab world or Jamāʿat-i Islāmī of South Asia, the Ḥizb is uncompromising in rejecting the nation-state and insistent, often to the chagrin of the many who might otherwise be sympathetic to its message, on restoring the caliphate as not just the final but an immediate and ever-present goal for all Muslims. Unlike the Muslim Brotherhood, which has been remarkable in its ability to compromise and adapt, the Ḥizb rejects both democracy and violence as methods of the desired transformation, and insists rather on the intellectual transformation of individuals as the only legitimate starting point, followed by the consolidation of a vanguard, which would then be able to transform the concepts and beliefs of the Muslim society at large, leading to the proper political transformation. This emphasis on intellect is found in the writings of al-Nabhānī, who was an Ashʿarī in theology, impressed with great classical theologians like al-Ghazālī (d. 1111), although the latter's embrace of Sufism as a way out of rational conundrums and doubt, as well as his critique of theology, are entirely absent in al-Nabhānī.

Bibliography

Ayoob, Mohammed. *The Many Faces of Political Islam: Religion and Politics in the Muslim World.* Ann Arbor: University of Michigan Press, 2008.

Cohen, Amnon. *Political Parties in the West Bank under the Jordanian Regime, 1949–1967.* Ithaca, N.Y.: Cornell University Press, 1982.

Jansen, G. H. *Militant Islam.* New York: Harper & Row, 1979.

Nabhānī, Taqī al-Dīn al-. *Niẓām al-Islām.* Jerusalem: Manshūrāt Ḥizb al-Taḥrīr, 1953.

Ovamir Anjum

Nadwat al-ʿUlamāʾ. Nadwat al-ʿUlamāʾ (Council of Muslim Religious Scholars was originally a convention of Indian Muslim scholars and subsequently a leading religious seminary based in Lucknow, Uttar Pradesh, with affiliations throughout India as well as in Pakistan and Nepal. Nadwat al-ʿUlamāʾ was founded in 1891 in Kanpur, Uttar Pradesh, with the aim of uniting the various streams of Islamic learning that had sprung up in India in the aftermath of the Great Revolt and the demise of the Mughal Empire in 1857–1858. Among the participants in the inaugural meeting in 1893 were modernists of Aligarh College, *qasba*-based Deobandīs, fundamentalist Ahl-i Ḥadīth, rationalist Farangi Mahallis, traditional Ṣūfī Barelwīs, and, for a while, even Shīʿī. A leading role in the formation of Nadwat al-ʿUlamāʾ was played by Shibli Nuʿmānī (d. 1914), a close associate of Aligarh's founder, Sir Sayyid Ahmad Khan, though the more consensual Naqshbandī *shaykh* Ali Mongiri (d. 1928) was elected first president.

The early annual meetings of Nadwat al-ʿUlamāʾ discussed the reformation of Indo-Muslim scholarship and the role of the Muslim scholars in colonial British India. Soon, however, it became apparent that the differences of opinions among the various *ʿulamāʾ* factions were too wide to overcome. The Shīʿī were the first to leave, followed by the Barelwīs, who found themselves excluded because of their adherence to "superstitious beliefs and practices." Following Mongiri's resignation in 1903 a new rupture developed within the Nadwah ranks, between the modernists led by Shibli, who called to form a new rational theology and historiography, and Mongiri's assistant Sayyid ʿAbd al-Ḥayy al-Ḥasanī of Rae Bareli (d. 1923), who adopted a more conservative agenda centered on the study of ḥadīth. ʿAbd al-Ḥayy eventually won the day and was nominated head of Nadwat al-ʿUlamāʾ in 1915. Thereafter he turned it into another Sunnī religious faction in India and a patrimony of his family, henceforth known as the Nadwīs.

The idea of establishing a model religious seminary (*dār al-ʿulūm*) under the supervision of Nadwat al-ʿUlamāʾ was first aired in 1896. Inaugurated two years later, it moved to its present site in Lucknow in 1908, to become the primary institution of the Nadwah and the basis of its political and social activity. Shibli was instrumental in shaping the initial reformist goal of the seminary, namely, to forge a new kind of proficient scholars capable of coping with the problems of the modern age and defending Islam against its Western and Hindu detractors. He demanded that the curriculum reflect modern knowledge and stressed the need to study English. Under ʿAbd al-Ḥayy and his successors the curriculum came closer to the Deobandī system, with the study of *ḥadīth* and the traditional sciences (*manqūlāt*) at the expense of the rational sciences (*maʿqūlāt*) that were not only advocated by Shibli but also imbedded in the *dars-i niẓāmī*, the customary curriculum created at Farangi Mahal. This was accompanied by a stress on the study of Arabic, which became the hallmark of Nadwat al-ʿUlamāʾ among Indian schools.

Nadwat leaders have generally shown little interest in politics as such. During the anticolonial struggle of the interwar period, ʿAbd al-ʿAlī al-Ḥasanī al-Nadwī (d. 1961), ʿAbd al-Ḥayy's eldest son and successor, refrained from supporting Jamʿīyatul ʿUlamāʾ-i Hind (the Association of Muslim Scholars of India) that, after the collapse of the Khilāfat movement, allied with the Indian National Congress against the separatist tendencies of the All-India Muslim League. He felt much closer to the Tablīghī Jamāʿat, an apolitical missionary movement that has directed its efforts toward marginalized Muslim populations. It was also during ʿAbd al-ʿAlī's term that the first Arabic journal *al-Diyaʾ* appeared in India and close ties were forged between Nadwat al-ʿUlamāʾ and Arab scholars, particularly of the Salafīyah trend.

These various activities were taken up and further elaborated by Abū al-Ḥasan ʿAlī al-Ḥasanī al-Nadwī (ʿAlī Miyān, d. 1999), ʿAbd al-ʿAlī's younger brother, whose term represented the peak of Nadwat al-ʿUlamāʾ's influence in India and beyond. As a true heir to the Nadwah ideology, Abū al-Ḥasan was initiated into the Naqshbandī

Ṣūfī brotherhood, studied with leading Deobandī scholars, served as one of the foremost missionaries of the Tablīghī Jamāʿat, and for a while associated with Abū al-Aʿlā al-Mawdūdī (d. 1979), leader of the Jamāʿat-i Islāmī movement—until he recognized the latter's excessive political propensity. Abū al-Ḥasan's was the way of religious propagation from below (*daʿwah*), rather than political change from above. He emphasized the central role of the *ʿulamāʾ* as the only legitimate transmitters of religious knowledge in the reform and propagation of Islam, and, to enhance Nadwat al-ʿUlamāʾ's position in these respects, in 1959, shortly before his appointment, he founded the Academy of Islamic Research and Publication on its premises. The Urdu mouthpiece of the institution, *Taʿmīr-i Ḥayāt* (Establishing the Pious Life), first appeared in 1963.

Abū al-Ḥasan's reputation in the Arab world rested on his writings, particularly his 1947 book *Mādhā khasira al-ʿālam bi-inhiṭaṭ al-muslimīn* (What Has the World Lost with the Decline of the Muslims?), which endeared him to Salafīs and Muslim Brothers in Egypt and Syria and led to his election as a founding member of the Saudi-based World Islamic League. As relations with the Wahhābī scholars soured, Abū al-Ḥasan established in 1984 the World League of Islamic Literature to support Indo-Muslim scholarship. He accepted the presidency with the stipulation that Nadwat al-ʿUlamāʾ should serve as the institutional core of the League and host its international gatherings. This helped him consolidate his position as the leading representative of Indo-Muslim scholarship and to harmonize the different approaches to religious education in India—the original goal of the Nadwat al-ʿUlamāʾ.

Today, with more than four thousand students, most of them boarders, and more than a hundred affiliated schools throughout India and the rest of South Asia, *dār al-ʿulūm* Nadwat al-ʿUlamāʾ is one of the leading institutions of higher education in India. Its current principal, ʿAbd al-Rabiʿ al-Nadwī, Abū al-Ḥasan's nephew and successor, shares the general concern with the contemporary association of *madrasahs* with terrorism and has called for incorporating an Islamized form of the modern sciences into the Indo-Muslim curriculum.

BIBLIOGRAPHY

Hartung, Jan-Peter. "The Nadwat al-ʿUlamāʾ: Chief Patron of *Madrasa* Education in India and a Turntable to the Arab World." In *Islamic Education, Diversity, and National Identity: Dīnī Madāris in India Post 9/11*, edited by Jan-Peter Hartung and Helmut Reifeld, pp. 135–157. New Delhi: SAGE, 2006.

Hartung, Jan-Peter. "Standardizing Muslim Scholarship: The Nadwat al- ʿUlamāʾ." In *Assertive Religious Identities: India and Europe*, edited by Satish Saberwal and Mushirul Hasan, 121–144. New Delhi: Manohar, 2006.

Malik, Jamal. *Islamische Gelhertenkultur in Nordindien*. Leiden: E. J. Brill, 1997.

Metcalf, Barbara Daly. *Islamic Revival in British India: Deoband, 1860–1900*. Princeton, N.J.: Princeton University Press, 1982.

Zaman, Muhammad Qasim. "Arabic, the Arab Middle East, and the Definition of Muslim Identity in Twentieth Century India." *Journal of the Royal Asiatic Society*, 3d ser., 8 (1998): 59–81.

ITZCHAK WEISMANN

NADWĪ, ABŪ AL-ḤASAN. Sayyid Abūl Ḥasan ʿAlīal-Ḥasan al-Nadwī (1914–1999) was a transnational Indian *ʿālim*, author, and educator. ʿAlī Miyān, as he is known affectionately by his South Asian admirers, was born in 1914 in the district of Rae Bareli, in Uttar Pradesh, India. His father, ʿAbd al-Ḥayy al-Ḥasanī (d. 1923), was a noted religious scholar and author of a prominent Arabic biographical dictionary on Indian Muslims (*Nuzhat al-khawāṭir wa-bahjat al-masāmiʿ wa-al-nawāẓir*) and two works on Islam in India (*al-Thaqāfah al-islāmīyah fī al-Hind* and *Al-Hind* *fī al-ʿahd al-islāmī*). Al-Nadwī's family was descended from the nineteenth-century revivalist Sayyid Aḥmad al-Shahīd (d. 1831).

During Nadwī's childhood his father died, leaving his mother and older brother to oversee his education, and he was enrolled in Lucknow's Darul Uloom Nadwatul Ulama (hence his moniker "Nadwī"). He also studied Urdu literature at Lucknow University and supplemented his religious and literary studies by studying English for three years. He furthered his religious training at Darul Uloom Deoband, studying *ḥadīth*, Qurʾānic studies, and *fiqh*.

In 1934, Nadwī was appointed lecturer at Darul Uloom Nadwatul Ulama and taught Qurʾānic exegesis, *ḥadīth*, Arabic literature, history, and logic. As a faculty member, he founded several journals in both Urdu and Arabic and was appointed to various posts in the college, the most important being director of education in 1954 and general secretary of the college in 1961, succeeding his brother. He held the latter position for the remainder of his life.

In addition to his post at Nadwa, he was president of the Dīnī Taʿlīmī Council (Uttar Pradesh) and a member of several Muslim organizations, including the standing committee of Dār al-Muṣannafīn (Azamgarh), Darul Uloom Deoband's Majlis-i Shūrā, and the board of directors of al-Rābiṭah al-Adab al-Islāmi al-ʿĀlamī (World Committee for Islamic Literature) in Jordan. He had strong ties with several Saudi institutes, including the World Muslim League, and served on the standing committee of Medina University. He was also a visiting professor in Medina, Damascus, and Marrakech. He received numerous awards, including the King Faisal Prize for Islamic Services in 1980. Nadwī was one of the trustees of the Oxford Centre for Islamic Studies, when it was established in 1983.

Nadwī's religious orientation reflected that of his alma mater. As one of the many Muslim educational institutions formed after the 1857 Sepoy Mutiny, Nadwatul Ulama sought to preserve and shape Indian Muslim culture and identity. Nadwa emphasized Arabic as a living language and stressed the strengthening of ties with the Arab world. In religious learning, Nadwa deferred to the authorities of Darul Uloom Deoband, and under Nadwī's influence the Tablīghī Jamāʿat came to have a strong presence at Nadwa.

As a student, Nadwī studied under prominent *ʿulama*ʾ, most notably the Moroccan Salafī Taqī al-Dīn al-Hilālī (d. 1987) and the Deobandī scholar-activist Ḥusayn Aḥmad al-Madanī (d. 1957). In a visit to Lahore in 1929, Nadwī met the Indian poet-philosopher Muhammad Iqbal (d. 1938) and wrote an Arabic study of Iqbal that popularized the latter's work in the Arab world. Perhaps his most notable relationship was with Abū al-Aʿlā al-Mawdūdī (d. 1979) and the Jamāʿat-i Islāmī. When Mawdūdī established the Jamāʿat in 1941 he sent letters of invitation to more than fifty Indian *ʿulamā*ʾ. While the senior *ʿulamā*ʾ did not respond, a few younger ones accepted and became founding members, among them Nadwī. Nadwī's formal relationship with the Jamāʿat was short-lived, and in October 1942 he parted ways with the organization. Despite this formal break, he maintained a working relationship with Mawdūdī through translating the latter's writings into Arabic, and he remained intimate friends with many of the Jamāʿat's senior members.

Upon leaving the Jamāʿat, Nadwī turned to the Tablīghī Jamāʿat, the Indian revivalist effort of Maulānā Muḥammad Ilyās Kāndhalavī (d. 1943), and the Ṣūfī teachings of Mawlānā ʿAbd al-Qādir Raipuri (d. 1962). Ilyās's vision of Islamic revival focused on individual and inter-Muslim moral reform through preaching. Nadwī wrote a biography of Ilyās and was greatly influenced by him, but he parted ways with the latter's successors, finding the focus of the group ill-suited to reaching educated Muslims. In all of his disagreements with his peers, Nadwī never severed relationships nor engaged in polemics, preferring to maintain ties with Muslim activists and scholars while giving counsel and advice on issues they disagreed on.

Nadwī's literary production was vast, including books and articles in both Urdu and Arabic, many of which have been translated into English and other Western languages. His first Arabic publication, at the age of seventeen, was an essay on Sayyid Aḥmad Shahīd that was published in *al-Manār*, the journal edited by Rashīd Riḍā (1865–1935). One of his most famous works is his 1950 *Mādhā khasira al-ʿālam bi inhiṭaṭ al-muslimīn* (What Has the World Lost with the Decline of Muslims?). In this book, Nadwī provides a narrative for the emergence of Islam and Islamic history that he contrasts with the history of Europe and European civilization, culminating in the domination of the latter over the former. This narrative is framed in terms of Islam and *jāhilīyah*, respectively, where the latter category is expanded beyond pre-Islamic Arabia to include the entire pre-Islamic world and, more importantly, modern Europe. The vision of revival that he articulates in this book assigns a central role to Arabs as leaders of the Islamic revival. It was thus influential on Arab Muslim activists in articulating a narrative of rise, decline, and revival, in addition to providing a counternarrative to Arab nationalist discourses. Islamists, particularly Sayyid Quṭb, were influenced by Nadwī's articulation of modern Arab nationalism as *jāhilīyah* and appropriated this idea in their own discourses.

Nadwī's vision of Islamic activism however differed significantly from Islamist ideologues. In a 1979 essay titled *Al-tafsīr al-siyāsī lil-Islām fī mirʿāt kitābāt al-ustādh Abī al-Aʿlāʾ al-Mawdūdī wa-al-shahīd Sayyid Quṭb*, Nadwī provides a critique of Islamist notions of religion as articulated in Mawdūdī's essay *The Qurʾan's Four Foundational Terms* and Quṭb's *Milestones*. A central point of Nadwī's critique is their notion of "establishing religion" (*iqāmat al-dīn*). Nadwī notes that Mawdūdī and Quṭb's texts make political ascendancy of a vanguard group of believers the key pillar in the establishment of religion. In this vision, political authority is made the ultimate telos of Islam in light of which all Islamic teachings, practices, and history become reinterpreted. While Nadwī did not deny a political dimension of Islam, the focus of his essay was to highlight and problematize Islamist reinterpretations of religion that he saw as breaking from normative Islamic teachings, highlighting in particular how Islamist interpretations instrumentalize religion and empty it of spiritual and ethical dimensions.

Nadwī's notion of Islamic revival and "establishing religion" is reflected in his influential four-part work on Islamic revivalism, *Rijāl al-fikr wa-al-daʿwah*, the first two volumes of which were delivered as lectures on a visit to Damascus. The first volume provides biographies of an eclectic collection of revivalists, containing entries on political leaders (ʿUmar ibn ʿAbd al-ʿAzīz), Ṣūfīs (al-Ḥasan al-Baṣrī, ʿAbd al-Qādir al- Jīlānī, and Jalāl al-Dīn al-Rūmī), and theologians-cum-jurists (Aḥmad ibn Ḥanbal, Abū al-Ḥasan al-Ashʿarī, al-Ghazālī). The remaining three volumes are dedicated to Ibn Taymīyah, Aḥmad Sirhindī, and Shāh Walī Allāh, respectively. A central aspect of this book is that Islamic revival is not conceived of as pertaining to the political sphere alone; it focuses instead on the ability of Islamic teachings to impact individual Muslims and society.

Nadwī opposed the partition of India, agreeing with his teacher Ḥusayn Aḥmad Madanī, who worked with the Congress Party for Indian independence. Nadwī's political activism developed in the 1960s and reflected the context of a religious and cultural minority in an ostensibly secular and democratic state. According to Nadwī, domination in a modern nation-state is all-pervasive, extending to virtually every aspect of life, education, and moral formation. Based on this observation about the reach of the state, he saw it as imperative for Muslims to be involved in the political processes in order to defend and preserve Indian Muslim culture. To this end, in 1964 Nadwī, along with other leading Indian religious figures, established the Muslim Majlis-i Mushāwarat (The Muslim Consultative Assembly). The Majlis was explicitly not a political party but an advisory group that sought to dialogue with existing parties on Muslim concerns and to facilitate intercommunal goodwill.

In 1973 Nadwī was part of a group that established the Muslim Personal Law Board, which aimed to maintain the sovereignty of the Muslim community on matters pertaining to personal law, which Nadwī led from 1983. The 1985 Shah Bano case brought the problem of personal status law into sharper focus. A divorced Muslim woman took her ex-husband to court to demand continued financial support. The husband argued that, according to Islamic law, her "waiting period" after the divorce had ended and that he was no longer financially responsible for her well-being. The High Court of Madhya Pradesh ruled in favor of Shah Bano, a verdict upheld by the Supreme Court. Muslim religious authorities of all stripes, under the Muslim Personal Law Board, came out in staunch opposition to this ruling, demanding that the government repeal the Supreme Court decision. Prime Minister Rajiv Gandhi met several times with Nadwī, and in 1986 the Muslim Women (Protection of Rights on Divorce) Bill was passed, overturning the Supreme Court's decision.

Though based at Nadwa, in Lucknow, Nadwī was an itinerant scholar, visiting virtually every Muslim-majority country in the Middle East, Asia, and Africa, in addition to Muslim communities in Europe and America. Through his travels, he came into contact with the most prominent figures of Islamic thought and activism in his lifetime, too numerous to list here. Of note are the *ʿulamāʾ* and activists of Syria, Egypt, Morocco, and Saudi Arabia, where he spent time writing and teaching. His mastery of spoken and literary Arabic endeared him to scores of Arab Muslim activists and to the Arab public. The prefaces and introductions that he wrote to numerous books were published in three sizable volumes and testify to the scope of his relationships, spanning the Arabic- and Urdu-speaking worlds.

Nadwī's influence as a transnational religious scholar and as a leader of Indian Muslims was substantial, extending well beyond India. In a period of tremendous contestation within Islamic activism on the interpretation of Islam, the reception of Nadwī's efforts has been overwhelmingly positive, with few detractors. His writings remain in print throughout the Muslim world and have been incorporated into the curricula of many educational institutions. What resonates most among Muslim activists and scholars are his indefatigable efforts in the cause of Islamic revival, his general lack of partisanship, and his saintly reputation. For many Muslims, this latter feature is testified to by the fact that on 31 December 1999 he died while reading the Qurʾān on a Friday morning in Ramaḍān.

Bibliography

Choughley, Abdul Kader. *Islamic Resurgence: Sayyid Abul Hasan ʿAli Nadwī and His Contemporaries.* New Delhi: DK Printworld, 2011.

Hartung, Jan-Peter. *Viele Wege und ein Ziel: Leben un Wirken von Sayyid Abūl-Ḥasan ʿAlī al-Ḥasanī Nadwī, 1914–1999.* Wurzburg, Germany: Ergon, 2004.

Nadwī, Muḥammad Akram. *Abū al-Ḥasan al-Nadwī: Al-ʿālim al-murabbī wa-al- dāʿīyah al-ḥakīm.* Damascus: Dār al-Qalam, 2006.

Sikand, Yoginder. *The Origins and Development of the Tablighi Jamaʿat, 1920–2000: A Cross-Country Comparative Study.* Hyderabad, India: Orient Longman, 2002.

Sikand, Yoginder. "Sayyed Abul Hasan ʿAli Nadwi and Contemporary Islamic Thought in India." In *The Blackwell Companion to Contemporary Islamic Thought*, edited by Ibrahim M. Abu Rabiʿ, pp. 88–1044. Malden, Mass.: Blackwell, 2006.

Zaman, Muhammad Qasim. "The Role of Arabic and the Arab Middle East in the Definition of Muslim Identity in Twentieth Century India." *Muslim World* 87, nos. 3–4 (1997): 272–298.

Zaman, Muhammad Qasim. *The Ulama in Contemporary Islam: Custodians of Change*. Princeton, N.J.: Princeton University Press, 2002.

JAWAD ANWAR QURESHI

NAHDATUL ULAMA. Nahdatul Ulama, or NU (Awakening of the Religious Scholars), is Indonesia's largest Islamic civil association. Established on 31 January 1926, it aims to preserve traditionalism and oppose modernism. It is a counter movement to the growing Muhammadiyah organization (Persyarikatan Muhammadiyah). From the second half of twentieth century, NU has been functioning as a socioreligious movement and political party. NU's purpose, as stated in its 1926 original charter, was to enhance relationships among Sunnī schools of thought and propagate Islam on the basis of their teachings; establish *madrasahs*; manage mosques; look after orphans and the poor; and organize the advancement of agriculture, trade, and industry under Islamic terms. NU's emblem, adopted in 1927, contains traditionalism, Sufism, and Javanese Muslim elements. From 1930 until World War II, NU grew rapidly, not only as a socioreligious movement but also as an agent for the internal transformation of the *pesantren*. During the Japanese occupation of 1942–1945 and also during the subsequent 1945–1949 war of independence, NU became part of an actively anticolonialist coalition, the Masyumi Party.

1952–1984. Withdrawing from Masyumi Party after seven years in 1952, the NU campaigned as an independent political party and was represented in a series of coalition governments. In the first parliamentary general elections of 1955, NU emerged, after receiving 18.4 percent of the total vote, along with the Nationalist Party (Partai Nasional Indonesia; PNI), Masyumi Party, and the Communist Party (Partai Komunis Indonesia; PKI), as one of the top four parties.

NU and other Islamic parties endeavored in the Constitutional Assembly to promote a new constitution that would make Indonesia an Islamic state. Failure to reach an agreement on the constitution led to controversy and, in 1958, to the dissolution of the assembly by President Sukarno, who declared a return to the 1945 constitution and formed the NASAKOM government, a coalition of nationalists, communists, and religious forces (including NU). In the NASAKOM government (1960–1965), NU became a much greater power, leading to its entrenchment in the religious administration.

Following a coup in 1967, Sukarno was replaced by Suharto (1921–2008), the second president of Indonesia, who ushered in a New Order (Orde Baru), expelling the communists and radical nationalists from national and local politics. In the 1971 general elections, NU was the only one of the four parties in the 1955 elections to have survived the tumult of 1965. Receiving an overwhelming 63 percent majority, the newly formed Golkar Party came to power, while NU secured second position by obtaining 18.3 percent, maintaining its popularity of 1955.

In 1971, NU campaigned as an independent party, as the New Order denied the NU its share of power, including cabinet seats. The number of political parties was reduced, to secure political stability, to three: Golkar, Partai Persatuan Pembangunan (PPP); United Development Party, and Partai Demokrasi Indonesia; Indonesian Democratic Party (PDI). In 1973, NU was forced to merge with PPP. Suharto's New Order regime, resulting in a decrease in the power of NU, thus promoted "depoliticization of Islam." After conflicts, the NU finally, in 1984, decided to withdraw from the PPP.

After 1984. The NU formally discarded its political role in 1984 and returned to its original position as a socio-religio-educational organization focused on education, community welfare, and socioeconomic development. This move allowed more opportunities for NU to build relationships with other political parties such as Golkar and the PDI-P (Partai Demokrasi Indonesia Perjuangan; Indonesian Democratic Party of Struggle). NU became more visible during the presidency of Abdurrahman Wahid (October 1999–July 2001) in efforts to involve *pesantren* in community development. This shift of focus exposed the NU's younger and more active members to nongovernmental-organization activities, creating an awareness among the *pesantren* of the relationship between religious discourse and social and economic activities.

Abdurrahman Wahid (1940–2009), the first democratically elected president of Indonesia after the resignation of Suharto in 1998, also served as the longtime president of NU and was the founder of the Partai Kebangkitan Bangsa (National Awakening Party; PKB). Under Wahid's leadership, NU broadened the playing field of politics where its socioreligious activities could generate political values. Understandably, the move was an attempt to seize the moment at a time when power politics was highly contested. This reentrance into party politics enabled Wahid to become Indonesia's fourth president. Two other leaders from NU's central board, Hasyim Muzadi and Salahuddin Wahid, ran as vice presidential candidates. Many more served in the cabinet, parliament, and regional administration.

NU also initiated the politics of counterbalancing the state, especially when the government was at the height of its hegemonic power. Cases in point include NU's criticism of the ICMI (Indonesian Muslim Intellectuals Association) as well as NU's pioneering role in forming Forum Demokrasi (Democratic Forum) in March 1991.

In the aftermath of Wahid's reign, NU has become an active codeveloper, in contrast with other parties, of a model for civil society, appropriate for the Indonesian context, by adapting to social change and modernity. NU has struggled with challenges such as religious liberalism and moderation, violence, and radicalism. By transforming NU into a movement for a more democratic, prosperous, and religiously harmonious Indonesia, a new generation of NU leadership personified by Wahid is responding to these and other challenges. At the same time, NU is facing a severe impasse when it comes to maintaining tradition and adjusting to these challenges and other current trends

Although the proper relationship between NU and politics has been an issue of concern, its leaders have tried to pay more attention to the socio-religious and cultural mission of the organization. This has also been a concern of the previous leaders as well; thus, whether or not NU will finally be able to design a new scheme with regard to its relationship with politics remains to be seen.

BIBLIOGRAPHY

Bush, Robin. *Nahdlatul Ulama and the Struggle for Power within Islam and Politics in Indonesia*. Singapore: Institute of Southeast Asian Studies, 2009.

Bush, Robin. "Redefining 'Political Islam' in Indonesia: Nahdlatul Ulama and Khittah '26." *Studia Islamika* 7, no. 2 (2000): 59–86.

Cederroth, Sven. "Indonesia and Malaysia." In *Islam Outside the Arab World*, edited by David Westerlund and Ingvar Svanberg, pp. 253–277. Richmond, U.K.: Curzon, 1999.

Falaakh, Mohammad Fajrul. "Nahdlatul Ulama and Civil Society in Indonesia." In *Islam and Civil Society in Southeast Asia*, edited by Nakamura Mitsuo, Sharon Siddique, and Omar Farouk Bajunid,

pp. 33–42. Singapore: Institute of Southeast Asian Studies, 2001.
Fealy, Greg. "The Political Contingency of Reform-Mindedness in Indonesia's Nahdlatul Ulama: Interest Politics and the Khittah." In *Islamic Legitimacy in a Plural Asia*, edited by Anthony Reid and Michael Gilsenan, pp. 154–166. London: Routledge, 2007.
Ismail, Faisal. *Islamic Traditionalism in Indonesia: a Study of the Nahdlatul Ulama's Early History and Religious Ideology, 1926–1950*. Jakarta: Departemen Agama R.I., 2003.
van Bruinessen, Martin. "New Leadership, New Policies? The Nahdlatul Ulama Congress in Makassar." *Inside Indonesia* 100 (2010). http://www.insideindonesia.org/weekly-articles/new-leadership-new-policies

TAUSEEF AHMAD PARRAY

NASSER, GAMAL ABDEL. Few Arab leaders made such a mark on the twentieth century as Gamal Abdel Nasser (Jamāl ʿAbd al-Nāṣir; 1918–1970). On the day the Egyptian statesman and proponent of Arab nationalism succumbed to a heart attack, on 28 September 1970, Cairenes displayed genuine emotion, as grown men openly wept for their fallen leader. His funeral procession marked Nasser's entry into the mythological sphere, with several million marching behind his coffin to honor their hero.

The leader of the group of Free Officers that overthrew King Farouk (Fārūq) on 23 July 1952, Colonel Nasser became chairman of the Revolutionary Command Council after a failed assassination attempt in Alexandria—suspected to be the work of the banned Muslim Brotherhood—which allowed him to consolidate power in December 1954. He was elected president of the Egyptian Republic on 23 June 1956, a post that he held until his death.

Nasser was one of the most renowned Third World leaders who had to face the demands of ruling postcolonial countries in the age of the superpowers and the Cold War, while at the same time coping with the problems of economic development in poor, overpopulated countries. In addition, Egypt under Nasser became the center of the Arab world and Arab nationalism, and Nasser was seen as the leader who would unite Arabs in the struggle to eliminate both the last vestiges of imperialism in the Middle East and the ally of the West, Israel. Importantly, a vast majority of anticolonial Arab elites looked up to him for guidance, and beyond the Arab world he was one of the key founders of the Non-Aligned Movement, along with India's Jawaharlal Nehru and Indonesia's Sukarno, which irked East and West alike.

Nasser came into office with no firm ideology or plans and made several attempts to provide a broader base of legitimacy for his rule. He decided on socialism as the best solution and, in the Arab Socialist Union, attempted to establish a vehicle to put his ideas into practice. Socialism, he believed, would foster development and provide a political framework for the country.

In the Charter of 1962 he set forth guidelines for Egypt's future based on ideas that were strongly influenced by the then widely held principles of Marxism. In the charter, religion was hardly mentioned, and Islam only once, as the historical determinant of Egypt's thought and spiritual development. Yet Nasser was not a Leninist atheist or a secularizing Atatürk. He valued Islam as an essential part of Egyptian life and believed that it should be enlisted to further the ends of his socialist revolution. Nothing he proposed conflicted with deeply held religious principles, yet he did not want these principles to be allowed to hinder the development of a progressive, modernizing society. Islamic values were to be applied positively to reinforce the legitimacy of the state political system.

Critically, and in order not to offend Christian Egyptians, the charter stressed the "eternal moral values of *religions*," (italics added) not solely of

Islam: "All religions contain a message of progress. Their essence is to assert man's right to life and freedom." But the religious leaders of al-Azhar University went further, stressing that the aims of Islam and socialism were identical—the achievement of social justice, equality, freedom, and dignity, and the elimination of want. Al-Azhar served as an organ of state propaganda, and Nasser himself used mosque pulpits as a platform from which to proclaim his policies whenever he sought to rally public opinion. After the 1967 Arab defeat in the Arab-Israeli War, when it seemed that Arab nationalism and socialism had failed, Nasser appealed more strongly than ever to Islamic values. Traditional Islamic themes and symbols were revived, and he made frequent references to Allāh in his speeches. By the time of his death he was trying to set Egypt on a different course, less socialist and more accommodating, in which religion would play a greater role.

Although Nasser's legacy highlighted his military defeats (in intra-Arab struggles, the Yemen Wars, and, most importantly, in successive Arab-Israeli confrontations), key domestic reforms, whether changes in the country's agrarian policies, its revamped education system (to offer free schooling to the poorer masses), support for the arts, or the introduction of major infrastructure projects, such as the Aswan High Dam, all helped build pillars of the modern Egyptian economy. Naturally, his military excursions proved grave errors, as did his systematic suppression of both political and religious opposition. Regrettably, it was under his rule that Egypt was transformed into a police state, a legacy exploited by each and every successor. Notwithstanding his pan-Arab penchants, Nasser lost the support of a significant segment of the Egyptian population, as al-Azhar University clerics opposed his regime. Among his most controversial decisions was the 1961 law limiting the power of al-Azhar religious leaders, which was the proverbial straw that broke the back of the camel, placing a permanent wedge between Nasser and the clerics.

[*See also* Arab Nationalism; Arab Socialism; *and* Egypt.]

BIBLIOGRAPHY

Ginat, Rami. *Egypt's Incomplete Revolution: Lutfi al-Khuli and Nasser's Socialism in the 1960s*. London: Routledge, 1997.

Gordon, Joel. *Nasser: Hero of the Arab Nation*. Oxford: OneWorld, 2006.

Gordon, Joel. *Nasser's Blessed Movement: Egypt's Free Officers and the July Revolution*. New York: Oxford University Press, 1992.

Hopwood, Derek. *Egypt, Politics, and Society, 1945–1990*. 3d ed. London: Routledge, 1991. An introductory survey.

McNamara, Robert. *Britain, Nasser, and the Balance of Power in the Middle East, 1952–1967: From the Egyptian Revolution to the Six-Day War*. London: Routledge, 2003.

Shafik, Viola. *Popular Egyptian Cinema: Gender, Class, and Nation*. Cairo: American University in Cairo Press, 2007.

Vatikiotis, P. J. *The History of Modern Egypt: From Muhammad Ali to Mubarak*. 4th ed. Baltimore: Johns Hopkins University Press, 1991. The standard history of the whole period.

Vatikiotis, P. J. *Nasser and His Generation*. London: Croom Helm, 1978. A good study by a keen observer.

DEREK HOPWOOD
Updated by JOSEPH A. KÉCHICHIAN

NATION. In modern times, nationalism emerged first in Europe and then on other continents. It was the ideological expression of complex political, economic, and social developments. By the eighteenth century English nationalism had already manifested itself in the works of John Milton and John Locke and later in those of William Blackstone and Edmund Burke. It was with the French Revolution, however, that a truly national state was created. Political and social institutions were secularized and transformed to serve the purpose of a national state. In other parts of Europe, Italians, Poles, Germans, Greeks, and Balkan Slavs gained national feeling and consciousness and strove toward creating, maintaining, and increasing the power of the national state.

The emergence of national consciousness and nationalism in a politically meaningful way among the Muslim peoples dates to the late nineteenth century; the formation of national states to the early twentieth century. Although linguistic, racial, and territorial notions regarding political entities, similar to Western perceptions, were known to Muslims earlier, the integrating factors remained their common identity as Muslims and their allegiance to dynastic rulers—sultans/caliphs. During medieval times, Muslims considered themselves members of the *ummah*, all brothers and sisters belonging to the community of Islam, even though the political philosophy of the state was based on distinct social estates with mutual obligations between the subjects and the ruler. Christians and Jews lived in Muslim lands as *dhimmīs*, protected members of the society, and had formal legal status.

In the Ottoman Empire (c. 1300–1918), the most powerful of the Muslim empires, the social estates, or *erkân-ı erbaa*, the division of the society into occupational groups, formed the economic and social foundations of the state. Concomitantly, from the rule of Mehmed II (r. 1451–1481) until the nineteenth century, the population was divided into religious-communal organizations known as *millets*. By the end of Mehmed II's reign, Orthodox Christian, Jewish, Armenian, and Muslim *millets* were organized. Each was headed by its highest-ranking religious leader—the Greek Orthodox patriarch, chief rabbi, Armenian patriarch, and *şeyhülislâm*, respectively. The heads of the *millets* and other officials were elected by their constituents; their positions were confirmed by the Ottoman government. *Millets* had the right to decide matters related to religion and personal status and establish their own social and cultural institutions. The system covered the entire empire.

The Ottoman Empire gradually declined beginning in the seventeenth century. Political and economic developments, both outside and within the empire, and European military successes affected the traditional social structure. By the end of the eighteenth century, the social estates had disappeared. In response to these changes, the Ottoman government first restructured its army and then reformed its educational institutions. Beginning early in the nineteenth century the reforms intensified and, with the Hatt-ı Şerif of Gülhane (the Rescript of the Rose Chamber) in 1839, the Ottomans entered the period of Tanzimat, or reorganization.

The Hatt-ı Şerif, which promised security of life, honor, and property for all and equality among Muslims and non-Muslims, ushered in fundamental administrative, educational, and financial reforms. Particularly after the Crimean War (1853–1856), it also furthered European influence and interference in Ottoman affairs. This often undermined the relations of the Porte with its non-Muslim subjects. The protection granted to Christians and the favorable economic privileges given to them by European powers subjected this segment of the population to socioeconomic forces different from those affecting Muslims. The Hatt-ı Hümayun (Imperial Edict) of 1856 reaffirmed the rights of all Ottoman subjects, Muslim and non-Muslim, and brought in further reorganization. The reforms also changed the structures of the *millets* so that the laity gained ground at the expense of the clergy, and ethnic affiliation and the use of the vernacular slowly overcame the universalist ideas of the church and its language. Thus secular ideas and increasing awareness of ethnic identity gave rise to nationalist ideals and movements first among Christian Ottomans.

Paradoxically then, the Tanzimat had created cultural and political crises. The Ottoman government, by issuing the law of nationality and citizenship in 1869, attempted to establish the concept of Ottomanism as the legal basis of the empire. The first cohesive response of the Muslim intelligentsia came through the Young Ottomans (1856–1876). Within the framework of Islamic precepts and Ottoman historical experience, they formulated a concept of fatherland (*vatan*; Ar. *waṭan*) and nation. In their writings, the liberal intellectuals İbrahim Şinasi (1824–1871), Ziya Paşa (1825–1880), and Namık Kemal (1840–1888) criticized the Tanzimat and argued that many of the reforms along Western lines had undermined basic Islamic values. They pointed out that the reforms had not answered the needs of the empire, and they demanded a constitutional system.

The constitution of 1876, promulgated by Abdülhamid II (r. 1876–1909), emphasized Ottomanism as the ideological basis of the empire. Parliament, which held only two sessions in 1877–1878 before it was prorogued, included deputies from all peoples of the empire. Yet it was during Abdülhamid II's reign that various Balkan provinces were lost and some other territories came under European control. This, combined with the influx of Muslims from Russian territories into the Ottoman lands, changed the composition of the population heavily in favor of Muslims.

These developments, along with increasing Western financial and political dominance, helped transform the ideology of the state. Ottomanism, which no longer appeared viable, gave way to Muslim nationalism. Increasingly, Islam became the social and political basis of the empire. Although the legal system, which recognized all subjects as equal, remained in effect both in theory and practice, Abdülhamid II's policies generated solidarity through Islam.

Early criticism of Abdülhamid II's repressive policies came from intellectuals, but most of them were exiled by the end of the nineteenth century. A new opposition was formed by students from military and military-medical schools, as well as from among young bureaucrats, together known as the Young Turks, who later established the Committee of Union and Progress.

Moreover, by the beginning of the twentieth century, the coastal regions of the Fertile Crescent had experienced economic and social development closely resembling that in the Balkans a few decades earlier. This gave rise to ethnic and linguistic awareness. The graduates of the new schools established in the major cities in Syria and Iraq had been exposed to new ideas and had gained political consciousness as well as pride in the Arabic language and history. Soon they expressed particularist and nationalist sentiments.

The Young Turk Revolution of 1908 brought about fundamental changes. In the newly established Ottoman parliament, the Union and Progress Party under the control of the Young Turks pursued secularist and, in certain important programs such as education, pro-Turkish policies. In addition, the Young Turks' efforts to centralize caused serious concern among Arab leaders who favored decentralization and even nurtured aspirations of independence. Arab nationalism, which was first expressed among the Christian Arab intellectuals very late in the nineteenth century, began playing a politically meaningful role in the first decade of the twentieth century. And the Arab revolt of 1916 against the Istanbul government during World War I clearly charted the course of nationalism in the Middle East. Arab nationalism, though still lacking cohesive expression and clear territorial definition, had now taken root. It would lead to the formation of the independent national states of Syria, Iraq, Lebanon, and Jordan after the British and French mandates of the interwar period.

Despite the emphasis Young Turks placed on Turkish identity, the ideology of the state remained

Ottomanist within an Islamic framework. Whereas Balkan nationalism did not inflame Turkish nationalism, the nationalist movements of non-Turkish Muslims, such as Albanians and Arabs, did; they influenced the emergence of Turkish nationalism with secular tendencies, which received sustenance from its chief ideologue, Ziya Gökalp (1876–1924), a sociologist. Early in the Turkish War of Independence (1919–1922), the "National Pact" (1920), although still couched in Ottoman terms, with its territorial definitions and expressions of popular will, set the agenda for the formation of a Turkish state, the Republic of Turkey, in 1923.

It was toward the end of World War I but particularly during the War of Independence between 1919 and 1922 that Turkish nationalism was also strongly expressed in terms of anticolonialism. The ideology and the policies followed by Turkey in the following years placing emphasis on Turkish language, history, and culture, and especially the personality and ideas of Mustafa Kemal (Atatürk), would have profound influences on some other nationalist leaders and their anti-imperialist aspirations in the Muslim world such as Reza Shah Pahlavi in Iran, Sukarno in Indonesia, and Mohammad Ali Jinnah in Pakistan.

In the development and expression of nationalism and the formation of nations among the Muslim peoples, a number of trends can be observed. First, certain economic and social formations are reached in order to allow nationalism to develop as an ideological force. As the medieval socioeconomic system disintegrated and modern conditions developed, individuals' identification with a particular social group lessened. The result of this process, with some variations, is indeed similar to nationalism in the West. Second, in the Muslim world, nation building received great impetus from religion, particularly from the anti-imperialist tendencies of Islam. As religious groups participated extensively in the nationalist movements from the Maghrib and Egypt to India and Indonesia, Islam lent a driving force to nation building. Thus, although the *ummah* was transformed into nations, Islam continued to be one of the major components of the ideologies of independent Muslim nations, as it continues to be today. And finally, the development of nationalism in the Middle East was closely associated with attempts to create a modern political system with territorial states. Yet the ideological orientations of nationalism differed among groups and nations. Arab nationalism directed against the Ottoman government in Istanbul for separation and independence between 1908 and 1916 was quite different from anti-British, anti-imperialist Egyptian nationalism after 1882 and the nationalism of Fertile Crescent after 1920. Hence it may be argued that owing to differences in the emergence and development of nationalism in various countries there, one cannot speak of a shared Middle Eastern ideology or political aspirations after World War I.

[*See also* Tanzimat; *and* Turkey.]

BIBLIOGRAPHY

Ahmad, Feroz. *The Young Turks: The Committee of Union and Progress in Turkish Politics, 1908–1914*. Oxford: Clarendon, 1969.

Badran, Margot. *Feminists, Islam, and Nation: Gender and the Making of Modern Egypt*. Princeton, N.J.: Princeton University Press, 1995.

Berkes, Niyazi. *The Development of Secularism in Turkey*. Montreal: McGill University Press, 1964.

Dawn, C. Ernest. *From Ottomanism to Arabism: Essays on the Origins of Arab Nationalism*. Urbana: University of Illinois Press, 1973.

Ghayasuddin, M., ed. *The Impact of Nationalism on the Muslim World*. London: Open Press, 1986.

Haddad, William W., and William Ochsenwald, eds. *Nationalism in a Non-National State: The Dissolution of the Ottoman Empire*. Columbus: Ohio State University Press, 1977.

Hourani, Albert. *Arabic Thought in the Liberal Age, 1798–1939*. London: Oxford University Press, 1962.

Karpat, Kemal H., ed. *Political and Social Thought in the Contemporary Middle East*. New York: Praeger, 1968.
Lewis, Bernard. *The Emergence of Modern Turkey*. 2d ed. London: Oxford University Press, 1968.
Mardin, Şerif. *The Genesis of Young Ottoman Thought: A Study in the Modernization of Turkish Political Ideas*. Princeton, N.J.: Princeton University Press, 1962.
Shaybānī, Muḥammad ibn al-Ḥasan al-. *The Islamic Law of Nations: Shaybānī's Siyar*. Translated and edited by Majid Khadduri. Baltimore: Johns Hopkins Press, 1966.

A. ÜNER TURGAY

NATION OF ISLAM. An American religious movement, consisting largely of African Americans. Master Wali Fard Muhammad led the Nation of Islam from 1930 to 1934; the Honorable Elijah Muhammad was the leader from 1934 to 1975; and the Honorable Louis Farrakhan has led from 1977 to 2013. The Nation is a "proto-Islamic" movement, using some of the symbols, rituals, and beliefs of Islam mixed with a core ideology of black nationalism.

Master Fard. On 4 July 1930 Master Fard appeared in a black ghetto of Detroit called Paradise Valley. He began teaching "true religion," or the religion of "Asiatic black man." The popularity of these meetings grew, and a hall was rented and named "Temple of Islam," which was later given the numeric designation "1." Mr. Farrad Muhammad, also known as Mr. Wali Fard, W. D. Fard, Wallace D. Fard, and Mr. Ford, was considered by some of his followers as a prophet. He later came to be recognized as the "Great Mahdi," or "Savior," who had come to bring a special message to the suffering blacks in America.

Master Fard instructed his followers that they were not Americans and therefore owed no allegiance to the American flag and urged them to refuse the American military draft. He wrote two manuals, *The Secret Ritual of the Nation of Islam*, which is transmitted orally to members, and *Teaching for the Lost-Found Nation of Islam in a Mathematical Way*, which is written in symbolic language and requires special interpretation.

Within three years, Fard had founded an effective organization, with a Temple of Islam that had its own worship style and rituals and a University of Islam with a special curriculum made up largely of Fard's teaching. He also established the Muslim Girls' Training Class to teach young women the principles of home economics and their proper role in the Nation of Islam. In 1933 he created the Fruit of Islam (FOI), a paramilitary organization of male Muslims who served as honor guards, ushers, and enforcers of internal discipline within the temples, as well as security agents for the minister of Islam and other leaders.

Elijah Muhammad. One of the earliest officers of the movement, who became Master Fard's most trusted lieutenant, was Elijah Poole, who was given the Muslim name Elijah Karriem and later Elijah Muhammad. Born on 7 October 1897, Poole was the son of Willie Poole, a rural Baptist minister and sharecropper, and his wife, Marie, from Sandersville, Georgia. The family moved to Cordele, Georgia, where, as a teenager, Elijah witnessed the public lynching of his good friend Albert Hamilton. Later, as head of the movement, Elijah would order that a picture of a black man lynched from a tree be placed in the front of every Nation of Islam temple.

In 1923 Elijah settled in Paradise Valley. After a dinner meeting with Master Fard, Elijah Poole converted to the Nation of Islam in 1931. Despite having only a third-grade education, Elijah's intelligence and devotion to Fard enabled him to rise rapidly through the ranks, and he was eventually chosen by Fard in 1933 to be the chief minister of Islam. In a short period of time, Fard's Temple of Islam had attracted more than eight thousand members.

After Master Fard mysteriously disappeared in 1934, rivalries and factions within the Nation of

Islam devolved into open hostilities. Part of the controversy involved Elijah Muhammad's proclamation that Master Fard was Allāh and that he himself was Allāh's Prophet or Messenger. As a result of the factional rivalries and death threats, Muhammad fled Detroit. Elijah was arrested for failing to register for the military draft on 8 May 1942 and sentenced to serve three years at the Federal Correctional Institute in Milan, Michigan. While Elijah was in prison, his wife Clara ran the affairs of the Nation of Islam. He was released from Milan on 24 August 1946.

Minister Malcolm X. Malcolm Little, born 19 May 1925, was introduced to the Nation of Islam in 1948 at the Norfolk Prison Colony by his younger brother Reginald. He dropped his "slave" surname and substituted it with "X," which represented his status as "undetermined," an unknown quantity as in mathematics, ex-slave, ex-Christian, ex-smoker, ex-drinker, and ex–mainstream American. Malcolm X later became Malik Shabazz.

The years between Malcolm X's release from prison and his assassination (1952–1965) mark the period of the greatest growth and influence of the Nation of Islam under Elijah Muhammad's leadership. Malcolm X added twenty-seven Muslim temples across the country to the existing seven by 1952. He established the Nation's newspaper, *Muhammad Speaks*, by printing the first issues in the basement of his home until it was taken over by Elijah Muhammad. Malcolm also made mandatory the sale of an assigned quota of newspapers for every male Muslim as a recruiting and fundraising device; failure to meet it often led to physical punishment. In his outreach to the black community, Malcolm preached on street corners in Boston and Harlem and often participated in "fishing" for lost souls in the bars and cafes and even in front of Christian churches as their Sunday services let out. In recognition of Malcolm's energetic preaching and organizing, Elijah Muhammad made him the minister of Boston Temple No. 11 in 1953, and in 1954 he rewarded Malcolm with the post of minister of Temple No. 7 in Harlem, the Nation's largest temple outside of Chicago.

Elijah Muhammad named Malcolm the national representative of the Nation of Islam, second in rank to the Messenger himself. Under his lieutenancy, the Nation of Islam achieved a membership estimated to have ranged from twenty to five hundred thousand.

Malcolm became one of the most important critics of the civil rights movement. He challenged Dr. Martin Luther King's central notions of integration and the nonviolent Christian ethic. Malcolm's biting critique of the "so-called Negro" (X, 1969, *Malcolm X Speaks*, pp. 184–185) and his emphasis on the recovery of black self-identity and independence provided the intellectual foundations for the Black Power and Black Consciousness movement that emerged in the late 1960s and early 1970s in American society.

While he often paid tribute to his teacher and mentor, the Honorable Elijah Muhammad, Minister Malcolm X felt personally constrained in his desire to participate actively in the politics and struggles of the civil rights movement. After resigning from the Nation in March 1964, Malcolm made the *ḥajj* (pilgrimage) to Mecca, where he underwent a conversion to Sunnī Islam, changing his name to El-Hajj Malik El-Shabazz. After returning to the United States, Malcolm created the Muslim Mosque, Inc. and the Organization for Afro-American Unity. He was assassinated on 21 February 1965 at the Audubon Ballroom in Harlem.

Minister Louis Farrakhan of Boston took over Malcolm's position as the minister of Temple No. 7 and was also appointed by Elijah Muhammad as the national representative. Farrakhan played a major role in stirring dissent against Malcolm. Farrakhan rebuilt the membership base of Temple No. 7 after a number of members left following Malcolm's death.

On 23 February 1975 the Honorable Elijah Muhammad died of congestive heart failure at the age of seventy-eight. Close advisers and family members decided to keep the leadership of the Nation of Islam within the Muhammad family and announced at the Savior's Day rally that Elijah's fifth son, Wallace Delaney Muhammad, would become the new leader of the organization. Within a few months of taking office, Supreme Minister Wallace Muhammad began making sweeping changes in the organization, getting rid of all of the black nationalist teachings of Master Fard and Elijah Muhammad and moving the Nation closer to orthodox Sunnī Islam

Minister Louis Farrakhan. As the national representative and second in command, Minister Louis Farrakhan was widely expected to become the next leader. When Farrakhan was asked to relocate to Chicago by Supreme Leader Wallace Muhammad, he quickly complied. Farrakhan was appointed to a small, run-down mosque. When Wallace began criticizing his father, the Nation's teachings, and organizations like the FOI, Farrakhan withdrew from the World Community of Al-Islam in the West in 1976 and began a series of travels abroad. During his travels in African countries and throughout the Middle East, Farrakhan learned about the continued oppression of black people and began to see the need for the special message of Elijah Muhammad and Master Fard to awaken their consciousness.

Beginning with a meeting in a Los Angeles hotel with Bernard Cushmeer (Jabril Muhammad) in September 1977 and later with other devoted followers in meetings in Florida and Las Vegas, Farrakhan began laying the groundwork for a rebirth of the Nation of Islam based on the work and message of the Honorable Elijah Muhammad, which he announced on 8 November 1977. Farrakhan attempted to purchase the licenses from the American Muslim Mission for Elijah Muhammad's books such as *Message to the Black Man*, *How to Eat to Live*, and *Our Savior Has Arrived*, as well as other Nation publications such as *Flag of Islam* and *Muslim Prayer Book*. In May 1979, Farrakhan began working on *The Final Call News*, taking its name from the first publication that Elijah Muhammad published in the 1930s, *The Final Call to Islam*. Farrakhan's newspaper was "dedicated to the resurrection of the Black Man and Woman of America and the world." The first Savior's Day event was celebrated in February 1981. On 12 September 1982 Farrakhan mortgaged his home to purchase the Final Call Administration Building at 734 West Seventy-Ninth Street in Chicago. During this rebuilding period, the Final Call building was used as the Nation's headquarters as well as the site for Farrakhan's speeches and meetings until Mosque Maryam was purchased.

After cooperating successfully to secure the release of Robert Goodman, an African American pilot, from the Syrian government in 1984, Minister Farrakhan and the Reverend Jesse Jackson began to work together during Jackson's presidential campaign. In 1985 Farrakhan released his economic vision, called People Organized and Working for Economic Rebirth (POWER), calling for the economic rebirth of black people. In the same year, he appointed five women ministers, breaking the tradition of having only males as ministers. The first woman appointed was his lawyer, Ava Muhammad (Atkinson). In 1998 he appointed Minister Ava Muhammad as the southern regional minister of the Nation of Islam and the minister of Mosque 15 in Atlanta. His appointment of women as ministers was evidence of a more progressive philosophy concerning the treatment of women than that of traditional Sunnī groups, which refused to have women imams.

On 12 January 1995 FBI agents informed Farrakhan of the arrest of Qubilah Shabazz, a daughter of Malcolm X, in a murder-for-hire plot against Minister Farrakhan. In a press conference, Farrakhan blamed the intelligence agencies for hatching this plot. Michael Fitzpatrick, a former member of the Jewish Defense League who had been convicted for a 1976 bombing of a Russian bookstore in New York City, who was both the informer and conspirator, tried to entrap Qubilah.

In October 1990, the Nation of Islam Ghana Mission information center was opened in Accra. International Minister Akbar Muhammad headed the mission. In the ensuing years, Akbar has established both a home and a Nation of Islam mosque in Accra. Under Farrakhan, the Nation has built upon its international outreach, establishing study groups and mosques in London and Paris and throughout the Caribbean. A study group was also established in South Africa.

From 1991 to 1995, Minister Farrakhan went on a national speaking tour of American cities. Part of the tour focused on the theme "Stop the Killing," which aimed to bring about peace among the Bloods, Crips, and other gangs. On 18 October 1992 he gave a lecture titled "A Torchlight for America," which was later published as a book, at the Georgia Dome to an audience of fifty-five thousand. He also had smaller meetings for men only, because that was the target audience for the Million Man March on 16 October 1995 in Washington, D.C. Although he had separate meetings for women, he made it clear that this march would focus on the needs and concerns of black men for apology, repentance, atonement, and reconciliation with black women, families, and the community.

More than a million people showed up for the Million Man March, largely men, but also including some women and children. The Million Man March was four times larger than the March on Washington in 1963, which featured Dr. Martin Luther King's "I Have a Dream" speech. As a result of the march, more than one million blacks registered to vote, and many church groups developed Million Man March committees that lasted more than a decade, trying to fulfill the pledge and work actively in their communities.

In 1996 Farrakhan began a World Friendship Tour of African nations and Muslim countries, visiting Nigeria, Zaire, Sudan, Egypt, Libya, Syria, and Iraq, among other countries. Due to the success of the Million Man March, he was often treated as a head of state.

In 1997 Minister Farrakhan was diagnosed with prostate cancer. In 1998 he opted for treatment with radiated seed implantation, which caused further health problems in ensuing years. In 1999 he claimed that he had a near-death experience from a severe infection caused by the implantation. This experience led him to move the Nation closer to Sunnī Islam. He changed the month of fasting from December, which Elijah Muhammad had chosen as a challenge to Christian celebrations, to the lunar-calendar tradition of the Sunnīs. For a while, Nation members fasted in December and again during the lunar month of Ramaḍān. Farrakhan also ordered that all members of the Nation learn how to do the orthodox prostration prayer, and all mosques were required to institute the Friday *jumʿah* prayer service.

On 15 October 2005, the tenth anniversary of the Million Man March, the Nation of Islam held the Millions More Movement, a march in Washington, D.C. This event, which also attracted about one million black people, was more inclusive and politically focused. Besides women and families and representatives from disempowered racial minority groups, the coalition also included representatives from African American gay/lesbian groups. In his seventy-five-minute speech, Minister Farrakhan criticized the Bush administration's mishandling of the Hurricane Katrina disaster in Louisiana and the disastrous war in Iraq. The Millions More Movement also issued a pamphlet listing its public policy initiatives and political direction.

After undergoing an hour-long operation for a severe infection in his lower intestine in December 2006, Minister Farrakhan took a leave of absence in 2007. Since then, the daily operations of the Nation of Islam have been handled by a selected leadership council.

BIBLIOGRAPHY

Breitman, George. *Malcolm X: The Man and His Ideas.* New York: Pathfinder, 1965.

Clegg, Claude Andrew, III. *An Original Man: The Life and Times of Elijah Muhammad.* New York: St. Martin's, 1997.

Curtis, Edward E., IV. *Black Muslim Religion in the Nation of Islam, 1960–1975.* Chapel Hill: University of North Carolina Press, 2006.

Curtis, Edward E., IV. *Islam in Black America: Identity, Liberation, and Difference in African-American Islamic Thought.* Albany: State University of New York Press, 2002.

Gardell, Mattias. *In the Name of Elijah Muhammad: Louis Farrakhan and the Nation of Islam.* Durham, N.C.: Duke University Press, 1996.

Lee, Martha F. *The Nation of Islam: An American Millenarian Movement.* Lewiston, N.Y.: Edwin Mellen, 1988.

Mamiya, Lawrence H. "From Black Muslim to Bilalian: The Evolution of a Movement." *Journal for the Scientific Study of Religion* 21, no. 2 (1982): 138–152. Reprinted in *Islam in North America: A Sourcebook,* edited by Michael A. Kőszegi and J. Gordon Melton, pp. 165–182. New York: Garland, 1992.

Muhammad, Elijah. *The Fall of America.* Chicago: Muhammad's Temple of Islam No. 2, 1973.

Muhammad, Elijah. *How to Eat to Live.* Chicago: Muhammad Mosque of Islam No. 2, 1967.

Muhammad, Elijah. *Message to the Blackman in America.* Chicago: Muhammad Mosque of Islam No. 2, 1965.

Muhammad, Elijah. *Our Saviour Has Arrived.* Chicago: Muhammad's Temple of Islam No. 2, 1974.

Toure, Muhammad. *Chronology of Nation of Islam History: Highlights of the Honorable Minister Louis Farrakhan and the Nation of Islam from 1977–1996.* Chicago: Toure Muhammad, 1996.

X, Malcolm. *By Any Means Necessary: Speeches, Interviews, and a Letter.* Edited by George Breitman. New York: Pathfinder, 1970.

X, Malcolm. *Malcolm X Speaks: Selected Speeches and Statements.* Edited by George Breitman. New York: Grove, 1969.

X, Malcolm, and Alex Haley. *The Autobiography of Malcolm X.* New York: Grove, 1965.

LAWRENCE H. MAMIYA

NATIONAL AWAKENING PARTY. The National Awakening Party (PKB, or Partai Kebangkitan Bangsa) was formed in 1999 at the end of the Suharto New Order authoritarian regime when the democratic process in Indonesia underwent a renewal. It was one of the many parties that drew strength from membership within the Nahdatul Ulama (Awakening of the Ulama, or NU) organization, a mass movement based upon traditional interpretations of Islam. While the NU officially remained aloof from electoral politics, the new party was led by Abdurrahman Wahid (known as Gus Dur), who came from a prominent NU and Islamic family, and was chairman of the coalition from 1984 to 1999, when he was elected the republic's fourth president. During the latter part of the New Order, Wahid supported the NU's divorce from national politics, as he sought to establish a grassroots foundation that would be ready to act. upon Suharto's fall. Toward that end, Wahid was at the forefront of the movement to oust Suharto and return Indonesia to democracy. While other minor parties had NU membership, the leadership of Wahid gave the PKB a particular status. Indeed, the PKB reflected the ideological tone of its leader, who was a strong supporter of democracy and political and religious pluralism. Importantly, he did not want the word Islam in the party's name, because it was multireligious, presenting a platform of national unity and social justice. In 2010, an Indonesian institute named the PKB as one of the two political parties most committed to human rights in the republic, noting that it stood alone in calling for reopening cases of alleged military and civilian human rights abuses as well as rejecting decrees to ban the Aḥmadīyah.

The PKB participated in all three post-Suharto elections of the national legislature, the People's Representative Assembly (DPR, or Dewan Perwakilan Rakyat), and won the third largest number of votes in the 1999 and 2004 elections, garnering 12.66 and 10.57 percent of ballots, respectively. It should be noted that, although the vast majority of Indonesians are Muslim, Islamic parties have not fared well in national elections, which have been dominated by secular parties. The PKB, however, participated in both Islamic and more secular coalitions. Wahid, who was impeached and lost the presidency in 2001, proved to be too erratic and was often ill, while NU members continued to divide their support among several political groups. The PKB fragmented by the middle of the decade and lost most of its support. It fell to the seventh lowest rank, receiving only 4.94 percent of the total vote in the 2009 elections, which resulted in a further disintegration into two separate groups, only one of which is recognized by the courts. The official party is led by Muhaimin Iskandar, dismissed by Wahid as secretary-general in 2004, while the second faction led by his daughter, Yenny Zannuba Wahid, proclaims loyalty to Wahid's memory.

BIBLIOGRAPHY

Bush, Robin. *Nahdlatul Ulama and the Struggle for Power within Islam and Politics in Indonesia*. Singapore: Institute of Southeast Asian Studies, 2009.

Manning, Chris, and Peter Van Dierman, eds. *Indonesia in Transition: Social Aspects of Reformasi and Crisis*. London: Zed, 2000.

FRED R. VON DER MEHDEN

NATIONAL ISLAMIC FRONT. The Sudanese Ikhwān (Muslim Brothers) movement was established in 1944 to fend off the Communists, who were active in Sudan. It gathered steam in the 1960s under Ḥasan al-Turābī, who made the Brothers independent from the trusteeship of the original Egyptian movement and modernized and reorganized it until it became the third major political party in 1986 elections.

In 1956, Sudan adopted an Islamic constitution to establish an Islamic republic, with a parliament democratically based on Islamic law and legislating according to the *Sharīʿah*. Muslims would be able to shape their lives in accordance with the dictates of their religion and to uproot social evils. Discrimination on the basis of race or religion would be forbidden and non-Muslim citizens would enjoy all rights granted under Muslim law.

The year 1964 was a turning point for the movement, when Ḥasan al-Turābī and several leading Brothers returned from their studies abroad. Al-Turābī, who had joined the Brothers while an undergraduate at Khartoum University College in 1954, had completed his Ph.D. in constitutional law in London and Paris and returned to teach law at Khartoum University. He was the most effective spokesman for the Brothers at the university. Most of the mass demonstrations of students and sympathizers in October 1964, which led ultimately to the downfall of General ʿAbbūd, were led by the Muslim Brothers from the university, where students founded the Islamic Charter Front (ICF) in October 1964, with al-Turābī as secretary-general.

Following the May 1969 military coup by Colonel Jaʿfar Nimeiri (al-Numayrī) some members of the Brotherhood were arrested, while others escaped. Al-Turābī, who was not exiled, met President Nimeiri following the abortive pro-Communist coup of July 1971 and asked for permission to resume the Brothers' activities. In an opportunistic move, Al-Turābī concentrated his efforts on purging the Brothers' leadership of its old guard, and replaced them with more sympathetic voices.

The Sudanese Brothers founded the National Islamic Front (NIF) following the failure of the anti-Nimeiri coup led by the Anṣār in July 1976. Gradually, the NIF gained power thanks to its financial supremacy from the remittances of the Sudanese migrant workers in the Arab oil-producing countries and to its control of the Islamic banking system.

Starting in 1977, the Muslim Brothers made inroads within the military, as members offered "Islamic ideology and instruction" (*da'wah*) courses for senior army officers, thus enabling them to infiltrate the officers' corps. Four members of the military council that ruled Sudan after the June 1989 coup, including its leader, 'Umar Ḥasan al-Bashīr (b. 1944), attended these courses. The post-1989 regime is an indication that the NIF's infiltration of the army paid the expected dividends, since the Islamist Revolution was not a popular uprising but a military coup brought about by al-Turābī and his NIF supporters with the military might of a group of officers led by 'Umar Ḥasan al-Bashīr. Following the 1989 coup, the NIF enacted the Special Courts Act to put in place an Islamist judicial system embracing civil and criminal courts. Al-Turābī believed that justice and the legal system for the whole of the Sudan, Muslim and non-Muslim, should be Islamic.

He also introduced the *shūrā* system, which he advanced as an alternative mode of governance to Western liberal democracy. According to Turābī, *shūrā* is the sole legitimate system of governance in an Islamic state; he viewed Western democracy as an acceptable system only after it became tailored to fit the values and norms of Islamic *Sharī'ah*. Turābī tried to replicate, in light of modern conditions, the original system developed by the Prophet Muḥammad and the Rightly Guided Caliphs, while adopting some of the modern aspects of Western democracy.

In theological matters, renewal and revival (*tajdīd*) were among al-Turābī's most cherished ideas, and he claimed that Islam had to be rethought on a permanent basis and be open to radical change by the whole Muslim community. There were eternal principles in Islam, but *fiqh*, the classical exposition of Islamic law inherited from earlier generations of Muslims, was a mere human endeavor that needed constant reevaluation in accordance with contemporary requirements.

Al-Turābī's contribution to women's rights is unique as well. According to the philosopher, Islam provides complete equality between male and female, and women are free to choose their partners, own property, and hold almost any public position. He admits that these principles had not been implemented in Islam since early times due to pre-Islamic (*jāhilīyah*) habits that prevailed in society, and he asserts that the early *Sharī'ah* judges misinterpreted these rules. As a result, women in Islam have experienced discrimination.

Under al-Turābī's leadership, the NIF organized and headed the Popular Arab and Islamic Congress (PAIC) in 1991, to coordinate anti-imperialist movements in the Muslim world and guide them toward Islamic revolution. After the first Gulf War, Sudan became a center for antiestablishment Muslim leaders, who viewed the Arab League and Saudi Arabia, which had cooperated with the West during that war, as having betrayed Arab and Islamic causes. In Khartoum this congress was hailed as the most significant event since the abolishment of the caliphate.

A group of Islamists in the Shura Council disseminated the "Memorandum of the Ten" in 1998, criticizing the experience of the NIF. They proposed granting some of al-Turābī's powers as secretary-general of the Congress Party to al-Bashīr. A year later al-Bashīr dissolved the parliament, discharged Turābī, and declared a state of emergency.

The subsequent conflict between the two men split the NIF into two separate camps: al-Bashīr's National Congress Party (NCP) and al-Turābī's Popular Congress Party (PCP). The NIF era was marked by the escalation of internal conflicts in the south and later on in Darfur. In 2005 the NIF signed the Comprehensive Peace agreement with the Sudan People's Liberation Movement, only to have South Sudan declare its independence after the 2011 popular referendum.

BIBLIOGRAPHY

Burr, J. Millard, and Robert O. Collins. *Revolutionary Sudan: Hasan al-Turabi and the Islamist State, 1989–2000.* Leiden, Netherlands: Brill, 2003.

Collins, Robert O. *A History of Modern Sudan.* Cambridge, U.K.: Cambridge University Press, 2008.

El-Affendi, Abdelwahab. *Turabi's Revolution: Islam and Power in Sudan.* London: Grey Seal, 1991.

Petterson, Don. *Inside Sudan: Political Islam, Conflict, and Catastrophe.* Boulder, Colo.: Westview, 2003.

Turābī, Ḥasan al-. *The Islamic Movement in Sudan: Its Development, Approach, and Achievements.* Translated by Abdelwahab El-Affendi. Beirut: Arab Scientific Publishers, 2008.

Turābī, Ḥasan al-. "The Islamic State." In *Voices of Resurgent Islam,* edited by John Esposito, pp. 241–251. New York: Oxford University Press, 1983.

Warburg, Gabriel. *Islam, Sectarianism, and Politics in Sudan since the Mahdiyya.* London: Hurst, 2003.

Weissbrod, Amir. *Turabi: Dover ha-Islam ha-ḳana'i.* Tel Aviv: Merkaz Mosheh Dayan le-Limude ha-Mizraḥ ha-Tikhon, 1999.

GABRIEL R. WARBURG
Updated by YOUNES ABOUYOUB

NATIONALISM. Nationalism is a distinctly modern ethos that comprises five assumptions: all humanity is naturally divided into unified societies (nations), each of which has a discrete identity; nations can be identified by certain characteristics (religion, language, common history), which all its members share; only national sovereignty can ensure that the interests of the nation and its citizens are protected; nations enjoy a special relationship with a particular territory that is the repository for that nation's history and memory; and nations retain their essential characteristics as they travel through time. Although historians differ about the initial site and time of nationalism's appearance in history, many, if not most, trace its origins to eighteenth-century Europe. Nationalism probably originated as a result of efforts made by rulers and statesmen to strengthen their states in the highly competitive European environment by making the state and sovereign the focal points of their subjects' loyalty and by mobilizing and harnessing the energies of those subjects in common endeavors and for the common interest. Hence, states organized conscript armies, standardized educational and legal institutions, and adopted strategies for "national" economic planning. Simultaneously, states attempted to eradicate institutions and social groups that blocked the central government's direct access to its population. Over time, in those places where governments imposed the new conception of state, populations internalized the notion that they were part of unified societies that had identities of their own and for whose benefit those populations had to direct their efforts.

In general, what might be called the "culture of nationalism"—the tendency for populations to view the aforementioned assumptions as self-evident and part of the natural order—spread to the Islamic world because, in a world in which the nation-state was increasingly the norm, there remained few other options for organizing sovereign political communities. Thus, even though the Ottoman Empire, for example, continued to call itself an empire, it increasingly took on the characteristics of a nation-state, and governing elites even promoted their own doctrines of Ottoman nationalism (*osmanlılık*). More specifically, however, it might be said that the culture of nationalism spread to the Islamic world in two ways. Sometimes, the imperialist powers of Europe established institutions there and engaged their subject populations in activities apposite to disseminating the culture of nationalism. Such was the case with the British in India and the French in Algeria. At other times, indigenous rulers directly borrowed eurogenic practices to strengthen state power and protect the domains they governed from outside interference. Such was the case in the Egypt of Mehmet Ali Pasha (r. 1805–1848), the Tunisia of Aḥmad Bey (r. 1837–1855), and the Ottoman Empire during and after the Tanzimat period (1839–1908).

Nationalist movements are a distinct form of political movement that draw from the assumptions of nationalism and thrive in an environment in which the culture of nationalism has taken root. By constructing a national narrative that privileges one or more characteristics its advocates claim to be intrinsic to the nation, nationalist movements create those nations, endow them with identities and histories, and define their rules for membership. Nationalist movements began to emerge in the Islamic world in the nineteenth century in four ways. In some cases, they were founded by social and cultural elites who had been exposed to the political culture of Europe through travel abroad, the proselytizing of foreign missionaries, or residence in cities (i.e., Beirut, Alexandria, Istanbul, and Algiers) in which a cultural cosmopolitanism flourished. Others—such as the previously mentioned *osmanlılık* and more recent "official nationalisms" such as Kemalism in Turkey—have enjoyed state support. Still others emerged in opposition to colonial powers (i.e., Egyptian and Indian nationalist movements) or rule by imperial elites whom nationalists identified as alien oppressors (i.e., the Balkan and Armenian nationalist movements in the case of the Ottoman Empire). Finally, there were nationalist movements that spread where a culture of nationalism had taken root but where a lack of state structure had created a political vacuum. Such was the case in the Asiatic provinces of the Ottoman Empire where a host of nationalist movements—including Arab and Greater Syrian nationalist movements—competed for support in the wake of the dismantling of that empire after World War I.

The nationalisms that nationalist movements promote are equivalent in form, and while the particular national characteristics and historical artifacts each nationalist movement uses to define the nature, reach, and boundaries of the national community are unique, the doctrines associated with the nationalisms that have emerged in the Islamic world commonly resemble those of contemporaneous movements that have emerged elsewhere. For example, during the two-decade period of decolonization that followed World War II, anticolonial struggles and the forging of new nations necessitated the construction of broad-based nationalist coalitions throughout the developing world, and the colonial legacy prompted nationalist elites to place rapid modernization and (frequently) economic populism at the center of their political platforms. Hence, the secular, modernizing nationalisms that dominated the Islamic world of the time—those identified with such anticolonial figures as Sukarno in Indonesia and Nasser in Egypt, with such anticolonial resistance movements as the National Liberation Front (FLN) in Algeria and the Palestine Liberation Organization (PLO) in Palestine, and with Baʿthism and Nasserism throughout the Arab world—were hardly unique to the Islamic world.

The one doctrinal innovation unique to the Islamic world might be found in those nationalisms that give the Islamic nature of the nation pride of place in their nationalist narrative and seek to reconstruct the state according to what they define as Islamic principles (although, of course, nationalisms outside the Islamic world have used religion as a national marker as well). The "Islamic nationalism" associated with such movements as Ḥamās in Palestine and the Taliban in Afghanistan is hardly new to the Islamic world; during the final quarter of the nineteenth century the Ottoman sultan Abdülhamid II sought to disseminate an Islamic *osmanlılık*, and *La Turquie*, the semiofficial journal in the empire once explained "Islam is not just a religion—it is a nationality." But the recent revitalization of "Islamic nationalist movements" might be attributed to a number of factors, including the failure of secular nationalisms to deliver on their promises, the "demonstration effect" of the Iranian revolutionary model, and the support they have received from conservative oil-rich states like Saudi Arabia. These movements work within the parameters of the international state system. For example, Article 12 of the Ḥamās charter states, "Hamas regards nationalism as part and parcel of the religious faith." Thus, although they privilege Islam as a national marker and base social reconstruction on so-called Islamic principles, they are consistent with prototypical nationalist movements.

[*See also* Arab Nationalism; Ḥamās; Palestine Liberation Organization; *and* Taliban.]

BIBLIOGRAPHY

Chatterjee, Partha. *Nationalist Thought and the Colonial World: A Derivative Discourse*. Minneapolis: University of Minnesota Press, 1993.

Gelvin, James. "'Arab Nationalism': Has a New Framework Emerged?" *International Journal of Middle East Studies* 41 (Winter 2009): 10–12.

Jankowski, James, and Israel Gershoni, eds. *Rethinking Nationalism in the Arab Middle East*. New York: Columbia University Press, 1997.

Malley, Robert. *The Call from Algeria: Third Worldism, Revolution, and the Turn to Islam*. Berkeley: University of California Press, 1996.

JAMES L. GELVIN

NECESSITY. *See* Sharīʿah.

NETHERLANDS. The Netherlands is most notable among European countries for its *poldermodel*, an active search for compromise, consensus, and tolerance in civil society.

Historical and Geographical Overview. Considering the geography, religious pluralism, and extensive trade of the Netherlands, the country provides a uique backdrop for examining the intersection of Islam and politics. The Netherlands is a small country (42,000 square kilometers) tucked between Belgium, Germany, and the North Sea. It is one of the six founding countries of the European Union and boasts one of the highest per capita gross national products in Europe. The Netherlands is densely populated, with 450 people per square kilometer. In the midst of its 16.6 million inhabitants are significant Muslim communities from Turkey, Morocco, Suriname, and other countries. The country is generally progressive on social issues and minority rights. As a water-rich country with distinctive waterways, the Netherlands has been in constant struggle with the sea and created exceptional technologies to reclaim land from water. With the arrival of the Dutch West Indian Company in Indonesia in the seventeenth century, the Netherlands would come to administer the largest Islamic country in the world until decolonization in 1945. The period of colonization has left an indelible imprint on Dutch culture, especially cuisine.

Politics and Religious Pluralism. The Netherlands has been markedly religiously plural since the late sixteenth century, including the Reformed Church, Mennonites, Catholics, Lutherans, Jews, and Huguenots. Even if benchmarks of religious tolerance are contested by historians, the philosophers Descartes and Spinoza were singing the praises of seventeenth-century religious tolerance in the Netherlands, which was unprecedented elsewhere in Europe during this period.

The period of colonization would also be marked by an attention to issues of religious pluralism. In 1854, the Dutch colonial administration in Southeast Asia issued a decree that gave the governor general the power to prohibit any Christian missionary activities, because they understood that these activities could undermine Dutch trade interests. In 1891, the administration in the Dutch Indies confronted the challenge of administering an Islamic population more directly by appointing a Muslim advisor to the consul general, Snouck Hurgronje. Hurgronje was the son of a pastor in the Reformed Church who throughout his life believed that the emancipation of Muslims within the Dutch kingdom, including the colonies, calling for a gradual assimilation of Muslims into Dutch society as early as 1900.

Two interlocking phenomena—pillarization (*verzuiling*) and depillarization (*ontzuiling*)—explain the rise of demands for equal religious rights and the formation of political agendas to achieve public funding for religious organizations in the twentieth century. First, the phenomenon of pillarization acted as a system of political pacification in a society organized into ideological pillars. Protestants, Catholics, and nonconfessionals have their own institutions—schools, cemeteries, media outlets, etc. This process started with the rise of mass politics in the late nineteenth century and ended in 1966. Depillarization took over during the 1960s, signaling more individualization and less identification with the pillar system owing to further modernization.

The arrival of Muslim guest workers at the end of pillarization and the start of a more individualized society led to a paradox, as the large Muslim minority initially had difficulty establishing itself in Dutch society without the benefits of pillarization. The ongoing establishment of Muslim communities reopened the public debate about the place of religion in society and issues of equity regarding newcomers. Articles of the constitution, especially Article 23, empowered the Muslim communities to push for religious, cultural, educational, and political demands and a subsequent politics of accommodation—from ritual slaughter, mosques, and cemeteries to Islamic media outlets and schools.

Muslim Communities. After the arrival of guest workers in the 1960s, most of the Muslims in the Netherlands are not from former colonies. After World War II the rebuilding of the Netherlands was undertaken with the aid of many guest workers, first from within Europe—Italians, Spaniards, Portuguese—and then expanding beyond Europe to Turks and Moroccans. The Muslim guest worker migration was male-dominated. Migrants utilized rudimentary venues such as old houses, garages, and hangars to conduct their religious practice. Eventually, the Council of Churches and many Dutch churches helped the Turkish and Moroccan workers establish the first prayer spaces in old churches. It was a significant gesture that led to the expansion of mosques and gave more confidence to the emerging Muslim community.

The number of people residing in the Netherlands from non-European countries, including Netherlands-born Muslims, has risen from 9 percent to 11 percent since 2000 to 1.9 million. Turks (392,923) form the largest group, followed by Indonesians (number unknown), Moroccans (362,954), and smaller groups such as Surinamese (45,000), Afghans (41,473), Iraqis (53,336), Iranians (34,226), and Somalis (18,150). One of every five Dutch citizens is foreign-born.

A quarter of the young people in the Netherlands are of foreign decent. Among the minority groups, Turks and Moroccans are the youngest. Half of the Turks and Moroccans in the Netherlands have only their original citizenship, and

80 percent of the second generation have dual citizenship.

As of 2010, there were 907,000 Muslims in the Netherlands, or 6 percent of the total population. According to data from 2007, 51 percent of the 475 mosques are Turkish (242), 38 percent are Moroccan (179), and 11 percent are Surinamese (52). Of the Turkish mosques, 143 belong to the Diyanet, the Turkish ministry of religious affairs; forty-eight mosques belong to the Süleymancı movement; and twenty-five are affiliated with the Milli Görüş movement. The majority of the 179 Moroccan mosques are members of the Union of Moroccan Mosques. Of the Surinamese mosques forty-one are Sunnī and eleven are Aḥmadī.

In the field of education, 9,331 students attend forty-three primary Islamic schools, and 1,179 students attend the two secondary Islamic schools, in Amsterdam and Rotterdam, all of which are fully funded by the state. There are two Islamic universities in the Netherlands: the Islamic University of Rotterdam and the Islamic University of Europe in Schiedam, neither being publicly funded or recognized. Imams and other Muslim spiritual workers are trained in a facility in Amsterdam, but the overwhelming majority are still imported from the countries of origin. The University of Leiden and the Vrije Universiteit in Amsterdam are starting master's programs in Islamic theology in collaboration with Muslim communities. Muslim organizations, both secular and religious, local and national, are thriving, including women's organizations such as Al Nisa and the National Muslim Women Network.

Publicly funded television and radio programs to accommodate the first-generation guest workers have existed since the 1970s in both Arabic and Berber. In 1986, the government facilitated the creation of the public Islamic Broadcasting Foundation. But the organization was fraught with internal power struggles among immigrant communities. In 1993, the organization was replaced by the Nederlandse Moslim Omroep, which was then replaced by the Nederlandse Islamitische Omroep in 2005. During this time, the power struggles were so intense that the Dutch government suspended the licenses of the Muslim broadcasting organizations in 2010. Following this decision in 2010, the Nederlandse Islamitische Omroep obtained a new license to broadcast 175 hours per year, which tripled the broadcast time. This increase in funded airtime has much to do with the politics of accommodation toward Muslims in the Netherlands.

Despite the rise of Muslim religious and political leadership, voter turnout among Muslims generally remains low, especially considering that the Dutch had granted noncitizens the right to vote at the municipal level in 1986. Most Moroccans vote for the Partij van de Arbeid (Labor Party). Even the Nederlands Moslim Partij (Dutch Muslim Party), which is active in some cities, can count on no more than 5 percent of the Turkish and Moroccan votes.

Radicalization. The Muslim population is identified by many media outlets and politicians as a source of tension in Dutch society. Public political debate in large cities often focuses on the role of Muslim youth in delinquency and petty crime such as pickpocketing. In 2006, 15 percent of accused criminals in the Netherlands were Turkish and Moroccan. Of youths between 18 and 25 accused of crimes, 10 percent were Moroccans and over 5 percent were Turks.

According to the Dutch Intelligence Service, in 2007 preachers considered to be radical were active in thirty of the total 475 mosques, and there are estimated to be 250 radical Muslims in the Netherlands. Despite the negative media and political drumbeat against Muslims in the wake of the 9/11 attacks, Muslim communities in the Netherlands have shown a concerted will to contain and oppose radicalism. There is also an intense debate surrounding the possibility of leaving the faith without being excommunicated.

Anti-Islamic sentiments were fueled by the rise of fundamentalist Islam in the Netherlands, especially after 9/11 and the killings of the famous right-wing politician Pim Fortuyn and filmmaker Theo van Gogh, and the trial surrounding a Muslim terrorist group founded in the Netherlands (the Hofstad Network). These developments contributed greatly to the rise in popularity of anti-Islam politics. The most notorious far-right politician is Geert Wilders, who made a movie called *Fitna* to draw attention to what he calls the dangerous and extremist character of Islam, and he compares Islam to dangerous ideologies like Nazism and communism. His outspoken opinions resulted in him being sued by Muslims, and the public trials gave him more exposure and notoriety. In the end, Wilders was not sentenced, and a number of Muslims, including a member of Parliament brought the issue to the Human Rights Committee of the United Nations, claiming that the government had not protected Muslims from politically backed hate speech.

Despite the challenges of adapting to a very liberal Dutch society, in less than fifty years of migration to the Netherlands Muslim communities have carved out a strong presence in Dutch society, even finding support in unlikely places. For instance, the Dutch Parliament voted in 2011 to ban *ḥalāl* slaughter. But by banning *ḥalāl* slaughter, they would also inadvertently ban kosher slaughter. The possibility of the ban becoming law has led to outrage in both the Muslim and Jewish communities, who have united to oppose the legislation.

BIBLIOGRAPHY

Andeweg, Rudy B., and Galen A. Irwin., eds. *Governance and Politics of the Netherlands*. New York: Palgrave Macmillan, 2002.

Centraal Bureau voor de Statistiek. *Integratie Rapport 2010*. http://www.cbs.nl/nl-NL/menu/themas/dossiers/allochtonen/cijfers/default.htm.

Cherribi, Sam. *In the House of War: Dutch Islam Observed*. Oxford: Oxford University Press, 2010 [2013].

Sengers, Erik, and Thijl Sunier, eds. *Religious Newcomers and the Nation State: Political Culture in France and the Netherlands*. Delft, Netherlands: Eburon Delft, 2010.

Sam Cherribi

New Media in the Muslim World. The introduction of new media in society is accompanied by subtle and gradual changes of cultural and religious norms and behavior. The new media are often embraced by certain groups before others, and those who master them will be able to spread their particular religious interpretation. More fundamentally, new media can also change the very way that believers perceive, engage, and express their religious sentiments and global views. In the Muslim world, new media have been instrumental in spreading new or oppositional versions of Islam, allowing innovative actors to come to the fore. In the twenty-first century, the spread of mobile phones, satellite TV, and the Internet have been important factors in the globalization of Muslim interactions and the engagement of millions of ordinary Muslims in the development of their faith.

The Significance of Printing. Revealed to a prophet who allegedly could not read, Islam has always been taught, transmitted, and propagated orally, and the recitation of the Qurʾān is a central ritual to this day. Writing and the written text, however, have also been of paramount importance and prestige, from the revelation onward. Over the centuries, literate scholars of Islam, the *ʿulamāʾ*, were the socially accepted transmitters of Islamic learning and authority. A significant part of the training of an *ʿālim* (sing. of *ʿulamāʾ*) was the meticulous copying (*taqlīd*) of texts that were recited orally by his *shaykh*.

Printed books appeared relatively late in the Muslim world, and for a long time mainly in the form of imports from Europe. A 1727 *fatwa* by the Ottoman Shaykh al-Islām, which permitted the establishment of a state press (which only operated for eighteen years) is evidence of a certain unease and opposition to printing on the part of the *ʿulamāʾ*. It was not until the second half of the nineteenth century that printing was fully established in the more advanced Muslim capitals, with a commercial book market and competing newspapers and cultural journals. This had a profound impact on Muslim religious knowledge, cultural production, and social and political life. As the first industrial mass medium, printing made the Muslim literary heritage available and more easily affordable. The introduction of new punctuation and indexing made the texts more easily readable and searchable. The *ʿulamāʾ*'s traditional teaching methods of memorization and copying were challenged by new and simpler ways of acquiring and storing Islamic learning (*ʿilm*) and an emphasis on interpretation of the basic sources of Islam (*ijtihād*) that would be in line with the progress of the age.

By 1900, the rise of national publics in various parts of the Muslim world was supplemented by a stress on the Muslim *ummah* as a transnational audience, as propagated by reformist publications. According to journals such as *al-Manār*, the *ummah* was living through difficult times, as it was afflicted by imperialism and Christian mission, but first and foremost by its own intellectual stagnation. Plans were hatched, and occasionally realized, for Pan-Islamic congresses with delegates from around the world discussing the challenges to the *ummah* and adopting strategies for overcoming them. The 1931 General Islamic Congress in Jerusalem alerted a broader Muslim world to the threat of Zionist immigration in Palestine and promoted the idea of Jerusalem as the third holy city of Islam. Many of the participants were not *ʿulamāʾ* in the strict sense, but belonged to a new category of intellectuals (*muthaqqafūn*) who made a living as publishers and writers. The spread of printing thus led to new ways of transmitting Islamic knowledge, and was accompanied by dynamic ideas of Islamic progress and reform.

New Media in the Twentieth Century. During the twentieth century, more new media were introduced in the Muslim world: the telephone, the gramophone, film, radio, television. These new media were technologically advanced, and industries arose to manufacture them, operate them, and produce content. On the reception side, however, these media did not require the literacy that was the precondition of print. Like the newspaper, the new media established themselves in urban centers long before they penetrated the countryside, and while the rich (including women) could enjoy them at home, poorer people encountered them in cafés. As elsewhere in the world, daily life with these media gradually changed the social mores, political awareness, and aesthetic sensibilities of audiences. Each new generation grew up with its own specific media diet.

For the most part there was often a certain apprehension toward a new medium in religious circles, either because the media posed a challenge to established ways of doing things, or because it seemed to make ordinary Muslims more oblivious to their religion. The introduction of films, in particular, was often seen to promote a Western lifestyle (both the content of the films, and the new habit of going to the cinema). With time, Muslim scholars and intellectuals took to the new media and employed them for specifically religious purposes. A standard twentieth-century argument would be to see the new media as an opportunity for *daʿwah* (mission among

Muslims), and to point to Christian missionary use of these media. For example, the first Arab epic film, set in Mecca at the time of the Prophet Muḥammad, *Ẓuhur al-Islām* ("The Emergence of Islam"), was finally allowed to be screened in 1950, partly as a response to the success of Hollywood's biblical films. Films and later TV drama were important in giving large audiences a twentieth-century version of Islamic history and personalities, but even more important was the ethical and emotional education found in family dramas about the right way to bring up a child, address a husband, or mourn a relative.

In most Muslim countries, radio and later television became a state monopoly. In the 1950s and 1960s, religious programming mainly took the form of sermons by top *ʿulamāʾ* during Ramaḍān and other religious holidays. Television could also provide factual and visual information about Islamic localities and rituals such as the *ḥajj*. From the 1970s onward, religious debate programs became popular, and their hosts would sometimes become national stars. The state monopoly meant that religious programs were given to regime loyalists, and sometimes gave religious endorsement to specific state policies, such as family planning. Still, with the religious awakening of the 1970s, which led to the establishment of Islamist opposition groups in many Muslim countries, the latter quickly realized how limited their access was to the most powerful media. Over time, most developed their own interpretations through the use of smaller media tools, such as the pamphlet and the audio tape, which state censors could only control with some difficulty.

Islam on Satellite TV. Technological advances in the late twentieth century led to the breakthrough of powerful media outlets that left profound impacts on Muslim religious activities.

More than anywhere else, broadcasting via satellite revolutionized television in Muslim countries. For one thing, it transformed key languages—Arabic, Persian, Turkish, Urdu—into global tongues, reconnecting the millions of immigrants in the Western world with audiences in their countries of origin. Secondly, it broke the state broadcasting monopoly, which had prevailed for decades. With a click of the remote control, viewers could access programs featuring opposition politicians and religious preachers who advocated messages that state channels would have seldom allowed.

A new public sphere evolved, transcending national borders. In the emerging Arab public sphere, spanning some twenty-three countries in addition to Arab immigrant communities in Europe, Australia, and the Americas, scant attention could be paid to local politics in any one country, and border conflicts between two Arab states could be difficult to handle. Conflicts between Arabs and non-Arabs, on the other hand, would be of interest to all the audience, and pan-Arab political stations such as Al Jazeera and Al-Arabiya successfully concentrated on conflicts with outside powers such as Israel or Iran, or even the United States. Although in general supportive of Western political values and institutions, pan-Arab channels regularly chastised Western governments for not living up to their own rhetoric of democracy and human rights and for pursuing self-interested and neo-imperialist policies in the Middle East. Many programs and debates implied that a cultural clash was raging between "the West" and "Islam."

By 2010 all major world powers had established television channels in Arabic, and some in Persian, to compete in what was known as "the battle for hearts and minds," but these were just a fraction of what became available over the airwaves. Al Jazeera, for example, acted as a forum for taboo-breaking debates along with nonconventional news coverage, especially from war zones in Afghanistan, Iraq, and Gaza. In turn, these broadcasts complemented the perspectives of major Western news channels, but always from a distinctly Arab perspective. Al Jazeera soon became one of the world's most recognized brands, and its English version was watched in non-Arab-speaking parts of the Muslim world such as Malaysia and India, which reinforced the notion that one the most powerful news channels was based in an Arab Gulf state. A few years later, Al-Arabiya added to the available choices, which further expanded their reach. Still, controversies emerged as to whether these media outlets—often owned by states or carefully vetted media moguls—were nothing more than "rentier media," since their income was generated from political investments. Because major Gulf audiences were attractive for some advertisers, producers naturally sought to cater to Gulf tastes, which may have slanted coverage.

From the turn of the century, specialized Islamic channels began to appear, some with an identifiable Salafī, Ṣūfī, or Islamist orientation. Aiming at becoming the default channels for Muslim families, these outlets developed Islamic versions of popular programming such as children's, cooking, reality, or quiz programs (*Who Wants to Be a Missionary?*). In contrast to the book market, where Islamic books held a dominant share of the market, Islamic channels accounted for less than 20 percent of the Arab television market.

Importantly, Islamic programming was never limited to Muslim channels and could be found on most of the popular stations. A good example of the impact of new media on religion is the way Ramaḍān in many countries became saturated with appealing TV programs. Many Muslims' recollections of Ramaḍān in their childhood would be of the family seated in front of the television from the hour of *ifṭār* until late at night. A special genre, the *musalsal*, a thirty-episode serial, evolved to cater to captive Ramaḍān audiences. Most of these were social or family dramas, but there were also biographical serials about famous caliphs or Islamic religious figures such as the founders of the law schools, Ṣūfī masters, or reformers such as Ibn Taymīyah or Jamāl al-Dīn al-Afghānī. In the 2000s, Egyptian state TV even produced a few *musalsalāt* about twentieth-century *ʿulamāʾ*. Serials such as these were opportunities for the producers to promote ideals of Islamic sanctity and propriety in an engaging way and, conversely, to depict representatives of competing visions of Islam as fanatics, hypocrites, and the like.

In the twenty-first century, the Islamic Republic of Iran emerged as a leading producer of *musalsalāt* on Qurʾānic figures such as Yūsuf, Maryam, ʿĪsā, and the People of the Cave. These serials were dubbed into other languages and exported. Consciously avoiding anything that would be dogmatically unacceptable to Sunnīs, they nevertheless preached typically Shīʿī themes of intense piety and sacrifice of God's chosen few in a world dominated by the unjust and ungodly.

Islam on the Internet. While satellite television enabled Muslim languages to become global, the Internet gave a boost to English as a Muslim language. Muslims in the West, as well as educated Muslims elsewhere, made use of the English-language Internet to communicate with each other about Islamic ethics and faith, and the challenges confronting Muslims in the digital age. In contrast to television, the Internet was from the outset a democratic medium allowing for individual believers to express themselves, and for more enterprising Muslim groups or individuals to build up their own platforms serving a broader "cyber-Muslim" community. A new Internet culture of news services, businesses, dating sites, blogs, and discussion forums specifically for Muslims evolved in the United States and United Kingdom and spread to the rest of the world. Followers of specific *shaykh*s or trends set up attractive sites to propagate their views and provide their followers with advice. Even militant groups sought to communicate and recruit new members via the Internet. Other Web sites in turn were set up by people, Muslim or non-Muslim, who wanted to warn against particular Islamic tendencies, or against Islam in general. And again, the individual Muslim and non-Muslim could surf and select, in the process learning about the diversity of contemporary Islamic views and visions.

By the early 2000s, major Internet portals for Muslims had evolved, often in several languages. Combining news and current affairs of Islamic interest with advice for everything from cooking and child rearing to finance, along with specifically Islamic services such as *ḥajj* instructions or prayer times, these Web sites aspired to be the default home page on the believing family's computers. These portals were major operations with hundreds of employees, mainly funded from the Arab Gulf as a part of *daʿwah* efforts engaged on fundraising on the site itself.

Islamic institutions were slow to make use of the new medium. Ministries of religion, and major Muslim educational institutions initially were content with a simple page of presentation, rarely updated. With time, many realized that they would need to defend their position by serving the community with relevant material, such as online versions of the Qurʾān and *ḥadīth*, or engaging services such as quizzes or vox-pops, to compete with popular Islamic Web portals.

As with Islamic television, these major Web sites were forced to deliver services that were popular on the broader Web in order to remain attractive to large audiences. Weather forecasts, general news, games, and cooking recipes could not be neglected. Other genres could be given an Islamic touch or a moralizing tone, such as on children's and women's pages. News would mainly be related to Muslim concerns, songs would be about religious subjects, and the date would be *hijrī* with a converter to avoid confusion.

But the classical Islamic cultural and literary genres were also represented. Theological and juridical treatises were published and downloadable for free. *Tafsīr* of the Qurʾān could be offered along with the verses. When computer speed and bandwidth allowed it, Qurʾān recitation, invocations (*duʿāʾ*) and pious songs (*anāshīd*) were broadcast. With the rise of YouTube, Friday sermons (*khuṭab*, sing. *khuṭbah*) and teachings (*durūs*) of important *ʿulamāʾ* became very popular and widely available.

Of special importance were *fatwa* services; Muslims from all over the world were invited to submit questions to be answered by scholars of Islamic jurisprudence. This was immensely popular, as many new social phenomena all over the world would get their first Islamic assessment in an Internet *fatwa*, and other Muslims could learn about their religion by reading the answers. Some institutions such as the Qatari Ministry of Awqāf offered searchable archives with hundreds of thousands of *fatwas*.

This was also an attractive way for scholars and activists to promote their versions of Islam and to combat misinterpretations that everyone recognized were "out there" on the Internet. Not only would various Islamic tendencies and schools have different interpretations of the same question, they might also engage in (easily accessible) polemics against other opinions, such as Sunnī versus Shīʿī, or Salafī versus Ṣūfī. Moreover, on the Internet there would extreme cases of permissive, intolerant, or militant *fatwas*, and muftis whom nobody had heard of before, and who might theoretically not even be Muslims. Hence, while in theory a Muslim could access a range of *fatwas* on any one question and compare them to reach his own considered opinion, the fear was that he would reach a confused or a self-serving one. By 2005, there were heated discussions about what to do about the "*fatwa* chaos" prevailing on the Internet and on satellite TV. Solutions varied from restricting *fatwa*-giving to a specific group of high *ʿulamāʾ* (implemented by Saudi Arabia in 2010) over specific mufti education to a voluntary code of conduct.

The Religious Significance of the New Media. Muslims have taken to the new media, and Islam has a prominence in it on a global scale that is vastly greater than its traditional presence in traditional outlets, whether in the Muslim world or beyond it. There are several reasons for this:

- Islam was newsworthy and provided drama. The attack on New York and Washington on 11 September 2001 was the single most important news item in the early twenty-first century. Many conflicts had a component of struggle between Muslims and non-Muslims: in Kashmir, Chechnya, the Balkans, Indonesia, Afghanistan, Iraq, and Sudan. Some Islamist media considered Muslims the victims of worldwide oppression, whereas some Western media spoke of a general "Islamic threat."
- For media with a global reach, Islam was an attractive common denominator. For audiences living in very different societies and under varying political arrangements, what might be of interest to some viewers would be of little interest to many others. Their Muslim identity, on the other hand, would be of interest to most consumers of media in Urdu, Arabic, Persian, or Turkish.
- Islam was raising general issues. It was not only with repsect to issues of violence and world politics that Islam grabbed the headlines. In most countries, the social coexistence of Muslims and non-Muslims suddenly raised many issues: on immigration policies, the treatment of minorities, or tolerance of diverging personal lifestyles.
- Muslims turned out to be not just engaged consumers of mass media but also dedicated producers of Islamic content on the Internet.

Much of the scholarship about Muslim use of the Internet has focused on this last point, of a democratization of Islamic cultural production, as individual users began to select and express their own versions of their faith. More than that, with the access of many more voices, new types of criticisms arose as well, including anticlericalism and radical skepticism.

While it is certainly true that the new media have empowered ordinary Muslims, it is less certain that this inevitably leads to a "fragmentation of authority in Islam," as has often been claimed. For the new media have also created "stars," by concentrating authority in the hands of individuals with a strong presence across the airwaves. This presence combines the Internet with smartphones, satellite television, and older media such as magazines and cassette tapes. The delivery of *fatwas* (*iftāʾ*), in particular, has seamlessly moved from media to media, from print to radio to phone-in services to Twitter, often promoting the same authorities across the board: Major Sunnī and Shīʿī *ʿulamāʾ* have their own important Web sites and their own television programs, and a few even own their radio or television stations. Similarly, Islamic movements such as Ḥizbullāh in Lebanon run major operations on all media platforms. So rather than merely fragmenting authority, new media tend to redistribute authority. In many settings, those who stand to lose are traditional seats of learning, state muftis, and other authorities, which were promoted by authoritarian states. If they are to reassert themselves, they will have to accept that authority in the context of new media outlets is no longer given to them by the state, or even by fellow scholars, but something they must establish with consumers directly.

Bibliography

Bunt, Gary R. *iMuslims: Rewiring the House of Islam.* Chapel Hill, N.C.: University of North Carolina Press, 2009.

Eickelman, Dale F., and Jon W. Anderson, eds. *New Media in the Muslim World: The Emerging Public*

Sphere. 2d ed. Bloomington: Indiana University Press, 2003.

Gräf, Bettina. *Medien-Fatwas@Yusuf al-Qaradawi: Die Popularisierung des islamischen Rechts*. Berlin: Schwarz, 2010.

Meyer, Birgit, and Annelies Moors, eds. *Religion, Media, and the Public Sphere*. Bloomington: Indiana University Press, 2006.

Salvatore, Armando, and Dale F. Eickelman. *Public Islam and the Common Good*. Leiden, Netherlands: Brill, 2004.

JAKOB SKOVGAARD-PETERSEN

NIGERIA. A federal republic, Nigeria comprises thirty-six states plus the Federal Capital Territory at Abuja. The most recent census, in 2006, did not ask questions of religious or ethnic identity, but put the total population at around 140 million. As of 2012, official figures put the population estimates for Nigeria at more than 160 million. According to the 2006 census, the state with the largest number of people was Kano, in the far north, with more than 9 million. (Note: Lagos State is normally regarded as having an even higher population.)

Religious Identity and Demographic Patterns. The last official census that asked about ethno-religious identity was in 1963. At that time the overall percentage of Muslim adherents was 49 percent, and Christian adherents 34 percent; the remainder identified with traditional forms of religion. Subsequently, the standard rendering of these data became: 50 percent Muslim, 40 percent Christian, 10 percent traditional. Thus, Nigeria is by far the largest country in the world with a population about half Muslim and half Christian. The major so-called ethnic identity groups were Hausa (Hausa-Fulani) at about 30 percent, Yoruba (20 percent), and Igbo (17 percent). Estimates of the number of language groups in Nigeria range from 350 to 400, with ten major groups accounting for about 90 percent of the population. With few exceptions, Nigerian Muslims follow the Sunnī tradition and the Mālikī legal school.

As of 2012, it is generally estimated that Nigeria is about half Muslim and half Christian, as both major world religions have gained since the late 1980s at the expense of traditional religions. However, traditional customs still affect the variety of forms in both Christian and Muslim communities. To some extent there is a regional pattern of religious distribution, with high percentages of Muslims living in the states associated with the nineteenth-century Sokoto caliphate and its twentieth-century successor states, such as Sokoto, Kebbi, Zamfara, Kano, Jigawa, Katsina, Bauchi, Kaduna (including Zaria), Niger, Kwara, Gombe, and Adamawa. In addition, the states of Borno and Yobe have been identified as Muslim states for about a thousand years and were never conquered during the Sokoto reformist period. Thus, Borno is one of the oldest continuous Muslim states in all of Africa.

In the southwest, there has been an indigenous pattern of Islamic culture throughout the nineteenth and twentieth centuries, especially in the Yoruba-speaking states of Oyo, Osun, Ogun, and Lagos. However, Yoruba patterns of religious identification are mixed, and even within the same extended family members may be Muslim, Christian, or traditionalist. City-state identities are generally regarded as the predominant factor in Yoruba political life. The "middle belt" of Nigeria—including such states as Kogi, Plateau, Benue, and the Federal Capital Territory at Abuja—has witnessed a significant number of Muslim converts in the past several decades. The identity of "Three-M-ers" (Muslim, Middle Belt, Minority) has become highly visible in recent years because Ibrahim Babangida, president from 1985 to 1993, was from that area. While the four geographical areas mentioned above form the bulk of the Muslim population in a zone stretching from northern Nigeria through southwest

Nigeria down to the coast, Muslim immigrants or converts can be found throughout Nigeria.

Much of the interpretation of these demographic patterns in relation to ethnicity, age, occupation, and education is a matter of speculation, since the period after the 1963 census has been one of considerable transformation in Nigeria. This includes the civil war of 1967–1970, the oil boom of the 1970s, the recession of the 1980s, the return to civilian politics in 1998–1999, the Fourth Republic (1999–present), and the elections of 2011. The Fourth Republic also saw the return to *sharīʿah* law in the criminal domain in the twelve far northern states.

Religious Organization and Thought. Several recognizable subcategories of identity within the Nigerian Muslim community may be noted: Ṣūfī brotherhoods, anti-innovation legalists, adherents of the caliphal/Medinan model, women's groups, and "big tent" national organizations. In addition, a large number of Nigerian Muslims of all ages and backgrounds simply identify themselves as "Muslim," without overt attachment to an organization or school of thought. More recently, since 2009, a movement in Borno called Boko Haram by outsiders has evolved, which has challenged the moderate Muslim establishment and the very idea of a secular state. As of 2012, the group's violence has increased, and a state of emergency has been declared in parts of four northern states, including Borno and Yobe.

In the nineteenth century Qādirīyah Ṣūfī affiliation became part of the identity of the Sokoto caliphal leadership. In addition, during the two decades after the death of Usuman Dan Fodio in 1817, the Tijānīyah brotherhood was spread in what later became northern Nigeria by ʿUmar al-Fūtī and his followers. Thus the Qādirīyah and the Tijānīyah became the two major Ṣūfī brotherhoods in the region, especially within the caliphal areas. By contrast, the leaders and scholars of Borno were not for the most part affiliated with Ṣūfī brotherhoods.

During the twentieth century the Tijānīyah spread extensively in Kano, the commercial and industrial capital of the north. Because of the social networks that extended out of Kano through the geographically extensive Hausa trading system, the Tijānīyah spread throughout Nigeria. A reformed version of Tijānīyah emerged that accommodated many of the modernizing developments of the era after World War II. The leader of this reform movement was Ibrahim Niass, of Kaolack, Senegal, but its Nigerian base was in Kano under the leadership of Tijjani Usman and others; the emir of Kano, Muhammadu Sanusi, eventually became the "caliph" in Nigeria. After World War II, the Qādirīyah also experienced a reformation, associated with Shaykh Nasiru Kabara of Kano. He reauthorized (through his own chains of authority) many of the emirate notables who had been associated historically with Qādirīyah, and he also attracted large numbers of young people to study and extend his networks.

In the period leading to independence (1949–1960) and in the early period of independence (1960–1966), the Ṣūfī brotherhoods were major vehicles for religious organization and identity. The system of social networks allowed for the expansion of the Muslim community and facilitated interethnic contact. Importantly, the brotherhoods facilitated the high rates of rural-urban migration occurring in many Nigerian cities.

In the 1970s, with the oil boom creating dramatic changes in Nigerian educational opportunities, many of the younger generation became interested less in brotherhood affiliation and more in Western education and, at the same time, returning to the basics of the Qurʾān and *ḥadīth*. Brotherhood affiliation is still significant, but it has been largely superseded by efforts to strengthen broader Muslim identity.

Another transformation during the oil boom of the 1970s, accompanying the enormous increase in higher educational opportunities, was the growth at Nigerian universities of Muslim student groups, especially the Muslim Students Society (MSS). Often the students in these groups were from families associated with brotherhood organizations, but the need to transcend Ṣūfī identities seemed imperative in the face of secular challenges.

Many of these students were influenced by Abubakar Gumi (1922–1992) from the village of Gumi in Sokoto, who had been grand *kadi* (Islamic judge; Ar., *qāḍī*) of northern Nigeria during the first republic and then retired to teaching from his home in Kaduna. Gumi had close connections with Saudi Arabian scholars and notables through his involvement in the pilgrimage. He began to preach a "return to basics"—the Qurʾān and *ḥadīth*—and came increasingly to regard Sufism as innovation.

Gumi formed a network called Izālah, which directly challenged many of the brotherhoods' leaders and practices, utilizing radio and television effectively. He was the first to translate the Qurʾān into Hausa; when he died in September 1992, it was estimated that his translation had sold millions of copies. His anti-innovation and legalist approach, combined with his emphasis on each person having direct access to the Qurʾān, became one of the major Muslim reformations in the 1970s and thereafter. He asked his students, many of whom were leaders in higher education, to interpret the Qurʾān in the light of modern times and not to adopt a literalist interpretation. A result in some quarters, however, was a revival of interest in re-creating some approximation of the Sokoto caliphal model or what they regarded as the earlier Medinan model in their personal lives or in the political communities of Nigeria. Many of the scholars and students who were exploring the ideals and relevance of these models to the contemporary situation were at the major universities within the current boundaries of the Sokoto caliphal states—Ahmadu Bello University in Zaria, Bayero University in Kano, and Usmanu Danfodiyo University in Sokoto. While many of these teachers and students participate in Nigerian affairs in various ways, their classical training creates a dynamic tension between present sociopolitical realities and the ideals of an earlier period.

The Izālah movement was particularly strong in the "new towns" of the north, that is, those without a strong legacy of traditional Muslim rulers. Thus, Kaduna and Jos became associated with the "back to basics" approach of Izālah. The decentralization of this movement was finally overcome in 2011, with the selection of the leader of the Jos faction (Sheikh Sani Yahaya Jingir) as the overall leader.

Another outcome of the focus on original sources was to provoke a reassessment of the role of women in Muslim society and a greater awareness of the Islamic emphasis on the education of girls and women. (Indeed, the daughter of Usman Dan Fodio, Nana Asmaʾu, was a distinguished scholar in her own right.) The opportunities for women in Western education during the oil boom were also strong incentives to consider women's issues.

Muslim women in Nigeria have usually reflected the ethnolinguistic cultures of which they were a part. Thus in the predominantly Hausa-Fulani emirates, urban women in the twentieth century have tended to be secluded. Muslim women in Borno have generally been less secluded and in recent years have been active in educational and commercial pursuits. Muslim women in Yoruba societies have not been secluded and are virtually indistinguishable from non-Muslim Yoruba women in many respects. In the Muslim/Middle Belt/Minority areas women have tended to be educated, and they have no tradition of seclusion.

In the mid-1980s the impact of the spread of education began to be felt more clearly among Muslim women. Some participated in organizations such as Women in Nigeria (WIN), which was widely regarded in Nigeria as "feminist." Others, educated through the secondary or university level, began to reclaim their own sense of Muslim identity. One result of this trend was the organization of the Federation of Muslim Women's Associations in Nigeria (FOMWAN). Established in the 1980s to give coherence to Muslim women's organizations throughout Nigeria, it has focused on the need to counteract the role of custom in Nigerian Muslim society.

After the return to civilian rule in 1999, there were about five hundred member organizations in FOMWAN, distributed throughout Nigeria but with a majority in the Yoruba-speaking areas. Each state selects representatives to a national committee, which publishes a magazine, *The Muslim Woman*, and holds annual conferences on topics of special concern. The main language of communication is English, and FOMWAN acts as a liaison with other national and international Muslim women's groups. Many of the leaders of FOMWAN are also active in state and national affairs. Latifa Okunnu of Lagos has served as president of FOMWAN and has also been the presidential liaison officer in Lagos State. In October 1992 she was appointed by the president of Nigeria to be the national organizer for one of the two political parties, the National Republican Convention, during the transition to civilian rule.

The emphasis on national-level activities reflects a widespread concern among Nigerian Muslims that they not be divided by sectarian loyalties. During the 1960s there was an attempt in northern Nigeria to form an ecumenical Muslim movement called the Society for the Victory of Islam (Jamʿīyatul Nasril Islam). Later, during the military periods, the ecumenical "big tent" approach was broadened to the national arena, mainly through the Nigerian Supreme Council for Islamic Affairs (NSCIA). The head of the Supreme Council was the sultan of Sokoto, the vice president was the *shehu* (*shaykh*) of Borno, and the secretary was a leading Yoruba Muslim lawyer. In a sense, this format reflected an emerging establishment with ties to the political, economic, and military sectors within Nigeria. With the succession of Ibrahim Dasuki (b. 1923) to the sultanship in 1988 (partly because of his close association with the Nigerian Supreme Council of Islamic Affairs), the council took on a new importance. It had to deal with a wide range of Nigerian Muslim identities and values and also try to serve as an effective liaison with its counterpart, the Christian Association of Nigeria (CAN). Dasuki was deposed for political reasons by General Sani Abacha (d. 1998) in 1996, and was replaced by Muhammadu Maccido (d. 2006). Following his death in a plane crash in October 2006, Maccido was succeeded by Sa'ad Abubakar (b. 1956), who had served for thirty-one years in the Nigerian army. Sultan Sa'ad Abubakar was installed on 3 March 2007. He has been very active in promoting interfaith dialogue, especially since the elections of 2011.

Relationships to Transnational Patterns. The nationally based federations of Muslim groups, such as FOMWAN and NSCIA, tend to mirror the existing international system and are often seen as an intermediate step toward closer cooperation within the global Muslim community (*ummah*). For their part, the Ṣūfī brotherhoods include transnational and national forms of community organization. Because of their grassroots nature and their connection with long-distance trade, the branches of the Tijānīyah in particular have close ties throughout West Africa—the reformed Tijānīyah is based on the mosque in Kaolack, Senegal—and North Africa (such as the tomb of Aḥmad al-Tijānī in Fez, Morocco). Likewise, the reformed Qādirīyah has ties to the Qādirī mosques in Iraq. Because of the traditional Nigerian pilgrimage routes through Sudan, there are connections to the Tijānī and Qādirī networks in Khartoum and elsewhere in Sudan.

Some members of the Sokoto caliphal dynasty had close ties to the Mahdī in the Sudan in the 1880s. Other members migrated to Sudan as a result of the British conquest of northern Nigeria at the turn of the twentieth century. In the late colonial period, the British encouraged contact between Nigeria and Sudan because the pilgrimage link was seen as a reinforcement of the policy of indirect rule. A number of distinguished Nigerian Muslim legalists studied the higher levels of Arabic in a school near Khartoum, and the Sudanese penal code was a model for reforms in northern Nigeria in 1959.

The anti-innovation legalists often have close ties to official religious circles in Saudi Arabia; Abubakar Gumi was central to this link. There is strong acceptance of the nation-state boundaries as appropriate units for international cooperation among Muslims, reflected in the model of the Organization of the Islamic Conference (OIC), which is often associated with a Saudi approach to international relations. On the other hand, the emphasis on non-Arabic Qurʾānic interpretation—especially through the Hausa language—creates a strong incentive for localism and Nigerian-based reforms rather than slavish imitation of Arab cultural models.

The adherents of the caliphal or Medinan model have a strong sense of *ummah*, or community of believers, but with due provision for trust (*amānah*) with people of the book and for tributary (i.e., taxation) relations with "pagans." Within the modern national state system, there is a strong sense of federalism with insistence on local autonomy, especially for Muslim communities that want to follow a *sharīʿah* model. Insofar as there are like-minded communities of believers throughout the world—whether in Africa, the Arab world, the Persian world, Asia, western Europe, or the Americas—a sense of solidarity that transcends nationalism and nation-state loyalties exists. The military regimes in Nigeria have often been suspicious of such sentiments, and since 9/11, these concerns have been transferred to civilian regimes. Yet the central tendency among Nigerian Muslims is "moderation in all things."

The national umbrella organizations in Nigeria, including women's groups, seem to welcome the national focus of their activities. They appear at ease in dealing with a variety of other national religious groups and nongovernmental organizations. The leaders of such organizations tend to have higher education and to be fluent in English. The national nature of the annual pilgrimage seems to reinforce the appropriateness of the nation-state unit and of international organizations like the OIC. The strength and the weakness of such national umbrella groups is their closer identification with national-level sources of political power than what characterizes the other types of Muslim organization in Nigeria.

The large-scale and complex nature of Nigerian society, combined with the rapid transformations associated with "riding the tiger" of an oil-based economy, makes it difficult to generalize about the Nigerian Muslim community. But what is clear is that a legacy of reformation continues as print and electronic media allow both vernacular languages and languages of wider communication to expand Nigerians' awareness of the larger changes going on within the Muslim world and the global economy as a whole.

Meanwhile in Borno and Yobe, as noted above, a fundamentalist group emerged after 2003 under the leadership of Muhammad Yusuf. After repeated clashes with the police, Yusuf was captured by the military and then killed by the police. This martyrdom set off the underground Movement for

Sunnah and Jihād (also called Boko Haram), which has challenged the police and other elements of the secular state.

After the presidential election of 2011, which split the country along ethno-religious lines, the Boko Haram became emboldened and has evolved into a loose coalition of elements, ranging from criminal gangs, to moderate believers, to radical and violent insurgents. While there is evidence of spillover involvement from neighboring countries such as Cameroon, Chad, Niger, and Mali (especially since the collapse of Libya), Boko Haram remains essentially a Nigerian rejectionist movement against the corruption of the modern state, including the moderate Muslim establishment. As of 2012 a state of emergency was declared in parts of the north, and questions lingered as to possible connections of Boko Haram to al-Qaʿida in the Islamic Maghrib elements in the Sahel.

BIBLIOGRAPHY

Bobboyi, Hamid, ed. *Principles of Leadership, According to the Founding Fathers of the Sokoto Caliphate.* Abuja, Nigeria: Centre for Regional Integration and Development, 2011.

Clarke, Peter B. *West Africa and Islam: A Study of Religious Development from the 8th to the 20th Century.* London: E. Arnold, 1982.

Coles, Catherine, and Beverly Mack, eds. *Hausa Women in the Twentieth Century.* Madison: University of Wisconsin Press, 1991.

Gbadamosi, T. G. O. *The Growth of Islam among the Yoruba, 1841–1908.* Atlantic Highlands, N.J.: Humanities Press, 1978.

Last, Murray. *The Sokoto Caliphate.* Ibadan History Series. Harlow, U.K.: Longman, 1967.

Olupona, Jacob K., and Toyin Falola, eds. *Religion and Society in Nigeria: Historical and Sociological Perspectives.* Ibadan, Nigeria: Spectrum, 1991.

Paden, John N. *Ahmadu Bello, Sardauna of Sokoto: Values and Leadership in Nigeria.* London: Hodder & Stoughton, 1986.

Paden, John N. *Faith and Politics in Nigeria: Nigeria as a Pivotal State in the Muslim World.* Washington, D.C.: United States Institute of Peace, 2008.

Paden, John N. *Muslim Civic Cultures and Conflict Resolution: The Challenge of Democratic Federalism in Nigeria.* Washington, D.C.: Brookings Institution Press, 2005.

Paden, John N. *Postelection Conflict Management in Nigeria: The Challenges of National Unity.* Arlington, Va: School for Conflict Analysis and Resolution, George Mason University, 2012.

Paden, John N. *Religion and Political Culture in Kano.* Berkeley: University of California Press, 1973.

Sulaiman, Ibraheem. *A Revolution in History: The Jihad of Usman dan Fodio.* London: Mansell, 1986.

JOHN N. PADEN

NIẒĀM AL-MULK. (1018–1092) Abū ʿAlī al-Ḥasan b. ʿAlī b. Isḥāq al-Ṭūsī, known by the honorific Niẓām al-Mulk (lit. "order of the realm"), was born in Rādkān, a village near Ṭūs, in the province of Khorāsān of northeastern present-day Iran. Little is known of his early life; his fame is due to his almost single-handedly governing the Turco-Persian Seljuk empire for a period of thirty years, as vizier of the Seljuk sultan Alp Arslan (r. 1063–1072) and of his teenage successor Malikshāh (r. 1072–1092); his establishing a series of colleges at which students boarded called Niẓāmīyah; and his authoring a work on governance that has been described as "the supreme work of its kind in Persian" (*Encyclopaedia of Islam* 1960–2004, vol. 7, p. 987b).

The period of Niẓām al-Mulk's vizierate coincided with the ascendancy of Seljuk power. As vizier Niẓām al-Mulk is said to have determined Seljuk policy to a large extent, going so far as to personally lead military campaigns. He is also said to have been behind the appointment of Malikshāh as Alp Arslan's successor, even though the former was not the eldest son; upon Alp Arslan's assassination, Niẓām al-Mulk was retained as vizier, whereupon he dominated the inexperienced sultan and reorganized state institutions along the line of the Sunnī Ghaznavids, in whose administration Niẓām al-Mulk and his father had worked.

The Niẓāmīyah colleges (*madrasahs*) the most famous of which was in Baghdad, were founded as strongholds of Sunnī orthodoxy in order to combat the encroaching Shīʿī Fāṭimid and Ismāʿīlī propaganda; their students, who lived at the complex and studied at the expense of the sultan, were taught Qurʾān, *ḥadīth*, law according to the Shāfiʿī school, scholastic theology (*kalām*) according to the Ashʿarī doctrine, Arabic language and literature, mathematics, and the law of inheritance (Boyle, ed. 1968, p. 216). Two renowned Shāfiʿī jurists and theologians, al-Juwaynī (d. 1085) and al-Ghazālī (d. 1111), taught at a Niẓāmīyah college.

Niẓām al-Mulk recorded for history his advice to rulers—a premodern Islamic literary genre known as "mirrors for princes"—in a treatise of fifty chapters entitled *Siyāsat-nāma* ("Book of Government"; in Persian it is better known as *Siyar al-mulūk*, "Ways of the Kings"), written between 1086 and 1091 (Niẓām al-Mulk 1960, p. xiv). In this work, Niẓām al-Mulk perpetuated the Iranian tradition of state government, reinforcing and strengthening the (Seljuk) sultanate vis-à-vis the caliphate. With his argument that the sultan was also endowed with divine authority, Niẓām al-Mulk argued against the Shāfiʿī jurist al-Māwardī (d. 1058), whose main objective was to empower the caliph alone. The practical advice in the treatise regarding how the sultan should govern and treat his people fairly is couched in and embellished by anecdotes and stories of a historical nature.

Niẓām al-Mulk was stabbed to death in 1092 by an Ismāʿīlī in Ṣūfī dress. Muslim historians speculated that the sultan Malikshāh had engineered the killing, in an effort to get out from under Niẓām al-Mulk's influence. The sultan himself died thirty-five days later, however, after which Seljuk power crumbled.

BIBLIOGRAPHY

Boyle, J. A., ed. *The Cambridge History of Iran*. Vol. 5: *The Saljuq and Mongol Periods*. Cambridge, U.K.: Cambridge University Press, 1968.

Encyclopaedia of Islam. 2nd ed., (Leiden: Brill, 1960–2004), s. vv. "Naṣīḥat al-Mulūk," "Niẓām al-Mulk".

Niẓām al-Mulk. *The Book of Government, or Rules for Kings: The Siyāsat-nāma or Siyar al-mulūk*. Translated by Hubert Darke. London: Curzon, 1960.

Safi, Omid. *The Politics of Knowledge in Premodern Iran: Negotiating Ideology and Religious Inquiry*. Chapel Hill: University of North Carolina Press, 2006.

PERI BEARMAN

NIẒĀMĪYAH COURTS. Until the nineteenth century the bulk of judicial activity in the Ottoman Empire took place in sharīʿah (Turk. *şeriat*) courts. In the mid-1860s, as part of the Tanzimat reforms, the government established a parallel judicial system, termed the Niẓāmīyah ("regular" [Arab. Niẓāmīyah]) courts, thus ending the centuries-old exclusive jurisdiction of the sharīʿah courts. According to the new division of labor, which remained in effect until the collapse of the empire, the Niẓāmīyah courts had jurisdiction over criminal matters as well as civil and commercial disputes, whereas the sharīʿah courts enjoyed exclusive competence in matters of personal status and pious endowments (*waqf*; Turk. *vakıf*). The institutional evolution of the Niẓāmīyah court system was completed in 1879 with the legislation of elaborate criminal and civil procedural codes and with the establishment of offices unprecedented in Ottoman law, such as those of public prosecution, examining magistrates, and professional attorneys.

Some historians have interpreted the establishment of the Niẓāmīyah courts as an indication of secularization, but recent scholarship has questioned this interpretation. The Niẓāmīyah statutory body of law can best be regarded as a typical case of legal borrowing, exhibiting an amalgamation of indigenous and received law. Large-scale incorporation of French Napoleonic law was evident, but it was quite selective. The Niẓāmīyah corpus stemmed from a process of codification that took place throughout the nineteenth century, consisting of codified Islamic–Ottoman law—such as the Civil Code (Mecelle-i Ahkâm-ı Adliye, 1869–1876) and the Land Law (1858)—along with codified adaptations of French statues—such as the Criminal Code (1858) and the procedural codes (1879). The French imprint was also evident in the administrative three-tiered structure of the courts: courts of first instance (*bidayet*), courts of appeal (*istinaf*) in the provincial capitals, and the court of cassation (*temyiz*) in the imperial capital. The law divided each court into civil and criminal sections. Although this division was upheld in appellate cases, in most courts of first instance the same panel addressed both civil and criminal cases. Commercial courts operated in major urban centers; elsewhere, the courts of first instance heard disputes of a commercial nature, applying the commercial codes.

Despite the formal division of labor between the Niẓāmīyah and the sharīʿah courts, a certain latitude for "forum shopping" was allowed in the civil domain of the Niẓāmīyah courts. Although these did not address disputes that belonged to the sharīʿah courts and the sharīʿah courts did not deal with criminal law, in some cases litigants could bring civil suits in the sharīʿah courts. Hence, a limited scope of legal pluralism was apparent.

The majority of Islamic legal-religious scholars (*ʿulamāʾ*) neither perceived the Niẓāmīyah courts as a threat to the status of the sharīʿah nor as a threat to their own position within the judicial sphere. Yemen was the only Ottoman province where the introduction of the Niẓāmīyah courts encountered fierce objection from the local *ʿulamāʾ*; as a result, the comprehensive jurisdiction of the sharīʿah courts was restored.

In most parts of the empire, the Niẓāmīyah judiciary consisted of a combination of specialized judges trained in Islamic educational institutions, together with graduates of the sole nonreligious law school (established 1878) and members of the local provincial elite. Also in most places, the lower courts of first instance and the civil sections of the higher courts of first instance were presided over by the local sharīʿah judge (*naib*, Ar., *nāʾib*). This phenomenon ended after the Young Turk Revolution of 1908, when the Ministry of Justice began staffing the position of court president with Niẓāmīyah judges.

The principle of the separation of the judicial from the administrative authorities was confirmed in the Provincial Law (*Vilâyet Nizamnamesi*, 1864) and was put into practice in 1879. The effort to secure the independence of the Niẓāmīyah courts encountered some resistance from provincial governors and foreign consuls, who were concerned about losing their influence in judicial matters. Yet, on the whole, independence of the Niẓāmīyah judicial system was accomplished with relative success.

The paradigm of legal formalism, which gained dominance in many parts of the world in the nineteenth century, was also evident in the legal culture of the Niẓāmīyah courts, especially after the introduction of the procedural codes (1879). Resorting to juridical and disciplinary means, the Ministry of Justice and the Court of Cassation enforced empire-wide standardization, expecting the Niẓāmīyah judiciary to adhere strictly to the codified clauses and to avoid doctrinal interpretation when sitting on the bench. The formalist legal culture typical of the Niẓāmīyah courts was also evident in the emphasis on procedure in court proceedings, a development that increased the dependency of litigants on professional legal advocacy.

[*See also* Courts; Secularism; *and* Tanzimat.]

BIBLIOGRAPHY

Demirel, Fatmagül. *Adliye Nezareti, Kuruluşu ve Faaliyetleri (1876–1914)*. Istanbul: Boğaziçi Üniversitesi Yayınevi, 2008. Provides the most detailed information on the administration of the Niẓāmīyah courts.

Miller, Ruth A. *Legislating Authority: Sin and Crime in the Ottoman Empire and Turkey*. New York: Routledge, 2005.

Rubin, Avi. *Ottoman Nizamiye Courts: Law and Modernity*. New York: Palgrave Macmillan, 2011. A study of the Niẓāmīyah court system from a sociolegal perspective.

AVI RUBIN

NŪRĪ, FAŻLULLĀH. Fażlullāh Nūrī (1843–1909), more fully Ḥājj Shaykh Fażlullāh ibn Mullā ʿAbbās Māzandarānī Nūrī Tihrānī, was a distinguished Iranian Shīʿī scholar. His father, Mullā ʿAbbās Nūrī, was a prominent jurist. Nūrī studied Shīʿī jurisprudence with Ḥājj Mīrzā Muḥammad Ḥasan Shīrāzī (d. 1894) in Najaf. Finishing his studies in Najaf, Nūrī returned to Tehran and became a *marjaʿ al-taqlīd* (source of exemplary conduct) in the Qājār capital. Among his writings is *Tadhkirat al-ghāfil wa-irshād al-jāhil* (Reminder to the Heedless and Guidance for the Ignorant), which contains a harsh condemnation of proconstitutional ideas and forces (see Hamid Dabashi's translation of this text in Arjomand, 1988, pp. 354–370; see also Hairi, 1977b).

Nūrī played an active but controversial part in the Constitutional Revolution of Iran (1905–1911). His role and that of the entire clergy have been debated extensively (for the nature of this debate, see Hairi, 1977a; cf. Lahidji, 1988). Most historians of the constitutional period are critical of his anticonstitutional stands. Some, including Aḥmad Kasravī and Farīdūn Ādamīyat, are moderate in their observations, although others, such as Nāẓim al-Islām Kirmānī, are extremely critical and even accuse him of greed and charlatanism (see Kirmānī, 1983, pp. 565–566; see also Qazvīnī, 1984, p. 880). Initially, he appears to have been one of the most active supporters of constitutional government, but he gradually shifted his position to oppose it (Kasravī, 1951, pp. 285–296; Kirmānī, 1983, pp. 535–537). Contrary to Muḥammad Ṭabāṭabāʾī and ʿAbd Allāh Bihbahānī, the two prominent proconstitutional clerics, Nūrī became increasingly concerned with the dangers that he felt constitutional government posed for Islam in general and for Islamic law in particular. The phrase *mashrūṭeh-yi mashrūʿeh* (constitutional government compatible with the Islamic law) is chiefly identified with Nūrī, who argued for tying the very foundations of a secular form of government to the requirements of Shīʿī law.

Historians of the constitutional period insist that personal rivalries between Nūrī and Bihbahānī were instrumental in Nūrī's opposition to constitutional government (Dawlatābādī, 1983, p. 185; Kasravī, 1951, pp. 285–286; Ādamīyat, 1976, pp. 429–430). Ādamīyat holds that their opposing positions cloaked their personal rivalries and a struggle for power. Kasravī, too, believes that none of the clerical antagonists "knew the precise meaning of constitutionalism, or the consequences of the propagation of European laws. They were not quite aware of the blatant incompatibility of constitutionalism with the Shīʿī faith" (Kasravī, 1951, p. 287). Nūrī emphasized the necessity for Islam of both *salṭanat* (monarchy) and *nīyābat dar umūr-i nabavīyah* (clerical vicegerency in matters of prophethood; see Martin, 1989, pp. 28–29).

Because of his anticonstitutional activities, Nūrī was captured and executed by the constitutionalist forces on 31 July 1909. One of Nūrī's sons, Shaykh Mīrzā Mahdī, was, against the wishes of his father, a staunch proconstitutionalist. He is reported to have been a militant advocate of constitutional government, and he was murdered by anticonstitutional forces in 1914 (Kirmānī, 1983, p. 566).

[*See also* Constitutional Revolution.]

BIBLIOGRAPHY

Ādamīyat, Farīdūn. *'Idi'ūlūzhī-yi nahẓat-i mashrūṭīyat-i Īrān*, vol. 1. Tehran: Payām, 1976.

Arjomand, Said Amir, ed. *Authority and Political Culture in Shi'ism*. Albany: State University of New York Press, 1988.

Dawlatābādī, Yahyā. *Ḥayāt-i Yaḥyā* (The Life of Yaḥyā), vol. 2. Tehran: Intishārāt-i 'Aṭṭār, 1983.

Hairi, Abdul-Hadi. "Shaykh Fażl Allāh Nūrī's Refutation of the Idea of Constitutionalism." *Middle Eastern Studies* 13, no. 3 (1977b): 327–339.

Hairi, Abdul-Hadi. *Shi'ism and Constitutionalism in Iran: A Study of the Role Played by the Persian Residents of Iraq in Iranian Politics*. Leiden, Netherlands: E. J. Brill, 1977a.

Kasravī, Aḥmad. *Tārīkh-i mashrūṭah-yi Īrān* (History of the Constitution of Iran). Tehran: Amīr Kabīr, 1951.

Kirmānī, Nāẓim al-Islām. *Tārīkh-i bīdārī-yi irānīyān* (History of the Awakening of the Iranians), vol. 1. Edited by 'Ali Akbar Sa'īdī Sīrjānī. Tehran: Āgāh, 1983. Originally published 1967.

Lahidji, Abdol Karim. "Constitutionalism and Clerical Authority." In *Authority and Political Culture in Shi'ism*, edited by Said Amir Arjomand, pp. 133–158. Albany: State University of New York Press, 1988.

Martin, Vanessa. *Islam and Modernism: The Iranian Revolution of 1906*. London: I. B. Tauris, 1989.

Nūrī, Fażlullāh. *Lavāyiḥ-i Aqā Shaykh Faẓl Allāh Nūrī*. Edited by Humā Riẓvānī. Tehran: Nashr-i Tārīkh-i Īrān, 1983.

HAMID DABASHI

NŪRĪ MOVEMENT. The Nūrī movement (Nurcu) encompasses loosely organized circles of followers of the spiritual leader Bediüzzaman Said Nursî. This Kurdish Sunnī scholar was born sometime in the 1870s in the eastern Anatolian village of Nurs, in the Ottoman province of Bitlis. At a young age, he became preoccupied with the central dilemma that vexed Ottoman rulers during the last decades of the caliphate, namely, how to incorporate elements of Western modernity without violating their faith or compromising their Islamic identity. His answer was to educate Muslims in ways that reconciled scientific thinking and religious tenets. In 1907, he presented his ideas to Sultan Abdülhamid II, only to be rejected and thrown into prison.

The bitterness of this encounter fueled Nursî's constitutionalist views, as a result of which he unwittingly supported the post-1908 Young Turks' modernizing regime, and joined the army on the eve of World War I. After a two-year stretch as a prisoner of war in a Siberian camp, he escaped and retuned to Allied-controlled Istanbul in 1918, to witness firsthand the humiliation of defeat. That trauma drove him to hastily join forces with Mustafa Kemal and his fellow mutinous officers.

In 1922, Nursî was invited to address the Grand National Assembly in Ankara, at a time when the caliph in Istanbul still considered its members nothing more than outlaws. Yet he was disenchanted by the religious irreverence of the soon-to-be master of Anatolia and his coterie, and considered the train ride back to his residence in Van a spiritual journey between the rebellious and politically engaged Old (*Eski*) Said, and the ascetic and withdrawn New (*Yeni*) Said.

In this new phase, Nursî deemphasized the necessity of an instant macro-transformation of his homeland in favor of building a group of pious individuals with a correct understanding of Islam and a healthy appreciation for science and material success, which he frequently referred to as an "intellectually able group." Only through spiritual renewal and reformed everyday practices could society achieve a new, more powerful Islamic consciousness, he argued, to gradually reflect these values in the sphere of politics.

From this point on, Nursî began disseminating his writings among a select group of students, though he made it clear that he was not establishing a new Ṣūfī order but rather a community of learning. Nursî's prolific writings (mostly in Arabic) include an exegesis of select verses of the Qurʾān, in addition to a voluminous compilation of religious commentaries, fragmented reflections, memoirs, and the long speeches he insisted on improvising and delivering in person during his numerous trials. These were all collected under the title of *Risale-i Nur Külliyatı* (The Complete Epistles of Light). Nursî's work was interrupted by detention and trial on several occasions, and he was falsely accused of inciting subversion. Inasmuch as the suffering associated with several prison stints and long periods of exile enhanced his mystical aura, they also reinforced the commitments of his followers.

Indeed, the ban on the private production of religious materials, enacted by Mustafa Kemal's aggressively secular republic, had a decisive influence on the character of the Nurcu movement. Being forced to produce and translate handwritten copies of his commentaries and circulate them door-to-door cemented his network of students. Moreover, the fact that Nursî was kept almost permanently under house arrest prompted his expanding base of followers to organize themselves in independent study groups (*dershane*) to examine his texts. As the republic moved to a multiparty system in the 1940s, the Nurcu movement was the best-organized section of Turkish civil society.

This political change marked the final transition of Said Nursî, to what he called the Third Said—the community activist who lent support to political leaders who would protect and promote Islam without formally belonging to one particular party or identifying with any faction. Not only did this become the model for future Islamist activists, it also made them flexible enough to weather the storms of military responses, which swept away political parties and cadres between 1960 and 1997. The Nurcu network was crucial to garnering enough votes to bring the Democratic Party to power in 1950, which was violently overthrown by the May 1960 coup, two months after Nursî passed away.

In its aftermath, the Nurcu study groups became more institutionalized, establishing branches all over the country (five thousand by the 1990s) and even spread abroad. Yet these networks of followers remained flexible enough to go underground during periods of secular backlash. Moreover, the diverse temperaments, backgrounds, and interpretations of Nurcu adherents (an estimated 6 million today) divided them into several groups rather than a single hierarchical organization, which made it difficult to repress them.

The most visible and politically influential group was the one that clustered around Fethullah Gülen (b. 1941), a teacher (*hocaefendi*) born in the town of Erzurum in eastern Anatolia, a historically insecure frontier zone that cultivated the young preacher's appreciation of a strong military. The Gülen group is really an evolution, rather than an extension, of the Nurcu movement. Its founder never met Said Nursî, but he combined Nursî's ideas with Western philosophy to produce a religious ideology that supported a powerful state, a free market economy, integration into the advanced (i.e., Western) world, and, most importantly, the need to stress Turkish nationalism and secularism. In other words, this neo-Nurcu group interpreted Islam in a way that appealed to both the Kemalist establishment and the intellectuals and business elites. Its "Turkish-Islamic synthesis" is credited with finally establishing a modus vivendi between the country's religious population and nationalist military, at the same time that its carefully crafted discourse on moderation and tolerance reassured secular elites.

Besides its potent and highly pragmatic ideology, the Gülen movement secured hegemony within the larger Nurcu trend, and among Turkish Islamists in general, through its formidable organizational resources, including a media empire with a prominent daily newspaper (*Zaman*), several periodicals, television and radio stations, a first-rate public relations company, and an impressive array of educational institutions (three hundred high schools, seven universities, and dozens of dormitories and summer camps), all funded by a giant business network backed by powerful homegrown financial intuitions. This was the intellectual and financial infrastructure that produced the "golden generation"—Gülen's version of Nursî's "intellectually able group." For some, the electoral triumphs of the Adalet ve Kalkınma Partisi (AKP) between 2002 and 2013, was partly a result of the influence of the Nurcu movement.

BIBLIOGRAPHY

Abu-Rabi', Ibrahim M., ed. *Islam at the Crossroads: On the Life and Thought of Bediuzzaman Said Nursi.* Albany: State University of New York Press, 2003.

Mardin, Şerif. *Religion and Social Change in Modern Turkey: The Case of Bediüzzaman Said Nursi.* Albany: State University of New York Press, 1989.

Nursî, Said. *Risale-i Nur Külliyatı*, vols. 1–2. Istanbul: Nesil, 1996.

Yavuz, M. Hakan. *Islamic Political Identity in Turkey.* New York: Oxford University Press, 2003.

HAZEM KANDIL

O

OFFICES AND TITLES: RELIGIOUS, SOCIAL, AND POLITICAL. This entry provides a brief description of religious, political, and social offices and titles encountered throughout Islamic history. It relies heavily on information contained in the second edition of *The Encyclopaedia of Islam*. Although the titles and responsibility of positions and functions differed from period to period and from dynasty to dynasty, depending on the historical circumstances of the time, officials generally had a combined religious-political stake in the successful functioning of the state. As has often been noted, the political and the religious are closely, if not symbiotically, integrated in Islam. Emblematic of this integration is the position of head of state, the caliph, sultan, shah, or king, who is also charged with upholding the Islamic faith.

The mutual and interdependent importance of the occupations of the "sword" and those of the "pen"—recognized as early as the ninth century—was stated clearly in the twelfth-century *Baḥr al-fawāʾid*, a work in the "mirror for princes" genre, according to whose anonymous author "the stability of the faith and of Islam depends on the religious scholars, who determine what is lawful and unlawful. The stability of religion and of the community depends on rulers, who distinguish between justice and injustice" (Marlow, 1997, p. 169). Nevertheless, the true hierarchy in Islam is between God and man, between the otherworldly and the this-worldly. Despite the recognition and acceptance of a hierarchical societal structure, as noted explicitly in the Qurʾān (e.g., 4:59 "[obey] those charged with authority among you"), Islam emphasizes the innate equality of believers in the Muslim community, *ummah*, and the merely temporal responsibility of those in position to sustain the Islamic ideal.

Aga, Agha. An eastern Turkish honorific (*ağa*, "elder brother") originating in Central Asia and used as a form of respectful address in Central Asia and Iran, from where it spread to Turkey. In Ottoman Turkish, it came to signify "chief, master; landowner." In early Ottoman times, it became a formalized title, generally signifying a low-ranking, uneducated army officer, in contrast to *efendi*, used for a literate person. In Ottoman times, the title was extended to two respected offices in the military and the palace: the commander in chief of the elite army of the Janissaries (*yeniceri ağası*) and the head of the eunuchs (*dar* *üs-saade ağası*, "aga of the abode of felicity") overseeing the imperial harem, below only the grand vizier and the grand mufti (*şeyhülislâm*) in stature. In the late Ottoman period, *ağa* was used for illiterate army officers occupying ranks up to a lieutenant colonel. The title was abolished upon the founding of the Turkish Republic and lives on in Turkey as a respectful term of address.

As a religious title, it is borne by the head of the Nizārī Ismāʿīlīs, the Aga Khan (Turkish *ağa* + Persian *khān*), having been bestowed by Shah Fatḥ ʿAlī in 1818 upon the forty-sixth Nizārī imam, Ḥasan ʿAlī Shāh (d. 1881). The present-day spiritual Ismāʿīlī leader is Karīm al-Ḥusaynī, Aga Khan IV (b. 1936).

ʿĀmil. In early Islam, an "agent" (active participle of the Arabic root *ʿ-m-l*, "to act"), a finance official who collected taxes. Although the office was usually associated with finance in one form or another, generally in tax or revenue collection, *ʿāmil* could refer to the governor of a province (more commonly, *amīr*; cf. the eleventh-century jurist al-Māwardī who, in his treatise on constitutional law, employs *ʿāmil* both as tax collector and as governor "invested with the general powers of administration"). This may have stemmed from the early caliphs' agent being delegated limited powers of representation while collecting revenue in districts far from the capital. In the early days of Islam, before the office of guardian of public morals (*muḥtasib*) was institutionalized, a market inspector was called *ʿāmil al-sūq*. The title of *ʿāmil* is still used in some Muslim countries.

Amīr. A governor, military commander, prince, or other individual invested with command (*amr*). In early Islamic history, the titles *amīr* (pl. *ʿumarāʾ*) and *ʿāmil* were often used synonymously. In the early centuries the *amīr* was appointed by the caliph, to whom he owed allegiance; his duties ranged from managing the armed forces in his province, to appointing subgovernors, to leading the prayer, to appointing judges, to collecting taxes—in short, the *amīr* stood in for the caliph in administrative and financial matters. Under the ʿAbbāsids, the functions of the *ʿumarāʾ* were reduced as the caliph took over the appointment of judges and created supplementary positions such as the finance official (*ʿāmil*). Some *ʿumarāʾ* established hereditary emirates, such as the Aghlabids in Ifrīqiya (r. 800–909), who were aided in their independence from the caliphate by the distance of North Africa from Baghdad and the caliphal succession disputes of the ʿAbbāsids. In modern-day Salafī political thought of, for example, Abū al-Aʿlā Mawdūdī (d. 1979) and others, the title of *amīr* is used for the head of state and Islamist community.

Amīr al-jund. Lit., "commander of the army." Originally of Persian origin, the term *jund* or its plural *junūd* is found in the Qurʾān twenty-nine times with the meaning of armed troop or military force. Under the Umayyads (r. 661–750), the term (with the plural form *ajnād*) took on the meaning of a settlement or district, in which soldiers were quartered, corresponding in Syria to the older Byzantine divisions.

Amīr al-Muʾminīn. Lit., "commander of the believers," the title that ʿUmar, the second Rightly Guided Caliph (r. 634–644), adopted and which became the standard caliphal title, understood to represent a united community of believers under one political aegis but still carried by leaders of minor dynasties after the ʿAbbāsid empire broke up.

Connected to the caliphal prerogative of calling for *jihād* against the unbelievers, the title *amīr al-muʾminīn* was taken by heads of movements to justify their legitimacy and wage *jihād*. Such commanders as Usuman Dan Fodio in Hausaland (northern Nigeria), who led an uprising against the Hausa sultanates in 1804 leading to the caliphate of Sokoto, and, more recently, Mullah Muhammad Omar, the leader of the Taliban in

Afghanistan, proclaimed themselves *amīr al-mu'minīn*. The title was less used among the Ottoman sultans, and is only given to ʿAlī ibn Abī Ṭālib among Twelver Shiites, although the Ismāʿīlīs and Zaydīs apply it less exclusively.

Ayatollah. Lit., "the (miraculous) sign of God (Ar. *āyat Allāh*)"; in Twelver Shīʿī Islam, a title from the twentieth century for the holder of the highest rank in the religious hierarchy.

Caliph. Ar. *khalīfah* ("successor"), a title of the leader of the Muslim politico-religious community after the Prophet's death in 632, adopted first by the four Rightly Guided Caliphs—Abū Bakr (r. 632–634), ʿUmar (r. 634–644), ʿUthmān (r. 644–656), and ʿAlī (r. 656–661)—and used most notably during the Umayyad and ʿAbbāsid caliphates.

Dervish. Pers. *darvīsh*; a mendicant, member of a Ṣūfī order.

Faqīh. Lit., "one possessing understanding (*fiqh*)"; in law, a jurist, a specialist in Islamic law.

Ḥājib. The office of palace chamberlain or guard (from the root *ḥ-j-b*, "to prevent [from entering]; to conceal"), who controlled access to the ruler. The exact responsibilities of the *ḥājib* fluctuated throughout the centuries and dynasties, at times equaling those of the vizier. The office first appears with the Umayyads, at whose court the *ḥājib* decided who among the caliph's visitors would be granted an audience. Under the ʿAbbāsids, the position became a high-ranking one, falling only under the vizier in importance. In addition to his supervising the domestic staff and organizing the caliph's audience, the *ḥājib* assisted the ruler with administrative and governing tasks, and was sometimes called upon to oversee or personally take care of the removal of persons whom the caliph deemed disloyal.

In Muslim Spain the *ḥājib* occupied a position of power; he was chosen from among the vizieral rank and controlled the court, the chancellery, and the financial department. The Party Kings (*reyes de taifas*), who ruled separate principalities during the last years of the weakened Umayyads and following their fall in 1031, either stemmed from the *ḥājib* class (e.g., the first ʿAmirid, Ibn Abī ʿĀmir) or titled themselves *ḥājib* in the absence of a caliph.

Ḥājib was a military title under the dynasties in the east, such as the Sāmānids (r. 395–1005), the Būyids (r. 945–1057), and the Ghaznavids (r. 977–1186), with the official taking on the duties of a general and apparently not being involved at all with the running of the palace. After this his responsibilities varied between military command, court officialdom, and judicial adjudication, a primary role for the *ḥājib* in the Mamlūk sultanate (r. 1250–1517).

Ḥujjat al-Islām. Lit., "proof of Islam"; in Twelver Shīʿī Islam, the title given to the second in importance in the religious hierarchy, under the ayatollah. Many religious scholars carry this honorific.

Imam. Both a religious and a political title; the imam in the early Islamic period was the leader of the Muslim community. The sources use *khalīfah* and *imām* interchangeably. Among Sunnīs the title was devalued, as the ʿAbbāsid caliphs lost control, and became more connected with the mosque and its prayer leader. In Shīʿī Islam, additionally, the imam is the descendant of the Prophet and the true leader of the Muslim community. According to the Twelvers, the largest Shīʿī branch today, the twelfth imam went into occultation in 874; he will return as the Mahdī to usher in the end of time.

Kātib. Lit., "writer" (active participle of the Arabic root *k-t-b*, "to write"); in the administration of the Umayyad caliphate and successive regimes, a "secretary" (Ar.; Pers. *dabīr*, *munshī*), whose function was to draft letters or other official documents. In addition to having beautiful orthography and rhetorical excellence, the powerful secretary had a close relationship with the ruler, whom he served. An abundance of books of secretarial etiquette and advice were written, one of the later and most famous ones being the encyclopedic work by the secretary al-Qalqashandī (d. 1418), *Ṣubḥ al-aʿshā*, which provides formulas and guides for writing documents, as well as samples of letters, along with a history of the chancery and chancery practice.

Khān. A Turkish title for a ruler or (tribal) chief; the sway of the Mongol dynasties under Genghis Khan (r. 1206–1227) spread the word to Persia and India. Its etymology is still uncertain, as similar terms are found in ancient Sumerian and Akkadian inscriptions and in Chinese (*kān*, *han*) for "ruler." Over the course of time, the term became devalued, surviving today in names—especially in Pakistan and India—as an honorific in the sense of "esquire" and as a common surname. The honorific Aga Khan (Turkish *ağa* + *khān*) was bestowed upon the forty-sixth imam of the Ismāʿīlī branch of Shīʿī Islam.

Khojah. A multipurpose title, from Pers. *khwāja*, applied in various periods and dynasties as an honorific to scholars, ministers, teachers, and merchants. In India it is used for Nizārī Ismāʿīlīs, and in Turkish (*hoja*) it is the common title of respect for a teacher.

Al-Mahdī. Lit., "the rightly guided one"; in a messianic sense, the last imam who will arrive at the end of time. The Mahdī eschatological doctrine is most visible in Twelver Shīʿī Islam, where it is attached to the twelfth imam who is believed to be in occultation and, known as al-Qāʾim (or Qāʾim Āl Muḥammad, "the one from the Prophet's family who will rise"), will rise against injustice and restore justice until the Day of Judgment.

In a noneschatological sense, al-Mahdī is the regnal title of two Sunnī caliphs: Abū ʿAbd Allāh Muḥammad, the third ʿAbbāsid caliph (r. 775–785), and Muḥammad b. Hishām, the eleventh Umayyad caliph of Spain (r. 976–1009/10).

Malik. Arabic for "king," of which there were none in the premodern Islamic period; the Qurʾān (40:15–16) claims kingship (*mulk*) for God (*dhū al-ʿarsh*, "Lord of the throne") alone. In the early period, the term was used by opponents of rulers as the opposite of *khalīfah* and *imām*, to show disdain for their corrupt and unrighteous ways. As Muslims came into contact with non-Arab custom, however, the term was adopted as a regnal epithet, mostly by non-Arab dynasties—such as the Būyids, Ghaznavids, and Seljuks—and usually with other honorific descriptors, such as *al-malik al-raḥīm* (the Būyid Khusraw-Fīrūz, r. 1048–1055) or *al-malik al-ṣāliḥ* (the Ayyūbid Najm al-Dīn, r. 1240–1248). The title *malik* lost out in supremacy to *sulṭān*, however, and by the rise of the Ottomans in the late thirteenth century had so diminished that it was revived only in the twentieth century.

Mamlūk. Lit. "something owned"; a military slave. Army regiments of captured or bought slaves were a basis of Islamic military power from the time of al-Maʾmūn, the seventh ʿAbbāsid caliph (r. 813–833), until the end of the nineteenth century. Most *mamlūk*s came from Central Asia and Eastern Europe; they converted to Islam and were trained in the art of the cavalry and made free men. While supplying a generally ferociously loyal contingent to the ruler who ensured their welfare, they could also turn against successive rulers. The Mamlūk sultanate, which reigned from the middle of the thirteenth century until 1516/1517 and consisted of *mamlūk*s who seized power from the Ayyūbids, is the most famous of the *mamlūk* regimes.

Marjaʿ-i Taqlīd. Lit., "source of imitation"; in Twelver Shiism, the highest jurisprudential authority, chosen as a model of emulation on account of his piety and wisdom. The singular religious office came into being in the middle of the nineteenth century, gradually becoming more and more enmeshed in politics.

Mawlā. One who is bound by patronage (*walā'*) to another, either as patron or as client, as master or as slave. The term (pl. *mawālī*) was often used in the early Islamic period for a non-Arab who had converted to Islam and become a client of the person who had converted him. This relationship was meant to ease the non-Arab into Arab society by providing him (or her) with a (tribal) lineage. With the overthrow of the Umayyad dynasty in 750 by the ʿAbbāsids and the founding of their capital and seat of power to the north in Baghdad, the emphasis on a society divided into Arab and non-Arab segments decreased and the *mawlā* distinction gradually fell away. In later times the term was used to address someone distinguished by great (religious) learning. In Persian the pronunciation of the Arabic *mawlā* became *mollā*, and in this form—commonly written "mullah" in English—it signifies a religious functionary in Turkish-, Iranian-, and Hindi-speaking communities.

In Sufism, the term *mawlā* designates a Ṣūfī master; the most famous is the poet-mystic Jalāl al-Dīn Rūmī (d. 1273), known as Mawlānā ("our master"), who founded the Mawlawī (Mevlevî) Ṣūfī order, which is known worldwide for its whirling dervishes.

Molla. *See* Mawlā.

Mullabashi. Lit. "head mullah" (Pers. *mollā* + Tur. *-bashi*, a suffix denoting "head, chief"), a title first held by Muḥammad Bāqir Khātūn-ābādī (d. 1715), who was appointed to this position upon the accession of his tutee, the Ṣafavid shah Sulṭān Ḥusayn (r. 1694–1722). The title denoted the head of all the *ʿulamā'*, and the office remained a respectable one deep into the nineteenth century, when it began its slide into oblivion.

Mufti. A specialist in Islamic law who issues an authoritative, but not binding, opinion (*fatwa*) on a legal matter. In classical legal doctrine, the mufti must be Muslim, have reached puberty, and be of good character, literate, and well versed in the law; he (rarely, she) could be consulted both by the layman on a question of individual importance and by the judge for advice on a difficult case. The mufti does not investigate the truth of a question posed to him; originally acting only in a private capacity, the mufti increasingly took on a semiofficial or official position as part of the state apparatus.

Muḥtasib. A functionary of the state whose responsibility was to keep the public place free of un-Islamic practices, whether offenses committed in the commercial sphere, for instance, the merchant who was hoarding, inflating prices, or cheating the customer; in the moral sphere, such as the mingling of sexes or the consumption of wine in the public space; or in the religious sphere, namely, a disregard for fasting during Ramaḍān or not closing one's shop for Friday prayer. Behind the *muḥtasib*'s duties was the Qur'ānic injunction to "command good and forbid wrong" (e.g., 9:71).

Mujaddid. Lit., "renewer"; a title given to the one who will appear at the turn of each century to renew Islam and revitalize religious practice, in accordance with a Prophetic saying to that effect. The first *mujaddid* to be acclaimed was at the end of the first Islamic century, the Umayyad caliph ʿUmar II (r. 717–720), praised generally as a pious and righteous ruler. At the turn of the first millennium, the Indian mystic Aḥmad Sirhindī developed the theory of the "renewer of the second millennium" (*mujaddid-i alf-i thānī*), whom he claimed to be himself, who was even more important in following the Prophet than centennial renewers. An important transmutation of the name Muḥammad into Aḥmad played a key role in the theory, cementing thereby Sirhindī's own ascendance to the rank.

Mujāhid. Lit., "striver"; a fighter for the faith. The *mujāhid* exerts him- or herself in *jihād*, the connotation of which today among Muslims and non-Muslims alike frequently lacks the nuance and multivalent quality of the Arabic, which means "struggle, exertion." There is a lesser and a greater *jihād*; the latter is derivative of the former and invokes the individual quest to perfection, to the banishment of one's lower passions. It can be extended to include a society ridding itself of its baser aspects, such as corruption or moral decline. The lesser *jihād* is the exertion undertaken in fighting an enemy of Islam and is the more common connotation.

Pīr. Lit., "old man"; a Persian title for the founder or head of a mystical order, equivalent to Ar. *shaykh*.

Qāḍī. A judge in a *Sharīʿah* court, appointed (and dismissed) by the ruler or his delegate. In addition to presiding over, adjudicating, and pronouncing decisions in a dispute brought before him, a *qāḍī* supervised trusts; led special prayers, such as the prayer for rain or the funeral prayer; and handled transactions, such as property deeds and tax payments, among other administrative and religious duties. The *qāḍī* was a Muslim male, learned in the law, pious, with an unblemished reputation; he was usually a local man, but under the ʿAbbāsids the judgeship was increasingly given to legal authorities of high standing who relied on deputies in the towns that fell under their jurisdiction.

Raʾīs. A leader of a group (Ar. *raʾs*, "head"), whether political, religious, social, tribal, or other; a mayor; in Ottoman Turkish (*reʾīs*), a sea captain. In the Ottoman Empire, the "leader of the men of the pen" or the chief scribe (*reʾisülkuttab* or *reʾis efendi*) was a position that began as chief of the chancery and developed into secretary of state.

Rasūl. The Arabic term for a messenger (of God), apostle; a prophet, synonymous with *nabī*. These two Qurʾānic terms are often used interchangeably, but it is often said that a *rasūl* is differentiated by having been sent by God with a written scripture, denoting thus in particular Moses, Jesus, and Muḥammad. In a nonreligious sense, *rasūl* can be used for diplomatic envoy, more often called *safīr*.

Ṣadr. Lit., "chest, breast"; a title used mostly in the Persian world for a high-ranking religious leader and in the Ottoman Empire for a high-ranking member of the *ʿulamāʾ* and, from the mid-sixteenth century on, as *ṣadr-i aʿẓam*, for the title of the grand vizier. In Mughal India, *ṣadr* was the title of an officer on the provincial level who was in charge of land grants.

Sayyid. Originally one of the terms for "master" and a tribal chief (now more commonly *shaykh*), in the early Islamic period *sayyid* acquired a specific sense denoting a descendant of the Prophet Muḥammad (especially the line through his grandson Ḥusayn, while *sharīf* was used for descendants through the line of Ḥasan). In the Sufism of mostly western Islamic lands, *sayyid* (often *sayyidī* or *sīdī*) has taken on a more general use for a holy person, saint; in contemporary Arabic, *sayyid* is used in the sense of "Mr."

Sharīf. Lit., "noble, eminent"; a person who can claim an illustrious ancestry (pl. *ashrāf*). In the early Islamic period, *sharīf* came to be used especially for descendants of the Prophet Muḥammad, in particular those through the line of his grandson Ḥasan (while *sayyid* was used in the same sense for descendants through the line of his grandson Ḥusayn). The term *sharīf*, denoting a person of noble and pure lineage, has endured as a social distinction throughout history; in South Asia its plural is used to distinguish well-bred Muslims of foreign ancestry (as opposed to *aṭrāf*, lower-class Muslims of local ancestry).

Shadow of God. Ar. *ẓill Allāh*; an epithet for a ruler, especially in the eastern Islamic lands, taken from a Prophetic saying, "The sultan is the shadow of God on earth"; as an expression, it goes back to Sasanid and Byzantine times. The first to call himself thus was the ʿAbbāsid caliph al-Mutawakkil (r. 847–861).

Shah. Persian *shāh* "king"; the title of the Persian monarch, going back to the Achaemenid king Darius I (r. 521–486 BCE). The last shah of Iran, Muhammad Reza Pahlavi (d. 1980), was deposed during the Iranian Revolution of 1979.

Shaykh al-Islām. An honorific given to *ʿulamāʾ* and mystics attesting to their deep knowledge of the principles of the religion. From its earliest mention, in the tenth century, it seems to have been borne by educators. It was the title of several scholars, including Ibn Taymīyah, the redoubtable Ḥanbalī jurist (d. 1328), who had the title bestowed on him by his followers, although he was not called this by his opponents. In its Ottoman usage, *shaykh al-islām* (T. *şeyhülislâm*) evolved into the state office of mufti of Istanbul and then grand mufti, appointed by the sultan. At its peak of influence in the sixteenth century, with the likes of Ebüssuʿûd Mehmet Efendi (d. 1574) holding the office, the *şeyhülislâm* taught at the Istanbul college (Ar. *madrasah*, T. *medrese*), appointed all the muftis in the larger cities, and controlled public policy with the issuance of state *fatwas*, such as Ebüssuʾûd's authorizing the capture of Cyprus from the Venetians in 1570 despite a peace treaty ratified by Selim II. The 131st and last officeholder was dismissed on 3 March 1924, and the office of *şeyhülislâm* was abolished, replaced by the Directorate of Religious Affairs (Diyanet İşleri Reisliği).

Supreme Leader. The position of highest religious power in Iran, first held by Ayatollah Khomeini after the 1979 Islamic Revolution and currently (2013) held by Ayatollah Khameneʾi. The supreme leader (Pers. *valī faqīh*) shares the executive with the president of Iran but holds considerably more power. He appoints six of the twelve members of the Guardian Council, which supervises the parliament and government elections (the other six are appointed by the head of the judiciary, one of the supreme leader's appointees), and all members of the Expediency Council, which decides disputes between the Guardian Council and the parliament, as well as the head of state radio and television and various heads of government, such as the above-mentioned head of the judiciary. He is commander in chief of the armed forces and has the sole authority to declare war. The supreme leader is chosen for life by an eighty-six member Assembly of Experts, which is an elected body (with the understanding that the Guardian Council chooses who may run for election).

Sultan. Arabic *sulṭān* "ruler"; lit., "one who holds power." The term, found in the Qurʾān with the meaning of an authority supported by a miracle, such as the authority of prophets, came to be used, in political terminology, as a title for both a provincial and an imperial ruler. It was also often prefixed to the proper name in families that traced their lineage to the Prophet, such as Sulṭān ʿAlī Mashhadī (d. 1513/1514), the celebrated calligrapher.

ʿUlamāʾ. Lit., "those who have (religious) knowledge (*ʿilm*)"; Arabic sing. *ʿālim*; in English, commonly ulama or ulema. This group of religious authorities—teachers, preachers, transmitters of Prophetic traditions, jurists—saw themselves as the heirs of the Prophet in terms of upholding Islamic belief and guarding the Muslim community against heresy and unbelief. Although in the early Islamic period it was used as a standard category for scholars or practitioners principally of the religious sciences, such as theology and law, the term has in contemporary times increasingly narrowed to describe only the professional religious establishment, especially as used in a Shīʿī context.

Valī Faqīh. *See* Supreme Leader.

Wālī. A person in authority, governor; in the Ottoman Empire, also called *pasha*, the governor of a province (*vilâyet*), such as Egypt.

Wazīr. In the Qur'ān (25:35: "We gave Moses the Book and made his brother Aaron a *wazīr* with him"), the term signified "helper," but under the ʿAbbāsids it evolved into an official position within the government, in English, "vizier" (from the Turkish pronunciation *vezir*). Appointed (and dismissed) by the ruler, the vizier reported to him and no other. He held extensive power as head of the administrative branch of government, including supervision of the collection of taxes and the distribution of revenue. His office was represented by an inkpot, which was given to him upon appointment, frequently gold-plated, and carried before him in ceremonial processions. In Sunnī constitutional theory, the vizier was the ruler's alter ego; the criteria for the positions were the same aside from the required Qurayshī lineage.

In Muslim Spain under the Umayyads, the workload was spread among several functionaries, each called a *wazīr*, who reported to the chief minister known as the *ḥājib*. The Ottoman Empire also saw multiple vizierate offices, headed by the *ṣadr-i aʿẓam*, or grand vizier.

Zaʿīm. Arabic for "(tribal) chief, leader." In contemporary political usage the term is particularly relevant in Lebanon, where the *zaʿīm*, usually a rural landowner or businessman and from a distinguished local family, trades support for the advancement of his political career with economic benefits for his client base, made up of those beholden to him for their livelihoods. The institution of *zaʿāmah* thus has strong feudal connections and is a system of political patronage that has brought with it graft and corruption and keeps the sectarian political system of Lebanon thriving.

BIBLIOGRAPHY

Bearman, P. J., Th. Bianquis, C. E. Bosworth et al., eds. *The Encyclopaedia of Islam*. 2d ed. 12 vols. Leiden: Brill, 1960–2004.

Lewis, Bernard. *The Political Language of Islam*. Chicago: University of Chicago Press, 1988.

Marlow, Louise. *Hierarchy and Egalitarianism in Islamic Thought*. New York: Cambridge University Press, 1997.

PERI BEARMAN

OMAR, MULLAH MOHAMMAD.

See Mullah Omar.

OPPOSITION.

Opposition is considered the most fundamental component of democracy as "there can be no real democracy without opposition" (Helms, 2008, p. 14). Democratic theory identifies opposition and inclusion/participation as two defining features of polyarchies (Dahl, 1971), although the recognition of the system of an institutionalized opposition vying to replace the ruling party is of relatively recent origin, developed mostly in the Western world. A leading theorist defines an opposition simply as those who are opposed to the conduct of a government and who may be in disagreement with those in power. Importantly, they present themselves to the populace as a viable alternative to the party in power, perhaps to gain legitimacy. An opposition is "a political grouping, party, or loose association of individuals who wish to change the government and its policies," another theoretician maintains (Robertson, 1993, pp. 357–358). Still others (Ionescu and Madariaga, 1972, p. 16) believe an opposition to be "the crowning institution of a fully institutionalized political society and the hallmark of those political societies that are variously called democratic, liberal, parliamentary, constitutional, pluralistic-constitutional, or even open or free." Thus defined, opposition refers to: (1) a political party that is (2) a minority and that (3) aims to garner majority support in the not too distant future to take over power from a ruling party. Two additional theoretical considerations were advanced in the mid-1960s at the height of the Cold War that fueled the debate on democratization and opposition: First, the opposition in a democracy opposes the government and not the political system within which it operates, which means that the opposition must uphold the sovereignty and the integrity of the country, refrain from activities subversive of the state, and be fair in the criticism of government policies. This differentiates it from other "irresponsible" antisystem parties that question the very legitimacy of the political system. Second, the opposition acts quietly and constructively, since it opposes rather than obstructs.

Opposition in the West. However, in Western democracies, the term opposition largely refers to parliamentary opposition, considering unconventional and unconstitutional opposition as deviations from the legitimate parliamentary type of opposition. The opposition has a formal status and its leader enjoys certain privileges. This, however, is not the case in the U.S.-type presidential system or the French semipresidential system, in which the president and his appointee, the prime minister, actively participate in the administration of the state. Such systems are characterized by the direct election of the head of the executive and the separation of powers between the executive and the legislative organs of the state. It is possible for a political party to enjoy widespread popularity and have its candidate elected as the president and also to have the support of the majority members in the legislature. However, it is quite often the case that the presidency is occupied by one party, while the legislative majority is enjoyed by another party. This is a case of two opposing organs of state and is referred to as "institutional opposition" and not "parliamentary opposition."

The major function of the opposition is to contest the government in power. The opposition works to persuade the electorate to vote out those in power and vote in the challenging party, presumably to pursue policies that it believes are in the best interest of the nation. Thus, the opposition provides alternative policies and presents itself as a substitute government. To this end, the opposition in a parliamentary system maintains a "shadow cabinet" with a list of shadow ministers and another of legislative programs that it promises to carry out once in power. In the Westminster model, the opposition is given recognition as "Her Majesty's Loyal Opposition." In many parliamentary systems, the leader of the opposition is accorded status almost equal to that of the prime minister. In carrying out the function of opposing, members of the opposition expose those aspects of the policies of the government that they believe are detrimental to the interest of the nation. It is quite common for the opposition to highlight the abuses of executive power, bureaucratic red tape and corruption, breaches of human rights, and the like. This watchdog function protects the society from executive excesses and helps institutionalize democracy.

The opposition performs other functions that are worth noting. The opposition airs the grievances and concerns of various groups and parties not represented in government. These complaints would otherwise go unheard, even though they might not be taken into account despite the opposition's efforts. At least it reassures citizens that their interests are ably expressed and hopefully attended to by members of the ruling party. It occasionally happens that the opposition joins with the party in power to reform the system. Additionally, the opposition serves as a channel of communication by informing the public on specific political issues. It can politicize a question by turning an apparent nonissue into a political matter, notably through public debate, and by so doing mobilize public opinion on a specific question.

The opposition, it must be pointed out, is assumed to operate in a free and democratic atmosphere, and, ideally, is not hampered in its efforts by restrictions on freedom of speech, movement, and assembly. It is also assumed that the opposition will have unhindered access to the state media and will receive similar treatment to that afforded government representatives. It will have the right to own media in order to articulate its views without any restrictions and have access to materials from official sources to enable it to make informed position statements on various policies. This requires the existence of laws on freedom of information and the protection of informants. Given the importance of the opposition and the functions they perform, opposition leaders in some countries, notably in Canada since 1905 and Britain since 1937, receive remunerations from the treasury.

Opposition in Islam. Political opposition is not inconsistent with Islam's principles of promoting virtue and prohibiting vice, decision making through consultation, and the necessity of dialogue and discourse, among others. The Qurʾān (3:104, 9:71, 9:112, 31:17) obligates believers to protect one another and to "enjoin what is right and forbid what is wrong." Believers are required to do everything possible to help improve the socioeconomic and political conditions of society. In this struggle, there is no room for passivity, because "Allah has preferred in grades those who strive hard and fight with their wealth and their lives above those who remain passive" (Qurʾān 4:95). According to Abū Dāʾūd (Sijistānī, 1988, vol. 3, p. 1207), the Prophet Muḥammad said: "I swear by Allāh, you must enjoin what is good and prohibit what is evil, prevent wrongdoer [*ẓālim*], bend him into conformity with what is right, and restrict him to what is right . . . or Allāh will mingle your hearts together and curse you as he cursed them."

The Qurʾān further designates believers as those who conduct their affairs through *shūrā* (mutual consultation) on an equal footing. *Shūrā* requires believers to render sound advice and provide constructive criticism to those in authority, as it is incumbent upon those in authority to implement the decisions arrived at through consultation. Similarly, the principle of *ikhtilāf* (disagreement) implies opposition. *Ikhtilāf* stems from the diversity inherent in human nature. God could have made mankind one people, but willed otherwise. The Qurʾān speaks of people who held divergent views and positions (11:118). Disagreement in Islam is considered a blessing; "It could help to expand perspectives and make us look at problems and issues in their wider and deeper ramifications, and with greater precision and thoroughness" (ʿAlwānī, 1994, p. 5). Therefore, differences of opinion should not lead to discord and conflict resulting in the disunity of the Muslim *ummah*, and these must not exceed their limits and must remain within the standard norms of ethics and proper behavior.

Thus, the Qurʾān leaves no room for oppression, tyranny, and injustice, and believers cannot justify wrongdoing in society by blaming the powerful or previous generations. Each person is obligated to stand for what is right to the best of his abilities (7:38–39, 33:67–68). An oft-quoted saying of the Prophet Muḥammad makes this obligation clearer: "If one of you sees something wrong, let him change it with his hand; if he cannot, then with his tongue; if he cannot, then with his heart, and this is the weakest faith" (Muslim, n.d., p. 50).

A small group of Muslim scholars, including the late Saudi mufti ʿAbd al-ʿAzīz bin Bāz, rejected the idea of opposition in an Islamic polity. They professed the idea that the sovereignty of God is absolute and that the unity of believers enjoined in the Qurʾān must be reflected in a polity characterized by a single leader uniting all believers under the banner of a single party enjoying the obedience of all. Opposition is permitted only if the imam (the leader) deviates from the *Sharīʿah*. Such scholars are opposed to democracy and to institutionalized opposition, although their views run contrary to that of the Qurʾān, which made obedience to rulers conditional.

The authority of governors and the responsibility of the governed are conveyed in the Qurʾān (4:59) as follows: "Obey Allāh and Obey the Messenger and those in authority among you." By meaningfully omitting the verb "obey" only in case of those having "authority," the verse makes obedience to them conditional and subservient to the Qurʾān and the *sunnah*. The rulers are obligated to have "right belief," perform the prescribed rites and rituals, seek the advice of the community, govern with justice (4:58), promote public interest, and look after the needy, and forbidden to benefit the rich at the expense of the community (59:7). There are several passages in the Qurʾān that categorically forbid obedience to someone who follows "the dictates of his own desires" (18:28) and "who oversteps the limits set by Allāh" (26:15). Indeed, the Qurʾān makes it obligatory for the believers to rebel against injustice; to defend themselves whenever tyranny afflicts them (13:39); and "to fight in the cause of Allāh and of the utterly helpless men, women and children" who are oppressed (4:75). Thus, Islam rejects passivism and affirms instead the *ummah*'s obligation to oppose those leaders who do not comply with divine law.

Consequently, most contemporary Muslim thinkers and Islamic movements subscribe, with minor variations, to the idea of political pluralism and of opposition to the ruler to safeguard the *Sharīʿah* and to promote the welfare of the *ummah* (the community of the faithful). The late Sayyid Abū al-Aʿlā Mawdūdī, the leader of the Jamāʿat-i Islāmī of Pakistan, held the same view. Yūsuf al-Qaraḍāwī, an Egyptian scholar associated with the Muslim Brotherhood, espouses this idea too. Taha Jabir al-Alwani, ʿAbd al-Qādir ʿAwdah, Khālid Muḥammad Khālid, and many others permit opposition and pluralism of parties in an Islamic state operating in conformity with the Qurʾān and the *sunnah*. Shaykh Rāshid al-Ghannūshī, the "intellectual leader" of Tunisia, explains that "the Islamists' preference of democracy is guided, by the teachings of their religion which encourages shura (consultation), justice and acquisition of good and wise things from any source" (Ghannushi, 1988, p. 9). It is conceivable that the Islamists, once in power, may not abide by these lofty ideals of Islam.

Opposition in Islam does not mean systematic rejection for the sake of opposition alone. Opposition in Islam involves correcting perceived errors of interpretation, suggesting alternatives, and working together for the achievement of the welfare within the general principles of the *Sharīʿah*. Opposition in Islam is an opposition with respect to details, not principles. Its aim is not, as in the Western system, to remove the government in power. Its primary concern is to help redress errors and indicate the right path. Consequently, opposition forces support the government if it is right, advise them if it is wrong, and try to remove those in power if their actions are contrary to the injunctions of the Qurʾān and the *sunnah*. Contemporary Muslim thinkers concur with the view that the function of the opposition is to check the arbitrary exercise of power by the government and to provide alternative policies for the welfare of the *ummah*.

Opposition in the Muslim World. Surveys conducted in Muslim-majority countries (MMCs) repeatedly affirm that there is strong Muslim support for popular sovereignty, Islamic values, and democracy as the key to a more just society and to progress. These surveys indicate that Muslims lament the lack of political freedom in their countries. They desire a system of government in which religious principles and democratic values coexist. Such a system, however, is not found in the Muslim world, which is characterized, among others, by the absence of democracy. In fact, governments in the Muslim world range from monarchies to illiberal democracies to states run by militaries, including those who don civilian garb. Legislative assemblies are either nonexistent or weak, acting as rubber stamps to approve executive decisions, and while political parties are more common, they operate under severe restrictions. Opposition parties are thus constantly under surveillance and their movements are very much restricted. They are often seen as being selfish, obstructive, and divisive. In most of the MMCs, citizens either have no right to vote or their right to vote is restricted by various factors. It is difficult for opposition forces to perform their function effectively under such systems, which means that their activities are prohibited by strictly political limitations rather than any theological considerations.

The Muslim world is characterized by relative authoritarianism with the concentration of power in the hands of political elites who are reluctant to accept newly organized groups into their political systems. Such intolerance results in severely restricted opposition activities, which are relegated to struggling for power rather than enhancing the level of civil societies to carry out democratizing functions. Most of the political parties, including opposition parties, are organized around personalities and not around policies or principles. These are the creations of the privileged few and thus do not command steadfast allegiance, which means that the majority of these parties can be easy to eliminate, and often are. There exists a culture of hostility leading to fragile political institution building and lack of institutionalization and integrity in the polity.

Bibliography

Ahmad, Mumtaz, ed. *State Politics and Islam*. Indianapolis, Ind.: American Trust, 1986.

ʿAlwānī, Ṭāhā Jābir al-. *The Ethics of Disagreement in Islam*. Translated by Abdul Wahid Hamid. Edited by A. S. al Shaikh-Ali. Herndon, Va.: International Institute of Islamic Thought, 1994.

Brack, Nathalie, and Sharon Weinblum. "'Political Opposition': Towards a Renewed Research Agenda." *Interdisciplinary Political Studies* 1, no. 1 (June 2011): 69–79.

Dahl, Robert A. *Polyarchy: Participation and Opposition*. New Haven, Conn.: Yale University Press, 1971.

David, Robertson. *The Penguin Dictionary of Politics*. 2d ed. London: Penguin, 1993.

Ghannushi, Rashid al-. "An-Nahda's Long March to Freedom." Interview by M. H. Faruqi. *Impact International*, December 1998, pp. 8–12.

Helms, Ludger. "Studying Parliamentary Opposition in Old and New Democracies: Issues and Perspectives." *Journal of Legislative Studies* 14, nos. 1–2 (2008): 6–19.

Ionescu, Ghita, and Isabel de Madariaga. *Opposition: Past and Present of a Political Institution*. Harmondsworth, U.K.: Penguin, 1972.

Muslim, Abū al-Ḥusayn ibn al-Ḥajjāj. *Al-Jāmiʿ al-ṣaḥīḥ*. Beirut: Dar al-Jeel, n.d.

Rahman, Fazlur. "The Principle of Shura and the Role of the Ummah in Islam." In *State Politics and Islam*, edited by Mumtaz Ahmad, pp. 87–96. Indianapolis, Ind.: American Trust, 1986.

Sartori, Giovanni. "Opposition and Control Problems and Prospects." *Government and Opposition* 1, no. 2 (1966): 149–154.

Shapiro, Ian. *Democracy's Place*. Ithaca, N.Y.: Cornell University Press, 1996.

Sijistānī, Abū Dāʾūd al-. *Sunan*. Edited by Muḥammad Muḥyī al-Dīn ʿAbd al-Ḥamīd. 4 vols. Beirut: Maktabah al-ʿAṣrīyah, n.d.

Abdul Rashid Moten

Organization of Islamic Cooperation. The Organization of Islamic Cooperation—formerly the Organization of the Islamic Conference—commonly known by its acronym, OIC—is the largest grouping of Muslim states. With fifty-seven states, including Palestine, spread over four continents as regular members, and another five states as observer members, it comprises almost one-third the total membership of the United Nations. The UN and several other international organizations also enjoy observer status at the OIC.

The OIC was created on 25 September 1969 at the first summit conference of the heads of state and governments of the Islamic countries in Rabat, Morocco. The conclave had been convened in response to an abortive arson attack on the al-Aqṣā Mosque, near the Dome of the Rock in Jerusalem, on 21 August 1969. It was decided at the meeting to found an organization that would aggregate the Muslim world's interests on all world forums, promote friendship and harmony among Muslim states, and improve relations between the Muslim world and the rest of the world. The charter was formalized in 1972 and the seat of the organization has temporarily been declared to be the Saudi port city of Jiddah, "pending the liberation of Jerusalem," which is intended to be the permanent seat of the OIC.

Structure. The OIC has a four-tiered structure. At the top, there are four principal organs, namely, the Conference of Heads of State, commonly called the Islamic Summit; the Islamic Conference of Foreign Ministers (ICFM); the General Secretariat; and, since 1981, the International Islamic Court of Justice (not yet operational for want of the necessary two-thirds ratification regarding its compulsory jurisdiction). In the second tier there are specialized organs, and the third tier consists of subsidiary organs. And in the last, there are several independent institutions like the Islamic Union of Parliaments and the Youth Dialogue Forum that are nominally affiliated with the organization.

Islamic Summit is the first principal organ and the highest authority of the Organization of Islamic Cooperation. The regular sessions are held triennially, although extraordinary sessions can be convened at any time at the request of no less than one-third of the membership. It sets the policy guidelines for the OIC.

The ICFM, as the second principal institution, holds its regular sessions annually and makes all operational decisions, such as appointment or election ofkey office holders, approval of OIC budget, induction of new member states, and the like.

The OIC General Secretariat is the executive and administrative organ of the organization. Headed by the secretary-general, it supervises the implementation of resolutions and recommendations of the summits and the ICFM conferences, assists subsidiary organs in carrying out their tasks, and coordinates their programs.

OIC Activities. The OIC mediates or offers its good offices in disputes between Muslim states, such as between Iran and Iraq (1980–1988), Pakistan and Bangladesh (1971–1973), and Mauritania and Senegal (1989), as well as during the civil wars in Afghanistan, Somalia, and Tajikistan, throughout the 1990s.

In conflicts where only one side is Muslim, as in Palestine, Cyprus, and Bosnia, the OIC becomes an advocate for "Muslim victims." The OIC gave recognition to the Palestinian Liberation Organization as the "government of Palestine" long before the United Nations accepted it as a legitimate interlocutor. It also recognized the government of (Turkish) Cyprus and the Muslim-dominated one of Bosnia and Herzegovina, giving them observer status in the OIC, thus providing the necessary diplomatic strength to sustain their own international existence.

Although the Muslim minorities in nonmember states have no status in OIC under the charter, since 1973 their issues have appeared on the agenda of every OIC conference in one form or the other, especially concerning Muslim ethnic minorities in the Philippines and Thailand and Muslim immigrants in Europe.

Politics is not the only arena for the OIC's activities. It is working in the fields of culture, information and communication, education, research in science and technology, tourism, and many other issues. Under the auspices of the General Secretariat, through early 2012 there have been eight conferences of OIC information ministers, seven of OIC tourism ministers, six of OIC agriculture ministers, and three each of the OIC culture ministers and OIC health ministers.

OIC Policies. The OIC's policies on nonalignment, colonialism, and similar issues since the late twentieth century clearly show that it has always stood for the principles of justice and freedom. It has struggled against racism and colonialism actively when the oppressed community is Muslim, and passively otherwise. It is also fairly obvious that during the Cold War, the Islamic Conference—as it was then called—retained a posture of strict nonalignment, if not outright antagonism, toward the two superpowers. In fact, it was this very radical rhetoric in the OIC resolutions that distinguished it from other nonaligned organizations, particularly the Non-Aligned Movement.

The OIC's concern with human rights also incorporates the humanitarian issues of refugees and war crimes, especially rape as an instrument of war and the proliferation of landmines. In fact, the OIC had been the only international organization to raise concerns on a number of human rights problems, such as those in Bulgaria, Kashmir, and the southern Philippines. The OIC has been instrumental in Muslim countries adopting a coordinated stand on human rights issues at the UN conferences. It has also tried to coordinate member-state activities in eliminating crimes like drug trafficking, illegal trafficking of women, and terrorism.

On the issue of nonproliferation and disarmament, it has been the OIC's consistent policy to oppose nuclear weapon proliferation all over the world, and it has repeatedly called for the establishment of nuclear-weapon-free zones in South Asia, Africa, and the Middle East. The OIC has also fought for the elimination of landmines and other destructive residual war materials.

The OIC's politico-diplomatic role in Muslim states is achieved through (1) harmonizing their foreign policies; (2) formulating an Islamic vision on international affairs of its own; and (3) becoming the spokesman of the Muslim world on issues of Islamic concern.

The changes in the OIC's name and Charter since 2011, according to its statement at the Thirty-Eighth ICFM conference held at Astana, Kazakhstan, symbolize the modernization, unanimity, and competitiveness of the Islamic world, as part of the goal of transforming the OIC into a rule-based modern outfit standing for good governance, human rights, and democracy. In the Arab Spring (2011–2012), the role of the OIC has clearly been pro-democracy, which is a welcome change in its orientation.

BIBLIOGRAPHY

Aḥsan, ʿAbdullah al-. *The Organization of the Islamic Conference: Introduction to an Islamic Political Institution*. Herndon, Va.: International Institute of Islamic Thought, 1988.

Baba, Noor Ahmad. *Organisation of Islamic Conference: Theory and Practice of Pan-Islamic Cooperation*. Karachi: Oxford University Press, 1994.

Khan, Saad S. *Reasserting International Islam: A Focus on the Organization of Islamic Conference and Other Islamic Bodies*. Karachi: Oxford University Press, 2001.

Moinuddin, Hasan. *The Charter of the Islamic Conferenceand Legal Framework of Economic Co-operation among Its Member States: A Study of the Charter, the General Agreement for Economic, Technical, and Commercial Co-operation, and the Agreement for Promotion, Protection, and Guarantee of Investments among Member States of the OIC*. Oxford: Clarendon, 1987.

OIC Secretariat. *Guide to the OIC*. Jiddah, Saudi Arabia: OIC, 1995.

Pasha, A. K. *India and OIC: Strategy and Diplomacy*. New Delhi: Centre for Peace Studies, 1995.

Pirzada, Sharifuddin. *Speeches and Statements of His Excellency Syed Sharifuddin Pirzada, Secretary-General, OIC*. Karachi: East & West, 1987.

Sarwar, Ghulam, ed. *OIC: Contemporary Issues of the Muslim World.* Rawalpindi, Pakistan: FRIENDS, 1997.
Selim, Mohammad El Sayed, ed. *The Organization of the Islamic Conference in a Changing World.* Cairo: Cairo University, 1994.

SAAD S. KHAN

ORIENTALISM. In historical hindsight the term "Orientalism" connotes both an academic field focused on the languages and cultures of a perceived region to the east of Europe, the "Orient," and also an ethnocentric ideology in the service of European colonialism. The sense of a unified cultural area as an Orient, even if divided into a Near, Middle, and Far East, waned in the latter part of the twentieth century. The demise of Orientalism as an academic field coincided with the rise of more sophisticated methodologies in a range of disciplines, but the final blow came with the publication of Edward Said's polemical work *Orientalism* in 1978. Said, a professor of comparative literature and a noted Palestinian intellectual, expanded the definition of the term to include almost any writing about a so-called Orient. Applying the ideological notion of "discourse" proposed by Michel Foucault, Said argued that Orientalist scholars were not objective observers but necessarily biased by their intellectual genealogy and underlying political agendas. For more than three decades the debate over the history of Orientalism has centered on Said's thesis and its relevance for understanding current political strategies of the United States and Europe about the Middle East and Islam.

In the opening paragraph of his *Orientalism*, Said famously suggests that the Orient was "almost a European invention." Linguistically, this Latin term denoting the east, or the place of the rising sun, was entirely a European view of the geography, imagined as well as real, to the east of Europe. The Egyptian pharaohs, the Islamic Caliphate, the Ottoman Empire, and the civilizations in India or China did not view themselves in a literal east. Said overlaid the binary of Europe vs. the world to its east onto political history, from the classical Greek battles with Persia through the development of Christianity and Islam to contemporary relations between the "West" and the modern state of Israel. As Said notes, Orientalism can accommodate Aeschylus, Karl Marx, and Henry Kissinger. Although widely criticized by many scholars whom Said had labeled Orientalists, his provocative approach to the subject inspired many students and young scholars in Middle East studies and the emerging field of cultural studies. Ironically, reception of his thesis by Arab intellectuals was limited, with the Syrian Ṣādiq al-ʿAẓm dismissing Said's notion of Orientalist discourse as "Orientalism in reverse." However, no contemporary survey of Orientalism can afford to ignore the influence of Said's work, whether seen as positive or negative.

Before Said, most intellectual histories of Orientalism or Oriental studies, such as those of A. J. Arberry, Gustave Dugat, and Johan Fück, focused on individual scholars who were fluent in the languages of the Middle East and Asia. One of the most important of these was the philologist William Jones, who arrived in India in 1783 and studied the local languages and the legal and religious texts in them. He inaugurated a British school of thought known as "Orientalism," which appreciated the local culture, in contrast to the inclination of the conservative Anglicists, who wanted to impose British values and rule India as a colony. In 1798 Napoleon invaded Egypt, in a maneuver to break British power in the Mediterranean, and brought with him more than one hundred civil engineers, artists, and scholars who recorded the antiquities and daily life. Although Napoleon's occupation of Egypt was brief, the first volume of the series *Description de l'Égypte* appeared in 1809. Said considered this the master text for modern Orientalism, although its distribution was limited because of its enormous size.

The academic term debuted as *orientalisme* in the encyclopedic *Bibliothèque orientale* of the French scholar Barthélemy d'Herbelot in 1697. As a compendium of translations from Arabic, Persian, and Turkish texts, this work established a field of study parallel to that of biblical and Judaic religious sources. The earliest academic societies devoted to Orientalism were nationally based, such as the French Société Asiatique (1822), the British Royal Asiatic Society of Great Britain and Ireland (1823), the American Oriental Society (1842), and the German Deutsche Morgenländische Gesellschaft (1845). The first International Congress of Orientalists convened in 1873 but was renamed exactly a century later when Orientalism came to be viewed as an outmoded paradigm. Tracing the intellectual history of Orientalism requires an examination of references in multiple European languages, as well as Russian. Said focused on sources in English and French; his failure to analyze the impact of Orientalists writing in German is a major flaw in his survey. Although Said examined a number of major works, primarily by nineteenth-century scholars, he neglected or ignored individuals, such as Ignaz Goldziher and Wilfred Blunt, who wrote against ethnocentric assumptions. Not having a thorough knowledge of the field he was writing against, he sometimes maligned other scholars, such as William Robertson Smith, on the basis of excerpts taken out of context. Said was not the first to challenge the utility of the concept of "Orient," and he was unaware of several important earlier critiques, especially that of Kurt Goldammer. Said also ignored the school of Orientalist art that flourished in the nineteenth century.

The most widely read part of Said's *Orientalism* is his introduction, where he lays out a threefold working definition. Instead of limiting the term to scholars who knew "Oriental" languages, he expands it from an academic field to "anyone who teaches, writes about, or researches the Orient," including literary figures such as Gustave Flaubert and scholars better known for contributions in other fields, such as Ernest Renan. Secondly, he homogenizes all this writing as a discourse "based upon an ontological and epistemological distinction" between a superior West and an inferior East. Even scholars he recognizes as sympathetic (e.g., Louis Massignon) are said to succumb to this underlying bias. Finally, Orientalism is viewed in politicized literary terms as "a Western style for dominating, restructuring, and having authority over the Orient." Recognizing the problems such a broad definition entailed, in his last chapter Said states that he is really making a distinction between "an almost unconscious (and certainly an untouchable) positivity," which he calls "latent Orientalism," and the various views and texts that make up "manifest Orientalism."

The reception of Said's rethinking of the idea of Orientalism was aided by his reference to two theoretical premises—an early application of Foucault's notion of discourse and an elaboration of Antonio Gramsci's concept of hegemony. Although Said cites Foucault, he insists that the imprint of individual authors is relevant. While Said had earlier written positively about Foucault in *Beginnings* (1975), he later was critical of Foucault's work. Several critics have questioned his use of both Foucault and Gramsci. Among these is Aijaz Ahmad, who is especially critical of Said's dismissal of Karl Marx as an Orientalist. The most vocal critic of Said was historian Bernard Lewis, who was vilified by Said in both *Orientalism* and public debate. Said responded to his critics in several essays and in both an afterword and foreword to later editions of his book, but he never revised the text. Even when criticism was constructive, Said insisted that his critics dismissed him because he was a Palestinian. As a result, the debate over the text became mired in a debate over what one thought of Edward Said.

The main criticism leveled against Said's *Orientalism* is that he homogenizes the field of Oriental studies and all the individuals he labels as Orientalists, in similar fashion to the discourse he proposes, pervaded all Western writing on the Orient. The power of his polemic is less about the details, which contain numerous historical flaws and literary lapses, than the inspiration to engage in what Said termed "worldly" criticism. The prejudice that he highlights deserved to be challenged, and as a result most Western scholars today are more aware of underlying cultural prejudices and utilize more effective methodologies. However, the prejudice that Said documents was equally distributed in other colonial contexts, such as the English wars in Ireland and the European colonial expansion into America and Africa. The lasting impact of Said's work is the importance of recognizing the ever-present politics in writing, whether academic or in the public media.

The term "Orientalism" has become so overgeneralized that it fails to have any significance today except in intellectual history. Said was primarily concerned with what he called the "Near Orient," more generally called the Middle East today. There was indeed cultural bias against Arabs and Turks, but there were also significant cultural clashes within Europe proper as evidenced by the bitter conflict between Catholics and Protestants and two world wars. Some of the prejudice was directed by Christians against Islam, similar to the trajectory of anti-Semitism within Europe. After World War I and the dissolution of the Ottoman Empire, the modern map of Middle Eastern states was fixed and determined the postcolonial and Cold War contexts after the World War II. The major conflict, one that especially engaged Edward Said, was over Western support for the creation of Israel and the resulting Arab-Israeli crisis. The establishment of the Islamic Republic of Iran and the more recent rise of terrorism in the name of Islam since 9/11 have further politicized the Middle Eastern foreign policy of the United States and Europe, but to lump all this conflict and ensuing bias under a single term like Orientalism ignores the complexity of the issues.

[*See also* Clash of Civilizations.]

BIBLIOGRAPHY

ʿAzm, Sadiq Jalal al-. "Orientalism and Orientalism in Reverse." In *Forbidden Agendas: Intolerance and Defiance in the Middle East*, edited by Jon Rothschild, pp. 349–376. London: Al Saqi, 1984.

Lewis, Bernard. "The Question of Orientalism." *New York Review of Books*, 24 June 1982, pp. 49–56; 12 August 1982, pp. 46–47.

Said, Edward W. *Orientalism*. New York: Pantheon, 1978.

Turner, Bryan, ed. *Orientalism: Early Sources*. 12 vols. London: Routledge, 1999.

Varisco, Daniel Martin. *Reading Orientalism: Said and the Unsaid*. Seattle: University of Washington Press, 2007.

Daniel Martin Varisco

Ottoman Empire. A multiethnic, multireligious, and multicultural entity, the Ottoman Empire was the last of the great Islamic empires. Starting in 1299, when various tribes united under Osman Bey in northwestern Anatolia, the empire enlarged its geographical realm. After Mehmed II conquered Constantinople in 1453, and until 1922, when it was formally abolished under Sultan Mehmed VI (r. 1918–1922), the empire ruled large areas of eastern Europe, North Africa, and the Arab World.

Conquest, 1300–1600. The Ottoman Empire was created by a series of conquests carried out between the early fourteenth and late sixteenth centuries by ten successive rulers of the Ottoman dynasty. Osman I and his successors in the fourteenth century expanded primarily into "Christian" lands of southeastern Europe as far as the Danube. The decisive defeat of the Byzantine army and the capture of the emperor Romanos IV Diogenes undermined Byzantine authority in Anatolia and Armenia and allowed Osmanlıs gradually to populate Anatolia. Conquests followed, facilitated by policies that left the defeated Christian princes in control of their states, as long as they accepted vassalage and provided tribute and warriors to assist further Ottoman occupations. The subordination gradually allowed Christian officials and soldiers to join the Ottoman government and army as mercenaries without being required to convert to Islam. This first Ottoman Empire incorporated territories that encompassed the modern states of Greece, Romania, Bulgaria, Macedonia, Serbia-Montenegro, Bosnia, and Croatia; it bypassed the Byzantine capital, Constantinople.

This initial period of Ottoman expansion came to an end during the reign of Bayezid I (r. 1389–1402), who replaced the *gazi* tradition of conquering Christian territories with seizure of the Turkoman Muslim principalities in Anatolia; simultaneously, Bayezid I substituted Byzantine for Muslim practices in his court and administration.

The Mamlūk Empire was then attempting to expand its influence north from Syria into the Armenian Kingdom of Cilicia and the headwaters of the Tigris and Euphrates, but it was by this time too weak to provide substantial military assistance to the Turkomans. Tamerlane (1336–1405), a Turkic ruler who referred to himself as the Sword of Islam and who founded the Timurid dynasty, preferred to move through Iran into India to restore the Mongol Empire of Genghis Khan, but fearing that Ottoman expansion eastward past the Euphrates might threaten his western provinces, he mounted a massive invasion of Anatolia that culminated in his rout of the Ottoman army and capture of Bayezid I at the Battle of Ankara (1402).

Bayezid I died in captivity, but enough of his sons survived to contest for power during the Ottoman Interregnum (1402–1413) that followed. Initially Prince Süleyman, based at Edirne, managed to retain Ottoman power in Europe with the assistance of the Christian vassal princes of southeastern Europe. Ultimately, however, his efforts to restore Ottoman rule in Anatolia were defeated by his brother Mehmed, supported by the Turkoman *gazis*. Mehmed I (r. 1413–1421) restored Ottoman rule between the Danube and the Euphrates, driving out Christian influences in the court and inaugurating a policy, continued by Murad II (r. 1421–1444, 1446–1451) and Mehmed II (r. 1444–1446, 1451–1481), instituting direct Ottoman administration in both Europe and Anatolia in place of the indirect rule through vassals that had characterized the previous century.

This restoration was accompanied in 1453 by Mehmed II's long siege and ultimate conquest of Byzantine Constantinople. Instead of following the Muslim tradition of sacking cities that resisted conquest, Mehmed II used his army to rebuild it and then carried out a policy of forced immigration (*sürgün*). Mehmed II repopulated the new capital with Christians, Jewish, and Muslim subjects.

The rapid expansion of Ottoman dominions created severe financial, economic, and social strains. These were, however, successfully resolved during the long and relatively peaceful reign of Sultan Bayezid II (r. 1481–1512), thus making possible substantial expansion in the first half of the sixteenth century beyond the boundaries of the first empire, across the Danube through Hungary to the gates of Vienna, and eastward into the territories of the classical Islamic empires of the Umayyads and ʿAbbāsids. Sultan Selim I (r. 1512–1520) "the Grim" (Yavuz), in response to the rise of the Ṣafavid empire in Iran starting about 1500 and its threat to Anatolia and to the regional balance of power, first defeated the Ṣafavids at Chaldiran (1514) in eastern Anatolia and went on to conquer the Mamlūk dominions during a rapid campaign through Syria and Egypt in 1516–1517, before adding the Arabian peninsula to his domains. The Ottoman Empire became the most powerful entity in the Islamic world.

Sultan Süleyman, "the Lawgiver" (Kanuni; called "the Magnificent" in Europe), who ruled from 1520 to 1566, went on to conquer Hungary (1526) and besiege Vienna (1529). With a stalemate in land warfare, the struggle between the Ottomans and Habsburgs was transferred to the Mediterranean Sea. Süleyman created a powerful navy under the leadership of the pirate governor of Algeria, Grand Admiral Hayruddin Barbarossa, who not only brought Algeria into the empire as a province whose revenues were set aside in perpetuity for support of the Ottoman navy but also transformed the entire Mediterranean into an Ottoman lake. Süleyman expanded Ottoman power further in the east, after conquering Iraq and the southern Caucasus from the Ṣafavids (1534). Under Süleyman, the Ottoman Empire became a world power.

Decline. In the second half of the sixteenth century, there emerged a series of external and internal challenges to the classical Ottoman system. The long and exhausting wars in the second half of the sixteenth century and early seventeenth century, often on two fronts, against the Habsburgs and Persians, both increased the financial burden and spoiled the classical military structure. Coupled with population growth in the sixteenth century, this led to social and political unrest, and rebellions both in the center and in the provinces. Structure of political elites and political culture changed, which weakened sultanic power.

Reform and Modernization. Under the leadership of Sultan Murad IV (r. 1623–1640) and the Köprülü dynasty of grand viziers, placed in power during the later years of the seventeenth century by Sultan Mehmed IV (r. 1648–1687), efforts were made to reform the political system to save the empire. This reform, however, was undertaken on the basis of the prevailing belief that Ottoman institutions and practices were superior to anything developed in Christian Europe; Ottoman leaders attributed the weaknesses of the system not to inferiority of its institutions but rather to a failure to apply them as had been done in the centuries of Ottoman greatness. Increasing losses to Russia and Austria during the eighteenth century, however, forced the sultans to modify this traditional reform, at least to the extent of acknowledging that European weapons and tactics were superior and to accept partial reforms of the Ottoman military.

From the late eighteenth century onward the Ottoman Empire faced three prominent challenges, and responses to these challenges paved the way for the Tanzimat period. The first was a strategic threat posed by the Russian Empire. In the eighteenth century, the emergence of Russia as a great power brought about a shift in the balance of power, at the expense of the Ottoman Empire. By then, the empire was in decline militarily, and Russia was eager to fill the vacuum that Ottoman weaknesses had created in the region. There was a series of Russo-Ottoman wars, resulting in the Russian invasion of Ottoman territory in the Balkans, southeastern Europe, and the Caucasus. Ottomans were repeatedly defeated by Russians (with the exception of the Crimean War of 1853–1856), and the very heart of the Ottoman Empire, the capital Constantinople, was often threatened by the Russian army. At the same time, the decline of the empire as well as the prospect of its disintegration created a power struggle among European Great Powers.

The second challenge was the emergence and spread of nationalist ideas and movements in the Ottoman Empire after the French Revolution, first among non-Muslim elements and then among non-Turkish Muslim elements. From the beginning of the nineteenth century until the end of World War I, the empire faced a series of nationalist and separatist uprisings, from different ethnic groups, seeking autonomy and self-determination.

The third challenge was the empire's slowly growing financial dependence on the West and the "peaceful penetration" of the major European powers. In the nineteenth century, European powers had succeeded in breaking through the Ottoman Empire to a considerable degree, interfering in its internal affairs, and recruiting networks of recruits among the sultan's own subjects. A number of factors facilitated this penetration. The European powers acquired certain legal rights of interference in Ottoman internal affairs. In addition, the considerable expansion of the Ottoman Empire's trade with the European powers, and the various economic concessions that had been awarded by the Ottoman government to European enterprises, enabled European powers to build up local commercial clienteles, particularly in the major ports and trading centers. The omnipresence of European political influence was assured through chains of consuls that were established in almost every important provincial center throughout the empire.

Militarization and Civilian Reforms. To save the empire, the foremost need was a better military; a better military required more revenue; more revenue required centralized administration and finance, and this required the rejection of decentralization and the elimination of the *âyâns*. Therefore, an administrative centralization process started along with military modernization. Military modernization in turn gave way to bureaucratic, administrative, and legal modernization, and the state underwent a period of Westernization in political, social, economic, and cultural fields throughout the nineteenth century.

These reforms during the Tanzimat period were planned under Sultan Mahmud II (r. 1808–1839), carried out under his sons Abdülmecid (r. 1839–1861) and Abdülaziz (r. 1861–1876), and brought to successful culmination under Sultan Abdülhamid II (r. 1876–1909). As proclaimed in 1839, the Tanzimat reforms promised an overall reorganization in every institution of state and society. Many of the proposed reforms were partially based upon European models, and they initiated an unprecedented, though slow, process of institutional and cultural Westernization. In another respect, too, the Islamic and Ottoman traditions were partially curtailed, with the promise of civil equality for the empire's non-Muslim subjects, to further placate growing internal discontent. Tanzimat reformers believed that the Ottoman Empire could only be saved by integrating the sick but still impressive empire into the Western political and economic systems. They argued that it would be wiser for the empire to join, rather than resist, Europe.

Centralization. Over a matter of a few short years, the Ottoman system became increasingly centralized. Constantinople extended its authority and activity to all areas of Ottoman life. The government was replaced with an increasingly complex system divided into executive, legislative, and judicial branches. The executive was organized into ministries headed by ministers who came together in a cabinet led by the grand vizier. The legislative function was given to deliberative bodies, culminating in a partly representative council of state in the last quarter of the nineteenth century and in the democratically elected parliament introduced initially in 1877–1878 and then again in the Young Turk constitutional period (1908–1918). Administration was turned over to a new hierarchy of well-educated bureaucrats (*memurs*) who dominated Ottoman governmental life until the end of the empire. The reforms introduced during the nineteenth and early twentieth centuries transformed the Ottoman Empire into a relatively well-governed and modern state. For all the difficulties and deficiencies in the implementation of government-sponsored reforms, it is clear that the Tanzimat era initiated a process of social and economic change without ever addressing intrinsic demands for added liberties.

Territorial Integrity and Abdülhamid II. Additionally, in the age of nationalism and imperialism, the most vital issue for the Ottoman elites was the effort to keep the independence and territorial integrity of the empire. From the 1830s until the end of the empire, heated political debates occurred among the elites, which consisted of different, and often opposing, solutions that aimed to prevent nationalist and separatist tendencies from gaining ground among the non-Muslims, who, it was important to note, constituted about 40 percent of the population at the beginning of the nineteenth century. To forestall nationalist challenges, Ottoman statesmen developed the policy of Ottomanism to promote the notion of one Ottoman nation, consisting of individuals with equal rights based on the law, sharing the same mother country, and loyal to the state and the sultan. Ottomanism underwent several phases: first, the state acknowledged basic rights for its citizens, Muslim and non-Muslim alike, as reflected in the 1839 Hatt-ı Hümayun of Gülhane; second, the Porte tried to create socioeconomic development together with a joint education system, especially in the Christian provinces of the Balkans after the 1856 Imperial Rescript of Reform; and third, as a last hope to curb separatist tendencies among Christian subjects, Constantinople gave its citizens political rights, turning the empire into a constitutional monarchy, with a new constitution and a fresh parliament in 1876.

Although the Ottoman Empire was weak in comparison with the European Great Powers, it remained a significant international actor whose independent decisions could materially influence the interests and behavior of more powerful states. After 1856, the Ottoman Empire was formally admitted by treaty into the European state system, and her status as a great European power was duly recognized.

From 1875 onward, the Tanzimat regime entered a period of profound crisis, marked by the bankruptcy of the treasury, a series of Christian rebellions in the Balkan provinces, a constitutionalist coup d'état, a major diplomatic confrontation with the European Great Powers, and a protracted and disastrous war with Russia that ended in 1878.

Sultan Abdülhamid II dissolved parliament in 1878 and established his own absolute control over the executive organs of government, which allowed him to control in some detail the initiation and implementation of policy. He ignored the rules of bureaucratic hierarchy, exerting personal authority over provincial as well as central officials, and, as a strong centralizer, determined to curb all tendencies toward provincial autonomy. Importantly, Abdülhamid II saw Islam and Muslim solidarity, expressed in a common loyalty to the Caliphate, as crucial to the empire's efforts to resist European expansion and to curb separatist aspirations among his non-Turkish Muslim subjects. These policies were expressed in much official deference to Islam and to religious leaders, and in an officially sponsored religious propaganda that, at times, assumed a "pan-Islamic" form by appealing to Muslim solidarity outside the Ottoman Empire. Abdülhamid II thus emphasized Islam at home to invoke the loyalty of his Muslim subjects, which betrayed earlier commitments to be more inclusive of non-Muslim subjects. While the reign of Abdülhamid II witnessed considerable achievements, it also set the stage for internal upheavals. The sultan encouraged improvement in finance, trade, mining, and agricultural export, as well as in education, civil administration, security, and military affairs, though financial caution significantly limited the extent of civil and economic reforms. Unlike the Tanzimat statesmen, Abdülhamid II avoided peacetime alliances with the Great Powers, maintained an overall diplomatic stance of "neutrality" or "noncommitment," and distanced the empire from its former protector, Great Britain. He harmonized relations with the empire's traditional enemy, Russia, initiating the longest period of peace in Russo-Ottoman relations in more than a century, and inaugurated a close relationship with Germany to restrain both Britain and Russia.

The sum total of these initiatives solidified opposition to Abdülhamid II's regime, which was led by the Young Turks. Their chief organization, the Committee of Union and Progress (CUP), demanded the restoration of parliament as a means to curb autocracy and preserve the integrity of the empire. Importantly, the CUP staged an uprising in Macedonia in the summer of 1908 that secured a sultanic proclamation that restored parliament on 24 July 1908. A counterrevolution broke out in Constantinople in April 1909 against the policies of the CUP, which crushed the rebellion and dethroned Abdülhamid II on 27 April 1909, falsely accusing him of having instigated the rebellion.

Democratization and Decay. During the second constitutional period (1908–1918), the Ottoman Empire experienced the most democratic era of its history, with myriad political parties electing deputies to the Ottoman parliament, which enacted major secular and liberal reforms. An initial period in which members of all the different nationalities worked to strengthen and preserve the empire was brought to an end by Austria's annexation of Bosnia, Bulgaria's annexation of East Rumelia, and Greece's annexation of Crete. Unrest in Macedonia and in other provinces resumed, with the forceful Ottoman military responses to restore order compounding the violence. Ottoman territorial losses continued, with Italy's invasion of the provinces of Libya in the Tripolitanian War (1911–1912) and the victory of the newly independent states of southeastern Europe during the First Balkan War (1912), which pushed Ottomans out of all their remaining European provinces and even threatened their control of Constantinople itself. As thousands of refugees flooded into the city, and as the remaining parts of the empire fell into increasing despair and chaos, CUP leaders Enver Pasha, Talat Pasha, and Cemal Pasha initiated a coup in January 1913 to establish a triumvirate that successfully defended Constantinople and took advantage of disputes among the Balkan states during the Second Balkan War (1913) to regain Edirne and eastern Thrace. They introduced major military, social, and economic legislation and suppressed internal opposition through deportation and massacres of the Armenian population.

In order to preserve the territorial integrity of the empire, the CUP was convinced that only an alliance with Britain (and the Entente) could guarantee the survival of what remained of the Empire and tried to seek support from London and Paris, but this proved impossible, and by the start of World War I the Ottoman government had failed to fulfill its objectives. CUP leaders were convinced that neutrality would be disastrous for the Ottoman Empire, since such would leave it isolated and at the mercy of belligerent states. In the end, the triumvirate formed an alliance with Germany and entered the war.

During World War I, the Ottoman Empire faced hostilities in eastern Anatolia against the Russians and in Mesopotamia, Arabia, and Palestine against the British and their allies. Although it successfully resisted an armada of British-French naval and land forces in the Dardanelles in 1915, it was less successful in other areas. Throughout the war, the Allies signed a number of agreements for the partition of the Ottoman Empire. As a result of the Anglo-Franco-Russian agreements of March–April 1915 (known as the Constantinople Agreement), Britain and France agreed that the question of Constantinople and the Straits would finally be solved by annexing the area to the Russian Empire. Under the secret 1916 Sykes-Picot Agreement, Russia was also given most of eastern Anatolia (including Erzurum, Trabzon, Van, and Bitlis), with France to receive Syria and Cilicia and Britain to gain control of Palestine and Mesopotamia in exchange. By 1917, Russian forces occupied territories east of the Trabzon-Van line; the Ottoman army was only able to regain eastern Anatolia after Russian forces evacuated as a result of the outbreak of revolution at home. As a consequence of Russia's withdrawal from the war, arrangements with Russia, including the Constantinople Agreement, were annulled.

After the 30 October 1918 Mudros Armistice, however, Britain, France, and Italy submitted their respective demands, based on previous agreements, to the Paris Peace Conference and began to occupy several parts of Anatolia. The peace treaty with the Ottoman Empire, known as the Treaty of Sèvres, dated 10 August 1920, was extremely severe; not only did it strip the empire of all its Arab provinces, it also deprived the Ottomans control of the Straits, and it envisaged the creations of two independent states for Armenians and Kurds, respectively, along with future Greek control over western Anatolia. Turkish nationalist forces, led by Mustafa Kemal Pasha (later Atatürk), organized an armed resistance movement against the Allies' occupation and successfully fought the Greeks, French, and Italians in western and southern Anatolia, thus leading to the establishment of the Turkish Republic in Anatolia and eastern Thrace. During the Turkish War for Independence (1919–1922), two rival governments appeared: one in Ankara under Mustafa Kemal, and one in Allied-occupied Constantinople. Accordingly, after the final victory of Mustafa Kemal over Greek forces in western Anatolia, and in the wake of peace negotiations at Lausanne, the Ankara government abolished the Ottoman sultanate on 1 November 1922, thus officially ending the Ottoman Empire.

[*See also* Abdülhamid II; Atatürk, Mustafa Kemal; Tanzimat; *and* Turkey.]

BIBLIOGRAPHY

Brown, L. Carl, ed. *Imperial Legacy: The Ottoman Imprint on the Balkans and the Middle East.* New York: Columbia University Press, 1996.

Butler, Daniel Allen. *Shadow of the Sultan's Realm: The Destruction of the Ottoman Empire and the Creation of the Modern Middle East.* Herndon, Va.: Potomac, 2011.

Davison, Roderic. *Reform in the Ottoman Empire, 1856–1876.* Princeton, N.J.: Princeton University Press, 1963.

Deringil, Selim. *The Well-Protected Domains: Ideology and the Legitimation of Power in the Ottoman Empire, 1876–1909.* London: I. B. Tauris, 1998.

Faroqhi, Suraiya, ed. *The Cambridge History of Turkey.* Vol. 3, *The Later Ottoman Empire, 1603–1839.* New York: Cambridge University Press, 2008.

Faroqhi, Suraiya. *The Ottoman Empire: A Short History.* Translated by Shelley Frisch. Princeton, N.J.: Markus Wiener, 2009.

Findley, Carter V. *Bureaucratic Reform in the Ottoman Empire: The Sublime Porte, 1789–1922.* Princeton, N.J.: Princeton University Press, 1980.

Finkel, Caroline. *Osman's Dream: The History of the Ottoman Empire.* London: John Murray, 2005.

Goffman, Daniel. *The Ottoman Empire and the Early Modern Europe.* New York: Cambridge University Press, 2002.

Hanioğlu, M. Şükrü. *A Brief History of the Late Ottoman Empire.* Princeton, N.J.: Princeton University Press, 2008.

Hanioğlu, M. Şükrü. *Preparation for a Revolution: The Young Turks, 1902–1908.* New York: Oxford University Press, 2001.

Imber, Colin. *The Ottoman Empire, 1300–1650: The Structure of Power*. New York: Palgrave Macmillan, 2002.

Inalcık, Halil. *The Ottoman Empire: The Classical Age, 1300–1600*. Translated by Norman Itzkowitz and Colin Imber. New York: Praeger, 1973.

Inalcık, Halil, and Donald Quataert, eds. *An Economic and Social History of the Ottoman Empire, 1300–1914*. New York: Cambridge University Press, 1994.

Karpat, Kemal H., ed. *The Ottoman State and Its Place in World History*. Leiden, Netherlands: E. J. Brill, 1974.

Karpat, Kemal H. *The Politicization of Islam: Reconstructing Identity, State, Faith, and Community in the Late Ottoman State*. Oxford: Oxford University Press, 2001.

Mantran, Robert, ed. *Histoire de l'Empire Ottoman*. Paris: Fayard, 1989.

McCarthy, Justin. *Muslims and Minorities: The Population of Ottoman Anatolia and the End of the Empire*. New York: New York University Press, 1983.

McCarthy, Justin. *The Ottoman Turks: An Introductory History to 1923*. New York: Longman, 1997.

McMeekin, Sean. *The Berlin-Baghdad Express: The Ottoman Empire and Germany's Bid for World Power*. Cambridge, Mass.: Belknap Press of Harvard University Press, 2010.

Quataert, Donald. *The Ottoman Empire, 1700–1922*. New York: Cambridge University Press, 2000.

Shaw, Stanford J. *Between Old and New: The Ottoman Empire under Sultan Selim III, 1789–1807*. Cambridge, Mass.: Harvard University Press, 1971.

Shaw, Stanford J. *History of the Ottoman Empire and Modern Turkey*. 2 vols. Vol. 2 by S. J. Shaw and E. K. Shaw. Cambridge, U.K.: Cambridge University Press, 1976–1977.

Suny, Ronald Grigor, Fatma Müge Goçek, and Norman M. Naimark, eds. *A Question of Genocide: Armenians and Turks at the End of the Ottoman Empire*. New York: Oxford University Press, 2011.

Turnbull, Stephen. *The Ottoman Empire 1326–1699*. London: Routledge, 2003.

Yasamee, F. A. K. *Ottoman Diplomacy: Abdülhamid II and the Great Powers, 1878–1888*. Istanbul: Isis, 1996.

STANFORD J. SHAW
Updated by GÖKHAN ÇETINSAYA
and JOSEPH A. KÉCHICHIAN

P

PAKISTAN. The Islamic Republic of Pakistan (Islāmī Jumhūrīya-e Pākistān), with a population of 193,238,868 million (2013 estimate), is the second largest Muslim state in the world, after Indonesia. Pakistan came into being as a result of the partition of British India on 14 August 1947.

The Nature of Islamic Politics in Pakistan. The political history of Pakistan has been characterized by rivalries and differences between three main Sunnī parties. Intense rivalry has existed between the Deobandī-oriented Jamʿīyatul ʿUlamāʾ-i Islām (JUI) and the Barelwī-oriented Jamʿīyatul ʿUlamāʾ-i Pākistān (JUP). The JUI was formed by pro-Pakistan *ʿulamāʾ* who had earlier differed with the staunchly anticolonial Jamʿīyatul ʿUlamāʾ-i Hind over its support for a united India. The conservative *ʿulamāʾ* of JUI insist on strict adherence to the *Sharīʿah* as interpreted by the founders of the four schools of Sunnī Islamic law, while the JUP's religious ideology is more populist, reflecting a Ṣūfī orientation that includes, among other things rejected by conservatives, the veneration of saints.

The third group, Jamʿīyat ʿUlamāʾ-i Ahl-i Ḥadīth (Society of the Religious Scholars of the People of the Ḥadīth), preaches uncompromising monotheism, rejects all notions of intercession by spiritual mentors, and condemns visitation of Ṣūfī shrines. The Jamāʿat-i Islāmī (Islamic Party; JI) founded by Sayyid Abū al-Aʿlā Mawdūdī (d. 1979) in 1941 represents the revivalist/fundamentalist Islam in today's Pakistan. However, since the early 1990s, the JI and other traditionalist parties such as the JUI and even the JUP have cooperated politically, and it has thus become increasingly difficult to differentiate between the revivalist and traditionalist streams.

In addition to adherents to the various schools of thought within Sunnī Islam, there are many Shīʿī Muslims in Pakistan. The Shīʿah in Pakistan have generally supported secular regimes, for fear of the Sunnī *ʿulamāʾ* who have shown increasingly anti-Shīʿī views since the 1990s. The Shīʿah have played a prominent role in Pakistan's politics: the country's first governor-general, Mohammad Ali Jinnah (r. 1947–1948), and three presidents—Iskander Mirza (r. 1956–1958), Agha Muhammad Yahya Khan (r. 1969–1971), and Asif Ali Zardari (r. 2008–)—belonged to the Shīʿah sect.

Other smaller Islamic sects in Pakistan include the Ismāʿīlīs and the Aḥmadīs. The Ismāʿīlīs, who belong to a subsect of the main Ithnā Ashʿarī Shīʿī sect, are numerous in Karachi and parts of northern Pakistan. The Ismāʿīlīs' spiritual leader, the Aga Khan, played a key role in the founding of the Muslim League at the beginning of the twentieth century. Some prominent members of the Punjabi political and bureaucratic elite adhere to the teachings of the small Aḥmadī (also known as Qādiānī) sect founded by Mirzā Ghulām Aḥmad (d. 1908). Pakistan's first foreign minister, Sir Zafaru'llah Khan, belonged to this sect.

Role of Islam in Pakistan, 1947–1970. Since 1947 Pakistan has faced critical economic, political, and ethno-regional problems that continue to shape political developments and contribute to its chronic sociopolitical instability. The ideological and political history of Pakistan has been marked by a continuous debate on the nature of the Islamic political system and its manifestation in constitutional structure and socioeconomic policies.

The ideological orientations and power imperatives of those who have controlled the state since its emergence—the higher echelons of the civil service, the military, the feudal landlords, and the urban-based capitalist class—did not always coincide with those of the *ʿulamāʾ* and the fundamentalists. At the state's conception, the majority of the political leadership of Pakistan agreed that its constitution and government should reflect the teachings and traditions of Islam. The problem was how to relate Islam to the needs of a modern state. The definition of an Islamic state formulated by the traditionalist and conservative fundamentalists or religious scholars assumed their own overarching authority in evaluating the Islamicity of all legislation. The most conservative insisted that laws and practices that conflicted with traditional interpretations of the Qurʾān and the *sunnah* should be repealed or amended. Mawlānā Shabbīr Aḥmad ʿUthmānī, a respected Deobandī *ʿālim* (scholar) who was appointed to the prestigious position of shaykh al-Islām of Pakistan in 1949, was the first to demand that Pakistan become an Islamic state. But Mawdūdī and his Jamāʿat-i Islāmī played the central part in the demand for an Islamic constitution. Mawdūdī demanded that the Constituent Assembly make an unequivocal declaration affirming the "supreme sovereignty of God" and the supremacy of the *Sharīʿah* as the basic law of Pakistan. Reformists and modernists advocated reinterpretation of Islamic laws in keeping with the needs of modern society.

The first important result of the combined efforts of the Jamāʿat-i Islāmī and the *ʿulamāʾ* was the passage of the Objectives Resolution in March 1949, whose formulation reflected compromise between traditionalists and modernists. The resolution declared the sovereignty of God over the nation, adherence to "the principles of democracy, freedom, equality, tolerance and social justice," and alignment with the "teachings and requirements of Islam as set out in the Holy Quran and the Sunnah." The Objectives Resolution has been reproduced as a preamble to the constitutions of 1956, 1962, and 1973.

Pakistan's political system from 1947 to 1958 was characterized by weak institutionalization and a lack of standards of accountability and commitment to pluralism. Pakistan's hostile relations with India—Pakistan has fought four armed conflicts with India, in 1947–1948, 1965, 1971, and 1999—and intermittent security threats coming from ethno-nationalist movements within the country gradually enabled the military to gain ascendancy over politicians by the late 1950s.

The chaos of Pakistani politics during 1951–1958, coupled with constant demands for regional autonomy by the smaller provinces, tilted the balance in favor of the military-bureaucratic establishment comprising senior military officials, civilian bureaucrats, and politicians hailing from the feudal classes. This facilitated the development of secular authoritarian rule backed by the military. Pakistan's first constitution (1956) reflected the influence of secular principles and laws on the administration of a parliamentary democratic form of government with broad Islamic ideology as its guiding but nonbinding basis. The constitution made the National Assembly responsible for deciding whether any law was in conflict with the Qurʾān and *sunnah*. The legal system of the country continued to be based on English common law, with Islamic law limited to private and family matters.

Pakistan witnessed its first coup d'état, by General Ayub Khan, in October 1958. The 1956 constitution was abrogated by the martial-law regime, and Ayub appointed himself president and announced a new constitution in 1962 that changed the name of the country from the Islamic Republic of Pakistan to the Republic of Pakistan. Later, however, as a result of pressure from religious groups, the constitution was amended to restore the word "Islamic." The new constitution retained most of the Islamic provisions of the 1956 constitution but did not make them mandatory.

During Ayub Khan's modernization of Pakistan (1959–1969), he launched intermittent intellectual assaults on the conservative *ʿulamāʾ* and the fundamentalist Jamāʿat-i Islāmī. The most controversial of these was the promulgation of the 1961 Muslim Family Laws Ordinance, which gave explicit rights to women in marriage, divorce, and inheritance but was considered to be un-Islamic by the conservative *ʿulamāʾ*. By the late 1960s, state power in Pakistan was essentially wielded by a military-bureaucratic establishment that accorded a privileged status to modernist interpretations of Islamic law. Pakistan's foreign policy in this period also reflected the perceptions of a mainly Westernized political elite as Pakistan aligned itself with the United States in the Cold War by joining anti-Communist U.S.-backed military alliances in Asia, such as the Central Treaty Organization (CENTO, dissolved in 1979) and South East Asia Treaty Organization (SEATO, dissolved in 1977).

General Ayub Khan was forced to resign in March 1969 as a result of protests led largely by prodemocracy secular parties and student groups. He handed over power to General Yahya Khan. The Yahya regime, which issued its own Legal Framework Order (LFO) replacing the 1962 constitution, was, like its predecessor, still essentially a secular regime.

The traumatic events of the 1971 civil war and subsequent secession of East Pakistan (forming independent Bangladesh) demonstrated that ethno-nationalism could override religious solidarity. The experience of East Pakistan became a rallying point for many Pakistanis, especially the religious groups, to call for a "return" to Islam as an ideological remedy to national malaise and to cultivate religious rejuvenation. The reemphasis on Islam was assisted by the civilian socialist-oriented Pakistan Peoples Party (PPP) government led by Zulfiqar ʿAli Bhutto (1929–1979), which came to power after the collapse of the Yahya regime. Bhutto used Pakistan's Islamic identity as a means of unifying a deeply divided nation. This post-1971 rediscovery of Islamic identity in Pakistan also had great impact on the new constitution (1973).

The 1973 constitution (still in effect albeit modified by successive regimes) placed greater emphasis on Islam than had previous constitutions. While the 1956 and 1962 constitutions had stipulated that only a Muslim could hold the office of president, the 1973 constitution extended that restriction to the office of the prime minister. The constitution also required government officials to "preserve the Islamic ideology." The constitution mandated compulsory Islamic studies in schools, promotion of the Arabic language, and publication of an "error-free" Qurʾān. The constitution provided that the state would endeavor to secure the proper organization of *zakāt* (obligatory charity tax) and *awqāf* (charitable endowments) and to eliminate *ribā* (interest). It also required that all existing laws should be brought into conformity with Islam, and reiterated that no law should be enacted that is against Islamic injunctions.

The Bhutto regime hosted the Second Islamic Summit Conference in Lahore in February 1974, a turning point in Pakistan's renewed efforts to forge new cultural, political, and economic ties with the Muslim Middle East. In 1977, in order to appease the *ʿulamāʾ* who had launched a mass movement to overthrow his government, Bhutto issued another set of Islamic reforms that included bans on alcoholic drinks, gambling, horse racing, and dance- and nightclubs.

In July 1977 the Pakistan army under the leadership of the Islamist-oriented General Muhammad Zia ul-Haq (1925–1988) overthrew the Bhutto regime. Zia was sympathetic to the Jamāʿat-i Islāmī. The JI and JUI had led the campaign against Bhutto. These two groups were an integral part of the right-wing Pakistan National Alliance (PNA) that opposed the PPP government. The JI, JUI, and other smaller Islamic groups had as an overt goal the establishment in Pakistan of an "Islamic system," Niẓām-i-Muṣṭafā (System of the Prophet Muḥammad Muṣṭafā), based on the *Sharīʿah*. The military had Bhutto executed in April 1979 on a dubious murder charge.

Coming in the wake of the worldwide Islamic resurgence exemplified by the Iranian revolution of 1979 and the *jihād* against the Soviet-backed regime in Afghanistan, General Zia's Islamization measures, introduced from 1977 to 1988 in a series of controversial laws and executive decrees, allowed him to create a network of state-sponsored institutional structures to translate what his administration considered to be the norms of the *Sharīʿah* into public policies. General Zia criticized democracy as an importation from the West and in its stead upheld Islam as the basis of legitimacy. The Hudood Ordinances, heralded as the foundation of this new system but essentially just a new penal code, focused on enforcing punishments for distinct kinds of crimes explicitly outlined in *Sharīʿah*, such as theft of private property, the consumption of intoxicants, and adultery and fornication (*zinā*). The most heated controversy concerned the latter, as the ordinance governing it made no legal distinction between adultery and rape. "Islamization" was being imposed by a military regime.

The years 1977–1988 witnessed the consolidation of the dominance of the armed forces over the state and its role as the protector of Pakistan's Islamic "ideological" and geographical frontiers. "The army" and "Islam" became synonymous for the preservation of Pakistani national integrity. General Zia and some of his senior military commanders died in a mysterious plane crash in August 1988, leading to the installation of a civilian government under Benazir Bhutto (1953–2007), daughter of Zulfiqar ʿAli Bhutto. Benazir Bhutto became the first female prime minister of a Muslim country. Nevertheless, her powers, like those of her successors, were restricted by the role of the military in the political process.

The post-Zia civilian regimes were unsuccessful in reconciling the demands of the *ʿulamāʾ* for imposition of Islamic law with reformist demands for a pluralistic multiethnic society. Prime Minister Nawaz Sharif introduced a *Sharīʿah* bill in April 1991, providing for a series of legislative and administrative measures to further Islamize education, the mass media, the economy, the bureaucracy, and the legal system; this bill was not approved by the parliament. Again in 1998, the Sharif government proposed a 15th Amendment to the 1973 constitution to impose the *Sharīʿah* as the supreme law of Pakistan. Despite strong pressure from the Islamists, a majority of the senate opposed this bill.

Besides Pakistan's conflict with India over Kashmir, the Pakistani military's association with

Afghan *jihād* contributed to the emergence of the Taliban movement in Afghanistan beginning in 1994. The Deobandī *madrasahs* at Akora Khattak in Khyber Pakhtunkhwa, and in Karachi, Baluchistan, and the tribal areas of the Khyber Pakhtunkhwa were the alma maters of more than half of the Taliban leadership.

On 12 October 1999 the Pakistan army under the leadership of General Pervez Musharraf carried out its third bloodless coup in the country's then-fifty-two-year history by arresting the prime minister, Nawaz Sharif, and declaring a state of emergency. General Musharraf portrayed his regime as reformist and determined to deal with the political and economic problems faced by Pakistan. Musharraf promoted a moderate form of Islam. He enunciated the concept of "enlightened moderation," which emphasized Islam as a moderate religion. The Musharraf regime supported the Taliban in Afghanistan until 11 September 2001.

The 9/11 terrorist attacks in the United States and Pakistan's subsequent alliance with the United States in the war on terror compelled the Pakistan army to curtail support for Islamic groups. Under U.S. pressure, the Musharraf regime took wide-ranging measures to assist the United States in apprehending hundreds of operatives belonging to Osama Bin Laden's al-Qaʿida organization. In January 2002 General Musharraf pledged to end Pakistani support for Islamic insurgents in Kashmir and Afghanistan and banned key Sunnī and Shīʿī militant groups, although some continued to function under changed names. The Pakistan army's action against al-Qaʿida suspects and their backers in the North-West Frontier Province's tribal areas between 2002 and 2007 led to a growing resentment against the Musharraf regime.

Most of the Islamic laws enacted during the Zia era remained largely intact under the Musharraf regime, with the exception of the Hudood Laws. With the passage of the Protection of Women Act 2006, the crimes of rape and adultery were placed once more under the jurisdiction of Pakistan's Penal Code. Despite General Musharraf's policy of "enlightened moderation," his regime's authoritarian rule backed by military coercion further eroded the vestiges of Pakistan's civil institutions and governance based on the rule of law and on parliamentary supremacy. The military's sidelining of the mainstream secular-oriented PPP and the Muslim League greatly benefited the Islamist groups, which remained among the best-organized political forces in Pakistan, although they lacked the unity and common ideological platform necessary to challenge the military-dominated state.

Fifty-five years after Pakistan's establishment, an Islamist political party won a significant election for the first time in 2002. The Mutahiddah Majlis-i-Amal (MMA) was voted into office in the provincial election in the North-West Frontier Province (now Khyber Pakhtunkhwa). It was also able to share power in a coalition government in the province of Baluchistan and came to head the opposition in the National Assembly. The provincial MMA was a coalition consisting of six Islamist parties: Jamāʿat-i Islāmī, Jamʿīyatul ʿUlamāʾ-i Islām (Fazlur Rahman group), Jamʿīyatul ʿUlamāʾ-i Islām (Samīul Ḥaq group), Jamʿīyatul ʿUlamāʾ-i Pākistān, Markazi Jamʿīyat Ahl-i Ḥadīth, and Taḥrīk-i Nifāz-i Fiqh-i Jaʿfarīyah (a Shīʿah party). The constituent political parties decided to make an alliance "to implement an Islamic system and to protect Islamic values," with the objective of ensuring the "supremacy of Islamic Law and enactment of legislation according to the recommendations of the Islamic Ideological Council." It introduced two controversial pieces of legislation, the provincial *Sharīʿah* Law and the Hisba Ordinance, to promote virtue (*amr bi-al-maʿrūf*) and eliminate evil.

In the context of foreign policy, the emphasis on the Islamic character of the state has given the

Pakistani political and military elites justification to confront India and enabled them to maintain relatively close relations with Muslim states having radically different political systems, such as Saudi Arabia, Turkey, and Iran. On the other hand, the assertion of "Islamic identity" since the 1970s has not significantly affected Pakistan's pro-Western foreign policy or its long-standing security relationship with the People's Republic of China. Even the growing U.S. engagement with India in the post–Cold War era has not substantially affected Pakistan's multifaceted relationship with the United States. The U.S. government's classification of Pakistan as a "major non-NATO ally" in 2004 was an acknowledgment of the country's pivotal role in the war on terror. However, after September 2001, the nature of U.S. assistance to Pakistan changed and was primarily aimed at inducing Pakistan's cooperation in counterterrorism. By late 2010 Pakistan had received around $20 billion in U.S. military and economic assistance.

Pakistan's Political Instability and Attempts at Democratic Governance. In October 2007 General Musharraf was reelected as president for a five-year term by the outgoing national assembly, further angering opposition groups, who considered his election unconstitutional. The contention was that he could not hold the office of president while retaining his rank as a military general. Increasing domestic instability and growing Islamic militancy in Pakistan compelled the United States and other Western states to pressure the Pakistani military to allow the return of Benazir Bhutto from exile. They perceived that Bhutto's return would facilitate democratic rule in Pakistan, which could assist in bolstering moderate, pro-Western secular forces in the country.

General Pervez Musharraf imposed a state of emergency, or de facto martial law, in Pakistan on 3 November 2007. He cited deterioration in law and order and the judiciary's interference in the running of the state as the prime reasons for this action. Replacing dissenting judges with handpicked appointees, Musharraf appeared to be seeking to retain personal power and his military position by gaining judicial approval for virtual martial law. Nevertheless, he gave up his position of army chief on 28 November 2007 under U.S. pressure.

On 27 December 2007 former prime minister Benazir Bhutto was assassinated in Rawalpindi. The government blamed Bhutto's murder on Taliban sympathizers, leading to violent countrywide protests.

Increased instability in Pakistan and persistent domestic and international pressure compelled the military-dominated regime to hold national elections on 18 February 2008. The PPP and Pakistan Muslim League (N) won over half the seats in the key province of Punjab and, with the support of many independents and other regional parties in the National Assembly, received close to the two-thirds majority needed to curb the president's powers and rekindle the prospect of a regrowth of civil society.

General Musharraf was forced to resign in August 2008 and was replaced by Asif Ali Zardari as president of the republic. The election of a "civilian" government in Pakistan, however, did not result in significant change in the country's foreign and security policies. Nevertheless, the PPP-led coalition under President Zardari and Prime Minister Yusuf Raza Gilani diminished the constitutional powers of the president accumulated during the Musharraf era under the 18th Amendment to Pakistan's constitution on 19 April 2010. The law transferred several presidential powers to the parliament, enhanced provincial autonomy, and formally repealed Musharraf's 17th Amendment, which concentrated sweeping powers in the office of his own presidency. Most importantly, the new law stripped the president of the power to dismiss the prime minister and dissolve the parliament. It also declared that neither the Supreme Court nor any high court could validate an "act of treason" (e.g., a military coup).

The United States maintained engagement with Pakistan in view of U.S. and NATO efforts to contain the more than a decade-long insurgency in neighboring Afghanistan. Since 2009, with the resurgence of the Afghan Taliban, the United States has increased pressure on Pakistan to do more to eliminate sanctuaries within its borders being used by the Afghan Taliban and its allies. At the same time, Pakistan has faced an increasingly complex insurgency waged by a network of Islamic militants under the banner of Tehrik-e-Taliban-e-Pakistan (TTP, Taliban Movement of Pakistan), also simply known as the Pakistani Taliban, distinct from the Afghan Taliban.

An earlier movement, the TNSM (Tehreek-e-Nefaz-e-Shariat-e-Mohammadi), was founded by Sufi Mohammad in the former princely state of Dir in 1989, with the goal of reinstating *Sharīʿah* as the primary legal system in Malakand Division and the Kohistan District of the Provincially Administered Tribal Areas (PATA). After the U.S. invasion of Afghanistan in October 2001, Sufi Mohammad left for Afghanistan with his son-in-law Fazlullah. After returning to Pakistan in 2002, they were both arrested, though Fazlullah was released relatively soon. He returned to his native Swat, where he founded the local faction of the TTP. He became known for his FM radio broadcasts, in which he preached an extremist version of Islam, as well as for his approval of violent practices toward women and his opposition to the Pakistani state. In May 2009 the Pakistan army launched an assault in Swat to remove the Taliban, although the threat of a resurgence remains.

Pakistan's relations with the United States entered a more difficult phase after U.S. Special Forces killed Osama Bin Laden, the leader of al-Qaʿida, near a Pakistani military base in Abbottabad in the Khyber Pakhtunkhwa province on 2 May 2011. Subsequent revelations that Osama Bin Laden had taken years-long refuge inside Pakistan led to intensive U.S. government scrutiny of the now troubled bilateral relationship. Nonetheless, the increasingly shaky U.S.-Pakistan engagement continued, with the U.S. government remaining committed to providing a nuclear-armed Pakistan $1.5 billion a year for five years in nonmilitary development assistance under the Kerry-Lugar-Berman Act of 2009.

Pakistan's politics remain deeply factionalized, elitist, and dynastic despite the return of overt civil rule. Elections alone have proved unable to allow civilian politicians to curtail the military's decades-long dominance over the state. Pakistan continues to be run by a military-dominated elitist state establishment, torn between moderate and extremist views and politically destabilized by the power imbalances between its civilian and military leadership.

[*See also* Aḥmadīyah; Aḥmad Khān, Sayyid; All-India Muslim League; Barelwīs; Bin Laden, Osama; Iqbal, Muhammad; Jamʿīyatul ʿUlamāʾ-i Pākistān; Jinnah, Mohammad Ali; Mawdūdī, Sayyid Abū al-Aʿlā; Qaʿida, al-; *and* Wahhābīyah.]

BIBLIOGRAPHY

Ahmad, Aziz. *Islamic Modernism in India and Pakistan, 1857–1964*. London: Oxford University Press, 1967.

Ahmad, Mumtaz. "Pakistan." In *The Politics of Islamic Revivalism: Diversity and Unity*, edited by Shireen T. Hunter, pp. 229–246. Bloomington: Indiana University Press, 1988.

Cohen, Stephen P. *The Idea of Pakistan*. Washington, D.C.: Brookings Institution Press, 2004.

Cohen, Stephen. P. *The Pakistan Army*. Rev. ed. Karachi: Oxford University Press, 1998.

Ewing, Katherine. "The Politics of Sufism: Redefining the Saints of Pakistan." *Journal of Asian Studies* 42, no. 2 (1983): 251–268.

Haqqani, Husain. *Pakistan: Between Mosque and Military*. Washington, D.C.: Carnegie Endowment for International Peace, 2005.

Hopkins, Benjamin D., and Magnus Marsden, eds. *Beyond Swat: History, Society and Economy along the Afghanistan-Pakistan Frontier*. London: Hurst, 2013.

Hussain, Rizwan. *Pakistan and the Emergence of Islamic Militancy in Afghanistan*. Aldershot, U.K.: Ashgate, 2005.

Jaffrelot, Christophe, ed. *Pakistan: Nationalism without a Nation?* London: Zed, 2002.

Jalal, Ayesha. *The State of Martial Rule: The Origins of Pakistan's Political Economy of Defence*. Cambridge, U.K.: Cambridge University Press, 1990.

Lieven, Anatol. *Pakistan: A Hard Country*. London: Allen Lane, 2011.

Lohdi, Maleeha, ed. *Pakistan: Beyond the "Crisis State."* New York: Columbia University Press, 2011.

Marsden, Magnus, ed. *Islam and Society in Pakistan: Anthropological Perspectives* Karachi: Oxford University Press, 2010.

McMahon, Robert J. *The Cold War on the Periphery: The United States, India, and Pakistan*. New York: Columbia University Press, 1994.

Nasr, Seyyed Vali Reza. *Mawdudi and the Making of Islamic Revivalism*. New York: Oxford University Press, 1996.

Nawaz, Shuja. *Crossed Swords: Pakistan, Its Army, and the Wars Within*. Karachi: Oxford University Press, 2008.

Qureshi, Ishtiaq Husain. *The Struggle for Pakistan*. Karachi: University of Karachi, 1965.

Qureshi, Ishtiaq Husain. *Ulema in Politics: A Study Relating to the Political Activities of the Ulema in the South-Asian Subcontinent from 1556 to 1947*. Karachi: Maʿaref, 1972.

Rizvi, Hasan Askari. *The Military and Politics in Pakistan, 1947–1997*. Lahore: Sang-e-Meel, 1999.

Rizvi, S. A. A. *A Survey of the History and Culture of the Indian Sub-Continent from the Coming of the Muslims to the British Conquest, 1200–1700*. Vol. 2 of *The Wonder That Was India*. London: Sidgwick & Jackson, 1987.

Sarila, Narendra Singh. *The Shadow of the Great Game: The Untold Story of India's Partition*. London: Constable & Robinson, 2006.

Sayeed, Khalid B. *The Political System of Pakistan*. Boston: Houghton Mifflin, 1967.

Shapiro, Jacob N., and C. Christine Fair. "Understanding Strong Support for Islamist Militancy in Pakistan." *International Security* 34, no. 3 (Winter 2010): 79–118.

Siddiqa, Ayesha. *Military Inc.: Inside Pakistan's Military Economy*. London: Pluto Press, 2007.

Smith, Wilfred Cantwell. *Islam in Modern History*. Princeton, N.J.: Princeton University Press, 1957.

Syed, Anwar Hussain. *Pakistan: Islam, Politics, and National Solidarity*. New York: Praeger, 1982.

Talbot, Ian. *Pakistan: A Modern History*. Rev. ed. London: Hurst, 2005.

Weiss, Anita M. "A Provincial Islamist Victory in Pakistan: The Social Reform Agenda of the Muttahida Majlis-i-Amal." In *Asian Islam in the 21st Century*, edited by John L. Esposito, John O. Voll, and Osman Bakar, pp. 145–173. New York: Oxford University Press, 2008.

Weiss, Anita M., and Saba Gul Khattak, eds. *Development Challenges Confronting Pakistan*. Sterling, Va.: Kumarian, 2013.

Wolpert, Stanley. *Zulfi Bhutto of Pakistan: His Life and Times*. New York: Oxford University Press, 1993.

RIZWAN HUSSAIN

PALESTINE. Islam in Palestine occupies a special place in the Muslim imagination and faith. Palestine, more specifically Jerusalem, holds the third most holy site in Islam, the original direction for Muslim prayer (*qiblah*). The Qurʾān and *ḥadīth* make reference to Jerusalem, from where the Prophet Muḥammad ascended to heaven during his Night Journey (*isrāʾ* and *miʿrāj*). In the Qurʾān it is related that the Prophet went on a journey by night from Mecca to Jerusalem; he reached the Ḥaram al-Sharīf, where the al-Aqṣā Mosque and the Dome of the Rock are situated. Thus, this location is revered by Muslims around the world and considered an important site for pilgrimage. This same site enjoys sanctity according to Jewish tradition as the location of the Second Temple.

The Semitic Canaanites, who developed an alphabet and other writing systems, were the earliest known inhabitants of Palestine during the third millennium BCE, living in cities, including Jericho. They immigrated from the Arabian Peninsula following a famine that devastated the area about two thousand years before the appearance of Moses and his followers. Located at the nexus of the roads connecting three continents, Palestine had a cultural and religious influence on Egypt, Syria, Mesopotamia, and Asia Minor. It was also a conflict arena for great powers that exerted various types of control. Ancient Egyptians occupied Palestine, then, during the second millennium BCE, two other newcomers settled on the same land as well: the Hebrews, a group of Semitic tribes, and the Philistines, Aegean peoples of possible Indo-European origin.

Arab Muslims entered Palestine in 638 CE, when the forces of Caliph ʿUmar (r. 634–644) conquered the country and its principal city, Jerusalem. According to Muslim tradition, Caliph ʿUmar entered Jerusalem on foot and received the keys to the city from Patriarch Sophronius. He then led the Muslim prayers at the site of the Prophet's Night Journey, which became known as the Ḥaram al-Sharīf. It is also believed that the caliph and Christian leaders reached a series of agreements known as the Umayyad Treaties. Caliph ʿAbd al-Malik (r. 685–705) commenced the building of the Dome of the Rock in 688 to commemorate the Prophet's Night Journey, and his son, the caliph Walīd (r. 705–715), built the al-Aqṣā Mosque.

Thus, under successive Umayyad, ʿAbbāsid, Ayyūbid, Mamlūk, and Ottoman periods of rule, the Islamic character of Palestine was established. Over centuries, Islamic institutions established mosques, schools, hospitals, seminaries, and endowment (*waqf*) properties. In time, the site of the Ḥaram al-Sharīf, along with many other locations throughout Palestine, was augmented by the construction of buildings, shrines, tombs, inns, fountains, palaces, homes, and courts.

Awqāf. Muslim rule in Palestine gave rise to a system of charitable endowments and trusts known as *awqāf* (sing., *waqf*). The third caliph, ʿUthmān (r. 644–656), acquired the spring of Silwan in Jerusalem and established it as the first *waqf* in Palestine, in perpetuity for the people of the city. *Awqāf* cannot be revoked and so were used as a means of maintaining Muslim governance throughout Palestine, as well as a form of charity. The establishment of *awqāf* in Palestine continued throughout Muslim rule of the country, with particularly fine examples of *awqāf* endowments founded during the Ayyūbid, Mamlūk, and Ottoman eras. During the Ayyūbid period, following Ṣalāḥ al-Dīn's defeat of the Crusaders, *waqf* endowments and institutions were a means of reestablishing the Muslim character of the country. They were proof of the Muslim attachment to Palestine as an Islamic center. These endowments further institutionalized Islam in Palestine, as various structures grew around them and their administrators formed the core of Palestine's notable classes and elites.

In Palestine, the importance of the *waqf* was connected to territoriality in terms of the lands and properties endowed and the social and political control derived from them. During the Ottoman era, state reforms and centralization meant that the authorities could use these endowments as a means to expand their power and influence over local elites. Under both the British mandate and Israeli occupation, authorities sought again to exploit *waqf* institutions and administration as a method of bringing their power to bear on a subject Palestinian Muslim population. Such methods have met with varying success.

Modern-day Palestinian Islamists have represented the issue of *waqf* in terms of the discourse on territoriality and conflict settlement with Israel. Conceptually, for example, the Ḥamās movement considers the whole of Palestine subject to *waqf*. They have stated in article 11 of their charter that, because the territory is being held in perpetuity for all Muslims, no party can renounce Muslim claim to it. With respect to resolution of the conflict with Israel, this rules out land-for-peace approaches. In the past, however, Ḥamās and its predecessors have also eschewed the formal institutions of the *waqf* administration. They have constructed their own mosques, paid their own preachers, and run their own charitable activities as if they are a form of endowment for the Palestinian people of the occupied territories.

Foreign Intervention. The Islamic character of Palestine was disrupted by foreign intervention in the country, beginning in the mid-nineteenth century. This intervention, Western and Christian in character, was manifested primarily as a "rediscovery" of Palestine. The picture of Palestine that was presented, however, was either devoid of a Muslim dimension or was one in which the majority Muslim population was portrayed negatively, as if Muslims were peripheral to the character of Palestine. This Orientalist approach was much approved of in political circles and added cultural legitimacy to the goal of subjecting Palestine to Western control, thus vanquishing Muslim governance and custodianship of the Holy Land. Muslim beliefs and practices were largely disdained as the Ottoman rulers of Palestine were dismissed.

The British occupied Palestine in 1917, during World War I, and thus brought to a close the continuous Muslim rule of the region that had lasted since the rout of the Crusaders by Ṣalāḥ al-Dīn in 1187. The newly formed League of Nations awarded Britain a mandate, which affirmed the commitments of the Balfour Declaration made in 1917, in which Jews were promised British assistance in the establishment of a "Jewish national home" in Palestine.

The majority Muslim population organized various forms of protest against both British authorities and the Zionist settlers who were intent on establishing a Jewish state in Palestine. Muslim national resistance strategies revolved around motifs of anticolonialism, nationalism, and Islamic nationalism. Notable Muslim families associated with major Islamic institutions such as the *awqāf* and Islamic courts split over how to respond to British tutelage and the Zionist influx. Some initially allied themselves with the Mandate authorities, while others resisted it by forming national political movements. Such movements and factions became embroiled in the Palestinian general strike and national revolt of 1936–1939.

The British attempted to bring Muslim institutions under their control through the establishment of the Supreme Muslim Council (SMC), which had responsibility for *awqāf* and the Muslim courts as well as the post of *muftī* of Jerusalem. This attempt was unsuccessful, however. The *muftī* opposed the British during the Palestinian revolt, and the SMC proved less than useful as a tool of divide-and-rule for the Mandate power. The SMC was dissolved in 1948, when the British terminated their mandate in Palestine.

Maintaining the Imprint of Islam. Following the 1947 partition of Palestine and the establishment of the state of Israel in 1948, the Muslim population of the region either became citizens of the new state or were subjected to the political leaderships of Jordan and Egypt. Israel's declaration of independence demanded that all of Israel's citizens, including Muslims, be treated equally in the eyes of the law. From 1949 to 1966 the Arab Muslim population of Israel was, however, ruled under strict martial law. Since the formation of Israel, Arabs in Israel have suffered legal discrimination, as McHenry and Mady noted, because the country's "Return Law" prohibited expelled Arabs from coming back, "while Jews have complete freedom to enter and receive automatic citizenship" (McHenry and Mady, 2006, p. 267). There is discrimination in land ownership, the provision of social services, housing, income, education, and political participation as well. Muslim resources derived from the *waqf* system and lands were also exploited and appropriated by the Israeli state and the Jewish National Fund.

Even before the formation of Israel, the Zionist movement sought to change the Palestinian demographic, cultural, social, and physical character to fit with its goals and ambitions in occupying Palestine. Israel continued this policy, known as "Judaization of Palestine," which allowed the Israeli government to use many means, including the demolition of houses, the building of Jewish settlements, the revocation of residency rights, and the replacement of Arabic place-names with Hebrew ones.

In the Jordanian-annexed territories of the West Bank and the Egyptian-administered Gaza Strip, the majority Muslim Palestinian population experienced different policies with respect to Muslim institutions and Muslim political activism. Under Jordanian rule, the Ministry of Awqāf became an important institution for legitimating the extension of Hashemite claims to the custodianship of the Ḥaram al-Sharīf. King Hussein's regime, however, regarded Palestinian Muslim activists with suspicion. In 1954 a law on "preaching and guiding" effectively banned the use of mosques for the propagation of Islamist ideas. Under Egyptian rule, members of the Muslim Brotherhood in the Gaza Strip were subject to cycles of repression, and activists were imprisoned.

In 1967, when Israel conquered the territories of the West Bank, Gaza Strip, and East Jerusalem, the Muslim majority population of Palestine found itself under occupation, subject to the legal jurisdiction of the state of Israel. East Jerusalem, including Islam's holy sites in the Old City, was also subject to Israeli occupying authority. The Maghribī quarter of the Old City, for example, which abutted the Jewish shrine of the Western Wall, was subject to demolition to allow for the creation of a plaza. Access to the Ḥaram al-Sharīf through the Maghribī gate fell into Israeli hands. The rest of the Ḥaram al-Sharīf complex, including the remaining gates, were managed and administered by the Ministry of Awqāf authorities, first through Jordanian and then Palestinian governance. Under Israeli control, the imprint of Islam in Palestine, through its formal institutions, was progressively erased.

Revivalism and Rebellion. Muslim Palestinians, however, established a revivalist tradition of Islamic thought that gave birth to Ḥizb al-Taḥrīr al-Islāmī (the Islamic Liberation Party) in Jerusalem in 1952. Its founder, Taqī al-Dīn al-Nabhānī, called for the reestablishment of a Muslim caliphate, not just in Palestine but across the Muslim world.

Palestinian Islamic thinkers and ideologues who succumbed to the influences and example of figures such as Ḥasan al-Bannā and Sayyid Quṭb, or movements such as the Muslim Brotherhood (Ikhwān al-Muslimīn) and the Mujāhidīn movement in Afghanistan, arose in the generation of new Islamic groups and movements such as the Groups (Mujama), Islamic Jihād (al-Jihād al-Islāmī), the Islamic Movement in Israel, and the Islamic Resistance Movement (Ḥamās). The organization of new groups and movements founded by Palestinian Muslims grew out of the wider regional Islamic resurgence. This resurgence had spiritual, political, economic, cultural, and social dimensions. In the Palestinian territories Israel encouraged some elements as a means of generating an antisecularist front in opposition to the Palestine Liberation Organization (PLO). In the late 1970s and early 1980s this expression of resurgent Muslim identity among Palestinians led to clashes and conflict with secularists and those associated with the leftist factions of the PLO.

During the first Palestinian *intifāḍah* (1987–1993), Muslim resistance in the form of the increasingly popular Ḥamās was representative of the progressive Islamization of Palestinian society. Indeed, the Islamic politicization of the national agenda with respect to the Israeli occupation and the demand for self-determination and independence gained ground. The PLO came to consider Ḥamās a serious rival for its claim to be the "sole legitimate representative of the Palestinian people." The campaign for Islamization led by organizations such as Ḥamās and Islamic Jihād had its impact on a number of dimensions of social, economic, and cultural life among the Muslim majority population in the West Bank and Gaza Strip. This was manifest in changing education curricula, dress codes, and social mores such as gender segregation, as well as welfare provision and burgeoning *zakāt* (alms tax) committees. Such activities also benefited from the support of the wider Muslim community outside of the Palestinian territories. The Muslim struggle in Palestine thus entered the discourse of contemporary Islam worldwide and has animated the work of many Muslim thinkers. *Fatāwā* (religious legal opinions), for example, issued by important Muslim theologians on the permissibility of *jihād* or, more specifically, what are commonly termed suicide missions against Israeli targets, have preoccupied Muslim discourse and created controversy and tension at the wider level of discourse on Islam and the West.

The Road to Muslim Statehood in Palestine. During the Oslo era of limited Palestinian autonomy, the Muslim institutions of Palestine were subject to a power struggle between the nascent Palestinian National Authority (PNA) and the Hashemite authorities in Jordan. The PNA, under the leadership of Fatah leader Yasir Arafat, won out, and the Muslim identity of the political institutions of the PNA was established. The Basic Law of the PNA underwrites the Muslim identity of this protostate institution by providing for *Sharīʿah* courts to address the realm of personal status issues. Article 4 of the Basic Law also declares that Islam is the official religion of Palestine and that due respect should be accorded to other religions. The laws of Islam are also the basis for Palestinian law under the PNA. (This article is problematic for secular Palestinians, who argue that faith should be restricted to the private realm and play no part in determining the nature of statehood and governance in the polity.)

Palestinian Islamists, however, rejected the Oslo Accords, the establishment of the PNA, and the principle of negotiations with Israel on the basis of land for peace. They adhered to the principle that all Palestine is considered Muslim territory, nonnegotiable and sanctified. PLO negotiators have been branded as traitors to Islam for their willingness to negotiate with Israel over territory in return for an independent state. While Islamists were part of the political opposition and marginalized, the Islamization project continued unabated throughout the 1990s and into the twenty-first century. The decision by Islamists to reinsert themselves into Palestinian politics resulted in the participation of Ḥamās (but not Islamic Jihād) in the elections for the Palestinian legislature in January 2006. Running on an electoral platform of "Reform and Change," Ḥamās swept to power, and many believed this would herald the establishment of a Muslim polity in Palestine and narrow the political vista with respect to peace with Israel.

Irrespective of the drive to attain Muslim-majority statehood in Palestine, Islamist groups such as Ḥamās and the movement for the resurgence of Islam more generally have established Islam as a permanent and primary feature of Palestinian identity and political discourse in the Palestinian territories of the West Bank and Gaza Strip, as well as in Israel and annexed East Jerusalem. Such elements have not always worked harmoniously with institutional Islam, but they represent much about Islam and Palestine in the twenty-first century. They also define Islam's meaning for a majority of Muslim Palestinians, whether they reside in Palestine or in the diaspora.

[*See also* Ḥamās; Israel; Jerusalem; Palestine Liberation Organization; *and* Waqf.]

BIBLIOGRAPHY

Armstrong, Karen. *Jerusalem: One City, Three Faiths.* New York: Alfred A. Knopf, 1996.

Awaisi, Abd al-Fattah Muhammad el-. *The Muslim Brothers and the Palestine Question, 1928–1947.* London: Tauris Academic Studies, 1998.

Dumper, Michael. *Islam and Israel: Muslim Religious Endowments and the Jewish State.* Washington, D.C.: Institute for Palestine Studies, 1994.

Grabar, Oleg. *The Shape of the Holy: Early Islamic Jerusalem.* Princeton, N.J.: Princeton University Press, 1996.

Kupferschmidt, Uri M. *The Supreme Muslim Council: Islam under the British Mandate for Palestine.* Leiden, Netherlands: E. J. Brill, 1987.

Lybarger, Loren D. *Identity and Religion in Palestine: The Struggle between Islamism and Secularism in the Occupied Territories.* Princeton, N.J.: Princeton University Press, 2007.

McHenry, Dean, Jr., and Abdel-Fattah Mady. "A Critique of Quantitative Measures of the Degree of Democracy in Israel." *Democratization* 13, no. 2 (2006): 257–282.

Milton-Edwards, Beverley. *Islamic Politics in Palestine.* London: Tauris Academic Studies, 1996.

Nüsse, Andrea. *Muslim Palestine: The Ideology of Ḥamās.* Amsterdam: Harwood, 1998.

Peled, Alisa Rubin. *Debating Islam in the Jewish State: The Development of Policy toward Islamic Institutions in Israel.* Albany: State University of New York Press, 2001.

Taji-Farouki, Suha. *A Fundamental Quest: Hizb al-Tahrir and the Search for the Islamic Caliphate.* London: Grey Seal, 1996.

BEVERLEY MILTON-EDWARDS
Updated by ABDEL-FATTAH MADY

PALESTINE LIBERATION ORGANIZATION. The Palestine Liberation Organization (PLO) was established in 1964 in Jerusalem. It was founded in response to a number of factors, including the growing salience of the Palestine question in inter-Arab politics; the increasing friction between the Arab states and Israel over water diversion projects and other issues; and the growth of underground, independent Palestinian nationalist activity, which Arab governments, notably that of Egypt, wanted to preempt.

Development of the PLO. The PLO quickly became the arena for much of this nationalist activity, which was increasingly directed at achieving independence of political action from the Arab regimes, in addition to the basic aim of liberating Palestine and securing the return of the approximately seven hundred thousand Palestinians who had been made refugees in 1948. In the wake of the June 1967 war, and the attendant shattering of the prestige of Arab regimes, control of the PLO was seized by independent Palestinian political formations with a more radical program than that of the original founders. These factions have dominated the organization ever since. Fatah stands for the Arabic Harakāt al-Tahrīr al-Watanī al-Filistīnī, or Palestinian National Liberation Movement; *fatāḥ* means "opening" or "conquest." It is by far the largest faction within the PLO, although leftist factions such as the Popular Front for the Liberation of Palestine (PFLP), the Democratic Front for the Liberation of Palestine (DFLP), and the Palestine Communist Party have also played key roles in the development of the PLO.

The PLO's first leader, the lawyer Aḥmad Shuqayrī, was a close ally of Egyptian president Gamal Abdel Nasser, and the PLO was strongly influenced by Egypt during its early years. However, in 1969, the organization signaled its emerging independence by choosing Fatah's leader, Yasir Arafat, as chairman of the Executive Committee of the PLO, the organization's guiding body. Arafat held the position until his death in November 2004. In 1968 the PLO's charter was amended to reflect the ideology of militant groups like Fatah, which advocated Palestinian-initiated "armed struggle" against Israel as the main vehicle for the liberation of Palestine. This ideology marks a contrast to the original approach of Shuqayrī and others of his generation, who believed that Arab states must play the leading role in dealing with Israel. The ideology of "armed struggle" was also a means by which the emergent middle-class leadership of the PLO could differentiate itself from the Palestinian elite, who were widely viewed as not suitably militant.

The new leaders of the PLO were younger, more radical, and generally of more modest social backgrounds than the old-line politicians from upper-class families who had dominated both the organization and Palestinian politics prior to 1969. These younger leaders also came from disparate political backgrounds. Arafat and his closest colleagues in Fatah, Ṣalāḥ Khalaf (Abū ʿIyāḍ) and Khalīl al-Wazīr (Abū Jihād), were deeply influenced during their time as students in Egypt by the Muslim Brotherhood. Others, such as Fārūq al-Qaddūmī (Abū Luṭf) of Fatah and George Habash, leader of the PFLP, were closer to Baʿthist or other Arab nationalist ideologies. They all agreed, however, on the principle of Palestinian agency—that Palestinians themselves must initiate political action and other forms of struggle—and all shared a profound skepticism regarding the professed commitment of Arab governments to act in support of the Palestinians.

After the Arab-Israeli War of 1967, the PLO rapidly became the central focus of Palestinian political activity, and by 1974 it was recognized as the "sole legitimate representative of the Palestinian people" by the Palestinians themselves, Arab and Islamic countries, and much of the rest of the world. "Armed struggle" by the PLO included some notorious acts, such as a wave of airplane hijackings spearheaded by Wadi Haddad and the PFLP, and the "Black September" attack by Fatah on Israel's Olympic team at the 1972 games in Munich. The insurgency against Israel inside the newly occupied West Bank and Gaza Strip and the international acts of violence failed to garner much success for the PLO, which gradually turned toward political solutions after the early 1970s. With the PLO's expulsion from Jordan in 1970–1971, it reestablished its operations in Lebanon, and increasingly focused on creating state-like institutions.

Beginning in 1974 with the twelfth meeting of the Palestinian National Council (PNC), the highest representative body of the PLO, the organization began to move away from its original maximalist policy of calling for the liberation of Palestine in its entirety and toward a two-state solution that called for a Palestinian state alongside Israel, in accordance with pertinent United Nations Security Council resolutions. This evolution was completed with the resolutions of the nineteenth PNC meeting in 1988 and the PNC's declaration of independence in the same year. This position firmly established the idea of a Palestinian state in the West Bank, Gaza Strip, and East Jerusalem (to be achieved via negotiations with Israel in an international forum) as the PLO's political objective.

This political evolution, while representative of majority Palestinian sentiment and welcome to most Arab states and much of the international community, met with the resistance of an important minority among Palestinians. Initially, the main advocates of this resistance were the so-called rejectionist groups of the PLO, backed by Arab regimes that claimed to be opposed to a negotiated settlement of the Arab-Israeli conflict or to the recognition of Israel. As these states waned in their opposition or their importance, and as the rejectionist trend within the PLO weakened, radical Islamic groups increasingly came to lead the Palestinian opposition to the PLO's policy of a negotiated, compromise settlement that would result in a Palestinian state in the West Bank and Gaza Strip alongside Israel.

The most important of these Islamic groups, Ḥamās (from the Arabic word meaning "zeal" or "enthusiasm" and an acronym for Ḥarakāt al-Muqāwamah al-Islāmīyah) was founded in 1988 in the Gaza Strip as an outgrowth of the Egyptian Muslim Brotherhood, which had long been a political force among Palestinians. Ḥamās soon spread to the West Bank and other areas. It was established in response to several factors, including the outbreak of the first *intifāḍah*, or Palestinian uprising, in the Occupied Territories in December 1987; the growth of militant, independent Islamic groups such as Islamic Jihād, which strongly criticized the moderate line of the Muslim Brotherhood vis-à-vis the Israeli occupation; and the PLO's political shift toward a compromise solution with Israel.

The Oslo Accords. In 1993 the PLO exchanged letters of recognition with Israel, and both signed a Declaration of Principles on Interim Self-Government Arrangements (DOP), commonly known as the Oslo Accords. The PLO accepted terms in the Oslo Accords that it had previously rejected, including a five-year interim period prior to the commencement of an unstated final status arrangement. The PLO probably accepted unfavorable terms because of its desperate organizational situation. Arafat's support for Iraq's invasion of Kuwait in 1990 led to the financial bankruptcy of the PLO (which had received the bulk of its funding from Kuwait and Saudi Arabia) and to its political marginalization regionally and internationally. The Oslo Accords were a surprise development that appeared to rescue the PLO from a critical situation, open up prospects of a change in the status quo in the Occupied Territories, and spark new Palestinian opposition.

The PLO's gambit in signing the DOP in 1993 and a series of other agreements with Israel throughout the 1990s failed to produce an independent Palestinian state. Indeed, Israeli colonization of the West Bank and East Jerusalem intensified during this period, with Jewish settlers doubling in number during the first decade of the Oslo peace process. The failure of the Oslo peace process gave more political clout to opponents of the PLO, especially Ḥamās. The inability of the PLO, Israel, and the United States to agree to terms of a final settlement at Camp David in the summer of 2000 ignited a second Palestinian uprising in September, the al-Aqṣā Intifāḍah. While Fatah initially controlled the Palestinians in this second *intifāḍah*, they gradually lost ground to Ḥamās, whose suicide bombings inflicted the most casualties on Israel.

The death of Yasir Arafat in November 2004 accelerated the fragmentation of Fatah and the PLO. By 1993 when it focused on creating a Palestinian state in the West Bank and Gaza, Fatah had already lost significant control over the Palestinian diaspora population. Palestinian refugee camps in Lebanon came to symbolize the often lawless character of this new reality, as PLO authority in the camps waned and the power of radical Islamists gained ground. Inside Palestine, the second Palestinian *intifāḍah* and its suppression by Israel led to the geographic fragmentation of the West Bank, where over five hundred permanent checkpoints and road closures made travel from town to town nearly impossible. As a result, local strongmen gained control over small fragments of Palestine; many of these men claimed allegiance to the PLO but in reality exerted power for their own interests. The widespread corruption of Fatah rulers while in power also contributed to discontent and opposition among Palestinians.

Israel unilaterally withdrew from the Gaza Strip in 2005, prompting Palestinian groups to jockey for power. Ḥamās effectively won the initial competition, first through its victory in the 2006 parliamentary elections and then in its 2007 plot to drive Fatah and the PLO out of Gaza. Whether Fatah in particular and the PLO in general can regroup and regain their preeminent position in Palestinian politics is unknown. Certainly, the era of Fatah one-party dominance over Palestinian politics is over, and a new era of political pluralism has begun.

[*See also* Arab-Israeli Conflict; Ḥamās; Intifāḍah; *and* Israel.]

BIBLIOGRAPHY

Aby Iyad and Eric Rouleau. *My Home, My Land: A Narrative of the Palestinian Struggle*. Translated by Linda Butler Koseoglu. New York: Times Books, 1981. A frank first-person account by one of the founders of Fatah.

Brand, Laurie A. *Palestinians in the Arab World: Institution Building and the Search for State*. New York: Columbia University Press, 1988. Careful examination of some of the major constitutive organizations of the PLO.

Brown, Nathan J. *Palestinian Politics after the Oslo Accords: Resuming Arab Palestine*. Berkeley: University of California Press, 2003. A careful analysis of Palestinian politics in the Palestinian Authority, with a focus on legal and constitutional issues.

Brynen, Rex. *Sanctuary and Survival: The PLO in Lebanon*. Boulder, Colo.: Westview, 1990. Study of the PLO's "Lebanese era," from 1969 to 1982.

Cobban, Helena. *The Palestinian Liberation Organisation: People, Power, and Politics*. Cambridge, U.K.: Cambridge University Press, 1984. Standard work on the history of the PLO during its first two decades.

Farsoun, Samih K., and Christina E. Zacharia. *Palestine and the Palestinians*. Boulder, Colo.: Westview, 1997. General history of the Palestinians with a sympathetic voice.

Gresh, Alain. *The PLO: The Struggle Within: Towards an Independent Palestinian State*. Translated by A. M. Berrett. London: Zed, 1985. Detailed and knowledgeable examination of the evolution of PLO policies.

Khalidi, Rashid. *Under Siege: PLO Decisionmaking during the 1982 War*. New York: Columbia University Press, 1986. Case study of how the PLO functioned during the Israeli invasion of Lebanon, based on primary sources.

Kimmerling, Baruch, and Joel S. Migdal. *The Palestinian People: A History*. Cambridge, Mass.: Harvard University Press, 2003. Excellent sociological and political overview of Palestinian history.

Maʿoz, Moshe. *Palestinian Leadership on the West Bank: The Changing Role of the Arab Mayors under Jordan and Israel*. London: Frank Cass, 1984. Examines key role of West Bank city mayors under Jordanian and Israeli rule.

Mishal, Shaul. *The PLO under ʿArafat: Between Gun and Olive Branch*. New Haven, Conn.: Yale University Press, 1986. Critical analysis of shifts in PLO strategy through the mid-1980s.

Parsons, Nigel. *The Politics of the Palestinian Authority: From Oslo to al-Aqsa*. New York: Routledge, 2005. A detailed analysis of Palestinian politics in the Palestinian Authority, including the breakdown of the Oslo Accords and the second uprising.

Quandt, William B., Fuad Jabber, and Ann Mosely Lesch. *The Politics of Palestinian Nationalism*. Berkeley: University of California Press, 1973. Valuable but dated study of different facets of Palestinian nationalism.

Robinson, Glenn E. *Building a Palestinian State: The Incomplete Revolution*. Bloomington: Indiana University Press, 1997. Case study of the first Palestinian uprising and its political aftermath, based on primary sources.

Rouleau, Eric. *Les Palestiniens: D'une guerre à l'autre*. Paris: Editions la Découverte, 1984. Acute analysis of the PLO and its leadership by a journalist.

Sahliyeh, Emile. *In Search of Leadership: West Bank Politics since 1967*. Washington, D.C.: Brookings Institute, 1988. Valuable overview of the PLO's rise in the West Bank in the first two decades following the 1967 war.

Sayigh, Yezid. *Armed Struggle and the Search for State: The Palestinian National Movement, 1949–1993*. Oxford: Clarendon, 1997. Single best source on the PLO, using unrivaled primary sources.

Shemesh, Moshe. *The Palestinian Entity, 1959–1974: Arab Politics and the PLO*. London: Frank Cass, 1988.

Examines the development of the idea of a Palestinian state up to 1974.

Smith, Charles D. *Palestine and the Arab-Israeli Conflict*. 8th ed. Boston: Bedford/St. Martin's, 2013. Best textbook on the conflict; includes essential documents.

GLENN E. ROBINSON

PAN-ISLAM. Pan-Islam emerged in the early days of Islam, although the European appellation for the ideology calling all Muslims to unite in support of their faith gained currency after 1878, as *ʿulamāʾ* and *fuqahāʾ* employed it repeatedly to encourage believers to display solidarity. Muslim scholars wished for a universally united Muslim community, and as Islam expanded, so has its Pan-Islamic element, chiefly since the 1860s and 1870s, when European colonialism reached a peak. It then became a defensive ideology, intended simultaneously to raise the morale of the foreign-dominated Muslims and save the few remaining independent Muslim states from a similar fate. Of these, Afghanistan and Morocco were rather peripheral geographically; Iran, overwhelmingly Shīʿī, was poorly suited to promote Pan-Islamic policy among preponderantly Sunnī populations. The Ottoman Empire, both centrally located and territorially the largest of the four, was decidedly more appropriate, especially as Arab lands languished under colonial rule.

Turkish intellectuals discussed and wrote about Pan-Islam (*ittiḥād-i Islām*) starting in the 1860s, developing ideas to utilize the concept as a potential political weapon capable of uniting all Muslims and saving the Ottoman Empire from fragmentation. However, it was only during the reign of Sultan Abdülhamid II (r. 1876–1909) that Pan-Islam became a favored state policy. Although Pan-Islam was adopted and promoted by some members of the ruling bureaucratic and intellectual elites of the empire, it was difficult to separate Pan-Islam from Pan-Turanism, especially as the latter confronted existential questions. In reaction to the loss of Cyprus (1878), Tunisia (1881), and Egypt (1882), both orthodox and secular intellectuals in the Ottoman Empire energetically strove to formulate political ideologies aiming at a Pan-Islam directed against European political, military, economic, and missionary penetration. It was consequently easier to market Pan-Islam, which made up for the loss of territories to powerful colonial entities.

The best known Pan-Islamist thinker was Jamāl al-Dīn al-Afghānī (1838–1897), an Iranian-born cleric who sought unity among Muslims to resist colonial occupation of Muslim lands. Al-Afghānī did not advocate constitutional government but simply envisioned "the overthrow of individual rulers who were lax or subservient to foreigners, and their replacement by strong and patriotic men" (Keddie, 1972, pp. 225–226). Others were subsidized by Abdülhamid, whose agents spread Pan-Islamic propaganda, openly and covertly, within and outside the Ottoman Empire. This sultan posed as the caliph, a would-be spiritual and temporal leader to whom all Muslims everywhere owed allegiance and obedience. The propaganda he fostered, intended to offset as much as possible the empire's military and economic weakness, had several policy objectives: to favor the central government over the periphery and the empire's Muslims over its non-Muslim subjects in education, office, and economic opportunities (particular attention being paid to Turks and Arabs, somewhat less to Albanians and Bosnians); to recruit the empire's Muslims and many outside it in response to the activities of some of the Great Powers; and to enable the sultan-caliph to threaten these powers with instigating Pan-Islamic activities among Muslims living under the rule of those powers.

Actions based on Abdülhamid's Pan-Islamic policies were modest, confined to expressions of support and fund-raising, especially during wars, such as the conflict with Greece over Crete in 1897. His efforts, however, were taken seriously enough by several European powers, which refrained from attacking the Ottoman Empire while he reigned. It was no coincidence that it was only after his deposition in 1909 and the general expectation that Pan-Islamic activities had come to an end that Italy invaded Tripolitania, and the Balkan peoples annexed Ottoman territories to bolster their own independence. The ruling Committee of Union and Progress (CUP, or, as they were popularly called, the Young Turks) were far less dedicated to Pan-Islam and so did not hesitate to exploit the concept then and later, during World War I. In fact, the Ottoman declaration of war on 11 November 1914 was accompanied by a proclamation of *jihād* and the pronouncement of five *fatwas* enjoining all Muslims everywhere to unite and join, with life and property, the Ottoman Empire in the *jihād* against Russia, Great Britain, and France (which, along with the Netherlands, then ruled most of the nonindependent Muslim populations).

But the intensive Ottoman Pan-Islamic propaganda, carried out with full German cooperation, failed to induce Muslims in the Allied forces to revolt, for several reasons: the limitations of Pan-Islamic organization; countermeasures by the Allied Powers; the reservations of Muslims, shocked by reports of the Young Turks' irreligiosity; the acquiescence of some Muslims (e.g., in India) in their foreign-dominated status; alternative priorities among some Muslims, such as Arab nationalist aspirations; the hidden Pan-Turanism agenda that was the CUP's real Pan-Islamic goal, to rid the empire of non-Muslim subjects, including Armenians, Greeks, and Jews; and the alliance of the Ottomans with Christian powers such as Germany and Austria-Hungary.

The failure of Pan-Islam in World War I and the defeat and dismemberment of the Ottoman Empire brought Pan-Islam nearly to a standstill in the following generation. The abolition of the caliphate in 1924 deprived it of its top leadership. Attempts at uprisings by Russia's Muslims (who had exhibited Pan-Islamic leanings since the late nineteenth century) were soon crushed by the Soviet army. A Pan-Muslim mass movement in India, in the 1920s, the Khilāfat, petered out with hardly a trace. Five Pan-Islamic conventions (Mecca, 1924; Cairo, 1926; Mecca, 1926; Jerusalem, 1931; Geneva, 1935) produced no follow-ups, highlighting organizational weaknesses. Further, Pan-Islam grappled with competing ideologies, including universalist ones, such as atheist communism in the Soviet Union and Pan-Arabism, and particularist ones, such as nationalism in Turkey and several Arab states, chiefly those that had adopted modernity and secularism as their creed and way of life.

After World War II, changing circumstances again favored Pan-Islam, although Arab nationalism overshadowed Islamism. At first, secular pan-Arab parties—such as the Baʿth—came to power in Egypt, Libya, Iraq, and Syria, while Islamist movements, led by Sayyid Quṭb, were repressed. Pan-Islam reversed its position of popularity relative to nationalism and pan-Arabism in 1967 after the devastating Arab defeat in the Six-Day War against Israel. In fact, rising Islamic fundamentalism comprised an element of Pan-Islam, as the preaching of Muslim solidarity as a step toward union found ready ears. Newly independent Muslim states with the political means to promote the fulfillment of Pan-Islam, and several with the economic capacity to do so, embarked on critical programs. The latter, Saudi Arabia foremost among them, set up Pan-Islamic international organizations for this purpose. The Muslim World League was founded in 1962 and served as an umbrella organization for many nongovernmental Islamic associations and groups. Likewise, the Organization of the Islamic Conference was established in 1969 to coordinate Islamic solidarity and promote Pan-Islamic political and economic cooperation internationally. In 1979 the Islamic Revolution in Iran ousted Shah Muhammad Reza Pahlavi from power, and a decade later the Afghan Mujāhidīn successfully forced the Soviet Union from Afghanistan. Indeed, the breakdown of the Soviet Union afforded Pan-Islam new opportunities to co-opt the newly independent former Soviet republics, while the futile attempts of Saddam Hussein of Iraq in 1990–1991 and Muʿammar al-Qadhdhāfī of Libya in 1992 to recruit all-Muslim support against "foreign aggression" indicated that Pan-Islam was still considered an important political tool. Remarkably, the dramatic events throughout the Muslim world mobilized Islamists, as various branches of the Muslim Brotherhood challenged both secular nationalist and monarchical governments. In Pakistan, the Jamāʿat-i Islāmī enjoyed popular support, while in Algeria the Front Islamique du Salut won the canceled elections of 1992. After the collapse of the Soviet Union, the Ḥizb al-Taḥrīr emerged as a Pan-Islamist force in Central Asia, and in the early twenty-first century, various Pan-Islamist groups emerged in Saudi Arabia and the Arabian Peninsula that further enlarged the gulf separating Muslim nations. Ostensibly one of the leading Pan-Islamic movements, al-Qaʿida positioned itself in Afghanistan, Iraq, and elsewhere, though its preference for violence limited its popularity. When al-Qaʿida leader, Osama Bin Ladin, was assassinated on 2 May 2011, the leading Pan-Islamist movement was significantly weakened.

[*See also* Abdülhamid II; Congresses; Khilāfat Movement; Organization of Islamic Cooperation; *and* Ottoman Empire.]

BIBLIOGRAPHY

Aziz, K. K. *The Indian Khilafat Movement, 1915–1933: A Documentary Record*. Karachi, Pakistan: Pak, 1972. Documentary record.

Charmes, Gabriel. *L'avenir de la Turquie: Le panislamisme*. Paris: Calmann Lévy, 1883. The first book informing Europe of Pan-Islam.

Donohue, John J., and John L. Esposito, eds. *Islam in Transition: Muslim Perspectives*. 2d ed. New York: Oxford University Press, 2007.

Fuller, Graham E. *The Future of Political Islam*. New York: Palgrave Macmillan, 2003.

Hegghammer, Thomas. *Jihad in Saudi Arabia: Violence and Pan-Islamism since 1979*. Cambridge, U.K.: Cambridge University Press, 2010. Provides an overview of the "rise of Islamist militancy" in Saudi Arabia and tackles the history of the global jihadist movement.

Keddie, Nikki R. "Pan-Islam as Proto-Nationalism." *Journal of Modern History* 41, no. 1 (March 1969): 17–28. Important historical analysis.

Keddie, Nikki R. *Sayyid Jamāl ad-Dīn "al-Afghānī": A Political Biography*. Berkeley: University of California Press, 1972.

Kidwai, Mushir Hosain. *Pan-Islamism*. London: Luzac, 1908.

Kramer, Martin. *Islam Assembled: The Advent of the Muslim Congresses*. New York: Columbia University Press, 1986. Pan-Islamic congresses.

Landau, Jacob M. "Al-Afghānī's Panislamic Project." *Islamic Culture* 26, no. 3 (July 1952): 50–54.

Landau, Jacob M. *The Politics of Pan-Islam: Ideology and Organization*. Oxford: Clarendon, 1990. Contains a detailed bibliography.

Levtzion, Nehemia. *International Islamic Solidarity and Its Limitations*. Jerusalem: Magnes Press, Hebrew University, 1979. Useful survey of then-active Pan-Islamic organizations.

Maududi, Sayyid Abul Aʿla. *Unity of the Muslim World*. Lahore, Pakistan: Islamic Publications, 1967. Distinguished Pakistani's thoughts on Pan-Islam.

Qureshi, M. Naeem. "Bibliographic Soundings in Nineteenth-Century Pan-Islam in South Asia." *Islamic Quarterly* 24, nos. 1–2 (1980): 22–34. Systematic bibliographic survey.

Qureshi, M. Naeem. *Pan-Islam in British Indian Politics: A Study of the Khilafat Movement, 1918–1924*. Leiden, Netherlands: E. J. Brill, 1999.

Sheikh, Naveed S. *The New Politics of Islam: Pan-Islamic Foreign Policy in a World of States*. London: RoutledgeCurzon, 2003.

JACOB M. LANDAU
Updated by JOSEPH A. KÉCHICHIAN

Partai Islam se Malaysia. The Islamic Party of Malaysia (Partai Islam se Malaysia; PAS) was established to promote Malay-Muslim interests. Its antecedents were small Malay-Muslim organizations, primarily the Muslim Party (Hizbul Muslimin) and the Pan Malayan Islamic Association (Persatuan Islam Se-Tanah Malaya; PMIA). However, it became institutionalized as a party in May 1955, when it registered itself as the Pan-Malayan Islamic Party (Partai Islam Se-Tanah Melayu; PMIP), later to become PAS. This initially small and loosely organized party stood in opposition to the multiethnic policies of the ruling Alliance coalition led by Malaya's largest Malay-Muslim party, the United Malay Organization (UMNO), and favored the realization of Islamic principles.

From its inception, PAS has stressed an Islamic agenda. It has called for the establishment of an Islamic state based upon the Qur'ān and *sunnah*. Although the party leadership initially did not delineate how such an Islamic-based system was to be formulated, it has more recently provided more specificity about how such a system should operate within a democratic society. It has rejected the UMNO declaration that Malaysia is already an Islamic state and asserted that the full implementation of criminal, personal, and commercial Islamic law is essential to such a state. Although PAS recognized that the federal government would not accept the establishment of criminal *ḥudūd* laws, efforts were made to promulgate in states under PAS control. A bill to attain that goal was passed unanimously in the state of Kelantan but was rejected by federal authorities as outside state powers. This has been part of a wider debate with PAS, arguing that the entire *Sharīʿah* should be implemented and attacking UMNO for supporting only some elements. PAS platforms have also called for banning vices such as gambling and limiting the sale of alcoholic drinks. UMNO has accused PAS of supporting violent militant Islam, and federal authorities have arrested party members for involvement in such activities, although PAS sees these charges as spurious. In foreign policy, it has vigorously criticized Israel and American actions in the Middle East, strongly supported the Palestinians, and praised suicide bombers as martyrs for Islam.

The party has not always been consistent in its policies. It initially criticized UMNO for working with other non-Islamic parties, but in 1999, 2008, and 2013, it formed electoral alliances with largely Chinese parties, notably the Democratic Action Party (DAP) and the ethnically pluralist People's Justice Party (Partai Keadilan Rakyat). The party now allows non–Malay Muslims to become members, although they may not hold top posts. In the face of criticism for not allying itself with its fellow Malay-Muslim party UMNO, PAS's leadership has declared that Islam embraces a pluralistic society and requires respect for non-Muslims. Efforts to ally with other ethnically based parties have also led PAS to play down its public demands for an Islamic state, a position negatively perceived by most non-Muslims in Malaysia.

BIBLIOGRAPHY

Kessler, Clive S. *Islam and Politics in a Malay State: Kelantan, 1838–1969*. Ithaca, N.Y.: Cornell University Press, 1978.

Liow, Joseph Chinyong. *Piety and Politics: Islamism in Contemporary Malaysia*. Oxford: Oxford University Press, 2009.

Means, Gordon P. *Malaysian Politics: The Second Generation*. Singapore: Oxford University Press, 1991.

Fred R. von der Mehden

Partai Keadilan Sejahtera. The Partai Keadilan Sejahtera (Prosperous Justice Party; PKS) has its roots in the Tarbiyah (education) movement, which was popular on college campuses during the New Order era. Suharto, the dictator who ruled Indonesia from 1967 to 1998, attempted a depoliticization of student life in the 1970s through the enactment of the Normalization of Campus Life Policy in 1978, which required all students to eschew political activity and focus on their studies. As a result of the regime's efforts to suppress political activity, dissent was channeled into a variety of religious clubs, which held regular meetings in mosques and faculty-level prayer rooms. The Tarbiyah movement was one of many religious study groups that met on university campuses during this period. Tarbiyah was inspired by the methods and teachings of the Muslim Brotherhood, particularly the teachings and methods of Ḥasan al-Bannā. Like al-Bannā, Tarbiyah members believed that Islamization of the state necessitated a long-term strategy that began with Islamic education and the encouragement of personal piety among individual Muslims.

With the fall of Suharto's New Order regime in 1998 and the subsequent lifting of restrictions on political party formation, Tarbiyah leaders decided to form the Justice Party (Partai Keadilan; PK). In the 1999 elections, PK was the only party with a cadre structure and a clearly delineated platform. In these first elections, it obtained 1.52 percent of the vote and seven seats in the legislature. It partnered with the National Mandate Party (Partai Amanat Nasional, PAN) to form the Reform Fraction. However, because it failed to pass the 2-percent electoral threshold, it reformed itself in order to contest the 2004 elections as the Prosperous Justice Party.

The PKS is the political wing of a mass Islamic movement with a clear religious mission of *dakwah* (Islamic propagation), *tarbiyah* (Islamic education), and service to the community, the nation, and the global Islamic *ummah*. The PKS cadre sees its primary goal as educating Muslims about Islam and specifically about how Islam offers comprehensive solutions to the political, economic, social, and societal challenges facing Indonesians. The party seeks not only to place its cadre in governmental institutions to introduce Islamic principles into policy and elect its cadre to public office but also to encourage Indonesian Muslims to accept Islamic policies. The PKS cadre regularly holds religious study groups targeting students and housewives; it establishes Islamic schools, creates publications, and hosts social welfare activities to show the universal applications of *Sharīʿah*. In these activities, the PKS employs religiously neutral language in order to raise awareness about Islamic principles and *Sharīʿah* without using the specific label of *Sharīʿah*.

In the 2004 elections, the PKS increased its share of the vote from 1.52 percent to 7.34 percent. This was attributed largely to the party elite's decision to deemphasize overtly Islamist themes like *Sharīʿah* in favor of universal messages stressing the need for a clean and caring government, social justice, and socioeconomic equality. This decision was based on a recognition of the preferences of Indonesian voters—specifically that their core political concerns centered on the economy and employment rather than religious or moral law—and that the PKS's religious goals would have to be reached incrementally over time and via popular socialization. In the 2004 and 2009 elections, the PKS has sought to project an inclusive image in order to earn the support of a wider array of voters. It has repeatedly formed electoral and legislative alliances with nationalist parties at the provincial and district levels. It also joined the governing coalition of President Susilo Bambang Yudhoyono in 2004, and again following the 2009 elections, despite protests from many members who believed the partnership comes at great cost to the party's integrity. In 2008 it declared itself an open party, invited non-Muslims to join, and ran non-Muslim candidates for the regional and district assemblies in majority non-Muslim areas.

The "openness strategy," as it has been termed, drew the ire of core supporters, who fear the party is compromising too much in pursuit of power. In 2009 the party largely maintained its share of the vote, with the percentage rising slightly to 7.88 percent and the total number of votes decreasing slightly, by 118,065.

The PKS's base among urban, educated, pious, young Muslims, particularly in the provinces of Jakarta, West Java, and Banten, remained steady. In 2004 they gained support from protest voters who were not necessarily Islamists but were disenchanted with the corruption and elitism of alternative candidates. Still, several PKS elites were implicated in corruption scandals, which cost it some of its core support. In 2009 they made inroads into rural farming communities in Central and East Java, as a result of social programs they ran through the Ministry of Agriculture.

BIBLIOGRAPHY

Hamayotsu, Kikue. "Beyond Faith and Identity: Mobilizing Islamic Youth in a Democratic Indonesia." *Pacific Review* 24, no. 2 (2010): 225–247.

Machmudi, Yon. *Islamising Indonesia: The Rise of Jemaah Tarbiyah and the Prosperous Justice Party.* Canberra: ANU E Press, 2008.

Julie Chernov Hwang

Partai Persatuan Pembangunan. The Partai Persatuan Pembangunan (Development Unity Party, abbreviated as Partai Persatuan, PPP, or P3) formed in 1973 through the merger of the four preexisting Islamic parties: the traditionalist NU (Nahdatul Ulama), the modernist Parmusi (Partai Muslimin Indonesia; Indonesian Muslim Party), and two other minor parties, the PSII (Partai Sarekat Islam Indonesia; Indonesian Party Union of Muslims) and Perti (Persatuan Tarbiyah Islam, United Islamic Education). The merger was imposed by the New Order government under General Suharto, who placed utmost importance on economic development, political stability, and national integration. The PPP was prohibited from pursuing an Islamic state as its goal and from using "Islam" or "Muslim" in its name. The government, to secure loyalty, also intervened in the selection of the PPP leadership.

In spite of these constraints, the PPP became increasingly confrontational vis-à-vis the government during the 1970s. The government had to revise its secular version of the Marriage Law bill in the face of Muslim criticism in 1973. Strong Islamic sentiments were mobilized in the 1977 general elections campaign for the PPP, who used the Kaʿbah as their party symbol. A number of charismatic *ʿulamāʾ* openly criticized the secularization, corruption, and inequality that the New Order had brought and urged Muslims to vote for the PPP as a religious obligation. The PPP received 29 percent of the national vote, obtaining the leading position in the capital city of Jakarta. The PPP staged a walkout from the parliament in 1978 in protest of the government's attempt to give Javanese mysticism (*aliran kepercayaan*) the same status as Islam. They maintained roughly the same level of popular support (28 percent) in the 1982 general elections.

Alarmed by the threat of political Islam, the government instituted a law requiring all social and political organizations to incorporate the state philosophy of Pancasila (Five Principles) as the sole foundation of their constitutions. The NU complied with this in 1983, followed by the PPP and others. The NU, however, was dissatisfied with the PPP leadership over the allocation of parliamentary seats and decided to withdraw its support from the PPP in 1984. In the 1987 general elections, the NU actively engaged in a "depression campaign" against the PPP; the results showed a drastic reduction in votes for the PPP, which received only 16 percent of the total. The replacement of the Kaʿbah with a star as the party symbol also contributed to this decline, symbolizing the fact that its constitution and statutes had become less explicitly Islamic. It received 17 percent of the total votes in the 1992 general elections.

Indonesian politics entered a new era after the collapse of Suharto's New Order regime in May 1998. Facing the 1999 general election, the PPP reinstated Islam as the sole foundation of the party, replacing Pancasila, in an attempt to rehabilitate the PPP's image and draw votes. The political reality saw a decline in the PPP's share of votes in three general elections, however, from 10.7 percent in 1999 to 8.15 percent in 2004 and 5.32 percent in 2009.

Scholars argue that the declining trend in votes for the PPP is related to two main factors. First, members of key traditional religious groups such as the NU and Masyumi, which had previously been the main constituents of the PPP, had swung their votes to the PKB (Partai Kebangkitan Bangsa, the National Awakening Party), PAN (Partai Amanat National, the National Mandate Party), and PKS (Partai Keadilan Sejahtera, the Prosperous Justice Party), and even voted for secular-nationalist parties such as Golkar, Partai Demokrasi Indonesia-Perjuangan, the Indonesian Democratic Party of Struggle, and Partai Demokrat, the Democratic Party. Second, the role of religion has become less significant in political life, and the role of political Islam in electoral politics remains minimal. The majority of Indonesian people disapprove of the use of religion, including Islamism and *Sharīʿah*-oriented ideology, in politics.

The PPP's leaders also have failed to support the values of pluralism in Indonesia. The PPP has become the icon of Islamic conservatism. Consequently, it fails to attract the young and moderate Muslim voters because they are unable to move upward in the PPP. Indeed, the future of the PPP is questionable. Scholars argue that the decline of the PPP and other Islamic parties can be seen as the end of political Islam in Indonesia. However, it would be fair to argue that the PPP's decline is due to its failure to respond to the changing political situation in Indonesia.

[*See also* Indonesia; *and* Nahdatul Ulama.]

BIBLIOGRAPHY

Bush, Robin. *Nahdlatul Ulama and the Struggle for Power within Islam and Politics in Indonesia*. Singapore: Institute of Southeast Asian Studies, 2009.

Fealy, Greg, and Sally White, eds. *Expressing Islam: Religious Life and Politics in Indonesia*. Singapore: Institute of Southeast Asian Studies, 2008.

Hamayotsu, Kikue. "The End of Political Islam? A Comparative Analysis of Religious Parties in the Muslim Democracy of Indonesia." *Journal of Current Southeast Asian Affairs* 30 (2011): 133–159.

Liddle, R. William, and Saiful Mujani. "Leadership, Party, and Religion: Explaining Voting Behavior in Indonesia." *Comparative Politics Studies* 40, no. 7 (2007) 832–857.

Sidel, John T. *Riots, Pogroms, Jihad: Religious Violence in Indonesia*. Ithaca, N.Y.: Cornell University Press, 2006.

Tanuwidjaja, Sunny. "Political Islam and Islamic Parties in Indonesia: Critically Assessing the Evidence of Islam's Political Decline." *Contemporary Southeast Asia* 32, no. 1 (2010): 29–49.

MITSUO NAKAMURA
Updated by MOHAMMAD SYAFI'I ANWAR

PARTY FOR DEMOCRATIC ACTION. The Party for Democratic Action (Stranka Demokratske Akcije, SDA) was founded in May 1990, on the eve of the first multiparty elections in Bosnia, then a socialist republic within the Socialist Federal Republic of Yugoslavia. The elections came in the wake of the weakening of the socialist political system and Communism in Yugoslavia and around the world.

Since its foundation, SDA has been a Muslim party because it sought to articulate political, state, economic, and cultural aspirations and interests of Muslims in Bosnia and throughout Yugoslavia. SDA is a national party and sees its political mission as reconciling Muslim communal interests with Bosnian multiethnic interests. Since Bosnia's independence, SDA has won a majority of Bosnian Muslim votes, even though the party's popularity and share of votes have been decreasing, especially since 2000. For this reason, the SDA was forced to seek coalition partners among other Bosniak parties, as well as among Bosnian Croats and Bosnian Serbs.

The SDA played a role in organizing resistance to Serbian aggression against Bosnia. It has also played a historical role in preserving Bosnia as a unified state and in building and bringing normality to postwar Bosnia.

In 1990, after his party won the majority of seats in the Bosnian Parliament, Alija Izetbegović was elected chairman of the presidency of the Republic of Bosnia and Herzegovina. Izetbegović's charisma ensured that the SDA remained the most influential political party in all general elections held between 1990 and 2002. Izetbegović served as SDA chairman between 1990 and 2001 before accepting the position of honorary chairman from 2001 to 2003.

Ideologically, many scholars regard the SDA to be partially an heir to the Young Muslim movement, which was founded in 1939 and made up of Muslim students in Sarajevo, Zagreb, and elsewhere. The movement was against both the Communists and the so-called Independent State of Croatia. Before it was outlawed in 1946, and before its leadership and members were arrested in 1949, the Young Muslims were a moral rather than political movement. This may explain some of the criticisms that the SDA has not yet evolved into a multiethnic party. Still, according to various analyses, the SDA's actions differed from those of the Islamic community, especially in the twenty-first century. Analysts insist that the tendency persisted, in light of the SDA's struggle to preserve Bosnia-Herzegovina's integrity, which was also reflected in the intensified participation in European projects to enhance European integration. Toward that end, the SDA cooperated with other parties, including the SDP (Social Democratic Party) and SzBiH (Stranka za Bosnu i Hercegovinu; Party for Bosnia-Herzegovina), which shared similar ideological orientations.

Still, neither the SDA nor other Bosnian parties were successful in solving the problem of corruption, which plagued the Balkan region. Over the course of its short lifespan, the SDA attained the role in the political system of Bosnia and Herzegovina of a champion pro-European party, anxious to secure the path toward Euro-atlantic integration.

[*See also* Bosnia and Herzegovina.]

BIBLIOGRAPHY

Filandra, Šaćir, and Enes Karić. *The Bosniac Idea.* Translated by Saba Risaluddin. Zagreb, Croatia: Nakladni Zavod Globus, 2004.

Izetbegović, Alija. *Inescapable Questions: Autobiographical Notes.* Leicester, U.K.: Islam Foundation, 2002.

Karić, Enes. *Prilozi za povijest islamskog mišljenja u Bosni i Hercegovini XX stoljeća.* Sarajevo, Bosnia: El-Kalem, 2004.

ENES KARIĆ
Updated by DŽENITA KARIĆ

PEACE AND PEACEBUILDING. In Arabic, *salām* and *silm* are the two main words used to refer to peace. They are both derived from the root *s-l-m*, whose different forms have the meanings of soundness, safety, and well-being. Neither *Islām* nor *al-Salām*, a term for God, is understood by classical Muslim exegetes or lexicographers as meaning "peace." Thus, when God is called *al-Salām*, according to Arab lexicographers and exegetes, it means that He is sound and without defect. *Islām* itself does not mean "peace" but "submission" (to God). Peace is a consequence of submission, either an inner peace of belief or a social peace of reconciliation among Arab tribes. Paradise, called *dār al-salām* in the Qurʾān, is the abode of perfection. Early Muslims used the words *silm* and *salm* for a treaty of reconciliation. In modern Arabic, the vocabulary of peace is enlarged. The word *amn*, which means "safety" and "security," is often used to refer to peace. Further, to render inner peace, intellectuals employ *ṭumaʾnīnah* (the tranquility [of the soul])—a Qurʾānic term. A sense of integrity, calm, and soundness is shared by these terms. Accordingly, the medieval Islamic conception tends to conceive of peace as harmony, protection, and confinement—a quest for a coherent and sound order. It is the opposite of *jāhilīyah*—a state of war, chaos, and turbulence. To be a Muslim is to disavow disbelief and to be sound, *barāʾah*, with a protective attitude of disengagement. Accordingly, the Muslim greeting, "peace be upon you" (*al-salām ʿalaykum*), is reserved for Muslims. The abode of disbelief, *dār al-kufr*, is also the abode of war, *dār al-ḥarb*, but peace is possible between the abode of Islam and the abode of war through a treaty of reconciliation, *ṣulḥ*.

In the famous verse 8:61, the Qurʾān uses the word *salm/silm* to denote peace, and Pickthall translates it as follows: "And if they incline to peace, incline thou also to it, and trust in Allah." In fact, here, the Qurʾānic peace is limited to reconciliation. It is not a call to a general peace or to prefer peace over war with non-Muslims. Hence, a majority of classical exegetes understand *salm/silm* to mean reconciliation initiated by non-Muslims. Few exegetes interpret *salm/silm* as a non-Muslim quest for safety and exoneration from war. That is, if they initiate submission, fearing the consequences of war, you should accept it. This interpretation inspires modern radical Salafīs. A group of exegetes see in *salm/silm* another term for Islam, which indicates in this case that Muslims should accept the formal conversion to Islam of non-Muslims without questioning their real intentions. The importance of the verse reemerged in modern Muslim discourse to justify peace treaties signed by Muslim leaders with non-Muslims. The popular Egyptian exegete Muḥammad Mutawallī al-Shaʿrāwī (d. 1998) epitomizes the modern scholarly Sunnī attitude of peace with non-Muslims. He claims accepting peace with others, if they lean toward it, is necessary. For him, religion wants social peace, and Islam should not be spread with force but by persuasion and wisdom. The outcome of Islamic radical violence in Egypt and elsewhere makes religious authorities favorable to peace.

In addition to *ṣulḥ*, denoting peace treaties, the jurists use the term *amān*. It is a contract, individual or communitarian, that bars hostilities with non-Muslims temporarily or for a longer period. This *amān* is of two sorts: the first is an *amān* contracted by the imam or his deputy. It could be temporary, such as a truce, *hudnah*; treaty, *muʿāhadah*; or agreement, *muwādaʿah*, in which the imam intervenes to stop fighting for a limited time. The *amān* can be a continuous one, *muʾabbad*, also called a protection contract, *ʿaqd al-dhimmah*. In the latter case, peace with non-Muslims is contracted in exchange for paying a tax, *jizyah*, and living under Muslim rule. The second sort of *amān* is issued by individual Muslims for a limited number of non-Muslims and length of time. Jurists attach a special importance to *amān*, as it assures the sanctity of life, religion, and property. Non-Muslims should enjoy peace through *amān*, they argue, which means that their lives, freedom, and property should be safe. Their protection is necessary for the credibility of Islamic law and order. For this reason, they require the imam to assume the function of guaranteeing the *amān* contract. The same teleological concern can be seen in the jurists' approval of war; it is usually justified by the preservation of religion, life, and property. In consequence, peace is interrelated with security.

The security-based conception of peace in Islamic jurisprudence is balanced by the Ṣūfī spiritual conception. Through self-discipline, nonviolence, and a quest for the divine, this conception promotes universality. Ṣūfī traditions encourage peace over war and conflict. Peace is said to be the means to righteousness and the gate of safety in the hereafter. Other traditions encourage adopting a peaceful attitude as a condition to adhere to the Ṣūfī way. For instance, Abū ʿAbd al-Raḥmān al-Sulamī (d. 1021) asserts that the Ṣūfī companionship, *ṣuḥbah*, mandates avoiding hatred, sticking to reconciliation, and forgiving companions. The disciple is also required to use the tongue rather than the sword to preach Sufism and to win over the enemy through benevolence. The perfect wisdom he should offer is a call to reconciliation.

In modern times, several Muslim thinkers have developed, in divergent manners, a theology of peace in Islam. The most popular among Muslim activists is *al-Salām al-ʿālamī wa-al-Islām* by Sayyid Quṭb (d. 1966). According to Quṭb, in Islam peace is a rule and war is a necessity. However, war is continuous and should be sustained until the achievement of divine order on earth. People would be free from slavery, except to God. His idea of a link between Islamic monotheism and peace is recurrent in the modern literature on the subject. There is a necessity to sustain war, Quṭb argues, because aggression on Islam by non-Muslims is to be driven out. Quṭb claims that the call to Islam, *daʿwah*, is universal and should be allowed to achieve its mission. Any attempt to prevent it would be seen as war on Islam. In case enemies prevent the call to Islam, like Quraysh did with Muḥammad, war should be launched. For Quṭb, peace is a unity of freedom, justice, and safety according to God's word. In his view, universal peace does not equal international peace. Rather, it is the sum of peace achieved at the levels of the individual, the family, and the community. At the individual level, Quṭb emphasizes tranquility of the believer, repentance, and unity of God. Any pious Muslim, not just Ṣūfīs, would subscribe to his description of inner peace here. According to Quṭb, peace in the family is realized through marriage, as he rejects gender mixing and unveiling (*tabarruj*). He supports divorce and polygamy. Further, he promotes family solidarity, which creates social peace through love, compassion, moral conduct, and cooperation. The Quṭbian family enjoys a conservative lifestyle that is seriously challenged by Western norms adopted in some Muslim societies. For him, peace and the Islamic way of life are interconnected, and any non-Islamic principle or mode is associated with the pre-Islamic period and chaos. As for the community, the relation between the subjects and the ruler should be based on consultation, *shūrā*. If the ruler applies *Sharīʿah*, peace will reign and corruption should vanish. *Sharīʿah* makes peace; it assures absolute justice and guarantees the human rights of life, property, honor, sustenance, and freedom. Thus, it creates a social balance where wealth is redistributed equitably for the public interest. Quṭb highlights Muslim economic principles such as the forbidding of usury, *ribā*, as well as the monopoly and establishment of *zakāt* to maintain social peace. With reference to the Muslim view of world peace, Quṭb asserts that its first principle is *jihād* in the way of God; *jihād* is both defensive (protecting the Muslim lands) and aggressive (defending the right to *daʿwah* and establishing God's word and justice on earth). Quṭb believes that Islam has a liberating message to humanity, and peace is secondary to the universality of this message. Islam is a continuous *jihād* to establish the divine order. Besides *jihād*, Quṭb thinks that Islam can offer the world tolerance and ethical transactions. In sum, world peace is not an objective state that should be sought by Muslims. Islam is peace itself and should be the key in peacemaking. Quṭb's conception is an example of the vision of peace among Salafīs and militant Islamism. It is a peace established as the outcome of an ideological total war; a sort of imperial peace as preached by Eastern and Western ideologues in the twentieth century. Quṭb certainly uses the core material of the medieval Muslim jurists and exegetes, but his horizon is modern and totalitarian. While medieval jurists were much more pragmatic, modern Islamists perceive peace as the end of history, in a similar vein to international socialism or neoliberalism. They belong to their time.

Quṭb's ideal of peace is increasingly challenged by Muslim peace thinkers in the Muslim world and the West. One outstanding example is the Syrian Jawdat Saʿīd (b. 1931). Living the ascetic life of a simple farmer in the Syrian village of Biʾr al-ʿAjam, he has developed a unique form of pacifist thought in the Muslim world, shaped by Gandhi (d. 1948), Muhammad Iqbal (d. 1938), and Mālik b. Nabī (d. 1973). Saʿīd discerns a lesson from prophetic disobedience. Since Adam, the prophets taught humanity to reject violence as a way of change. He asserts, in particular, that Muḥammad's experience with moral, social, and political issues was based on persuasion rather than violence. In his view, the *khilāfah* (632–661) is as peaceful as Muḥammad's order. Willing to idealize the holy figures of Islam, he falls into a defense of *jihād* as well. For him, *jihād* is war for a just society and should be preceded by persuasion in a peaceful society. That is, only an elected government can wage war. Saʿīd does not see in Islam a universal message that should be spread, as Quṭb does. Reason is universal and all humans should make their own peaceful and just societies. He claims early Muslims did not use violence for the sake of worldly goals. They endorsed the Qurʾānic view of peace and violence that consists of fighting unjust violence with justice. Saʿīd supports his claim by citing Muḥammad's refusal to use violence in the Meccan period. He wanted to transmit a peaceful message by peaceful means. Saʿīd undermines the importance of the Medinan prophetic *jihād*. In his view, prophetic violence was a tool to establish justice in Medina. Saʿīd's thought is subtle. Peace is the primary attitude Muslims should adopt; they should not start conflict in any case. Calling to Islam should be peaceful, and peace should be the basis of an Islamic society. Violence is only permissible if a society agrees to use it to establish justice and to end persecution. In this case, violence should only be employed by a mature and rational authority. Force should be used proportionally to remove injustice. He thinks that peace creates spiritual force, science, democracy, and justice. In international relations, Saʿīd criticizes Muslim attitudes toward external occupation and American hegemony. He thinks world peace is only relevant if Muslims make peace essential to their societies. Although he vehemently rejects American hegemony, based on violent policies, he focuses on building a Muslim rationalist and humanist ethos. He often calls on followers to learn from the Japanese experience after World War II: coping with the American hegemony through science, democracy, and economic development rather than passion and violence. For current Muslim societies, he preaches peaceful resistance to occupation and despotism. Naturally, this idea is resisted by many opponents. However, he also dismisses the policies of current regimes. Further, he totally rejects the Islamic movements, which he compares to *khawārij*—violent Muslim dissidents in early Islam.

Similarly to Saʿīd, Asghar Ali Engineer (b. 1939), an Indian Muslim reformist based in Mumbai, combines a call to peace with promotion of justice. In his view, violence is inherent in the human condition, and Islam, as a religion, is peaceful by nature. The Qur'ān tries to regulate violence, but does not encourage it. Engineer interprets *jihād* verses as defensive. During the history of Islam, violence is either caused by Arabian society or is the result of the struggle for power among leaders. In his thought, Islam is, above all, a spiritual experience. His interpretation draws on Ṣūfī teachings and Islamic ethics to put forward self-control as the true *jihād*. Addressing an audience of Muslims in southeast India, consumed by ethnic and religious violence, he exploits a set of pacifist Indian ideas, especially ones based on Hinduism and Buddhism. In addition to Indian influences, his criticism of power, greed, and domination attest to his socialist tendencies as well.

With regard to peacebuilding, Mohammed Abu-Nimer, a Palestinian academic and expert on peace, based in the United States, draws on many principles of Islam to formulate an Islamic philosophy of peacemaking. His concern is to transform Islamic teachings into a means of peacebuilding. For example, Muslim rituals such as prayers and fasting could serve as opportunities to train for nonviolent actions. Hunger strikes, uniformity, and discipline, to name but a few, are forms of struggle that could be encouraged. Religious chanting could be a channel for peaceful marches and meetings. This moral interpretation of Islam is inspired by Sufism and Asian philosophies. It selects some principles within Islamic traditions and avoids militant aspects of Islam.

In recent years, a group of Muslim scholars undertook a distinguished peace initiative, most notably in "A Common Word between Us and You," the famous open letter addressed by 138 Muslim scholars to Pope Benedict XVI on 13 October 2007. They emphasize the necessity of peace and justice between Muslims and Christians as a necessary process for world peace. This peace should be based on the common love of the one God and of one's neighbors. The document draws on inner peace as well, inspired by Ṣūfī scholars who took part in the initiative, but it has not yet spread widely within the Muslim world. At local levels, a noteworthy example of a peace initiative is the Algerian post-civil-war Charter for Peace and National Reconciliation, affirmed by referendum on 29 September 2005 (accepted with 97 percent of the vote). Nonetheless, the apparent electoral support should not hide the superficial character of the initiative. It was promoted by a contested regime who annulled the results of a democratic election. Further, the initiative exonerates governmental violence and punishes radical Islamists. Above all, peace is seen as an end of hostilities and not the beginning of development and democracy. An Equity and Reconciliation Commission, a similar Moroccan initiative, was proposed by the King Muḥammad VI in 2004 in the aftermath of several oppressive years under Ḥasan II. Both initiatives instilled a positive environment but failed to address the root causes of violence: autocracy and social inequality.

Bibliography

Books

Engineer, Asghar Ali. *On Developing Theology of Peace in Islam*. Delhi: Sterling, 2003.

Ibn Fāris al-Qazwīnī, Aḥmad. *Muʿjam maqāyīs al-lughah*. Edited by Shihāb al-Dīn Abū ʿAmr. Beirut: Dār al-Jīl, 1991.

Ibn Manẓūr, Muḥammad ibn Mukarram. *Lisān al-ʿArab*. Edited by ʿĀmir Aḥmad Ḥaydar and ʿAbd al-Munʿim Khalīl Ibrāhīm. 18 vols. Beirut: Dār al-Kutub al-ʿIlmīyah, 2003–2005.

Quṭb, Sayyid. *Al-Salām al-ʿālamī wa-al-Islām*. Cairo: Dār al-Shurūq, 1989.

Shaʿrāwī, Muḥammad Mutawallī al-. *Tafsīr al-Shaʿrāwī*. 24 vols. Cairo: Akhbār al-Yawm, 1991–1993.

Sulamī, Abū ʿAbd al-Raḥmān al-. *Ādāb al-ṣuḥbah wa-ḥusn al-ʿishrah*. Edited by Majdī Fatḥī al-Sayyid. Ṭanṭā, Egypt: Dār al-Ṣaḥābah lil-Turāth, 1990.

Ṭabarī, Abū Jaʿfar Muḥammad ibn Jarīr al-. *Jāmiʿ al-bayān fī taʾwīl al-Qurʾān*. Edited by Aḥmad Muḥammad Shākir. Beirut: Muʾassasat al-Risālah, 2000.

Zuḥaylī, Wahbah al-. *Al-fiqh al-islāmī wa-adillatuh.* Damascus: Dār al-Fikr, 2008.

Journal Articles

Abu-Nimer, Mohammed. "A Framework for Nonviolence and Peacebuilding in Islam." *Journal of Law and Religion* 15 (2000–2001): 217–265.

Larcher, Pierre. "Le concept de paix et ses expressions en arabe." *Cahiers de la Paix* 8 (2001): 95–105.

Said, Jawdat. "Law, Religion, and the Prophetic Method of Social Change." Translated by Afra Jalabi. *Journal of Law and Religion* 15 (2000–2001): 83–150.

Abdessamad Belhaj

Personal Status Codes. Personal status codes in Muslim countries show a large amount of variation both in form and substance. While in many countries rules pertaining to personal status are codified separately—as is the case in Egypt, Morocco, Sudan, Pakistan, Malaysia, Indonesia, Mali, and Nigeria (in Egypt, the codification of Islamic personal status law has been partial)—in other countries personal status law forms part of the civil code (as is the case in Afghanistan and Iran). In Saudi Arabia there is no codified personal status law since here, as in many other areas of law, *Sharīʿah* itself constitutes the national law. In federations such as Malaysia and Nigeria a secular code of family law falls under the jurisdiction of the federal government, whereas Islamic and customary personal status laws fall under the jurisdiction of individual states. It is therefore difficult to use "personal status code" as the unit of comparison for all Muslim countries—indeed, in most Muslim countries Muslims and non-Muslims are likely to refer to different laws. Whatever the form of codification, the substance of personal status law must be regarded as a contemporary, national interpretation—and adaptation—of values and norms derived from classical Islamic law.

Different Schools of Islamic Thought. National personal status laws bear the marks of differing Islamic schools of thought (sing. *madhhab*) as source of law. By way of example, the family law of Egypt, Afghanistan, and Pakistan is based on the Ḥanafī school of *fiqh* (jurisprudence); Morocco, Mali, and Nigeria take inspiration from the Mālikī school; Saudi Arabia's legal system draws on the Ḥanbalī *fiqh* books; Indonesia and Malaysia look to Shāfiʿī jurisprudence; and Iran's legal system refers to Shīʿī jurisprudence of the Twelver school. Though these schools of thought share many provisions, they have also led to differences between the national legal systems. For example, Shīʿī inheritance law grants a more egalitarian position to females as legal heirs than does Sunnī law.

In modern times, these schools have become less exclusive. During the drafting of personal status laws, reformers made increasing use of the *fiqh* principle of selectivity (*takhayyur*). *Sharīʿah* norms that were drafted and enacted as statute law—which was premised on European legal structures and concepts—were often based on a mixing of "some general and partial principles or views from one school of Islamic jurisprudence with those derived from other schools, without due regard to the methodological basis or conceptual coherence of any of the schools whose authority was being invoked" (An-Naim, 2008, p. 332). For example, in Sudan the Muslim Personal Act of 1991 is predominantly based on the Ḥanafī school, but in order to introduce reforms, solutions from the other three Sunnī schools of law, especially the Mālikī school, have been inserted (Köndgen, in Otto, 2010, p. 205). Similar developments have taken place in Egypt, where in 2000 a law was introduced that allowed for a divorce requested by the wife without the need for consent of the husband. This nonconsensual form of *khulʿ* meant a radical break with the *khulʿ* as commonly defined by classical Islamic jurisprudence (Berger and Sonneveld, in Otto, 2010, p. 76).

Dual or Triple Foundation. Generally speaking, legal systems in most Muslim majority countries are built on either a dual or triple foundation, with national (civil/common) law, *Sharīʿah*, and customary law being the main sources of law. It is in the area of personal status law—compared, for example, to constitutional law, administrative law, criminal law, and property law—that *Sharīʿah* has had the most influence. With the notable exceptions of countries that have a secular family law according to a Western European model, such as Turkey, or where uncodified *Sharīʿah* is applied in marital affairs, such as Saudi Arabia and in northern Nigeria, the personal status laws of most Muslim countries show varying levels of incorporation of classical *Sharīʿah* into their national law of personal status.

Until the twentieth century *Sharīʿah* functionaries—*muftīs*, *qāḍīs*, and other ulama—in most Muslim countries occupied important positions in political and social life. However, rule-enacting and adjudication were gradually transferred to state institutions governed by a new legal elite. After gaining independence during the twentieth century, most Muslim states did not particularly favor parallel legal systems, and *Sharīʿah* was therefore usually incorporated into the laws and infrastructure of the state itself.

Coverage of Personal Status Codes in Muslim Countries. Personal status codes, characteristically, include all procedural and substantive rules pertaining to marriage (rules for validity, interreligious marriage, marriage age, marriage registration, dowry, bride price, maintenance during marriage, rights of wife and husband); polygamy; divorce (by mutual consent or repudiation, financial compensation after divorce); custody (guardianship, support). Taken together with inheritance matters, these topics comprise what is often referred to as the legal status of women in the Muslim world.

The status of women under Islamic law has emerged as one of the main symbols of political struggle between social and religious groups throughout the Muslim world. Social, political, and legal struggles have been fought in every Muslim country about each of these topics. Personal status laws can therefore be regarded as the temporary outcomes of the confrontations and reconciliations of sociopolitical and religious forces.

Reforms of Personal Status Laws: Trends. The Iranian Islamic Revolution of 1979 marked the beginning of almost a decade of reforms, notably in Iran and Sudan, that undid many earlier legal reforms that had liberated women from traditional patriarchal dominance. It also led to a global outcry against the Islamization of laws. However, it did not affect the personal status laws in populous Muslim countries such as Pakistan, Indonesia, and Egypt, whose relatively liberal marriage laws of 1961, 1974, and 1979, respectively, remained largely intact. In the personal status laws of these latter countries, male unilateral divorce and polygamy were restricted by procedural and substantive requirements, which had been implemented in case law and in (standard) marriage contracts. Such restrictive provisions vary in their comprehensiveness and effectiveness. In recent decades Egypt and Morocco have enacted new laws that further improve the legal status of women in marital affairs. A closer look at legal developments in several Muslim countries shows that as a result of political give-and-take, the legal status of women has improved in some aspects while worsening in others. Such changes can take place simultaneously or consecutively. In the case of Iran, Ziba Mir-Hosseini (in Otto, 2010, p. 353) notes that patriarchal mandates of classical jurisprudence are validated while attempts are made to protect and compensate women in the face of them. Such ambiguity characterizes the legal systems in many Muslim countries. When compared to the areas of marriage and divorce, fewer reforms seem to have taken place in regard to inheritance and/or custody.

In recent decades international monitoring of compliance with the 1979 Convention for Elimination of All Forms of Discrimination Against Women has increased pressure on national governments to modernize their personal status laws. At the same time Islamist forces, both domestic and transnational, have stepped up efforts to Islamize national laws in Muslim countries. These diametrically opposed developments have led to increased discord within (inter)national political discussions about personal status laws. In most Muslim countries this debate flares up a few times a year, especially when attention is called to specific events and issues, such as a new bill, a court case, a public statement by an official, or a personal tragedy covered by mass media, or at times an election. Otherwise, the debate keeps simmering in the background.

Political Configurations Regarding the Islamization of Personal Status Codes. Political configurations concerning issues of personal status law vary de facto according to space and time. Major roles in most countries are played by the government, the religious establishment, Islamist groups and parties, traditional (tribal) leaders, legislature, legal professions, human rights and feminist organizations, Ṣūfī groups, and international donor organizations. In most Muslim countries the government performs a balancing act between "orthodox" and "modernist" groups—or, to borrow Khaled Abou El Fadl's (2005) terms, between puritans and moderates—and naturally, the extent to which one group has the upper hand over the other varies per country. The political situation is often reflected in changes in personal status codes. For example, in Iran the Protection of the Family bill, which was drafted by Mahmoud Ahmadinejad's government in 2007 and which inter alia made it easier for men to be polygamous, led to such protests among women's movements that members of Parliament were persuaded to withdraw the bill in 2008. However, following the unrest after the 2009 election, the article on polygamy (Art. 23) was modified and reintroduced. In January 2010 Parliament ratified the bill, using the closure of the reformist press and the imprisonment of a number of women activists to its advantage. In the following years, however, it was not ratified by the Guardian Council (cf. Mir-Hosseini, in Otto, 2010, pp. 356 f.).

Similarly, in Morocco, when far-reaching reforms in family law were drafted by the government in 1999, which led to fierce confrontations between Islamists and those supporting the reforms, it is significant that the debate was almost fully waged in Islamic terms (Buskens, in Otto, 2010, p. 108). Progressive groups frequently referenced the applicability of universal human, women's, and children's rights, and the importance of complying with international women's conventions, but they never dared frame Moroccan family law in secular terms.

The Complex Relationship between *Sharīʿah* and Custom. As stated above, in many Muslim countries matters pertaining to personal status are often not only ruled by national law infused with Islamic law, but customary law usually also plays an important role. Customary rules were often already present before the rise of *Sharīʿah*, and in certain areas a consensus emerged through mutual acceptance and adaptation. In other areas, tension grew between local leaders and Islamic authorities.

There is evidence from several countries in both Africa and Asia that there is a strong demand by women for *Sharīʿah* as a substitute for tribal justice. Amid much contemporary criticism of *Sharīʿah*, it is often forgotten that the only available alternative in many places is not an effective and fair, state justice system but rather a semi-functional customary system. Western media often do not distinguish precisely between Islamic court rulings and mob justice or abuse of power by local clan leaders, policemen, or other officials. If clan members kill a woman accused of fornication (*zinā*) by stoning, as has happened repeatedly in Pakistan, one needs to remember that these ordeals take place in flagrant violation of the procedural and evidential rules of both *Sharīʿah* and national law.

Country Surveys. The following sections look more closely at the issues at stake and the actual changes and content of personal status codes in a number of Muslim countries. For a comprehensive examination of each country, see the respective chapters in Otto, 2010.

Egypt. The first major reform of personal status law in Egypt since the 1920s took place in 1979 when Anwar Sadat passed a progressive Marriage Law in favor of women. The act was so controversial that some judges refused to implement it. After the Supreme Constitutional Court annulled this law, the government, then under Hosni Mubarak, pushed through a slightly more moderate version of the same law. Still, this 1985 law was far more progressive and pro-women's rights than the personal status laws of the 1920s had been (El Alami, 1994, pp. 116–130). For example, the law introduced a payment of compensation in cases where a woman was divorced against her will and without any cause on her part.

The first years of the new millennium witnessed several substantive reforms. Article 20 of Law 1/2000 provides women with the right to apply for divorce without the husband's consent through a court procedure called *khulʿ*. Although *khulʿ* was presented as being in accordance with the *Sharīʿah*, as such it is not part of the corpus of any of the four Sunnī schools of jurisprudence (which recognize *khulʿ* as a divorce initiated by the wife but requiring the husband's consent). With this law therefore the legislature further expanded its authority to interpret the *Sharīʿah*.

Also in 2000 a new standard marriage contract was adopted by law, which confers on women the right to insert conditions such as the right to an automatic divorce in the event the husband takes another wife and the right to work and education. In November 2000 another law was enacted that allowed women to apply for a passport—and thus travel—without their husbands' consent. Also since 2000, deadbeat ex-husbands can be punished with jail sentences of up to thirty days.

Morocco. Patriarchy was until recently the touchstone for the basis of Moroccan family law, which required a wife's obedience to her husband and allowed polygamy on the part of husbands, the marrying off of daughters by their male guardians, and male unilateral divorce. In 1992–1993 King Hassan II introduced some modest reforms, but a more significant reform occurred in 2004 when King Mohammed VI proclaimed the new Family Code (*Mudawwanat al-usra*). The new law promotes the stability of a nuclear family, within which men and women are to act as equals. Article 4 states that the goal of marriage is "the creation of a stable family under the supervision of both spouses."

According to the 2004 law, adult Moroccan women can marry without a male guardian, if they choose to do so. The minimum marriage age for women rose from fifteen to eighteen years, which equals the minimum age for men (Art. 19). Article 20 allows the judge to exempt women from this requirement. Polygamy by men is further restricted: a man can only marry another woman with permission from the judge, his current wife, and his future wife (Arts. 40–46). If he violates his promise not to take a second wife, his first wife can apply for a judicial divorce.

Some traditional patriarchal elements remained in the 2004 law. For example, unilateral divorce by the husband (*ṭalāq*) continues to exist, but now requires judicial approval. However, in addition to *ṭalāq*, a new set of rules was introduced that allows both spouses to ask for a judicial divorce. On the other hand, the husband's traditional duty to provide maintenance to his wife and children was kept intact (Arts. 194, 197, 198).

Iran. In the case of Iran, the 1967 Family Protection Law (FPL) introduced substantive reforms to the 1935 Civil Code, whose provisions on family law were basically those of Shīʿī *fiqh*. Courts known as "FPL Courts" were created, men's right to *ṭalāq* was eliminated, women's grounds for divorce were expanded, and polygamy was restricted. These reforms were dismantled shortly after the 1979 revolution by the Special Civil Courts Legislation, which abolished the FPL Courts and created courts presided over by religious judges. At the same time, some of the earlier reforms were retained, such as the need for a court order for divorce. By the mid-1990s many of the dismantled reforms were reinstated, although in a different guise. In 1992 a bill called Amendments to Divorce Laws abolished all extra-judicial divorces and entitled women to demand "wages in kind" at the time of divorce. During the presidency of Khatami (1997–2005) and when reformists had a majority in Parliament (2000–2004), a number of bills were introduced with the object of reducing gender inequality. Almost all were rejected by the Guardian Council, however. In 2007 under Ahmadinejad, Parliament introduced the Protection of the Family bill, which allows a man to register additional marriages if he can establish certain conditions, including financial guarantees. It also relaxes regulations for the registration of temporary marriages, requires tax payments from women at the time of marriage if they ask for a marriage gift that exceeds a certain limit, and limits compensation payments if the husband wants a divorce. This bill, as said, was heavily contested and has now been pending for years.

Pakistan. While family-related matters in Pakistan are in general governed by the Muslim Family Laws Ordinance (MFLO) of 1961, the Protection of Women Act of 2006 has had some impact on the position of women within this legal system. Section 7 of the MFLO recognizes the traditional unilateral divorce initiated by the husband, but subjects him to a compulsory procedure that will invalidate the divorce if not followed strictly. This particular clause was complicated by the Zina Ordinance of 1979, which criminalized sexual relations outside of marriage. Abandoned wives who had since remarried were thereupon accused of adultery by their former husbands, who claimed that because they had not followed the compulsory procedure outlined in Section 7 of the MFLO, they were still married to their wives. The 2006 Protection of Women Act solved the issue by stating that it was sufficient for a woman to believe herself to be validly married to avoid the charge of adultery.

The right of divorce by repudiation can be delegated to the wife by the husband at the time of the marriage, in accordance with Section 8 of the MFLO. Recent case law has also given Muslim women the right to seek a judicial dissolution of their marriage. "Women are now able to procure a divorce solely on the basis of their own testimony to the effect that their marriage has broken down and that they can no longer live with their husbands 'within the limits of Allah'" (Lau, in Otto, 2010, p. 416).

Indonesia. In Indonesia, the world's most populous Muslim country, marriage, divorce, and matrimonial property are all regulated by the Marriage Act 1/1974. Since 1974 two government regulations (GR 9/1975 and GR 10/1983) have been added and in 1991 the Compilation of Islamic Law (*Kompilasi Hukum Islam di Indonesia*), addressing marriage and inheritance law, was introduced. In terms of its rules and provisions, the Compilation only differs from the 1974 Marriage

Act in that some Indonesian terms are replaced with equivalent Arabic terminology. The 1974 Marriage Act curbs the right of Muslim husbands to divorce their wives unilaterally. It also grants wives a variety of instruments through which to obtain divorce and sets clear limits on polygamy. GR 10 of 1983 makes unilateral repudiation more difficult for state civil servants than for ordinary people, and even forbids two state officials from concluding a polygamous marriage. Lastly, upon entering marriage, both husband and wife have the right to joint marital property—a concept that is unknown in classical *Sharīʿah*. These provisions demonstrate the state's preference for equal rights for men and women.

[*See also* Egypt; Family; Fiqh; Indonesia; Iran, Islamic Republic of; *and* Morocco.]

BIBLIOGRAPHY

Abou El Fadl, Khaled. *The Great Theft: Wrestling Islam from the Extremists*. New York: HarperCollins, 2005.

An-Naim, Abdullahi Ahmed. *Islamic Family Law in a Changing World: A Global Resource Book*. London: Zed, 2002.

An-Naim, Abdullahi Ahmed. "Shari'a in the Secular State: A Paradox of Separation and Conflation." In *The Law Applied: Contextualizing the Islamic Shariʿa. A Volume in Honor of Frank E. Vogel*, edited by Peri Bearman Wolfhart Heinrichs and Bernard G. Weiss. London: Tauris, 2008.

El Alami, D. S. "Law No. 100 of 1985 Amending Certain Provisions of Egypt's Personal Status Laws." *Islamic Law and Society* 1, no. 1 (1994).

Esposito John, with Natana J. DeLong-Bas. *Women in Muslim Family Law*. Syracuse, N.Y.: Syracuse University Press, 2001.

Otto, J. M., ed. *Sharia Incorporated: A Comparative Overview of the Legal Systems of Twelve Muslim Countries in Past and Present*. Leiden: Leiden University Press, 2010. For this article, the chapters by Leon Buskens (Morocco), Ziba Mir-Hosseini (Iran), Martin Lau (Pakistan), and Jan Michiel Otto (Indonesia) have been heavily consulted.

Sonneveld, Nadia. "*Khulʿ* Divorce in Egypt: Public Debates, Judicial Practices, and Everyday Life." Unpublished PhD diss., University of Amsterdam, 2009.

Welchman, Lynn. *Women and Muslim Family Laws: A Comparative Overview of Textual Development and Advocacy*. Amsterdam: Amsterdam University Press, 2010.

JAN MICHIEL OTTO
and HANNAH MASON

PESANTREN. *See* Education, Muslim.

PHILIPPINES. The Philippines has often been described as Asia's Catholic country, with about 85 percent of its people professing the religion. There is, however, a Muslim minority that constitutes about 5 percent of the estimated 2011 Philippine population of 101,833,938. The majority of Muslims are concentrated in the central and western parts of Mindanao and in the Sulu archipelago and among thirteen ethnic groups, the major ones being Maranao, Maguindanao, Tausug, Yakan, and Samal. However, an internal migration spurred by the Muslim-government military conflict in the 1970s and the search for better economic opportunities have driven Muslims to traditionally Christian areas in other parts of the Philippines. In addition, Philippine labor export to the Middle East, especially to Saudi Arabia, has contributed to the growing number of converts. Known as Balik Islam (those who "return" to Islam), they are former Catholics and members of other Christian denominations whose conversion took place either in the Middle East or upon their return to the Philippines. The Balik Islam groups include organizations such as the Fi Sabilillah Dawah and Media Foundation, Islamic Information Center, Darul Hijrah, Islamic Wisdom Worldwide, and the Islamic Studies Call and Guidance. There are, however, some Balik Islam groups, such as the Rajah Solaiman

Movement, which had been engaged in militant activities and were under government surveillance.

Philippine Muslims are overwhelmingly Sunnīs, but there are also Shīʿahs and Aḥmadīyah. The Tablīghī Jamāʿat, which was brought by Pakistani Muslims to the Philippines in the 1970s, has also become more visible in recent years as members pursue *daʿwah* in various parts of the country.

Introduction of Islam; Spanish and American Rule. Muslim traders and preachers brought Islam to the southern Philippines around the thirteenth century. Coming by way of Malaysia, they established mosques, introduced the Qurʾān, intermarried with local people, and settled in the Philippines. Other Muslims from the Malay area founded principalities in the southern Philippines. By the time the Spaniards colonized the country in 1565, there were already established Muslim principalities in Sulu, Maguindanao, and Buayan. Spanish authorities succeeded in conquering and Christianizing other parts of the country, but not the south, where these three principalities offered formidable resistance.

The three hundred and fifty years of Spanish rule in the Philippines were punctuated by warfare between Spaniards and Moros (the Spanish name for Muslims), with Christianized natives serving Spain. Although the wars were fought for conquest, for purposes of retaliation, or for economic reasons, they were viewed as wars between Muslims and Christians, since Christianization was one of the goals of Spanish conquests. Colonial policies and literature privileged Christianity, and in time religion became a salient feature of Filipino identity.

In the latter half of the nineteenth century, Spain's efforts were directed more toward maintaining colonial control than toward Christianization. Spain became more concerned with defining and securing its Philippine borders amidst Dutch and British activities. With increasing economic losses, decline in agricultural productivity, and a reduction in maritime commerce resulting from Spanish incursions, the sultans and *datus* (chieftains) who had earlier resisted the colonizers were left with little choice but to sign treaties with the Spanish government making the Muslim areas part of Spanish colonial territory.

In 1898 Spain ceded the Philippines to the United States. Muslims continued their resistance, this time against the United States, but later capitulated to the militarily superior Americans. Agreements between American administrators and sultans defined the status of the latter and required them to relinquish temporal sovereignty in exchange for land grants and monetary compensation. The Americans left Islam and customary law untouched except those that ran counter to the U.S. Constitution and laws governing such things as slavery and polygamy.

Independence. When the Philippine Republic was established in 1946, Muslims found themselves included in a political structure without their consent. In 1951 a Senate committee studying the causes of an alarming breakdown of law and order in Muslim regions concluded that most Muslims did not identify themselves as Filipinos or agree with national policies.

Meanwhile, signs of a heightened Islamic awareness were becoming evident as hundreds of Muslims made the pilgrimage (*ḥajj*) to Mecca and returned with elevated prestige and increased religious fervor. New mosques and *madrasah*s (schools) were built, often with the aid of Middle Eastern Muslim organizations. The Egyptian government offered scholarships for Muslims to study at al-Azhar University in Cairo. This offer was matched by other Middle Eastern governments, so that by the 1990s Filipino Muslims were attending schools and universities in Saudi Arabia, Libya, Jordan, Kuwait, and other Arab countries. A new sense of pride and achievement arose among Moro youth, as a class of younger and better-educated local *ʿulamāʾ* (religious scholars) emerged.

Simultaneously, the conflict in Mindanao was being exacerbated by several factors: the influx of Christian settlers into traditionally Muslim lands, often with government support; continued national neglect of Muslim economic and educational aspirations; subtle discrimination against Muslims serving in top national offices; Muslim leaders' loss of political power in their former areas of influence; and severe land conflicts between Muslims and Christian settlers. These led to an increase in armed clashes between Christian and Muslim bands, in which the military usually sided with the former. Muslim claims of genocide elicited sympathy from the Muslim world. The proclamation of martial law by President Ferdinand Marcos in 1972, followed by military attempts to confiscate Muslim arms, led to open revolt. The most popular liberation front was the Moro National Liberation Front (MNLF), whose military arm was the Bangsamoro Army (BMA) under the leadership of Nur Misuari, a former instructor at the University of the Philippines. In 1977 the MNLF was given observer status in the Organization of the Islamic Conference (OIC).

Pressure from the OIC and mediation by Libya led the Philippine government and the MNLF to sign the 1976 Tripoli Agreement, which provided for some autonomy for thirteen provinces with sizable Muslim populations. Neither the autonomy granted by the Marcos government in 1977 nor that under the administration of Corazón Aquino in 1989 satisfied OIC expectations or MNLF demands. In early 1989 the MNLF renewed its demand for secession while seeking membership status in the OIC.

The Muslim uprising, along with diplomatic pressure from Muslim countries, persuaded the government to make various concessions, including the use of Arabic as a medium of instruction in schools attended by Muslims, the proclamation of Muslim religious feast days as legal holidays for Muslims, the codification of Muslim personal laws, and the creation of *Sharīʿah* courts. The top MNLF field commanders who had pledged their loyalty to the republic were rewarded with political positions or economic opportunities. In 1981 a Ministry of Islamic Affairs (now the Office of Muslim Affairs) was created, which regulates and facilitates the annual *ḥajj* and oversees mosque administration. Since 1982 the Department of Education and Culture has been involved in institutionalizing and integrating the *madrasah* curriculum into the regular Philippine curriculum. *Sharīʿah* courts are now functioning, with training programs for *Sharīʿah* lawyers. These were called for by the promulgation of the Code of Muslim Personal Laws during the rule of President Marcos.

In 1996, during the term of President Fidel Ramos, the MNLF signed a peace agreement with the Philippine government, but the agreement did not end the conflict, because Muslims perceived the inability of the government to follow up with development programs. This, coupled with internal politics among Muslims, contributed to the growth and expansion of other Muslim movements that also sought the establishment of an independent state, like the Moro Islamic Liberation Front (MILF), organized by Hashim Salamat, and the Abu Sayyaf group, organized by Abdurazak Janjalani. The MILF, which has replaced the MNLF as the largest organized Muslim movement, established various camps, organized as Muslim communities, in Mindanao. The government launched a major attack on the camps in 2000. There were several peace negotiations between the government and the MILF, but issues on terms of agreement continued to arise. In 2008 the government and the MILF were about to sign a Memorandum of Agreement on Ancestral Domain that would create a Moro homeland known as Bangsamoro Juridical Entity (BJE), but the Supreme Court declared the agreement unconstitutional. Peace talks have resumed, with Malaysia again serving as mediator. The Abu Sayyaf Group, which had claimed to be fighting for the establishment of an Islamic state, was listed as a terrorist group because of its kidnapping for ransom and its links with international terrorism.

Socioeconomic development projects and refugee rehabilitation are continuing in Muslim areas. The early twenty-first century witnessed the growth of Muslim nongovernmental organizations, which are involved in issues like women's empowerment, political participation, promoting peace, and livelihood projects. Many of these programs receive funding from international agencies like the U.S. Agency for International Development, United Nations Development Programme, UNICEF, World Food Program, and others. Although Philippine government programs in Muslim areas have already started to reduce agitation for secession, both the government and Muslims are aware that much remains to be done.

[*See also* Islam and Politics in Southeast Asia; Moro Islamic Liberation Front; Moro National Liberation Front; *and* Organization of Islamic Cooperation.]

BIBLIOGRAPHY

Abinales, Patricio N., and Nathan Gilbert Quimpo. *The US and the War on Terror in the Philippines.* Manila: Anvil, 2008.

International Crisis Group. *Philippine Terrorism: The Role of Militant Islamic Converts.* Asia Report 110. Brussels: International Crisis Group, 2005.

Lacar, Luis Q. "Balik-Islam: Christian Converts to Islam in the Philippines, c. 1970–98." *Islam and Christian-Muslim Relations* 12, no. 1 (2001): 39–60.

Majul, Cesar Adib. *The Contemporary Muslim Movement in the Philippines.* Berkeley, Calif.: Mizan, 1985.

Majul, Cesar Adib. *Muslims in the Philippines.* 2d ed. Quezon City: University of the Philippines Press, 1973.

Tan, Samuel K. *Internationalization of the Bangsamoro Struggle.* Rev. ed. Quezon City: University of the Philippines Center for Integrative and Development Studies, 2003.

Tuazon, Bobby M., ed. *The Moro Reader: History and Contemporary Struggles of the Bangsamoro People.* Quezon City: Center for Empowerment in Governance, 2008.

CESAR ADIB MAJUL
Updated by VIVIENNE SM. ANGELES

PĪR. *See* Sufism.

PLURALISM. Religious pluralists believe that their faith is not the sole and exclusive source of truth. Many pluralists believe that variations between different faiths are actually expressions of a universal truth. Pluralism denotes an attitude of coexistence between people of different faiths and practices. Tolerance and pluralism have been important characteristics of Islam from its origins in the seventh century. The protected status of non-Muslim minorities, or *dhimmī*, in Islamic law is well established. Often religious minorities, dependent on the protection of those in power, held positions of high prestige in the courts of sultans and rulers. In many instances, however, the *dhimmī* were treated as second-class citizens and not provided with the same rights and privileges as Muslims. Under traditional Islamic law, for instance, the *dhimmī* are required to pay a special poll tax, or *jizyah*. Nonetheless, some scholars, such as Mahmoud Ayoub, have claimed that the word *dhimmī* did not imply second-class status but rather a special "covenant." More recently, Muslim intellectuals and reformers such as Fahmī Huwaydī, Fatima Mernissi, Tariq Ramadan, Nurcholish Madjid, Abdulaziz Sachedina, Fathi Osman, Farid Esack, and others have embraced the ideas of pluralism and democratization, even using Muslim scripture and the *ḥadīth*, or sayings of the Prophet, to argue that the Qur'ān supports pluralism and the equality of all humans. Often cited is the famous Qur'ānic verse 5:48: "To each of you we prescribed a law and method. Had Allāh willed, He would have made you one nation [united in religion], but [He intended] to test you in what he has given you." Also frequently cited is 2:256, "There shall be no compulsion in [acceptance of] the religion [Islam]."

Yet along with more pluralistic views of religion, there have also been defensive, traditionalist perspectives. This defensiveness is not exclusive to Islam. Indeed, the three major religions of the Middle East, Judaism, Christianity, and Islam, have developed exclusive scriptural notions of faith in one God, that God communicated with humanity through a final, revealed scripture that some claim to be exclusively their own. Despite the general theology of scriptural exclusivity used by those interested in political power and resistance to change, coexistence and pluralism remained the historical norm of Middle East politics and society. This coexistence often persisted despite the determined efforts of some with a more exclusivist view of religion.

During the Muslim conquests, for instance, the Arab armies would encamp outside major cities but not compel infidels to convert. In fact, there was an incentive to allow Christians and Jews to maintain their religion: as non-Muslims, they could add more revenue to the Caliphate through the special *jizyah* tax. Also, in the first decades of the conquest those who wished to convert were expected to become *mawālī* (clients) of an Arab Muslim guardian who could guide them in the faith. The idea of spreading the faith through forced conversion or persecution was certainly foreign to the first Muslims. Even during the Crusades and in the midst of aggressive Christian expansion, most Muslim rulers maintained a tolerant attitude to Arabized Christians and Jews. Itinerant Ṣūfī preachers who spread Islam throughout much of Central Asia and Southeast Asia were highly tolerant of different religions, some like the famed poet and religious thinker Ibn al-ʿArabī (d. 1240) displaying highly pluralistic attitudes towards different religions: "My heart has become capable of every form: it is a pasture for gazelles and a convent for Christian monks, and a temple for idols and the pilgrim's Kaʿbah [the sacred shrine at the heart of Mecca]." Ibn al-ʿArabī's ideas, as well as those of pluralistic thinkers such as Jalāl al-Dīn Rūmī (d. 1273), exemplified highly universalist and ecumenical ideas. "The domain of Love has a different religion of all religions—For Lovers God alone is their religion." Such ideas have had a profound influence on the Islamic world. Followers of tolerant forms of Sufism remain numerous and influential even in regions that have seen the rise of more radicalized forms of Islam, such as Pakistan.

The Ottomans also actively protected Christians, often under treaty obligations with European powers. In the later years of the Ottoman Empire some Christian communities, such as the Armenians, did experience persecution, though less for sectarian reasons than is often assumed. The Wahhābī sect did, however, bar Christian and Jewish worship in Mecca and Medina.

Since the late twentieth century the rise of nationalism and the persistence of foreign intervention in the region have led to unfortunate backlashes against some religious minorities in the Muslim world. The plight of Christian minorities in modern Iraq is one example. In the absence of a powerful state to enforce pluralism and security, many have opted to leave the country as refugees, despite millennia of history in the Mesopotamian region. The creation of the state of Israel and the fear of Nazi encroachment in North Africa and the Middle East during World War II encouraged thousands of Jews from Yemen, Morocco, Tunisia, Iran, and elsewhere to move to the new Jewish state or to Western countries.

These migrations, often voluntary, occurred to the dismay of many Muslims who valued their Jewish compatriots. In South and Southeast Asia, religious minorities in Muslim countries and Muslims as minorities under non-Muslim rule are much more numerous. Pluralism in many of these countries is well established. Ibn Baṭṭūṭah, the medieval Maghribī scholar and traveler who went as far as China and Indonesia, spoke of Islam in places where it was the minority religion. He noted the high degree of diversity among the Muslims of the Indian Ocean region. Famously, he was particularly appalled at the practice of Muslim women of the Maldives Islands who walked about bare-breasted as their non-Muslim ancestors had before being converted by Muslim merchants. In India, where religious differences were apparent on a daily basis, the influential Ṣūfī Shāh Walī Allāh promoted understanding of other religious traditions. In Indonesia and Pakistan, for instance, there are many diverse voices, with moderate Muslims and Christians seeking to preserve tolerance despite an Islamist surge. There is also an effort to preserve pluralism within Islam, including the coexistence of Shīʿī and Sunnī.

Contrary to most media depictions of "radical Islam," modern Muslim proponents of various forms of religious pluralism are numerous. This entry will only discuss some of the more famous advocates. In each case, the views of Muslim intellectuals and political leaders, as in the West, are variable. Although criticized recently for his role in suppressing secular parties in Tunisia, Rāshid al-Ghannūshī, for instance, has written extensively about pluralism in Islam, often from the relative comfort of exile in Europe. Although the "intellectual" head of the dominant Nahḍah Party played a leadership role in Tunisia, however, some of his ideals have been compromised as he deals with internal pressures from more traditional members of his own party and the Ḥizb al-Taḥrīr, a largely antipluralist, Islamist organization. Another ambiguous figure is Yūsuf al-Qaraḍāwī, the highly influential Egyptian Islamic theologian who currently resides in Doha with the support of the emir of Qatar. He is known for advocating dialogue with non-Muslims even as he calls Shīʿīs heretics. He claimed that Jews who believe in the authentic Torah are very close to Muslims even as he also is identified with anti-Israeli remarks, especially reacting to settlement activity. But at the same time he is also on record against theocracy, although he believes homosexuality should be punishable by death. Thus, although certainly not an ideal pluralist according to Western standards, he is a very influential voice who does advocate coexistence and dialogue between different faiths.

Muḥammad Salīm al-ʿAwwā, who often criticized Qaraḍāwī for his anti-Shīʿī views, belongs to the moderate, democratic strain of Islam. He calls not only for coexistence but also for active, new interpretations of what Islam could mean in a modern society. Although he declared his candidacy for president of Egypt, an act that may push some intellectuals to one political extreme or another, he is a staunch advocate of *al-wasaṭīyah*, or moderation. His liberal and pluralist standards are high, and he famously criticized the pope for not upholding his predecessor's ideals of Christian pluralism. Also from Egypt, Ahmed Aboulmagd, a renowned lawyer and Islamic intellectual, and a large number of other influential scholars have advocated strongly for "dialogue, not confrontation."

There are a large number of Muslim intellectuals and leaders trained or teaching in the West who are very strong advocates of democratic pluralism. Fathi Osman, a member of the Muslim Brotherhood of Egypt who completed his doctorate at Princeton, has written numerous influential works on religious pluralism including *Human Rights in Western Thought and Islamic Law* (1981).

He moved to the University of Southern California's Center for Muslim-Jewish Engagement.

The Swiss academic and writer Tariq Ramadan is one of the most influential European Muslim intellectuals. His work is also known in the Middle East. His grandfather was Ḥasan al-Bannā, founder of the Muslim Brotherhood, a group that sought to bring Islam back into the political realm. He focuses on the heterogeneous nature of Islam in Europe. Rejecting the idea of the "abode of Islam" and the "abode of war," the way some Muslim radicals describe the West, Ramadan advocates for a more open interpretation of the Qurʾān and Islam's other fundamental texts. Some Western scholars see him as a Muslim Martin Luther and as a person with legitimacy in both Western and Islamist circles. Tariq Ramadan, and other academics who can speak to multiple audiences and points of view, are essential for the shaping of pluralism. It is through such figures that effective dialogue can often occur.

The American academic Abdulaziz Sachedina was condemned by Ayatollah Sistani for holding views that challenged the closed and conservative views of modern political Shiism in Iran. Thus, although he resides in the United States and is a professor at the University of Virginia, his views are widely known. Rather than suggesting that Islam must change in accordance with Western models, Sachedina sees the Islamic roots of democratic pluralism itself. Other American Muslims include Mahmoud Ayoub, a strong advocate of pluralism who also writes in the West but for a global audience.

In Indonesia, a country with a Muslim majority but many significant and diverse minority groups, several advocates of pluralism emerged. Nurcholish Madjid, known as Cak Nur, advocated for modernization in Islam and delved into politics as a presidential candidate. He called for Islam but not Islamic parties, and suggested that Islam must embrace pluralism if it is to survive the onslaught of diverse, globalizing perspectives. Like Sachedina, he found the origins of pluralism not simply in the West but in Islam as well. In his case, he embraced Indonesian Islam as a model for religious coexistence and understanding and showed that pluralism is not merely an option for Islam, it is a necessity if Islamic thought is to survive globalization intact.

Pluralism has roots in Islamic history. Recognizing this factor, most contemporary Muslim advocates of pluralism have pointed to the pluralizing tendencies of their faith. While most Muslim intellectuals point first to these Islamic roots of pluralism, some also advocate new interpretations that challenge Islamic thinking at a fundamental level. On the other hand, there are certainly extremists who reject the very notion of pluralism, as in every religion, and desire to make Islam compatible with democracy, as became evident during the Arab Spring. These ideas are not entirely new. Many of the young protestors in the major cities of the Arab world were influenced by a long tradition of Islamic pluralistic thought. At the same time, the rise of democratic Islam and the power of the conservative, rural, less-educated voter have sparked fears of popular majority will being imposed on religious minorities such as Christians, Yazīdīs, or Jews. Thus, even as the potential and necessity of pluralistic thinking remain strong, the future of pluralism in the Middle East is not guaranteed in the midst of change.

BIBLIOGRAPHY

Ayoob, Mohammed. *The Many Faces of Political Islam: Religion and Politics in the Muslim World.* Ann Arbor: University of Michigan Press, 2008.

Esack, Farid. *Qurʾān, Liberation, and Pluralism: An Islamic Perspective of Interreligious Solidarity against Oppression.* Oxford: Oneworld, 1997.

Esposito, John L. *The Future of Islam.* Oxford: Oxford University Press, 2010.

Hirji, Zulfikar, ed. *Diversity and Pluralism in Islam: Historical and Contemporary Discourses amongst Muslims*. London: I. B. Tauris, 2010.
Mandaville, Peter. *Global Political Islam*. London: Routledge, 2007.
Osman, Fathi. *The Other: A Restructuring of the Islamic Concept*. Los Angeles: Pharos Foundation, 2009.
Sachedina, Abdulaziz. *The Islamic Roots of Democratic Pluralism*. Oxford: Oxford University Press, 2001.
Safi, Omid, ed. *Progressive Muslims: On Justice, Gender, and Pluralism*. Oxford: Oneworld, 2003.

ALLEN FROMHERZ

POLITICAL PARTIES. Political parties are considered essential tools of democracy. Developments of modern democracies have been paralleled by the emergence of political parties such that modern democracies are "unthinkable save in terms of parties" (Schattschneider, 1942, p. 124). However, parties may and do exist in a wide range of political systems, including semidemocratic or nondemocratic. Essentially, a political party is an association of individuals with a common set of beliefs and political goals, sharing a desire to take control of the government under a specific label. It is "a formal organization whose self-conscious, primary purpose is to place and maintain in public office persons who will control, alone or in coalition, the machinery of government" (La Palombara and Weiner, 1966, p. 3). Thus defined, parties are groups of people. They are organized, with labels. That is, they deliberately act together to achieve common goals. They seek to acquire power by winning political office (Heywood, 2002, p. 248). They provide the voters with a brand name so that they can identify with a general approach to public questions and to make an informed choice with ease.

Political parties emerged with the development of democracy, the extension of popular suffrage and parliamentary power (La Palombara and Weiner, 1966). The growth of parliamentary power in Europe and in the United States led members of parliament who shared similar views on important issues to organize themselves into groups (called factions). Over time, the parliamentary and electoral groups cooperated to form mass parties to capture support from newly enfranchised voters. Not all political parties were internally created, however. In fact, beginning around 1900, parties were created from outside parliament. For example, trade unions sometimes developed into or helped create socialist political parties; this is how the British Labour Party developed. The nationalist movements, like the Muslim League in Pakistan, that ended colonial regimes were organized to influence colonial policies. Externally, parties may also be formed as a result of social modernization of the country. The modernizing nationalist reform parties in newly independent societies, such as the National Liberation Party of Costa Rica, the Republican Party of Turkey, and the Destourian Socialist Party of Tunisia, were created to absorb the shocks resulting from rapid—modernization, communications, economic development, mass education, and the disruption of traditional social forms and attitudes.

The core function of political parties is to nominate candidates for public office and to try to get them elected. This involves two steps. The first is to nominate winnable candidates for the election. By so doing, parties not merely control the voter's range of choices but severely limit the number of those eligible for public office. The second step is to mobilize the partisans to vote and to motivate the nonpartisans or "independent voters" to support their candidates. This function distinguishes a political party from other groups. To underscore its importance, Sartori (1976, p. 64) provides the famous "minimal definition" of a party, as "any political group that presents at elections, and is capable of placing through elections, candidates for public office." Once the elections are over, parties form and sustain governments in office and determine the legislation and execution of policies. This involves selecting members of the cabinet, appointing qualified men and women with interest and experience in public policy deliberation and formulation of public relations, media, and political strategies. Political parties not in power assume the role of the opposition by overseeing government programs, presenting critiques of policies, and offering themselves as alternative government. Additionally, parties provide a link between people and government. They are the channels of expression communicating the needs and wishes of the citizens to the government and conversely keeping the citizens informed about the decisions made by the government. Parties also perform an interest aggregation function. They bring together a number of different interest groups under the banner of the party and transform a multitude of specific demands into a manageable package of proposals. This is different from the interest articulation function largely performed by the interest groups. Political parties are mechanisms for social integration as they enable citizens to participate effectively in the political process and to feel they have a vested interest in its perpetuation. Finally, in some societies, parties provide a range of nonpolitical benefits including social activities and recognition and status for people and groups.

The political parties functioning in a political system taken together make up a party system. This refers to the interaction of parties with each other and with the overall political system. The distinction between party systems is generally in terms of the number of parties with such categories as single party, two-party, and multiparty systems. The set of relationships is wholly internal in a single party system and is exemplified by, among others, the Communist Party of China, the Communist Party of Cuba, and the Communist Party of Vietnam. The two-party system is characterized by two parties that share the major part of the electoral vote, and these two major parties alternate in the exercise of power. The United States of America, United Kingdom, and Canada have a dominant two-party system. Frequently in the multiparty system no party is able to obtain the majority of the legislative seats to form the government, often requiring the parties to form coalitions to form a government. The parties in competition vary in size and support base. There are some seventeen to twenty political parties in France, and Spain has up to fifty-five parties. Indonesia has more than thirty political parties.

Political Parties and Islamic Thought. Political parties, with the exception of monarchies and military dictatorships, form important components of the political system in the Muslim world. Given overwhelming Western dominance, understandably most of the political parties are secular and hence have been subjected to severe criticisms by some Muslim scholars and activists. Emphasizing certain vital Islamic values and principles and yearning for the immediate establishment of a single, united Muslim *ummah*, these scholars refuse to recognize the role of political parties in an Islamic political system. They argue that Muslims are one *ummah* guided by the Qurʾān and the *sunnah*, and that the Qurʾān (3:105; 6:159; 8:46) repeatedly asks Muslims not to be divided among themselves. Political parties are perceived as divisive in nature, detrimental to the welfare of the *ummah*, and hence forbidden in an Islamic polity. They further point out that the Qurʾān disapproves of the formation of alliances specifically in the chapter entitled "The Parties" (al-Ahzab).

The majority of Muslim scholars are, however, of the opinion that political parties are not in conflict with the democratic spirit of the Islamic political system. Islamic scholarship looks with favor on *ikhtilāf*, or disagreement, among the believers and plurality of views on matters that have not been determined by the Qur'ān and the *sunnah*. Indeed, the Qur'ān enjoins unity of the *ummah*, which implies belief in the unity and sovereignty of Allāh, and to be engaged in continuous worship as prescribed in the Qur'ān and the *sunnah*. The unity of the *ummah* does not imply political unity and disapproval of disagreement. Islam supports political pluralism, which means tolerating and respecting differences, which is a fact of human existence. However, any party or association that defies the teachings of Islam is indeed *ḥizb al-Shayṭān* (the party of the Devil).

Thus, instead of being repugnant to Islam, political parties are helpful in achieving the goals set by Islam. The need of the hour is to institutionalize them after weeding out some minor elements that are in conflict with Islamic principles. The Qur'ān asks the believers to "cooperate in righteousness and piety, and [not to] cooperate in sin and transgression" (5:2). It obligates believers to establish from among themselves a "group calling to the Goodness [*al-khayr*] and enjoining what is good [*al-ma'rūf*] and forbidding what is evil *al-munkar*]" (4: 104). Ibn Taymīyah (1922–1930, 141) argued that the parties that promote people's welfare are not merely allowed but are considered in the Qur'ān as "the party of the God [*ḥizb Allah*]," and "they are the successful" (58:19). Muḥammad al-Ghazālī concurred with Ibn Taymīyah and added that any party that aims at destroying the unity of the *ummah* is unlawful and hence forbidden.

Muslim scholars and activists seem to have accepted the legitimacy and desirability of political parties participating in the promotion of good for the Muslim *ummah*. However, the debate shifted to minor issues like the naming of the party and the modalities of taking part in elections. Since the term *ḥizb* used in the Qur'ān carries a negative connotation (as well as positive connotation), early Muslim political leaders shied away from naming their political parties *ḥizb*. *Ḥizbīyah*, or partisan difference, has been an especially negative condition to be avoided. Leaders opted instead for such terms as *jamā'ah*, *jam'īyah*, or *ḥarakah*, meaning association, society, and movement, respectively. Thus, the Muslim Brotherhood established in 1928 called itself Jam'īyatal-Ikhwān al-Muslimūn (the Society of Muslim Brothers). Other examples include the Jamā'at-i-Islāmī of Pakistan (Pakistan Islamic Society); al-Jamā'at al-Islāmīyah of Syria (Syrian Islamic Society); and Ḥarakat al-Muqāwamah al-Islāmīyah (the Islamic Resistance Movement, or Ḥamās), the Palestinian political party that governs Gaza. The early reluctance gradually waned and the word *ḥizb* gained increasing currency. Thus, the Islamic Liberation Party in Jordan is called Ḥizb al-Taḥrīr al-Islāmī. The Pashtun-based Islamic Party in Afghanistan is named E, and in Lebanon there is Ḥizbullāh (the Party of God). The prime ministers elected after the ousting of Saddam Hussein in Iraq, Ibrahim Ja'afari and Nouri al-Maliki, came from the Shī'ī Islamist party, Ḥizb al-Da'wah al-Islāmīyah (Party of the Call to Islam). Interestingly, al-Ittijah al-Islami (Mouvement de la Tenedance Islamique) of Tunisia adopted a new name in 1998, Ḥizb al-Nahḍah (Renaissance Party).

The other issue debated among Muslim scholars and activists was the function of political parties. They all agreed that the political parties must perform two tasks as specified in the Qur'ān (3:104; 3:110): to call people to all that is good (i.e., to Islam); and to enjoin virtue (i.e., performing all activities prescribed by Islam) and forbid vice (i.e., restraining corrupt influences that violate the principles of Islam). They also agree that the parties in Islam cannot function as simply electoral devices to get a group of leaders elected. The parties would take part in elections, if necessary, to replace the corrupt leadership with that of the pious and upright. They must, however, act continuously to provide leadership and initiative in promoting virtue and prohibiting vice. Political parties should not just be an electoral instrument but should take part in a massive socioeconomic revolution along Islamic lines. Islam, as Ayatollah Khomeini pointed out, "is a religion where worship is joined to politics and political activity is a form of worship" (Algar, 1981, p. 275).

The debate whether Islam approves of political parties has somewhat become obsolete. Scholars and leaders have successfully made the transition from debating the issue to creating parties and taking part in elections to wrest power in order to implement the Islamic welfare system with or without calling their endeavors Islamic. Parties of secular and Islamic persuasion operate side by side, occasionally forming alliances to implement their agreed upon policies. Tunisia's al-Nahḍah party, which won a plurality with 41 percent of the popular vote in 2011, opted to form a new government with two secular parties. Earlier in 2006, Ḥizbullāh formed an alliance with a right-wing Christian party. In Bangladesh, the Jamāʿat-i-Islāmī joined the coalition government with the Bangladesh Nationalist Party under the leadership of the wife of the slain president Ziaur Rahman.

Political Parties in the Muslim World. Political parties in the Muslim world emerged in response to the crises of legitimacy, integration, and participation (La Palombara and Weiner, 1966). The Muslim elites questioned the legitimacy of colonial rule, which did not meet the demand of the majority of people, and hence felt the need to establish a government of their own. However, this required integrating the masses, who were ethnically divided and geographically dispersed with limited or nonexistent communication systems. The masses, additionally, were politically apathetic. The national elites thus faced integration and penetration crises and were forced to respond to these crises. Most political parties emerged as nationalist movements aimed at ending colonial rule by mobilizing the masses against it. The colonial powers tried to weaken these movements by introducing limited self-government, which taught them the art of bargaining and electioneering. Sometimes, the colonial government assisted the local elites to form parties in order to "divide and rule." Thus, the Muslim League, which struggled for Pakistan, was created with the support of British officers.

The independence of the colonies did not result in the resolution of the crisis of legitimacy, integration, and participation. This gave rise to various factions within the parties, which eventually metamorphosed into separate parties. In some countries, these parties functioned for a while. In some others, party activity was short-lived. Parties were banned under military regimes. In some countries, only a single party was allowed to operate.

A two-party system characterized by alternation of two major parties in control of government is virtually nonexistent in Muslim-majority states. Instead, there are a few states with no parties at all. In Bahrain and Kuwait, all political parties are illegal, but candidates across the political spectrum compete in elections with the support of political societies that have some similar functions to political parties. Parties are also illegal in Oman, Qatar, Saudi Arabia, and the United Arab Emirates (UAE), which is a federation of seven emirates. Independent candidates run for posts in parliaments with limited powers in Oman and the UAE. Saudi Arabia does not hold legislative elections, but independent candidates participated in the country's first municipal elections in 2005.

One reason for the persistence of nonparty politics, according to many scholars, is the existence of populations satisfied with the status quo in these states. In the language of political culture, the people are apathetic, and hence there is no demand for reforms or political change in these countries. An additional reason that has been suggested is the prevalence of rent-based economies. The ruling elites consolidate their power by distributing oil and gas revenues among the population, thereby preempting any calls for representation that might have followed from the imposition of taxes. Even if this was true in the past, this argument may not hold for long in an era of low prices and increasing unemployment.

Most Muslim-majority states have multiparty systems. Examples of such countries include Bangladesh, Bosnia, Indonesia, Iraq, Maldives, Morocco, Turkey, Yemen, and others. In the legislative elections held in Indonesia on 9 April 2009 for 132 seats of the Regional Representative Council (DPD) and 560 seats of the People's Representative Council (DPR), a total of thirty-eight political parties, including many Islam-based ones, participated. The Islamic parties fared rather poorly in the election. There are about fifteen political parties competing for seats in the Grand National Assembly of Turkey. They range from religious-based parties, to those based in regional groups, to ideologically based parties. The Justice and Development Party, a center-right conservative party, has been winning elections since 2002 under the leadership of Recep Tayyip Erdoğan, who has been the prime minister of Turkey since 2003.

The extent to which a multiparty system in Muslim-majority countries exists is debatable. Most scholars suggest calling these parties "groups" rather than political parties. These parties are neither sanctioned nor supported by the state. These parties do not consider each other legitimate competitors. Quite often, these parties are created with the announcement of forthcoming elections, and they die immediately if the individual or group sponsoring the party fails to garner enough votes or seats in the parliament. Thus, multiplicity is a function of low-level institutionalization. The lives of component parties are episodic and their political role is quite marginal. Multiplicity is also a reflection of a body politic characterized by the low level of political tolerance and uncompromising attitude of various partisans.

In some countries, a multiparty system prevails but one party almost always wins the election. Malaysia is one country where several parties exist and elections are held at regular intervals. However, a coalition of political parties known as Barisan Nasional (BN, the National Front), which is registered as a single party, won a two-thirds majority of seats in the national parliament until 2008, when the opposition parties, composed of the Islamic Party of Malaysia, the Chinese-dominated Democratic Action Party, and the centrist People's Justice Party, denied it its customary overwhelming majority. The BN nevertheless rules with a majority in the parliament, making Malaysia a single dominant party system.

Most of the Islamic parties that have participated in national elections have gradually adopted liberal electoral platforms. Before the 1990s, a majority of the Islamic parties campaigned promising implementation of the *Sharīʿah* and the establishment of an Islamic state. In the twenty-first century, these parties promise a welfare state, good governance, the principles of human rights, equality, and the rights of minorities. The Justice and Development Party in Turkey refers to itself as a conservative party and has removed almost every reference to Islam from its electoral platforms (Yavuz, 2009). The Renaissance Movement in Algeria, the Islamic Action Front in Jordan, the Jamāʿat-i-Islāmī in Bangladesh, and the Justice and Development Party in Morocco have dropped their support for *Sharīʿah*. Likewise, the Muslim Brotherhood in Egypt, the Jamāʿat-i-Islāmī in Bangladesh, and the Yemeni Congregation for Reform offer secular justifications for democracy. They see no major contradictions between democratic politics and piety. This is not to deny that these parties are still conservative and occasionally move away from liberalization. Yet the overall trend toward publicly embracing global norms of democracy and human rights is well worth noting. They are considered to be the most dynamic political force across the Arab world. Compared to secular parties, Islamic political parties are better organized. By 2012 more than fifty Islam-based political parties succeeded in mobilizing millions of supporters in a dozen Arab countries. At least three of these parties won the right to form governments in Egypt, Tunisia, and Morocco.

BIBLIOGRAPHY

Heywood, Andrew. *Politics*. New York: Palgrave Macmillan, 2002.

Ibn Taymīyah, Taqī al-Dīn. *Majmuat al-Rasailwa al-Masail*. 4 vols. Edited by Muḥammad Rashīd Riḍā. Cairò: Matba'atal-Manar, 1922–1930.

Khomeini, Ruhollah. *Islam and Revolution: Writings and Declarations of Imam Khomeini*. Translated by Hamid Algar. Berkeley, Calif.: Mizan, 1981.

La Palombara, Joseph, and Myron Weiner, eds. *Political Parties and Political Development*. Princeton, N.J.: Princeton University Press, 1966.

Sartori, Giovanni. *Parties and Party Systems: A Framework for Analysis*. Cambridge, U.K.: Cambridge University Press, 1976.

Schattschneider, Elmer Eric. *Party Government*. New York: Holt, Rinehart & Winston, 1942.

Yavuz, M. Hakan. *Secularism and Muslim Democracy in Turkey*. Cambridge, U.K.: Cambridge University Press, 2009.

ABDUL RASHID MOTEN

POLITICAL SCIENCE. For Muslim scholars, political science as a distinct discipline is of relatively recent origin. Traditionally, Muslim scholars studied matters pertaining to politics such as the nature and need of the state, qualifications and installations of the chief executive, functions of ministers, and responsibilities and rights of the rulers and the ruled as part of the *Sharīʿah* (the Islamic legal system) or as *siyāsah sharʿīyah*. This is due to the fact that in Islam religion and politics are intertwined, and as such ethics sets the tone for politics, and the rules of political activities are deduced from the ethical norms of Islam. Almost all Muslim scholars dealt with political problems but couched them in religious terms. Some thinkers, however, did directly confront the questions relating to political science and its essential features. For instance, Abū Naṣr al-Fārābī (d. 950) wrote about the "attainment of happiness" through political life in *Kitāb ārāʾ ahl al-madīnah al-fāḍilah* (The Book of Opinions of the People of the Ideal City). Abū al-Ḥasan al-Māwardī (d. 1058) blended reasoning derived from the Qurʾān, *sunnah*, and other Islamic sources with political deductions from the period of the Prophet and the first four caliphs in his *al-Aḥkam al-sulṭānīyah* (Ordinances of Government), and Abū Ḥāmid Muḥammad al-Ghazālī (d. 1111) wrote about the necessity of a properly constituted authority in *al-Iqtiṣād fī al-iʿtiqād* (Moderation in Belief). Abū Yūsuf (d. 798) wrote on government and authority in his *Kitāb al-kharāj* (Book on Taxation). ʿAbd al-Raḥmān Ibn Khaldūn (d. 1406) explained the necessity of social organization and the rise and fall of civilization in his *Muqaddimah* (Prolegomenon).

Defining Political Science. Political science, according to al-Fārābī, examines the various kinds of actions and behavior that lead to the appointment of virtuous leaders and the formation of virtuous societies. The purpose of politics is to lead man to true happiness (*saʿādah*) through right modes of conduct—virtue and good deeds. Such modes of conduct are instilled by virtuous leadership, which, in turn, brings about ultimate happiness. The true happiness is to be found in the hereafter. Fārābī's *Fī al-ʿilm al-madanī wa ʿilm al-fiqh wa ʿilm al kalām* (On Political Science,

Science of Jurisprudence, and Science of *Kalām*) is in the arena of a manual on political science. To al-Ghazālī, political science deals with the proper order for administering the affairs of men. Such an order is derived from books revealed by God to His prophets. Politics is a science that aims at ensuring man's welfare in this world and bliss in the next. This "happiness" can be attained only if the government is based upon religious sciences and political sciences. Al-Māwardī conceives of political science rather narrowly as government that, to him, is instituted to maintain religion and to administer the world. This government is necessitated by divine will and not by reason. Variations and emphases notwithstanding, all the Muslim scholars based their formulations upon the assumptions that the state is ordained by God to administer the world, and its function is to apply the Islamic law (*Sharīʿah*) so as to create happiness in this world and in the hereafter (Rosenthal, 1968).

Methods Used to Study Politics. Muslim scholars have used several approaches to study politics. The works of Muslim political thinkers can be grouped under three categories: philosophical works, works by jurists, and administrative handbooks and "Mirrors for Princes" (Rosenthal, 1968).

The philosophers considered politics as a craft and were very much influenced by Greek philosophy. They began their formulation by laying down the rationale for political association and by explaining the constituents of an ideal state. Their approach was normative and utopian. The foremost among the philosophers was al-Fārābī, who sought to reconcile Greek philosophy with Islam, or philosophy with revelation. Central to the work of philosophers is the law that is the foundation of the state and regulates it. Happiness to al-Fārābī can be found only in an ideal state led and administered by an imam who is likened to a philosopher-king. The ideal authority promotes true happiness; the corrupt authority promotes supposed happiness composed of wealth, honor, or pleasure. Al-Fārābī influenced many others, including Ibn Sīnā (Avicenna d. 037) and Ibn Rushd (Averroes, d. 1198).

The juristic formulations stressed the need to implement divine will as laid down in the two divine sources of Islam, the Qurʾān and the *sunnah* of the Prophet Muḥammad. They also relied upon the practices of the first four caliphs of Islam (Khulafāʾ al-Rāshidūn) since they ruled by following the guidance of the Prophet. They believed in the centrality of the ruler or the caliph, who had to fulfill certain conditions, the most important of which was justice (*ʿadālah*), which also require knowledge. The ideal state is defined as the one where *Sharīʿah* is implemented and where the legitimate authority carries out the duty of promoting virtue and prohibiting vice. The prominent thinkers who produced juristic works include al-Māwardī, al-Ghazālī, Ibn Taymīyah (d. 1328), and others.

The administrators and writers of manuals of conduct for rulers may be considered as political realists. They emphasized the divine right of kings and assumed a symbiotic relationship between "kingship and righteousness" on the one hand and "prosperity with right religion" on the other. They advocated obedience to the ruler but pointed out that the true ruler is the one who is strong, who practices justice, and who maintains the social order. Unlike the philosophical works that discussed the principles of government, the administrators dealt with the art of government. *Siyāsat nāmah* (Book of Government) by Niẓām al-Mulk (d. 1092), *Naṣīḥat al-mulūk* (Advice to the Kings) by al-Ghazālī, and *Akhlaq-e-Muhsini* (The Morals of the Beneficent) by Ḥusayn Vāʿiẓ Kāshifī (d. 1505) are prominent examples of the "mirrors for princes."

Political Science in Modern Times. As noted earlier, Muslim scholars wrote about politics and all other matters by subsuming these under their discussion of jurisprudence and *Sharīʿah*. The situation changed with the nineteenth-century European encroachment on the Muslim world, the dissolution of the Ottoman Empire and the Caliphate, and the spread of Western ideas and influence throughout Muslim societies. These threats not only gave birth to various Islamic movements but also led scholars to embark upon writing separate works on sociological and particularly political topics. The early writers wrote using the language of the Islamic sciences. Over time, a group of intellectuals admiring Western culture and civilization replaced the traditional scholars and expressed their thought in Western languages and redefined political science in modern terms. The able representatives of this group include Sir Sayyid Ahmad Khan (d. 1898), Jamal al-Din Asadabadi (d. 1897), ʿAlī ʿAbd al-Rāziq (d. 1966), and others.

The new elites considered earlier definitions of politics to be too restrictive, since they tied it to state organizations. They replaced the classical or medieval preoccupation with the search for happiness with a search for the laws of behavior. They saw nothing wrong in Robert Dahl's definition of political science as a study of "any persistent pattern of human relationships that involves, to a significant extent, power, rule or authority" (Dahl, 1970, p. 6). They also agreed with David Easton that political acts are those that "authoritatively allocate values in a society" (Easton, 1953, p. 134). Easton's definition is similar to Dahl's in conceiving of politics as a set of human interactions. Easton, however, limits it by emphasizing "authoritative allocations" for an entire society and focuses attention on the distribution of scarce resources or values in a society as well as on the authority or power relationships involved in it. Muslim scholars took Easton's definition as a "conventional guide" for political analysis. Many, however, realized that no political theory or idea will ever be acceptable to the broader Muslim community unless their stress on the value allocation process, power, and conflict in the distribution process and policy outcomes are shown to be in conformity with the dictates of the Qurʾān and the *sunnah*. Consequently, defining politics as a struggle for power, they added that in Islam power is sought to serve the Lord Almighty and thus to serve humanity and to attain a blissful eternal life. Power is sought to repudiate all those who claim absolute right and power that are due only to Allāh and, therefore, to banish oppression and injustice from the face of the earth. Thus they made the ethical, normative content of power, which was made irrelevant and redundant by the triumphant march of materialism and behaviorism, relevant. Likewise, they stressed that the essence of politics is the striving for the "good life," but this good life is given a social, economic, and material connotation along with a life lived in worship and in seeking the pleasure of the One and only Allāh. ʿAlī ʿAbd al-Rāziq, according to Rosenthal (1968, p. 100), was "obviously unaware of the political treatise of al-Fārābī ... and of others," those who conceived of good life in both temporal and spiritual terms.

Along with the definition of political science, much has also been written on methods of research to produce pertinent political theories. Sayyid Abū al-Aʿlā Mawdūdī (d. 1979), Sayyid Quṭb (d. 1966), and other twentieth-century scholars have advocated the universality of Islam. They do not object to the philosophical method, the historical method, or the juridical method. They appreciate, however, Ibn Khaldūn's approach of asking questions and of verifying the truth or falsity of statements through reliable records, observation, and experience. They stress the need to observe actual behavior through systematic research and statistical applications, if need be. They aim at providing explanations for political action as well as providing recommendations to help improve the conditions of the Muslim community (*ummah*) and humanity at large. Their research is rooted in divine revelation, but they see reason and revelation as complimentary to each other. They suggest obtaining knowledge through revelation or divinely ordained absolute knowledge (*ḥaqq al-yaqīn*), rationalism or inference based upon judgment and appraisal of evidence (*ʿilm al-yaqīn*), historical reports, description of life experiences, and the like (*ʿayn al-yaqīn al-yaqin*). Thus, they suggest studying politics by turning to experience and experiment and to rational and intellectual inquiry within the circumference of revealed knowledge.

Bibliography

Crone, Patricia. *Medieval Islamic Political Thought.* Edinburgh: Edinburgh University Press, 2004.

Dahl, Robert A. *Modern Political Analysis.* Englewood Cliffs, N.J.: Prentice-Hall, 1970.

Donohue, John J., and John L. Esposito, eds. *Islam in Transition: Muslim Perspectives.* 2d ed. New York: Oxford University Press, 2007.

Easton, David. *The Political System.* New York: Alfred A. Knopf, 1953.

Enayat, Hamid. *Modern Islamic Political Thought: The Response of the Shīʿī and Sunnī Muslims to the Twentieth Century.* Kuala Lumpur, Malaysia: Islamic Book Trust, 2001.

Esposito, John L., ed. *Voices of Resurgent Islam.* New York: Oxford University Press, 1983.

Lambton, A. K. S. *Theory and Practice in Medieval Persian Government.* London: Variorum, 1980.

Moten, Abdul Rashid. *Political Science: An Islamic Perspective.* Houndmills, U.K.: Macmillan, 1996.

Rosenthal, Erwin I. J. *Political Thought in Medieval Islam: An Introductory Outline.* Cambridge, U.K.: Cambridge University Press, 1968.

Abdul Rashid Moten

Politics and Ethics. The word *politics*, because it so widely employed in diverse situations, is multivalent. It is typically taken to mean the self-interested struggle for competitive advantage that inevitably goes on in all societies or groups. In the Western tradition, we may identify two (often overlapping) ways of engaging in discourse about politics. Political philosophy, in its idealistic form, is the art of purposeful management of public affairs based on the ultimate knowledge of the unchanging essences of political objects. This type of discourse about politics is best idealized by Plato, who thought of politics as "soulcraft"—good public life depends on the creation, according to the wise philosopher, of a good citizen. Ethics, in this model, are inextricably connected to politics, for the good life is unimaginable except in a community, in the good city. Modern political science, taking its cue from Aristotle rather than Plato, sees political knowledge as the empirical science of systematic observation of political life. This view focuses not on human moral self, beliefs, or conscience, but on "statecraft," that is, the conditions and institutions that would facilitate the desired end of collective life. Theorization about politics is often carried out in times of unusual instability and disorder, and nearly always in order to address some problem of politics—to reign in disorder, injustice, tyranny, or weakness of a community—and hence relies on some vision of the collective good.

Ethics, understood as the discourse that addresses moral value of actions, differentiating good from bad conduct, address the micro or individual level of human conduct. Collective and individual goods need not necessarily be linked, and an ethical philosophy may choose to turn away from politics (as many otherworldly ones do), and, much more rarely, a political philosophy may require no ethical commitment of its citizens other than self-interested, even instinctive action (as Hobbes or Mill). But in most cases, certainly in Islam, ethics and politics are interdependent; in particular, good politics in Islamic tradition has been primarily good ethics on the part of the ruler.

Early Islamic ethics are eminently political in one sense, since the individual is enjoined to be concerned with the well-being of the community and, secondarily, with all human beings as well as other creatures of God, including animals, plants, and the environment. This concern with the whole, and even requirement in certain situations to sacrifice personal gains, interests, and preferences, even legitimate ones, for others in general and for the Muslim community in particular, is a crucial virtue that enables politics and a strong sense of "citizenship" (understood as membership in the *ummah*).

Unlike the Hellenic tradition, the ultimate good in Islamic ethics is not defined by the good of the whole, or the political good. Ultimately, it is the consequences of one's actions that reflect in the divine reckoning in eternal afterlife that matter; this-worldly existence being only a transient one. The ultimate reckoning, the Qurʾān teaches, is addressed to the individual soul, not the community: "None shall [in the afterlife] bear the burden of another. And that there is nothing for man except for what he strives" (53:39), and "The pious man shall avoid [the divine chastisement], the one who gives his wealth, seeking to purify himself. He expects favors [in return] from none, except his desire for the Face of God, the Highest. And he shall be pleased" (92:19–21). Yet the collectivist ethics of the Qurʾān are so intense as to add a clearly communal dimension even to this essentially individualist judgment: people will be called to their eternal abodes, good or bad, in groups or nations (7:38; 38:71, 73, etc.), and the company one keeps in this world may be decisive in the choices one makes and hence in the afterlife (25:28). Prophetic *ḥadīth*s evince a similar view.

An additional feature of early Islamic ethics that accentuates their political character is that they are action-oriented rather than theoretical, mystical, or gnostic, and actions acquire their meaning invariably in a community. More specifically, in Islamic scriptural teachings, individuals must strive within a community in a mission to humankind that mirrors the mission of the Prophet himself: "Thus we have made you a community of the golden mean [*ummat wasaṭ*], that you be witnesses unto people and the Messenger witness unto you" (2:143), and "You are the best community ever brought forth to humankind: you command what is right, forbid what is evil, and believe in God" (3:110). What connects the communal nature of this-worldly struggle of the believers to the individualist nature of divine reckoning in eternal life is the concept of intention (*nīyah*), which interiorizes Islamic ethics, creating a dual plane for the evaluation of any act, one based on its external propriety and accordance with the law—this being the subject of Islamic jurisprudence (*fiqh*)—and the other based on its internal sincerity and meaning—this being unknown except to God alone, not liable to any earthly judgment, thus being the subject of Islamic disciplinary and pietistic discourses, in particular Sufism.

Social ethics appear to have been the central concern of Islamic tradition right from the beginning, as the earliest short chapters of the Qurʾān ask their Meccan audience to be kind and charitable toward the weak, the orphans, the poor, and the prisoners, and to free the slaves; thus social justice and charity are the chief ethical concerns in the early period. Over time, the preaching of Islam obviously produced a radical change in moral values as well, based on the worldview and commandments of the new message, grounded in particular in the fear of God and of the Last Judgment. Kindness, fairness, mercy, generosity, self-restraint, courage, sincerity, and moral fellowship of the believers were among the new virtues that replaced or altered the existing tribal morality. The thrust of the Qur'ānic discourse is geared toward creating an overwhelming consciousness of God's presence and active involvement in the world, linking acts of charity and worship to each other and to God: "Prayer forbids promiscuity and evil" (29:45); "[Take alms from the wealthy] lest it [wealth] circulate [merely] within the rich among you" (59:7), and so on.

The specific term that came to be used for ethics is *akhlāq*. Its cognate *khuluq* is employed in the Qur'ān to refer generally to behavior or conduct: "You [O Prophet], indeed are of a lofty character" (68:4), and once more in a similar sense in 26:137. A bulk of *ḥadīth* literature is richly focused on ethics and exhorts good character in general as well as a host of particular virtues.

Classical Period: Legal Formalism and Political Ethics. Despite Islam's political beginning and prophetic model, certain important strands of Islamic tradition developed in apolitical, if not antipolitical, directions, such as mysticism, various forms of theological predestinarianism that effectively denied free will, legal formalism, and so on.

One strand was Sufism. To draw on Max Weber's distinction between mysticism and asceticism, we may identify two types of ethics that came to be incorporated in different strands of Sufism (Weber, 1978). Early Islamic asceticism was highly self-abnegating, defiant of authority, and warlike, and shunned dependence on others in any form, whereas mystical Sufism preached a highly esoteric ethic, and strands of it denied causality, responsibility, and public decorum, focusing solely on interiority at the expense of collective ethics (*malāmatīyah*, who publicly engaged in self-deprecating behavior; mendicants, who lived on charity or leftovers and refused to work to earn a living). The Sunnī *'ulamā'* typically embraced a strong collective and social ethics (e.g., al-Ḥārith al-Muḥāsibī and Aḥmad ibn Ḥanbal, themselves prominent ascetics), and wrote against such kinds of renunciation.

Another central strand starting in the tenth century was legalistic. After the demise of the central caliphate, the predominant aim in the classical era was to live between memory and desire and accept the poverty of the present. Accepting that politics in reality was always "corrupt and corrupting" was concomitant with an ideal of politics that was so lofty that it could be fulfilled only in the distant past or messianic future. In the present, one lived with piety and law, seeking solace in one's family and religion, doing what God or one's kin and clients required. A typical Muslim scholar of classical Baghdad would have seen engagement with power as disdainful and ephemeral. The rulers and the ruled, like the two banks of a river, flowed together but seldom met. Elitism and even disdain for the commoner alongside sanctification of kingship were nothing new in the Near Eastern intellectual traditions. But in the religion of the "Unlettered Prophet" (Qur'ān 7:157), which had been based in collectivist and action-oriented ideals, common sense, and egalitarianism, the accommodation to elitism was far from easy. The conservatism of the period was reflected in the growing legal formalism and cynicism regarding the ethical capacity of human reason that was not strictly grounded in analogical scriptural reasoning. Although there existed strong countercurrents, such as Ibn Taymīyah (d. 1328), the dominant mood of the medieval period against the validity of independent political and ethical reasoning persisted, leaving such reasoning to take place often outside the confines of strict Islamic reasoning (Anjum, 2012). This probably explains why the bulk of *akhlāq* works addressed to rulers and other government officials was written mostly in the Persianate tradition while drawing on a host of other, foreign traditions, with Islamic scriptures treated merely as one among many mines of wisdom, rather than with any systematic attention.

Ethics in Islamic Political Advice Literature. A work devoted to *akhlāq* addresses the cultivation of personal virtue, or, more generally, ethics. Scores of *akhlāq* works have been written, primarily in Arabic initially and then in Persian, and translated between Arabic, Persian, Turkish, and Urdu. Advisory compositions reflect their historical context and the concepts of legitimacy that were current at the time. Earlier ones are written in the tradition of Islamic consultation, *shūrā*, for giving and seeking advice; *shūrā* was both a mode of imparting ethics and a crucial Qurʾānic ethical imperative in itself. Later ones reflect the development of increasingly specialized bureaucracies and highly stratified societies and near-complete separation between the ruler and the ruled.

Plato's *Republic* and Aristotle's *Nicomachean Ethics*, as well as some Neoplatonic writings, were appreciated by authors whose books fall within the ethical branch of advice literature known as *ʿilm al-akhlāq*, "the science of moral characteristics." The earliest Arabic works on ethics, such as the *Fī tahdhīb al-akhlāq* of Miskawayh (d. 1030), address the cultivation of virtue in the individual; later works add sections devoted to the household, family, and the polity. The later works thus treat ethics, economics, and politics, the three divisions of practical philosophy (*al-ḥikmah al-ʿamalīyah*) derived from the Aristotelian tradition and assimilated into philosophical discourse in the medieval Islamic and European worlds. Another significant contribution to Arabic ethics literature was made by the popular genre of the gnomologium, a collection of aphorisms transmitted from or attributed to Greek philosophers and sages (Marlow, 2010).

The most widely disseminated of Persian-Sassanian works was the *ʿAhd Ardashīr* (Testament of Ardashīr), which was incorporated into several Arabic histories and anthologies and cited extensively in works of advice literature for over a millennium. The testament is addressed by Ardashīr, founder of the Sassanian dynasty, to his successors or son, and it offers a lengthy presentation of the principles and practical aspects of kingship. Translations of books dealing with the culture and customs of the Sassanian court also contributed to works of Arabic advice literature. The only such fully extant work that has been widely read in courts of Muslim rulers is the *Kitāb al-tāj* of Muḥammad b. al-Ḥārith al-Taghlibī (or Thaʿlabī, d. 864), which treats topics such as the conduct of the ruler, the organization of the court, and the proper behavior of the ruler's boon companions.

The ʿAbbāsid secretary of Persian extraction Ibn al-Muqaffaʿ (d. c. 757) introduced *Kalīlah wa-Dimnah*, a collection of allegorical fables of Indian origin in which various animals portray the roles of king and courtiers. The frame tale involves a king and his counselor, who, when asked to explicate a point, reply with a brief statement followed by an illustrative story. Each chapter in the *Kalīlah wa-Dimnah* repeats this model interaction before proceeding to the next story. The *ʿUyūn al-akhbār* of Ibn Qutaybah (828–889) and the *ʿIqd al-farīd* of Ibn ʿAbd Rabbihi of Córdoba (860–940), both open with a "Book of Authority" (*Kitāb al-sulṭān*), which explores the qualities necessary for rulership. Ibn Miskūyah, in his *al-Ḥikmah al-khālidah* and other works, brought together and integrated ideas derived from multiple cultural strands.

An example of literature intended to guide the ruler to Islamic political ethics is *Kitāb al-kharāj* of Abū Yūsuf (d. 798), a treatise on taxation submitted to Hārūn al-Rashīd (r. 786–809), which emphasizes the caliph's accountability before God and his responsibilities toward his subjects. He portrays those placed in authority as deputies (*khulafāʾ*) on God's earth (not "God's deputies," as some mistaken translations state; Anjum, 2012, p. 86), recipients of a light by which they are able to elucidate for their subjects certain obscure matters and explicate the duties incumbent upon them. Among the tasks of those in authority are the upholding of legal provisions and penalties and the revival of the established practices (*sunan*) of the pious Muslims of old (*salaf*). Abū Yūsuf cites numerous *ḥadīths*, many of which stress the high standing of the just ruler and his reward in the life to come, and the corresponding abasement and punishment that await the unjust ruler. He also urges the caliph to cultivate a close relationship with the *ʿulamāʾ*, perhaps with a view to encouraging the participation of religious scholars in the administration (Zaman, 1997, pp. 91–101).

One such widely circulated and admired document of the early period that draws on Islamic scriptural sources was the "testament" of the caliph al-Maʾmūn's provincial regent Ṭāhir b. al-Ḥusayn (r. 775–822), founder of the largely independent Ṭāhirid dynasty in eastern Iran. Ṭāhir's testament offers an extensive and comprehensive model of rulership to which those in authority should aspire. He takes as his premise the Qurʾānic pronouncement that sovereignty belongs to God alone and that earthly rulers find themselves in authority only by His permission (cf. 3:26); he invokes the Qurʾān and *sunnah* and asserts repeatedly the need for the ruler to consult jurists and other bearers of religious knowledge. Ṭāhir's testament emphasizes piety and remembrance of humanity's ultimate return to God; it urges its recipient to promote justice among his subjects, to observe moderation (*iqtiṣād*) in all matters, to be mindful of God in all his actions, to apply the statutory penalties, to keep agreements, to be just, to control his temper, and to expend his wealth for the prosperity of Islam and its people. Ṭāhir shows a particular concern that the common people should be treated with equity and kindness. A notable feature of his testament is that after offering each piece of advice, Ṭāhir expatiates on its significance in attaining the overall objectives of promoting religion, sovereignty, and prosperity, as well as the ruler's own felicity in this world and the next.

Mirrors for Princes. The earliest extant book-length works of advice, to which the term "mirror" has been applied, are written in Arabic and date from the tenth century. Many such works have been written since. A common theme is the indispensability of personal virtue for the ruler, on whose sound governance the well-being of all his subjects, entrusted to his care by God, depends. Others are the centrality of justice to the harmonious working of all components of the realm, if not the cosmos; the need for the ruler to uphold Islamic law and abide by it in his own rulings and in his personal conduct; to cultivate learning and patronize the learned; to solicit advice from scholars and sages and pay heed to their counsel; to control his temper and refrain from meting out punishments in haste; and to study the ways of past kings. Other recurrent elements include certain Qurʾānic quotations, such as 4:59, "Obey God, obey the messenger, and those in authority among you," and 38:26, "O David! We have created you as a deputy [*khalīfah*] in the earth; therefore judge truthfully among people," and certain *ḥadīths*, such as "religion is sincere counsel" (*al-dīn al-naṣīḥah*). The maxims "The ruler is the shadow of God on earth" and "Religion and sovereignty are twins" also appear with regularity. Several metaphors for the ruler's relationship to his subjects occur across numerous cultures; they include the head (or heart) to the body, the physician to his patient, or the shepherd to his flock (Marlow, 2010).

The eminent Sunnī jurist and chief judge of Baghdad al-Māwardī (974–1058), in his *Tashīl al-naẓar wa-taʿjīl al-ẓafar*, draws on Islamic, Greek, Persian, and other sources and presents rulership, like his contemporary scholars, in the context of the differences among people and their resultant needs for cooperation. The beginning of virtues, he writes, is reason, and the last or highest of them, justice.

Niẓām al-Mulk (d. 1092), vizier to the Seljuk rulers Alp Arslān (r. 1063–1072) and Malik Shāh (r. 1072–1092), in his celebrated *Siyāsatnāma*, also known as *Siyar al-mulūk*, portrays sovereignty, in the Persian-Sassanid tradition, as the result of divine appointment, symbolized by the "divine aura" (or effulgence; *farr-i ilāhī*). The ruler is responsible for the upholding of religion and the suppression of heresy and rebellion, topics that particularly preoccupied the author; the ruler should rule in accordance with justice, and the subjects owe him obedience. This Persianate model, rather than Islamic scripture, undergirds much of subsequent literature on the ethics of governance.

Abū Ḥāmid al-Ghazālī (1058–1111) wrote several such works. The *Kitāb al-mustaẓhirī* is a theological polemic against the Ismāʿīlī doctrine of the imamate, a legitimation of the ʿAbbāsid caliphate, and apparently an accommodation of the Seljuk sultanate as well. More widely read was al-Ghazālī's *Kīmiyā-yi saʿādat*, a Persian abridgement of his *Iḥyāʾ ʿulum al-din* addressed to the commoners. The *Kīmiyā* is structured according to four headings (knowledge of the self, knowledge of God, knowledge of this world, and knowledge of the world to come) and four pillars (acts of worship, social transactions, the removal of impediments to religion, and personal prayers). Personal piety and striving for moral excellence are emphasized throughout the work. The *Kīmiyā* also incorporates materials not found in the *Iḥyāʾ*; among these additions is a mirror addressed to the ruler, strongly Ṣūfī in tone, which outlines ten instructions for rulers emphasizing the necessity of justice, the perils of injustice, and the need for rulers to consult pious scholars (Hillenbrand, 1988). Of special importance is another treatise, *Naṣīḥat al-mulūk*, attributed to al-Ghazālī. This Persian work consists of two parts, only the first of which is by al-Ghazālī; the second part is by an unknown author whose cultural and political orientations contrast with those of al-Ghazālī (Hillenbrand, 1988). The first part portrays rulership as a divine gift, for which the ruler will be held accountable at the Last Day; it places great emphasis on the ruler's personal virtue. The second part, by contrast, exhibits a perspective reminiscent of that of Niẓām al-Mulk and a Persianate milieu, in which the king occupies a preferential position in the divine order.

An influential mirror written in the Shīʿī and philosophical traditions was that of Naṣīr al-Dīn al-Ṭūsī (1201–74), which came to be eminently influential in Persianate cultures. The *Akhlāq-i Nāṣirī* was written first for an Ismāʿīlī prince and later redacted for the Mongol ruler Hülegü (r. 1256–1265). Ibn Miskūyah's work *Fī tahdhīb al-akhlāq* constitutes the basis for al-Ṭūsī's first discourse, on the refinement of moral characteristics. Al-Ṭūsī, however, added two further discourses, on household management (*tadbīr-i manzil*) and the governance of polities (*siyāsat-i mudun*); these two last discourses draw on the works of Bryson, the second-century CE Neopythagorean, and al-Fārābī (d. 950), respectively. In the first discourse, al-Ṭūsī discusses the faculties of the soul, its perfection and deficiency, the nature and alterability of the human disposition, the cultivation of moral characteristics, virtues and vices, justice, the acquisition of virtues, and preserving the health of the soul and treating its sickness. The second discourse covers households, property and stores, wives, children, parents, servants, and slaves. The third discourse treats the need for cooperation among human beings; love, by which societies are connected; the divisions of societies and the conditions of cities; the manners of courtiers; friendship; behavior toward the different categories of people; and testaments attributed to Plato.

Al-Ṭūsī's philosophical vision is a comprehensive one, in which the various aspects of individual, familial, and political experience, including rulership, are situated in an ordered and rational system. The *Akhlāq-i Nāṣirī* enjoyed a very broad circulation almost from the moment of its composition, and in its conception established a new model for works of advice.

The writing of advice literature also flourished in Muslim communities in South Asia, where Fakhr al-Dīn Mubārakshāh (Fakhr-i Mudabbir) composed the *Ādāb al-mulūk va-kifāyat al-mamlūk*, in Persian, at the request of Sulṭān Shams al-Dīn Iltutmish (r. 1210–1236) of Delhi. Like some other works of advice literature written for Muslim audiences in northwestern South Asia during the period of the sultanates, the *Ādāb al-ḥarb va-al-shajāʿah* also addresses the status of non-Muslims, whose protection and just treatment Fakhr-i Mudabbir commends (Marlow, 2010).

BIBLIOGRAPHY

Anjum, Ovamir. *Politics, Law and Community in Islamic Thought: The Taymiyyan Moment.* Cambridge, U.K.: Cambridge University Press, 2012.

Hillenbrand, Carole. "Islamic Orthodoxy or Realpolitik? Al-Ghazālī's Views on Government." *Iran* 26 (1988): 81–94.

Hourani, George F. *Reason and Tradition in Islamic Ethics.* Cambridge, U.K.: Cambridge University Press, 1985.

Karamustafa, Ahmet T. *Sufism: The Formative Period.* Berkeley: University of California Press, 2007.

Marlow, Louise "Advice and Advice Literature." *Encyclopaedia of Islam.* 3d ed. Leiden, Netherlands: Brill, 2010.

Weber, Max. *Economy and Society: An Outline of Interpretive Sociology.* 4th ed. Berkeley: University of California Press, 1978.

Zaman, Muhammad Qasim. *Religion and Politics under the Early Abbasids: The Emergence of the Proto-Sunni Elite.* Leiden, Netherlands: Brill, 1997.

OVAMIR ANJUM

POSTCOLONIALISM. Postcolonialism in the Muslim world was ushered in at the end of World War II and refers to political developments that happened after the end of the colonial period. Major events within the Muslim world can be explained in terms of a native-colonial struggle over forms of political organization. In this struggle the territorial modern nation-state was imposed by colonial powers and preserved by an international system of states established and defended by such powers, while native precolonial political identities expressed themselves in various forms ranging from Islamism to tribal affiliation. Relations between these two identities were consistently radicalized with the passage of time. Attempts at reconciliation between the two started in the early years of the Ottoman Empire and continued through the establishment of secular liberal modern states following the various colonial military interventions up until World War I. With the end of the interwar period and the establishment of the state of Israel, socialism presented itself as an alternative noncolonial paradigm, while socialist nationalist movements succeeded it by redefining the colonial state, further attempting to reconcile it with native sentiment, culture, and public opinion. The failure of these nationalist movements resulted in the rise of a spectrum of Islamic movements, most of which were more hostile to the European colonial project than all preceding arrangements.

When Graham Fuller wrote that political Islam was the only popular political force in the Middle East and Central Asia in the 1990s and when Samuel Huntington wrote that Islam was the most likely force with which liberal democracies had to clash, they were not referring to a coherent Islamic movement. The Islamic movements to which these authors referred were mainly a shared public opinion expressed through movements that differed in their structure, function, strategy, and tactics. There was no overarching institutional power, state or non-state, to unite or even mediate between these movements.

This phenomenon became more visible with the failure of colonially created nation-states to achieve the goals they promised constituencies. In most cases these goals involved independence from Western control, economic development, and military invulnerability to colonial intervention. In the case of the Arab Muslim majority countries, this was coupled with a drive for unity. Territorial nation-states were compromises between colonial and native identities and agendas. While Britain's agenda in creating an Egyptian nation-state was, in the words of Evelyn Baring, Earl of Cromer, the British proconsul in Cairo, to create a skillfully constructed automaton that would govern Egypt in the manner Britain would like to be governed, the Egyptian population demanded "full independence or else, imminent death." The Egyptian nationalist movement promised both goals to both sides. After World War II, when Egyptian public opinion, according to Gershoni and Jankovski, had grown more pan-Arab and Islamist, the Nasserist regime promised the Egyptian people Arab unity and the liberation of Palestine, yet as a member of the United Nations accepted the very state system it promised to change. In Iran Shah Reza and his son Muhammad promised an independent nation of Iran to their constituencies and oil to Britain and the United States. In Turkey successive Kemalist governments promised the ultimate expression of the Turkish national identity, while altering that identity beyond recognition by changing everything about popular culture from the script to religion to headgear. Such impossible compromises originated from the contradiction embedded in the colonial process itself. The compromise was expressed in the very structure of the state and the very independence of the Muslim state. According to the literature of movements such as the Muslim Brotherhood, the al-Gamāʿa al-Islāmīyah, and the Front Islamique du Salat (Islamic Salvation Front), the sovereignty of these states was a sign of their servitude. From Pakistan to Morocco, one would easily find in the constitutions of Muslim nations articles referring to their belonging to the larger Islamic *ummah*, and in some instances, especially in Arab Islamic countries, a declared will to dissolve the colonially created state in a larger entity, in this case a united Arab nation-state.

Nascent Arab nationalism emerged when several literary groups were created in the nineteenth century. This search moved hand in hand with Turkish nationalism but was also a reaction to it within the strictly defined parameters of political discourse in the Ottoman Empire. After Napoleon's invasion of Egypt, a central province of the Ottoman Empire, elites in both Cairo and Istanbul came to realize the necessity of administrative economic and political reforms, with the primary purpose of military self-defense. Egypt, the site of the invasion, was the first to modernize under Muḥammad ʿAlī (r. 1805–1849). Muḥammad ʿAlī's system of centralized government abolished a class of tax-collecting local administrators, a remnant of the ruling medieval military caste of warrior slaves called the Mamlūks. It was not long before Muḥammad ʿAlī found himself expanding his domain against the will of his employer, the Ottoman sultan. That threat in and by itself hastened the Ottoman will to modernize and the era of administrative reforms known as the Tanzimat followed. The administrative centralization of the Tanzimat alienated many of the ethnic and religious groups in the empire because it changed the terms of the social contract; while people accepted the Ottoman Islamic caliphate in which no Muslim ethnicity had supremacy over the other, many were not as welcoming of a Turkish national empire. Among the Arab subjects this resistance expressed itself in literary and cultural groups aimed at the revival of the Arabic language and cultural heritage, as well as a political party calling for the decentralization of the Ottoman Empire. Some colonial powers, especially France, adopted the demands of many Arab nationalists and hosted the first Arab nationalist conference in Paris in 1913. Attendees redefined Arab nationalism to fit France's colonial interest, so much so that discussing the situation in Algeria, an Arab French colony, was not allowed. With World War I imminent, Arab nationalism seemed a middle ground between the native population and colonial powers; it could retain some of the region's cultural identity while breaking down the Ottoman Empire, now the enemy and target of colonial powers. After the war ended, the first failure of that compromise came to light when both France and Britain refused to allow Arab national unity and independence, carving out their own colonial spheres of influence instead.

The British played a greater role than the French in that disappointment. They had promised a unified Arab state, denied it, and helped establish a Jewish state in part of the land promised to the Arabs: Palestine. During the war Great Britain and the Ottoman governor of Mecca, Sharif Hussein bin Ali of Hejaz, had agreed to the latter's rebellion against the empire, in return for a united Arab state in Ottoman lands west of the Suez. The *sharīf*, who presented himself as king of the Arabs to the British, presented himself to the Muslims as the potential new caliph. He justified his rebellion by arguing that its aim was to save the caliphate from the corrupting effect of the secular Turkish nationalists, and to save the holy sites of Islam in Mecca and Medina from being overrun by the British. After the war, the *sharīf* was not given his promised state and had to spend the rest of his life in exile in Cypriot, sent there by his former British allies, to prevent him from attempting to achieve that unity. He was nonetheless rewarded by granting two of his sons the thrones of the newly created states of Jordan and Iraq. His own province of Hejaz was awarded to another British ally, Abdul Aziz bin Abdul Rahman bin Saud, the founder of Saudi Arabia. The regimes established in the Arab world east of Suez after World War I were therefore incomplete compromises. The loss of Palestine was uncertain until the war of 1948 and the establishment of the state of Israel. While Arab countries were supportive of the war, the pro-British orientation and colonial nature of the Arab states were blamed for the defeat and punishment of Arab leaders was swift: in 1949 the prime minister of Lebanon was killed, the president of Syria overthrown, the king of Jordan assassinated in 1951, the king of Egypt deposed in 1952, and the king of Iraq deposed in 1958. In a decade the face of the Middle East had changed. What followed was another form of Arab nationalism, one that kept the structure of the colonial state, yet drove it east away from Britain and France toward the Soviet Union. Socialism represented an alternative modernity, an alternative nationalism that was not colonial in orientation and function. Alliance with the Soviet Union meant getting rid of the remnants of British and French colonial influence, the most visible of these remnants of course to most Arabs was the state of Israel. In 1955 Egypt's president was buying weapons from the Soviet Union, and the next year he was at war with Britain, France, and Israel over the nationalization of the Suez Canal, emerging triumphant from that war; expectations regarding Palestine were high. Arab socialist nationalist regimes were either promised or were expected to engage the plight of Arab, mostly Muslim, Palestinian refugees and the restoration to the Arabs of the territories lost in the war of 1948. Such a victory was therefore a function of the will of the superpowers supplying the Arabs with weapons. Among the very few matters of consensus among the Soviets and the Americans, heirs to Britain and France in the region, was that Israel should survive. The Arab defeat in the war of 1967 sealed the fate of Arab nationalist socialist projects and paved the way for an Islamism that deconstructed the foundations of the colonially created system ruled outside the state.

Persian nationalism was defeated by the West in 1953, with the coup against Iran's nationalist prime minister Mohammad Mossadegh. Iran was allowed all the symbols of ancient Persian imperial grandeur, but not control of its oil revenues. While the state of Iran was not carved out by colonial officers like its neighbors in British India-Pakistan and the Arab world, the structures of the state and the coming to power of Reza Shah, founder of the Pahlavi two-man dynasty, were greatly influenced by colonial powers. Just like the Arabs, from the late nineteenth to the early twentieth century the two political trends of Islamism and modern nationalism were in conflict. While many clerics supported the constitutional movement of 1906, some under the leadership of Ayatollah Nouri opposed the establishment of a national constitution on the basis of it being a replacement for the Qur'ān and a threat to Iran's Islamic identity. As in the case of the Arab world, a Western colonial defeat of local secular nationalism resulted in the rise of a version of Islamism that deconstructed the Western-inspired modernist structure to replace it with something else. Khomeini was able, through meticulously traditional methodologies of exegesis, to argue that Shīʿī Islam, based on the doctrine of divine choice of the leader of the community, actually called for a republic ruled by scholars who balanced each other's powers. Iran could therefore boast the first significant modern innovation in Islamic political theory to be put into practice on a large scale, as well as the first popular revolution in the Middle East. The eight-year war with Iraq showed how solid this regime was, the loss of legitimacy Iraqi president Saddam Hussein suffered among his Shīʿī citizens, and the military campaigns he conducted against them, could not be compared with any insurrection or rebellion against the regime in Iran. Despite the fact that Iraq claimed victory, the Islamic republic's legitimacy was unharmed, if not strengthened by the war, while Saddam Hussein's decline in legitimacy, especially among his Shīʿī citizens, led him to use military force against them. The fallout between Iraq and its allies in 1991 and the subsequent destruction, siege, and occupation of the country by the United States left Iran's Islamic republic with the opportunity to fill the political vacuum, increasing its influence in Iraq, the Gulf, and subsequently the rest of the Arab world. The Islamic legitimizing discourse of the Iranian regime also put it on a direct collision course with Israel over Jerusalem. Not only was Iran's position on Palestine a doctrinal imperative and a domestic course of legitimacy, it was also a way to win over many Arabs. Ḥizbullāh's victory over Israel during the war of 2006 advanced the cause of Islamism throughout the region and made evident that non-state actors could perform the state's most important function, defense, much better than the state itself.

A compromise similar to that offered to the Arabs was offered to the Turks after World War I. Unlike the Arabs, however, Turkey had neither oil nor Jerusalem. The territorial integrity of Turkey did not contradict the colonial interests of the victors of World War I, including the United States. Hence, unlike the Arab lands, Turkey was not partitioned and Turkish secular nationalism was not forced to suffer humiliating defeats through the manipulation of arms supplies. Therefore the Turkish secular nationalist project lasted longer, and the Europeanization of Turkish society went further than attempts to the south and the east. Europeanization included turning Istanbul's grand mosque into a museum, *scratching* Islamic decorations to reveal the Christian Orthodox icons of the church beneath, and changing the script of the Turkish language from Arabic to Latin alphabets. It was that Europeanization that made the rejection of Turkey's admittance to the European Union more insulting. Turkey's importance as a NATO ally in the Cold War against Soviet expansion into the Mediterranean was contrasted with its lack of importance as a sharing member of the economic affluence that came with membership in such an alliance. By the end of the Cold War there was political vacuum in the Middle East. Allies of the Soviet Union, such as Syria, found it was too late to bargain gainfully for a switch to the Western camp and hence were left without a patron and looking for allies. Imposed military expansion by the United States in the Persian Gulf in 1991 and 2003 was met with violence. This made the political choice of Turkey to be yet another ally of the now ally-saturated West even less attractive; a Turkey capitalizing on its Islamic Ottoman heritage had a chance to expand south and southeast in terms of influence, much more than its chance to be integrated to the north and northwest. Being active to the south and to the east was also an important bargaining chip, improving Turkey's strategic value to the Western alliance.

Both Iran and Turkey suffered less direct colonial pressure than their Arab neighbors. The leadership in both countries understood that the war to win over the Middle East would not be won fighting Iraq, but rather by opposing Israel. With the political opportunity for leadership in the Middle East, a form of Islamism developed in Turkey, which is still the closest form of compromise between Islamism and Western-imposed identities.

The revolutions in Tunisia and Egypt came as an expression of the inability of the state structure, formal parties, and even trade unions to achieve self-determination and independence. The struggle with colonialism was made clear through consecutive defeats. While Turkey showed that compromise, even after having worked for a long time, failed, Iran showed that rebelling against compromise worked. Iraq, Lebanon, Afghanistan, and Gaza showed that while formal modern armies cannot protect independence and self-determination, the people can frustrate the political ambitions of the mightiest superpowers. The revolutions in Tunisia, Egypt, and the rest of the Arab world therefore hold the possibility of redefining the terms of that compromise.

BIBLIOGRAPHY

Arquilla, John, and David Ronfeldt, eds. *Networks and Netwars: The Future of Terror, Crime, and Militancy.* Santa Monica, Calif.: RAND, 2001.

Blake, Kristen. *The U.S.-Soviet Confrontation in Iran, 1945–1962: A Case in the Annals of the Cold War.* Lanham, Md.: University Press of America, 2009.

Fuller, Graham E. *The Future of Political Islam.* New York: Palgrave Macmillan, 2003.

Gasiorowski, Mark, and Malcolm Byrne, eds. *Mohammad Mosaddeq and the 1953 Coup in Iran.* Syracuse, N.Y.: Syracuse University Press, 2004.

Gershoni, Israel, and James P. Jankowski. *Redefining Egyptian Nationhood, 1930–1945.* New York: Cambridge University Press, 1995.

Hale, William, and Ergun Özbudun. *Islamism, Democracy and Liberalism in Turkey: The Case of the AKP.* London and New York: Routledge, 2010.

Jones, David Martin, Ann Lane, and Paul Schulte, eds. *Terrorism, Security and the Power of Informal Networks.* Cheltenham, U.K.: Edward Elgar, 2010.

Khomeini, Ruhollah. *Islamic Government.* Translated by the Joint Publications Research Service. New York: Manor Books, 1979.

Mahaza, Ali. *Al-fikr al-siyāsī fī al-Urdunn* [Political Thought in Jordan]. Amman: Markaz al-Kutub al-Urdunī, 1991.

Rabasa Angel, and F. Stephen Larrabee. *The Rise of Political Islam in Turkey.* Santa Monica, Calif.: RAND, 2008.

Tibi, Bassam. *Arab Nationalism: A Critical Inquiry.* Edited and translated by Marion Farouk-Sluglett and Peter Sluglett. 2d ed. Houndmills, U.K.: Macmillan, 1990.

Yavuz, Hakan. "Turkish-Israeli Relations Through the Lens of the Turkish Identity Debate." *Journal of Palestine Studies* 27, no. 1 (Autumn 1997): 22–37.

TAMIM AL-BARGHOUTI

POWER. Power, defined as the ability to make someone do something which he or she otherwise would not do, plays a central role in Islam. Power is essential to maintain order and progress in the society (Qur'ān 4:59, 43:32). The Qur'ān states categorically that power can be exercised for the good of a person or the society, just as it can be used to create and perpetuate injustice, oppression, and stagnation (6:123, 20:24, 27:34, 33:67, 34:34, 43:23–24, etc.). The Qur'ān abhors the abuse of power and enjoins the believers to use power for the good of the self and the society. Power could be used as an end in itself, just as it can be used as a means to an end. In Islam, the emphasis has always been to use power as a means to earn the pleasure of Almighty Allāh. Power must not be used for aggression. It must be used to respond to aggression. Islam permits waging of war by those "who are fought against, because they have been wronged" (22:39–40). However, the believers are enjoined to explore and exhaust all possible peaceful means of resolving the problem before resorting to war. The Qur'ān nevertheless requires of believers to "make ready against them all you can of power, including steeds of war to threaten the enemy of Allah and your enemy" (8:60).

In Islam, absolute right and power belong only to Allāh, who has no partner (2:165, 5:17, 12:40, 13:31 etc.). Allāh is omnipotent and is dominant over all His creation. He achieves whatever He wills. No human being, as such, has an inherent right to exercise power over others except as a servant of Allāh. It is obligatory for Muslims to continue ceaseless struggle to repudiate those who arrogate power to themselves and thus to banish oppression and injustice from the face of earth. The Qur'ān requires Muslims to shatter the absolutism of demigods and false deities; to divest them of any leadership roles; to wrest power for the righteous; and to reinstate good in place of evil. Power in Islam has only one function, and that is to "establish regular prayers and practice regular charity and enjoin the right and forbid the wrong" (22:41). Thus, power must be underpinned by legitimacy and used only for the purposes sanctioned in the divine sources of Islam.

Islam is thus actively concerned with power, a power through which the world should be transformed to be in accord with Islamic tenets and principles to benefit humanity as a whole. *Jihād fī sabīl-Allāh* (utmost exertion in the way of Allāh) is but another name for the effort to establish the divine order. Power is sought in Islam not for personal or collective aggrandizement but as a means to serve Allāh and to earn His pleasure. Thus, the reason to strive to control the state structure and to wrest power for the righteous is to root out evil and bring about the good life in this world as a means to attain salvation in the hereafter.

Power and Prophethood. Given such a clarion call, the Prophet Muḥammad had no alternative but to fight all those who rebelled against his guidance. Similarly, all the earlier prophets were engaged in conveying divine guidance and reminding the faithful to eschew *ṭāghūt* (Qur'ān 16:36). Prophet Muḥammad lacked military and political power in Mecca, but he had the loyalty of and authority over the handful of companions who accepted Islam. The Prophet was endowed with divine legitimacy. The Qur'ān proclaims: "We have sent you with legitimacy, as a bearer of good news and a Warner" (2:119). Verse 4:170 announces: "O Mankind, the Apostle has now come unto you with legitimacy from Your Sustainer."

One of the momentous events in the life of the Prophet Muḥammad is the migration (*hijrah*) to Medina undertaken in order, among other reasons, to restructure power relationships and make them subservient to the divine will. He reorganized the tribal society by creating a bond of brotherhood between the immigrants and the hosts in Medina, created strategic alliances with several tribes, and drafted in the first year of the Hijrah, according to Muhammad Hamidullah (1986), the first written constitution in the world. This constitution enshrined the principles of freedom and justice. It contains provisions relating to the prerogatives and obligations of the ruler and the ruled and other requirements, including what may be termed social insurance for the needy. Thus was established the first Islamic polity, of which the Prophet Muḥammad was the spiritual and temporal head. He led public prayers, commanded the army, acted as a judge, and formulated public policies. He led his followers into battle but only when diplomatic options failed to resolve the problem and only when enemies resorted to aggression.

The Prophet, however, did not arrogate all power to himself. Under divine instruction, he empowered the people through the establishment of *shūrā*, or decision making through consultation. The Qurʾānic verse 42:38, "Their affairs are decided by consultations between them," emphasizes the principle of *shūrā*. The Prophet himself was commanded to "consult them in their affairs" (3:159). The Qurʾān places *shūrā* on the same footing as establishing prayer and paying *zakah*. According to the text and context of the Qurʾān and the *sunnah*, *shūrā* means a decisive participation of the people in governing themselves. *Shūrā* not only ensures the participation of the people in public affairs, but it acts as a check against tyrannical rule as well.

The Rightly Guided Caliphs (Khulafāʾ al-Rāshidūn, r. 622–659 CE), who headed the four successive postprophetic polities, emulated the Prophet in every detail. Their selection and that of all those in positions of power were conducted by *shūrā*, whether it was carried out directly or indirectly through selected or elected representatives. They, as leaders of the community, executed the *Sharīʿah*, maintained the purity of religion, and expanded the frontiers of Islam. By the time of the third caliph, ʿUthmān, Islamic civilization had extended from Transoxiana to the shores of the Atlantic in the west.

Power in the Post-Rashīdah Period. There is unanimity among scholars that the political system established in Medina is a model (defining the principles to implement an Islamic polity) for all Muslim societies to adopt and follow. With the emergence of the Umayyads, however, there ensued a new model in Muslim history—dynastic rule, which sometimes degenerated into unbridled monarchy. The authority of these rulers, for all practical purposes, was arbitrary. Power during most of Muslim history has not always been subject to divine will and has been exercised for ends other than establishing justice among the people. This led some Ṣūfī teachers (mystics) to disengage from politics, but some were also actively engaged in politics, often coming into conflict with the rulers, and eventually generated powerful sociopolitical movements. The intellectual disciple of al-Ghazālī, Muḥammad Ibn Tūmart (d. 1130), preached a doctrine that formed the basis of the Almohad Empire (1130–1269), which encompassed the whole of the Maghrib. Their predecessors, the Almoravids, meaning those who dwell in a *ribāṭ* (a place where warriors of faith live and worship), waged a successful *jihād* and founded the Almoravid Empire (1056–1147), which extended from Senegal to Algeria.

The degeneration and decline of caliphal power and the emergence of "sultans" as the de facto rulers of their regions also led to the emergence of a discourse or power among prominent Muslim scholars. Abū al-Ḥasan al-Māwardī (d. 1058), Abū Ḥamīd Muḥammad al-Ghazālī (d. 505/1111), Badr al-Dīn Muḥammad Ibn Jamāʿah (d. 1333), and others wrote treatises that discussed the nature of the caliphate, the duties of the caliphs, the rise and power of sultans, and their impact on the government. Al-Māwardī, in *al-Aḥkām al-sulṭānīyah,* recognized the power of the sultans but called upon them to show allegiance to the caliphs, which would give a moral and legal basis to their rule. Al-Ghazālī argued that military power is the sole basis of the government and that a caliph is the person who obtains the allegiance of the person with military power. Ibn Jamāʿah took the final step by abandoning the theoretical suzerainty of the caliph and declaring that military power is the essence of rulership. However, it is Ibn Khaldūn (d. 1406) who recognized the will to power and domination as the principal driving force in the society and accordingly "propounded a theory of the power-state" (Rosenthal, 1958, p. 84). He was also concerned with questions relating to political legitimacy in societies desiring to be Islamic.

BIBLIOGRAPHY

Browers, Michaelle L. *Democracy and Civil Society in Arab Political Thought: Transcultural Possibilities.* Syracuse, N.Y.: Syracuse University, 2006.

Esposito, John L., ed. *Voices of Resurgent Islam.* New York: Oxford University Press, 1983.

Hamidullah, Muhammad. *The First Written Constitution in the World: An Important Document of the Time of the Holy Prophet.* Karachi: Kazi, 1986.

Lambton, Ann K. S. *State and Government in Medieval Islam: An Introduction to the Study of Islamic Political Theory: The Jurists.* Oxford: Oxford University Press, 1981.

Rosenthal, E. I. J. *Political Thought in Medieval Islam: An Introductory Outline.* Cambridge, U.K.: Cambridge University Press, 1958.

Saeed, Abdullah, ed. *Islamic Political Thought and Governance: Critical Concepts in Political Science.* London: Routledge, 2011.

Siddiqui, Kalim. *Political Dimensions of the Seerah.* Toronto: Institute of Contemporary Islamic Thought, 1998.

ABDUL RASHID MOTEN

PROFESSION OF FAITH. *See* Religious Beliefs.

Q

QADARITES. The term *Qadarite* refers to a partisan in the controversy over free will versus predestination during the first two centuries of Islam. More often, it refers to an advocate of human free will in opposition to absolute divine omnipotence and predeterminism (a doctrine known as *jabr*). The Qurʾān constantly asserts divine justice and righteousness on the one hand and divine omnipotence on the other. On the human side, divine justice entails moral responsibility, while divine omnipotence undergirds to a large extent the very rationale of worship and prayer. Although political motivations have been asserted for each side of the controversy in early Islam by modern scholars, no obvious causal link can be established between Qadarite theology and politics. Although at times Qadarism did become associated with anti-Umayyad movements, so did its opposite, the doctrine of *jabr*, as noted below. Both traditional detractors and modern scholars have suggested that Christian influence may be the source of the Qadarite doctrine. However, outside influences cannot reconcile the inherent paradox between divine justice and omnipotence. As in other Near Eastern monotheistic traditions, the two ideas often seem contradictory and have given rise to considerable theological speculation.

The term *Qadarite* was always used in a pejorative sense, never applied to oneself, due possibly to the circulation of a prophetic *ḥadīth* condemning Qadarites as the "Majūs (Magians) of this *ummah*," in so far as they attributed the creation of evil to other than God, resembling Zoroastrians (known as the Majūs to the Arabs) who posited another god of evil. Accordingly, this term was employed early on by the advocates of free will to label their predeterminist opponents. During the second century, the Qadarite tendencies became incorporated into the Muʿtazilah, a more developed theological sect with free will as one of its essential doctrines.

According to the lists of Qadarites provided in traditionalist (proto-Sunnī and Sunnī) accounts, their major concentration was in Basra (totaling forty names); next in Syria (fifteen names), which is also the only region where the Qadarites can be associated with anti-Umayyad political activism; followed by half a dozen or fewer names each in Mecca, Medina, Kufa, and Yemen; and none in Egypt or Iran (van Ess, 2011).

Qadarite Writers. The early history of the notion of *qadar* (which can hardly be equated with a "movement" or "sect") is still elusive. Several major figures stand out.

Maʿbad b. ʿAbd Allāh al-Juhānī of Basra was the first writer to discourse on *qadar*. He allegedly learned this doctrine from a Christian who had converted from the Magian religion of Persia. He held office in the Umayyad government, but took part in the revolt of Ibn al-Ashʿath and was executed in 703. It is unclear whether his Qadarite leanings were relevant to his politics or his fate.

Ḥasan al-Baṣrī (d. 728) is the author of an epistle (*risālah*) in response to questions from the caliph ʿAbd al-Mālik or his governor. This is possibly the most important and earliest document on the issue, composed between 694 and 699, according to van Ess (2011). It advocates "moderate Qadarism" in that it asserts God's foreknowledge of human acts, but attributes evil human acts to the doer or Satan. Van Ess regards the letter as authentic; others, such as Judd (1999), question its authenticity. Ḥasan's disciples split over the true interpretation of his teachings on *qadar*; van Ess speculates that the anti-Qadarites among them, who later came to constitute the Sunnī orthodoxy, attributed Qadarism and its political consequences to Maʿbad to clear Ḥasan of the charge. Ḥasan's own participation in Ibn al-Ashʿath's revolt, which included anti-Umayyad scholars from all doctrinal leanings, is debated.

The followers of the Khārijite Shabīb (fl. c. 718) adhered to an extreme version of Qadarism that denied God's foreknowledge.

The Umayyad caliph Sulaymān b. ʿAbd al-Mālik (d. 717), the predecessor of ʿUmar II, discoursed on *qadar*.

ʿUmar II, an anti-Qadarite, wrote a refutation of extreme Qadarism but also employed Qadarites in his administration. Since he tolerated dissidents generally, including the Khārijites, little can be deduced from this fact (Murad, 1991; Judd, 1999).

Ghaylān al-Dimashqī (d. probably 743), possibly of Coptic origin, is seen as a founder of Qadarism after Maʿbad. He associated with revered figures such as ʿUmar II and Ḥasan al-Baṣrī (soft Qadarite), as well as with heretics such as Maʿbad (the "first" Qadarite) and al-Ḥārith b. Surayj (d. 746—a Jabrite, a Murjiʾī, and an anti-Umayyad rebel [Judd, 1999]). Ghaylān was reportedly debated by the Syrian proto-Sunnī traditionalist al-Awzāʿī, condemned as a heretic, and executed by Hishām (Alajmi). Van Ess correctly observes that Ghaylān's politics were independent of his Qadarite leanings; as a non-Arab member of the *mawālī*, he rejected the Umayyad and traditionalist claim of Qurayshite exclusivity for the caliphate and supported al-Ḥārith, which may better explain his execution. It appears that al-Ḥārith's threat (couched in terms of a call for justice and righteousness) made the Umayyad caliph Hishām wary of doctrinal innovation and therefore, about this time, anti-Qadarite punishments were meted out.

The pro-Qadarite and pro-*shūrā* caliph, Yazīd III (d. 744), who presumably followed Ghaylān's ideas, mounted a revolt against his decadent cousin al-Walīd II. The role of ideological factors in this revolt led to another rise in political executions in the reign of Marwān II. For example, ʿUmar b. Hāniʾ al-ʿAnsī was executed in 744–45 because of his participation in Yazīd III's revolt (Murad, 1991).

Qadarism and Politics. The historical data do not support the commonly held association of Qadarism with political nonconformism; neither the revolt of Ibn al-Asʿath nor of al-Ḥārith, in which some Qadarites participated, can be explained as a result of Qadarism. Nor did the Umayyads endorse anti-Qadarism as a consistent state theology or fear Qadarism's political threat. It seems, however, that dissident groups who held strong political positions also held strong theological opinions. In its logically extreme forms, total divine omnipotence undermined human agency, just as total human agency in the name of divine justice undercut the very purpose of worship, humility, and prayer. The theological debates, therefore, could have been fierce for their own sake, and the caliphs naturally would have become involved, at some times for ideological reasons and at others because a doctrine became associated with rebellion. But the caliphs had no strong reason to hold or enforce any one doctrine consistently, for whereas predestinarian sentiments may have helped people cope at times of great injustice or desecration (such as the bombardment of the Kaʿbah by al-Ḥajjāj in 692), they might also have undermined a caliph's sense of credit for accomplishments and conquests.

Theological Aspects. As a theological doctrine, Qadarism emphasizes moral responsibility and God's justice, but only rarely did its adherents reach the logical extreme of denying God's omnipotence. Conversely, the denial of free will, in either extreme or moderate form, was not necessarily used to excuse moral laxity or political passivism, as the cases of ʿUmar II and al-Ḥārith b. Surayj illustrate.

Qadarism can be better understood as a tendency shared by a variety of religious thinkers who held other (at times ostensibly incompatible) doctrines, such as Khārijites, Murjiʾah, proto-Sunnīs, and even Umayyads. It could not be regarded as a sect until it was claimed by the Muʿtazilah.

[*See also* Umayyad Caliphate.]

BIBLIOGRAPHY

Bearman, P. J., Th. Bianquis, C. E. Bosworth, E. van Donzel, W. P. Heinrichs, eds. *The Encyclopaedia of Islam*. 2d ed. 12 vols. Leiden: Brill, 1960–2004.

Judd, Steven. "Ghaylan al-Dimashqi: The Isolation of a Heretic in Islamic Historiography." *International Journal of Middle East Studies* 31, no. 2 (1999): 161–184.

Murad, Hasan Q. "*Jabr* and *Qadar* in Early Islam: A Reappraisal of Their Political and Religious Implications." In *Islamic Studies Presented to Charles J. Adams*, edited by W. Hallaq and D. Little, pp. 117–132. Leiden and New York: Brill, 1991.

ṭabarī, Ibn Jarīr al-. *Tʾrīkh al-rusul waʾl-mulūk*. 15 vols. Leiden: Brill, 1879–1901.

Watt, W. Montgomery. *The Formative Period of Islamic Thought*. Oxford: Oneworld, 1998.

OVAMIR ANJUM

QADHDHĀFĪ, MUʿAMMAR AL-. *See* Libya.

QĀḌĪ. *See* Courts.

QĀḌĪ AL-QUḌĀT. *See* Courts.

QAʿIDA, AL-.

Al-Qaʿida, "the base" in Arabic, is regarded as the first global terrorist group of the twenty-first century. Since its attacks of 11 September 2001 against the World Trade Center in New York and the Pentagon near Washington, D.C., al-Qaʿida has become known as the new face of terrorism. It was allegedly founded in 1988/1989 by two veterans of the anti-Soviet civil war in Afghanistan, Dr. Abdullah Azzam and Osama Bin Laden, with the goal of replicating the victory of Islam in Afghanistan in other theaters of Muslim conflict around the world. When Azzam was killed in 1989 as the result of internal rivalry and disagreement over tactics and objectives, Bin Laden is believed to have assumed full control of the group until his death on 2 May 2011. Bin Laden's purpose was to spread *jihād* worldwide with the objective of liberating the *ummah*, the global community of all Muslims, from the suffering inflicted by U.S. foreign policy and imperialism through its cooperation with Israel and support for corrupt authoritarian regimes that oppress and abuse their own people. Although al-Qaʿida is widely considered to pose a serious threat to U.S. and Western interests, there is no consensus among scholars and security experts regarding the organizational structure of the group and its ideology.

Ideology. The events of 9/11 triggered a variety of assessments of the rationale and motivation for the attacks and of the ideology of al-Qaʿida. The theories included suggestions that the terrorists were completely irrational and probably suffering from mental illnesses; that the religious posturing was hypocritical, with the religious rhetoric being a veil for political ambition; or that this was religious fanaticism, born of some form of Islamist extremism and laying claim to origins in the early history of Islam. As anti-Muslim sentiments grew in the post 9/11 climate, particular effort was made by Muslim moderates to distinguish al-Qaʿida's ideology of destruction as unrepresentative of Islam or majority Muslim religious opinion, making particular reference to the widely acknowledged prohibitions under Islamic law of attacks upon civilians, especially women and children, and of engaging in wholesale destruction of property. Many of the theories propounded in the immediate aftermath of 9/11 focused on explaining al-Qaʿida's violence with little recourse to the broader message conveyed through its public statements, limiting much of the discussion to the condemnation of the means without addressing the larger political dimension at stake.

Bin Laden's leadership and ideology were, and to some extent still are, fundamental to both al-Qaʿida's existence and its strategy. While Bin Laden's—and, therefore, al-Qaʿida's—rationale has evolved over time in response to sociopolitical developments, the central theme of his statements, from open letters and video messages to interviews and training manuals issued from the late 1980s until his death, is the suffering and humiliation of the *ummah* at the hands of the United States and its allies, especially Israel. At the core of his messages lies a Pan-Islamic worldview, according to which God's favored community faces an existential threat from the modern arch-enemies of Islam, the Zionist-Crusader alliance. Tapping into a strong and widely shared sense of Muslim grievances, the primary means of communicating this message is the evocation of Muslim anguish by reference to profoundly significant situations such as in Palestine, Iraq, Chechnya, Kashmir, and Saudi Arabia, where American political influence and military forces allegedly occupy and control the holy places of Islam. The only way to effectively defend the *ummah* against this perceived aggression is through violent confrontation with America, which Bin Laden presents in highly emotive terms as the rightful *jihād* of the present time against the principal enemy of the *ummah* and, by extension, Islam itself, with the ultimate goal of reestablishing the caliphate. Although Bin Laden did not stipulate how the community of Muslims should be structured and organized, al-Qaʿida's ideology—the raison d'être for its promotion of violent *jihād*—represents the latest, most aggressive presentation of Pan-Islamism. In practice, and in response to the hostile circumstances in which al-Qaʿida-affiliated groups (e.g., al-Qaʿida in Iraq, al-Qaʿida in the Maghrib, and al-Qaʿida in the Arabian Peninsula) find themselves operating since 9/11, the rationale communicated by local leaders has become increasingly factious and nationalistic, resulting in attacks against the governments of Yemen and Algeria and a bloody confrontation with Iraqi Shiites, among others. While these have been justified as the first steps toward the liberation of the *ummah*, the last of these in particular has triggered disagreement within the ranks of al-Qaʿida as to which objectives should be pursued and by what means, reflecting an overall shift toward local agendas.

Al-Qaʿida has expanded the definition of "defensive" *jihād* beyond the classical interpretation, which focuses on a specific community defending itself against physical attack, to include the idea that the attack upon the *ummah* includes economic and political elements, including cultural offenses, all of which warrant the defense of the Muslim community. Yet reinterpreting Islamic concepts and practices in the context of sociopolitical changes, often described as the selective utilization and (mis)interpretation of Scripture, is not unique to al-Qaʿida. Rather, al-Qaʿida's reasoning stands in a long tradition of Islamists who have identified Muslim grievances and called for a response, such as the Egyptian political activist Sayyid Quṭb (1906–1966), who envisioned unending, uncompromising *jihād* as a reflection of the cosmic conflict between good and evil.

Arguably the strongest influence on Bin Laden and the future ideology of al-Qaʿida was exercised by Abdullah Azzam, a disciple of Quṭb and leading Islamist of his time, who promulgated much of the jihadist propaganda in defense of Afghanistan. His particular contribution was his reinterpretation of the need to defend a Muslim country against invasion by non-Muslim forces. Where this was traditionally considered an obligation of the community, or "collective duty" (*farḍ kifāyah*), Azzam turned it into a personal obligation (*farḍ ʿayn*) for every Muslim, in which there could be no legitimate reason for failure to participate. He also considered Afghanistan to be merely the first stage in a worldwide *jihād* to recapture Muslim lands lost to infidels, a rationale that sets al-Qaʿida's global agenda apart from the nationalist, and hence more parochial, projects of previous Islamist groups. Although Azzam was an aggressive advocate of *jihād*, he refrained from demanding the overthrow of secular Muslim governments on the grounds of apostasy and strongly rejected internecine Muslim conflicts. His views would later clash with the ambitions of Ayman al-Ẓawāhirī and other members of the Egyptian Islamic Jihād, who aimed to overthrow the Egyptian government and in whose minds condemnation of the apostasy of secular Muslim states was inseparable from true Islamic faith. Following Azzam's death, al-Qaʿida adopted a harder line: *takfīr*, the practice of one Muslim declaring another Muslim an unbeliever, has become central to al-Qaʿida's justification for its use of violence against Muslim states and institutions. Thus Muslims deemed to be outside the faith are viewed as legitimate targets or acceptable collateral damage, for example, Iraqi Shiites, Yemeni soldiers, and Muslims living in the West. More recently, the Arab Spring of 2011, in which peaceful public uprisings resulted in the removal of a number of dictatorial regimes, has seen al-Qaʿida left on the political margins in the Middle East. Its call for holy war as the means of change has been comprehensively challenged, with its public statements conceding that peaceful protest is an equally acceptable option.

Organization and Structure. Considerable ambiguity and disagreement exist as to the precise organizational structure of al-Qaʿida at every stage in its development, from its inception in the late 1980s to the present day.

1986–1991: The Birth of al-Qaʿida. Most accounts of the origins of al-Qaʿida begin with the legacy of the Soviet invasion of Afghanistan and the well-documented Afghan National Resistance Movement that attracted young Muslims from around the world to join what was portrayed as a holy war against a godless invader. Among these volunteers were the Saudi Osama Bin Laden, who would become the emir (leader) of al-Qaʿida; the Egyptian Dr. Ayman al-Ẓawāhirī, former leader of the Egyptian Islamic Jihād and al-Qaʿida's number two, considered by some to have been the real leader and mastermind of the group; and the Jordanian-Palestinian Dr. Abdullah Azzam, a disciple of Sayyid Quṭb and mentor of Bin Laden. Azzam and Bin Laden together set up the Maktāb al-Khidmāt (MAK), also known as the Service Bureau, which channeled international recruits and funding into Afghanistan. Although it is considered to be the organizational forerunner from which al-Qaʿida emerged, information about the precise nature and extent of the MAK is ambiguous, with detailed, albeit often unsubstantiated descriptions of a sophisticated undertaking funded by Western aid standing in marked contrast to more modest accounts of an informal network of mosques, schools, and boarding houses. Consequently, there is no agreement as to the nature of the organization that would become al-Qaʿida, giving rise to two schools of thought that continue to shape the debate into the present. One of these holds that al-Qaʿida was from its inception a tightly knit organization, with distinct divisions of labor among different branches and with recognized forms of entry such as an oath of allegiance to Bin Laden. The contrasting theory holds that the essence of al-Qaʿida was something more vague: a network of individuals affiliated with different Islamist groups that could well have aspired to become highly organized and boast a strong chain of command, but which in fact consisted of much looser associations.

1992–1996: Al-Qaʿida in Sudan. It is generally agreed that, in the aftermath of the Gulf War and Bin Laden's exile from Saudi Arabia, al-Qaʿida's seat of power moved to Sudan with Bin Laden and Ẓawāhirī, at the behest of Sudanese Islamist Ḥasan al-Turābī, possibly in the hope of bringing money and investment to the impoverished country. This period has generated plenty of speculation as to how much money Bin Laden had, what amounts he invested in Sudan, and whether his ventures were profitable or in fact a significant waste of money. Agreement exists only on the fact that Bin Laden invested a great deal of his own money in Sudan, with estimates ranging from $25 million to $350 million. The question of whether these funds later ran out remains unresolved.

1996–2001: Gaining Strength in Afghanistan. Bin Laden's expulsion from Sudan and return to Afghanistan under the protection of the Taliban regime in 1996 marked another widely acknowledged change in al-Qaʿida's geographic base. Views as to the nature of its relations with the Taliban depend largely on the position taken on the funding situation, whether Bin Laden used his wealth to further his interests with the Taliban or merely provided an ideology and a vision that fed into a preexisting infrastructure. There is agreement that the group gained significant strength during this period, preceding the attacks of 9/11. Attempts were made to establish a public profile through different forms of propaganda, featuring Bin Laden as the public face of what was portrayed as an increasingly potent group determined to strike the United States and the West. The increased outreach to the public included interviews with Western journalists, open letters, and the issuing of two key *fatwas*, *Declaration of Jihad against Americans Occupying the Land of the Two Holy Mosques* (1996) and *Jihad against the Jews and Crusaders*, better known as the "1998 *Fatwa*," issued by the newly formed World Islamic Front on 23 February 1998.

By almost all accounts, 1998 witnessed significant progress in al-Qaʿida's attempts to establish itself as a global player. In particular, the 1998 *Fatwa*, unlike previous decrees, bore four cosignatories in addition to Bin Laden: Āyman al-Ẓawāhirī, leader of Egyptian Islamic Jihād; Abu Yasir Rifa'i Ahmad Taha, representing al-Jamāʿat al-Islāmīyah; Mir Hamza, secretary general of Jamʿīyatul-ʿUlamāʾ-i Pākistān; and Fazlur Rahman, leader of the Jihād Movement in Bangladesh. That each signatory retained his affiliation with his original group suggests that the World Islamic Front was designed to act as an umbrella organization to promote regional cooperation, although the extent of cooperation between these groups remains unclear. While they appear to have agreed on objectives and tactics on paper, they did not necessarily pledge obedience or loyalty to Osama Bin Laden or join the official al-Qaʿida network. These issues are most apparent in the 9/11 attacks, the level of al-Qaʿida's involvement in which has remained a matter of contention. The purported mastermind of the attacks, Khālid Shaykh Muḥammad, has claimed full responsibility for conceiving and planning the 9/11 attacks under the auspices of his own jihādist organization, the Pakistani-based Jaysh-i Muḥammad. Although he admitted to having requested and received the approval and financial and logistical support of al-Qaʿida, he has consistently denied having pledged loyalty or obedience to Osama Bin Laden, asserting his independence of action. Several analysts have thus interpreted Bin Laden's position as a main feature of al-Qaʿida as an organization, pointing to a number of preceding attacks, including, in the year 2000 alone, the attacks on the USS *The Sullivans* and the USS *Cole*, the Christmas Eve bombings in Indonesia, and the Rizal Day bombings in Manila, as examples of a strategy embracing the centralization of decision and the decentralization of execution. During the period 1998–2001, al-Qaʿida is seen as being at its most organized, potent, and well-financed, having spread its reach into several countries.

2001–2009: The War on Terror and the Ongoing Controversy over Potency and Structure. The attacks of 9/11 are widely regarded as al-Qaʿida's most significant success, making the group a global household name. Yet the U.S. military response largely destroyed whatever infrastructure existed in Afghanistan by early 2002, delivering a major blow to the organizational makeup and capacity of al-Qaʿida. The surviving leadership went into hiding, further shifting responsibility for action to affiliated activists in other locations, resulting in the decentralization of the funding and logistical support for proposed attacks. Consequently, there appears to have been a shift from seeking prior approval for attacks to demonstrating the ability to carry out attacks and seeking al-Qaʿida's seal of approval afterward. While most analysts concluded that subsequent attacks, such as the Bali nightclub bombing in 2002, were initiated locally rather than planned by the core leadership, the U.S. government continued to advance the idea of the immense threat posed by a centralized, global organization.

The question of the potency and organizational makeup of al-Qaʿida post-9/11 remains contentious. Since 2005, two distinct narratives have emerged. One maintains that al-Qaʿida is on the rise, with new centers of leadership emerging in different locations, including Iraq, the Maghrib, and the Arabian Peninsula. Its proponents point to a continued ability to influence and facilitate smaller-scale attacks. Prominent examples include the 30 November 2009 Fort Hood shooting, the failed attempt to detonate a bomb aboard an airliner on Christmas Day 2009, and the failed plot to blow up two commercial aircraft en route from Yemen to the United States on 29 October 2010. Advocates of this view, such as Peter Bergen and Bruce Hoffman, maintain that al-Qaʿida consists of a hierarchically organized inner core leadership, surrounded by a second level of loyal cadres and a wider network of supporters and links to other groups. The other narrative asserts that al-Qaʿida's central leadership, to the extent that such a center of control ever existed in the first place, is getting weaker and is no longer able to plan and carry out large-scale attacks. Supporters of this position point to the shrinking number of al-Qaʿida fighters in Afghanistan as a result of the ongoing counterinsurgency campaign, the fact that its funding has all but dried up, its perceived lack of operational capacity to execute attacks on the scale of 9/11, and, chiefly, the marginalization of the group by the events of the Arab

Spring, in which al-Qaʿida has played no role. Prominent advocates of this position include Marc Sageman, with his theory of "leaderless *jihād*," and Jason Burke, with his theory of "free-lance combatants," who argue that the main threat no longer comes from the organization called al-Qaʿida, but from radicalized individuals and groups who meet and plot in their neighborhoods or via the Internet, who act independently and without any ties to a central organization beyond a shared ideological connection, as has indeed been the case in the aforementioned attacks of 2009 and 2010.

Against this unresolved controversy, the killing of Osama Bin Laden on 2 May 2011 has widely been viewed as a major blow to al-Qaʿida, with most of the coverage reinforcing the idea of a structured organization of sorts. This was further supported by a statement issued by "the al-Qaʿida Organization—General Leadership" pledging to avenge his death, forecasting attacks more severe than those seen before, and calling on believers across the globe to take up the fight. The extent to which these statements amount to mere posturing—a display of rhetoric rather than actual strength—remains unclear. Yet, while real and thorough analysis of how al-Qaʿida's true nature and strength can be determined has not yet begun, it seems clear from current trends that any justifications for its claims of being a worldwide movement for Islamic *jihād* diminish with each day that does not see another attack.

BIBLIOGRAPHY

Atwan, Abdel Bari. *The Secret History of al Qaeda.* Berkeley: University of California Press, 2006.

Behnke, Andreas, and Christina Hellmich, eds. *Knowing Al-Qaeda: The Epistemology of Terrorism.* Farnham, U.K.: Ashgate, 2012.

Bergen, Peter L. *The Osama bin Laden I Know: An Oral History of al-Qaeda's Leader.* New York: Free Press, 2006.

Bin Laden, Osama *Messages to the World: The Statements of Osama bin Laden.* Edited by Bruce Lawrence. Translated by James Howarth. London: Verso, 2005.

Burke, Jason. *Al-Qaeda: The True Story of Radical Islam.* 3d ed. London: I. B. Tauris, 2007.

DeLong-Bas, Natana J. *Wahhabi Islam: From Revival and Reform to Global Jihad.* Rev. ed. New York: Oxford University Press, 2004.

Esposito, John L. *Unholy War: Terror in the Name of Islam.* New York: Oxford University Press, 2002.

Gerges, Fawaz A. *The Rise and Fall of Al-Qaeda.* Oxford: Oxford University Press, 2011.

Gunaratna, Rohan. *Inside Al Qaeda: Global Network of Terror.* New York: Columbia University Press, 2002.

Hellmich, Christina. *Al-Qaeda: From Global Network to Local Franchise.* London: Zed. 2011.

Nasiri, Omar. *Inside the Jihad: My Life with Al Qaeda; A Spy's Story.* New York: Basic Books, 2006.

Sageman, Marc. *Leaderless Jihad: Terror Networks in the Twenty-First Century.* Philadelphia: University of Pennsylvania Press.

Ẓawāhirī, Āyman al-. *His Own Words: A Translation of the Writings of Dr. Ayman al-Zawahiri.* Translated by Laura Mansfield. Old Tappan, N.J.: TLG, 2006.

NATANA J. DELONG-BAS
Updated by CHRISTINA HELLMICH

QARAḌĀWĪ, YŪSUF AL-. Yūsuf al-Qaraḍāwī (1926–) is an Egyptian-born theologian and preacher, who resides in Qatar. Qaraḍāwī is regularly voted among the world's foremost public intellectuals and has a large following throughout the world, but he has also been an extremely polarizing figure throughout his career. He was born in Saft at-Turab, Upper Egypt, in 1926. His family background was modest and his father died when he was two. Beginning his education in a village Qurʾānic school, he went on to study Islam and the Arabic language, achieving a doctorate at al-Azhar in 1974 for his dissertation on *zakāt* (alms). He was strongly influenced by Ḥasan al-Bannā (1906–1949) and Muḥammad al-Ghazālī (1917–1996), while acknowledging a special debt to the great Ṣūfī scholar Abū Ḥāmid al-Ghazālī (d. 1111). His political activities led to his arrest several times during the reign of King Farouk and after the 1952 revolution. He has always been close to the Muslim Brothers and later twice declined an invitation to become their supreme leader. Since 1961 he has resided in Qatar, founding several Islamic institutions in that state and using it as a base for the spread of his intellectual influence all over the Muslim world. His major study, *Fiqh al-zakāt* (1971; Eng. trans. *Fiqh Al Zakah: A Comparative Study of Zakah, Regulations, and Philosophy in the Light of Qur'an and Sunnah*, n.d.), provided the main theological basis for the formation of modern Islamic charitable organizations. He has built up connections with many key Islamic institutions in different spheres—academic, financial, judicial, educational, and charitable—not only in Muslim-majority countries but in Britain, Ireland, and Switzerland. His career has embodied his doctrinal commitment to Islam as a comprehensive way of life (*shumūlīyat al-Islām*).

He has succeeded in becoming the most influential religious authority in the Sunnī Muslim world, not only through the publication of over 120 books but also by his use of the media, including the Arabic and English website Islam-Online, founded in 1999. Since 1970 he has hosted his own program, *Hadī al-Islām* (Guidance of Islam), on Qatar's national television, and after the foundation of the Al Jazeera television channel in 1996 he has been the mainstay of its religious program *Sharia and Life*, winning a huge global audience. He is an impressively gifted orator in Arabic, his only language.

One of Qaraḍāwī's guiding principles is *wasaṭīyah*, or centrism, which he calls "the soul of Islam," aiming to reconcile the intellectual conflict of the twentieth century between renewal (*tajdīd*) and conservatism—but always within current Islamic orthodoxy. He criticizes, on the one hand, those interpreters of religious texts who try to accommodate them to secular ideologies and, on the other, those who dwell on the letter rather than the meaning of the texts and are subservient to the four classical Sunnī schools. This tendency was evident in his early book *al-Ḥalāl wa-al-ḥarām fī al-Islām* (1960; Eng. trans. *The Lawful and the Prohibited in Islam*, 2003), translated into more than twenty languages, which sought to free Islamic jurisprudence (*fiqh*) from the pedantry and negativity of the old jurists. His authority extends throughout the Islamic world, and he has even been ascribed the status of *marjiʿīyah*, an authoritative reference, which is a Shīʿah concept when applied to persons. Whereas his youthful ambition was to be the Shaykh al-Azhar in Egypt, a political appointment, he is seen by many followers as the *shaykh* of the entire *ummah*.

Controversy. Qaraḍāwī's endorsement of a middle way has not protected him from sharp controversy. Indeed, the polemics surrounding his name are paradigmatic of the crisis of authority in Islam today. From the Salafī perspective (though he is respected by some Salafī tendencies), he has been criticized for arguing that "offensive" *jihād* has been made obsolete by the new media, which allow the message of Islam to be disseminated peacefully, and also on the grounds that he is too lenient toward infidels. But liberal and secular Muslims take issue with him vigorously, especially on the questions of religious freedom, gender, violence, and Judaism. Study of the positions he has taken on such issues reveals many ambiguities.

On religious freedom, Qaraḍāwī condemns apostasy as a capital offense under *Sharīʿah*, but insists that the punishment should be inflicted only by the Islamic state and only if the offender publicizes the act. He urges dialogue with other religions and has defended the rights of the Coptic minority in Egypt. He has rejected the classical division of the world into *dār al-Islām* and *dār al-ḥarb* (domain of war), sketching a theory of *fiqh al-aqallīyāt*, or law of Muslim minorities, which would facilitate integration of Muslims in non-Muslim societies such as Europe without abandoning what are seen as the essentials of the religion. On blasphemy he has been emphatic, intervening, for instance, in the Danish cartoon crisis of 2005–2006, calling for a "day of anger" against the Danish and Norwegian governments but swiftly condemning the violence that ensued.

On gender issues, Qaraḍāwī stresses the complementarity between male and female, sidestepping the question of gender equality and proclaiming that women have a "natural disposition" (*bi ḥukm al-fiṭrah*) to domesticity, wifehood, and motherhood, but he also encourages women to fulfill their potential in education and public life. He supports women's right to vote and stand for election, and even to engage in paramilitary operations in the Palestinian cause. Such emancipatory steps are validated, for Qaraḍāwī, by their contribution to the collective interest and only secondarily by their implications for the individual. He is intransigent in abominating homosexuality and in defending the practice of wife beating (albeit only lightly and when reasoning has failed).

Qaraḍāwī is strongly opposed to al-Qaʿida-style violent extremism and immediately condemned the 11 September 2001 attacks on the United States. He has also dismissed as extremist the teaching of Sayyid Quṭb (1906–1966), during the final, radical stage of his life, when he preached violence against infidels and morally corrupt Muslims alike. But the position for which Qaraḍāwī is most attacked in the West has been his doctrine of "defensive *jihād*," according to which when Muslims are under attack—as in Israel, Chechnya, or Kashmir—resistance is obligatory and suicide-bombing legitimate. He grants this permission only within the territories in dispute, but in the case of Israel he defends Palestinian attacks on civilians, including children, on the grounds that the entire Israeli society is militarized. This position reflects widespread opinion in the Arab world, but is contradicted by many other *ʿulamāʾ*. It is doubtless the principal reason he was banned from entering the United States in 1999, the United Kingdom in 2008, and France in 2012. Qaraḍāwī's image as a conciliator, deserved in some other contexts, comes under greatest strain when he has, on occasion, praised Hitler for his treatment of the Jews.

Qaraḍāwī's Rhetoric. In a study of Islamist rhetoric, Jacob Høigilt has analyzed illuminatingly the literary style of Qaraḍāwī's publications dating back to 1998. Qaraḍāwī has "a pyramidal vision of the Islamic field" (Høigilt, 2011, p. 64). At the base are the ordinary people, *al-nās*; above them is a stratum of religiously aware Muslims; he is at the apex as the final judge of things Islamic. Abstaining from detailed rebuttals of other *ʿulamāʾ*'s interpretations, he adopts a measured, impersonal tone, respectful of the Arabic rhetorical tradition and colored by allusions to the great thinkers and poets of the classical Islamic age. It is not Muslims who act, but a personified Islam that ordains and performs the Good—opposed by extremists, conservatives, secularists, and imperialists. All who fall outside the school of *wasaṭīyah* are disqualified. Høigilt concludes that the result is to boost Qaraḍāwī's own authority while disempowering the reader.

Since the "Arab Awakening." In February 2011 Qaraḍāwī returned to Egypt—for the first time after he was banned from leading the Friday prayers there thirty years earlier—and preached in Tahrir Square, Cairo, to hundreds of thousands. He has been hailed by many as a great reformist religious leader and was likened by Ken Livingstone, the former mayor of London, to Pope John XXIII. Controversy continued to erupt, however, with regard to his alleged double standards. Though he gave his approval to the antigovernment forces in Egypt, Libya, and Syria, he withheld it from those in Bahrain, dismissing them as sectarian, although the Shī'ah constitute a majority of the population. His critics charge that this view reflects the bias of the petromonarchies, including Qatar, his adopted country.

In 2013, Qaraḍāwī denounced the Lebanese Ḥizbullāh and the Iranian Shī'ah government for their support of the Bashār al-'Asad regime in Syria. More consistently with his previous positions, he called on the Egyptian people to oppose the July 2013 military coup and the deposition of president Muḥammad Mursī.

Bibliography

Gräf, Bettina, and Jakob Skovgaard-Petersen, eds. *Global Mufti: The Phenomenon of Yusuf al-Qaradawi*. London: Hurst, 2009. Excellent collection of articles by ten authors considering Qaraḍāwī's life and work from many angles, with a bibliography of his texts.

Høigilt, Jacob. *Islamist Rhetoric: Language and Culture in Contemporary Egypt*. London: Routledge, 2011.

Qaradawi, Yusuf. *The Lawful and the Prohibited in Islam*. London: Birr Foundation, 2003. English translation of his first and best known book, published in Arabic in 1960.

Qardawi, Yusuf Al. *Fiqh Al Zakah: A Comparative Study of Zakah, Regulations and Philosophy in the Light of Qur'an and Sunnah*. Translated by Monzer Kahf. Jiddah, Saudi Arabia: Scientific Publishing Centre, King Abdulaziz University, n.d. http://monzer.kahf.com/books/english/fiqhalzakah_vol1.pdf.

Jonathan Benthall

Qur'ān Exegesis and Hermeneutics.

The Qur'ān, according to traditional Muslim belief, is the literal word of God that was sent to Muḥammad over the course of his prophetic career (610–632 CE). The Prophet Muḥammad was a mouthpiece, passively and involuntarily receiving the "speech of God" (*kalām Allāh*, 9:5) via the angel Gabriel. The humanity of Muḥammad was neither transformed nor influenced by the revelatory process. According to Muslim tradition, the Prophet reliably narrated the Qur'ān to his people as it was revealed to him. His followers used it for recitation (*tilāwah*) in ritual prayer (*ṣalāt*) and for inspiration in their struggles (*jihād*), both spiritual and against forces of opposition and disbelief.

The Qur'ān is the first Arabic book in history, and the last scripture of the world's global religions. From the seventh to fifteenth centuries, it became the intellectual, spiritual, and cultural axis of peoples from Spain to India and beyond. Until the present day, Arabic has preserved its place at the center of Islamic education and ritual for both Arabs and non-Arabs, from Muslim majority countries like Turkey, Iran, and Indonesia to minority populations such as in India, China, or the United States.

Qur'ānic studies has traditionally consisted of several branches: *tafsīr* is the interpretation and explanation of the Qur'ān; *asbāb al-nuzūl* is a study of the occasions for revelation of various sets of verses; *i'jāz* is the concept of the Qur'ān's inimitability, which is investigated linguistically through rhetoric (*balāghah*) and more recently through other perspectives such as science; *'ilm al-qirā'ah* is a study of the multiple accepted modes of recitation, including *tajwīd*, which is the art of its oral recitation with proper enunciation of each letter in measured tone. Contemporary Muslim scholars of the Qur'ān have continued to focus on its linguistic, legal, theological, and spiritual aspects, but the emphasis has shifted in Western scholarship toward historicity, reception, chronology, and function.

For Muslims, the Qur'ān embodies God's final revelation to humanity for guidance until the end of time. Throughout history and to all peoples, God has sent prophets and scriptures in their own languages. Muḥammad is the last of these messengers to arrive on the stage of history. His primary mandate was for the nation of the Arabs but with a general commission for all of humanity. The Qur'ān is referred to by many names. Among them are: *al-kitāb* (the book, the scripture), *al-tanzīl* (the bringing down), *al-waḥy* (the revelation), *al-dhikr* (the reminder), and *al-furqān* (the criterion). According to Muslim tradition, the Qur'ān has been transmitted across the ages via an unbroken chain of transmission from God, to the angel Gabriel, to the prophet Muḥammad, to his companions (*ṣaḥābah*), with enough members in each generation successively transmitting to the next (*tawātur*) as to render its authenticity beyond doubt.

The Qur'ān is organized into thirty parts (*juz'*) to help the devoted complete a recitation of the entire book in one month. A more natural division is into *sūrahs*, of which there are a total of one hundred and fourteen, and *āyahs*, of which there are over six thousand. A *sūrah* is analogous to but not synonymous with a chapter. Each one is distinct, yet the overall arrangement is non-linear and anachronistic. An *āyah* is analogous to a verse, but may consist of a single letter, series of letters, phrases, a complete sentence, or several sentences put together. Muslims believe the *sūrah-āyah* divisions to be *tawqīfī*, coming directly from the authority of the Prophet. The order of the *sūrahs* is considered to have been either from the Prophet or the result of the collective reasoning (*ijtihād*) and agreement (*ijmā'*) of the companions.

Muslim history records a process of compilation that took place after the death of the Prophet (632 CE) and was completed before the death of the third caliph, 'Uthmān (656 CE). However, alternative or "variant" readings have been preserved in the vast repository of *tafsīr* literature, along with differences, mostly minor, among the private Qur'ān codices (*muṣḥafs*) of a few of the companions. An official "'Uthmānic" codex was compiled, according to Muslim tradition, during the reign of 'Uthmān (r. 644–656). Modern Western scholars have attempted to mine the storehouse of Muslim literature in order to construct revisionist accounts of the textual history of the Qur'ān. There is no evidence of any attempt to conceal variants in traditional Muslim scholarship, where they have been preserved and appropriated within a sacred narrative.

The arrangement of the Qur'ān in its present form is not according to the chronological order of revelation. Both Muslim tradition and modern Western scholarship—with the exception of revisionist scholarship—have adopted the paradigm of Meccan and Medinan parts of the Qur'ān to contextualize the verses within the life of the Prophet. Textual analysis in the West, spearheaded by Theodor Nöldeke in the nineteenth century, has argued for three distinct periods of "revelation" in Mecca (610–622 CE) and one in Medina (622–632 CE). Some Muslim scholars, particularly Ḥamīd al-Dīn Farāhī (d. 1930) of India, came up with a similar scheme but without reference to Western scholarship.

Major Themes. In *The Jewels of the Qur'ān*, al-Ghazālī (d. 1111) puts forward six thematic divisions of the Qur'ān. Three of these divisions are primary and three are secondary. The following three sections correspond to the primary divisions: 1) knowledge of God, 2) the path to God (as illuminated by the institution of prophethood), and 3) the life hereafter. Belief and reflection on these categories became a central feature of Muslim creed and theology in Islamic intellectual history.

God. It is possible to identify various themes running through the Qur'ān, but none as prominent as God's unity. There is no god but God (e.g., Q 20:14, 64:13), "His is the dominion of the heavens and the earth" (57:2 and passim). "He is the first, and the last, and that which is most apparent, and what which is most hidden" (57:3). He has power over everything (57:2 and passim), is knower of the "seen" and "unseen" realities (59:22 and passim), planner of affairs (10:3, 31; 13:2, 32:5), and closer to humans than their jugular veins (50:6), yet there is nothing comparable to Him (42:11 and 112:4).

Most importantly, for the purpose of political thought, "there is no command or judgment except by God" (Q 12:40). "Whoever does not judge by what God has revealed—it is those who are disbelievers" (5:44). "It is not for a believing man or a believing woman, when God and His Messenger have decided a matter, that they should have any choice about their affair" (33:36). Believers are to "obey God and His messenger, as well as those in authority" among them (4:59), while putting their complete trust in God (64:13 and passim). They are to strive in God's path, with their wealth and belongings (e.g., 9:111, 49:15, 61:11), so that the "way of life" *(dīn)* is entirely for God (2:193) and the light of God is perfected even though the polytheists (*mushrikūn*) may detest it (9:33, 61:8). Toward this end, Muḥammad and his companions were compassionate among themselves but stern against the unbelievers (48:29), and the believers are commanded to "help God" (47:7) and His messenger (57:25).

The verses above have been strung together to provide the reader with a glimpse of how modern-day Islamists read the Qur'ān with political ambition. For them, a direct implication of God's unity is in the arena of politics on the world stage. Humankind will continue to drift, with some groups treating others unjustly, unless God's final message is established (*iqāmat al-dīn*, Q 42:13). Adherents of past scriptures went astray precisely because they failed to establish or to maintain the kingdom of God on earth: "O People of the Book! You have no ground to stand upon unless you establish the Torah and Gospel and that which has been revealed to you from your Lord" (5:68). After all, it is only God who can be just to all groups, because He created everything and we return to Him for final judgment—man and woman, capitalist and laborer, gay and straight.

Although believers of all stripes refer to these same verses, the types of hermeneutics that one brings to bear greatly influence the ultimate meaning that is drawn. For example, verses may be identified as specific rather than general, or as being applicable only in a prophetic context. Pluralism may be accepted as a fact, with rules derived from rational principles to govern conduct among peoples in a framework that supersedes that of any particular revelation. In addition, Muḥammad's Meccan ethical context may be taken as universal, with his Medinan one as a particular manifestation of the prophetic ethics in a specific historical moment, as expounded by Fazlur Rahman (d. 1988), a Pakistani-American scholar at the University of Chicago, and the Sudanese scholar-activist Maḥmūd Muḥammad Ṭāhā (executed 1985).

Traditionally, the sovereignty of God and concomitant application of the *Sharī'ah* was a given in Islamic societies. The ruler—whether caliph, *amīr*, *imām*, or sultan—was bound by the law as interpreted by an independent class of jurists with popular appeal. The advent of modernity, nation-states, secularization of law, and displacement of traditional *'ulamā'*, who not only were jurists but also mediators of authority between the rulers and the populace, has resulted in the rise of totalitarian Islamist hermeneutics and movements as a direct response to the totalitarian nature of the modern nation-state. The notion of people as sovereign lawmakers in a democracy vs. God as sovereign of the universe and its affairs are seen as being in essential and irreconcilable tension by Islamists. As a consequence, the imperative of establishing God's sovereignty over political institutions is a paramount religious obligation for believers. For modernists and traditionalists, the agenda of Islamists will lead to tyranny in the name of God. Instead, it is the piety of a religious public (guided by a class of properly trained *'ulamā'* for traditionalists and by public reason for modernists) that should indirectly influence political institutions.

Prophecy. A second theme that threads the Qur'ān is the idea of prophecy. God chooses from among angels and men (Q 22:75) whom He pleases to convey His message. The Qur'ān employs two words for His emissaries: *nabī* refers to a prophet, and *rasūl* refers to a messenger. Whereas both words are considered synonymous and interchangeable for all practical purposes, when used in contradistinction, a prophet is considered to be the one who receives revelation from God but merely interprets and preaches the teachings of a messenger, who receives not only revelation but also scripture and law.

There are five major messengers in the Qur'ān: Noah, Abraham, Moses, Jesus, and Muḥammad, all of whom were commanded to "establish the *dīn*" (Q 42:13). The missions of Qur'ānic prophets and messengers are presented in a unified narrative with the following elements: they are sent to their people to invite them to serve and to worship one God; except for a few followers, the people, foremost among them by the political elite (*mala'*), reject the call of the prophets; the prophets and their followers are persecuted to test the strength of their conviction; the prophets and their followers are ultimately saved, while those who rejected them are annihilated by divine command.

The life of Muḥammad, when viewed along this pattern, provides glimpses into the political nature of his struggle. There are two points of significant difference between Muḥammad and the previous prophets and messengers, however: (1) Muḥammad prevailed by establishing God's rule in his city and throughout Arabia in his own lifetime, which enabled him to exercise political authority and to leave a practical example in this field for the generations that have believed in his message across the ages, and (2) Muḥammad's engagement with his opponents was largely the result of human stratagem, even occasional error, and his enemies were vanquished at the hands of believers rather than through a divine cataclysmic act, such as a flood or earthquake, reinforcing the notion that followers today are to engage in a similar struggle at the human level.

Two other Prophets with distinctive elements in their narrative are Abraham, the patriarch of all three major monotheistic religions, and Joseph, the one responsible for settling the Israelites in Egypt. The unique aspect introduced by Abraham is his method of argument. The Qur'ānic accounts of Abraham portray him as a staunch monotheist, both inquisitive and quarrelsome. He asks God to show him how He resurrects the dead so that his heart may be at ease (Q 2:260), and challenges the beliefs of his father, tribe, and ruler by engaging in debate on the terms of his opponents rather than by quoting revelation (2:258, 6:75–83), until he is ordered to be thrown into fire (21:51–69) and ultimately exiled (37:99). Joseph, on the other hand, agrees to serve in the administration of one of the ancient Pharaohs of Egypt (cf. *sūrah* 12). These varying prophetic dispositions in the Qur'ān are all capable of inspiring either confrontational or accommodationist political thought.

Afterlife. It is not possible to find a single page in any conventional printing of the Qur'ān without some sort of reference to the life hereafter. Chronologically, the early verses tend to combine an apocalyptic tone, promise of judgment in the life to come, and a strong moral imperative in this life. The *sūrahs* from the early Meccan period are short, with rhythmic and rhyming verses. The Qur'ān juxtaposes an appeal to moral conscience, or "the reproaching soul" (75:2), with resurrection in the afterlife in a message that carries strongly social and political overtones. Qur'ān 81:1–10 speaks of a moment "when the sun is rolled up, when the stars are dimmed, when the mountains are set in motion... when the seas boil over... when the baby girl buried alive is asked, for what crime she was killed." This is an obvious critique of the practice of female infanticide prevalent in Arab society at the time. Qur'ān 83:1–5 declares: "Woe to those who give short measure, who demand of other people full measure for themselves, but when it is they who weigh or measure for others give less than they should; do these people not realize that they will be raised up, on a mighty day?" These verses criticize fraudulent business practices. Another *sūrah* (107:1–3) reads: "Have you considered the one who denies the Judgment? It is he who pushes aside the orphan, and does not urge others to feed the needy."

Although these verses have no explicit political directives, they have the potential to be read politically, so that it becomes a religious duty to work in the political arena to regulate social practices as well as business and commerce in light of moral teachings. The manner of such an engagement—whether implicitly, through a virtuous citizenry, or explicitly, through direct political organization and action—is a matter of debate between Islamists, traditionalists, and modernists.

Biography of Muḥammad. When these central themes of the Qur'ān are read in light of the biography of Muḥammad, the Qur'ān may be seen as a manual for holistic political revolution, beginning with a transformation of the individual and then moving to society. Although the varying prophetic models of engagement (from Abraham to Joseph) provide openings for multiple approaches, the thrust of the text revolves around a central message: there is only one God, to whom all allegiance belongs; prophets have been sent by God to guide humanity to His submission and worship; there will be a final day of resurrection when everybody will be taken into account and rewarded or punished for their deeds.

The struggles that a believer must undergo in this world in the path of God are pivotal for a meaningful religious life. The Qur'ān explains that true faith (*īmān*) and struggle (*jihād*) are the twin requisites of salvation, *falāḥ* or *najāḥ* (Q 49:15 and 61:10–11). Believers are not simply to be "left alone" by God on a mere declaration of faith, but tested on a pattern similar to previous prophets and generations (29:1–7). "Do you think that you will enter Paradise while God has not yet made evident those of you who strive in His cause and made evident those who are steadfast?" (3:142).

A theme of justice undergirds the prophetic mission and Qur'ānic call for struggle: For example: "We send Our messengers with clear signs, the Scripture, and the Balance, so that people could uphold justice" (Q 57:25), and "Let those of you who are willing to trade the life of this world for the life to come, fight in God's way.... Why should you not fight in God's cause and for those oppressed men, women, and children, who cry out, 'Lord, rescue us from this town whose people are oppressors! By your Grace, give us a protector and give us a helper!'?" (4:74–75). In the Qur'ān, the Prophet Muḥammad is commanded to say: "I am commanded to bring justice between you" (42:15).

The Qur'ān mandates for the entire community of believers (*ummah*) the collective obligation of bearing witness to all of humanity (Q 2:143, 22:78). These verses and themes, if not restricted in their applicability to the context of the Prophet and his companions, when viewed in the grand narrative of Muḥammad's biography, provide a general agenda with political implications, but no specific policies or structure for governance. For that, guidance must be taken from the life of Muḥammad, the practices of the early community, and reason. In Mecca during the first half of his prophetic career, Muḥammad remained nonviolent, was persecuted, and was commanded to respond kindly to offenses (41:34). In Medina, Muḥammad established a stronghold, gained strength, took up arms, and overcame all who resisted. This pattern of peaceful missionizing followed by emigration (*hijrah*) to a sanctuary and then armed conflict is one followed by some Islamist movements today.

Interpretation. The Qur'ān has been interpreted—now and in the past—through a myriad of lenses. For Twelver Shī'ah, the sayings of the *imāms* provide a definitive guide for the meaning of the text. For Ismā'īlīs and other esotericists, including many mystics, the inner meaning of the Qur'ān as interpreted by an accepted living authority or through true dreams overrides literal meanings. For modern secularists and academics, the Qur'ān is read historically and through the lens of any one or combination of contemporary theories in gender studies, anthropology, or religious studies. Those engaged in movements for independence or resistance to foreign occupation and other political Islamists read the Qur'ān from the point of view of pragmatic necessity or political expediency. Traditional Sunnī Muslims draw on a long history of interpretation based, to varying degrees, on the literal meaning of the text according to the classical Arabic lexicon, *ḥadīth*, and opinions of the companions and sound authorities of the past, followed by reason on the basis of empirical evidence and rationality, typically in that order.

The traditional style of systematic exegesis proceeds verse-by-verse according to the present arrangement of the Qur'ānic text. Historically, works of political exegesis (*tafsīr*) are nonexistent before the modern period. Although works on political theory and governance abound in the classical age, they draw on the Qur'ān selectively and through one or another interpretive framework. By contrast, leaders of Islamic movements today have generated *tafsīrs* of the entire Qur'ān from the vantage of politics. Two prominent examples are *Fī ẓilāl al-Qur'ān* (*In the Shade of the Qur'ān*) by the Egyptian Sayyid Quṭb (d. 1966) and *Tafhīm al-Qur'ān* (*Towards Understanding the Qur'ān*) by the Indian/Pakistani Abū al-A'lā Mawdūdī (d. 1979). Quṭb was an intellectual pillar of the Muslim Brotherhood in the heart of the Arab world, whereas Mawdūdī became influential among the masses in the Indian subcontinent. These works attempt to read both the Qur'ān and Muslim tradition in light of contemporary political contexts. As such, traditionalists accuse them of betraying the spirit of that very tradition and modernists accuse them of being radical fundamentalists.

Conclusion. In Muslim culture the Qur'ān is omnipresent. It is present orally in recitation, visually in calligraphy, physically on shelves and in talismans, and symbolically at ceremonies and festivals. It is the foundation of traditional thought and scholarship as well as of efforts for reform (*iṣlāḥ*) and renewal (*tajdīd*). It is generally against etiquette to place it on the floor or to come into contact with it when not in a state of ritual purity. It is recited by individual believers and in gatherings, often accompanied by effects of amplification and echo that have been introduced by modern technology. It is preserved in the hearts of men and women who have memorized it in its entirety in schools (*madrasas*) of Qur'ān learning and memorization (*ḥifẓ*). It is the primary source of Muslim creed (*'aqīdah*), law (*Sharī'ah*), theology (*kalām*), and spirituality (*taṣawwuf*). It carries a civilizational legacy that spans over a millennium and influences a sizeable share of the earth's inhabitants, embodied in texts, architecture, art, science, ritual, philosophy, law, spirituality, melody, theology, and politics.

Bibliography

Bowering, Gerhard. "Qur'an." In *The Princeton Encyclopedia of Islamic Political Thought*, edited by

Gerhard Bowering, 448–456. Princeton, N.J.: Princeton University Press, 2013.
Cook, Michael. *The Koran: A Very Short Introduction.* Oxford: Oxford University Press, 2000.
Ghzālī, Abū Ḥāmid al-. *The Jewels of the Qurʾān: Al-Ghazālī's Theory: A Translation, with an Annotation and Introduction of al-Ghazālī's Kitāb Jawāhir al-Qurʾān.* Trans. Muhammad Abul Quasem. London: Kegan Paul International, 1983.
Izutsu, Toshihiko. *Ethico-Religious Concepts in the Qurʾān.* Montreal: McGill University Press, 1966.
Mattson, Ingrid. *The Story of the Qurʾān: Its History and Place in Muslim Life.* Malden, Mass.: Blackwell, 2008.
McAuliffe, Jane Dammen, ed. *The Cambridge Companion to the Qurʾān.* Cambridge: Cambridge University Press, 2006.
McAuliffe, Jane Dammen, ed. *Encyclopaedia of the Qurʾān.* 6 vols. Leiden: Brill, 2001–2006.
Rahman, Fazlur. *Major Themes of the Qurʾan.* Minneapolis, Minn.: Bibliotheca Islamica, 1980.
Rippin, Andrew, ed. *The Blackwell Companion to the Qurʾān.* Malden, Mass.: Blackwell, 2006.
Robinson, Neal. *Discovering the Qurʾan: A Contemporary Approach to a Veiled Text.* London: SCM, 1996.
Saleh, Walid A. *The Formation of the Classical Tafsīr Tradition: The Qurʾān Commentary of al-Thaʿlabī (d. 427/1035).* Boston: Brill, 2004.
Watt, W. Montgomery. *Muhammad's Mecca: History in the Qurʾān.* Edinburgh: Edinburgh University Press, 1988.
Wild, Stefan, ed. *The Qurʾan as Text.* Leiden: Brill, 1996.

MAHAN MIRZA

QUṬB, SAYYID.

Sayyid Quṭb (1906–1966), was a literary critic, novelist, and activist of the twentieth century, exceeding in reputation even the founder of the Muslim Brotherhood, Ḥasan al-Bannā (1906–1949). His passionate writings contain powerful images of the maladies of contemporary Islamic societies and an idealization of the faith through the words of the sacred texts. In his overall standing as an Islamic thinker and activist, he may be compared with Turkey's Bediüzzaman Said Nursî (1873–1960), Pakistan's Abū al-Aʿlā Mawdūdī (1903–1979), and Iran's ʿAlī Sharīʿatī (1933–1977) and Ayatollah Ruhollah Khomeini (1902–1989).

Early Life. Quṭb was born on 9 October 1906 in the village of Musha, near the city of Asyut in Upper Egypt. His family was in economic decline at the time of his birth, but it remained prestigious owing to his father's educated status.

Quṭb was a frail child, which may have influenced his tendencies toward deep spirituality. He is reported to have memorized the entire Qurʾān by the age of ten. Although he attended the village *kuttāb* (elementary religious school), he soon transferred to the government school, from which he graduated in 1918. Quṭb moved to Helwan (a suburb of Cairo) in either 1919 or 1920. In 1930 he was admitted to Dār al-ʿUlūm, established in 1872 as a modern Egyptian university on the Western model, and graduated in 1933 with a bachelor's degree in arts education. In recognition of his accomplishments, he was appointed instructor at the Dār al-ʿUlūm, but he mainly earned his living between 1933 and 1951 as an employee of the Ministry of Education, where he later held the post of inspector for some years.

During the 1930s, Quṭb wrote works of fiction, literary criticism, and poetry. He was influenced by such modernists as Ṭāhā Ḥusayn (d. 1973), ʿAbbās al-ʿAqqād (d. 1964), and Aḥmad Ḥasan al-Zayyāt (d. 1968). Al-ʿAqqād in particular introduced Quṭb to editors of various newspapers, and he wrote scores of articles over the course of his career for the Egyptian press. Ṭāhā Ḥusayn, who was the minister of education (1950–1952), also encouraged him, at one time introducing his lectures to the Officers' Club after the July 1952 coup that overthrew the monarchy. However, Quṭb turned against both al-ʿAqqād, whose writings he deemed overly intellectualized, and Ḥusayn, on account of his Western orientations. Eventually, Quṭb left the Ministry of Education over disagreements with the government's educational policies as well as its submissiveness to the British. Quṭb joined the opposition Wafd Party of Saʿd Zaghlūl but eventually abandoned it to enter the breakaway Saʿdist Party on its emergence in 1937, only to break with it in 1942.

In 1948, still in the ministry's employ, Quṭb was dispatched to the United States to study Western methods of education. He studied at Wilson Teacher's College (now the University of the District of Columbia); the Colorado State College of Education, where he earned a master's degree in education; and at Stanford University. Quṭb spent about three years abroad, leaving America in the summer of 1950 and visiting England, Switzerland, and Italy on his way back to Egypt in 1951. His trip to the United States was a defining moment for him, marking a transition from literary and educational pursuits to intense religious commitment. Although he acknowledged the economic and scientific achievements of American society, Quṭb was appalled by its racism, sexual permissiveness, and pro-Zionism.

Political Involvement. Back in Egypt, Quṭb refused a promotion to the position of adviser in the Ministry of Education and began writing articles for various newspapers on social and political themes. In 1953, Quṭb joined the Muslim Brotherhood and was appointed editor of its weekly paper, *al-Ikhwān al-Muslimūn*. Not long afterward, he became the director of the Muslim Brotherhood's propaganda section and was chosen to serve on the organization's highest bodies, the Working Committee and the Guidance Council.

It is said that Quṭb was a key liaison between the Muslim Brotherhood and the Free Officers, who overthrew the monarchy in 1952. Some of these men, including Gamal Abdel Nasser, visited his house just before the coup, and Quṭb was the sole civilian to attend meetings of the Revolutionary Command Council (RCC) after the seizure of power. He agreed to be an adviser to the RCC in cultural matters and was briefly the deputy secretary-general of the Liberation Rally, the government-sponsored mass mobilization organization. However, relations between the Free Officers and the Brotherhood soon deteriorated as it became clear that each side had a different agenda. The Brotherhood called for a referendum on the new constitution, anticipating that Egyptians would demand the application of Sharīʿah (Islamic law), but the RCC refused. The Muslim Brotherhood condemned the RCC's agreement with Britain in July 1954 to end the occupation, because that agreement allowed the British to return their troops at any time during the next seven years if they perceived a threat to their interests. The Brotherhood demanded a plebiscite on the agreement, but it, too, was rejected out of hand. A tense standoff prevailed until October 1954, when shots were fired at Nasser during a speech.

The Muslim Brotherhood has always maintained that this incident was a provocation engineered by the regime to justify a sweeping crackdown against it. Quṭb, whom the regime had already detained for three months in early 1954 but then released, was caught in the net of arrests. Although he suffered from poor health, Quṭb was brutally tortured. In May 1955 he was transferred to the prison hospital. In July, the court sentenced him to fifteen years in prison, most of which he spent in the hospital. He witnessed continued torture of his colleagues in jail, with perhaps the worst episode occurring in 1957, when more than twenty Muslim Brotherhood inmates were killed outright and dozens injured. Accordingly, Quṭb set in motion steps for the creation of a disciplined secret cadre of devoted followers whose task was originally limited to self-defense. Without declaring it publicly, however, Quṭb came to believe in using violence against the government if it used force against his organization. Still later, he came to the view that violence was justified even if the regime were merely deemed unjust and refused to alter its behavior.

Quṭb was released in May 1964, but in August 1965 he was rearrested on charges of terrorism and sedition. The authorities initially permitted media coverage of the trial, but when the defendants talked about their torture, the proceedings were moved behind closed doors. Incontrovertible evidence against Quṭb was apparently not presented, as his revolutionary tract, *Maʿalim fī al-ṭariq* (*Milestones*, 1964)—the chief document upon which the prosecutors relied—did not explicitly call for armed overthrow of the government. Rather, it urged resistance by encouraging believers to turn away from existing society and create a model *ummah* (Islamic community) that would eventually establish true Islam. Despite great international pressure, including from the Vatican, the government executed Quṭb on 29 August 1966. Ever since, his supporters have considered him a martyr.

Political Thought. Perhaps more than any other post–World War II Sunnī Muslim thinker, Sayyid Quṭb personifies the determination of Islamist movements to oppose the West, Israel, and leaders in Islamic societies whom they consider to be disregarding God's law. Quṭb regarded the leaders of Islamic societies of whom he disapproved, and the societies they ruled, as living in a state of *jāhilīyah* (literally, ignorance [of the truths of revelation]). His most important political work, *Milestones*, contains trenchant attacks on *jāhilīyah*, which he perceived to pervade contemporary life throughout the world. The symbolism of this concept is highly charged, because it is the term used to describe pagan Arabia prior to the revelation. Quṭb's writings have been translated into Persian, Turkish, Urdu, English, and other languages.

Quṭb's writings show his uncompromising commitment to the sacred text. It is self-evident to him that if the Qurʾān contains a message, then human beings must obey that message. Quṭb was so clear on this in his own mind that it did not occur to him that Muslims, living in historical time, might reinterpret their traditions and their past in the context of their contemporary historical circumstances, nor that earlier understandings of scripture by the pioneers of Islam were themselves interpretations of texts whose true meanings could not be categorically determined. Quṭb plainly held that Islam is a timeless body of ideas and practices whose import is self-evident. Thus, in his mind, people have no excuse to fail to adhere to God's word. This failure is a brazen refusal, as he saw it, to accept God's commands and is not due to ambiguities that must be explored via hermeneutical discourse.

One key to Quṭb's overall social and political program is its organic view and connotations of corporatism. This is interesting in view of his explicit rejection of Greek thought and Islamic Neoplatonic philosophy, themselves steeped in corporate and organic assumptions about society. More specifically, Quṭb believes that Muslims cohere in a dynamic entity that he calls *tajammuʿ ḥarakī*. This entity is, in fact, the embodiment of the *ummah*, which he sees as a living organism with attributes of thought and behavior. The success of this dynamic entity lies in its acceptance of the trust given to it by God to master the world and benefit from its resources, but the purpose of this mastery is to obey the sovereign commands (*ḥākimīyah*) of God. Quṭb holds that the dynamic community of believers is a real entity acting in society and the world, and that it experiences change, has practical purposes, and is thoroughly enmeshed in the immediacy of everyday existence. The sources for its existence and behavior lie entirely outside itself and are rooted in revelation (Binder, 1988, pp. 178–179).

Reflecting the ideas of Mawdūdī, Quṭb focused on the so-called *ḥākimīyah* (sovereignty) verses of the Qurʾān (5:44, 45, 47; 12:47, 60). Qurʾān 5:44,

45, and 47 are nearly identical and have been classically understood by commentators across the centuries to state: "And those who do not judge according to what God has revealed are unbelievers ... oppressors ... sinners." Qurʾān 12:47 and 60, according to these commentators, state: "Verily, judgment is God's alone." Like Mawdūdī, Quṭb understands the verb in Q. 5:44, 45, and 47 to be "rule," and the noun in Q. 12:47 and 60 to be "rulership." Rendered in this innovative way, the verses implicitly sanction collective action to dismiss rulers who fail to apply God's revelations. Quṭb invoked the precedent of Taqī al-Dīn Aḥmad ibn Taymīyah (d. 1328), who anathematized the Mongols, despite their adoption of Islam, for their impious beliefs and actions. Just as the fourteenth-century jurist had advocated disobedience to Mongol leaders, so Quṭb and his supporters came to the view that Islam made armed resistance not only permissible or commendable but mandatory against nominally Muslim rulers who were deemed to be anti-Islamic in their beliefs and conduct.

Influence. Among the groups that Quṭb's writings have inspired are the Egyptian groups known as al-Fannīyah al-ʿAskarīyah (the Technical Military Academy Group); Jamāʿat Takfīr wa-al-Hijrah (Excommunication and Exile); Tanẓīm al-Jihād, the group that claimed responsibility for the assassination of Anwar al-Sadat in 1981; and al-Jamāʿah al-Islāmīyah (the Islamic Group). A reading of *al-Farīdah al-ghāʾibah* (The Neglected Duty, written 1979–1980, first published in December 1981), by Muḥammad ʿAbd al-Salām Faraj on behalf of Tanẓīm al-Jihād, reflects that organization's indebtedness to Quṭb's ideas about *jāhilīyah*, *ḥākimīyah*, and *jihād*. Groups outside Egypt have claimed Quṭb's legacy as well. His writings are frequently read by Sunnī opposition groups, such as Jabhat al-Inqādh al-Islāmī (Islamic Salvation Front) in Algeria; the Tunisian Islamic Tendency Movement (al-Ittijāh al-Islāmī), now called Ḥizb al-Nahḍah; the Muslim Brotherhood in Sudan, Syria, and Jordan; Ḥamās in the Gaza Strip and West Bank; the Taliban in Afghanistan; and, among others, several Islamist groups across Turkey, Pakistan, Malaysia, Indonesia, the Philippines, and Africa. The transnational al-Qaʿida also considers itself a legatee of Quṭb's tradition. Shīʿī groups, including Ḥizbullāh in Lebanon, the Ḥizb al-Daʿwah in Iraq, and even the Iranian clerical establishment, have taken certain cues from Quṭb, although they disagree with him on the question of leadership. It can thus be concluded that Quṭb's role in inspiring Islamic revivalist movements since the late 1960s might be even greater than that of comparable figures such as Mawdūdī and Khomeini.

Critiques of Quṭb's Thought. Ultimately, Quṭb's worldview rests on a manifest historicity. He is not interested in a historically grounded analysis of the development of law in Islam, for example. Rather, one finds repeated references to the primary sacred texts, the Qurʾān and, to a lesser extent, the *ḥadīths*. Quṭb does not acknowledge that Qurʾānic and *ḥadīth* texts might not be self-evident and that, as they are interpreted over the centuries, people might come to different conclusions as to their meanings.

The tone of Quṭb's writings is exhortatory and didactic. As a professional educator, Quṭb adopted the role of tutor instructing students in the verities of the true faith: the enemy is at the gates in the form of international neo-Crusaders seeking to destroy the identity of Muslims and domestic despots who set up their own laws in defiance of what God has revealed. He believed both the capitalist and communist systems were materialistic, spiritually bankrupt, and hostile to Islam. The former, he believed, fell victim to rampant and grotesque individualism while the latter brutally enslaved the human being.

Despite his unreconstructed rejection of "Western" values, Quṭb, as is often the case with twentieth-century Islamic thinkers, does not hesitate to invoke concepts rooted in the Western tradition. He does not acknowledge the Western provenance of such ideas, reaching into the early Islamic period instead to argue that they in fact are endemic to Islam, but many of these concepts derive either from the ancient Greek tradition or otherwise emanate from the period of the Enlightenment and the French Revolution and its aftermath.

An example of the Western roots of Quṭb's thought can be seen in his concept of democracy. No Arabic word for this term exists, so the cognate *al-dīmuqrāṭīyah* has been devised. Despite Quṭb's sensitivity to language issues, he never asks why Muslims use the word in this borrowed form. He is satisfied to find two brief references to *shūrā* (consultation) in the Qurʾān (3:159 and 42:38), from which he constructs a full-blown system of (Islamic) "democracy." Although commentators on the Qurʾān have for centuries understood these two verses to mean something different from the modern notion of political democracy in its twin attributes of individual freedom and social equality, as institutionalized in representative bodies endowed with sovereign authority, Quṭb is not deterred from vindicating the Islamic roots of democracy.

The same can be said of social justice. It was not until the twentieth century that the phrase *al-ʿadālah al-ijtimāʿīyah* (social justice) was used by jurists in Islamic law, although medieval writers such as Abū Bakr al-Ṭurṭūshī (d. 1127), Najm al-Dīn al-Ṭūfī (d. 1316), Ibn Taymīyah, and Ibn Khaldūn (d. 1406) focused on the justice and injustice of rulers and the requirement that the state pursue justice to ensure the *maṣlaḥah* (public interest) of the Muslims. Quṭb's method is to find verses in the Qurʾān referring to God bidding people to "justice" (16:90) or verses pertaining to the perfection of God's words in "justice" (6:115). The view of justice that emerges from the scripture is a highly abstract and idealized interpretation of what can be termed "divine justice," perceived without regard to social reality as captured in the historical record.

In contrast, social justice, as understood in modern discourse, comes from the tradition of natural law and the philosophy of law, which are anthropocentric. The very phrase "social justice" implies equity considerations in the context of the development of human societies in historical time, rather than a reified category that is theocentric at its very core. Accordingly, the phrase "social justice," so important for Quṭb, contains within it the subversion of his project, which is based on the belief that truth is to be found immediately in revelation, not by references to human endeavors in history.

Nevertheless, a critique of Quṭb that is made only at this level, such as that of the Iranian ʿAlī Sharīʿatī (d. 1977), misses the point. His advocacy of revolutionary change to restore a pure Islamic order has resonated powerfully among those disgusted with the system that the leaders of the Muslim world have erected. Quṭb's evocations and invocations of concepts that seemingly come from Western traditions are apparently one of the ironies of the Islamic resurgence that has developed since the mid-twentieth century. But the measure of Quṭb's contributions will no doubt be the impact that he has had in this period as the nonpareil exemplar of collective protest against those deemed to be the enemies of Islam.

BIBLIOGRAPHY

Akhavi, Shahrough. "The Dialectic in Contemporary Egyptian Social Thought: The Scripturalist and Modernist Discourses of Sayyid Qutb and Hasan Hanafi." *International Journal of Middle East Studies* 29 (August 1997): 377–401.

Akhavi, Shahrough. "Sayyid Qutb: The 'Poverty of Philosophy' and the Vindication of Islamic Tradition."

In *Cultural Transitions in the Middle East*, edited by Şerif Mardin, pp. 130–152. Leiden, Netherlands: E. J. Brill, 1994.

Bergesen, Albert J., ed. *The Sayyid Qutb Reader: Selected Writings on Politics, Religion, and Society*. New York: Routledge, 2008.

Binder, Leonard. *Islamic Liberalism: A Critique of Development Ideologies*. Chicago: University of Chicago Press, 1988.

Euben, Roxanne. *Enemy in the Mirror: Islamic Fundamentalism and the Limits of Modern Rationalism*. Princeton, N.J.: Princeton University Press, 1999.

Haddad, Yvonne Yazbeck. "The Qur'anic Justification for an Islamic Revolution: The View of Sayyid Quṭb." *Middle East Journal* 37 (Winter 1983): 14–29.

Haddad, Yvonne Yazbeck. "Sayyid Qutb: Ideologue of Islamic Revival." In *Voices of Resurgent Islam*, edited by John L. Esposito, pp. 67–98. New York: Oxford University Press, 1983.

Jansen, Johannes J. G. *The Neglected Duty: The Creed of Sadat's Assassins and Islamic Resurgence in the Middle East*. New York: Macmillan, 1986.

Kepel, Gilles. *Muslim Extremism in Egypt: The Prophet and the Pharaoh: Muslim Extremism in Egypt*. Translated by Jon Rothschild. Berkeley: University of California Press, 1985.

Mitchell, Richard P. *The Society of the Muslim Brothers*. London: Oxford University Press, 1969.

Moussalli, Ahmad S. *Radical Islamic Fundamentalism: The Ideological and Political Discourse of Sayyid Quṭb*. Beirut: American University of Beirut, 1992.

Qutb, Sayyid. *Milestones*. Damascus: Dar al-Ilm, 2007.

Qutb, Sayyid. *Social Justice in Islam*. Oneonta, N.Y.: Islamic Publications International, 2000.

Shepard, William. "The Development of the Thought of Sayyid Quṭb as Reflected in Earlier and Later Editions of 'Social Justice in Islam.'" *Die Welt des Islams*, n.s., 32 (1992): 196–236.

SHAHROUGH AKHAVI
Updated by NAEL SHAMA

R

Rahman, Omar Abdel. Omar Abdel Rahman, (b. 1938), a well-known Egyptian religious scholar and Islamic fundamentalist leader, was born to a poor rural family in the village of al-Jamālīyah, in Lower Egypt. According to some sources, he was blinded in an accident at ten months of age, although he may have lost his eyesight to childhood diabetes. A dedicated student, Omar received a traditional religious education in regional urban centers, memorized the Qur'ān, and developed an interest in the works of leading purists such as Ibn Taymīyah and Sayyid Quṭb. He enrolled at al-Azhar University in Cairo in 1960 and graduated with honors in 1965 from the Faculty of Fundamentals of Religion. Frustrated that he failed to secure a teaching post at the university—when he was appointed by the state as a mosque preacher in a poor rural village in Upper Egypt—Omar quickly returned to al-Azhar, where he obtained a master's degree in 1967. He fulfilled his lifelong dream with a faculty appointment in 1968.

Abdel Rahman made the pilgrimage to Mecca in 1968 and there met Saʿīd Ramaḍān, an expatriate leader of the Egyptian Muslim Brotherhood who opposed the government of Gamal Abdel Nasser. Ramaḍān persuaded him to carry funds back to Egypt for the families of jailed Brotherhood members, but he was arrested on his return. This first run-in with the law ended his academic career, and he accepted a less than desirable bureaucratic position in late 1969. It was in the late 1960s that he emerged as an outspoken critic of secular ideas.

A critic of Nasser, Abdel Rahman was detained for eight months, and he honed his preaching skills behind bars. To better manipulate opposition forces, the Anwar el-Sadat regime granted amnesty to jailed Islamic fundamentalists, with the aim of enlisting them as a counterweight to leftist forces. After completing his doctorate in 1972, he briefly held a professorship at al-Azhar before moving to Asyūṭ, a center of Islamic fundamentalist activity.

In 1977 Abdel Rahman married ʿIshaʿ Hasan Judah, the daughter of a Brotherhood member, and left for Saudi Arabia, where he taught at King Saud University. Soon after his return, he was arrested for his involvement in the fundamentalist Islamic *jihād* organization, then led by Ayman al-Zawāhirī, a future lieutenant of Osama Bin Laden. Following Sadat's assassination in 1981, Abdel Rahman was accused of leading the organization that plotted and carried out the assassination but was acquitted on both counts, released in 1984, and expelled from his native country.

During his protracted trial (1981–1984), three factors led to Abdel Rahman's emergence as a leading figure in Islamist circles. First, as clearly discussed in his book *Mīthāq al-ʿamal al-Islāmī* (Charter of Islamic Action), was his explanation of correct Islamic conduct. It marked a departure from the more moderate wing of the Brotherhood, as he argued for an overthrow of the secular state to restore fundamental principles of holy scriptures. Second, he married Fātin Shuʿayb, a kinswoman of several important activists, affirming his solidarity with the Jamāʿah al-Islāmīyah in Upper Egypt and lending weight to his religious status as *muftī al-jihād*. Third, as major leaders of the *jihād* organization were executed or imprisoned for life, Abdel Rahman filled the leadership power vacuum.

In the late 1980s, Omar visited Afghanistan, although his primary motive then was opposition to the Soviet occupation. In July 1990, Abdel Rahman was issued a visa for the United States in Khartoum. He settled in the New York area, where he preached and assembled a core group of devoted followers. It was in those meetings that individuals who carried out the 1993 World Trade Center bombing came under his influence.

With the assistance of an Egyptian informant wearing a listening device, the FBI managed to record Rahman issuing a *fatwa* (religious decree) that favored acts of violence against civilian targets. Washington alleged that one of the plans was to carry out simultaneous attacks on the United Nations, the Lincoln and Holland tunnels, the George Washington Bridge, and a federal building housing FBI offices. Abdel Rahman was arrested in 1993 along with nine of his followers, tried, and convicted of seditious conspiracy in October 1995. He was sentenced to life in prison and was incarcerated in the Federal Administrative Maximum Penitentiary in Florence, Colorado.

The cleric's imprisonment rallied Islamists, who demanded his release. In 1997, the Jamāʿat al-Islāmīyah attacked European tourists near Luxor, killing fifty-eight. Leaflets were found at the scene linking the atrocity to Abdel Rahman's detention. Ironically, a member of his legal team, Lynne Stewart, was convicted in 2005 of facilitating communication between the imprisoned cleric and his followers. According to the FBI, Abdel Rahman was seriously ill with a liver tumor, but was given medical attention to stabilize his condition. Following the rise of Islamists in post-Mubarak Egypt, supporters of Abdel Rahman organized several demonstrations in front of the U.S. embassy in Cairo to call for his release. To Egyptian hard-line Islamists, Abdel Rahman still remains a spiritual guide with uncompromising views.

[*See also* Egypt; Jamāʿat al-Islāmīyah, al-; Jihād Groups; *and* Muslim Brotherhood.]

BIBLIOGRAPHY

Fawzī, Maḥmūd. *ʿUmar ʿAbd al-Raḥmān al-shaykh al-amrīkī al-qādim*. Cairo: n.p., n.d.

Jacquard, Roland. *In the Name of Osama Bin Laden: Global Terrorism and the Bin Laden Brotherhood*. Edited by Samia Serageldin. Translated by George Holoch. Durham, N.C.: Duke University Press, 2002.

Kepel, Gilles. *Jihad: The Trail of Political Islam*. Translated by Anthony F. Roberts. Cambridge, Mass.: Harvard University Press, 2002.

McCarthy, Andrew C. *Willful Blindness: A Memoir of the Jihad*. New York: Encounter, 2008.

GEHAD AUDA
Updated by JOSEPH A. KÉCHICHIAN
and NAEL SHAMA

RASHĪD RIḌĀ, MUḤAMMAD. Islamic revivalist and reformer, (1865–1935), was born in a village near Tripoli, then part of Syria, to a family that claimed a line of descent from the prophet Muḥammad. After his early education in a traditional religious school, Riḍā attended an Islamic school established by an enlightened scholar, Shaykh Ḥusayn al-Jisr (d. 1909), who believed that the way to the progress of the Muslim nation was through a synthesis of religious education and modern sciences. Riḍā thus acquired a thorough education in the doctrine and traditions of Islam and a fair knowledge of the natural sciences and languages (Turkish and French). He studied the works of al-Ghazālī (d. 1111) and Ibn Taymīyyah (d. 1328), which inspired him with the need to reform the declining conditions of Muslims and purify Islam from degenerate Ṣūfī practices.

By the end of the nineteenth century a broader movement of reform, the Salafīyah movement led by Jamāl al-Dīn al-Afghānī (d. 1897) and Muḥammad ʿAbduh (d. 1905), was under way in Egypt. This movement stressed the need for the exercise of reason and the adoption of modern natural sciences, for agitation against tyranny, despotism, and resistance to foreign domination, as well as the promotion of Muslim solidarity. The tenets of this movement were expounded in *al-ʿUrwah al-wuthqā* (The Indissoluble Bond), which al-Afghānī and ʿAbduh published in Paris in 1884.

In 1897 Riḍā left for Egypt to join ʿAbduh, to become one of his close associates and, in time, a leading disciple. In Cairo Riḍā published his own magazine, *al-Manār* (The Lighthouse), which first appeared in 1898 as a weekly and, subsequently, as a monthly until his death in 1935. The objectives of *al-Manār* were to articulate and disseminate the ideas of reform to preserve the unity of the Muslim nation. A prolific writer Riḍā produced far more than ʿAbduh and al-Afghānī, which sealed his own legacy.

Riḍā, like ʿAbduh, believed in the compatibility of Islam and modernity. Still, while ʿAbduh emphasized *ijtihād* (independent judgment) in an effort to reinterpret Islamic doctrines and give Islam a new vitality, Riḍā insisted on certain criteria for Islamic reform. Riḍā witnessed the disintegration of the Islamic caliphate, the fragmentation of the Muslim world, and the ascendancy of the advocates of wholesale adoption of Western models.

Concerned with the unity of the Muslim community and the preservation of its identity and culture, Riḍā viewed the original Islamic sources, the Qurʾān, *sunnah*, and *ijmāʿ* (consensus of the companions of the Prophet), as the basis of reform. Nevertheless he distinguished between acts of worship (*ʿibādāt*) and matters concerning interaction with others (*muʿāmalāt*). Since the *ʿibādāt*, which organize human behavior, were revealed in the Qurʾān, and were laid down by authentic *ḥadīth*, they cannot be changed. But human relations, in the absence of an explicit, authentic, and binding text, can be reinterpreted according to the interest (*maṣlaḥah*) of the community.

Throughout his intellectual career Riḍā was preoccupied with the issue of reform. He believed the decline of the Muslim nation was due to the stagnation of its scholars and the tyranny of its rulers. He viewed European dominance over the Muslims as a result of the latter's weakness, which he attributed to the Muslims' inability to master the sciences, form organized political institutions, and restrict the power of their governments. Considering education a precondition for political reform and independence, Riḍā urged the Muslim peoples to acquire the commendable aspects of Western civilization, such as science, technical skill, and wealth.

Central to Riḍā's scheme of thought was the concept of the caliphate and its indispensability to the coherence of the Muslim community. On the eve of the breakup of the Ottoman caliphate in 1923, Riḍā wrote a treatise, "The Caliphate, or the Supreme Imamate," which included an elaborate discussion of the caliphate and a plan for its restoration. Realizing the obstacles surrounding the revival of a proper Islamic caliphate of *ijtihād*, Riḍā proposed a caliphate of necessity, a temporary one, to preserve Muslim solidarity. Essential to this caliphate were the issues of *shūrā* (consultation), *Ahl al-Ḥall wa-al-ʿAqd* (those who loose and bind), and *ijtihād* to ensure the adaptability of Islamic laws and the sovereignty of the Muslim nation.

Riḍā's ideas, particularly in the interwar period, gave an Arab emphasis to the Islamic reform movement. His contributions to the preservation and dissemination of the ideology of Islamic reform were also significant, as he clearly perceived the challenges and threats that led to the disintegration of the Muslim nation. These constituted a link between al-Afghānī and ʿAbduh and succeeding generations of Muslim activists and thinkers who appeared in the third decade of the twentieth century. Riḍā's most direct heir was Ḥasan al-Bannā, the founder and spiritual leader of the Muslim Brotherhood group, who developed his own thoughts and elaborated a specific and systematic doctrine of Islamic laws and policies. In his later years, Bannā's ideas drew close to the Ḥanbalī school of law, thereby closing the great reform circle with Riḍā.

[*See also* ʿAbduh, Muḥammad; Afghānī, Jamāl al-Dīn al-; Modernity; *and* Salafī Movements.]

BIBLIOGRAPHY

Works by Muḥammad Rashīd Riḍā

al-Khilāfah aw-al-imāmah al-ʿuẓmā [The Caliphate, or The Supreme Imamate]. Cairo: Maṭbaʿat al-Manār, 1923.

The Muhammadan Revelation. Translated by Yusuf DeLorenzo. Alexandria, Va.: Al-Saadawi Publications, 1996.

Christian Criticisms, Islamic Proofs: Rashid Rida's Modernist Defence of Islam. Translated and analysis by Simon A. Wood. New York: OneWorld Publications, 2007.

Secondary Sources

Adams, Charles C. *Islam and Modernism in Egypt: A Study of the Modern Reform Movement Inaugurated by Muhammad ʿAbduh*. London: Oxford University Press, 1933.

Arslān, Shakīb. *Al-Sayyid Rashīd Riḍā wa-ikhāʾ arbaʿīn sanah* [Rashīd Riḍā and Forty Years of Brotherhood]. Damascus: Maṭbaʿat Ibn Zaydūn, 1937.

Enayat, Hamid. *Modern Islamic Political Thought*. Austin: University of Texas Press, 1982.

Hourani, Albert. *Arabic Thought in the Liberal Age, 1798–1939*. London and New York: Oxford University Press, 1970.

Kerr, Malcolm H. *Islamic Reform: The Political and Legal Theories of Muḥammad ʿAbduh and Rashīd Riḍā*. Berkeley: University of California Press, 1966.

Al-Manār magazine (1898–1935).

Safran, Nadav. *Egypt in Search of a Political Community: An Analysis of the Intellectual and Political Evolution of Egypt, 1804–1952*. Cambridge, Mass.: Harvard University Press, 1961.

Shahin, Emad Eldin. "Muḥammad Rashīd Riḍā's Perspectives on the West as Reflected in al-Manār." *Muslim World* 79, no. 2 (April 1989): 113–132.

Soage, Ana Belen. "Rashid Rida's Legacy." *Muslim World* 98, no. 1 (January 2008): 1–23.

Willis, John. "Debating the Caliphate: Islam and Nation in the Work of Rashid Rida and Kalam Azad." *International History Review* 32, no. 4 (December 2010): 711–732.

EMAD EL-DIN SHAHIN
Updated by NAEL SHAMA

REBELLION. Acts of rebellion against recognized political authority have been a commonplace throughout Islamic history. The meaning of rebellion, however—how it was justified, defined, and countered—has varied dramatically, reflecting both changing political circumstances and the Islamic tradition's capacity to accommodate and rationalize these changes. As in any other religious tradition or political order, rebellion in Islam must be seen in light of the struggle over power and the authority to use power. To define rebellion is to outline the limits of internal dissent and the proper response to it. For this reason, talk about rebellion in classical Islamic sources parallels talk about other threats to the Islamic state—unbelievers, sectarians, apostates, and brigands—and the conditions of waging war (*jihād*) against them.

Tribes and Tribalism. The earliest rebellions in Islam grew out of tensions between Arab tribes, as an emerging Islamic elite tried to impose its authority on recalcitrant tribal groups. Evidence of such tension was apparent during the life of the Prophet Muḥammad, specifically during the Medinan phase of his preaching and tribal consolidation. After his death in 632 CE, conflict broke out when tribes that had recognized Muḥammad as a tribal leader, prophet, or both renounced their allegiance and refused loyalty to Abū Bakr, Muḥammad's caliphal successor. Abū Bakr spent his entire reign (632–634) fighting these rebellious tribes and unifying the power of the new Islamic state. Later tradition labeled this fighting the *ridda* wars or the wars of apostasy, a stark reminder of the religious framework imposed on political matters to legitimize just rule. Abū Bakr's success at subduing the "apostate" tribes freed Arab Muslim fighters to pursue the conquests, but it did not eliminate the impact of tribalism, which made compromise over leadership difficult and rebellion somewhat natural, on later society and politics.

Deeply embedded tribal interests continued to hamper efforts to create an identity and community based solely on Islam, an ideal at the heart of Muḥammad's message. The danger posed by these interests was addressed in prophetic tradition, which identifies tribalism (*ʿaṣabīyah*) as a threat to the Muslim community and condemns those who fight and die under its banner as deserving a pagan's death (Muslim, *Ṣaḥīḥ*, Kitāb al-imāra). Legal sources list tribalism as a type of rebellion (*baghy*) but one that lacks legitimacy, unlike other types, and must be fought without mercy (Abou El Fadl 2001, 205–206). Elements of tribalism have also been mentioned in connection with the defining period of rebellion in early Islam, the first civil war.

Leadership Conflict. Of all the challenges faced by the nascent Islamic empire, none proved as daunting and damaging as the one over the rightful *imām* or ruler. It led to two civil wars (sg. *fitna*) and gave rise to entrenched sectarian divisions. The first civil war spanned the period of ʿAlī's rule as caliph, 656–661, and consisted of a series of rebellions against his authority. It began on the heels of the murder of the third caliph, ʿUthmān, who had gained numerous enemies because of his attempts to centralize power and enrich his clan, the Umayya. Upon ʿAlī's succession as caliph, two groups emerged immediately to challenge him. The first represented an old guard of Meccan leaders, under the direction of Ṭalḥa, Zubayr, and ʿĀʾisha, the Prophet's favorite wife. The second challenge came from Muʿāwiyah, the governor of Syria and ʿUthmān's cousin, who refused to recognize ʿAlī until ʿUthmān's murderers had been brought to justice. ʿAlī defeated the first group at the Battle of the Camel in 656; he spent the remainder of his caliphate dealing with the second. During a skirmish between the forces of ʿAlī and Muʿāwiyah at Ṣiffīn, in 657, ʿAlī was tricked into agreeing to an arbitration process that put his status as caliph in question. A body of ʿAlī's supporters, angered over his willingness to arbitrate what they regarded as God's decision, withdrew from his ranks, declaring both ʿAlī and Muʿāwiyah, along with ʿUthmān, unfit leaders and apostate Muslims and taking up arms against them. These defectors, known as the Khārijīs because they "went out" (from the Arabic verb *kharaja*) or rebelled against Alī's forces, became the first Islamic sect; they continued to instigate violent raids and threaten caliphal authority well into the ninth century. The arbitration process failed to produce an agreement, mainly because neither ʿAlī nor Muʿāwiyah was prepared to step aside. Low-grade conflict continued between the two until ʿAlī was assassinated by a lone Khārijī swordsman in 661, after which Muʿāwiyah became caliph.

While the first civil war came to an end, it did not do away with factions contending for power and thus rebellion remained an ongoing reality. Supporters of ʿAlī, the Shia (from *shīʿat ʿAlī*, "the faction of ʿAlī"), continued to nurture hopes that one of ʿAlī's descendants would become leader. Meccans had also not given up their claims to an office that, with the reign of Muʿāwiyah and the advent of the Umayyad dynasty, had moved to Damascus. Muʿāwiyah's death in 680 and the succession of his son Yazīd awakened these factions, marking the beginning of the second civil war. By the time this war ended in 692, three distinct leadership orientations had taken hold—Sunni, Shii, and Khārijī—and each saw itself as the sole inheritor of Muḥammad's mantle of authority. Like Muḥammad, the leaders of these factions were viewed as religious guides whose thought and actions were worthy of emulation. To adhere to a particular *imām* at this time was not simply to join a party; it meant linking oneself to the community of the saved with God's representative at the top (Crone 2004, 25–30). Much was at stake, which accounts for the violent contestations and the vehemence of the denunciations the factions leveled at one another. It also accounts for the gradual rethinking of the necessary link between political authority and religious purity that informed the early factions and their notions of the Muslim community.

What Muslims, or the majority of those who acted and spoke on behalf of the faith, came to reject was a set of attitudes toward the ruler that seemed to invite *fitna* and undermine political order. Rejected were both the Shiite notion of the ruler as an infallible, prophet-like source of God's continuing justice in the world and the Khārijī view of the ruler as a tribal leader who, once compromised by sin or a failure of duty, could be removed from office. Thus the rebellions associated with the civil wars gave rise, over time, to a practical compromise about the character of the ruler and the possibility of rebellion against him—a compromise that emerged as the basis of Sunni political authority.

It is important to bear in mind, however, that the Islamic sources that are used to understand rebellion were themselves composed after the events they purport to explain. The Sunni winners in the struggle over power and authority also won the right to identify rebellion and define its meaning. The problem of sorting out actual motives for rebellion in early Islam, then, is itself influenced by the struggle over, and ability to control, the Islamic state.

Could this intense period of rebellion have been avoided if Muḥammad had made clear preparations for a successor? Perhaps. But other factors were also in play. As a result of the conquests, Arabs found themselves ruling over regions—in Iraq, Syria, Palestine, and Egypt—with more advanced social and political structures than had been the case in Arabia. There was clearly much to gain for those Arabs in positions of power and much to lose for those who failed to assert themselves. Moreover, when the tribal ethos merged with the newly minted divine mandate to "command right and forbid wrong," rebellion of some sort was inevitable.

Classical Framework. Sunnī dominance did not rid the community of rebellion, but it did provide an organizing principle for dealing with disobedient Muslims. At the heart of that principle lay a number of insights learned from the civil wars and often articulated by early factions that took positions on the rebellions but were themselves later deemed sectarian, such as the Qadarīs, Murjiʾīs, and Muʿtazilīs. These insights fused the distinction between religion and politics, like much of the discourse and debate in early Islam. But they did so with the purpose of establishing an "orthodox" view that avoided the earlier dangers. Thus the Sunnī compromise recognized that the ruler, in particular his office (imamate or caliphate), had the political responsibility to enforce Islamic law, but he was not viewed as a religious figure above the law or without the human frailties of other Muslims. Moreover, although obedience to the ruler was a religio-legal requirement, it was religious specialists (*ʿulamāʾ* or *fuqahāʾ*), not rulers, who established the boundaries of true faith. Put simply, the orthodox fusion of religion and politics was actually a separation of political and religious responsibilities and the institutions that carried them out—institutions that sometimes collaborated and sometimes conflicted. The political well-being of the Muslim community rested in the hands of rulers who may or may not embody the pious ideal of leaders like Muḥammad or the first four Rightly Guided Caliphs; its spiritual well-being was in the hands of religious experts who interpreted God's law in daily life. Both institutions operated under a divine mandate and were ideally linked in service to the community, but breaches of this ideal were not uncommon.

Credal Statements. Early confessional statements, such as *Fiqh Akbar I* (mid-eighth century) and *Fiqh Akbar II* (mid-ninth century), clearly rejected the rebellious impetus of the civil wars in an attempt to impose political harmony. It became a matter of faith for Muslims to support the first four caliphs, to avoid judgment about their rule, and thus to reject Khārijī and Shiite factionalism. In a specific reproach to the Khārijīs, sinful Muslims were included among the community of faithful. Moreover, difference of opinion among Muslims, which had stoked the fires of rebellion, was deemed a blessing from God (Wensinck 1965, chapters six and eight).

Legal and Theological Perspectives. Perhaps the best known legal work on the treatment of rebels is *al-Aḥkām al-sulṭāniyya* (translated as "The Ordinances of Government") by Abū al-Ḥasan al-Māwardī (d. 1058). The treatise purports to be an instruction manual, culled from the best legal advice, for those in positions of political authority. Al-Māwardī's treatment of rebels falls under a section on *jihād*—namely, the fighting of believers who live within the "Abode of Islam" (*dār al-Islām*), not of enemies of Islam who typically reside in the "Abode of War" (*dār al-ḥarb*). Following common usage, al-Māwardī calls rebels *bughāt* or *ahl al-baghy*, a term derived from a Qurʾānic verse (49:9) that speaks of the need to fight believers if during a dispute one side "wrongs" another. According to al-Māwardī, rebels are one of three categories of believers who must be fought, the other two being apostates and brigands. It was ʿAlī's interactions with the Khārijīs that provided al-Māwardī, and most other writers, with the raw material for mapping the rules of engagement with rebels. According to al-Māwardī, those who simply adopted a sectarian view but did not openly rebel against the ruler, either by taking up arms or by refusing to pay taxes, were left in peace. Those who continued to rebel, after receiving the required warning of impending warfare, were fought until they returned to obedience; they were not killed if taken prisoner, nor was their property taken as booty or their wives and children sold into slavery (al-Māwardī 1996, 64–67).

For al-Māwardī, rulers were both legally empowered and obligated to fight unrepentant rebels, unless they constituted a force that the state was unable to subdue—then their sovereignty over a given territory had to be recognized and a peace treaty was valid. Here legal theory reflected the political reality of an empire already divided into petty sultanates. In practical terms, then, rebels were as likely to be cross-border neighboring Muslims living under autonomous political authority as they were disobedient believers in need of the state's disciplinary hand.

Not all writers agreed on who fit into the category of *bughāt*, and the distinction between rebel, brigand, and apostate often blurred when religious interpretation was not an issue and the means of dissent seemed self-serving (Abou El Fadl 2001, 248). In legal sources, for example, *bughāt* was used to describe those rebelling against a just or rightful ruler (Abou El Fadl 2001, 241); in his famous work on Islamic sects, the Sunnī theologian al-Shahrastānī (d. 1153) used much the same description to define a Khārijī, though he added that this rebellion might take place at any time period (al-Shahrastānī 1923, 85). Such transhistorical usage of the name "Khārijīs" as a generic substitute for Muslim rebels was not uncommon in historical sources and shows the extent to which specific reasons for rebellion were glossed in later tradition (Kenney 2006, chapter one).

The legitimacy of deposing a ruler was also a matter of dispute. Certainly those identified in Sunni sources as rebels, such as Khārijīs and Muʿtazilīs, argued in favor of rising up against a ruler. But isolated, otherwise mainstream Sunnī figures also made a case for it. Some jurists, for example, participated in the rebellions and were killed in battles. Of particular note is the Andalusian Ẓāhirī Ibn Ḥazm (d. 456/1064), who maintained that a ruler could be challenged for even minor acts of injustice and unseated if he failed to reform. Other jurists spoke of obedience to unjust rulers as a necessity simply by virtue of the improbability of rebellion leading to anything other than further chaos or anarchy, which can be read as permitting or at least sympathizing with rebellion if it is efficient and allows for the prompt reestablishment of order. Thus alternative views have survived in the literature, although in the end the weight of Sunnī opinion on how to deal with an errant ruler was clear: "Rebuke is endorsed while rebellion is rejected" (Cook 2000, 479).

Modern Developments. Political modernization changed the rules of rebellion in Muslim societies. Nation-states and the political economies that defined them created new reasons to rebel and new understandings of rebellion. Traditional Islamic rhetoric about rebellion continued to find a place in the political discourse of Muslim societies, but it was typically expressed in support of or opposition to secular political realities.

Accommodation, Resistance, Revolution. The Muslim experience of modernity parallels its encounter with and resistance to Western power and its legacy in Muslim societies. In the historical progression of this encounter, differences between resistance, rebellion, and revolution often blurred, only becoming clear after events were settled. The instability and questionable legitimacy of governments during the colonial period, even when these governments had local support, make rebellion difficult to assess. Suffice it to say that colonial incursions and accommodative Muslim leaders sparked uprisings during the nineteenth century in Africa, the Middle East, and Asia. It was not until the twentieth century, after having absorbed the material and intellectual results of Western modernity, that Muslim peoples began to throw off their colonial occupation and gain independence. In some cases, such as Turkey, it was not a colonial power but an *ancien régime* that revolutionary forces confronted. The common thread was the recognized need for violence—for rebellion—to unseat established powers and create a new political order. This attitude was captured in Kemal Atatürk's recounting of his 1921 address to the Turkish Assembly: "Sovereignty has never been given to any nation by scholarly disputation. It has always been taken by force and with coercion.... The Turkish nation has now taken back its usurped sovereignty by rebellion.... That is a fact" (quoted in Berkes 1964, 450). In like manner, Gamal Abdel Nasser, Egypt's first president after the 1952 revolution, linked the notion of progress to the people's need for "a political revolution by which it wrests the right to govern itself from the hand of tyranny" (Nasser 1955, 39–40).

Nationalism and State Politics. Nasser and Atatürk were political rebels who made good, successfully establishing new nation-states, and their retrospective status was that of national heroes. But in the build-up to independence during the first half of the twentieth century, many countries experienced intense periods of nationalist ferment, in which groups across a range of political ideologies—communism, socialism, capitalism, Islamism—competed for popular support. The fallout from this competition determined the new holders of state power and the new opposition, including those deemed rebels. Like the medieval rules of rebellion, the modern ones revolved around winners and losers, with the winners employing control over state institutions to ensure their uncontested power.

The authoritarian politics that came to dominate many Muslim societies after independence ensured sizable political opposition and, in some cases, continuing paroxysms of political violence. Single-party states, in places like Syria, Iraq, Egypt, and Algeria, pushed through fast-paced development programs. Initially, populations were prepared to sacrifice political rights for economic stability and the material benefits of modern life. But over time, as economic growth faltered and the benefits proved fleeting to all but a limited few, states resorted to the standard array of authoritarian tactics to deal with critics: propaganda, restrictive civil society, sham elections, conspiracies, secret police, and prisons. Such an atmosphere made it easy for regimes to elide distinctions between critics, opponents, and traitors.

The classical language of rebels—*bughāt* and Khārijīs—did not fit the modern political landscape because, in large part, both the regimes in power and their opponents were steeped in secular political ideas. The one exception to this linguistic practice was Islamist groups.

Islamists as Modern Muslim Rebels. After having lost out to secularists in the competition for power, Islamists went into political opposition, continuing their struggle through a variety of means, most peaceful, some violent. Convinced that Islam offered a viable total system of modern life, one that surpassed any Western ideology, Islamists challenged the legitimacy of secular leaders and governance. It was the radical tactics of some Islamist groups that drew the anger and strong arm of states and that reawakened classical references to *bughāt* and Khārijīs in public discourse. But the accusation of being modern or neo-Khārijīs was not restricted to militant Islamists alone—in part because Islamists shifted their methods depending on political circumstances and in part because regimes often preferred to eliminate the political competition by whatever means necessary.

Deployed by regime-friendly religious authorities and state-controlled media, the discourse was intended to anathematize Islamists in the eyes of Muslim citizens and undermine their cause. It arose initially in response to the actions and writings of members of the Society of Muslim Brothers, the first Islamist movement, founded in Egypt in 1928. The most prominent Muslim Brother accused of being a Khārijī was Sayyid Quṭb (d. 1964), who argued forcefully for the need to take up *jihād* against secular, un-Islamic rulers. Many others Islamists were labeled with the same broad brushstroke, especially as militant offshoots of the Muslim Brothers and violent episodes multiplied. Indeed, starting in the mid-1960s the Middle East witnessed a thirty-year surge of "Muslim rebel" discourse (Sivan 1990, 92, 105–11; Kenney 2006, 97 ff.).

While Muslim populations firmly rejected Islamist radicalism, the questions Islamists raised about the failure of Muslim leaders resonated—a trend that grew stronger as tyranny, corruption, and economic deprivation increased. Since Islamists were often the only opposition group willing to openly challenge authoritarian regimes, they won grudging respect for their efforts, if not for their larger cause of creating an Islamic state and implementing Islamic law. Islamist criticism of secular regimes often emerged in response to the charge of being Khārijī, for once the interpretive judgment of Khārijī rebellion and extremism was awakened, other normative possibilities emerged.

For example, during his trial for providing the Jihād Group with religious sanction for killing Egyptian President Anwar el-Sadat in 1981, ʿUmar ʿAbd al-Raḥmān was accused of Khārijī-like behavior; in response, he teasingly asked the civil prosecutor: "Where is the rightful leader against whom to rebel? Where is ʿAlī b. Abī Ṭālib today?...Was his rule based on socialism or democracy?...Was ʿAlī among those who separated religion and politics?" (ʿAbd al-Raḥmān 2002, 105). Perhaps the most effective line of reasoning is that of Yūsuf al-Qaraḍāwī, a traditionally trained religious scholar with an international following, who acknowledges that some have taken a turn toward the Khārijīs but asks why. He then proceeds to explore a myriad of social, economic, and political problems that plague the lives of Muslims: unemployment, expensive housing, crime, political corruption, substandard education, television, and lack of effective religious and political leaders (al-Qaraḍāwī 1983, 110–150). In short, he turns the Khārijī accusation into an accusation against the state and its inability to fulfill its obligations.

Current Moment. The actions of Islamist radicals and the resulting public debates about political violence have reintroduced the classical problem of rebellion into a modern political setting. Does Islam demand political quietism as a matter of faith? Is rebellion never a legitimate response, even in the face of tyranny or a leader incapable or unwilling to secure social justice for citizens? And even more to the point, does the traditional, passive stance toward political leaders comport with modern understandings of open societies and representative government?

Tangible responses to these questions were on public display throughout the Arab Muslim world starting in January 2011 and continuing into the summer, as citizens in Tunisia, Egypt, Syria, Libya, Bahrain, and Yemen took to the streets to demand new governments and improvements in living conditions. The initial organizers of these uprisings were tech-savvy, secular-oriented youth, though they were quickly joined by others, including Islamists. This so-called Arab Spring has turned the streets into a democratic forum, a place to transcend rigged elections and to force leaders to listen and respond to their people's voices.

Two authoritarian governments have already fallen during this Spring, in Tunisia and Egypt, and democratic elections are in the offing. The "rebels," then, have won and are preparing to assume positions of political authority and power. It is too simplistic to conclude that one person's rebel is another person's freedom fighter and future democrat. Clearly much remains unsettled, including the capacity of Islamists to conform to democratic rules of engagement. But the classical notion of political quietism—that tyranny is better than chaos—has been seriously challenged, and rebellion has a new legacy.

[*See also* Commanding Right and Forbidding Wrong; Fitnah; Qaraḍāwī, Yūsuf al-; Quṭb, Sayyid; *and* Tyranny].

BIBLIOGRAPHY

ʿAbd al-Raḥmān, ʿUmar. *Kalimat ḥaqq* (Word of Truth). Cairo: Dār al-Iʿtiṣām, 2002.

Abou El Fadl, Khaled. *Rebellion and Violence in Islamic Law*. Cambridge, U.K.: Cambridge University Press, 2001.

Berkes, Niyazi. *The Development of Secularism in Turkey*. Montreal: McGill University Press, 1964.
Cook, Michael. *Commanding Right and Forbidding Wrong in Islamic Thought*. Cambridge, U.K.: Cambridge University Press, 2000.
Crone, Patricia. *God's Rule: Government and Islam*. New York: Columbia University Press, 2004.
Donner, Fred McGraw. *The Early Islamic Conquests*. Princeton, N.J.: Princeton University Press, 1981.
Kenney, Jeffrey T. *Muslim Rebels: Khārijītes and the Politics of Extremism in Modern Egypt*. New York: Oxford University Press, 2006.
Kraemer, Joel L. "Apostates, Rebels and Brigands." *Israel Oriental Studies* 10 (1980): 35–73.
Lambton, Ann K. S. *State and Government in Medieval Islam*. Oxford: Oxford University Press, 1981.
al-Māwardī, Abū al-Ḥasan. *The Ordinances of Government*. Translated by Wafaa H. Wahba. Reading, U.K.: Garnet Publishing, 1996. English translation of *al-Aḥkām al-sulṭāniyya wa-l-wilāyāt al-dīniyya*, written c. 1045–1058.
Muslim ibn Hajjaj. [al-Jami' al-] Sahih, ed. M. F. 'Abdul Baqi. Cairo, 1955–6.
Nasser, Gamal Abdel. *Egypt's Liberation: The Philosophy of the Revolution*. Washington, D.C.: Public Affairs Press, 1955.
al-Qaraḍāwī, Yūsuf. *al-Ṣaḥwa al-islāmiyya bayn al-juḥūd wa-l-taṭarruf*. Cairo: Dār al-Shurūq, 1983.
al-Shahrastānī, Muḥammad b. 'Abd al-Karīm. *Kitāb al-Milal wa-l-nihal* (Religious Sects and Divisions). Edited by William Cureton. Leipzig: Otto Harrassowitz, 1923.
Sivan, Emmanuel. *Radical Islam: Medieval Theology and Modern Politics*. Enlarged ed. New Haven, Conn.: Yale University Press, 1990.
Wensinck, A. J. *The Muslim Creed: Its Genesis and Historical Development*. London: Frank Cass and Co., 1965.

Jeffrey T. Kenney

Refâh Partisi. The strictly secular character of the Turkish republic was relaxed after the 1960 pro-democracy coup. Within a decade later peasants and merchants in the countryside, and artisans and petite bourgeoisie in the cites gathered around an engineering professor by the name of Necmettin Erbakan to form Turkey's first Islamist party, the National Order Party (Milli Nizam Partisi, MNP). The party was dissolved in the aftermath of the 1971 coup, but its members immediately regrouped in Erbakan's newest institution, the National Salvation Party (Milli Selâmet Partisi, MSP), which participated in the weak coalitions of the 1970s, though its modest share of the national vote (12 percent in 1973; and 9 percent in 1977) highlighted its political marginalization. The Islamists' chances increased following the 1980 coup even if their party, the MSP, was dissolved once again. Coup instigators were set on eradicating communism from Turkey, and checking the rise of Islamic militants (after the 1979 Islamic Revolution in Iran), while moderate Islamists presented themselves as alternatives to both.

Erbakan was thus allowed to return to political life with the stronger and more vigorous Islamist Welfare Party (Refâh Partisi, RP). The new party benefited from the fragmentation of the political landscape after the coup as Islamists were the only faction that maintained their ideology, members, and organization, and thus managed to position Refâh as the mainstream party in Turkey. Remarkably the new party benefited from the disorienting effect of Turkey's neoliberal restructuring in the 1980s, and Islamism appeared as an alternative to both the social democratic politics of the left, as well as the conservative liberals on the right. Refâh distinguished itself from social democracy by its emphasis on free enterprise and individual initiative as the engines of growth (which attracted aspiring businessmen), and from conservative liberals in its stress on social justice (which was encouraging for the poor). Members of both the lower and middle classes espoused the religious identity provided by Refâh as a unifying framework, a sort of class compromise among believers that could guard Turkey from polarization and social violence. What finally shifted the balance, nevertheless, was demography rather than economic ideology. Islamist leaders encouraged their supporters to move from the countryside to the city to benefit from the new economic opportunities, offered newcomers food, healthcare, casual employment, cheap credit, and temporary residence, and aimed to help them move up the social ladder so that they would have more of a say (and a stake) in politics. In addition to these structural reasons, Islamist success was greatly enhanced by their first-rate grassroots organization and face-to-face contact with voters.

Refâh's ascendancy began with its signal success in the 1994 municipal elections, when the party carried Turkey's most important cities, including Istanbul and Ankara. Control of municipal administration helped the party achieve popularity on the national level, as reflected by its increased share in the national vote from 8 percent in 1987, to 17 percent in 1991, to an impressive 21 percent in 1995. Slowly but surely Erbakan pushed his party from being a junior partner in the cabinet to the leader of a government coalition. In June 1996 he became the first Islamist prime minister in the history of the republic.

Shortly thereafter, however, security and media reports accused Islamists of undermining secularism by packing the bureaucracy with like-minded employees, accumulating substantial funds through Islamic holding companies and banks, organizing a national campaign to reinstall *Sharīʿah* law, and peppering their rhetoric with militant statements, such as Erbakan's comment that Islamists would remain in power "either through normal channels or by shedding blood." (Heper and Güney, 2000, pp. 640–641) Erbakan seemed adamant on subordinating the military as well. Few were thus surprised when, on 28 February 1997, the military leadership presented Refâh with a list of eighteen recommendations for immediate adoption, including restrictions on religious education and controls against the spread of religious orders. Erbakan was forced to endorse the measures, but his halfhearted attitude toward implementing them pushed the generals to pressure Refâh's political partners to defect, forcing Erbakan's resignation on 18 June 1997. By mid-January 1998 Refâh was dissolved by a court order, and Erbakan was forced to try his luck with yet another political party, the Virtue Party (Fazilet Partisi). This successor party maintained the same ideology and membership, although it tried to be more cautious about alienating the secular elite or the military. Still, in the 1999 elections, Fazilet obtained barely 15 percent of the votes, coming fourth in the parliamentary race, and was expectedly marginalized during the formation of government.

Notwithstanding this setback Fazilet's insistence on avowedly Islamist politics prompted another court ban in July 2001, when the reformist wing of the party broke off to form the Justice and Development Party (Adalet ve Kalkınma Partisi, AKP). Erbakan regrouped in what turned out to be the last and weakest chain of Islamist parties: the Felicity Party (Saadet Partisi), which performed poorly in national elections as its share of the vote fell from 2.5 percent in the 2002 to a negligible 1.24 percent in 2011. After Erbakan's death in 2011, its fortunes were unlikely to be reversed.

That being said, Erbakan deserves credit as the most prominent author of Turkish Islamism and the man who prophesized, in 1998, that Islamists would eventually install themselves firmly in power: "They [the ruling elite] have dissolved the MNP so we created the MSP, which was much more popular and allowed Islamists to participate in government for the first time. Then they dissolved MSP, so we created Refâh, which became the largest Turkish political party and led a coalition government. If they dissolve Refâh, then our next party will dominate government alone." (Helal, 1999, p. 220) Nonetheless, it was AKP, which branched off from Erbakan's movement—rather than his last two political renditions—that finally fulfilled his prophecy.

BIBLIOGRAPHY

Helal, Reda. *Al-Saif wa-al-Helal: Turkiya min Ataturk ela Erbakan: Al-Sera' bein al-mu'assasa al-'askariya wa-al-Islam al-siyassi* [The Sword and the Crescent: Turkey from Atatürk to Erbakan: The Struggle between the Military Institution and Political Islam]. Cairo: Shorouk Books, 1999.

Heper, Metin, and Aylin Güney. "The Military and the Consolidation of Democracy: The Recent Turkish Experience." *Armed Forces & Society* 26, no. 4 (2000): 635–657.

Narli, Nilufer. "The Rise of the Islamist Movement in Turkey." In *Revolutionaries and Reformers: Contemporary Islamist Movements in the Middle East*, edited by Barry Rubin, pp. 125–140. Albany: State University of New York Press, 2003.

Tugal, Cihan. "NATO's Islamists: Hegemony and Americanization in Turkey." *New Left Review* 44 (2007): 5–34.

Hazem Kandil

Religious Beliefs. The carefully cultivated image of a Muslim community united around a simple set of basic beliefs masks a history of vigorous debate about God, creation, humanity, prophethood, ethics, salvation, and the Muslim community itself. In order to understand the religious discourse of Muslims, it is helpful to imagine Islam not as a static and monolithic core of essential beliefs but as a continuing story of inquiry and argument around these seven topics. The terms in which they are discussed have changed over time, but the fundamental questions over which Muslims grapple remain the same.

At each stage in its history the Muslim community can be carved up into named groups that are associated with opposing views on one or more of these topics. Muslims of the first few Islamic centuries are often labeled Murjiʾī, Khārijī, or Qadarī, depending on their answers to certain questions about salvation and the Muslim community. For later periods this division is replaced by the categories of Sunnī and Shīʿī. Since the rise of *kalām* (a form of theology elaborated through rational argument), its practitioners, the theologians, are distinguished from its opponents, the traditionalists. Theologians are classified principally as Muʿtazilī, Ashʿarī, or Māturīdī. (These Arabic terms ending in -ī should be used only to characterize individuals and ideas, as in "a Muʿtazilī doctrine," "a Shīʿī thinker," or simply "a Shīʿī," i.e., a Shīʿī individual. The corresponding substantives, which often end in -ah or -īyah, should be used only to designate entire groups, e.g., "among the Shīʿah," "the Ashʿarīyah believed. . . ." Anglicized forms ending in -ite may be used both ways: "Shiite thought," "a Shiite thinker," "the Shiites.")

Alongside the traditionalists and the several schools of theologians we may distinguish the philosophers, who developed Islamic versions of Neoplatonic thought, as well as laypeople without formal training in religious thought, whose "popular" beliefs sometimes coincide with those of traditionalists, and sometimes depart from them markedly. Many theologians, philosophers, traditionalists, and laypeople are simultaneously Ṣūfīs, meaning that they belong to one of many Islamic traditions of mysticism or spiritual practice. In modern times Muslims are often classified as traditionalist, modernist, Islamist, or secularist; in this classification "traditionalist" has a new sense, designating those who believe classical theology and law are still relevant and adequate for the modern world. There are, of course, many other terms used to make finer distinctions among Muslims, but these are the most common terms for the most prominent groups, whose views will be sketched in what follows.

God. The Qurʾān calls human beings to worship and serve wholeheartedly the God who created them, who sustains them, and who will someday resurrect and judge them. It presents this God as both powerful and compassionate, vengeful yet forgiving, utterly transcendent but intimately involved in the affairs of his creatures. Above all, the Qurʾān insists that God is one—unique and unrivalled, without peer, partner, or offspring.

On all this Muslims agree. With remarkably little dissent they have worked out long lists of the ninety-nine "most beautiful names" of God, dividing them into "names of beauty" and "names of majesty." The former include names like Merciful, Peace, Forgiving, Provider, Generous, Gentle, Loving, and Patient; the latter include King, Mighty, Victorious, Powerful, Forceful, Avenger, Judge, Reckoner, and Afflicter. Theologians have developed shorter lists of God's essential attributes, such as eternity, self-subsistence, power, knowledge, life, will, hearing, and sight. These are typically distinguished from God's attributes of action, which include creating, sustaining, justice, and mercy. What is remarkable about all these lists is how much they coincide. Minor differences in how Muslims enumerate or classify God's attributes do not substantially change their portrait of him. What distinguishes Muslims is how they conceive of these attributes—what they think it means for God to be one, powerful, or just. For some Muslims, God's justice is inscrutable, his power is arbitrary, and his oneness makes him incomprehensible. Others imagine God as intimately bound up with his creatures, completely dedicated to their welfare, connected and accessible to them mentally, spiritually, or even physically.

Indeed, some early Muslims claimed that God actually has some kind of physical body. Such views eventually became historical curiosities, remembered only as outlandish heresies, but they were not without scriptural support. The Qurʾān itself refers to God's hand, face, and eyes, and says that he sits upon a throne and will be seen by humans in the afterlife. Some theologians, wishing to protect God's transcendence, developed metaphorical interpretations of these anthropomorphisms: God's hand means his power, his face means his existence, his eyes mean his watchfulness, and so on. Traditionalists and some Ashʿarī theologians, however, felt that the Qurʾān's statements about God should not be reinterpreted so lightly. They insisted that God really does have a face and hands, but qualified this by saying that they are not like a human face and hands. When pressed, they refused to say what those words actually mean when applied to God; they would only affirm them "without explanation" or "without [asking] how" (*bi-lā kayf*). Opponents of this position labeled it *tashbīh*—"making God like" created beings—but, in fact, it put God beyond the grasp of human comprehension and language.

For Muʿtazilī theologians, God was necessarily comprehensible, because they started with human concepts such as existence, power, life, and knowledge, and then sought to demonstrate through rational inference which of those attributes God must have. For them God's character was, in effect, a human construct. At the other end of the spectrum, proponents of "negative theology" responded that if God is one and without peer, he cannot be like his creatures in any respect, so even his essential attributes such as power and knowledge must be unlike human power and knowledge. Such words do not express God's nature in terms that humans can understand; they are just names that God has ascribed to himself in revelation, which humans must repeat without really grasping what they mean.

Those who made God incomprehensible were motivated by God's oneness (*tawḥīd*)—a central doctrine that Muslims have interpreted in many creative and contrasting ways. In the Qurʾān this doctrine was a simple condemnation of Arab polytheism and the Christian doctrine of the Trinity, but eventually it had to be refined. Muslims were compelled to explain how they could affirm God's eternal attributes of life, knowledge, and power without positing a multiplicity of eternal beings or persons as the Christians did. Some early Muʿtazilīs accomplished this by denying that God has distinct qualities called attributes at all; he is simply God, and his attributes are nothing but his own essence. Ashʿarī theologians responded that the Muʿtazilah had shorn God of his attributes, and insisted instead that God is knowing and powerful because there are entities called knowledge and power that subsist eternally in his essence; but they had to clarify that these entities are neither identical to God nor yet other than God. Another explanation was that some of God's attributes are merely states of his being: God does not have knowledge, he just "is knowingly."

One especially troublesome attribute was God's speech. The Muʿtazilah argued that God's speech should be defined as a sequence of sounds produced in time by the speaker, just like human speech. This makes the Qurʾān one of God's created acts, thus neatly avoiding the Christian notion that God has an eternal Word. This doctrine was officially adopted by the ʿAbbāsid caliph al-Maʾmūn (r. 813–833), but it was widely rejected. Traditionalists felt that it diminished the Qurʾān's status as divine revelation, and affirmed that the Qurʾān must be eternal. The Ashʿarīyah and Māturīdīyah sought to have it both ways: they argued that the words and letters of the written and recited Qurʾān are indeed created, but they are not themselves God's attribute of speech; they are merely an expression of the meanings or ideas that constitute his "inner speech" (*kalām nafsī*), which is an attribute subsisting eternally in God's essence, neither identical with God nor yet distinct from him.

For the theologians, rightly affirming God's oneness meant figuring out how to talk about God's attributes without positing multiple eternal beings. For Ṣūfīs, rightly affirming God's oneness means recognizing that only God truly exists, and losing all independent sense of selfhood in an experience of union with God. Some Ṣūfīs have emphasized the personal side of this doctrine: the soul's love and longing for God, and its quest to overcome its grievous sense of separation from God. Ṣūfīs with philosophical inclinations developed God's oneness into a more systematic doctrine of "the unity of being" (*waḥdat al-wujūd*). Drawing on Islamicized versions of Neoplatonic thought, they argued that the created world is merely a manifestation, at a less abstract and more particular level, of God's eternal being. In this metaphysical system, God is unknowable in and of himself, but his attributes can be grasped by the human mind, not because they are human rational constructs, as in the Muʿtazilī system, but because human categories of thought are reflections of God's attributes. This way of affirming God's oneness made God accessible to his creation both intellectually and experientially, but many Muslim traditionalists and theologians have argued that it undermines God's uniqueness by identifying creation with its creator.

In modern times this Neoplatonic understanding of God's oneness continues to find eloquent exponents among heirs of the Iranian Ishrāqī philosophical tradition, such as Seyyed Hossein Nasr. The more technical theological debates about God's attributes, however, have been replaced by more modern concerns. At a popular level, the doctrine of God's oneness has been interpreted as a critique of the modern "idolatries" of materialism and consumerism. It has also been interpreted as a social and political doctrine, most strikingly by Sayyid Quṭb (d. 1966), who argued that to affirm God's oneness means above all to submit unquestioningly to God alone, which requires eliminating all forms of human legislation in favor of a purely Islamic government. For him, as for many prior thinkers, God's oneness makes him an imperious Other unaccountable to the human intellect.

Another attribute that Muslims affirm unanimously but understand in diverse ways is God's power. The Qurʾān asserts God's unqualified sovereignty over his creatures, yet simultaneously asserts that humans have control of their own choices and will be held responsible for them. Some early Muslims, labeled the Qadarīyah, insisted that humans bring about their own actions freely, while their critics argued that since only God can create things, human actions can only result from God's decree and power. The Qadarī position became a central doctrine of the Muʿtazilah, and remained common among Shīʿī theologians, but among Sunnīs it came to be considered a grave heresy. Traditionalists, the Ashʿarīyah, and (in their own way) the Māturīdīyah affirmed that God determines all events—not only the circumstances of peoples' lives but also their responses to those circumstances. God even wills and decrees the impiety and unbelief of the infidels and creates their sinful actions and their unbelief, yet commands them to believe, and punishes them for failing to do so. The Ashʿarīyah sought to explain this with their doctrine of acquisition (*kasb*): human actions are created solely by God, but when God creates a person's action he also simultaneously creates in that person a certain kind of power over that action, so that the person "acquires" it in the sense of taking on moral responsibility for it, even though he or she did not have the power to do otherwise.

Islamic Neoplatonic philosophy likewise entails a strict determinism: nothing could be otherwise than the way it is, because no part of creation has any independent existence; particular historical facts are simply reflections of a single timeless and necessary Truth, which is God himself. For these philosophers, and for the Ṣūfīs who share their vision of the world, determinism is inescapable but not unwelcome; in fact, it can have great spiritual significance. Since the Ṣūfī quest aims at identifying one's own will and attributes with God's will and attributes, an important step along the path is to recognize that what one takes to be one's own actions are in fact God's.

Many Muslims today, however, are wedded to a modern individualism and existentialism that require personal choice and decision as the sine qua non of spiritual and moral life. They may readily affirm that God determines the circumstances of a person's life, but they typically insist that humans have full control over their responses to those circumstances. Lay Muslims seldom recognize how starkly their belief in free will contradicts what was formerly considered orthodox Sunnī doctrine, but some modern thinkers have explicitly acknowledged their agreement with the Muʿtazilah on this issue, arguing that Ashʿarī doctrine encouraged fatalism and contributed to the intellectual and economic stagnation of Muslim societies, and that only a robust doctrine of free will can promote needed social, political, and economic reforms. Like the question of how to interpret God's oneness, the question of whether and how humans share God's attribute of power has become a sociopolitical issue.

A related debate revolves around God's attribute of justice. The most compelling argument for free will is that a just God cannot punish people for sinful actions they have no choice but to perform. This argument holds God accountable to a human conception of justice, which fits the Muʿtazilī view that God's attributes are analogous to human attributes. In this world a wise and just person only does what is good, and since God is necessarily wise and just and self-sufficient (so that he has no need to do anything for his own benefit) he can only do what is in the best interest of his creatures. He cannot cause suffering without ensuring that it results in an even greater blessing in this life or in the hereafter, and he cannot impose obligations without knowing that they are ultimately for the benefit of his servants. The world God has created must be the best of all possible worlds, and any evil in it can only result from the free actions of human beings.

The problem with this view, according to many traditionalists and Ashʿarī theologians, is that it puts a transcendent God in a box constructed by humans. No one denied that God is, in fact, just; they denied that God has to measure up to some human conception of justice. Whatever God does is just, simply because God does it. Whatever God wills people to do they do, whether good or evil, and God rewards or punishes that good or evil as he chooses, and this is justice on his part. This view of justice, which came to be regarded as Sunnī orthodoxy, preserved the transcendent unpredictability and arbitrariness of God's actions and decrees and laws, against those who wanted to make God more accessible to human understanding.

Contemporary Muslim thinkers have raised again the question of God's justice, this time with an eye to its implications for human life and society. While traditionalists continue to view God's justice as inscrutable at least in principle, Islamists and modernists alike have been quick to project their own conceptions of justice onto God, interpreting his commands in keeping with their own diverse visions of social justice. Muslim liberation theologians such as the South African antiapartheid activist Farid Esack have chosen to understand God's justice through the lens of their own experience of struggling against oppression, and have made that very concrete and human conception of God's justice their key to interpreting the Qurʾān. Once again an old discussion of one of God's attributes has been revived as a matter of sociopolitical import, and the old orthodox view of God as an imperious Other imposing his inscrutable will is being challenged by Muslims who imagine God instead as a sympathetic reflection of their own concepts, values, and aspirations.

Creation. A similar distinction runs through Muslim conceptions of God's creation: some regard it as a world of independent particulars disconnected from each other and from God; others see it as a seamless whole, connected to God as part of an integrated spiritual and material universe.

The Qurʾān echoes the Bible's account of creation but does not elaborate upon it. It tells the story mainly to define humanity as God's earthly vice-regents, endowed by their creator with a special knowledge and responsibility that were not given to either the angels (heavenly beings important mainly for their role in delivering God's revelations to his prophets) or the *jinn* (genies, ethereal beings made from fire who inhabit the earth alongside humans as a separate species of rational and religious beings). The Qurʾān points out the goodness of humanity's physical environment, but its main thrust is to get humans to look beyond the horizons of their present experience, to see the natural world in light of the supernatural power that sustains and controls it, and to consider this earthly life (*al-dunyā*) in light of a future life after death (*al-ākhirah*) that makes this world pale in significance. The Qurʾān repudiates materialism in every sense, condemning materialistic cupidity, a naturalistic worldview, and the attitude (called *dahrīyah*) that this life is all there is. While it does not disparage the natural world, the Qurʾān presents it primarily as a set of signs that point to a supernatural reality.

Because the Qurʾān does not articulate a systematic theory of physical and spiritual reality, Muslims have been free to develop their views of the universe in very different directions. Theologians developed integrated metaphysical systems that allowed them to discuss the earthly and supernatural realms using one consistent vocabulary. They used the terminology of the Greek philosophical traditions not only to discuss God and his attributes but also to explore notions of time, space, causality, and the relationship between universal categories and particular things, using words such as substance, atom, essence, attribute, and accident. For a time there was sharp competition between several ways of talking about the material world, but the theory that finally prevailed among theologians was atomistic: all material beings are composed of indivisible units called atoms, which are characterized by properties called accidents. The dominant theory was also occasionalist: each atom and all its properties are created anew by God at every occasion, that is, at every moment in time. This atomistic and occasionalist theory eliminated all direct physical causality: things are the way they are not because of past events but only because God chooses to create them as they are at the present moment. God habitually chooses to create things in predictable patterns and sequences—if he creates a person in the act of dropping a glass at one moment, he usually creates broken shards of glass the next—but he could just as well proceed to create an intact glass floating in the air, or no glass at all. Such unusual events are miracles, which God occasionally creates in order to validate his prophets' claims of divine revelation; but apart from this special religious significance, miracles are no different from ordinary mundane events, because both are equally possible and depend equally on God's decision to create them. This atomistic natural philosophy, like the doctrine of God's predetermination of events, contributes to the concept of a transcendent, imperious, and inscrutable God who controls his creation without being bound to it in any way.

The most enduring alternative to this atomistic view of the universe was formulated on the basis of Greek Neoplatonic thought by Muslim philosophers and mystics such as al-Fārābī (d. 950), Ibn Sīnā (Avicenna, d. 1037), and Ibn ʿArabī (d. 1240). These thinkers viewed the universe as a great chain of being, of which God is the ultimate cause and the unifying principle. This cosmic chain comprises several levels of being, from intellectual abstractions down to the concreteness of unformed matter; but all these dimensions of reality are actually manifestations of God. In this vision of the universe, God and creation are not different beings, for there is only one Being. In this system, as in the Ashʿarī metaphysic, everything that happens is fully determined by God, but in this case everything is determined by God's necessary and unchanging nature, not by God's inscrutable and unpredictable will. The more radical and philosophical Ṣūfī mystics who adopted this theory of the "unity of being" (*waḥdat al-wujūd*) viewed their life in this created realm as a participation in the nature and will of God. Their spiritual struggle was not to change the course of their lives through moral effort but to recognize more clearly that even the most mundane events reflect, in a veiled way, some aspect of God's character.

This integrative metaphysic, which links nature to God and the spiritual world, has gained some popularity in the modern period. Seyyed Hossein Nasr, for example, has argued that the modern natural sciences deal not with what is most real but with what is least real—observable material phenomena that simply mirror what occurs in the spiritual realm. In this view, miracles are not violations of natural law that modern people should dismiss as superstitious fables; they are reflections of spiritual realities that scientists cannot account for because of their materialist presuppositions.

A more common direction in modern Muslim thought has been to adopt the naturalistic discourse of science while asserting that it is compatible with the Qurʾān's claims about both the natural and supernatural realms. The Indian modernist Sayyid Aḥmad Khān (d. 1898), for instance, argued that, although the Qurʾān appears to affirm prescientific beliefs such as a geocentric model of the universe, it can always be reinterpreted from the perspective of each new scientific advance, so that it always turns out to be compatible with, or even to have anticipated, each new discovery about nature. This line of thinking has been developed by fundamentalists who mine the Qurʾān for intimations of scientific discoveries such as the water cycle, embryonic biology, and nuclear energy. By embracing modern science, and by abandoning both the atomistic occasionalism of the theologians and the Neoplatonic cosmology of the philosophers, modernists and fundamentalists alike have lost the ability to talk about God and creation using a single vocabulary, and have split theology and natural philosophy into separate and incommensurate discourses.

Humanity. The Qurʾān sets human beings within the natural world as God's vice-regents, equipped and authorized to rule creation—not according to their own desires but in obedience to God. The Qurʾān tells how the first man, Adam, and all his descendants (while still "in Adam's loins") entered into a primordial covenant with God, recognizing his authority over them and their duty to worship, obey, and give him thanks. Adam and his wife broke that covenant by disobeying, and consequently were banished from paradise to dwell on earth for a time, but they were not cursed or cut off from God; on the contrary, God forgave their sin, which the Qurʾān presents as due to their inattentiveness and the temptations of Satan rather than any inherent human rebelliousness. Their descendants still possess a basically sound and upright nature (*fiṭrah*) and are still just as capable as Adam and Eve of resisting temptation, following God's instructions, and earning his reward. What they fundamentally need, therefore, is not transformation but information: guidance to keep them on the straight path.

Muslims tend to emphasize either the spiritual or the moral dimension of that path. Ṣūfīs seldom deny the importance of outward morality, but they see the most crucial human struggles as inward and psychological. They tend to have a more dramatic sense of the soul's true nature—its primordial state of communion with God, to which it will ultimately return—and also of its present experience of sinfulness and alienation from God. They emphasize the individual's inner struggle, not only against the temptations of Satan but also against the lower part of the human soul, the *nafs*. They have developed elaborate and subtle theories of the human psyche, and have charted in detail the spiritual practices and stages through which the soul must pass as it struggles to recover its true nature and overcome its illusory sense of separation from God. According to this Ṣūfī vision of the human condition, what people need most is the guidance of a spiritual master who knows his or her disciples intimately and tailors their course of meditative practice to the particular ills of the heart from which they suffer.

The most pervasive emphasis of Islamic thought, however, is the moral path. The whole edifice of Islamic law, or *Sharīʿah*, is grounded in a vision of God as a lawgiver and humans as his servants. This vision presupposes that humans are by nature capable of fulfilling God's commands, and that what they need most is simply knowledge and awareness of God and his law. Muslims disagree sharply, however, about whether humans are by nature capable of achieving that knowledge on their own, or whether they are utterly dependent on God to grant them that knowledge through revelation.

Neoplatonic philosophers argued that knowledge of God and of the good is an intellectual achievement and that revelation is only an aide for lesser minds. The Muʿtazilah agreed that human reason and experience are sufficient to reach a great deal of truth about God and his requirements. They argued that revelation must be interpreted in conformity with the dictates of reason and that it cannot even be trusted until reason has first established that God exists, that he is wise, that he cannot lie, that he has revealed his will through prophetic books, and that the Qurʾān is one such book.

The Qurʾān itself suggests that reflection upon the evidence of nature and history should be sufficient to teach humans about God and justice, but it also asserts that God has revealed himself through prophets and scriptures, including Muḥammad and the Qurʾān. In the centuries following the Prophet's death, some Muslims (including the Khārijīyah) argued that the Qurʾān should be Muslims' sole source of guidance. The Shīʿah emphasized the need for living interpreters of revelation who could continue to function as guarantors of truth, just as the Prophet had; they therefore sought authoritative pronouncements on matters of belief and behavior from their imams, descendants of the Prophet whom they regarded as endowed by God with infallible knowledge. Other Muslims appealed to the community itself as an infallible criterion: Muslims should believe and do what the community has always believed and done. This epistemology was formalized as adherence to the *sunnah* (way or practice or precedent) and *ijmāʿ* (consensus) of the community—whence their claim to be *ahl al-sunnah wa-al-jamāʿah* (the people of the way and of the community), from which is derived the label "Sunnī." Eventually Sunnīs shifted their emphasis to the authority of *ḥadīth* (reports about the *sunnah* of the Prophet Muḥammad), especially those selected and compiled by the scholars al-Bukhārī and Muslim. In this way Sunnī Muslims came to view the textual record of prophetic revelation, consisting of both the Qurʾān and *ḥadīth*, as the principal, or indeed the only, source of religious knowledge.

Traditionalists were most adamant about humanity's complete dependence on revelation, while theologians sought various ways of integrating revelation and reason. Eventually the Muʿtazilah came to accept even *ḥadīth* as an important supplementary source of legal knowledge. The Māturīdīyah held that human reason could, in principle, lead to knowledge of God, but that in fact humans depended on revelation. The Ashʿarīyah admitted that basic religious truths should be validated and defended through rational argument, but only because this was commanded in revelation. To the great Ashʿarī theologian and mystic al-Ghazālī (d. 1111), rational argument was valid but beside the point; true knowledge was not a human achievement but a divine gift, conveyed through revelation and, for the spiritually advanced, through the mystical experience of "unveiling."

As Muslims came into contact with Enlightenment thought, however, reliance on revelation was called into question. Some Muslims pointed out that the Qurʾān itself urged reflection on the evidence of nature, and argued that Islam represented a natural and rational religion that Europeans were finally rediscovering. Modernists decried the decline of creative Islamic reasoning, denounced the tradition of reliance on the views of prior generations (*taqlīd*), and called for fresh interpretive reasoning (*ijtihād*), still grounded in the revealed scriptures, to apply Islamic principles to modern life. Islamists too called for *ijtihād* but regarded this as a return to a literal reading of revelation, not a renewed dedication to human reasoning. More recently, postmodern Muslims have begun to assert their right to reinterpret the Qurʾān and reconstruct Islamic knowledge from the perspective of particular identities and experiences: to be an African American Muslim woman, for example, entails a duty to reinterpret the Qurʾān with the explicit aim of overcoming the forms of injustice one has experienced. Although the assumption that knowledge of God's requirements is the most basic human need remains central to Islamic thought, Muslims continue to debate just how much humans can rely on their own reasoning and experiences to guide them, and how closely they must adhere to the words of revelation.

Prophethood. Revelation takes place exclusively, or at least principally, through prophets; but prophets are not merely channels of revelation. The Prophet Muḥammad is an object of affection and devotion for all Muslims, but his significance is multifaceted. For some he is primarily a source of information about God's law, but for others he is the pinnacle of human leadership, and for still others the pinnacle of the created universe.

The Qurʾān characterizes Muḥammad as the continuation of a Near Eastern tradition of prophethood that includes numerous biblical figures from Adam to Jesus, all of whom were sent by God to warn their communities about a coming judgment, to urge them to worship the one true God, and to guide them in the path of righteousness. Some of them brought revealed books (the Torah of Moses, the Psalms of David, and the Gospel of Jesus) containing God's very own speech, spelling out the same consistent message for each community in its own language, along with the particular laws God has prescribed for that community. The Prophet Muḥammad, therefore, is not presented as founding a new religion; he brings the same message as the previous prophets, in a new divine book, the Qurʾān, in the language of his own people, Arabic.

The Qurʾān hinted, and Muslims soon asserted, that Muḥammad was the final prophet, that the Qurʾān superseded earlier revelations, and that Islam was a religion not only for the Arabs but for all humanity. Theologians therefore sought ways to convince non-Muslims of the truth of Islam. They were able to demonstrate the existence and attributes of God by rational argument, but to prove Muḥammad's prophethood they had to appeal to his miracles. There were numerous reports of minor signs and wonders that they could cite, but the miracle upon which they chiefly rested their case was the Qurʾān itself, whose content, they argued, could never have come from a human mind, and whose elevated style had never been matched by any poet. Such a feat of inimitable eloquence was clearly a miracle confirming Muḥammad's claim to prophethood—all the more so because Muḥammad was said to be illiterate.

One of the Qurʾān's functions, therefore, is to serve as a miraculous sign of its own veracity. It also has ritual and aesthetic functions: it is recited during prayers, chanted in a variety of highly formalized styles, and incorporated into architecture, literature, and everyday speech. One of its functions, however, has overshadowed all the others: its role as a source of law. This function was emphasized most forcefully by the Muʿtazilah, who argued that the only purpose God could possibly have for revealing the Qurʾān is to convey some beneficial information to his servants, and this information can only consist of those legal details humans are unable to discover for themselves, since relying on the Qurʾān presupposes that one already knows God, his attributes, and the nature of good and evil. Few Muslims would have stated this view so starkly, but in practice many came to regard the communication of law as the main point not only of the Qurʾān but of Muḥammad's entire life. His actions and words are a pattern to be imitated by all Muslims, and even his inaction or silence in response to someone else's action is a revealed indication that it is permissible. This view of Muḥammad required that he be regarded as sinless, so theologians developed the doctrine that prophets are protected from sins, or at least from serious sins, though not necessarily from mistakes in nonreligious matters. This view of the Prophet as a source of law fits well with the Qurʾān's depiction of human nature as essentially sound and upright, needing only God's guidance to earn his pleasure and reward.

Some Muslims, however, have given the Prophet a grander role. Neoplatonist philosophers regard prophets as consummate intellectuals who not only grasp the highest all-encompassing Truth but are also capable of expressing it in vivid stories and practical rules that common people can understand, and are able to impose those beneficial rules through skillful leadership. Ṣūfīs have given Muḥammad a cosmic dimension, calling him the ontological origin of the universe, the "Light of Muḥammad" from which all creation proceeds. In Ṣūfī and popular devotion Muḥammad is the perfect human being and the beloved of God, who saves his community from the punishment their sins deserve by interceding on their behalf. He is venerated through song, poetry, and a festival celebrating his birth (*mawlid*). Similar veneration, albeit on a smaller scale, is extended also to numerous Ṣūfī saints (sing., *walī*), to whom local shrines are often erected after their death and to whom petitions are addressed for healing, protection, and all manner of concrete assistance.

The Shīʿah extended this exalted view of the Prophet to Muḥammad's daughter Fāṭimah and son-in-law ʿAlī, who, with their descendants, were likewise said to be primordial sources of light from which derive the sun, moon, and stars. The Shīʿah placed special emphasis on the Prophet's role as a political leader, which they refused to separate from his role as bearer of revealed knowledge. Viewing both leadership and revelation as a continuing necessity, they claimed that his authority and infallibility had devolved upon a series of imams—ʿAlī, his sons al-Ḥasan and al-Ḥusayn, the latter's son ʿAlī Zayn al-ʿĀbidīn, and further descendants whose identity was disputed by different Shīʿī factions. The largest group, known as the Imāmī or Twelver Shīʿah, regard their twelfth imam as still ruling the world in principle, though not visibly, so that actual political leaders are at best temporary substitutes.

The Imāmī Shīʿah expect that the twelfth imam will return shortly before the day of judgment to restore the ideal of life under a charismatic leader who embodies both the political and religious authority of the Prophet. Other Muslims have similar expectations of a coming figure called the Mahdī, whose role is variously imagined, in keeping with their various understandings of prophethood. A paramount expectation of Sunnīs is that the Mahdī will finally perfect and implement the *Sharīʿah*—which was, after all, the main point of Muḥammad's prophethood in Sunnī thought.

Ethics and Law. Since the ninth century, almost all Muslims have agreed that the *Sharīʿah* is an important aspect of the Prophet's legacy, but they have held profoundly different understandings of what that *Sharīʿah* is. Is it an exhaustive system of detailed rules imposed arbitrarily by God? Or is it just a supplement to natural law? Alternatively, is the *Sharīʿah* just a set of basic moral principles that can be applied differently in different contexts? Or is it not a set of rules or principles at all, but an ongoing personal quest for a moral life?

The Qurʾān begins its moral message with a simple imperative to pursue justice, often assuming that its Arabian audience already knows what justice is. It builds upon pre-Islamic Arabian and Jewish practices and modifies some of them significantly. Early Muslim leaders continued to adopt local practices in the areas they conquered, sometimes modifying them in light of the Prophet's example. As Islam came to be viewed as a distinct religion, however, it became increasingly important to assert the specifically Islamic nature of law by tying it to prophetic revelation.

Some Muslims, including the Khārijīyah and some early Muʿtazilah and Ẓāhirīyah, preferred a minimal religious law consisting only of the few explicit provisions found in the Qurʾān, to which some added provisions from the most widely accepted *ḥadīth*. This left most areas of personal and social life to the discretion of individuals and rulers. Other Muslims, however, sought to develop comprehensive legal systems. The first concern of these systems was to prescribe in detail how to carry out basic ritual duties—the five daily prayers (*ṣalāt*), fasting (*ṣawm*) during daylight hours throughout the lunar month of Ramaḍān, the alms tax (*zakāt*) paid each year on various forms of wealth, and a once-in-a-lifetime pilgrimage (*ḥajj*) to Mecca. Beyond those rituals—which, with the profession of faith (*shahādah*), are known as the pillars of Islam—the legal systems also regulated *jihād* (warfare to expand Islamic rule), oaths and religious vows, marriage and divorce, commerce, slavery, crimes, court procedures, inheritance, and personal behavior such as dress, manners, and diet. These sets of rules were developed and disputed within scholarly circles, which eventually coalesced into several Shīʿī legal traditions and four Sunnī schools of law (Ḥanafī, Mālikī, Shāfiʿī, and Ḥanbalī), each with its own distinctive tendencies but all sharing the same basic rules and overall structure. By the time these schools were firmly established, most Sunnī legal scholars had adopted the view articulated by al-Shāfiʿī (d. 820) that every rule had to be traceable not to some pre-Islamic precedent but to the Qurʾān and prophetic *ḥadīth*. Islamic law had become a revealed law.

Muslims have disagreed profoundly, however, about what it means for God to reveal such a law. The Muʿtazilah regarded it as a revealed extension of a natural law grounded in the intrinsically beneficial or harmful properties of human actions; human reason is able to discern many of these properties on its own, but the moral and legal properties of some actions (such as prayer) are known only from revelation.

Philosophers took a quite different view of the *Sharīʿah*: it is not a truth in its own right, but merely an aid in the quest for truth. They argued that prayer is not a universal mandate whose benefits are built into the structure of the universe, but merely a practical measure imagined by a prophet to help his followers escape the bondage of bodily desires and progress toward the knowledge of God. True philosophers, therefore, do not need the law. Nor do the most advanced mystics, according to a few radical antinomian Ṣūfīs, who likewise regarded the law as a means to a higher end.

The Ashʿarīyah and traditionalists argued that law is neither a natural fact nor a spiritual tool, but simply a divine command. It is conducive to human welfare—indeed, one of its basic principles is never to impose undue hardship—but it cannot be reduced to utilitarian considerations, nor can it be known by reasoning about the properties of human actions. Actions are good if God declares them good, and they are obligatory if he commands them, promises to reward them, and threatens to punish those who fail to perform them. God is just and wise, but the wisdom behind his commands remains inscrutable unless he chooses to reveal it. God's commands are part of his speech, and are therefore known only through revelation, not through reason. Where revelation is silent, humans must extrapolate from revelation using the principle of reasoning by analogy (*qiyās*): for example, since revelation explicitly prohibits grape wine, and date wine shares with it the property of being intoxicating, date wine must likewise be prohibited. Such reasoning, however, is legitimate only because God has specifically commanded it, not because of any necessary rational coherence or predictability in God's demands.

This view, which eventually became mainstream, appears to make the law eternally fixed and independent of social context, because revelation itself is now fixed in the Qurʾān and the canonical collections of *ḥadīth*. It has long been claimed that the law is largely settled and that the "gates of *ijtihād*" are now closed. In fact, the law has never been immune from incremental changes, but the sudden social transformations brought on by the encounter with modern Europe pressed upon Muslims more forcefully the question of the law's adaptability, leading to calls by modernists and Islamists for renewed *ijtihād* to legitimate reforms through fresh readings of the Qurʾān and *ḥadīth*. Such reform programs retain the classical assumption that *Sharīʿah* should be comprehensive and based on revelation. Secularists, however, have preferred to limit revealed law to the small domain of private religious practice, thus leaving most social regulation to the legislative efforts of human governments—much like some of the earliest Muʿtazilah and Ẓāhirīyah. And some progressive Muslims have come to affirm (rather like the later Muʿtazilah) that there exist natural legal principles, such as universal human rights, which revelation upholds and elaborates, and which must be used as a criterion for interpreting revelation. Some have argued that interpretation can even go against the language of revelation, because the detailed rules spelled out in the Qurʾān and *ḥadīth* are not actually meant to be permanently binding; they reflect just one way of implementing, in a particular historical context, the more fundamental moral imperatives that really constitute God's law. (This view has some classical precedent among a minority of jurists, such as Abū Isḥāq al-Shāṭibī (d. 1388), who argued that the entire revealed law should be made to support five objectives—the preservation of religion, life, reason, property, and family lineage.) Finally, in the spirit of the philosophers, some Muslims have come to view the rules of law as just a means in the pursuit of a higher personal quest. Khaled Abou El Fadl, for example, argues that the law is not a set of rules but a process of seeking after God's will, in which the conclusions one reaches are less important than the integrity of one's quest for a moral life.

Each of these responses to the challenge of modernity reflects some aspect of prior Islamic thought. The range of viewpoints on specific points of law has expanded greatly in the last century, but the vibrant debate between different conceptions of revealed law is nothing new.

Salvation. The goal of law, as formulated by mainstream classical jurists, is to avoid God's punishment and gain his reward in the afterlife. This otherworldly orientation is firmly rooted in the Qurʾān, which warns Muḥammad's opponents that they face physical destruction in this life, but puts much greater emphasis on a coming day of resurrection and judgment, followed by eternal bliss in paradise or agony in hell. That day is described using vivid images of cataclysmic upheavals of the natural order: mountains crumbling to dust, the skies being rent asunder, and society falling apart so that each individual is left to stand utterly alone before God as the record of his or her deeds is examined and weighed in the balance, each deed being rewarded or punished to within a fraction of an ounce. The resulting sentence of heaven or hell is described in equally graphic but more familiar imagery drawn from the landscape and life of Arabia: cool shade, flowing water, refreshing drinks, luxurious couches, and virginal companions on the one hand and fire, scalding water, bitter food, and everlasting torment on the other.

This is the vision of salvation to which Islamic law refers when it spells out which acts will be rewarded and which will be punished. This simple legal arithmetic, however, does not adequately capture the Qurʾān's teaching about salvation, because the Qurʾān makes paradise contingent not only on deeds but also on faith, which is inextricably bound up with deeds and yet distinguishable from them. If believers are promised paradise, and paradise is a place of unmitigated bliss, how can they also be punished for their sins? One response to this problem was to try to define who is actually a believer and how faith is affected by sins. We will return to this topic in the next section. Another response was to develop a more complex account of the resurrection, judgment, heaven, and hell. Numerous reports (sing., *ḥadīth*) were attributed to the Prophet on this subject, describing the questioning of the soul in the grave by two angels, punishment for sins while still in the grave (while the soul is still in an intermediate pre-resurrection state known as the *barzakh*), then a physical reconstitution and resurrection of the body, a vast assembly for judgment, the enumeration and weighing of each person's deeds, a walk over a narrow bridge from which some will fall into the fire of hell while others cross over to a refreshing pool, and the final destination, one of several levels of heaven or hell. Additionally, it was reported that God, in his mercy, would allow the Prophet to intercede on behalf of his followers, so that believers might enter heaven in spite of their sins, or at most would have to endure temporary punishment in hell. Some of the Muʿtazilah questioned these reports, and denied the bodily nature of the resurrection, the Prophet's ability to intercede, and the idea of temporary hell. Some philosophers argued that the soul's ultimate destiny of escape from matter precluded physical resurrection and eternal hellfire. But traditionalists and many theologians took literal acceptance of these detailed reports as a litmus test of orthodoxy.

Mainstream Sunnī orthodoxy thus developed a very physical, eschatological view of salvation, making it hinge on a combination of individual faith, good deeds, and God's mercy. The most rigorous religious scholars tended to make salvation dependent on meticulous adherence to the law, or faith arrived at through personal intellectual exertion. At a more popular level, salvation has often been seen to depend rather on one's membership in the Muslim community, and on God's mercy, which makes up for individual deficiencies. For Shīʿī Muslims, salvation has also been tied to recognition of the imams. Ṣūfīs, while usually affirming orthodox teachings about faith and deeds, the bodily resurrection, and eternal reward, have tended to regard those aspects of salvation as secondary to the personal journey of return to union with God, meaning either annihilation (*fanāʾ*) of the self or subsistence (*baqāʾ*) of the soul in loving communion with God; indeed, some Ṣūfīs have denigrated the preoccupation with eternal reward or punishment as a self-centered distraction from the soul's focus on God himself. In the modern world, a literal understanding of the traditional account of human destiny remains widely popular, but interaction with liberal Christians and a resurgence of Sufism and Neoplatonism have led some Muslims to pursue more psychological views of ultimate salvation, and to consider the possibility that even some non-Muslims might achieve it.

The Faithful Community. To define who will enter paradise is to also define who is a believer, and thus to define the boundaries of the believing community. Perhaps no theological question has been more vexed than this: Who is a true believer, and, if that cannot be determined, who should at least be treated as a Muslim?

The Prophet Muḥammad preached to his seventh-century Arabian audience a monotheistic piety for all peoples. At first he used the term believer (*muʾmin*) broadly, to include not only his own immediate followers but also those Jews and Christians whom he regarded as sharing his concern for ethical and worshipful living. Over time his movement grew into a distinct community, the *ummah*, consisting only of Muslims (Ar.

muslim, one who submits) and held together by a religion called Islam (*islām*, submission). Even during the Prophet's lifetime, however, the unity of his community was strained by internal dissent and by varying degrees of commitment, to the point that the Prophet declared some of his followers to be hypocrites (*munāfiqūn*), nominal members of the community who professed belief but were shown by their actions not to be true believers.

The question of how to identify and demarcate the community of true believers became one of the most pressing concerns of early Islamic thought. From the power struggles that followed Muḥammad's death there emerged several competing ways of imagining and defining this community. That argument subsided somewhat as Sunnīs reached an uneasy consensus on a fairly inclusive and tolerant social vision, but it resurfaced in modern times as colonization and globalization forced the *ummah* to reassess its identity and its relationship to non-Muslims. Today, as in the early centuries of Islam, some Muslims choose to draw the boundaries of the community in sharp and uncompromising terms, admitting only the most zealous and impeccable believers, while others adopt more pragmatic standards to accommodate the community's diversity and imperfections. Some have even blurred the boundary between Muslims and adherents of other religions.

The narrowest and most exclusive definition of who is a true believer was articulated by a number of early groups known collectively as the Khārijīyah. They originated as a political opposition movement, fighting first against ʿAlī, whom they had previously supported, and then against the Umayyad caliphs (r. 661–750). They argued that a person who has committed a grave sin (*fisq*) is no longer a believer (*muʾmin*) but an apostate (*murtadd*); such a grave sinner (*fāsiq*) is ineligible to lead the Muslim community and, indeed, should be killed, according to some of them, without any possibility of repentance. This was their ground for opposing ʿAlī and several other claimants to the caliphate: they had all committed grave sins, and had therefore lost their status as believers and their legitimacy as leaders. The Khārijīyah assumed, perhaps without articulating it explicitly, the uncompromising view that faith (*īmān*) is not just a matter of inner belief (*taṣdīq*) and verbal profession (*iqrār*) but also of righteous action (*ʿamal*)—a definition that drew a very tight circle around the Muslim community. They would follow only irreproachable leaders, whom they selected by vote without regard for ethnicity or lineage; they called others to leave society and come join their encampments; and some conducted raids against other less stringent Muslims, whose life and property they thought it legitimate to take because they considered them unbelievers.

A much more inclusive definition of the community came to be associated with the label Murjiʾah. At first this name designated movements that refused to declare who had been right and who had been wrong in the early disputes over the caliphate, and that consequently were at odds with the Khārijīyah, the early Shīʿah, and the Umayyads. In time, however, the Murjiʾah came to be associated with the view that faith consists simply in knowing and verbally confessing, in a very general way, that God is one and that the Prophet Muḥammad's message is true. They refused to question any professing Muslim's faith on the basis of his or her actions because they considered actions entirely distinct from faith, and they believed that God would forgive believers even for grave sins, or would punish them only temporarily in hell. All believers, therefore, will eventually be admitted to paradise, and all who profess faith must be treated as full members of the believing community on earth. Eventually, the Murjiʾah's refusal to criticize any of the early caliphs became a common Sunnī trope, and their conception of faith was widely adopted, in one form or another, by Māturīdī and Ashʿarī theologians. Their views bolstered the common Sunnī argument that even an impious ruler can lead the community in spite of his sins, and therefore should not be deposed violently, as long as he professes Islam and hails from the Prophet's tribe, the Quraysh.

Sunnī traditionalists generally shared the orthodox theologians' quietist attitude toward political authority, but felt that their Murjiʾī definition of faith did not recognize the importance of pious works. They therefore articulated a compromise definition: faith requires outward works as well as inner knowledge and verbal profession, but faith is not an all-or-nothing affair; it can increase and decrease in accordance with one's works. This means that sinful actions affect faith but do not make the sinner an unbeliever; they just make him or her a lesser believer. This view, which was especially associated with the Ḥanbalīyah and became quite popular among Sunnīs, combined a very inclusive view of the community of believers and a tolerant view of political leaders with a personal challenge to pursue higher levels of piety.

Similar concerns led the Muʿtazilah to a similar compromise, which they articulated somewhat differently. They shared the traditionalist view that faith includes actions and increases or decreases in keeping with a person's deeds, but they believed God was bound by his own word to punish grave sins with eternal hellfire. Consequently, anyone who commits a grave sin and fails to repent can never enter paradise, and therefore cannot be a believer. Yet the Muʿtazilah did not wish to exclude such people from the earthly community of Muslims, so they denied that such people are rendered unbelievers by their sins. Grave sinners, they said, are neither believers nor unbelievers; they stand in an "intermediate position" (*al-manzilah bayn al-manzilatayn*) and should be called simply "grave sinners." They will be punished eternally in hell, but in this world they should still be treated as full members of Muslim society. This avoided the radical exclusivism and revolutionary implications of the Khārijī doctrine, while still allowing the Muʿtazilah to hold rulers' feet to the fire for their behavior, thus fulfilling what they felt was a binding mandate to "command right and prohibit wrong" (*al-amr bi-al-maʿrūf wa-al-nahy ʿan al-munkar*).

These arguments over faith, sin, and divine judgment expressed a tension between uncompromising idealism and resigned pragmatism in Muslims' view of their own community and its leadership. The pragmatism of the classical Murjiʾī and traditionalist positions eventually came to dominate Sunnī thought, but the yearning for a separate and more uncompromisingly pious community lived on in the form of occasional Khārijī revolts, and also among the Shīʿah. The latter's vision of leadership required not just mere competence but an almost prophetic charisma and immunity from error that God granted only to certain descendants of the Prophet, the imams. Like the Khārijīyah, the Shīʿah came to view themselves as a community apart, the only true followers of the Prophet's legacy; but for the most part they did not translate this idealistic vision into exclusivism or political revolt. The largest Shīʿī movement, the Imāmīyah, translated their aspirations into an eschatological vision in which the hidden imam will return to establish an ideal community. The desire to belong to a distinct community called to a higher level of personal piety also found an outlet in Ṣūfī orders—communities of masters and initiates pursuing varying levels of personal and group spiritual practices. These orders were usually well integrated into Muslim society, but occasionally became potent forces of political opposition, as during the colonial period when several resistance movements were led by Ṣūfī orders.

In the twentieth century the vision of a pure community of true believers reemerged among radical Islamist movements, motivating and validating their sometimes violent opposition to Muslim governments, which they regard as agents of unbelief. This puritanical vision is not unprecedented, but it is a radical departure from the pragmatism that has long dominated Sunnī views of the community, and from the more eschatological and spiritual visions of ideal community that have animated Shīʿīs and Ṣūfīs. As Islamists have raised again the question of how to define the community, others have responded, reopening old debates about the nature of *īmān* (faith) and *islām* (submission). For example, Farid Esack's experience of struggling against apartheid in South Africa, shoulder to shoulder with Christians but often in direct opposition to fellow Muslims who maintained a pragmatic political quietism, let him to redefine the words *īmān*, *islām*, and *kufr* (unbelief) so that the community of believers is defined in terms of solidarity with the oppressed; in consequence, that community sometimes includes Christians, and it excludes some Muslims. Others have argued that the term *islām* should be understood to refer to a personal quality of submission to God that can be shared by non-Muslim monotheists, effectively opening the boundaries of the Muslim community to those of other religions who recognize and submit to God's all-encompassing oneness.

The broad and pragmatic Sunnī definition of the community that dominated classical thought still stands as the default measure of who is and who is not a believer, and most Muslims still affirm that no Muslim should question the faith of another. But that definition is now being challenged, because the Muslim world is no longer as insulated from the non-Muslim world as it was before colonization and globalization. If nothing else, the sheer immediacy of daily contact with non-Muslims has forced Muslims to reexamine the boundaries of the faith and the community. They still share some basic concepts such as faith and paradise, but they interpret those concepts in very different ways, echoing disputes that have divided Muslims throughout their history. In this as in other aspects of Muslim belief, understanding Muslims today requires viewing them not as adherents of a simple set of essential beliefs but as participants in an ongoing conversation about God, creation, humanity, prophethood, ethics, salvation, and the boundaries of their own community.

BIBLIOGRAPHY

General Overviews

Denny, Frederick Mathewson. *An Introduction to Islam.* 4th ed. Upper Saddle River, N.J.: Pearson Prentice Hall, 2011.

Fakhry, Majid. *A History of Islamic Philosophy.* 3d ed. New York: Columbia University Press, 2004.

Frank, Richard M. *Texts and Studies on the Development and History of Kalām.* Edited by Dimitri Gutas. 3 vols. Aldershot, U.K.: Ashgate/Variorum, 2005–2008.

Goldziher, Ignaz. *Introduction to Islamic Theology and Law.* Translated by Andras Hamori and Ruth Hamori. Princeton, N.J.: Princeton University Press, 1981.

Hodgson, Marshall G. S. *The Venture of Islam: Conscience and History in a World Civilization.* 3 vols. Chicago: University of Chicago Press, 1974.

Watt, W. Montgomery. *Islamic Philosophy and Theology: An Extended Survey.* 2nd ed. Edinburgh: Edinburgh University Press, 1985.

Winter, Tim, ed. *The Cambridge Companion to Classical Islamic Theology.* Cambridge, U.K.: Cambridge University Press, 2008.

Works on Specific Schools and Thinkers

Frank, Richard MacDonough. *Beings and Their Attributes: The Teaching of the Basrian School of the Muʿtazila in the Classical Period.* Albany: State University of New York Press, 1978.

Gimaret, Daniel. *La doctrine d'al-Ashʿarī*. Paris: Cerf, 1990.

Goldziher, Ignaz. *The Ẓāhirīs: Their Doctrine and Their History; A Contribution to the History of Islamic Theology.* Translated and edited by Wolfgang Behn. Leiden, Netherlands: E. J. Brill, 2008. English translation of *Die Zâhiriten: Ihr Lehrsystem und ihre Geschichte; Ein Beitrag zur Geschichte der muhammedanischen Theologie*, first published in 1884.

Hourani, George F. *Islamic Rationalism: The Ethics of ʿAbd al-Jabbār.* Oxford: Clarendon, 1971.

Momen, Moojan. *An Introduction to Shiʿi Islam: The History and Doctrines of Twelver Shiʿism.* New Haven, Conn.: Yale University Press, 1985.

Rapoport, Yossef, and Shahab Ahmed, eds. *Ibn Taymiyya and His Times.* Karachi: Oxford University Press, 2010.

Schimmel, Annemarie. *Mystical Dimensions of Islam.* Chapel Hill: University of North Carolina Press, 1975.

Taji-Farouki, Suha, and Basheer M. Nafi, eds. *Islamic Thought in the Twentieth Century.* London: I. B. Tauris, 2004.

Watt, W. Montgomery. *The Formative Period of Islamic Thought.* Oxford: Oneworld, 1998.

Suggested Primary Texts in English Translation

ʿAbd al-Jabbār. "*Kitab al-usul al-khamsa* (Book of the Five Fundamentals)." In *Defenders of Reason in Islam: Muʿtazilism from Medieval School to Modern Symbol*, by Richard C. Martin and Mark R. Woodward, pp. 90–115. Oxford: Oneworld, 1997.

Aḥmad Khān, Sayyid "Sir Sayyid Aḥmad Khān's Principles of Exegesis: Translated from his *Taḥrīr fī uṣūl al-tafsīr.*" Translated by Muḥammad Daud Rahbar. *Muslim World* 46 (1956): 104–112 and 324–335.

Ashʿarī, Abū al-Ḥasan al-. *The Theology of al-Ashʿarī.* Translated by Richard J. McCarthy. Beirut: Imprimerie Catholique, 1953.

Ghazālī, Abū Ḥāmid al-. *The Faith and Practice of al-Ghazālī.* Translated by W. Montgomery Watt. London: G. Allen & Unwin, 1953; repr. Oxford: Oneworld, 1994.

Ibn Sīnā, Abū ʿAlī al-Ḥusayn ibn ʿAbd Allāh. *Avicenna on Theology.* Translated by Arthur J Arberry. London: J. Murray, 1951.

Kurzman, Charles, ed. *Liberal Islam: A Source Book.* New York: Oxford University Press, 1998.

The Qurʾan. Translated by M. A. S. Abdel Haleem. Oxford World's Classics. Oxford: Oxford University Press, 2004.

Quṭb, Sayyid. *Milestones.* Indianapolis: American Trust, 1993.

Sells, Michael A., ed. and trans. *Early Islamic Mysticism: Sufi, Qurʾan, Miʿraj, Poetic and Theological Writings.* New York: Paulist Press, 1996.

Swartz, Merlin, ed. and trans. *A Medieval Critique of Anthropomorphism: Ibn al-Jawzī's Kitāb Akhbār aṣ-Ṣifāt.* Leiden, Netherlands: Brill, 2002.

Watt, William Montgomery, trans. *Islamic Creeds: A Selection.* Edinburgh: Edinburgh University Press, 1994.

DAVID R. VISHANOFF

RENAISSANCE MOVEMENT. *See* Ḥizb al-Nahḍah.

REPRESENTATION. Representation in politics refers to an arrangement whereby one is enabled to speak and act with authority on behalf of some other. Any theory of representation must address the questions of who or what is to be represented, who or what is to do be the representing and how, and where the limits, if any, to that representative authority lie. While today the notion of "representative government" tends to be equated with "representative democracy," and the legitimacy of a democratic order is said to stand on the idea that a democratic government gives effect to the will of a sovereign people through representation, the concept of political representation in Islamic political thought emerges in the context of God's revelation, and the representative's primary obligation is to implement divine law.

According to classical Islamic political thought, the Prophet Muḥammad was the messenger of God and the first leader of the Islamic community. He represents God only insofar as he transmits and gives effect to God's will as exemplified by God's law. In regard to rule after the death of the prophet, Shīʿī theory holds that the power and authority transmitted from God to the Prophet is entrusted to the person of the imam, who is considered infallible, whereas Sunnī thought maintains that it is left to any worthy (but fallible) successor to the prophet (*khalīfah rasūl Allāh*) to apply God's laws as expounded by the Prophet.

However, as Khaled Abou El Fadl notes, early Muslim jurists, such as Bāqillānī (c. 950–1013) and Ibn Taymīyah (1263–1328), "did not completely sever the connection between the ruler and the people" (Abou El Fadl, 2007, p. 261). Rather, "a person who fulfills certain conditions (*mustawfi al-shurut*) must come to power through a contract entered into with *ahl al-ʿaqad* [the people who have the power of contract] pursuant to which the Caliph is to receive the *bayʿah* [oath of allegiance] in return for his promise to discharge the terms of the contract" (261), although the contract is more implied than explicit, and the people who have the power to contract were most often understood to be those who could ensure the people's obedience to the ruler. As a result, Abou El Fadl concludes, "consent in pre-modern Muslim discourses appears to be the equivalent of acquiescence" (262).

Many Islamic thinkers writing during the Nahḍah (Renaissance), or modernist, period of the late nineteenth and early twentieth centuries proved more willing to draw equations between the institution of the Caliphate and modern institutions of representations. The Shīʿī religious scholar Muḥammad Ḥusayn Nāʾīnī (1860–1936) argues that in the absence of a just ruler (since only the imam is infallible) one must design good institutions to strengthen the principle of accountability and stave off corruption. The main institution is the legislature, which he likens to "'the public representatives' of the Hidden Imam during his occultation," and which is to act as a supervisory branch to the executive and remains "responsible to every individual in the nation" (Na'ini, 2002, p. 120). The Egyptian Muḥammad ʿAbduh (1849–1905) drew parallels between Western notions of public utility and the notion of public interest (*maṣāliḥ mursalah*) in Islamic thought to argue that the governing power is responsible for establishing laws in a just and beneficial manner that does not exclude the voice of the people (*ummah*) or public opinion (*raʾy ʿam*) (see Rashīd Riḍā, 1931, *Tārīkh al-ustādh*, pp. 52–54). For ʿAbduh and a number of other Islamic modernists the Qurʾānic principle of consultation (*shūrā*) is a further condition placed on the ruler's power and a central principle of representative government. ʿAbduh's disciple, Muḥammad Rashīd Riḍā (1865–1935) argues that, according to Islam, decision making is to be conducted through *shūrā*, and that the ruler is to implement Islamic law with the aims of preserving religion and serving the public interest (Rashīd Riḍā, 1922, *al-Khilāfah*, p. 9). Abū al-Kalām Azād (1888–1958), a theoretician of the pan-Islamic Khilāfat movement in British India maintains that not only the caliphs but also the Prophet Muḥammad constituted "a perfect conception of democratic equality," which "could only take shape with the whole nation's will, unity, suffrage, and election. This is the reason why the sovereign or a president of a republic is like a designated caliph; caliphate means nothing more nor less than representation" (Azad, 2002, p. 329).

Perhaps this too easy equation between the principles of Islam and the institutions of modern representative democracy were challenged by a number of Islamist thinkers. Abū al-Aʿlā Mawdūdī (1903–1979), founder of the Jamāʿat-i Islāmī in still-united India (in 1941) reasserted that sovereignty belongs to God (*al-ḥākimīyah lil-Allāh*). God "alone is the law-giver" and "no man, even if he be a prophet, has the right to order others in his own right to do or not do things" (Maudoodi, 1964, p. 26). People must obey the Prophet, Mawdūdī argues, not because he represents them (as in a democracy), but because he enforces the laws of God and only in so far as he does so. The Prophet is a representative of the God. However,

Mawdūdī notes that the Qur'ān (45:12, 13) states that not only the Prophet but "anyone who holds power and rules in accordance with the laws of God would undoubtedly be the vicegerent [*khalīfah*] of the supreme ruler" and, further, "the power and rulership of the earth has been promised to the whole community of believers" (44). Mawdūdī identifies this "popular vicegerency" as the "real foundation of democracy in Islam."

Mawdūdī affirms the classical conception of who or what is to be represented (God or divine law). At the same time, he seems to give the people a greater role in the selection of the representative. In the Islamic state the "Muslim public" is to elect as leader the one who is most respectable and virtuous. After the election, Mawdūdī maintains that the leader will exercise full authority and be completely obeyed so long as he follows God's law (51). If he violates God's law the people can remove him, but it is unclear how Mawdūdī envisions this coming about. He states that the leader should seek council, but in all matters regarding his rule the leader's judgment is supreme, even if it goes against the opinion of the majority—or even unanimity—of his council (53).

Mawdūdī's ambiguous relationship to the notion of democracy and his clarification that it is God's laws (not popular will) that are represented in the just Islamic state is reflected in later writings. While some continue to reject democracy as a system where popular whim is a threat to divine law, many contemporary Islamic thinkers embrace democracy as central to insuring that modern states represent the interests of Islam. For example, the Qatar-based Egyptian thinker Yūsuf al-Qaraḍāwī (b. 1926) notes how Islamic movements "have never flourished or borne fruit unless in an atmosphere of democracy and freedom, and have withered and become barren only at times of oppression and tyranny that trod over the will of the people which clung to Islam" (Qaraḍawi, 2000, *Priorities of the Islamic Movement*, p. 187). Addressing contexts in which Muslims have not been permitted to perpetuate their message and compete fairly in majoritarian elections, Qaraḍāwī expresses confidence in democratization as a means of better realizing Islamic values in society. Whereas Mawdūdī placed his confidence in a ruler once elected, Qaraḍāwī seems to have greater confidence in the majority opinion of the Muslim people. However, to ensure the Islamic basis of a majoritarian rule, Qaraḍāwī clarifies that it is necessary to check popular whim with a constitutional provision "stipulating that any legislation contradicting the incontestable provisions of Islam shall be null and void" (Qaraḍawi, 2000, *Priorities of the Islamic Movement*, pp. 188–189). Here too, we see that what is to be represented is God's will, not popular will, though with greater faith placed on the people in a Muslim-majority country to transmit that will through democratic processes.

Qaraḍāwī's assertion that representative democracy is the best system for the perpetuation of Islamic values assumes a Muslim majority that it is presumed will elect a good Muslim ruler. But do Muslims need to be represented by Muslims—or can they be represented by non-Muslims? Qaraḍāwī is clear on this issue: non-Muslims can only hold government positions that have no direct bearing on the religious lives of Muslims. Thus, he excludes non-Muslims from holding positions of imam and caliph, as well as positions involving the collection of *zakāt* or in an Islamic judiciary, and as head of the army, since he considers these positions to require the implementation of Islamic rules. While Qaraḍāwī's seems to be the predominant view among Islamists, other Islamic intellectuals, such as Ṭāriq al-Bishrī (Egypt, 1933–), argue that even if the idea of a Christian becoming president in a democratic election in a Muslim majority country like Egypt remains impossible, in the interests of national unity, one should not deny a minority population, such as

Copts, their full political rights (Bishrī, 1980, pp. 712–713; see also Browers, ch. 2).

Some Islamist thinkers have argued that, in the absence of Islamic governance, even in Muslim-majority contexts, Islamic movements should seek alliances, power-sharing arrangements, or other piecemeal means of realizing the aims of the Islamist movements. Even Qaraḍāwī cites approvingly the example of the Ḥasan al-Turābī, who, through accepting an appointment to a senior post in the Sudanese Socialist Union under Numairi's government, was able to bring about the establishment of Islamic law in Sudan (Qaraḍāwī, 1991, *Islamic Awakening*, pp. 50–51). Similarly, the leader of Tunisia's Nahḍah party, Rāshid al-Ghannūshī (1941–), wrote while in exile in Europe that Islamic movements must participate in those areas that remain available to them in existing states, working for Islamic reform through power sharing with secular forces. Like Qaraḍāwī, Ghannūshī defends this strategy through two principles: the principle of "necessity" (*ḍarūrah*) engendered by the "exceptional" circumstances of the present, where Muslims are unable to establish Islamic rule directly and with reference to the Islamic principle of public interest (*maṣlaḥah*). Where the choice is not between Islamic and non-Islamic rule but between dictatorship and democracy, Muslims must actively pursue the implementation of Islamic laws and values, even if only in part, to serve the necessities and interests of mankind. Here is where Ghannūshī seems to go beyond Qaraḍāwī—at least in the sense of acknowledging that the outcome of a democratic election in a Muslim-majority context might not be an Islamic state, and, thus, Muslims should recognize the interests that can be achieved through the establishment of a "secular democratic system." In other words, Ghannūshī puts forth the notion of "power sharing" not just with an aim toward bringing about a democratic system that will allow the election of an Islamist group that will then implement Islamic government. Rather, he seems to acknowledge a broader benefit of working with non-Islamist groups to achieve interests that he terms "national" and "humanistic," such as "independence, development, social solidarity, civil liberties, human rights, political pluralism, independence of the judiciary, freedom of the press, or liberty for mosques and Islamic activities" (Ghannouchi, 1998, p. 92).

With the changes brought about by the Arab uprisings that toppled authoritarian leaders and permitted Islamist groups to fully compete in elections in both Egypt and Tunisia—elections in which Islamist parties won the greatest share—the question arises as to whether the principles of necessity of and interest in working in alliance with non-Islamist groups in an ideologically plural political sphere still apply.

Bibliography

Abou El Fadl, Khaled. "Islam and the Challenge of Democratic Commitment." *Oriente Moderno*, n.s., 87, no. 2 (2007): 247–300.

Azad, Abu'l-Kalam. "The Last Word." In *Modernist Islam, 1840–1940: A Sourcebook*, ed. Charles Kurzman, pp. 325–333. New York: Oxford University Press, 2002.

Bishrī, Ṭāriq al-. *Al-Muslimūn wa-al-Aqbāt fī iṭār al-jamāʿah al-waṭanīyah*. Cairo: al-Hay'ah al-Miṣriyah al-ʿĀmah lil-Kitab, 1980.

Browers, Michaelle L. *Political Ideology in the Arab World: Accommodation and Transformation*. Cambridge, U.K.: Cambridge University Press, 2009.

Ghannouchi, Rachid. "Participation in Non-Islamic Government." In *Liberal Islam: A Sourcebook*, ed. Charles Kurzman, pp. 89–95. New York: Oxford University Press, 1998.

Maudoodi, Abul Ala. *Political Theory of Islam*. Delhi: Markazi Maktaba Jamat-e-Islāmī, Hind, 1964.

Na'ini, Muhammad Husayn. "Government in the Islamic Perspective." In *Modernist Islam, 1840–1940: A Sourcebook*, ed. Charles Kurzman, pp. 116–125. New York: Oxford University Press, 2002.

Qaraḍāwī, Yūsuf al-. *Islamic Awakening between Rejection and Extremism*. Herndon, Va.: International Institute of Islamic Thought, 1991.

Qaraḍāwī, Yūsuf al-. *Priorities of the Islamic Movement in the Coming Phase*. Rev. ed. Edited by Hasan al-Banna. Swansea, U.K.: Awakening, 2000.

Rashīd Riḍā, Muḥammad. *Al-khilāfah, aw-al-imāmah al-ʿUẓmā*. Cairo: al-Manār, 1922.

Rashīd Riḍā, Muḥammad. *Tārīkh al-ustādh al-Imām al-Shaykh Muḥammad ʿAbdūh*, vol. 2. Cairo: al-Manār, 1931.

Michaelle Browers

Republic. The concept of a republic, similar to the concept of democracy, is rooted in the Western political tradition, yet Muslim societies have embraced a republican (*jumhūrīyah*) form of government that enjoys widespread legitimacy throughout much of the Muslim world today. The overwhelming majority of the fifty-seven members of the Organization of Islamic Cooperation (OIC) are republics, albeit with considerable variation that includes republics that are Islamic, Arab, socialist, and secular.

While the 1923 Turkish Republic, founded on the ruins of the Ottoman Empire by Mustafa Kemal Atatürk, is the best-known and most influential form of republicanism in the Islamic world, the first independent republic in a Muslim-majority society emerged in May 1918 in Azerbaijan. It was a short-lived experiment that ended with the conquest of Azerbaijan by the Red Army in April 1920 and its subsequent incorporation into the Soviet Union.

Similarly, the Tripolitanian Republic (*al-Jumhūrīyah al-Trabulsiya*) was proclaimed in November 1918 by Sulayman Pasha al-Baruni, a journalist and former member of the Ottoman parliament, in the country now known as Libya. Its declaration of independence invoked both Islamic themes and modern forms of republican government in justifying its existence. This was the first republican experiment in the Arab world, but it gained little support from the great powers, and by 1923 it was incorporated into Italy's colonization of Libya.

The model of French republicanism was bequeathed to those parts of the Middle East that France controlled after World War I. The Lebanese Republic was proclaimed in May 1926 and the Syrian Republic was proclaimed in May 1930, although it was more than a decade before these countries obtained full independence.

The end of World War II coincided with the decolonization of large parts of Asia and Africa. This resulted in the emergence of many new independent republics with Muslim-majority populations. The Republic of Indonesia was proclaimed in August 1945; Pakistan became independent in 1947 and declared itself an Islamic republic in November 1953. In Africa, Sudan became a republic in January 1956, and Tunisia abolished the monarchy and became a republic in May 1959.

A series of military coups led by junior military officers led to the creation of new republics in the Arab world based on a blend of Pan-Arab nationalism, socialism, and nonalignment with the great powers. After the overthrow of King Farouk, Egypt was declared a republic in June 1953 under the leadership of Gamal Abdel Nasser. In July 1958, a similar military coup toppled the Hashemite monarchy in Iraq, and a republic was declared in its stead. A brief experiment in Arab unity saw the emergence of the short-lived United Arab Republic (*al-Jumhūrīyah al-ʿArabīyah al-Muttaḥidah*) from February 1958 to September 1961. The tide of Arab nationalism swept away the monarchy in Yemen in September 1962 and led to the emergence of the Yemen Arab Republic. Colonel Muʿammar al-Qadhdhāfī declared the Libyan Arab Republic in 1969 after a military coup that toppled the pro-British monarchy. This new regime was based on similar Arab nationalist and socialist themes.

The 1979 revolution in Iran marked a departure from the dominance of secular nationalism in Muslim countries and led to the creation of the first Islamist-controlled state, albeit a Shīʿah one based on the writings of Ayatollah Ruhollah Khomeini. After a popular referendum in March 1979, Iran proclaimed an Islamic republic that sought to balance clerical rule with popular representation.

Historical Roots of the Term. The word for republic in Arabic, Persian, Turkish, and Urdu is, with minor phonetic variations, *jumhūrīyat*. In tracing the origins and first use of the term, Bernard Lewis observes that the Ottoman Turks needed a word to facilitate their relations with the republics of Venice and Ragusa. As a result they adopted the Arabic term *jumhūr*, which referred to the general public or masses. The use of the term became more frequent after the French Revolution, when Turkish documents used it to describe the French Republic and other republics in Europe that were based on a similar model.

The use of the word *jumhūr* for "republic" in the late 1870s in Turkish and Arabic was still abstract, however, without a clear distinction between public and republic. It took on a more precise definition in Turkey during its modernization process, when the word *jumhūrīyat* appeared in a Turkish dictionary in the late nineteenth century. It was defined as "the principle of government by the public—the mass." From here, this meaning of the term caught on and gradually spread eastward to Arabic-, Persian-, and Urdu-speaking populations.

Political Authority in Muslim Societies. The political theory and history of Islam contains no reference to the concept of a republic or republicanism. The ideal form of political authority was the caliphate, and after its breakdown in the eleventh century, the de facto form of rule became the sultanate, which was effectively a military autocracy. In contrast to a republic, these forms of government located political sovereignty in the rule of one person who became the head of state. According to classical Islamic jurisprudence, legitimate rule should be based on a social contract between ruler and ruled, and the head of state should obtain a pledge of allegiance from the influential members of society as well as the majority of his constituency. In theory, rulers are supposed to consult with Islamic jurists as well as representatives of society, and only after these consultations are complete should the head of state act in the best interests of society. In reality, however, after 660 both the caliphate and the sultanate were dynastic and authoritarian. A system of political patronage and nepotism was widespread and consultation was pro forma and limited to the circle of ruling elites. Some of the key dynasties where this form of political rule manifested itself were the Umayyads (661–750), ʿAbbāsids (750–1258), Ottomans (1299–1923), Ṣafavids (1501–1737), and Mughals (1526–1857).

The reason a republican form of government gradually became popular and mainstream in Muslim societies during the twentieth century has both a normative theological dimension and a practical political one. Islamic political theory and practice contains elements that are potentially supportive of democratic and republican authority. In theory, the caliph is not an absolute ruler, and he is bound to uphold Islamic law, to which he is also subject. In the Qurʾān, the idea of mutual consultation (*shūrā*) is praised. In classical jurisprudential theory governance should be based on a civil contract (*ʿaqd*) between the ruler and the ruled, and a pledge of support (*bayʿah*) from influential members of the community should be obtained. There is also the longstanding Islamic juridical concept of consensus (*ijmāʿ*), while the equality and fraternity of believers, regardless of race or class, is emphasized in Islamic theology. All of these are conducive to the development and promotion of republicanism.

After World War I most of the Islamic world fell under the control of external powers. The struggle for political independence against colonial and imperial domination became the most powerful organizing theme, dominating political life and shaping the modern history and identity of Muslims from Morocco to Indonesia. This struggle for political freedom naturally entailed the idea of popular rule, which contrasted with the elite control of Muslim societies by European powers and their allies in Muslim lands, many of whom were monarchs. The influx of new ideas of secular nationalism from the West also played a part in the modernization of Muslim societies and led to the establishment of new nation-states based on republican ideals.

Conclusion. In thinking objectively about the various republics that have existed in the Muslim world, it is important not to equate these republics with representative government or liberal democracy. For most of the twentieth century, a republic simply meant a state with a nondynastic head, and republicanism suggested the end of the institution of monarchy. The term does not indicate the location of political power, who wields it, or the processes by which the head of state attains office or the manner in which authority is discharged.

Until recently, most republics in the Muslim world were nondemocratic regimes. These postcolonial states were republics only in theory. In reality, they varied from soft authoritarian regimes to hard totalitarian ones. In terms of human rights, republics have been more repressive than monarchies, particularly in the Middle East. The human rights record of the Islamic Republic of Iran, for example, is far worse than that of the Pahlavi monarchy. The secular republics in Iraq under Saddam Hussein and in Syria under the Assad family have a human rights record that has been described by leading human rights organizations as "genocidal" in the case of Iraq and the Kurds and tantamount to "crimes against humanity" in the case of Syria and its response to the Arab Spring protests.

The Arab Spring, however, holds considerable promise that the era of authoritarian republics is at an end. While the future is unknown, these democratic revolutions provide an opportunity, arguably for the first time in the modern history of the Arab world, for the realization of concepts such as civic virtue, universal political participation, representative government, and the rule of law, all of which are founding ideals of republicanism.

BIBLIOGRAPHY

Abou El Fadl, Khaled. *Islam and the Challenge of Democracy.* Edited by Joshua Cohen and Deborah Chasman. Princeton, N.J.: Princeton University Press, 2004.

Abou El Fadl, Khaled. "Islam and the State: A Short History." In *Democracy and Islam in the New Afghan Constitution*, edited by Cheryl Benard and Nina Hachigian, pp. 13–16. Santa Monica, Calif.: Rand Corporation, 2003.

Enayat, Hamid. *Modern Islamic Political Thought.* Austin: University of Texas Press, 1982.

Lapidus, Ira M. *A History of Islamic Societies.* 2d ed. Cambridge, U.K.: Cambridge University Press, 2002.

Lewis, Bernard. "The Concept of an Islamic Republic." *Die Welt des Islams*, n.s., 4, no. 1 (1955): 1–9.

Lewis, Bernard. "Djumhurriyya." In *The Encyclopaedia of Islam*, edited by P. J. Bearman et al., vol. 2, pp. 594–595. Leiden: Brill, 1960.

Schulze, Reinhard. *A Modern History of the Islamic World.* Translated by Azizeh Azodi. New York: New York University Press, 2000.

NADER HASHEMI

REVOLUTION. *See* Rebellion.

RIBĀṬ. *Ribāṭ* is a concept with a diverse history. The basic meaning of the root *r-b-ṭ* is "to bind." Via the idea of "binding a mount" there developed the meaning "to muster the mount," which led to a general military connotation of many word forms derived from the root. Today, *ribāṭ* is customarily used to designate an establishment with both a religious and military character occupied by a garrison of ascetic volunteers dedicated to the defense of Islam; in other words, a fortified convent. This has become the usage since the publication of the relevant entry in the first edition of *The Encyclopaedia of Islam* (1934), in which Georges Marçais defined *ribāṭ* as "a fortified Muḥammadan monastery" on the frontiers of Islam.

The most commonly cited extant buildings of *ribāṭs* are those in Sousse and Monastir (in Tunisia). The Almoravid Berber movement and dynasty that conquered western North Africa and southern Iberia in the eleventh century derives its name (al-Murābiṭūn) from its supposed origin in a *ribāṭ* situated on the Senegal River. In 1984 and in 2002 remnants of alleged *ribāṭs* were identified near Guardamar del Segura on the Spanish coast near Alicante and in Arrifana on the Portuguese coast near Aljezur. Yet as early as 1966, Albrecht Noth raised serious doubts about the conventional use of the term *ribāṭ*, and in 1995, Jacqueline Chabbi refuted it categorically as an illegitimate conflation of spatially, chronologically, and conceptually dissociated references in the sources.

According to Chabbi it, is crucial to distinguish between *ribāṭ* as an action, as a place, and as a convent. In the first use, *ribāṭ* could take on the meaning of performing voluntary military service on the frontier starting in the ninth century. In the second use, as a place, *ribāṭ* could designate, among other things, a site where one could do *ribāṭ* in the first sense. Tenth-century writers mention thousands of *ribāṭs* on the Islamic frontiers in the Middle East and the Mediterranean as starting points for idealized *jihād* action. Yet these places are not to be understood as a certain type of building or institution. Thirdly, the urban establishments where Ṣūfīs lived together in late medieval Islamic cities were also occasionally dubbed *ribāṭs*. But they had no connection at all with the places or actions described by that term in earlier ages, and the notion of the Ṣūfī *ribāṭ* as a convent must therefore not be transferred to those earlier occurrences of the term.

The modern conventional understanding of the *ribāṭ* as a fortified convent populated by religiously motivated volunteers is a construction of Western scholarship leaning on idealized representations of border warfare in medieval Islam. It was conceived in the terms of Christian monasticism and especially of the military orders, to which the *ribāṭ* and its men were compared from the beginning of Oriental studies. First raised in a passing comment in a footnote in José Antonio Conde's *Historia de la dominación de los árabes en España* (Madrid, 1820–1821), the analogy of the *ribāṭ* and its garrison with the Templars and other chivalrous orders is strongly present in the works of the colonial French Orientalist school of Algiers (notably Georges Marçais). Historians of Spain (notably Américo Castro) positing the idea of a fusion of cultures in medieval Iberia then elaborated this into a hypothesis that the *ribāṭ* had been the model for the military orders. The existence of the Christian monastic militias is thus explained as a cultural borrowing from Islam, against the background of the imputation that mixing religion with violence was originally alien to medieval Christianity but essential to Islam.

Bibliography

Castro, Américo. *The Structure of Spanish History*. Translated by Edmund L. King. Princeton, N.J.: Princeton University Press, 1954. English translation of *España en su historia: Cristianos, Moros y Judíos*, first published in 1948.

Chabbi, Jacqueline. "Ribāṭ." In *The Encyclopaedia of Islam*, rev. ed., edited by C. E. Bosworth, E. van Donzel, W. P. Heinrichs et al., vol. 8, pp. 493–506. Leiden: Brill, 1995.

Feuchter, Jörg. "The Islamic Ribāt: A Model for the Christian Military Orders? Sacred Violence, Concepts of Religions, and the Invention of a Cultural Transfer." In *Religion and Its Other: Secular and*

Sacral Concepts and Practices in Interaction, edited by Heike Bock, Jörg Feuchter, and Michi Knecht, pp. 115–141. Frankfurt: Campus Verlag, 2008.

Marçais, Georges. "Ribāṭ." In *E. J. Brill's First Encyclopaedia of Islam, 1913–1936*, edited by M. Th. Houtsma et al., vol. 6, pp. 1150–1153. Leiden: Brill, 1987.

Noth, Albrecht. *Heiliger Krieg und Heiliger Kampf in Islam und Christentum: Beiträge zur Vorgeschichte und Geschichte der Kreuzzüge*. Bonn: Rohrscheid, 1966.

JÖRG FEUCHTER

RIDDAH. *See* Apostasy.

RUSSIA. Islam first entered the territory of the modern Russian Federation (RF), in the northern Caucasus as early as the seventh century, following the Arab conquest of the Sassanid Persian Empire in 642 CE. In 685/86, the Arabs took the city of Derbend, which subsequently became the focus for the Islamization of the northeast Caucasus, referred to as *bāb al-jihād* (the gateway of *jihād*). In the central part of modern Russia, the Upper Volga basin, Islam gradually took root through trade and other economic relations with the Muslim world. The first independent Muslim state in the Volga-Urals region was the Bulgar Kingdom (eighth century–1236), which voluntarily recognized Islam as an official state religion in 922 in the presence of a delegation sent by the ʿAbbāsid caliph Jaʿfar al-Muqtadir Billāh (r. 908–932). From there, Islam spread to other parts of what is now Russia, including Siberia.

The next wave of the spread of Islam in Russia took place during the period of the Golden Horde, a western province of the Chinggisid Empire, established in 1242 as a result of the Mongol invasion of the Bulgar Kingdom and other neighboring territories including the Kievan Rus in 1237–1240. Under the rule of Öz Beg Khan (r. 1312–1342), Islam became the official religion of the entire kingdom, while the Volga Bulgar elite dominated its cultural and Islamic discourse. Under Chinggisid rule, the Russian Orthodox Church was given a preferential legal status, which enabled it to strengthen its economic and political positions in Russia (Pilkington and Yemelianova 2003, p. 21). Yet the Russian perception of an Islamic threat had been intensified around the time of the demise of the empire in 1437.

The political status of Islam had changed radically by the mid-sixteenth century, when a pattern of conquest and incorporation was reversed by the Russian state under the Ivan IV, "the Terrible," who invaded the states of Kazan (1552) and Astrakhan (1556). Over the next three centuries, Russia continued its expansion into Muslim-inhabited lands in Siberia, the Caucasus, and Central Asia. Thus, at the beginning of the twentieth century, the Russian Empire (aside from the protectorates of Bukhara and Khiva), included more than 14 million Muslims, or more than 11 per cent of the total population.

Under Russian rule, Muslim inhabitants were treated as Russian subjects to whom the rights reserved to Christians were entirely denied. The suppression of Islam, accompanied by coercive Christianization and Russification, was central to Moscow's policy of integrating non-Russian territories into a centralized Russian state, except during the reign of the Catherine II (Pilkington and Yemelianova, 2003, p. 6). Such a hostile atmosphere and forceful Christianization policies resulted in systematic uprisings of Muslims under the banner of Islam, culminating in the second half of the eighteenth century with the Batyrsha Revolt and Pugachev's Rebellion.

The emergence of relative religious, intellectual, and economic freedom owing to the imperial reforms of the late eighteenth and nineteenth centuries initiated an Islamic renewal movement. Muslim Tatar intellectuals such as ʿAbd al-Naṣr al-Qursawi (1776–1812), Shihab al-Din Marjani (1818–1889), Abdülkayyum Nasiri (1824–1902), and others emphasized the creative and flexible potential of Islam and its compatibility with modern progress. In the beginning of the twentieth century, this religious-educational movement evolved into a broader sociopolitical and cultural phenomenon that was also referred to as Jadīdism.

After the Bolshevik Revolution in 1917, the antagonistic policies of the Communist regime undermined the traditional religious, social, economic, and political foundations of the Muslim society.

The Muslim Population of the Russian Federation. There is no official record of the number of Muslims in the RF, as the 2010 census did not include a question about religious beliefs. Nevertheless, most estimates put the number of Muslims in the RF between 18 and 20 million, which is about 14–15 percent of the total population (about 143 million in January 2012).

Muslim populations exist in all of the territorial divisions of the RF, and ethnic Muslims predominate in seven of the twenty-one republics: Bashkortostan and Tatarstan in the Volga-Urals region, and Chechnya, Ingushetia, Daghestan, Kabardino-Balkaria, and Karachay-Cherkessia in the northern Caucasus. Other parts of Russia, including large cities such as Moscow, Nizhniy Novgorod, and Saint Petersburg, also have significant Muslim populations. The Muslim community of Moscow alone is estimated to be more than 2 million (about 20 percent of the total), and Saint Petersburg's Muslim population is approximately 700,000 (out of a population of about 4.78 million, according to the 2010 census). Major cities with large Muslim populations in Siberia and the Far East include Omsk, Tyumen, Tobolsk, Novosibirsk, Vladivostok, Khabarovsk, and Urengoy.

Russia's Muslims belong to more than forty ethnic groups, such as the Volga Tatars, the Siberian Tatars, Chechens, Ingush, Bashkirs, Dargins, Balkars, Avars, Karachays, Lezgins, Kabardins, and many others. The majority of them follow two Sunnī schools of Islamic jurisprudence—the Ḥanafī and Shāfiʿī *madhhabs*. Muslims of the Volga-Urals region and the Nogays, Karachays, and Balkars in the northern Caucasus follow the Ḥanafī *madhhab* (school of law), while Muslims of Daghestan, Chechnya, and Ingushetia are Shāfiʿī. Shiites are a small minority found almost exclusively in the Caucasus, among Azeri Turks and part of the Lezgins, a small Muslim ethnic group in Daghestan.

Experts on Russia's demographic development predict Muslim a majority in Russia in the second half of the twenty-first century. They observe the decline in the ethnic Russian population and the rapid growth among the country's ethnic Muslims. A significant gap exists between the birthrates of ethnic Russians and Russia's predominantly Muslim ethnic groups: 1.7 births per 100 women for ethnic Russians annually, which is below the replacement rate, and 4.5 births per 100 women for Muslim ethnic groups (Hunter, 2004, *Islam in Russia*, 45). In addition, Muslim immigration from Central Asia and the south Caucasus is increasing because of higher demand for labor in Russia.

Identity. The process of Islamic revival, which began in the early 1990s, made Muslims of Russia keenly aware of being part of the Islamic civilization and belonging to the worldwide Muslim *ummah*; it helped them to overcome the inferiority complex developed during their time in the Russian Empire and later, during the Soviet period. Their religious awareness and appreciation of being Tatars, Bashkirs, Ingush, or Chechens not just as an ethnic group but a part of the great civilization had significantly increased. In Tatarstan, Islam contributed significantly in reshaping the identity of Tatars, the second largest nationality in Russia, during the independence movement in the 1990s. In Chechnya, the separatists tried to impart a religious foundation to their struggle and employed the Islamic slogan of *jihād*. In general, the post-1990 increase in expression of Islamic identity among Russia's Muslim groups is not an anti-Russian phenomenon. The majority of Muslims feel committed to the integrity and survival of Russia, and their leaders promote loyalty to and cooperation with the secular Russian state.

Islam and the State. As a result of the introduction of religious freedom in the 1990s and the subsequent appearance of an Islamic renaissance, Russian society adapted to the fact that it is not only a multiethnic entity but one with religious diversity. A preamble to the 1997 Law on Freedom of Conscience, a supplemental law on religion, identifies Russian Orthodoxy, Judaism, Islam, and Buddhism as traditional religions of the RF. Islam is repeatedly asserted by the Russian authorities to be the part of Russian society (Akhmetova 2010). Nonetheless, the attitude of the Russian ruling establishment to Islam is somewhat reserved. The Kremlin wants a conformist Islam and reacts negatively to any deviations from conformism, particularly since the 1990s, when Islam not only served as the banner of the Chechen resistance but was also employed by the opposition in other Muslim regions.

The Islamic factor played a minor role in the declaration of war by the Russian government against Chechnya in 1994 and 1999. Yet the horrible consequences of these wars, together with the 9/11 attacks in the United States, played a fundamental role in creating a negative image of Islam and Muslims in Russia. In the wake of the Russian Extremist Law of 2002, adopted after the declaration of the U.S.-led global "war on terror," cases of discrimination and violation of Muslims' rights have significantly increased. Dozens of mainstream Islamic books, and organizations and movements such as Ḥizb al-Taḥrīr, Tablīghī Jamāʿat, Nurdzhular, Salafīyah, Wahhabism, and others had been banned as being "extremist" and "contradictory to the traditional Ḥanafī *madhhab*," marking a slow erosion of religious freedom in Russia (Akhmetova 2010).

Muslims in Russian Politics. The history of Russian Muslim political activism dates back to the early 1900s. During the years of the First Russian Revolution of 1905–1907, Muslims formed a political party called Ittifak-i Müslümin (Union of Muslims), which represented the liberal opposition and adhered to peaceful, parliamentary methods of political struggle. The Muslim Fraction participated in four state Dumas between 1906 and 1916. Political goals of Muslims were frustrated by the reassertion of tsarist authoritarianism and, later, by the establishment of the Soviet Union and its brand of nation building.

With the political opening presented by Gorbachev's reform agenda, Islam again became a factor in the political life of Russian society, including several important aspects such as the establishment of political organizations and parties with the principle of belonging to Islam and making appropriate religious demands (for instance, that the necessary conditions be created for every Muslim to lead "an Islamic way of life"); an active involvement of Muslim clergymen in politics; getting secular politicians, members of the central and regional elites, to turn to Islam; the employment of Islam by political opposition parties and movements, including separatist ones; and, lastly, taking Islam into account as a foreign-policy factor.

Islamic political organizations have been active in Russia during the last decade of the twentieth century. The first of them was the All-Russia Islamic Rebirth Party, established in June 1990. It advocated the creation of an Islamic government in Daghestan through peaceful and gradual means, without, however, demonstrating separatist tendencies. It failed to register for the 1993 parliamentary elections and shortly faded away. Although the ARIRP was not destined to become one of Russia's influential parties, it gave an impetus to the politicization of Islam during the remainder of the Soviet era and later, after the disintegration of the USSR.

In 1995 three important Muslim parties were created: the All-Russia Muslim Social Movement Nur ("Light"), the Union of Muslims of Russia, and the Islamic Committee of Russia. During the 1995 parliamentary elections Nur got 0.58 percent of the votes in Russia as a whole (with a total of 393,500 votes). In Chechnya and Ingushetia it got 23 percent, in Tatarstan 5 percent, and in Bashkortostan 1.25 percent of the vote.

Another important Muslim organization was Refakh, which supported the pro-Putin Unity Movement in the 1999 elections and managed to get twenty seats in the Duma. However, in 2001 the Russian parliament passed the Law on Political Parties, banning parties based on religion. Moreover, tougher requirements for political parties, such as having branches in at least forty of the regions, effectively meant the end of Muslim political parties (Hunter, 2009, "Russia").

At present Russia's Muslim population does not have a policy-making voice, any influential political figure, or analytical and lobbyist centers. Their voice is mainly represented by the so-called official *'ulamā'*; three institutions of the *Muftiyét*: the Sovet Muftiyev Rossii (Russian Council of Muftis—RCM; founded in July 1996 in Moscow), the Tsentral'noe Dukhovnoe Upravlenie Musul'man Rossii i Evropeĭskiĭ Stran (Central Spiritual Board of Muslims of Russia and European Countries of the Commonwealth of Independent States—CSBM, founded in 1992 in Ufa) and the Koordinatsionniy Tsentr Musul'man Severnogo Kavkaza (Muslim Coordination Centre in the Northern Caucasus, established in 1998).

The Islamic factor in foreign policy serves to corroborate the claim about Russia's special place in global politics, its "intermediary" situation as a Eurasian state, which enables it to serve as a bridge between the Muslim world and the West. On 29 June 2005, the RF was granted the status of "an observer" at the Organization of Islamic Conference (OIC).

BIBLIOGRAPHY

Akhmetova, Elmira. "Russia." In *Yearbook of Muslims in Europe* 2 (2010): 435–456.

Bennigsen, Alexandre, and S. Enders Wimbush, eds. *Muslims of the Soviet Empire: A Guide*. London: Hurst, 1986.

Bukharaev, Ravil. *Islam in Russia: The Four Seasons*. Richmond, U.K.: Curzon, 2000.

Hunter, Shireen T. *Islam in Russia: The Politics of Identity and Security*. Armonk, N.Y.: M. E. Sharpe, 2004.

Hunter, Shireen. "Russia." In *The Oxford Encyclopedia of the Islamic World*, edited by John L. Esposito, vol. 4, pp. 562–565. New York: Oxford University Press, 2009.

Malashenko, Alexei. "Islam and Politics in Present-Day Russia." Learning Ace http://www.learningace.com/doc/2231255/60d036e0487424e5c477081a33c6de55/wp_russiaseries_malashenko

Pilkington, Hilary, and Galina Yemelianova, eds. *Islam in Post-Soviet Russia: Public and Private Faces*. London: RoutledgeCurzon, 2003.

Elmira Akhmetova

S

Ṣabrī Efendi, Mustafa. (1869–1954), Mustafa Ṣabrī Efendi was an Ottoman Islamic scholar and a political activist during the period of Turkey's change from Ottoman monarchy to Turkish Republic. He is known especially for his blistering criticisms of Atatürk's political movement (Ankara Hükümeti) against the Ottoman government, which resulted in the collapse of the latter in 1923.

Born in the Tokat Province of Middle Anatolia, Ṣabrī followed the classical *medrese* (Ar. *madrasah*) curricula of the Ottoman education system, and as a brilliant student he successfully achieved his educational goals at an early age. Ṣabrī's political life began when he was selected as a member of parliament, after the announcement of the Second Constitution (İkinci Meşrutiyet) in 1908. He took part in several political parties and organizations and afterward had the chance to work with other noteworthy Islamist activists such as İskilipli Mehmed Atıf and Bediüzzaman Said Nursî (the pioneer of the Gülen movement in modern Turkey). He became *şeyhülislam* (the highest official rank in religious affairs) during the government of Damat Ferid Paşa in 1919. Circumstances began to change drastically for Ṣabrī after the government was taken over by Atatürk and his anti-Ottoman group. In 1924 Ṣabrī was stripped of his Turkish citizenship, along with other members of the royal family of the Ottoman state, some of whom were included in the notorious list of 150 (*Yüzellilikler*, i.e., 150 people to be removed from the new Turkish land). He remained in exile for the rest of his life, mainly in Egypt, where he died.

Mustafa Ṣabrī was a Muslim scholar in the classical sense, one who struggled to cope with the values of modernity. A scholar who once held the highest religious position in Muslim society, Ṣabrī lived in an age in which he saw the political and social decline of the religion of Islam. Neither the Islamic world he adhered to nor the West in its ideological and political aspects escaped the criticism of this loyal protector of Islamic tradition; in fact, he was angrier with Muslim society than with the West, since he thought that it was due to the weakness and the disloyalty of the former that Islam fell into the hands of anti-Islamic powers. To him, the most catastrophic mistake of Muslim people was the abolishment of the caliphate in 1924. He severely criticized those who saw in the event the salvation of Muslim world.

Ṣabrī defines "Islamic democracy" as divine rule that primarily set its starting point as responsibility before God. Social benefits come automatically, after the authority of God is accepted. Islamic democracy thus distinguishes itself from other artificial democracies, which are nothing more than manipulations of poor people by groups such as communists and Bolsheviks. In order to apply the just system of Islam, the principle of the integrity of religion and state should be strictly observed. As a formidable opponent of the idea that religion (Islam) and state must be separated, he is of the opinion that the separation of religion and state does not mean simply the autonomy of the one from another, a situation that Islam will not tolerate. Having personally observed the cases of Turkey and Egypt, he comments that the application of the separation principle refers only to the control of religion and religious people by the political power.

In keeping with his stance on political issues, Ṣabrī thinks that it was a mistake to deviate from the conventional status of women in Islam and that modern Muslims failed to understand the position of women in society. He observes that Muslims' enthusiasm for their women vanished with their lack of enthusiasm for Islam. He was deeply distressed to witness the changing manners and corruption of women in Islamic countries. One example of this corruption which he regretted was that Muslim women dressed in the streets the way they would dress in their bedrooms and disobeyed the rules of Islam about *ḥijāb*.

Mustafa Ṣabrī also engaged in the popular discussions brought by contemporary Muslim thinkers to their home countries from the West. With respect to the value of modern science, Ṣabrī expresses his astonishment that the West has, in modern times, restricted the scope of science to the experimental approach, because the relation of science to the theoretical side (reason) is basically more secure and robust than its relation to the experimental side (five senses). He even goes so far as to regard the hegemony of the experimental over the theoretical as the reason that modern Western philosophy went into collapse in terms of philosophy. Ṣabrī's attitude can be explained by his adherence to the classical stance of Islamic theology, which is based to some extent on Aristotelian logic, a logic that principally assumes the superiority of deductive reasoning over induction.

He contends that the conflict between science and religion in the West emerged from the nature of the religion of Westerners (i.e., Christianity); therefore, any attempt to look for a similar debate in Islam would be the work of those misguided Muslim thinkers who desperately engage in imitation (*taqlīd*) of the West. In this point, he separates the "true" Christianity that, like Islam, contradicts neither reason nor science from the Christianity that evolved after Jesus.

As for the future, Ṣabrī was extremely pessimistic, as was shown in his banned book, *Dini müceddidler*, which was written to evaluate the intellectual level of the new Muslim reformists. He maintains that the new *mujtahids* of Islam are not capable of what they intend to do, namely, to revive Islam. In his opinion, this is due to their lack of correct understanding of the Islamic tradition and their lack of proper respect for the authorities of classical Islamic disciplines. Expressing his doubts about the sincerity of reformers' belief in Islam, he states that "true Muslim scholars would not allow Islam to become a toy in the hands of these reformers" (Sabri, 1969) who see Islam as a religion that is expected to conform to every new ideological trend.

BIBLIOGRAPHY

Bein, Amit. *Ottoman Ulema, Turkish Republic: Agents of Change and Guardians of Tradition*. Stanford, Calif.: Stanford University Press, 2011.

Karabela, Mehmet Kadri. "One of the Last Ottoman Şeyhülislâms, Mustafa Sabri Efendi (1869–1954): His Life, Works and Intellectual Contributions." M.A. thesis, McGill University, 2003. http://digitool.Library.McGill.CA:80/R/-?func=dbin-jump-full&object_id=79952&silo_library=GEN01.

Sabri, Mustafa. *Dini müceddidler* (Religious Reformists). Istanbul: Sebil Yayınevi, 1969. First published 1919–1921.

Sabri, Mustafa. *Mawqif al-ʿaql wa-al-ʿilm wa-al-ʿālam* (The Position of Reason, Science, and the Universe). 4 vols. Cairo: ʿĪsā al-Bābī al-Ḥalabī, 1949.

Sabri, Mustafa. *Qawlī fī al-marʾah* (My Opinion on Women). Beirut: Dār Ibn Ḥazm, 1990. Collected articles.

Yavuz, Yusuf Şevki. "Mustafa Sabri Efendi." In *Türkiye Diyanet Vakfı İslam Ansiklopedisi*, vol. 31, pp. 350–353. Istanbul: Türkiye Diyanet Vakfı, 2006.

VEYSEL KAYA

SADAQA. *See* Charity.

ṢADR, MUḤAMMAD BĀQIR AL-. (1935–1980), Muḥammad Bāqir al-Ṣadr was an innovative and influential Iraqi Islamic thinker and political leader. "An important figure not only in Iraq but in the life of the Shiʿi world, and indeed in the Muslim world as a whole" (Albert Hourani), Muḥammad Bāqir al-Ṣadr was both a prominent scholar of Islamic law and its contemporary applications and a political leader whose writ transcended his native country to reach Iran and the rest of the Middle East.

Thought. Muḥammad Bāqir al-Ṣadr's output is probably the most varied of any Muslim author of the twentieth century. Ṣadr wrote books on philosophy, Qurʾānic interpretation, logic, education, constitutional law, economics, and interest-free banking, as well as more traditional works of *uṣūl al-fiqh* (principles of Islamic jurisprudence), compilations of devotional rites, commentaries on prayers, and historical investigations into early Sunnī-Shīʿī controversies.

With Ṣadr an innovative thinker on the issue of the ideal shape and structure of a contemporary Muslim society, his most important work, which established his fame early in his career, is a book on Islamic economics, which was published in two volumes in 1959–1961. This book *Iqtiṣādunā* (Our Economics), probably remains the most scholarly twentieth-century study of Islamic economics as an alternative ideological system to capitalism and communism.

Methodologically, Ṣadr acknowledges, in *Iqtiṣādunā*, that there is no scientific discipline in Islam that can be identified as economics and that the main elements in the approach to an Islamic economy must be derived from what he calls the "legal superstructure." The resultant process leads to the well-known process of *ijtihād*, which is understood by Ṣadr in its wider sense as an intellectual endeavor in the law and jurisprudence of classical Islam and is consequently acknowledged as prone to human error. For Ṣadr, "Islamic economics is not a science" and will only stand as an original and serious discipline after a long process of legal discovery. Only after this research is done can one speak of an original Islamic discipline of economics, in which the moral imperative derived from the law is clear but in which there is also a painstaking and patient scholarly investigation into the riches of the classical *fiqh* (jurisprudence) tradition.

From a substantive point of view, Ṣadr introduces in *Iqtiṣādunā* a detailed critique of Marxist socialism and Western capitalism before proceeding with the presentation of his alternative system. Because of the particular strength of communist ideology in Iraq at the time *Iqtiṣādunā* was composed, the book is devoted primarily to refuting various brands of Marxist socialism. Ṣadr's arguments against capitalism rest on the usual criticism of the hollowness of the concept of liberty when applied to unequal parties in economic exchange. Against socialism, Ṣadr develops an informed, if long-winded, argument demonstrating the fallacies of Marxist periodization of history, its overemphasis on the class struggle, and its unrealistic prescriptions against the basic (and natural) instincts of economic self-interest in mankind. Subsequently, Islamic economics as a discipline is introduced by a series of principles, mostly of a methodological nature, which the author follows with a dirigiste (i.e., involving extensive state intervention) and generally egalitarian reading of the concept of property in a predominantly agricultural context.

Without going into the intricacies of his theory of landed property, Ṣadr's thesis can be presented as a call for systematic intervention by the state to ensure that land ownership depends as directly as possible on the actual laborer who works on it. The central concept of labor in *Iqtiṣādunā* requires an interventionist and welfarist stance of the ruler (called in that book *walī al-amr*), who combines two tools to redress the "social balance": one is the guidance of legal principles of property that connect ownership of land and means of production with labor; the other is "need," and the state is free, according to Ṣadr, to fill in the discretionary area with measures adequate to suppress what Ṣadr did not shy from calling, on the eve of the Iranian Revolution two decades later, "the exploitation of man by man."

Beyond these general principles, Ṣadr elaborately develops the guiding rules for property within the frame of what he calls "distribution in the phase that precedes production." Both in this phase and in the actual productive process, the most original dimension of *Iqtiṣādunā* appears in the method of uncovering Islamic economics. By quoting classical jurists of the *fiqh* tradition, Ṣadr engages the field with the most serious such investigation among Muslim authors in the twentieth century, by basing it on the books of a millennium-old legal tradition.

The detour through classical law is also Ṣadr's path to a lengthy treatise on Islamic banking. Here again, he is a forerunner in a field that by a decade after his *Al-bank al-lā-ribawī* (The Interest-Free Bank) was published in 1969 had become fashionable and controversial. Islamic finance is premised on a narrow interpretation of the ban on *ribā* (a word that for Ṣadr means "interest"), which has led Islamic banks to create arrangements allowing access to their coffers by depositors, in return for the bank's pooling these resources for investment arrangements that do not bear a predetermined or fixed rate of return.

The system devised by Muḥammad Bāqir al-Ṣadr needs to be appraised against the common practice of present-day Islamic institutions. If a deposit invested by an Islamic bank in a successful venture is profitable, the depositor and the bank (as entrepreneur) will share the profit according to a predetermined rate—for example, a 50-50 or 60-40 split. But the endeavor can also be a total failure, eating up the deposit as capital. In this case, under the classical contract of *muḍārabah*, which is also known as *commenda*, or partnership for profit and loss, the depositor has no recourse against the bank in normal circumstances.

Under classical Islamic law, *muḍārabah* operates as a two-party contract, with the agent-entrepreneur endeavoring to make money entrusted to him by the owner of capital. The arrangements of a modern Western bank, in contradistinction, involve as a matter of course three parties: the depositors, the bank, and the borrowers. The answers of present-day Islamic banks, although based in theory on the idea of *muḍārabah*, have to accommodate the original two-party contract of *muḍārabah* to the three parties. They sever the tripartite relationship by fictitiously considering the arrangement as consisting of a double contract entered into by the bank on the one hand and the depositor and the borrower on the other as separate parties. In the first contract, the depositor would be the owner of capital, and the bank the agent-entrepreneur. In the second contract, the bank would be the owner of capital, and the borrower the agent-entrepreneur.

Ṣadr has a more original and elaborate scheme in *Al-bank al-lā-ribawī*: he considers the bank to actually be only a mediator in a single *muḍārabah* contract between the pool of depositors and the pool of entrepreneurs. He goes on to elaborate the rights and duties of each of the three parties and to provide interesting, if not altogether convincing, arithmetic formulas to assess the rate of profit and the resulting shares in the profits and losses of the three parties to the arrangement.

Beyond the rearrangements of contracts to avoid interest, the problem facing theoreticians and practitioners of Islamic banking can be summed up in the crucial question of whether a bank can refuse to tie itself down to a fixed interest rate offered to its depositors while guaranteeing the safety of these deposits. For present-day Islamic banks, the answer is generally negative. Guarantees on deposits cannot be offered, as the bank operates on the basis of a partnership for profit and loss. Ṣadr, in the main, embraces this idea, although he seems to be inclined to acknowledge, in a treatise written ten years after his *Al-bank al-lā-ribawī*, the necessity of preserving the depositor's capital, even if the venture it is used for fails.

A third area of innovation in Ṣadr's thought is related to the concept of an Islamic state: How would the constitution of such a state be conceived in theory and practice? Here, the influence of Ṣadr on the Iranian Revolution is remarkable, and there is an identifiable link between his 1979 treatise on the subject and the constitution ratified in the Islamic Republic of Iran a few months later.

The thrust of Ṣadr's idea is a two-tiered separation of powers, and in the Iranian constitution onto the traditional separation of powers between the three branches of government (executive, legislative, and judicial) was grafted an Islamic scheme that combines features of Shīʿī scholarship and the representation of the Platonic figure of the philosopher-king in the form of a jurist. The guardian of the city became the classical *faqīh* (jurisprudent), hence the concept of *vilāyat-i faqīh* (guardianship of the jurisconsult), which Ayatollah Ruhollah Khomeini (1902–1989) had outlined in his Najaf classes of 1970 and which was brought into a more precise constitutional rendering by Ṣadr in 1979. As for the Shīʿī imprint, it was obvious in the remodeling of the elaborate Marjaʿīyah system in modern Shīʿī society, which grants a power of broad guidance to the most learned jurists of the tradition. These are called *marjaʿs* (lit., reference) represented by the top *mujtahids* (those who practice *ijtihād*) or *ʿulamāʾ* (scholars) in the clerical system known for this reason as Marjaʿīyah. In the Western world, the better-known word for *marjaʿ* is "ayatollah" (Ar. *āyat Allāh*).

But whether in Ṣadr's system or in the Iranian constitution, the power of the ayatollahs in the Islamic state stood alongside more Western-type offices, such as a president and parliamentarians who are elected under universal suffrage. The Iranian system has struggled with the two-tiered separation of powers since its inception, although the inevitable tug-of-war had been best described on the eve of the revolution by Muḥammad Bāqir al-Ṣadr.

Political Leadership. Considering the influence of his ideas in the Shīʿī milieu at large, it is not surprising to see Ṣadr in 1979–1980 being referred to as the "Khomeini of Iraq." The sobriquet came about as the result of a slow assertion of his leadership, first on the scholarly level and then directly on the political scene.

Ṣadr, who was born in 1935, showed early signs of intellectual superiority. His father, who died when Ṣadr was very young, was, like his older brother and uncles, versed in traditional legal scholarship. Ṣadr grew up in the southern Iraqi holy city of Najaf in an Iraq that was witnessing a combination of mistrust of a system perceived as corrupt and prone to Western influence and domination and a sharp rise in radical doctrines, most remarkably Baʿthism and communism.

It is because of this tidal wave of communism that the *ʿulamāʾ* of Najaf, Ṣadr's seniors, were most exercised when the monarchy was overturned in 1958. But it was the Baʿth Party that proved to be their worst nemesis. Ṣadr had countered the communist appeal by trying to expound a rational Islamic system, including such arcane topics as philosophy, banking, and economics. His more direct political appeal can be traced back to the early and mid-1960s, among small circles of militant *ʿulamāʾ* who proved extremely influential across the Shīʿī world in the 1980s. With the accession of the Baʿth party of Aḥmad Ḥasan al-Bakr and Saddam Hussein to power in the summer of 1968, the relatively sheltered world of the schools of law and *ʿulamāʾ* in Najaf came under direct attack by a massive system of absolute repression that was combined with an increased "Sunnization" of the regime in Baghdad. This repression culminated inside Iraq in 1980 in the execution of Ṣadr and his sister and outside Iraq in an all-out war against Iran.

The development of the antagonism between Saddam Hussein's Baghdad and Muḥammad Bāqir al-Ṣadr's Najaf between 1968 and 1980 has yet to be fully chronicled, but the occasion of ʿĀshūrāʾ (the yearly day of mourning for the martyrdom of Imam Ḥusayn in 680) often proved to be violent. Especially in 1974 and in 1977, and more abruptly after the accession of Khomeini to power in February 1979, the antagonism flared up in full-fledged rioting. It was reported that already during the 1977 riots, the security agents of the Baʿthist government would question those detained about their relationship with Ṣadr. Later, after Ṣadr was clearly turning into a major threat to the government, the rulers of Iraq moved directly to curb his activities and influence.

Ṣadr was arrested several times through the 1970s, but in June 1979, as he was reportedly getting ready to lead an Iraqi delegation to congratulate Khomeini in Tehran, he was forbidden to leave his home in Najaf. The tension continued to rise, until grenade attacks against leading Baʿthists in Baghdad led to the removal of Ṣadr from Najaf on the evening of 5 April 1980. He and his sister Bint al-Hudā were taken to Baghdad, where they are believed to have been killed on 8 April.

In the last years of his life, Ṣadr had tried to take advantage of the Shīʿī network to strengthen his appeal, but the organization was not effectively structured, and the government had been alerted by the success of the Iranian precedent. But his death marked the real beginning of the spread of his influence across the Middle East, in the midst of a confrontation between Tehran and Baghdad that turned into the bloodiest war in the Middle East of the twentieth century.

In Iran, the debates on constitutional law and economics and banking bore the mark of Ṣadr's reasoning. In Iraq, Pakistan, and Lebanon, the Najaf network of Ṣadr's companions and students produced several leaders whom the Shīʿī community looked up to. But the intellectual influence of Ṣadr can also be seen in other areas of the Middle East, where his thought was received despite the skepticism of the Sunnī world toward Shīʿī legal scholarship. In Egypt and Jordan, his books were taught in universities, and critical works were published. In Algeria, where the Islamic movement lacked an original thinker to rest its views on, *Iqtiṣādunā*'s concepts could be found in the literature of the Front Islamique du Salut (FIS).

It is in Iraq, however, that Ṣadr will be best remembered. For a few days after the Gulf War, in March 1991, as Najaf was freed from Baʿthist rule,

Ṣadr's pictures were paraded in his native city. The government of Saddam Hussein brutally regained control immediately afterward. But whatever the future of central rule in Baghdad, it is only a matter of time before Ṣadr gains the respect of all Iraqis for a legacy with which they may or may not agree from an ideological point of view but that must be acknowledged as formidable in modern Islamic thought.

[*See also* Iraq.]

BIBLIOGRAPHY

Works by al-Ṣadr

Al-bank al-lā-ribawī fī al-Islām. 8th ed. Beirut: Dār al-Taʿāruf, 1983. Ṣadr's book on the structure of an interest-free bank. First published 1969.

Falsafatunā. 10th ed. Beirut: Dār al-Taʿāruf, 1980. Translated by Shams C. Inati as *Our Philosophy* (London: Routledge & Kegan Paul, 1987). First published 1959.

Iqtiṣādunā. Rev. ed. Beirut: Dār al-Kitāb al-Lubnānī, 1977. First published 1959–1961. Available in English as *Our Economics*, 2 vols. (Tehran, 1982–1984), but a better translation of the most important sections of the text was serialized as "The Islamic Economy, I–VII," in the Shīʿī journal *al-Sirat* from 1981 to 1985.

Khilāfat al-insān wa-shahādat al-anbiyāʾ and *Lamḥah fiqhīyah tamhīdīyah ʿan mashrūʿ dustūr al-jumhūrīyah al-islāmīyah fī Īrān*. Beirut: Dār al-Taʿāruf, 1979. Constitutional pamphlets.

Lessons in Islamic Jurisprudence. Translated by Roy Parviz Mottahedeh. Rev. ed. Oxford: OneWorld, 2005.

Al-majmūʿah al-kāmilah li-muʾallafāt al-Sayyid Muḥammad Bāqir al-Ṣadr. 15 vols. Beirut: Dār al-Taʿāruf, 1980– . Ṣadr's collected works.

Secondary Sources

Mallat, Chibli. *The Renewal of Islamic Law: Muhammad Baqer as-Sadr, Najaf, and the Shiʿi International*. Rev. ed. New York: Cambridge University Press, 2004.

Ṣadr, Muḥammad Bāqir al-. *Unsere Wirtschaft: Eine gekürzte kommentierte Übersetzung des Buches Iqtiṣādunā von Muḥammad Bāqir aṣ-Ṣadr*. Translated by Andreas Rieck. Berlin: K. Schwarz, 1984. German translation of *Iqtiṣādunā*, which includes a good introduction by Rieck.

CHIBLI MALLAT

ṢADR, MŪSĀ AL-. Born in Qom, Iran, on 15 May 1928, the son of Ayatollah Ṣadr al-Dīn al-Ṣadr, one of Lebanon's most prominent *mujtahids* (qualified theologians empowered to render independent legal interpretations). Originally from Tyre (Ṣūr), his father moved to Qom to study in one of Shīʿah Islam's most renowned centers of learning, where the young Mūsā attended primary and secondary school. Although he was thoroughly familiar with seminary life, and was repeatedly prodded to follow in his illustrious father's footsteps, Mūsā matriculated in the School of Political Economy and Law at Teheran University in 1948. At the time, he was not particularly interested in becoming a cleric but changed his mind after his father fell ill, and he returned to Qom to study Islamic jurisprudence. Ayatollah Ṣadr al-Dīn al-Ṣadr died in 1953, and Mūsā moved to Najaf, Iraq, in 1954 to continue his religious education with ayatollahs Muḥsin al-Ḥakīm and Abol-Qāsem al-Khoʾi.

Mūsā al-Ṣadr first set foot in Lebanon in 1957, where he met distant relatives and several Tyre officials, including a cousin, Sayyid ʿAbd al-Ḥusayn Sharaf al-Dīn, then a prominent Shīʿah official. After Sharaf al-Dīn died in 1958, and on the strong recommendation of his mentor Muḥsin al-Ḥakīm, Mūsā was invited to accept Tyre's vacant position, which he filled in 1960. He was granted Lebanese citizenship by presidential decree in 1963, a rare and extremely complicated procedure that required simultaneous signatures from the president of the republic (Fuʾad Shihāb [Maronite]), the Speaker of Parliament (Sabri Hamadé [Shīʿah]), and the prime minister (Rashid

Karami [Sunnī]]. In 1969 he was appointed the first head of the Supreme Islamic Shīʿah Council, a political entity that wished to secure Shīʿah positions in the state, especially after Palestinian fighters flocked to Lebanon in the aftermath of both the 1967 Six-Day War and the 1970 Jordanian massacres. Although al-Ṣadr warned of the dangers of Israeli aggression against Lebanon, he was equally preoccupied with the dangers that armed Palestinians posed to the fragile state, which prompted him to forge even closer ties across sectarian lines. In 1971, for example, he established a joint Muslim/Christian coalition of all southern spiritual leaders to direct critical political and social activities that affected ordinary peoples' lives.

Al-Ṣadr and six companions departed for Libya in August 1978, ostensibly to meet with senior officials there, but were never heard from again. More than thirty years after their probable assassinations and even after the fall of the Muʿammar al-Qadhdhāfī regime in September 2011, it was still unclear what motivated the party to travel to Libya and what exactly happened in the Libyan capital. Some Lebanese Shīʿahs believed that, as unlikely as it was, Sadr remained secretly in jail in Libya, which meant that the disappearance blocked any reconciliation between Beirut and Tripoli. In the event, his disappearance transformed Mūsā al-Ṣadr into a legendary martyr.

Political Awakening. Mūsā al-Ṣadr was widely perceived as a moderate religious figure who demanded that the two historically dominant religious communities in Lebanon, the Maronites and the Sunnīs, relinquish some of their power to create a more equitable system. Toward that end, he pursued ecumenism and peaceful relations among all Lebanese, and though he was a vocal opponent of Israel, he insisted that the Lebanese put their country—not their religious affiliation—first. According to an eminent biographer who authored a pioneering study on the Shīʿah, the Imam, as Mūsā al-Ṣadr came to be known, often noted: "For us Lebanon is one definitive homeland" (Norton, 1987, p. 144). He never contemplated a coup d'état against Beirut and rejected any suggestions that the Shīʿahs' growing numerical strength should grant them unconstitutional privileges, simply because he understood that each community added value to the whole.

This ambitious individual, who mastered several languages and was a prominent intellectual, was a reformer who worked tirelessly to improve the people's standard of living. Although his Iranian birth confused some and raised doubts about his "nationality," Mūsā al-Ṣadr understood that Lebanese Shīʿahs needed fellow Sunnīs and Christians, because they were Lebanese and Arabs first, not Persians. A physically imposing man, al-Ṣadr won over not only his Shīʿah constituency but also many of Lebanon's cosmopolitan non-Shīʿah citizens. Most succumbed to his intellectual charm and welcomed the opportunities to contribute financially to his sorely needed vocational institutions. In Tyre, al-Ṣadr first witnessed the economic injustices that prevailed and, with financial support from Shīʿah expatriate workers toiling in Africa throughout the 1940s and 1950s, founded the first of several vocational institutes to train unemployed youths. Resources were limited, but the charismatic cleric cajoled and persuaded many to donate to his various causes, hoping to penetrate and change the tightly controlled *zuʿamāʾ* system in place, which protected a privileged class under the authority of sectarian warlords.

Given his intrinsic capabilities and willingness to confront established patronage mechanisms that served the few, Mūsā al-Ṣadr made many enemies. Even if pragmatism defined his every move, the cleric clashed with Kamal al-Asaʿad, the immensely powerful Shīʿah political boss who became speaker of the parliament. Asaʿad quickly understood that the connected cleric could easily upset his entire power base and, conversely, Mūsā al-Ṣadr saw the *zaʿīm* as the epitome of what was wrong in Lebanon. Remarkably, the energetic cleric saw beyond the patronage system, including within his Shīʿah community, and developed a keen sense of nationalism. In successive speeches throughout the 1960s, Mūsā stood above intrinsic sectarian divisions, wishing to distance his supporters from victimization to focus on earned value.

In 1975 the Imam delivered a Lenten sermon at a Catholic church in Beirut, when he prayed:

> God, the God of Moses and Jesus and Muhammad, the God of the weak and of all creatures ... [thank you] for uniting our hearts with your love and mercy. We are assembled here today in a house of yours, at a time of fasting.... Our hearts yearn for you; our minds derive light and guidance from you.... We have come to your door, we have gathered together to serve man. It is man that all religions aspire to serve.... All religions were once united; they anticipated one another; they validated one another. They called man to God and they served man. The then different religions diverged when each sought to serve itself, to pay excessive attention to itself to the point that each religion forgot the original purpose—the service of man. Then discord and strife were born, and the crisis of man deepened. (Ajami, 1986, p. 134)

Like most naturalized citizens, al-Ṣadr developed a love of country that was taken for granted by native-born nationals, and while a deeply spiritual individual, the cleric knew enough about religion to understand its manipulative features.

The Amal Party. As Baʿthism flourished among impoverished Shīʿahs, al-Ṣadr appropriated leftist slogans to mobilize his flock in what became on 18 March 1974 the Ḥarakat al-Maḥrūmīn (Movement of the Disinherited), a popular mass association that pressed for better economic and social conditions. A series of demonstrations against Beirut's neglect of rural areas were well attended as the Palestinians simultaneously enhanced their presence in Lebanon.

After 1970 Mūsā al-Ṣadr warned the Palestine Liberation Organization not to establish a state within the state and vehemently opposed the 1969 Cairo Accords that granted Palestine Liberation Organization (PLO) fighters exceptional rights in Lebanon. In just a few years, "natural allies" (neglected Shīʿahs and disenfranchised Palestinians) became bitter enemies, especially since PLO leaders, including Chairman Yasir Arafat, mistakenly concluded that the Imam was on the army's payroll as a spy. As anticipated by Mūsā al-Ṣadr, Lebanon plunged into its protracted civil war in 1975, which prompted him to seek to prevent full-scale violence. Out of necessity, he first aligned himself with the Lebanese National Movement (LNM), the leftist Druze militia, but quickly concluded that Kamal Jumblatt was exploiting the Shīʿah. Reportedly, he once noted that the LNM was willing "to combat the Christians to the last Shīʿah," and implied that Jumblatt was responsible for the prolongation of the war. The two men fell out, and al-Ṣadr established the Afwāj al-Muqawāmah al-Lubnānīyah (Lebanese Resistance Detachments), better known by the acronym Amal (which also means "hope"). While Amal militiamen were trained by Palestinians and aligned themselves with the PLO and other leftist groups until 1976, Mūsā al-Ṣadr pulled his Amal forces out of the coalition, after Syria intervened in June 1976 to prevent the defeat of the Maronite-dominated Lebanese Front.

While Mūsā al-Ṣadr was a friend and confidant of President Hafez al-Assad, he mistrusted Syrian motives in Lebanon, and, unlike several successors, never depended on Damascus. In fact, four months before Syria dispatched troops to Lebanon, al-Ṣadr participated in critical discussions with Lebanese president Suleiman Frangiyeh over an updated constitution. The nascent framework redefined the prerogatives of the head of state, allocated new powers to the prime minister, and called for an increase in the proportion of Muslim parliamentary seats. It was this document that formed the basis of the 1989 Ṭā'if Accord, which updated the constitution and was approved by Imam Mūsā al-Ṣadr. Revisionist historians have neglected to mention that al-Ṣadr wished to implement a Lebanese solution to the country's problems, although Syria was by then a privileged interlocutor, having become well entrenched in internal Lebanese affairs. The many assassinations of major political figures, including Kamal Jumblatt and Rachid Karami, as well as the disappearance of Imam Mūsā al-Ṣadr thus served the interests of supranational elements along with emerging Shīʿah lieutenants who wished to restore a weakened patronage system under Syrian protection.

Legacy and Impact on Lebanon. One of al-Ṣadr's most remarkable attributes was his outreach to Lebanon's Christian communities, whose undeniable contributions transformed the country into a sophisticated and cosmopolitan society. To further enhance religious tolerance and coexistence, he cofounded, with the Maronite archbishop Grégoire Haddad, a spiritual gathering known as the Social Movement in 1960. For the next few years, al-Ṣadr participated in Muslim-Christian dialogues, going so far as to lecture in several churches during Easter services. When former president of the republic Charles Helou introduced Mūsā al-Ṣadr to a group of Catholic worshippers gathered for an ecumenical service in 1975, he declared that believers were gathered "to hear the word of God from a non-Catholic religious guide." "It is only natural that Lebanon is the country in which this deed is taking place" (Ajami, 1986, p. 134), chimed the erudite Helou, which was an acknowledgment of al-Ṣadr's intellectual and spiritual capacities. As the excerpts from the speech quoted above illustrate, his entreaty's Christian tone was unmistakable, in "homage to Christ as an apostle of the weak and the oppressed, the preaching against 'love of the self.'" Indeed, the declaration had "that tone of deliberation and calm that [was] so much a mark of Catholicism and its ritual" (Ajami, 1986, p. 134).

This was the legacy of this visionary imam. Mūsā al-Ṣadr managed to focus the Shīʿah plight through the lens of justice. His slight Persian accent notwithstanding, al-Ṣadr managed to be viewed as a genuinely spiritual leader of all Lebanese, including Christians, a feat that has not been duplicated since. At a time when martyrs proliferated the Middle East, the "vanished imam" gave Lebanon much more than a party, which evolved in a direction he rejected. He left Beirut persuaded that national unity would be attainable when everyone believed in a just country where institutions were upheld, and all strove to defeat poverty and ignorance.

BIBLIOGRAPHY

Ajami, Fouad. *The Vanished Imam: Musa al Sadr and the Shia of Lebanon*. Ithaca, N.Y.: Cornell University Press, 1986.

Halawi, Majed. *A Lebanon Defied: Musa al-Sadr and the Shiʿa Community*. Boulder, Colo.: Westview, 1992.

Miri, Seyed Javad. *Reflections on the Philosophy of Imam Musa Sadr*. Bloomington, Ind.: Xlibris, 2007.

Norton, Augustus Richard. *Amal and the Shiʿa: Struggle for the Soul of Lebanon*. Austin: University of Texas Press, 1987.

Shaery-Eiselohr, Roschanack. *Shiʿite Lebanon: Transnational Religion and the Making of National Identities*. New York: Columbia University Press, 2008.

Theroux, Peter. *The Strange Disappearance of Imam Moussa Sadr*. London: Weidenfeld & Nicolson, 1987.

JOSEPH A. KÉCHICHIAN

ṢAFAVID DYNASTY. The Ṣafavid dynasty ruled Iran from 1501 to 1722. That period formed a bridge between Iran as a premodern society and the emergence of a country with global connections and the attributes of the modern nation-state. The Ṣafavid period included the beginning of frequent and sustained diplomatic and commercial interactions between Iran and Europe. Most importantly, the Ṣafavids introduced a concept of patrimonial kingship, combining territorial authority with religious legitimacy that, with modifications, would endure until the twentieth century. The political system that emerged under them had overlapping political and religious boundaries and a core language, Persian.

Of Kurdish ancestry, the Ṣafavids started as a mystical order centered in Ardabīl, Azerbaijan. Their religious beliefs were an intricate mixture of Christian, pre-Islamic Turkish, and Muslim cults and beliefs, centering on a messianic devotion to Imām ʿAlī and his family and a shah who was venerated as an incarnation of God. Instrumental in the evolution of the Ṣafavids were the Qizilbash, seminomadic Turkmen tribal groups who had migrated eastward from Syria and Anatolia.

The dynasty's political rule began with Ismāʿīl, the first of the Ṣafavid shahs, who in 1499 defeated his rivals and set out to wrest western Iran from the Ak-Koyunlu. Barely fifteen years old, Ismāʿīl in 1501 proclaimed himself shah in Tabrīz. He also declared Shiism the official faith of the realm, thus solidifying his own status as divinely appointed and endowing his new state with a strong ideological basis while giving Iran overlapping political and religious boundaries that would last until modern times. In the next decade, Ismāʿīl set out to subdue large parts of Iran, most notably Khorāsān and Iraq.

Ismāʿīl encountered his most formidable enemy in the Sunnī Ottomans, who felt threatened by the establishment of a militant Shīʿī state on their border and by its propaganda among their own Turkmen. Mutual vilification and pro-Ṣafavid rebellions in Anatolia led to war, which culminated in the Ṣafavid defeat at the battle of Chaldiran in 1514. The most dramatic outcome of this defeat was the doubt it cast on the invincibility and thus the divine aura of the Ṣafavid ruler, which led to the dynasty's search for different ideological moorings under Shah Ismāʿīl's successors.

Shāh Ismāʿīl died in 1524 and was succeeded by his ten-year-old son Ṭahmāsp. Shāh Ṭahmāsp extended his authority and influence over various areas that, under his father, had been buffer regions or vassal states, but he was less successful against the Ottomans. Provoked by the militantly anti-Sunnī Ṣafavids, the Ottomans invaded Iran three times between 1534 and 1554, taking Iraq and forcing the Iranians to move their capital from Tabrīz to Qazvīn.

Shāh Ṭahmāsp's reign was followed by that of two interim rulers, Ismāʿīl II, known as much for his erratic, cruel behavior as for his Sunnī leanings, and the purblind, feeble Shāh Khudābanda. The resulting weakness led to renewed Qizilbash revolts and the Ottoman annexation of Iran's northwestern territories. A turning point came with the rule of Shāh ʿAbbās I (r. 1587–1629). Universally seen as the greatest Ṣafavid ruler, he oversaw a crucial phase in the evolution of Ṣafavid Iran, from a steppe polity to a (quasi-)bureaucratic state. Shāh ʿAbbās was above all an outstanding strategist, keen to regain the territories that had been lost to enemy forces or internal sedition. Lacking the resources to fight on two fronts at once, he initially concluded a disadvantageous peace with the Ottomans in order to take on the Uzbeks and regain Khorāsān. He also took Qandahār, established control over the Caspian provinces, and extended Ṣafavid authority to the Persian Gulf, eventually ousting the Portuguese from Hormuz. He reestablished Ṣafavid control over Iraq in the same period.

Dynasty

1501	Ismāʿīl I
1524	Ṭahmāsp I
1576	Ismāʿīl II
1588	ʿAbbās I
1629	Ṣafī I
1642	ʿAbbās II
1666	Sulaymān
1694	Ḥusayn I
1722	Ṭahmāsp II
1732	ʿAbbās III

Securing Iran's borders was intimately linked to the shah's main objective—maximizing personal control and centralizing power. To this end, Shāh ʿAbbās embarked on a series of internal reforms designed to break the power of the Qizilbash.

Conventional wisdom portrays Shāh ʿAbbās's death, in 1629, as the beginning of Ṣafavid decline. There is no question that, even though the country appeared relatively stable for the next few decades, its resource base grew weaker and the quality of its leadership deteriorated. This is in part attributable to the inherently fragile economic base of Iran and to some of Shāh ʿAbbās's policies. In 1638 the Ṣafavids bowed to Ottoman military supremacy and concluded a definitive peace with Istanbul, giving up Iraq.

Shāh ʿAbbās's immediate successors, Shāh Ṣafī (r. 1629–1642) and ʿAbbās II (1642–1666), continued to be roving warriors, keen to quell tribal revolts and resist external aggression. This changed with Sulaymān (r. 1666–1694) and Sulṭān Ḥusayn (r. 1694–1722). Both reigned as stationary monarchs who, aside from occasional hunting parties and pilgrimage journeys, preferred to live within the confines of the palace, invisible to all but the most intimate of courtiers. Under these weak rulers, factionalism, endemic to the system, spun out of control and paralyzed decision making. The last third of the seventeenth century saw economic retrenchment, most strikingly reflected in a fall in agricultural output and growing numbers of bankruptcies among merchants. The flow of precious metals from Ottoman lands decreased and led to the closing of numerous mints and to a deteriorating currency.

By the time Sulṭān Ḥusayn ascended the throne in 1694, the Ṣafavid polity, once driven by millenarian energy, had lost its ideological direction. Exceedingly pious and impressionable, Sulṭān Ḥusayn lacked the requisite fortitude to inspire both loyalty and fear. The attendant religious and fiscal policy alienated many groups, among them the country's large Sunnī population, which was concentrated near the exposed borders. Armenians, a group with a disproportionately large role in the economy, reacted to the increasing fiscal burden by leaving the country in growing numbers.

Even as the peace with the Ottomans endured, outside threats multiplied at the turn of the eighteenth century. Outward domestic stability began to deteriorate as well. Sulṭān Ḥusayn organized a military campaign in 1718, but problems with the recruitment and payment of soldiers doomed the effort, and even the decision to have the gold from Shīʿī shrines minted into coins failed to yield the requisite funds.

The decisive blow came from the east and had its origins in the brutal repression of the population of Qandahār by the local Georgian governor, fueling rebellion by the Ghilzai Afghans. In 1721 their leader, Maḥmūd, took Kermān, where he was welcomed by the hard-pressed Zoroastrian population. Moving on to Isfahan, the Afghans were even encouraged by members of the Qizilbash embittered about the Georgians and the high positions they had concentrated in their hands. After defeating a hastily assembled Ṣafavid (Georgian) army near Isfahan, the Afghans took the suburbs and, unable to breach the city walls, resorted to a siege. After six months, starvation brought the city down, and Sulṭān Ḥusayn in

October 1722 submitted to Maḥmūd, conferring on him the title of shah. As the Ṣafavid regime crumbled, both the Ottomans and the Russians took advantage of Iran's weakened state to invade the north and northwest.

[*See also* Iran, Islamic Republic of.]

BIBLIOGRAPHY

Aubin, Jean. "L'avènement des Safavides reconsidéré." *Moyen Orient et Océan Indien* 5 (1988): 1–130.

Babaie, Sussan, Kathryn Babayan, Ina Baghdiantz, et al. *Slaves of the Shah: New Elites of Safavid Iran.* London: I. B. Tauris, 2004.

Babayan, Kathryn. *Mystics, Monarchs, and Messiahs: Cultural Landscapes of Early Modern Iran.* Cambridge, Mass.: Harvard University Press, 2003.

Bacqué-Grammont, Jean-Louis. *Les Ottomans, les Safavides et leurs voisins: Contribution à l'histoire des relations internationales dans l'Orient Islamique de 1514 à 1524.* Istanbul: Nederlands Historisch-Archaeologisch Instituut te Istanbul, 1987.

Calmard, Jean, ed. *Études Safavides.* Paris: Institut Français de Recherche en Iran, 1993.

Floor, Willem. *The Economy of Safavid Persia.* Wiesbaden, Germany: Reichert, 2000.

Floor, Willem. *Safavid Government Institutions.* Costa Mesa, Calif.: Mazda, 2001.

Jackson, Peter, and Laurence Lockhart, eds. *The Cambridge History of Iran.* Vol. 6, *The Timurid and Safavid Periods.* Cambridge, U.K.: Cambridge University Press, 1986.

Lockhart, Laurence. *The Fall of the Ṣafavī Dynasty and the Afghan Occupation of Persia.* Cambridge, U.K.: Cambridge University Press, 1958.

Matthee, Rudi. *The Pursuit of Pleasure: Drugs and Stimulants in Iranian History, 1500–1900.* Princeton, N.J.: Princeton University Press, 2005.

Matthee, Rudolph P. *The Politics of Trade in Safavid Iran: Silk for Silver, 1600–1730.* Cambridge, U.K.: Cambridge University Press, 1999.

Mazzaoui, Michel, ed. *Safavid Iran and Her Neighbors.* Salt Lake City: University of Utah Press, 2003.

Melville, Charles, ed. *Safavid Persia: The History and Politics of an Islamic Society.* London: I. B. Tauris, 1996.

Newman, Andrew J. *Safavid Iran: Rebirth of a Persian Empire.* London: I. B. Tauris, 2006.

Newman, Andrew J., ed. *Society and Culture in the Early Modern Middle East: Studies on Iran in the Safavid Period.* Leiden, Netherlands: Brill, 2003.

Savory, Roger. *Iran under the Safavids.* Cambridge, U.K.: Cambridge University Press, 1980.

Savory, Roger. *Studies on the History of Ṣafawid Iran.* London: Variorum, 1987.

Biancamaria Scarcia Amoretti
Updated by Rudi Matthee
and Khaled M. G. Keshk

Salafī Movements. In its simplest definition, Salafism is Islam as understood and practiced by the *salaf,* the forefathers of the Muslim community. While it is true that any Muslim can claim that his understanding of Islam is based on its spirit as understood by the *salaf,* Salafīs are generally distinguished by their strict adherence to the practice of the *salaf* and their "literal" understanding of the foundational texts of Islam. According to a statement attributed to the Prophet Muḥammad, the best of Muslims were the first three generations of the Muslim community, namely, the Companions of the Prophet Muḥammad, their followers (the Successors), and the followers of their followers. Thus, unlike those who seek to understand Islam by direct reference to the transmitted foundational religious texts (i.e., the Qurʾān and the *ḥadīth*), Salafism proceeds on the assumption that the earliest Muslim generations were in a much better position than later generations to interpret these religious texts and safeguard the true Islam from corruption. These generations practiced pristine Islam; later, Islam was adulterated by alien cultures that Islam was meant to subvert rather than be influenced by. In holding this view about the first three Muslim generations, Salafīs can exercise more freedom in critiquing and rejecting views held by later generations, but can also disregard the historical context of the early generations and sidestep the fact that an indefinite number of conflicting views on many religious issues were attributed to them. And while these conflicting views can be taken to indicate that disagreement in religious issues is not un-Islamic, Salafīs generally tend either to seek to synthesize conflicting views attributed to these generations—at times ingeniously, as done by the Ḥanbalī scholar Taqī al-Dīn Ibn Taymīyah (d. 1328), who is, together with Aḥmad ibn Ḥanbal (d. 855) and Ibn Qayyim al-Jawzīyah (d. 1350), the most esteemed scholar for the Salafīs—through the exercise of reasoning or selectively rely on some of them to present their own, often one-sided, views of Islam as the correct, original understanding of Islam. Because of this selectivity, generalizations about Salafī movements do not always do justice to the diversity that characterizes their religious views and, consequently, political persuasions. Other factors in this diversity are the regional, social, and religious settings in which Salafī movements operate and their understanding of these settings. For example, whereas Salafism in some parts of the Muslim world is concerned with demarcating sharp lines between Sunnī and Shīʿī Islam or between Muslims and non-Muslims, Salafīs in other parts are more preoccupied with combating mystical forms of Islam (Sufism) or the contamination of Islam with alien "modern" cultural influences. Because of this diversity, it is not surprising that Salafī groups, each one seeing itself as the guardian of true religion, accuse each other of deviating from the true path of Islam, for they all agree that the cultural context does not and should not play a role in the understanding and practice of Islam, and, despite some exceptions, do not therefore accept diversity and disagreement.

Salafīs thus do not distinguish between the religious texts and how they were interpreted by the earliest Muslim generations. Understood in these terms, Salafism is as old as Islam itself. The Arab culture in which Islam arose venerated "traditional" views, such that the Prophet's message was rejected for its incompatibility with the views of the forefathers of the Arabs. Medieval scholars, therefore, would call someone Salafī who was not an innovator (*mubtadiʿ*) in religious matters and whose understanding of Islam was similar to those of the *salaf*. This uncritical approach toward the *salaf* has led Salafī movements to disregard the historical context; the acts of earlier generations are eternally valid regardless of the environment and culture in which they lived. For example, following what they believe was the appearance of early Muslims, Salafīs can be identified in some parts of the Muslim world by their relatively short white garments and usually untrimmed beards (and head and face covering for women), unlike many non-Salafī Islamist groups who cannot be distinguished easily on the basis of their outfit (they simply wear either traditional national or local clothes or even Western-style attire).

The origin of modern Salafī movements is usually traced to the rise of Wahhabism—named after Muḥammad ibn ʿAbd al-Wahhāb (d. 1792) and regarded by Salafīs and some non-Salafīs as a reform movement that sought to purge Islam of alien cultural elements—in Arabia in the second half of the eighteenth century CE. Saudi Arabia has been the stronghold of Salafism since the early twentieth century, and it has played a pivotal role in spreading a Salafī vision of Islam through the publication and dissemination of important medieval and modern religious works that Salafīs cherish. Salafīs from various parts of the Muslim world were given jobs in Saudi educational and legal institutions, which also led to diversity and conflict on the Salafī scene in Saudi Arabia, especially after the first Gulf War in 1991. Some scholars believe that it was Wahhabism, with its "inflexible" interpretation of Islamic law and the institutionalization of "moral" policy to enforce Islamic moral and dress codes in society, that has earned Salafism the reputation of being a backward, ultraconservative social and political movement. Like Wahhabism, Salafī movements in other parts of the Muslim world that stressed the purity of the Islamic creed and the authenticity of its ritual practices, and showed great interest in studying reports about the way the Prophet Muḥammad and the first Muslim generations led their lives, are also seen as prototypes of modern Salafī movements, such as the Ahl-i Ḥadīth in the Indian subcontinent.

While Salafī views have the potential to be radicalized, and despite the fact that there are Salafī movements that are militant in nature (known as jihādist Salafīs, involved in "holy war" against foreign powers and their domestic allies in various parts of the Muslim world), Salafīs typically adopt a quietist approach that can put them in conflict with other Islamist groups (for instance, Salafīs are reportedly suppressed in the Gaza strip by Ḥamās, a Muslim Brotherhood group). It has been rightly pointed out that the term "Salafī" is a religious rather than a political term, for which reason it says little about the political views of Salafī individuals or groups or their position on whether and how to take part in politics. However, rather than resorting to violence or participating in the electoral process (which some of them do, while others reject it, believing that democracy and Islam are incompatible) to establish a state that rules according to their understanding of Islam, Salafīs typically focus on spreading their views by peaceful, quiet preaching, mostly in mosques that they build and fund, and, when possible, try to correct what they regard as religious wrongs by available means (which could be violent, if the use of violence does not lead to a greater evil). In fact, during the wave of political unrest that took place in many Arab countries in 2011, Salafī scholars were vocal in opposing popular demonstrations against Arab regimes, following in the footsteps of some early religious authorities who preached political quietism and obedience to Muslim rulers, including those not ruling according to the teachings of Islam, to avoid schism and bloodshed. In Egypt, this quietism led them to approve President Mubarak's plans to transfer power to his son a few years before his downfall by a popular uprising in 2011; hereditary rule, after all, was tolerated by the early Muslim generations when it was instituted some thirty years after the death of the Prophet Muḥammad.

Salafī movements almost certainly exist in all Muslim and some non-Muslim countries. While we do not possess enough data on their popularity in different societies, we can identify some factors that contribute to it. Due to their quietism, Salafī groups are in a much better position to be tolerated by ruling regimes than other Islamist groups and are therefore favorite options for Islamists unwilling to clash with their societies. However, they are definitely less favorable for the jihādi-minded Islamists who believe in the inevitability of violent overthrow of "un-Islamic" regimes that rule Muslim countries, or those willing to work for the gradual establishment of the Islamic state through participation in political life (like the Muslim Brotherhood). The traditional animosity of the Salafīs toward all forms of institutional Ṣūfī and "popular" Islam, however, has put them at odds with the large segments of Muslim populations who often, for example, pay visits to the tombs of Ṣūfī saints and descendants of the Prophet Muḥammad, a practice that Salafīs regard as tantamount to idolatry. Therefore, the presence and influence of Salafī movements as political actors depend to a large extent on the views of each movement and the social, political, and religious contexts in which it operates.

BIBLIOGRAPHY

ʿAbbāsī, Muḥammad ʿĪd. *Al-daʿwah al-salafīyah wa-mawqifuhā min al-ḥarakat al-ukhrā*. Alexandria:

Dār al-Īmān, 2002. With a commentary by Nāṣir al-Dīn al-Albānī.

Egerton, Frazer. *Jihad in the West: The Rise of Militant Salafism*. Cambridge, U.K.: Cambridge University Press, 2011.

Meijer, Roel. *Global Salafism: Islam's New Religious Movement*. New York: Columbia University Press, 2009.

Metcalf, Barbara Daly. "Alternative Tendencies within Sunni Islam: The Ahl-i Hadis and the Barelwis." In *Islamic Revival in British India: Deoband, 1860–1900*. Princeton, N.J.: Princeton University Press, 1982.

ʿUthmān, Muḥammad Fatḥī. *Al-salafiyah fī al-mujtamaʿāt al-muʿāṣirah*. Kuwait: Dār al-Qalam, 1993.

Wiktorowicz, Quintan. "Anatomy of the Salafi Movement." *Studies in Conflict and Terrorism* 29 (2006): 207–239.

Amr Osman

SALVATION. *See* Religious Beliefs.

SANHŪRĪ, ʿABD AL-RAZZĀQ AL-. (1895–1971), an Egyptian jurist, legal scholar, and architect of civil codes in several Arab countries. The academic and professional life of Sanhūrī is a reflection of the time during which the need for legal reform arose. For some Muslim countries, this meant the codification and modernization of the *Sharīʿah*, and for others the replacement of imported legislation by national and Islamic laws. Sanhūrī drafted the modern civil codes of various Arab countries and attempted to reinvigorate the *Sharīʿah* in light of contemporary legal developments and to incorporate it into the study of comparative jurisprudence.

Born in Alexandria, Egypt, in 1895, al-Sanhūrī received a modern education and graduated from the Khedevial School of Law in Cairo in 1917. He was appointed assistant prosecuting attorney and by 1920 had joined the School of Sharīʿah Judges as a lecturer. The following year he went to France for postgraduate studies. He wrote two theses, *Les restrictions contractuelle à la liberté individuelle de travail dans la jurisprudence anglaise* and *Le califat*, obtaining dual doctorates in law and political science from the University of Lyon. He was also awarded a diploma from the Institut des Hautes Études Internationales in Paris.

In 1926 al-Sanhūrī returned to Egypt and began teaching civil law at the Law School, where he became dean a decade later. His involvement in politics led to his dismissal in 1936. He then served as dean of the law college in Baghdad and began drafting the Iraqi civil code. Al-Sanhūrī went back to Egypt in 1937 and served in various cabinet posts, becoming president of the Council of State in 1949.

He supported the movement of the Free Officers in 1952, and in his capacity as president of the council he provided the legal advisory opinion that gave a constitutional basis to the Revolutionary Command Council's (RCC) exercise of power. Following a falling out among RCC members, al-Sanhūrī was ousted from the Council of State in 1954 and was later deprived of his political rights. He devoted the rest of his life to teaching, research, and writing.

Sanhūrī articulated his theoretical approach of legal reform in *Le califat: Son évolution vers une société des nations orientales* (Paris, 1926). Unlike ʿAlī ʿAbd al-Rāziq, who claimed that political authority was not an integral part of Islam, al-Sanhūrī considered the restoration of the Caliphate a necessity, signifying the unity of Muslims and the preservation of the law. To reflect prevailing conditions, he made a distinction between an irregular (temporary) and a regular caliphate. He proposed that the Caliphate develop into an "Eastern League of Nations," with the caliph presiding over a body exercising only religious authority until a similar body with executive functions could be established. The exercise of executive and legislative authority would be the prerogative of individual governments and heads of state.

The restoration of the regular Caliphate, al-Sanhūrī maintained, must be preceded by an evolution of Islamic law. Despite his genuine belief in the relevance and significance of the *Sharīʿah* to the judicial and social institutions of the Muslim world, he was more concerned with maintaining the stability of legal practices and relationships. In an effort to make legal reforms acceptable to all citizens, he differentiated the immutable and temporal parts of the *Sharīʿah* and claimed that only the variable rules of the temporal portion were subject to change. His proposed modernization of Islamic law would involve two phases. The first would be that of scientific research, during which the *Sharīʿah* would be thoroughly studied in light of modern comparative law. The second, the legislative phase, would include the gradual revision of existing codes. These new legislative reforms would take into account the historical, social, and legal experience of each country.

Al-Sanhūrī put these ideas into practice in the revisions of the Egyptian and Iraqi codes, enacted in 1949 and 1951, respectively. He selected provisions—Islamic or Western—according to their merit, but he often concluded that the *Sharīʿah* was more effective. In Egypt, where the existing code was based on foreign laws, he added provisions that made it more Islamic. In Iraq, however, the code was based largely on the Mecelle, and he introduced Western provisions that made it more modern. His final objective was a modern comparative legal system that would gradually come to emphasize Islamic rather than Western values and thus would become the basis for a unified Arab code.

Al-Sanhūrī was responsible for laying the foundation for modern legislation in the Arab world. The codes he drafted for Egypt and Iraq have become models for other countries: they were adopted with minor modifications by Syria, Libya, and Jordan. His voluminous work on civil codes and Islamic law remains the main reference for Islamic scholarship in comparative law and codification to this day.

BIBLIOGRAPHY

Arabi, Oussama. "Intention and Method in Sanhūrī's Fiqh: Cause as Ulterior Motive." *Islamic Law and Society* 4, no. 2 (1997): 200–223.

Arabi, Oussama. "Al-Sanhūrī's Reconstruction of the Islamic Law of Contract Defects." *Journal of Islamic Studies* 6, no. 2 (1995): 153–172.

Bechor, Guy. *The Sanhūrī Code, and the Emergence of Modern Arab Civil Law, 1932 to 1949*. Leiden: Brill, 2007.

Hill, Enid. "Islamic Law as a Source for the Development of a Comparative Jurisprudence, the 'Modern Science of Codification': Theory and Practice in the Life and Work of ʿAbd al-Razzāq Aḥmad al-Sanhūrī (1895–1971)." In *Islamic Law: Social and Historical Contexts*, edited by Aziz al-Azmeh, pp. 146–197. London: Routledge, 1988. Insightful analysis of al-Sanhūrī's contribution to codification and legal reform.

Hill, Enid. *Al-Sanhuri and Islamic Law: The Place and Significance of Islamic Law in the Life and Work of ʿAbd Al-Razzaq Aḥmad Al-Sanhuri, Egyptian Jurist and Scholar, 1895–1971*. Cairo: American University in Cairo, 1987. The most thorough study to date in English on al-Sanhūrī's life and work, with an extensive bibliography of his works.

Khadduri, Majid. *Political Trends in the Arab World: The Role of Ideas and Ideals in Politics*. Baltimore: Johns Hopkins Press, 1970. See pp. 239–244.

Sanhūrī, ʿAbd al-Razzāq al-. *ʿAbd al-Razzāq al-Sanhūrī min khilāl awrāqihi al-shakhsīyah* (ʿAbd al-Razzāq al-Sanhūrī through His Journals). Edited by Nādiyah al-Sanhūrī and Tawfīq al-Shāwī. Cairo: Zahrāʾ lil-Iʿlām al-ʿArabī, 1988. Collection of al-Sanhūrī's personal journals and his views on various issues, arranged chronologically.

Sanhūrī, ʿAbd al-Razzāq al-. "ʿAlā ayy asās yakūnu tanqīḥ al-qānūn al-madanī al-Misrī?" (On What Basis Will the Egyptian Civil Code Be Revised?). *Al-Kitāb al-Dhahabī lil-Maḥākim al-Ahlīyah* 2 (1938): 106–143.

Sanhūrī, ʿAbd al-Razzāq al-. "Al-qānūn al-madanī al-ʿArabī" (The Arab Civil Code). *Majallat al-Qadāʿ* 20, nos. 1–2 (1962): 7–33.

Sanhūrī, ʿAbd al-Razzāq al-. "Wujūb tanqīḥ al-qānūn al-madanī" (The Necessity of Revising the Civil Code). *Majallat al-Qānūn wa-al-Iqtiṣād* 6, no. 1 (January 1936): 3–144.

Ziadeh, Farhat. *Lawyers, the Rule of Law, and Liberalism in Modern Egypt*. Stanford, Calif.: Hoover Institution on War, Revolution, and Peace, Stanford University, 1968. See pp. 137–147.

EMAD EL-DIN SHAHIN

SANŪSĪYAH. Founded by Muḥammad ibn ʿAlī al-Sanūsī (1787–1859), the Sanūsīyah is a Ṣūfī brotherhood based in Libya and the central Sahara. The Sanūsī brotherhood is well known for its role in the resistance to French and Italian colonialism, but it was formed as a strictly religious brotherhood based on the doctrine of the Shādhilīyah order. The founder was born near Mostaganem in Algeria. In his early life, Muḥammad ibn ʿAlī al-Sanūsī studied Sufism and Islamic sciences, including law and tradition, in the reformist environment of Fez, Morocco. In 1823 he moved to Cairo, and later to the Hejaz to extend his studies. In Mecca he met the very influential Ṣūfī teacher Aḥmad Ibn Idrīs, and his Ṣūfī doctrine was from then on virtually identical to that of Ibn Idrīs. When Ibn Idrīs left Mecca for Yemen shortly afterward, al-Sanūsī was put in charge of his students in Mecca and built the first lodge at Abū Qubays, outside Mecca, in 1827. However, Ibn Idrīs never formed a structured order around his teachings, and after his death in 1837 several of his students set up independent orders like the Khatmīyah and the Rashīdīyah. Al-Sanūsī moved back to North Africa, and after an apparent period of indecision he settled in Cyrenaica (northeastern Libya) in 1841, founding his new organization.

The Sanūsīyah is commonly known as a "revivalist" brotherhood, but its doctrine shows little variation from traditional Sufism. It disapproves of excesses in ritual, such as dancing and singing. The founder put great emphasis on the role of the Prophet and on following his example. Al-Sanūsī was more controversial in his views on Islamic law; he wrote several books arguing for the right to *ijtihād*, the interpretation of dogma in the light of original sources. He put this into practice by incorporating elements commonly found in the Shāfiʿī school of law into the prayer ritual of the Sanūsīyah, while still continuing to rely on Mālikī traditions.

The brotherhood was, in its internal organization, typical of some newer orders of the eighteenth and nineteenth centuries. Its structure was simple and centralized, as the local lodge had little autonomy and was ruled by three or four officials appointed by the center, each with specific tasks and answering to the center. Shortly before al-Sanūsī's death, a central lodge was established in Jaghbūb, on the Libya-Egypt border.

Because the Sanūsīyah was primarily a desert order, its core area was that of the Bedouin of Cyrenaica, and the larger part of the population there came to identify with it. Still, the order was not confined to this area, because it also had a number of urban lodges and spread into non-Bedouin areas such as Tripolitania and Fezzan in western Libya, as well as in the Hejaz on the Arabian Peninsula. Toward the end of the nineteenth century it spread across the Sahara to the area east (and partly northwest) of Lake Chad, where it gained adherents from among other population groups.

The brotherhood was, in this period, not at all militant; rather, it promoted learning and piety among its adherents. It also had a strong work ethic, in particular relating to the building and upkeep of new lodges and development through agriculture. The guild became an important agent in the development of trans-Saharan trade, as various lodges provided safety as well as a network of resting places and contacts for traders who joined the order.

Through its internal organization and the increasing identification of the local population with the order, the Sanūsīyah acquired the capacity for political leadership in the eastern Sahara. In spite of this, there is no indication that the brotherhood was grown and spread with a conscious political objective. Although relations with the Ottoman rulers of the region may have cooled toward the end of the nineteenth century, this was not the major reason that the center of the order was moved from Jaghbūb to Kufrah, in the middle of the Libyan desert, in 1895. This was more likely a result of the order's increasing importance in the south, beyond the desert, and a wish to be closer to that region. However, the French, who were moving toward Lake Chad, saw the Sanūsīyah as an activist and inimical force and opened hostilities at the Bir Alali lodge in Kanem in 1901. Sanūsī leaders were caught unaware and withdrew. However, they quickly took up arms, and the population in the region fought the French in the name of the brotherhood and under its leadership until the Sanūsīyah were forced to withdraw around 1913–1914.

At the same time, Italian troops invaded Libya in 1911. Although they did not initially target the Sanūsī brotherhood as enemies, the Sanūsī leader Aḥmad al-Sharīf raised the call for *jihād* and led a largely Bedouin force against the invaders after Turkey, then the protectorate power in North Africa, withdrew from Libya in 1912. The Ottomans granted independence to Libya before their withdrawal, which led to the proclamation of the Sanūsī state in 1913. Politically emboldened Sanūsīs engaged in anticolonial rebellions in Fezzan and Jabal between 1914 and 1922, which quickly spread elsewhere. What altered the equation, however, was Italy's entry into World War II, which allowed Sanūsī leaders to pursue their quest for independence. An attack on British forces in Egypt mobilized London and led it to provide superior military equipment to Rome, leading eventually to the brotherhood's defeat. Al-Sharīf was replaced by his cousin Muḥammad Idrīs, and a settlement was reached whereby the Sanūsī retained a large degree of autonomy. After the rise of fascism in Italy, the agreement broke down, and hostilities recommenced. At this stage, however, the struggle became a battle for independence as ʿUmar al-Mukhtār rallied tribal leaders to fight the occupiers, while the Sanūsī hierarchy led by Idrīs remained in exile in Egypt. In the course of this struggle, which lasted until 1932, the Sanūsī organizational structure of lodges was largely destroyed. When the modern state of Libya was created, Muḥammad Idrīs was brought back as amir of Cyrenaica and in 1951 was made king of Libya; he was removed by the coup of Muʿammar al-Qadhdhāfī in 1969. The order showed some signs of revival under his patronage, but essentially the religious brotherhood had become a monarchical order. Most of the organization was destroyed in the conflicts in Egypt and Chad as well as in Cyrenaica. While the order was not tolerated in Libya under Qadhdhāfī's rule, changes triggered by the revolution in 2011 may translate into a revival, though only a few lodges remain outside Libya, including the oldest one at Abū Qubays near Mecca.

[*See also* Mukhtār, ʿUmar al.]

BIBLIOGRAPHY

Ayyūb, Muḥammad Ṣāliḥ. *Al-dawr al-ijtimāʿī wa-al-siyāsī lil-Shaykh ʿAbd al-Ḥaqq al-Sanūsī al-Tarjamī fī dār Wādī-Shād, 1853–1917*. Tripoli, Libya: Jamʿīyat al-Daʿwah al-Islāmīyah al-ʿĀlamīyah, 2001.

Dajānī, Aḥmad Ṣidqī al-. *Al-ḥarakah al-sanūsīyah: Nashaʾatuhā wa-numūʾuhā fī al-qarn al-tāsiʿ ʿashar*. Beirut: Dār Lubnān, 1967.

Evans-Pritchard, E. E. *The Sanusi of Cyrenaica*. Oxford: Clarendon, 1949.

Peters, Emrys L. *The Bedouin of Cyrenaica: Studies in Personal and Corporate Power*. Edited by Jack Goody and Emanuel Marx. Cambridge, U.K.: Cambridge University Press, 1990.

Vikør, Knut S. *Sufi and Scholar on the Desert Edge: Muḥammad b. ʿAlī al-Sanūsī and His Brotherhood.* Evanston, Ill.: Northwestern University Press, 1995.

Vikør, Knut S., and R. S. O'Fahey. "Ibn Idrīs and al-Sanūsī: The Teacher and His Student." *Islam et Sociétés au Sud du Sahara* 1, no. 1 (1987): 70–83.

KNUT S. VIKØR
Updated by JOSEPH A. KÉCHICHIAN

SAREKAT ISLAM. Indonesia's first mass political party, Sarekat Islam at one time claimed more than one million adherents. It was the successor to Sarekat Dagang Islam, a primarily commercial Muslim organization initially formed to oppose Chinese competition in the batik industry. It was succeeded by Sarekat Islam in 1912 under the leadership of H. O. S. Tjokroaminoto.

Sarekat Islam's leadership tended to reflect Islamic socialist and modernist views. The party emphasized Javanese nationalism, the unity of Indonesian Muslims, and Pan-Islamic principles, and demanded economic and political reform. The organization never had a strongly centralized administration, and its various branches often reflected diverse patterns of economic, social, political, and religious interests. This diversity aided its expansion by drawing a wide range of members into the party. It was also a hindrance, because the radical Marxist statements and actions of some branches antagonized the Dutch colonial administration, and far-left elements competed with the religious socialist leadership for control of the party. In particular, Sarekat Islam became locked in a crippling struggle for dominance of the nationalist movement with the newly formed Communist Party of Indonesia, which controlled some Sarekat Islam branches.

Sarekat Islam reached its height in the years immediately after World War I, when it was the largest nationalist movement in the East Indies. It had its own newspapers, national congresses, and membership in the colonial legislature, and was the target of Dutch colonial administrators, who feared its influence and religious views. However, the colonial system provided only limited political participation for indigenous political parties. Sarekat Islam declined throughout the 1920s because of internal divisions, poor organization, secular competition, and Dutch repression. It first changed its name to the Partai Sarekat Islam, then in 1929 to the Partai Sarekat Islam Indonesia to emphasize its move toward a more nationalist and less Muslim platform. By that time, however, it had only 1 percent of its former membership and was overshadowed by other nationalist and religious organizations.

The party became moribund, only to be reinvigorated after World War II, but in the 1955 national elections it received only 2.9 percent of the vote. In the 1970s, when the Suharto government consolidated all Muslim parties into one coalition (the PPP, or Partai Persatuan Pembangunan), it became a charter member of that organization. After Indonesia returned to democracy in 1999, the party won only 0.3 percent in the first national legislative elections. It split into the Partai Syarikat Indonesia and Partai Syarikat Islam Indonesia 1905 and has had very limited influence on the twenty-first-century Indonesian political scene.

[*See also* Indonesia; *and* Partai Persatuan Pembangunan.]

BIBLIOGRAPHY

Blumberger, J. Th. Petrus. *De nationalistische beweging in Nederlandsch-Indië.* Haarlem, Netherlands: Willink & Zoon, 1931.

Korver, A. P. E. *Sarekat Islam, 1912–1916: Opkomst, bloei en structuur van Indonesie's eerste massabeweging.* Amsterdam: Historisch Seminarium van de Universiteit van Amsterdam, 1982.

Laffan, Michael Francis. *Islamic Nationhood and Colonial Indonesia: The Umma below the Winds.* London: RoutledgeCurzon, 2003.

von der Mehden, Fred R. *Religion and Nationalism in Southeast Asia: Burma, Indonesia, and the Philippines.* Madison: University of Wisconsin Press, 1963.

FRED R. VON DER MEHDEN

SAUDI ARABIA. The first Saudi state was founded in 1744 upon a partnership between Muḥammad Ibn Saʿūd and Muḥammad Ibn ʿAbd al-Wahhāb. The former was the emir of Diriyah; the latter was a religious scholar who promoted the oneness of God in its absolute form, disallowing the then common practices of intercession, shrine visitations, and praying to saints. The devout supporters of Ibn ʿAbd al-Wahhāb became known as Wahhābīs, but his supporters do not identify with this term; to them, it is derogatory, and they prefer the label *ahl al-tawḥīd* (the people of monotheism) or *muwaḥḥidūn* (unitarians).

The first Saudi state collapsed in 1818 with the sacking of Riyadh by Ottoman forces. The second Saudi state was established in 1824 by Turkī ibn ʿAbd Allāh Āl Saʿūd and lasted until 1891. It was a weaker state than its predecessor, but it continued to rely on the teachings of Ibn ʿAbd al-Wahhāb for its theological foundations. The second state failed mainly because of internal power struggles. The Rashīdīs of Ḥāʾil attacked Riyadh in 1887, forcing ʿAbd al-Raḥmān ibn Fayṣal (then the ruler of the house of Saʿūd) and his son ʿAbd al-ʿAzīz to escape to Kuwait, where they resided until 1902.

ʿAbd al-ʿAzīz, popularly known as Ibn Saʿūd, returned from Kuwait in 1902 and recaptured Riyadh. In order to bring the Arabian Peninsula under his control, Ibn Saʿūd needed a strong military force. He successfully gathered the Bedouins under one banner and established the Ikhwān movement by advocating the Islamic revivalism preached by Ibn ʿAbd al-Wahhāb more than a century before. The Wahhābī doctrine was appealing to the Bedouins, who previously lived in the deserts of Arabia without any strong religious or political convictions. The Ikhwān became a military tool for Ibn Saʿūd to consolidate his power and conquer the whole of Arabia. The modern Saudi state, consisting of 80 percent of the peninsula, was thus officially formed in 1932. It included four culturally and geographically diverse regions: Nejd, in central Arabia, the ancestral home of the Saʿūd family; the Asir in the southwest of the country, which shares a border with Yemen; the Hejaz, which hosts the two Muslim holy cities, Mecca and Medina, where Muslims travel to perform *ḥajj* and *ʿumrah* (pilgrimages); and, finally, the Eastern Province, located on the Gulf coast, rich in oil and hosting the largest number of the kingdom's Shīʿah minority. There are other small Shīʿah communities living in Medina and Najrān (a province in the south of Saudi Arabia that borders Yemen). The exact number of the Shīʿah residing in Saudi Arabia remains unknown. Estimates of their population range between around 7 and 20 percent of the country as a whole; the wide variation betrays the controversy associated with such estimates.

Institutionalization of Islam. The partnership between the ruling family and the religious establishment has continued through each of the three Saudi states. The children and grandchildren of Ibn ʿAbd al-Wahhāb inherited his religious teachings and established a long-standing alliance with the House of Saʿūd. They also played a significant role in spreading his teachings. Traditionally, the *ʿulamāʾ* were derived from the Āl al-Shaykh family, who were descendants of Ibn ʿAbd al-Wahhāb, but over time, non–Āl al-Shaykh *ʿulamāʾ* of "Wahhābī" religious orientation began to permeate the Saudi religious establishment. The Āl Saʿūd family has ruled the Saudi kingdom based on the legitimacy that the *ʿulamāʾ* have given to their rule.

In the 1950s, the Saudi government slowly bureaucratized Saudi religious institutions, which led to the creation of "establishment *'ulamā'*." These *'ulamā'* are on the government payroll, are part of the kingdom's state apparatus, and act generally in the interests of the Saudi ruling family. The establishment *'ulamā'* vary in seniority. Senior *'ulamā'* hold high positions in the religious bureaucracy and are influential both in state affairs and with the general public. There are five organizations of senior religious figures that differ in influence and role. The Board of Senior 'Ulamā' (BSU) (Hay'at Kibār al-'Ulamā') is at the peak of the Saudi religious pyramid and is responsible for issuing *fatāwā* on matters of public concern. The BSU is also the ultimate authority on the interpretation of the *Sharī'ah* in Saudi Arabia. The BSU has over time issued many *fatāwā* in support of the ruling family, one of the most notable examples being one that legitimized the execution of more than sixty participants in the siege of Mecca's Grand Mosque in 1979. The second organization is the Permanent Committee for Scientific Research and Legal Opinion (CRLO, al-Lajnah al-Dā'imah lil-Buḥūth al-'Ilmīyah wa-al-Iftā'), which conducts research and provides administrative support for the BSU. The third is the Office of the Grand Muftī, who serves as the president of the BSU and the CRLO. The fourth and the fifth organizations are the Supreme Council of Islamic Affairs (al-Majlis al-A'lā lil-Shu'ūn al-Islāmīyah) and the Council for Islamic Mission and Guidance (al-Majlis lil-Da'wah wal-Irshād). These two organizations provide guidance for Saudis outside the kingdom, are responsible for the moral behavior of the Saudi public, and oversee the conduct of mosque functionaries.

The *'ulamā'* who are members of these organizations are the most influential in the Saudi state. On the other hand, the less senior *'ulamā'*, who number in the thousands, hold less significant positions in various governmental religious organizations. These include the Ministry of Islamic Affairs, Endowments, Instruction, and Preaching (Da'wah wa-al-Irshād) and the Committee of Commanding Right and Forbidding Wrong (Hay'at al-Amr bi-al-Ma'rūf wa-al-Nahī 'an al-Munkar, also known as Muṭawi'ah). The members of the latter organization are tasked with enforcing the guidelines to regulate public morality promulgated by the BSU, including monitoring public compliance with dress codes, identifying alcohol and drug users, and ensuring that shops halt business activities during prayer times. Some of the less senior *'ulamā'* also function in the Muslim World League (Rābiṭah al-'Ālam al-Islāmī), a government body that aims to spread Wahhabism globally. This organization was established in 1962, during the reign of King Fayṣal, who promoted Pan-Islamism to counter the influence of Arab nationalism championed by Gamal Abdel Nasser. Mainly funded by Saudi Arabia, it is known for its charity activities in the Muslim world. Less senior *'ulamā'* also hold positions as *qāḍīs* under the Higher Council of Qāḍīs, Muftīs, and Sharī' (judges and lawyers).

The Saudi government needs clerical endorsement to secure its legitimacy to govern. Yet at times the government has pursued modernization despite clerical opposition. The ruling family has generally allowed the religious establishment to control education and social behavior within the state, though these powers have been stripped in recent years. For example, women's education now falls under Ministry of Education, while reserving to itself the power to make economic and political decisions. Societal evolution therefore takes place largely within the boundaries established by the clerics.

Internal Opposition. The bureaucratization of the religious establishment, coupled with the rapid modernization of the country, has created unintended consequences for the ruling family. Disillusioned by what they see as "un-Islamic" practices among the ruling family, some *'ulamā'* have dissociated themselves from the ruling family and the establishment *ʿulamāʾ*. The siege of the Grand Mosque of Mecca in 1979, led by Juhaymān al-ʿUtaybī, signified the discontent with the ruling family. With the uprising crushed, the ruling family, under the leadership of King Khālid Ibn ʿAbd al-ʿAzīz, granted more power to the religious establishment to further secure its support and restore its legitimacy, which had been tainted by the siege. Instead of containing the fundamentalist elements within the kingdom that contributed to the uprising, the king did the exact opposite. The religious establishment began to ban many practices that they deemed un-Islamic, for example, by shutting down cinemas and outlawing photographs of females in newspapers. The intense promotion of religious education led to the expansion of religious faculties in Saudi universities, while nonreligious courses came under scrutiny.

During the first Gulf War, the Saudi government was heavily criticized by a group of clerics for its positive relations with the United States of America and allowing American troops on Saudi soil. These *ʿulamāʾ* embarked on a difficult political path and created a voice of dissent to challenge the legitimacy of the ruling family. Their opposition to the ruling family has at times caused their political intimidation, including imprisonment. *Ṣaḥwah al-islāmīyah* (Islamic awakening) was a binding ideal that circulated among scholars and preachers to combat what was seen as the growing trend of secular behavior in Saudi Arabia in the 1990s. *Ṣaḥwah al-islāmīyah*'s original focus was Western-educated Saudis, but the first Gulf War saw the inclusion of political issues in the *ṣaḥwah* platform, in which the *ʿulamāʾ* were critical of the ruling family, especially concerning its alliance with the United States in the Gulf War. Many of its leaders, including the prominent clerics Salmān al-ʿAwdah and Safar al-Ḥawālī, were imprisoned. The rise to prominence of this movement of non-establishment clerics threatened to undermine the ruling family's religious credibility. Many radical jihādists, including Osama Bin Laden, expressed admiration for the *ṣaḥwah* clerics and questioned the House of Saʿūd's commitment to upholding Islam. The establishment *ʿulamāʾ*, on the other hand, continued to support the ruling family, issuing *fatāwā* in favor of the Saudi government's policies; the most notable was the *fatwa* permitting the presence of U.S. forces on Saudi soil.

The 9/11 attacks damaged the international reputation of Saudi Arabia, because, according to United States, fifteen out of the nineteen hijackers were Saudi citizens. The ruling family's inability to control radicalism within the kingdom became the subject of discussion in the West. A series of attacks in 2003 and 2004 targeting Western workers angered not only the Saudi government but also much of the Saudi public. The culprits were Saudi citizens who were forced to leave Afghanistan following the removal of the Taliban regime after 9/11. The House of Saʿūd responded to these attacks by quickly asserting control, hunting down and killing the terrorists. The clerical establishment supported the government's efforts, and, more importantly, *ṣaḥwah* clerics including al-ʿAwdah began to endorse the government's positions against radicalism. Saudi Arabia, under the leadership of Prince Nayef, who was the interior minister at the time, introduced programs designed to rehabilitate arrested terrorists.

National Dialogue. In 2003 Crown Prince ʿAbd Allāh established the King Abdulaziz Center for National Dialogue, which aimed to foster debate and the exchange of ideas on various subjects including religious pluralism, the rights and duties of citizens, the public's relationship with the ruling family, and women's rights. The dialogue was very much ʿAbd Allāh's personal initiative, and at times it included debates on sensitive religious and political matters.

The ruling family has also run the risk of offending the *ʿulamāʾ* through its gradual process of democratization. Saudi citizens were given the vote in municipal elections in 2005, which saw conservative candidates winning most seats. However, women were excluded, and half of the available seats were reserved for government appointees. In 2011 King ʿAbd Allāh announced that women would be able to participate in the 2015 municipal elections as both candidates and voters. Although this decision was supported by members of the BSU, it dismayed hard-line clerics.

The Arab Spring. The demonstrations that swept through the Arab world in 2011 affected many countries, but mostly those struggling with high unemployment rates and economic hardship. King ʿAbd Allāh and his administration were quick to act to allay any latent public discontent about the kingdom's economic circumstances, handing out over $110 billion in social benefits. However, this was not enough to pacify the Shīʿah community of the Eastern Province, who had struggled for a long time for equality with their Sunnī counterparts for freedom of religion and economic prosperity. The Shīʿah in the Eastern Province, who are mainly Twelvers, staged protests calling for reform. Their opposition became more intense as the Saudi ruling family decided to intervene to assist the Bahraini ruling family, which was the subject of more intense protests from a largely Shīʿah movement. Saudi Shīʿah leaders pledged solidarity with the Bahraini coreligionists. Meanwhile, members of the ruling family including the late Prince Nayef blamed Iran for interfering and sponsoring uprisings in both Saudi Arabia and Bahrain. They were supported by the kingdom's *ʿulamāʾ*, who largely blamed Iran and Shiism as the cause of the unrest. Similarly, Saudi Arabia and other Gulf countries have condemned the Assad regime in Syria and its allies Ḥizbullāh and Iran.

BIBLIOGRAPHY

Al-Atawneh, Muhammad K. *Wahhābī Islam Facing the Challenges of Modernity: Dār al Iftā in the Modern Saudi State*. Leiden: Brill, 2010.

Bachar, Shmuel, Shmuel Bar, Rachel Machtiger et al. *Establishment Ulama and Radicalism in Egypt, Saudi Arabia, and Jordan*. Research Monographs on the Muslim World 1, no. 4. Washington, D.C.: Hudson Institute, 2006.

Habib, John S. *Ibn Saʿud's Warriors of Islam: The Ikhwan of Najd and Their Role in the Creation of the Saʿudi Kingdom, 1910–1930*. Leiden: Brill, 1978.

Hegghammer, Thomas. *Jihad in Saudi Arabia: Violence and Pan-Islamism since 1979*. New York: Cambridge University Press, 2010.

Kechichian, Joseph A. *Succession in Saudi Arabia*. New York: Palgrave Macmillan, 2001.

Lacey, Robert. *Inside the Kingdom: Kings, Clerics, Modernists, Terrorists, and the Struggle for Saudi Arabia*. London: Hutchinson, 2009.

Lacroix, Stéphane. *Awakening Islam: The Politics of Religious Dissent in Contemporary Saudi Arabia*. Translated by George Holoch. Cambridge, Mass.: Harvard University Press, 2011.

Nelles, Wayne. "Theoretical Issues and Pragmatic Challenges for Education, Terrorism, and Security Research." In *Comparative Education, Terrorism and Human Security: From Critical Pedagogy to Peacebuilding?*, edited by Wayne Nelles, pp. 11–32. New York: Palgrave Macmillan, 2003.

Al-Rasheed, Madawi. *A History of Saudi Arabia*. New York: Cambridge University Press, 2002.

Al-Yassini, Ayman. *Religion and State in the Kingdom of Saudi Arabia*. Boulder, Colo.: Westview, 1985.

RAIHAN ISMAIL

SCANDINAVIAN STATES. This entry provides a short overview of the history of Islam and Muslims in the Nordic countries (i.e., Finland, Sweden, Norway, and Denmark, excluding Iceland). The focus is on historical developments and so-called church-state relationships, that is, how the state views religion and how religious organizations (in this case, Muslim organizations) are given access to and take part in the public sphere.

Even though we have archaeological, textual, and numismatic evidence for sporadic contacts between peoples from northern Europe and various Muslim groups during the Viking period (late eighth to mid-eleventh centuries), especially with the Iberian Peninsula and the Volga region, it is clear that the Nordic countries have come into contact with the so-called Muslim world mostly since World War II. Apart from early diplomatic contacts with the Ottoman Empire and some minor expeditions to the Orient in the eighteenth century, it was mostly through labor migration in the 1960s and 1970s that Muslims started to arrive in the Nordic countries. Because—unlike Great Britain, France, the Netherlands, and Germany—the Nordic countries had no (or only minor) experience of colonialism, migration patterns there are not linked to former colonies. Migration from the so-called Muslim world is therefore very heterogeneous in the Nordic countries. Personal contacts and family ties have generally been more important in the migration process than a colonial connection with the new country, especially after the restrictions on migration that were imposed in the first half of the 1970s after the oil crisis and the economic recession. Although diversity (for example, of language, educational background, ethnicity, and religious preference) is significant among Muslims in the region, it is clear that Norway, for example, has attracted more people from Pakistan than the other Nordic countries have. Today all international and transnational Muslim organizations and religious divisions are present in the region, and it is possible to find all of the major Muslim organizations represented in the Nordic countries. For example, the Muslim Brotherhood, Jamāʿat-i Islāmī, Tablīghī Jamāʿat, the Aḥmadī community, many Ṣūfī orders, major reform movements (such as the Deobandī and Barelwī), and a growing presence of converts and Shīʿah Muslim organizations are today found in Denmark, Norway, and Sweden. Turkish movements, such as the Diyanet, Süleymancı, and Milli Görüş, are also important for the establishment and building of mosques in the Nordic countries. Private donors and Islamic foundations from the Persian Gulf and Saudi Arabia have also funded many mosques. As in many other countries in western Europe, the Aḥmadīyah community was the first Muslim organization to arrive and build mosques in the region, whereas Denmark is the only country in the region that has an organized and established branch of the Hizb ut-Tahrir, a movement that has caused controversies and conflicts between Muslims and non-Muslims, especially when it comes to questions of religion and democracy, but also the Israel-Palestinian conflict.

While the first Sunnī Muslim mosques and umbrella organizations were established in the 1980s and 1990s, the Aḥmadīyah community built the Nusrat Djahan Mosque in Hvidovre (Copenhagen, Denmark) in 1966–1967 and the Nur Mosque in Gothenburg, Sweden, in 1975–1976, but the first mosques in the Nordic countries were built in Finland. The wooden Tatar mosque in Järvenpää was built in 1942, and a basement has functioned as a mosque in central Helsinki since the 1960s. In total, the Tatar community in Finland has five mosques, in Helsinki, Järvenpää, Kotka, Tampere, and Turku. Following the general European pattern, the building of new mosques in the region tends to be met with suspicion, hostility, and even hatred in the Nordic countries. Opposition to mosques is often transnational, and anti-Muslim groups in Denmark have, for example, taken part in protests in Sweden. A great variety of support groups and antiracist organizations, ranging from political youth groups to Christian churches to autonomous left-wing groups, however, have supported the building of new mosques.

Finland differs from Sweden, Norway, and Denmark in respect to the history of Muslims for two reasons. First, Finland had, after Finnish independence in 1917, already recognized as a religious minority the Tatar Muslims from the Nizhniy Novgorod region, who had arrived in the country starting in the 1870s. This group of Muslims was granted citizenship from the 1920s, and in 1923 they were given the right to practice their religion in full. Second, Finland did not receive migrants before the 1980s. Before that, more people left Finland for economic reasons, and the country attracted no migrants. Also, since the 1980s Finland's migration policy has been stricter than that of the other Nordic countries. Hence, the number of Muslims in Finland is much lower than in Norway, Sweden, or Denmark.

The number of Muslims in the Nordic countries is nonetheless debatable and open to criticism, as there are no reliable official statistics. According to data provided by the *Yearbook of Muslims in Europe* (2012), the Muslim population is estimated at 50,000–60,000 Muslims in Finland (roughly 1 percent of the total population of 5.4 million), 236,300 in Denmark (4.2 percent of the total population of 5,543,453), 180,000 in Norway (3.5 percent of the total population of 4.9 million), and 350,000–400,000 Muslims in Sweden (3.8–4.4 percent of the total population of 9.1 million). All these figures are rough estimates based on ethnicity; because religious adherence and belief are a private affair in the Nordic countries, the state is not allowed to keep records of religious preferences. It is nonetheless possible to acquire information about how many Muslims are members of Muslim organizations that are recognized by the state in Norway and Sweden. The figures for organized Muslims in Sweden suggest, for example, that the great majority of people with a Muslim cultural background are not members of Muslim organizations. Of the estimated 350,000–400,000 Muslims in Sweden, only 110,000 are members of Muslim organizations recognized by the Swedish state. The large parts of the Muslim community that are only vaguely religious—for example, observing special holidays or life-cycle rituals such as birth, marriage, and death—or those who are indifferent to religious matters are seldom addressed in public discussions about Islam and Muslims.

The constitutions of the Nordic countries provide for freedom of religion, and there are generally no restrictions on practicing any religion so long as the specific beliefs or practices concerned do not violate the law. In Denmark and Norway, however, the Lutheran Church is still the state church, which gives it specific privileges, including subsidies from the state directly through the tax system. However, other religious organizations can be recognized by the state, and Muslims can also benefit from other forms of support from the state. The Norwegian system is under review, and in 2000 Sweden changed the relationship between the state and the Lutheran Church. Denmark was the first country in the region to pass a law guaranteeing freedom of religion (included in the 1849 constitution). Freedom of religion was added to the Finnish constitution in 1923, but the Evangelical Lutheran and Finnish Orthodox Churches have a special status. The Lutheran Church in all of the Nordic countries is privileged for historical reasons, but there is a growing debate over this issue, and many different groups in Nordic countries stress the importance of treating all religious groups and organizations equally.

As in the rest of Europe, it is clear that public discussion about religion and its role in society is heated in the Nordic countries. Islam and Muslims are often the focus of this debate. For example, controversies followed the translation and publication of the British Indian author Salman Rushdie's book *The Satanic Verses* in 1988–1989 and the attack on his Norwegian publisher, the publication of cartoons depicting Muḥammad by *Jyllands-Posten* in 2005 (later republished several times), the drawing of the Prophet Muḥammad as a so-called roundabout dog ("Rondellhund") in Sweden in 2007 (with several republications), and the failed terror attack in Stockholm, Sweden, by a Muslim man in 2010. Norway and Denmark both have political parties with seats in parliament that have voiced strong anti-Muslim sentiments, and, since the 2010 elections, Sweden also has had a party with strong anti-Muslim opinions. Both Muslim and non-Muslim organizations and governmental bodies have addressed the problems of Islamophobia, racism, and discrimination in the Nordic countries. With the terror attack of Anders Behring Breivik in Oslo, Norway, on 22 July 2011, the debate over anti-Muslim politics and opinions has become even stronger.

Bibliography

Jacobsen, Christine M. *Islamic Traditions and Muslim Youth in Norway*. Leiden: Brill, 2011. This book gives an outline of the history of Muslims in Norway, with a special focus on Muslim youth.

Larsson, Göran, ed. *Islam in the Nordic and Baltic Countries*. London: Routledge, 2009. An edited volume that contains texts that analyze the history and current situation of Muslims in both the Nordic and Baltic countries. The book includes chapters on Sweden, Norway, Denmark, Finland, Iceland, the Faroe Islands, Estonia, Latvia, and Lithuania.

Larsson, Göran, and Åke Sander. *Islam and Muslims in Sweden: Integration or Fragmentation? A Contextual Study*. Berlin: Lit, 2008. Besides providing an outline of the history of Muslims in the country, the book contains discussions on integration, migration, and equal rights in Sweden.

Nielsen, Jørgen S., ed. *Islam in Denmark: The Challenge of Diversity*. Lanham, Md.: Lexington, 2012. Contains a detailed analysis of the history and current situation of Muslims in Denmark.

Sakaranaho, Tuula. *Religious Freedom, Multiculturalism, Islam: Cross-Reading Finland and Ireland*. Leiden: Brill, 2006. A comparative study that provides information on the situation of Muslims in Finland and Ireland.

Yearbook of Muslims in Europe. Leiden: Brill, 2009– . One of the most useful reference works on Muslims in Europe, published annually since 2009.

Göran Larsson

Schools of Jurisprudence.

This entry contains four subentries:

Shīʿah Schools of Jurisprudence: Imāmī School, The
Shīʿah Schools of Jurisprudence: Ismāʿīlī School, The
Shīʿah Schools of Jurisprudence: Zaydī School, The *and*
Sunni Schools of Jurisprudence.

The great majority of Muslims belong to one of several *madhāhib* (pl. of *madhhab*, lit. "manner of going"; "movement"; "ideology"), schools of Islamic legal doctrine whose jurisprudence developed beginning about a century after the death of the Prophet Muḥammad, in 632. The following subentries describe the Shīʿī and the Sunnī (*madhāhib*), respectively.

Iza Hussin

Shīʿah Schools of Jurisprudence: Imāmī School, The

The origins of the Imāmī school of law (*madhhab*) can be traced to Imām Muḥammad al-Bāqir (d. 743) and Jaʿfar al-Ṣādiq (d. 765), the fifth and sixth Imams of Twelver Shīʿī Islam, respectively. A large body of legal doctrine is traced to the latter in particular, and hence the school is sometimes referred to as the Jaʿfarī *madhhab* (or as the Twelver school). Jaʿfar was an accomplished jurist, who disputed with (and supposedly bested) Abū Ḥanīfah (d. 765). From its beginnings in Medina, where Muḥammad al-Bāqir and Jaʿfar al-Ṣādiq were based for much of their lives, the school spread to their followers in Iraq and Iran. Baghdad and Qom became centers of Imāmī legal thought, particularly after the disappearance (*ghaybah*) of the Twelfth Imam in 940. Under both the Umayyads and the early ʿAbbāsids, the Imams were seen as political threats and were suppressed. Under the Shīʿī Būyid dynasty (945–1055), however, Imāmīs succeeded in gaining some political power, and the developing Imāmī school of law influenced some decisions in the Būyid courts. In positive law, the Imāmī school was based on the *ḥadīth* reports from the Imams, mainly those related from al-Bāqir and al-Ṣādiq, but also some from ʿAlī al-Riḍā (d. 818, the Eighth Imam). The distinctive doctrines of the Imams included, for example, a system of inheritance law in which the Sunnī concept of *ʿaṣabah* (male relatives who inherit after the Qurʾānic heirs) was rejected and male and female relatives were given greater equality. The "marriage of pleasure" (*mutʿah*), which is contracted for a limited period, was considered licit by Imāmīs, though forbidden by the Sunnīs. The absence of an Imam also implied the illegitimacy of all current political power. Hence, the duty to pay religious taxes (*zakāt* and *khums*) was thought by some early Imāmī jurists to have lapsed (*sāqiṭ*), because there was no legitimate power to collect and distribute them. The legal system that emerged was, however, similar to that of the rival Sunnī schools in many respects.

Early Imāmī scholars collected legal traditions (sing. *ḥadīth*) and were not concerned with constructing a practical legal system as such. Later jurists were more concerned with coherence and hence developed a science of legal theory (*uṣūl al-fiqh*) that, similar to that of the Sunnī jurists, attempted to present a comprehensive theory of law. In the early period Imāmīs rejected personal juristic effort (*ijtihād*) and the uncertainty that it inevitably engendered in the jurist's mind. Al-ʿAllāmah (d. 1325), however, argued for *ijtihād* and adopted elements of Sunnī jurisprudence. Subsequent Imāmī jurisprudence followed al-ʿAllāmah's model, even through the Ṣafavid and Qājār periods in Iran, where it was partially instituted in the court system. Those qualified to perform *ijtihād* (sing. *mujtahid*) faced opposition from the traditionalist Akhbārī school, which rejected reliance by the jurist on anything but the revealed sources, but by the end of the nineteenth century, al-ʿAllāmah's *mujtahid* theory dominated the Imāmī Shīʿī world.

When the Ṣafavids came to power in 1501, they proclaimed Imāmī Shiism the state religion. The lack of centralized policy that had characterized the breakdown of Timurid rule was replaced with the clear dynastic power of the Ṣafavids and the enforcement of Imāmī doctrine throughout the land. This changeover to Shiism took some time, and influential non-Imāmī thinkers continued to operate in Iran well into the sixteenth century, but political and judicial influence was reserved for Imāmī Shīʿīs, and the Ṣafavids began to develop their own distinctive state-controlled judicial system. They inherited the position of *ṣadr* from their Sunnī predecessor dynasties, but they expanded the remit of the office. The *ṣadr* took control of mosques, religious schools, courts, and endowments and was charged with appointing local chief judges, giving them the title *shaykh al-Islām*, an honorific title for a position that had been elevated to a state-appointed, local official, religiously trained and legally qualified, who was in charge of the local court system in a town or province. A *shaykh al-Islām* was appointed for every major city during the Ṣafavid period. It was through this hierarchy of state-appointed religious scholars, from the Ṣafavid court down to the village chief, that the spread of Imāmī Shiism was achieved in the first century or so of Ṣafavid rule.

The Imāmī Ṣafavid jurists set about establishing a court system that would maintain their legal prerogative within the Ṣafavid administration. Religiously trained judges implemented Imāmī law in the *Sharīʿah* courts, and government bureaucrats oversaw the courts that applied the law of customary practice (*ʿurf*). This dual system survived the fall of the Ṣafavids in 1722, the rise of the Sunnī-oriented Nādir Shāh, and the power of the tribal Shīrāz-based Zand dynasty. Historical records suggest that the two jurisdictions worked closely together. There was a general division of labor, as trade and land disputes were covered by the *ʿurf* courts, while personal law and strictly religious matters (e.g., apostasy, endowment cases) were dealt with by the *Sharīʿah* judge.

Alongside these practical developments in the Iranian court system, the Imāmī religious scholars established for themselves a secure financial base through the remittance of religious taxes entirely separate from the state. This enabled them to continue the development of their own jurisprudence. This independence manifested itself in opposition to the policies of the Qājār shahs during the Constitutional Revolution (1905–1907) and in the call by some jurists for a *Sharīʿah*-based legislature as a device whereby the arbitrary imperial decree of the shah might be controlled. The call for a religious legislature did not survive the civil tumult of the Constitutional Revolution, as more secularized elements of the revolutionary movement took control.

Elements of Imāmī doctrine were included in Iranian legal codes in the early twentieth century. This was the case primarily in the areas of personal law (marriage, divorce, and inheritance), as public law was under the control of the Pahlavi shahs. Although nominally Shīʿī, the Pahlavi shahs pursued a modernizing agenda, abolishing the headscarf and suppressing the influence of Imāmī jurists. The marginalization of religion in juridical matters, linked to the general secularization of the public sphere, led to popular discontent beginning in the early 1960s. This discontent grew under the Imāmī jurists, who, given their financial independence, operated as a focus for opposition to the Pahlavis. Several scholars, including Ruhollah Khomeini, were expelled in the mid-1960s for antigovernment activities.

After the Iranian Revolution of 1979, Imāmī jurisprudence gained a renewed influence in the Iranian legal system. Iranian judges were religiously trained jurists, who made judgments in both personal and public law on the basis of their traditional training. In southern Lebanon and in Pakistan, the Imāmī community has its own court system, primarily dealing with personal law. Even the secular Iraqi Baʿthist government under Saddam Hussein attempted to include elements of Imāmī law in its personal codes. After the 2003 invasion of Iraq, the Iraqi Shīʿah proposed a system of courts staffed by traditionally trained jurists, and the future may well see the reemergence of traditional Imāmī jurisprudence in the Iraqi court system.

[*See also* Imamate, Theories of the; Iran, Islamic Republic of; Khomeini, Ruhollah al-Musavi; Muslim Political Thought; *and* Ṣafavid Dynasty.]

Bibliography

Gleave, Robert. *Inevitable Doubt: Two Theories of Shīʿī Jurisprudence*. Leiden: Brill, 2000. An examination of the conflict between traditionalism and rationalism within Imāmī Shīʿī jurisprudence.

Modarressi Tabātabāʾī, Hossein. *An Introduction to Shīʿī Law: A Bibliographical Study*. London: Ithaca, 1984. A primarily bibliographical resource of works in Shīʿī law from the earliest period to the modern day, with useful introductory chapters.

Stewart, Devin J. *Islamic Legal Orthodoxy: Twelver Shiite Responses to the Sunni Legal System*. Salt Lake City: University of Utah Press, 1998. A thorough resource for the history of Imāmī Shīʿī law, which concentrates on the influence of Sunnī jurisprudence upon Shīʿī legal thought.

Robert Gleave

Shīʿah Schools of Jurisprudence: The Ismāʿīlī School

Like the Imāmī Shīʿī, the Ismāʿīlīs accept Jaʿfar al-Ṣādiq (d. 765) as an imam, that is, an infallible source of law. It is only after Jaʿfar's imamate that the Ismāʿīlīs differ from the Imāmīs concerning the identity of the imam, arguing that Jaʿfar's son Ismāʿīl, rather than Mūsā, was the next imam. Ismāʿīlī law, most evident in the works of the great Fāṭimid Egyptian jurist al-Qāḍī al-Nuʿmān (d. 974), resembles Imāmī law in some respects, being derived from Jaʿfar's teachings. Ismāʿīlī law is, however, distinctive in the role it permits the imam of adjusting the dictates of the *Sharīʿah* to the exigencies of the time. Hence the largest contemporary Ismāʿīlī group, the Nizārīs, follow a code of religious law (in terms of ritual and worship) that is very different from that of the Imāmīs and Sunnīs.

After the collapse of the Fāṭimids (1171), the Ismāʿīlī movement fractured between rival claims to the imamate. The Nizārī (Agha Khani) Ismāʿīlīs had split earlier from the Fāṭimids and survived in small communities in Iran and Syria, and later in India. Most of the remnants of Fāṭimid Ismāʿīlīsm were located first in Yemen and then in India. The prominence given to the imam, or for some sects the imam's representative (*dāʿī muṭlaq*, "the supreme propagator"), meant that legal scholarship was of secondary importance. Since the imam was the source of law, he had the power to abrogate or change it. Legal interpretation, and hence jurists, were, to a certain extent, superfluous. For this reason, the study of the *Sharīʿah* has not been a major element of Ismāʿīlī scholarship since the time of al-Nuʿmān. Today, Ismāʿīlī communities have both codes of ethics and recommended ritual and community practice. These have the imprimatur of their various imams or *dāʿī muṭlaq*s, but there is no mature science of legal exegesis: a living, omniscient guide renders interpretation unnecessary.

BIBLIOGRAPHY

Daftary, Farhad, ed. *Medieval Ismāʿīlī History and Thought*. New York: Cambridge University Press, 1996. An edited collection of essays tracing the important elements of Ismāʿīlī thought, including jurisprudence in the Middle Ages.

Madelung, Wilferd. "The Sources of Ismāʿīlī Law." *Journal of Near Eastern Studies* 35 (1976): 29–40.

ROBERT GLEAVE

SHĪʿAH SCHOOLS OF JURISPRUDENCE: THE ZAYDĪ SCHOOL

The Zaydīs are a sect of Shīʿī Islam that takes its name from Zayd ibn ʿAlī (d. 740), a great-great-grandson of the Prophet Muḥammad. Zayd led an abortive revolt in Kūfa against Umayyad rule in 740 and died a martyr. His political example, as a rebel against unjust rule, has remained a cornerstone of Zaydī self-definition. On questions of law, the most significant repository of his learning is the work known as the *Majmūʿ* of Zayd ibn ʿAlī. It has been claimed by Zaydīs, and by some Western scholars, to be the earliest work of Islamic law. Zayd's authorship, however, is a disputed matter. Wilferd Madelung, for example, has argued that the work represents the Kūfan legal tradition and that Zayd is unlikely to have had a significant part in it.

Throughout the ages, very few Zaydīs have claimed to be followers of Zayd on questions of law. Rather, the Zaydī tradition has spawned several legal schools, each tracing its origin to an individual imam in the tradition. Of these imams, those with the most significant historical followings were the Medinan Ḥasanid al-Qāsim ibn Ibrāhīm (d. 860); his grandson al-Hādī ilā al-Ḥaqq Yaḥyā ibn al-Ḥusayn, the founder of the Zaydī state in Yemen; and the Caspian imam al-Nāṣir li-Dīn Allāh al-Ḥasan ibn ʿAlī al-Uṭrūsh. Zayd's unimportance as a legal eponym has generated much controversy within Zaydī circles, as well as polemics with non-Zaydīs, about what specifically defines Zaydism. The classical response of the Zaydīs has been to state that Zaydism is defined by a commitment to a set of theological and political beliefs, and they have downplayed the importance of law. Furthermore, they have justified the diversity in legal opinions that characterizes their schools by stating that their imams, as *mujtahids* (independent jurists), are all correct in their views. This is known as the doctrine of infallibilism (*taṣwīb*), and it has played a major role in resolving tensions arising from differences of opinion within the sect.

The Zaydīs have survived into modern times in the northern highlands of Yemen, where the legal school (called al-Hādawiyya) of al-Hādī Yaḥyā, the founder of the first Zaydī state in Arabia, has dominated. Al-Hādī's most important legal text is the *Kitāb al-Aḥkām*, but his views were set in canonical fashion by Aḥmad ibn Yaḥyā al-Murtaḍā (d. 1436) in *Kitāb al-Azhār*. The latter remains the standard work of reference for Zaydī law in Yemen.

A legal tradition emerged around al-Hādī's teachings, and it is common to recognize three ranks of legal activity. The first consists of the explicit statements of the eponymic imams (*aṣḥāb al-nuṣūṣ*), for example, al-Hādī for the Hadawī *madhhab*. The second rank, the so-called *muḥaṣṣilūn*, is occupied by those who sifted and clarified these statements and articulated the principles upon which the imam's decisions rested, a process that is sometimes referred to as *takhrīj*. The third rank is that of the *mudhākirūn* who apply these principles to new cases. To the extent that the Zaydī *madhhab* in Yemen was identical to the elaboration of the teachings of al-Hādī by many generations of scholars, it had come to acquire an impersonal character. This in turn challenged its followers to provide a satisfactory theoretical explanation of how adherence to the *madhhab* constituted actual "emulation" (*taqlīd*) of the eponym.

In the fifteenth century, at the time that *Kitāb al-Azhār* was written, the Zaydī school came under attack from internal critics who rejected the fundamental principles of the existing legal schools, including their own. The first scholar in this anti-*madhhab* tradition was Muḥammad ibn Ibrāhīm al-Wazīr, and perhaps the most famous in this lineage is Muḥammad ibn ʿAlī al-Shawkānī (d. 1834). Given that the theory of *taqlīd* would require reliance on a *mujtahid*, one of the most troubling questions that emerged from the attack on the *madhhabs* is where, in the complex scholastic tradition that emerged around al-Hādī's doctrine, could his followers find the requisite authority on which to base their *taqlīd*. The solution that the opponents of the *madhhabs* proffered was a total rejection of *taqlīd* and, with it, the whole *madhhab* structure, to be replaced by a reliance on the perpetual practice of *ijtihād* (independent judgment). By this they intend a constant citation by qualified scholars of revelatory texts, especially the canonical Sunnī *ḥadīth* collections, when elaborating legal opinions. The legal methodology of these *madhhab* opponents is the strict constructionism of the Sunnī traditionists (*ahl al-ḥadīth*), which in contemporary times is associated with the Salafīs and Wahhābīs.

In the eighteenth century, the Zaydī state dominated most of Yemen and was headed by the imams of the House of Imām al-Manṣūr al-Qāsim ibn Muḥammad (d. 1620). These sought to establish dynastic and patrimonial forms of rule, which clashed directly with the traditional Zaydī political doctrine that only persons fulfilling strict qualifications could become imams. A convergence of interests arose between the Qāsimīs and the anti-*madhhab* jurists, and this was concretized when al-Shawkānī assumed the post of chief judge from 1795 until 1834. In return for state patronage, al-Shawkānī developed a Sunnī-oriented legal and ideological framework that legitimized Qāsimī rule. In this period the majority of the state's subjects were Shāfiʿī Muslims, and these found favor under, and would identify with, al-Shawkānī's Sunnī teachings.

In the twentieth century, the Zaydī state was reconstituted under the Ḥamīd al-Dīn imams (r. 1918–1962), after the defeat of the Ottomans in

World War I. These imams perpetuated the forms of rule established by the Qāsimīs while maintaining the Hadawī *madhhab* as the official school of law. A process of legal codification, influenced by Ottoman reforms as well as traditional Imāmī "choices" (*ikhtiyārāt*), was initiated by the Ḥamīd al-Dīn imams, but it remained unaccomplished in 1962, when the dynasty was overthrown by republican revolutionaries. The modern Republic of Yemen has codified its laws, basing them primarily on Egyptian codes and processes. Officially, Zaydism is one of the recognized schools of law in Yemen, but the state has decided de facto to abandon its doctrines and rulings, which are applied ever more infrequently by an aging generation of judges who were trained in its legal manuals.

[*See also* Yemen.]

Bibliography

Haykel, Bernard. *Revival and Reform in Islam: The Legacy of Muhammad al-Shawkānī.* Cambridge, U.K.: Cambridge University Press, 2003.

Haykel, Bernard, and Aron Zysow. "What Makes a Madhab a Madhab: Zaydī Debates on the Structure of Legal Authority." In *Arabica* 59 (2012): 332–371. A special issue of *Arabica* devoted entirely to the Zaydī school of law.

Madelung, Wilferd. *Der Imam al-Qāsim ibn Ibrāhīm und die Glaubenslehre der Zaiditen.* Berlin: Walter de Gruyter, 1965.

Messick, Brinkley. *The Calligraphic State: Textual Domination and History in a Muslim Society.* Berkeley: University of California Press, 1993.

Würth, Anna. *Aš-Šarīʿa fī Bāb al-Yaman: Recht, Richter, und Rechtspraxis an der familienrechtlichen Kammer des Gerichts Süd-Sanaa (Republik Jemen), 1983–1995.* Berlin: Duncker & Humblot, 2000.

Bernard Haykel

Sunni Schools of Jurisprudence

Islamic jurisprudence developed from about a century after the death of the Prophet Muḥammad in 632, with the result that the great majority of Muslims belong to one of a number of *madhāhib* (movements, schools of Islamic legal doctrine). The Sunnī *madhāhib* (sing. *madhhab*) emerged in the ninth and tenth centuries, giving form to the legal thought and legacy of particular authoritative figures or communities of the eighth and ninth centuries. This occurred after the schism between the followers of the Prophet's Companions (*ahl al-sunnah wa-l-jamāʿa*, the people of tradition and community) and the followers of the Prophet's son-in-law and cousin ʿAlī (*shīʿat ʿAlī*, in short Shīʿa, the partisans of ʿAlī) over the question of political succession after the Prophet's death. This led to the emergence of the Shīʿī *madhāhib*, which is identified with various imams. For example, the Imāmī, or Twelver, school of law, which encompasses most Shiites, emerged after the Occultation of the twelfth imam in 941.

The implications of the difference between the Sunnī and Shiites over the question of succession extended to the development of schools of law, since the Sunnī did not develop a clerical hierarchy with clear authority to pronounce and interpret law, whereas the Shiites did. It became the role of master jurists (sing. *mujtahid*) to articulate the doctrine and scholarship of the *madhāhib* for both jurists and lay Muslims to follow. Sunnī judicial authority was built gradually by generations of scholars around multiple centers, both geographic and personal. Sunnī *madhāhib* were organized first around particular locales and then around prominent scholars. By the tenth and eleventh centuries, the Mālikī school (named after Mālik ibn Anas, d. 795), the Ḥanafī school (named after Abū Ḥanīfa, d. 767), the Shāfiʿī school (named after Muḥammad ibn Idrīs al-Shāfiʿī, d. 820), the Ḥanbalī school (named after Ahmad ibn Ḥanbal, d. 855), and the Ẓāhirī school (which followed Dāʾūd ibn Khalaf, d. 883) represented distinct schools of thought and jurisprudence. By the twelfth century, almost all jurists had aligned themselves with the doctrine of a particular school.

These schools also came to dominate in different geographic regions—the Mālikī in North Africa, the Ḥanafī in South and Central Asia, the Shāfiʿī in Egypt and Southeast Asia, and the Ḥanbalī in North and Central Arabia. Together, the Sunnī *madhāhib* encompass most Muslims today, and although they differ on matters of doctrine, method, and substantive law, they recognize each other's validity and have continued to interact in legal debate and discourse.

Development of the Schools of Law. The sources of jurisprudence (*uṣūl al-fiqh*) for the Sunnī *madhāhib* are the Qurʾān, *Sunnah* (authoritative custom of the Prophet), *ijmāʿ* (consensus of the jurists), and *qiyās* (analogical reasoning). Despite the principle of mutual recognition, the Sunnī *madhāhib* differed in, and continued to be elaborated on the basis of, their approach to the authoritative sources of law, their methods of interpretation of those sources, their stance on the permissibility of applying human reasoning in jurisprudence, and their substantive rulings on specific local problems in law. Within each school there existed multiple ethnic, regional, intellectual, and scholarly variations, and a large part of the tradition of the *madhāhib* involves scholarly debates and disagreement over matters of substantive law and legal philosophy.

The Mālikī school of law, also known as the school of Medina or the school of the Hejaz, counts within its fold some of the first to follow the Prophet Muḥammad, such as his wife ʿĀʾishah and the second caliph ʿUmar ibn al-Khaṭṭāb. Accordingly, the school's rules emphasize the customs and practices of the people of Medina and the early Companions of the Prophet. Mālik's *al-Muwaṭṭaʾ* ('The Well-Trodden Path') is itself a compilation of traditions of the Prophet, the Companions, and the early Medinan Muslims, and his jurisprudence relied explicitly on these. This reliance on *Sunnah*, or custom, and not on authoritative *ḥadīth* until a later period, has also meant that Mālikī opinion on some matters reflected the practice of the time. Thus, on the personal status of women, it required a male guardian to consent to a woman's marriage and gave male guardians the right to contract marriages without the woman's consent. Mālikī influence spread from the Hejaz to Andalusia and North Africa because of contacts established during the *ḥājj* (pilgrimage to Mecca), and it replaced the Ẓāhirī school in these places under the patronage of the Umayyad dynasty. The Mālikī school is still dominant in these areas, as well as in many states of the Arabian Gulf.

The Ḥanafī school, originating in Kūfa (Iraq), combined an emphasis on human reasoning with a preference for the autonomy of the individual believer, which resulted in an approach to law that has widely been seen as the most liberal of the schools of law. The Ḥanafī *madhhab* was the first to develop rules on the performance of contracts. Its concepts of *qiyās* and *istiḥsān* (preference), which allowed pragmatic considerations to be a basis of jurisprudence, served to broaden the foundations on which Islamic law could rest. In this school, the autonomy of the Muslim individual extended to granting adult women the right to contract marriages for themselves (without the consent of a male guardian). The initial prominence of the Ḥanafī school can be traced to its elaboration by key actors in the ʿAbbāsid state who were students of Abū Ḥanīfa, in particular, by Abū Yūsuf (d. 798) and Muḥammad al-Shaybānī (d. 804). Later it became the dominant school in both the Mughal and Ottoman empires, and today it covers the broadest swath of the world's Muslim regions, from China to the Levant.

Al-Shāfiʿī, one of Mālik's students, embraced in his legal doctrines a synthesis between the traditionalism of the Mālikīs and the rationalism of the Ḥanafīs. His treatise *Kitāb al-Umm* ('The Basic Book') contains both the positive rules of his school and comparisons with the other schools of law, and it elaborates al-Shāfiʿī's insistence upon the traditionalist approach in matters of legal theory (*uṣūl al-fiqh*). The Shāfiʿī *madhhab* became prominent in Egypt with the rise of the Ayyūbids and later the Mamlūks, is dominant in Southeast Asia, and has significant numbers of adherents in South Asia, Iran, the Levant, Egypt, Iraq, Yemen, and the Hejaz.

Aḥmad ibn Ḥanbal, a student of al-Shāfiʿī, compiled more than forty thousand traditions of the Prophet and his Companions in his *Musnad*. This traditionalism is reflected in the Ḥanbalī definition of legal theory as containing five sources of law, arranged in order of priority: the Qurʾān and *sunnah*, fatwas of the Companions, narrations by individual Companions, traditions with weaker chains of transmission (*isnād*), and analogy (*qiyās*). Taking a strong stance against the rationalist doctrine that the Qurʾān was created, rather than eternal, Ibn Ḥanbal defied the ʿAbbāsid caliph al-Maʾmūn despite torture and imprisonment during the *miḥna* (the inquisition of Baghdad, from 833 to 861). Always the smallest of the four Sunnī *madhāhib*, two followers of the Ḥanbalī school, Ibn Taymiyya (d. 1327) and Muḥammad ibn ʿAbd al-Wahhāb (d. 1792), have been credited with its revival in more recent times. The jurisprudence of the Wahhābiyya movement rejects later scholarship and opinion in favor of such sources as the Qurʾān, *sunnah*, and a vision of a pure Islam from the time of the Prophet. It has gained popularity as a form of global Islamic reformism, being associated in particular with Saudi Arabia. The Ḥanbalī *madhhab* is also dominant in Qatar and parts of Iraq, Palestine, and Syria.

Traditionalism and Rationalism. The Ḥanbalī and Shāfiʿī *madhāhib* have been known as traditionalist, and its members as "followers of *ḥadīth*" (*ahl al-ḥadīth*), in contrast with the Ḥanafīs, who have been called rationalists and "followers of opinion" (*ahl al-raʾy*). In the writings of Mālik ibn Anas, the practice of the Medinan Muslims represented the most authoritative tradition (*sunnah*). The Ẓāhirī *madhhab* rejected all human opinion and analogical reasoning as a valid tool in jurisprudence in favor of the "literal" (*ẓāhir*) meanings of revealed text. Both the most rationalist of the *ahl al-raʾy* (the Muʿtazilī movement of theologians) and the most literalist of the *ahl al-ḥadīth* (the Ẓāhirīs) eventually declined in prominence, the latter being no longer considered a *madhhab*, although their approaches to law continue to exert influence.

Al-Shāfiʿī himself played a major role in the development of the *madhhab*, his synthesis of the traditionalist and rationalist approaches to law providing both the systematic basis for the elaboration of rules and the theoretical foundations on which later scholars could build. Al-Shāfiʿī placed these sources in a hierarchy of four. He prioritized (1) the Qurʾān and (2) the *sunnah* of the Prophet when transmitted by an authoritative chain of narrators (*isnād*), defined (3) *ijmāʿ* as the consensus of scholars, and replaced *raʾy* (human opinion) with the more constrained (4) *qiyās* (human reasoning that drew analogies between existing rules and new situations for law). Such followers of al-Shāfiʿī as Abu al-Abbas ibn Surayj (d. 918) taught his texts and methods and trained generations of important scholars, who in turn further established the techniques and legitimacy of this *madhhab* throughout much of the Muslim world.

Political Implications of the *Madhāhib*. Scholars affiliated with a *madhhab* were often supported by a private endowment (*waqf*). Such endowments funded colleges of higher Islamic learning (sing. *madrasa*) where scholars were trained in law and where debate was fostered. The *madhāhib* thus became institutionalized within regimes, supplying judges, jurists, and other legal officials who acted both for the state and independently. The *madhāhib* became recognized both as bodies of legal doctrine and interpretation and as communities of scholars of law and religion.

The relationship between scholars of Islamic law and the political power of the state has involved, at least since the ʿAbbāsid period, a delicate balancing act: it was the scholar (*ʿulamāʾ*, sing. *ʿālim*, henceforth, ulema) who interpreted the texts and made authoritative laws pronounced by the state, and it was adherence to and propagation of the law that made the state Islamic. The institutionalization of the legal schools and their affiliation with ruling regimes led to pressures to conform to earlier opinions and traditions within each school, but also to the development of legal doctrine to respond to new challenges. While later legal scholarship in each *madhhab* did tend to lean on commentaries on existing texts, which led to increasing doctrinal deference to established *madhhab* opinion (*taqlīd*), each *madhhab* also had mechanisms by which new legal ideas were authorized and legitimized. The Ḥanafī *madhhab*, for example, developed the concept of juristic preference (*istihsān*) beyond the four foundational sources of law.

Some Muslim imperial states favored particular *madhāhib* and extended their reach over localities that had previously been dominated by other schools. The ʿAbbāsids and Ottomans favored the Ḥanafī school—hence its large geographic spread. Efforts by Ḥanafī scholars to develop a jurisprudence with clear hierarchies among opinions and increasing standardization of doctrine lent their school to state administration and the extension of imperial power. The articulation of Ottoman or other imperial law over Muslim subjects of a different *madhhab* itself required new techniques and theories to reconcile multiple systems or prioritize the imperial *madhhab*. The needs of the state and calls for reform in Islamic law also occasioned new kinds of exchanges between the *madhāhib*. Thus, the methods of *talfīq* ("patching" rules from different *madhāhib* together) and *takhayyur* ("choosing" to apply rules from different *madhāhib*) came into common use. The Ottomans in 1876 codified portions of Ḥanafī law relating to contracts, procedures, and torts in the Mejelle (civil code), and in 1917 promulgated a family law based upon an amalgamation of doctrines of marriage, divorce, and personal status from various *madhāhib*.

Colonial and Contemporary Times. European colonialism and the development of modern states, with their near-monopoly on law-making and jurisdiction, have posed serious challenges to the juristic integrity of the *madhāhib* and their influence on legal practice. European colonial powers often sponsored and supported the translation of particular texts of Islamic law and extended their application to all areas under their jurisdiction, to the exclusion of other texts and interpretations, thus contributing to a sense of Islamic law as being rigid and unchanging. One example of this development was the nineteenth-century English translation and use of *Al-Hidāya* (divine guidance), by Burhān al-Dīn al-Farghānī al-Marghīnānī (d. 1196), as a textbook of Ḥanafī law in British India—a text that excised ambiguities from the original text and in many cases replaced local experts with the letter of the law as taken from the Anglo-Muḥammadan *Hedaya*.

The reorganization of Islamic legal institutions, including the institutions of learning and adjudication that housed scholars of Islamic law, and their incorporation into the colonial state had profound implications for the modern development of the *madhhab* system. Some, such as the Deoband school in India, which followed Ḥanafī law, have developed in competition and cooperation with the modernizing state, while others have seen their influence wane as the institutions and resources on which they relied became marginalized and replaced by state administration. The *madhāhib* have also faced the challenge of adapting doctrine to new issues that face increasingly mobile communities of Muslims, with the result that global issues of immigration, communications, and other problems have transformed the regional character of the *madhhab*.

While the *madhāhib* continue to find expression in the national legal systems of many Muslim states, their jurisdiction, with a few notable exceptions (such as Saudi Arabia), has been limited mostly to the domain of personal status, family law, and some areas of ritual practice. In addition, national laws and state legal institutions have exercised increasing amounts of control over legal interpretation, with non-*Sharīʿah*-trained judges, lawyers, and policymakers taking over the domain of the *Sharīʿah* scholar in the elaboration of law, and the state legal academy encroaching on the domain of the Islamic scholar in the development of legal theory. In the contemporary period, national legal practice and state law, rather than the *madhhab*, have come to determine much of Muslim legal practice, and the influence of the *madhāhib* in each jurisdiction depends on the position of local ulema and Islamic institutions in the national system. Some ulema, such as those in Indonesia, have responded with calls for a new, national *madhhab*, while others rely less on the formal doctrine of a particular *madhhab* and more on the formulation of new rules based on the Qurʾān and *sunnah* alone.

Islamic movements that are global, rather than nation-state–focused, have drawn upon various *madhāhib* to appeal to Muslims worldwide, often characterizing local practices as "impure" Islam and offering an interpretation of Islam based strictly on the Qurʾān and *sunnah*. The Ḥanbalī *madhhab* in particular has been represented as a version of Islam whose strong adherence to the *sunnah* of the Prophet offers an antidote to both impure local Islamic traditions and the ills of modernization and Westernization. This variant of Ḥanbalī practice has been labeled, often pejoratively, as Wahhabism because of its perceived sponsorship by Saudi Arabia. Other movements, such as networks of ulema based in Indonesia who belong to the Shāfiʿī school but distance themselves from the doctrine of Indonesian state-based ulema, and some scholars based in the United States and other non-Muslim-majority states, offer a liberal interpretation of Islamic law aimed at solving problems faced by contemporary Muslims without the focus on the jurisprudence of a particular *madhhab* or region.

[*See also* Colonialism and the Muslim World; Deobandīs; Fiqh; Kānūn; Jurisprudential Council of North America; Minorities in Muslim States; *and* Mughal Empire.]

BIBLIOGRAPHY

Bearman, Peri, Rudolph Peters, and Frank Vogel, eds. *The Islamic School of Law: Evolution, Devolution, and Progress*. Cambridge, Mass.: Harvard University Press, 2005.

Hallaq, Wael. *The Origins and Evolution of Islamic Law*. Cambridge, U.K.: Cambridge University Press, 2005.

Hallaq, Wael. *Sharia: Theory, Practice, Transformations*. Cambridge, U.K.: Cambridge University Press, 2009.

Kamali, Mohammad Hashim. *Principles of Islamic Jurisprudence*. Cambridge, U.K.: Islamic Texts Society, 1991.

Kozlowski, Gregory C. *Muslim Endowments and Society in British India*. Cambridge, U.K.: Cambridge University Press, 1985.

Mahmassani, Subhi. *The Philosophy of Jurisprudence in Islam*. Translated by Farhat J. Ziadeh. Leiden, Netherlands: Brill, 1961.

Melchert, Christopher. *The Formation of the Sunni School of Law, 9th–10th Centuries C.E.* Leiden, Netherlands: E. J. Brill, 1997.

Rahman, Fazlur. *Islam*. 2d ed. Chicago: University of Chicago Press, 1979.

Schacht, Joseph. *The Origins of Muhammadan Jurisprudence.* Oxford: Clarendon Press, 1953.
Weiss, Bernard G. *The Spirit of Islamic Law.* Athens: University of Georgia Press, 1998.
Wheeler, Brannon. *Applying the Canon in Islam: The Authorization and Maintenance of Interpretive Reasoning in Hanafi Scholarship.* Albany: State University of New York Press, 1996.

IZA HUSSIN

SECULARISM. Political secularism has distinct European roots. It emerged in response to the problem of religion in political life. Islam has long been viewed as a religious tradition that is uniquely anti-secular. Influential scholars in the social sciences have argued that Islam's early formative historical experience and its inner theology have prevented secularism from developing. The strength of these arguments was enhanced by the writings of political Islamists in the twentieth century who rejected any separation between *dīn wa-dawlah* (religion and government) in their normative theories on what constituted a just political order.

The problems with secularism in Muslim societies are rooted in the lived experiences of Muslim communities since the early nineteenth century. The most politically salient part of this lived experience has been the encounter with European (and later American) imperialism. The 2003 American-Anglo invasion and occupation of Iraq is just the latest chapter in a long series of interventions that has shaped the moral context in which debates on modernization and secularism have taken place. In broad terms, the Muslim experience has been marked by a perception of secularism as an alien ideology initially imposed from outside by invaders and then kept alive by the postcolonial states and the ruling elites who came to power after World War II. As a result, secularism in the Muslim world has suffered from weak intellectual roots and, with a few exceptions, most notably Turkey, it has never penetrated the mainstream of Muslim societies.

For generations of Muslims growing up in the postcolonial era, despotism, dictatorship, and human rights abuses came to be associated with secularism. Muslim political activists who experienced oppression at the hands of secular national governments concluded that secularism is an ideology of repression.

The Ottoman Empire and Its Legacy. Ottoman Turkey, as a bureaucratic empire, had institutionalized both civil and religious authority in the imperial administration and in the figure of the sultan. During the nineteenth century, a state-sponsored modernizing reform movement created secular institutions intended to introduce Western educational methods, legal systems, and military techniques. This process of reform, called the Tanzimat (reorganization), encountered resistance throughout the century.

After World War I and the defeat of the Ottoman Empire, the new state of Turkey emerged under the leadership of Mustafa Kemal, later known as Atatürk. He abolished both the political sultanate and religious caliphate, opening the way for a secular state on the French model in which Islam would be relegated to the private sphere. The Muslim calendar was replaced by the Gregorian and Arabic script by Latin, and the veil was discouraged. This top-down secularization process created an authoritarian secular state, but it could not erase Islam as a religion followed by the masses. With the advent of a multiparty democratic system after World War II, secular politicians often won elections by appealing to mass religiosity, thus appearing to threaten the legacy of Atatürk. Military intervention in Turkish politics has been frequent throughout the twentieth century. In 1997 the military once again intervened to topple a coalition government led by an Islamist-based party, thus highlighting the ongoing political tensions in Turkey over the boundaries of Islamic expression. The rise of a series of religious-based political parties in the 1990s has placed the question of secularism at the center of Turkish politics. The controversy is between contrasting interpretations of the concept of secularism: an Anglo-American version, which allows for religious participation in public life, versus a more draconian French secularism, which views such participation as a threat to social order and which is championed by the Kemalist establishment and the Turkish military. The overwhelming landslide victories for the Adalet ve Kalkınma (AK) Party in the 2002, 2007, and 2011 elections and the election of Abdullah Gül, a senior leader of the AK Party, as president suggest a victory for proponents of Anglo-American secularism in Turkey.

The Arab World and Iran. A range of governments exist in the Arab Muslim world, from the Wahhābī-sanctioned Saudi Arabian state to the avowedly secular socialist regimes in Algeria and Syria. Saudi Arabia, because of the two-centuries-old link of the House of Saud to the Wahhābī reform movement, proclaims itself an Islamic state. Technically, its rulers are secular officials governing in accordance with the *Sharīʿah* as interpreted by the *ʿulamāʾ* (clergy). Islam legitimizes the state, which is governed by a strict interpretation of Islamic law. Saudi officials finance Islamic movements in other states against governments that are deemed hostile to Saudi Arabia's interests. Nevertheless, the Saudi ruling family has come under attack from more fundamentalist Muslim groups for its supposed deviation from Islamic norms.

At the opposite end of the spectrum are the secular regimes in Syria, Algeria, Tunisia (under Ben Ali), Egypt (under Mubarak), and Yemen (under ʿAlī ʿAbd Allāh Ṣāliḥ), each ruling in the name of various forms of Arab nationalism, although in the final years of the last three rulers they attempted to shore up their legitimacy in the face of Islamist opposition by claiming to respect and uphold religious values. Concessions have been made to religious groups in society in the hope of pacifying opposition to the state. The future of many of these regimes is uncertain due to the tumultuous events related to the Arab Spring.

In Iraq, following the overthrow of Saddam Hussein, Islamist parties and militias flourished. Despite their differences and the competition for resources and political power, these parties were united by an explicit rejection of secularism. This was in large part because of the perception of Baʿthist rule as an outgrowth of secularist ideology. Even the once powerful Communist Party, decimated under Saddam Hussein, adopted the politics of religion to spread its message. In the constitutional meetings that sought to draft a new Iraqi constitution, the majority of the delegates, reflecting popular opinion, insisted on assurances that the principles of Islam would not be violated and that Islam would be the state religion and a source of legal opinion. A similar set of events occurred in Afghanistan during its post-Taliban constitutional process.

A condemnation of the concept of secularism and secularist intellectuals has been a staple of Islamic revolutionary discourse in Iran since the 1979 revolution. The perception of a close association between secularism, imperialism, and the foreign policies of the great powers has been a staple of official ideology of the Iranian regime since its rise to power.

In the second decade after the Iranian Revolution, a gradual indigenization of political secularism took place in Iran, led by religious intellectuals and some dissenting clerical figures. The enveloping context that gave force to this intellectual transformation was Iran's negative experience with clerical rule after the revolution and the failures of the Islamic Republic to meet the aspirations of many members of the educated and middle-class segments of society who desired more freedom, rights, and accountability in government. Most of Iran's leading intellectuals and political dissidents, including prominent figures such as Shirin Ebadi, Abdolkarim Soroush, Akbar Ganji, Mohsen Kadivar, Ibrāhīm Yazdī, and many others support a separation of religion from state, although not a separation of religion from politics.

The Arab world is currently in the midst of a momentous political transformation known in the West as the Arab Spring. In 2011 three longstanding dictators were toppled (Zine el Abedine Ben Ali, Tunisia; Hosni Mubarak, Egypt; and Muʿammar al-Qadhdhāfī, Libya) while two others, Bashar al-Assad in Syria and ʿAlī ʿAbd Allāh Ṣāliḥ in Yemen, clung to power in the face of massive nonviolent protests. To the extent that these countries undergo democratic transition, the questions of religion-state relations and political secularism will inevitably emerge as points of contention that will be strongly debated and hotly contested. Events in Tunisia and Egypt post-2011 have demonstrated this point.

South and Southeast Asia. India's Muslim population is estimated at 140 million, which is only 12 percent of the total population. With independence in 1947, the Indian polity proclaimed itself a democratic secular state with religious identities presumably subsumed under the common bond of Indian nationalism. The dominant Congress Party had long claimed to embrace all religious and ethnic groups as Indian. Although still a secular state, India has fallen victim to sectarian passions, Sikh as well as Hindu. Hindu revivalism has focused on a desire to erase India's Islamic past. Hindu sectarianism, encouraged by poverty and illiteracy, has become a political force threatening the basis of Indian citizenship.

In principle, Pakistan has always been an Islamic republic; however, it was governed for years as a secular state. The 1956 constitution, though making obeisance to Islamic thought, was not bound by Islamic statutes. It contained secular laws creating a parliamentary democracy on the British model with the parliamentary right to ensure that no laws were passed that undermined Islamic legal principles. The distinction between adherence to Islamic legal principles versus a strict application of Islamic law is the classic modernist position. It essentially permits the existence of a secular state and the tolerance of a secular urban culture in a Muslim society whose constitutional framework and popular culture would remain Islamic.

Pakistani history in the twenty-first century has reflected the tensions inherent in its past struggles between democracy and state enforcement of an Islamic system, as well as between conflicting visions of Islam. The struggle between Islamic modernism and traditionalism continues, buffeted by external factors such as Afghan resistance to Soviet occupation, which became a popular Sunnī Muslim cause and strengthened traditionalist as well as fundamentalist Islam during the 1980s. NATO intervention in Afghanistan after 11 September 2001 has strengthened this trend to a considerable degree.

The South Asian experience has produced two social movements with opposing philosophical orientations with respect to society and the state, the Jamāʿat-i Islāmī and Tablīghī Jamāʿat. On an organizational level, the politically activist Jamāʿat-i Islāmī has succeeded in influencing political debate in Pakistan but has failed to win popular electoral backing; the Tablīghī Jamāʿat in contrast rejects political activism, opting for individual preaching and moral reform. In essence these movements reflect the two poles of Islamic *daʿwah*, or propagation of the faith. The first group rejects secularism outright; the second views its political manifestation as a necessary evil to be tolerated in order to fulfill personal religious goals. They both claim to return to the same source, early Islam, for inspiration, as do Islamic modernists and Islamic fundamentalists.

Analogous differences appear in the two sharply contrasting approaches to Islam and secularism found in Malaysia and Indonesia, which are a result of their different histories and colonial experiences. As Manning Nash has observed, both Malaysia and Indonesia are "Islamic nations but secular states," but their concepts of nationhood are quite different.

Indonesia is home to more than 242 million people, with a population that is nearly 88 percent Muslim. It is the largest Muslim country in the world, but the state is based on the concept of Pancasila, whose first principle, enshrined in the constitution, is "belief in the one and only God." Secular and Islamic educational systems are both state-sponsored, and secular and *Sharīʿah* courts coexist, but this duality does not mean that the products of the secular education system are antireligious. Many, like their counterparts in Northern Africa, are devout Muslims who accept a quasi-secular state as preferable to a religious one so long as all mainstream religions are respected. Infringement can arouse protest, as occurred in the mid-1970s when the government was forced to withdraw a proposed family status/marriage law that would have permitted Muslim women to marry non-Muslim men and granted civil courts final authority in cases regarding divorce or polygamy. Strong public opposition led to a reassertion of Muslim statutes and legal authority in such cases and banned interreligious marriages for Muslim women. Indonesian tolerance and pluralism regarding manifestations of Islam could easily change if the state were perceived as trying to Westernize at the expense of Islamic norms.

Indonesia, like the rest of the Muslim world, experienced an Islamic resurgence in the latter half of the twentieth century. This resurgence played a central role in opposing the authoritarianism of the Suharto regime (1966–1998) and in the democratic transition that followed his ouster. A distinguishing feature of this religious resurgence—in contrast to the rest of the Muslim world—has been its tolerant and democratic orientation; "civil Islam," in the words of Robert Hefner.

Malaysia is over 50 percent Muslim. Islam serves as a source of national identity to Malays in a country with Chinese and Indian minorities amounting to 37 and 11 percent of the population, respectively. Nevertheless, Malaysian Islam is itself fragmented. Though there is a national government and Islamic officialdom, there are thirteen states, nine of which have their own bureaus, legal officials, and religious courts. With such official fragmentation, Islamic revivalism has taken root in the *dakwah* (missionary) movement. Many young Malays of the *dakwah* desire an Islamic state. They are quite similar in aspiration to the Muslim Brotherhood. The achievement of their goals would signify the end of the current Malaysian secular state unless explicit guarantees for ethnic minorities were given. The main political party that embodies these aspirations is the Pan-Malaysian Islamic Party (PAS).

In both Malaysia and Indonesia there has been a growing movement for the implementation of *Sharīʿah* law. This poses a major challenge to the secular state and has mobilized a coalition of groups composed of feminists, human rights activists, religious minorities, lawyers, and intellectuals who oppose this trend.

The Secular States and Its Elites. The historical relationship between secularism and Islam has passed through several stages that have varied according to the particular Islamic society in question. Muslim governing elites were often attracted to Western secular values in the nineteenth century, because Western culture had proved superior militarily. In the early twentieth century, a new generation mostly educated in Western schools more readily turned to European values in the context of struggles for national independence that produced various forms of secular nationalisms.

In many Muslim-majority societies the early postcolonial states were ruled by secular nationalist leaders who attempted to rapidly modernize their societies. While the case of Mustafa Kemal in Turkey was certainly unique in terms of its harsh secularization polices, most ruling elites in the Muslim world followed this developmental model. What these regimes all had in common was their authoritarian nature, and their policies eventually produced a backlash. Summarizing the trend, Vali Nasr has noted:

> Secularism in the Muslim world never overcame its colonial origins and never lost its association with the postcolonial state's continuous struggle to dominate society. Its fortunes became tied to those of the state: the more the state's ideology came into question, and the more its actions alienated social forces, the more secularism was rejected in favor of indigenous worldviews and social institutions—which were for the most part tied to Islam. As such, the decline of secularism was a reflection of the decline of the postcolonial state in the Muslim world. (Nasr, 2003, p. 69)

Asef Bayat has identified an emerging trend in Islamic politics called "post-Islamism." Based on a specific trajectory of mainstream Islamist thought, it seeks to reconcile tradition with modernity, especially democracy and human rights. According to Bayat, "post-Islamism is not anti-Islamic or secular; a post-Islamist movement dearly upholds religion but also highlights citizens' rights. It aspires to a pious society within a democratic state" (Bayat, 2011). He lists Iran's Green Movement, Turkey's AK Party, Morocco's Justice and Development Party (PJD), and Egypt's Ḥizb al-Wasat Party as embodying this trend. Tunisia's Ennahda Party, led by Rāshid al-Ghannūshī, arguably could also be added to this list. The internal debates on religion-state relations and secularism within this broad intellectual trend will likely dictate how Muslim societies will approach the concept of secularism in the coming decades.

[*See also* Jamāʿat-i Islāmī; Mawdūdī, Sayyid Abū al-Aʿlā; *and* Tablīghī Jamāʿat.]

BIBLIOGRAPHY

An-Na'im, Abdullahi Ahmed. *Islam and the Secular State: Negotiating the Future of Shari'a.* Cambridge, Mass.: Harvard University Press, 2008.

ʿAẓmah, ʿAzīz. *Al-ʿalmānīyah min manẓūr mukhtalif.* Beirut: Markaz Dirāsāt al-Waḥdah al-ʿArabīyah, 2008.

Bayat, Asef. "The Post-Islamist Revolutions." *Foreign Affairs,* 26 April 2011. http://www.foreignaffairs.com/articles/67812/asef-bayat/the-post-islamist-revolutions.

Calhoun, Craig, Mark Juergensmeyer, and Jonathan VanAntwerpen, eds. *Rethinking Secularism.* New York: Oxford University Press, 2011.

Farha, Mark. "Global Gradations of Secularism: The Consociational, Communal, and Coercive Paradigms." *Special Issue: Heterogeneity and Democracy; Comparative Sociology* 11, no. 3 (Winter 2011): 354–386.

Hashemi, Nader. "The Multiple Histories of Secularism: Muslim Societies in Comparison." *Philosophy and Social Criticism* 36, nos. 3–4 (2010): 325–338.

Keddie, Nikki R. "Secularism and Its Discontents." *Daedalus* 132 (Summer 2003): 14–30.

Nasr, Vali. "Lessons from the Muslim World." *Daedalus* 132 (Summer 2003): 67–72.

Roy, Olivier. *Secularism Confronts Islam.*Translated by George Holoch. New York: Columbia University Press, 2007.

Tamimi, Azzam, and John L. Esposito, eds. *Islam and Secularism in the Middle East.* New York: New York University Press, 2000.

NADER HASHEMI

SELJUK DYNASTY. The original Seljuks (or "Great Saljūqs," 1038–1194) were part of the broad grouping of Turks who were converted to Islam in the late tenth century, probably by traveling Ṣūfī missionaries, while still living by the Syr Darya River, on the borders of the *dār al-Islām* (Muslim lands). They and their followers were hired as mercenaries by the Sāmānid and Karakhanid rulers of Transoxiana and then moved into the eastern Iranian province of Khorāsān in 1035, under the leadership of two brothers, Toghril Beg and Chaghri Beg. They defeated the dominant power in the region, the Ghaznavid *sulṭān* Masʿūd, at Dandānqān in 1040. Chaghri was left to hold the east while Toghril marched westward, entering Baghdad in 1055, bringing to an end the rule of the Shīʿī Būyids.

Toghril Beg's arrival in Baghdad signaled major changes in the political situation in the ʿAbbāsid capital. It is from this period that formal recognition of the Seljuk leader as *sulṭān* (meaning ruler in temporal affairs) created a situation responding to political reality; while the caliph remained the symbolic holder of religious legitimacy, *sulṭāns* would henceforth vie for control of the reins of the government and the military.

By the time of Toghril's death in 1063, the Seljuk Empire included Iran and Iraq as well as parts of Syria. By about 1100—and despite regional declarations of continued broad Seljuk dynastic control from the original core of the sultanate—the rise of the Seljuks of Rum in Asia Minor, or Anatolia (c. 1077–1307), appeared to overshadow the importance of Seljuk dominions to the east. Alp Arslan precipitated clashes with Emperor Romanus Diogenes in Christian-dominated Asia Minor. The famous battle of Manzikert in 1071, during which the emperor was taken prisoner, opened Anatolia to gradual occupation by Turkic groups united under the Seljuk banner.

THE GREAT SELJUK DYNASTIC LINE (IRAQ AND PERSIA)

Ṭughril (r. 1038–1063)
Alp Arslan (r. 1063–1072)
Malik Shāh I (r. 1072–1092)
Maḥmūd I (r. 1092–1094)
Barkiyāruq (r. 1094–1105)
Malik Shāh II (r. 1105)
Muḥammad I (r. 1105–1118)
Sanjar (r. 1118–1157)

The impact of the First Crusade on Seljuk dominions varied between regions. In Syria, although there are recorded instances of Seljuk-sponsored local confrontations with Christian intruders, one cannot say that an actual coordinated policy emerged that drew systematic attention from Baghdad. In Anatolia, by contrast, the recurring presence of Roman Catholic crusading forces both in the Levant and in Anatolia itself contributed to a complex set of military and political relationships affecting the Seljuk sultanate at Konya. By the twefth century, control was passing back and forth between the Seljuk *sulṭāns* and their main Muslim rivals in Anatolia, the Danishmendids. The most successful Danishmendid chief, Amīr Ghāzī (d. 1134), managed to prop up his son-in-law Masʿūd as commander of a sort of "protectorate" over a geographically limited Seljuk sultanate in Konya. This situation of dependency allowed the Byzantine emperor John II to isolate and temporarily defeat Seljuk forces at key points on the Byzantine border, while Emir Ghāzī essentially left the Seljuks to their fate, engaging his main forces against the Duke of Trabzon on the Black Sea. Ghazi's eventually serious interest in Konya came when he invaded Cilicia to reverse the advance of Christian Crusaders from Syria. Because of this service and until his death in 1134, Ghāzī enjoyed open recognition from the Seljuk *sulṭān* Sanjar of Baghdad, who bestowed upon him the title of Malik (king) Ghāzī—thus apparently setting aside Seljuk claims to Konya. Ghāzī passed this title on to his son Mehmed, but Danishmendid fratricidal struggles soon allowed the Seljuk claimant Masʿūd to retake the dynasty's former domains and to reverse Byzantine advances by 1147. Masʿūd then demonstrated his loyalty to the Muslim cause in Syria by repeating Emir Ghāzī's earlier campaigns to retake the key centers of the Anatolian southeast (Maraş, Aintab) from Crusader infiltration of Syria.

THE DYNASTIC LINE OF THE SELJUKS OF RUM

Sulaymān ibn Qutalmısh (r. 1077–1086)
Interregnum Qılıch Arslan I (r. 1092–1107)
Malik Shāh (r. 1107–1116)
Masʿūd I (r. 1116–1156)
Qılıch Arslan II (r. 1156–1192)
Kay Khusraw I (r. 1192–1196)
Sulaymān II (r. 1196–1204)
Qılıch Arslan III (r. 1204)
Kay Khusraw I (second reign, 1204–1210)
Kay Kāʿūs (Kāwūs) I (r. 1210–1219)
Kay Qubādh I (r. 1219–1237)
Kay Khusraw II (r. 1237–1246)
Kay Kāʿūs (Kāwūs) II and Qılıch Arslan IV (r. jointly, 1248)
Kay Kāʿūs (Kāwūs) II, Qılıch Arslan IV, and Kay Qubādh II (r. jointly, 1249–1257)
Qılıch Arslan IV (r. 1257–1265)
Kay Khusraw III (r. 1265–1282)
Masʿūd II (r. 1282–1284)
Kay Qubādh III (r. 1284)
Masʿūd II (r. 1284–1293)
Kay Qubādh III (r. 1293–1294)
Masʿūd II (r. 1294–1301)
Kay Qubādh III (r. 1301–1303)
Masʿūd II (r. 1303–1305)
Kay Qubādh III (r. 1305–1307)
Masʿūd III (r. 1307)

Sulṭān Masʿūd's death in 1155 ushered in the long reign of his son Qılıch Arslan II (r. 1156–1192) and, by the middle of the next century, the establishment in Konya not only of effective ruling institutions and administration but also of an impressive array of monumental structures. Among these the best known was (and remains) the mausoleum of the mystic poet Jalāl al-Dīn Rūmī (born in what is now Tajikistan but resident in Konya from c. 1230) and several major *madrasahs* (schools), including the Karatay Madrasah (now a museum), the Ince Minareli Madrasah, and the Sircali Madrasah.

It was the rising pressures of Mongol advances from the east that presaged an end to Seljuk ascendancy, already a fact in Iran and then, in stages following the battle of Köse Dagh near Sivas in 1243, ushering in the last stages of the Sultanate of Rum.

BIBLIOGRAPHY

Golombek, Lisa. "The Saljuq Monuments of Kirman." In *T. Cuyler Young, Jr. Festschrift 2005: March 30, 1934–February 7, 2006*. Toronto: Canadian Society for Mesopotamian Studies, 2005.

Ibn al-Athīr, ʿIzz al-Dīn. *The Annals of the Saljuq Turks: Selections from al-Kāmil fī'l-Taʾrīkh of ʿIzz al-Dīn ibn al-Athīr*. Translated and edited by D. S. Richards. London: RoutledgeCurzon, 2002.

Schnyder, R. "Political Centres and Artistic Powers in Saljuq Iran." In *Islamic Civilisation, 950–1150*, edited by D. S. Richards, pp. 201–209. Oxford: Cassirer, 1973.

BYRON D. CANNON
Updated by KHALED M. G. KESHK

SEXUALITY. "Sexuality in Islam" and "sexuality in the Muslim world" sometimes overlap. Their relationship is analogous to that between "what people do" and "what people say." Any definition of sexuality in Islam and/or Muslim society must describe the relationship inscribed in the pendulum between discourse and practice, text and context, theory and praxis, while taking into consideration how time, space, labor, and capital are divided and gendered, how power relations are sexualized, and how sexual intercourse is politicized.

In the Muslim world, sexuality is both more exposed, as it is the subject of extensive Islamic discourse, and more confined, as Islam often stresses the regulation of sexuality and the control of one's body. This ambivalence between the "openness" and "closedness" of Islamic sexuality is embodied in a dualism between opposing genres. On one hand, Orientalist literature puts the stress on "libertinism," "sexual freedom," and "boy-love" in Islam (e.g., the old and new translations of *One Thousand and One Nights*, the poems of Abū Nuwās, and the texts of Shaykh Nafzāwī).

On the other hand, pseudo-academic or populist literature emphasizes the negative side: how sexuality is repressed, women are sexually exploited, men and women are sexually frustrated by gender separation, and the like, or, on the contrary, it focuses only on an extraordinary Muslim man/woman who dares to expose his/her "deviant" sexuality. Note that, for instance, most of the time women's sexuality in Muslim societies is debated either in a lesbian context or one of family honor and shame. It is seldom that a woman is given the opportunity to speak freely about her body, sexuality, and physical pleasures.

In the mid-1970s academic literature started to take interest in the subject of sexuality in Muslim societies and in the Islamic written tradition in general. Efforts were made to present a balanced picture compatible with the equilibrium that exists between religious texts and sexual practices in Muslim societies. In this sense Abdelwahab Bouhdiba showed how some social and cultural practices, such as the *ḥammām* (steam bath), "temper" sexual frustration and tensions between sexes. On a similar note, Fatima Mernissi argued, based on her experience in a bourgeois household in the city of Fez, that Moroccan women try frequently to transgress the sexualized boundaries and challenge the gender segregation imposed by tradition and some "false" *ḥadīth* used to control women and their sexualities. Both authors call for a return to the origins of Islam to look for an essence of "Islamic feminism," as Mernissi called it, while Bouhdiba dubbed the same phenomena the "idyllic sexuality in the Golden Age of Islam."

Islamic canonic texts, in general, promote licit sex within marriage and recognize that the purpose of sex is not restricted to procreation, as pleasure is taken into account as well; for this reason contraception has always been tolerated, both in its more primitive forms, such as coitus interruptus (*ʿazl*), and in its scientific medical forms, such as birth-control pills, male and female condoms, vaginal rings, the cap or diaphragm, and so on, including abortion. Islam prohibits *zinā*ʾ (adultery), such as pre- and extramarital sex, but does allow in some cases various means to circumvent the restrictions of the *Sharīʿah*, such as *zawāj al-mutʿah* in Arabic, or *sīgheh* in Farsi—temporary marriage recognized by Shīʿī Islam—or polygamy in Sunnī Islam. Homosexuality is not regarded as *zinā*ʾ, as it is outside the equation of licit/illicit; it is categorically forbidden and severely punished, at least de jure. In practice, homosexuals, effeminate men, and lesbians are tacitly tolerated on the society's margins. A woman's virginity is a major consideration for marriage, and early marriage is encouraged to avoid *zinā*ʾ and illicit relationships. Teenagers are not encouraged to engage in romantic relationships owing to the possibility that they will lead to sexual relations. Regardless, the practices of everyday life in a given Muslim society are far from the puritan regulations prescribed by *Sharīʿah* texts.

In the 1980s several academic monographs, aware of this dissymmetry between religious statutes and actuality, tried to bridge this gap. Basim Musallam's 1983 monograph on contraception in medieval Muslim societies and texts is a groundbreaking study, followed by Judith Tucker's *Women in Nineteenth-Century Egypt*, which showed the darker aspects of the modernization process and how the introduction of new technologies to Egypt exposed women to slavery rather than liberating them.

Sexuality, Gender, and Islamic Feminism. Relationships between men and women in Muslim societies are determined by several factors: (a) how space, time, labor, and capital are divided and gendered; (b) the fact of biology that men are physically stronger than women; (c) the banality of the practices of everyday life; and, lastly, (d) what God and other Islamic texts say.

The last becomes significant when people have recourse to justice, religious authority, or the state in general as arbiter in issues that concern *qānūn al-aḥwāl al-shakhṣīyah*, personal status or family law.

Generally, the Qurʾān is more generous with men than with women, especially regarding inheritance, polygamy, and control over one's body. However, there are several instances in which this generosity has been accentuated not by the enforcement of religious text, but by societal traditions. Thus, while men are expected to protect their wives and provide for their needs and desires, women are required to obey their husbands. Moreover, the gender-segregated organization of everyday life through the regulation and limitation of interactions between the sexes is common in Muslim societies. Women are expected to adhere to the rules of modesty in the public sphere; dress codes, including veiling, are common ways of controlling the presence of women in the social spheres of many Muslim countries.

The division of space and time is also dictated by societal logic: the indoors are for women, outdoors for men; housework for women, outside work for men; public space for men, private space for women; nighttime is not for women, daytime and nighttime are both for men. These divisions are always challenged, contested, and transgressed by the conditions of the societal milieu (urban/rural, agrarian/industrial), ecological factors (nomadic/sedentary/transhumant), the necessities of modern life, and the will of women to emancipate their self.

The 1990s and the first decade of the twenty-first century witnessed the emergence of several feminist activist voices, from outside as well as from within Muslim societies, which asked for parity and equality between sexes and political recognition of "deviant" identities that stem from "illicit" sexual relations, such as male and female homosexuality. Several studies have tried to understand the impact of these movements on their societies, while others turned directly to studying societal phenomena that were regarded as deviant and taboo. The trend took advantage of the fact that the 1990s were the heyday of the American academic and ideological movements of feminism, gender studies, gay and lesbian studies, subaltern studies, and postcolonial theory. Many of these methodologies and theories were imported into Middle Eastern studies and gave researchers and scholars a sophisticated analytic arsenal. The use of postmodernist and poststructuralist theoretical framework is an efficient way to argue for liberating bodies and freeing identities that were born from all kind of "deviant" or "illicit" sexual relationship.

Normal and Abnormal Sexuality. The 1990s feminist wave opened venues for sensitive topics and subjects that were and still are considered taboo (e.g., homosexuality, masturbation, oral sex, eroticism, pornography, sadomasochism, virginity, women's sexual desire, etc.), not only in academic literature but also in the popular press, mass culture, and yellow press, and through digital technologies of communication and social networks. Thus, several daily newspapers in countries like Morocco, Egypt, and Lebanon added "sexual education" supplements in which youngsters could ask questions about their sexualities and have them answered by professional sexologists and psychotherapists, a trend that became popular not only among youths but also among parents who felt the need, like their children, to understand their sexuality. This socio-psychological situation reached its apogee with the emergence in 2008 in Beirut, Lebanon, of the first Arabic erotic cultural magazine, *Jasad*, which was founded by a young intellectual Lebanese woman, Joumana Haddad. The articles, which bear the real names of the authors—no pseudonyms are allowed—are in Arabic, because sex and sexuality are usually debated in today's Arab-Muslim societies in foreign languages, especially English and French.

In this vein, at the level of academic discourse, several interesting studies have been carried out: Stephen O. Murry and Will Roscoe's *Islamic Homosexuality* offered a historical and cross-cultural synthesis of different discourses and practices of homosexuality in medieval Muslim societies—trying to put an end to the orientalist discourse on boy-love in medieval Arab-Islamic literature—and refuted the prejudice that men slept with men because women were "hard to get" in Muslim societies. Through historical, anthropological, and literary studies and texts documenting the conceptions and organizations of homosexual desire and conduct in Islamic societies, their book successfully dealt with the subject outside the Islamic canonical texts. In his *Before Homosexuality in the Arab-Islamic World, 1500–1800*, Khaled El-Rouayheb investigated the state of "homosexuality" in premodern Muslim societies in a large Arab-Muslim corpus of written tradition, including medieval literature, theology, jurisprudence, chronicles, and the like. He came to the conclusion that there was no concept of "homosexuality" in premodern Muslim societies: the one who played the "active" role was not regarded as someone who was transgressing any gender role, whereas the love for beardless men or beautiful boys was a platonic metaphor for beauty used by the urban elite whose aesthetic taste was very sophisticated. Joseph Massad's *Desiring Arabs* took on the subject with a militant tone, positing the influence and monopoly of an abstract and corrupting sexual Western cultural that he called the "gay international" that operates through nongovernmental organizations (NGOs) and influences the mores or norms, and forms Arab-Muslim youth's perception of their sexuality. Based on a conference at the American University of Beirut, *Sexuality in the Arab World* includes chapters that attempt to address the subject with an anthropological approach, focusing on how Arab youths live, practice, and talk about their sexual practices (heterosexuality and homosexuality alike) in everyday life. Although the case studies try to focus on local contexts, such as youth in Tunis, Beirut, and Damascus, the framework of the study deals with sexuality in the Arab world in the context of globalization, new technologies, traveling, satellite TV, and the Internet. The general conclusion of the conference's panels and the book is that, despite the growing awareness of the importance of sex and sexuality in Arab societies, there hasn't been any open or informal public debate or exploration in this context, a vacuum that the researchers and the editors of the book think that NGOs may fill—the same NGOs that Joseph Massad accuses of corrupting Arab youth's sexuality on the levels of both discourse and practice.

In his *Producing Desire*, Dror Ze'evi also accuses the West of exporting to the Ottoman Middle East, along with imperialism and colonialism, the Judeo-Christian Puritan spirit, which was silent on the practice of sodomy, a tendency that in return silenced Ottoman literature and other written traditions on the subject of sexuality in general and homoerotism in particular.

The thesis, which accuses European Puritanism of repressing the Arab-Muslim libido through imperialism and colonialism, was adopted by a large number of studies, most of which are from the first decade of the twenty-first century. Their common denominator is the attempt to bridge the premodern and the modern throughout the long nineteenth century.

By the start of the second decade of the twenty-first century, it seems as if there are two opposing approaches fighting to lead the study of the history of sexualities and gender in Muslim societies. The first attempts to look inside Muslim societies to grasp their peculiarity in this context. The second tries to understand the peculiarity of sexualities in Muslim societies in their plurality, that is, through a synthesis of inter-influences or a cultural system borrowing mutually between East and West; its ultimate aim is not to define what "Islamic sexuality" is but to explore what kind of sexualities have been born as a cultural product of the encounter of East and West and, more importantly, how individuals experienced and felt these "new" forms and norms of sexuality in regard to their bodies and everyday practices in a given Muslim society.

BIBLIOGRAPHY

Dror, Ze'evi. *Producing Desire: Changing Sexual Discourse in the Ottoman Middle East, 1500–1990*. Berkeley: University of California Press, 2006. See pp. 167–173.

Habib, Samar. *Female Homosexuality in the Middle East: Histories and Representations*. New York: Routledge, 2007.

Ḥaddād, al-Tāhir. *Muslim Women in Law and Society*. Edited and translated by Ronak Husni and Daniel L. Newman. New York: Routledge, 2007. See esp. pp. 45–52.

Keddie, Nikki R. *Women in the Middle East: Past and Present*. Princeton, N.J.: Princeton University Press, 2007.

Khalaf, Samir, and John Gagnon, eds. *Sexuality in the Arab World*. London: Saqi, 2006.

El-Rouayheb, Khaled. "Introduction." In *Before Homosexuality in Arab-Islamic World, 1500–1800*, pp. 1–12. Chicago: University of Chicago Press, 2005.

Massad, Joseph A. *Desiring Arabs*. Chicago: University of Chicago Press, 2007. See esp. pp. 160–164.

Najmabadi, Afsaneh. *Women with Mustaches and Men without Beards: Gender and Sexual Anxieties of Iranian Modernity*. Berkeley: University of California Press, 2005.

Rogan, Eugene, ed. *Outside In: On the Margins of Marginality in the Modern Middle East*. London: I. B. Tauris, 2002.

Thompson, Elizabeth. "Public and Private in Middle Eastern Women's History." *Journal of Women's History* 15 (2003): 52–69.

Tucker, Judith E. "Women and Men in Gendered Space." In *Women, Family, and Gender in Islamic Law*, pp. 175–217. Cambridge, U.K.: Cambridge University Press, 2008.

Samir Ben-Layashi

Shafi'i, al-. *See* Sunni Schools of Jurisprudence.

Shaltūt, Maḥmūd. Maḥmūd Shaltūt (1893–1963) was a religious scholar, teacher, jurist, and reformist rector of al-Azhar. He was one of several celebrated *shaykhs* who undertook the reform of the institution, to reverse the mosque-university's decline, which occurred during the nineteenth century, and to recapture its role as the guide that defined Egypt's educational, cultural, and political destiny. Although best known and esteemed for his vast knowledge of Islamic *fiqh* (jurisprudence) and Qur'ānic interpretation, Shaltūt made his mark as the shaykh of al-Azhar (1958–1963). It was during his tenure that al-Azhar began its modern reincarnation. Although compromising with the state over administrative control, Shaltūt managed to bring about the partial realization of the dreams of past religious reformers of al-Azhar, including *shaykh*s Rifā'ah al-Ṭahṭāwī, Muḥammad 'Abduh, and Muṣṭafā al-Marāghī.

Born in 1893 in the village of Minyat Banī Manṣūr (Buḥayrah Province) in Lower Egypt, Shaltūt memorized the Qur'ān as a child, entered the Alexandria Religious Institute in 1906, and later joined al-Azhar, where he received the *'ālimīyah* (erudition) degree in 1918. After teaching at the Alexandria Religious Institute for some years, Shaltūt joined al-Azhar in 1927 under the auspices of Shaykh Muṣṭafā al-Marāghī. When al-Marāghī was fired by King Ahmed Fu'ād in 1930, Shaltūt and seventy other Azharīs who supported his reform plans were also dismissed. At the time, Shaltūt had backed al-Marāghī's opposition to Fu'ād's efforts to have himself elected the new Islamic caliph, following Atatürk's abolition of the Ottoman Empire in 1924.

On his return to the leadership position in 1935, al-Marāghī asked Shaltūt, who had turned to the practice of law, to rejoin the university. He was soon accepted as one of al-Azhar's chief *ʿulamāʾ* (religious scholars), after presenting a highly acclaimed study, "Civil and Criminal Responsibility in the Islamic *Sharīʿah*," at the Second International Congress of Comparative Law at the Hague in 1937. In his study, Shaltūt outlined his vision of a reformed Islam.

In 1946 he was one of the few intellectuals selected as members of the newly formed Majmaʿ al-Lughah al-ʿArabīyah (Academy of the Arabic Language) and was invited to teach *fiqh* and *sunnah* (Prophetic traditions) at Cairo University's Faculty of Law in 1950, where he became general supervisor for the Murāqabat al-Buḥūth al-Islāmīyah (Inspectorate of Islamic Research), an office that allowed him to travel widely throughout the Islamic world to promote better relations between Muslim nations. In 1957 he became the secretary-general of the Islamic Conference and undersecretary of al-Azhar. In the following year he was chosen *shaykh* of al-Azhar, a position he held until his death, in 1963.

Shaltūt became the head of al-Azhar during the most radical phase of Egypt's 1952 revolution. At the time, most standing institutions were undergoing fundamental reorganizations, and, by 1961 a law reorganizing al-Azhar was passed by a reluctant Majlis al-Ummah. Even though Shaltūt shared credit as architect of the law, he was not entirely happy with it, because it brought al-Azhar under the direct control of the state. After 1958 power over al-Azhar had been shared with a secular authority in the form of a minister of al-Azhar and religious affairs, the Wizārat al-Awqāf (Ministry of Religious Endowments).

Shaltūt may have had mixed feelings about the 1961 law, but he came from the generation that had participated in the 1919 revolution. Al-Azhar scholars and students participated heavily in this revolution and were somehow influenced by its liberal and pro-reform tendencies. His book *The Azhar in a Thousand Years* (1964) shows that he had long stood for an activist al-Azhar that could play a greater international role in fighting religious fanaticism and uniting the Islamic *ummah* (community) with its various schools of thoughts. Reorganization, and the budgetary allowances that came with it, meant the partial fulfillment of the goals of his teacher, Shaykh Muḥammad ʿAbduh, and his collaborator, al-Marāghī: reopening the door of *ijtihād* (individual inquiry in legal matters); reforming education at al-Azhar through the introduction of modern subjects; and ending the religious fanaticism that kept the Islamic world divided by narrowing the differences among the Muslim *madhhabs* (legal schools).

The reformed al-Azhar would graduate *ʿulamāʾ* with an all-around education. Thus, to the university's traditional religious education were added modern departments for training doctors, engineers, and scientists, and even a college for women for the first time in its thousand-year history. A new division, Idārat al-Thaqāfah wa-al-Buʿūth al-Islāmīyah (Department of Culture and Islamic Missions), dispatched al-Azhar graduates to teach and preach in Islamic countries and supervised foreign students studying at al-Azhar. Cairo's Madīnat al-Buʿūth al-Islāmīyah (City of Islamic Missions) enabled thousands of students from all over the Islamic world to study at the institution as well. Primary and secondary *maʿāhid Azharīyah* (Azhar institutions) became active in graduating *dāʿīs* (missionaries) to work throughout the Islamic world. Even women graduates of the *maʿāhid* and al-Azhar's Kullīyat al-Banāt (Girl's College) could act as *dāʿīs* among Egyptian and other Arab women.

Throughout his life, Shaltūt was preoccupied with the unity of the Muslim nation. In 1947 he established Dār al-Taqrīb bayna al-Madhāhib al-Islāmīyah (House of Promoting Proximity between the Schools of Islam) with the aim of bringing Sunnī and Shīʿī scholars closer together and reducing sectarian divisions among Muslims. In 1958 he recognized the Shīʿī Jaʿfarī school of thought and introduced the study of Jaʿfarī jurisprudence to the curriculum of al-Azhar, considering it to be a legitimate sect of Islam.

Other achievements of Shaltūt's tenure with a long-term impact on Egypt and the Islamic world included the formation of al-Majlis al-Aʿlā li-al-Shuʾūn al-Islāmīyah (Supreme Council for Islamic Affairs), which brought together for the first time representatives of eight Islamic *madhhabs* (Ḥanafī, Mālikī, Shāfiʿī, Ḥanbalī, Jaʿfarī, Zaydī, Ibāḍī, and Ẓāhirī) to meet in Cairo in 1962 for theological discussions. The meeting resulted in the publication of the first encyclopedia to cover the various interpretations of *muʿāmalāt* (acts concerned with relations among people) according to the eight sects, *Mawsūʿat Jamāl ʿAbd al-Nāṣir fī al-fiqh al-Islāmī.*

One other institution attributed to Shaltūt, the Majmaʿ al-Buḥūth al-Islāmīyah (Islamic Research Center), has had a deep impact on Egyptian intellectual life. Meant as a scholarly center to assure the accuracy of religious works, it has turned into an organ of censorship that monitors the purity of literature, declaring what is heretical, demanding the removal of publications from the market and libraries, and calling for the punishment of authors it considers "innovators" and "heretical enemies of Islam."

Shaykh Maḥmūd Shaltūt authored twenty-six works, including a treatise on the Qurʾān and fighting, an interpretation of the Qurʾān, an assortment of religious *fatwas* (verdicts), an analysis of international relations in Islam, and a study of women and the Qurʾān. He received four honorary doctorates, from universities in Chile, Indonesia, and the Philippines, and was given awards by the leaders of Afghanistan, Cameroon, Morocco, and Sudan.

[*See also* Azhar, al-.]

BIBLIOGRAPHY

Shaltūt, Maḥmūd. *Al-fatāwā*. Cairo: Dār al-Shurūq, 1986.

Shaltūt, Maḥmūd. *Ilā al-Qurʾān al-karīm*. Cairo: Dār al-Shurūq, 1978.

Shaltūt, Maḥmūd. "A Modernist Interpretation of Jihad: Maḥmûd Shaltût's Treatise *Koran and Fighting*." In *Jihad in Classical and Modern Islam: A Reader*, edited and translated by Rudolph Peters, pp. 59–102. Princeton, N.J.: Markus Wiener, 1996.

Shaltūt, Maḥmūd. *Tafsīr al-Qurʾān al-karīm*. 10 vols. Cairo, 1982.

Zebiri, Kate. *Maḥmūd Shaltūt and Islamic Modernism*. Oxford: Clarendon, 1993.

Zebiri, Kate. "Shaykh Maḥmūd Shaltūt: Between Tradition and Modernity." *Journal of Islamic Studies* 2, no. 2 (1991): 210–224.

AMIRA EL AZHARY SONBOL
Updated by NAEL SHAMA

SHAMS AL-DĪN, MUḤAMMAD MAHDĪ.

Shaykh Muḥammad Mahdī Shams al-Dīn (1936–2001) was an Iraqi-born Shīʿī *mujtahid* of Lebanese decent. Born in Najaf, which is generally regarded by Shīʿah as the holiest city in Islam after Mecca and Medina, Muḥammad Mahdī Shams al-Dīn was the son of ʿAbd al-Karīm Shams al-Dīn, a native of the Jabal ʿĀmil region of southern Lebanon who had traveled to Iraq to complete his religious studies. Najaf and Jabal ʿĀmil have for centuries enjoyed a rich and vibrant exchange of scholars and clerics.

Upon his father's return to Lebanon in 1948, Shams al-Dīn opted, at age twelve, to remain in Najaf to pursue his own training as a *mujtahid*. There, he studied with the prominent clerics Abol Qāsem al-Khoʾi, Muḥsin al-Ḥakīm, Muḥammad Taqī al-Ḥakīm, and ʿAbd al-Raʾūf Faḍl Allāh, among others. From 1961 to 1969, Shams al-Dīn served as a representative of Muḥsin al-Ḥakīm in al-Dīwānīyah, today the capital of Iraq's al-Qādisīyah Governorate.

In 1969 Shams al-Dīn returned to his native Lebanon to join Mūsā al-Ṣadr, also a student of

Muḥsin al-Ḥakīm, in the establishment of the Supreme Shīʿī Council (al-Majlis al-Shīʿī al-Aʿlā). The establishment of the council, headed by its first president, al-Ṣadr, and recognized by the government of Lebanon, bestowed a new degree of autonomy on the country's Shīʿah, who had hitherto been subject to the Islamic Council and the Sunnī *muftī* of the Lebanese Republic. Soon thereafter, Shams al-Dīn was elected to the position of vice president of the council. With al-Ṣadr's 1978 disappearance in Libya, however, Shams al-Dīn became, in effect, the acting president of the council. He was succeeded in this position upon his death in 2001 by ʿAbd al-Amīr Qablān, who likewise often styles himself as "deputy" president of this religious body—a reference to the unknown fate of the body's president, al-Ṣadr.

The Role of the Jurist. Unlike Sunnī Muslims, Shīʿahs generally believe that the interpretation of the faith must be the responsibility of a qualified cleric of the Jaʿfarī school of Islamic law. Such a cleric is referred to as a *marjaʿ* (reference for emulation). Titles for a *marjaʿ* include "ayatollah," "imam," or, less commonly, "allamah." A *marjiʿīyah* (the authority or institution of a *marjaʿ*) is recognized by a consensus of students, less credentialed clerics, and believers who turn to the *marjaʿ* for matters of interpretation, for example, for a legal decision (*fatwa*). Historically, the majority of the Lebanese Shīʿah have followed the *marjaʿ* of Najaf in most matters, for example, the *marjiʿīyah* of Muḥsin al-Ḥakīm until his death in 1970, Abol Qāsem al-Khoʾi until his death in 1992, and ʿAlī Ḥusaynī al-Sistānī currently. However, following Khoʾi's death, an increasing number of Lebanese Shīʿah in the late 1990s began to refer to a *marjaʿ* closer to home. This is the period in which Shams al-Dīn's *marjiʿīyah* was recognized by his followers in Lebanon, as were the *marjiʿīyah* of Ḥizbullāh secretary-general Ḥasan Naṣrallāh. Shams al-Dīn's *marjiʿīyah*, however, differed from Naṣrallāh's conceptually, in that it was based on a historic, or traditional, understanding of the role of the jurist, whereas Naṣrallāh's authority derived from his position as the representative (*wakīl*) of the Iranian Ayatollah ʿAlī Khameneʾi. Naṣrallāh and his followers fully embraced Ayatollah Ruhollah Khomeini's teachings on "the guardianship of the jurist" (*vilāyat-i faqīh*).

Shams al-Dīn did not reject the Iranian model of *vilāyat-i faqīh* outright, and his earliest writings on Islam and governance—from his days in Najaf—did not differ greatly from those articulated by Khomeini. Before moving to Lebanon and assuming his position in the Supreme Shīʿī Council, Shams al-Dīn too imagined a "divine human state" (*dawlah ilāhīyah basharīyah*), in which a religious leader was chosen by the people to rule. In *Niẓām al-ḥukm* (System of Governance), Shams al-Dīn enumerated the merits of this uniquely Shīʿī approach to governance, at the same time downplaying the parallel that some Sunnī scholars had drawn between democracy and the juridical idea of *shūrā*, which referred to the consensual process by which the companions of the Prophet chose leaders.

The role he played in the administration of the Supreme Shīʿī Council in Lebanon, along with his partnership with Mūsā al-Ṣadr, however, tempered this rather exclusionary vision of governance. Confronting the Lebanese reality of a highly diverse and sectarian society, Shams al-Dīn acknowledged that rule by an imam was not feasible for the country, and he became a vocal proponent of Muslim-Christian dialogue. Even through the years of the civil war, the cleric met regularly with local and world Christian leaders. In these exchanges, he often sought to build common ground between the two faiths based on a shared aversion to antireligious currents in society, including secularism and communism. Shams al-Dīn argued in *Niẓām al-dīmuqraṭiyah al-ʿadadīyah al-qaʾīmah ʿalā mabdāʾ al-shūrā* (The System of Democratic Pluralism Based on the

Principle of Consultation, published in 1985, three years after the Israeli occupation of southern Lebanon) not for the replacement of Lebanon's consociational democratic system but for its reform, so that the Shīʿah would no longer be excluded from state institutions dominated by Maronite Christians.

Civil Resistance. Before 1982 Shams al-Dīn described the conflict in Palestine as an Arab-Israeli, rather than a Muslim-Jewish, conflict and held that the Arab states should be united in their cultural opposition to the state of Israel. After the occupation of southern Lebanon, however, Shams al-Dīn began to use an increasingly Islamic vocabulary to describe the means of resistance available to his followers, and in 1983 he issued a *fatwa* calling for full civil resistance to the Israeli occupation. Actions included sit-ins at mosques and widespread protests, but also, on occasion, the harassment of individuals perceived to have collaborated with Israel.

Shams al-Dīn was well known for his position that one was Lebanese first, Arab second, Muslim third, and Shīʿī only fourth. This maxim shaped his response to both the Lebanese civil war and Israeli occupation. In addition to advocating Christian-Muslim dialogue, Shams al-Dīn wrote prolifically on uniquely Shīʿī aspects of the practice of the faith, including the role of the *marjaʿ*, the centrality of the commemoration of the martyrdom of Ḥusayn, and the permissibility of visiting tombs (*zayārah*). These practices had long set the Shīʿah apart from Sunnīs in Lebanon, and he sought to explain their history and significance to a non-Shīʿī readership.

The Rising of al-Ḥusayn was perhaps Shams al-Dīn's most influential work of scholarship. It was, on the surface, both a historical account of the martyrdom of Ḥusayn at Karbala and a defense of Shīʿī rites of commemoration during the month of ʿĀshūrāʾ. However, the work also provided a framework for revolutionary civil action, and throughout it there are parallels between the revolt of Ḥusayn and contemporary Shīʿī resistance to both Lebanese oppression and Israeli occupation. The history of the revolution, he observes, "may be a mirror of the spirit of the present time, through which the *umma* is living now, and a justification for the situation to which it is shackled" (Shams al-Dīn, 1985, p. 11).

Shams al-Dīn was generally critical of the use of violence by Islamic movements. He argued that terror tactics were prohibited in Islam and that the use of violence isolated an Islamic movement, discouraged cooperation across multiparty platforms, and could lead a movement to ally with unjust regimes in order to obtain financing or other resources. This may be read as a critique of the militarization of Amal, Islamic Amal, and Ḥizbullāh through the 1980s. In contrast, he argued, "Peaceful political action may be slow in achieving results and may demand greater expenditure of effort and more sacrifice, but it leads certainly to more permanent results and sounder consequences" (Shams al-Dīn, 2001).

Legacy. Shams al-Dīn is remembered as a moderate Shīʿī cleric who promoted dialogue between Muslims and Christians and between Sunnīs and Shīʿah. Widely regarded as a conduit for political and religious exchange among the sects of Lebanon, he was, during the years of the civil war, sometimes asked to intervene to secure the release of Western hostages, for example, during negotiations regarding the fate of Jean-Louis Normandin, who was kidnapped by a group calling itself the Revolutionary Justice Organization in 1986 and released two years later. The cleric also established the Islamic University in Lebanon, which is today managed by the Supreme Shīʿī Council and associated with a number of charity organizations.

Bibliography

Abisaab, Rula Jurdi. "The Cleric as Organic Intellectual: Revolutionary Shiʿism in the Lebanese *Hawzas*."

In *Distant Relations: Iran and Lebanon in the Last 500 Years*, edited by H. E. Chehabi, pp. 231–258. London: I. B. Tauris, 2006.

Kawtharānī, Wajīh. *Bayna fiqh al-iṣlāḥ al-Shīʿī wa-wilāyat al-faqīh: Al-dawlah wa-al-muwāṭin*. Beirut: Dār al-Nahār lil-Nashr, 2007.

Mallat, Chibli. *Shi'i Thought from the South of Lebanon*. Oxford: Centre for Lebanese Studies, 1988.

Mūsā, Faraḥ. *Al-Shaykh Muḥammad Mahdī Shams al-Dīn: Bayna wahaj al-Islām wa-jalīd al-madhāhib*. Beirut: Dār al-Hādī, 1993.

Shams al-Dīn, Muḥammad Mahdī. "On the Political Utility of Using Armed Violence." Translated by John J. Donohue. In *The Fiqh of Armed Violence in Islam*. Beirut: International Foundation for Study and Publication, 2001.

Shams al-Dīn, Muḥammad Mahdī. *The Rising of al-Ḥusayn: Its Impact on the Consciousness of Muslim Society*. Translated by I. K. A. Howard. Bury St. Edmunds, U.K.: Muhammadi Trust of Great Britain and Northern Ireland, 1985.

TAYLOR LONG

SHARĪʿAH. Most often translated as "Islamic law," the term *Sharīʿah* describes both Muslim practices that relate to law in Western understanding and others that do not. It is better understood as the Muslim conception of a life in conformity with God's will. Thus it includes both the rules that regulate the Muslim's relationship to God, such as the ritual practices of worship (prayer, fasting, pilgrimage, etc.) and the rules that regulate the worshippers' relationships to one another and to society. The first are called *ʿibādāt* ("acts of worship"), the latter *muʿāmalāt* ("transactions"). The divide largely coincides with the definition of legal as "concerning cases that are brought before a court of law," which applies to the *muʿāmalāt*, but some legal infractions, as those falling under the category of *ḥudūd*, below, are considered to be crimes against God and fall under *ʿibādāt*.

Muslims follow the *Sharīʿah* because it is instituted by God. While following the *ʿibādāt* rules simply conveys an acceptance of God's will and needs no further rationalization, the *muʿāmalāt* were put into place by God in order to promote the well-being (*maṣlaḥa*) of the Muslims and their society. Thus God had an intention with the law (*maqāṣid al-sharīʿa*) that is knowable to the believer and can be expressed as a "just society." For many Muslims therefore, the word "sharīʿah" simply means "justice," and they will consider any law to conform to the *Sharīʿah* as long as it promotes justice and social welfare.

However, for most Muslim believers and scholars the term refers to rules developed on the basis of the divine revelation through a legal methodology known as *fiqh*. The sources of revelation did not provide a corpus of rules that could be applied directly by the believers, but instead in most cases provided only indications (*dalālāt*) from which those specifically trained in the methodology of law could derive and develop positive rules of law.

Classical Sharīʿah. In traditional Muslim belief the *Sharīʿah* is based directly on God's revelations to the Prophet Muḥammad in the Qurʾān, and on the latter's normative practices (*sunnah*). Historically, however, the law developed over time in the first centuries of Islam. How fast and to what degree it relied on pre-Islamic legal tradition in the regions the Muslims came to control (such as the semi-nomadic Arabian Peninsula, the formerly Byzantine Syria and Egypt, and the formerly Sasanid Iraq) are a matter of considerable controversy among scholars. It is commonly held that the early Muslim governors of Syria and Iraq largely left pre-Islamic administrative and legal practices untouched as far as the non-Muslim populations were concerned. In the new communities of conquering Arabs that settled there, however, the rulers began to implement rules that marked their identity as Muslims.

These rules were often made ad hoc, and may have been amalgams of practices of the Arab nomads or of previous rulers of the conquered regions, and/or new understandings of what the early community of believers considered to be pious and moral behavior. Thus local law regulated both affairs overseen by state authorities (governors, military commanders) and customs of society that were outside political control. In the first century or so it was most likely only in the urban centers, and perhaps only in the largest of them, that the state was the effective legal authority. As long as the original inhabitants remained non-Muslim, they mostly kept their legal autonomy, while Muslims outside the major towns would most likely also have continued the middleman or arbiter (*ḥākim*) system that they were familiar with from the Arabic Peninsula, and not involve the new authorities unless they had to. This middleman would, of course, have continued the customary legal practices from the pre-Islamic past.

In the urban centers there came together people particularly concerned with religion, whether it was their full-time profession or not. Some of them came to discuss the practical matters of what Muslims should or should not do, as to ritual but also to legal aspects of the believers' behavior. These scholars were not necessarily linked to the state (the caliph and governor), although some were. For many of them it was an intellectual and pious exercise, but also an attempt to answer practical questions arising in the community as a new society was being formed, for which they wished to provide a "correct" solution increasingly based on religious views.

These new scholars of law often did not agree with one another, and the elaboration of law often took the form of sharp *munāẓarāt* (literally, "examinations" of matters), that is, disputes between individual scholars in various parts of the Muslim world. Disagreement was thus rife, but the scholars agreed on one thing: If formulating "correct practice" for the believers was to be based on religion, it had to be a matter for those who knew about religion—in other words not for the caliph or other officers of the state, who had no authority over religion. Although he was the "commander of the faithful," the caliph was not and could not be a "commander of the faith." In law his task was to implement the law of Islam, to "command good and prevent evil" but not to formulate it. In this the scholars, not the caliph, were the "heirs of the Prophet." Thus whatever vague attempts there were—and they were only tentative—to establish the caliph as a legislator and establish one particular law as an official "caliphal" code were nipped in the bud.

Therefore, while the law of the Muslim lands was probably first based more on "accepted practice" than on religious ideas (although this is contested), in the course of the first three centuries it became more and more clear to the community of scholars that the law had to be firmly based on the divine revelation. The process of legislation must in fact be a process of uncovering the divine will for each and every act, based on what God had commanded. This, however, required the intellectual efforts of specialized scholars (the *fiqh* scholars, or *fuqahāʾ*). After a period of perhaps three centuries, a science of the methodology of this process, *uṣūl al-fiqh*, developed, and came in broad terms to be agreed upon by the scholars. This is often called the "four roots" of Islamic law—after the scholar al-Shāfiʿī (d. 820 CE)—but when understood as a process of discovering the divine law, it may perhaps be easier to conceive of it as "three stages": revelation, formulation, and confirmation.

The Theory of *uṣūl al-fiqh*.

Revelation. God's will, the basis of the sharīʿah in Muslim belief, is expressed in the two forms of the Qurʾān and the *sunnah*. These two provide the "raw material" for the law, because God's will does not necessarily appear in a form directly comprehensible to the believers in these two sources. Only a minor part of the Qurʾān is relevant to the *Sharīʿah* (estimates vary according to definition, but it is reasonable to consider some 350 verses out of the total of 6,200 to be of direct legal relevance, most of them dealing with a few particular areas, especially inheritance). The Qurʾān is much more important as a general reference for rules and principles expounded on elsewhere. Thus the verse 4:59 "Obey those in authority among you" can be read to give divine sanction to any number of particular legal rules, according to how one interprets "those in authority" (parents, sultans, scholars?), and what is implied in "obeying."

On the other hand, the text of the Qurʾān is clearly demarcated; all Muslims agree on its veracity and its textual content. That is not the case for the *sunnah*, as preserved in the enormous and amorphous body of orally transmitted stories (*ḥadīths*, or Prophetic traditions) relating of the Prophet and his contemporaries. The *ḥadīths* are far more concrete and practical than the often general statements of the Qurʾān. However, not all of the vast number of stories that were told could be genuine—some contradicted each other and others could not possibly have stemmed from the Prophet. As they were written down about one to two centuries after the death of the Prophet, Muslim scholars developed a methodology of separating the true stories, which were legally binding, from the spurious, which had to be ignored. A number of *ḥadīth* scholars undertook this work and established a hierarchy of probability, from traditions that were considered to be absolutely true ("sound," primarily by being *tawātur*, so widespread among the earliest scholars that it was inconceivable that they all shared an untruth), through "probable" in various degrees, to "weak" or false.

Not all of the *ḥadīth* scholars agreed on the selection of true versus probable traditions. Some collections of *ḥadīth* were generally accepted to have a higher normative status (the figure "six" for authoritative canonical collections is often used, although nine or ten of them did in fact gain particular authority). A *ḥadīth* that is included in both the collection of al-Bukhārī (d. 870) and of Muslim ibn Ḥajjāj (d. 875) is as close as one can get to absolute certainty in this field.

By and large, however, the development of *ḥadīth* studies left open vast areas of scholarly disagreement both in the relative merit of the texts and in how to interpret them, not least because the same *ḥadīth* could appear in very many variants and forms with minor but crucial differences in wording, either including a context that might limit its application, or omitting it, which would make the tradition's pronouncement universally valid. As this was the most practically important source of revelation (the *sunnah* explains the Qurʾān, as the expression goes), such variations allowed legal scholars considerable leeway in formulating alternative rules, all of which could claim a basis in the divine revelation.

Formulation. The process of formulating the divine law was therefore clearly the result of human scholarly endeavor. This introduced a duality in the authority of the law: If correctly understood, it represents God's will and is absolute, undoubted by the pious believer. But in as far as it is the result of fallible human intellect, it cannot directly represent God's will, and is only at best so close to it as can be humanly attained. The scholar cannot put himself in God's place and give divine authority to his interpretation; he must—as every legal opinion does—conclude with "God knows best" (*wa-Allāh aʿlam.*)

Yet the scholars did begin a process of formulating a consistent set of legal rules on the basis of the revealed sources. This process of formulation is called *ijtihād*, and it was open to every scholar who had the competence in terms of scholarship and knowledge. *Ijtihād* encompasses a number of specialized methodologies, of which perhaps the most important and the best known is analogy, *qiyās*. *Qiyās* is the process by which the content of a single Qurʾānic verse or *ḥadīth* is generalized into a legally consistent rule—for example, from the verse stating that "*khamr* (wine) is Satan's handiwork" (Qurʾān 5:90), the rule "the consumption of any substance that is intoxicant in any amount is forbidden" is produced. There were also many other methods of legal elaboration open to the scholars, some of which (*istiḥsān* or *istiṣlāḥ*, among others) were also intended to mollify or nullify the very same rules produced through *qiyās* in cases where these would lead to socially unacceptable results.

Confirmation. Evidently, when many scholars using a variety of methodologies are producing laws based on a source material that is itself without clear limitations, numerous disputes and disagreements are bound to arise. The majority of scholars came to consider such disagreement (*ikhtilāf*) as a natural consequence of human fallibility and, indeed, as one of God's bounties to mankind; not all scholars agreed and these insisted that as God's will was only one, there could also be only one valid interpretation.

If the law was to be enforceable, such a benevolent variety was impracticable. In a court of law, each party could not claim for itself the interpretation that served its cause best without the judge being able to say that one was correct and the other incorrect. Thus out of all the possible interpretations and formulations of each rule that was, or could be, provided through *ijtihād*, a subset had to be established that could become the positive law that the court and the authorities could enforce as "the *Sharīʿah*."

The problem was the question of who was to decide which was the "correct" view. It had already been established that the ruler—the caliph or sultan—did not have the authority to intervene in what was still considered to be a religious area, to put himself in the place of the Prophet or, indeed, God. Therefore the "state" could not be the legislator; only God is the legislator in Islam. But there was also no organized religious establishment to make such decisions, no pope or ecclesiastical council; all such formal structures were unknown to Islam.

What came to be the answer, then, was again typically pragmatic and vaguely defined: The correct interpretation of the law was that which was approved as such by the community of scholars through consensus (*ijmāʿ*). But what would that mean? A consensus encompassing all living (and perhaps also dead) scholars? Or only a majority at any given moment? And how is such a consensus established in the amorphous body of scholars in the far-flung reaches of the Muslim world? The theorists disagreed over these issues. A concept of absolute *ijmāʿ*—to include every single scholar in any particular generation (a unity so miraculous that it must be a proof of God's will, thus a third source for revelation)—was developed, but by its nature it had little practical impact on legal development.

A more pragmatic use of the concept of consensus came to be that the clear majority opinion among the scholars on a legal issue, established at one particular point in time, constituted positive law on that issue, although it might not convey the absolute divine truth. A rule thus established was final and could not be reopened for later discussion.

The Development of Different Legal Schools. Even this more pragmatic unity was impossible to achieve, however. Instead, the *Sharīʿah* was formulated in several slightly different variants, each stemming from a different "school of law" (*madhhab*). These variants share many—perhaps most—of the basic rules, but differ substantially on some points. While they also have many points of methodology in common, they are clearly distinct even in their theory of how to develop the law. Thus the schools must primarily be seen as four parallel legal systems that share many features. A scholar in the classical period was not expected to seek answers outside of his own school. Yet the schools recognized each other's authority: a judge should not seek to overturn a verdict made in another *madhhab*'s court, even if his own school would have ruled differently. Modern reformers, however, often try to transcend the *madhhab* divisions in order to create a "unified" *Sharīʿah*.

Classical Muslim historians emphasized the normative link from the Prophet's historical practices to the establishment of the *madhhab*s. Learned scholars who excelled in collecting information attesting to the Prophet's example sought in the best possible way to follow in his footsteps. Around the best of these legal scholars there formed groups of students who transmitted their views to succeeding generations, thus laying the foundation for the *madhhab*. Some modern historians, however, question this normative chronology and believe that the views of these early scholars were rather based on established practice in their own region which they distilled into conceptions of the "best way," the original meaning of the word *sunnah*. For these scholars this was the Muslim way of behavior, in that the community represented the religious ideal. Only later was this behavior personalized into the authority of the Prophet, at which time support for the already established opinions of the jurists had to be sought in the *ḥadīth*, as far as that was possible.

The historical development of the law can thus be seen through two partly, but not completely, separate processes: On the one hand, the necessities of government forced the new state authorities to develop legal institutions and to try to universalize common rules for the empire rather than letting each province maintain its diverse pre-conquest practices. On the other, independent scholars developed discursive traditions that were also localized, albeit specifically Muslim. These were developed partly by logical reasoning and partly by conceptions of "justice" that were influenced by custom. Thus there were both individual variations between scholars in each town and more systematic differences between regions (for example, the distinctions between the "new" Arab towns of Iraq and the "old" Roman towns that the Muslims took over in Syria). However, as over time religious authority came to be vested more and more in the persona of the Prophet Muḥammad—common to all Muslims—the authority behind the laws became increasingly universal in theory even though they always retained local variety in their application.

The governors did try to recruit some of these scholars as judges in their courts or as advisors, and while it is a pious fiction that scholars sought to distance themselves from the "tainted" touch of political power, it was clearly an avenue for material and social promotion to take such a position. They were initially subservient to the governor but in the course of time established an independent role that allowed them to maintain control over the content of the laws they applied, even though each judge was always in danger of being deposed, or worse, by his political master.

While, in each major town, groups of scholars formed that may have agreed on a number of legal issues and also discussed the methodology of how exactly one discovered the most proper practice, they cannot yet be called formalized schools before the ninth century CE. A scholar could agree on some matters with his peers and disagree on others, and in most cities—as in Kufa, the intellectual center of the time—there were a number of different such scholarly groups, some of which found fellow supporters in other major towns. The transmission of learning was informal and oral—groups of students would gather around a renowned scholar sitting in his mosque, listen to him expound on a topic of law or recite a series of *ḥadīth*s, and, perhaps, note them down for later memorization.

In the ninth and particularly the tenth century, it appears that transmission changed to a written form, when students were allowed to copy over the texts directly. This changed the nature of the law, as it imposed a much greater conformity on the conclusions. As long as teaching was only oral, it was easier for students to introduce additions to the transferred readings—for example, in order to counter arguments from opposing groups. From the mid-tenth century on, at the latest, the basic legal texts became "frozen" in the form they are today, which helped to solidify the scholars who based their views on them into separate groups.

Over time these groups of scholars became further institutionalized. Proper schools of thought, with locally recognized leaders, were now clearly identified, and individual scholars were noted as belonging to one and only one of these groups. While they earlier might have been known as the "people of Kufa" or the "the people of Medina" (vague descriptions that might have included only some of the scholars of these towns), these schools now began to trace their lineage to legal scholars of the previous centuries and see themselves as "followers of the views of" such and such a departed figure. These early authorities became the "founding fathers" of schools that actually came into existence a century or more after their death. Initially, there were many such schools, each with its own eponymous founder, but by the twelfth or thirteenth century most had faded away or merged into the four major schools within Sunnī Islam.

These four—named after Abū Ḥanīfa (d. 767), Mālik b. Anas (d. 795), Muḥammad b. Idrīs al-Shāfiʿī (d. 820), and Aḥmad b. Ḥanbal (d. 855)—came into being in the major cities of the central Middle East: Kufa, Baghdad, and [old] Cairo. In the course of time, however, they came to be distributed geographically across the Muslim world so that each *madhhab* dominated one region—the Mālikīs in North and West Africa east to Upper Egypt; the Shāfiʿīs in parts of the central Middle East (Lower Egypt, Syria) and along the coasts of the Indian Ocean from East Africa over the Arabian Peninsula to southeast Asia; and the Ḥanafīs mostly in the north, in particular in areas governed by the Turks and Mongols, that is, in Central Asia, Mughal India, and any area later falling within the Ottoman Empire. The Ḥanbalīs, the fourth and smallest of the schools, was mostly present as a minority in some of the cities of the central Middle East, but came to dominate parts of the Arabian Peninsula with the Wahhābī movement from the eighteenth century onwards.

These four schools of law, which are mutually accepting, are all Sunnī and are not specifically linked to any differences in theology. From the tenth century on, the minority Shīʿīs also gained political ascendance in certain regions of the Islamic world; *madhhab* formation among the Shīʿa mostly followed its theological differences and three separate *madhhab*s were formed, one each for the Twelvers (Imāmīs), Ismāʿīlīs, and Zaydīs. The Ibāḍī minority, which came to rule in Oman, also has its own *madhhab*. Although there are differences of opinion between all these schools, mostly found in details, the clearest distinction may be in the less complex Twelver (Jaʿfarī) inheritance law, which developed later than its Sunnī counterpart. This last school of law was embroiled in a methodological dispute in the early modern period that pitted those who emphasized the importance of scholarly *ijtihād* against those who relied only on the *ḥadīth* of the Prophet and the Shīʿī imams—the Uṣūlīs and the Akhbārīs, respectively; the former largely won out and now dominate Shīʿī law.

The Law as Literature. The law was thus not codified in any fixed form as there was no authority that could do so. It existed rather in the form of a scholarly literature and through the efforts of jurists to extract judgments (*aḥkām*, sing. *ḥukm*) from it. Islamic law is thus often called a "jurist's law" as opposed to European civil- and British common-law systems. The views and statements of the early "founders" of the schools of law were collected in basic works purportedly composed by them or by their closest students. These were then commented upon and expanded through commentaries (*shurūḥ*, sing. *sharḥ*) as well as later super-commentaries (*ḥāshiyāt*), in a complex system of interconnected texts with which the scholar had to be familiar. The commentaries aimed to explain the views stated by the founders and if necessary defend them against criticisms, but could in effect also be used by later scholars to introduce new understandings and points of view under the cover of explaining a statement by the early founders. The authority of the *madhhab* was thus based on the stature given to its founder, and later real developments would have to be sanctioned through a link to him.

This linking of authority of *madhhab* rules to the person of the founder echoes in many ways the earlier linking of the law to the authority of the Prophet himself. Both of these personal identifications are essential to the credibility of the law, and the same way Muslim scholars generally will insist that sharīʿah rules are based on the Prophet's example and the divine revelation, the followers of any particular *madhhab* will most often defend their school's view on the authority of the founder, even when the actual rule may have been elaborated later and take later contexts into consideration.

It is likely that in both cases the authority and perceived status of the early authoritative figure grew as the lifetime of the individual in question receded into the past. There is no reason to doubt that contemporaries of the Prophet remembered his words and actions and that these memories were passed down. Similarly, the statements of famous early scholars such as Mālik and Abū Ḥanīfa were noted, discussed, and remembered after their time. However, this does not mean that these stories necessarily had the absolute authority that they later came to have. Studies have shown that many of the views later ascribed to Mālik did in fact circulate among his contemporary group of scholars in Medina and Cairo. But other scholars of that group did not link these views particularly to Mālik nor accord him any special veneration. Thus while these certainly may have been views that Mālik actually subscribed to, they were when they later became identified with the school that took Mālik's name primarily presented as views that Mālik had pronounced, and later Mālikīs therefore had to accept and follow. As the identity and internal authority of the schools increasingly came to be focused on the founder, their perceived status rose over time such that they came finally to be seen as almost infallible. Some late jurists with mystical tendencies even regarded the founders as having received supernatural knowledge by meeting directly with the Prophet himself. If such was the case, no latter-day scholar could, of course, expect to question or amend the views that had this stamp of approval.

The *fiqh* literature was initially mainly argumentative, comprising disputes between the schools or within them; in their presentation of different opinions and support for each, it was a literature for and by scholars. As the opinions on the various issues eventually settled into a more or less established set of rules that had attained consensus within the school, the need arose for simpler and more practical manuals that could be used by judges and understood by nonscholars. These were called "abridgments" (*mukhtaṣarāt*), and appeared from the fourteenth century onwards. The most famous of them was possibly the *Mukhtaṣar* of the Egyptian Khalīl b. Isḥāq (d. 1350) from the Mālikī school. The *mukhtaṣarāt* did not discourse on the topics or present alternate views, but simply stated that on a certain issue the agreed opinion was the following *ḥukm*. These abridgements were not properly codified laws since they had no formal authority to back them. A judge was free to (and often did) deviate from the consensual opinion if he had sufficient competence and knowledge to find another opinion that could also be supported within the school. But the rules of the abridgment did increasingly come to be seen as the views of the school.

There were also other types of legal literature, such as the succinct *qawāʿid*, short formulas that were meant to aid the student by summing up principles important for the law, as in "acts are [evaluated according] to intention." Another very important genre of legal literature collected together judicial opinions (sing. *fatwa*) of the specialized legal scholar (*muftī*).

The Judge and the Legal Scholar. The Islamic legal system includes two kinds of scholars who had structurally different tasks: the judge (*qāḍī*) who was in charge of the *Sharīʿah* court (*maḥkama*), and the jurist or legal scholar (*muftī*) who expounded on the law. It was the job of the *qāḍī* to establish the facts of the case before him, to evaluate the veracity of the evidence, and to make a decision in favor of one of the parties. The *qāḍī* was not to interpret the law to be applied if there was any doubt. In everyday cases he would, of course, know the relevant legal rule and needed no help in this. But if the use of the law was unclear or there were disagreements as to how the legal texts of the school should be understood, then he should consult a *muftī*.

The *muftī* on his part had no responsibility for the actual case or its facts, nor did he pass judgment; his role was only to elaborate on the law. He would often not be told any material facts such as the names of the parties involved, but only posed a question in the form, "If a case has such and such properties, what is then the appropriate ruling," to which he answered, "If that is the case, then the most appropriate is such." Such an answer is known as a *fatwa*, and is thus completely conditional upon the supposition of facts made in the question. Whether these facts are actually correct or not is the judge's responsibility. Thus both parties to a conflict may approach a *muftī* of their choice, present the case as they understand it, and turn up in court with conflicting *fatwas*. The judge cannot reject a *fatwā* due to its content (this is the *muftī*'s authority), but he can reject its relevance to the case in question and thus ignore it.

In this sense, the *muftī* was an aide to the judge, but also his superior in knowledge of the law. However, in practice the distinctions between the two offices were not always so sharp. Going from one position to the other—in either direction—would often be a step on a jurist's career path that was decided on the size of the salary or the importance of the town he moved to; these factors determined whether the change in position was a promotion or a demotion. Also, while in theory the *muftī* had no place in the courtroom itself, a resident *muftī* might in many cases be present. Often a verdict in serious criminal cases required the approval of a senior *muftī*, even if the legal basis for the decision was unproblematic. This was applied in particular to death sentences, which generally required a second opinion from a *muftī*, who then evidently knew and could evaluate the actual facts of the case. At the other end of the scale, a local *muftī*, perhaps meaning anyone with some religious learning, could himself settle disputes between parties in small villages that did not have a court. Such a solution would then not carry the authority of the state, but the social pressure of the community would compel the parties to accept the *muftī*'s decision.

The *Sharīʿah* does not actually recognize the distinction between private and public law. Thus criminal cases and arbitration between private parties are treated in the same manner, most often in the same court. There is no public prosecution, every criminal case beginning with an injured party suing the suspected perpetrator. Most of the court procedures are identical in civil and criminal cases, with the plaintiff making a claim against the defendant and having the onus of presenting evidence for his case. The judge may make his own inquiries by asking expert witnesses to testify or in other ways, but the burden of proof rests squarely on the plaintiff. If the plaintiff is not able to prove his case satisfactorily, the defendant is acquitted; he is asked to swear to his innocence, and having done so has won the case. But if the judge finds the evidence compelling, it is the plaintiff who is "given the oath" and by swearing to the truth of his claim wins the case. In criminal cases, the judge then passes judgment, and it is up to the court officials, police, or prisons to effectuate the sentence.

The judge thus decides between right and wrong, but he can also have an important role as a middleman and effect a compromise between civil parties, continuing the older function of *ḥākim*, arbitrator. The judge also had a number of other functions, such as officiating at marriages, authorizing marriage contracts, overseeing religious trusts (*waqf*s), and the like.

The rules of procedure in Islamic law were very strict and it was often difficult to get convictions even when the facts of the matter appeared to be evident. Short of admission, the main type of evidence was the testimony of witnesses. To prove a case, a plaintiff had to provide the required number of firsthand witnesses, normally two, to give identical evidence. The witnesses had to be morally upright and free Muslims, normally male (although in most cases two Muslim females could substitute for one male). Many court disputes were about the status of witnesses: their moral standing, whether their statements coincided—both had to be the same type of witnesses, not one having heard and the other seen the act—and so on. In some cases, policemen could not be accepted because their closeness to the state made them morally suspect; a witness need not be a notable—a morally unblemished laborer was fully acceptable.

If the required number of witnesses was provided and they could not be challenged, the case was proven and closed. If not, the judge could use circumstantial evidence to reach his conclusion, such as documents or material objects, but it had to supported by witness statements as to its relevance. Particularly in criminal cases, however, if the strict rules of procedure were not met, the case had to be dismissed as inconclusive.

Who Was the Law For? The *Sharīʿah* is intended to regulate a Muslim community in a Muslim state. Thus at least in theory, religious affiliation is paramount for its application. Accepted religious minorities (*dhimmī*s) had legal autonomy, that is, the Muslim state did not intervene in intracommunity affairs, but in disputes between Muslims and *dhimmī*s, as well as between parties of different religions (e.g., Jew against Christian), the Muslim *Sharīʿah* was applied by a *qāḍī*. Otherwise, non-Muslims could not be admitted to a *Sharīʿah* court and could not, for example, be used as witnesses in a case between Muslims.

The application of this exclusion clearly varied. Sometimes it was strictly upheld, while in other periods or towns it appears that all members of the local community used the same court without much regard for the religious affiliation of the parties involved. The same variation probably applied in relation to women. Free Muslim women did have access to the court, and were in many cases very active on their own behalf; in family matters the court was often seen as a way to protect the wife's rights against the capricious will of the husband. But women might also avoid this public arena and let themselves be represented, as plaintiffs or defendants, by a male spokesman, unlike male parties who had to attend in person. The *Sharīʿah* does not assume an equality of individuals. Both the rules of civil cases and the application of criminal penalties distinguished between male and female, Muslim and non-Muslim, free and slave, and in many cases even between social classes.

Non-qāḍī Courts. In cases where the *Sharīʿah* court could not reach a verdict, the aggrieved party could often go to other courts. Although the *Sharīʿah* was the only law of the Islamic state, the *qāḍī*'s court was not the only court. These other tribunals were generally linked more closely to the state, and thus provided the ruler with the legal institution that the legal scholars had deprived him of by insisting that the sultan or caliph had no business in deciding on God's law.

These courts were often called the "sultan's council" (*majlis*), but in the literature they are subsumed under the concept of *maẓālim* courts. They certainly meant to apply the *Sharīʿah*, but were freed from some of the procedural constraints of the actual *qāḍī*'s courts. Their rationale was to "right wrongs" that the *Sharīʿah* courts proper were unable to address. The sultan's council was generally considered to work hand in hand with the *Sharīʿah* courts. Thus the sultan would normally have *qāḍīs*, *muftīs*, or both sitting in attendance to his council and the sultan's judgment was to conform to the "spirit of the *Sharīʿah*" if not the letter of the law. Other courts also, such as the "magistrate courts" of the police (*shurṭa*), applied the "content" of the *Sharīʿah* norms without being fettered by its procedures.

Areas of Law. All *Sharīʿah* cases are grouped into one of five categories known as "the five decisions" (*al-aḥkām al-khamsa*). An act may be mandatory (*wājib* or *farḍ*), meaning that it is a sin or crime not to perform it. A *mandūb* act is recommended, but it is not a sin to omit it. An act that is neither recommended nor disliked is neutral (*mubāh*), that is, God has no particular opinion about it. If an act should be avoided, but is not an actual sin, it is "despised" (*makrūh*). Finally, an act that is a sin or a crime to commit is *ḥarām*. The term *ḥalāl*, "allowed," covers the first three or four categories; there is disagreement about whether the despised *makrūh* acts are included in *ḥalāl*. The law of the courts, however, is only concerned with the mandatory, the forbidden, and the neutral. Acts that are *mandūb* or *makrūh* are matters between the believer and God, not for the court to decide upon. An act may also be committed out of necessity, *ḍarūra*, such as one to prevent a greater sin, which also influences its legal as well as moral verdict.

Criminal Law. The *Sharīʿah* encompasses all areas of human activity, but can be separated into different fields. What we call "criminal law" falls in the *Sharīʿah* into three or four categories that are treated in widely divergent ways. Five specific crimes are considered "crimes against God" and fall into the category of *ʿibādāt*. They are set apart because the punishment for them is based directly on the revealed text, and thus cannot be subject to human interpretation, notwithstanding the *fiqh* process that went into formulating their legal form. They are known as the *ḥudūd* crimes. There is some disagreement as to which crimes fall under the *ḥudūd* category, but the normal list is: theft (penalty is amputation of the right hand), "highway robbery" (*ḥirāba*, often translated as "rebellion"; death), drinking wine (80 lashes), committing fornication (100 lashes or death), and unsubstantiated accusation of fornication (*qadhf*, 80 lashes).

On the basis of a *ḥadīth* asking for restraint in applying these rules, jurists developed various sets of restrictions (*shubuhāt*, or "similarities") that specified in what cases the *ḥudūd* rules should *not* be applied. In many cases these restrictions, along with the general restrictions on evidence in *Sharīʿah* courts, became so stringent that it was virtually impossible to convict anyone under these rules (except for *qadhf*, which was not restricted by *shubuhāt*). However, if there was political and judicial will, we find in periods a greater willingness to apply them.

Murder or other crimes that relate to bodily harm are not part of the *ḥudūd*. They are judged according to a version of *lex taliones* called *qiṣāṣ*. If the death or harm was caused intentionally, the victim (or his heirs) was given the choice between retaliation or recompense. If he chose the former, a disfigurement similar to that the victim received was applied to the culprit, for example, an eye removed for an eye blinded. If the victim chose recompense, he was free to ask for whatever sum of money he wanted. In the event of accidental harm, only recompense (*diya*, "blood money") was allowed, and here the court followed established *fiqh* guidelines that determined the rate for each type of injury.

All criminal cases that were neither *ḥudūd* nor bodily harm were termed *taʿzīr*, where the verdict was largely left to the *qāḍī*'s discretion, thus allowing adjustments to the custom and expectations of the time and place. Theft that did not fall under *ḥudūd* rules (because of the *shubuhāt* restrictions, i.e., the item stolen had been left in the open, was of little value, etc.) was often treated as "unlawful appropriation" (*ghasb*), whereby the aim was primarily to restore the stolen object to its owner in its original state rather than to sanction the act of appropriation.

Family Law. The largest area for conflict concerned the family, personal status, and inheritance. As marriage and divorce were primarily seen as legal matters where the content of the marriage contract was of paramount importance, the courts were often used to resolve conflicts within families. The *qāḍī* was regularly asked to intervene in issues such as economic maintenance or the domicile of husband and wife. In these fields the gendered nature of the *Sharīʿah* stands out clearly. While a marriage may be described as an exchange of (differentiated) rights and duties between husband and wife, divorce was without a doubt a male prerogative, even if all *madhhab*s allowed the wife some options to seek dissolution of a marriage (the Ḥanafī school hardly so, while the Mālikī applied a fairly wide interpretation of "harm," *ḍarar*, that allowed the *qāḍī* to dissolve the union).

Ottoman Sharīʿah. The Ottoman Empire expanded the state's intervention into legal affairs, not just by applying the law but also by influencing its content. The early sultans began to apply rules, *kanun* (Ar. *qānūn*), that were collected into a separate law book, *kanun-name*, which dealt with primarily administrative and economic matters but also criminal law. The *kanun*s were by definition subservient to the *Sharīʿah* and were only meant to fill those gaps where the *Sharīʿah* did not provide clear answers. However, it soon became clear that judges in Ottoman-controlled lands had to give the *kanun* precedence but could apply *Sharīʿah* according to the *fiqh* literature if the *kanun* did not provide an answer. In many matters, such as in criminal law, the *kanun* followed the content of the *Sharīʿah* fairly closely, so the difference may not always have been dramatic.

The Ottomans also reinforced state control by drawing the legal professions closer under its management. *Qāḍī*s had always been appointed by the state and could be deposed by the governor or sultan at will (often, however, through the intermediary of a chief judge, *qāḍī al-quḍāt*). *Muftī*s, on the other hand, were as religious scholars generally only recognized through the acceptance of their peers and through the public seeking them out for *fatwā*s. Some earlier rulers did draw certain renowned *muftī*s into closer contact by appointing them as advisors in their council, but the Ottomans made the *muftī*s akin to state employees. They were salaried and a hierarchy was established, with a chief *muftī* (*shaykh al-islām*) at the top. Scholars had to pass formal exams to gain access to this source of remuneration. These Ottoman reforms were most influential in the central regions of the empire; in the provinces as well as on the local village level, *muftīs* continued to be recruited informally as before.

The Ottomans also favored the Ḥanafī *madhhab* and made this the official school of law of the empire to be applied in the court (alongside *kanun* and local custom, *örf*). In Anatolia and the northern parts of the empire, this school was dominant anyway, but in many of the Arab lands it was not. Other *madhhabs* were still adhered to in matters of religious ritual, so believers maintained their identication with Mālikism or Shāfiʿism. Jurists of these schools also continued to practice—either in separate courts, which parties could choose to consult, or attached to the state courts as assistant judges, advisors to the main Ḥanafī judge, or in other ways. The central cities of the Middle East had for centuries known a cosmopolitan mixture of *madhhabs*, which the Ottomans continued, but now with one *madhhab* in clear preference, unlike in earlier periods where a balance between the four was sought in the large towns.

Modern Developments. The advent of European influence in the nineteenth century furthered the development of greater state control over the legal arena. As before, state courts and *Sharīʿah* courts continued to exist alongside each other. But while the sultanic courts were in theory and largely also in practice subservient to the ideals of the *Sharīʿah* and should implement those, the Europeans brought new legal norms that were in no way related to the *Sharīʿah* and Islam, and in the course of time these came to dominate over the *Sharīʿah*. Criminal law, which the political authorities had always kept a grip on, was transferred to new laws inspired by Europe. Foreign traders refused to submit to Islamic economic regulations, so the finance-starved Middle Eastern states soon came to apply European, in particular French, law. Judicial administrative procedures were also brought into line with European practice. Appeals courts, new to the *Sharīʿah* court system, were set up. In the *Sharīʿah* courts, the parties presented their own cases and the judge ensured their rights. Now, professional lawyers and barristers, increasingly educated in Western law only, were introduced to plead the cases. While Islamic terms such as *qāḍī* and *maḥkama* were preserved, these now mainly came to mean judge and court in the Western sense. Only in family law were the *Sharīʿah* rules largely preserved. In the course of the twentieth century, most countries finally abolished the parallel *Sharīʿah* courts altogether and brought all legal matters under the "civil" state court system.

Thus family and personal matters remained in many Muslim countries the last stronghold for the *Sharīʿah*. This meant that in this field (but sometimes also in other fields related to religious identity, such as the permission to serve alcohol), the classical divisions along religious lines were preserved. Most Muslim countries with Christian or Jewish minorities allowed these to maintain a separate family law, codified by the state or, more usually, left to each religious authority to define. Some countries (such as Lebanon) also allowed different Islamic currents—e.g., the Shīʿīs and Druze—to apply their own family law, while others (such as Syria) had only one, state-determined Muslim family law.

While the governing law related to family and personal status matters was based on the *Sharīʿah* to a much greater extent than in other fields of law, there was also a fundamental shift in who defined this law. In most countries family and personal status laws were codified in the same way as other laws by a legislative body of some kind. Thus they were subject to the authority of the state, unlike the autonomous control of the *fiqh* scholars of premodern times. The state as legislator also had the opportunity to influence the content of the law, insofar as the community was willing to recognize and adopt such changes.

In this way most modern states have introduced amendments and modernizations to family law. Often this is done by drawing upon the differences between *madhhabs*. While the classical law did not—or only to a very limited degree—allow a *madhhab*'s interpretation to be influenced by the views of other schools, modern states often use a "cut-and-paste" (*talfīq*) method, picking the rules or interpretations most in line with their wishes from whichever *madhhab* they want, for example, the more liberal view on divorce from the Mālikī school and the more liberal view on marriage from the Ḥanafī school. Thus they may end up with a hybrid "state *madhhab*" unlike any of the original four, even though each individual rule may be based on *fiqh*. By the same process, each modern Muslim state ends up with its own, national "*Sharīʿah*" law that differs at least in detail from the *Sharīʿah* of other states, rather than the universal *madhhabs* of the classical period that transcended political frontiers. Still, the main lines of classical *Sharīʿah* family law can be said to persist in this development, and most actors will accept these laws as variations of the *Sharīʿah*.

The Islamic resurgence of the last quarter of the twentieth century brought this issue to the fore again, with renewed calls by Islamist groups for full implementation of the *Sharīʿah*. By this is meant expanding the *Sharīʿah*'s scope from personal status law to all fields of law, and for many the symbolic and key aspect is to implement Islamic criminal law, in particular the *ḥudūd* rules. Since they are considered to be directly based on the divine text rather than on the jurists' interpretation or *ijtihād*, it is particularly important—at least symbolically—to follow God's direct statements in these matters. The *ḥudūd* are thus seen by Islamist groups as the core of the divine *Sharīʿah*, and the restraints that later jurists built in to limit their application (the *shubuhāt* rules) are often rejected, at least in theory. Several Muslim countries under Islamist influence have thus reintroduced the *ḥudūd*, such as Iran, Sudan, certain states in Nigeria, and others. This is in many cases, however, more a matter of symbolism—the rules had to be on the books and some cases brought to trial to show they were enforced—for they are in practice often used only sparingly or not at all. Clearly, this varies in accordance with the political vagaries of each country, as well as with the enthusiasm of the legal institutions to prosecute and convict such cases.

Thus the role of the *Sharīʿah* has become a contested topic in many countries, and may have, for example, been a contributing factor to the breakup of at least one Muslim state, Sudan. While the term clearly has more of a symbolic value than a real value for many—calling up a purity of religious ideals—it has also brought about actual legal reform in a more conservative direction in some Muslim countries. Only Saudi Arabia may be said to follow a classical *qāḍī* court system, but other countries have established review boards of some sort, composed of religious scholars, in order to vet proposed laws. On the other hand, secular forces and in particular women's movements have argued for either a reinterpretation of the *Sharīʿah* to allow for greater flexibility in application or a reduction in impact of classical *Sharīʿah* rules altogether. In some countries, such as Morocco, such argumentation has resulted in considerable revisions to the family law, despite their still being drawn from concepts and principles derived from the *Sharīʿah*. While most Muslim countries continue to refer in their constitution to the *Sharīʿah*, or use formulations such as "based on the principles of the *Sharīʿah*" to describe the basis for their legal system, the actual interpretation and content of the *Sharīʿah* seem to allow for greater variation, with some developments embracing traditionalism and others modernized reform.

[*See also* Courts; Fatwa; Fiqh; Justice; Kānūn; Schools of Jurisprudence; *and* Siyāsah *Sharīʿah*.]

BIBLIOGRAPHY

Studies

Brockopp, Jonathan E. *Early Mālikī Law: Ibn ʿAbd al-Ḥakam and His Major Compendium of Jurisprudence*. Leiden: Brill, 2000.

Brown, Nathan J. *The Rule of Law in the Arab World: Courts in Egypt and the Gulf*. Cambridge, U.K.: Cambridge University Press, 1997.

Cook, Michael. *Commanding Right and Forbidding Wrong in Islamic Thought*. Cambridge, U.K.: Cambridge University Press, 2000.

Calder, Norman. *Studies in Early Muslim Jurisprudence*. Oxford: Clarendon, 1993. A very controversial thesis on the dating of early law.

Gleave, Robert. *Inevitable Doubt: Two Theories of Shīʿī Jurisprudence*. Leiden: Brill, 2000.

Hallaq, Wael B. *Authority, Continuity, and Change in Islamic Law*. Cambridge, U.K.: Cambridge University Press, 2001.

Hallaq, Wael B. *A History of Islamic Legal Theories: An Introduction to Sunnī* uṣūl al-fiqh. Cambridge, U.K.: Cambridge University Press, 1997. An in-depth study of the thinking behind the *Sharīʿah*.

Hallaq, Wael B. *Sharia: Theory, Practice, Transformations*. Cambridge, U.K.: Cambridge University Press, 2009.

Imber, Colin. *Ebuʾs-suʿud: The Islamic Legal Tradition*. Edinburgh: Edinburgh University Press, 1997. On the most famous Ottoman *shaykh al-islām*.

Jackson, Sherman A. *Islamic Law and the State: The Constitutional Jurisprudence of Shihāb al-Dīn al-Qarāfī*. Leiden: Brill, 1996. Puts the later development of the *madhhabs* into new perspective.

Masud, Muhammad Khalid. *Shāṭibī's Philosophy of Islamic Law*. Islamabad: Islamic Research Institute, 1995. Important for the concept of *maṣlaḥa*, God's intentions with the law.

Melchert, Christopher. *The Formation of the Sunni Schools of Law, 9th-10th Centuries CE*. Leiden: Brill, 1997. A basic work for the historical dating of early law.

Messick, Brinkley. *The Calligraphic State: Textual Domination and History in a Muslim Society*. Berkeley: University of California Press, 1996. Classical study of how legal texts meet practice in modern Yemen.

Motzki, Harald. *The Origins of Islamic Jurisprudence: Meccan Fiqh before the Schools*. Translated by Marion H. Katz. Leiden: Brill, 2002.

Müller, Christian. *Gerichtspraxis im Stadtstaat Córdoba: Zum Recht der Gesellschaft in einer mālikitisch-islamischen Rechtstradition des 5./11. Jahrhunderts*. Leiden: Brill, 1999. The most detailed modern study on "state courts" in medieval Islam.

Peters, Rudolph. *Crime and Punishment in Islamic Law: Theory and Practice from the Sixteenth to the Twenty-First Century*. Cambridge, U.K.: Cambridge University Press, 2005.

Powers, David S. *Law, Society, and Culture in the Maghrib, 1300-1500*. Cambridge, U.K.: Cambridge University Press, 2002.

Schacht, Joseph. *An Introduction to Islamic Law*. Oxford: Clarendon Press, 1991. Still the unavoidable basic study in the field.

Schacht, Joseph. *The Origins of Muhammadan Jurisprudence*. Oxford: Clarendon Press, 1979. A classical work of the "revisionist" history of the *Sharīʿah*.

Shaham, Ron. *Family and the Courts in Modern Egypt: A Study Based on Decisions by the Sharīʿa Courts, 1900–1955*. Leiden: Brill, 1997.

Skovgaard-Petersen, Jakob. *Defining Islam for the Egyptian State: Muftis and Fatwas of the Dār al-iftā*. Leiden: Brill, 1997. On the modern state's use of the traditional *muftī* office.

Tillier, Mathieu. *Les cadis d'Iraq et l'état abbasside (132/750-334/945)*. Damas: IFPO, 2009.

Tucker, Judith E. *Women, Family, and Gender in Islamic Law*. Cambridge, U.K.: Cambridge University Press, 2008.

Tyan, Emile. *Histoire de l'organisation judiciaire en pays d'Islam*. Leiden: Brill, 1960. Still the basic study on courts and classical court practice.

Vikør, Knut S. *Between God and the Sultan: A History of Islamic Law*. London: Hurst, 2005.

Vogel, Frank E. *Islamic Law and Legal System: Studies of Saudi Arabia*. Leiden: Brill, 2000. Fundamental study on the state today that follows classical *Sharīʿah* practices most closely.

Zubaida, Sami. *Law and Power in the Islamic World*. London: Tauris, 2003. A political sociologist's essay on the modern history of Islamic law.

Articles and Edited Works

Bearman, Peri, Rudolph Peters, and Frank E. Vogel, eds. *The Islamic School of Law: Evolution, Devolution, and Progress*. Cambridge, Mass.: Islamic Legal Studies Program, Harvard Law School, distributed by Harvard University Press, 2005.

Hallaq, Wael B. "From *fatwās* to *furū*ʿ: Growth and Change in Islamic Substantive Law." *Islamic Law and Society* 1 (1994): 29–65.

Krawietz, Birgit. "Cut and Paste in Legal Rules: Designing Islamic Norms with *talfīq*." *Die Welt des Islams* 42 (2002): 3–40.

Layish, Aharon. "The Transformation of the Sharia from Jurists' Law to Statutory Law in the Contemporary Muslim World." *Die Welt des Islams* 44 (2004): 85–113.

Masud, Muhammad Khalid, Brinkley Messick, and David S. Powers, eds. *Islamic Legal Interpretation: Muftis and Their Fatwas*. Cambridge, Mass.: Harvard University Press, 1996. Comprehensive studies on *fatwas* in theory and practice.

Masud, Muhammad Khalid, Rudolph Peters, and David S. Powers, eds. *Dispensing Justice in Islam: Qadis and Their Judgments*. Leiden: Brill, 2006.

Melchert, Christopher. "Religious Policies of the Caliphs from al-Mutawakkil to al-Muqtadir, AH 232–295/AD 847–908." *Islamic Law and Society* 3 (1996): 316–342.

Peters, Rudolph. "From Jurists' Law to Statute Law or What Happens When the Shariʿa Is Codified." *Mediterranean Politics* 7 (2002): 82–95.

Welchman, Lynn. "Islamic Law: Stuck with the State?" In *Religion, Law and Tradition: Comparative Studies in Religious Law*, edited by Andrew Huxley, pp. 61–83. London: RoutledgeCurzon, 2002.

KNUT S. VIKØR

SHARĪʿATĪ, ʿALĪ.

ʿAlī Sharīʿatī was born in in 1933 in the village of Mazinan, near the town of Sabzevār, on the edge of the Dasht-i Kavīr Desert in Khorāsān province, northeastern Iran. He came from a well-known family whose paternal line included clergymen active in the religious circles of Mashhad, the city that houses the shrine of the eighth imam, ʿAlī al-Riḍā (d. 818).

Much of Sharīʿatī's life remains obscure. His grandfather Ākhūnd Hakīm was a respected *ʿalim* (pl. *ʿulamāʾ*, religious cleric) whose fame apparently had extended beyond Iran to Bukhara and Najaf, and he had spent some time at Tehran's Sipah Sālār mosque, though he returned to his native district, declining the shah's posts and honors. Ākhūnd Hakīm's brother ʿĀdil Nīshabūrī had also earned a reputation as a religious scholar.

Sharīʿatī's father Muḥammad Taqī Sharīʿatī was of the same ilk, but he was a modernist who had lost patience with the traditional perspectives of the *ʿulamāʾ*, which he saw as suffused with abstract scholasticism. Muḥammad possessed a large and comprehensive library that ʿAlī fondly regarded as the wellspring of his thought, from which he nourished his mind and soul. Muḥammad Taqī not only taught students of the religious sciences in Mashhad, he was also the founder of the city's Kānūn-i Nashr-i Ḥaqāʾiq-i Islāmī (Society for the Promulgation of Islamic Verities), a lay organization dedicated to the revival of Islam as a religion of social obligation and commitment.

Education and Early Career. Little is known of ʿAlī Sharīʿatī's early years, except that he attended government (as opposed to seminary) schools in Mashhad, and also took lessons from his father. On graduating from secondary school, apparently in 1949, Sharīʿatī enrolled in a two-year program at Mashhad's Teachers' Training College (Dānishsarāy-i Tarbiyat-i Muʿallim).

He seems to have begun teaching at the age of eighteen or nineteen (1951–1952), probably in one of the government village schools near Mashhad. Both he and his father were involved in pro-National Front rallies in support of Prime Minister Mohammad Mossadegh (Muḥammad Muṣaddiq) held by the Mashhad branch of the National Resistance Movement (Nahẓat-i Muqāvamat-i Millī) after the August 1953 royalist coup d'état that overthrew Mossadegh. The movement was founded by Mehdi Bazargan and the social-activist clergyman Sayyid Maḥmūd Ṭāleqānī. Apparently, Sharīʿatī had entered Mashhad University as an undergraduate in 1956 and married that same year. He was arrested in September 1957 for his role in a

National Front demonstration and was jailed at Tehran's Qizil Qalʿah prison until May 1958. He is also said to have affiliated himself with a political movement known as the Movement of Socialist Believers in God (Junbish-i Khudāparastān-i Sūsiyālist).

Sharīʿatī was therefore about twenty-seven at the time he received his degree, with honors, in French and Persian literature in 1960. He left immediately for Paris to study at the Sorbonne. Since he later frequently alluded to his training under the Orientalist Louis Massignon, the sociologist Georges Gurvitch, the historian Jacques Berque, and the philosopher Jean-Paul Sartre, many of his supporters believed that he had been formally trained in philosophy and social sciences, but his doctoral dissertation was a translation of and introduction to a medieval book, *Faẓāʾil-i Balkh* (The Notables of Balkh), under the supervision of the philologist Gilbert Lazard. If, therefore, he had received such training, it was not reflected in his dissertation.

Political Activity. During his years abroad, Sharīʿatī participated actively in the anti-shah student movement and came to know Ibrāhīm Yazdī, Ṣādiq Quṭbzādah, Abol-Hasan Bani Sadr (Abū al-Ḥasan Banī Ṣadr), and Muṣṭafā Chamrān, all of whom became principals in Iran's early postrevolutionary government. During the 1962 Congress of the National Front in Europe in Wiesbaden, Germany, Sharīʿatī was elected editor of the organization's newly established newspaper, *Īrān-i Āzād* (Free Iran). He also contributed articles to the Algerian revolutionary resistance newspaper *al-Mujāhid* (The Struggler).

Sharīʿatī returned to Iran in 1964 and was immediately arrested at the Turkish frontier and jailed for six months for his political activities in France. After his release, he returned to Mashhad and taught briefly in a regional secondary school before securing an obscure post as instructor in humanities at Mashhad University's Faculty of Agriculture. Shortly thereafter, he transferred to the Faculty of Arts. Sharīʿatī's lectures attracted students from outside the university as well. As he became popular, the government engineered his dismissal, although he continued to receive invitations to lecture from university student organizations on campuses in various cities.

Meanwhile, in Tehran, a group of religious reformers had established the Ḥusaynīyah-i Irshād in 1965. This religious institution, like the Kānūn-i Nashr-i Ḥaqāʾiq-i Islāmī of Mashhad, granted no degrees but sponsored lectures, discussions, seminars, and publications on religious subjects. Sharīʿatī joined the Ḥusaynīyah-i Irshād in 1967 and not long after became its most popular instructor. For six years, his lectures were packed with students eager to hear a new interpretation of Islam and its role in society. His activities angered orthodox clergymen, who saw him as an untutored agitator who was undermining respect for the seminary and its scholars. The younger generation, however, was enthralled by his innovative approach.

Because of pervasive censorship, Sharīʿatī had to couch his discussions in elliptical language. One of the leading intellectuals of the Iranian Revolution of 1979, Murtaẓā Muṭahharī (d. 1979), remarked that he and Sharīʿatī's other colleagues at the Ḥusaynīyah-i Irshād believed that his talks were too overtly political and feared a government crackdown. By mid-1973 the regime had indeed come to regard Sharīʿatī as a dangerous radical, and he was again arrested and jailed. Sharīʿatī was released on 20 March 1975 because of pressure from the Algerian government. The Iranian press published his essay "Marxism and Other Fallacies: A Critique of Marxism from the Perspective of Islam" without his permission, in a transparent attempt to suggest that Sharīʿatī had sold out his leftist supporters.

After being under virtual house arrest for about two years, Sharīʿatī was finally allowed to go abroad in the spring of 1977. His plans were to meet his wife and family in Europe and then to proceed to the United States, where his son Iḥsān was a student, but the government prevented his family's departure, and Sharīʿatī, who had already flown to Brussels, went to England to stay with his brother pending resolution. On 19 June 1977 his body was discovered at his brother's house in southern England. The official ruling was that he died from a heart attack, but many believe he had been assassinated by the shah's secret police.

Sharīʿatī's body was transferred to Iranian authorities in London, and the Iranian government sought to persuade his wife to go claim the body and return it for burial at state expense. However, she refused to participate in this blatant attempt to exploit her husband's death for the shah's own propaganda purposes, and Sharīʿatī instead was buried in Damascus, near the tomb of Zaynab, the Prophet's granddaughter and sister of the third imam, Ḥusayn ibn ʿAlī (d. 680)—Shiism's foremost martyr, whose struggle against impiety and tyranny had been the subject of many lectures by Sharīʿatī. Officiating at the funeral was Mūsā al-Sadr (who vanished under mysterious circumstances in Libya during a 1978 visit), leader of the Lebanese Shīʿah.

Writings. Sharīʿatī was less a disciplined scholar than a social and political activist. By the time of his final arrest, he had given over two hundred lectures at the Ḥusaynīyah-i Irshād, many of which had been prepared for publication and sold thousands of copies in several printings. His early works include *Maktab-i vāsiṭah* (the Middle School of Thought), which he wrote while at the Teachers' Training College and which upheld Islam as the virtuous path between capitalism and communism, and *Tārīkh-i takāmul-i falsafah* (History of Philosophy's Perfection), written in 1955. He was deeply impressed by the biography titled *Abū Dharr al-Ghifārī* by Jūdah al-Saḥḥār, whose protagonist, Abū Dharr (d. 657), symbolized Muslim resistance to injustice. In fact, Sharīʿatī's admirers affixed to his name upon his death the sobriquet "Abū Dharr-i Zaman" (the Abū Dharr of the Age).

Sharīʿatī's Critics. Sharīʿatī's detractors, mainly scripturalists with an ahistorical view of the sacred texts, felt that he had diffused and distilled the Qurʾān, the *sunnah* (practices and sayings) of the Prophet, and the traditions of the imams into a mere vulgate, with debasing appeals to "enlightened thinkers" to overturn the existing social arrangements for the sake of an anthropocentric "new order." This view, however, ascribing to Sharīʿatī no more than a merely instrumental approach to the faith, falls apart in light of the role he ascribed to religious belief in the spiritual life of the individual. For Sharīʿatī, it was religion that enabled freedom for the people, not freedom that made possible the verification of religious truths.

There might be a limited basis for the scripturalists' concerns, however, because Sharīʿatī did invoke a central theme of the humanistic, Enlightenment tradition: the individual's enormous potential for living a life of emancipation, harmony, and well-being through the exercise of reason. For all of Sharīʿatī's ecstatic paeans to Allāh's majesty and love, his system did seem to assume the vision of those who believed in history's progressive march toward the liberation of mankind from the evils of superstition, obscurantism, and mystification. His scheme did at least imply the possibility that human reason was uniquely capable of achieving the individual's emancipation and enfranchisement.

Sharīʿatī's critics blamed him for opening the door to the emergence of a human community that would vanquish the forces of evil through dedication to its own confraternity. Even if this community submitted itself to Allāh, Sharīʿatī's critics implied, such submission would be suspect because it appeared to be contingent rather than categorically compelling in the first instance. Whether his critics are right in suspecting that, in his worldview, Allāh's role appears to be reduced to merely providing comfort from personal doubts, one thing is clear: Sharīʿatī was concerned, perhaps more than anything else, about human injustice, which he viewed both as a symptom and as an integral consequence of a failed human emancipation. He therefore dedicated his life to fighting it. How can the Shīʿah, who are devoted to Imams ʿAlī (d. 661) and Ḥusayn, acquiesce to injustice? he demanded. Rulers have oppressed the faithful, often in the name of Shiism itself. But the traditional clergy must share the blame, because they have for centuries encouraged stoic acceptance of despotism, some for opportunistic reasons, others in the expectation that the Hidden Imam would one day return to purge all the accumulated wrongs visited on the righteous. In this refusal to wait passively for the redeemer, Sharīʿatī once again had much in common with Ayatollah Khomeini. Nonetheless, Khomeini was not an admirer of Sharīʿatī and doubtless shared his fellow *mujtahids*' views that he was an ignorant hothead who made gratuitous attacks on the Shīʿī clergy.

Principal Concepts. Although he was a controversial figure, almost all agree that Sharīʿatī's was an urgent voice. Despite the prevalence of Shīʿī symbols, his cause was humanity in general, especially the masses of the Third World. He believed that Western imperialism sought to transform the masses into slaves. Islam was, in his view, the answer to both Marxism and capitalism. Some of the key concepts in Sharīʿatī's writings and speeches were *shahādat* (martyrdom); *intiẓār* (anticipation of the return of the Hidden Imam); *ẓulm* (oppression of the imam's justice); *jihād* and *iʿtirāẓ* (struggle for God's sake and protest); *ijtihād* (independent judgment to determine a legal rule); *rūshanfikrān* (enlightened thinkers); *tārīkh* (the movement of history); *masʾūlīyat* (responsibility); and *ʿadālat* (social justice).

From Marxism, Sharīʿatī borrowed the notion of dialectical conflict and appropriated the term *jabr-i tārīkh* (historical determinism). But he preferred Hegel's primacy of contradictions among ideas along the path to an Absolute Truth to Marx's insistence on the precedence of social contradictions and class conflict. From Western liberal thought, Sharīʿatī adopted the Enlightenment's stress on reason as the corrective for the maladies of society. From both Marxism and "bourgeois" Enlightenment philosophy, he seems to have gained an appreciation of the dangers that institutionalized religion can pose. And from romantic philosophy, which he may or may not have formally studied, he gained an appreciation of the shortcomings of positivism and ratiocination.

In the matter of institutionalized religion, Sharīʿatī believed that *ijtihād* is the purview not merely of the experts in religious law but of every individual. All persons have the responsibility to exercise *ijtihād* on substantive, nontechnical matters. He likened the emulation of putative experts—the *mujtahids*—in regard to such basic problems as authority, justice, mobilization, and participation to abdication of individual responsibility, choice, and will. We can see, then, the manifest influence of existentialist and Marxist philosophy on Sharīʿatī. From the former, he adopted the notion that the individual must take responsibility for his or her actions. (The French philosopher Jean-Paul Sartre is said to have asserted: "I have no religion, but if I were to choose one, it would be that of Shariʿati"). And from Marx's understanding of the Prometheus legend, Sharīʿatī absorbed the humanistic admonition that religion can be made to serve despots, that the eternal truths represented by religion must be determined by individuals appropriating true knowledge from those seeking to monopolize it for non- or even antihumanistic ends.

Influence. Sharīʿatī's contributions are many. At the time of the Iranian Revolution, his portraits were held high by many of the younger revolutionary groups, and while ideologues who dominated Iranian political culture thereafter marginalized his ideas in the media and educational institutions, they have not been able to suppress his voice. His example may well have inspired lay religious activists outside Iran for example, the Syrian engineer Muḥammad Shuhrūr, whose ideas on *ijtihād* are strikingly similar to those of Sharīʿatī.

[*See also* Iran, Islamic Republic of; Jihād; *and* Khomeini, Ruhollah al-Musavi.]

BIBLIOGRAPHY

For a comprehensive list of Sharīʿatī's works, see Yann Richard, "A Bibliography of the Writings of Ali Shariati." *Abstracta Iranica* (supplement to *Studia Iranica*) 1–2 (1978–1979).

Abrahamian, Ervand. "Ali Shariʿati: Ideologue of the Iranian Revolution." *MERIP Reports* 102 (January 1982): 24–28.

Aḥmadī, Ḥamīd, ed. *Sharīʿatī dar jahān: Naqsh-i Duktur ʿAlī Sharīʿatī dar bīdārgarī-i Islāmī az dīdgāh-i andīshmandān va muḥaqqiqān-i khārijī*. Tehran: Shirkat-i Sihāmī, 1986.

Akhavi, Shahrough. "Shariati's Social Thought." In *Religion and Politics in Iran: Shiʿism from Quietism to Revolution*, edited by Nikki R. Keddie, pp. 125–144. New Haven, Conn.: Yale University Press, 1983.

Algar, Ḥamīd. "Islām bi ʿunvān-i yak īdiyūlūzhī." In *Sharīʿatī dar jahān: Naqsh-i Duktur ʿAlī Sharīʿatī dar bīdārgarī-i Islāmī az dīdgāh-i andīshmandān va muḥaqqiqān-i khārijī*, edited by Ḥamīd Aḥmadī. Tehran: Shirkat-i Sihāmī, 1986.

Bayat-Philipp, Mangol. "Shiʿism in Contemporary Iranian Politics: The Case of Ali Shariʿati." In *Towards a Modern Iran: Studies in Thought, Politics and Society*, edited by Elie Kedourie and Sylvia Haim, pp. 155–168. London: F. Cass, 1980.

Dabashi, Hamid. "Ali Shariʿati: The Islamic Ideologue Par Excellence." In *Theology of Discontent: The Ideological Foundations of the Islamic Revolution in Iran*, pp. 102–146. New York: New York University Press, 1993.

Hanson, Brad. "The 'Westoxication' of Iran: Depictions and Reactions of Behrangi, Āl-e Ahmad, and Shariʿati." *International Journal of Middle East Studies* 15 (1983): 1–23.

Hermansen, Marcia K. "Fatimeh as a Role Model in the Works of Ali Shariʿati." In *Women and Revolution in Iran*, edited by Guity Nashat, pp. 87–96. Boulder, Colo.: Westview, 1983.

Malushkov, V. G., and K. A. Khromova. *Poiski puteĭ reformatsii v islame: Opyt Irana*. Moscow: Nauka, 1991.

Rahnema, Ali. *An Islamic Utopian: A Political Biography of Ali Shariʿati*. 2d ed. London: I. B. Tauris, 2000.

Sachedina, Abdulaziz. "Shariʿati: Ideologue of the Iranian Revolution." In *Voices of Resurgent Islam*, edited by John L. Esposito, pp. 191–214. New York: Oxford University Press, 1983.

Shariʿati, Ali. *On the Sociology of Islam: Lectures*. Translated by Hamid Algar. Berkeley, Calif.: Mizan, 1979.

SHAHROUGH AKHAVI

SHŪRĀ. Many of the scholars and activists who see democratic principles in Islam have singled out the principle of *shūrā* to illustrate their point. *Shūrā* is a consultative decision-making process that is considered either obligatory or desirable by Islamic scholars. Those scholars who choose to emphasize the Qurʾānic verse "and consult with them in affairs [of the moment]" (3:159) consider *shūrā* obligatory, but other scholars, who emphasize the verse that says that "those who conduct their affairs by counsel" (43:38) are praised, consider *shūrā* desirable. The first verse directly addresses a particular decision of the Prophet and speaks to him directly, but the second verse is more in the nature of a general principle. Perhaps this is the reason that traditional Islamic scholars have never considered consultation as a necessary and legitimizing element of decision making. Also, the second verse may have been given more significance because it occurs in the chapter entitled "al-Shūrā."

There is no doubt that *shūrā* is an Islamic way of making decisions, but one thing remains unsettled: Is it necessary and obligatory? Will an organization or a government that does not implement a consultative process become illegitimate? Muslim scholars have not provided a definitive answer, although a growing number of Muslim intellectuals agree that consultative and consensual governance is the best governance. Experts in jurisprudence, however, are often conservative or ambivalent on the topic. This reluctance may be the result of an inadequate definition of those who deserve to be consulted, the specialists or the general population. Some of the jurist specialists provide consultation for authoritarian rulers, and this may serve as an alternative or obstacle to the development of mechanisms for consultation involving the general population more democratically.

Parliaments in Muslim countries increasingly use the term *shūrā* in their names. Pakistan, Egypt, Iran, Saudi Arabia, and Oman have used the phrase *majlis al-shūrā* (consultative council) in the names of their parliaments.

Shūrā as an Islamically privileged idea provides an important means of legitimizing the establishment of parliamentary democratic practices in the Muslim world. It is important to note, however, that there are some fundamental differences between *shūrā*—as currently understood by Muslim scholars—and parliamentary processes.

Unlike *shūrā*, democracy allows modification of foundational texts. One can amend a constitution but not the Qurʾān or the *sunnah*. On the face of it, this should not be a problem, because Muslims are by definition supposed to accept the primary sources of Islam. In practice, however, one is dealing not with the sources but with interpretations of the sources, and the process of *shūrā* may be subordinated to a historical understanding of Islamic texts.

Muslim organizations, international and local nongovernmental organizations (NGOs), and even mosque management committees are relying increasingly on the idea and the process of *shūrā* in making both important and routine decisions. The word *shūrā* is proliferating in Islamic management discourses. Muslims in the West, especially in North America, have merged *shūrā* and democracy in the bylaws and the procedures that govern their organizations.

[*See also* Democracy.]

BIBLIOGRAPHY

El-Awa, Muhammad S. *On the Political System of the Islamic State*. Translated by Ahmad Naji al-Imam and edited by Anwer Beg, pp. 89–90. Indianapolis, Ind.: American Trust Publications, 1980.

Esposito, John L., and John O.Voll. *Islam and Democracy*. New York: Oxford University Press, 1996.

M. A. MUQTEDAR KHAN

SHUʿŪBĪYAH. A literary movement of the early period of Islamic civilization that contested the Arabs' cultural hegemony and proclaimed the superiority, for the most part, of the Persians. It emerged in the late eighth century, was in full bloom in the ninth, and continued to the end of the tenth, coinciding with the cultural efflorescence of the ʿAbbāsids, who appropriated major elements of Greek and Sassanian cultures while fashioning a new Arab-Islamic civilization. By the eleventh century, the Shuʿūbīyah movement had disappeared from the eastern part of the Islamic empire where it had originated. It manifested itself with various degrees of ideological intensity and remained strongly expressive of the particular social and historical realities of its time and place. Because the Shuʿūbīyah touched upon some universal elements of strife between ethnic groups, it lent itself inevitably to interpretations along universal rather than historical lines. In this article, the Shuʿūbīyah is depicted in its social and historical contexts, and some of the universalist readings it triggered are addressed insofar as they constitute part of its legacy.

Context. Although no evidence exists of the articulation of Shuʿūbīyah sentiments prior to the ʿAbbāsids, the earliest Arab conquests had already fomented reflections on the relationship and hierarchy among various groups shaping the nascent Islamic empire, which, in turn, provided the Shuʿūbīyah movement with some of its tools. By refuting the assumption that the leader of the Muslim community had to be from the Quraysh, the early Khārijī sect proclaimed the equality of people based on their religious merit and rejected blood ties or lineage as a criterion for measuring their merit. By referring to the Qurʾānic verse "And We have made you into peoples [*shuʿūb*] and tribes" (49:13), the Khārijī coined the term *shuʿūbīyah*, from the word *shuʿūb* (people), to express egalitarianism, clearly not the same meaning that the term came to acquire later under the ʿAbbāsids, with the Shuʿūbīyah movement proper. This early meaning of *shuʿūbīyah* persisted to a limited extent under the ʿAbbāsids; its proponents were known as *ahl al-taswīyah* (the people of equality). Another precursor to the Shuʿūbīyah can be found in members of the southern Arab tribes who expressed their bitter discontent with their northern counterparts, favored by the Umayyads, who gave them political monopoly in the new empire. Many of the motifs used by the southern Arabs to defame the northerners were later adapted by the Shuʿūbīyah authors for their own purposes. Such motifs include cowardice, depravity, and, of course, absence of a civilized past.

The Shuʿūbīyah movement was ushered in by two new major ʿAbbāsid policies: the establishment of new cities, most importantly the city of Baghdad, that brought together in geographical and cultural proximity non-Arab and Arab Muslims; and the implementation of equality between Arab and non-Arab Muslims (*mawālī*). The immediate impact of these two new policies on the development of Shuʿūbīyah can be observed, for example, among the class of the secretaries of Persian descent. Though the Umayyads employed Persian secretaries at their court, none of the latter had voiced Shuʿūbīyah sentiments, despite the discriminatory policy of the Umayyads against non-Arab Muslims. Paradoxically, however, when the ʿAbbāsids offered equality to Persians and other non-Arab Muslims, Shuʿūbīyah sentiments emerged among the same class of secretaries. Thus the secretaries in particular and Shuʿūbīyah proponents in general had to compete with the proponents of the Arab-Islamic humanism that was emerging at the same time from the ʿAbbāsid courts. Some scholars have highlighted the purely socioeconomic reasons behind the secretaries' frustrations with these competitors at the court, but the roots of these frustrations certainly ran much deeper.

Doctrine. No Shuʿūbīyah treatise survives, so all that we know about its doctrine comes from references to it in hostile sources, where its proponents are presented as voices of criticism and resistance to Arab customs, practices, and language. There is no reference in these sources to a centrally organized movement with a specific agenda. On one level, we encounter an attack against pre-Islamic Arabic lore and poetry as it came to be represented and glorified under the ʿAbbāsids. The targets include pre-Islamic literary motifs such as standing on the ruins of the encampments of the beloved, pride in lineage, and the poet's description of his camel. This criticism of pre-Islamic Arabic culture constitutes a resistance to its ʿAbbāsid construction, perception, and glorification, which became institutionalized in Arab-Islamic sciences such as grammar and lexicography. On this level, their criticism can be viewed as a mere literary motif. But the testimony of al-Jāḥiẓ (d. 869), the master of Arabic prose and famous theologian, suggests that, on another level, the Shuʿūbīyah was also perceived as an ideological threat, nothing less than an attack on Islam itself. Indeed, al-Jāḥiẓ associated proponents of Shuʿūbīyah with Manichaeanism (Zandaqah) and heresy. Given the centrality of al-Jāḥiẓ not only as a literary figure but also as a theologian and major representative of Arab-Islamic humanism, his testimony reflects the perceived ideological threat of the Shuʿūbīyah as a counterculture.

Although it is evident that the Shuʿūbīyah was not purely a literary movement with no ideological intent, it was also far from a political or military movement, let alone one that was associated with separatist activities in Iranian territories. Not only are there no sound grounds for such an assumption, but, given what we know of the Shuʿūbīyah members' social status and their advanced literacy, it hardly seems plausible that they would engage in the destruction of the very system in which they thrived.

Two social and linguistic elements further our understanding of this movement as a product of Arab-Islamic civilization. One is that not all authors of Persian descent were advocates of the Shuʿūbīyah. One illustrative example is Ibn Qutaybah (d. 889), who was of Persian descent. Other figures in the Shuʿūbīyah movement were, in fact, of southern Arab descent, such as the poet Abū Nuwās (d. between 813 and 815), who was known for his adoption of modern poetry (*muḥdaṭ*) and his attack on pre-Islamic Arabian lore. The second element is that all Shuʿūbīyah authors expressed their views eloquently in the very language that they attacked for its limitations and primitiveness. Therefore, the Shuʿūbīyah was as much a product of the civilization it criticized as the Persian identity that it praised and from which it claimed descent.

Legacy. In sparking a counterliterature, the Shuʿūbīyah had, paradoxically, a crucial role in fashioning and accentuating a self-consciously Arab-Islamic *adab* (belles lettres) tradition, most importantly expressed in the works of al-Jāḥiẓ and Ibn Qutaybah. Moreover, since all Shuʿūbīyah figures expressed themselves in eloquent Arabic, they also, in turn, became part of *adab*. Thus the Shuʿūbīyah movement helped to form the ʿAbbāsid cultural identity.

The Shuʿūbīyah also made long-term impressions on the consciousness of Islamic peoples, influencing the composition of independent works as well as movements. We find in the epistle of Ibn Garcia, a secretary of Basque origin at the court of Denia in al-Andalus in the eleventh century, a testimony to the inspiration the Shuʿūbīyah had on later authors of different geographical and intellectual circumstances. Although there is no evidence of a larger movement in which this text can be placed, and despite the demographic and social differences between the eastern part of the ʿAbbāsid Caliphate in which the Shuʿūbīyah emerged and al-Andalus, this epistle of Ibn Garcia is considered by some scholars as a manifestation of a larger phenomenon of Andalusian Shuʿūbīyah. This claim is mainly based on Ibn Garcia's use of Shuʿūbīyah themes to defame Arabs in favor of the merits of Slavs and Berbers. Furthermore, with the rise of modern nationalist movements in Iran and the Arab world at the turn of the twentieth century, there arose a view of the Shuʿūbīyah as a form of Persian nationalism. Although some themes of criticism of Arab customs familiar from the Shuʿūbīyah writings may appear in twentieth-century Iranian nationalism, such as denigration of the Arabs' lack of culture and their barbaric habits such as eating lizards, the Shuʿūbīyah had little to do with nationalist aspirations themselves. What remains worthy of note for the historian about the nationalists' grounding of their cause in the Shuʿūbīyah is the value that this movement seems to have retained as an inspiration for new movements in Islamic history.

[*See also* ʿAbbāsid Caliphate; Andalusia; *and* Iran, Islamic Republic of.]

BIBLIOGRAPHY

Carter, Michael. "The Kātib in Fact and Fiction." *Abr-Nahrain* 11 (1971): 42–55. This article highlights the economic rather than ideological concern behind the secretaries' Shuʿūbīyah sentiments to strengthen their status at the court of the ʿAbbāsid caliphs.

Enderwitz, Susanne. "Al-Shuʿūbīyah." In *Encyclopaedia of Islam*, 2d ed., edited by P. Bearmann et al., vol. 9, pp. 513–516. Leiden, Netherlands: E. J. Brill. Identifies the major primary sources for the study of the Shuʿūbīyah, one of which Enderwitz had studied at great depth in a single monograph that remains unparalleled in its comprehensive study of one of the founding sources on the Shuʿūbīyah: her *Gesellschaftlicher Rang und ethnische Legitimation: Der arabische Schriftsteller Abū ʿUṭmān al-Gāḥiẓ (gest. 868) über die Afrikaner, Perser und Araber in der Islamischen Gesellschaft* (Freiburg, Germany: Schwarz, 1979).

Gibb, H. A. R. "The Social Significance of the Shuʿūbīyah." In *Studies on the Civilization of Islam*, edited by Stanford J. Shaw and William R. Polk, pp. 62–73. Boston, Beacon: 1962. This article is influential in distancing from separatist military activities in Iran the Shuʿūbīyah proponents that Gibb identifies as figures related to the centralized ʿAbbāsid court. The relationship between the two was a hypothesis assumed by Ignaz Goldziher.

Goldziher, Ignaz. "The Shuʿūbīyah." *Muslim Studies* 1 (1967): 137–163. This earliest piece of modern scholarship on the Shuʿūbīyah is memorable for identifying the role of the ʿAbbāsids toward non-Arab Muslims (*mawālī*) in the rise of this movement.

Madelung, Wilferd. "Review." *Journal of Near Eastern Studies* 33 (1974): 431–432.

Monroe, James. The *Shuʿūbiyya in al-Andalus: The "Risāla" of Ibn García and Five Refutations*. Berkeley, Calif.: University of California Press, 1970. Translation and study of the work of the Andalusian Ibn Garcia, who used the themes of the Shuʿūbīyah for the new cause of Berbers and Slavs. Monroe's work remains crucial in calling attention to the Shuʿūbīyah echoes in al-Andalus, but, as pointed out by Wilfred Madelung, the legitimacy of speaking of an Andalusian Shuʿūbīyah based on this single work is questionable.

Mottahedeh, Roy P. "The Shuʿûbîyah Controversy and the Social History of Early Islamic Iran." *International Journal of Middle Eastern Studies* 7 (1976): 161–182. This article is crucial in the way it looks at *tafsīr* (Qurʾānic exegesis) as a new source for the study of the Shuʿūbīyah movement, where locality, rather than lineage or language, emerges as a basic trait for the self-identification of the proponents of the Shuʿūbīyah. Furthermore, Mottahedeh dispels any lingering notion of the Shuʿūbīyah's historical connection to modern Iranian nationalism.

Norris, H. T. "Shuʿūbīyah in Arabic Literature." In *ʿAbbasid Belles-Lettres*, edited by Julia Ashtiany, pp. 32–47. Cambridge History of Arabic Literature 4. Cambridge, U.K.: Cambridge University Press, 1990. This article covers the various levels of the Shuʿūbīyah, ranging from literary themes to its cultural, ideological, and theological manifestations, and articulates the legacy of this movement on the formation of a distinctly ʿAbbāsid literary self-consciousness, namely *adab* (belles lettres).

RACHA EL OMARI

SIBĀʿĪ, MUṢṬAFĀ AL-. (1915–1964), Syrian intellectual, educator, activist, politician, and founder of the Syrian Muslim Brotherhood. Born in western Syria, in the city of Homs (also spelled Hims), al-Sibāʿī was born into a prominent family of religious scholars, or *ʿulamāʾ*, who instilled in him a strong sense of both religious devotion and public activism. Under the tutelage of his father, a *shaykh* in the local community, al-Sibāʿī was immersed in religious learning from a very young age, culminating in his eventual completion of a doctorate in Islamic Law at Cairo's prestigious al-Azhar University. While a student in Egypt in the 1930s, al-Sibāʿī quickly became involved in the political developments of the day, which were heavily preoccupied with gaining independence from European imperial control. Al-Sibāʿī joined the newly created Egyptian Muslim Brotherhood, where he became a close follower and acquaintance of the movement's founder and leader, Ḥasan al-Bannā. Al-Bannā, in particular, and the Egyptian intellectual environment, more generally, proved to have a profound impact on the development of al-Sibāʿī's own intellectual maturation and political thought. Al-Sibāʿī's political activism, however, resulted in various confrontations with Egyptian and British authorities, which eventually resulted in his forced departure from Egypt. Following his imprisonment for participating in anti-British protests in 1934, al-Sibāʿī was forced to leave the country in 1940, having been charged with subversion, and he was shipped off to a prison camp in Palestine.

By the age of twenty-five, al-Sibāʿī had served at least four prison terms, founded a secret society, been convicted of subversion, and acquired a reputation as a staunch opponent of colonial rule. In 1941 he returned to his hometown in Homs and established a group known as Shabāb Muḥammad ("Muḥammad's Youth"), an Islamic movement that later merged with Syria's Muslim Brotherhood. As in Cairo, al-Sibāʿī's political activism frequently led to confrontation with the local authorities. Shortly after his return to Syria, which was then under French control, he was detained by French authorities for two and a half years, during which time he was repeatedly tortured, resulting in serious damage to his health. Nevertheless, al-Sibāʿī emerged from prison in 1943 with renewed vigor, launching into a two-decade-long period of untiring political, educational, religious, and leadership activity. He became a high school teacher of Arabic and Islamic studies, an editor of three Islamic magazines (*The Civilization of Islam, The Muslims,* and *The Lighthouse*), a professor of Islamic law at the University of Damascus, a university dean, a drafter of the Syrian constitution, a parliamentarian, and a founder of the *Encyclopedia of Islamic Law.* Moreover, throughout his exceedingly active political and public life, al-Sibāʿī remained a prolific writer and political philosopher, shaping and transforming the political-religious ideologies of his day.

Of all his many contributions and accomplishments, al-Sibāʿī is best known for creating the Syrian Muslim Brotherhood (al-Ikhwān al-Muslimūn), which he accomplished by merging various existing Islamic movements and serving as its elected leader (*al-murāqib al-ʿAmm*) during its formative years. Under his successful leadership, the Brotherhood, which was known in Syria as the Islamic Socialist Front, grew in numbers, strength, and influence, including regional influence, particularly following Gamal Abdel Nasser's suppression of the Egyptian Muslim Brotherhood in the mid-1950s. Despite its comparatively small size and generally elitist membership, the Syrian Brotherhood under al-Sibāʿī's watch remained politically active and publicly influential until its dismantling by the Syrian authorities in 1952.

Despite such heavy political involvement, al-Sibāʿī conceived of the Brotherhood in a religiously oriented, philosophical way, viewing it not as a political party or even a political movement, but as a *ruh*, or a spirit, seeking to raise awareness of the need for comprehensive reform on the basis of Islamic ideals. Such philosophical-religious musings are contained in the many books written and published by al-Sibāʿī, the most influential among them being *Ishtirakīyat al-Islām* (The Socialism of Islam). Considered his masterpiece, *Ishtirakīyat al-Islām* represents al-Sibāʿī's defense of the compatibility between Islam and socialism. According to al-Sibāʿī, socialism, which aims to provide for the needs of every individual within society, perfectly complements Islam, which guarantees to all individuals five core rights: the right to life, freedom, knowledge, dignity, and ownership. To ensure that all of these rights are protected, al-Sibāʿī introduces the concept of *al-takāful al-ijtimāʿī* (mutual social responsibility), a concept that was fully realized during Islam's golden age and, according to al-Sibāʿī, needs to be reintroduced today. To do this, every Muslim society is responsible for following the *qawanin al-takāful al-ijtimāʿī* (the laws of mutual social responsibility), a set of twenty-nine enumerated laws backed by *muʿayyidāt* (sanctions) that describe the individual recipients of, as well as the funds necessary for financing, the extensive social responsibilities dictated by Islam.

Al-Sibāʿī's political thought clearly reveals a belief in the natural blending of Islam and politics. Throughout his writings, he characterizes the *ʿulamāʾ* as the best guardians over a nation's rights, deeming their participation in politics both critical and dictated by the Qurʾān. And God is considered the ultimate owner over all things, material and immaterial, with humans ideally acting as honest and careful vice-regents of God's possessions, which rightfully belong to society at large and thus should never be monopolized by any one individual or group. This blending of Islam and politics, according to al-Sibāʿī, must come about slowly, secretly, and pacifistically. Persuasion, not force, and secrecy, not public imposition, are the means of ensuring that society returns to the Islamic straight path.

Al-Sibāʿī's life of political activism, academic intellectualism, and religious devotion is an example of the ways in which Islam and politics merged seamlessly in the lives of many reformers of the colonial and postcolonial period. For al-Sibāʿī, the only way to reform society was through Islam; and Islam, alone, provided all the answers. Since his death in 1964, other Muslim ideologues and movements have embraced his vision of reform, on the basis of Islamic principles and the example of the Prophet, through clandestine persuasion, education, and pacifism.

BIBLIOGRAPHY

Abd-Allah, Umar F. *The Islamic Struggle in Syria*. Berkeley, Calif.: Mizan Press, 1983.

Dekmejian, R. Hrair. *Islam in Revolution*. Syracuse, N.Y.: Syracuse University Press, 1985.

Donohue, John J., and John L. Esposito, eds. *Islam in Transition*. 2d ed. New York: Oxford University Press, 2007.

Hanna, Sami. "Al-Takaful al-Ijtimai and Islamic Socialism," *The Muslim World* 59, no. 3–4 (1969): 275–286.

Hatina, Meir. "An Earlier Sunni Version of Khomeini's Rule of the Jurist: Mustafa l-Sibai on Ulama and Politics." *Arabica* 57, no. 4 (September 2000): 455–476.

Ruth, Roded. "Lessons by a Syrian Islamist from the Life of the Prophet Muhammad." *Middle Eastern Studies* 46, no. 6 (2006): 855–872.

Salt, J. "An Islamic Scholar-Activist: Mustafa al-Sibāʿī and the Islamic Movement in Syria 1945–1954." *Journal of Arabic, Islamic and Middle Eastern Studies* 3, no. 1 (1996): 103–115.

Teitelbaum, Joshua. "The Muslim Brotherhood and the 'Struggle for Syria,' 1947–1958 Between Accommodation and Ideology." *Middle Eastern Studies* 40, no. 3 (2004): 134–158.

CHRYSTIE SWINEY

SIRHINDĪ, AḤMAD. (1564–1624), Indian Ṣūfī *shaykh* and scholar, founder of the Mujaddidī branch of the Naqshbandīyah brotherhood in South Asia. Sirhindī was born into a scholarly family of the Punjab. After a thorough religious education he left at the age of twenty for the Mughal capital, Agra, and established contacts with leading scholars at the court. He then returned to follow the Ṣūfī path under the guidance of his father ʿAbd al-Aḥad. Passing through Delhi on the way to perform the pilgrimage in 1599, Sirhindī was introduced to the Afghan Naqshbandī *shaykh* Bāqī Billāh (d. 1604); after completing the Ṣūfī path with him, within a mere three months Sirhindī was nominated as his deputy. He authorized numerous disciples throughout India and kept in contact with them through letters, which were collected in his magnum opus *al-Maktūbāt*. Sirhindī regarded himself as the renovator of the second millennium of Islam (*mujaddid-i alf-i thānī*), hence the name of his branch in the Naqshbandī brotherhood, the Mujaddidīyah.

The Naqshbandīyah had emerged in central Asia in the fourteenth century. From the time of its eponymous founder Bahāʾ al-Dīn Naqshband

(d. 1389), the brotherhood rested on two pillars: strict adherence to the orthodox tenets of Islam and active involvement in worldly affairs. These were embodied in the life of ʿUbaydullāh Aḥrār (d. 1490), who exerted much influence on the Tīmūrid rulers of his day. Aḥrār was also responsible for the spread of the Naqshbandīyah beyond Transoxiana, to the Ottoman lands, the Indian subcontinent, and China. The major mystical principle that guided the Naqshbandī *shaykhs* in the political sphere was *khalwat dar anjuman*, or "seclusion within the crowd." It reflected the deep concentration that the followers of this path attained, while at the same time emphasizing their duty to associate with the people.

Sirhindī's work as a Naqshbandī *shaykh* coincided with the last years of the reign of Akbar (d. 1605), the founder of the Mughal Empire in India, and that of his son and heir Jahāngīr (d. 1627). Sirhindī was deeply averse to the syncretic religion that Akbar had instituted at his court, the *dīn-i ilāhī*, and tried to convince the Mughal nobles to prevail upon Jahāngīr to eschew the "heresies" of his father. It was in this context that he formulated another major political principle, according to which it is incumbent upon the Naqshbandī master to approach the ruler in order to guide him on the straight path.

Sirhindī stressed the Naqshbandī dictate to strictly follow the *sunnah* of the Prophet and to comply with the precepts of the *Sharīʿah*. In the realities of India, these were translated into an unabashed hostility toward the Hindu majority. He called upon the rulers to treat the Hindus like dogs, to levy from them the poll tax (*jizya*) in humiliating terms, and to slaughter cows. Sirhindī was likewise opposed to all manifestations of Shīʿī influence upon the Sunnī character of the Mughal state, though his attitude toward the Shīʿah was more conciliatory, and he generally avoided calling them infidels.

Sirhindī's call upon the Naqshbandī *shaykhs* to guide the rulers proved paradoxical. On the one hand, it necessitated their seeking contact with state dignitaries in order to gain influence at the court, while on the other hand, it demanded their rejecting any official position or support in order to avoid compromising their mission. Sirhindī himself remained ambivalent on this issue. Along with the letters he dispatched to top officials of the Mughal Empire in which he tried to impress upon them his strict orthodox views, there are letters in which he solicited help or made recommendations on behalf of his community. He also received material support for the running of his Ṣūfī hospice (*khānqāh*).

Contrary to the claims made by contemporary Indian historians that Aḥmad Sirhindī paved the way for the gradual shift of the Mughal dynasty from the heresy of Akbar to the strict orthodoxy of Awrangzīb (d. 1707), it seems that the impact he exercised over the evolution of Mughal religious policies was rather limited. Following a letter in which he deplored the slackening of the observance of *Sharīʿah* law in the state, Sirhindī was summoned to the presence of Jahāngīr in 1619. The emperor recorded in his memoirs that the *shaykh* behaved arrogantly and made presumptuous claims that necessitated his imprisonment. Released a year later, Sirhindī chose to remain in the emperor's camp "to bless the royal army." He returned to Sirhind shortly before his death in 1624.

The Naqshbandī-Mujaddidī brotherhood spread throughout India in the course of the seventeenth century under the direction of Sirhindī's heirs and descendants. Yet none of them had any pertinent impact upon the Mughal court. On the contrary, Sirhindī's extravagant statements about his lofty spiritual position embarrassed orthodox circles, and in 1679 these prevailed upon Awrangzīb to issue a decree banning the *Maktūbāt*.

It was mainly in the Sunnī Muslim-majority countries to which the Mujaddidī brotherhood subsequently spread that the orthodox and activist dimensions of Sirhindī's political teaching were put into practice. This was especially the case with the Kurdish *shaykh* Khālid al-Shahrazūrī (d. 1827), founder and head of the Khālidī offshoot, who disseminated the path in the Ottoman lands in the early part of the nineteenth century. The deputies whom Khālid sent to Istanbul joined the local Mujaddidīyah in backing Sultan Maḥmūd II's (d. 1839) efforts to consolidate and revitalize the Ottoman Empire in the face of the mounting Western threat. At the same time, other deputies instigated and led the resistance movement to the Russian occupation of the northern Caucasus.

Mujaddidī and Khālidī masters continued to play a conspicuous political role in the course of the twentieth century and beyond. In Turkey, the major uprising against the institution of the secular Kemalist regime was led by the Khālidī *shaykh* Saʿīd (d. 1925), while roots of the present Islamic government of Recep Tayyip Erdoğan (2003–) lie in the Naqshbandī-Khālidī tradition of western Anatolia. Other branches played a role in the resistance to the Soviet invasion of Afghanistan in 1979 and to Saddam Hussein's rule over Iraqi Kurdistan.

[*See also* Mughal Empire; *and* Sufism.]

BIBLIOGRAPHY

Friedmann, Yohanan. *Shaykh Aḥmad Sirhindī: An Outline of His Thought and a Study of His Image in the Eyes of Posterity.* Montreal: McGill Queen's University Press, 1971.

Haar, Johan G. J. ter. *Follower and Heir of the Prophet: Shaykh Aḥmad Sirhindī (1564–1624) as Mystic.* Leiden: Het Oosters Instituut, 1992.

Habib, Irfan M. "The Political Role of Shaikh Ahmad Sirhindi and Shah Waliullah." In *Proceedings of the Twenty-Third Session of the Indian History Congress, Aligarh 1960*, Pt. 1, pp. 209–223. Calcutta, 1961.

Rizvi, S. A. A. *Muslim Revivalist Movements in Northern India in the Sixteenth and Seventeenth Century.* New Delhi: Munshiram Manoharlal, 1965.

Weismann, Itzchak. *The Naqshbandiyya: Orthodoxy and Activism in a Worldwide Sufi Tradition.* London: Routledge, 2007.

ITZCHAK WEISMANN

SĪSTĀNĪ, ʿALĪ AL-. Born in Mashhad, Iran, on 4 August 1930, ʿAlī al-Sīstānī is a leading grand ayatollah, or *marjaʿ*, of the Shīʿah world who played an important role in democratic transition in Iraq after the U.S.-led invasion and subsequent toppling of the Baʿthist regime in 2003.

Al-Sīstānī was born into a clerical family and, at the age of five, began theological training under his father's supervision. In 1951 al-Sīstānī migrated to the shrine city of Najaf, Iraq, where he studied Shīʿah jurisprudence under Ayatollah Abol-Qāsem al-Khoʾi (1899–1992). Al-Sīstānī returned to Mashhad in 1960 with the title of *mujtahid.* At thirty, he was one of only three *mujtahids* granted permission to practice jurisprudence by a high-ranking cleric.

In 1961 al-Sīstānī returned to Najaf to pursue scholarship, teaching, and writing. During the 1960s he refused to become involved with politics, and maintained a cordial though distant relationship with Ayatollah Ruhollah Khomeini (1900–1989). After the 1979 Islamic Revolution in Iran and the Iran-Iraq war (1980–1988), al-Sīstānī kept a low profile, while the Baʿthist regime kept close watch over Najaf and his mentor Ayatollah Khoʾi until the early 1990s, especially after the failed 1991 Shīʿah uprising. Al-Sīstānī succeeded Ayatollah Khoʾi after the latter's death and was endowed with a vast income from religious taxes and other institutions, including the seminary school. Between 1992 and 2003 al-Sīstānī was under the surveillance of the Baʿthist regime and survived several assassination attempts by government security forces.

In the summer of 2003, just months after the U.S.-led invasion, al-Sīstānī advocated the institutionalization of elections and political parties, while attempting to distance himself from direct involvement in daily political affairs. The 15 November agreement between the Coalition Provisional Authority (CPA) and the Iraqi Governing Council (IGC), appointed by Paul Bremer, then the U.S. representative in Iraq, called for a speedy transfer of power in the form of council-based elections by 30 June 2004. The CPA's vision was to establish a seven-step process in which the Americans would maintain control over the transfer of power to the Iraqis. Elections were to take place after a succession of caucuses to elect an assembly and design a constitution that would be ratified by a national referendum. Al-Sīstānī opposed the caucus plan for two reasons: first and foremost, the caucus system would not immediately empower ordinary Iraqis to participate directly in the election of official representatives; second, the nonpopular electoral system, regulated and organized by a foreign occupying force, would make the transition process illegitimate in the eyes of both the religious establishment and ordinary Iraqis. For al-Sīstānī, direct popular elections were essential for the formation of a democratic Iraq, and a caucus system would only lead to the replacement of one illegitimate government by another.

Al-Sīstānī's most significant contribution to participatory politics in Iraq was his call for active citizenship. In 2004 he informally supported a Shīʿī-dominated political party, the United Iraqi Alliance (UIA), which in elections in January 2005 and December 2005 won a majority of the 275 available seats in parliament. He persisted in his call for electoral participation despite popular dissatisfaction with governance at the local level. During the drafting of the constitution in 2005, al-Sīstānī also advocated a system of governance based on accountability and the creation of legitimacy based on the ideals of popular sovereignty.

Al-Sīstānī's June 2003 and November 2004 *fatwas* on the doctrine of the guardianship of the jurist further highlighted his innovative conception of democratic governance, which differed fundamentally from Ayatollah Khomeini's conception of *vilāyat-i faqīh*, or "rule of the jurisconsult," which grants leading jurists considerable power over state affairs. In his *fatwas*, al-Sīstānī endorsed increased clerical involvement in political affairs, which included the explicit responsibility of the jurist to protect and guide the community, while it implicitly excluded absolutist rule of the supreme jurist at the state level. In other words, for al-Sīstānī the authority of the leading jurist ought to be limited to the defense of Islam and the community and not extended to state policies as in the case of Iran.

With the 2006 sectarian civil war in Iraq, al-Sīstānī's presence in politics decreased further, as the clergyman disapproved of the growing factionalism within and among Shīʿah parties. Al-Sīstānī has nevertheless left the Shīʿah world a legacy of engaged quietism, as the leading cleric who acted as both the promoter of civic participation in electoral politics as well as the model of religious emulation for everyday concerns.

[*See also* Khomeini, Ruhollah al-Musavi.]

BIBLIOGRAPHY

Al-Rahim, Ahmed H. "The Sistani Factor." *Journal of Democracy* 16, no. 3 (2005): 50–53.
Khalaji, Medhi. *The Last Marja: Sistani and the End of Traditional Religious Authority in Shiism*. Policy Focus 59. Washington, D.C.: Washington Institute for Near East Policy. 2006. See pp. 22–23.
Rahimi, Babak. *Ayatollah Sistani and the Democratization of Post-Baʿathist Iraq*. United States Institute of Peace Special Report 187. Washington, D.C.: United States Institute of Peace, 2007.
Rahimi, Babak. "Democratic Authority, Public Islam, and Shiʿi Jurisprudence in Iran and Iraq: Hussain Ali Montazeri and Ali Sistani." *International Political Science Review* 33 (2012): 193–208.

BABAK RAHIMI

SIYĀSAH SHAR'ĪYAH. *Siyāsah shar'īyah* means state policy (*siyāsah*) established in accordance with the religious law of Islam. The two terms, *siyāsah* and *shar'īyah*, are not always understood to belong together, but since early Islamic times it was accepted that the ruler had the prerogative to make policies deemed appropriate for stable government and social order that were not based on juristic (*fiqhī*) principles. To understand the concept of *siyāsah shar'īyah*, it is necessary to recall the historical development of *siyāsah* and its interaction with the religious law. The following remarks refer mainly to Sunnī political and legal thought.

The Historical Development of *Siyāsah* and Its Interaction with the *Sharī'ah*. The term *siyāsah* was used in Umayyad and early 'Abbāsid writings in the expression *ḥusn al-siyāsah*, denoting good government and good political administration. Under the influence of Sassanian conceptions of government, *siyāsah* acquired the meaning of discretionary power of the sovereign in matters of policy making, an authority distinct from that of religious leader (*imām*) of the community. Until the end of the ninth century, the caliph as head of the Islamic state represented the authority of the spheres of both religion (*dīn*) and politics (*siyāsah*). The two spheres were considered to be the provinces of different agents. *Dīn* was the subject matter of the religio-legal scholars ('*ulamā'*) and *siyāsah* that of the bureaucratic class of "men of the pen" (*kuttāb*, often translated as "secretaries"), though overlapping concerns always existed; a good civil official needed to be well acquainted with the religious sciences, and a judge had to keep political realities in mind when adjudicating. Although separate, religion and politics were seen to complement one another. The Sassanian adage that religion and state are twins with religion being the foundation and political authority the guardian, neither able to prosper without the other, became deeply absorbed into Islamic thought. However, even the '*ulamā'* recognized that the state can survive without "good religion" (Islam), whereas religion cannot survive without good *siyāsah*.

Throughout most of Islamic history, the '*ulamā'* considered *siyāsah* in the service of the religious law, tying the legitimacy of the political ruler to upholding the *Sharī'ah*. Nevertheless, many scholars, such as al-Māwardī (d. 1058) and al-Ghazālī (d. 1111), acknowledged that as part of *siyāsah* the ruler and his delegates held discretionary power, which allowed them, for instance, to mete out punishments that did not fully comply with *Sharī'ah*-determined limits (*ḥudūd*, sing. *ḥadd*), or to try enemies of the state and heretics without following the procedures of Islamic criminal law. These discretionary powers became associated with law enforcement to such an extent that the term *siyāsah* became applied to severe, especially capital, punishment. Such measures were often seen to belong to *maẓālim*, an extra-*Sharī'ah* jurisdiction directly under the authority of the ruler. Its procedures were not specified, and its decisions were often based on equity as well as political expedience. The conception of *siyāsah* as a distinct discipline that informed successful governance of the state, independent of *Sharī'ah* considerations, was continuously articulated in Islamic political thought, often espoused by those with close ties to the state apparatus.

The Rise of the Concept of *Siyāsah Shar'īyah*. With the declining power of the caliphate, particularly after the tenth century, and the rise of military dynasties as de facto rulers, the notion of separate spheres of religio-spiritual authority and politico-military power emerged. The new constellation encouraged Muslim thinkers to bring *siyāsah* more explicitly in line with the *Sharī'ah*.

Key in this development was the ascent of the '*ulamā'* as representatives of religious authority. They considered themselves the "heirs to the

Prophet," responsible for the perpetuation of the Islamic mission and as providers of social stability. This view is expressed, for example, by al-Juwaynī (d. 1085), who writes in *Ghiyāth al-umam* that in the absence of an *imām* capable of independent reasoning in religio-legal matters (*ijtihād*), affairs are entrusted to the interpreters of the law (*'ulamā'*) (al-Juwaynī, 1981, p. 392). The role of *'ulamā'* as leaders of society became especially apparent when political-military authority was weak or absent. Then it was not uncommon for a local judge or preacher to temporarily organize the political affairs of a locality.

The weakness of the caliphate also resulted in efforts on the part of the ruling military dynasties to assume religious influence and legitimacy, independent of the caliph's investiture. This was largely done by courting those who enjoyed religious authority (religious scholars and mystics). Starting with the Seljuks in the eleventh century, political patronage for the religious sciences expanded, with rulers giving generous endowments to law colleges (sing. *madrasah*) and to institutions teaching *ḥadīth* (sing. *dār al-ḥadīth*), employing religious personalities as emissaries in state affairs, and using Friday sermons to propagate state policies. During the Mamlūk period (1250–1517) in particular, religious knowledge could lead to a career as a teacher, preacher, or functionary in the state judiciary.

As a result of the changed status of religious scholars in society and of their increasingly influential role in shaping state policy, *siyāsah* was more explicitly imbued with *Sharī'ah* principles. The legitimacy of state policies was scrutinized against the demands of the religious law. While earlier scholars had already articulated that *siyāsah* is subject to the *Sharī'ah* (al-Ghazālī) and that *Sharī'ah* is *siyāsah* perfected (Sibṭ ibn al-Jawzī, d. 1256), the concept of *siyāsah shar'īyah* is associated in particular with the names of Ibn Taymīyah (d. 1328) and his disciple Ibn Qayyim al-Jawzīyah (d. 1351). The novelty in Ibn Taymīyah's thought was that he reinterpreted what constitutes *Sharī'ah* and turned back from the elaborate law-finding procedures that were in use by Muslim jurisprudents since at least the ninth century for the meaning of the sacred texts as interpreted by the first generations of Muslims. Grappling with the reality of a politically fractured Islamic community, Ibn Taymīyah sought to unify Muslim experience through the political implementation of the *Sharī'ah*. In his view, the revealed law did not prescribe a particular form of government but rather a particular way of life—God-fearing, pious, and guided by the principles of Islam. According to Ibn Taymīyah and Ibn Qayyim al-Jawzīyah, *Sharī'ah* was applied most correctly by the revered elders (*al-salaf al-ṣāliḥ*). Hence, they called for following the practice of the early Muslim community when interpreting the law as opposed to abiding by the formalistic procedures and abstract systematization developed by later generations of jurists. The formalized approach to legal reasoning, they believed, had distorted the meaning of the texts of the Qur'ān and *ḥadīth*, made permissible what is prohibited and vice versa, and was, like political decisions generally, driven primarily by utility.

In their approach to *siyāsah*, Ibn Taymīyah and Ibn Qayyim followed their fellow Ḥanbalī Ibn 'Aqīl (d. 1119), who saw the sole function of politics as bringing human beings closer to salvation. Contrary to earlier thinkers such as al-Māwardī, they did not authorize the ruler to deviate from the demands of the revealed law to achieve effective *siyāsah*. In their view, all public offices have a religious dimension and must serve a meaningful religious purpose, namely, to command good and forbid evil (*amr bi-l-ma'rūf wa-nahy 'an al-munkar*), and all state functionaries are obliged to apply and judge by the revealed law. However, as Baber Johansen (2002, p. 182) points out, when all public officials are subject to the *Sharī'ah* and working toward the same end, their precise area of competence is not necessarily fixed. If officials are to be judged only by whether they perform their job honestly and piously, not by how they practice their profession, the application of Islamic law is not restricted to those trained in *fiqh*. Thus, in the name of commanding good and forbidding evil (*ḥisbah*), military authorities, instead of the *qāḍī*, may adjudicate persons suspected of a crime. Similarly, the doctrine of *siyāsah sharʿīyah* propounded by Ibn Taymīyah calls for the active participation of religious scholars, or more generally of religious-minded persons, in public affairs. Hence, Ibn Taymīyah felt entitled to tell the Mamlūk ruler al-Malik al-Nāṣir (r. 1293–1341) to wage *jihād* against the Mongols, arguing that the *Sharīʿah* forbids infidels to set foot on Muslim soil.

Subjecting political decisions to the demands of the *Sharīʿah* gave Islamic law and its practitioners more influence in guiding state policies, expanded their area of jurisdiction, and frequently served as a restraining force against state abuses. Yet, when combined with rejecting the formal procedures of law established by classical Islamic jurisprudence and the lack of a clear definition of judicial competence, the close association of *siyāsah* and *Sharīʿah* could also lead religious scholars to legitimize practices previously deemed illegitimate by most *ʿulamāʾ*. For example, Ibn Taymīyah and Ibn Qayyim held that a *qāḍī*'s decision could be based on circumstantial evidence, without supportive oral testimony of witnesses—usually the primary source of evidence. They thereby endorsed beating, imprisoning, and torturing persons suspected of a crime in order to extract confessions, a practice al-Ghazāli had vehemently rejected (1995, vol. 1, p. 260). The well-established legal principle that a coerced confession is inadmissible in court was thereby reversed. Ibn Taymīyah's interpretation of *siyāsah sharʿīyah* meant that legal procedures accepted by the majority of Muslim jurists could be set aside as long as the outcome commanded good, forbade evil, and served the public interest.

This articulation of *siyāsah sharʿīyah* was aided by the rise of the concept of *maṣlaḥah* in Islamic legal thought. *Maṣlaḥah*, loosely translated as well-being or public interest, had become widely acknowledged as a valid procedure of law finding ever since al-Ghazālī defined it as that which preserves humankind's religion, life, intellect, offspring, and property. Whatever promotes and benefits these necessary values of human existence was considered commensurate with the divine law. *Maṣlaḥah* came to represent the primary purpose of the *Sharīʿah*: to ensure humanity's well-being and protect it from harm. Depending on a jurist's interpretation, considerations of *maṣlaḥah* could serve even without concrete textual evidence (*maṣlaḥah murasalah*) to find rulings for legal cases on which the Qurʾān and *sunnah* were silent. Although Ibn Taymīyah adamantly denied the legal validity of such textually unattested *maṣlaḥah*, his rejection of formal criteria to identify what constitutes *maṣlaḥah* allows for pronouncing a wide range of policy-driven rulings in the name of public interest and the *Sharīʿah*'s higher objective.

The Development of *Siyāsah Sharʿīyah* after Ibn Taymīyah. After Ibn Taymīyah, the concept of *siyāsah sharʿīyah* continued to flourish in two broad interpretations. Jurists who followed Ibn Taymīyah's and Ibn Qayyim's understanding of the concept focused on the spirit of the law and the practice of the early Muslim community, subjecting political and military decisions to scrutiny by the interpreters of the *Sharīʿah*. One finds jurists as diverse as Ibn Farḥūn (d. 1397) and al-Ṭarābulusī (d. 1440) espousing ideas in the same vein as Ibn Taymīyah. The spread of Wahhabism in the eighteenth and nineteenth centuries, which consciously drew upon Ibn Taymīyah's work, gave his political thought renewed impact, and today Saudi Arabia upholds the notion that its policies are in accordance with the demands of the *Sharīʿah*. A second line of interpretation of *siyāsah sharʿīyah* follows the ideas articulated by al-Ghazālī and others that allow the ruler to issue ordinances and laws but closely subject them to the principles, methods, and procedures established in Islamic jurisprudence, trying to ensure that these policies are not contrary to people's *maṣlaḥah*, or well-being.

The concept of *siyāsah sharʿīyah* also influenced the constitutionalist movements of the nineteenth and twentieth centuries, which insisted that the state receives its power for all-inclusive authority only by wielding it in the public interest (*maṣlaḥah*) within the limits and the prescriptions of the *Sharīʿah*. It may only deviate from established practices of *fiqh* when serving a beneficial purpose. For instance, the Egyptian jurist ʿAbd al-Wahhāb Khallāf (d. 1956) approved the state legislature imposing a minimum marriage age (as opposed to the onset of puberty) because it protects the individual.

The regime of *siyāsah sharʿīyah*, in association with *maṣlaḥah*, can be seen as one that allows for a flexible and adaptive interpretation of Islamic law, which gives religious scholars a voice in political affairs and the ability to restrain state authorities from violating the rights of their citizens. However, the close cooperation between political and religious authorities also implicates the latter in vesting policies driven by political expedience with the mantle of religious legitimacy. One example of such rubber stamping is the Syrian jurist al-Būṭī's justification for the state's right to restrict freedom of speech, stating that people's intellect is thereby preserved from deviation and error.

[*See also* Commanding Right and Forbidding Wrong; Ḥisbah; *and* Māwardī, Abū al-Ḥasan al-.]

BIBLIOGRAPHY

Primary Sources

Ghazālī, Abū Ḥāmid Muḥammad al-. *Al-Mustaṣfā min ʿilm al-uṣūl*. 2 vols. Beirut: Dār al-Ṣādir, 1995.

Ghazālī, Abū Ḥāmid Muḥammad al-. *Book of Counsel for Kings (Naṣīḥat al-Mulūk)*. Translated by F. R. C. Bagley. London: Oxford University Press, 1964. Expresses many of al-Ghazālī's ideas in the literary genre of "mirror for princes," although it is doubtful that al-Ghazālī authored the second part of this book.

Ibn Qayyim al-Jawzīyah, Muḥammad ibn Abī Bakr. *Al-Ṭuruq al-ḥukmīyah fī al-siyāsah al-sharʿīyah*. Edited by Muḥammad Jamīl Aḥmad Ghāzī. Cairo: Maṭbaʿat al-Madanī, 1978. English translation: *The Legal Methods in Islamic Administration*. Translated by Alaeddin Kharofa. Kuala Lumpur: International Law Book Services, 2000.

Ibn Taymīyah, Aḥmad ibn ʿAbd al-Ḥalīm. *Kitāb al-siyāsah al-sharʿīyah fī iṣlāḥ al-rāʿī wa-l-raʿīyah*. Beirut: Dār al-Afāq al-Jadīda, 1993. English translation: *Ibn Taimiyya on Public and Private Law in Islam: Or, Public Policy in Islamic Jurisprudence*. Translated by Omar A. Farrukh. Beirut: Khayats, 1966.

Juwaynī, ʿAbd al-Malik ibn ʿAbdallāh Imām al-Ḥaramayn al-. *Ghiyāth al-umam fī iltiyāth al-ẓulam*. Edited by ʿAbd al-ʿAzīz al-Dīb. Cairo: Maṭbaʿat Nahḍa, 1981.

Māwardī, Abū l-Ḥasan ʿAlī ibn Muḥammad al-. *Al-Aḥkām al-sulṭānīyah wa-l-wilāyāt al-dīnīyah*. Cairo: Maktaba wa-Maṭbaʿa Muṣṭafá al-Bābī al-Ḥalabī, 1966. English translation: *The Ordinances of Government*. Translated by Wafaa H. Wahba. Reading, UK: Garnet, 1996.

Secondary Sources

Bosworth, C. E., I. R. Netton, and F. E. Vogel. "Siyāsa." In *Encyclopaedia of Islam*, edited by H. A. R. Gibb, 693–696. 2d ed. Vol. 9. Leiden, Netherlands: E. J. Brill, 1960–2004.

Johansen, Baber. "Signs as Evidence: The Doctrine of Ibn Taymiyya (1263–1328) and Ibn Qayyim al-Jawziyya (d. 1351) on Proof." *Islamic Law and Society* 9 (2002): 168–193. A critical evaluation of Ibn Taymīyah's legal thought, pointing to its implications institutionally and for the rights of the individual in criminal law.

Khalidi, Tarif. *Arabic Historical Thought in the Classical Period*. Cambridge, U.K.: Cambridge University Press, 1994. Chapter 5, "History and *Siyasa*" (pp. 182–231), addresses specifically the development of *siyāsah* between the eleventh and fifteenth centuries.

Lewis, Bernard. "Siyasa." In *In Quest of an Islamic Humanism: Arabic and Islamic Studies in Memory of Mohamed al-Nowaihi*, edited by A. H. Green, pp. 3–14. Cairo: American University of Cairo Press, 1984. An account of the historical development of the term *siyāsah* and its usage in various types of literature.

Najjar, Fauzi M. "*Siyasa* in Islamic Political Philosophy." In *Islamic Theology and Philosophy: Studies in Honor of George F. Hourani*, edited by Michael E. Marmura, pp. 92–110. Albany: State University of New York Press, 1984. A comparison of the constitutional theories of Muslim religious scholars and philosophers.

Opwis, Felicitas. "*Maṣlaḥa* in Contemporary Islamic Legal Theory." *Islamic Law and Society* 12 (2005): 182–223. An overview of various interpretations of the concept of *maṣlaḥa* and their premodern precursors.

FELICITAS OPWIS

SLAVERY. Slaves played formative roles in the evolution of Islamic politics. From the mid-seventh through the nineteenth century, from the geographical center of the Middle East to far-flung African and Asian countries, similar administrative, military, and social institutions developed within the ruling dynasties. All had origins in pre-Islamic Byzantine and Persian societies.

Islam was to bring about social reform, not revolution in the Arabian Peninsula: slaves were society's most vulnerable, exploited persons in need of protection; they were also property in need of management. The rapid expansion of Islam into new cultures challenged Muslim jurists, even as they attempted to codify the law; in addition to questions of appropriate treatment of slaves and legal rights and responsibilities of masters, the issue of what constituted "legitimate enslavement" repeatedly posed itself.

The Qurʾān reminded masters that, in the eyes of God, slaves were their equals: they had a duty to feed, clothe, and educate slaves in the ways of Islam. The treatment of slaves was a measure of a master's personal piety. Several reasons (including a slave's honorable or brave behavior) urged masters to emancipate slaves; specific contraventions of Islamic law required freeing of a stipulated number of slaves as penance. A master's duty extended to assisting slaves in their post-emancipation lives.

Although as "property," slaves could be bought, sold, and inherited and did not exist legally—could not by law bring cases, give evidence, or inherit—they had rights, including the right to complain of abuse and demand new masters. They could marry (with approval), have children, and request purchase of their own freedom (acceptance of which was a pious action for masters). Female slaves frequently became concubines; Islam limited the number of legal wives to four but placed no limitation on a master's concubines. These understandings on the part of masters and slaves were integral to the functioning of "Islamic slavery" for many centuries across the multicultural Muslim world. They were also the framework for the development of "royal slavery" across this same time and space.

Royal Slavery: Slave Soldiers. The central pillar of this institution was the slave soldier. In the 660s, the Umayyad dynasty adopted the Byzantine and Persian practice of buying young Turkish slaves and incorporating them into the army alongside prisoners captured in battle. By the late ninth century, the Umayyads' successors (the ʿAbbāsids) formalized the use of these *ghilman* (sing., *ghulman*), later known as *mamlūk*; they moved from a system in which individual masters trained slaves and sometimes freed them in return for military service, to one in which 60,000 such "slaves of the caliph" were trained and educated in the capital, subsequently converted, and were freed.

Following the ʿAbbāsids, subsequent dynasties (e.g., the Fāṭimids, Seljuks, Ayyūbids, Būyids, and ʿAbbāsids in Iraq) developed their dependence on slavery, increasingly turning to the market for supplies; *mamlūks* (unlike *ghilman*) were exclusively "purchased." This posed a problem for their Islamic masters: enslaving non-Muslim prisoners was legitimate—non-Muslims and "people of the book" (Jews and Christians) who refused to convert or submit could be enslaved. Purchasing slaves whose origins could not be proven challenged legitimacy. Centralizing the process such that Islamic education, conversion, and freeing were assured, as it was with the *mamlūk*, satisfied the *ʿulamāʾ*.

The *mamlūks* became the best-known of the slave soldiers, because they exploited their Muslim slave-soldier identity even when freed; rather than assimilate with local populations, they reproduced with purchased slaves (soldiers and wives). They succeeded in establishing their own sultanates in thirteenth-century India, Egypt, and Syria that replicated those of their former masters; they enjoyed de facto autonomy under the Ottomans in eighteenth- and nineteenth-century Iraq and Egypt.

The Ottomans developed a variation on slavery in the fourteenth century, responding to the needs of a rapidly expanding state. Janissaries (*yeniciri,* "new troops"), Christian prisoners who later converted to Islam, served the traditional "slave-soldier" role of providing unchallenged loyalty to Sultan Murād I. Like *mamlūks*, they were trained to be professional soldiers, initially kept celibate and confined to army barracks. By the late fourteenth century, their importance to Ottoman military strength demanded more regular recruitment; the *devşirme* ("gathering") was implemented. This state-directed exaction (of "one in forty") every three to seven years sent Christian boys (initially from Balkan villages) between eight and twenty years old for military and administrative training and Islamic education in Istanbul. Recruits performed as ordinary slaves during early years; later, they took on senior administrative positions (including that of *vezir-i âzam,* or grand vizier) and joined the janissaries—for which they became the only source.

In the new North African ʿAlawid dynasty, Sultan Mawlāy Ismāʿīl's seventeenth-century attempt to emulate the "slave-soldier" institution likewise stirred controversy among local *ʿulamāʾ*. In the African context, the issue took on the added nuance of race. Black slaves from sub-Saharan Africa came from *dār al-kāfir* ("land of the unbeliever") or *dār al-ḥarb* ("land of war"); blacks, therefore, were liable to enslavement. But by the sixteenth century, most of these lands had become *dār al-Islām,* and this assumption disintegrated.

Royal Slavery: The *Ḥarīm* and Eunuchs. Islam's blessing of concubines in the household and the "free" status that Islam conferred on concubines' children, combined with the special treatment and ultimate freedom that the *umm al-walid* received, meant that the *ḥarīm's* social significance grew rapidly. In the royal context, it rapidly acquired a political role famously perfected under the Ottomans. By the late sixteenth century, royal concubines had replaced free women in political marriages, the most important of which was with the sultan himself—following Süleyman the Magnificent, heirs to the throne were produced in the *ḥarīm.* Concubines were converted to Islam and groomed as (manumitted) wives for court and provincial administrators. The sultan's mother (*valide sultan*), herself a freed slave, controlled the *ḥarīm* and, increasingly, palace politics; she also became a public voice and supporter of royal charities. The position of *ḥarīm* women mirrored the special status of household concubines but translated it into enormous political influence; in the seventeenth century, *ʿulamāʾ* spoke critically of the "sultanate of women," a reference to the *ḥarīm* having usurped the power of the sultan.

The eunuch, also a fixture of pre-Islamic courts, rapidly entrenched himself in Islamic politics. A castrated slave who had no family and could not physically produce one, the eunuch was uniquely valuable to perenially suspicious sultans. Moreover, a fully castrated eunuch could be trusted in the *ḥarīm*, where adult male slaves were not permitted. The Ottomans developed parallel hierarchies under "white" and "black" chieftainship: the former managed *devşirme* and administrative affairs, the latter, the *ḥarīm*. The chief black eunuch's power grew in tandem with the women he guarded; in the seventeenth century he was the center of palace espionage and managed valuable religious endowments. However, the eunuch was problematic for a religion that rejected physical alteration of "natural" (God-given) gender: ownership of such a slave was permissible, but "producing" him was not. In the early days, surgery was carried out by non-Muslims in Saharan oases considered to be just "outside" *dār al-Islām*; under the Ottomans, a Coptic monastery specialized in the procedure.

Variations on these institutions spread from the early Arab caliphates across North Africa and into India; the Ottomans' five-century dominance of the Muslim world encompassing (parts of) Europe, Asia, and Africa furthered their proliferation. The Omani move to Zanzibar (East Africa) in the mid-nineteenth century replicated the politics of the *ḥarīm* (including eunuchs) on the island and slave soldiers in the spread of empire that took Islam to Central Africa. In West Africa, nineteenth-century *jihāds* followed in the wake of eighteenth-century reformism: echoing earlier controversies, scholars debated whether those deemed to practice "corrupt" Islam and refusing reform were liable to enslavement. Variations on this structure were mirrored in each of the emirates that comprised the state.

Contemporary Legacies. Islam has been important in shaping former slave-holding Muslim societies that are now becoming democracies. Whereas the abolitionist policies of colonial rule everywhere transformed slavery, in Muslim societies this transformation was often mitigated by the fact that secular emancipation was not accepted by masters or slaves. Many slaves remained with masters until they could secure "legal" Islamic freedom. And they remained in post-emancipation relations of interdependency in which masters' obligations provided security that often translated into financial and material assistance.

This has changed in most of the Muslim world, but its political meaning is not yet clear. In Mauritania (West Africa), for example, in April 2012 a freed slave, leader of an abolitionist party, publicly burned the writings of Muslim jurists who had initially articulated Islam's position vis-à-vis slavery. He argued that while the Islamic Republic of Mauritania abolished slavery, the "Islam" of the state is rooted in medieval Sharīʿah. This contradiction poses an overt political challenge for Mauritania but also represents an implicit threat to social stability in other Muslim societies where the legacies of slavery—elite or otherwise—pertain.

BIBLIOGRAPHY

Hunwick, John O., and Fatma Harrak. *Mirʿaj al Suʿud: Ahmed Baba's Replies on Slavery*. Rabat: Institute of African Studies, 2000. Translated and annotated edition.

McDougall, E. Ann. "Islam: An Overview." In *Macmillan Encyclopedia of World Slavery*, edited by Paul Finkleman and Joseph C. Miller, vol. 1, pp. 434–439. New York: Macmillan Reference, 1998.

McDougall, E. Ann. "North Africa: Morocco." In *Macmillan Encyclopedia of World Slavery*, edited by Paul Finkleman and Joseph C. Miller, vol. 2, pp. 643–646. New York: Macmillan Reference, 1998.

McDougall, E. Ann. "The Politics of Slavery in Mauritania: Rhetoric, Reality and Democratic Discourse." Special Issue; Mauritania (1–2). Edited by Pierre

Bonte and Sébastien Boulay. *Maghreb Review* 35, nos. 1–2, 3 (2010): 259–286.
McDougall, E. Ann. "The Sahara." In *Macmillan Encyclopedia of World Slavery*, edited by Paul Finkleman and Joseph C. Miller, vol. 2, pp. 646–649. New York: Macmillan Reference, 1998.
Toledano, Ehud. *As If Silent and Absent: Bonds of Enslavement in the Islamic Middle East.* New Haven, Conn.: Yale University Press, 2007.
Toru, Miura, and John Edward Philips, eds. *Slave Elites in the Middle East and Africa: A Comparative Study.* London and New York: Kegan Paul International, 2000.

ANN MCDOUGALL

SOCIAL JUSTICE.

See Justice.

SOCIAL MOVEMENTS.

The term "social movement" broadly describes collective action by individuals who organize themselves into a group to attain social, economic, or political gains. The history of social movements in Islam is a long one, arguably Islam itself started as a social movement that attempted to induce wide-ranging changes in the Arabian Peninsula. Since then, there have been a wide variety of social movements that are grounded in Islam. These include but are not limited to the Muslim Brotherhood, Ḥamās, Ḥizbullāh, Hizb ut-Tahrir, the Iranian Green Movement, and Tablīghī Jamāʿat.

Social Movement Analysis. Contemporary analysis of social movements can be generally divided into three broad approaches: structural theories, social movement theory (SMT), and rational choice theory, each differing in the unit of analysis. To analyze social movements, structural theories tend to focus on the larger "structure," where the unit of analysis is the state and the international system, granting less agency to individual actors. At the other end of the spectrum, rational choice theory uses the individual as a unit of analysis and gives much credit to individual actors, their thought processes, and their individualistic choices with minimal agency afforded to the structure of the system. SMT lies in the middle between these two approaches, as it uses the group as a unit of analysis while acknowledging the agency of both the structure and the individual.

SMT is the dominant social movement paradigm, currently widely used to investigate social movements, and has three main tenets: resource mobilization theory, political opportunity structure, and cultural framing. Resource mobilization theory (RMT) focuses on the ability of groups to mobilize the resources necessary to be able to take collective action. In this view, actors are seen as rational individuals who organize and mobilize accordingly to air their grievances. In RMT, group action is not haphazard but is calculated in its organization and manifestation (Tilly, 1978; Jenkins, 1983; Zald and McCarthy, 1987).

Political opportunity structure attempts to encapsulate the different conditions that precipitate social mobilization such as access to legitimate political participation, state repression, availability of allies, instability of elite alignments, and the strength of the state. Social movement theorists working within this framework investigate the opportunities and constraints that actors face in the political system. To work effectively, movements require organization and resources, though organizations can acquire and then deploy resources to achieve their well-defined goals. Some versions of the resource mobilization theory hold that movements operate similarly to capitalist enterprises, which make efficient use of available resources. Scholars have suggested a typology of five types of resources: material (money and physical capital); moral (solidarity, support for the movement's goals); social-organizational (organizational strategies, social networks); human (volunteers, staff, leaders); and cultural (prior activist experience, understanding of the issues, collective action know-how) (Edwards and McCarthy, 2004).

Relative deprivation theory argues that social movements have their foundations among people who feel deprived of some good(s) or resource(s). According to this approach, individuals who are lacking some good, service, or comfort are more likely to organize a social movement to improve (or defend) their conditions. Adding to this theory, social strain theory, also known as value-added theory, proposes factors that encourage social movement development: First, structural conduciveness—people come to believe their society has problems. Second, structural strain—people experience deprivation. Third, growth and spread of a solution. Discontent usually requires a catalyst (often a specific event) to turn it into a social movement. Fourth, a lack of social control—the entity that is to be changed must at least be somewhat open to the change; if the social movement is quickly and powerfully repressed, it may never materialize. Lastly, mobilization—this is the actual organizing and active component of the movement; people do what needs to be done. This theory is also subject to circular reasoning, as it incorporates, at least in part, deprivation theory and relies upon it, along with social/structural strain for the underlying motivation of social movement activism. However, social movement activism is, as in the case of deprivation theory, often the only indication that there was strain or deprivation (Smelser, 1962).

Increasing Use of Social Movement Analysis in Understanding Contemporary Islamic Movements. Islamism, or political Islam, is a contemporary form of Islamic social movements. The term Islamists (*al-Islāmīyūn*) is used by Muslim activists to refer to the adherents of the "Islamic Movement," and the term Islamism is used in the English language to denote political Islam in contemporary discourse. Some scholars have described collective action by social forces in Muslim states as "Islamic activism" (Wiktorowicz, 2004). Earlier scholarship on social movements in the Middle East and Muslim world focused on socioeconomic transformations and the psychological stress they cause as the root cause of collective action by the people through stressing the common socioeconomic background of Islamist. Scholars in the 1990s began to view Islamic activism as a response to cultural imperialism. Many earlier narratives viewed Islamism within a narrow religious lens, not as a set of dynamic social movements. Since then, a variety of scholars have adopted SMT in their research of contemporary Islamic movements.

How Certain Islamic Movements Exhibit the Dynamics of Social Movements. A key phenomenon in the contemporary Muslim world is the rise of Islamist groups and organizations. Some Islamists have utilized peaceful means to reach their goals, while others have utilized violent means. Among the Islamic movements that have chosen to follow legitimate paths of political participation is the Egyptian Muslim Brotherhood (MB), which despite its past association with militancy has accepted working within the existing political framework and has fielded candidates for parliamentary elections for decades. The MB has utilized "political opportunities" and sought to reemphasize its role in civil society by seeking election in trade unions and student unions on various university campuses, utilizing narrow but legitimate avenues of participation. On the extremist front, some Islamic groups have appeared to adopt the ideology of *takfīr* (accusing others of apostasy) and expressed their ideology through violence, most notably, the Islamic Jihād (Jamāʿat al-Jihād) organization, which assassinated the Egyptian president Sadat, and the Jamāʿat al-Islāmīyah, which was the driving force behind some of the most violent terrorist attacks against the state and society in Egypt throughout the

1990s. There are other Islamic movements like the Tablīghī Jamāʿat that are transnational and apolitical, focusing on incremental changes in society through creating more observant Muslims. Many of these groups exhibit the main features and dynamics of social movements. Many of these movements have become prominent in contemporary debates in the Muslim world, and SMT has been increasingly applied by scholars to analyze Islamic social movements.

Contemporary Islamic Social Movements. The Ḥarakat al-Muqāwamah al-Islāmīyah (Islamic Resistance Movement), better known as Ḥamās, was founded in 1987 (during the First Intifada) as an offshoot of the Egyptian Muslim Brotherhood. Cofounder Shaykh Aḥmad Yāsīn stated in 1987, and the Ḥamās Charter affirmed in 1988, that Ḥamās was founded to liberate Palestine from Israeli occupation and to establish an Islamic state in the area that is now Israel, the West Bank, and the Gaza Strip. Ḥamās has elicited distinct reactions from American policymakers and academics. Books by Khaled Hroub (2006), Ziad Abu-Amr (1994), and Shaul Mishal and Avraham Sela (2000) have presented a comprehensive picture of Ḥamās to the English-speaking world. Ḥamās is particularly popular among Palestinians in the Gaza Strip, though it also has a following in the West Bank, and to a lesser extent in other Middle Eastern countries. Its popularity stems in part from its welfare wing, which provides social services to Palestinians in the Occupied Territories where these services are not generally provided by the Palestinian Authority. It is estimated that most of Ḥamās' activities revolve around social welfare, cultural, and educational activities. Social services provided include schools, orphanages, mosques, health clinics, soup kitchens, and sports leagues.

Another noteworthy example is the Iranian Green Movement, which was founded after a series of uprisings following the 2009 Iranian presidential election, when protesters demanded the removal of President Mahmoud Ahmadinejad from office. The Iranian government claimed a two-thirds majority for Ahmadinejad, before the vote count was finalized. Supporters of his main challengers, Mīr Ḥusayn Mūsavī and Mehdi Karroubi, accused the government of tampering with the votes. "Where is my vote?" was a widely used motto during the 2009 protests. Mūsavī and Karroubi are recognized as political leaders of the Green Movement, while Grand Ayatollah Hossein-Ali Montazeri was named as the spiritual leader of the movement. Witnesses to Green Movement protests often claim that protests of this size had not been seen in Iran since the 1979 revolution.

An equally interesting organization is the Hizb ut-Tahrir (Party of Liberation), an international Sunnī-based Pan-Islamic group that was founded in 1953 in Jerusalem by Taqī al-Dīn al-Nabhānī, an Islamic scholar and appeals court judge (*qāḍī*) from Palestine. Hizb ut-Tahrir has now spread to more than forty countries. The group is commonly associated with the goal of unifying Muslim countries as an Islamic state or caliphate ruled by Islamic law and with a caliph as head of state elected by Muslims. Hizb ut-Tahrir is also strongly anti-Zionist and calls for Israel to be dismantled. Accused by some of the use of violence, Hizb ut-Tahrir states on its U.K. Web site that it has adopted the methods employed by the Prophet Muḥammad, who limited his struggle for the establishment of the Islamic state to intellectual and political work. Observers believe Hizb ut-Tahrir is the victim of false allegations of connections to terrorism, pointing out that the organization explicitly commits itself to nonviolence. Bangladesh banned Hizb ut-Tahrir on 22 October 2009 for "destabilizing" the country. The organization is also banned in Russia and Germany. Hizb ut-Tahrir is outlawed in Turkey but is still in operation. Hizb ut-Tahrir also works openly in

Malaysia, Indonesia, the United Arab Emirates, Lebanon, and Yemen.

Perhaps the best-known organization in the contemporary Middle East is Ḥizbullāh, which first emerged in response to the 1982 Israeli invasion of Lebanon at the height of the 1975–1990 Lebanese civil war. Ḥizbullāh's 1985 manifesto listed its four main goals as Israel's final departure from Lebanon, ending any imperialist power in the country, submission of the Phalangists to just rule and bringing them to trial for their crimes, and giving the people the chance to choose their government without hiding its commitment to the rule of Islam. Ḥizbullāh leaders have also made numerous statements calling for the destruction of the state of Israel, which they refer to as the "Zionist entity" (Rabinovich and Reinharz, 2008). Ḥizbullāh was largely formed with the aid of the Ayatollah Khomeini's followers in the early 1980s in order to spread Islamic revolution and follows a distinct version of Islamic Shīʿī ideology (*wilāyat al-faqīh*, or guardianship of the Islamic jurists) developed by Ayatollah Ruhollah Khomeini. Although Ḥizbullāh originally aimed to transform Lebanon into a formal *faqīhī* Islamic republic, this goal has been abandoned in favor of a more inclusive approach (Saad-Ghorayeb, 2002). Since the 1990s, with Ḥizbullāh's entry into parliament, the party is thought to have conveyed a more lenient stance toward the Lebanese state and began to engage in dialogue with Lebanese Christians. However, there is still much conjecture regarding the true aspirations of the group.

The Muslim Brotherhood (al-Ikhwān al-Muslimūn), one of the largest Islamic movements, gained significant attention in the aftermath of the Egyptian revolution of 25 January 2011. It was founded in Egypt in 1928 as a pan-Islamic, religious, political, and social movement by Ḥasan al-Bannā and by the end of World War II boasted an estimated two million members (Hallet, 1974). The Muslim Brotherhood began as a religious social organization, preaching Islam, teaching the illiterate, founding hospitals, and even launching commercial ventures. Its stated goal is to instill the Qurʾān and *sunnah* as the "sole reference point for . . . ordering the life of the Muslim family, individual, community . . . and state" (Lia, 1998, p. 53), and its most famous slogan, used worldwide, is "Islam is the solution." The MB officially opposes violent means to achieve its goals, although it included a paramilitary wing under the Nasser government (1952–1970). The MB is financed by contributions from its members, who are required to allocate a portion of their income to the movement. On 29 June 2011 the Brotherhood's political power became more apparent and solidified its presence, while the United States announced that it would reopen formal diplomatic channels with the group, with whom it had suspended communication as a result of suspected terrorist activity. The MB's leadership welcomed this move. On 24 June 2012 the MB candidate for the office of president of the republic, Mohamed Morsi, won with 51.73 percent of the vote.

BIBLIOGRAPHY

Abu-Amr, Ziad. *Islamic Fundamentalism in the West Bank and Gaza: Muslim Brotherhood and Islamic Jihad*. Bloomington: Indiana University Press, 1994.

Al Jazeera English. "Poll Results Prompt Iran Protests." 14 June 2009. http://www.aljazeera.com/news/middleeast/2009/06/2009613172130303995.html.

Bayat, Asef. "Islamism and Social Movement Theory." *Third World Quarterly* 26, no. 6 (2005): 891–908.

Commins, David. "Taqī al-Dīn al-Nabhānī and the Islamic Liberation Party." *Muslim World* 81, nos. 3–4 (1991): 194–211.

Edwards, Bob, and John D. McCarthy. "Resources and Social Movement Mobilization." In *The Blackwell Companion to Social Movements*, edited by David A. Snow, Sarah A. Soule, and Hanspeter Kriesi, pp. 116–152. Malden, Mass.: Blackwell, 2004.

Eyerman, Ron. "Social Movements and Social Theory." *Sociology* 18, no. 1 (1984): 71–82.

Gurney, Joan Neff, and Kathleen J. Tierney. "Relative Deprivation and Social Movements: A Critical Look at Twenty Years of Theory and Research." *Sociological Quarterly* 23 (1983): 33–47.

Hallett, Robin. *Africa since 1875: A Modern History*. Ann Arbor: University of Michigan Press, 1974.

Hizb ut-Tahrir Britain. "What Is Khilafah?" http://www.hizb.org.uk/category/what-is-khilafah.

Hroub, Khaled. *Hamas: A Beginner's Guide*. London: Pluto, 2006.

Ibrahim, Saad Eddin. "Anatomy of Egypt's Militant Islamic Groups: Methodological Note and Preliminary Findings." *International Journal of Middle East Studies* 12, no. 4 (December 1980): 423–453.

Jenkins, J. Craig. "Resource Mobilization Theory and the Study of Social Movements." *Annual Review of Sociology* 9 (1983): 527–553.

Karagiannis, Emmanuel, and Clark McCauley. "Hizb ut-Tahrir al-Islami: Evaluating the Threat Posed by a Radical Islamic Group That Remains Nonviolent." *Terrorism and Political Violence* 18, no. 2 (2006): 315–334.

Lia, Brynjar. *The Society of the Muslim Brothers in Egypt: The Rise of an Islamic Mass Movement, 1928–1942*. Reading, U.K.: Ithaca, 1998.

Mishal, Shaul, and Avraham Sela. *The Palestinian Hamas: Vision, Violence, and Coexistence*. New York: Columbia University Press, 2000.

Morris, Aldon. "Reflections on Social Movement Theory: Criticisms and Proposals." *Contemporary Sociology* 29, no. 3 (2000): 445–454.

Rabinovich, Itamar, and Jehuda Reinharz, eds. *Israel in the Middle East: Documents and Readings on Society, Politics, and Foreign Relations pre-1948 to the Present*. 2d ed. Waltham, Mass.: Brandeis University Press, 2008.

Saad-Ghorayeb, Amal. *Hizbu'llah: Politics and Religion*. London: Pluto, 2002.

Smelser, Neil. *Theory of Collective Behavior*. New York: Free Press, 1962.

Tilly, Charles. *From Mobilization to Revolution*. Reading, Mass.: Addison-Wesley, 1978.

Wiktorowicz, Quintan, ed. *Islamic Activism: A Social Movement Theory Approach*. Bloomington: Indiana University Press, 2004.

Zald, Mayer N., and John D. McCarthy, eds. *Social Movements in an Organizational Society: Collected Essays*. New Brunswick, N.J.: Transaction, 1987.

ADEL ABDEL GHAFAR
and LISA WORTHINGTON

SOROUSH, ABDOLKARIM. (1945–), Iranian philosopher and reformer. Abdolkarim Soroush was born in 1945 into a religious family. He attended the Alavi high school, where he combined modern and traditional learning and continued his traditional education while obtaining a doctorate in pharmacology from the University of Tehran. Soroush was pursuing a Ph.D. in the philosophy of science in Britain when the Islamic Iranian Revolution occurred. Upon his return to Iran, he appeared on national television as an esoteric interpreter of Jalāl al-Dīn Rūmī and an ideological defender of the newly established Islamic Republic, against its Marxist detractors. He served briefly as a member of the Central Committee of the Cultural Revolution, an appointment that continued to inspire controversy long after he resigned to begin his career as an independent Islamic reformer and dissident.

Soroush's initial philosophical project was a rationalist endeavor to reconcile the contradictions of faith and reason. He labeled as "derivationism" Islamic liberals' efforts to discover bases of human rights and democracy in Islam. Inspired by Muhammad Iqbal (1877–1938), Soroush called for the reconstruction of Islamic thought through a fundamental overhaul of the old intellectual apparatus of Islamic philosophy, theology, and law. This reconstructionism acknowledges that the sphere of values be autonomous from religion. A modern, autonomous reason, he averred, was the basis of all intellectuality, religious or otherwise. No longer were reason, morality, and freedom to be treated as handmaidens of the legalistic decrees of Muslim jurists. In his reappraisal of these human endowments, Soroush did not stop at critique of their theological restrictions. He also warned against the misapplication of transrational views of mystical poets and sages of Iran: "I shudder every time I evoke the impassioned poetry of Rumi and Hafez in my lectures, lest their ecstatic odes to love and their contempt for reason be used as a weapon by the enemies of reason and freedom. I am afraid this will lead us to spurn the small measure of reason that we have been given at the sight of a mirage.... Indeed we love humanity for the sake of these few examples. But the rest of us who are not so blessed must use our God-given gift of reason and engage in rational discourse" (Soroush, 2000, p. 93).

Soroush's audacious theories made him vulnerable to charges of eclecticism. Criticisms impelled him to undertake an ambitious philosophical project (published in "The Hermeneutical Contraction and Expansion of the Shariah"), where he privileged the discussion of modern philosophy of religion and sociology of knowledge over traditional, hypothesized investigations of Islamic theology. He argued that knowledge of religion (a collective and fluid affair that reflected the current zeitgeist and the disputations of the reigning intellectual elites) must not be conflated with the essence of divine revelation. Publication of this book constituted a paradigm shift in Iranian reformist thought in the twentieth century. Hundreds of articles and no fewer than fourteen books were written to refute it.

In a subsequent book (*Expansion of the Prophetic Experience*) Soroush observed that the Qurʾān is replete with tropes of caravan trade and slavery, signifying a vanished cultural world that has nonetheless left its imprint on religion. The length of the Qurʾān depended on that of the Prophet's life, and its content was partially determined by its accidents (e.g., rumors against ʿĀʾishah, the Prophet's wife, in one of the expeditions of the Prophet, occasioned Qurʾānic injunctions against the calumny of adultery). These considerations led Soroush to the separation of the "essential" and "accidental" aspects of religion.

One of Soroush's most controversial arguments is his contention that a clerical caste must not claim an interpretive monopoly on religion or impose political hegemony in its name. In a funeral oration, he praised Mehdi Bazargan, in effect the first prime minister of the Islamic Republic and a prominent Islamic thinker, because he lived for, rather than off, religion. The obvious implication that there cannot be an "official interpretation" of religion prompted the Supreme Leader of the Islamic Republic of Iran, Ayatollah Khameneʾi, to proclaim that there does indeed exist an official and correct interpretation of religion.

In the late 1990s Soroush was banned from teaching and subsequently was dismissed from his positions at the Academy of Philosophy and the Iranian Academy of Sciences. Under threats of assassination, Soroush was constrained to leave Iran for stints at various universities in Southeast Asia, Europe, and the United States. He returned to Iran for short periods until the controversial elections of 2009. In the aftermath of that radical split between the reform movement (both political and intellectual wings) and the apparatus of the right-wing state in the Islamic Republic of Iran, Soroush took increasingly strident stances against the Islamic Republic in his articles and open letters to the Supreme Leader, ʿAlī Khamaneʾi. Consequently, the intelligence apparatus of the Islamic Republic put his son-in-law under pressure to publicly denounce his wife and father-in-law, which Soroush bitterly condemned as an inhumane and tyrannical method of coercion. In an open letter that takes its title from the first words his son-in-law spoke in a telephone conversation after his escape from Tehran: "I Swear by God That There Is No God... None."

[*See also* Iqbal, Muhammad.]

BIBLIOGRAPHY

"Soroush, Abdolkarim." http://www.drsoroush.com. Official website.

Soroush, Abdolkarim. *Reason, Freedom and Democracy in Islam: Essential Writings of Abdolkarim*

Soroush. Translated, edited, and with a critical introduction by Mahmoud Sadri and Ahmad Sadri. Oxford and New York: Oxford University Press, 2000.

Soroush, Abdolkarim. "Reason and Freedom in Islamic Thought." *Muslim Democrat* 4, no. 1 (January 2002): 2–3. Published by the Center for the Study of Islam and Democracy in Washington, D.C.

Vakili, Valla. *Debating Religion and Politics in Iran: The Political Thought of Abdolkarim Soroush*. Occasional Paper Series No. 2. New York: Council on Foreign Relations, 1996.

AHMAD SADRI
and MAHMOUD SADRI

SOVEREIGNTY. Broadly speaking, all sovereignty within Islam stems from the principle of *tawḥīd* (unity of God), whereby God is recognized as the sovereign of sovereigns, and all peoples and all things belong to Him. As God rules everything for all times, Islam does not recognize any partition between political, social, or cultural life and that which is controlled by Islam.

Sovereignty in an Islamic state does not therefore belong directly to the human ruler—rather, it belongs to God, and the mortal rules only through a vice regency (*khilāfat*), implementing what has already been legislated in the Qurʾān and protecting the Islamic community on earth. If the character of the governance conflicts with Islamic principles as laid down in the Qurʾān, its commands (theoretically) no longer bind its subjects. As such, the ruler cannot create laws that conflict with those of God, and while he or she can create laws on which the Qurʾān says little, every state law is ultimately subservient to God. *Sharīʿah* (the ideal of God's law) thus outweighs *fiqh* (law based on human interpretation of Islamic texts). At the same time, Islam recognizes the importance of *ʿilm* (knowledge) and believes that people are imbued with the faculties of creativity, individuality, and reasoning in order to sustain the Islamic community through changing contexts. This means that sovereignty in Islam is flexible; it can be used to legitimate and shape diverse governance structures from autocracies to democracies. Within this, Islamic practices such as *shūrā* (consultation) and *ijmāʿ* (consensus) are applied very differently, depending on the interpretation of Islamic sovereignty.

Islamic sovereignty does not conform to territorial or political borders; rather, it claims dominion over the entire Muslim community (the *ummah*). Islam rejects popular sovereignty in favor of the rule of God and the vice regency of the *khilāfat*. However, it is important to remember that the vice regent is also subject to the sovereignty of God. There is no official church or accepted hierarchical power structure within Islam, and some Islamists—such as the influential Abū al-Aʿlā Mawdūdī—argue that this protects the direct relationship between the worshipper and God, guarding against the flawed leadership of man. The ultimate allegiance of the people is, according to Islamic doctrine, not to the *khilāfat* but to God, and the people are therefore (theoretically) protected from the tyranny of a mortal ruler.

Islamic Sovereignty in Practice. The first application of Islamic sovereignty was during the Rashīdūn caliphate (632–661 CE) led by Abū Bakr, the first successor of Muḥammad's political leadership according to Sunnī tradition (contested by Shīʿī Muslims). Drawing from the example of the Prophet, the caliphs emphasized their *khilāfat* status and, as Islam was a new religion and relatively territorially cohesive, they were able to actually rule over most of the *ummah*. Moreover, these early caliphates stressed their Islamic roots, emphasizing *Sharīʿah* and *fiqh*. Early Islamic unity, however, was short-lived; as rival claims to the title of *khilāfat* grew and the religion split between Sunnī and Shīʿī, competing dynasties vied for control over the *ummah*. The Umayyad, ʿAbbāsid, Fāṭimid, and Ottoman caliphates successively claimed sovereignty over the Muslim community, although none was ever universally accepted as *khilāfat.*

By claiming sovereignty over the entire *ummah* and ruling over vast geographic regions, Islamic sovereignty has also applied to non-Islamic peoples. Islamic doctrine states that non-Muslim practices, culture, and religion must be respected. These rules were particularly directed at "people of the pact" (Jews and Christians) and allowed them, in principle, to live according to their own rules under Islamic sovereignty. In reality, however, non-Muslims in the caliphate period were often accorded only second-class citizenship. Christians and Jews in the Ottoman Empire, for example, were not permitted to hold political office, paid higher taxes, and their testimony in court was overruled by that of a Muslim.

By the late nineteenth century, the Ottoman Empire (which had itself used the title *khilāfat* only sporadically) was waning. European states had grown considerably more powerful and had begun to encroach on Ottoman sovereignty. The Europeans introduced a fundamentally different concept of sovereignty that would challenge and transform the Islamic world.

Islamic versus Western Conceptions of Sovereignty. Unlike Islamic sovereignty, the European construct was based on the Westphalian system of nation-states and the sovereignty of the people. Ultimate loyalty was accorded to the human monarch, and the populace was expected to respect the rule of human law, even where it clashed with religious laws. Moreover, Westphalian sovereignty was territorially bounded. While the last bastion of Islamic *khilāfat*s—the Ottoman Empire—declined, European powers established dominance over many parts of the Islamic community, from Morocco to Indonesia, through colonialism. They imposed their concept of sovereignty, with the bureaucratic structures that accompanied it, on the Muslim community. Islamic responses to the imposition of Westphalian sovereignty ranged from rejection of the West and reassertion of Islamic sovereignty to acceptance of Western political systems and the advantages they offered.

In particular, leaders of Muslim states increasingly implemented secularist policies, exiling Islam from state to society. Mustafa Kemal Atatürk, for example, abolished the position of *khilāfat* in the Ottoman Empire, opting instead for secular, Western-inspired state structures. Previously Islamic countries such as Egypt, Algeria, Tunisia, Iraq, and Syria likewise attempted to build states based on the principles of Westphalian, not Islamic, sovereignty. Even after the end of colonialism, nationalist leaders of newly independent states, such as Gamal Abdel Nasser in Egypt, redefined the basis of the state as the nation rather than Islam, rejecting Islamic sovereignty in favor of the Western construct. In some cases, Islam became merely a formula of legitimation for authoritarian rulers. As time passed, the populations of many of these countries grew accustomed to Westphalian sovereignty and the nationalist identity that accompanied it.

However, increasing acceptance of Westphalian sovereignty and the exile of Islam from the state by no means extinguished the influence of Islamic sovereignty. While nationalist leaders have been quick to repress nascent Islamic movements that could challenge the secular nature of the state, since the late twentieth century these movements have grown in frequency and power. Islamic movements are driven by two broad and contested understandings of Islamic sovereignty, outlined below.

Contested Understandings of Sovereignty within Islam. While the basic tenets of Islamic sovereignty are generally agreed upon, the flexibility of Islam has produced diverse interpretations of sovereignty among Islamic groups and political actors. In particular, two influential interpretations have emerged, which emphasize different aspects of Islamic sovereignty and contest how it should apply to issues of governance, state structures, and social movements.

The first interpretation is "Jihād-i sovereignty," which appeals to those whom Amin Saikal (2008) terms "Jihād-i Islamists," who adhere to a strict interpretation of Islamic sovereignty, stemming from a literal interpretation of the Qur'ān and *sunnah*. They strongly assert the universal authority of God and do not recognize any division between public and private life. They often appeal to the wider *ummah* rather than the citizens of any particular state. The only acceptable government in their view is an Islamic structure that implements *Sharī'ah* and *fiqh* in line with a strict understanding of Islam. They emphasize the *khilāfat* status of the human ruler and that the ultimate loyalty of all Muslims should be to God. The practices of *shūrā* and *ijmā'* are affirmed, but only within a strict Islamic framework. Rather than an adaptable view of sovereignty, Jihād-i sovereignty advocates governance as a reflection of God's rule on earth and argues that it should be closely based on the example set by the Prophet Muḥammad. This view of sovereignty lends itself to authoritarianism, autocracy, and other political structures that favor top-down, unilateral rule. Prominent Islamic proponents of this understanding of sovereignty include figures such as Sayyid Quṭb, a leading Egyptian activist and theologist who was imprisoned and hanged during the presidency of Gamal Abdel Nasser in 1966. Another example, the international Islamic party Hizbut-Tahrir, has called for the re-creation of the sovereignty over the Islamic *ummah* under a *khilāfat*. Importantly, proponents of Jiḥād-i sovereignty believe that *tawḥīd* provides a clear and single direction and demands a unified spirit from the *ummah*. Jihād-i sovereignty is thus far more inflexible than the understanding of sovereignty promulgated by Ijtihād-i Islamists.

Ijtihād-i sovereignty is a liberal interpretation of Islamic sovereignty. Ijtihād-i proponents strive to adapt Islamic sovereignty to the modern world. They maintain that Islam does not provide a "blueprint" for Islamic systems of governance so much as general guidance and direction. Ijtihād-i sovereignty thus emphasizes the importance of *'ilm* and creativity. Ijtihād-i Islamists generally view Islam as compatible with democracy, emphasizing the Islamic practices of *shūrā* and *ijmā'*. There is less consensus on whether Ijtihād-i sovereignty applies to the entire *ummah* or should recognize the political reality of Westphalian nation-states. Often, Ijtihād-i Islamists will attempt to adapt Islamic sovereignty to the nation-state system, creating nation-states that emphasize their Islamic character. Prominent Islamic scholars who have interpreted Islamic sovereignty relatively liberally include the influential Pakistani theologian Abū al-A'lā Mawdūdī, former Indonesian president Abdurrahman Wahid, and the former Iranian president Mohamed Khatami.

Across the Islamic world, states have carefully balanced Islamic and Western forces. Although they have increasingly done so within the framework of Westphalian sovereignty and the international nation-state system, Islamic interpretations of sovereignty continue to influence the thinking of rulers, clerics, and the general population throughout the Islamic world.

BIBLIOGRAPHY

Esposito, John. *Voices of Resurgent Islam*. New York: Oxford University Press, 1983.

Mawdūdī, Abū al-A'lā. *Political Theory of Islam*. Edited and translated by Khurshid Ahmad. Lahore: Islamic Publications, 1960.

Piscatori, James. *Islam in a World of Nation States*. Cambridge, U.K., and New York: Cambridge University Press, 1986.

Saikal, Amin. "Westphalian and Islamic Concepts of Sovereignty in the Middle East." In *Re-envisioning Sovereignty: The End of Westphalia?*, edited by Trudy Jacobsen, Charles Sampford, and Ramesh Thakur, pp. 73–81. Aldershot, U.K.: Ashgate, 2008.

Steunebrink, Gerrit. "Sovereignty, the Nation State, and Islam." *Ethical Perspectives: Journal of the European Ethics Network* 15, no. 1 (2008): 7–47.
Yilmaz, Hakan. "Islam, Sovereignty, and Democracy: A Turkish View." *Middle East Journal* 61, no. 3 (Summer 2007): 477–493.

JESSIE MORITZ

SPAIN. *See* Andalusia.

SUCCESSION. Succession concerns were problematic in Muslim countries because of ingrained power struggles that, for better or worse, determined how the mighty ruled. In Europe, where dynasties flourished, succession was formerly determined by a show of strength among a ruler's sons. In time, however, it reverted to primogeniture, in which a ruler's oldest male descendant acceded to the throne. For a variety of reasons, chiefly because of religious and tribal traditions, primogeniture failed to develop among Muslim dynasties in similar fashion, because under *Sharīʿah* law, all of a man's sons are equal and legitimate, even if they were born from illicit marriages. Moreover, in pre-Islamic tribal norms, while the throne could have passed from one generation to the next within a particular family, it was not necessarily passed from father to son. Rather, authority was sometimes entrusted to a ruler's brother, uncle, or cousin, depending on which of these oldest male relatives was seen to possess "the qualities of nobility, skill in arbitration, *hazz* or 'good fortune,' and leadership" (Helms, 1981, p. 57).

The inherent fragility of the succession principle in Muslim states was mitigated by the traditional prerogative of rulers to designate their successors, starting with the Prophet himself. In the absence of an institutionalized state structure, which complicated matters, it was difficult for a designated heir to guarantee his succession and deter challenges, or even to maintain his position once he assumed rulership. Therefore, the power of a Muslim governor stemmed from the complicated personal loyalties that he established with relatives and advisers. Moreover, the absence of formal state institutions did not mean that dynastic rulers operated in a vacuum, but that despite rich tribal traditions—which ensured the survival of a particular dynasty—monarchical rulers in the Arab and Muslim worlds assumed additional burdens after the advent of the state system.

Whether the Prophet Muḥammad ever envisaged a process for legitimate and orderly succession, the absence of a male heir ensured that there would be no dynasty to perpetuate the first "Islamic state." In fact, the first four caliphs who succeeded the Prophet—Abū Bakr (632–634), ʿUmar (634–644), ʿUthmān (644–656), and ʿAlī (656–661)—not only were related to him through marriage but also were members of the Quraysh tribe. Indeed, the first three successors were chosen by tribal acclamation, though the struggle did not culminate until 656 with the assassination of ʿUthman, and the accession of ʿAlī. ʿAlī himself was challenged by Muʿāwiyah, the Umayyad governor of Syria, who demanded vengeance for the murder of the previous caliph, his cousin ʿUthmān. What unfolded was the first schism in Islam that would later lead to major sectarian divisions. This problem of succession, impeachment, legitimacy, and authority would plague the Islamic empire and the Muslim world with some periods of respite (some very long, such as under the ʿAbbāsids and the Ottomans) when a system of succession was put in place.

In 661, after the assassination of ʿAlī by the Khārijī Ibn Muljam, the empire came under the control of Muʿāwiyah (661–680), and for the next nineteen years there was no succession dispute. It was after the death of Muʿāwiyah that the next succession dispute came about. This was finally solved by a second civil war in which the victors, the Umayyads (692–749), under Abd al-Malik ibn Marwān, instituted a system of succession that outlasted the dynasty itself. The ʿAbbāsid dynasty (750–1258) in Baghdad utilized the same method of succession, which was the sitting ruler designating his successors in public and private; usually it was one son, but there were many times two sons were named to rule one after the other.

These problems of succession were not so pervasive with regard to the Shīʿī dynasties; still, once they arose, the ramifications were much more permanent. Thus, the Ismāʿīlī/Shīʿī Fāṭimid dynasty (909–1171) that started in North Africa had only two incidents of succession disputes, but these two resulted in the permanent split of Ismāʿīlī Shiism.

In the tenth century, the ʿAbbāsid caliphate lost its secular power to warlords in Baghdad, and in 1258 their reign was eradicated altogether by the Mongol invasion, which earned the wrath of various scholars, including Taqī al-Dīn Aḥmad Ibn Taymīyah (1263–1328). Various military powers then emerged whose leaders were astute enough to rule in the name of Islam and, ostensibly, by applying *Sharīʿah* law. Over time, Sunnī jurists elaborated their interpretation and opined that rule seized by force was legitimate, provided that rulers declared their support for the *Sharīʿah*. Such explanations, while expedient and perhaps even necessary, certainly hindered the development of proper succession mechanisms in the Muslim world in general and the Arab world in particular. Still, extenuating circumstances, including tribal and regional politics, played critical roles as well.

For the next six hundred years, succession patterns within most of the Muslim world were set by the behavior of Ottoman rulers, who, more often than not, were innovative and bloody.

From the thirteenth to the sixteenth centuries, twelve sultans ruled the Ottoman Empire following a lineal setup, with authoritative governance passing from a ruler to his eldest son. Despite this seemingly orderly pattern, there was no clearly defined system of primogeniture, and the strongest male offspring routinely eliminated rival siblings. Under the rule of Mehmed I (1413–1421), a "law of fratricide" was introduced, which gave the conqueror the right to execute any surviving brothers to eliminate potential uprisings. This approach was violently followed by Mehmed III, who acceded to the throne in 1595 and, conveniently, had nineteen surviving brothers executed. His own children were not spared, being executed for alleged court conspiracies, which left prospects for succession rather dim. Mehmed III died in 1603 with two minor heirs, Ahmed I and Mustafa I, and, fittingly, both ruled, but more as the result of a winnowing of ranks than through any merit in their intrinsic capabilities. In 1617 Sultan Ahmed I instituted a new mechanism, known as the *khafes* (cage), to further isolate his own sons and nephews from the seat of authority in Constantinople. The *khafes* were isolated courts—often spread in remote parts of the empire—serviced by deaf mutes and sterilized concubines to further control the production of undesired offspring. If and when the performances of a particular eligible "successor" was required, the sultan would fetch one, but naturally the practice weakened whatever institutions the empire could support. Moreover, isolation often nurtured mediocrity, which in time affected the quality of successors. Several sultans subjected to the *khafes* treatment in their youths suffered from personality disorders and other psychological problems that affected their putative rules. This loss of quality did not escape the notice of shrewd rulers, and in the case of Sultan Abdülhamid (1774–1789), the suspension of the *khafes* system was deemed necessary. Sadly, as his own son was not particularly promising, Abdülhamid retrieved his nephew Selim III (1789–1807), because the latter was allegedly bright. Sultan Selim III, although responsible for the organization of military institutions, proved to be less enlightened than his uncle because, once in power, he reinstituted the *khafes* system, ostensibly to limit palace intrigues.

To their credit, none of the tribes on the Arabian Peninsula instituted fratricide or cage methods, although most were aware of such practices. Even if tribal traditions—steeped in family honor and the survival of the entire community—prevented behavior similar to the ones practiced by Ottoman sultans, succession struggles were not eliminated in toto. Largely because of widespread poverty, the struggles for survival on the peninsula meant that intrigues and clashes were intended not only to retain power but also to ensure that a strong leader would safeguard tribal members from harm and utter destitution. This was certainly the case with the Rashīd dynasty that ruled Ḥā'il in Saudi Arabia from 1835 to 1921. In the case of the Āl Rashīd, a series of weak leaders failed to maintain order, which plunged the dynasty into chaos. Similar changes occurred in Abu Dhabi in 1966, when Zāyid bin Sulṭān Al Nahayān replaced his brother Shakhbut, with full family consent. In this instance, the violence was very limited, but winnowing potential challengers was largely completed by the time Zāyid assumed rulership just as oil production filled the emirate's coffers. To be sure, vengeance fueled successive murders in Abu Dhabi and elsewhere in the Lower Gulf, but underlying weaknesses were equally important. Tribal customs, especially the contest over meager landholdings, determined the extent to which conflicts evolved. Moreover, the belief that all were equal, even when that was not the case, prompted those who possessed military resources to challenge rulers, in search for legitimizing authority. Equally important were the influences of outside forces, especially the Ottoman and British Empires, which slowly aligned themselves with several Arabian Peninsula tribes. Importantly, the Āl Rashīd failed because several rulers were too narrowly concerned with internal disagreements, and because they slowly lost the ability to compromise and govern through consensus. This was a major lesson to the equally ambitious Āl Saʿūd leaders, who gained ground from their stronghold of Nejd.

Among the legacies of the Arab and Ottoman Empires were two main characteristics. First, monarchical principles were applied without official Islamic legitimacy, as the title *malik* (king) was regarded as non-Islamic and therefore unlawful. In fact, until the twentieth century, Islamic rulers did not even assume this title, as a ruler's emphasis was on fulfilling the task of a *khalīfah* (the Prophet's substitute, ruling over a community of believers, or *ummah*), claiming his right to rule according to *Sharīʿah* law. However, throughout all of Islamic history, Muslim rulers practiced at least two fundamental models of monarchic rule: individual-absolutist and dynastic-hereditary. A social system based on kinship, as well as ethnic, religious, and other unifying characteristics, was arrayed in hierarchical divisions. They also adopted additional monarchical facets, such as royal entourages and household trappings that created significant retinues that benefited from royal largesse. The ruler wielding these prerogatives in hereditary fashion within a family or a dynasty held the helm. Second, without an official religious sanction, adoption and exercise of these qualities did not develop into a desired norm or into an official doctrine of monarchical rule. Monarchical principles in the Arab and Ottoman Empires evolved more haphazardly, typical of a regime created by a forceful seizure of government following Persian, Greek, and Byzantine examples as well as local practices and arbitrary rulers' interests. To some extent, this was the legacy of empire, which left undeniable marks on nascent dynasties. In Asia and Africa, monarchical rule evolved along lines of ethnicity, kinship, religion, and several other attributes within specifically defined tribal and hierarchical divisions. Still, few survived the political ravages of the nineteenth and twentieth centuries, with the remaining ruling families galvanized by their rapid declines.

Astonishingly, in the post–World War II period, when most North African and Muslim monarchs were toppled and replaced by republican forms of government, military dictators and presidents for life pursued more or less the same pattern in securing power for the next generation of leaders. This phenomenon was evident in Syria, Egypt, Yemen, Libya, and Azerbaijan. Nevertheless, the future composition and stability of the decision-making elite in the fourteen surviving Arab monarchies nestled in eight independent countries (Bahrain, Jordan, Kuwait, Morocco, Oman, Qatar, Saudi Arabia, and the seven federation Sheiykhdoms within the United Arab Emirates—Abu Dhabi, Ajman, Dubai, Fujairah, Ras al-Khaimah, Sharjah, and Umm al-Qaiwain) were subjected to dramatic changes too, even if complex interfamily realignments were carefully controlled.

BIBLIOGRAPHY

Bendix, Reinhard. *Kings or People: Power and the Mandate to Rule.* Berkeley: University of California Press, 1978.

Coulson, Noel J. *A History of Islamic Law.* Edinburgh: Edinburgh University Press, 1964.

Firdawsī. *Stories from the Shahnameh.* Translated by Dick Davis. 3 vols. Washington, D.C.: Mage, 1998–2004.

Gibb, H. A. R. "Al-Mawardi's Theory of the Caliphate." In *Studies on the Civilization of Islam*, edited by Stanford J. Shaw and William R. Polk, pp. 151–165. Princeton, N.J.: Princeton University Press, 1982.

Helms, Christine M. *The Cohesion of Saudi Arabia: Evolution of Political Identity*, Baltimore: Johns Hopkins University Press, 1981.

Kéchichian, Joseph A. *Power and Succession in Arab Monarchies: A Reference Guide.* Boulder, Colo.: Lynne Rienner, 2008.

Kéchichian, Joseph A. *Succession in Saudi Arabia.* New York: Palgrave, 2001.

Niẓām al-Mulk. *The Book of Government, or Rules for Kings: The 'Siyar al-muluk' or 'Siyasat-nama' of Nizam al-Mulk.* Translated by Hubert Darke. 2d ed. London: Routledge & Kegan Paul, 1978. Originally published in Arabic c. 1110.

Rashīd Riḍā, Muḥammad. *Le califat dans la doctrine de Rašīd Riḍā.* Translated by Henri Laoust. Paris: Librairie d'Amérique et d'Orient, 1986.

Sachedina, Abdulaziz Abdulhussein. *The Just Ruler (Al-Sultān al-ʿĀdil) in Shīʿite Islam: The Comprehensive Authority of the Jurist in Imamite Jurisprudence.* New York: Oxford University Press, 1988.

JOSEPH A. KÉCHICHIAN

SUDAN. *Bilād al-Sūdān* means "lands of the Blacks" in Arabic. It is a generic term for sub-Saharan Islamic Africa (also known as the Sahel) and has been the name of the modern nation since 1898. Islam entered Sudan in the sixteenth century and an overwhelming majority of the 25.9 million people living in Sudan in 2012 are Muslims, while a large majority of the 10.6 million people living in the newly created South Sudan are Christian. After twenty-two years of renewed civil war between the "Muslim" north and the "Christian" south (1983–2005), sparked by the introduction of *Sharīʿah* as national law, a Comprehensive Peace Agreement (CPA) was signed by the Government of Sudan (GoS) and the Sudanese People's Liberation Movement (SPLM) in January 2005. The CPA granted the southern rebels autonomy for six years followed by a referendum on independence for southern Sudan. When the referendum was held in January 2011 the southerners voted overwhelmingly in favor of independence. South Sudan became independent on 9 July 2011.

Arrival of Islam. The distinctive cultural pattern of African Islam, grounded in the Mālikī school of law and its traditions, that prevails in

Sudan spread in from the west, where African kingdoms had been Islamized since the twelfth century, and from the north, especially after the fall of the Christian kingdoms in Nubia in the fifteenth century. From the fifth to the twelfth centuries Christian Nubia blocked the introduction of Islam through a unique treaty of nonaggression and trade known as the Baqṭ. It was by turns a peace treaty, a slave-trade accord and schedule of tribute payments, and a recognition of mutual political autonomy. Islam finally reached Nubia peacefully in the sixteenth century—later in West Africa—when Kenzi Muslim traders and preachers intermarried with Christian Danagla as the Christian kingdoms fell into decline.

The first Muslim state in Sudan, the Funj Sultanate, was established at Sinnar in 1504. Arabization and Islamization followed quickly after the fall of the Nubian Christian kingdom. Islam spread southward along the Nile while a separate migration of Muslims followed *ḥajj* and caravan routes from West Africa into Kordofan and Darfur. The Funj, also known as the "Black Sultanate," attracted holy men from the Hejaz and from Egypt who introduced Islamic theology and Shariʿah and established the first religious courts. Pilgrimage routes to Mecca, following the vast system of trans-Saharan routes, were an important source of continuous contact and influence of West African Islam on Sudan. By the nineteenth century Islam was well established in Sudan through this infusion of religion and culture from West Africa, Egypt, and to a lesser extent, Arabia.

Turkish Rule and Resistance, Mahdism, an Early Islamist State. Modern Sudanese history begins with the Ottoman Turkish-Egyptian invasion of 1821, resulting in an occupation that lasted until 1881. Known as the Turkīyah, Turco-Egyptian rule is recalled even today by Sudanese as harsh, with oppressive taxes, forced conscription of soldiers, and slaving expeditions. However there was no general rising until the sixth decade of the Turco-Egyptian occupation, when Muḥammad Aḥmad of Dongola, known as the Mahdī (the expected one), unified this resistance and led a successful revolt that ended Turco-Egyptian rule.

Across linguistically Sudanic Africa, several successful jihādist movements flared in the nineteenth century in response to foreign intervention. Among the most famous of these movements was that of the Sudanese Mahdī. His resistance ended Turkish rule, and for seventeen years (1881–1898), in a period known as the Mahdīyah, prevented the English from colonizing the country.

Muḥammad Aḥmad, the Mahdī, was educated in a traditional *khalwah* (religious school) in northern Sudan and joined the Sammānīyah Ṣūfī order after studying with the grandson of its founder, Muḥammad Sharīf Nūr al-Dāʾim. He practiced a vigorous asceticism and criticized the immorality and corruption of the political and social leaders of his day. His personal zeal blended with the Islamic concept of an expected deliverer (comparable to the Judaic and Christian idea of a Messiah), and in May 1881 he proclaimed himself the Mahdī. His support grew rapidly in northern and western Sudan among diverse ethnic groups through his use of the idea of *ummah* (Islamic community). In January 1885 the Mahdī's forces seized Khartoum and killed General Charles George Gordon, setting the stage for the conquest of Mahdist Sudan by the British Empire.

The Mahdī died soon after the fall of Khartoum and was succeeded by Caliph (Khalīfa) Abdallahi al-Taʿishi, who ruled from Omdurman. A zealous movement, it continued its military campaigns to extend the Dār al-Islām (the abode of Islam) southward to the Nuba Mountains and Bahr al-Ghazal, attempting to convert the animists living there. This early form of Islamic revival presaged the move toward an Islamic state after 1983, and in the south it is recalled as the beginning of Muslim domination. The fall of Mahdism and the military conquest of Sudan occurred in 1898 when British troops under the command of General Horatio Herbert Kitchener massacred an estimated ten thousand Mahdist Anṣār outside Omdurman.

ʿAbd al-Raḥmān al-Mahdī, son of the Mahdī, led the Anṣār during the early decades of colonial Anglo-Egyptian Sudan. The Anṣār later developed into one of the nationalist organizations, the Ummah Party, led by ʿAbd al-Raḥmān's son Ṣadiq. Ṣiddīq's son, al-Ṣādiq al-Mahdī, served twice as prime minister of Sudan (1965–1969 and 1986–1989).

Darfur. Controlling the lucrative "forty-days road" for trade with Egypt and occupying the neighboring region of Kordofan for much of the eighteenth century, the sultanate of Darfur dominated western Sudan until it was conquered by Turco-Egyptian forces in 1874, a half-century after their initial invasion of Sudan. During the Mahdist period a core group of the Anṣār al-Mahdī came from Darfur, especially from the Taʿaīsha Baqqārah, the ethnic group of the Mahdī's successor, Khalīfa Abdullahi ibn Muḥammad (d. 1899). Darfur regained some measure of independence under the last sultan, ʿAlī Dinār, who ruled from 1898 to 1916.

As peace negotiations ending the civil war between north and south were being finalized in 2003, rebel groups in Darfur—notably the Sudanese Liberation Movement (SLM) and the Justice and Equality Movement (JEM)—mounted an offensive against the GoS in an effort to gain their share of political and economic representation in the central government. The GoS responded with a counteroffensive that was aided by irregular militias—infamous Janjawīd (raiders on horse- or camelback)—that led to raiding, ethnic cleansing, and allegations of genocide. The Western press simplistically characterized the conflict as between government-backed "Arabs" and "Black" African Darfuris, while scholars noted the complexities of race, identity, and ethnic-ecological rivalries in the region. Unlike the north-south dispute, religion is not a factor in the Darfur conflict, unless it emerges in a future redistribution of power and wealth among this historically marginalized region.

Ṣūfī Traditions. The Ṣūfī tradition parallels and at times conflicts with state Islam. Populist Ṣūfī orders were the main agents of Islamization from the sixteenth century on. With their style of religious performance in the form of *dhikr* (remembrance [of God]), and the use of drumming, chanting, and dancing led by a local *shaykh*, the Ṣūfīs blended with and enhanced local traditions without threatening them. In Sudan Ṣūfī brotherhoods are egalitarian and decentralized in organization and so eschew the formalism of such Islamic institutions as *Sharīʿah* courts or state-supported official interpretations issued by the *ʿulamāʾ*. With the introduction of the colonial state and the official administration of Islam, the local Ṣūfī leaders were undermined; in response they withheld their support from the state. At times the state further antagonized the orders by declaring them to be outside the boundaries of orthodox Islam because of their veneration of local holy men and unrestrained modes of worship. However both major post-independence parties—the Ummah of the Anṣār al-Mahdī and the Democratic Unionist Party of the rival Khatmīyah sect—are rooted in the Ṣūfī tradition. After the National Islamic Front—which had evolved from the Muslim Brotherhood and was led by Dr. Ḥasan al-Turābī—seized power in 1989, the Ṣūfī orders were recruited to the "Islamic project," lessening the historical tension between "orthodox" or official state Islam and its deeply populist rival, the Ṣūfī orders.

The Colonial and Independent States. Anglo-Egyptian Sudan was created after the pacification of Mahdist forces between 1898 and 1902. Taking a cautious approach toward Islam, the British erected semiautonomous Islamic institutions, finding reliable agents to govern on their behalf. Carefully selected *ʿulamāʾ* were placed strategically in a new structure that was, on one hand, Muslim and familiar, and, on the other, foreign and colonial.

A "Mohammedan" legal system, with its own system of jurisdiction, courts, and appeals, was separated from the English-derived civil and criminal courts and law. These *Sharīʿah* courts adjudicated the personal status of Sudanese Muslims—marriage, divorce, child custody and support, inheritance, wills, and religious bequests (*waqf*). In 1982 Islamic and civil courts were combined into a single system with one chief justice. In 1991 a new *Sharīʿah* penal code was enacted, codifying Islamic law for the first time.

The Muslim Brotherhood, founded in Egypt in 1928, spread its influence to neighboring Sudan in the 1940s, establishing a branch there in the 1950s. In the mid-1960s the Muslim Brotherhood began to exert political influence when its Islamic Charter Front entered electoral politics and attempted to build a mass organization. From the earliest days the leader of the Muslim Brotherhood in Sudan has been Ḥasan al-Turābī, widely recognized as the architect of Sudan's Islamism and a leader of resurgent Islam.

Since gaining independence in 1956, Sudan has been governed by secular nationalist, military, and Islamist regimes that often combined all three elements. The issue of religion and the state—that is, the status of Islam and its institutions—was always a part of political agendas. In 1983 President Jaʿfar Nimeiri (1969–1985) declared *Sharīʿah* national law, reigniting the civil war between the north and south. Popular discontent with the direction of the Nimeiri government increased when the regime executed Maḥmūd Muḥammad Ṭāhā, the elderly leader of the Republican Brothers, a reformist Muslim movement based in Ṣūfī thought and dating to the pre-independence era. Within a matter of months a popular revolution and coup d'état overthrew Nimeiri and restored democracy to the country in 1985.

During the transitional period al-Ṣādiq al-Mahdī served as prime minister a second time, from 1986 to 1989. He was unable to resolve the two critical issues facing the country, the war in the south and the modification of the *Sharīʿah* as state law. A second coup d'état in 1989 brought an Islamist regime to power, headed by General ʿUmar al-Bashīr (b. 1944) but supported by the Islamist leader Ḥasan al-Turābī. This regime codified *Sharīʿah* criminal law, abolished all political parties, repressed Muslim dissenters in the north, and pressed for a military victory in the south. Eventually, they responded to international pressure, war fatigue, and domestic economic growth from oil revenues to reach the CPA in 2005.

Since independence, both Sudans have faced numerous internal and external challenges to peace as they seek to accommodate marginalized populations and to agree on sharing infrastructure and oil revenues. There has been ongoing violence in the disputed Abyei region along the new border, as well as in Southern Kordofan and Blue Nile states, both of which lie in Sudan but contain inhabitants aligned with South Sudan. In the western region of Darfur a separate conflict that broke out in 2003 has displaced nearly 2 million people and caused upwards of 400,000 deaths. The situation has become regional in scope, fomenting instability in Chad while Sudan has been faced with large refugee influxes from Chad and Ethiopia. Religious differences remain an element in the north-south disputes; however ethnic and tribal differences and the control of scarce resources now fuel the conflicts.

[*See also* Muslim Brotherhood; Sanūsīyah; *and* Turābī, Ḥasan al-.]

BIBLIOGRAPHY

ʿAbdel Rahim, Muddathir. *Imperialism and Nationalism in the Sudan: A Study in Constitutional and Political Development, 1899–1956*. Oxford: Clarendon Press, 1969.

Beshir, Mohamed Omer. *Revolution and Nationalism in the Sudan*. New York: Collings, 1974.

Cockett, Richard. *Sudan: Darfur and the Failure of an African State*. New Haven, Conn.: Yale University Press, 2010.

El-Affendi, Abdelwahab. *Turabi's Revolution: Islam and Power in the Sudan*. London: Grey Seal, 1991.

Flint, Julie, and Alex DeWaal. *Darfur: Short History of a Long War*. London: Zed Books, 2005.

Fluehr-Lobban, Carolyn. *Islamic Law and Society in the Sudan*. London: Cass, 1987.

Johnson, Douglas H. *The Root Causes of Sudan's Civil Wars*. Bloomington: Indiana University Press, 2003.

Voll, John O., ed. *Sudan: State and Society in Crisis*. Bloomington: Indiana University Press, 1991. The Sudan Studies Association (www.sudanstudies.org) promotes the scholarly study of Sudan.

CAROLYN FLUEHR-LOBBAN
Updated by RONALD BRUCE ST JOHN

SUFISM. Sufism (*taṣawwuf*) is often described as the mystical tradition in Islam, which is an unavoidable simplification. Views on its nature and relation to Islam are diverse and nuanced, but we can distinguish its proponents who accept some form of Sufism within Islamic orthodoxy from those who consider it heterodoxical (including those who oppose and those who promote it for this reason). Orthodoxy, here, refers broadly to anyone who holds the Qurʾān and *sunnah* as the ultimate criteria of Islamic legitimacy.

Sufism encourages individuals with higher spiritual aspirations. Muslim jurists have distinguished the minimally adequate Islamic obligations from the supererogatory, and the Qurʾān distinguishes the "companions of the right hand" from the "foremost" as destined for different levels of paradise. A *ḥadīth* describes someone who comes nearer to God with supererogatory worship until God loves him: "And when I love him, I am his hearing with which he hears, his sight with which he sees, his hand with which he seizes, and his foot with which he walks. If he asks Me, I will surely give to him, and if he seeks refuge in Me, I will surely protect him" (*Ṣaḥīḥ al-Bukhārī*). To be loved by God in this way is the goal of the Ṣūfī aspirant, known as a *sālik* (traveler). Sufism thus claims to offer a conception of and *ṭarīqah* (path) to what the Islamic sources describe as the best possible form of human life—that of a *walī* (friend, saint).

One rationale offered by Sufism's orthodox proponents is a *ḥadīth* according to which the Prophet Muḥammad, when questioned regarding *islām*, *īmān*, and *iḥsān*, explained the five pillars, or core obligatory deeds, of being Muslim (*islām*); the six pillars or core principles of Islamic belief (*īmān*); and described *iḥsān* ("most beautiful") as "worshipping God as if you see him." From this, Muslim scholars explicated a tripartite division of Islamic sciences, relating, respectively, to behavior, belief, and spirituality. While the first category is the concern of jurisprudence, the second is the concern of theology, and *iḥsān* is the concern of Sufism. Thus, it is treated as a subject matter integral to a comprehensive Islamic education, rather than a specific sectarian stance, as the "ism" in "Sufism" might be taken to mean.

Crucially, this gives Sufism a divine origin by associating it with God's Messenger. Opponents of Sufism have questioned these credentials, and accused it of having foreign (Neoplatonic, Christian, or Buddhist) origins. But the textual bases of Sufism drawn from the Islamic sources are rich, and while some Ṣūfī discourse is informed by "foreign" ideas, it is usually with a critical eye to conformity to Islamic revelation, which remains the ultimate criterion. However, the Ṣūfī approach to religious knowledge, where the question of origin is not necessarily historical, allows for more openness toward the "foreign" than its detractors appreciate.

Ṣūfī doctrine affirms the possibility of being divinely graced with a unique access to religious knowledge that outstrips the normal epistemological faculties. This *maʿrifah* ("recognition") or *dhawq* ("tasting") is granted by God, in various forms and degrees, to an elect few, the *awliyāʾ* ("friends," "saints"), qualified as guides to the inner dimension of religious belief and practice. This concept potentially precludes any monopoly on religious authority by those who depend on purely exoteric claims to religious knowledge. Thus, the chain (*silsilah*) connecting the disciple (*murīd*) to the *shaykh* (or *pīr*, "elder" or spiritual guide), and leading back ultimately to the Prophet Muḥammad, functions like the transmission chain (*isnād*) of an authenticated *ḥadīth* by establishing for the orthodox a connection to the ultimate source of religious knowledge. This has been a source of friction between Ṣūfīs and others who have based competing claims to religious authority on strictly textual epistemologies.

The exoteric and esoteric forms of religious knowledge and authority are not necessarily mutually exclusive. The commitments of Sufism's orthodox proponents entail placing the knowledge of prophets on a higher level than any possible for nonprophets: *maʿrifah* can never contradict the revealed sources, which alone form the basis of *Sharīʿah*. Most renowned Ṣūfīs were also trained scholars in the "exoteric" fields, and carefully kept everything in its place. But even if not contradicting purely exoteric readings, Sufism can radically reframe them.

This tendency is evident in the ethical element of Sufism, which places special emphasis on the morally decisive role of the conscious state with which the Muslim conforms to the outward injunctions of the *Sharīʿah*. Muslims generally understand that the deed is judged by the intention and that the act of worship done out of insincere motives is actually sinful. But Ṣūfīs emphasize such matters, and follow their implications through to a degree that some fear can threaten to turn the apparent values of things upside down. The image of the dervish, the wandering Ṣūfī who out of absolute trust and dedication to God leads a life of material poverty but spiritual wealth, can represent an indictment of the materialistic values that often determine the structure of ostensibly conservative religious societies. In a cultural context where social position and political legitimacy depend greatly on the public's assessment of one's piety, this emphasis can deflate efforts by the state or wealthy classes to build political capital on an outward application of religious rules.

Maʿrifah implies that the way things truly are can be radically different from how they appear to be. To some, it reveals that only God truly exists and that everything else, inasmuch as it can be said to exist at all, does so only relatively. Consequently, anything other than God has only relative value. This world (or its appearance) is only a transitory phase of collecting provisions for the journey to the Real. Outward conformity in religious practice, therefore, finds its sole purpose in another, more real world, in relation to which the independent value and reality of the apparent world (including its political order) are negated. The Real is not simply a future condition, but exists timelessly. This renders possible the recognition of a true moral and spiritual order, over and above any political order that apparently obtains.

For the Sunnī orthodox, the true moral order of things coincided with the political order under the Prophet and the first four caliphs. When the two orders began to come apart during the reign of the Umayyads (661–750), a religious opposition was inevitable and would take different forms. The tenth-century authors of the earliest explicitly Ṣūfī manuals describe their own social environment as an inversion of values from their true order, comparing it to the oppression of the family of the Prophet Muḥammad by the Umayyads. After the Prophet and companions, most Ṣūfīs include the Prophet's early descendants in their spiritual lineage—all of them figures of opposition, in some form, against Umayyad abuses.

Early accounts of this lineage (which includes notables like al-Ḥasan al-Baṣrī and the four eponyms of Sunnī jurisprudential schools) display a righteous contempt for most existing political figures, alongside a strategy of passive resistance. Wary of the spiritually corrupting influence of politics, they stayed above the fray of open political revolt and avoided proximity to political authority and the danger of cynical manipulation it posed to religious scholarship. In more dramatic instances that called for "speaking truth to power," the aim was not to overthrow or even primarily reform the political order but to preserve and protect the means by which recognition of the moral order could be preserved.

This describes the general political posture of the Sunnī *'ulamā'* of repute throughout this early phase, and not just that of adherents of Sufism, which either had not been explicitly articulated as a category within Sunnī orthodoxy (when it was a "reality without a name" before becoming a "name without a reality," as some proponents explain), or had not yet been "innovated" (as its detractors charge). However it may be, the Sunnī religious classes were busy during these centuries building nonstate systems of religious and moral authority, with which the state was forced to contend.

Meanwhile, a number of early Ṣūfī personalities emerged that would test Sufism's relation to the public religious boundaries of the Islamic political order. Rābi'ah al-'Adawīyah (d. 801) spoke of a love of God so powerful that divine punishment and reward become insignificant. Abū Yazīd Bisṭāmī (d. 874), the first of the "intoxicated" Ṣūfīs, made shocking, seemingly heretical utterances while in the throes of ecstatic spiritual states. Abū al-Qāsim al-Junayd (d. 910), the first organizer of Ṣūfī disciples, was a more tactful public representative of Sufism. He excused Bisṭāmī's ecstatic utterances as an effect of legitimate religious experience, but maintained that they only represent temporary, subjective states of mind that may be experienced by an aspirant on the Ṣūfī path, rather than its ultimate goal. He advised sobriety and care in what is publicly expressed about spiritual experiences. Manṣūr al-Ḥallāj (d. 922), a student of al-Junayd's, may represent the culmination of the relation between Sufism and the political order in this period. He did not follow Junayd's advice, and after attracting some disciples of his own from high places in Baghdad, he was executed on charges of heresy. This became a seminal event in early Ṣūfī history.

When 'Abbāsid central authority began to disintegrate, scholars in Khorāsān were developing nonstate religious institutions, including the *madrasah* and *khānqāh* (Ṣūfī lodge, also known as *zāwiyah*, *ribāṭ*, or *tekke*). Ṣūfīs were among the *'ulamā'*, and *taṣawwuf* was on the *madrasah* curriculum, along with exoteric disciplines. At this time, elements of organized Ṣūfī life began to appear. These include the formalization of the hierarchical, personal relationship connecting the *murīd* to the *pīr*'s *silsilah*, sealed with a pledge of loyalty, the granting of the initiate's ceremonial initiatory cloak (*khirqah*), and the prescription of a daily litany (*dhikr*, "remembrance"). Organized Sufism's ability to inspire and guide religious aspirations and to form wide networks across political and ethnic lines became instrumental in unifying a transnational Sunnī cultural identity.

Niẓām al-Mulk (d. 1092) considered Sufism vital to his project of organizing the Seljuk system of administration. Through a network of state-funded religious institutions, including the *khānqāh*, he facilitated a Sunnī consensus by defining a scope of pluralism within Sunnī thought and pursuing a policy of nonpartisanship toward the four Sunnī schools of jurisprudence. He enlisted Abū Ḥāmid al-Ghazālī (d. 1111) at the Niẓāmīyah College in Baghdad to articulate the project's epistemological paradigm. After experiencing a profound moral crisis, al-Ghazālī gave up his post for a period of solitude in pursuit of the Ṣūfī path. During this time he wrote *The Revival of the Religious Sciences*, setting out a comprehensive spiritual-intellectual paradigm that organized the whole range of religious disciplines, philosophy, and even the natural sciences within an orthodox Sunnī framework in the service of an ultimately Ṣūfī agenda of spiritual transformation. In this work he severely criticized religious scholars who served the political aims of corrupt princes. He warned against associating with the rulers of the time and even suggested a boycott of state-appointed judges. But he acknowledged the value of economic and political activity insofar as is necessary for establishing the conditions under which people can pursue the true purpose of life to which Ṣūfīs aspire. The moral and intellectual power of his work helped establish an enduring, global Sunnī cultural order. Sufism continued to enjoy Seljuk support, and Ṣūfī orders proliferated. ʿAbd al-Qādir al-Jīlānī (d. 1166), a powerful personality in Ṣūfī history, inspired the formation of the Qādirīyah order, which eventually spread to all corners of the Muslim world.

Al-Nāṣir li-Dīn Allāh (d. 1225), the last effective ʿAbbāsid caliph, was a *murīd* of ʿUmar al-Suhrawardī (d. 1234), himself a spiritual descendant of al-Jīlānī. The caliph attempted to use Sufism as a religio-political program to reestablish caliphal power. He was given the status of a Ṣūfī *shaykh* by al-Suhrawardī, and rulers in Egypt, Syria, and Anatolia accepted his invitation to become his disciples. In this way the Sunnī world in the east might have been politically reunified as virtually a Ṣūfī order had it not been cut short by the Mongol invasion. But the Suhrawardīyah order did live on in Central Asia, India, and Anatolia, and it was under the spell of Sufism that many of the Mongol conquerors later converted to Islam.

Another Ṣūfī order, the Naqshbandīyah, inspired by Bahāʾ al-Dīn Naqshband (d. 1389), associated with political power to great effect. Between the fourteenth and seventeenth centuries, Naqshbandīs cultivated relationships with centers of Timurid power in Central Asia, enjoying patronage and serving as mediators between the rulers and the people. Their political agenda was to bring rulers under their influence in order to unify and protect the Muslim community from oppression. Timurid rulers were *murīds* of Naqshbandī *shaykhs*, who sometimes took political positions. The Naqshbandīyah were marginalized in favor of the Chishtīyah by the Mughal emperor Akbar, who also presented himself as a Ṣūfī *shaykh* as part of an effort to unify his Muslim and Hindu subjects under an all-embracing state religion. In opposition to the effects of this project, the Naqshbandī Aḥmad al-Sirhindī (d. 1654), called the renewer (*mujaddid*) of the second millennium, set about to reestablish the identity of the Muslim community in India along Sunnī orthodox lines.

A wave of reform movements swept across the Muslim world in the eighteenth century. The Wahhābī movement reduced Sufism to its popular practices, such as visiting the graves of saints, labeling that an act of worship and thus effectively accusing many Muslims of idolatry. When Wahhābīs occupied Mecca and Medina at the beginning of the nineteenth century, they destroyed tombs and massacred people until their defeat by the Ottomans. New Ṣūfī orders also appeared at this time, describing themselves (as did the Wahhābīs) as a *ṭarīqah Muḥammadīyah*. They were concerned with revitalizing rather than destroying Sufism, sharing an emphasis on reaffirming the *sunnah*. There were objections to some popular excesses, including the veneration of saints, but views on their degree of continuity with or departure from older Ṣūfī orders differ.

Their effects were felt most profoundly on the geographic periphery of the Muslim world, especially in Africa, far from the centers of culture and power where the older Ṣūfī establishment was strong. After a waking vision in which he met the Prophet, in 1782 Aḥmad al-Tijānī founded the Tijānīyah order, which spread throughout Africa. Aḥmad Ibn Idrīs, a Moroccan Ṣūfī and founder of the Idrīsīyah order, defended Sufism from both the hostility of the Wahhābīs and the decadence of existing orders. Several of his disciples were influential in this period. Muḥammad ibn al-Sanūsī (d. 1859) founded the Sanusīyah as a network of self-sufficient communities integrated into the tribal structure of the remote regions of the Sahara. In India, a similar reform effort was inspired by Shāh Walī Allāh al-Dihlawī. Aḥmad Barelwī (d. 1831) claimed to have synthesized the "esoteric" elements of India's three dominant orders with a new exoteric element he also called *ṭarīqah Muḥammadīyah*, representing a renewed emphasis on *Sharīʿah*.

Political activity among Ṣūfīs on the Muslim periphery increasingly aimed at consolidating Islamic order and resisting colonial advances. The Qādirī *shaykh* Usuman Dan Fodio (d. 1817) established an Islamic state in West Africa. The Qādirī emir ʿAbd al-Qādir fought the French in Algeria for fifteen years before he was imprisoned in France and later exiled to Damascus. Under ʿUmar al-Mukhtār, the Sanusīyah were vital in the Libyan resistance to Italian occupation. And under Imām Shāmil, the Naqshbandīyah fought the Russians in the North Caucasus. With their foothold in China since the sixteenth century, they were also involved in a series of nineteenth-century anti-Qing revolts there. In the Malay Archipelago, notably Aceh and Singapore, Ṣūfī networks engaged in continuous intrigue against Dutch and British colonial administrators.

As it became more vigorous in the Muslim periphery, Sufism came under concerted attack in the center. Wahhābīs accused Sufism of idolatry and innovation (*bidʿah*). For the modernist Salafī movement, the *bidʿah* issue doubled as an apologetic for the inherent modernity of Islam, held back only by "foreign" Ṣūfī ideas. In Turkey, Egypt, and the Levant, where relations between political authority and various Ṣūfī orders had become thick and complex, governments found themselves defending against some Ṣūfī groups or trying to bring them under control while depending on others for legitimation and influence in return for legitimation and influence going the other way. Thus, for anyone looking for the cause of the "ailment" of Muslim society, there were Ṣūfīs well-positioned to take the blame.

Atatürk abolished the Ṣūfī orders in Turkey in 1925. In the Wahhābī-dominated Arabian Peninsula they were largely destroyed or driven underground. In other places, such as Egypt, Ṣūfī orders were either brought under centralized government control or remained outside the law. This meant that proponents of government-inspired reform efforts could blame Sufism for obstruction, while antigovernment reformists (e.g., Salafī Islamists) could label Ṣūfīs as tools or enablers of corrupt dictators.

With the perceived failure of Arab nationalism and the resurgence of Islamic movements, Sufism is being remarketed as a counter to extremism. But this has appealed to divergent political sensibilities. In Western democracies, where Sufism has gained some following, it represents a more palatable, socially acceptable Islam than the picture of tyranny and terrorism presented in Western media. But an oppressive regime hoping that the influence of a cooperative Ṣūfī order will dissuade the public from organized political activity operates under a decidedly less liberal moral paradigm. The Arab Spring's more assertive demand for democracy and human rights makes this tension more explicit. While some Ṣūfī figures lent their support and advice to the uprisings, others backed the entrenched regimes. Though motivated to no small degree by fear of their Islamist enemies, these followed Sunnī historical precedent in opposing resistance to the established order except under very limited circumstances. Ṣūfīs who embraced the revolutions are in the process of developing an unprecedented relationship to power under a regionally unprecedented framework of political legitimacy. The future political role of Sufism will turn on the course of current changes in the Middle East and how Ṣūfī leaders and constituencies respond.

BIBLIOGRAPHY

Black, Antony. *The History of Islamic Political Thought: From the Prophet to the Present*. Edinburgh: Edinburgh University Press, 2001.

Buehler, Arthur F. *Sufi Heirs of the Prophet: The Indian Naqshbandiyya and the Rise of the Mediating Sufi Shaykh*. Columbia: University of South Carolina Press, 1998.

de Jong, F. *Ṭuruq and Ṭuruq-Linked Institutions in Nineteenth-Century Egypt: A Historical Study in Organizational Dimensions of Islamic Mysticism*. Leiden: E. J. Brill, 1978.

Gilsenan, Michael. *Saint and Sufi in Modern Egypt: An Essay in the Sociology of Religion*. Oxford: Clarendon, 1973.

Heck, Paul. "The Politics of Sufism: Is There One?" In *Sufism Today: Heritage and Tradition in the Global Community*, edited by Catherina Raudvere and Leif Stenberg, pp. 13–30. London: I. B. Tauris, 2009.

Johansen, J. E. A., and Mohammad Talib. "Sufism and Politics." In *The Oxford Encyclopedia of the Modern Islamic World*, edited by John L. Esposito. New York: Oxford University Press, 1995.

Rahman, Fazlur. "Revival and Reform in Islam." In *The Cambridge History of Islam*, edited by P. M. Holt, Ann K. S. Lambton, and Bernard Lewis, vol. 2, pp. 632–656. Cambridge, U.K.: Cambridge University Press, 1970.

Trimingham, J. Spencer. *The Sufi Orders in Islam*. Oxford: Clarendon, 1971.

van Bruinessen, Martin. "Sufism, 'Popular' Islam, and the Encounter with Modernity." In *Islam and Modernity: Key Issues and Debates*, edited by Muhammad Khalid Masud, Armando Salvatore, and Martin van Bruinessen, pp. 125–157. Edinburgh: Edinburgh University Press, 2009.

Voll, John O., and Kazuo Ohtsuka. "Sufism." In *The Oxford Encyclopedia of the Islamic World. Oxford Islamic Studies Online*. http://www.oxfordislamicstudies.com/article/opr/t236/e0759.

Wright, Zachary Valentine. *On the Path of the Prophet: Shaykh Ahmad Tijani (1737–1815) and the Tariqa Muhammadiyya*. Atlanta, Ga.: African-American Islamic Institute, 2005.

EDWARD MOAD

SUICIDE BOMBING. *See* Martyrdom.

SUNNA. *See* Sunni Schools of Jurisprudence.

SUWARI, AL-HAJJ SALIM. A prominent Muslim intellectual who lived under the Songhay Empire in the Middle Niger region in the first half of the sixteenth century. He made the pilgrimage to Mecca no less than seven times, according to oral tradition; this was extraordinary, because the journey to the Holy Lands was long and arduous. Suwari was renowned for his piety and learning. Tradition puts his early life in the old town of Ja (sometimes written Diakha or Zagha), in the inland delta of the Niger (the region of Masina), and his later life in Jahaba (also written Diakhaba) in Bambuhu or Bambuk, the eastern part of today's Senegambia. His linguistic affiliation was with the Soninke, an ethnic group with a strong and early identification with Islam in West Africa.

Suwari was a distinguished teacher and writer, but his writings are not extant. He lived at a time when Islam was practiced mainly by merchants and scholars in the main cities of the Sahel or western Sudan and, to some degree, by royal families. Islam was still a minority religion among the diverse practices of ethnic groups such as the Soninke, Songhay, Mandinka, Fulbe, and others. Suwari consequently focused his teaching on the dilemma of the Muslim who lived among people who did not share the faith or shared it in very limited ways. He built a pedagogical tradition around the study of three major works. The most important was the *Tafsīr al-Jalālayn* of Jalāl al-Dīn Maḥallī, which he probably acquired from the Egyptian scholar Jalāl al-Dīn al-Suyūṭī during one of his pilgrimages. The other was the *al-Muwaṭṭa'* of Imam Mālik ibn Anas and *al-Shifa' bi-al-ta'rif ḥuqūq al-Muṣṭafā* by Qāḍī 'Iyad ibn Mūsā.

Suwari's teaching was transmitted across generations of teachers and Muslims, and is particularly strong among the Jahanke, clerics and practitioners in the Futa Jalon and eastern Senegambia, and the Juula, Muslim merchants who are best known for their settlements and trading connections in the southern (forested) portions of today's West Africa, and especially in today's Ghana and Ivory Coast. His guidance for Muslims living in non-Muslim societies became more pertinent in the south, while his own Sahel region moved increasingly toward Muslim majorities and some Islamic states in recent centuries.

In his works Suwari drew upon North African and Middle Eastern jurists and theologians who had reflected upon the situations of Muslims living among non-Muslim majorities, situations that were frequent in the centuries of Islamic expansion. According to this understanding, Muslims must nurture their own learning and piety, and thereby furnish good examples to the non-Muslims who lived around them. They could accept the jurisdiction of non-Muslim authorities, as long as they had the necessary protection and conditions to practice their faith. Suwari followed a strong predilection in Islamic thought for any government, albeit non-Muslim or tyrannical, as opposed to none. The military jihād was a resort only if the faithful were threatened. Suwari esteemed that God would bring non-Muslims to convert in His own time, and that it was not the responsibility of the Muslim minorities to decide when ignorance or unbelief would give way to faith. This tradition was widely practiced in the years before African rulers gave way to British and French authorities and colonial rule during the late nineteenth century.

BIBLIOGRAPHY

Robinson, David. *Muslim Societies in African History*. Cambridge, U.K., and New York: Cambridge University Press, 2004.

Sanneh, Lamin O. *The Jahanke: The History of Islamic Clerical People of the Senegambia*. London: International African Institute, 1979.

Wilks, Ivor. *Asante in the Nineteenth Century: The Structure and Evolution of a Political Order*. Cambridge, U.K., and New York: Cambridge University Press, 1975.

Wilks, Ivor. *Forests of Gold: Essays on the Akan and the Kingdom of the Asante*. Athens: Ohio University Press, 1993.

Wilks, Ivor. "The Juula and the Expansion of Islam into the Forest." In *The History of Islam in Africa*, edited by Nehemia Levtzion and Randall L. Pouwels. Athens: Ohio University Press, 2000.

Wilks, Ivor. "The Transmission of Islamic Learning in the Western Sudan." In *Literacy in Traditional Societies*, edited by Jack Goody. Cambridge, U.K.: Cambridge University Press, 1968.

DAVID ROBINSON

T

Tablīghī Jamāʿat. The Tablīghī Jamāʿat of the South Asian subcontinent is one of the most important grassroots Islamic movements in the Muslim world. From a modest beginning in 1926 with missionary (*daʿwah*) work in Mewat near Delhi under the leadership of the Islamic scholar Mawlānā Muḥammad Ilyās (1885–1944), the Tablīghī Jamāʿat today has an estimated 12 to 15 million followers throughout the Muslim world and in several Western countries. The Tablīghī Jamāʿat's international headquarters are located in the Nizamuddin West district of south Delhi, and has country headquarters in over two hundred countries. Its three major annual congregations (*ijtimāʿ*), held in India, Pakistan, and Bangladesh, are regularly attended by 1 to 2 million Muslims. Tablīghī elders claim that these meetings are the second largest religious congregation of the Muslim world, after the *ḥajj*.

The emergence of the Tablīghī Jamāʿat as a movement for the reawakening of faith and reaffirmation of Muslim religio-cultural identity can be seen as a continuation of the broader trend of Islamic revival in North India in the context of British colonial and cultural domination. One manifestation of this trend was the rapid growth of the *madāris* (*madrasah*s, religious educational institutions) that sought to reassert the authority of Islam and reconnect ordinary Muslims with Islamic institutions. The reformist intentions of the Tablīghī Jamāʿat, along with its pietistic and devotional aspects, owe their inspiration to South Asian Islamic thinkers and activists such as Shaykh Aḥmad Sirhindī (d. 1624), Shāh Walī Allāh (d. 1762), and the founder of the Mujāhidīn movement, Sayyid Aḥmad Shahīd (d. 1831). The Tablīghī Jamāʿat has been described as a reinvigorated form of Islamic orthodoxy and as a reformed Sufism. Since the 1930s its activities have been generally associated with the reformist teachings of the orthodox Deobandī seminary, which seeks to establish "true" Islam and correct Islamic practices according to its interpretation.

The appearance of the Tablīghī Jamāʿat was a direct response to the rise of Hindu proselytizing movements like the Shuddhi (Purification) and Sangathan (Consolidation), which launched massive efforts in the early twentieth century to "reclaim" Muslims whose ancestors had converted from Hinduism and retained some of its customs. Initially, the Tablīghīs were concerned with Mewat, a Gangetic plateau in North India inhabited by Rajput tribes known as Meos. Mawlānā Ilyās established a network of mosque-based religious schools to educate local Muslims about correct Islamic beliefs and practices. But he became disillusioned with this approach, realizing that these institutions produced "religious functionaries," not preachers. Mawlānā Ilyās resigned from his teaching position at in Saharanpur and moved to the old quarters of Delhi to begin his missionary work through itinerant preaching.

Physically frail and intellectually unassuming, Mawlānā Ilyās was not an outstanding religious scholar, public speaker, or charismatic leader. Yet he was persistent in what he described as "the mission of the prophets," calling people to "the path of God." He wanted to make Muslims better believers. For this purpose he organized units or groups of ten people and sent them to various localities to spread the mission of the Jamāʿāt.

The ideology of the Tablīghī Jamāʿāt is structured on six principles:

1. A Muslim must be able to recite the *shahādah* ("There is no God but Allāh and Muḥammad is His Prophet") in Arabic and know its meaning; this is interpreted as asserting the unity of God, rejecting all other deities, and emphasizing obedience to the Prophet Muḥammad.
2. A Muslim must learn how to say and perform the obligatory ritual prayer (*ṣalāt*) correctly and in accordance with its prescribed rituals; this emphasizes the external and internal submission by prostration before God in humility.
3. A Muslim must be knowledgeable about the fundamental beliefs and practices of Islam and perform ritual remembrance of God (*dhikr*) regularly.
4. Muslims should be respectful and polite toward fellow Muslims and show deference toward them. This idea of respect for Muslims (*ikrām-i Muslim*) is considered not only a religious obligation but also a basic prerequisite for effective *daʿwah* work. Included in this principle is an obligation to recognize and respect the rights of others with special emphasis on the elders, the young, the poor, neighbors, and even adversaries.
5. A Muslim must always be honest and sincere, with pure intention (*niyāt*). Everything is to be done for the sake of God and not for any worldly benefit.
6. A Muslim should spend time preaching with the Tablīghī groups.

During its formative days the new movement met with success and thousands of Muslims joined Mawlānā Ilyās to propagate the message of Islam throughout Mewat. Many new mosques and *madāris* were established. People began to observe the more formal obligatory rituals of Islam. The most visible change was in dress and in the customs associated with birth, marriage, and burial rituals. By the time Mawlānā Ilyās died in 1944, Mewat had come to be seen as a symbol of this new approach to Islamic preaching. The Jamāʿat then extended its activities into other parts of India. Since the Tablīghī method of preaching did not require any degree of religious scholarship, formal training, or lengthy preparation, everyone who joined the Jamāʿat became an instant preacher (on the basis of his familiarity with the six simple principles of *daʿwah*). Thus the number of itinerant preachers multiplied quickly, and the Jamāʿat was able to send its Tablīghī missions all over northern India, from the Northwest Frontier Province to East Bengal.

After the death of Mawlānā Ilyās, his son Mawlānā Yūsuf was selected by the elders of the Jamāʿat as his successor. Mawlānā Yūsuf was a strong organizer and an untiring worker. He extended the movement's operations beyond the northern provinces and mobilized thousands of groups to tour all over India. It was during his tenure that the Jamāʿat's activities reached Southeast Asia, the Middle East, Africa, Europe, and North America. After Mawlānā Yūsuf's death in 1965 and until 1995, Mawlānā Inʿāmul Ḥasan led the movement; under his leadership the movement expanded further, consolidated its international operations, and established independent national organizations in many countries.

The Tablīghī Jamāʿat can now be considered part of the Muslim mainstream. This development has spawned several consequences. Internally the movement developed a strong policy of leadership and guidance. In what used to be a highly egalitarian movement, the administration, although largely obscured from ordinary followers, has become more elaborate, bureaucratic, and hierarchical. Questioning the decisions and intentions of elders is strongly discouraged. Appointments of senior leaders and council members are submitted for approval to the headquarters in Delhi or to the Pakistan center in Raiwind.

The success of the Jamāʿat owes much to the dedicated missionary work of its members and followers, its simple message, and its direct, personal appeal to and contacts with individual Muslims. Younger followers have also delved into new media. Tablīghī leaders are reconciled with their speeches being widely distributed on cassettes and CDs. Enthusiasts discuss moral issues and organizational matters in internet forums, and provide related reading material at internet sites. Women have come to play an increasingly important role in the movement. They have developed their own format of preaching, which they do accompanied by a male guardian (*maḥram*).

In matters of religious beliefs and practices the Tablīghī Jamāʿat consistently follow the orthodox Deoband tradition and emphasize *taqlīd* (following the established schools of Islamic law) over *ijtihād* (independent reasoning). It rejects such popular expressions of religion as the veneration of saints, visiting shrines, and observing the syncretic rituals associated with popular Sufism. Jamāʿat workers are rigid in following orthodox rituals and practices and in observing the rules of the Sharīʿah. Like other Sunnī groups the Tablīghīs shun the members of sects seen as heretical, such as the Aḥmadīyah. As such, it has spread a much more orthodox interpretation of Islam—more consistent with Ḥanbalī practices (dominant in Arabia) than with Ḥanafī practices (historically dominant in South Asia)—than that traditionally adhered to in South Asia and elsewhere.

When the Tablīghī Jamāʿat was founded, its leaders sought to stay away from politics and political controversies. Mawlānā Ilyās believed that the Jamāʿat would not be able to achieve its goals if it got embroiled in partisan politics. The reform of individual Muslims was more important than reforming social and political institutions. His later years coincided with a great schism in Indian Muslim religious circles: most of the Deoband *ʿulamāʾ* opposed the idea of a separate homeland for Muslims and supported the All-India National Congress in calling for a united India; other *ʿulamāʾ* joined the Muslim League in its demand for Pakistan. Mawlānā Ilyās asked his followers not to take sides with either camp and to continue their essentially nonpolitical *daʿwah* work among Muslims of all political persuasions.

Tablīghī elders have tried to maintain this nonpolitical posture, but the Jamāʿat's involvement in politics has become ambiguous. While the Jamāʿat's leaders have refused to take public positions on political issues, they have allowed politics to seep into the movement. It is widely perceived today that much funding for the movement now comes from Saudi Arabia, which results in a distinct doctrinaire message but a political one as well.

[*See also* Aḥmadīyah.]

BIBLIOGRAPHY

Aḥmad, Mumtāz. "Islamic Fundamentalism in South Asia: The Jamaat-i-Islami and the Tablighi Jamaat." In *Fundamentalisms Observed*, edited by Martin E. Marty and R. Scott Appleby, pp. 457–530. Chicago: University of Chicago Press, 1991.

Masud, Muhammad Khalid, ed. *Travellers in Faith: Studies of the Tablīghī Jamāʿat as a Transnational Islamic Movement for Faith Renewal*. Leiden: Brill, 2000.

Reetz, Dietrich. "Sufi Spirituality Fires Reformist Zeal: The Tablīghī Jamāʿat in Today's India and Pakistan." *Archives de Sciences Sociales des Religions* 51, no. 135 (2006): 33.

Sikkand, Yōgīndar. *The Origins and Development of the Tablīghī Jamāʿat, 1920–2000: A Cross-Country Comparative Study*. Hyderabad: Orient Longman, 2002.

DIETRICH REETZ
Original article by MUMTAZ AHMAD
Updated by FARAH JAN

TAGHUT. *See* Tyranny.

ṬĀHĀ, MAḤMŪD MUḤAMMAD. (1909–1985), one of the central figures of Sudanese Islam during the twentieth century. Ṭāhā's approach to Islamic reform is a synthesis of republican-liberal-socialist ideas and Ṣūfī interpretations of law and Muslim traditions. He transformed the secular Republican Party into a radical Ṣūfī reformist movement under the name of the Republican Brothers. Though he lived an ascetic life, he adopted very progressive ideas about Islam, society, and politics. As a political activist, he struggled for human rights, secularism, democracy, women's empowerment, and religious pluralism. His critical hermeneutics of the Qurʾān and Islamic law led him to confrontation with conservatives, Islamists, and the military regime of Jaʿfar al-Numayrī. A law of apostasy adopted by the latter paved the way for his execution in 1985, making him the martyr of modern Sudan.

During his life, Ṭāhā was involved in major turning points of modern Sudanese history. In the years 1936–1956, he opposed British colonial rule and monarchism, founding the Republican Party in 1945. In 1955, he launched a campaign for a constitution in which he called for a presidential, federal, democratic, and socialist republic of Sudan. After independence and until his execution, he opposed the increasing militarization and Islamization of Sudan. His resistance to al-Numayrī was his last struggle in a life of risk-taking.

His clash with other Islamist groups and with traditional Islamic elements in Sudan became evident in 1960 when he published his book *Islam*. His neo-mystic interpretation of Islam, with liberal and socialist connotations, made him a dissident. Although some of his insights are deeply developed, most of his statements are written in a more cursory, popular style. Generally speaking, he does not use consistent arguments or rely on mainstream medieval interpretations of Islamic sources. For example, he states that the *sunnah* of the Prophet Muḥammad is limited to his actions and statements of a purely personal nature. It does not include the Prophet's public teachings and actions, which should be considered Sharīʿah. Ṭāhā's combination of the unity of existence (between material environment and human morals) and equality appear to be central in his early writings. He often defends universal values (freedom, equity, etc.), but he does not provide any solid rationalization or argumentation for his claims.

Ṭāhā's most systematic ideas can be found in *The Second Message of Islam*. In this book, he distinguishes between a legal, dogmatic, and historical Islam (the first message), which developed from the fixation of the *ʿulamāʾ* on the Medinan period of the Prophet's life, and a spiritual, scientific, and universal Islam (the second message), which he sees as the essence of the Islam preached by Muḥammad during the first part of his mission, the lengthy Meccan period. This allows him to reinterpret Islamic teachings in theology and ethics. He states that "in Islam, the individual is the end. Everyting else, including the Qurʾān and the religion of Islam itself, are means to that end."

(Taha, 1996, p. 62) Thus, free will is seen as a premise for human rights and democracy. Conversely, he advocates socialism and justice in sharing resources. Ṭāhā also supported pacifism and rejected the assertion that *jihād* (in the sense of a holy war) is foundational in Islam. Likewise, he discarded polygamy, established gender equity, and called for the protection of women's rights in divorce. His final purpose was to remove all boundaries between classes and genders and to achieve absolute social equality. Thus, he has been described as a utopian, liberal, republican, progressive, spiritualist, neo-Ṣūfī, dissident, and feminist thinker.

Ṭāhā's political and intellectual impact during his life was limited to his followers among students and intellectuals in Sudan. However, after his death, his ideas became widely known and read throughout the Muslim world. His critical interpretation of Islamic law, particularly his criticism of how Sharīʿah is understood and implemented, is a major reason for his popularity. His idea of using Islam as a liberating religion has inspired a number of progressive Muslim intellectuals (such as Abdullahi Ahmed An-Naʿim). His open vision toward non-Muslims also has inspired inter-religious relations based on norms of equal citizenship, and his hermeneutics have influenced critical thinkers such as the Syrian intellectual Muḥammad Shahrour. Ṭāhā's devotion, courage of conviction, and martyrdom are still relevant and challenge Islamist calls to implement Sharīʿah.

BIBLIOGRAPHY

Mahmoud, Mohamed. *Quest for Divinity: A Critical Examination of the Thought of Mahmud Muhammad Taha*. Syracuse, N.Y.: Syracuse University Press, 2007.

Taha, Mahmoud Mohamed. *The Second Message of Islam*. Edited and translated by Abdullahi Ahmed An-Naʿim. Syracuse, N.Y.: Syracuse University Press, 1996.

ABDESSAMAD BELHAJ

TAKAFUL. *See* Islamic Finance.

TAL, ʿUMAR IBN SAʿĪD. (c. 1797–1864), prominent West African writer and Tijānī leader. ʿUmar ibn Saʿīd Tal, or al-Ḥājj ʿUmar, as he is often called, exerted a profound influence on the spread of Islam and one of the Ṣūfī orders—the Tijānīyah—across a broad swath of West Africa in the nineteenth century. Through his writings, charisma, and military achievements, as well as through his descendants, he remains a prominent figure for Muslims in Senegal, Guinea, Mali, and other parts of West Africa.

ʿUmar was born in the late 1790s (1794 and 1797 are most frequently used) in the middle valley of the Senegal River, near the town of Podor. He was the son of a local cleric and teacher in a Muslim society dominated by the Fulbe (Fulani) people, who played a leading role in the spread of Islam across West Africa in the eighteenth and nineteenth centuries. These particular Fulbe often go by the name of Tokolor, which is probably derived from Takrūr, the name that Arab geographers gave to a Muslim state in the middle valley in the eleventh century. The people prefer to call themselves Haal Pulaar, "speakers of Pulaar" or Fulfulde, the language of the Fulbe. In the late eighteenth century, these Haal Pulaar created an Islamic state to which they gave the name Almamate (derived from *imām*, the "one who stands in front" and leads in prayer).

ʿUmar showed a strong aptitude for learning as he pursued a curriculum in the conventional peripatetic pattern. In addition to his studies in Islamic law, theology, and literature, he accepted initiation into the Tijānīyah Ṣūfī brotherhood, which had begun in Algeria and Morocco in the late eighteenth century, under Aḥmad al-Tijānī. ʿUmar then performed the pilgrimage to Mecca and Medina, a feat that had to be accomplished overland and was extremely rare for West Africans at the time.

He fulfilled this Muslim obligation in three successive years, 1828–1830. During this time, he apprenticed himself to the leading Tijānīyah authority in the Holy Lands, Muḥammad al-Ghali, and he emerged with an appointment as the *khalīfah* (deputy) of the order, charged with spreading it in West Africa.

During his journey to and from Mecca, ʿUmar spent significant time in most of the main Muslim centers of West Africa, particularly in the areas where Fulbe Muslims had taken power through the military *jihād*: the Almamate of Futa Jallon, the Caliphate of Hamdullahi or Masina, and the Sokoto Caliphate. On his return journey, as pilgrim and *khalīfah*, he enjoyed great prestige and formed communities of Tijānīyah that survive to this day. In Sokoto and other parts of Nigeria, he acquired the wives who formed a kind of instant lineage of Tal by the mid-nineteenth century. He spent at least five years in the 1830s in Sokoto during the reign of Muḥammad Bello, and he obtained considerable military and political experience while he was there.

ʿUmar spent the 1840s in Futa Jallon developing a loyal group of disciples and writing his major work, *al-Rimāḥ*, or *Kitāb Rimāḥ Ḥizb al-Rahīm ʿala Nuhūr Ḥizb al-Rajīm*, an important resource for Tijānīyah today and the main source of information on his pilgrimage.

Between 1852 and his death in 1864 ʿUmar enlisted his disciples and many other Muslims in a *jihād* against several predominantly non-Muslim kingdoms in the upper Senegal and middle Niger river valleys. Most of the recruits were Fulbe from the area of Futa Jallon, Futa Toro, and Senegambia; most of his opponents were Mandinka and, especially, Bambara living in the western part of present-day Mali. His greatest triumph was the defeat of the formidable Bambara kingdom of Segu in 1861. In the late 1850s, he also fought against the French expansion in Senegal led by Governor Louis Faidherbe.

In 1862, ʿUmar went beyond his mission of destroying "paganism" when he issued an ultimatum to Hamdullahi to cease its support of the Bambara regime of Segu and hand over its refugee king. He conquered this Fulbe Muslim regime, but its inhabitants soon joined forces with the influential Timbuktu cleric Aḥmad al-Bakkāʾī, overturned the new regime, and brought ʿUmar's life to an end in 1864 in the cliffs of Degembere.

ʿUmar has left his imprint on the societies of Senegal, Guinea, and Mali in particular. His works, especially *al-Rimāḥ*, are widely used in Tijānīyah teaching. Many of his descendants are well placed in the elite political and religious classes today. By the Senegalese, he is remembered as a hero of Islamic expansion and resistance to the French, while many Malians see him as an invader who destroyed indigenous states and weakened their social structures.

BIBLIOGRAPHY

Ly-Tall, Madina. *Un Islam militant en Afrique de l'Ouest au XIXe siècle.* Paris: Éditions l'Harmattan, 1991.

Robinson, David. *The Holy War of Umar Tal: The Western Sudan in the Mid-Nineteenth Century.* Oxford: Oxford University Press, 1985.

DAVID ROBINSON

TALIBAN. The Taliban, an Afghan Islamic militia movement that coalesced in 1994 amid the civil war that followed the Soviet withdrawal (1989), grew to control most of Afghanistan's major cities and provinces. Ruling until 2001, they have been described as the product of a society at war for over twenty years during which 1.5 million people were killed and the country devastated.

The English word "Taliban" is from the Pashto *tālibān* (students), which comes in turn from the Arabic *ṭālib* (student): many of the early recruits into the movement were Afghan refugee students at Islamic religious schools in Pakistan.

The Taliban's State-Building Project, 1994–2001. The 1978–1992 *jihād* against a communist government and Soviet intervention occasioned a general mobilization of Afghan society. In the *jihād* around the southern city of Kandahār several fronts operated which mainly recruited religious students and young clerics as fighters. After the collapse of the communist government in 1992 most of these clerical veterans of the *jihād* stood aloof from the chaotic new provincial administration that the other *mujāhidīn* established in Kandahār (Linschoten, 2012). Growing discontent with prevailing insecurity prompted the clerical veterans in Kandahār to launch a movement, which rapidly became known as the Taliban. The Taliban launched their campaign in 1994 with a series of attacks on roadside checkpoints. Harassment of wayfarers at these posts by former *mujāhidīn* fighters had come to epitomize the anarchy prevailing in southern Afghanistan. The first administrative center captured by the Taliban, in October 1994, was Spin Boldak, close to the Afghan-Pakistan border. Shortly thereafter, the Taliban seized Kandahār, Afghanistan's second-largest city. This was followed by assaults on Herāt in March 1995, and in September Herāt fell to the Taliban. After a ten-month siege and bombardment of Kabul, the capital city fell on 26 September 1996.

During their period in power, from the capture of Kabul to 2001, the Taliban referred to their political system as the Islamic Emirate of Afghanistan. Shortly before the siege of Kabul in April 1996, the movement's supreme leader, Mullah Muhammad Omar Akhund, claimed the caliphal title of Amīr al-Muʾminīn (commander of the faithful). To signify the religious dimension of the movement, he appeared in public on one occasion wearing a relic considered by Afghan Pashtuns to be the cloak of the Prophet Muḥammad.

The Taliban in power retained the basic structure of the Afghan state. Mullah Omar, based in Kandahār, exercised many of the powers of an Afghan president. A council of ministers, based in Kabul, ran the administration. The Taliban did not adopt a constitution, but, through a series of decrees developed under the supervision of Justice Minister Nuruddin Turabi, they embarked upon an ambitious program of legislation for the Islamization of state and society. One of the most practical changes that they introduced was an expansion of the role of the clergy, as they appointed clerics associated with the movement to most senior government positions.

Human Rights Watch and others have documented massive violations of human rights under the rule of the Taliban. Among these was the killing of civilians and noncombatants in the northern city of Mazār-i Sharīf. In August 1998, the Taliban attacked the city and its Hazāra Shīʿī minority, killing an estimated two thousand civilians. On 8 January 2001, in Yakaolang, approximately 170 Hazāra Shīʿī were massacred by the Taliban.

Pakistan recognized the Taliban regime on 25 May 1997, and Saudi Arabia and the United Arab Emirates did so a year later. There was initially also limited Western political support for the Taliban, as some U.S. diplomats believed that the Taliban would bring peace to a country wracked by internecine violence.

In March 2001, the Taliban destroyed the Buddhist statues at Bāmiān, despite intense worldwide opposition. The regime also ordered the smashing of other ancient sculptures in the country's museums, claiming statues were idols. In May 2001, it was decreed that the few Hindus residing in Kabul should wear an identifying yellow patch.

The Taliban after the International Intervention. In the aftermath of al-Qaʿida's 9/11 attacks against New York and Washington, the

Taliban regime was attacked militarily by the United States. On 7 October 2001, the United States launched Operation Enduring Freedom with a massive aerial bombardment of Taliban and al-Qaʿida infrastructure. Under intense bombing by the United States and a ground assault by Northern Alliance fighters, the Taliban collapsed almost immediately.

For over a year after the international intervention in Afghanistan it appeared as if the Taliban would no longer be a major factor in Afghan politics. There was no Taliban participation in the November 2001 Bonn Conference or the new government that the conference helped establish. However, those members of the leadership who escaped arrest relocated to Pakistan, and by 2003 they had decided to organize armed resistance to the new Afghan authorities and the NATO forces. The Taliban movement was by far the largest component of the decade-long insurgency that NATO faced during its presence in Afghanistan.

Taliban members referred to a "new movement" to stress the contrast between their organization before and after the international intervention. By 2013, although some of the original companions of founder Mullah Omar remained active, the bulk of the Taliban fighting forces consisted of young men whose whole adult experience consisted of the fight against NATO and who had no experience of the Taliban's period in power. The new movement was more clandestine and depended on a tight chain of command where every Talib was expected to obey his immediate *amīr*, or "leader," unquestioningly. The Taliban established a countrywide shadow administration, appointing district and provincial governors and judges. In areas where the Taliban achieved military influence, some of the population looked to them to adjudicate property issues and other disputes in rural life.

The new movement was noticeably more media-savvy than the Taliban had been while in government. Former education minister Amir Khan Motaki headed a "Cultural Commission" that used spokesmen, press statements, propaganda videos, websites, online magazines, and social media. The Taliban's communications effort sought to portray the movement as engaged in legitimate resistance to foreign occupation, an approach that helped the Taliban in their attempt to broaden their base of support.

The Taliban military rapidly adapted to the challenge of fighting a stronger enemy by adopting techniques of unconventional warfare. To this end they used assassinations, built up expertise in the use of improvised explosive devices (IEDs), and developed the use of suicide bombers, including in *fidāʾyūn* operations, in which multiple fighters mounted suicide attacks on high-profile government targets. The Taliban managed to sustain the tempo of their operations even in the face of a U.S. military surge from 2010. This led the Kabul-based Afghan political leadership and NATO to conclude that complete military defeat of the Taliban was impossible.

The Taliban's new movement after 2001 continued to style itself the Islamic Emirate of Afghanistan and its leader Mullah Omar as the Amīr al-Muʾminīn. A leadership council, popularly known as the Quetta Shura, ran the movement and its military campaign. As a sequel to the legislative decrees of the 1990s, the new movement adopted a *lahya* (rule book) to define the roles and responsibilities of fighters and officials. Obedience to the *amīr* continued to be the Taliban's main operating principle, but after about 2009, the lack of authenticated communication with the supreme leader posed an increasing challenge to the legitimacy of the leadership council.

The Ideology of the Taliban. The genealogy of the movement can be traced to the anti-Soviet *jihād* in Afghanistan and to Afghan refugee camps in neighboring Pakistan. The political scientist

William Maley suggests that their values were "not the values of the village, but the values of the village as interpreted by refugee camp dwellers or madrassa students who typically had not known normal village life," and moreover, a worldview that "conspicuously omitted the pragmatic moderation which historically had muted the application of tribal and religious codes in Afghan society" (Maley, 2002, p. 223).

The Taliban movement, drawn primarily from Pashtun tribes, professes an Islamic ideology, but Pashtun ethnicity played a role in the Taliban's chauvinism and in the construction of ideological boundaries between it and the country's non-Pashtun ethnic groups such as Tajiks, Hazāras, and Uzbeks. Pashtunwali, the Pashtun tribal code, informs the Taliban's highly traditional and patriarchal interpretation of Islamic ideology.

The avowed goal of the Taliban is to implement a pure Islamic state that has extirpated foreign influences deemed to be un-Islamic. The Taliban's primary religious and ideological influence is a form of Deobandī Islam. This particular Deobandī understanding of Islam is derived largely from the Jamʿīyatul ʿUlamāʾ-i Islām (JUI) in Pakistan.

In the 1980s, the JUI had established hundreds of religious seminaries in Pakistan's North-West Frontier Province (NWFP) and Baluchistan, where Afghan refugees were offered a free education alongside Pakistanis. With a lack of centralized religious authority, numerous JUI factions emerged, the most prominent of which was that led by Samīul Ḥaq.

Ḥaq's principal *madrasah* is the Darul Uloom Haqania, which is located in Akora Khattak, in the NWFP. Haqania trained eight cabinet ministers of the previous Taliban regime. Ḥaq has also recruited Pakistani students from Haqqania to fight for the Taliban. During one Taliban military campaign in 1997, the entire student body was sent to join the militia.

Shortly after taking Kabul, the Taliban enforced the most drastic interpretation of Sharīʿah law ever seen. Among the more controversial acts of the Taliban were bans on all music, movies, television, women's magazines, pigeon keeping, and kite flying. Women were not to wash clothes in streams. Tailors were not to take measurements of females. Men were to grow beards, and Western-style haircuts were forbidden. Dancing and singing, common at Afghan wedding celebrations, were proscribed. Television sets, radios, cassettes, and photographs were destroyed.

Taliban and Women. The Taliban's treatment of women provoked an international outcry. They rigorously enforced a rule that women had to wear a garment called a *chadari* (*chādor*) or burqa, which covered them from head to toe.

The Taliban's religious police (Ministry for the Enforcement of Virtue and Suppression of Vice) banned girls from going to school and women from working. According to one estimate, the Taliban, after capturing Kabul, shut down sixty-three schools, affecting 103,000 girls and 148,000 boys. Illiteracy, a grave problem in Afghan society, was made worse. The most pronounced effects were on women in urban areas, such as Kabul, Herāt, and Mazār-i Sharīf, where women were most involved in education and enforcement of the ban was most rigorous.

The Taliban issued a series of decrees forbidding women to work outside their homes and prohibiting them from traveling except when accompanied by a male family member. It is estimated that 40,000–150,000 working women in Kabul alone were negatively affected by the prohibition. The Taliban later issued decrees requiring separate hospitals for women and men. Women were supposed to be examined by male physicians only when a male family member was present. Women without a male family member, and especially war widows, faced onerous obstacles to health care. Many war widows—an estimated fifty thousand in Kabul alone—were reduced to dependence on United Nations assistance or begging in order to provide for their children. Women who did not comply with these policies faced threats, harassment, and beatings.

The Taliban and International Terror. One of the main controversies surrounding the Taliban movement has been its relationship with al-Qaʿida and other groups involved in international terrorism. In power, the Taliban sheltered the Saudi radical Osama Bin Laden and his followers who had been in Jalālābād since May 1996. Capitalizing on his financial support, Osama Bin Laden increasingly gained influence over Taliban leader Mullah Omar, and militants from across the Muslim world congregated in Taliban Afghanistan.

The movement's leadership has repeatedly declared itself to be committed only to achieving objectives within Afghanistan, but in both the pre- and post-2001 periods, the Afghan Taliban cooperated closely with al-Qaʿida, regional terrorist groups such as the Islamic Movement of Uzbekistan (IMU) and Pakistani terrorist groups such as Lashkar-i Tayyiba and Lashkar-i Jhangvi. During their period in power in Afghanistan the Taliban drew up to 30 percent of their army from these Pakistani groups, plus eight to fifteen thousand other foreign fighters. They incorporated the fighters into their army and deployed them in their campaigns against the anti-Taliban resistance. During their period of insurgency against the post-2001 government, militants from these organizations joined the fighting, conducted military training, and supplied some of the movement's funding. Since 2000 the Taliban movement has been under a regime of United Nations Security Council sanctions in response to the movement's foreign terror links. The primary rationale given by the United States for its involvement in Afghanistan since 2001 has been the campaign against international terrorism rather than objections to the Taliban's treatment of the Afghan population. Scholars have long debated whether the Taliban movement's dealings with international terrorist groups reflect a pragmatic need for backing in its campaigns or a more profound identification with the cause of international *jihād*.

Pakistan's Support for the Taliban. Support for the Taliban came from a variety of Pakistani institutions including the military, intelligence services, political leaders, and religio-political parties such as the JUI.

Pakistani clerics disseminated propaganda in favor of the Taliban and helped mobilize students of their *madrasahs* to go and join the movement. The clerics saw the Taliban's victory in Afghanistan as an opportunity to be involved in applying their ideas for Islamic state building. It is unsurprising therefore that when a coalition of religious parties came to power in Pakistan's North-West Frontier Province in 2002, they legislated similar measures to promote adherence to Islamic norms (but failed to achieve any fundamental transformation of society).

The Pakistani military's support for the Taliban was predicated on their desire to maintain what was called "strategic depth" and also to have a stake in the turbulent internecine Afghan conflicts roiling the country during the early 1990s. Support from the Pakistani military and intelligence apparatus was to prove vital to the success of the Taliban. The rapid expansion of the Taliban across southern Afghanistan in 1994 and 1995 prompted Pakistan to abandon its previously preferred proxy, Ḥizb-i Islāmī. The Pakistani military support operation was covert but probably included funding, military advice, and coercion of Taliban opponents. The issue of Pakistani support to the Taliban became even more controversial in the post-2001 period when the Taliban's ability to access "safe havens" in Pakistan was one of the key factors enabling them to mount such a successful insurgency in Afghanistan. From 2001 the United States put pressure on General Pervez Musharraf and subsequent Pakistani leaders to end support of the Taliban, but, throughout the NATO presence in Afghanistan, the Taliban leadership operated from inside Pakistan.

The Pakistani Taliban Movement. In 2007 several militant groups that had emerged in Pakistan along its frontier with Afghanistan merged and styled themselves the Pakistan Taliban Movement, or TTP. The TTP went on to wage a violent campaign against the Pakistani state and those in the population who refused to submit to Taliban authority. The TTP also targeted what it considered to be symbols of alien modernization, including schools and polio vaccination campaigns. One of its most infamous attacks was the 9 October 2012 assassination attempt on Malala Yousafzai, the young advocate of girls' education. The TTP espoused no sophisticated political agenda. It called for the Pakistan state to end its cooperation with the United States and support the cause of *jihād* in Afghanistan and elsewhere. Several of the founders of the TTP, such as Abdullah Mahsud and Baitullah Mahsud, had served as volunteers in the Afghan Taliban army before 2001, and they declared their loyalty to the Afghan Taliban supreme leader, Mullah Omar. However, the movements were separate and differed in their origin and approach. The TTP lacked the close association with the clergy that had characterized the Afghan movement. Whereas the Afghan movement instructed its members to avoid actions against the Pakistan security forces, the TTP directly challenged them. The border tribes from which the TTP has recruited have extensive migratory networks, with communities established in all major cities of Pakistan and in many places in the Gulf and wider Middle East. Since 2012 the TTP has expanded its presence in Karachi using these networks.

Another significant development in militancy within Pakistan has been the rapid increase in the scale of sectarian violence, especially targeting the Shīʿī community. For example, Human Rights Watch reported over four hundred Shīʿī dead in targeted attacks during 2012. Virulently anti-Shīʿī groups from the Punjab, including Lashkar-i Jhangvi, have conducted such killings. Although Punjabi militant groups did not formally join the TTP, some of them have been associated with the Afghan Taliban since 1998 and are suspected of participating in the movement's massacres of Shīʿī in Afghanistan. Those who have now established a presence alongside the Taliban in Waziristan are known locally as "Punjabi Taliban." The high rates of sectarian killings in Pakistan provide a potent example of blowback. Previous covert military support to the Afghan Taliban helped create the conditions in which *jihādī* groups such as Lashkar-i Jhangvi could thrive and launch campaigns in Pakistan.

The TTP's adoption of the term "Taliban" reflected a recognition of the way in which the Afghan movement had become associated with rigid enforcement of a conservative interpretation of Islamic norms and violent resistance to the Western powers. The term has gradually come to be used loosely, beyond the movement led by Mullah Omar, to describe those involved in militant puritanism and resistance to modernity. Similarly, Pakistani journalists have used the term "Talibanization" to refer to forcible Islamization.

[*See also* Bin Laden, Osama; Deobandīs; Mullah Omar; *and* Pakistan.]

BIBLIOGRAPHY

Ahmad, Eqbal. *The Selected Writings of Eqbal Ahmad.* Edited by Carollee Bengelsdorf, Margaret Cerullo, and Yogesh Chandrani. New York: Columbia University Press, 2006.

Bergen, Peter, ed. *Talibanistan: Negotiating the Borders between Terror, Politics, and Religion*. New York: Oxford University Press, 2013.
Clark, Kate. *The Layha: Calling the Taleban to Account*. Kabul: Afghanistan Analysts Network, 2011.
Crews, Robert D., and Amin Tarzi, eds. *The Taliban and the Crisis of Afghanistan*. Cambridge, Mass.: Harvard University Press, 2008.
Flood, Finbarr Barry. "Between Cult and Culture: Bamiyan, Islamic Iconoclasm, and the Museum." *Art Bulletin* 84, no. 4 (December 2002): 641–659.
Giustozzi, Antonio, ed. *Decoding the New Taliban: Insights from the Afghan Field*. New York: Columbia University Press, 2009.
Giustozzi, Antonio. *Koran, Kalashnikov, and Laptop: The Neo-Taliban Insurgency in Afghanistan*. London: Hurst, 2007.
Goodson, Larry. *Afghanistan's Endless War: State Failure, Regional Politics, and the Rise of the Taliban*. Seattle: University of Washington Press, 2001.
Gutman, Roy. *How We Missed the Story: Osama Bin Laden, the Taliban, and the Hijacking of Afghanistan*. Washington, D.C.: United States Institute of Peace Press, 2008.
Human Rights Watch. "The Crisis of Impunity: The Role of Pakistan, Russia and Iran in Fueling the Civil War." *Human Rights Watch Report* 13, no. 3(C), July 2001.
Hussain, Rizwan. *Pakistan and the Emergence of Islamic Militancy in Afghanistan*. Aldershot, U.K.: Ashgate, 2005.
Maley, William. *The Afghanistan Wars*. New York: Palgrave, 2002.
Nojumi, Neamatollah. *The Rise of the Taliban in Afghanistan: Mass Mobilization, Civil War, and the Future of the Region*. New York: Palgrave, 2002.
Rashid, Ahmed. *Descent into Chaos: The United States and the Failure of Nation Building in Pakistan, Afghanistan, and Central Asia*. New York: Viking, 2008.
Rashid, Ahmed. *Taliban: Militant Islam, Oil, and Fundamentalism in Central Asia*. New Haven, Conn.: Yale University Press, 2000.
Rubin, Barnett R. *The Fragmentation of Afghanistan: State Formation and Collapse in the International System*. 2d ed. New Haven, Conn.: Yale University Press, 2002.
Rubin, Barnett R. "Saving Afghanistan." *Foreign Affairs* (January/February 2007)): 57–78.
Semple, Michael. "The Revival of the Afghan Taliban 2001–2011." *Orient* 53, no. 2 (March 2012): 58–67.
Sinno, Abdulkader H. *Organizations at War in Afghanistan and Beyond*. Ithaca, N.Y.: Cornell University Press, 2008.
Strick van Linschoten, Alex, and Felix Kuehn. *An Enemy We Created: The Myth of the TalibanAl Qaeda Merger in Afghanistan, 1970–2010*. New York: Oxford University Press, 2012.

EMRAN QURESHI
and MICHAEL SEMPLE

TANZIMAT. The Turkish term Tanzimat (regulation) denotes a period of social and political reform intended to reorganize the Ottoman Empire starting in 1839. While the failed effort ended with the First Constitutional Era in 1876, it was nevertheless the goal of the Tanzimat to secure the empire's territorial integrity against nationalist movements. Although Ottoman leaders wished to create institutions deliberately copied from those of Western Europe, Tanzimat reforms encouraged the rise of Turkish nationalism as various attempts at integrating non-Muslims and non-Turks by enhancing civil liberties and granting equality clashed with Turkish interests. It is generally agreed that the period began with the proclamation of the quasi-constitutional Charter of Gülhane in 1839, but its end date is harder to determine. Still, the effort was slowed in 1877, when Sultan Abdülhamid II suspended the 1876 Ottoman Constitution, even as he continued elements of the Tanzimat's social programs. An equally valid end point was the granting of special privileges to Ottoman Christians in 1856, predominantly Armenians and Greeks, which overemphasized the importance of external pressures on a movement that was in fact driven by internal nationalist concerns.

The origins of the Tanzimat lie in the latter half of the eighteenth century, which saw successive efforts to modernize the Ottoman Empire, especially the modernization of the military and the establishment of a school of military engineering (1776–1794), which started a trend among the bureaucratic elite of imitating Western upper classes. After the first printing press in the empire was installed in 1729, and translations of Western scientific texts on medicine, botany, astronomy, and mathematics appeared throughout the rest of the century, an increasing appreciation of the material aspects of Western culture gained momentum among the elite. Although the ideas of the French Revolution, especially its quest for liberty, had little influence among Ottoman elites, they clearly affected the empire's Christian communities. In fact, the political theory that most noticeably underlay later Ottoman reforms was a variation on the idea of enlightened despotism known as cameralism.

Nevertheless, the reform movement was at once an attempt at modernization and an effort to prevent the disintegration of a multiethnic, multireligious empire by insisting it become something it could not possibly be. At the inception of the Tanzimat, the Ottoman Empire comprised, or at least effectively controlled, the present territories of Albania, northern and eastern Greece, Crete, Serbia, Bosnia, Bulgaria, Romania, Syria, Iraq, Jordan, Saudi Arabia, Egypt, and Libya and had loose ties with Tunisia.

Sultan Mahmud II (r. 1808–1839) had already linked these two goals of Ottoman policy in his efforts to quell rebellions by ambitious provincial dynasties such as the Kurdish Babans and by regional Ottoman notables such as Ali Pasha of Janina and Muḥammad ʿAlī of Egypt. On the advice of some of his younger councilors, in 1837 the sultan established two new bodies: an embryonic Council of Ministers (Dâr-i Şurâ-yı Bâb-ı Âli) and the Council of Judicial Ordinances (Meclis-i Vâlâ-yı Akam-ı Adliye). Indeed, the evolution of these bodies during the nineteenth century eventually led to the separation of the executive from the judiciary. (The Assembly of Provincial Notables that convened in Istanbul in 1845 did not, however, much affect the administration of the empire.)

The charter known as the 1839 Gülhane Rescript (named for the imperial garden where it was first proclaimed), was authored primarily by Minister of Foreign Affairs Mustafa Reşid Paşa, who wrote that it was "only intended to introduce a complete security of life, property and honor of individuals and regulate the internal and military expenditures of the Porte" (Mardin, 2000, p. 157). In fact, the Rescript was framed to protect the advantages of Ottoman bureaucrats who resented the sultan's power over them.

Foreign conflicts marked the first years of the Tanzimat period. The first was the attempt by Muḥammad ʿAlī to detach Egypt and Syria from the empire; this was resolved by a European-driven compromise in 1841 that left Muḥammad ʿAlī and his heirs in possession of Egypt but forced him out of Syria. The second was the Crimean War, which had complex origins involving Russian assertions of the right to protect Ottoman Orthodox Christians as well as the interests of European alliances. In 1856 Britain, France, and their allies forced Russia to accept preliminary peace terms.

In February 1856 the Ottoman government proclaimed the second important document of the Tanzimat, the Edict of Reforms (Islâhat Fermanı), which guaranteed under the law that Muslims and non-Muslims would have equal rights and obligations in regard to military service, the administration of justice, taxation, admission to educational institutions, and public employment. The edict revoked the civil powers formerly held by the heads of Christian congregations under the *millet* system, which had provided for the separate administration of certain minority communities. Instead, the churches were to be governed by a synod of clergy and a national council of laymen. These features, which were widely resented in both Muslim and Christian communities, were made public by the Ottomans in the days preceding the 1856 congress that convened in Paris and confirmed this engagement. The congress also resulted in Turkey's admission to the European alliance, which, at least nominally, guaranteed its territorial status.

The first generation of Tanzimat reformers, the supporters of Reşid Paşa, were succeeded by a second generation after 1856. The leading officials of the new era, Âli Paşa and Fuad Paşa, alternated in holding the highest offices and continued efforts to erode the sultan's powers and transfer them to the higher bureaucracy. They in turn were accused of autocratic malfeasance by a new movement, the Young Ottomans, who would eventually give rise to the Young Turks, who promoted constitutionalism and parliamentary government.

The Young Ottomans rose out of newly established institutions such as the Bureau of Translation and the Ministry of Foreign Affairs, where they had ongoing contact with Western institutions and publications. Most of their adherents came to adulthood during a period when a nascent Turkish journalism opened windows on current events and scientific advances in the West. The foundation for the movement was laid by the Istanbul journalist and bureaucrat İbrahim Şinasi, who founded the successful periodical *Tasvir-i Efkâr* (Herald of Ideas) in 1862, the first publication to address not merely the elite but a wider audience of readers from all classes. It and its successors subtly transformed Turkish opinion, preparing the way for the Young Ottomans to espouse lofty ideals of liberty and equality. That organization apparently originated in intellectual, primarily bureaucratic circles in the 1860s, with an inaugural meeting held in 1865 under the leadership of Mehmet Namık Kemal, a young official who was also a poet and a contributor to *Tasvir-i Efkâr*. The Young Ottomans later founded their own journal, *Hürriyet* (Liberty).

While bureaucratic reformers were interested in representative government, there was religious ferment among the *ʿulamāʾ*, who concluded that Tanzimat reforms undermined their role as social arbiters and that secular schools founded under the Tanzimat had a similar effect on their control of education. In particular, the *rüşdiye*, a primary and middle school on the Western model, gained popularity and replaced the traditional religious curriculum with such new subjects as arithmetic, geography, composition, and secular history, which, presumably, hampered the authority of the clergy. Unlike extended theological courses in *madrasahs* (Turk. *medrese*), more practically oriented forms of education became popular, which further alarmed the *ʿulamāʾ*, whose grievances were articulated by such luminaries as Ali Suavi, a seminarian with a bureaucratic career who preached at the Şehzade Mosque and who wrote for the journal *Muhbir*. He approached the Young Ottomans when he was forced to join some of their leaders in exile in Europe, but they found little common ground with Suavi, and the alliance was short-lived.

The core of the Young Ottomans was forced by the regime into exile in Europe, where the movement nearly disintegrated, even if the ideas of Namık Kemal appear, at least in retrospect, to be its most cogent and influential result. Both Enlightenment contractual theories and nineteenth-century European constitutional currents inspired Kemal. Whether out of respect for the ferment among the conservative *ʿulamāʾ* or out of a more general consciousness of the Islamic nature of Ottoman culture, Kemal combined his Western influences with an Islamic foundation. From the West he adopted the idea of a representative government—a novel concept in the Islamic world—but proposed that such a body be based on Islamic values. Also novel was the idea of Ottoman (Turkish) patriotism, which inspired some of Kemal's most trenchant articles and his most moving poems. There were serious practical obstacles to both of Kemal's innovations: he did not clarify how Islam was to inspire legislators, nor how Ottoman patriotism could take hold in an empire characterized by deep ethnic and religious divisions. Nevertheless, during his widely fluctuating career (he returned to Turkey and was alternately employed and jailed by the government) he appears to have had some influence in the process leading up the 1876 Ottoman Constitution.

The major factor leading to the 1876 constitution, however, was the general setting of the Tanzimat. It established a series of reforms that set the stage, notably the evolution of consultative and judicial bodies, the codification of civil law (the Mecelle) based on *şer'i* (Ar. *sharʿī*; religious) logic, the modernization of education, and the application of the Law on the Administration of the Provinces (1864–1871). Ironically, the Mecelle represented the only concession granted by the Tanzimat to religion, which hinted at a more sinister agenda for non-Muslim subjects. The Law on the Administration of the Provinces was based on the French administrative system; it rationalized central administration by dividing the empire into *vilâyets* (departments) and sub-*vilâyets* (*kaza*). Mithat Paşa, the Ottoman governor of the Danube province, furthered this legislation by strengthening government in the provinces at the same time as he expanded local representative institutions.

The 1876 revolutionary movement originated among Islamic seminary students, who protested the submissive policies of Grand Vizier Mahmud Nedim toward Russia. These agitations enabled a group of ministers, including Minister of Military Education Süleyman Paşa, to depose Sultan Abdülaziz and enthrone Prince Murād, who was known to support more liberal ideas. When it became obvious that Murād V was mentally incompetent, the young Prince Abdülhamid was installed as Sultan Abdülhamid II (r. 1876–1909).

With the empire facing dual crises of war with Russia and massive foreign debt, a committee was formed to work on a draft constitution. It included Mithat Paşa, now grand vizier, as well as leading Young Ottomans and members of the deposing junta. Working quickly under pressures from the war and Western creditor nations, they proclaimed the Ottoman Constitution on 3 December 1876. Constantinople was finally endowed with a duly constituted parliament, whose multiethnic membership met and debated openly for five months in 1877, which, not surprisingly, irritated an increasingly challenged monarch. The sultan dismissed Mithat Paşa and suspended the constitution in late 1877, which prompted a new crisis with leading Western powers engaged in conflict with the Ottoman Empire. The resolutions of the Congress of Berlin, convened in 1878 to settle the outcome of the war, parceled out the peripheral territories of the empire among the new Balkan states, with Russia acquiring Kars, Ardahan, and Batum. Most of the architects of the constitution were soon exiled; Süleyman Paşa was tried for treason and involvement in the death of Sultan Abdülaziz, and Mithat Paşa was murdered in exile.

The rule of Sultan Abdülhamid II has generally been characterized as despotic, and only recently have scholars noted his support for the main reforms of the Tanzimat, especially its nationalist features. Although the democratic thrust of the 1860s was extinguished after 1878, the modernization of Turkey under the Young Turks (1908–1918) and the Republic (after 1923) can be seen as an uninterrupted movement proceeding from the Tanzimat, facilitated by the internal policy of the sultan, and nurtured by Young Turk idealisms.

The foreign policy of the Tanzimat and its architects proved less successful. In Lebanon, for example, the Sublime Porte mishandled the upheavals, which, in turn, encouraged local elites to misinterpret the Tanzimat. As a result, Ottoman forces clashed with Western powers in the Levant, which resulted in misery for all. Likewise, in Palestine, land reforms, especially the change in land ownership structure via the 1858 Ottoman Land Law, allowed Russian Jews to buy land, which enabled many to immigrate under the First Aliyah (return). It was after this first wave, and in order to boost revenues, that Ottoman officials required Arabs in Palestine to "register" their lands. Largely illiterate and easily manipulated by relatively educated mayors (*mukhtars*), many Palestinians embarked on the first wave of collective decision making that gradually stripped them of land ownerships, setting the stage for Jewish immigrants to buy from parvenu landowners anxious to secure their newly acquired wealth. In Constantinople, the Young Turks were unable to prevent the empire from being broken up into a number of successor states. The policy of uniting the subjects of the empire under a law applied equally to all was unsuccessful largely because few actually believed in its egalitarian goals. This was due in part to the slow pace of reform, but more importantly the immense and ultimately intractable task of unifying an extremely diverse society proved to be overwhelming, especially when the ultimate goal of the Tanzimat was to promote Turkish nationalism.

[*See also* Ottoman Empire *and* Turkey.]

BIBLIOGRAPHY

Ahmet Cevdet Paşa. *Tezâkir*. Edited by Cavid Baysun. 4 vols. Ankara: Türk Tarih Kurumu Basımevi, 1953–1967.

Davison, Roderic H. *Nineteenth Century Ottoman Diplomacy and Reforms*. Istanbul: Isis, 1999.

Engelhardt, Ed. *La Turquie et le Tanzimat; ou, Histoire des réformes dans l'Empire Ottoman depuis 1826 jusqu'à nos jours*. Charleston, S.C.: Nabu, 2010.

Karal, Enver Ziya. *Osmanlı Tarihi VI: Islahat Fermanı Devri 1856–1861*. Ankara: Türk Tarih Kurumu Basımevi, 1954.

Karal, Enver Ziya. *Osmanlı Tarihi VII: Islahat Fermanı Devri 1861–1876*. Ankara: Türk Tarih Kurumu Basımevi, 1956.

Karpat, Kemal H. *The Politicization of Islam: Reconstructing Identity, State, Faith, and Community in the Late Ottoman State*. Oxford: Oxford University Press, 2001.

Lewis, Bernard. *The Emergence of Modern Turkey*. 3d ed. New York: Oxford University Press, 2002.

Mardin, Şerif. *The Genesis of Young Ottoman Thought: A Study in the Modernization of Turkish Political Ideas*. Rev. ed. Syracuse, N.Y.: Syracuse University Press, 2000.

Riedler, Florian. *Opposition and Legitimacy in the Ottoman Empire: Conspiracies and Political Cultures*. London: Routledge, 2011.

Shaw, Stanford J., and Ezel Kural Shaw. *History of the Ottoman Empire and Modern Turkey*. Vol. 2. *Reform, Revolution, and the Republic: The Rise of Modern Turkey, 1808–1975*. Cambridge, U.K.: Cambridge University Press, 1977.

Weismann, Itzchak, and Fruma Zachs, eds. *Ottoman Reform and Muslim Regeneration: Studies in Honour of Butrus Abu-Manneb*. London: I. B. Tauris, 2005.

ŞERIF MARDIN
Updated by JOSEPH A. KÉCHICHIAN

TAWḤĪD. *See* Religious Beliefs.

TAXATION. Islam makes specific provision for taxation, the payment of which is viewed as a religious duty. The most important tax is *zakāt*—an alms tax paid by all free adult Muslims based on assets—which is one of the five pillars of Islam. *Zakāt* is a transfer payment, as it is designed to be paid by those with surplus liquid wealth for the benefit of the poor and needy. The essential purpose is redistribution, and the funds raised are earmarked for social and humanitarian spending. The proceeds cannot merely be paid into the treasury and used to finance such commitments as expenditure on defense or even infrastructure investment. The collection is usually organized separately from other taxes; the receipts are often not counted with fiscal revenue, and balances are accounted for independently.

The issue of whether taxation should be limited to *zakāt* obligations has been debated by Muslim scholars since the time of the Prophet. In the early Islamic period, a poll tax called *jizyah* (as sanctioned in Q 9:29) was imposed on non-Muslims. This was justified on the grounds that non-Muslims did not pay *zakāt*, yet they received government protection if they resided in a Muslim state. *Jizyah* was not therefore not perceived as a punishment of the conquered who refused to convert to Islam but as an assurance that all residents of an Islamic state contributed to its maintenance on a non-discriminatory basis. Throughout history, however, many non-Muslims viewed it as a burden and a humiliating means of subjugation.

Unlike the above two taxes, the Islamic land tax (*kharāj*) was applied to both Muslims and non-Muslims. The tax was levied on conquered lands according to the acreage of the land, but the rate depended on the output potential. Higher rates applied on irrigated lands, better soils, and fields suitable for higher-value crops. The maximum rate was half the value of the crop. In the event of crop failure owing to climatic factors, at the discretion of the ruler the tax was not applied. If low yields were the result of negligence, the owner was still obliged to pay. In such circumstances, the land could be sold to another farmer, who, it was hoped, would make better use of it. *Kharāj* meant that landowners had a responsibility to use their land effectively and realize its potential, as land is a gift from God and should not be wasted.

In the Ottoman Empire, land taxes were a major source of state revenue, and all land was registered so that an accurate assessment could be made. This land registration proved very useful, as uncertainties were removed about boundary demarcation, and the security of tenure with land title encouraged productive investment by landowners in irrigation and other farm improvements. State-owned land (*mīrī*) was auctioned to private operators under the *muqaṭṭaʿah* system, with successful bidders given the right to farm the land for a three-year period. This system was extended to mining, the minting of coinage, and even the collection of customs revenue. This franchising out to private operators of former government-run activities resembled in many respects the privatization methods increasingly adopted by Western governments. *Kharāj* as a special land tax was abolished by decree in Ottoman-governed lands in 1856.

In the nineteenth century, the European imperial powers tended to undermine traditional Islamic methods of tax collection. Secular taxes were introduced as Ottoman control weakened, customs duties being a major source of revenue. Income tax was also introduced in many parts of the Islamic world, although this never proved popular, and in practice often only government employees paid the tax. In such countries as Iran, tax evasion was widespread under the secular regimes of the shahs, although *zakāt* was administered independently by the mullahs through the mosques. There were frequent attempts at government interference, but these were resisted by the clerics, who had little faith in the states provision of social welfare.

Recent years have witnessed a resurgence of interest in the Islamic tax of *zakāt*, which in most Muslim countries exists in parallel with conventional tax structures. The latter often function ineffectively owing to the reluctance of businesses and individuals to pay. In Saudi Arabia, *zakāt* is the main form of taxation, and, although contributions are voluntary, most Muslims pay willingly. In Sudan, most domestic social-welfare expenditure is financed from *zakāt* funds, the government spending most of its unearmarked budget on the military. In Pakistan, Islamic taxation is increasingly important, although much remains to be done if the economic system is to be fully Islamized.

[*See also* Charity.]

BIBLIOGRAPHY

Abdul Mannan, Muḥammad. *Islamic Economics: Theory and Practice*. Cambridge, U.K.: Islamic Academy, 1986. Examines tax structures in the early Islamic period, including taxes on non-Muslims and land taxes.

Iqbal, Zafar, and Mervyn K. Lewis. *An Islamic Perspective on Governance*. Cheltenham, U.K.: Edward Elgar, 2009.

Kahf, Monzer. "Fiscal and Monetary Policies in an Islamic Economy." In *Monetary and Fiscal Economics of Islam*, edited by Mohammad Ariff, pp. 125–137. Jiddah: International Centre for Research in Islamic Economics, 1982. Concise outline of Islamic taxation for those with some knowledge of public finance.

Wilson, Rodney. "Macroeconomic Policy and the Islamic State." In *Islamic Business: Theory and Practice*. London: Economist Intelligence Unit, 1985. Examines fiscal policy objectives and the role of *zakāt* as a wealth tax.

RODNEY WILSON

TAʿZĪYAH. *Taʿzīyah* are the Shīʿī Muslim commemorative theatrical performances that depict dramatically the martyrdom of the grandson of the Prophet Muḥammad (c. 570–632)—Imam Ḥusayn ibn ʿAlī (c. 626–680)—and his followers at Karbala, Iraq, in 680. The ceremonies span the first ten days of the Islamic month of Muḥarram, when the story of the battle of Karbala is theatrically reenacted, primarily by male members of the local neighborhood, while others mournfully watch the ceremonies as both religious experience and communal festivity. *Taʿzīyah* originates from the larger body of Muḥarram rituals, which were institutionalized on a large scale by the Ṣafavid state (1501–1722) in the early sixteenth century, when Shiism was declared the state religion in Persia. As an elaborate form of theatrical display, *taʿzīyah* most likely appeared in the late seventeenth century in Ṣafavid Persia, as the Muḥarram commemorations evolved into complex and sumptuous religious festivals of communal significance.

In the post-Ṣafavid period Muḥarram rituals grew so popular and widespread throughout Iran that they became an aspect of everyday life. Probably under the Zands (1750–1794), *taʿzīyah* first emerged in public squares and neighborhood centers, fusing civic and sacred identity on a calendar basis. Under the Qājārs (1796–1924), especially Naṣīr al-Dīn Shāh Qājār (r. 1848–1897), *taʿzīyah* developed into elaborate theatrics of processional and stationary ceremonies, performed around melodic eulogy and recitation of the Karbala event, known as *rowzeh-khwani (raw ḍah-khwānī)*, reaching its height in popularity with the construction of the royal theater, the Takkiya Dowlat, in 1868–1869. Tied to the construction of city spaces, such as boulevards and royal buildings, the Takkiya Dowlat represented a massive ceremonial site, the largest in the capital city, Tehran, where *taʿzīyah* plays were organized and performed by actors with considerable preparation, performance sophistication, and visual richness that underlined the splendor and dramatic effect of the plays.

Ḥusaynīyah is the name of the building constructed for the performance of Muḥarram commemorative rites, in particular the *taʿzīyah* performances. Found in many Shīʿī communities around the world, *ḥusaynīyahs* were originally part of the mosque complex and later, probably during the Ṣafavid era, evolved into independent ceremonial sites for the commemorative rituals. In Iran, where they can be found in urban neighborhoods, *ḥusaynīyahs* are built around a courtyard around which the participants congregate to watch *taʿzīyah* performances. In other Shīʿī communities, especially in India, Iraq, and Lebanon, *ḥusaynīyahs* also serve as communal spaces of ritual significance, though with varied architectural designs. Throughout modern Iranian history *ḥusaynīyahs* have constituted distinct civic spaces where political activists gather for dissident activities, many of which occurred in the course of the Muḥarram ceremonies. In the late 1960s and early 1970s in Iran *ḥusaynīyahs* expanded from civic-religious into intellectual-political centers. The Ḥusaynīyah-Irshad in Tehran became a major forum for antigovernment intellectuals such as ʿAlī Sharīʿatī (1933–1977) and clerics such as Ayatollah Murtażā Muṭahharī (1920–1979), both of whom were prominent thinkers behind the Islamic Revolution of 1979. In post-revolutionary Iran *ḥusaynīyahs* became major civic spaces for government supporters to propagate the Islamic Republic's theocratic ideology.

BIBLIOGRAPHY

Aghaie, Kamran Scot. *The Martyrs of Karbala: Shiʿi Symbols and Rituals in Modern Iran*. Seattle: University of Washington Press, 2004.

Chelkowski, Peter J., ed. *Eternal Performance: Taʿziyeh and Other Shiite Rituals*. London: Seagull Books, 2010.

Rahimi, Babak. *Theater State and the Formation of Early Modern Public Sphere in Iran: Studies on Safavid Muharram Rituals, 1590–1641 CE*. Leiden, Netherlands, and Boston: Brill, 2012.

BABAK RAHIMI

TERRORISM. Terrorism is a deliberate, unjustifiable, and random use of violence for political ends against protected persons. Obviously, there is no inextricable connection between Islam, or any other religion, and terrorism. In fact, there is often a great confusion between the phenomenon of political violence and terrorism. The term terrorism applies to a special category of opprobrious acts rather than to all acts of politically inspired violence. Muslims have engaged in terrorism in the modern era, and just as Jews and Christians engaging in terrorism, they have sometimes claimed a justification based in religion. In point of fact, however, the Sharīʿah (divine law) does not condone the use of violence except to combat injustice, and noncombatant immunity is a prominent feature of Islamic literature on *jihād* (religiously sanctioned warfare). In warfare, necessity might justify putting noncombatants at risk, but harm to innocents should be neither intentional nor excessive. Thus, phrases such as "Islamic terrorism" significantly misrepresent the religious roots of violence committed by Muslims and encourage Islamophobia.

Nationalist Rationales for Terrorist Acts. Since World War II, the Middle East has become infamous as a cockpit for terrorism, although many of the perpetrators have not purported to act in the name of Islam. Arguably, the first modern act of political terrorism in the region was the bombing of the King David Hotel in 1947, an act carried out by Jewish terrorists led by Menachem Begin, then leader of the Irgun. Following the creation of the state of Israel in 1948, Begin became leader of the political opposition, and in 1977 acceded to the prime ministership of Israel. In the 1960s and 1970s, Palestinian guerrillas (*fidāʾyūn*) launched dozens of horrendous acts of violence against innocent bystanders, all in the name of gaining recognition for Palestinian nationalism. These acts included the slaughter of Israeli athletes at the Munich Olympics in 1972, a long series of hijackings, including four in 1970 that helped precipitate the civil war in Jordan, and several bloody attacks on air travelers both inside Israel and in Europe. Significantly, the Palestinian perpetrators were inspired by a secular irredentist ideology, not by religion. The same can be said for Kurdish guerrillas who, in the 1980s and early 1990s, committed a number of vicious acts of violence in Turkey as part of their quest to win an independent Kurdistan.

Political Violence with Islamic Rationales. Muslims claiming a religious rationale for their violence are also noteworthy. In Egypt, in 1954, the Muslim Brotherhood (al-Ikhwān al-Muslimīn) allegedly attempted to assassinate Gamal Abdel Nasser, who then accelerated his suppression of the organization. In 1981, Egyptian President Anwar el-Sadat was assassinated by extremist Muslim conspirators serving in the army. Muslim revolutionaries, who were intent on toppling the regime of Hosni Mubarak, had engaged in escalating acts of violence, including terrorism, to destabilize the Egyptian government since the late 1980's. Many of these acts have been egregiously indiscriminate, targeting innocent foreign tourists in addition to state officials, soldiers, and police officers. These acts illustrate the scope of activities that constitute contemporary political violence; whether they all constitute acts of terrorism is another question.

Thus, terrorism is notoriously difficult to define, since the term is often used to refer to generic acts of violence committed by political adversaries. Nevertheless, it is a useful epithet with which to bludgeon one's adversaries, even if the moral indictment is often debased by a tendency to apply the label selectively to foes while turning a blind eye to equally contemptible acts carried out by friends or allies pursuing congenial goals.

The quest for a definition of terrorism has bedeviled diplomats and international lawyers, and there is no internationally accepted definition. Although terrorism is frequently decried, the standard practice in international law has been to proceed inductively, criminalizing specific acts such as air piracy, attacks on diplomats, or the theft of nuclear materials. Nonetheless, there is general agreement that hijacking of commercial aircraft or vessels constitutes a form of terrorism when carried out by nonstate perpetrators.

Acts of violence carried out within the borders of a state are more problematic to characterize, since illegal acts of violence might be legitimate, especially when the state authorities harshly repress dissent and when the illegal acts do not target protected persons. To argue that an act of political violence is unlawful (a factual statement) is not the same as arguing that it is illegitimate (a normative conclusion). It is important to distinguish between those political systems in which citizens can effectively voice their demands and those in which whole categories of citizens are disenfranchised. In the second category of states, which are deaf to its citizens and residents, violence might be justifiable and legitimate even though it is deemed illegal by the authorities. In contrast, in the first category of states, political violence is both illegal and illegitimate, because the enfranchised citizen need not resort to violence to be heard or to enjoy the protection of the state.

Legality and Legitimacy. Of course, legality and legitimacy are not always easy to disentangle, as the case of Algeria illustrates. The Islamic Salvation Front, often referred to by its French acronym, FIS, was on the verge of attaining an overwhelming parliamentary majority following its impressive victory in the first stage of a two-stage set of elections. Instead of allowing FIS its electoral victory, the Algerian army, fearful of Islamist intentions that were supported by approximately half of the Algerian population, seized power in January 1992. Understandably, the membership of FIS reacted with fury to the army's action, and a civil war ensued, with thousands of FIS adherents arrested and detained under martial-law conditions. Moderate leaders in FIS were thoroughly discredited, and the Islamists launched a campaign of insurrection and violence that respected few moral boundaries and targeted not only government officials but also intellectuals deemed unsympathetic to the Islamists, as well as individuals who favored Western dress or styles of behavior. Some have accused government forces of instigating, or at least condoning, violence that was then blamed on the Islamists. In a striking throwback to the Algerian revolution of the 1950s and early 1960s, when French rule was overthrown, terrorism again became the coin of the realm for both sides in Algeria, thoroughly polarizing Algerian society.

The right of a people to resist foreign occupation is widely, if somewhat erratically, upheld. A clear majority of world governments—including Egypt, France, Iran, Saudi Arabia, and the United States—supported Afghan Muslims struggling violently against Soviet occupation. Relatively few observers outside the Soviet Union described the Afghani *mujāhidīn* as terrorists, even though their attacks were often condemned as terrorism by the Soviet Union. As long as the Mujāhidīn directed their efforts against the Soviet presence in Afghanistan, right was literally on their side. By the same token, though agreement is less general, the resistance by Lebanese Muslims and Christians to the Israeli occupation of a portion of southern Lebanon, which it had occupied between 1978 and 2000, was similarly sanctioned, despite Israel's description of those who attacked its soldiers and client militiamen as terrorists.

A sounder test addresses the moral legitimacy of the means rather than the technical legality of the ends. If the Afghan or the Lebanese resistance forces broadened their campaigns to encompass as targets protected categories of noncombatants, their actions tended to lose privileged status. Whatever the politics of the observer, it is significant to distinguish between attacks on soldiers occupying foreign lands and attacks on persons in universally accepted protected categories, such as children or, more broadly, noncombatants. As long as a resistance force is discriminate in its methods and targets, it is not objectively justified to affix the terrorist label.

A Definition of Terrorism. Deliberate and random uses of violence for political ends against protected groups constitute terrorism. This is a functional and nonpolemical definition that has the merit of parsimony and universality. The perpetrators can be states, agents of states, or individuals acting independently. Indeed, the Iraqi government's al-Anfal Campaign in the 1980s to intimidate and exterminate major segments of its Kurdish population or the actions taken by the Tunisian, Egyptian, Yemeni, and Syrian governments against civilians during the spring 2011 uprisings in those countries clearly constituted acts of state terrorism. The record shows, sadly, that states have often been able to commit murderous feats with impunity—acts that dwarf the deeds of horror committed by nonstate terrorists. There are many examples, including Indonesia's bloody suppression of East Timor in the early 1960s; Syria's annihilation of more than twenty thousand people in Hama in 1982; and Sudan's savage campaign in the south to quash resistance to Islamization in the 1990s.

In general, militant opposition movements of Muslims have focused their violence domestically on the authoritarian state, which is typically characterized as thwarting the imposition of the Sharīʿah as the sole legitimate source of law. The writings of Sayyid Quṭb (executed in 1966 by the Egyptian government) and his rejuvenation of the terminology of *jāhilīyah* (literally, a state of ignorance of the truths of Islam) as a description of contemporary Muslim societies have provided some contemporary groups with a rationale for acts of violence as part of a *jihād* to reestablish Islamic society.

Although most militant movements of Muslims have concentrated on domestic goals, the revolution in Iran spawned an ideology that has been used to justify the use of violence on the international stage since the late 1980s. Not only has the Iranian government been implicated in widespread assassinations and plots against political and intellectual opponents, it has also lent material support to militant Islamist groups. This can be observed in the case of the Lebanese Shīʿī group Ḥizbullāh (Party of God).

Ḥizbullāh. Ḥizbullāh is an Iranian-funded party that came to light following the Israeli invasion of Lebanon in 1982. Ḥizbullāh has proven to be a competent, dedicated, and well-led challenger to the more moderate Amal movement of the early 1970s, although Ḥizbullāh spokespersons are keen to dissociate the party from acts such as the kidnappings of Westerners in the 1980s—the Islamic Jihād organization claimed credit for many of the kidnappings, which conveniently masked Ḥizbullāh involvement. Ḥizbullāh played a major role in inflicting a chain of humiliations on the United States. They precipitated the 1984 departure of the American marines from Lebanon with the truck bombing of the marine barracks, helped to scuttle the U.S.-brokered 17 May 1983 agreement between Lebanon and Israel, and held the world in thrall over the fate of foreign hostages (including Terry Waite, the personal envoy of the archbishop of Canterbury). Equally impressive was the success of the Islamic Resistance (al-Muqāwamah al-Islāmīyah) in forcing an Israeli withdrawal from most of Lebanese territory in January 1985, and completely by 2000.

In effect, the Islamic Revolution in Iran provided the substance for a new ideological framework that served to explain the causes of deprivation and suffering among the Muslim masses. This framework legitimized and commended the use of violence against the enemies of Islam, particularly the West. This comes through clearly in the remarkable "Open Letter" of Ḥizbullāh released in February 1985.

This open letter explains and justifies the use of violence by Ḥizbullāh, which, it is argued, has been trivialized in the West as "a handful of fanatics and terrorists who are only concerned with blowing up drinking, gambling, and entertainment spots.... Each of us is a combat soldier when the call of *jihād* demands it and each of us undertakes his task in the battle in accordance with his lawful assignment within the framework of action under the guardianship of the leader jurisprudent." (Norton, 1987, p. 15)

The letter emphasizes that the 1978–1979 revolution in Iran was an inspiration to action, a proof of all that can be accomplished when the faithful gather under the banner of Islam. "We address all the Arab and Islamic peoples to declare to them that the Muslim's experience in Islamic Iran left no one any excuse since it proved beyond all doubt that bare chests motivated by faith are capable, with God's help, of breaking the iron and oppression of tyrannical regimes" (Norton, 1987, pp. 12–13). The letter described a world in which "the countries of the arrogant world," and especially the United States and the Soviet Union, struggle for influence at the expense of the Third World. As a commentator in *al-ʿAhd*, the Ḥizbullāh newspaper, noted: "The Soviets are not one iota different from the Americans in terms of political danger, indeed are more dangerous than them in terms of ideological considerations as well, and this requires that light be shed on this fact and that the Soviets be assigned their proper place in the... forces striving to strike at the interests of the Moslem people and arrogate their political present and future" (*al-ʿAhd*, 9 May 1987, p. 12). Nonetheless, pride of place belonged to the United States, which directly or indirectly through its "spearhead," Israel, has inflicted suffering on the Muslims of Lebanon: "Imam Khomeini, the leader, has repeatedly stressed that America is the reason for all our catastrophes and the source of all malice. By fighting it, we are only exercising our legitimate right to defend our Islam and the dignity of our nation." The French were also singled out for attack, largely because of their longstanding sympathy for Christians in Lebanon and their arms sales to Iraq.

Ḥizbullāh also positioned itself as a force resisting the designs and games of Israel and the superpowers, whose jockeying for power, in its view, has led to subjugation and oppression throughout the Third World. "Thus, we have seen that aggression can be repelled only with the sacrifice of blood, and that freedom is not given but regained with the sacrifice of both heart and soul" (Norton, 1987, p. 14). The objective is to free Lebanon from the manipulation and chicanery of the malevolent outside powers and, at the same time, to combat internal enemies, such as the Christian Phalange, who have, according to Ḥizbullāh, unjustly enjoyed privilege at the expense of Muslims. Ḥizbullāh has been especially intolerant of competitors for Shīʿī recruits. Moreover, the Communist Party, an especially appealing target given its alien and atheistic ideology, has been singled out for attacks. Dozens, if not hundreds, of party members were killed in a brutal, bloody campaign of suppression and assassination in 1984 and 1985.

Fallout of Terrorism. The cost of terrorism is obviously most severe for its immediate victims, but there are heavy costs for the perpetrators' society as well. The use of terrorism stereotypes a community, thereby reducing rather than enhancing international support for its claims. The heavy moral baggage of past outrages can be a burden. Not surprisingly, many Lebanese Shīʿī have come to resent the kidnapping of foreigners, sometimes on moral grounds, but often simply on practical grounds. Many acts of terrorism are patently counterproductive. Rather than weakening the resolve of the target population, terrorists—whether agents of a state or acting independently—supply the argument, and all too often the means, for their own eradication.

Scholars are wont to emphasize that terrorism is the weapon of the weak. Although there is some truth in this observation, as illustrated by the bombing of the World Trade Center in New York City in 1993 by a band of militant Muslims, the major perpetrators are not individuals or nonstate actors inspired by a vision of Islam but strong, authoritarian governments intent on maintaining or extending their power, or punishing their adversaries.

Throughout the 1990s, several serious incidents were recorded that fit the terrorist label but are not necessarily associated with Islam: In 1993 a series of bombings killed 250 and injured more than seven hundred in a reaction to the 1992 Bābarī Mosque attack; in July 1994 a Jewish community center in Buenos Aires was destroyed, killing eighty-five people; the Aum Shinrikyo sect released an impure form of sarin gas in the Tokyo Metro in March 1995, killing twelve; on 19 April 1995 Gulf War veteran Timothy McVeigh and several associates blew up the Oklahoma City Federal Building, killing 168 and injuring more than eight hundred; on 7 August 1998 simultaneous attacks on U.S. embassies in Kenya and Tanzania resulted in the deaths of 213 in Nairobi and twelve in Dar es Salaam, while more than four thousand were injured in these attacks, for which al-Qaʿida claimed responsibility. Then, on 11 September 2001, the attacks against the World Trade Center in New York and the Pentagon in Arlington County, Virginia, resulted in the deaths of 2,973, with twenty-four missing and several thousand injured.

Post-9/11. Terrorism as it had existed until 11 September 2001 changed dramatically when the United States declared a perpetual war on terrorism. Washington first retaliated against al-Qaʿida and the Taliban regime in Afghanistan, with significant attacks on that hapless country beginning in October 2001, followed by a worldwide hunt of "terrorists," or what were called "enemy combatants" when it was necessary to bypass normal procedures and whisk them past European and Middle Eastern airports in "rendition" flights to secure facilities. The second Gulf War in Iraq began in 2003, ostensibly to prevent the Ba'thist regime from using weapons of mass destruction. One of the reasons for the war that started in 2003 was to prevent terrorist activities from migrating to the U.S. "Homeland"—in the words of the often quoted slogan: "If we don't fight them there, they'll follow us home."

It must be emphasized that 9/11 was not the only terrorist act that mobilized international attention. Several other terrorist activities occurred after 2001, including the Beslan school siege by Chechen rebels in North Ossetia that killed 344 and injured several hundred more. This was followed on 12 October 2002 by an attack on a nightclub in Bali, Indonesia, which killed 202 and injured another 209; on 11 March 2004 an attack on the Madrid Metro killed 191 and injured 2,050; and on 7 July 2005, London transportation vehicles were targeted, with a total of fifty-two killed and more than seven hundred injured. In 2003, Saudi authorities launched a massive hunt for terrorists who attacked civilian housing complexes or plotted to blow up oil facilities throughout the kingdom. Many other attacks occurred throughout the world, including dozens of killings in ongoing military confrontations between Israel and the Palestinians as well as between Ḥizbullāh and Israel, which have resulted in thousands of deaths. Clearly, most terrorist attacks are designed to kill as many people as possible, although most fail or fall short. Yet what changed dramatically after 9/11 was the concerted effort by Western as well as Muslim governments to respond in kind or even more forcefully in the name of "security." On 2 May 2011, American Navy SEAL commandos raided a compound in Abbottabad, Pakistan, where they killed Osama Bin Laden, the alleged leader of al-Qaʿida. Attempts on other putative leaders followed, as terrorism progressively evolved into an asymmetric war, given the scarce resources available to transnational movements.

[*See also* Ḥizbullāh; *and* Islamic Salvation Front.]

BIBLIOGRAPHY

Chaliand, Gérard, and Arnaud Blin, eds. *The History of Terrorism: From Antiquity to al Qaeda.* Translated by Edward Schneider, Kathryn Pulver, and Jesse Browner. Berkeley: University of California Press, 2007. A classic study that covers centuries of key developments that led to asymmetric violence.

Esposito, John L. *Unholy War: Terror in the Name of Islam.* New York: Oxford University Press, 2002.

Faḍl Allāh, Muḥammad Ḥusayn. *Al-Islām wa-manṭiq al-qūwah.* 2d ed. Beirut: Dār al-Islāmīyah, 1981.

Geaves, Ron, Theodore Gabriel, Yvonne Haddad, et al., eds. *Islam and the West Post-9/11.* Burlington, Vt.: Ashgate, 2004.

Hamzeh, Ahmad Nizar. *In the Path of Hizbullah.* Syracuse, N.Y.: Syracuse University Press, 2004.

Harik, Judith Palmer. *Hezbollah: The Changing Face of Terrorism.* London: I. B. Tauris, 2005.

Kepel, Gilles. *Jihad: The Trail of Political Islam.* Translated by Anthony F. Roberts. Cambridge, Mass.: Belknap Press of Harvard University Press, 2002.

Kepel, Gilles. *Muslim Extremism in Egypt: The Prophet and Pharaoh.* Translated by Jon Rothschild. Berkeley: University of California Press, 1985.

Kepel, Gilles. *The Roots of Radical Islam.* Translated by Jon Rothschild. London: Saqi, 2005.

Kepel, Gilles. *The War for Muslim Minds: Islam and the West.* Translated by Pascale Ghazaleh. Cambridge, Mass.: Belknap Press of Harvard University Press, 2004.

Khan, L. Ali. *A Theory of International Terrorism: Understanding Islamic Militancy.* Leiden: Martinus Nijhoff, 2006.

Martin, David C., and John Walcott. *Best Laid Plans: The Inside Story of America's War against Terrorism.* New York: Harper & Row, 1988.

Mohaddessin, Mohammad. *Islamic Fundamentalism: The New Global Threat.* Washington, D.C.: Seven Locks, 1993.

Norton, Augustus Richard. *Amal and the Shi'a: Struggle for the Soul of Lebanon*. Austin: University of Texas Press, 1987.

Rabasa, Angel M. *Political Islam in Southeast Asia: Moderates, Radicals, and Terrorists*. Oxford: Oxford University Press, 2003.

Ranstorp, Magnus. *Hizb'allah in Lebanon: The Politics of the Western Hostage Crisis*. Houndmills, U.K.: Macmillan, 1997.

Schmid, Alex P., ed. *The Routledge Handbook of Terrorism Research*. New York: Routledge, 2011. A major reference guide that synthesizes scholarly research and provides a comprehensive overview of terrorism studies.

Selbourne, David. *The Losing Battle with Islam*. Amherst, N.Y.: Prometheus, 2005.

Shanahan, Rodger. *The Shi'a of Lebanon: Clans, Parties and Clerics*. London: Tauris Academic Studies, 2005.

Ṭaleqānī, Maḥmūd, Murtaḍa Muṭahhari, and ʿAlī Sharīʿatī. *Jihād and Shahādat: Struggle and Martyrdom in Islam*. Edited by Mehdi Abdi and Gary Legenhausen. Houston, Tex.: Institute for Research and Islamic Studies, 1986.

Thornton, William H. *New World Empire: Civil Islam, Terrorism, and the Making of Neoglobalism*. Lanham, Md.: Rowman & Littlefield, 2005.

White, Jonathan. *Terrorism and Homeland Security*. 7th ed. Belmont, Calif.: Wadsworth, 2011.

Wright, Robin. *Sacred Rage: The Wrath of Militant Islam*. Rev. ed. New York: Simon & Schuster, 2001.

AUGUSTUS RICHARD NORTON
Updated by JOSEPH A. KÉCHICHIAN

THAILAND. About 90 percent of the Thai population of approximately 67 million adheres to the Theravada Buddhist faith. The second-largest religious affiliation is Islamic. Approximately 4 million people in Thailand profess the Islamic faith and maintain about twenty-seven thousand mosques. The Muslims in Thailand comprise two broad, self-defined categories, Malay Muslims residing primarily in southern Thailand and Thai Muslims residing in central and northern Thailand.

The approximately 3 million Malay-speaking Muslims are concentrated in the southern provinces of Narathiwat, Pattani, Satun, and Yala; they were incorporated into the Thai polity during the latter part of the nineteenth century. Despite the aggressive assimilationist policies of the Thai authorities, the vast majority of Malay Muslims maintain a strong ethnoreligious identity. Thai government assimilationist policies have resulted largely in irredentist and separatist ethnic and religious movements in South Thailand.

The Thai Muslim population is a much more heterogeneous group than the Malay Muslim populace of Thailand. The Thai-speaking Muslims include descendants of Iranians, Chams, Indonesians, Indians, Pakistanis, Chinese, and Malay Muslims who reside in the predominantly Thai Buddhist regions of central and northern Thailand. Most Thai Muslims reside in Bangkok and the surrounding communities of central Thailand. The population of Muslims in Bangkok alone is approximately four hundred thousand. Smaller communities of Chinese, Indian, and Pakistani Muslims reside in the northern provinces of Chiang Mai, Chiang Rai, and Lamphun.

With the exception of a few descendants of Indians and Iranians who maintain Shīʿī traditions, most Muslims in Thailand are Sunnī. Traditional Islamic thought, beliefs, and practices in both the Malay Muslim and Thai Muslim communities of Thailand were suffused with Hindu-Buddhist and folk-animistic accretions. Charms, amulets, magical beliefs, and some aspects of Hindu-Buddhist teachings regarding merit-making were interwoven with Islam in both the rural and urban regions of Thailand.

Beginning in the early twentieth century, a reformist, Sharīʿah-minded form of Islam stemming from the renowned Salafīyah movement associated with Muḥammad ʿAbduh of Cairo (1849–1905) influenced the urban Muslim intellectuals, primarily in Bangkok. Islamic reformism reached Bangkok in the 1920s through an Indonesian political refugee, Ahmad Wahab, who helped establish organized centers of reformism that encouraged more orthodox Islamic beliefs and campaigned against popular forms of Islam in Thailand. These reformists viewed many of the popular Islamic beliefs as *shirk*, the association of other beings with Allāh, and emphasized the use of *akal* (Ar. *ʿaql*; rational thought) and *ijtihād* (independent judgment) rather than a reliance upon *taqlīd* (authoritative teachings). Along with increases in education, printing technology and literacy, urbanization, economic development, and more opportunities to travel to the Middle East, the reformist movement has had a substantial influence on Islamic belief and practice in Thailand.

Since the 1970s and the emergence of Islamic resurgence movements in the Middle East and elsewhere, some Muslims in Thailand have participated in *dakwah* (Ar. *daʿwah*) movements similar to those that have influenced Malaysia and Indonesia. *Dakwah* leaders support the reinforcement of Islamic values and institutions in an era of rapid secularization and change. In addition to the *dakwah* movement, a small but active Jamāʿat Tablīghī movement has also been successful in recruiting young Muslims, especially in South Thailand.

As part of the globally based Islamic revival, some Middle Eastern countries have been involved in granting scholarships to young Muslims from Thailand to study in Saudi Arabia, Egypt, and elsewhere. These developments have had consequences for the content of Islamic curricula within the Islamic schools in Thailand. In particular, the Saudi government has been active in sponsoring Islamic education and Islamic institutional development. The Wahhābī-inspired programs of Saudi-trained educators have created some tensions within the more traditional Muslim communities in Thailand. However, the Wahhābī influences have had very little effect in fomenting militant forms of Islam in Thailand.

The Muslim communities of Thailand interact with the Thai government through a religious bureaucracy headed by the Office of the Chularajmontri, the Central Islamic Committee, and the representatives of the Provincial Islamic Committee, which is constitutionally established within the Ministry of the Interior. These representative institutions regulate and manage mosque and educational affairs at the local level. The mosque and Islamic school (*pondok*) are the key institutions of socialization in Muslim communities. They are the center of Ramaḍān activities, ʿĪd prayers, weekly *khuṭbah*s (Friday sermons), Qurʾānic recitations, and other religious activities. A mosque committee manages its *waqf* (endowed property) and acquires legal recognition and government subsidies through the Islamic bureaucracy and Ministry of Interior.

A major challenge facing both the Buddhist majority and Muslim minority population in Thailand is whether the nation can become a truly pluralistic society that recognizes the equality of all religious faiths and ethnic minorities. Since 2001, this challenge has been sorely tested. In October 2001, following the U.S.-led strikes in Afghanistan, thousands of Muslims in Thailand gathered for demonstrations against these actions. The Chularajmontri, the religious and government representative of the Muslims in Thailand, and other Muslim leaders spoke out against the Thai government's support of the U.S. "War on Terror" and the invasion of Afghanistan and Iraq.

Increasing tensions between Muslims and Buddhists have led to sporadic violence in southern Thailand since January 2004, and Thai Buddhists, including some Buddhist monks, have been killed by Muslims. Violence continued for over four months in the southern region until it resulted in a massive day-long siege against a series of planned attacks on police and army installations on 28 April 2004, resulting in the deaths of 112 Muslims. The Thai military surrounded the Muslim militants, who were armed with machetes and cleavers, in a predawn raid. Some of the young Muslims hid in the historic Krue Se mosque in Pattani which was firebombed, killing some thirty-two young assailants who were crying out the *takbīr* (Allāh is Great). On 26 October 2004, thousands of Muslim protestors assembled at a police station, demanding the release of Muslims accused of supplying weapons to insurgents. The Thai military arrested thirteen hundred Muslims and fired bullets and water cannons into the crowd. The arrested Muslims were packed into army trucks headed for prison, and eighty-five prisoners suffocated and died.

Since 2004 there have been more than five thousand deaths and at least eight thousand related injuries of Buddhists and Muslims in the largest insurgency outside of Iraq and Afghanistan. The Thai government has imposed martial law on the territory of South Thailand, and this has had some troubling consequences. For example, the government has indirectly sponsored an aggressive Buddhist-based nationalism in South Thailand in opposition to the Islamic groups and institutions. In some cases, Buddhist monks have acted as covert military officers and have equipped themselves with weapons. As a result of these religious-political tensions and violent incidents, some Thai universities and educational institutions, Buddhist and Islamic-oriented nongovernmental organizations, and government-sponsored projects have been active in promoting peaceful relations between Buddhists and Muslims in Thailand.

It is to be hoped that, as Muslims have more opportunities to participate in political, educational, and cultural activities geared toward developing a more open, tolerant, and pluralistic society, ethnic and religious tensions in the country will subside.

[*See also* Daʿwah; *and* Islam and Politics in Southeast Asia.]

BIBLIOGRAPHY

Askew, Marc. *Conspiracy, Politics, and a Disorderly Border: The Struggle to Comprehend Insurgency in Thailand's Deep South.* Policy Studies 29. Washington, D.C.: East-West Center Washington, 2007. This is a recent study of the tensions between the Buddhist and Muslim communities in South Thailand.

Forbes, Andrew D. W., ed. *The Muslims of Thailand.* 2 vols. Gaya, India: Centre for South East Asian Studies, 1988–1989. Essays by both Western and non-Western authorities on Muslims in Thailand.

Fraser, Thomas M., Jr. *Fishermen of Southern Thailand: The Malay Villagers.* New York: Holt, Rinehart & Winston, 1966. Classic ethnography of a coastal Malay Muslim population.

Gilquin, Michel. *Les Musulmans de Thaïlande.* Paris: Harmattan, 2002. A historical and ethnographic overview of Islam in Thailand.

Jerryson, Michael K. *Buddhist Fury: Religion and Violence in Southern Thailand.* New York: Oxford University Press, 2011. A study of how Buddhist nationalism and monastic organizations have heightened religious-political tensions in South Thailand.

Joll, Christopher. *Muslim Merit-Making in Thailand's Far South.* Muslims in Global Societies Series, vol. 4. New York: Springer, 2012. An in-depth ethnographic portrait of Muslim rituals and practices in an urban Malay community of Cabetigo, in Pattani Province.

K. Che Man, W. *Muslim Separatism: The Moros of Southern Philippines and the Malays of Southern Thailand.* Singapore: Oxford University Press, 1990. Comprehensive comparative analysis of the cultural, political, and religious movements of the minority Muslims of the southern Philippines and the Malay-speaking Muslims of South Thailand in a broad international context.

Liow, Joseph Chinyong. *Islam, Education, and Reform in Southern Thailand: Tradition and Transformation.* Singapore: Institute of Southeast Asian Studies, 2009. An excellent in-depth account that demonstrates that Islamic militancy is not an integral aspect of Islamic education in South Thailand.

Madmarn, Hasan. *The Pondok and Madrasah in Patani.* Bangi, Malaysia: Penerbit Universiti Kebangsaan Malaysia, 2002. A comprehensive account of the role of the Islamic school and education in Muslim communities in South Thailand.

McCargo, Duncan, ed. *Rethinking Thailand's Southern Violence.* Singapore: National University of Singapore Press, 2006. A comprehensive overview and analyses of the problems in South Thailand.

McCargo, Duncan. *Tearing Apart the Land: Islam and Legitimacy in Southern Thailand.* Ithaca, N.Y.: Cornell University Press, 2008. A book by a well-known political scientist who specializes in Thai affairs that offers a perceptive analysis of the politics and religious tensions and developments in South Thailand.

Pitsuwan, Surin. *Islam and Malay Nationalism: A Case Study of the Malay-Muslims of Southern Thailand.* Bangkok: Thai Khadi Research Institute, Thammasat University, 1985. The most comprehensive treatment of the Malay-Muslim situation in southern Thailand, written by an insider.

Teeuw, A., and D. K. Wyatt. *Hikayat Patani.* 2 vols. The Hague: Martinus Nijhoff, 1970. Translation and account of the early indigenous narratives regarding the religious center of Patani in southern Thailand.

Thomas, M. Ladd. *Political Violence in the Muslim Provinces of Southern Thailand.* Singapore: Institute of Southeast Asian Studies, 1975. Thorough monograph depicting the political situation of the Muslim minority in southern Thailand in the 1970s.

Yusuf, Imtiyaz, and Lars Peter Schmidt, eds. *Understanding Conflict and Approaching Peace in Southern Thailand.* 2d ed. Bangkok: Konrad Adenauer Stiftung, 2006. Explores the development of peace strategies to reduce Buddhist-Muslim tensions in South Thailand.

RAYMOND SCUPIN

TOLERANCE. "Tolerance" has been defined as a "double negation": a negative appraisal of something others do, followed by a decision not to interfere with it, despite one's capacity for doing so. Comments on tolerance in Islam arise in a polarized political situation. The clash-of-civilizations narrative posits the "West" in conflict with an incompatible Islam, often painted as intolerant, illiberal, and hostile. Underlying assumptions about a monolithic Islam and a Muslim cultural essence are repeatedly questioned in academic scholarship but remain entrenched in public discourses. Assertions emphasizing Islam's compatibility with "Western" values risk reinforcing simplistic assumptions. A widespread postcolonial narrative paints Muslims as disempowered underdogs in a struggle against non-Muslim neocolonial forces. Here "tolerance" appears as a euphemism for submitting to an oppressive alien order rather than revolting against it. Advocates of Islamic tolerance risk being accused of serving imperial religion-building projects that seek to defang troublesome Muslim publics and convert them into accommodating subjects. Challenging these assumptions while discussing tolerance in Islam is necessarily complex, and, where concision is required, cannot be entirely satisfactory.

A practice may be described as "Islamic" to the extent that "it is authorized by the discursive traditions of Islam, and is so taught to Muslims" (Asad, 1986, p. 15). Diverse pronouncements on tradition, ostensibly contradictory at times, constitute what claimants have termed "Islamic." Because the juristic tradition permits interpretative contestation, it is difficult to describe a particular jurisprudential position as "the" Islamic position on the matter. Yet claims that Islam is tolerant abound. Toleration, according to Emad Shahin (2008), is grounded normatively in the Islam's sacred sources, and is a moral duty and religious obligation; it was particularly apparent in the tenth-century Islamic "Renaissance" and in modern humanistic trends in political Islam. While Khaled Abou El Fadl (2002) notes that the Qurʾān celebrates and sanctifies human diversity, he also asserts that the Qurʾān, like any text, will be read in ways that reflect the moral sensibility the reader brings to it. Although Abou El Fadl believes that the text does not "command" intolerant readings, he acknowledges that people can read intolerance into it.

Teachings regarding tolerance can be categorized into those relating to Muslims who have different understandings of Islam, those who belong to the recognized revealed faiths, those who belong to other religions, and those who reject religion altogether or do not belong to an identifiable religious tradition. With respect to diversity within the Islamic fold, Abou El Fadl summarizes the juristic tradition as having great acceptance of heterodox views. Nevertheless, there are theological limits to tolerance among Muslims. Key questions of who claims the authority to judge what those limits are, and how these are delineated and where they are implemented, remain contextually dependent. A prime example may be the escalating communal tensions that culminated in the push to have the Aḥmadīs in Pakistan declared non-Muslims, while other minority sects were not targeted. The Munir Report, commissioned as an inquiry into the anti-Aḥmadī disturbances in Pakistan in the early 1950s, found that defining who counted as a "Muslim" was nearly impossible, given disagreement among the *ʿulama*ʾ on the question.

Takfīr—declaring a person or group to be outside the fold of Islam—has spread in the contemporary Muslim world as a virulent, incendiary instrument in conflicts, often serving to mobilize sectarian groups. In response, prominent religious figures offered the Amman Message in 2005. Purporting to be a consensus statement, it seeks to curtail rampant *takfīr* statements, and, by pointing to eight broadly defined categories, offers an inclusive approach to answering the question: "Who is a Muslim?" How precisely one is determined to belong to one of these categories or outside the fold remains open to question.

From the standpoint of juristic efforts to interpret Sharīʿah and to generate rulings of *fiqh*, the position of non-Muslims according to the sacred law is a matter of interpretative contestation. Some argue that an exclusive salvific claim in the Qurʾān has superseded other revelations, rendering them obsolete as sources of salvation. In itself, however, this theological position does not necessarily mean that religiously prescribed legal protections for non-Muslim minorities are eliminated. Some jurists in later centuries tried to place social and political constraints on non-Muslims, but social attitudes and practices remained more tolerant, according to Shahin. Jeremy Benthall (2005) describes a concentric Islamic doctrine of toleration. At the center is Islam; on the periphery are *shirk* and *kufr*. In the liminal areas are the Peoples of the Book, mainly Jews and Christians, who have legal status.

A prominent recent effort at interreligious understanding and collaboration, the 2007 Common Word document, claims to offer an authoritative interpretation of a Qurʾānic verse (3:64) referring to relations with People of the Book. The document is a broadly endorsed letter addressed to Christian leaders. It invites Christians to collaborative and mutually respectful coexistence with Muslims based on the core commandments to love God and one's neighbor found in the Christian and Muslim traditions. The document represents an effort at improving relations between the two communities by emphasizing common ground and may be unprecedented in the diversity of its signatories. Depending on how the document is received by both Muslims and Christians, it may be a significant step in promoting tolerant practices.

Polytheists are often considered the least tolerable, yet, as Benthall notes, prominent "conciliatory" positions can be found. Hinduism, often characterized as polytheistic, was included by some in the ambit of recognized religions.

Al-Bīrūnī, the eleventh-century Iranian Indologist, asserted in his *Kitāb al-Hind* that the Hindu elites worshipped God alone, while the common people needed idols. Dārā Shukūh, son of the Mughal emperor Shāh Jahān, argued that the Vedas are a heavenly text. Arab conquerors of Sindh treated Hindu temples on a par with synagogues and mosques. The Ḥanafī school of law in India came to accept Hindus as *dhimmī*. The Ṣūfī traditions tend to be particularly open to recognizing alternative paths to salvation. Ibn al-ʿArabī (d. 1240) saw potential for divine truth in vast spaces; Rūmī (d. 1273) and Ḥāfiẓ (d. 1390) suggested that there are as many paths to God as there are persons.

With respect to those who express doubts about religious truth, Sohail Hashmi (2002) suggests that a tolerant spirit can be found in the Qurʾānic narrative about Abraham asking God to show how the dead were revived. Regarding the stark divide between those who profess belief in Islam, and those who openly reject it, the chapter "al-Kāfirūn" of the Qurʾān (*sūrah* 109) instructs the believer to say: "... to you be your way, and to me mine." The translator Abdullah Yusuf Ali interprets that as meaning that even though "in matters of Truth, we can make no compromise, but there is no reason to persecute or abuse anyone for his faith or belief" (Ali, n.d., p. 2020).

One entry into the discussion of tolerance in Islam rests on the presumed dichotomy between "modernity" and "tradition." Some have argued for reinterpretations of religious texts to reflect the modern context. Abdullahi Al-Naʾim (2008), for example, argues that the state is necessarily a secular institution and that Sharīʿah should be excluded as a rationale for policy advocacy in the public sphere. Al-Naim's suggestion is that political advocacy be based instead on "civic reason," which would maximize the space for public deliberation, allowing the incorporation of diverse voices without fear of allegations of impiety. Farid Esack (2002) argues for a reading of the Qurʾān based on a South African hermeneutic of religious pluralism for liberation. These approaches imply that tolerance results from a less traditional reading of Islam, although each deploys a method of relating to religious sources that they would argue is authentic.

Others, such as Abou El Fadl, argue that the erosion of tradition, the advent of the modern state, and the rise of intolerant puritan movements are related. Puritanical doctrines have historically arisen but over time been marginalized by tradition. The capacity of *ʿulamaʾ* to mediate between governing authorities and the public, checking the state, has been compromised as *waqf* endowments have come under state control, and as *ʿulamaʾ* have become state employees. Authoritarian movements have presumed that they can discern the true understanding of religion and implement it as public law in a manner untainted by human interpretation, reminiscent of the Khārijites, Restoring the tradition and the independence of *ʿulamaʾ* would enhance tolerance in this view.

BIBLIOGRAPHY

Abou El Fadl, Khaled. "The Place of Tolerance in Islam." In *The Place of Tolerance in Islam* by Khaled Abou El Fadl, et al., edited by Joshua Cohen and Ian Lague, chapter 1. Boston: Beacon Press, 2002.

A Common Word Signatories. *A Common Word Between Us*. 2007. https://www.acommonword.com.

Ali, Abdullah Yusuf. *The Holy Quran: English Translation of the Meanings and Commentary*. Revised and edited by The Presidency of Islamic Researches, IFTA, Call and Guidance. King Fahd Holy Qur-an Printing Complex, n.d.

Al-Naʾim, Abdullahi. *Islam and the Secular State: Negotiating the Future of Shariʿa*. Cambridge, Mass.: Harvard University Press, 2008.

Asad, Talal. "The Idea of an Anthropology of Islam." Occasional Papers Series, 1986. Georgetown University, School of Foreign Service, Center for Con-

temporary Arab Studies. http://ccas.georgetown.edu/story/1242687906497.html.
Benthall, Jeremy. "Confessional Cousins and the Rest: The Structure of Islamic Toleration." *Anthropology Today* 21, no. 1, "Policy and Islam" (February 2005): pp. 16–20.
Esack, Farid. *Quran, Liberation and Pluralism: An Islamic Perspective of Interreligious Solidarity against Oppression*. Oxford: OneWorld, 2002.
Hashmi, Sohail. "A Conservative Legacy." In *The Place of Tolerance in Islam* by Khaled Abou El Fadl, et al., edited by Joshua Cohen and Ian Lague, pp. 31–36. Boston: Beacon Press, 2002.
Shahin, Emad. "Toleration in a Modern Islamic Polity: Contemporary Islamist Views." In *Toleration on Trial*, edited by Ingrid Creppell, Russell Hardin, and Stephen Macedo. Lanham, Md.: Lexington Books, 2008.
The Amman Message. 2007. http://www.ammanmessage.com.

Anas Malik

TREATIES. The modern Arabic term for treaty is *muʿāhadah*, which denotes both the act of concluding a contract and the ensuing contract. In Islamic international law, a *muʿāhadah* is a contract between two or more sovereign states designed to normalize relations among them. Philologically, it shares the same root as *ʿahd*, which is used in the Qurʾān with a variety of meanings, among which are God's covenant with man (e.g., 2:124; 16:91) and a contractual agreement (e.g., 17:34; 18:8). *ʿAhd* also encompasses the classical concept of protection given to an enemy or to a non-Muslim, as a pledge of security for a limited time (*amān*) or with more permanent status (*dhimmah*). The parties to the covenant are called *ahl al-ʿahd*.

Four basic and interrelated concepts of Islamic international law determine relations with the non-Muslim world. These principles are: *jihād*, *dār al-Islām* (the territory of Islam), *dār al-ʿahd* (or *dār al-ṣulḥ*, the territory of the covenant), and *dār al-ḥarb* (the territory of war). Other technical terms also represent types of relations with non-Muslim states and their subjects, such as *hudnah* (ceasefire or temporary peace), *muwādaʿah* (peace agreement), *ṣulḥ* (truce), and *mīthāq* (covenant or pact). All these relations are contractual (*ʿaqd*, "contract") and are considered binding, provided they do not stipulate anything that contradicts Islamic law. These contracts or treaties can be either written or oral, depending on the circumstances under which they are concluded.

In modern international law, the *muʿāhadah* is restricted to significant political agreements such as peace treaties or affiliations or alliances between nations or supranational agencies. In the case of economic international treaties, as in agreements with world organizations such as the International Monetary Fund, the World Bank, and the Asian Development Bank, the term *ʿahd* or *mīthāq* is normally used.

In Classical Islamic Law. The majority of jurists define *muʿāhadah* as a *muhādanah* (conclusion of a truce). For the Ḥanafī al-Shaybānī (d. 804), a *muʿāhadah* is a peace agreement between Muslims and non-Muslims for a fixed period of time. Many Ḥanafī jurists adopted this definition, including ʿAlāʾ al-Dīn al-Samarqandī (d. 1144), who added that it involved the paying of tribute or other conditions. Mālikī jurists, such as Ibn ʿArafa, Dardīr, and al-Wansharīsī, define *muʿāhadah* as a truce between Muslims and non-Muslims, concluded to end physical conflict for a fixed period of time under Islamic law, while Shāfiʿī jurists—including al-Bahūtī, al-Muṭarrizī, al-Fīrūzābādī, and al-Fayūmī—define it as a contract concluded for the sake of ending fighting for a fixed time period with or without compensation. Ḥanbalī jurists define it as an abstention from fighting for a fixed time period with or without compensation.

Some scholars try to define further the distinctions between these terms; according to Abū Hilāl al-ʿAskarī (d. 1005), for example, an *ʿaqd* is more elastic than an *ʿahd*, for when a person or a party concludes the latter with another person or party, it means that each is bound to that particular agreement, while in the case of the former, the person or party is bound by conditions that can be waived under certain circumstances.

According to al-Shaybānī, there are two sets of circumstances for a *muʿāhadah* with non-Muslims. The first situation occurs when the Muslims are in a position of power, in which case they should not seek a treaty with non-Muslims, especially if it is not in the best interests of the greater Muslim community. This condition is made explicit in the Qurʾān: "So lose not heart, nor fall into despair. For ye must gain mastery if ye are true in Faith" (3:139), and "Be not weary and faint-hearted, crying for peace, when ye should be uppermost; for Allah is with you, and will never put you in loss for your [good] deeds" (47:35).

The second situation occurs when Muslims are not in a position of advantage over non-Muslims, at which time it is permissible to seek a peace agreement, since in these circumstances it serves the interests of Muslims to do so. Further justification of concluding a peace agreement is found in the Qurʾān: "But if the enemy incline towards peace, do thou [also] incline towards peace, and trust in Allah; for He is One that heareth and knoweth [all things]" (8:61).

Qurʾānic verse 4:92 addresses cases in which a Muslim has killed a person with whom a preexisting treaty or alliance had been established. It encourages the parties to seek redress within the confines of that particular treaty or understanding. The verse also indicates and encourages the concept of a treaty, referring to it as a *mīthāq*—a confirmed contract.

When the Qurʾān exhorts Muslims to fight, it also stipulates that Muslims not take up arms against those who have established a treaty (*mīthāq*) with them, stating, for example, "[Slay them] Except those who join a group between whom and you there is a treaty [of peace], or those who approach you with hearts restraining them from fighting you as well as fighting their own people" (4:90).

Another source for the understanding of a *muʿāhadah* with non-Muslims arises from the conduct of the Prophet as spelled out in the *ḥadīth*. When the Prophet entered Medina, he concluded a treaty (strictly speaking, a *muwādaʿah*) with the various Jewish tribes living there. This agreement illustrates the validity of a treaty with non-Muslims at a time of weakness on the part of Muslims. The Prophet's act in this instance became another source for validating a peace agreement under special circumstances.

In Islamic History. The Battle of the Trench (in 627), in which the Meccan Quraysh allied with other Arab and Jewish tribes laid siege to the Muslims in Medina, marked another type of treaty; on that occasion the Prophet received an envoy from the non-Muslims, ʿUyayna ibn Ḥiṣn, who demanded that the Prophet hand over all of the date harvest of Medina for one year in return for the Meccans' renouncing of hostilities. The Prophet consulted two community leaders from the Aws and Khazraj tribes, Saʿd ibn Muʿādh and Saʿd ibn ʿUbāda, regarding the offer. The Prophet and his two consultants agreed to give half of the produce. However, instead of a peace agreement, only an agreement to restore relations between parties (*murāwaḍah*) was achieved, since such a concession had not been revealed to Muḥammad nor had it ever been agreed to before; realizing the possible effect a peace treaty would have on the inhabitants of Medina, the Prophet decided not to change the custom.

Another event that provided a precedent for future treaties was the truce of al-Ḥudaybīyah (in 628) concluded between the Prophet and the Meccan chiefs. The truce came with conditions stipulating a fixed duration of ten years (some historians, such as Ibn ʿAdī, Ibn al-Ḥākim, al-Ṭabarānī, and Abū ʿUbayd, say four years), and imposed a further condition in proscribing theft or betrayal by either party. Whoever left for or escaped to Medina from Mecca after the truce was concluded would be handed back, even if a Muslim, whereas whoever left Medina for Mecca would not be returned to the Prophet.

In the Modern Period. Modern treaties that were concluded between Muslim and non-Muslim countries in the twentieth century include the Anglo-Iraqi treaty (1930), Anglo-Egyptian treaty (1936), the agreement between Egypt and Israel known as the Camp David Peace Accord in 1978, the Oslo agreement between the Palestinians and the Israelis in the early 1990s, and between Jordan and Israel, known as Wadi ʿAraba, in 1994.

The Anglo-Iraqi treaty of 1930, which was signed on behalf of the two ruling monarchs, George V and Faisal I, lasted until 1947; it was dictated by and overwhelmingly favored Britain, and was broken by a 1947 coup led by the Iraqi national Rāshid ʿAlī that ended the monarchy. The only Islamic aspect of the treaty is the Islamic *hijrī* date that was used.

The ultimate purpose of the Anglo-Egyptian treaty of 1936 was to end the British occupation of Egypt. However, twelve conditions were imposed by the British whereby full independence was not assured. The treaty was abrogated in October 1951 by the Wafd Party, which had been elected into the government in 1950. This treaty was not fully in accordance with the precedent set by the Ḥudaybīyah treaty between Muslims and non-Muslims, yet despite its weakness in supporting the Muslim side, it did propel an end to the British colonization of Egypt and led to the appointment of the first indigenous Egyptian leader in 1952, Muhammad Naguib.

[*See also* International Law.]

Bibliography

Bsoul, Labeeb Ahmed. *International Treaties (Muʿāhadāt) in Islam: Theory and Practice in the Light of Islamic International Law (Siyar) according to Orthodox Schools*. Lanham, Md.: University Press of America, 2008.

Ghunaymī, Muḥammad Ṭalʿat al-. *Aḥkām al-muʿāhadāt fī l-sharīʿah al-islāmīyah*. Alexandria, Egypt: Munshaʾat al-Maʿārif, 1977.

Ḥamīdallāh, Muḥammad. *Majmūʿat al-wathāʾiq al-siyāsīyah li-l-ʿahd al-nabawī wa-l-khilāfah al-rāshidah*. Beirut: Dār al-Irshād, 1969.

Kasānī, ʿAlāʾ al-Dīn Abū Bakr ibn Masʿūd al-Ḥanafī al-. *Badāʾiʿ al-ṣanāʾiʿ fī tartīb al-sharāʾiʿ*. Beirut: Dār al-Kutub al-ʿIlmīyah, 1968.

Khadduri, Majid. *War and Peace in the Law of Islam*. Baltimore: Johns Hopkins Press, 1955.

Kruse, Hans. "The Islamic Doctrine of International Treaties." *Islamic Quarterly* 1 (1954): 152–158.

Landau, J. M. "Muʿāhada." In *The Encyclopaedia of Islam*, edited by H. A. R. Gibb, vol. 7, pp. 250–253. Rev. ed. Leiden, Netherlands: E. J. Brill, 1993.

Sarakhsī, Abū Bakr Muḥammad ibn Aḥmad ibn Sahl al-. *Kitāb al-mabsūṭ*. Beirut: Dār al-Maʿrifa, 1906.

Shaybānī, Muḥammad ibn Ḥasan al-. *Sharhḥ kitāb al-siyar al-kabīr*. Cairo: Maṭbaʿat Sharikat al-Iʿlānāt al-Sharqīyah, 1971.

Zaydān, ʿAbd al-Karīm. *Aḥkām al-dhimmīyīn wa-al-mustaʾminīn fī dār al-islām*. Beirut: Muʾassasat al-Risālah, 1976.

LABEEB AHMED BSOUL

TRIBES. In both historical and contemporary times tribes have played important roles in the Islamic world. Tribal groups facilitated the rapid spread of Islam across vast territories in the early Islamic period. They contributed to the demise and rise of empires and states throughout the premodern period. Their political and military support of rulers at the local, regional, and wider levels helped to sustain many regimes in power, and their defiance and opposition weakened these entities and contributed to their collapse. In modern times tribal groups have continued to exert influence on many regimes. Foreign and occupying military forces—such as those in Afghanistan and Iraq in the early twenty-first century—have discovered that they needed to take seriously the tribal systems there. Rebels fighting against Muʿammar al-Qadhdhāfī and his regime in Libya in 2011 drew effectively on their tribal connections for organizational and logistical strength.

The English term "tribe" is one that scholars and others use inconsistently to depict what they perceive as a group of people, a political entity, a form of social organization, or a structural type. Although they often equate tribes with nomads and pastoralists, not all nomads or pastoralists have been tribally organized, and more tribal peoples have been settled than mobile. Often negatively, scholars and others associate the adjective "tribal" with certain cultural systems, ideologies, attitudes, modes of behavior, and material culture. For some the term "tribal" invokes primitive and traditional traits as compared to modern ones. The expression "tribes with flags" conveys the notion that even nation-states in the modern era (such as Somalia and Yemen) might be little more than tribes disguised as complex polities. Scholars usually neglect to consider tribal entities as part of a vibrant civil society in the Islamic world, but such polities have sometimes proven to be vital parts of postcolonial, modernizing, and democratizing societies, as witnessed, for example, by some tribally based sectors of Kurdish society in urban Turkey, Iraq, and Iran.

Many settled people have viewed the tribes they feared as synonymous with outlaws and rebels. For their part tribespeople have feared the loss of autonomy and have considered themselves fiercely independent and loyal to their own groups. Settled people have often perceived tribal society as inferior to urban society (*ḥadārah*), the so-called civilized Islamic ideal. They have seen cities as centers of government and order and tribes as rebellious and destructive. From an urban perspective "tribe" has often meant nomads or other rural people beyond the government's reach. State and colonial officials have tended to reify the concept of tribe in order to facilitate their own administration. Declaring tribes to be identifiable corporate bodies with fixed memberships and territories, they have produced lists of the tribes under their supposed authority and have acted in terms of those entities. Such attitudes and the resulting policies have created and fortified political, social, and physical boundaries.

Formation of Tribes. Tribes have emerged when people, their strategic location, and their vital resources have intersected with the interests of external powers and mediating agents. These resources have included land for pastoralism and agriculture, water, raw and processed materials, labor forces, migratory routes, trade routes, and markets. The mediating agents have been tribal leaders, governmental officials, regional elites, foreign powers, and outside analysts. The people so organized, their leaders, and external powers and agencies could all benefit by this association.

Tribally organized people have created their local ties voluntarily by centering them on residential communities within certain territories and drawing upon the principles and processes of kinship, marriage, co-residence, economics, and political affiliation. Their ties with wider sociopolitical entities—their tribal groups—have tended to be less concrete and more abstract than their local ones.

Individuals and groups have formed tribes when they affiliated politically with local and sometimes higher-level groups and leaders. Various factors explain the extent of supralocal, wider tribal ties: the geopolitical and strategic setting, the value placed internally and especially externally on local resources and labor, the extent of external pressures (from foreign invaders, colonists, state governments, and urban-linked institutions), the ability of groups to organize and act in their own interests, and the level of military expertise and power. As each of these circumstances has changed, so, too, have the characteristics of tribal groups, leadership systems, and identities. For millennia tribal people have associated with more complexly organized society, in particular the state, the market, and urban-centered institutions; no local group has remained isolated. The main stimulus for tribal formation has related to this wider association, and tribal leaders and governmental officials have served as the principal mediating agents. Tribal leaders have represented state power for tribal members while they simultaneously acted on behalf of the interests of the tribal polity for the state.

Tribal groups have expanded and contracted. Small groups have joined larger ones when, for example, state officials attempted to restrict their access to essential resources or a foreign power sent troops to attack them. Large groups have divided into smaller entities in order to be less visible to the state and escape its reach. Intertribal mobility—the movement of people from one tribe to another—has been a common process in tribal formation and dissolution.

Tribes and States. A state in any historical period can be characterized by multiple traits: territorial borders (not necessarily secure or clearly delineated), a bureaucratic apparatus, some success at monopolizing physical coercion (especially for suppression), some degree of legitimacy, rules for the succession of leadership, extraction of resources (especially taxes), maintenance of order associated with the distribution of goods and services (such as constructing and policing roads), occupational specialization (such as artisans and priests), and a socioeconomically stratified population. Asserting centralizing goals, state rulers have tried to control the territories they claimed and to subjugate or integrate any autonomous or rebellious groups within them. They have not always succeeded. Problems with legitimacy and rules of succession have meant that rulers were vulnerable to competitors, especially those having independent military resources, such as tribal leaders.

Rigid definitions and models of states do not necessarily apply to the early Islamic era and the premodern period and can be problematic as well for modern times. Few states in the early period could claim recognized, legitimized power, and rulers did not always succeed in achieving territorial control. The polities represented by Afghanistan and Iraq in 2012 demonstrated few similarities with nearby established nation-states such as Iran and Turkey. Premodern and modern states should be distinguished, although certain so-called traditional or premodern elements have persisted in modern times. Kinship and tribal ties including genealogies extending back to the Prophet Muḥammad, for example, have enhanced the legitimacy of rule in modern-day Saudi Arabia, Jordan, and Morocco. Constitutional regulations in a newly independent Kazakhstan (formed after the dissolution of the Soviet Union in 1991) required citizens who sought major political offices to speak the Kazakh language fluently. All Kazakhs had been members of clan and tribal groups, and these affiliations (at least superficially) have continued to be important in the running of the new state.

Modern nation-states are legal and international entities to be defined, also, in these terms. Modern rulers coming to power have usually relied on Western-style militaries and bureaucracies. Through state centralization they have aimed to cause changes in government and society by supporting a nationalist ideology, economic development and control, modernization (including such features as the expansion of formal education), and some secularization.

States in history have ranged from fragmented polities lacking autonomous structures of authority, to decentralized polities with rudimentary institutions, to centralized states maintained by a functioning bureaucracy and standing army and claiming a monopoly of the legitimate use of power.

The structure, organization, and leadership of tribal groups have reflected their relationship with states. Thus they have also ranged from being small, loosely organized, diffuse, noncentralized entities; to fragmented and ephemeral tribal confederacies; to large state-like confederacies with centralized hierarchical leadership. From before Islam until the mid-twentieth century (and in some locales into the early twenty-first century), challengers to state rule as well as founders of states have often required the military and technological prowess of tribal groups, while established state rulers have needed tribal support for levies, revenue, and regional security. Tribes have always offered a reservoir of military force. State rulers have often needed to share power with tribes, and their ability to penetrate the countryside has often depended on the extent of their ties to the tribal elite there.

Even in the early twenty-first century tribal leaders and structures have continued to facilitate the rise, survival, and demise of state rulers and institutions. Afghanistan and Iraq offer recent examples of the ways that tribal entities (and others) could disrupt state-building efforts by foreign occupiers. Tribal polities have both coordinated with and opposed the Taliban (itself based partly on tribal and ethnic ties) in Afghanistan, and they have both assisted and impeded international al-Qaʿida forces in Afghanistan, Pakistan, and Iraq. Even in more stable, established states such as Morocco, tribes have thwarted the government's efforts to control its vital border regions.

Tribal formations have enabled the integration of people into state structures, while at the same time preventing these peoples from being subordinated to or assimilated within the state. Tribal structures have emerged as components of state rule while simultaneously facilitating people to resist certain forms of state interference. A loosely formed, noncentralized tribal group has been as much a response to external pressures as has been a complexly organized, centralized one; both entities have exhibited adaptive strategies. A loosely organized group, protected by its structural diffuseness, has offered little to state agents to manipulate, while a centralized group has used its complex organization to resist state pressure as well as to benefit from being an instrument of state control.

As a result of these formative and functional relationships, tribes and states through history have demonstrated interdependence and have maintained each other as a single (yet complex) system. Tribes and states have represented alternative polities, each creating and solving political problems for the other. State rulers especially have depended on tribes for military power, revenue, and regional security. They have exploited and strengthened the polities they encountered, which often required minimal effort and expense on their part and yet provided some order and security. Tribal people in turn have sometimes depended on state intervention in regional competition and conflict, and their leaders have drawn power, authority, and wealth from their connections with states. A weak state has facilitated the emergence of strong tribes; strong tribes in turn have helped to ensure a weak state. Strong states and strong tribes have also coexisted with tolerance or antagonism. Especially in the premodern era many states had begun as tribal dynasties from which emerged state-like confederacies and eventually empires, such as the Ottoman Empire.

At any time up to the mid-twentieth century what was "tribe" and what was "state" depended on prevailing political circumstances, especially when foreign powers interfered. Eager to influence the policies of states, foreign powers supported tribal leaders and buttressed tribal structures in order to threaten state rulers into complying or to force changes in state leadership. Some complex polities demonstrated both tribal and state features, for example, Kalat (1638–1955) and Swat (1849–1969) in the territory of modern-day Pakistan. In general the term "state" is best used to refer to a higher level of political, economic, and social complexity than has usually been found in tribal groups.

Tribal Leaders. Tribal leaders have emerged from local, regional, and state relationships and processes. High-level tribal leaders have drawn power and authority from their contacts with the state and other external forces, but they also have depended on support and allegiance at the local level. They have often based their legitimacy on ideologies and systems of values that they shared (or claimed to share) with their political supporters.

Various symbolic systems have linked tribal leaders of all levels with supporters. For some notions of shared beliefs in Islam have united them, especially when these beliefs have differed from those of surrounding nontribal societies. Shīʿī Muslim tribes in southern Iraq differentiated themselves from the tribal and nontribal Sunnī Muslims who supported the regime of Saddam Hussein (and they suffered violence and discrimination because of their Shīʿī identity). Common affiliations as members of Ahl-e Ḥaqq (a Shīʿī sect) in eastern Turkey unified some Kurdish tribespeople against the secularized, nontribal Sunnī Muslims who controlled the Turkish government and aimed to force dissident minority groups to integrate themselves in the state.

Other symbolic systems include notions of a shared history (often invoking past military exploits), genealogies (political charters), rituals, language, notions of territory, tribal names, sentiments of honor, and conventions of residence, mobility and migration, dwellings, apparel, and expressive arts. Tribal people have recognized and supported leaders more because of shared beliefs than because of threats of coercion.

Leaders have often been limited in their ability to apply force because tribespeople could "vote with their feet," deny allegiance to them, and ally with other groups and leaders. High-level tribal leaders have also played economic roles in a regional, often nontribal, context and have developed a base of power there as well. Such contacts may have benefited their tribal supporters. The most successful leaders have simultaneously cultivated the allegiance of their political followers and their regional and governmental contacts.

Tribal leaders who have wanted to expand their power and authority beyond immediate tribal boundaries have often needed to invoke wider Islamic, linguistic, ethnic, national, or state notions. For example, the Bakhtiārī tribal khans in the nineteenth and early twentieth centuries shared Iranian, Shīʿī values and notions of kingship with many nontribal, urban Iranians. In Turkey, Iraq, and Iran in the past several centuries, Kurdish tribal leaders drew on the institutions and ideologies of Sunnī, Shīʿī, and Ṣūfī Islam, particularly religious brotherhoods and saintly lineages, in order to transcend local tribal sources of authority. In the early 1950s the paramount Qashqaʾi tribal khans supported the nontribal National Front, an Iran-wide political association espousing liberal, secular, democratic, and nationalist goals. In these and other ways such tribal leaders relied on extralocal, nontribal connections, which also could enhance their internal, tribal links.

The scholarly literature and media reports on the Muslim world often regard tribes negatively, despite the corruption and abuse of power characterizing the states in which many tribal people lived. Instead, by understanding the perspectives of people who fell under the ruthless policies of states, a consideration of alternative polities (such as tribes) proves informative. The persistent failure of many modern states to provide equality and justice for the majority of their citizens suggests that scholars and others could benefit by examining other kinds of political formations without succumbing to false, alarming, or stereotyped notions.

[*See also* Ethnicity; *and* Nation.]

BIBLIOGRAPHY

Beck, Lois. "Ethnic, Religious, and Tribal Minorities in Iran." In *Sectarian Politics in the Gulf*, edited by Lawrence Potter. New York: Hurst, 2013.

Beck, Lois. *Nomad: A Year in the Life of a Qashqa'i Tribesman in Iran*. Berkeley: University of California Press, 1991.

Cronin, Stephanie. *Tribal Politics in Iran: Rural Conflict and the New State, 1921–1941*. London and New York: Routledge, 2007.

Eickelman, Dale F. *The Middle East and Central Asia: An Anthropological Approach*. 4th ed. Englewood Cliffs, N.J.: Prentice Hall, 2002.

Hourani, Albert. "Conclusion: Tribes and States in Islamic History." In *Tribes and State Formation in the Middle East*, edited by Philip S. Khoury and Joseph Kostiner, pp. 303–311. Berkeley: University of California Press, 1990.

Huang, Julia. *Tribeswomen of Iran: Weaving Memories among Qashqa'i Nomads*. London: Tauris Academic Studies, 2009.

Khoury, Philip S., and Joseph Kostiner, eds. *Tribes and State Formation in the Middle East*. Berkeley: University of California Press, 1990.

Lavie, Smadar. *The Poetics of Military Occupation: Mzeina Allegories of Bedouin Identity under Israeli and Egyptian Rule*. Berkeley: University of California Press, 1990.

Schatz, Edward. *Modern Clan Politics: The Power of "Blood" in Kazakhstan and Beyond*. Seattle: University of Washington Press, 2004.

Shahrani, M. Nazif. *The Kirghiz and Wakhi of Afghanistan: Adaptation to Closed Frontiers and War*. Seattle: University of Washington Press, 2002.

Tapper, Richard, ed. *The Conflict of Tribe and State in Iran and Afghanistan*. London: Croom Helm, 1983.

Tapper, Richard. *Pasture and Politics: Economics, Conflict, and Ritual among Shahsevan Nomads of Northwestern Iran*. London and New York: Academic Press, 1979.

Wedeen, Lisa. *Peripheral Visions: Publics, Power, and Performance in Yemen*. Chicago: University of Chicago Press, 2008.

LOIS BECK
and JULIA HUANG

TRUCES. *See* Treaties.

TURĀBĪ, ḤASAN AL-. Ḥasan al-Turābī (1932–) was born in Kassala, Sudan, on the border with Eritrea, and became one of Sudan's leading Islamist political leaders. Growing up in a particularly devout Muslim family, he received an Islamic education from his father as well as a standard modern education, going on to study law at the universities of Khartoum, London, and the Sorbonne. He joined Sudan's Muslim Brotherhood as a student in the early 1950s and rose to prominence during the popular uprising of October 1964. The brotherhood subsequently founded a small but vociferous party, the Islamic Charter Front, through which al-Turābī pushed for an Islamic constitution.

Although the 1969 military coup that brought to power President Jaʿfar Nimeiri was a setback, al-Turābī accepted Nimeiri's 1977 reconciliation overtures and returned from exile along with his brother-in-law al-Ṣādiq al-Mahdī. Al-Turābī became minister of justice in 1979 and encouraged the Muslim Brothers to move into many areas of public life, including the newly established Islamic banks, various government offices, as well as the armed forces. Many Sudanese believed al-Turābī was behind Nimeiri's introduction of Islamic law in September 1983; however Nimeiri broke with al-Turābī and imprisoned him shortly before the popular uprising of 1985 in which Nimeiri was overthrown.

In the 1986 elections al-Turābī's party, now known as the National Islamic Front (NIF), came in third, but was clearly the rising force in Sudanese politics. For the next three years the NIF was in and out of al-Ṣādiq al-Mahdī's weak coalition governments, though the party remained determined to develop Sudan as an Islamic state, even at the expense of perpetuating the civil war in the south. It was widely believed that the prospect of a secularizing compromise with the south was the cause that precipitated the NIF-backed coup of 30 June 1989, the so-called National Salvation Revolution, which brought him to power (although al-Turābī was briefly imprisoned along with other leaders of the officially banned parties, the coup was carefully orchestrated by the longtime hard-line ideological leader from his prison cell). After 1989 he was the mastermind behind Sudan's efforts to establish an Islamic state, even though al-Turābī held no formal position in any government.

Al-Turābī survived an attack by a disgruntled Sudanese exile, Hashim Bedreddin, in Ottawa, Canada, on 26 May 1992. Bedreddin, a Ṣūfī opponent of the NIF, opposed al-Turābī's efforts to introduce Islamic rule. Severely wounded by the assault al-Turābī suffered from slurred speech problems and required the use of a cane. Notwithstanding his injuries the ideologue remained active in political circles, which earned him imprisonment terms in March 2004, on the orders of his one-time ally President ʿUmar al-Bashīr. Although he was released on 28 June 2005 al-Turābī returned to jail many times thereafter, most recently on 17 January 2011, following civil unrest across North Africa, allegedly for inciting Sudanese to rise against Khartoum.

Al-Turābī has never published a comprehensive account of his thoughts, but his various writings and pronouncements presented a relatively liberal interpretation of Islam, including a belief in democracy and pluralism. Remarkably he seldom repudiated this line of thought, although successive Sudanese governments were widely seen as the most restrictive since independence in 1956. Parliamentary democracy was abolished by the military, which in promoting its Islamic revolution forcibly repressed not only political parties but also many independent groups in civil society. The Muslim Brotherhood, for example, became dominant not only in government but also in the civil service, the professions, and the economy. Feared by neighboring Arab states as a promoter of radical Islamic activism, the new regime cooperated in turn with Libya, Iraq, and Iran; Iran in particular supported government victories in the civil war in the south in 1992.

Still al-Turābī maintained his progressive ideas, such as embracing democracy, healing the breach between Sunnīs and Shīʿī, integrating art, music, and singing into religion, and even expanding the rights of women, where he noted: "The Prophet himself used to visit women, not men, for counseling and advice. They could lead prayer. Even in his battles, they are there! In the election between Othman and Ali to determine who will be the successor to the Prophet, they voted!" (Wright, 2006, p. 165). His avant-garde views on women shocked conservative clerics, though he remained steadfast by declaring "I want women to work and become part of public life" because "the home doesn't require much work anymore, what with all the appliances." He even opined that the requirement for hijab was outdated too, because, according to his 2006 Al-Arabita Television interview, the tradition only applied to the Prophet's wives. An equally controversial position was his opposition to the death penalty for apostasy, which rejected the Iranian *fatwa* issued by Ayatollah Ruhollah Khomeini against the author Salman Rushdie. Such views angered many, though his vision for Sharīʿah was truly enlightened, as he insisted that the law ought to apply only to Muslims, especially as the latter were called upon to share power with Christians in his contemplated federal system for Sudan.

Building on his principles of tolerance, al-Turābī issued his own *fatwa* in 2006, which allowed Muslim women to marry non-Muslim men and even allowed consumption of alcohol in certain situations. He was promptly imprisoned on 12 May 2008, along with other members of his Popular Congress Party (PCP), but released after about twelve hours in detention. Ostensibly Khartoum objected to certain political documents he carried that, allegedly, placed him in league with Salva Kiir Mayardit, the first vice president of Sudan and the first president of the government of Southern Sudan after 9 July 2011, although Bashīr seldom perceived al-Turābī as a genuine threat to his rule. Critically, however, al-Turābī called on Bashīr to surrender himself to the International Criminal Court (ICC) on 12 January 2009, after it held the Sudanese president responsible for war crimes in Darfur. In ill health and of advanced age—he was seventy-seven when he reentered jail in 2011—al-Turābī stood as a maverick in Muslim affairs. A pragmatic thinker who was flexible in the pursuit of a resurgent Islam, which he sought to see expand not only in Sudan but also in neighboring African and Arab countries. His success in building the Muslim Brotherhood in Sudan before 1989 enabled the military regime to pursue its Islamizing policies. These actions entrenched the Brotherhood within the country and made it a wider force for the promotion of radical Islamic fundamentalism throughout North and East Africa, although al-Turābī knew that South Sudan's loss was a direct result of Khartoum's intransigence.

[*See also* Muslim Brotherhood; *and* Sudan.]

BIBLIOGRAPHY

Works of Ḥasan al-Turābī

"The Islamic State." In *Voices of Resurgent Islam*, edited by John L. Esposito, pp. 241–251. New York: Oxford University Press, 1983.

"Principles of Governance, Freedom, and Responsibility in Islam." *American Journal of Islamic Social Sciences* 4, no. 1 (1987).

Women in Islam and Muslim Society. London: Milestones, 1991.

Secondary Works

El-Affendi, Abdelwahab. *Turabi's Revolution: Islam and Power in Sudan*. London: Grey Seal, 1991. Fullest account of al-Turābī's work and thought.

Burr, J. Millard, and Robert O. Collins. *Sudan in Turmoil: Hasan al-Turabi and the Islamist State, 1889–2003*. Princeton, N.J.: Markus Wiener Publishers, 2009.

Esposito, John L., and John O. Voll. *Makers of Contemporary Islam*. New York: Oxford University Press, 2001. Contains a biography of al-Turābī.

Lowrie, Arthur L., ed. *Islam, Democracy, the State, and the West: A Round Table with Dr. Hasan Turabi, May 10, 1992*. Tampa, Fla.: World and Islam Studies Enterprise, 1993.

Sidahmed, Abdel Salam. *Politics and Islam in Contemporary Sudan*. Richmond, Surrey, U.K.: Curzon, 1996.

Voll, John O., ed. *Sudan: State and Society in Crisis*. Bloomington: Indiana University Press, 1991.

Wright, Lawrence. *The Looming Tower: Al Qaeda and the Road to 9/11*. New York: Knopf, 2006.

Peter Woodward
Updated by Joseph A. Kéchichian

TURKEY. One of the successor states created from the ruins of the Ottoman Empire after World War I, Turkey became the first secular state in the Muslim world. The new state was declared a republic in October 1923 after the defeat of the Greek army and the sultan's forces in a bitter civil war. The abandonment of the Sharīʿah and the adoption of a secular legal system based on

Western codes of law, as well as the declaration of a secular republic in 1928, were radical departures from tradition. The new Turkey was predominantly Muslim, with non-Muslims accounting for only 2.6 percent of the population in 1927. There were many who argued that retaining such Islamic symbols as the caliphate would provide legitimacy for the new regime. Until 1924 Turkey had been the seat of the caliphate, and from the very genesis of the Ottoman Empire, the Turkish state and society had been deeply influenced by Islamic traditions and culture, especially the tradition of the *gazi* (Arabic, *ghāzin*) warrior. Not surprisingly, Mustafa Kemal Atatürk, the founder of the republic, enjoyed the honorific "Gazi" into the 1930s.

The Early Republic. The Islamic component of Turkish nationalism was bound to be strong because the majority of the new nation's people were Muslims. The composition of the population within the borders of the new republic changed dramatically between 1914 and the census of 1927; the non-Muslim population had declined from 20 to 3 percent and continued to decline thereafter. But secularization might not have been so radical or so swift had the conservatives not used Islam to challenge Kemalist leadership. After dissolving the sultanate in 1922 the Kemalists toyed with the idea of retaining the caliph as a symbolic figurehead; however the ambitions of Caliph Abdülmecid, supported by Mustafa Kemal's opponents, forced the government to act swiftly and abolish the caliphate on 3 March 1924. All educational institutions were placed under the jurisdiction of the Ministry of Public Instructions, and a Directorate of Religious Affairs under the prime minister was given charge of "all cases and concerns of the exalted Islamic faith which relate to dogma and ritual."

The Kurdish rebellion of February 1925 led by the Naqshbandī Shaykh Said prompted the creation of an extraordinary regime that lasted until 4 March 1929. The Kemalists used these four years to launch a program of reforms that effectively removed Islam from political life and secularized society. The dervish orders and sacred tombs were closed in November 1925, and practices such as fortune-telling, magic, and cures by breathing performed by *shaykh*s, *babas* (elders of religious orders), *seyyids* (descendants of the Prophet), *mürşid*s (Arabic, *murshids*, spiritual guides), *dedes* (dervish leaders), and *çelebis* (leaders of religious orders) became illegal. The wearing of the fez, a symbol of Muslim identity, was outlawed, and men were required to wear hats. The Gregorian calendar was adopted, along with the twenty-four-hour clock. The Swiss civil code, adapted to Turkey's conditions, replaced the Sharīʿah in 1926, depriving the *ʿulamāʾ* of their traditional source of influence. In 1928 the Assembly voted to remove the words "The religion of the Turkish state is Islam" from Article 2 of the constitution, completing the disestablishment of Islam. Meanwhile a committee set up to study the implementation of an "Islamic reformation" presented its findings. It recommended, among other things, introducing pews into mosques and sacred instrumental music into the service. These proposals were too radical, and the committee was quickly disbanded, suggesting that the government had no intention of alienating Muslim opinion. However the committee's proposal to replace Arabic with Turkish as the liturgical language of Islam was adopted a few years later.

The purpose of these radical reforms was not anti-Islamic but political: to remove from the jurisdiction of religious leaders and their political allies all legal, social, and educational institutions and place them in the hands of the Directorate of Religious Affairs. The state would then direct religious energy toward its own socioeconomic program. One of the reformers defined a secular government as "one which transfers the leadership in religious affairs from the ignorant to the enlightened," and the Kemalist daily *Hakimiyet-i Milliye* (30 December 1925) editorialized "We can sincerely claim that our Revolution has more of a religious than an irreligious character as it has saved consciences from harmful tyranny and domination.... To think that a nation can live without any religion is nothing less than denying humanity, sociology, and history."

Islam and Political Parties. The National Order Party (Millî Nizam Partisi [MNP]) was led by Necmettin Erbakan, an engineer trained in Germany, who also enjoyed the support of the Naqshbandīs. He was a new politician who emerged in the 1960s to fill the vacuum left by the Democrats, disqualified from political life by the junta. He was provincial rather than cosmopolitan in outlook and had nothing in common with the old elite except the ambition to develop the country. Such people were willing to adopt Western technology to create a modern, capitalist economy, but they were at home in the culture they associated with Islam and were contemptuous of the imported Western culture they identified with loose morals and decadence. The MNP never called for the restoration of the Sharīʿah; they campaigned only for a national economy independent of foreign control and a national culture based on Ottoman-Islamic traditions and free of corrupting fashions imported from the West.

The party was banned by the military regime in 1971 but regrouped as the National Salvation Party (Millî Selamet Partisi [MSP]) in 1973. In the next general election the MSP garnered 11 percent of the vote and became the coalition partner of the social democratic Republican People's Party (Cumhuriyet Halk Partisi [CHP]), as both shared a similar economic program. When the coalition broke up Erbakan continued to play a significant role in new coalition governments led by the Justice Party. This gave him considerable powers of patronage, which he exercised on behalf of his supporters, especially the Naqshbandīs. As a result Islamists were soon entrenched throughout the bureaucracy, posing a threat to secular education.

The MSP was banned again by the military junta that seized power in September 1980. When political activity was partially restored in 1983, the Motherland Party (Anavatan Partisi) led by Turgut Özal, a former member of the MSP, assumed the mantle of political Islam. But Muslim opinion in Turkey, radicalized by the Iranian revolution, wanted a more militant party to support. Initially the Welfare Party (Refâh Partisi [RP])—the MSP reincarnated—attempted but failed to meet these radical expectations. After failure in the 1987 election the party changed its strategy and emphasized "the struggle against feudalism, imperialism, and fascism." The strategy paid off, and the RP, in coalition with the neofascist Nationalist Labor Party (Milliyetçi Çalısma Partisi), won 17 percent of the vote in 1991. It also fared well in the local elections of 27 March 1994, winning municipalities in squatter and working-class areas, but it was still far from winning power throughout the country. However it was accused of strengthening its position by colonizing the state bureaucracy with its loyalists. The party was said to be entrenched in the Interior Ministry, holding some seven hundred of the fifteen hundred key executive posts such as provincial governors and inspectors.

The parties of the center-right and center-left remained divided, allowing the Welfare Party to become the leading party in the general election of December 1995 with 21 percent of the vote and 158 seats in parliament. As no party had the electoral strength to form a government, they were forced to negotiate a coalition. The secular parties refused to form a coalition with the Islamists even though Erbakan declared that he had no interest in changing the constitution in order to institute the Sharīʿah, and that his party wanted work for the state and the welfare of the people.

Finally, on 6 March 1996 the center-right parties—Motherland and True Path—formed a coalition that was rendered unstable by the rivalry between the leaders. On 6 June Prime Minister Mesut Yilmaz resigned, and another round of negotiations followed. On 29 June Erbakan and Tansu Çiller, leader of True Path, announced the formation of a coalition—after both leaders agreed to shelve investigations of corruption against each other. The coalition, between an Islamist and a self-declared secularist, and based on pure opportunism was bound to be unstable. The secular media constantly scrutinized and criticized Erbakan, especially after his visit to Iran and Qadhdhāfī's Libya. Erbakan wanted to strengthen Turkey's links with the "Islamic world" and balance his country's pro-Western foreign policy. He was humiliated by the generals, who signed a Defense Industry Cooperation Agreement with Israel without the approval of his government on 28 August 1996.

Erbakan had also to appease his party's base. He did so by such gestures as inviting Islamic leaders to his residence and promising to build mosques in Taksim, the very center of secular Istanbul. But the rank and file was not so easily appeased, and in January 1997 the Welfare Party's mayor of Sincan organized a Jerusalem Day rally to protest Israel's occupation of that city. The generals responded by sending tanks through Sincan, a surburb of Ankara, and having the mayor arrested. On 28 February the National Security Council, dominated by the generals, ordered the government to clamp down on Islamist activity, especially the wearing of headscarves by women working in the public sphere. This event came to be known as "the post-modern coup" or the "February 28 Process." In August parliament passed a law extending secular education from five to eight years so as to weaken the hold of Islamists on the youth. A new law placed independent mosques under government control, another measure to curb Islamic radicalism. Under such pressure Erbakan decided to resign in June hoping that that the Welfare Path would continue under Tansu Çiller, the coalition's deputy prime minister. But President Süleyman Demirel accepted his resignation and appointed Mesut Yilmaz to lead the new coalition.

Even before the constitutional court ordered the dissolution of the Welfare Party in January 1998 for violating the principles of the secular republic, the Islamists had founded the Fazilet Partisi (Virtue Party) in December 1997. The new party had learned that there was no point in defying the army and no longer talked of withdrawing from NATO or introducing Islamic banking. But there were still many hardliners in the party who wanted to challenge the dress code by supporting the headscarf.

The Islamists had been marginalized, and Turkey was led by a nationalist coalition until the election of 18 April 1999. Thanks to the capture of Abdullah Ocalan, the leader of the Kurdistan Workers' Party, the nationalists emerged the winners while parties of the center-right and left collapsed. Although the vote of the Virtue Party also declined, it still managed to win almost 16 percent of the vote and performed even better in local elections. The center had collapsed because the voters were tired of the bickering between the parties and their leaders and therefore preferred to vote Islamist or in this case nationalist.

The Kavakçı Affair. When the new parliament convened on 2 May, it erupted in fury when the Virtue Party's Merve Kavakçı entered wearing a headscarf. Bülent Ecevit, soon to be the prime minister, declared: "No one may interfere with the private lives of individuals, but this is not a private space. This is the supreme foundation of the state. It is not the place to challenge the state." Merve Kavakçı was not allowed to take her oath and was disqualified from being a deputy on the technicality that she had not made her dual Turkish-U.S. citizenship public. Her party was described as a "cancer-producing metastasis," and, on 22 June, the constitutional court dissolved the Virtue Party. The Islamists were now irrevocably divided between Erbakan's "traditionalists," and those described as moderate reformers. The Kavakçı affair was the last attempt of the traditionalist to challenge the system so openly.

The nationalist coalition, though marred by corruption, seemed stable. But on 19 February 2001 an ailing Ecevit created a crisis when he stormed out of the National Security Council meeting, accused by President Ahmet Necdet Sezer of turning a blind eye to corruption in the government and obstructing investigations. Ecevit's refusal to resign and allow a younger man to take over the leadership of the party and the government meant that a general election was the only way out of the political impasse.

In July 2001 the traditional wing of Islamists around Erbakan responded by forming the Felicity Party (Saadet Partisi). The party's emblem, five stars floating within the crescent, was interpreted as either the five pillars of Islam or the party's reincarnation of the four earlier parties of political Islam—National Order (Millî Nizam), National Salvation (Millî Selamet), Welfare (Refâh), and Virtue (Fazilet)—plus Felicity (Saadet).

The "moderate" Islamists countered by forming the Justice and Development Party (Adaletve Kalkınma Partisi [AKP]) on 14 August. Its leader was Recep Tayyip Erdoğan and its emblem a light bulb symbolizing enlightenment. Though its roots lay in the Erbakan movement, Erdoğan did not see it as the continuation of the earlier parties. It represented new elements in the country and was described as "democratic-conservative," rather like Christian Democrats in Europe. While some of its supporters called for the Sharīʿah (23 percent), the majority (44 percent) were opposed, suggesting that the demand for the Sharīʿah in Turkey was falling.

Erdoğan was also a new kind of leader, someone who did not come out of "the system" as had Menderes, Demirel, Erbakan, and Özal. He was a product of Kasımpaşa, a rough and ready, lower-middle-class district of Istanbul, and had made his reputation as the dynamic mayor of Istanbul. His earlier political career suggested that he was a militant Islamist, and in April 1998 he was even sentenced to ten months for reciting lines from a Mehmet Ziya Gökalp poem: "The mosques are our barracks, / the domes our helmets, / the minarets our bayonets, / and the believers our soldiers."

The Election of 2007. Erdoğan, more confident after his electoral victory, was determined to strengthen his control over the state structure. He was able to use the EU's agenda that called for civilian control over the armed forces. Before the presidential election Erdoğan told the generals politely to stay out of politics. Nevertheless, on 27 August Chief of Staff General Büyükanıt declared that the armed forces would continue to protect a social, democratic, secular republic. Next day Abdullah Gül, the JDP's candidate, was elected president. With a majority in parliament and the party's man in the presidency, the prime minister began to assert greater control over the state.

In June 2007 prosecutors began to investigate a military conspiracy—called Ergenekon—whose aim was to overthrow the JDP government. Initially, retired generals were called to give testimony, but in January 2008 the court ordered the arrest of thirteen suspects. Thereafter and for the next four years, waves of arrests of hundreds of senior officers, journalists, and university professors allegedly involved in this conspiracy followed. They were kept in prison until their inconclusive trials. In January 2010 the neo-liberal daily *Taraf* published a story about a coup in preparation between 2002 and 2003. Again there were dozens of arrests but no resolution of this case, dubbed "Sledgehammer" (Balyoz), despite claims that the evidence had been fabricated. By the beginning of 2013 there was still no end in sight in either case. The wheels of Turkish justice move extremely slowly; a case against Dev-Yol, a militant leftist faction, that opened in the early 1980s was not closed until December 2009. Apart from these cases, which undermined the position of the military, in January 2012 the civil National Intelligence Organization took over much of intelligence gathering from the armed forces. A new balance had been established and the government was now dominated.

The judiciary came next. On 21 January 2008 Erdoğan issued a warning against judicial interference in matters like the turban or headscarf issue. The next day parliament began to legislate against the powers of the judiciary. These were slowly whittled down and on 6 May 2010 parliament passed a law to overhaul the board that appointed judges who became party appointees. Observers noted that the separation of powers so vital to a democracy was no longer present in Turkey.

In 2009 the state launched an attack on the press, imposing a half-billion-dollar fine on the Doğan media group. The Turkish Journalists' Association described the huge fine as a way of silencing the media the government disliked. The U.S. government's Human Rights Report also criticized the JDP for putting pressure on both the judiciary and the media. In October the EU's annual progress report criticized the government for its campaign against the press, as well as for closing down four Kurdish newspapers. Such actions, it noted, were obstacles in Turkey's bid to join the EU. Such was Turkey's record of human rights violations that in 2009 the European Court of Human Rights found Turkey guilty and sentenced it to pay a fine of 297,000 euros, but the governing party did not take the report seriously, and establishing its control over state and society was, for the moment, more important than joining the EU.

The lack of strong opposition parties made the JDP's task easier, but neither the Republican People's Party (RPP) nor the Nationalist Action Party was up to the task of opposition. Despite the change in leadership in the RPP in 2010 after eighteen years under Deniz Baykal's leadership, the party was riddled with factionalism; by 2013 it had made no progress in challenging the government on any significant issue.

During these years commentators observed that the national view (*milligörüş*), the Islamist ideology of JDP's predecessor, had gradually taken over the ruling party. There was creeping Islamization of society; municipalities no longer permitted alcohol to be served on premise; taxes were increased on alcoholic drinks; education was becoming more religious and the teaching of Darwin's theory of evolution was discouraged. By the end of 2008 the government began to appoint Islamist university rectors close to the party. Even TÜBİTAK—the Scientific Research Council of Turkey—was directed by an anti-Darwinist. Later that year the Istanbul municipality restored the lodges of mystical Ṣūfīs, banned in 1925.

Another feature of these years was the deterioration of the Turkish-Israeli relationship. The process began in Davos on 30 January 2009. Erdoğan rebuked Prime Minister Shimon Peres, declaring: "When it comes to killing, you know very well how to kill [in Gaza]." The relationship deteriorated further after 31 May 2010, when Israeli commandoes attacked the *Mavi Marmara*, a Turkish ship taking international volunteers to the Gaza strip. The relationship had not been repaired by the beginning of 2013.

The Kurdish problem had plagued Turkey's governments since 1984. Prime Minister Erdoğan made concessions to the Kurds such as permitting Kurdish to be used in courts, opening a state radio station broadcasting in Kurdish, and allowing

Kurdish classes in some schools and a university. He talked of a "Kurdish opening," going as far as to permit secret talks between the imprisoned leader, Abdullah Öcalan, and his own emissaries. However by the beginning of 2013 no results had been achieved and the insurgency of the PKK, the Workers Party of Turkey, continued.

Ever since Erdoğan came to power the economy has flourished, because his government has followed the IMF prescription under a finance minister who worked for Merrill Lynch. That was perhaps the single most important factor in the party's success. Foreign investment and privatization aided in the country's economic growth. But there has been steady unemployment, especially among the young, and a growing gap between rich and poor. How long the JDP can remain in power after winning three general elections will depend on continuing economic growth. It will also depend on the opposition party's ability to resolve its own problems and then present a program to the electorate that offers a better future than the incumbent can.

[*See also* Abdülhamid II; Anavatan Partisi; Atatürk, Mustafa Kemal; Cumhuriyet Halk Partisi; Demokrat Parti; Erbakan, Necmettin; Justice and Development Party; Ottoman Empire; *and* Tanzimat.]

BIBLIOGRAPHY

Allen, Henry Elisha. *The Turkish Transformation*. New York: AMS Press, 1968.

Barnes, John Robert. *An Introduction to Religious Foundations in the Ottoman Empire*. Leiden: E. J. Brill, 1986.

Berkes, Niyazi. *The Development of Secularism in Turkey*. Montreal: McGill University Press, 1964.

Birge, John Kingsley. *The Bektashi Order of Dervishes*. New York: AMS Press, 1982.

Finkel, Andrew. "Turkey: Torn Between God and State." *Le Monde Diplomatique* (English ed.). May 2007.

Gibb, H. A. R., and Harold Bowen. *Islamic Society and the West: A Study of the Impact of Western Civilization on Moslem Culture in the Near East*. London and New York: Oxford University Press, 1950–1957.

Göle, Nilüfer, and Ludwig Ammann, eds. *Islam in Public: Turkey, Iran, and Europe*. Istanbul: İstanbul Bilgi University Press, 2006.

Lewis, Bernard. *The Emergence of Modern Turkey*. 3d ed. London and New York: Oxford University Press, 2002.

Rustow, Dankwart A. "Politics and Islam in Turkey, 1920–1955." In *Islam and the West*, edited by Richard N. Frye, pp. 69–107. The Hague: Mouton, 1957.

Smith, Wilfred Cantwell. *Islam in Modern History*. Princeton, N.J.: Princeton University Press, 1957. Has a stimulating chapter on "Turkey: Islamic Reformation?"

Tapper, Richard, ed. *Islam in Modern Turkey: Religion, Politics, and Literature in a Secular State*. London and New York: I. B. Tauris, 1991.

Toprak, Binnaz. *Islam and Political Development in Turkey*. Leiden: E. J. Brill, 1981.

White, Jenny B. *Islamist Mobilization in Turkey: A Study in Vernacular Politics*. Seattle: University of Washington Press, 2002.

Yavuz, M. Hakan. *Islamic Political Identity in Turkey*. Oxford and New York: Oxford University Press, 2004.

FEROZ AHMAD

TYRANNY. A word with a rich history in the Western lexicon, "tyranny" is today usually translated into Arabic and other languages spoken by Muslims as *istibdād*. This has become the usage since the publication at the turn of the twentieth century of *Ṭabā'iʿ al-istibdād wa-maṣāriʿ al-istiʿbād* (The Characteristics of Tyranny and the Struggles against Enslavement) by ʿAbd al-Raḥmān al-Kawākibī (1849–1902). Before that time tyranny (oppressive and unjust government; despotism—to cite a current English dictionary definition) was usually conveyed in Arabic by such terms as *jawr* (turning aside, straying from the path), *ṭughyān* (insolence; exceeding bounds), and especially *ẓulm* (oppression; injustice), which in its various verbal and nominal forms appears almost three hundred times in the Qurʾān (especially in the plural active participle *ẓālimūn*, meaning the wicked, the oppressors). *Istibdād* appears not at all in the Qur'ān. There are also numerous Qur'ānic references to Pharaoh and Haman as epitomizing tyranny. Although such words as *jawr*, *ṭughyān*, and *ẓulm* have not disappeared as descriptions of tyranny in the languages of Muslims, the emergence of *istibdād* is of more than semantic interest. Al-Kawākibī's book was inspired by, indeed leans heavily on, *Della tirannide* (On Tyranny) by the Italian Vittorio Alfieri (1749–1803), playwright and fervent Italian nationalist. The publishing history of *Della tirannide*, beginning in 1787 is complicated, but it seems that al-Kawākibī consulted the Turkish translation by Abdullah Cevdet published in Geneva in 1898 (this being the time of Hamidian censorship). In short, the Turkish *istibdād* and the Arabic *ṭabā'i' al-istibdād* serve as milestones marking the intrusion of Western-inspired notions of liberty, nationalism, and constitutionalism into the traditional Muslim understanding of tyranny.

The traditional understanding of the tyrant or despot (the terms may be used interchangeably, even though one should be on guard against exaggerated Western notions of "Oriental despotism") was usually presented in terms of the single ruler vis-à-vis the undifferentiated ruled. What constituted tyranny remained vague, usually hardly more than that the tyrant's rule offered not justice (*'adl*) but oppression (*ẓulm*). A more precise explication emerges, however, if one understands the traditional notion of tyranny as the obverse of maxims for just rule set out in the Muslim "mirrors for princes" literature as composed by, for example, al-Ṭurṭūshī, Niẓām al-Mulk, al-Ghazālī, and the anonymous author of *Baḥr al-favā'id* (The Sea of Precious Virtues). Addressed more fully was the thorny question of whether the despot was to be resisted, answers to which were clustered into two camps: the majority position of those championing political quietism versus those supporting active resistance. Arguments for the former camp ranged from viewing the tyrant as God's punishment of a sinful people to the more prevalent idea that *fitnah* (anarchy, disorder) must at all costs be avoided. Thus was created the memorable maxim, "Better sixty years of tyranny than one hour of anarchy." The activist camp was represented by certain Mu'tazilites and others supporting the 'Abbāsid overthrow of the Umayyads, but even here the thrust of their arguments sought to justify this regime change while not leaving the door open for others to follow suit. The basic principle set out in Qur'ān 3:104 enjoining Muslims to "command the good and forbid the evil" may also be said to support active resistance to tyranny, but if so it is sharply scaled down by the corollary maxim that one is to resist evil with the hand, if possible, failing that with the tongue, and if not even that then with the heart (i.e., from the sword to speech to silence). This idea of what to do about tyranny may be said to accord chronologically and contextually with what has been studied much more by scholars: the trajectory from caliphate to kingship, as set out so bleakly in Ibn Jamā'ah's virtual acceptance of might makes right. Even Ibn Taymīyah, ironically a major inspiration of today's Islamists, insisted that "if somebody from among unjust kings becomes ruler, this would be better than there being none." In sum, classical Islamic political thought offers a majority view that the need for stability trumps demands for justice and a minority view that resistance to tyranny is acceptable, but usually this is narrowly circumscribed.

Today, by contrast, the idea that to avoid *fitnah* one must be resigned to despotic rule, however prettied up in the presentation, is rarely advanced in Islamic political thought. This change from ideological quietism to activism has grown out of the confrontation between the West and the

Muslim world in modern times and may be said to have developed during the second half of the nineteenth century, predating al-Kawākibī's *Ṭabā'i' al-istibdād* by several decades. Here, concentrating on the more strictly Islamic (and Islamist) aspects of this ideological change, one might cite the following developments in roughly chronological order:

(1) The encroachment of the state into society—before, during, and after colonial rule—shattered the earlier accommodation of a despotism mitigated by limited demands made by government on society.

(2) A small but growing elite within the Muslim world found European ideas of constitutionalism attractive, and although efforts at implementation in Tunisia, Egypt, the central Ottoman Empire, and Iran all failed, the ideology took root. The writings of the Tunisians Khayr al-Dīn Pasha and Aḥmad ibn Abī Ḍiyāf are examples of fitting European liberalism into an Islamic frame. It is also noteworthy that the Shiite cleric Mīrzā Muḥammad Ḥusayn Nā'īnī published *Tanbih al-Ummah wa-Tanzih al-Millah* in 1909, a book championing the Constitutional Revolution in Iran that drew on al-Kawākibī's *Ṭabā'i' al-istibdād*.

(3) The meteoric, if not quixotic, activities of Jamāl al-Dīn al-Afghānī (which included the encouragement to assassinate despots, costing Nāṣir al-Dīn Shāh his life in 1896), and the more moderate Salafī thought of Muḥammad 'Abduh all gave religious valorization to action in this world.

(4) Throughout the period since about the end of World War I, almost all governments have been seen by its people as either foreign (colonial rule) or despotic (e.g., the Mukhabarat state). Moreover, the various ideologies that, one way or another, might have justified a form of authoritarianism (whether communist, fascist, Ba'thist, praetorian, or an adaptation of European "enlightened despotism") failed in practice or lost favor in other ways.

Hence, in recent decades and certainly by the turn of the twenty-first century, ideologies based on political quietism in the face of despotism have been superseded by those advocating either democracy or radical Islamism, both being opposed to tyranny but otherwise dissimilar, if not polar opposites. This juxtaposition of democracy and Islamism at least suggests how much the discourse about tyranny has changed. The very prominence of the word *istibdād* since al-Kawākibī's book appeared over a century ago (with its terminology and basic ideas soon available in Persian and Turkish as well as Arabic) is indicative of the change. A random library search shows some thirty books appearing as recently as 2000 in those three languages on the subject of *istibdād* with publishers ranging from Algiers (indeed, even Bethesda, Maryland) to Qom. One intriguing title published in Cairo in 2000 reads *Miṣr bayna l-istibdād al-fir'awnī wa l-'awlama l-amrīkiyya* (Egypt between the Tyranny of Pharaoh and American Globalism). This highlighting of *istibdād* is connected with other lexical changes in modern times wherein *thawrah* (revolution), once viewed suspiciously as *fitnah*, becomes laudable, and tyranny becomes not so much the obverse of justice as of liberty (*ḥurrīyah*, which in modern times has expanded its meaning beyond simply indicating "not enslaved").

Other examples confined to those who claim to speak or act in the name of Islam would include:

(1) Ayatollah Khomeini's insisting in his *Islamic Government* that "it is our duty to overthrow the *ṭāghūt*, that is, the illegitimate political powers that now rule the entire Muslim world."

(2) Anwar Sadat's assassin proudly proclaiming, "I have killed Pharaoh."

(3) Shaykh Yūsuf al-Qaraḍāwī asserting publicly, soon after Hosni Mubarak was forced from his long-term presidency in

> February 2011, that the revolt undertaken by Egypt's youth was of the very essence of the religion and in no way a *fitnah*, adding that Islam commands resistance to oppressors for "the tyranny (*ẓulm*) that the rulers exercise is among the most hateful of their traits." A few days later, reacting to the news in Libya, al-Qaraḍāwī issued a fatwā ordering that it was incumbent upon any Muslim able to do so to kill Qadhdhāfī of Libya in order to stop and avenge that leader's sinful acts against his own people.

It would seem that all Muslims today—whether jihadists who fold their actions against the tyrannical ruler into the larger mandate of fighting both governments and peoples mired in their *jāhilīyah* (ignorance of, or resistance to, Islam and its precepts), plus crusaders and Zionists; moderate Islamists such as the Muslim Brothers who insist on their determination to play by democratic rules; or those of diverse secularist orientations—are as one in opposing tyranny and not taking into account the classical dogma to avoid *fitnah*. Yet shortly after demonstrations broke out in Syria in March 2011, a government statement justified the crackdown on demonstrators in terms of suppressing *fitnah*.

[*See also* Commanding Right and Forbidding Wrong; Fitnah; *and* Māwardī, Abū al-Ḥasan al-.]

BIBLIOGRAPHY

Ayalon, Ami. "From Fitna to Thawra." *Studia Islamica* 66 (1987): 145–174.

Haim, Sylvia G. "Alfieri and al-Kawakibi." *Oriente Moderno* 34 (1954): 321–334 (see also pp. 335–337 for the Turkish translation of Alfieri's *On Tyranny*).

Hairi, Abdul-Hadi. *Shīʿīsm and Constitutionalism in Iran: A Study of the Role Played by the Persian Residents of Iraq in Iranian Politics*. Leiden, The Netherlands: E. J. Brill, 1977.

Ibn Abī al-Ḍiyāf, Aḥmad. *Consult Them in the Matter: A Nineteenth-Century Islamic Argument for Constitutional Government*. Translated by L. Carl Brown. Fayetteville: University of Arkansas Press, 2005.

Lewis, Bernard. *The Political Language of Islam*. Chicago: University of Chicago Press, 1988. See esp. chap. 3, "The Ruler and the Ruled."

Lewis, Bernard. *Political Words and Ideas in Islam*. Princeton, N.J.: Markus Wiener, 2008. See esp. chap. 5, "Usurpers and Tyrants: Notes on Some Islamic Political Terms."

L. CARL BROWN

U

ULŪ AL-AMR. Originating as a phrase in the Qurʾān (4:59), *ulū al-amr* (lit. those vested with authority) was understood differently throughout Muslim political history. In the Sunnī world today the standard view posits *ulū al-amr* as the executive leadership of a state, viz., the heads of state, the monarchy, etc. Contemporary Sunnī thinkers and jurists often discuss the limits of obedience to the leadership (*ṭāʿat ulī al-amr*). However *ulū al-amr* was earlier accepted as both the executive and the religious leadership, *al-umarāʾ wa-al-ʿulamāʾ*. Muḥammad al-Ṭāhir ibn ʿĀshūr (d. 1973), a modern exegete, summarizes the inherited view of *ulū al-amr* as that, after the Prophet, all were leaders, from the caliph to the inspector of morals to the commanders of the army, the jurists, the Prophet's Companions, and the people of religious knowledge. In other words the term covered all legislative, executive, and judiciary authorities. For Ibn ʿĀshūr it was synonymous with the representative leaders of the community (*ahl al-ḥall wa-al-ʿaqd*). This conciliatory interpretation embodies the compromise between the later sultans, especially Mamlūk and Ottoman ones, and the religious scholars to share at least formally authority over the community.

The earliest Muslim accounts of *ulū al-amr* present a different picture from later Islam. Two contrasting views were held, pointing to opposing visions of the people of the pen and the people of the sword. The first view was represented by Ibn ʿAbbās (d. 687), al-Ḥasan al-Baṣrī (d. 728), and Mālik ibn Anas (d. 795), along with a large group of Companions and traditionists. For them, *ulū al-amr* were the jurists and the religious scholars (*fuqahāʾ wa-ʿulamāʾ*). Because the scholars were pious and virtuous teachers of the essence of religion—commanding good and forbidding wrong—they should lead the community, they argued. Mālik ibn Anas narrowed this group even further, to the Qurʾānic scholars as the leaders meant by the term in the Qurʾān. Others interpreted the term to mean only the Companions.

The opposing view claimed that *ulū al-amr* pointed exclusively to the executive leadership, particularly the military commanders. This interpretation was supported by a group of renowned exegetes in the seventh to eighth centuries, led by the Companion Abū Hurayrah (d. 681), a pro-Umayyad religious scholar. It was propounded by early and later exegetes such as Muqātil ibn Sulaymān (d. 767), al-Ṭabarī (d. 923), and Fakhr al-Dīn al-Rāzī (d. 1210). The Sunnī exegete al-Ṭabarī supports the view that the leaders were, above all, the sultans. Appointed officials (*wulāt*) could be considered *ulū al-amr* inasmuch as they held an office under the authority of the sultan in a matter of either religion or state. This included the judiciary, because it had also an official responsibility to assure peoples' rights. Al-Ṭabarī's understanding presents a more complex state where the various levels of administration report to the sultan, its chief leader. Al-Rāzī included in his interpretation of *ulū al-amr* both military commanders (*umarāʾ*) and sultans (*salāṭīn*). This extension of the concept can be explained by the context of the period in which he lived, when the sultans had limited authority compared to military chiefs. Al-Rāzī argued against the interpretation of the phrase as denoting religious scholars, maintaining that leadership entails ruling people. Since the jurists have no authority over the people, leadership can be only executive. Al-Māwardī (d. 1058) allowed for both interpretations but seems to use *ulū al-amr* for the executive leaders, the princes. He avers twice in his treatise *al-Aḥkām al-sulṭānīyah* that leaders are those who rule the community. The Ḥanbalī jurist Ibn Taymīyah (d. 1328) also supports this interpretation. His comparison of executive leadership with the market is revealing: leaders are like the market, in that the quality of goods determines the quality of the generated profit. If one invests sincerity, goodness, justice, and honesty, one can expect a similar benefit.

Increasingly, a synthetic view emerged in the juristic and Ṣūfī circles from the tenth century onward. For example, al-Jaṣṣāṣ (d. 980), a Ḥanafī jurist, interpreted *ulū al-amr* to mean both the jurists and the executive leaders (*umarāʾ*). Anticipating objection, he justified the inclusion of the jurists because they were knowledgeable in the commands of God and His prohibitions. Thus, he understood "command" (*amr*) to be a divine command. Although the Ṣūfīs believed that the masters of Ṣūfī education were the true leaders, they contributed to this binary understanding of *ulū al-amr*. In this regard al-Qushayrī (d. 1074) states that, in the terminology of the jurists, the leader is the sultan, but, in the Ṣūfī way, he is the one who knows God (*ʿārif*), who has authority over the beginner. Furthermore he affirms that the Ṣūfī master or *shaykh* is the chief of the disciples and the head of any Ṣūfī community. Thus a de facto secularism dominated the later interpretations of *ulū al-amr*.

For the Shīʿī it is obvious that *ulū al-amr* are the imams, who are both religious leaders and rulers. For instance, an account attributed to Muḥammad al-Bāqir (d. 733) and Jaʿfar al-Ṣādiq (d. 765) clearly lays out this understanding. Their argument is that the Qurʾān requires absolute obedience to the leaders; nobody should be followed unless he is infallible. Neither military commanders nor scholars can be leaders, as they could be neglectful and erring, and the scholars have no real authority. Some accounts, such as *al-Anwār al-bahiyya* of ʿAbbās al-Qummī (d. 1941), even mention the names of the twelve imams as the *ulū al-amr*. Ismāʿīlī (Sevener Shīʿī) authors also rebut the notion that scholars or commanders could be the *ulū al-amr*. As al-Qāḍī al-Nuʿmān (d. 974) argues, scholars and commanders cannot be better than the imams who appointed them. And the scholars disagree among themselves; obeying some would imply disobedience to others. The *ulū al-amr* are, he concluded, the imams who have all the authority for they are the only infallible leaders—the belief in the infallibility of the leaders being the cornerstone of Shīʿī thought.

[*See also* Ahl al-Ḥall wa-al-ʿAqd.]

BIBLIOGRAPHY

Afsarruddin, Asma. "Obedience to Political Authority: An Evolutionary Concept." In *Islamic Democratic*

Discourse: Theory, Debates and Political Perspectives, edited by M. A. Muqtedar Khan, pp. 37–60. Lanham, Md.: Lexington Books, 2006.

Ibn ʿĀshūr, Muḥammad al-Ṭāhir. *Tafsīr al-taḥrīr wa-al-tanwīr*. Tunis: al-Dār al-Tūnisīyah lil Nashr, 1973.

Ibn Taymīyah, Aḥmad ibn ʿAbd al-Ḥalīm. *al-Siyāsa al-sharʿiyya fī iṣlāḥ al-rāʿī wa-al-raʿiyya*. Edited by Ibrāhīm Ramaḍān. Beirut: Dār al-Kutub al-ʿIlmiyya, 1992.

Jaṣṣāṣ, Aḥmad ibn ʿAlī al-. *Aḥkām al-Qurʾān*. Edited by Muḥammad al-Ṣādiq Qamḥāwī. Beirut: Dār Iḥyāʾ al-Turāth al-ʿArabī, 1985.

Lambton, Ann K. S. *State and Government in Medieval Islam: An Introduction to the Study of Islamic Political Theory: The Jurists*. Oxford and New York: Oxford University Press, 1981.

Māwardī, ʿAlī ibn Muḥammad al-. *The Ordinances of Government* [*Aḥkām al-sulṭānīyah wa-al-wilāyāt al-dīnīyah*]. Translated by Wafaa Hassan Wahba. Reading, U.K.: Garnet, 2000.

Nuʿmān ibn Muḥammad, Abū Ḥanīfah. *Daʿāʾim al-Islām*. Edited by Asaf Ali Asghar Fyzee. 2 vols. Cairo: Dār al-Maʿārif, 1960–1963.

Qummī, ʿAbbās ibn Muḥammad Riḍā al-. *al-Anwār al-bahīyah fī tawārīkh al-ḥujaj al-ilāhīyah*. Beirut: Dār al-Aḍwāʾ, 1984.

Qushayrī, ʿAbd al-Karīm ibn Hawāzin al-. *Laṭāʾif al-tafsīr* Edited by ʿAbd al-Laṭīf Ḥasan ʿAbd al-Raḥmān. Beirut: Dār al-Kutub al-ʿIlmiyya, 2000.

Rāzī, Fakhr al-Dīn Muhammad ibn ʿUmar al-. *Mafātīḥ al-ghayb*. Edited by Aḥmad Shams al-Dīn. Beirut: Dār al-Kutub al-ʿIlmiyya, 2000.

Ṭabarī, Muḥammad ibn Jarīr al-. *Jāmiʿ al-bayān fī taʾwīl al-Qurʾān*. Edited by Aḥmad Muḥammad Shākir. Beirut: Muʾassasat al-Risāla, 2000.

ABDESSAMAD BELHAJ

ʿUMAR IBN AL-KHAṬṬĀB. ʿUmar ibn al-Khaṭṭāb (r. 634–644) was the second of the Rightly Guided Caliphs. Before his death, Abū Bakr designated ʿUmar as his successor, a decision that apparently met little resistance from the larger community. ʿUmar had undergone a dramatic conversion in the early days of the Muslim community in Mecca, which turned him from a persecutor of Muslims into an avid practitioner of the new faith. His reign is held up as paradigmatic by later generations for several important reasons. A primary reason is the general consensus among the majority of Muslims that ʿUmar best exemplified and implemented the moral, social, and political objectives envisioned by the Qurʾān for the post-Prophetic Muslim polity. This evaluation of ʿUmar and his farsighted policies is captured in a statement attributed to the Prophet, "If God had wished that there be a prophet after me, it would have been ʿUmar."

A frequent epithet applied to ʿUmar is al-Farūq, roughly "one who distinguishes between right and wrong." It is commonly understood to point to his role as a prolific interpreter of the evolving religious law (Sharīʿah). As ruler ʿUmar appears to have been called, at first, Khalīfat Abī Bakr (the successor to Abū Bakr), but he later adopted the title Amīr al-Muʾminīn (Leader of the Faithful), which henceforth became the title of the legitimate ruler after him. The title *khalīfat Allāh* (deputy of God) is said to have been rejected by both Abū Bakr and ʿUmar as presumptuous, implying the arrogation of an absolutist religious authority that no Muslim ruler had the right to claim. When a man once addressed ʿUmar as "O Deputy of God," the annoyed caliph exclaimed, "May God prove you wrong!"

Among other civil and legal acts ʿUmar established the Islamic (*hijrī*) calendar dating from the beginning of the Islamic era to the Prophet's emigration in 622. He abolished the practice of temporary (*mutʿah*) marriage, a pre-Islamic custom that continued to be practiced sporadically during the Prophet's time. He established the office of the *qāḍī* (judge), designated official muezzins (callers to prayer), and appointed professional reciters of the Qurʾān for men and women. ʿUmar also continued the territorial expansion of the realm of Islam into Sassanian and Byzantine territories in Iraq, Syria, and Egypt. As these lands came within the orbit of Muslim control, ʿUmar established garrison cities (*amṣār*) in Fusṭāṭ (Egypt) and in Basra and Kufa (Iraq). The Pact of ʿUmar that is thought to discriminate toward the Christians of Syria is certainly spurious and was drawn up in a later period.

In 644 ʿUmar was attacked by a Persian Christian slave named Abū Lūʾlūʾ and died three days later from the serious wounds inflicted on him. While he hovered between life and death, ʿUmar appointed a six-man advisory council called the *shūrā* which eventually elected ʿUthmān ibn ʿAffān as his successor.

[*See also* Companions of the Prophet.]

BIBLIOGRAPHY

Ibn Saʿd, Muḥammad. *al-Ṭabaqāt al-kubrā.* Edited by Muḥammad ʿAbd al- Qādir ʿAṭā. Beirut: Dār al-Kutub al-ʿIlmīyah, 1997.

Ṭabarī, Muḥammad ibn Jarīr al-. *Tārīkh al-rusul wa-al-mulūk.* Selections translated and annotated by Michael Fishbein as *The Victory of Islam.* Albany: State University of New York Press, 1997.

ASMA AFSARUDDIN

UMAYYAD CALIPHATE. Although it is generally accepted that the first Umayyad to come to the position of the caliphate was ʿUthmān ibn ʿAffān (r. 644–656), because of his status as a very close Companion of the Prophet, he is not seen as the precursor of the dynasty that started to rule in earnest around 658. At that time, Muʿāwiyah ibn Abī Sufyān (d. 680) became recognized by a sizeable portion of the Islamic Empire as caliph. But it was not until the death of the fourth caliph, ʿAlī, in 661 that the whole of the community came under Muʿāwiyah's rule. Muʿāwiyah had been appointed governor of Syria by the second caliph, ʿUmar; after 656, at the beginning of the first *fitnah* (civil war), an attempt by ʿAlī as caliph to replace him led to intermittent hostilities between the two. After the assassination of ʿAlī in 661, Muʿāwiyah gained control of the whole caliphate and was recognized as caliph. By the time of his death in 680, he had established a system of administration for the caliphate, with Damascus as the capital, that gave it a degree of stability.

Muʿāwiyah's successor, his son Yazīd I, defeated at Karbala an attempt by ʿAlī's son Ḥusayn to become caliph. When Yazīd died in 683, leaving only a young son, Muʿāwiyah II, ʿAbd Allāh ibn al-Zubayr in Mecca claimed the caliphate. Most of the Syrians and the Umayyad clan were about to recognize ʿAbd Allāh ibn al-Zubayr when the son of the former governor of Iraq, ʿUbayd Allāh ibn Ziyād ibn Abīh, persuaded another Umayyad, Marwān ibn al-Ḥakam, to vie for the caliphate. In the famous battle of Mardj Rāhiṭ in 684, Marwān was able to recover Syria and become caliph; his son ʿAbd al-Malik (r. 685–705) restored Umayyad rule over the whole caliphate, though it was not until 692 that ʿAbd Allāh ibn al-Zubayr was defeated and this second civil war ended. Before the defeat of ʿAbd Allāh ibn al-Zubayr, the Umayyads had a very important meeting that solved the problem of succession, at least until the caliphate of al-Walīd II. It is from within this particular conflict that the seeds of tribal rivalries were sprouted. The rivalry between the Qays and the Yemen was to plague the Umayyad dynasty until its demise in 750. ʿAbd al-Malik, during his rule, strengthened the organization of the empire. Up to this time, administrators from the previous Byzantine and Sassanian regimes had continued to work for the caliphs, but he now made Arabic the official language of government and replaced the Byzantine and Sassanian coinage with one with Arabic inscriptions. ʿAbd al-Malik was able to secure the reign not only to one but to four of his sons with little or no resistance.

Although the caliphate of al-Walīd (r. 705–715) was a period of continuing prosperity, ongoing rivalry between two groups of Arab tribes, the Qays and the Yemen, threatened the unity of the empire. Al-Walīd is famous for his building efforts in and around Syria. He also tried to appoint his own son, ʿAbd al-ʿAzīz, to succeed him, counter to his father's wishes, which were that his brother Sulaymān would succeed him. Sulaymān (r. 715–717) did in fact succeed al-Walīd, and it was his appointment of his cousin ʿUmar ibn ʿAbd al-ʿAzīz, or ʿUmar II (r. 717–720), that would have long-term repercussions for the dynasty and the empire. This was his reward for refusing to accept al-Walīd's wishes to forsake his brother in favor of his own children.

ʿUmar II tried to reform the empire by introducing many reforms that were meant to curtail some of the ongoing threats to the empire. Only two of these reforms, the stopping of the official cursing of ʿAlī and the writing of history, outlasted his reign. The remainder—his fiscal reforms, which were designed to redress the inequity of the taxes paid by the new non-Arab converts (*mawālī*) and the Arabs; an attempt at bringing back to the fold many of the groups that had broken off during the first and second civil war; and the halting of the expansionist policy of the empire—were all reversed immediately after his death by his successor, Yazīd II b. ʿAbd al-Malik (r. 720–724).

It was during the long reign of the next caliph, Hishām b. ʿAbd al-Malik (r. 724–743), that the empire began to wane. His reign saw a number of defeats at the hands of outsiders, as well as large rebellions that were eventually put down, but at a high cost. After Hishām there were no fewer than three caliphs in a period of one year, two of whom were removed by force by other members of the Umayyad dynasty. By the time the thirteenth and final caliph, Marwān II b. Muḥammad b. Marwān I (r. 744–750), was able to ascend to the caliphate, a rebellion was brewing in the eastern part of the empire. The ʿAbbāsids, descendants of Muḥammad's uncle al-ʿAbbās, raised an army in Khorāsān in Iran, which included many *mawālī*. The Umayyads were unable to offer effective resistance, and Marwān II was killed in Egypt in 750. One member of the Umayyad family escaped and in 755 founded in Spain the Umayyad emirate of al-Andalus, which was never incorporated into the ʿAbbāsid Empire.

The Umayyads were responsible for a great expansion of the Islamic state. By 661 the Arabs occupied Egypt, Syria, Iraq, and most of Iran. The Umayyads continued the westward advance through North Africa until they reached the Atlantic. In 711 they crossed into Spain and rapidly conquered most of the country, establishing a forward base at Narbonne in southern France. In 732 their defeat by Charles Martel between Tours and Poitiers checked the advance, but Narbonne remained in Arab hands until 759. The Umayyads pressed on eastward, from Iran into Central Asia (Bukhara and Samarqand) and into northwest India. In the north, however, despite frequent expeditions, little progress was made because of the strength of the Byzantine Empire. A long, unsuccessful siege of Constantinople began in 672; when Sulaymān b. ʿAbd al-Malik attacked that city, the Arabs were repulsed and lost almost all of their fleet and army.

This great expansion was primarily military and political, not religious. Indeed, there was a short period when conversion to Islam was discouraged because it reduced the amount collected in taxes. Non-Arabs who became Muslims were also required to become *mawālī* of an Arab tribe; the *mawālī*, who were often called "clients," were persons incorporated into the tribe and reckoned as belonging to it, but without having the rights of those who were members by birth. Christians and Jews who kept their religion normally became *dhimmī* (protected minorities with limited autonomy). In the conquered provinces the center of government was sometimes a city, such as

Kairouan (Qayrawān), which had first been a forward army base and then a garrison town, which increased in size as many of the local population settled around it to serve the needs of the army. Originally the armies were exclusively Arab and Muslim, but in time numerous *mawālī* were added, mostly of Iranian and Berber/Amazigh origin.

Most of the histories related to this period originated under the ʿAbbāsids and accuse the Umayyads of being irreligious, which has led some modern scholars to view the Umayyads as a "secular" dynasty. Recent scholarship has shown this picture to be highly problematic and indicates that the Umayyads in fact relied on and cultivated religious foundations to champion their cause. The Umayyads claimed to be upholders of Islam, as demonstrated in the works of court poets and private secretaries of the time.

[*See also* ʿAbbāsid Caliphate.]

BIBLIOGRAPHY

Brockelmann, Carl. *History of the Islamic Peoples.* New York: G. P Putnam, 1944.

Donner, Fred McGraw. *The Early Islamic Conquests.* Princeton, N.J.: Princeton University Press, 1981.

Hitti, Philip K. *History of the Arabs.* London: Macmillan, 1937.

Holt, P. M., Ann K. S. Lambton, and Bernard Lewis, eds. *The Cambridge History of Islam.* Vol. 1, *The Central Islamic Lands.* Cambridge, U.K.: Cambridge University Press, 1970.

Shaban, M. A. *Islamic History: A New Interpretation.* Vol. 1, *AD. 600–750 (AH. 132).* Cambridge, U.K.: Cambridge University Press, 1971.

Ṭabarī, Abū Jaʿfar Muḥammad ibn Jarīr al-. *Tārīkh al-rusul wa-al-mulūk*, vols. 18–27. Albany: State University of New York Press, 1996.

Wellhausen, Julius. *The Arab Kingdom and Its Fall.* Translated by Margaret Graham Weir. Beirut: Khayats, 1963. Deals with the Umayyad period in detail. First published in 1927.

WILLIAM MONTGOMERY WATT
Updated by KHALED M. G. KESHK

UMMAH.

The Arabic term *ummah* refers to a people or a community united by certain features that they share in common, such as customs, ethnicity, history, language, and, particularly, religion. It is often used to refer to the *ummah al-Muḥammadīyah* (community of Muḥammad) or *ummah al-Islāmīyah* (community of Islam). Although its meaning has developed throughout history, it has often been used to express the essential unity of Muslims in diverse cultural settings.

Use in Qurʾān and *Ḥadīth*. The term *ummah* occurs sixty-four times in the Qurʾān. In most of these cases, the term is used to designate a people to whom God sends a prophet, or a people who are part of a divine plan of salvation. Hence, in these contexts in the Qurʾān the term *ummah* refers to a single group sharing some common religious orientation. In Qurʾānic usage, however, the connotations of community and religion do not always converge, and the word has diverse meanings.

In several instances *ummah* refers to an unrestricted group of people. *Sūrah* 28:23, for example, reads, "And when he [Moses] came to the water of Madyan, he found on it a group of men [*ummah min al-nās*] watering." The term can also mean a specific religion or the beliefs of a certain group of people (43:22–23), or an exemplar or model of faith, as in the reference to Abraham as an "*ummah*, obedient to God" (16:120). *Ummah* also refers to the followers of a particular prophet, there being, the Qurʾān says, no people who have not been sent such messengers by God (10:47); to a group of people adhering to a specific religion in terms of rules, rituals, and practices (5:48); to a smaller group within the larger community of adherents (3:113); to the followers of Muḥammad who are charged with a special responsibility (2:143); or to a subgroup of these followers (3:104).

The term *ummah* is often used in the Qurʾān in reference to a misguided group of people (43:33) or a misguided party from among the followers of a prophet (27:83; 23:44). *Ummah* could mean (an indefinite) period of time (11:8) and an order of being (6:38).

The occasional rift between the civil and religious notions of *ummah* in Qurʾānic usage has parallels in *ḥadīth* literature. In several traditions Muḥammad is said to use "my *ummah*" to mean the group related to him by lineage rather than by religion. It is the *ḥadīth* literature, however, that provides the concept of *ummah* with its precise and focused meaning. Besides the Qurʾān, the earliest extant source available is a set of documents written by Muḥammad shortly after his arrival at Medina. These documents, commonly referred to in modern scholarship as the "Constitution of Medina," comprise several practical provisions designed to regulate social and political life in Medina under Islam. Most scholars agree that the main purport of the constitution is political and not religious. It defines treaty relations among the different groups inhabiting Medina and its environs, including the Muslim tribes of Medina, Muslims who emigrated from Mecca, and Jews.

The "constitution" starts with the pronouncement that all these groups constitute "one distinct community [*ummah*] apart from other people." In the forty-seven clauses of the constitution the term *ummah* appears in only one other instance, when the Jews of Banū ʿAwf are said to constitute "an *ummah* with the believers." The same clause goes on to state that the Jews have their religion and the Muslims have theirs. The meaning of the term *ummah* in the constitution is clearly not synonymous with religion. The constitution also delineates relations of mutual aid among the different constituent tribal groups, actions to be taken against those who violate the terms of the agreement, and actions to be taken against criminals belonging to the incipient community in Medina. Rather than supplanting or abolishing tribal bonds, the constitution regulates relations among tribes, and between them and the outside world, on the basis of the higher order of the *ummah*. *Ummah* here is a concept of daily life that also stands for a certain kind of identity and defines a social and political unit.

While the Constitution of Medina seems to sanction diversity within the Islamic *ummah*, the Qurʾān sanctions differentiation among various *ummahs* as a norm decreed by God. *Sūrah* 10, verse 19, reads, "People were once a single *ummah*; but they differed (and followed different ways). Had it not been for the word proclaimed by your Lord before, their differences would have been resolved" (see also 2:213, 5:48, 11:118, 16:93, and 42:8). There is a sense, therefore, in which the concept of the *ummah* refers to an ideal state, an original all-encompassing unity that is always invoked but never completely recovered.

This rudimentary concept of the *ummah*, however, is complemented by the narrower concept of the *ummah* of believers. This is the "justly balanced *ummah*" (2:143), which is further qualified in the Qurʾān as "the best *ummah* evolved for mankind, enjoining what is good, forbidding what is wrong, and believing in God" (3:110; see also 4:41 and 16:89). This specific *ummah*, or the followers of Muḥammad, is further differentiated from the followers of earlier messengers and prophets; whereas the latter's sphere of influence is restricted to particular peoples, the former's scope is all of humanity. When referring to prophets before Muḥammad, the Qurʾān says, "To every *ummah* We have sent an apostle [saying:] Worship God" (16:36; see also 10:47). In reference to Muḥammad, however, the Qurʾān adds, "Say: O men, I am verily the apostle of God to you all" (7:158). The universality of Muḥammad's mission was thereby asserted, and the "justly balanced *ummah*" shouldered the central role in the fulfillment of this mission after him.

Development in Legal and Political Thought. The concept of *ummah* underwent important developments immediately after Muḥammad's death. Different circumstances accompanied the selection of each of the first four caliphs after Muḥammad who are recognized in the Sunnī tradition, yet in each case the appointment was conferred by the majority of the *ummah*, thereby investing ultimate political authority in the *ummah* and its consensus. It was argued that, to preserve its unity, the *ummah* needed leadership consolidated in the person of one imam. The second caliph, ʿUmar, relinquished the distribution of conquered land to Muslim conquerors, considering it public property, the property of the whole *ummah*. The idealization of the period of the first four Rightly Guided Caliphs is not a mere creation of the historical imagination of later generations of Sunnī Muslims; it was a period in which important Islamic ideals were actually conceived. These include the principles of the unity of the *ummah*, the *ummah* as the ultimate source of political authority, and the related principles of the unity of political leadership and the unity of the land of Islam.

Under Umayyad rule the need for a unified political authority was overemphasized and used to justify exclusive Arab dynastic rule at the expense of the Islamic ideal of the unity of the *ummah*. Under the ʿAbbāsids the inclusive Qurʾānic notion of the *ummah* was revived, and the political dominance of the ʿAbbāsid family did not preclude the participation of other ethnic groups. This participation, however, eventually led to the gradual loosening of political centralization. As the ʿAbbāsid caliphs wielded less control over an increasingly decentralized state, they continued to function as symbols of the unity of its *ummah*. This unity was corroborated by an Islamic cultural tradition that was well developed by the end of the second century of Islam.

Traditionalists and *ḥadīth* scholars argued that Islam could only be preserved by safeguarding the unity of the *ummah*. The standard legal formulations of the classical period defined it as a spiritual, nonterritorial community distinguished by the shared beliefs of its members. This concept was not a mere abstraction; it had legal consequences. The distinction in later Muslim jurisprudence between the "land of Islam" (*dār al-Islām*) and the "land of war" (*dār al-ḥarb*) was based on the conceptual division of people into believers and nonbelievers, although this notion of the two types of "land" does not, strictly speaking, have any Qurʾānic sanction. Nonbelievers were further classified on the basis of their relation to the *ummah* of believers. There were no formal conditions or ritual requirements for joining the *ummah*, aside from being born to Muslim parents or freely choosing to become a Muslim. Membership in this *ummah* can thus be viewed as a sort of citizenship that guarantees, at least theoretically, equality among all Muslims. One expression of the treatment of the *ummah* as a legal entity is the distinction in Islamic jurisprudence between religious obligations that fall on individuals and other obligations that the *ummah* shoulders collectively as one unit. As late as the early twentieth century, French courts, for example, had to deal with the implications of a Muslim's membership in the *ummah* as a reality with substantive legal consequences.

In legal theory—for example, in the writings of Shāfiʿī (d. 820) on the principles of jurisprudence—the consensus of the community (*ijmāʿ*) was elevated into the status of a source of law second only to the Qurʾān and the traditions of Muḥammad. The *ḥadīth* stating "My *ummah* would never agree on an error" (*lā tajtamiʿu ummatī ʿalā ḍalālah*) was perceived in the legal classics as evidence of the infallibility of the *ummah* and its unrivaled authority. The literature of the classical period thus viewed the *ummah* as a socioreligious reality with legal and political import.

Beginning with the third century of Islam, some scholars suggested a distinction between religious forms of human association (*millah*) and sociopolitical forms (*ummah*). A more significant distinction was promoted by political theoreticians working during periods of political fragmentation. The celebrated al-Māwardī (d. 1058), for example, conceded the possibility of having more than one executive organ of political power, but he insisted on the unity of the *ummah* and on the symbolic unity of the office of the caliph.

From the ninth century, Islamic literature also conferred a distinguished status on the Arabs within the larger *ummah* of Muslims. This literature emphasized the centrality of the Arabs and their language to Islam, in response to the Shuʿūbīyah movement, which denigrated the Arabs in favor of other ethnic identities. Al-Shāfiʿī, for example, lists in his *Risālah fī uṣūl al-fiqh* (Treatise on the Principles of Jurisprudence) the Qurʾānic references to Arabic and its prominence, and Aḥmad ibn Ḥanbal (d. 855) collects numerous *ḥadīths* that enumerate the virtues of Arabs and reprimand their foes. In various genres of writing, including jurisprudence, philosophy, histories, poetry, and prose, the Arabs are said to be privileged by speaking the language of the Qurʾān and of paradise, and by being the core community to whom Muḥammad was sent. As the political hegemony of the Arabs receded, so did the cultural tensions between them and other ethnic groups. The tradition of praising the Arabs, however, did not subside; rather, the initial reactive defense gave way to independent self-conscious reflections on Arabness as a cultural identity, and on its unique and organic link to the religious, political, and social identity of the Islamic *ummah*.

Era of Nationalism. The social reality of the unified *ummah* and the related concept of *dār al-Islām* were not undermined by political decentralization in the Islamic world, but, under the pressure of European colonial encroachment on Muslim domains, this social identity was seriously challenged. Islamic resistance movements defending the *ummah* against European intrusions emerged throughout the Muslim world. The attempts of the Ottoman sultan Abdülhamid II (r. 1876–1909) to restore Muslim unity by reviving the idea of *ummah* were extremely popular among Muslims from India to Morocco. Equally popular was the call by Jamāl al-Dīn al-Afghānī (1839–1897) for Islamic solidarity to reinvigorate the *ummah*. On the other side of the confrontation, European powers were making progress both on the military front and in the concessions ("capitulations") imposed on the Ottoman Empire. Moreover, the European idea of the secular nation-state had some appeal among Muslim elites.

The earliest forms of nationalism in the Islamic world, however, conceived of Islam as a central component of the nationalist project. With few exceptions, the early nationalists, including the non-Muslims among them, appropriated the Islamic concept of *ummah*. Although nationalist movements, in the guise of Islamic reform, often disrupted the actual political unity of the *ummah*, they did not challenge the theoretical authority of the concept. Moreover, the symbols of Arab nationalism retained their religious weight, in contrast to the Turkish nationalism of Mustafa Kemal Atatürk, who dissociated Turkey from its Islamic tradition. In India, some nationalist *ʿulamāʾ* who opposed the Muslim League's demand for a separate land for the Indian Muslims, later to be named Pakistan, developed the notion of "composite nationalism," arguing that the Hindus, Muslims, and other religious communities of India were, all taken together, members of a single nation. For this purpose, they cited the Constitution of Medina, referred to above, which recognized all parties to the treaty, Muslims and non-Muslims, as members of a single *ummah*. This usage of the concept of *ummah* sought to counter exclusivist understandings of the term that were championed by forceful advocates of pan-Islamism as well as Indian Muslim leaders who were behind the movement for Pakistan.

In reaction to the political vacuum created by Atatürk's elimination of the caliphate in 1924, several Islamic conferences were held to discuss the political situation of the Muslim *ummah*. These conferences failed to achieve significant results because of the conflicting loyalties between the sovereign secular nation-states and the religious *ummah*. These competing loyalties eventually led to greater separation between Islam and nationalism. Beginning in the 1960s, even Arab nationalists began to speak in favor of a complete separation of religious and national identities. In reaction, many Islamists argued that loyalty to the Islamic *ummah* negates any loyalty to other ethnic, linguistic, or geographical entities. Still, the idea of the Islamic *ummah*, as it is used in contemporary political discourse, carries the imprint of the nation-state with which it is competing. The gradual secularization of public life has curtailed political and legal expressions of the idea of the *ummah*, but its significance as a source of social identity persists in the Islamic world.

[*See also* Nation; *and* Pan-Islam.]

BIBLIOGRAPHY

Aḥsan, ʿAbdullāh al-. *Ummah or Nation? Identity Crisis in Contemporary Muslim Society*. Leicester, U.K.: Islamic Foundation, 1992.

Darrow, William R. "Ummah." In *The Encyclopedia of Religion*, vol. 15. Edited by Mircea Eliade, pp. 123–125. New York: Macmillan, 1987.

Denny, Frederick Mathewson. "The Meaning of *Ummah* in the Qurʾān." *History of Religions* 15, no. 1 (1975): 35–70.

Denny, Frederick Mathewson. "*Ummah* in the Constitution of Medina." *Journal of Near Eastern Studies* 36, no. 1 (1977): 39–47.

Faruqi, Maysam J. al-. "*Umma*: The Orientalists and the Qurʾānic Concept of Identity." *Journal of Islamic Studies* 16 (2005): 1–34.

Giannakis, Elias. "The Concept of *Ummah*." *Graeco-Arabica* 2 (1983): 99–111.

Gibb, H. A. R. "The Community in Islamic History." *Proceedings of the American Philosophical Society* 107, no. 2 (1963): 173–176.

Gibb, H. A. R. "The Islamic Congress at Jerusalem in December 1931." In *Survey of International Affairs, 1934*. Edited by A. J. Toynbee, pp. 99–109. London: Oxford University Press, 1935.

Grunebaum, G. E. von. "Nationalism and Cultural Trends in the Arab Near East." *Studia Islamica* 14 (1961): 121–153.

Hourani, Albert. *Arabic Thought in the Liberal Age, 1798–1939*. London: Oxford University Press, 1962.

Kramer, Martin. *Islam Assembled: The Advent of the Muslim Congresses*. New York: Columbia University Press, 1986.

Madnī, Maulana Ḥusain Aḥmad. *Composite Nationalism and Islam*. Translated by Mohammad Anwer Hussain. New Delhi: Manohar, 2005.

Naṣṣār, Naṣīf. *Mafhūm al-ummah bayna al-dīn wa-al-tārīkh*. Beirut: Dār al-Ṭalīʿah, 1978.

Naṣṣār, Naṣīf. *Taṣawwurāt al-ummah al-muʿāsirah: Dirāsah taḥlīlīyah li-mafāhīm al-ummah fī al-fikr al-ʿArabī al-ḥadīth wa-al-muʿāṣir*. Kuwait: Muʾassasat al-Kuwayt lil-Taqaddum al-ʿIlmī, Idārat al-Taʾlīf wa-al-Tarjamah, 1986.

Nieuwenhuijze, C. A. O. van. "The Ummah: An Analytic Approach." *Studia Islamica* 10 (1959): 5–22.

Paret, Rudi. "Umma." In *Encyclopaedia of Islam*, new ed., vol. 4. Edited by H. A. R. Gibb, pp. 1015–1016. Leiden, Netherlands: E. J. Brill, 1978.

Roy, Olivier. *Globalized Islam: The Search for a New Ummah*. New York: Columbia University Press, 2004.

Sayyid, Riḍwān al-. *Mafāhīm al-jamāʿāt fī al-Islām: Dirāsāt fī al-sūsyūlūjiyā al-tārīkhīyah lil-ijtimā ʿal-ʿArabī al-Islāmī*. Beirut: Dār al-Muntakhab al-ʿArabī, 1993.

Sayyid, Riḍwān al-. *Al-ummah wa-al-jamāʿah wa-al-sulṭah: Dirāsāt fī al-fikr al-sīyāsī al-ʿArabī al-Islāmī*. Beirut: Dār Iqraʾ, 1984.

ʿUmarī, Akram Ḍiyāʾ al-. *Al-mujtamaʿal-madanīfīʿahd al-nubūwah, khaṣāʾiṣuhu wa-tanẓīmātuhu al-ūlā: Muḥāwalah li-taṭbīq qawāʿid al-muḥaddithīn fī naqd al-riwāyāt al-tārīkhīyah*. Medina: Al-Jāmiʿah al-Islāmīyah, 1983.

AHMAD S. DALLAL
Updated by YOGINDER SIKAND
and ABDUL RASHID MOTEN

UNION DES ORGANISATIONS ISLAMIQUES DE FRANCE. The Union des Organisations Islamiques de France (UOIF) is France's largest political Islamic federation. It was founded by Islamist exiles from Morocco and Tunisia in 1983, and later incorporated Islamisists from Algeria. Composed of a network of 250 cultural, religious, and political associations, it influences perhaps a hundred others and, in addition to contributions by local affiliated associations, the UOIF receives financial assistance from the Muslim World League and from private individuals from Saudi Arabia, Kuwait, and the United Arab Emirates.

Before 2003 the UOIF was active in mobilizing on behalf of Muslim causes in France but gained more influence after Nicolas Sarkozy, then Minister of the Interior, created the Conseil Français du Culte Musulman (CFCM). The UOIF was given the vice presidency, and gained representation for mosques it shepherded. As a result the organization became a mediator—rather than an organizer—of conflict, evidenced when it issued a *fatwa* to condemn the inner-city rioters of October 2005. In contrast to the mobilizations of 1989, in 1998 it stopped granting financial support to lawyers who were making appeals on behalf of girls who wore headscarves, and refused to support protests against the 2004 legislation that banned foulards in public schools. In 2009, as the French government began to gather support to pass legislation to ban the burqa, the UOIF opposed the legislation, but spoke about legislative reforms rather than protests. When a French magazine republished the offensive Danish cartoons mocking Muḥammad, the UOIF did not organize streets protests but instead joined a lawsuit that was unsuccessful.

Thus, within the institutional constraints that the organization accepted, the UOIF became a force for moderation within the Muslim community in France. On 10 January 2008 it cosigned with the other twenty-six associations of the Federation of Islamic Organizations in Europe (FOIE) a Charter of European Muslims, to support more effective participation of Muslims in their relations with states and societies throughout Europe. The text echoed a 1995 Charte de Culte Musulman en France (as well as other similar charters in other countries), and refers to a moderate Islam—to "enhance the values of mutual understanding, work for peace and the welfare of society, moderation and inter-cultural dialogue, removed from all inclinations of extremism and exclusion." It calls for a balance between preserving Muslim identity and the duties of European citizenship. In this way the charter defines the emerging role of the UOIF in France and Europe today.

Since 2011, however, the UOIF has moved to loosen the constraints imposed by the CFCM. It boycotted the elections for representatives in June 2011, and since then has "frozen" its relations with the council, as has the Grand Mosque of Paris. Since then both organizations have demanded "reforms" that would give them greater independence from the ministry of the interior, and that would decentralize the structure of the CFCM. In 2012 the new minister of the interior, Manuel Vals reaffirmed his commitment to the structure of the council, and called for "Islam in France to organize itself and fulfill its responsibilities."

BIBLIOGRAPHY

Bowen, John R. *Why the French Don't Like Headscarves: Islam, the State and Public Space.* Princeton, N.J.: Princeton University Press, 2007.

Cesari, Jocelyne. *L'Islam à l'épreuve de l'Occident.* Paris: Découverte, 2004.

Fregosi, Frank. "La représentation institutionnelle de l'Islam en France." In *Histoire de l'Islam et des musulmans en France du Moyen Age à nos jours*, edited by Mohammed Arkoun, pp. 837–855. Paris: Albin Michel, 2006.

Laurence, Jonathan. *The Emancipation of Europe's Muslims: The State's Role in Minority Integration*. Princeton, N.J.: Princeton University Press, 2012.
Sellam, Sadek. *La France et ses musulmans: Un siècle de politique musulmane, 1895–2005*. Paris: Fayard, 2006.
Wihtol de Wenden, Catherine, and Jocelyne Cesari. *Musulmans d'Europe*. Cahiers du CEMOTI 33 (October, 2002).

MARTIN A. SCHAIN

UNITED DEVELOPMENT PARTY. The United Development Party (Partai Persatuan Pembangunan [PPP], sometimes called the Development Unity Party) was formed in 1973, part of efforts by the then military-dominated Suharto "New Order" to control Islamic political activities in Indonesia. The government forced four Islamic parties into the PPP: the traditional Islamic organization Nahdatul Ulama (Awakening of Muslim Scholars, NU); the Islamic Association of Indonesia (Partai Sarekat Islam Indonesia, PSII); the Muslim Party of Indonesia (Partai Muslimin Indonesia Permusi, PMI); and the Islamic Educational Movement (Parti). The two major partners were the traditional Nahdatul Ulama and the modernist-oriented PMI, which was an outgrowth of the Masyumi, a modernist organization banned by President Sukarno in 1960.

The structure of the New Order effectively weakened the political role of Islam in Indonesia. National elections in which the PPP participated were dominated by the government party, Golkar, and were gerrymandered to elect members to a weak national legislature controlled by Golkar and military appointees. State power was further reinforced by questionable electoral systems, government selection of candidates, and other measures to insure the political dominance of the military. To further emasculate Islamic political strength, the PPP ultimately was prohibited from running on religious platforms. In the first years of the New Order the coalition did campaign with the ka'abah as its symbol, but this was banned in the mid-1980s. The PPP could never successfully confront the government-supported party, Golkar, at the polls. In the six national elections during the New Order, Golkar received between 62.1 percent and over 74 percent of the votes. In contrast the PPP only managed between 16 percent to 29.3 percent of cast ballots. Higher percentages were recorded in earlier elections before the NU abandoned politics, although it increasingly found its electoral base to lie outside of Java, the country's most populated region.

The New Order sought to establish the Pancasila (Five Principles) as the national ideology, which Muslim groups were suspicious of, ever since President Sukarno proclaimed its virtues in the 1950s. Their main objection was the religious tenet, which they termed as being agnostic since it gave equal importance to all religions, including Javanese mysticism. These differences surfaced in the 1983 elections when religious parties confronted Pancasila. At the time the government demanded that all organizations proclaim Pancasila as their sole ideology, which the PPP refused to do. A PMI-dominated PPP national council, however, acquiesced to government requirements and accepted the Pancasila. Rather than submit to Jakarta's whims, Nahdatul Ulama opted to withdraw from active political affairs and return to its social, religious, and educational roots. The NU declared that it was no longer part of the political process, and that participation in the PPP was an individual decision for its members, further weakening the coalition.

Following the return of democracy in Indonesia in 1999, the PPP continued to be active, now as a vehicle for conservative Islam and as defender of Muslim causes. It placed members in the several cabinets and President Megawati Sukarnoputri appointed a member of the PPP, Hamzah Haz as her vice president, although Haz originally rejected the idea of a female president, a position held by most PPP *'ulamā'*. While a member of Islamic coalitions it has differed from more pluralist Islamic parties in its requirement that all members be Muslim. It also was part of acrimonious electoral confrontations with one of those parties, the National Awakening Party (Partai Kebangkitan Bangsa, PKB) leading to violence in the 1999 elections. The PPP's conservatism was exemplified when the question of establishing Sharīʿah law in the northern Sumatra province of Aceh arose in the national legislature. This was when the PPP called for the Sharīʿah to be applicable to all citizens of the province, the only exception for non-Muslims being Islamic family law. In the 1999 general elections for representatives to the national house of representatives (Dewan Perwakilan Rakyat, DPR) the party received 10.72 percent of the ballots cast but has shown a precipitous drop ever since. In 2004 the percentage was 8.15 and in 2009 just 5.3 percent. Slippage was in large part due to leadership problems and personality and power splits within the party, as well as a general weakening of the credibility of Islamic parties in the republic.

Bibliography

Budiman, Arief, Barbara Hatley, and Damien Kingsbury, eds. *Reformasi: Crisis and Change in Indonesia*. Clayton, Australia: Monash Asia Institute, 1999.

Manning, Christopher, and Peter Van Dierman, eds. *Indonesia in Transition: Social Aspects of Reformasi and Crisis*. London: Zed Books, 2000.

Vatikiotis, Michael. *Indonesian Politics under Suharto: The Rise and Fall of the New Order*. London: Routledge, 1998.

Fred R. von der Mehden

United Malays National Organization. The United Malays National Organization (UMNO) has been the dominant member of the ruling coalition of Malaysia (previously Malaya) since independence in 1957. UMNO was formed on 12 May 1946 and sought to establish itself as the paramount party in the colony during the next eleven years of colonial rule. When independence was gained in 1957 UMNO was the dominant member of the ruling Alliance, a coalition of Malays, Chinese, and Indian parties. The Alliance and its successor, an expanded coalition called the Barisan Nasional (National Alliance), has won every national election since independence. With the exception of the 1969, 2008, and 2013 general elections, the coalition has held over two-thirds of the members of parliament, allowing it to pass changes to the constitution without opposition votes. The two top offices go to the winners of party elections. Malaysia is a federal system and since independence the party has won a majority of state elections, the opposition gaining no state in the first national elections in 1957 and one state to five since.

UMNO's policy positions have changed in focus since independence. Initially the emphasis was on national development. National politics tended to be secular in nature although there was always attention given to its Malays Muslim constituency. To rise within UMNO it has been necessary to reinforce the candidate's ethnic and religious legitimacy. However national politics has meant compromises with other members of multiethnic and multireligious coalitions. After racial riots in 1969 the UMNO-led government inaugurated a program to support the advancement of the *bumiputra* (sons of the soil, i.e., Malays and other indigenous peoples). Muhammad Mahthir became prime minister in 1981, and his long tenure (1981–2003) bought continued support for development, but with an increased emphasis upon Islam.

UMNO's position with regard to Islam has been primarily based upon three foundations, its

Malays Muslim constituency, the focus of its top leadership, and its electoral and ideological confrontation with the other major Malays Muslim party, Partai Islam Se-Malaysia (PAS, Islamic Party of Malaysia). Initially Malays Muslims were almost 90 percent rural and less involved in the modern urban economy than the Chinese and Indians. While the New Economic Policy (NEP) and economic modernization has fostered a growing Malays Muslim urban middle class and elite, this constituency continues to have strong ties to Islam and UMNO has sought to proclaim itself as the defender of Islam. Since being a Malays is to be a Muslim, religion and development have been able to target the same electorate, although Malays support for UMNO has been weakening.

The personal foci of prime ministers have also helped to frame UMNO's policies toward Islam. While all have given strong verbal support to Islamic principles and the country's Muslims, the first three prime ministers were far more secular in their tone and policy. After Mahathir came to power he pressed Islamic symbols and rhetoric at both the domestic and international level. This effort included the fostering of Islamic banking, the establishment of the International Islamic University, and strengthening national government control over Islamic issues. While the constitution states that Islam is the official religion of the country, Mahthir asserted that, as a result of Malaysia's increasing Islamization, it had become an Islamic state. This was negatively perceived by non-Islamic parties and declared a sham by PAS.

The third factor effecting UMNO's Islamic stance has been its electoral rivalry with its major Malays Muslim competitor, PAS, particularly in the last three decades. In the early years after its official registration in 1955, PAS did not seriously challenge UMNO's paramountcy. It received only one representative out of fifty-two members of parliament and was even part of the coalition from 1974 to 1977. However continued PAS criticisms of UMNO as insufficiently Islamic, its victories in Malays Muslim majority states, and its attempts to forward Sharīʿah law in those states, have pressed UMNO to emphasize its own Islamic credentials.

Under UMNO leadership there has been a concerted effort to centralize religious authority. In part to counter PAS's state and local power, institutions and policies have been established to define and control religious teaching in the schools, to determine the legitimacy of Islamic organizations, to foster the conversion of non-Muslims, and to control religious deviancy and encourage UMNO's interpretation of Islam in society. In addition, there has been a long history of government support for the building of mosques and religious schools, culminating in the establishment of the International Islamic University. This has all been part of an increased role of the federal government led by UMNO to further the Islamization of Malaysia.

Bibliography

Crouch, Harold. *Government and Society in Malaysia.* Ithaca, N.Y.: Cornell University Press, 1996.

Liow, Joseph. *Piety and Politics: Islamism in Contemporary Politics*. Oxford and New York: Oxford University Press, 2009.

Milne, R. S., and Diane K. Mauzy. *Malaysian Politics under Mahathir*. London: Routledge, 1999.

Fred R. von der Mehden

Universities. In the classical Islamic world the primary educational institution was the *madrasah*, established by an individual founder through a *waqf* (endowment). The founder was allowed to designate beneficiaries and successors and even to impose his will on the administration, similar to the colleges of late medieval Europe, which were established in a similar manner.

Between 1100 and 1200 there was an influx of new knowledge into western Europe, much of it through the Arab scholars of Spain. In order to explore this knowledge and to free scientific investigation from the control of the church, new universities were formed. By the thirteenth century, this secular orientation and dependence on science rather than on revealed truth had become the basis of educational principles in these institutions.

In Muslim education there had never been any dissociation between secular learning and divinely revealed knowledge. With the expansion of the Islamic world, however, Muslim scholars came into contact with the Hellenistic traditions of knowledge in Syria and Alexandria. Instead of becoming secularized, they assimilated and Islamized this philosophy, and thus expanded the sphere of Islamic educational activity. This was possible because the Muslims believed that God is the source of all knowledge. Muslim scholars therefore considered all knowledge to be a basic trust (*amānah*, Qurʾān 33:72) given to humankind. Thus it is a duty to explore, learn, understand, and teach all kinds of knowledge.

Muslim educationalists, however, maintained a dual hierarchy of knowledge. Revealed knowledge was directly transmitted from the divine source to the prophet Muḥammad, through whom this message was transmitted to humanity. Acquired knowledge was gained by means of human beings' God-given intellect and reason. The former category was known as "transmitted sciences" (*al-ʿulūm al naqlīyah*) and the latter as "intellectual sciences" (*al-ʿulūm al-ʿaqlīyah*). Wisdom acquired through vision (*kashf*) and the direct perception of truth (*dhawq*) but tested with reference to the Qurʾān was also regarded as a form of knowledge that could be acquired and transmitted to others. The first and second categories of knowledge were taught in the *madrasahs*; the last category was taught mainly in *khanqahs* and *zāwiyahs*.

Muslims brought the Hellenistic sciences into Islamic parameters in order to harmonize reason and revelation. Al-Kindī's *Fī aqsām al-ʿulūm* (On the Types of the Sciences) and al-Fārābī's *Iḥṣāʾ al-ʿulūm* (The Enumeration of the Sciences) are two works that integrate religion and science. Al-Ghazālī, in volume two of his *Iḥyāʾ ʿulūm al-Dīn*, had by this time simplified the classification of knowledge. According to him, basic knowledge of the *Sharīʿah* must be regarded as obligatory (*farḍ ʿayn*) for all Muslims; the rest of knowledge was optional for individuals but obligatory for a society, which ensured that other knowledge would be pursued by at least some (*farḍ kifāyah*). The new and existing forms of science that were developing in the Islamic world, as well as the sciences acquired from other civilizations, were fitted into the hierarchy based on Islamic concepts drawn from the Qurʾān and *sunnah*. These concepts were metaphysically, philosophically, and rationally justified with reference to the order of life and the universe enunciated by God.

Trend toward Secularization. In the Western world, by contrast, there developed a rift between the theological and secular approaches, a rift characterized by T. S. Eliot as "the dissociation of sensibility." Western universities, established with the intention of keeping the quest for knowledge free from the control of the church, emphasized a secular scientific approach to external nature and internal human nature. The formulations of philosophers further strengthened scientific thinking along pragmatic and empirical lines. Scientific activity and its mode of operation acquired credibility, prestige, and power. Religious thinkers had not developed new intellectual tools to combat the enthronement of reason as the only means of gaining truth and knowledge, to show the limits of scientific knowledge, or to demonstrate the moral and spiritual needs that faith can fulfill.

The secularist educational system based on this approach entered the Muslim world in earnest early in the nineteenth century. Much of the impetus for this came from the fact that many Muslims lived in countries controlled or dominated by European colonial powers. The Europeans had started establishing modern secular schools, colleges, and universities. Some of these were technical schools; others were medical colleges or teacher training institutes. Resistance from the Muslim *'ulamā'* and other traditional elements was ignored or suppressed. It was not long before the colonial governments started granting Muslim students access to the universities in the mother countries, and then began to establish similar institutions in their colonies, which served to create a new elite who would control, guide, and modernize society. The British established the first university in Calcutta in 1850, but only a few Muslims were admitted.

Perceiving the advancement of Hindu university graduates in India, Sir Sayyid Ahmad Khan founded the Anglo-Mohamedan Oriental College in 1875, in Aligarh, southeast of Delhi. It was renamed Aligarh Muslim College later in 1875, and in 1920 it became Aligarh Muslim University, with the goal of educating a modern elite who would be able to compete successfully with Hindus and assume new leadership in politics and economics. Sir Sayyid Ahmad had been influenced by the reformer Jamāl al-Dīn al-Afghānī, and he applied a Western scientific, rational, and empirical approach to the interpretation of the Qur'ān. Although his influence was resisted by the *'ulamā'*, some of whom were teaching at Aligarh, the new elite that emerged was less conversant with Islam but had gained more secular knowledge. In order to bring about some sort of synthesis, the British government in Bengal introduced the "New Scheme Madrasah," where modern subjects such as history, geography, and mathematics—but not the natural sciences—were taught along with traditional religious subjects. Their students could be directly admitted to universities like the University of Dhaka, which started taking such students in 1921, without taking the examination in English usually required of *madrasah* students seeking entrance to universities.

The educational policy of the British colonial power in India was otherwise entirely secular. Religion was not taught in government schools, but by allowing the Calcutta Alia Madrasah to be run along orthodox Islamic lines, they maintained a dual education system, and Muslims had to choose one system or the other. A clear-cut division arose in the Muslim community of India: one group, basically traditional and orthodox in attitude, had little knowledge of modern education or modern science; the other, more or less secularist, had little in-depth knowledge of their own Islamic faith.

When Pakistan came into existence, the subject of Islamic studies was introduced into all secondary schools. In Karachi Federal University, founded in 1951, it became an obligatory subject for all Muslim undergraduates, and for non-Muslim students "moral education" was introduced. In other subjects the secular philosophical basis remained unchallenged. As a result, the course in Islamic studies could not offset the secularization of minds as had been hoped.

From Morocco to Iran modern secular school systems were introduced in the nineteenth century, although modern universities were not established until the twentieth. This modernization started with military schools in Turkey in the early eighteenth century, but it received a national color after Napoleon's conquest of Egypt and his attempt to remodel the education and legal systems after those of France.

In method and substance Cairo's al-Azhar—established as a mosque in 970 CE and declared a *jāmiʿat* in 988—retained its original *madrasah* character in spite of the influence of al-Afghānī and later of Muḥammad ʿAbduh. The addition of modern sections and the attempt to modernize continued under Gamal Abdel Nasser. It then gained faculties of education, medicine, and engineering. Although English was listed in the curriculum in 1901, it was not until 1958 that the first course was actually offered, after Nasser's drastic reform, with the structure overhauled and changed in 1961. Al-Azhar did not attempt to produce Islamic analogies for modern branches of knowledge in order to Islamize the modern education system; it simply resisted all attempts to modernize its own system. The government in Egypt initiated modern primary and secondary education, and private and foreign-supported schools acquired prestige. A College of Arts was established in 1909. Other higher institutions of law, medicine, engineering, agriculture, and commerce were all incorporated into the University of Cairo in 1925.

The private American University in Cairo was established in 1919. The second state-run university in Egypt was not opened until 1942, in Alexandria, with a third, Ain Shams University, Cairo, in 1950. Conflict between al-Azhar and these universities and the government-backed education system resulted in conflict between their graduates in terms of both thought and action. The transformation of the administration of the university and the introduction of faculties beyond the traditional trio of jurisprudence, theology, and Arabic studies did expand the role of al-Azhar graduates; however, the new faculties and the new Institute of Languages and Translation were purely modern, and there was no attempt to Islamize the basic philosophical concepts of these different branches of knowledge. Hence this university did not contribute to the resolution of the conflict between traditionalism and modernism in Egypt or abroad.

Nationalism. Besides the conflict between tradition and modernity and between orthodox religious consciousness and modern secularist ideas, there was also the politically influential contribution that modern higher education, including university education, made in giving birth to Arab nationalism. Foreign missionary schools and universities in the Levant—Syria, Jerusalem, Lebanon, and Jordan—led to an Arabic cultural revival. By the end of the nineteenth century the philosophy of Arab nationalism had repercussions throughout the region. The Jesuit University of St. Joseph (1875) at Ghazir, Lebanon, and the American University of Beirut (first opened as the Syrian Protestant College in 1866) contributed immensely to the modernization process and later to the propagation of Arab nationalism and anti-imperialism, as did the University of Damascus, founded in 1903.

Turkey. In Turkey, the first university was established in 1453 as a school to train civil servants and in 1871 became a university in the modern sense of the word. It was closed soon afterword, then reopened by Sultan Abdülhamid II in 1900 and restructured in 1908 after the Young Turk revolution. It became Istanbul University in 1923 after Mustafa Kemal took power, being restructured in 1933 and again in 1946.

The dismemberment of the Ottoman Empire after World War I was attended by the growth of nationalism in various Muslim countries; this was especially true in Turkey, where modern Western education had been particularly influential. In Turkey higher educational institutions produced an elitist generation that supported Mustafa Kemal Atatürk's Turkish nationalism. Like Egypt, Turkey also had private schools, missionary schools, and foreign schools that contributed to the generation of nationalist sentiment and served as channels for the transmission of Western educational and cultural principles. Ankara University was established in 1933.

Mustafa Kemal banned all traditional *madrasahs*. In 1948, after his death, the Democrat Party came to power, and courses in Islamic studies were initiated in ten provinces. The University of Ankara started teaching Islamic studies in 1949, and the University of Istanbul established the Islamic Research Institute in 1954. In 1971 Erzurum Atatürk University opened a Faculty of Islamic Studies. Religious education was introduced into elementary schools in 1949, and Qurʾānic courses were being actively organized by the government education system by 1971. Secondary-school textbooks had also been thoroughly revised by that time. In the late 1960s and the 1970s the universities were the center of the antigovernment protest movement. Since the late 1980s there have been protests at all universities in Turkey in support of and opposition to the wearing of headscarves by women students and staff members.

India. Modern Western education generated a narrow nationalistic spirit in other Islamic communities. An example is the Young Bengal Movement in Calcutta University in the nineteenth century, which became the precursor of a Hindu nationalist movement and later a Muslim nationalist movement in India.

Iran and Iraq. In Iran, Reza Shah tried to follow Kemal's secularizing policy with Iran's modernization of higher education beginning in 1921. The same pattern seen in Turkey and in Egypt was repeated. Established colleges were integrated into the University of Tehran, and the universities were expected to reinforce the process of secularization. Religious instruction was abolished in schools in 1941. In the same year, Reza Shah abdicated under pressure from the British and Russians. During the reign of his son four more universities were established, and these soon became centers of political unrest. What was seen as an anti-Islamic educational and social policy was modified. The *ʿulamāʾ* came to power in Iran in 1979 after the shah was overthrown by Ayatollah Ruhollah Khomeini's revolutionary movement. Since the revolution, a process of Islamizing curricula and textbooks has taken place, and the universities have been divided into religious and secular institutions. In neighboring Iraq, the regime of Saddam Hussein enforced strict secularism in school education; the University of Baghdad (founded 1957) has a Faculty of Islamic Sciences.

South Asia and Southeast Asia. In South and Southeast Asia there has been a repetition of the same pattern. Until 1977 most of the universities had been established during the colonial period and hence were liberal and secular in approach. In Malaysia and Indonesia, a system of Islamic schools—the *pesantrens*—coexisted with secular universities.

The move to establish Islamic universities in Malaysia and Pakistan began in earnest after the World Conference on Islamic Economics held in Jiddah in 1976 and the First World Conference on Muslim Education held the following year in Mecca. At the latter, S. A. Ashraf's theory of formulating Islamic concepts for all branches of knowledge as substitutes for secular theories was unanimously accepted. Ismāʿīl al-Fārūqī suggested certain methods to achieve this end in his 1982 book *Islamization of Knowledge*. Ashraf's Islamic education theory and revision of the university curriculum, especially in the field of teacher education, has been the source for the revision of teacher education and teaching methodology at the International Islamic University of Kuala Lumpur.

In Indonesia, the Islamic University of Indonesia was founded in 1945 and has about twelve thousand students. The Islamic University of North Sumatra (founded 1952), the Islamic University Nusantara at Bandung (founded in 1959 as the Nahdlatul Ulama University), and the Islamic University of Riau (founded 1962) all have sizable student bodies. The University of Brunei Darussalam has declared the gradual

Islamization of knowledge as their education policy; to this end, the Sultan Haji Omar Ali Saifuddien Institute of Islamic Studies at the University of Brunei Darussalam was founded in 1985.

Other Islamic Universities. In Pakistan the International Islamic University (founded 1980) is experimenting with Islamizing the whole area of jurisprudence and the legal system. The Islamic University of Gaza has a large student body. The Islamic University at Kushtia, Bangladesh (1980), the Islamic University of Niger (1987), and the Islamic University in Uganda, at Mbale (1988) all have relatively small numbers of students. So do the newer Islamic universities in Indonesia: the Islamic University of Jakarta and the Islamic University of Indonesia in Cirebon. Al-Quds University in Jerusalem has a Higher Institute of Islamic Archaeology. Mention should also be made of the Islamic College for Advanced Studies in London, the Oxford Centre for Islamic Studies, and the Oxford branch of Azad University (Tehran). There are also many universities with faculties of Islamic studies, such as the Faculty of Arts and Islamic Studies at the Usmanu Danfodiyo University in Nigeria; there are many more that have centers of Islamic studies.

Saudi Arabia, the Middle East, North Africa. In Saudi Arabia traditional *madrasahs* have been almost entirely replaced by modern schools with Islamized curriculum and texts, especially in literature and history, and with intensive teaching of Islam at the primary and secondary levels. At the university level four courses in Islamic culture are taught over the four years to reinforce the Islamic approach to life and knowledge. The deep religious ethos of the society counteracts the secularist tendencies and ideas acquired through modern subjects such as economics and natural sciences. In addition there is the Islamic University of Medina, founded in 1961, which is mainly a theological school where the teaching methodology is modern, but the subjects are the same as in the old *madrasahs*.

Jordan and the Gulf States have modern universities, but they have also introduced Islamic culture courses. The same is true of universities in Morocco, Algeria, Tunisia, and Libya.

Future Directions. The six World Conferences on Muslim Education (Mecca, 1977; Islamabad, 1980; Dhaka, 1981; Jakarta, 1982; Cairo, 1987; Cape Town, 1996) have given Muslim educationalists a new method of solving the conflict between the knowledge to be acquired and the theories to be formulated. Unless Muslim scholars meet the challenge of secular philosophies—as al-Ghazālī did in his *Tahāfut al-falāsifah* (Incoherence of Philosophy)—and establish Islamic concepts, producing textbooks in different branches of knowledge based on those concepts, it will not be possible to counteract the secularization process. Many Muslim scholars in both Western and Eastern universities have become conscious of this fact, and attempts are being made.

[*See also* ʿAbduh, Muḥammad; Afghānī, Jamāl al-Dīn al-; Aḥmad Khān, Sayyid; Azhar, al-; Education, Muslim; Fārūqī, Ismāʿīl Rājī al-; *and* Zaytūnah.]

BIBLIOGRAPHY

Ashraf, Syed Ali. *New Horizons in Muslim Education.* London: Hodder & Stoughton, 1985. Criticizes the secularist philosophy of education and suggests Islamic principles for the design of curriculum, textbook preparation, and teaching methodology at all levels.

Banani, Amin. *The Modernization of Iran, 1921–1941.* Stanford, Calif.: Stanford University Press, 1961. Critical analysis of the condition of Iran under Reza Shah.

Bilgrami, H. H., and S. A. Ashraf. *The Concept of an Islamic University.* Cambridge, U.K.: Islamic Academy, 1985. Historical survey followed by suggestions for the present and future.

Makdisi, George. *The Rise of Colleges: Institutions of Learning in Islam and the West.* Edinburgh: Edinburgh University Press, 1981. Valuable historical survey that contains a detailed description of the principles and methods of establishing universities and other educational institutions in both Islamic countries and the West.

Al-Naguib al-Attas, Syed Muhammad, ed. *Aims and Objectives of Islamic Education.* Jiddah, Saudi Arabia: King Abdulaziz University, 1979. Publication of the First World Conference on Muslim Education, held at Mecca in 1977, containing articles dealing with the conflict between the Western secularist approach and the Islamic approach, with suggestions for resolving them through education.

Nasr, Seyyed Hossein. *Islamic Science: An Illustrated Study.* London: World of Islam Festival, 1976. Contains chapters on Islam and the rise of sciences and the Islamic educational system, along with essays on the early contribution of Muslims to the natural sciences.

Qubain, Fahim I. *Education and Science in the Arab World.* Baltimore, Md.: Johns Hopkins University Press, 1966.

Rosenthal, Franz. *Knowledge Triumphant: The Concept of Knowledge in Medieval Islam.* Leiden, Netherlands: E. J. Brill, 1970. Authoritative analysis of the meaning of *ʿilm* (knowledge).

Szyliowicz, Joseph S. *Education and Modernization in the Middle East.* Ithaca, N.Y.: Cornell University Press, 1973. Thorough analysis of the spread of modern Western education in the Middle East, fully supportive of secularist education.

Tritton, A. S. *Materials on Muslim Education in the Middle Ages.* London: Luzac, 1957. Historical survey of Muslim education.

SYED ALI ASHRAF
Updated by JUSTIN CORFIELD

UṢŪL AL-DĪN. *See* Religious Beliefs.

ʿUTHMĀN IBN ʿAFFĀN. ʿUthmān ibn ʿAffān (r. 644–656) was the third of the caliphs identified as "rightly guided" by Sunnīs. He was a prominent member of the Umayyad clan in the tribe of Quraysh. By all accounts, ʿUthmān was a pious, self-effacing man despite his wealthy, privileged background; he embraced Islam early and emigrated first to Abyssinia and then to Medina—all of which established his precedence in Islam. After becoming Muslim he was first married to Ruqayyah and then, upon her death, to Umm Kulthūm, two daughters of Muḥammad. For this distinction he earned the honorific Dhū al-Nurayn (He of the Two Lights).

The sources tend to divide ʿUthmān's tenure as caliph into six good years in the beginning and six bad years at the end. Under ʿUthmān, new frontiers were opened in North Africa through carefully planned expeditions, and the remnants of the Sassanian Empire fell to Muslim control. The third caliph was concerned with asserting his control over the provinces that had seen fresh new waves of tribesmen immigrating from the Arabian Peninsula. Part of his policy was to appoint relatives from his own clan as governors. Such appointments made ʿUthmān vulnerable to charges of nepotism and disregard of the Qurʾānic principles of precedence and moral excellence in making political appointments. These grievances eventually came to a head in 656.

The achievement for which ʿUthmān is forever remembered and which proved to be a milestone in the consolidation of the Muslim polity as a religious, scripture-based community, was the final recension of the Qurʾān, completed around 651, as the sources overwhelmingly report. ʿUthmān appointed an editorial committee headed by Zayd ibn Thābit to collate the various textual versions already in existence and cull disparate verses and sections committed to memory by various Companions in order to produce a final canonical edition. The ʿUthmānic codex (*al-muṣḥaf al-ʿUthmānī*) was meant to supersede all other extant manuscripts, because it was feared that variant versions would lead to sectarian divisiveness, as had happened in earlier religious communities.

Once the text was finalized, ʿUthmān ordered that variant copies be destroyed and a copy of the canonical text be sent to all the major garrison cities.

Because of his bid to exercise greater control over the provinces, particularly Iraq and Egypt, ʿUthmān earned the ire of the settlers there who increasingly resisted his policies. In the last year of his reign, a few hundred embittered tribesmen from Iraq and Egypt arrived in Medina to present their grievances before ʿUthmān. Negotiations and debates were held for almost fifty days, with the caliph practically under siege in his own house. Sometime in June 656, while ʿUthmān sat reciting the Qurʾān in the mosque at Medina, a cabal of angry Egyptians burst in and assassinated him. His blood is said to have spilled onto the pages of the sacred text and his wife, Naʾilah bint al-Furāfiṣah, was wounded while trying to protect him. The third caliphate ended with ʿUthmān's secret burial in the middle of the same night.

[*See also* Companions of the Prophet.]

BIBLIOGRAPHY

Ibn Abī Dawūd. *Kitāb al-maṣāḥif.* In *Materials for the History of the Text of the Qurʾān: The Old Codices*, edited by Arthur Jeffrey. Leiden: Brill, 1937.

Ṭabarī, Muḥammad ibn Jarīr al-. *The Crisis of the Early Caliphate* (*Tāʾrīkh al-rusul wa-al-mulūk*). Translated and annotated by R. Stephen Humphreys. Albany: State University of New York Press, 1990.

ASMA AFSARUDDIN

UZBEKISTAN. Within the territory of largely Sunnī Uzbekistan lie the most prestigious centers of Islamic culture and influence in Central Asia: the ancient cities of Bukhara, Samarqand, and Khiva, where the religion took root in the seventh century. With European colonial expansion and the spread of European ideas to other Islamic realms in Asia and North Africa, "holy" Bukhara (Bukhārā-yi sharīf)—which retained a quasi-independent status under its emirs even after Russian conquest of Turkestan in the nineteenth century—was an object of special veneration in Muslim eyes, as a locus of uncontaminated belief. Bukharan *madāris* attracted students from other Muslim areas of the Russian Empire and beyond. Baymirza Hayit, an Uzbek Muslim who reached the West during World War II, described (1956) his homeland prior to 1917 as "a land of Islamic dervishes" and superstition, with four active Ṣūfī orders (the Naqshbandīyah, Qādirīyah, Kubrawīyah, and Qalandārīyah).

Tashkent, the capital of modern Uzbekistan, was the dominant political center of the region during both the tsarist and Soviet periods. Following establishment of Soviet rule after 1917, anti-Islamic policies prevailed, despite initial resistance to them even from within the ranks of Uzbek and other Central Asian Communists. A few years later, however, party discipline had been restored. Yet despite harsh measures against Islam, official media attacks on Islamic "survivals" throughout the Soviet period revealed that a substantial number of Uzbek Muslims continued to defy or circumvent strictures by continuing to observe religious life-cycle rituals and making forbidden pilgrimages to the graves of holy men.

During World War II a Muslim "Spiritual Board" under a *muftī* was created in Tashkent, with official sanction and along the lines of Russian Orthodox hierarchical structures. Its jurisdiction extended throughout the four Central Asian republics and Kazakhstan (always regarded by Soviet officials as a separate geographic entity). Any hope that this was a step toward legitimation of Islam was soon dashed, however, when the persecution of religion resumed at the end of the war. The Spiritual Board emerged as an official instrument for controlling Islamic activity within Central Asia, and as a handmaiden of the regime for foreign political purposes. Tashkent became a showcase used in attempts to impress foreign Muslims with the supposed superiority of the Soviet system.

With fluctuation, anti-Islamic policies remained intact after Joseph Stalin's death in 1953, but erosion of Moscow's control over the republics in the period of stagnation under Brezhnev was marked by a de facto softening. It became possible for Uzbek social scientists to collect and publish data on the extent of Islamic practice. The Uzbek researcher Talib S. Saidbaev published a book (*Islam i obshchestvo*, Moscow, 1982) showing that in traditional Muslim areas of the Soviet Union religion was far more pervasive, especially among the young and the educated, than in Christian parts of the country. Saidbaev found that the structure of society, with tightly knit extended families that cut across socioeconomic lines and remained loyal to age-old tribal and clan affiliations, led to increased social pressures to conform to religious obligations. Officials charged by the Communist Party with responsibility for atheist indoctrination warned that their work was being frustrated by a widespread public tendency to identify Islamic rituals with national tradition.

Members of Uzbekistan's Soviet-educated professional elite joined in global efforts to reform Islam to make it more acceptable. The Uzbek Encyclopedia (*Ozbek Sovet Entsiklopediyasi*, vol. 5, Tashkent, 1974) listed some of the aspects of "Islamic modernism," among them portrayal of Muḥammad as a democrat and reformer, identification of Islam with socialism and communism, equation of religious and communist morality, and modernization of Sharīʿah rules governing women, the family, and daily life.

When Mikhail Gorbachev first came to power in Moscow in 1985 he viewed elimination of religion as an essential ingredient of a program of reform. This was manifested in especially brutal fashion in Uzbekistan, where in Tashkent in 1986 Gorbachev made a speech so anti-Islamic that it was never published. His visit was followed by mass expulsions from the Uzbek Communist Party of members accused of participation in religious events. Ironically relaxation of central controls over the Soviet republics produced an effect opposite to his intent. In February 1989 the *muftī* of Tashkent, Shamsuddin Baba Khan (Shams al-Dīn Bābā Khān), a mainstay of the regime and grandson of the original *muftī* appointed in 1943, was ousted from office following a demonstration by members of the *ummah*. In June 1989 a new Uzbek Communist Party chief, Islam A. Karimov (subsequently president of independent Uzbekistan), came to power and presided over the inception of a more flexible policy toward Islam.

The new *muftī*, Muḥammad Ṣādiq Muḥammad Yūsuf, became a highly visible public figure, appearing on state-controlled television. He also published articles containing liberal advice on such matters as family relations and women; the newspaper that carried these (*Ozbekistan adabiyati va sanati*) had until recently been a vehicle of attacks on Islam. As part of his new public role the *muftī* refrained from appearing as spokesman for the aspirations and grievances of the *ummah* or of Uzbeks in general, avoiding any criticism of secular power. This led to discontent among some segments of the *ʿulamāʾ* and *ummah*, who repeatedly attempted to depose him. On one occasion he managed to hold on to office in the face of accusations that he had enriched himself unjustly through the sale of Qurʾāns donated by Saudi Arabia.

Uzbekistan's declaration of independence on 31 August 1991 removed the remaining impediment to such manifestations of spiritual life as public worship and religious education. In new and ancient mosques newly restored to religious control, Qurʾān classes began for adults of both sexes and for children. Once-forbidden religious publications now appeared on sale at kiosks, and bus tours advertised taking Uzbeks on pilgrimages to religious shrines. The state imposed limits on Islamic political activity, however; the government denied registration to the Islamic Revival Party (as it had to secular opposition parties).

At the same time increased religious leverage and visits by emissaries of such conservative Muslim countries as Iran and Saudi Arabia led many Uzbeks, including believers, to fear that the tyranny of Soviet rule might be replaced by the tyranny of Islamic fundamentalism, which became a household phrase. Muslims welcomed toleration of their religion after many decades of persecution, but some, especially the better-educated, were alarmed by the perceived danger of an Islamic republic in which the country's moderate, Ṣūfī-influenced religious tradition would be submerged. The Karimov government played on these fears to repress all dissent, branding even secular critics as "Islamic extremists." This became a self-fulfilling prophesy: restrictions on legal dissent drove many critics of the regime underground, where the Islamist influence was strongest.

Ironically, many of the social and economic problems that the Uzbeks had blamed on the Soviet regime continued or were exacerbated under independence, especially the cotton monoculture. Even with international assistance efforts to halt the drying up of the Aral Sea due to diversion of its water sources to irrigation, the sea continued to shrink. Education continued to be disrupted by the drafting of school children to help with the cotton harvest. Against a backdrop of problems the climate of repression enhanced the potential of Islam as champion of the poor and downtrodden and increased the leverage of radical elements seeking to destabilize secular institutions. One group that emerged was the Islamic Movement of Uzbekistan (IMU), which had a base in neighboring Afghanistan under the Taliban. In the fighting that followed US invasion, many IMU members were killed or imprisoned. One who perished was the IMU's field commander, Juma Namangoni. To judge from statements of the Uzbek government, remnants of the IMU are still active. Another Islamic organization, the illegal Hizb ut-Tahrir (al-Ḥizb al-Taḥrīr, Party of Liberation), which has adherents in many countries as well as Central Asia, is also a force in Uzbekistan. Ḥizb al-Taḥrīr seeks to abolish secular governments and establish a global caliphate. Reportedly the thousands of political prisoners being detained in Uzbekistan are predominantly supporters of Ḥizb al-Taḥrīr.

The source of two powerful bombs that exploded in Tashkent on 16 February 1999 was shrouded in mystery, but President Karimov blamed Islamic militants. There were arrests and a closed trial, after which some of the defendants were executed on the basis of "confessions." In May 2005 a major protest took place in the Fergana Valley city of Andizhan, triggered by the arrest of twenty-three local businessmen. Armed demonstrators attacked the prison and liberated the businessmen, as well as many other prisoners. The regime responded with massive force, killing hundreds. Once again, Islamic extremists were blamed. Such repressions clouded the Uzbek government's relations with other countries, although Russia and China supported its actions. A British ambassador to Uzbekistan, Craig Murray, sacrificed his diplomatic career in order to publish a book on human rights abuses in the country.

[*See also* Islam and Politics in Central Asia and the Caucasus.]

BIBLIOGRAPHY

Barthold, V. V. *Istoriia kul'turnoĭ zhizni Turkestana.* Leningrad: Izd-vo Akademii nauk SSSR, 1927.

Bennigsen, Alexandre, and Chantal Lemercier-Quelquejay. *Islam in the Soviet Union.* New York: Praeger, 1967.

Critchlow, James. "Islam and Nationalism in Central Asia." In *Religion and Nationalism in Soviet and East European Politics*, edited by Pedro Ramet, 2d ed., pp. 196–217. Durham, N.C.: Duke University Press, 1989.

Critchlow, James. "Islam in Soviet Central Asia: Renaissance or Revolution?" *Religion in Communist Dominated Areas* 29 (Autumn 1990): 196–211.

Critchlow, James. *Nationalism in Uzbekistan: A Soviet Republic's Road to Sovereignty*. Boulder, Colo.: Westview Press, 1991. See chapter entitled "The Islamic Factor."

Hayit, Baymirza. *Turkestan im XX. Jahrhundert*. Darmstadt, Germany: C. W. Leske, 1956.

Murray, Craig. *Murder in Samarkand: A British Ambassador's Controversial Defiance of Tyranny in the War on Terror*. Edinburgh: Mainstream Publications, 2007.

Ramiz, Mannan. "Khayaldan Haqiqatqha. Tashkent-Samarkand, 1928." Uncataloged manuscript in the Near East Division, Library of Congress, described in James Critchlow, "Religious-Nationalist Dissent in the Turkestan Communist Party: An Old Document Resurfaces." Report on the USSR, 19 January 1990.

Schuyler, Eugene. *Turkistan: Notes of a Journey in Russian Turkistan, Kokand, Bukhara, and Kuldja* (1878). Abridged by K. E. West. New York: Praeger, 1966.

James Critchlow

W

WAHHĀBĪYAH. An eighteenth-century movement of religious revival (*tajdīd*) and reform (*iṣlāh*) founded in Najd in Saudi Arabia by the scholar and jurist Muḥammad ibn ʿAbd al-Wahhāb (1702/3–1791/2). Although originally founded as a religious movement designed to purify society of un-Islamic practices, it took on a political dimension in 1744, when an alliance was formed between Ibn ʿAbd al-Wahhāb and Muḥammad ibn Saʿūd (d. 1767) that placed religious scholars in an advisory and legitimating role to political authority. This symbiotic relationship between the Al-Saʿūd and the Al Al-Shaykh (descendants of Ibn ʿAbd al-Wahhāb) has remained intact and continues in the present Saudi state. Also known popularly and pejoratively as "Wahhābism," this movement has been accused in the contemporary era of inspiring militant extremism and global jihād, particularly in connection with al-Qaʿida and Osama Bin Laden.

Eighteenth-century adherents of the movement referred to themselves as Muwaḥḥidūn, reflecting their central belief in absolute monotheism (*tawḥīd*) and rejection of association of anyone or anything with God (*shirk*). Ibn ʿAbd al-Wahhāb's most famous treatise, *Kitāb al-tawḥīd*, detailed the implications of belief in *tawḥīd*, outlining behaviors to be followed and avoided. Particularly prominent were the prohibition of requesting intercession from saints, veneration of saints, shrines, and tombs, and worship of or prayer to anyone or anything other than God. These issues became flashpoints for disagreement, debate, and conflict both with other Muslims, notably Shīʿīs and Ṣūfīs, and with non-Muslims historically, particularly in extreme cases of the destruction of objects considered to be sacred or to contain special blessing. Ibn ʿAbd al-Wahhāb's emphasis on *tawḥīd* had historical precedent in the writings of the medieval Ḥanbalī jurist Ibn Taymīyah (1263–1328) but was more nuanced in focusing on debate, dialogue, and persuasion, as opposed to punishment, as the appropriate means of redressing incorrect behaviors. Ibn ʿAbd al-Wahhāb's discussion was also focused on practice, rather than on the philosophical, mystical, or metaphysical debates about *tawḥīd* that had occurred historically among groups such as the Muʿtazilah and the Ashʿariyah.

Of most concern historically has been the question of appropriate treatment of *mushrikūn* (associationists, or those committing shirk) and *kuffār* (unbelievers, those committing *kufr*). Ibn ʿAbd al-Wahhāb taught that the appropriate method of addressing *shirk* was to engage in education and discussion in order to explain why the practice was incorrect. He distinguished between *shirk* and *kufr*, noting that *shirk* might be committed accidentally, out of ignorance, whereas *kufr* was a deliberate action that could be undertaken only by someone who had received proper instruction, declared belief in it, and then made a conscious decision to reject the teaching. Consequently, while a person committing *shirk* was to be reprimanded, the person was nevertheless considered to remain within the Muslim community (*ummah*). On the other hand a person committing *kufr* was considered, on the basis of their deliberate rejection of Islam, to be outside the Muslim community. Nevertheless the commission of *kufr* did not result in a declaration of jihād against such a person or community or in the imposition of the death penalty. Instead, Ibn ʿAbd al-Wahhāb permitted Muslims to live among *kuffār* (unbelievers) and engage in business relations with them, provided that the Muslims were free to practice their faith.

Beginning in the nineteenth century, many Wahhābīs no longer made this distinction between *shirk* and *kufr*, using the terms interchangeably and creating a new ideology of *takfīr* that justified declaring jihād as holy war against such persons. Prominent examples of this include the attacks on the Shīʿī shrines and populations of Karbala and Najaf in 1802. This ideology of *takfīr* is considered one of the hallmarks of Wahhābīyah in the contemporary era, particularly because of its presence in some Saudi textbooks. The practical expression of this ideology varies from hatred or disapproval within one's heart to militant opposition, raising concerns about the ability of Wahhābīs to live peacefully with non-Wahhābīs.

In contrast with the traditionalists and other regional *shaykhs*, Ibn ʿAbd al-Wahhāb argued against literal and decontextualized interpretations of the Qurʾān and *sunnah* (examples of the Prophet, recorded largely in the *ḥadīth*). Instead, he called for a multilayered interpretation that considered the historical context in which a verse was revealed or *ḥadīth* occurred, the broader context of Qurʾānic teachings about a topic in order to determine the underlying value, and analysis of the intent of the action undertaken. His focus on intent, in particular, provided the legal structure for circumventing more literal interpretations in favor of consideration of public welfare (*maṣlaḥah*), as in the case of permitting a delay in required charitable giving (*zakāt*) in the event of a drought so as not to overburden Muslims already suffering its economic consequences. He taught a methodology of *ḥadīth* criticism that focused on content (*matn*) rather than chains of transmission (*isnād*) in order to assure consistency between the Qurʾān and *ḥadīth* and attention to Qurʾānic values, with the Qurʾān holding absolute authority in the event of conflicting values or information. Although literalism and concern for ritual correctness permeated Wahhābī thought and practice in the twentieth century, attention to contextualized, nuanced, and value-oriented interpretation is apparent in some twenty-first-century Saudi thought, particularly legal opinions (*fatāwā*) issued by the Permanent Committee of Iftaʿ.

In his legal theory, Ibn ʿAbd al-Wahhab rejected the practice of blindly imitating past legal scholarship (*taqlīd*) in favor of an ongoing practice of independent reasoning (*ijtihād*) in the interpretation of Islamic law. His legal writings reflect broad knowledge of the four major and two extinct Sunnī law schools (*madhāhib*), as well as of the Shīʿī legal tradition. His methodology considered the opinions of various jurists on legal matters but concluded with his own opinion. Thus the writings of other jurists were deemed important to study and consider, but were neither authoritative nor binding. Such authority was reserved for the Qur'ān and *sunnah* alone. Ibn 'Abd al-Wahhāb asserted the right and responsibility of every Muslim to personally and directly study the Qur'ān and *sunnah* in order to know their content and to be able to discern when a religious leader might be leading people astray. Thus the education of both men and women in the Qur'ān and *sunnah* became a hallmark of the early Wahhābīyah.

Over time, Wahhābī scholars came to consider certain jurists particularly authoritative, most notably Ibn Taymīyah. The incorporation of Ibn Taymīyah's writings into the Wahhābī tradition is evident by the nineteenth century. Ibn Taymīyah's justifications for the overthrow of a political leader deemed to have failed in his responsibilities as a Muslim ruler, whether by failure to implement Islamic law as the only law of the land, to protect Muslims from physical harm, or to abide personally by the Islamic code of conduct, were particularly important in the Wahhābī declaration of jihād against the Ottoman Empire in the late eighteenth century and the subsequent conquest of the Hejaz. Some contemporary Wahhābīs have used similar justifications to protest the rule of the Saudi royal family, arguing that secular or Western laws have been used to circumvent Islamic law, that the personal lifestyles of certain members of the royal family are objectionable, or that the kingdom has failed to provide effective defense for itself, despite the expenditure of millions of dollars for defense. Osama Bin Laden raised these concerns during the 1990s through his Advice and Reform Committee, particularly with respect to the invitation to 500,000 American troops to defend the kingdom following Saddam Hussein's invasion of Kuwait. When the king repeatedly refused to make the requested reforms, Bin Laden called for the overthrow of the royal family, using Ibn Taymīyah's writings as support.

Although contemporary concerns about Wahhābīyah tend to focus on terrorism and extremism, the theme of jihād is not prominent in Ibn 'Abd al-Wahhāb's writings. He dedicated only one treatise to jihād, outlining restrictions and limitations and focusing on ending the conflict, preferably through the establishment of a treaty between the previously warring parties. Following the classical interpretation of jihād, Ibn 'Abd al-Wahhāb specified that jihād as armed conflict was to be purely defensive in nature: only if a geographically specific Muslim community was attacked or faced with the threat of an imminent attack by an armed group was jihād justified. The purpose of jihād was to end conflict, not to annihilate the enemy. Ibn 'Abd al-Wahhāb specified that civilians were never to be attacked or killed, abject destruction of life and property were prohibited, military actions undertaken had to be proportionate in nature and focused on specific strategic objectives, and jihād was to be undertaken as a communal duty (*farḍ kifāyah*), not as an individual duty (*farḍ 'ayn*). These teachings stand in marked contrast to the ideology of global *jihādī* organizations like al-Qa'ida that do not limit their jihād geographically or in terms of the destruction of life and property, particularly where civilians are concerned. Additionally, al-Qa'ida has declared the carrying out of jihād to be an individual, rather than communal, duty and cites broad categories of people, such as "Christian Crusaders" and "Zionist Jews" to be subject to jihād, rather than limiting the conflict to parties directly involved in an attack against a particular geographic community. Al-Qa'ida has also expanded the definition of "defense" to include nonmilitary "aggressions," such as economic sanctions, and has declared its right to engage in aggressive jihād, raising questions about its purported connection to Wahhābism.

In contemporary Saudi Arabia, debate has revived over the legacy of Ibn 'Abd al-Wahhāb and the teachings of Wahhābism as it developed historically as the realities of living in a global political system and economy have required reexamination of issues such as *takfīr* and appropriate relations with non-Wahhābī Muslims, Christians, and Jews, among others. Distinctions are increasingly being made between religion and politics, so that commonalities of belief can be acknowledged between Muslims, Christians, and Jews, while particular political issues, such as the existence of Israel, remain contested. Since the accession of King Abdullah to the throne in 2005, official emphasis has been placed on moderation in religious interpretation and the importance of dialogue, rather than conflict, between different religions and cultures. Although there remain highly conservative and literal interpreters within Saudi Arabia, there is also an increasing number of scholars calling for a more nuanced and inclusive vision of Islam and recognition of the difference between religion and culture, particularly where women's rights and access to public space are concerned.

[*See also* Saudi Arabia.]

BIBLIOGRAPHY

Works by Muḥammad Ibn ʿAbd al-Wahhāb

Muʿallafāt al-Shaykh al-Imām Muḥammad ibn ʿAbd al-Wahhāb. 5 vols. Riyadh: Jāmʿiat al-Imām Muḥammad ibn Saʿūd al-Islāmīyah, 1981.

Muʿamalāt al-Shaykh al-Imām Muḥammad ibn ʿAbd al-Wahhāb: Mulḥaq al-muṣannafāt. Riyadh: Jāmʿiat al-Imām Muḥammad ibn Saʿūd al-Islāmīyah, 1981.

Muʿamalāt al-Shaykh al-Imām Muḥammad ibnʿAbd al-Wahhāb: Qism al-ḥadīth. 4 vols. Riyadh: Jāmʿiat al-Imām Muḥammad ibn Saʿūd al-Islāmīyah, 1981.

Secondary Works

Algar, Hamid. *Wahhabism: A Critical Essay*. Oneonta, N.Y.: Islamic Publications International, 2002. A critique of Wahhābīyah as it developed historically, written by a prominent Shīʿī scholar.

Al-Rasheed, Madawi. *Contesting the Saudi State: Islamic Voices from a New Generation*. Cambridge, U.K., and New York: Cambridge University Press, 2007. Examination of the political uses of religion in Saudi Arabia, including the increasingly contested labels of Wahhābī and Salafī.

Al-Yassini, Ayman. *Religion and State in the Kingdom of Saudi Arabia*. Boulder, Colo.: Westview Press, 1985. Outlines the relationship between religion and state in Saudi Arabia.

Commins, David. *The Wahhabi Mission and Saudi Arabia*. London and New York: I. B. Tauris, 2005. A comprehensive analysis of the nineteenth-century Wahhābīyah and the homogenization of religious scholarship in Saudi Arabia.

DeLong-Bas, Natana J. *Jihad for Islam: The Struggle for the Future of Saudi Arabia*. New York: Oxford University Press, 2013. Analysis of contemporary Saudi thought and practice related to theology, Islamic law, women and gender, jihād, and relations with non-Muslims and non-Wahhābī Muslims.

DeLong-Bas, Natana J. *Wahhabi Islam: From Revival and Reform to Global Jihad*. Oxford and New York: Oxford University Press, 2004. Analysis of the writings of Muḥammad ibn ʿAbd al-Wahhāb on theology, Islamic law, women and gender, and jihād and outlining the differences between Wahhābīyah as originally founded and global jihādism.

Doumato, Eleanor Abdella. "Saudi Arabia: From 'Wahhabi' Roots to Contemporary Revisionism." In *Teaching Islam: Textbooks and Religion in the Middle East*, edited by Eleanor Abdella Doumato and Gregory Starrett. Boulder, Colo.: Lynne Rienner Publishers, 2007. Addresses the teaching of Islam in Saudi Arabia's school system, including changes that have occurred in the aftermath of 9/11.

NATANA J. DELONG-BAS

WAQF. The Arabic word *waqf* (pl. *awqāf*) means "the holding and preservation of a certain property for the confined benefit of a philanthropy with prohibiting any use or disposition of the property outside that specific purpose." The definition indicates the perpetual nature of *waqf* as it broadly relates to land and buildings, although there is *waqf* of books, agricultural machinery, cattle, shares and stocks, and cash. In North and West Africa, *waqf* is called *ḥabs*.

Waqf in Islamic History. In the history of Islam, the first religious *waqf* was the mosque of Qubāʾ in Medina. It was built upon the arrival of the Prophet Muḥammad in 622. Six months later it was followed by the Mosque of the Prophet in the center of Medina. Mosques, as well as real estate that provides revenues for mosque maintenance and expenses, are in the category of religious *waqf*.

Philanthropic *waqf* aims at supporting the poor segments of society and the public interest of the community by funding such institutions as hospitals, orphanages, nursing homes, libraries, scientific research, education, public services, and care of animals and the environment. There are also *awqāf* for interest-free loans to small businesses and for maintenance of parks, roads, bridges, and dams. This started during the time of the Prophet Muḥammad. On advice from the Prophet, ʿUthmān, a well-to-do Companion, bought the Well of Rumah and made it into *waqf*, to provide everybody with free drinking water. This was followed by the *waqf* of ʿUmar. When he asked the Prophet what to do with a palm orchard he acquired in the city of Khaybar, the Prophet said, "If you like, you may hold the property as *waqf* and give its fruits as charity."

A third kind of *waqf* was initiated shortly after the death of the Prophet, during the caliphate of ʿUmar (635–645). When ʿUmar confirmed his *waqf* in a written document and released it, the Companion Jābir said that many real-estate owners made *awqāf*. Some of them added a condition to ensure that fruits and revenues first be given to their own children and descendants and only the surplus, if any, should be given to the poor. This kind of *awqāf* is called posterity or family *awqāf*. Unlike foundations in America, *awqāf* in Islamic society can be for one's own family and descendants.

Characteristics of Waqf. "Perpetuity" is the most important characteristic of *waqf*. This means that once a property, often real estate, is assigned as *waqf*, it remains *waqf* forever. Except in cases of corruption and mishandling, perpetuity implies that *waqf* properties should grow continuously, with new founders adding new properties. Perpetuity is also interpreted as durability or long life of a property. Accordingly, books, weapons, machinery, cattle, and money can be made *waqf*.

To preserve *waqf* properties, both founders and courts took extra precautions in documenting and preserving *waqf* deeds. They often insisted on recording these deeds in courts and having them witnessed by renowned people. Courts in many cities and towns kept detailed records of *waqf* properties as early as the fifteenth and sixteenth centuries. Many of these records are still preserved, and historians study them in the archives of Istanbul, Cairo, Fez, Damascus, Jerusalem, Isfahan, and other ancient cities.

Since *waqf* is a voluntary act, its second characteristic is abiding by conditions of the founder. This implies that revenues of *waqf* should be used exclusively for the purpose decreed by the founder. It also implies that purpose of *waqf* cannot be changed by management or supervisory courts as long as it is still achievable. If the purpose of a particular *waqf* becomes impossible to achieve, the revenue should be spent on the most similar achievable goal; otherwise, it goes to the poor and needy. The condition of permanence covers all the founder's stipulations whether they relate to purpose, distribution of revenues, management, or supervisory authority.

Conditions to Create Waqf. *Waqf* creation requires certain conditions, of which the most important are the following:

1. The property must be real estate or a durable asset. Muslim societies have as *waqf* such things as land, buildings, livestock, books, jewelry, swords, and agricultural tools.

2. The property should be given on a permanent basis.
3. The *waqf* founder should be legally fit and able to make an act of donation.
4. The purpose of the *waqf* must be an act of goodness or benefit.
5. Finally, beneficiaries must be alive and legitimate.

Management of *Waqf*. The founder determines the type of management of *waqf*. The *waqf* manager is usually called *mutawallī* or *nāẓir*. A *mutawallī* is responsible for administering the *waqf* in the best interest of the beneficiaries. This includes preservation of the property and maximizing its revenues. The *waqf* document usually mentions how the *mutawallī* is compensated. If not, the *mutawallī* either volunteers his work or seeks compensation from courts. The judicial system is the authority of reference with regard to *waqf*. In the eighth century, a judge in Egypt established a special register and office for *awqāf*. This culminated in the establishment of an *awqāf* office that was linked to the chief justice, called the "judge of judges."

In 1863 the Ottoman Empire enacted the Law of Awqāf to regulate their management and supervision. It remained in effect in several countries (Turkey, Syria, Iraq, Lebanon, Palestine, and Saudi Arabia) for many years after the disintegration of the Ottoman Empire in 1918. Most Muslim countries today have either ministries or departments of *awqāf* and religious affairs combined. These ministries control the *waqf* properties and use their revenues for financing the maintenance of mosques.

Muslim communities in other countries have organized their *awqāf* in accordance with Sharīʿah. For instance, in India, a federal *waqf* act was adopted in 1954, and the Indian minister of law was made the supervisory authority on *waqf*.

In the United States and Canada, Muslim communities administer their *waqf* properties in accordance with the acts and regulations of foundations and nonprofit organizations. In 1975, the North American Islamic Trust (NAIT) was registered in the state of Indiana. Its main objective is to hold titles of the *awqāf* of Muslims in North America. A few years later, a sister organization with the name Canada NAIT was registered in Ontario. NAIT and its Canadian counterpart hold the property titles of many mosques, Islamic centers, and Islamic schools in North America.

Socioeconomic Role of *Waqf*. Information extracted from the registers of *awqāf* in Istanbul, Jerusalem, Cairo, and other cities indicates that *waqf* lands cover a considerable fraction of total cultivated area. For instance, a survey of land in Egypt in 1812 showed that *waqf* represented 600,000 *feddan* (570,000 acres) out of a total of 2.5 million *feddan* (2.375 million acres). In Palestine the number of *waqf* deeds recorded up to middle of the sixteenth century is 233, containing 890 properties, compared to only ninety-two deeds of private ownership containing 108 properties.

The primary recipients of *waqf* revenues are mosques. Educational institutions are the second largest recipient of *waqf* revenues. Even government financing of education used to take the form of constructing a school and assigning certain property as *waqf* for its operating expenses. For instance, historical sources on Palestine mention that Jerusalem had sixty-four schools at the turn of the twentieth century, all of which were *awqāf* and supported by *waqf* properties in Palestine, Turkey, and Syria. The oldest university in the world, al-Azhar, continued to be financed by its *waqf* revenues until the government of Muḥammad ʿAlī in Egypt confiscated the *awqāf* in 1812.

In addition to providing freedom of education, this financing approach helped create a learned class not derived from the rich and ruling classes. At times, the majority of Muslim scholars were from poor and former-slave segments of the society, and they often strongly opposed the repressive policies of the rulers.

The third major beneficiary of *waqf* is the poor and needy population. *Waqf* revenues also fund health services, including the construction of hospitals and funding for physicians, apprentices, and patients. One example of a health *waqf* is the Şişli Children's Hospital in Istanbul, founded in 1898.

***Waqf* in the Twentieth Century.** The general underdevelopment and backwardness prevalent in the Muslim world also affected the *waqf* properties. With the independence of most Islamic countries in the middle of the twentieth century and establishment of national states, many *waqf* properties in Syria, Egypt, Turkey, Tunis, and Algeria were annexed to the public property of the government or distributed through land reforms and other measures. The institution of *waqf* is now confined mostly to mosques. Some countries have enacted new laws of *awqāf*, which help recover, preserve, and develop the *awqāf* properties and encourage people to create new *awqāf*.

BIBLIOGRAPHY

Dallal, Ahmad. "The Islamic Institution of Waqf: A Historical Overview." In *Islam and Social Policy*, edited by Stephen P. Heyneman, pp. 13–43. Nashville, Tenn.: Vanderbilt University Press, 2004.

Islamic Research Center for History, Culture, and Arts. *Awqāf wa-amlāk al-Muslimīn fī Filasṭīn*. Istanbul: Markaz al-Abḥāth lil-Tārīkh wa-al-Funūn wa-al-Thaqāfah al-Islāmīyah, 1982.

Qureshi, M. A. *Waqfs in India: A Study of Administrative and Legislative Control*. New Delhi: Gian, 1989.

Sabra, Adam. *Poverty and Charity in Medieval Islam: Mamluk Egypt, 1250–1517*. Cambridge, U.K.: Cambridge University Press, 2000.

Singer, Amy. *Constructing Ottoman Beneficence: An Imperial Soup Kitchen in Jerusalem*. Albany: State University of New York Press, 2002.

van Leeuwen, Richard. *Waqfs and Urban Structures: The Case of Ottoman Damascus*. Leiden: Brill, 1999.

MONZER KAHF

WASAT PARTY, AL-. When former Egyptian president Hosni Mubarak's government introduced an aggressive policy against Islamist activism in 1996, several members of the younger generation within the Muslim Brothers left the movement and officially applied to found a political party, which they called the Ḥizb al-Wasaṭ al-Jadīd (the New Center Party, which became known as the al-Wasat Party). Several centrist activists, of whom the engineer Abul Ela Mady and the lawyer Essam Sultan were the most prominent, adhered to the path of peaceful, democratic change and wished to create a moderate Islamic political party in Egypt. Mady concluded that the established Muslim Brotherhood was politically limited, which naturally drew the ire of the Ikhwān. The latter went so far as to accuse al-Wasat of secession, especially because most of its membership drew most heavily from the Brothers. Still, unlike the Ikhwān, al-Wasat differentiated itself as a civil party that included Muslims and Copts (two Copts and three women were among the party's twenty-four senior members in 2011) and sought to address the concerns of all Egyptians with new and creative interpretations of Islam's message for the global age. Ironically, along with the Brothers, the Mubarak regime perceived al-Wasat in negative terms too, trying the two founders in front of a military court for setting up an illegal Islamist group. Cairo rejected al-Wasat's applications for an official license on at least on four separate occasions between 1996 and 2009, probably because of a conspiracy between the Brothers and members of the ruling National Democratic Party. Understandably, the collusion was due to an official ban under the Egyptian constitution—article 5 as amended in 2007—that prohibited the creation of political institutions on the basis of religion. The party's manifesto accepted the right of a Christian Copt to become head of state a Muslim-majority country, which was anathema to most Egyptians.

Irrespective of false accusations, complex New Islamist concepts, drawing on the work of such major centrist figures as Muḥammad al-Ghazālī, Yūsuf al-Qaraḍāwī, and Muḥammad Salīm al-ʿAwwā, found expression in the party platform. Indeed, the core substantive notions of civilizational Islam and appreciation for the historical roots of the broad *wasaṭīyah* (Islamic mainstream) trend, expressed al-Wasat ideology. In the clearest terms, the party platform stated that the civilizational project went "beyond religion and all artificial divisions" to emphasize Islam's inclusive, tolerant character. Importantly, Islam was understood in terms broader than those of religion, and the platform made the explicit point that the Islamic civilizational project embraced both constituent elements of the Egyptian national community, Copts and Muslims. "Everybody is called upon to join this project, which unifies groups without eliminating their differences," the founding document declared.

With its strong commitment to nonviolent political action aimed at democratizing and developing Egypt, the Wasat Party stood as a clear and compelling alternative to both Islamist extremism and the National Democratic Party. Parallel developments of centrist movements occurred elsewhere in the Arab Islamic world, notably the Justice and Development Party in Morocco and the Jordanian Islamic Action Union. Long before the spring 2011 uprisings, an informal network of centrists that shared an Islamic civilizational worldview combined with a commitment to a gradualist, democratic politics and a foreign policy of vigilant, lawful resistance to Western, especially American, intrusions in the Islamic world emerged. In the West these centrist groups and parties attracted nowhere near the attention of the violent extremists with whom they competed, although their weight in their respective societies was far greater, as the collapse of several Arab regimes illustrated.

Although the Wasat Party was blocked from lawful participation in public life since 1996 on legal technicalities, it was granted official recognition on 19 February 2011 after a court in Cairo approved its formal establishment. While the court's ruling came in the wake of the 2011 Egyptian Revolution, the mere fact that al-Wasat endured for all of these years compelled authorities to accept its legality shortly after Hosni Mubarak resigned. To be sure, during those dark years party activists continued to develop ideas and to find outlets for their constructive, creative energies in a variety of civil-society activities Yet the full measure of this embodiment of the promise of the broader *wasaṭīyah* was tested in several parliamentary elections as this and other parties with an Islamic background competed more or less freely.

BIBLIOGRAPHY

Baker, Raymond William. *Islam without Fear: Egypt and the New Islamists*. Cambridge, Mass.: Harvard University Press, 2003.

Mikhail, Sarah, and Tom Perry. "New Party Shows Deep Political Change in New Egypt." *Reuters*, 19 February 2011, http://www.reuters.com/article/2011/02/19/us-egypt-idUSTRE70O3UW20110219.

Norton, Augustus Richard. "Thwarted Politics: The Case of Egypt's Hizb al-Wasat." In *Remaking Muslim Politics: Pluralism, Contestation, Democratization*, edited by Robert W. Hefner, pp. 133–160. Princeton, N.J.: Princeton University Press, 2005.

Wickham, Carrie Rosefsky. "The Path to Moderation: Strategy and Learning in the Formation of Egypt's *Wasat* Party." *Comparative Politics* 36, no. 2 (January 2004): 205–228.

RAYMOND WILLIAM BAKER
Updated by JOSEPH A. KÉCHICHIAN

WETU TELU. Wetu Telu, literally "Three-Time" Islam, usually contrasted with Wetu Lima, "Five-Time" (orthodox) Islam, is a syncretic form of Islam among the Sasak people of Lombok Island, Indonesia, whose roots go back to the sixteenth century, when Islam arrived in Lombok. It has survived down to the present, albeit with declining significance because of the influence of Islamic reform movements.

The Sasak people, who represent well over 90 percent of the population of Lombok, are almost all Muslim. However, Sasak religion shows a remarkable variety ranging from nominal adherence to the faith to an enthusiastic embrace of strict reformist Islam. The conversion of the Sasak to Islam was a gradual process, and the period of slow adaptation to Islamic practices resulted in remarkable religious syncretism. Dominated politically by non-Muslim outsiders—first by the Balinese and later by the Dutch—for the last few centuries, the Sasak developed their own Islamic religious institutions and customs, largely undisturbed by outside influences up to the modern era.

There are no great differences of belief between Wetu Telu and Wetu Lima, the distinction being based on religious practice rather than theology. Religious holidays are also largely identical. Non-Islamic elements in Wetu Telu religion include the worshipping of holy places (*kemaliq*) under the control of specialized ritual experts (*pemangku*). The veneration of the graves of ancestors is an important element of Wetu Telu practice, and the blessing of ancestors is sought by living descendants at special ceremonies (*gawe*). Other types of holy places, such as the shrines of early Muslim missionaries, sacred trees or rocks, or the majestic volcano Rinjani, are also revered. The most distinctive feature of Wetu Telu is the existence of a specialized class of religious leaders (*kiai*) responsible for carrying out all religious rites. The right to read the Qurʾān is also reserved to the *kiai* class, and they alone are responsible for their followers' spiritual well-being and eventual entry into paradise. The exact nature of the ritual obligations of the *kiai* class varies greatly from one community to another. As the very name suggests, Wetu Telu followers embrace only three of the five main pillars (*arkān*) of Islam, namely the creed (*shahādah*), prayer, and fasting, and even the latter two are incumbent only on the *kiai*.

According to Sasak tradition, Islam originally entered Lombok in the sixteenth century from Java. Shortly thereafter, the western—and later also the eastern—half of Lombok came to be ruled by the Hindu Balinese. The new rulers had no intention of changing the religious traditions of the Muslim Sasak, and later on the Dutch colonizers would largely continue this tradition of noninterference in local religious affairs. Nevertheless, it is in the late colonial period that the religious landscape of Lombok began to change.

Growing numbers of Sasak Muslim leaders made the *ḥajj* and initiated a movement of religious reform, which effectively meant the elimination of the unorthodox practices associated with the Wetu Telu. Sasak *ḥājjīs* returning from Mecca, bearing the honorific title *tuan guru haji*, were instrumental in the reform movement, starting schools, disseminating orthodox Islamic teachings, and propagating the Sharīʿah. Reformist scholars tended to reside in their own rural communities and dominated village-level politics. The Islamic reform movement provided ambitious individuals in the commoner class with a means of increasing their opportunities and power at the expense of the traditional nobility, which dominated Wetu Telu rituals. The growing influence of the discourse of Islamic reform is thus as much a reflection of social change as a religious phenomenon.

In 1935 an Islamic educational institute and movement called Nahdlatul Wathan (Arabic *nahḍat al-waṭan*, "Renaissance of the Homeland") was founded in Pancor (East Lombok) by Haji Zainuddin Abdulmajid, popularly known as

Maulana Syekh or Tuan Guru Pancor. Aiming at religious reform and the eradication of *bidʿah* (reprehensible innovation), it drew its main support from the *ʿulamāʾ* establishment. Ironically, however, many traditional *ʿulamāʾ* regarded certain features of the educational system established by Nahdlatul Wathan—such as the use of the Latin script and students sitting at Western-style school desks—as instances of *bidʿah*. Its progress hindered by such attitudes and by the conservatism of the rural population, Nahdlatul Wathan took off only after World War II, and after Indonesian independence it gained more momentum. Events causing political and social upheaval—especially the horrific anticommunist mass murders following an abortive coup attempt by communists in 1965, as well as a famine in the subsequent two years—have strengthened the new, reformist Muslim elite, who provided villagers with food, political patronage, and protection. Perceived as a belief system incompatible with communist sympathies, orthodox Islam was thought to be more acceptable by the political establishment, and gained influence accordingly. Independent Indonesia is a secular state, but the government of Lombok has tended to be dominated by reform-minded Muslims, including many *tuan guru*, with obvious consequences for Wetu Telu.

The spread of literacy and mass education has also furthered the cause of religious reform. Rural Islamic schools open their doors to every child, not just to the traditional *kiai* class as among the Wetu Telu, and in tandem with the spread of religious instruction came reformist ideas and participation in Islamic rites. After independence the Nahdlatul Wathan opened the first modern-style *pesantren* (Islamic boarding school) in Lombok, which featured classrooms, students' dormitories, and a curriculum including modern disciplines along with Islamic religious ones, all novelties in Lombok at the time. Today, Nahdlatul Wathan maintains a thriving network of *madrasahs* and other educational establishments, including a university.

The followers of Wetu Telu now form a small minority among the Sasak, limited to the town of Bayan and a number of rural communities, mainly in remote mountainous areas. Even in these places they are heavily targeted by orthodox Islamic mission (*dakwah*, Arabic *daʿwah*). Wetu Telu, or some of its aspects, may yet survive as a kind of sanitized folklore (and a tourist attraction) rather than a religion. An example is the yearly festival held at the temple complex at Lingsar (West Lombok), one of the holiest places for Wetu Telu adherents. All Sasak participants at the festival now take part in Islamic communal prayers, a sign of the efforts of Wetu Telu adherents to conform to a more orthodox Islam.

Bibliography

Budiwanti, Erni. *Islam Sasak: Wetu telu versus waktu lima*. Yogyakarta: LKiS, 2000.

Cederroth, Sven. *The Spell of the Ancestors and the Power of Mekkah: A Sasak Community on Lombok*. Gothenburg, Sweden: Acta Universitatis Gothoburgensis, 1981.

Ecklund, Judith Louise. "Tradition or Non-Tradition: Adat, Islam, and Local Control on Lombok." In *What Is Modern Indonesian Culture? Papers Presented to the Conference on Indonesian Studies, July 29–August 1, 1976, Indonesian Studies Summer Institute, Madison, Wisconsin*, edited by Gloria Davis, pp. 249–267. Athens: Ohio University, Center for International Studies, 1979.

Krulfeld, Ruth. "Fatalism in Indonesia: A Comparison of Socio-Religious Types on Lombok." *Anthropological Quarterly* 39, no. 3 (1966): 180–190.

Zoltan Szombathy

Wilāyat al-Faqīh. The term *wilāyat al-faqīh* in Arabic, or *vilāyat-i faqīh* in Persian, gained wide currency in the Shīʿī world when it was used as the title for the published version of lectures delivered by Ayatollah Ruhollah Khomeini (1902–1989) in 1969 to his students in Najaf. It means "the guardianship of the jurist," and when the "jurist" Khomeini came to power in 1979, he became the supreme arbiter of all matters of government in Iran. It was henceforth clear to the Islamic world that such guardianship was one route to an ideal espoused by many contemporary Muslims, namely, the establishment of an Islamic government.

The term resonated in the example of the first imam, ʿAlī ibn Abī Ṭālib (d. 661), who is called by Shīʿīs "Walī Allāh," which means both "the Friend of God" and "the Vicegerent of God." Moreover, the phrase highlighted the kinship to the saying attributed by many Muslims, both Sunnī and Shīʿī, to the prophet Muḥammad: "The *ʿulamāʾ* [religious scholars] are the heirs of the prophets." Some Muslims assume that this saying implies the inheritance by the *ʿulamāʾ* of direct government by the Prophet.

Origins of the Concept. The specific background of the theory of *wilāyat al-faqīh*, however, is to be found in developments in eighteenth- and nineteenth-century Twelver Shīʿī thought, which made the issue of central leadership more prominent. The Uṣūlī school of Twelver Shiism, which developed in the middle of the eighteenth century and achieved predominance by the middle of the nineteenth, gave the exclusive right to interpret Islamic law to *mujtahids*, experts who claim that their authority extends back in an unbroken chain of teacher-disciple recognition to the infallible imams. As the rank of *mujtahid* was passed on to only a very few pupils by practicing *mujtahids*, it was seldom—if ever—held by as many as two hundred people. Among the *mujtahids*, a few of the most prominent published manuals interpreting basic practice for ordinary believers, who are obliged by Uṣūlī legal theory to choose one of these few as a *marjaʿ al-taqlīd* (source of emulation). Shaykh Murtaḍā al-Anṣārī, for example, achieved wide recognition as the leading source of emulation before his death in 1864, thanks to his intellectual predominance. He therefore received from all over the Twelver Shīʿī world the contributions payable to the Hidden Imam, which, according to Uṣūlī theory, went in his absence to the "sources of emulation." Another "source of emulation," Mirzā Ḥasan Shīrāzī (d. 1896), showed the political muscle of this office when, following his 1891 ruling, he forced the ruler of Iran, Nāṣir al-Dīn Shāh (r. 1848–1896), to cancel a tobacco concession to the British. However, it was only while Ayatollah Moḥammad Ḥosayn Borujerdi was the "source of emulation" from 1947 to 1962 that it became clear that a single individual could turn this office into a source of ultimate authority over the overwhelming majority of Twelver Shīʿīs.

If this office represented the authority of the absent Twelfth Imam, who is, according to Twelver Shīʿīs, their infallible leader, this meant that the supreme "source of emulation" assumed the worldly authority of the Twelfth Imam in his absence. Ḥājj Mullā Aḥmad Nirāqī (d. 1828 or 1829) drew this conclusion very early in the nineteenth century, and Khomeini often referred to Nirāqī. Shaykh Murtaḍā al-Anṣārī, supported it, as he honed his own political scheme. Both were aware of the political implications of the newly expanded role of the "source of emulation" (which called for continuity with traditional Islamic legal sources, the *faqīh*, or jurist), though al-Anṣārī devoted a lengthy discussion in his masterwork, *al-Makāsib*, to refute the theory of the guardianship of the jurist.

Khomeini's Political Interpretation. Because *al-Makāsib* was a work on commercial law, it became a tradition to treat this subject in the context of discussions concerning the authority of the jurist-judge over financial expenditure. Remarkably, Khomeini, in a section of his *Kitāb* *al-Baʿyah* (Book on Trade), opens the discussion with a direct quote from al-Anṣārī: "Among the guardians over the expenditure of money of the person who does not have independence in the expenditure of his or her money [e.g., a minor] is the judge. He is the jurist with all the qualifications to issue a *fatwa* [authoritative opinion]." To these words Khomeini adds: "It would not be wrong to turn one's attention to the guardianship of the jurist in general, in a summary way. A detailed discussion would require devoting an independent treatise to this subject, which the present scope of our work does not permit us to do." The lectures he delivered on this subject were published simultaneously in a somewhat more popular form in Najaf, first as pamphlets, then in book form.

The resulting book, *Vilāyat-i faqīh*, which bears the subtitle *Ḥukūmat-i Islāmī* (Islamic Government), argues that it is incumbent on Muslims to establish such government and that it is incumbent on jurists to assume all the tasks that the Prophet Muḥammad performed, including direct rule. In the version published in pamphlets, Khomeini restated the traditional view of Uṣūlī Twelver Shīʿīs that every *mujtahid*, the exact equivalent for *faqīh* in this context, ought to follow his own judgment, which would imply that no *mujtahid* need defer to another in matters of government. The book version, however, states that if one *faqīh* possessing knowledge and moral integrity undertakes the task of government, "he will possess the same authority as the Most Noble Messenger [of God, i.e., Muḥammad], and it will be the duty of all people to obey him."

Uṣūlī theory ideally embodied leadership in a single person, such as Ayatollah Borujerdi, who was called "the absolute source of emulation" and hence made it conceivable (if not necessary) that a *faqīh* be the final source of all authority. Yet Khomeini's assertion that everyone, even *mujtahids*, should submit to such a *faqīh* continues to be a contested point among Shīʿī clergymen. For example, the Iraqi clergyman Muḥammad Bāqir al-Ṣadr, in one of the lectures written shortly before his death in April 1980, developed a similar interpretation of the role of the *faqīh*, and Ṣadr's eloquent exposition of this theme, alongside the success of the Iranian Revolution of 1979, made the theory of the guardianship of the jurist well-known in the Sunnī world.

Ayatollah Khomeini's influence after the 1979 Iranian Revolution was evident in the new constitution for the country, with articles 5 and 107 (which are not fully consonant with each other) treating the leadership of a single *faqīh* as the norm. The document says that "only in the event that no *faqīh* should be so recognized by the majority" should a "source of emulation possessing outstanding qualification" be chosen for this position. If such a candidate cannot be found, three or five "sources of emulation" would form a leadership council. When Khomeini found that his chosen successor as supreme *faqīh*, Ayatollah Ḥusayn ʿAlī Muntaẓirī, often opposed his policies, he got Muntaẓirī to withdraw from the succession. Such a withdrawal might imply that the *faqīh* recognized by so many as possessing qualities of knowledge and leadership suddenly no longer possessed these qualities. Khomeini, recognizing the strain that such change put on the clergy and ordinary believers, called for a revision of the constitution some months before his death in 1989. He also advised that the qualification that the religious leader be a "source of emulation" be dropped from the constitution.

The updated constitution, presented to Iranians shortly after Khomeini's death, duly dropped this qualification as the circle around Khomeini reported that on his deathbed he recognized an important political figure, ʿAlī Khameneʾi. Because Khameneʾi was short of the highest levels of training as a theological student, his qualifications as a mere *mujtahid*, now the sole requirement for a national spiritual leader of Iran, allowed him to assume the position. Given the problem inherent in the disjunction between the political theory of the guardianship of the jurist and the actual hierarchy among Shīʿī clergymen, the Iranian government attempted to persuade the public that they should accept Ayatollah Muḥammad ʿAlī Arākī, a very pious *mujtahid* in his nineties, to be the leading "source of emulation." In the event, Arākī had not previously aspired to be recognized as a "source of emulation" by even a minority of Shīʿīs, beginning an interesting discussion of the meaning of the guardianship of the jurist, in which some theorists argued that the voice of the people was the voice of God and the true source of the authority of the *faqīh*.

Reevaluations. In the early twenty-first century, Muḥsin Kadīvar has written the most discussed book on the guardianship of the jurist. In it he considers the subject from all aspects of Shīʿī learning, including the *ḥadīth* ascribed to the Prophet and the Imams, theology, mysticism, and jurisprudence. In none of these areas does he find substantiation for the claim that the guardianship of the jurist is more than a trusteeship for legally incapable persons, such as minors. Even in this narrower sense, there is no consensus among the jurists, as Kadīvar shows that the presumption of Islamic law has been that there is no guardianship except for a few cases, such as administration of the estate of a deceased person. Attempts to legitimize the guardianship of the jurist on theological grounds such as God's justice, which in the Shīʿī view requires the existence of an Imam, implying the need for a just *faqīh* in the absence of the Imam, would undermine the theory of the imamate, as there would be no distinction between a fallible jurist and an infallible Imam. The thrust of Kadīvar's argument is that there is no specific form of government mandated by Islam. If there is to be an element of *wilāyah* in the government, it should be "elective" (*intikhābī*) and not, as earlier, "mandated" (*intiṣābī*).

There have been many defenders of the guardianship of the jurist. One of the most prominent is Ayatollah ʿAbdallāh Javādī-āmolī, one of the conservative young clergymen favored by Khomeini, who connects the theory of *wilāyat al-faqīh* with theological and philosophical themes in order to make it a primary necessity of religion. Still, later echoes of the theory of the guardianship of the jurist that have been heard among the Muslim Brothers, a Sunnī organization, indicate that the theory in a diffuse form has caught the attention of the broader Muslim World. The difficulty of transferring the theory to the Sunnī world, however, is that there are very few parallels to the comparatively hierarchical clergy of Twelver Shīʿī.

[*See also* Khomeini, Ruhollah al-Musavi.]

BIBLIOGRAPHY

Anṣārī, Murtaḍā al-. *Kitāb al-makāsib.* Vol. 2. Qom, 1991. Contains his refutation of the guardianship of the jurist (pp. 80–100).

Dabashi, Hamid. "Early Propagation of Wilāyat-i Faqīh and Mullā Aḥmad Nirāqī." In *Expectation of the Millennium: Shiʿism in History*, edited by Seyyed Hossein Nasr, Hamid Dabashi, and Seyyed Vali Reza Nasr, pp. 287–300. Albany: State University of New York Press, 1989. Presents the early history of the theory.

Javādī-āmolī, ʿAbdallāh. *Vilāyat-i faqīh: Vilāyat-i fuqāhat va ʿadālat.* Qom: Markaz-i Nashr-i Isrāʾ, 1999.

Kadīvar, Muḥsin. *Ḥukūmat-i vilāyī.* Tehran: Nashr-i Nay, 1998.

Khomeini, Ruhollah al-Musavi. *Islam and Revolution: Writings and Declarations of Imam Khomeini.* Translated and annotated by Hamid Algar. Berkeley, Calif.: Mizan, 1981. Contains a complete translation of Khomeini's treatise on government, which includes his assertion that *mujtahids* should defer to the jurist who has actual leadership (p. 62).

Khomeini, Ruhollah al-Musavi. *Kitāb al-bay'ah*. 5 vols. Qom, n.d. See esp. vol. 2, pp. 459–539.

Maghnīyah, Muḥammad Jawād al-. *Al-Khumaynī wa-al-dawlah Islāmīyah*. Beirut: Dār al-'Ilm lil-Malāyīn, 1979. Critiques the guardianship of the jurist from a traditional standpoint.

Mallat, Chibli. *The Renewal of Islamic Law: Muhammad Baqer Sadr, Najaf, and the Shi'i International*. Cambridge, U.K.: Cambridge University Press, 1993. Compares the ideas of Ṣadr and Khomeini on Islamic government.

Modarressi, Hossein. "The Just Ruler or the Guardian Jurist: An Attempt to Link Two Different Shi'ite Concepts." *Journal of the American Oriental Society* 111, no. 3 (1991): 549–562.

Moussavi, Ahmad Kazemi. "A New Interpretation of the Theory of Vilayat-i Faqih." *Middle Eastern Studies* 28, no. 1 (1992): 101–107. Revisionist approach to the concept.

Muntaẓirī, Ḥusayn 'Alī. *Dirāsāt fī wilāyat al-faqīh wa-fiqh al-dawlah al-Islāmīyah*. 4 vols. Qom, 1988–1992. Revisionist treatment.

Muṭahharī, Murtaḍā. *Valā'hā va vilayāthā*. Qom: Daftar-i Intishārāt-i Islāmī, 1983. Discusses the concept of *wilāyah* in Shiism.

Sachedina, A. A. *The Just Ruler (al-Sulṭān al-'Ādil) in Shī'ite Islam: The Comprehensive Authority of the Jurist in Imamite Jurisprudence*. New York: Oxford University Press, 1988. Contains a discussion of the concept of *wilāyah* in Shiism; should be read in conjunction with Modarressi (1991).

Tehrani, Mahdi Hadavi, and Hossein Pirnajmuddin. *The Theory of the Governance of Jurist (Wilayat al-Faqih)*. London: Islamic Centre of England, 2004.

ROY P. MOTTAHEDEH
Updated by JOSEPH A. KÉCHICHIAN

WIZĀRA. The term *Wizāra* (vizierate) designates the office of the *wazīr* (vizier), or minister of state. It became fixed in Islamic political vocabulary only in the early 'Abbāsid period (after 750 CE). Qur'ān verses 20:29 and 25:35 give *wazīr* in the sense of "helper"—Hārūn is *wazīr* to Mūsā. Other words based on the root *w-z-r* in the Qur'ān refer to a burden of responsibility, often moral, or its bearer (e.g., 6:31).

Certain supporting participants in seventh-century sectarian revolts (e.g., al-Mukhtār in Kufa, d. 687) were called *wazīrs*. The first 'Abbāsid caliphs seem to have called associates by this title, but not until the time of the caliph al-Mahdī (r. 775–785) was there a formal office or institution called the *Wizāra*. The theoretical duties and limits later attached to the office developed in dialogue with practice. Thus there was little that was strictly "Islamic" about the *Wizāra* as discharged by its most famous early occupants, the powerful Barmakid family, whose forebears had been Buddhist priests in Balkh. The sudden fall of the Barmakids occurred under the caliph Hārūn al-Rashīd in 803, but the institution was by then firmly established. In the next 140 years the 'Abbāsid *Wizāra* was occupied by a series of powerful figures who, like the Barmakids, were often raised from marginal social or religious groups, and who, like them, might fall precipitously at a ruler's discretion. These two features have been shared broadly by the Islamic *Wizāra* throughout history, despite great diversity across time and space. After the Barmakids, the two Faḍls, *wazīrs* who served Hārūn's rival heirs, were, respectively, a convert from Zoroastrianism and the son of a slave. The great scribal families that monopolized the *Wizāra* in the late ninth and early tenth centuries were recent converts from Christianity (the Banū al-Jarrāḥ and Banū Makhlad) or Shī'ah (the Banū al-Furāt). Members of these families were in factional competition with one another and with other factions in 'Abbāsid society, notably the military, to which they effectively lost when the Būyids took Baghdad in 945. From this time on and with few exceptions, *wazīrs* of note served military rulers.

What would become of the classical theory of the *Wizāra* was expounded by al-Māwardī (d. 1058) late in the Būyid period. This theory bore some resemblance to practice in most places, but nowhere does it seem to have served as a strict prescriptive blueprint. Māwardī drew a critical distinction between the *Wizāra* of *tanfīdh* (execution) and that of *tafwīḍ* (delegation). The former was charged only with carrying out the directives of the imam. Less was formally required of a candidate for the *Wizāra* of *tanfīdh*; he—Māwardī barred women from the office—might be a non-Muslim, an uneducated Muslim, or a slave. The *wazīr* of *tafwīḍ*, however, could assume delegated powers nearly equal to those of the imam himself. This distinction, which was probably not entirely original to Māwardī, preserved for Islamic legal and political theory some influence on practice by formally condoning a degree of deviance from Islamic ideals in the appointment of underqualified candidates.

The *Wizāra* in the successor states to the ʿAbbāsid empire took diverse forms. Perhaps the most significant unifying factor was the *wazīr*'s responsibility for state finances. In al-Andalus the institution was distinguished by its flexibility and frequent informality and by the large number of people who might occupy it concurrently. Under the Umayyads of Córdoba, rivalry for appointment often flared between native-born candidates (*baladīyūn*) and those from the east (*shāmīyūn*). The second Fāṭimid caliph in Egypt, al-ʿAzīz (r. 975–996), appointed the Jewish convert Ibn Killis to the *Wizāra*. Thereafter, the Fāṭimid office (sometimes called the *wāsiṭah*) was characterized by the sectarian diversity of its occupants, the multiplicity of the roles they played (including the judiciary and the missionary efforts of the *daʿwah*), and, after 1075, a strongly military cast that occasionally saw the *wazīr* act as effective ruler. The Ayyūbid and Mamlūk *Wizāra* also included certain military duties, though it rarely rivaled the supremacy of the sultan. Its particular institutional forms and unprecedented liaisons with Sunnī religious scholarship can be traced to the architect of the Great Seljuk *Wizāra* Niẓām al-Mulk (d. 1092). Niẓām al-Mulk's legacy was also felt in post-Seljuk Persia; here *wazīr*s often coexisted at multiple levels of the administration. The quintessential *Wizāra* in Persia was the official in charge of the *dīvān-i aʿlā*. The Ottoman *Wizāra*, though of course a multifarious, evolving entity, developed immense institutional complexity and was typically occupied by individuals recruited as slaves on the peripheries of the empire and trained for administrative service. Today the term *Wizāra* is applied to government ministries (of defense, the interior, etc.) in many Muslim countries.

BIBLIOGRAPHY

Goitein, S. D. "The Origin of the Vizierate and Its True Character." In *Studies in Islamic History and Institutions*, pp. 168–191. Leiden: Brill, 1968.

Yūzbakī, Tawfīq Sulṭān al-. *Muʾassasat al-Wizāra fī al-dawlah al-ʿAbbāsīyah*. Baghdad: Dār al-Shuʾūn al-Thaqāfīyah al-ʿĀmmah, 1989.

Zaman, Muhammad Qasim, Anne-Marie Eddé, A. Carmona, et al. "Wazīr." In *The Encyclopaedia of Islam*, rev. ed., edited by P. Bearman, Th. Bianquis, C. E. Bosworth et al., fasc. 181–186, vol. 11, pp. 185–197. Leiden: Brill, 2002.

LUKE YARBROUGH

WOMEN IN POLITICS. Throughout Islamic history, women have been actively involved in politics in Muslim societies. During the twentieth and twenty-first centuries, their engagement evolved through several intertwined and overlapping phases: debates over the discursive interpretation of Islamic texts dealing with women's rights, women's participation in nationalist struggles and modern political violence against occupying forces, state-sponsored feminism, contestation of women's status following the rise of Islamism in several Muslim states, and women's involvement in the Arab Spring. Important debates over women's rights in Islam first emerged in the nineteenth century. Male and female reformers disputed the narrow orthodox interpretation of Islamic passages and history that was often used to legitimize women's exclusion from education and full veiling. These debates expanded to other aspects of women's roles in public life, affording them greater opportunities in a gradual fashion, especially for upper-class women and in combination with state-led reforms. As such, beginning in the nineteenth century and continuing into the twenty-first century, women participated in social movements and organizations involved in nationalist, charitable, gender-centered, political, economic, or religious activities. With the rise of Islamism came a reaction to the earlier modernist view of sex-role expansion and reform, as well as a new activism by some Islamist women. Also, women continued organized efforts to reform laws as well as social practices affecting women's rights. In the early twenty-first century, women played a remarkable role in the massive wave of political revolts that have swept the Arab world and are continuing to consolidate the role of women in rebuilding their nations.

The Nineteenth Century. From the mid-nineteenth century onward, women and men began to discuss the need for social, educational, and political reform. Western colonialist figures had highlighted Muslim women's oppression as an area requiring reform; hence, debates about women and gender relations among Muslims also raised questions concerning the role of the West in the Muslim world. Several intellectuals and social reformers questioned the legal and social restrictions on women, especially in regard to education, female seclusion (known as purdah in the Indian subcontinent), strict veiling of the face, polygamy, the marriage of very young women to much older men by family arrangement, and enslavement of women.

Discussions of women's involvement in politics began in the form of discursive engagements among contending interpreters of the Islamic scriptures. The aim was to challenge the exclusion of women from politics and declare it against the principles of Islam. Citing accounts of female leadership in the Qurʾān, such as the queen of Sheba, and from Islamic history, such as ʿĀʾishah's leadership in the Battle of the Camel in 656, they challenged gender-biased interpretations of Islam.

Muslim reformers argued that it was not the tenets of Islam that subordinated women but rather incorrect interpretations of sacred texts. A number of Egyptian male reformers wrote on women's behalf, among them Aḥmad Fāris al-Shidyāq, author of *Leg Over Leg* (1855); Rifāʿah Rāfiʿ al-Ṭahṭāwī (1801–1871); Muḥammad ʿAbduh (1849–1905), a founder of the Salafīyah (Islamic reform) movement; Qāsim Amīn, whose book *Women's Emancipation* (The Liberation of Women) (1899) unleashed furious discussion; and Aḥmad Luṭfī al-Sayyid, publisher of *al-Jarīdah*. In Iraq, too, before World War I, Jamil Sidqi al-Zahawi (1863–1936) wrote a controversial attack on veiling and women's treatment under Sharīʿah. Turkish counterparts included Namık Kemal (1840–1888), Ahmet Mithat (1844–1912), and Halil Hamit, who in 1910 published the book *İslam'da Feminizm* (Feminism in Islam) in support of women's suffrage. In Iran, too, several male intellectuals of the 1880s and 1890s took up the cause of women's rights. Many of them were associates of the famous reformer Jamāl al-Dīn al-Afghānī (1838–1897), among them Mīrzā Malkom Khān (1833–1908), Mirza Aqa Khan Kermani (1854–1886), Shaykh Ahmed Ruhi (1855/56–1896), and Fatḥ ʿAlī Akhūndzādah (1812–1878). These four writers favored women's emancipation, supported their right to education, and opposed polygamy.

Educated women, such as Wardah al-Yāzijī (1838–1924) and Wardah al-Turk (1797–1874) in Syria and ʿĀʾishah al-Taymūrīyah (1840–1902) in Egypt, began writing to each other in the 1860s and 1870s regarding reform for women, as women later did for women's publications.

In this period, women in various Muslim countries established schools for girls. Women's presses also witnessed unprecedented growth. Hind Nawfal (1860–1920), a Syrian immigrant to Alexandria, published and edited *al-Fatāh*, a women's Arabic monthly; Zaynab Fawwāz (1860–1914), who immigrated from Tibnin to the same city, founded the newspaper *al-Nīl* in 1891. Malak Hifni Nassif (1886–1918) wrote under the pen name of Bāḥithat al-Bādīyah (Searcher in the Desert) in the contemporary press criticizing Muslim women's seclusion. In Iraq, too, a small elite group of feminists were active in the reign of King Faysal (1921–1933).

The first woman to offer a detailed reinterpretation of Islamic texts in favor of women's rights was probably the Lebanese writer Naẓīrah Zayn al-Dīn in her 1928 book *al-Sufūr wa-al-ḥijāb* (Unveiling and Veiling), followed in 1929 with a bold response to her critics in *al-Fatāh wa-al-shuyūkh* (The Girl and the Shaykhs). Persian women also started writing and publishing women's journals, the earliest being *Danesh* (1907). In Turkey, early feminists included the well-known Halide Edib Adıvar (1884–1964), Atatürk's advisor, and Fatma Âliye Hanım (1862–1936), who published in 1896 *Nisvan-i İslam* (Women of Islam) and regularly contributed articles between 1895 and 1908 to *Hanımlara Mahsus Gazete* (Ladies' Own Gazette).

Somewhat earlier, some Iranian women had participated in the Bābī movement, an offshoot of Shiism; its leaders included Rustam-ʿAli (killed in 1850) and the martyr Qurrat al-ʿAyn (1815–1851), who appeared unveiled and preached against polygamy and the veil. In Indonesia a famous advocate of women's education and emancipation was Raden Adjeng Kartini (1879–1904). She wrote and founded a school for the daughters of Javanese officials, becoming more influential after her death.

Women's Participation in Nationalist Struggles and Modern Political Violence. Early nationalist leaders and reformers like Muṣṭafā Kāmil (1874–1908) and Talʿat Ḥarb (1867–1941) in Egypt were against any idea of women's emancipation. Similarly, in 1882, Sayyid Aḥmad Khān of India felt that *purdah* should be maintained and female education postponed. The turn of the century, though, saw a rise in women's political activity, continuing after World War I.

In Iran, women took part in the Tobacco Rebellion (1890–1892) and in the Constitutional Revolution (1905–1907) and its aftermath, when mainly upper-class women organized separate *anjumans* (political societies), seeking education and the right to vote. Among the influential women in the Iranian constitutional movement is Bibi Khānoom Astarābādi (1858/59–1921), who in 1907 founded Madreseh Dooshizegan (School for Girls), the first school for girls in the modern history of Iran, and wrote numerous articles in defense of the right of girls to receive universal education. Another leading activist of the period is Sadiqa Daultabadie (1881–1961), who took a strong nationalist stance on political issues and protested very strongly against Iran's treaty with Britain in 1919.

In Egypt, too, Egyptian women played a key role in the 1919 revolution against the British occupation. The women were led by Safiya Zaghlūl (1878–1946), wife of Wafd Party leader Saʿd Zaghlūl; Hudā Shaʿrāwī (1879–1947), originator of the Egyptian Feminist Union; and Muna Fahmi Wissa. Egyptian women's participation in the 1919 nationalist movement eroded the custom of female seclusion, allowing women to enter for the first time various public forums. Upper-class women ventured to meetings in elite salons—Eugénie Le Brun's in Egypt, and later the literary salon of May Ziada (1886–1941). Wafd members' wives established the Wafdist Women's Central Committee (Lajnat al-Wafd al-Markazīyah lil-Sayīdat) in 1920, and Hudā Shaʿrāwī was elected president of the committee. The Wafdist Women's Central Committee solidified links between various women's associations in Egypt, such as the New Women Society (Jamʿīyat al-Marʾah al-Jadīdah, founded by Shaʿrāwī in 1919), the Society of the Renaissance of the Egyptian Woman (Jamʿīyat Nahḍat al-Sayīdatal-Miṣrīyat), and the Society of Mothers of the Future (Jamʿīyat Ummahāt al-Mustaqbal). The members of the Wafdist Women's Central Committee were disappointed when Wafdist men did not consult them on a proposal for independence. They published a critique of the Wafdist men's actions and eventually founded the Egyptian Feminist Union (al-Ittiḥād al-Nisāʾī al-Miṣrī) in 1923.

Palestinian women, too, have a long history of involvement in national political struggles. After the dispersal of the Palestinian people in 1948, middle-class women conducted relief efforts until the establishment of the United Nations Relief and Works Agency (UNRWA) refugee camps and facilities. In exile and at home, charitable associations formed the major focus for Palestinian women's organized activities until the 1967 war. More recently, women were crucial to the waging of the first and second Intifadas in the occupied West Bank and the Gaza Strip. They participated at the grassroots level and through the four women's committees of the Palestine Liberation Organization (PLO), founded in 1981, which have sponsored economic, health, and political projects.

Despite women's active engagement in liberation movements, many observers noted that women's gain from struggles are disproportional to their effort. Invariably, the primacy of the nationalist struggle forced feminist issues onto the back burner. An example of this is the later arrival of female suffrage in various countries, which all but Saudi Arabian women have now attained. In addition to Egypt's 1919 revolution, the Algerian liberation struggle, the Omani movement, and the Lebanese resistance are oft-cited cases demonstrating the contradictions between women's role in and gains from nationalist movements. The Algerian National Liberation Front incorporated women in its rebellion against French authority that lasted from 1954 to 1962. The Front's leadership was male, but so many men were imprisoned or in hiding that women served as fighters, intelligence operatives, and liaison agents, as well as in nursing and supply operations. Initially, the veil provided cover, as the French were reluctant to search women, who became increasingly involved in carrying bombs and arms. Later, women were imprisoned and tortured, and in the process some became national heroines, but the postrevolutionary government paid only lip service to their heroism. The government required the registration of their activities, and many lost benefits and recognition because they were illiterate or because, as women, they were designated "civilian" rather than "military" participants.

During the Israeli occupation of Lebanon in the 1980s, women were impelled to make use of political networks in the absence of their imprisoned or fighting men. Women resisted the Israeli occupiers when possible and were harassed, attacked, and arrested. Most adopted the *ḥijāb* and a more actively anti-Western stance in reaction to the Israeli occupation and in order to assert communal identity. In postwar Lebanon, a small reformist women's movement campaigned unsuccessfully for an optional civil law of personal status, and successfully against a law permitting reduced sentences for honor killings. That movement contrasts with the less-organized emphasis on public piety as "women's *jihād*" in the Shīʿī community in Beirut.

The modern nature of political struggles created new and more radicalized roles for women. Women in several Muslim societies entered the stage of modern political violence by carrying out suicide attacks against occupying forces. Sanaʿa Mehaidli (1968–1985), a member of the Syrian Social Nationalist Party, was the first female suicide bomber. In 1985, Mehaidli blew herself up next to an Israeli convoy during the Israeli occupation of south Lebanon. Since then, female suicide bombings have occurred in places like Afghanistan, Chechnya, Iraq, India, Israel, Lebanon, Pakistan, Palestine, Russia, Sri Lanka, Turkey, and Uzbekistan.

Postwar State Feminism. Nationalist movements and the new states that emerged in the post–World War I period perceived women's and gender issues as crucial to modernization. An important element of the regimes' visions of modernization was the emancipation of women, which was closely integrated with the ideology of Westernization. Atatürk of Turkey, Reza Shah of Iran, and later Habib Bourguiba of Tunisia—leaders with unassailable nationalist credentials—initiated new policies to reform the status of women and weaken the power base of the *ʿulamāʾ*. The case of Turkey became one of the most discussed issues in the Muslim world, and efforts were made to emulate it in Iran and Afghanistan. Atatürk introduced the 1926 civil code in place of Sharīʿah. Under the new law, polygamy and marriage by proxy were illegal, and women were given equal rights regarding divorce, custody, inheritance, and marriage with non-Muslims. Furthermore, Turkish women were requested to abandon the veil and adopt Western clothes and secular education. These actions were controversial, as were, in Afghanistan, Amānullāh Khan's reforms of the family code in 1921, the banning of polygamy for state employees, and the public appearance of his wife, Queen Suraya, unveiled.

Later amendments in Iran, Tunisia, and Egypt addressed various areas of personal status, including divorce, child custody, women's rights to the family home, and alimony, as did the Family Law Ordinance (1961) in Pakistan. State-controlled education and laws provided women with at least a basic education. State policies enabled groups of women to enter the male-dominated political sphere and professions previously closed to them. Egyptian women were accorded voting rights in 1956, in part as a consequence of long-term advocacy, but also through unprecedented public activism by feminists such as Durrīyah Shafīq (1908–1975).

Feminist policies enacted by the state in the name of promoting women's rights caused popular and religious hostility to state intervention in matters of gender. In several cases, state-sponsored feminism came at the expense of independent feminist movements. In Egypt, following the 1952 coup, the Free Officers associated women's rights with the aristocratic activities of the Feminist Union and the social agendas of the old regime. Under the new regime, Egyptian feminists such as Durrīyah Shafīq, Inji Aflatun (1924–1989), and Zaynab al-Ghazālī (1917–2005) were imprisoned, and several feminist organizations were dissolved.

Furthermore, Muslim women who gained the most from state-advocated feminism primarily benefited as individuals. Many Turkish female political scientists, who were themselves the products of these reforms, such as Nermin Abdan-Unat, Şirin Tekeli, and Fatima Mansur questioned these benefits. According to them, state-advocated feminism is a purely urban bourgeois phenomenon. It only brought superficial changes and did not reflect any fundamental change in society. In both Iraq and Syria, the Baʿth Party featured women's associations, yet these movements were not able to translate their goals successfully or equally among all classes of society. Marriage remained essential to women's status, and thus many postponed their careers.

State-sponsored feminism has also been criticized for empowering a small group of elite older women, who have dominated official political life and associations in many Muslim countries. The elitist background of women in political life meant that women's issues might be promoted, but the activists were often isolated from lower-class women, who did not necessarily favor changes to current practices, such as the suggested reduction of *mahr* (the bridegroom's dower to the bride), the listing of the bride's property, the insertion of stipulations in marriage contracts, or, in Egypt, the custom of female circumcision.

Not only did state-sponsored feminism introduce superficial solutions to complex problems in many countries, many argue it also heightened state control over women's associations. In Iran, Ashraf Pahlavi headed the Higher Council of Women's Organizations. Similarly, Sūzān Mubārak, Egypt's former first lady, was the head of the National Council for Women's Rights. Skeptics argue that advancements in women's political rights were used to cover up political frauds. For instance, the allocation of sixty-four seats for women in Egypt's 2010 parliamentary election is believed to have enforced the regime's domination. The majority of the seats—fifty-six out of sixty-four—went to women who were members of the ruling party.

Women and Islamist Politics. Women have played important roles in various Islamist movements around the world. In Egypt, the Association of Muslim Women was established by Zaynab al-Ghazālī as a female wing of the Muslim Brotherhood. These Islamist women wore the veil and eventually adopted a white *khimār* (head cover). They held that women must preserve their modesty, morals, and loyalty to their role in the home. The Muslim Brotherhood spread in the Arab world, opposing the female vote and coeducation in the 1950s, but later proposing reforming the status of women in an Islamic manner.

Similar to the Muslim Brotherhood, Jamāʿat al-ʿAdl wa-al-Iḥsān (JSA; the Justice and Charity Society) was the leading Islamist opposition movement to the Moroccan monarchy. The movement was founded by Abdessalam Yassin (1928—2012), the father of Nadia Yassin. Nadia Yassin (1958) headed the female wing of the JSA and emerged as the foremost public leader of the movement. Yassin's prominent role as a public figure has led to the creation of a wealth of material on her views on woman's role in governance and public life. In Yassin's view, the Islamic movement offers real participation for women, because Islam, Yassin forcefully contends, affords women the right to speak and participate in politics at the highest levels.

Women have also been important in religious opposition groups in Syria, including the outlawed Muslim Brotherhood. Among the activists' tactics in Syria was displaying their Islamic beliefs through wearing *ḥijāb* and urging other women to follow suit, in a sign of defiance of the state's secularist policies. When urban Sunnī women adopted the *ḥijāb*, some were met by officially organized demonstrations of ʿAlawī Baʿthī women, who unsuccessfully protested the wearing of *ḥijāb* in school and work settings.

In Malaysia, the discussion of gender involves matters of national identity, as the Malay majority coexists with other communities (Chinese, Indian, and aboriginal) who are legally free to observe their own faiths. The religious revival was propagated by several organizations, including the Islamic Youth League of Malaysia, Darul Arqam, and the more traditional Jemaat Tabligh. Clusters of adherents to revivalist groups had formed same-sex "family" groups (*usrah*). Islamization, including that of the laws in some areas, has continued. Women's participation in student movements has been a feature of Islamic revival in Malaysia, known generally as *dakwah* (Ar. *daʿwah*). Dissension arose over the increase in veiling, particularly when universities required it. Similarly, debate continues over the appropriate level of female participation in the public sphere, ranging from sermons emphasizing a strong Muslim family life, to the complete segregation of female *dakwah* communal members, to the activism of other women such as those in the Sisters of Islam. Sisters of Islam is an Islamic group in Malaysia that advocates for equal rights for women, human rights, and justice within the framework of Islam.

In Indonesia the Muhammadiyah organization, founded in 1912, typifies apolitical educational and service activities. The Aisyiyah was the women's branch of this party, allowing for mobilization beyond the traditional teacher-peasant dynamic in place in Indonesia as well as Malaysia. After the Sukarno era, religious political parties were banned under Suharto, and the four existing Islamic parties were combined into the Partai Persatuan Pembangunan (PPP). Nonetheless, religiosity has been on the rise in Indonesia, along with contemporary Islamic dress. Groups such as the Association of Islamic Students eschew militancy but view gender issues as integrally tied to Muslim identity.

Like in Indonesia, informal attempts to "Islamize" public spaces by pushing women to private space could be seen in Algeria and Iraq. After the Algerian revolution, the linkage of Sharīʿah with the constitution meant that women were harassed in the streets, beaten, and secluded, and legal reforms such as the minimum age for marriage were not enforced. With time, Islamist parties gained large followings, including women who espoused a more conservative view of gender. During the 1990s, feminists and women not wearing *ḥijāb* came under attack. In the same vein, in post-Saddam Iraq, many international projects that aimed to provide income or other aid to women were interrupted by violence. Kidnappings and attacks on women forced many into exile, or to cease attending school, and many adopted the *ḥijāb* out of fear of attacks when unveiled women, those driving, and some with businesses were targeted. In response, the Organization of Women's Freedom in Iraq (OWFI) was founded in June 2003 by Yanar Mohammed, Nasik Ahmad, and Nadia Mahmood. The organization challenged both Islamic extremism and the American troops' presence in Iraq. Iraqi women were also successful in blocking a law that would require them to attend the family courts of their own sect.

In Sudan, the Islamization of Muslim society, both organized and informal, increased in the 1980s. Women were fully involved in the process, whether by personal choice, familial loyalties, or active recruitment. Sondra Hale describes in *Women Activists of the National Islamic Front—Sudan* (1992) the ways in which many Muslim men positioned "their" women, at least temporarily, at the forefront of Sudanese public life, making them in the 1980s among the most visible and active women in Sudan. Women were organizing for the Islamic revolution in the schools, in the nurseries, in the mosques, and in the medical clinics, where most employees are women.

The rise of Islamist movements has sharpened controversies involving women's legal status and public role. Governments often claim an Islamic character as an affirmation of their independence from Western domination. For instance, the Islamic governments in Afghanistan, Pakistan, Iran, and the Gaza Strip frame their policies as countering secularization and Western gender identity with Muslim notions of modesty and piety. Feminism is viewed as a form of neocolonialism, and calls for women's rights are accused of encouraging Western intervention. When the Taliban took over Afghanistan's capital in September 1996, they immediately imposed severe restrictions on Afghan women. They were forbidden to work, leave the house without a male escort, or seek medical help from a male doctor and forced to cover themselves from head to toe. These restrictions were couched within an anti-Western frame and were presented as a defense against what are seen as corrupting Western ideologies and forces.

In Pakistan, the most important locus of Islamist activity, prior to the emergence of al-Qaʿida and the Taliban, was the Jamāʿat-i Islāmī and the Tablīghī Jamāʿat. Both proposed countering Western domination and gender identity with Muslim notions of modesty and piety. With the rise of Islamist parties and individuals in politics, disputes over gender issues increased, including legal debates over whether rape victims can be prosecuted as adulteresses. Veiling and separation of the sexes have continued, though tempered by the changing fortunes of the various political actors and parties, and with al-Qaʿida supporters backing much stricter regulations on women. However, several spectators believe that the 2007 assassination of Benazir Bhutto and the rising concerns over radicalism after 9/11 could mean more support for women's rights in Pakistan. Their speculations appear overly optimistic in light of the 2012 attempted assassination of Malala Yousafzai. This fourteen-year-old Pakistani girl was targeted and nearly killed by the Taliban for championing education for girls.

In Iran, women, Islamist and non-Islamist, had been involved in opposition to Shah Muhammad Reza Pahlavi and had protested the Western commodification of women. However, when the Islamic Republic imposed Islamic dress and removed women from legal, judicial, and other offices, many Iranians fled. Nonetheless, women actively participated in the Mujāhidīn-i Khalq, an organization of Marxist-Islamic orientation not fully defeated in Iran until 1981–1982. In addition to the Mujāhidīn-i Khalq, a patrol and information division called the Zaynab Sisters and other women's associations began operating in Iran. A penal and family code revised along Islamic lines was imposed, but women, though now excluded from holding judgeships and other positions, kept alive a debate about fairer treatment of women under the law. Women parliamentarians in the Sixth Majlis (2000–2004)—notable among whom are Jamileh Kadivar and Elahe Kulayi—challenged certain discriminatory laws and struggled to bring the Majlis to pass a bill making Iran a party to the Convention on the Elimination of All Forms of Discrimination against Women (CEDAW). The eleven women of the Sixth Majlis were banned from running for office in the Seventh Majlis, which ended up including only conservative female figures and reversed some legal reforms. Between 2003 and 2007 an Iranian movement for women's rights reasserted itself in the Abolish Stoning Forever and the One Million Signatures for the Repeal of Discriminatory Laws campaigns. In a blow to these efforts, four of the One Million Signatures' leaders, Mariam Hossein-khah, Nahid Keshavarz, Jelveh Javaheri, and Parvin Ardalan, were sentenced to jail in 2008 for contributing to banned websites.

In Palestine, the rise of Islamists to power created debates among female activists. Secularist and religious women joined forces in the struggle against Israel but diverged over their attitudes toward Ḥamās and Islamic Jihād. Following the victory of Ḥamās, tension has arisen between liberal activists and conservative women who supported Ḥamās and Islamic Jihād when attempts were made to impose the *ḥijāb* in Gaza and elsewhere. Although these attempts were thwarted, Islamist women's associations and agendas have come to parallel the efforts made by non-Islamist women, though they have different aims.

International Trends. Tensions between transnational feminist goals and those of local groups, whether Islamic feminists or those who disavow a feminist agenda altogether, have continued since the 1980s. With global migration, large groups of Muslim women are now living outside historically Muslim lands. Some explicitly Muslim groups have begun to organize, such as the North American Association of Muslim Women (founded 1992) or the Women's Islamic Initiative in Spirituality and Equality (launched 2006), an endeavor of the American Muslim Society for Advancement. Western branches of the longstanding General Union of Palestinian Women did not deal with specifically Muslim issues but with national ones. A Muslim feminist group in France, Ni Putes Ni Soumises (Neither Whores nor Repressed), organized to battle violence against women, obligatory *ḥijāb* wearing, and forced marriage—thus, some say, enacting the French New Right's agenda.

Many women's organizations ranging from Islamic feminist to profession-oriented or human-rights groups now exist in Muslim countries. Other issue-oriented groups, such as al-Marʾah al-Jadīdah (The New Woman), the Bint al-Ard (Daughter of the Earth), and Egypt's female-genital-mutilation task force, operate in Egypt. Numerous conferences and events in the region display the activities of gender-oriented nongovernmental organizations, among them the Turkish-based Women for Women's Human Rights, working on the issue of sexual rights, which the group defines as the proper focus for women's rights. Some attention has also been given to women *mujahidāt* and *shahīdāt* (suicide bombers), in various incidents from Iraq to Jordan to Palestine, as a social phenomenon.

Women and the Arab Spring. Women were an integral part of the Arab Spring, which led to political change in Tunisia, Egypt, Yemen, and Libya and which is still playing out in Syria and Bahrain. Women such as Tawakkol Karman, a Yemeni Nobel laureate; Asmaa Mahfouz and Israa Abdel Fattah, Egyptian Internet political activists; and Zainab Hasan Ahmed al-Jumaa, a Bahraini political activist who died during the protests, participated in the demonstrations demanding changes, calling for justice, and fighting for human rights. Muslim and Christian, religiously conservative and liberal, veiled and unveiled women fought courageously despite social norms and faced governmental cruelty. Some women actively participated in agitation or reported and blogged on the situation. Other women supported domestic and economy-sustaining services for protestors and provided logistical support and health care for supporters.

However, there is uncertainty regarding the position of women in the wake of the Arab Spring. In Egypt, Libya, and Yemen, women have been excluded from important decision-making bodies. Egypt's transitional military council excluded women from the decision-making process, and women won less than 2 percent of seats in the new parliament. Similarly, the Transitional National Council in Libya has given women only a limited role in the formal transition process. In Yemen, the exit of President ʿAlī ʿAbd Allāh Ṣāliḥ was brokered exclusively by men representing the political opposition and the country's Arab neighbors. Shirin Ebadi, the winner of the 2003 Nobel Peace Prize, published an article in the *Wall Street Journal* titled "A Warning for Women of the Arab Spring." In it, Ebadi compares the revolutions of the Arab Spring to the 1979 revolution in Iran, warning that revolutionary men often take advantage of women's participation during the movements but then neglect them in constructing post-revolutionary orders.

Despite the limited presence of women in the official political structure, the post–Arab Spring period is witnessing a flourishing of grassroots activities of feminists and female political activists. Female activists, though, share among themselves different visions of women's rights and roles in rebuilding their nations and reshaping their future. The young generation of activists is displaying resilience and determination for change, yet they see no contradiction between national and women's rights issues. For activists such as Nawara Negm and Dalia Ziada, the younger generation of female activists in Egypt, the general trend of political reform and democratization in the region will protect women's rights. Meanwhile, older feminists such as Nawāl al-Saʿdāwī prefer to single out women's rights as a separate issue that should be highlighted and fought for. Skeptics view the failed International Women's Day march in Tahrir Square in March 2012, the exclusion of women from the formal political structure, and the rise of Islamic groups to power as warning signs that women are being pushed out of the public sphere of political participation and social visibility and forced back into the private, domestic sphere.

BIBLIOGRAPHY

Abu El-Komsan, Nehad. *The Freedom of the Square: Reflections on the Course of the Egyptian Revolution and the Participation of Women.* United Nations Entity for Gender Equality and the Empowerment of Women (UN Women), 2012.

Al-Ali, Nadje. *Secularism, Gender, and the State in the Middle East: The Egyptian Women's Movement.* Cambridge, U.K.: Cambridge University Press, 2000.

Al-Jawaheri, Yasmin Husein. *Women in Iraq: The Gender Impact of International Sanctions.* London: I. B. Tauris, 2008.

Amin, Qasim. *The Liberation of Women: A Document in the History of Egyptian Feminism.* Translated by Samiha Sidhom Peterson. Cairo: American University in Cairo Press, 1992.

Arat, Yesim. *Rethinking Islam and Liberal Democracy: Islamist Women in Turkish Politics.* Albany: State University of New York Press, 2005.

Ariffin, Rohana. "Feminism in Malaysia: A Historical and Present Perspective of Women's Struggles in Malaysia." *Women's Studies International Forum* 22, no. 4 (1999): 417–423.

Badran, Margot. *Feminism in Islam: Secular and Religious Convergences.* Oxford: OneWorld, 2009.

Badran, Margot. *Feminists, Islam, and Nation: Gender and the Making of Modern Egypt.* Princeton, N.J.: Princeton University Press, 1995.

Brand, Laurie A. *Women, the State, and Political Liberalization: Middle Eastern and North African Experiences.* New York: Columbia University Press, 1998.

Bullock, Katherine, ed. *Muslim Women Activists in North America: Speaking for Ourselves.* Austin: University of Texas Press, 2005.

Chatty, Dawn, and Annika Rabo, eds. *Organizing Women: Formal and Informal Women's Groups in the Middle East.* Oxford: Berg, 1997.

Cooke, Miriam. "Islamic Feminism Before and After September 11th." *Duke Journal of Gender Law and Policy* 9 (2002): 227–235.

Deeb, Lara. *An Enchanted Modern: Gender and Public Piety in Shīʿī Lebanon.* Princeton, N.J.: Princeton University Press, 2006.

Emadi, Hafizullah. *Repression, Resistance, and Women in Afghanistan.* Westport, Conn.: Praeger, 2002.

Haeri, Shahla. "Obedience versus Autonomy: Women and Fundamentalism in Iran and Pakistan." In *Fundamentalisms and Society: Reclaiming the Sciences, the Family, and Education,* edited by Martin E. Marty and R. Scott Appleby, pp. 181–213. Chicago: University of Chicago Press, 1993.

Hale, Sondra. *Women Activists of the National Islamic Front–Sudan.* Tucson, Ariz.: Middle East Studies Association of North America, 1992.

Hamit, Halil. *İslam'da Feminizm.* Istanbul: Okumus Adam Puplications, 2001.

Hijab, Nadia. *Womanpower: The Arab Debate on Women at Work.* Cambridge, U.K.: Cambridge University Press, 1988.

Hiltermann, Joost R. *Behind the Intifada: Labor and Women's Movements in the Occupied Territories.* Princeton, N.J.: Princeton University Press, 1991.

Jayawardena, Kumari. *Feminism and Nationalism in the Third World.* London: Zed, 1986.

Joseph, Suad, ed. *Gender and Citizenship in the Middle East.* Syracuse, N.Y.: Syracuse University Press, 2000.

Kandiyoti, Deniz, ed. *Women, Islam, and the State.* Philadelphia: Temple University Press, 1991.

Keddie, Nikki R. *Women in the Middle East: Past and Present.* Princeton, N.J.: Princeton University Press, 2007.

Khan, Shahnaz. *Zina, Transnational Feminism, and the Moral Regulation of Pakistani Women.* Vancouver: UBC Press, 2006.

Mahmood, Saba. *Politics of Piety: The Islamic Revival and the Feminist Subject*. Princeton, N.J.: Princeton University Press, 2005.

Nelson, Cynthia. *Doria Shafik, Egyptian Feminist: A Woman Apart*. Gainesville: University Press of Florida, 1996.

Ng, Cecilia, Maznah Mohamad, and tan beng hui. *Feminism and the Women's Movement in Malaysia: An Unsung (R)evolution*. London: Routledge, 2006.

Nouraei-Simone, Fereshteh, ed. *On Shifting Ground: Muslim Women in the Global Era*. New York: Feminist Press at the City University of New York, 2005.

Peteet, Julie M. *Gender in Crisis: Women and the Palestinian Resistance Movement*. New York: Columbia University Press, 1991.

Sabbagh, Suha, ed. *Palestinian Women of Gaza and the West Bank*. Bloomington: Indiana University Press, 1998.

Schweitzer, Yoram, ed. *Female Suicide Bombers: Dying for Equality?* Tel Aviv: Jaffee Center for Strategic Studies, Tel Aviv University, 2006.

Shaarawi, Huda. *Harem Years: The Memoirs of an Egyptian Feminist, 1879–1924*. Translated and edited by Margot Badran. London: Virago, 1986.

Shidyaq, Ahmad Faris al-. *Leg Over Leg*. Translated by Humphrey Davies. New York: New York University Press, 2013.

Talhami, Ghada Hashem. *The Mobilization of Muslim Women in Egypt*. Gainesville: University Press of Florida, 1996.

Verveer, Melanne. "Women and the Arab Spring." *Foreign Service Journal* 89, no. 5 (May 2012): 24–26.

Worden, Minky, ed. *The Unfinished Revolution: Voices from the Global Fight for Women's Rights*. New York: Seven Stories, 2012.

Zuhur, Sherifa. "The Mixed Impact of Feminist Struggles in Egypt during the 1990s." *MERIA Journal* 5, no. 1 (2001): 78–89.

Sherifa Zuhur
Updated by Nermin Allam

Y

YĀSĪN, ʿABD AL-SALĀM. ʿAbd al-Salām Yāsīn (1928–2012) was the leader of an illegal but tolerated Moroccan Islamist political movement, Justice and Benevolence (al-ʿAdl wa-al-Iḥsān). The movement originated after the failed military coups of 1971 and 1972 against the monarchy, when Yāsīn sent a letter, "Islam or the Deluge," admonishing King Ḥasan II, asking him to "repent" and to become a just ruler. The king interned Yāsīn in a psychiatric institution for six years and placed him under house arrest in Salé, near Rabat, until 1978. From that day forward, the religious leader spent time either in jail or under house arrest until Ḥasan's successor, his son Muḥammad VI, freed him in 2000. Unrepentant, Yāsīn addressed a new missive to the monarch titled "Memorandum: To Whom It May Concern," in which he advised the young ruler to "redeem his father from torment by restoring to the people the goods they are entitled to." Yāsīn believed that the Sharīfī throne was guilty of amassing fortunes that, according to him, were equivalent to the country's foreign debt and that needed to be restored to the people.

Yāsīn was born in a modest farming household in the Haha region, not far from the hamlet of Essaouira (Ar., al-Ṣawīrah; Berber, Taṣṣurt) in the Sūs region, not far from Marrakech. A native speaker of Tashelhit, a dialect of Tamazight (Berber), Yāsīn had attributed to him by fellow clerics an Idrīsid genealogy, which elevated him to Sharīfī title, with prophetic lineage, even if he recognized that his father was a peasant of Berber origins. He studied at the Yūsufīyah *madrasah* in Marrakech and made his career as a former regional inspector in the Ministry of National Education where in 1948 he became a teacher of Arabic in public schools and later inspector of Arabic teaching. He traveled to the United States and France in 1959 to receive specialized educational training, spending forty-five days in each country, though the experiences left him unimpressed. In 1967, he retired for medical reasons, although his cathartic crisis of faith in 1965 led him to become a disciple of Ḥājj ʿAbbās al-Qādirī and join a Ṣūfī brotherhood, the Būshīshīyah, near the city of Berkane, and followed the authority of al-Qādirī. After the death of Shaykh ʿAbbās in 1972, Yāsīn left the *ṭarīqah* (brotherhood) and politicized his Ṣūfī understanding and practice of Islam. The political movement he created in 1987 was reminiscent of a *ṭarīqah* as well.

Yāsīn's political thought was influenced by the writings of Ḥasan al-Bannā (d. 1949) and Sayyid

Quṭb (d. 1966). He belonged to the tradition of political Islam that distinguishes between *jāhilīyah* as an ontological category and the Islamic state. However, Yāsīn articulated his thought within the framework of Sufism, distinguishing his movement from other Islamist movements in the Middle East and North Africa. It bore continuities with the old Moroccan model of the saint-chastiser, such as Hassan Lyousi (born 1631), or Muḥammad ibn ʿAbd al-Kabīr al-Kattānī (1873–1909). The mystical and messianic aspects of Yāsīn's ideology prevented him from unifying the Moroccan Islamist movements, which disagreed with his movement's Ṣūfī orientation and authoritarian nature. Yāsīn's stance toward violence was ambiguous. Clashes often pitted militants against police, and his writings contained revolutionary ideas, often adapted from leftist ideologies and Khomeinism. His scathing criticisms of the monarchy, for example, and his strong opposition to official religious scholars and Westernized elites preoccupied followers who blamed all of Morocco's ills on those who were alleged to be working to de-Islamize and secularize society.

Justice and Benevolence militants were Yāsīn's primary disciples. They considered him a living saint, and while the movement organized their individual lives and rituals in a detailed way, most of the followers sought the association's social services. The organization's structure was rigid and authoritarian, and observers stated that it had about thirty thousand members, an unconfirmed figure.

Yāsīn did not recognize the legitimacy of the monarchy, and the state never recognized his movement as an association or political party. The liberalization of the regime after the mid-1990s weakened Yāsīn's movement, because Islamist movements were now participating in elections and attracting voters and members at the expense of Justice and Benevolence. In part to stem this loss of influence, Yāsīn called for a reconciliation of the state and *daʿwah*, as well as for the implementation of the prophetic model that envisaged the restoration of the caliphate, even if the project was largely theoretical in the nation-state–dominated twenty-first century. Yāsīn's movement nonetheless remained important as a defined sphere in the fragmented opposition to the monarchy, and it wielded a significant ability to mobilize.

In addition to twenty books, several of which were translated into French, he published a now-banned monthly magazine, *al-Jamāʿah*. A moderate supporter of the Amazigh (Berbers), he published in 1997 *Ḥiwār maʿa ṣadīq amāzīghī* (Dialogue with an Amazigh Friend), in which he objected to the political dimension of Amazigh cultural and linguistic revival. He claimed that the revival of the ancient Berber script of Tifinagh and the demand for constitutional change to recognize Tamazight as an official language in Morocco would serve postcolonial interests but also represented blasphemous attacks on the Qurʾān and Islam. On 17 June 2011, King Muḥammad VI issued a constitution comprising 180 articles, which called for making the Tamazight language the second official language of the kingdom alongside Arabic—and to reinforce the Ḥassānī culture, which was a characteristic feature of the Saharan provinces in the south. Yāsīn's reactions were muted. He died on 13 December 2012, at the age of 84.

[*See also* Morocco.]

BIBLIOGRAPHY

Munson, Henry, Jr. *Religion and Power in Morocco*. New Haven, Conn.: Yale University Press, 1993.

Tozy, Mohamed. *Monarchie et Islam politique au Maroc*. Paris: Presses de la Fondation Nationale des Sciences Politiques, 1999.

Yāsīn, ʿAbd al-Salām. *Al-Islām aw al-ṭawafān: Risālah maftūḥah ilā Malik al-Maghrib*. Beirut: Dar al-Afaq, 2000.

Zeghal, Malika. *Les islamistes marocains: Le défi à la monarchie*. Paris: Découverte, 2005.

Malika Zeghal
Updated by Joseph A. Kéchichian

Yemen. Yemen is an Abrahamic country where Judaism, Christianity, and Islam have been the primary religions for many centuries. Islam was introduced to Yemen during the lifetime of the Prophet Muḥammad, who sent some of his close companions to call Yemenis to Islam. Yemenis often express pride that their country was once described by the Prophet Muḥammad as being a land of faith and wisdom. Yemen is the home of diverse Islamic schools, but the Zaydī and Shāfiʿī *madhāhib* (sg. *madhhab*, school of Islamic jurisprudence) remain the most commonly practiced. The predominant Ṣūfī schools, which have existed for centuries throughout South Yemen, belong to the Shāfiʿī *madhhab*, but the small town of Tarim, in Ḥaḍramawt, has remained the unofficial but undisputed capital of Sufism. Ṣūfī scholars and preachers from Tarim and surrounding areas played a significant role in spreading Islam to such distant areas as Jakarta in Indonesia, where generations of Ḥaḍramawt descendants have been living for centuries. However, the Ṣūfī influence on the overall social and political life of South Yemen was diminished by the strengthening of the Yemeni Socialist Party (YSP) beginning in the late 1960s. The unification of Yemen in 1990 and the defeat of the YSP during the 1994 civil war prompted a resurrection of Ṣūfī learning institutions that began to attract both Yemeni and international Muslim students, primarily from Southeast Asia.

Although the intellectual roots of the Zaydī *madhhab* were planted outside Yemen, this *madhhab* has become NorthYemen's major contribution to the history of Islamic jurisprudence. The Zaydī *madhhab* is a branch of the Shīʿī tradition, but is considerably different from Ithnā Ashʿarīyah (Twelver) Shiism in Iran, Iraq, Lebanon, and other parts of the Islamic world. One key difference between these two major Shīʿī schools is that the school of Ithnā Ashʿarīyah considers the first three Rightly Guided Caliphs (Abū Bakr, ʿUmar, and ʿUthmān) to be the de facto government and believes that the twelve Shīʿī imāms have the right to rule, based on clear designation, and that they are infallible. However, the Zaydī *madhhab* recognizes the legitimacy of the first Rightly Guided Caliphs, while believing that Imām ʿAlī ibn Abī Ṭālib is the best Muslim, after the Prophet Muḥammad. This belief is called *imāmat al-mafḍūl*, accepting the right of the less qualified to rule, even in the presence of a much more qualified person. This intellectual position aligns the Zaydī *madhhab* more closely with Sunnī Islam.

Zaydī imāms brought the Zaydī *madhhab* to North Yemen beginning in the ninth century. Several Zaydī learning centers were established in such areas as Sanaa, Ṣaʿda, and Dhamār. The later Zaydī Imamate (1918–1962) used Islam to effectively obstruct any attempts to modernize Yemen, viewing political and economic modernization as a threat to its grip on power. The revolution of 26 September 1962 ended the imamate regime, and Islam has since been viewed as compatible with modernization. In the south, Islam was excluded almost entirely from public political life during the 1970s and 1980s, when Marxism was the dominant and ruling ideology.

Modern Yemen. On 22 May 1990, as the Cold War dissipated, the Republic of Yemen was founded, unifying North and South Yemen. North Yemen was the first Arab country to gain independence from the Ottoman Empire in 1918, and was ruled from that time until 1962 by a traditional imamate that promoted complete isolation from the rest of the world. The north had paid a heavy price for this isolation in terms of lack of infrastructure or economic and political development. Many parts of South Yemen, in contrast, fell under either direct or indirect British rule for more than a century. Aden, the only British colony in the Arabian Peninsula from 1839 to 1967, enjoyed a remarkable modernization process. Not long after gaining independence, however, the south fell under the rule of the YSP and remained under its control until 1990. In 1994, the civil war caused a tremendous setback to the democratic transition that began in 1990, and while the initial success of the 2011 Yemeni uprisings offered a new glimmer of hope for a transition toward democracy and modernization, conditions deteriorated.

Key Islamist Actors. A number of key Islaimist actors had emerged on Yemen's political scene after the unification of Yemen in 1990. Although they all call for promoting the Islamic political agenda, significant differences exist among them along ideological and political lines.

Iṣlāḥ (Reform). The Yemeni Congregation for Reform (Iṣlāḥ) was established in 1990 and became Yemen's key Islamic political party. However, the establishment of the Iṣlāḥ should be regarded as part of the political development of the Islamic movement in Yemen, which goes back to the 1940s. The founder of the Muslim Brotherhood Movement in Egypt, Ḥasan al-Bannā, directed special attention to Yemen by sending al-Faḍīl al-Wartalanī, an Algerian member of al-Bannā's movement to the country. Al-Wartalanī succeeded in recruiting a few influential and educated Yemeni youth and participated in the revolution of 1948, which failed to establish a constitutional imamate. During this revolution, Imām Yaḥyā was assassinated, but his son Imām Aḥmad succeeded in aborting the revolution and killing its leaders, including al-Wartalānī. Nevertheless, Imām Aḥmad was not able to entirely eradicate Yemen's Islamic movement.

After the 1962 revolution, Muḥammad Maḥmūd al-Zubayrī (1910–1965), a renowned Islamist and freedom fighter, continued his efforts to emphasize the Islamic nature of the new republic. However, he was soon assassinated in a shadowy conspiracy that has continued to puzzle many Yemenis until the present time. The golden era of Yemen's pre-1990 Islamic movement occurred during the reign of former president Ṣāliḥ, who became president of North Yemen in 1978 and served as the first president of the unified Yemen from 1990 until 2012. Yemen's Islamic movement played a significant role in supporting Ṣāliḥ at various critical junctures, such as his war against the National Democratic Front in the Central Region during the late 1970s and early 1980s. Nevertheless, following the unification of Yemen, the Islamic movement established its own political party, Iṣlāḥ, which is an alliance between the Muslim Brotherhood, some tribal leaders, and the business community. Yemen's current constitution stipulates that Islam is the main source of all legislation, in part because of political pressure exercised by Iṣlāḥ.

The strong electoral performance of Iṣlāḥ in the first democratic parliamentary elections of 1993 made the Iṣlāḥ a key player in Yemen's overall politics. Iṣlāḥ continued its good relations with Ṣāliḥ, in part through the powerful tribal leader Shaykh ʿAbd Allāh Ḥusayn al-Aḥmar (1933–2007), who headed the party from its inception until his death. The party sided with Ṣāliḥ during the civil war of 1994 against the YSP and was part of a government coalition with his party, the General Popular Congress (GPC), until the parliamentary elections of 1997. However, political mistrust arose between the Iṣlāḥ and Ṣāliḥ when the former officially joined the main opposition parties and formed the Joint Meeting Parties (JMPs) in 2005, with the primary objective of bringing about significant political reforms. The JMPs organized an unprecedented political challenge to Ṣāliḥ during the 2006 presidential election with its support for the late Fayṣal bin Shamlān, an independent and widely respected opposition politician. In 2011, the JMPs, including Iṣlāḥ and YSP, joined youth and student activists in the Yemeni uprisings that forced Ṣāliḥ out of the presidency and further propelled Yemen along its path of shaky democratic transition.

Salafists. The rise of Salafism in Yemen is attributed to three broad factors. First, with the oil boom of the 1970s, hundreds of thousands of Yemeni workers moved to Saudi Arabia to work in various infrastructure projects and for small businesses, enjoying the special guest-worker status extended to them by the Saudi government. This favorable Saudi labor policy toward Yemeni workers ended in 1990 with the eruption of the First Gulf War. In Saudi Arabia, these workers were exposed to Salafī teachings that some subsequently carried back to Yemen. Second, the establishment of scientific institutes across North Yemen, with their focus on Sunnī Islam, helped weaken the dominance of Zaydī traditions and thus paved the way for Salafī learning centers. Third, the intellectual influence of late Muqbil al-Wādiʿī (1930–2000), a prominent Salafī scholar, further promoted the teachings of Salafism. Muqbil al-Wādiʿī returned to Ṣaʿdah, the home of his ancestors in northern Yemen, after receiving his religious education in Saudi Arabia. In Ṣaʿdah, al-Wādiʿī founded Dār al-Ḥadīth, which became an important seat of Salafī learning.

Al-Wādiʿī followed a very literalist and strict interpretation of Salafism, which embroiled him in a number of intellectual battles with prominent Yemeni Islamists. For example, he disapproved of establishing political parties or participating in democratic elections and aggressively criticized Iṣlāḥ for its political organization and participation. His death, however, created a considerable intellectual vacuum within Salafī groups and led to the rise of a new generation of Salafī leaders who later established the first Yemeni Salafī political party, al-Rashād (Upright), in 2012. The political development of the Salafī movement has steadily evolved from its early focus on Islamic education to the establishment of the al-Ḥikmah (Wisdom) and al-Iḥsān (Virtue) charity organizations by two predominant groups within the Salafī movement to promote active political participation during the Arab awakening. However, there are still strong leaders within the Salafī movement who remain opposed to the idea of establishing political parties and participating in democratic elections.

Militant Islamic Groups. Two Yemeni Islamist actors resorted to violence to achieve political objectives and their militant activism has threatened the overall fragile security in the country since the last decade.

Al-Qaʿida in Yemen. Following the tragic attacks of 11 September 2001 in the United States, Yemen became a key front in the War on Terrorism. Extremists came to Yemen after the end of the Soviet occupation of Afghanistan, with the return of hundreds of former Islamist fighters. Later a group of Islamic extremists formed the Islamic army of Abyan, which was crushed by the Yemeni military under former president Ṣāliḥ. The attacks on the US Navy destroyer USS *Cole* in the Gulf of Aden during October 2000 was a remarkable and bold move by al-Qaʿida elements in Yemen. Soon after the pronouncement of the War on Terrorism by the George W. Bush administration, al-Qaʿida affiliates established in the Arabian Peninsula in both Yemen and Saudi Arabia were accused of plotting many attacks against the United States, including the failed terrorist incident of Umar Farouk Abdulmuttalib who attempted to blow up a commercial plane en route from Europe to Detroit in the United States on Christmas Day 2009. The Obama administration has since increased its aggressive use of unmanned aircraft targeting al-Qaʿida leaders in Yemen, including the assassination of the American-born Yemeni Islamic cleric Anwar al-Awlaki (1971–2011). After signing the Gulf Initiative of 2011, which helped shift Yemen away from the brink of total civil war, President Abdu Rabbu Manṣūr Hādī authorized more American attacks on Al-Qaʿida leaders in Yemen. He also made targeting al-Qaʿida strongholds in Abyan Province a security priority. Despite president Hādī's initial military successes, al-Qaʿida will remain a security threat for both Yemen and the international community for many years to come.

The Houthis. The Houthis was established in 1992 as the Believing Youth (al-Shabāb al Muʾmīn) in Ṣaʿdah, a northern Yemeni province. The Believing Youth began as a peaceful movement with the objective of reviving Zaydī traditions. Ṣāliḥ encouraged most religious groups during the 1990s, including the Believing Youth and Salafī groups, in order to weaken Iṣlāḥ. The Believing Youth later became al-Ḥūthī Group (or the Houthis), named after its founder, Husayn al-Ḥūthī, son of a prominent Zaydī scholar. Husayn al-Ḥūthī once served as a member of parliament, but after 2004 his group increasingly used violence against Ṣāliḥ's regime. The Houthis have been very critical of U.S. intervention in Yemen's domestic politics. Like Ḥizbullāh in Lebanon, the Houthis blame both the United States and Israel for the problems of the Muslim world. Despite several civil wars with Ṣāliḥ, the Houthis remain a reasonably strong Islamic militant group with broad political ambitions aimed at restoring the pre-1962 political influence of the Zaydī *madhhab*. The Houthis succeeded in expanding their base beyond Ṣaʿdah during the Yemeni uprisings; however, their opponents argue that they are a destabilizing force in Yemen's democratic transition and have increased Iranian influence in Yemen.

BIBLIOGRAPHY

Carapico, Sheila. *Civil Society in Yemen: The Political Economy of Activism in Modern Arabia*. Cambridge, U.K.: Cambridge University Press, 1998.

Day, Stephen W. *Regionalism and Rebellion in Yemen: A Troubled National Union*. Cambridge, U.K.: Cambridge University Press, 2012.

Dresch, Paul. *A History of Modern Yemen*. New York: Cambridge University Press, 2000.

Haykel, Bernard. *Revival and Reform in Islam: The Legacy of Muhammad al-Shawkānī*. Cambridge, U.K.: Cambridge University Press, 2003.

Johnsen, Gregory D. *The Last Refuge: Yemen, al-Qaeda, and America's War in Arabia*. New York: W. W. Norton, 2013.

Phillips, Sarah. *Yemen's Democracy Experiment in Regional Perspective: Patronage and Pluralized Authoritarianism*. New York: Palgrave Macmillan, 2008.

Schwedler, Jillian. *Faith in Moderation: Islamist Parties in Jordan and Yemen*. Cambridge, U.K.: Cambridge University Press, 2006.

Weir, Shelagh. *A Tribal Order: Politics and Law in the Mountains of Yemen*. Austin: University of Texas Press, 2007.

GAMAL GASIM

YEMENI CONGREGATION FOR REFORM. The Yemeni Congregation for Reform (al-Tajāmmuʿ al-Yamanī lil-Iṣlāḥ), or Iṣlāḥ Party—commonly known simply as al-Iṣlāḥ—was established on 13 September 1990. It quickly emerged as a prominent party, endorsing democracy and participating in all elections, and playing an active role in the educational and social sectors (through the network of teaching institutes it controlled until 2002 and through the (formally independent) al-Iṣlāḥ Charity Society. Although its base of membership is complex, as it draws from various social groups and has no fixed ideological corpus, it is often described as the local branch of the Muslim Brotherhood. Al-Iṣlāḥ is said to comprise two distinct branches: Muslim Brothers or ideological Islamists such as

ʿAbd al-Majīd al-Zindānī, Muḥammad Qaḥṭān, and Muḥammad al-Yādūmī, and tribesmen such as ʿAbd Allāh al-Aḥmar (who headed the party until his death in December 2007 and was simultaneously paramount chief of the large Ḥāshid tribal confederation) and Sinān Abū Luḥūm.

Inside al-Iṣlāḥ, such an alliance of different groups appears as the result of the historical specificities of contemporary Yemen, where tribes continue to play an important role and where the alliance between Muslim Brothers and tribal *shaykhs* in the 1960s managed to rally the people around the republic (an accomplishment the nationalist revolutionaries were incapable of achieving on their own). Bluntly describing al-Iṣlāḥ as an Islamist party is therefore inaccurate, as it is a heterogeneous alliance drawing together different strains, some of which have been accused of supporting terrorism in the framework of the "global war against terror."

Calling al-Iṣlāḥ an opposition party has also long been inexact, as its relations with the government of President ʿAlī ʿAbd Allāh Ṣāliḥ were ambivalent. Indeed, in the context of the unification of North and South Yemen in the early 1990s, al-Iṣlāḥ became an alternative ally of the General People's Congress (GPC), the ruling party, which experienced tensions with the Socialists. Between 1993 and 1997, al-Iṣlāḥ participated in government, controlling important ministries. Its leader, ʿAbd Allāh al-Aḥmar, was consistently elected speaker of Parliament between 1993 and 2007 with the support of the ruling party, and in 1994, al-Iṣlāḥ militants assisted the national army in its war against southern secessionists headed by former socialist rulers.

Starting at the end of the 1990s and becoming more overt in the mid-2000s, al-Iṣlāḥ experienced a slow and hesitant transformation, accepting its role as an opponent of ʿAlī ʿAbd Allāh Ṣāliḥ's rule. A common platform, called the Joint Meeting (al-Liqāʾ al-Mushtarak), was elaborated with the various opposition groups, including the former socialist enemies. During the 2003 parliamentary elections, local agreements were signed, and in 2006, the opposition parties chose a common candidate to compete in the presidential election. Fayṣal bin Shamlān managed to win more than 22 percent of the vote. Yet some inside al-Iṣlāḥ rejected such an alliance: ʿAbd Allāh al-Aḥmar as well as ʿAbd al-Majīd al-Zindānī never formally endorsed the candidate designated by their party. Such opposition illustrated the reluctance of some Islamists to cooperate with "impious" socialists and also exposed a generation gap that could well be overcome with the emergence of a new generation of activists after ʿAbd Allāh al-Aḥmar's death in late 2007.

[*See also* Yemen.]

BIBLIOGRAPHY

Bonnefoy, Laurent, and Marine Poirier. "The Yemeni Congregation for Reform (al-Islâh): The Difficult Process of Building a Project for Change." In *Returning to Political Parties? Partisan Logic and Political Transformations in the Arab World*, edited by Myriam Catusse and Karam Karam, pp. 61–99. Beirut: Lebanese Center for policy Studies, 2010.

Schwedler, Jillian. *Faith in Moderation: Islamist Parties in Jordan and Yemen*. Cambridge, U.K.: Cambridge University Press, 2006.

LAURENT BONNEFOY

Z

ẒĀHIRĪYA. *See* Schools of Jurisprudence, *subentry* Sunni Schools of Jurisprudence.

ZAKĀT. *See* Charity.

ẒAWĀHIRĪ, AYMAN AL-. Born in al-Maʿādī (a residential suburb of Cairo), Ayman Muḥammad Rabiʿ al-Ẓawāhirī (b. 19 June 1951), was the former head of the Egyptian militant group Islamic Jihād and succeeded Osama Bin Laden as the commander of al-Qaʿida on 2 May 2011. A medical doctor and surgeon, al-Ẓawāhirī hailed from an upper-bourgeois family that combined two central Islamic traditions: the institutional scholarly Islam of al-Azhar University (headed in the 1930s by his paternal grandfather) and Sufism (in which his maternal grandfather, ʿAbd al-Wahhāb ʿAzzām, was very active). In 1979 Ẓawāhirī married ʿIzzat Aḥmad Nuwayr, a graduate in philosophy, and fathered five children, three of whom—along with his spouse—were killed an American air strike on Afghanistan in late 2001, immediately after the 11 September attacks on the World Trade Center in New York and the Pentagon in Arlington County, Virginia.

His early commitment to a revolutionary and elitist strategy can be related to three major events in his personal and public life. First was the execution of Sayyid Quṭb in 1966, when Ẓawāhirī was fifteen. It was at this time that Ẓawāhirī created his first activist cell, aimed at establishing an Islamic state through a coup d'état against President Gamal Abdel Nasser. The second event that marked Ẓawāhirī was the 1967 defeat in the Six Day War, which constituted a very strong blow to the credibility of Arab nationalism. Nasser's successor, Anwar el-Sadat, chose to support the young Muslim activists of the emerging Jamāʿat al-Islāmīyah in the early 1970s against a possible Nasserist opposition. However, Sadat's later policies—including his personal journey to occupied Jerusalem and the Camp David agreement in 1978—were seen as a betrayal by Ẓawāhirī and others. Third, and equally important, was Ẓawāhirī's 1981 arrest, which associated him, albeit indirectly, with the president's assassins. Ẓawāhirī was tortured in Hosni Mubarak's jails, which led him to betray his companions (including his closest friend, ʿIssam al-Qamari) and testify against them in court in 1982. He was freed in 1984 after only three years in jail (possibly a result of his influential family) and embarked on various travels that took him to Tunisia, Saudi Arabia, Pakistan, and twice to Afghanistan. As a physician in an Islamic non-governmental organization, he was impressed by Afghanistan, which, unlike Egypt, experienced limited Western influence and was in the middle of a major uprising against an occupying superpower.

Ẓawāhirī's philosophy, as detailed in *The Bitter Harvest*, a pamphlet written in 1988 in which he denounced the sixty-year struggle of the Muslim Brotherhood as futile, was clearly influenced by Sayyid Quṭb's binary vision. Ẓawāhirī saw no possible connections between the normative system inherited from the colonial period and the genuine ethical practices (the Sharīʿah) of Islamic culture. Until 1998, although convinced of the limited ties between international and local politics, he gave priority to the armed struggle against the "near enemy" represented by Arab regimes that he considered the main allies of the former colonial powers as well as the state of Israel. Ẓawāhirī argued that opposing both Israelis and Arab leaders would be counterproductive and accomplish neither a victory against regimes aligned with Western powers nor Israel; in this situation, the latter took practical precedence.

In 1992, at a time when internal dissent transformed the victory of the Afghan Mujāhidīn over the Soviet Union into civil war, Ẓawāhirī moved to Khartoum, where a more stable Islamic regime offered opportunities for traveling to Europe and Asia as well as acting against the Egyptian regime. From Sudan, he initiated at least three actions against Egyptian interests: he failed in assassination attempts against the minister of interior and former prime minister ʿĀṭif Ṣidqī and President Hosni Mubarak (during his 1995 visit to Addis Ababa), but succeeded in blowing up the Egyptian embassy in Islamabad. In 1996, he refused to follow the Jamāʿat, which halted its armed struggle ("to prevent weakening the capacity of the Egyptian state in its efforts against Israel"). The victory of the Taliban and their agreement with Osama Bin Laden, over whom he acquired a strong influence, allowed him to settle in Afghanistan.

While his activities at the Egyptian level were weakened by a series of repressive blows, Ẓawāhirī switched from a local to a global strategy to mobilize efforts against the "distant enemy," America. In February 1998, in the name of his Jihād organization, he joined the newly created World Islamic Front for Jihād against Crusaders and Jews, and fully engaged in the al-Qaʿida strategy of striking Americans—in Africa, then in Saudi Arabia, then inside their own territory—who were considered occupiers of the holy land (Saudi Arabia) of all Muslims. A month after the 11 September attacks Ẓawāhirī made his strategy and motives explicit in his memoirs (first circulated by the London-based newspaper *Asharq Alawsat*) under the title *Knights under the Banner of the Prophet*. Strongly involved in post-9/11 pronouncements of al-Qaʿida, he was often considered Bin Laden's successor, particularly when he was silent for long periods of time; this turned out to be accurate.

Although his whereabouts remained unknown, Ẓawāhirī was generally thought to be in the tribal regions of Pakistan, even if he seldom appeared alongside Bin Laden after 2003. In 2004, the Pakistani army launched an attack on the city of Wana, with reports alleging that he was trapped in the center of the conflict by the Pakistani army. Ẓawāhirī either escaped or was never among the fighters, but as the conflict spread into the tribal areas of western Pakistan, he became a prime target of the Pakistani Inter-Services Intelligence, which failed to capture him. On 13 January 2006, the U.S. Central Intelligence Agency launched yet another airstrike on a village near the Afghan border where it was believed Ẓawāhirī was hiding, with initial reports that he was killed. Ẓawāhirī was unhurt, although dozens lost their lives in the raids, as the rebel taunted George W. Bush to "come and get him." Ẓawāhirī allegedly fell ill in

2009, with an urgent request for a physician, although this turned out to be a hoax. Dr. Humam Khalil al-Balawi, a thirty-two-year-old Jordanian triple agent was reportedly the doctor who would deliver Ẓawāhirī in a carefully mounted sting operation. Instead, al-Balawi detonated his powerful explosive vest at the CIA operations base in Khost, Afghanistan, killing himself along with his handler, an allegedly unsuspecting member of the Jordanian royal family, Ali bin Zeid; four CIA officers; and their three contracted bodyguards. In mid-2009, Ẓawāhirī emerged as the operational and strategic commander of al-Qaʿida with a formal appointment on 16 June 2011, as confirmed by several Islamist Web sites. Still, al-Qaʿida was significantly weakened, with desperate calls by Ẓawāhirī on Muslims to be loyal while inciting most to oppose diabolical Western hegemons.

[*See also* Bin Laden, Osama; Qaʿida, al-; *and* Quṭb, Sayyid.]

BIBLIOGRAPHY

Mansfield, Laura. *His Own Words: Translation and Analysis of the Writing of Dr. Ayman Al Zawahiri*. Old Tappan, N.J.: TLG, 2006.

Parker, William, and Heidi J. Bridges. *Jihadist Strategic Communication: As Practiced by Usama bin Laden and Ayman al-Zawahiri*. Bloomington, Ind.: AuthorHouse, 2008.

Warrick, Joby. *The Triple Agent: The al-Qaeda Mole Who Infiltrated the CIA*. New York: Doubleday, 2011.

Wright, Lawrence. *The Looming Tower: Al-Qaeda and the Road to 9/11*. New York: Knopf, 2006.

Ẓawāhirī, Ayman al-. *Knights under the Banner of the Prophet: Reflections into the Jihad Movement. Asharq al-Awsat*, December 2001. The full text in English is available at http://azelin.files.wordpress.com/2010/11/6759609-knights-under-the-prophet-banner.pdf.

Zayyat, Montasser al-. *The Road to al-Qaeda: The Story of Bin Laden's Right-Hand Man*. Translated by Ahmed Fekry. Edited by Sara Nimis. London: Pluto, 2004.

FRANÇOIS BURGAT
Updated by JOSEPH A. KÉCHICHIAN

ZAYTŪNAH.

According to one view, put forward by the French scholar Lucien Golvin, the Zaytūnah mosque in Tunis was built in 734 by ʿUbayd Allāh Habhab, the governor of Ifrīqīyah (as Tunisia was called by the Arabs). Other historians have maintained that the Zaytūnah mosque was built earlier, around 698, by Ḥussān ibn al-Nuʿman al-Ghassānī, the Arab conqueror of Tunis and Carthage. A more recent thesis, however, has been put forward by Muḥammad al-Bājī Bin Māmī, who holds that the Arab conquerors built the Zaytūnah mosque on the remains of an existing Byzantine construction and within the ramparts of a fort.

Whatever its origin, al-Zaytūnah was, until the twelfth century, primarily a place of worship, and the Kairouan mosque was the major center of Islamic thought and learning in North Africa. When the Ḥafṣid dynasty (1207–1534) came to power and made Tunis its capital, the Zaytūnah emerged as one of the most important Islamic institutions of higher learning in the Muslim world. Its famous library, al-ʿAbdalīyah, expanded to house a large collection of books and rare manuscripts that attracted Islamic scholars and men of learning from many nations. Students were taught Qurʾānic exegesis, *ḥadīth*, and *fiqh*, as well as history, grammar, science, and medicine, in its *madrasah*s (Islamic schools), which in turn produced great scholars such as the historian and philosopher ʿAbd al-Raḥmān ibn Khaldūn.

In 1534, the Ḥafṣid dynasty was ousted and the Spaniards occupied Tunis until 1574. They ransacked its libraries and mosques and burned or removed many of the Zaytūnah's precious books and manuscripts. With the expansion of the Ottoman Empire into North Africa, there emerged in the seventeenth century two local Turkish dynasties, the Murādids and the Ḥusaynids, who restored and expanded the Zaytūnah mosque, its libraries, and its *madrasah*s, and made it once again a major center of Islamic learning and culture.

The French occupation of Algiers in 1830 revealed the political, economic, and military weaknesses of North African states and led Aḥmad Bey I and his grand vizier, Khayr al-Dīn al-Tūnīsī, to begin reforming the government and the educational system of Tunisia. Between 1840 and 1875, they introduced major administrative and curricular changes that included placing the Zaytūnah under the control of two *qāḍī*s and two *shaykh*s *al-Islām*, representing the Mālikī and Ḥanafī schools of jurisprudence, to accommodate the Ottoman preference for the Ḥanafī school while maintaining Zaytūnah's Mālikī traditions. With the establishment of the French protectorate in 1881, the pace of change increased, with Zaytūnah students organizing to demand reforms in the curriculum and the methods of teaching. New courses were introduced in 1896, including physics, political economy, and French as a foreign language, and in 1912 the reforms were extended to the regional branches of the Zaytūnah in Kairouan, Sousse, Sfax, Tuzir, and Gafsa.

The reforms of 1958 that unified the educational system in independent Tunisia and the creation of the University of Tunis in 1960 undermined the status of the Zaytūnah as a university. In 1965, its role as an independent educational institution was officially abolished, and it became the school of theology and Islamic studies of the University of Tunis.

Bibliography

Abdel Moula, Mahmoud. *L'université zaytounienne et la société tunisienne*. Paris: Maisonneuve & Larose, 1971.

ʿAyyāshī, Mukhtār. *Al-Zaytūnah wa-al-Zaytūnīyūn: Fītārīkh Tūnis al-muʿāṣir, 1883–1958*. Tunis: Jamʿīyat al-Zaytūnah, 2003.

Daoulatli, Abdelaziz. *Al-Zaytūnah: ʿAshrat qurūn min al-fann al-miʿmārī al-Tūnisī*. Tunis: Turāth lil-Nashr, 1996.

Green, Arnold H. *The Tunisian Ulama, 1873–1915: Social Structure and Response to Ideological Currents*. Leiden: Brill, 1978.

Mary-Jane Deeb

Topical Outline of Entries

Biographies
Education
Institutions and Structures
International Relations
Islam and Politics in Regions and Select Countries
Islamic Finance
Islamic Law
Modern Movements, Associations, and Parties
Muslim Communities, Sects, Schools of Thought
Muslim Political History
Muslim Political Thought
Offices and Titles
Political Theorists, Thinkers, and Reformers
Religious Beliefs
Society
Terms and Concepts
Theories of the State

Biographies

ʿAbd al-Rāziq, ʿAlī
Abdülhamid II
Abū Bakr
Ahmad, Eqbal
Ahmad, Israr
Ahmadinejad, Mahmoud
Atatürk, Mustafa Kemal
Āzād, Abū al-Kalām
Bin Laden, Osama
Chirāgh ʿAlī
Faraj, Muḥammad ʿAbd al-Salām
Ḥasan II of Morocco
Ḥawwā, Saʿīd
Ḥusayn ibn ʿAlī
Izetbegović, Alija
Jinnah, Mohammad Ali
Kāshāni, Abol-Qāsem
Khameneʾi, ʿAlī
Kishk, ʿAbd al-Ḥamīd
Kishk, Muḥammad Jalāl
Mossadegh, Mohammad
Mukhtār, ʿUmar al-
Mullah Omar
Nasser, Gamal Abdel
Niẓām al-Mulk
Nūrī, Fażlullāh
Rahman, Omar Abdel
Ṣabrī Efendi, Mustafa
Ṣadr, Mūsā al-
Shaltūt, Maḥmūd
Sīstānī, ʿAlī al-
Suwari, Al-Hajj Salim
Tal, ʿUmar ibn Said
ʿUmar ibn al-Khaṭṭāb
ʿUthmān ibn ʿAffān
Ẓawāhirī, Ayman al-

Education

Azhar, al-
Education, Muslim
Humanism
Islamization of Knowledge and Society
Khuṭbah
Nadwat al-ʿUlamāʾ
Universities
Zaytūnah

Institutions and Structures

Administration
Arab League
Bayt al-Ḥikmah
Bayt al-Māl
Congresses
Council(s) of Senior ʿ*Ulamā*ʾ
Courts
Dār al-Iftāʾ
Dīwān
Dīwān al-Maẓālim
Dīwānīyah
Executive
Gulf Cooperation Council
Ḥawzah
Imārah
International Institute of Islamic Thought
Jurisprudential Council of North America
Loya Jirga
Majlis
Masjid Jāmiʿ
Ministry of Islamic Affairs
Monarchy
Niẓāmīyah Courts
Organization of Islamic Cooperation
Ribāṭ
Slavery
Waqf
Wizāra

International Relations

Crusades
Globalization
International Islamic Organizations
International Law
International Relations and Diplomacy
Islamophobia
Just War
Muslim-Christian Relations
Muslim-Jewish Relations
Peace and Peacebuilding
Treaties

Islam and Politics in Regions and Select Countries

Islam and Politics in Africa

Ethiopia
Horn of Africa
Islam and Politics in Africa
Nigeria

Islam and Politics in Central Asia and the Caucasus

Afghanistan
Azerbaijan
Chechnya
Iraq
Islam and Politics in Central Asia and the Caucasus
Israel
Kazakhstan
Lebanon
Palestine
Uzbekistan

Islam and Politics in Europe

Balkan States
Bosnia and Herzegovina
France
Germany
Great Britain
Islam and Politics in Europe
Netherlands
Russia
Scandinavian States

Islam and Politics in North America

Council on American-Islamic Relations
Islam and Politics in North America
Islamic Society of North America
Malcolm X
Muslim Students Association of North America
Nation of Islam

Islam and Politics in South Asia

China
India
Islam and Politics in South Asia
Pakistan

Islam and Politics in Southeast Asia

Australia and Oceania
Indonesia
Islam and Politics in Southeast Asia
Malaysia
Philippines
Thailand

Islam and Politics in Sub-Saharan Africa

Islam and Politics in Sub-Saharan Africa

Islam and Politics in the Middle East and North Africa

Algeria
Egypt
Iran, Islamic Republic of
Islam and Politics in the Middle East and North Africa
Jordan
Libya
Morocco
Saudi Arabia
Sudan
Turkey
Yemen

Regions and Sites

Andalusia
Jerusalem

Islamic Finance

Islam and Economics
Islamic Finance
Taxation

Islamic Law

Fiqh

Fatwa
Fiqh
Minority Fiqh

Legal Schools

Schools of Jurisprudence
- Shīʿah Schools of Jurisprudence
- Sunni Schools of Jurisprudence

Sharīʿah

Kānūn
Personal Status Codes
Sharīʿah

Modern Movements, Associations, and Parties

Aal al-Bayt Institute for Islamic Thought, The Royal
Adalet ve Kalkınma Partisi
African Muslim Party
Aḥbāsh, al-
Al-Khoei Benevolent Foundation
All-India Muslim League
Al-Wefaq National Islamic Society
Amal
Anavatan Partisi
Baʿth Parties
Barelwīs
Constitutional Movement
Constitutional Revolution
Cumhuriyet Halk Partisi
Darul Islam Movement
Demokrat Parti
Dewan Dakwah Islamiyah
Fedāʾīyān-i Islām
Freedom Movement of Iran
Groupe Islamique Armé
Ḥamās
Ḥizb al-Daʿwah al-Islāmīyah
Ḥizb al-Nahḍah
Ḥizb al-Taḥrīr al-Islāmī
Ḥizb-i Islāmī Afghānistān
Ḥizbullāh
Ḥojjatīyeh Society
Indonesian Mujahidin Council
Iranian Revolution of 1979
Islamic Action Front
Islamic Constitutional Movement
Islamic Republican Party
Islamic Salvation Front
Islamic Supreme Council of Iraq
Islamic Youth Movement of Malaysia
Jamāʿat-i Islāmī
Jamāʿat al-Islāmīyah, al-
Jamāʿat Izālat al-Bidʿa wa Iqāmat al-Sunna
Jamʿīyat al-Shubbān al-Muslimīn
Jamʿīyatul ʿUlamāʾ-i Hind
Jamʿīyatul ʿUlamāʾ-i Pākistān
Jihād Groups
Justice and Benevolence Party
Justice and Development Party
Khilāfat Movement
Laskar Jihad
Majlis Ulam Indonesia
Masyumi Party
Moro Islamic Liberation Front
Moro National Liberation Front
Movement for National Reform
Movement for the Society of Peace
Muhammadiyah
Mujāhidīn-i Khalq
Muslim Brotherhood
Muttahida Majlis-i Amal
Nahdatul Ulama
National Awakening Party
National Islamic Front
Nūrī Movement
Partai Islam se Malaysia
Partai Keadilan Sejahtera
Partai Persatuan Pembangunan
Qaʿida, al-
Refâh Partisi
Salafī Movements
Sarekat Islam
Tablīghī Jamāʿat
Taliban
Union des Organisations Islamiques de France
United Development Party
United Malays National Organizations
Wasat Party, al-
Yemeni Congregation for Reform

Muslim Communities, Sects, Schools of Thought

Abangan
Alevis
Ashʿarīs
Bahāʾī
Brethren of Purity
Deobandīs
Druze
Khārijites

Kurds
Murji'ites
Muʿtazilah
Qadarites
Sanūsīyah
Wahhābīyah
Wetu Telu

Muslim Political History

Arab Nationalism
Arab Spring
Combat
Expansion of Islam
Historiography

Colonialism and the Muslim World

Arab-Israeli Conflict
Capitulations
Clash of Civilizations
Colonialism and the Muslim World
Cultural Invasion
Intifāḍah
Orientalism
Palestine Liberation Organization
Postcolonialism
Secularism

Empires, Dynasties, Kingdoms and Sultanates

ʿAbbāsid Caliphate
Būyids
Fāṭimid Dynasty
Mamlūk State
Mughal Empire
Ottoman Empire
Ṣafavid Dynasty
Seljuk Dynasty
Umayyad Caliphate

Islamic Reform

Islamic Reform
Tanzimat

Modernity

Civilization
Modernity
New Media in the Muslim World

Muslim Political Thought

Amānah
Equality
Freedom
Human Rights
Jihād
Martyrdom
Mirrors for Princes
Muslim Political Thought
Political Science
Politics and Ethics
Rebellion
Siyāsah Sharʿīyah
Succession
Terrorism
Tolerance
Tyranny

Offices and Titles

Offices and Titles: Religious, Social, and Political

Political Theorists, Thinkers, and Reformers

Classical

Abū Yūsuf, Yaʿqūb ibn Ibrāhīm al-Anṣārī
Bāqillānī, Abū Bakr Muḥammad ibn al-Ṭayyib al-
Fārābī, Abū Naṣr al-
Ghazālī, Abū Ḥāmid al-
Ibn Bājjah, Abū Bakr
Ibn al-Farrā', Abū Yaʿlā
Ibn Ḥazm, ʿAlī Ibn Aḥmad
Ibn al-Muqaffaʿ, ʿAbd Allāh
Ibn Qutaybah, ʿAbd Allāh
Ibn Rushd, Abū al-Walīd Muḥammad Aḥmad
Ibn Sīnā, Abū ʿAlī
Ibn Ṭufayl, Abū Bakr
Juwaynī, ʿAbd al-Mālik al-
Kindī, Abū Yūsuf Yaʿqūb ibn Isḥaq al-
Māwardī, Abū al-Ḥasan al-

Medieval

Aqḥiṣārī, Ḥasan Kāfī al-
Baranī, Ḍhiya' al-Dīn al-
Çelebi, Kâtip
Ibn Jamā'ah, Badr al-Dīn
Ibn Khaldūn, 'Abd al-Raḥmān
Ibn Qayyim al-Jawzīyah
Ibn Taymīyah, Taqī al-Dīn Aḥmad
Karakī, 'Alī al-
Sirhindī, Aḥmad

Modern

'Abduh, Muḥammad
Abū Zahrah, Muḥammad
Afghānī, Jamāl al-Dīn al-
Aḥmad Khān, Sayyid
Arslān, Shakīb
Azzam, Abdullah Yusuf al-
Bannā, Ḥasan al-
Bennabi, Malek
Bishrī, Ṭāriq al-
Erbakan, Necmettin
Faḍlallāh, Muḥammad Ḥusayn
Fārūqī, Ismā'īl Rājī al-
Fāsī, Muḥammad 'Allāl al-
Ghāmidī, Jāved Aḥmad
Ghannūshī, Rāshid al-
Ghazālī, Muḥammad al-
Gülen, Fethullah
Haron, Imam Abdullah
Iqbal, Muhammad
Kawākibī, 'Abd al-Raḥmān al-
Khaled, Amr
Khālid, Khālid Muḥammad
Khan, Maulana Wahiduddin
Khatami, Mohamed
Kho'i, Abol-Qāsem al-
Khomeini, Ruhollah al-Musavi
Mahathir bin Mohamed
Mahdī, al-Ṣādiq al-
Majlisī, Muḥammad Bāqir al-
Mawdūdī, Sayyid Abū al-A'lā
Montazeri, Hossein 'Alī
Muṭahharī, Murtażā
Nabhānī, Taqī al-Dīn al-
Nadwī, Abū al-Ḥasan
Qaraḍāwī, Yūsuf al-
Quṭb, Sayyid
Rashīd Riḍā, Muḥammad
Ṣadr, Muḥammad Bāqir al-
Sanhūrī, 'Abd al-Razzāq al-
Shams al-Dīn, Muḥammad Mahdī
Sharī'atī, 'Alī
Sibā'ī, Muṣṭafā al-
Soroush, Abdolkarim
Ṭāhā, Maḥmūd Muḥammad
Turābī, Ḥasan al-
Yāsīn, 'Abd al-Salām

Religious Beliefs

Apostasy
Muḥammad
Qur'ān Exegesis and Hermeneutics
Religious Beliefs

Society

Charity
Commanding Right and Forbidding Wrong
Ethnicity
Family
Sexuality
Shu'ūbīyah
Social Movements
Sufism
Tribes
Ummah
Women in Politics

Terms and Concepts

Companions of the Prophet
Da'wah
Fitnah
Ḥirābah
Ḥisbah
Hypocrites
Islamism
Ta'zīyah

Theories of the State

Ahl al-Ḥall wa-al-'Aqd
Arab Socialism
Authority and Legitimation
Caliphate, Theories of the

Citizenship
Constitutions and Constitutionalism
Dawlah
Democracy
Elections
Governance
Imamate, Theories of the
Individualism
Justice
Minorities in Muslim States
Nation
Nationalism
Opposition
Pan-Islam
Pluralism
Political Parties
Power
Representation
Republic
Shūrā
Ulū al-Amr
Wilāyat al-Faqīh

Directory of Contributors

Deina Abdelkader
Department of Political Science, University of Massachusetts Lowell
International Institute of Islamic Thought; Jurisprudential Council of North America

Mohammad A. Abderrazzaq
Department of Near Eastern Studies, University of Michigan, Ann Arbor
Bāqillānī, Abū Bakr Muḥammad ibn al-Ṭayyib al-; Ibn Qayyim al-Jawzīyah

Shukri B. Abed
The Middle East Institute, Washington D.C.
Arab-Israeli Conflict

Reem Abou-El-Fadl
Department of Politics and International Relations, Oxford University
Egypt

Younes Abouyoub
Middle East Institute, Columbia University
Al-Wefaq National Islamic Society; National Islamic Front

Peter Adamson
Ludwig-Maximilians-Universität München
Kindī, Abū Yūsuf Yaʿqūb ibn Isḥaq al-

Asma Afsaruddin
Department of Near Eastern Languages and Cultures, Indiana University
Abū Bakr; Companions of the Prophet; ʿUmar ibn al-Khaṭṭāb; ʿUthmān ibn ʿAffān

Feroz Ahmad
Yeitepe University, Istanbul
Anavatan Partisi; Demokrat Parti; Turkey

Mumtaz Ahmad
Hampton University, Virginia
Tablīghī Jamāʿat

Engin Deniz Akarli
Washington University in St. Louis
Abdülhamid II

Shahrough Akhavi
Distinguished Professor of Political Science Emeritus, University of South Carolina; Adjunct Professor of Political Science, Columbia University, New York
Dawlah; Khameneʾi, ʿAlī; Quṭb, Sayyid; Sharīʿatī, ʿAlī

Elmira Akhmetova
Russia

Mustafa Aksakal
Department of History, Georgetown University
Constitutional Movement

Abdullah A. Al-Arian
School of Foreign Service at Qatar, Georgetown University
Bannā, Ḥasan al-; Muslim Brotherhood

Muhammad Al-Atawneh
Department of Middle East Studies, Ben-Gurion University of the Negev
Council(s) of Senior ʿUlamāʾ

Tamim Al-Barghouti
Postcolonialism

Kelly Al-Dakkak
St. Anthony's College, University of Oxford
Abū Zahrah, Muḥammad

Abdullah M. Alhajeri
History Department, Kuwait University
Dīwānīyah

Nermin Allam
Department of Political Science, University of Alberta
Women in Politics

Chris Allen
Birmingham Race Action Partnership (BRAP) UK
Islamophobia

Audrey L. Altstadt
Department of History, University of Massachusetts Amherst
Azerbaijan

Biancamaria Scarcia Amoretti
Università degli Studi di Roma "La Sapienza"
Ṣafavid Dynasty

Vivienne SM. Angeles
Department of Religion, La Salle University
Moro Islamic Liberation Front; Moro National Liberation Front; Philippines

Ovamir Anjum
Department of Philosophy, University of Toledo
Administration; Globalization; Governance; Ibn Jamāʿah, Badr al-Dīn; Imamate, Theories of the; Juwaynī ʿAbd al-Mālik al-; Māwardī, Abū al-Ḥasan al-; Muslim Political History; Nabhānī, Taqī al-Dīn al-; Politics and Ethics; Qadarites

Etin Anwar
Hobart and William Smith Colleges
Laskar Jihad

Syed Ali Ashraf *(deceased)*
Islamic Academy, Cambridge
Universities

Gehad Auda
Center for Political and International Development Studies, Cairo
Rahman, Omar Abdel

Mahmoud M. Ayoub
Temple University
Ḥusayn ibn ʿAlī

Mohammad Syafi'i Anwar
School of International Studies, Universiti Utara Malaysia
Partai Persatuan Pembangunan

Christopher Anzalone
Institute of Islamic Studies, McGill University
International Islamic Organizations; Islamic Action Front

Osman Bakar
International Islamic University of Malaysia
Malaysia

Raymond William Baker
Trinity College, Connecticut
Ghazālī, Muḥammad al-; Wasat Party, al-

Kilian Bälz, Attorney at Law
Partner at Amereller Legal Consultants, Berlin, Dubai, Cairo
Islamic Finance

Amatzia Baram
University of Haifa, Israel
Ḥizb al-Daʿwah al-Islāmīyah

Joyce N. Baram
Ḥizb al-Daʿwah al-Islāmīyah

Peri Bearman
Harvard Law School, Retired
Dār al-Iftāʾ; Dīwān al-Maẓālim; Fitnah; Ḥirābah; Majlis; Masjid Jāmiʿ; Niẓām al-Mulk; Offices and Titles: Religious, Social, and Political

Lois Beck
Department of Anthropology, Washington University in St. Louis
Tribes

William O. Beeman
University of Minnesota
Iranian Revolution of 1979

Abdessamad Belhaj
Pázmány Péter Catholic University
Abū Yūsuf, Yaʿqūb ibn Ibrāhīm al-Anṣārī; Ashʿarīs; Bayt al-Māl; Fārābī, Abū Naṣr al-; Fāsī, Muḥammad ʿAllāl al-; Ibn Qutaybah, ʿAbd Allāh; Imārah; Minority Fiqh; Peace and Peacebuilding; Ṭāhā, Maḥmūd Muḥammad; Ulū al-Amr

Samir Ben-Layashi
Tel Aviv University, Middle Eastern Department
Sexuality

JONATHAN BENTHALL
University College, London
Charity; Qaraḍāwī, Yūsuf al-

MAURITS S. BERGER
Institute for Religious Studies, Faculty of Humanities, Leiden University, Netherlands
Fatwa

ROBERT BRENTON BETTS
University of Belamand, Lebanon
Druze

KAMRAN BOKHARI
Strategic Forecasting, Inc. (STRATFOR)
Jamāʿat-i Islāmī; Jamʿīyatul ʿUlamāʾ-i Pākistān

LAURENT BONNEFOY
University of Provence, France
Jihād Groups; Yemeni Congregation for Reform

CATERINA BORI
Alma Mater Studiorum, University of Bologna
Aqḥiṣārī, Ḥasan Kāfī al-

MEHRZAD BOROUJERD
Syracuse University
Ḥizbullāh

JAMES BROUCEK
Department of Religion, Florida State University
Combat

MICHAELLE BROWERS
Wake Forest University, Department of Political Science
Citizenship; Democracy; Representation

L. CARL BROWN
Department of Near Eastern Studies, Princeton University, Emeritus
Colonialism and the Muslim World; Tyranny

FRANÇOIS BURGAT
CNRS Institut de Recherches et d'Études sur le Monde Arabe et Musulman, France
Ẓawāhirī, Ayman al-

KEN BURNSIDE
Independent Scholar, Cedar Falls, Iowa
ʿAbbāsid Caliphate

LABEEB AHMED BSOUL
Khalifa University, Abu Dhabi
Mossadegh, Mohammad; Treaties

KETRINA ÇABIRI
Researcher, Group for Legal and Political Studies
International Relations and Diplomacy

BYRON D. CANNON
History, University of Utah
Baʿth Parties; Chechnya; Seljuk Dynasty

OLIVIER CARRÉ
Centre d'Etudes et de Recherches Internationales, Paris
Bannā, Ḥasan al-; Faḍlallāh, Muḥammad Ḥusayn

GÖKHAN ÇETINSAYA
Istanbul Technical University
Ottoman Empire

ABDIN CHANDE
Department of History, Adelphi University
Africa Muslim Party; Haron, Imam Abdullah; Islam and Politics in Africa

W. K. CHE MAN
Moro National Liberation Front

SAM CHERRIBI
Department of Sociology & MESAS, Emory University
Netherlands

DAVID COMMINS
Dickinson College
Modernity

DAVID COOK
Department of Religious Studies, Rice University
Jihād

ELVIRE CORBOZ
Department of Near Eastern Studies, Princeton University
Al-Khoei Benevolent Foundation; Ḥizb al-Daʿwah al-Islāmīyah; Khoʾi, Abol-Qāsem al-

JUSTIN J. CORFIELD
Geelong Grammar School, Australia
Khārijites; Universities

JAMES CRITCHLOW
Davis Center for Russian and Eurasian Studies, Harvard University
Uzbekistan

HAMID DABASHI
Columbia University
Nūrī, Fażlullāh

Farhad Daftary
The Institute of Ismaili Studies, London
Fāṭimid Dynasty

Ahmad S. Dallal
Yale University
Ummah

Mary-Jane Deeb
Chief, African and Middle Eastern Division, the Library of Congress
Zaytūnah

Adrian De Gifis
Department of History, Loyola University New Orleans
Caliphate, Theories of the; Hypocrites

Vanessa De Gifis
Asst. Prof. of Islamic Studies, Graduate Advisor in Near Eastern Studies, Wayne State University
Bayt al-Ḥikmah

Natana J. DeLong-Bas
Boston College
Bin Laden, Osama; Qaʿida, al-; Wahhābīyah

Abdul Rahman I. Doi *(deceased)*
Rand Afrikaans University, Melville, South Africa
Ḥisbah

Dale F. Eickelman
Department of Anthropology, Dartmouth College
Ethnicity

Nader El-Bizri
Institute of Ismaili Studies
Brethren of Purity

Sarah Eltantawi
Berlin Graduate School of Muslim Societies and Cultures, Freie Universitat
Islam and Politics in Sub-Saharan Africa

Nader Entessar
University of South Alabama
Ḥizbullāh

Aykan Erdemir
Middle East Technical University
Alevis: Turkey

Haggai Erlich
Tel Aviv University
Aḥbāsh, al-; Ethiopia; Horn of Africa

John L. Esposito
Georgetown University
Fārūqī, Ismāʿīl Rājī al-

Mohammad H. Faghfoory
Department of Religion, The Middle East Institute and The Elliott Center for International Affairs, George Washington University
Kāshāni, Abol-Qāsem

Elizabeth Warnock Fernea
University of Texas, Austin
Family

Jörg Feuchter
History Department, Humboldt University Berlin
Ribāṭ

Carolyn Fluehr-Lobban
Rhode Island College
Sudan

David M. Freidenreich
Franklin & Marshall College
Muslim-Jewish Relations

Yohanan Friedmann
Institute of Asian and African Studies, The Hebrew University, Jerusalem
Aḥmadīyah

Allen Fromherz
History Department, Georgia State University
Civilization; Islam and Politics in the Middle East and North Africa; Jerusalem; Pluralism

Richard N. Frye
Harvard University
Būyids

Douglas H. Garrison
Center for Middle East Studies, Josef Korbel School of International Studies, University of Denver
Elections

Gamal Gasim
Grand Valley State University
Yemen

James L. Gelvin
University of California, Los Angeles
Nationalism

Adel Abdel Ghafar
CAIS, Australian National University
Social Movements

Sahar Ghumkhor
Islamic Studies, University of Melbourne
Australia and Oceania

Dru C. Gladney
Pomona College
China

Robert Gleave
University of Exeter
Shīʿah Schools of Jurisprudence: Imāmī School, The; Shīʿah Schools of Jurisprudence: Ismāʿīlī School, The

Ellis Goldberg
University of Washington
Bishrī, Ṭāriq al-

Kadir Gömbeyaz
Uludağ University
Çelebi, Kâtip

Matthew S. Gordon
Miami University, Ohio
Jamʿīyat al-Shubbān al-Muslimīn

Peter Gottschalk
Wesleyan University
Jamʿīyatul ʿUlamāʾ-i Hind

Matthew Gray
The Australian National University
Druze

Jeroen Gunning
University of Wales, Aberystwyth
Intifāḍah

Najam Haider
Department of Religion, Barnard College, Columbia University
Muʿtazilah

Aaron Albert Haley
University of Washington
Majlisī, Muḥammad Bāqir al-; Muṭahharī, Murtażā

Wael B. Hallaq
Avalon Foundation Professor in the Humanities at Columbia University, Department of Middle Eastern, South Asian, and African Studies
Ahl al-Ḥall wa-al-ʿAqd

Kikue Hamayotsu
Department of Political Science, Northern Illinois University
Indonesian Mujahidin Council; Islamic Youth Movement of Malaysia

Shadi Hamid
University of Oxford
Ḥasan II of Morocco

Haider Ala Hamoudi
University of Pittsburgh School of Law
Iraq

Eric J. Hanne
Department of History, Florida Atlantic University
Ibn al-Farrāʾ, Abū Yaʿlā

Judith Harik
Matn University, Beirut
Amal

Nader Hashemi
University of Denver, Josef Korbel School of International Studies
Human Rights; Republic; Secularism

Sohail Hashmi
Mount Holyoke College
Iqbal, Muhammad

Tawfiq Y. Hasou
Applied Science University, Amman, Jordan
Arab League

M. Kamal Hassan
International Islamic University Malaysia, Petaling Jaya
Malaysia

Rachel Havrelock
University of Illinois at Chicago
Muslim-Jewish Relations

Bernard Haykel
Princeton University
Shīʿah Schools of Jurisprudence: Zaydī School, The

Robert W. Hefner
Institute on Culture, Religion and World Affairs, Boston University
Education, Muslim

Christina Hellmich
Department of Politics and International Relations, University of Reading, UK
Qaʿida, al-

Jocelyn Hendrickson
Emory University
Andalusia

Derek Hopwood
St. Anthony's College, University of Oxford
Nasser, Gamal Abdel

Ishtiaq Hossain
International Islamic University Malaysia (IIUM)
Arab Spring

Julia Huang
Yale University
Tribes

Rizwan Hussain
Australian National University, Canberra
Ahmad, Israr; Jam'īyatul 'Ulamā'-i Hind; Jam'īyatul 'Ulamā'-i Pākistān; Mullah Omar; Pakistan

Shakira Hussein
Australia and Oceania

Iza Hussin
University of Chicago
Schools of Jurisprudence: Sunni Schools of Jurisprudence

Julie Chernov Hwang
Goucher College
Partai Keadilan Sejahtera

Ibrahim Ibrahim
Georgetown University
Jamā'at al-Islāmīyah, al-

Raihan Ismail
Saudi Arabia

Abbas Jaffer
Harvard University
Ghāmidī, Jāved Aḥmad

Farah Jan
Tablīghī Jamā'at

Johannes J. G. Jansen
Utrecht University
Kishk, 'Abd al-Ḥamīd

Mustafa Kabha
Open University of Israel
Aḥbāsh, al-

Cemal Kafadar
Harvard University
Dīwān

Monzer Kahf
Islamic Development Bank, Jeddah, Saudi Arabia
Waqf

Hazem Kandil
Department of Sociology, University of California, Los Angeles
Adalet ve Kalkınma Partisi; Capitulations; Cultural Invasion; Nūrī Movement; Refâh Partisi

Klodiana Kapllani (née Çabiri)
Legal Expert
International Relations and Diplomacy

Dzĕnita Karić
Philological Department, Oriental Institute in Sarajevo
Party for Democratic Action

Enes Karic
Faculty of Islamic Studies, University of Sarajevo
Balkan States; Bosnia and Herzegovina; Party for Democratic Action

Serdar Kaya
Simon Fraser University, Canada
Islamic Society of North America

Veysel Kaya
Uludag University
Ṣabrī Efendi, Mustafa

Joseph A. Kéchichian
King Faisal Center for Research and Islamic Studies
Aal al-Bayt Institute for Islamic Thought, The Royal; Aḥbāsh, al-; Ahmadinejad, Mahmoud; Amal; Arab League; Arab Nationalism; Arab Socialism; Arslān, Shakīb; Atatürk, Mustafa Kemal; Azhar, al-; Ba'th Parties; Citizenship; Da'wah; Erbakan, Necmettin; Faḍlallāh, Muḥammad Ḥusayn; Ghazālī, Muḥammad al-; Groupe Islamique Armé; Gulf Cooperation Council; Ḥamās: Overview; Ḥamās: Parliamentary Reform; Ḥizb al-Nahḍah; Ibn al-Muqaffa', 'Abd Allāh; Ibn Rushd, Abū al-Walīd Muḥammad Aḥmad; Ibn Sīnā, Abū 'Alī; Ibn Taymīyah, Taqī al-Dīn Aḥmad; Islamic Action Front; Islamic Constitutional Movement; Islam and Politics in the Middle East and North Africa; Jamā'at al-Islāmīyah, al-; Jam'īyat al-Shubbān al-Muslimīn; Jihād Groups; Khuṭbah; Kishk, 'Abd al-Ḥamīd; Kurds; Martyrdom; Mawdūdī, Sayyid Abū al-A'lā; Ministry of Islamic Affairs; Mirrors for Princes; Movement for National Reform; Mukhtār, 'Umar al-; Muslim-Christian Relations; Nasser, Gamal

Abdel; Ottoman Empire; Pan-Islam; Rahman, Omar Abdel; Ṣadr, Mūsā al-; Sanūsīyah; Succession; Tanzimat; Terrorism; Turābī, Ḥasan al-; Wasat Party, al-; Wilāyat al-Faqīh; Yāsīn, ʿAbd al-Salām; Ẓawāhirī, Ayman al-

NIKKI R. KEDDIE
University of California, Los Angeles
Afghānī, Jamāl al-Dīn al-; Constitutional Revolution

JOHN KELSAY
Florida State University
Just War

HUGH KENNEDY
University of St. Andrews, Scotland
ʿAbbāsid Caliphate

JEFFREY T. KENNEY
DePauw University
Rebellion

KHALED M. G. KESHK
DePaul University
Būyids; Fāṭimid Dynasty; Ibn Ḥazm, ʿAlī Ibn Aḥmad; Ibn Qayyim al-Jawzīyah; Kishk, Muḥammad Jalāl; Mahdī, al-Ṣādiq al-; Mamlūk State; Ṣafavid Dynasty; Seljuk Dynasty; Umayyad Caliphate

AS'AD ABU KHALIL
Jihād Groups

MUHAMMAD ATIF KHAN
Science PO, Grenoble, France
Jamāʿat-i Islāmī

M. A. MUQTEDAR KHAN
University of Delaware
Khan, Maulana Wahiduddin; Shūrā

SAAD S. KHAN
International Islamic University, Islamabad and *United Nations Habitat*
Organization of Islamic Cooperation

CHARLES A. KIMBALL
Wake Forest University
Muslim-Christian Relations

BAHGAT KORANY
University of Montreal
Arab Nationalism

MARTIN KRAMER
The Shalem Center, Jerusalem
Congresses; Ḥizbullāh

CHARLES KURZMAN
University of North Carolina, Chapel Hill
Modernity

JACOB M. LANDAU
The Hebrew University of Jerusalem
Pan-Islam

RICARDO LAREMONT
SUNY Binghamton
Justice and Benevolence Party; Justice and Development Party; Movement for the Society of Peace

BRENDAN LAROCQUE
Carleton College, Asian Studies
Baranī, Ḍhiyaʾ al-Dīn al-

GÖRAN LARSSON
University of Gothenburg, Sweden
Scandinavian States

FRED H. LAWSON
Millis College
Gulf States

B. TODD LAWSON
University of Toronto
Martyrdom

OLIVER LEAMAN
University of Kentucky
Apostasy; Ibn Rushd, Abū al-Walīd Muḥammad Aḥmad

JEAN-FRANÇOIS LEGRAIN
Centre National de la Recherche Scientifique, Amman
Ḥamās: Overview

JAMES LIDDELL
Ḥasan II of Morocco

MEIR LITVAK
Tel Aviv University
Ḥawẓah

TAYLOR LONG
University of Michigan, School of Social Work, Department of Political Science
Lebanon; Shams al-Dīn, Muḥammad Mahdī

ABDEL-FATTAH MADY
Alexandria University, Department of Political Science
Palestine

MOJTABA MAHDAVI
Department of Political Science, University of Alberta, Canada
Iran, Islamic Republic of

Cesar Adib Majul
University of the Philippines (Emeritus)
Philippines

William Maley
Asia-Pacific College of Diplomacy, The Australian National University
Ḥizb-i Islāmī Afghānistān; Loya Jirga

Anas Malik
Xavier University (Cincinnati) and Vincent and Elinor Ostrom Workshop in Political Theory and Policy Analysis, Indiana University (Bloomington)
Humanism; Individualism; Tolerance

Hafeez Malik
Villanova University
Aḥmad Khān, Sayyid; Iqbal, Muhammad

Chibli Mallat
University of London
Ṣadr, Muḥammad Bāqir al-

Lawrence H. Mamiya
Paschall-Davis Professor of Religion and Africana Studies, Vassar College
Nation of Islam

Andrew F. March
Department of Political Science, Yale University
Justice

Şerif Mardin
American University
Tanzimat

Andrew Marsham
University of Edinburgh
Monarchy

Hannah Mason
Personal Status Codes

Muhammad Khalid Masud
Council of Islamic Ideology, Islamabad
Daʿwah

Rudi Matthee
University of Delaware
Ṣafavid Dynasty

Ann McDougall
Department of History and Classics, University of Alberta
Slavery

James McDougall
Trinity College, University of Oxford
Algeria

Nicola Melis
Department of Social Sciences, University of Cagliari
Minorities in Muslim States

David E. Merrell
University of Washington School of Law
Islam and Politics in Central Asia and the Caucasus

Barbara D. Metcalf
Professor of History Emerita, University of California, Davis
Deobandīs; India

Murat Metinsoy
Assistant Professor, Istanbul University, Political Science and International Relations, Istanbul-Turkey
Executive

Ali Altaf Mian
The Graduate Program in Religion, Duke University
Historiography

Beverley Milton-Edwards
Queens University in Belfast
Palestine

Gail Minault
Khilāfat Movement; Chirāgh ʿAlī

Mahan Mirza
Zaytuna College
Muḥammad; Qurʾān Exegesis and Hermeneutics

Edward Moad
Department of Humanities, Qatar University
Ibn Bājjah, Abū Bakr; Ibn Ṭufayl, Abū Bakr; Sufism

Valentine M. Moghadam
Professor of Sociology and International Affairs, Northeastern University
Clash of Civilizations; Family

Moojan Momen
Independent Scholar
Bahāʾī

Jessie Moritz
Australian National University
Jordan; Sovereignty

Scott Morrison
ʿAbduh, Muḥammad; Ibn Khaldūn, ʿAbd al-Raḥmān

Abdul Rashid Moten
Department of Political Science, International Islamic University Malaysia
Islamophobia; Mahathir bin Mohamed; Opposition; Political Parties; Political Science; Power; Ummah

Roy P. Mottahedeh
Harvard University
Wilāyat al-Faqīh

Ahmad Moussalli
American University of Beirut
Ḥawwā, Saʿīd; Islamic Reform; Lebanon

Hadia Mubarak
Department of Islamic Studies, Georgetown University
Khaled, Amr; Khuṭbah

Akbar Muhammad
State University of New York, Binghamton
Malcolm X

Henry Munson Jr.
University of Maine, Orono
Morocco

Muhammad Muslih
Democracy

Abdul Rahman Mustafa
Islam and Politics in South Asia

Mitsuo Nakamura
Partai Persatuan Pembangunan

Seyyed Vali Reza Nasr
Naval Postgraduate School, California
Mawdūdī, Sayyid Abū al-Aʿlā

Phillip C. Naylor
Department of History, Marquette University
Bennabi, Malek

Ronald L. Nettler
University of Oxford and Mansfield College
Ibn Taymīyah, Taqī al-Dīn Aḥmad

Jørgen S. Nielsen
Centre for European Islamic Thought, Faculty of Theology, University of Copenhagen
Great Britain; Islam and Politics in Europe

Mehdi Noorbaksh
Freedom Movement of Iran

Augustus Richard Norton
Boston University
Amal; Lebanon; Terrorism

Kirill Nourzhanov
Australian National University
Kazakhstan

Kerem Öktem
St Antony's College, University of Oxford and Faculty of Oriental Studies
Germany

Martha Brill Olcott
Colgate University and *Foreign Policy Research Institute*
Kazakhstan

Robert Olson
University of Kentucky
Kurds

Racha el Omari
Muʿtazilah; Shuʿūbīyah

Felicitas Opwis
Department of Arabic and Islamic Studies, Georgetown University
Siyāsah Sharʿīyah

Amr Osman
Department of Humanities, Qatar University
Amānah; Equality; Freedom; Murji'ites; Salafī Movements

Jan Michiel Otto
Director Van Vollenhoven Institute for Law, Governance, and Development; Leiden
Personal Status Codes

H. Ozan Ozavci
Izmir University, International Relations Department
Cumhuriyet Halk Partisi

John N. Paden
George Mason University
Nigeria

Tauseef Ahmad Parray
Aligarh Muslim University, India
Nahdatul Ulama

Frank Peter
European University Viadrina Frankfurt, Germany
France

F.E. Peters
New York University
Jerusalem

Rudolph Peters
University of Amsterdam
Jihād

Carl F. Petry
Northwestern University
Mamlūk State

James Piscatori
Australian National University
Elections; International Relations and Diplomacy

Emin Poljarevic
University of Edinburgh
Islamism

Alexandre Popovic
Centre National de la Recherche Scientifique, Paris
Balkan States

Mezna Qato
St. Antony's College, University of Oxford
Ḥizb al-Taḥrīr al-Islāmī

Emran Qureshi
Harvard Law School
Ahmad, Eqbal; Human Rights; Taliban

Jawad Anwar Qureshi
University of Chicago-Divinity School
Nadwī, Abū al-Ḥasan

Intisar A. Rabb
Princeton University
Fiqh

Babak Rahimi
University of California, San Diego
Khomeini, Ruhollah al-Musavi; Montazeri, Hossein ʿAlī; Sīstānī, ʿAlī al-; Taʿzīyah

Hisham M. Ramadan
Constitutions and Constitutionalism

Dietrich Reetz
Centre for Modern Oriental Studies, Berlin
Tablīghī Jamāʿat

Donald Malcolm Reid
Georgia State University
Azhar, al-

Elie Rekhess
Northwestern University
Israel

Hamid Rezai
Visiting Assistant Professor, American University in Cairo
Mujāhidīn-i Khalq

D. S. Richards
St Cross College, University of Oxford
Fāṭimid Dynasty

Paola Rivetti
School of Law and Government, Dublin City University
Fedāʾīyān-i Islām

David Robinson
Michigan State University
Suwari, Al-Hajj Salim; Tal, ʿUmar ibn Saʿīd

Francis Robinson
Royal Holloway College
Mughal Empire

Glenn E. Robinson
Naval Postgraduate School, California
Palestine Liberation Organization

Elaheh Rostami-Povey
London Middle East Institute; School of Oriental and African Studies, University of London
Afghanistan, 2001 U.S. Invasion of

Avi Rubin
Department of Middle East Studies, Ben-Gurion University of the Negev, Israel
Niẓāmīyah Courts

Abdulaziz Sachedina
University of Virginia
Al-Khoei Benevolent Foundation; Khatami, Mohamed

Ahmad Sadri
Lake Forest College
Soroush, Abdolkarim

Mahmoud Sadri
Texas Woman's University
Ḥojjatīyeh Society; Soroush, Abdolkarim

Abdullah Saeed
University of Melbourne
Apostasy

Louay M. Safi
Georgetown University
Islamization of Knowledge and Society; Muslim Political Thought

BARAK A. SALMONI
Marine Corps Training and Education Command, Quantico, VA
Iraq

ELIZ SANASARIAN
Islamic Republican Party

USHA SANYAL
Rutgers University
Barelwīs

LAITH SAUD
Religious Studies, DePaul University
ʿAbd al-Rāziq, ʿAlī; Islam and Politics in North America

MARTIN A. SCHAIN
New York University
Union des Organisations Islamiques de France

IRENE SCHNEIDER
Fiqh

JOHN S. SCHOEBERLEIN
Harvard University
Islam and Politics in Central Asia and the Caucasus

RACHEL M. SCOTT
Virginia Tech
Faraj, Muḥammad ʿAbd al-Salām

REINHARD SCHULZE
Otto-Friedrich-Universität Bamburg, Germany
Daʿwah

RAYMOND SCUPIN
Center for International and Global Studies and Department of Anthropology and Sociology, Lindenwood University
Thailand

RÜDIGER SEESEMANN
Northwestern University
Islam and Politics in Sub-Saharan Africa

MICHAEL SEMPLE
Taliban

EMAD EL-DIN SHAHIN
The American University in Cairo
Ghannūshī, Rāshid al-; Kawākibī, ʿAbd al-Raḥmān al-; Kishk, Muḥammad Jalāl; Rashīd Riḍā, Muḥammad; Sanhūrī, ʿAbd al-Razzāq al-

M. NAZIF SHAHRANI
Indiana University
Afghanistan: Overview

NAEL SHAMA
Political researcher and columnist with a special interest in the international relations and comparative politics of the Middle East region
Afghānī, Jamāl al-Dīn al-; Ahmadinejad, Mahmoud; Ḥasan II of Morocco; Jamāʿat al-Islāmīyah, al-; Kawākibī, ʿAbd al-Raḥmān al-; Khatami, Mohamed; Quṭb, Sayyid; Rahman, Omar Abdel; Rashīd Riḍā, Muḥammad; Shaltūt, Maḥmūd

DAVID SHANKLAND
University of Bristol
Alevis: Overview

STANFORD J. SHAW
University of California, Los Angeles
Ottoman Empire

WILLIAM E. SHEPARD
University of Canterbury (Retired)
Abangan; Expansion of Islam; Khālid, Khālid Muḥammad; Muhammadiyah

YOGINDER SIKAND
Associated with the Centre for the Study of Social Exclusion at the National Law School, Bangalore, India
Ummah

JAKOB SKOVGAARD-PETERSEN
New Media in the Muslim World

PETER SLUGLETT
University of Utah
Arab Socialism

CHARLES D. SMITH
University of Arizona
Arab-Israeli Conflict

AMIRA EL AZHARY SONBOL
Georgetown University
Shaltūt, Maḥmūd

RONALD BRUCE ST JOHN
Independent Scholar
Andalusia; France; Libya; Morocco; Sudan

KRISTEN A. STILT
Northwestern University
Commanding Right and Forbidding Wrong; Ḥisbah

CHRYSTIE FLOURNOY SWINEY
The College of William and Mary
Ḥamās: Parliamentary Reform; Ḥirābah; Islamic Constitutional Movement; Sibāʿī, Muṣṭafā al-

Zoltan Szombathy
Department of Arabic Studies, Eotvos Lorand University, Budapest
Jamā'at Izālat al-Bid'a wa Iqāmat al-Sunna; Wetu Telu

Anara Tabyshalieva
Department of History, Marshall University
Kazakhstan

Suha Taji-Farouki
University of Exeter and *The Institute of Ismaili Studies, London*
Ḥizb al-Taḥrīr al-Islāmī

David Taylor
Institute of Commonwealth Studies, University of London
All-India Muslim League

Fehrullah Terkan
Department of Islamic Philosophy, Faculty of Divinity, Ankara University
Ghazālī, Abū Ḥāmid al-

Jörn Thielmann
Erlangen Centre for Islam and Law in Europe EZIRE, Friedrich-Alexander-University Erlangen-Nuremberg
Islamic Salvation Front

Bassam Tibi
University of Göttingen, Germany
Authority and Legitimation

Mathieu Tillier
Institut français du Proche-Orient, Beirut; Aix-Marseille Université
Courts

Binnaz Toprak
Boğaziçi University, Istanbul
Erbakan, Necmettin

Christian W. Troll
Philosophisch-Theologische Hochschule S.J., Sankt Georgen, Frankfurt am Main, German
Āzād, Abū al-Kalām

John Trumpbour
Harvard Law School
Ahmad, Eqbal; Crusades

Mete Tunçay
Ankara University
Cumhuriyet Halk Partisi

Naim M. Turfan
University of London
Atatürk, Mustafa Kemal

A. Üner Turgay
McGill University
Citizenship; Nation

Nada Unus
Harvard University
Izetbegović, Alija; Jerusalem

Emrullah Uslu
University of Utah
Ḥizbullāh

Dirk Vandewalle
Dartmouth College
Libya

Daniel Martin Varisco
Department of Anthropology, Hofstra University
Orientalism

Knut S. Vikør
University of Bergen
Mukhtār, 'Umar al-; Sanūsīyah; Sharī'ah

David R. Vishanoff
University of Oklahoma
Religious Beliefs

Fred R. von der Mehden
Department of Political Science, Rice University
Darul Islam Movement; Dewan Dakwah Islamiyah; Indonesia; Islam and Politics in Southeast Asia; Laskar Jihad; Majlis Ulam Indonesia; Malaysia; Masyumi Party; National Awakening Party; Partai Islam se Malaysia; Sarekat Islam; United Development Party; United Malays National Organization

Sabina von Fischer
Institute of Advanced Study in the Humanities and the Social Sciences, Philosophical-Historical Faculty, University of Bern (Universität Bern)
Council on American-Islamic Relations; Muslim Students Association of North America

Paul E. Walker
University of Michigan, Ann Arbor
Da'wah

SUSAN WALTZ
Florida International University
Ḥizb al-Nahḍah

GABRIEL R. WARBURG
University of Haifa, Israel (Emeritus)
Mahdī, al-Ṣādiq al-; National Islamic Front

DAVID J. WASSERSTEIN
Vanderbilt University
Ibn Ḥazm, ʿAlī bn Aḥmad

WILLIAM MONTGOMERY WATT
University of Edinburgh (Emeritus)
Umayyad Caliphate

ITZCHAK WEISMANN
University of Haifa
Nadwat al-ʿUlamāʾ; Sirhindī, Aḥmad

ANITA WEISS
University of Oregon, Department of International Studies
Muttahida Majlis-i Amal

DAVID A. WESTBROOK
University at Buffalo Law School, State University of New York
International Law

JOYCE N. WILEY
University of South Carolina Upstate
Islamic Supreme Council of Iraq; Khoʾi, Abol-Qāsem al-

JOHN ALDEN WILLIAMS
College of William and Mary
Fitnah

RODNEY WILSON
Emeritus Professor and Founder of Islamic Finance Program, Durham University, England
Islam and Economics; Taxation

STANLEY WOLPERT
University of California, Los Angeles
Jinnah, Mohammad Ali

PETER WOODWARD
Arizona State University
Turābī, Ḥasan al-

LISA WORTHINGTON
Religion and Society Research Centre, University of Western Sydney
Social Movements

LUKE YARBROUGH
History Department, Saint Louis University
Dīwān; Wizāra

HAKAN YAVUZ
University of Utah
Gülen, Fethullah

WALTER EDWARD YOUNG
Institute of Islamic Studies, McGill University
Karakī, ʿAlī al-

MALIKA ZEGHAL
University of Chicago
Morocco; Yāsīn, ʿAbd al-Salām

NAHED ARTOUL ZEHR
Western Kentucky University, Department of Philosophy and Religion
Azzam, Abdullah Yusuf al-

MADELINE C. ZILFI
University of Maryland, College Park
Kānūn

SHERIFA ZUHUR
The Institute of Middle Eastern, Islamic, and Strategic Studies
Women in Politics

Index

Page references in boldface indicate the main entry on the subject. Page references in italics refer to tables.

A

Aal al-Bayt Institute for Islamic Thought, The Royal, **1:1–2**
Aaron, 1:245
Abacha, Sani, 2:192
abangan, **1:2–4,** 483, 486
Abbas, Mahmoud, 1:391
ʿAbbās I (Ṣafavid shah), 2:359–360
ʿAbbās II (Ṣafavid shah), 2:360
ʿAbbās III (Ṣafavid shah), 2:360
ʿAbbās VIII al-Muʿ taṣim (ʿAbbāsid caliph), 2:60
ʿAbbās, ʿAbd Allāh ibn, 1:693
ʿAbbās, Ferhāt, 1:153, 203–204
ʿAbbāsid Caliphate, **1:4–8,** 170–172; 2:123–125
  Abū Yūsuf on, 1:17–18
  ʿAlid rebellion, 1:344
  amīrs, 2:202
  Andalusia, 1:75
  Ashʿarīs and, 1:105–106
  authority in, 2:121
  bayt al-māl, 1:151
  Brethren of Purity and, 1:164–165
  Būyids and, 1:166–167
  citizenship, 1:188
  civilization, 1:193
  combat and, 1:206
  commanding right and forbidding wrong, 1:208
  daʿwah and, 1:246
  on *dawlah,* 1:250
  dīwān of, 2:266
  on ethics, 2:276
  in expansion of Islam, 1:308
  Fāṭimids and, 1:170–172, 332
  Ghazālī on, 1:360–362
  governance, 1:372
    administration, 1:24–25
    executive, 1:305
  ḥājīb, 2:203
  Ḥanafī school of law, 2:381, 383
  on *ḥirābah,* 1:398–399
  historiography of, 1:404
  humanism of, 1:425
  Ibn al-Farrāʾ on, 1:445
  Ibn Qutaybah, 1:456–458
  international relations, 1:500–501
  judges, 1:228, 229
  Juwaynī on, 1:673–674
  khuṭbah, 1:705
  Kindī, 1:707–708
  Kurds in, 1:712
  Mamlūks and, 2:30
  maẓālim court, 1:230–231
  ministry of Islamic affairs, 2:48
  minorities under, 2:50
  mirrors for princes, 2:60–61
  monarchy, 2:70, 71
  Ottomans and, 2:218–219
  Palestine, 2:233
  revivalism, 1:280
  Seljuks and, 2:126
  Shīʿīs on legitimacy of, 1:230
  Shuʿūbīyah movement and, 2:419–420, 421
  siyar, 1:498
  slave soldiers, 1:6; 2:432–433
  succession system, 2:445
  translation of literature in, 1:149–150
  tribal model in, 2:127
  Umayyads defeated by, 2:513
  ummah, 2:516
  vizierate, 2:546
  weakening of, 1:562
ʿAbbās al-Qādirī, Ḥājj, 1:666
ʿAbbūd, Ibrāhīm, 2:109, 110, 176
ʿAbdalīyah, al-, 2:569
ʿAbd al-ʿAll, Aḥmad, 1:39
ʿAbd al-ʿAll, Maḥmūd, 1:39
ʿAbd al-ʿAll, Walīd, 1:39
Abdalla, Mohamad, 1:108–109
ʿAbd Allāh (King of Saudi Arabia), 1:89; 2:116, 371, 372
ʿAbd Allāh b. ʿUbayy b. Salūl, 1:440
ʿAbd Allāh Ḥasan, Muḥammad, 1:203
Abdallahi al-Taʿishi (caliph), 2:448
Abdan-Unat, Nermin, 2:551
ʿAbd al-ʿAzīz, Shah, 1:118, 706
ʿAbd-al-Bahāʾ, 1:129, 130
Abd Elk-Meguid, Ahmad Esmat, 1:88
Abdesalam, Ahmad, 2:83
ʿAbd al-Ḥalīm, Ṣalāḥ al-Dīn, 2:55

C

F

H

I

J

K

L

M

O

S

T

U

V